Television
1970– 1980

Also by Vincent Terrace

Complete Encyclopedia of Television Programs 1947–1979
Radio's Golden Years: The Encyclopedia of Radio Programs 1930–1960

Television
1970–1980

Vincent Terrace

San Diego
A. S. Barnes & Company, Inc.
In London:
The Tantivy Press

First Edition
Manufactured in the United States of America

For information write to:
A.S. Barnes & Company, Inc.
P.O. Box 3051
La Jolla, California 92038

The Tantivy Press
Magdalen House
136-148 Tooley Street
London, SE1 2TT, England

Library of Congress Cataloging in Publication Data

Terrace, Vincent, 1948–
      Television, 1970–1980.

      Includes index.
      1. Television programs — Plots, themes, etc. — Dictionaries.   I. Title.
PN1992.18.T4   791.45′75   81-3580
ISBN 0-498-02539-X (Papercover)   AACR2
ISBN 0-498-02577-2 (Hardcover)

1   2   3   4   5   6   7   8   9   84   83   82   81

Contents

Illustrations

Acknowledgments

The author wishes to thank the following people for their help in making this book possible:

Alvin H. Marill, Robert Reed, Patricia Anne Anders, Laura Stuart, Sylvia Lawler and Rena Terracuso.

And, Kevin Schluter, of *TV Times* magazine, Sydney, Australia, for his help in compiling information on *Dad's Army, The Expert, For the Love of Ada, George and Mildred, Man About the House, Nearest and Dearest, Porridge, Steptoe and Son* and *Till Death Us Do Part.*

Preface

Television 1970–1980 is an encyclopedic listing of more than 1,910 entertainment programs. It is the most thorough chronicle of a television decade ever published.

The book covers in great detail the network and syndicated entertainment series broadcast between January 1, 1970 and October 26, 1980 (a program addendum covers October 27, 1980 through March 1, 1981); network and syndicated pilot films broadcast from January 1, 1970 through October 31, 1980; and the British series on which American programs are based: *For the Love of Ada* (America's *A Touch of Grace*), *George and Mildred (The Ropers), Love Thy Neighbour (Love Thy Neighbor), Man About the House (Three's Company), Miss Jones and Son (Miss Winslow and Son), Nearest and Dearest (Thicker Than Water), On the Buses (Lotsa Luck), Porridge (On the Rocks), Steptoe and Son (Sanford and Son), Till Death Us Do Part (All in the Family)*, and *Whodunit? (Whodunit?)*.

While an index has been provided for easy access to personalities, programs also have been divided into four sections for easy reference:

Section 1: 1,356 regular network and syndicated series (both American and foreign imports) of the following type: adventure, animated cartoon, anthology (with new examples), children, comedy, crime drama, drama, game, human interest, miniseries, musical variety, mystery, science fiction, sequential special series, serial (soap opera), talk-variety, thriller, variety, and western.

Entries, which are arranged alphabetically, contain the following information: type, story line, complete casts (major, minor and semi-regular performers), character relationships, announcers, credits (e.g., producer, director, writer), program openings, theme vocal credits, length, network or syndication information, complete running dates, episode numbers, and trivia information (e.g., addresses). In situations where a new version of a series broadcast prior to 1970 has been aired, both versions have been included for comparison.

Section 2: 516 pilot films. Program types and content are the same as those listed for Section 1. See the introduction to the Pilot Films section for additional information.

Section 3: Variety Specials. An alphabetical listing of the 425 variety specials broadcast between January 1, 1970 and January 1, 1981.

Section 4: Program Addendum: An alphabetical listing of the series broadcast from October 27, 1980 through March 1, 1981.

In short, with the addition of more than 140 photographs, *Television 1970–1980* is the ultimate encyclopedia of television programming. It is not only a fascinating trip down memory lane, but is a compilation of information that cannot be found elsewhere.

New York   V.T.
March 1981

Author's Notes

An explanation of the program terminology used in the listings:

ABC: The American Broadcasting Company.

BBC: The British Broadcasting Corporation.

CBS: The Columbia Broadcasting System.

Golden Circle: A system whereby local, independent stations pool their resources and purchase top-quality, first-run programs.

ITC: The Independent Television Corporation, an independent British producer of syndicated television series.

London Weekend Television: A British television network.

NBC: The National Broadcasting Company.

Operation Prime Time: The premiere system whereby local, independent stations pool their resources to purchase top-quality, first-run programs.

PBS: The Public Broadcasting Service.

Pilot Film: A filmed or videotaped sample episode that is used to sell a potential series. See the introduction to Pilot Films in Section 2 for additional information.

Syndicated: A term for off-network reruns or first-run programs produced especially for non-network use by local, independent stations. When the term Syndicated appears after a network listing, it indicates that the program has been placed into syndication.

Thames: An independent British network whose programs are seen in the United States as both network and syndicated offerings.

Running Dates: The running dates listed after each network program are based on New York City station broadcasts, which are the official network broadcast dates. Dates will vary in certain areas of the U.S. where affiliated stations delay, cancel or reschedule certain network programs to accommodate their own local schedules.

Syndicated programs, which are sold to local stations, are listed by their first year of syndication. While most network programs are seen in all parts of the U.S., syndicated programs are not, and those listed have aired and have been made available for national distribution.

Golden Circle and Operation Prime Time programs are listed by month and year, based on comparisons with New York and Los Angeles air dates. (While a station may be associated with Golden Circle or Operation Prime Time, it is not obligated to run a program on a specific date. Generally speaking, though, member stations will air programs within the same month, but not necessarily on the same dates.)

Program Exclusions: Excluded are religious programs, sports programs and news broadcasts.

Section 1
Network and Syndicated Series
January 1, 1970 – October 26, 1980

Alice. From left: Vic Tayback, Diane Ladd, Beth Howland, Linda Lavin.

CBS

CBS

Archie Bunker's Place. Danielle Brisebois, Carroll O'Connor (front). Rear, from left: Jason Wingreen, Martin Balsam, Danny Dayton, and Bill Quinn.

CBS

The Beverly Hillbillies. Donna Douglas and Buddy Ebsen (front). Irene Ryan and Max Baer (back).

A

01 THE ABC AFTERNOON PLAYBREAK

Anthology. A monthly series of varying dramatic, suspense and comedic productions.

Music: Al Kasha, Joel Hirschhorn, Jack Elliott, Allyn Ferguson.
Producers: Ira Barmek, Lila Garrett, Alan Landsburg, Laurence D. Savadove, Kay Hoffman.

Included:

Oh, Baby, Baby, Baby ... The story focuses on the preparations taken by an intern and his expectant wife when it is discovered that she may give birth to quintuplets.

Cast: Stacy Stoner: Judy Carne; Rick Stoner: Bert Convy; Dr. Fisher: King Moody; Dr. Roth: Henry Corden; Dr. Burkeholder: Parley Baer; Ms. Phillips: Laura Kaye; Mrs. Hoffman: Reva Rose.

The Girl Who Couldn't Lose. The story of Jane Darwin, a plain-looking librarian whose knowledge of esoterica makes her a winner on a TV game show—but a potential loser in the game of love.

Cast: Jane Darwin: Julie Kavner; Jackie Leroy: Jack Carter; Florence Darwin: Fritzi Burr; Charlie Darwin: Milton Selzer; Susan Miller: Beverly Sanders; Rosalie: Candice Azzara; Andy Martin: Dennis Dugan; Judd Moore: Oliver Clark.

The Gift of Terror. The story of a woman whose sudden visions of death become reality.

Cast: Laura: Denise Alexander; Steve: Michael Callan; Donny: Christopher Connelly; Ben: Will Geer; Les Parker: Edd Byrnes; Marian: Linda Kaye Henning; Mrs. Cummings: Jeff Donnell; Aunt Caroline: Carmen Zapata.

Can I Save My Children? A story of survival as a mother and her two children, stranded in a wilderness area when their plane crash lands, seek help.

Cast: Diana Hansen: Diane Baker; Melanie Hansen: Tammi Bula; Peter Hansen: Todd Glass; Clay Hollinger: David Hedison; Harry Hansen: Jack Ging; Doug Powell: Kenneth Tobey.

This Child Is Mine. A courtroom melodrama that centers on the custody battle between a child's natural and foster parents.

Cast: Elizabeth Thatcher: Rosemary Prinz; Shelley Carr: Robin Strasser; Martin Thatcher: Don Galloway; Judge Hendrick: Marjorie Lord; Jay Lawrence: John Conte; Max Dettmen: Milt Kamen; Mae Dayton: Royce Wallace.

THE ABC AFTERNOON PLAYBREAK—90 minutes—ABC—October 30, 1973–May 20, 1976. 16 programs.

02 THE ABC AFTERSCHOOL SPECIAL

Anthology. A bimonthly series of outstanding dramatic specials.

Theme Music: John Morris.
Music: Jay Smith, Maurice Jarre, Kenyon Hopkins, Neiman Tillar, Doug Goodwin, Eric Rodgers, Glenn Paxton, Hoyt Curtin, John Morris, Dean Elliott, Brad Fiedel, Michel Legrand.
Executive Producer: Daniel Wilson, Robert Guenete, David DePatie, Friz Freleng, Richard Gottlieb, Linda Gottlieb, Alan Landesburg, William Hanna, Joseph Barbera.
Producer: Linda Marmelstein, Diane Baker, Diane Asselin, Paul Asselin, Martin Tahse, Jon Kubichan, Tom Biener, Albert Waller, Robert Chenault, Evelyn Barron, Daniel Wilson, Doro Bachrach, Fran Sears, Iwao Takamoto, Alan Handley, Bill Schwartz, Arthur Barron.
Writer: Jan Hartman, Howard Rayfield, Albert Waller, Arthur Heinemann, Jeffrey Kindley, Durrell Royce Crays, Gloria Banta, George Malko, Larry Spiegel, Arthur Barron.
Director: Anthony Lovell, Harry Winer, Tom Blank, Bruce Malmuth, Wes Kenney, Albert Waller, Larry Elikann, Robert Liberman, Stephen Gyllenhaal, Robert Fuest, Charles A. Nichols, Alan Handley, Herbert Klein, Arthur Barron.

Included:

Dear Lovey Hart: I Am Desperate. The story centers on Carrie Wasserman, a pretty high school girl who becomes the paper's advice to the lovelorn columnist—a job she doesn't take seriously until she learns that her flip answers have caused more harm than good.

Cast: Carrie Wasserman: Susan Lawrence; Skip Custer: Meegan King; Marty: Stephen Liss; Linda: Elyssa Davalos; Susan: Barbara Timko; Jeff: Al Eisenmann; Cindy: Jane Alice Brandon; Freddie: Bruce Caton; Bernice: Bebe Kelly; Marc: Del Hinkley.

Very Good Friends. A tender story about the loving relationship between a sensitive teenager named Kate and her younger sister Joss, an irrepressible scamp. The heart of the program shows how their togetherness is shattered by Joss's accidental death, a tragedy that also shatters Kate, leaving her bitterly grieving and desperately searching for meaning.

Cast: Kate: Melissa Sue Anderson; Joss: Kay Kurtzman; Father: William H. Bassett.

The Late Great Me: Story of a Teenage Alcoholic. A sensitive drama about a suburban high school student who becomes an alcoholic. The story focuses on Geri Peters, a 15-year-old girl with few friends and few interests. When Dave Townsend, a new student takes a liking to her, Geri decides to keep his attentions by sharing one of his avid pursuits: drinking. The program details her rapid decline—and desperate attempts to seek help.

Cast: Geri Peters: Maia Danziger; Dave Townsend: Charles Lang; Ms. Laine: Kaiulani Lee; Ginger Peters: Teri Keane; George Peters: Michael Miller; Jack Peters: Al Corley; Carolyn: Amy DeMayo; B.J.: Jo Lynn Sciarro.

Sara's Summer of the Swans. A heartwarming story that follows the transformation of Sara Godfrey from a self-conscious young girl to a young adult.

Cast: Sara Godfrey: Heather Totten; Aunt Willie Godfrey: Priscilla Morrill; Wanda Godfrey: Betty Ann Carr; Charlie Godfrey: Reed Diamond; Joe: Christopher Knight; Mary: Doney Oatman; Gretchyn: Eve Plumb.

A Movie Star's Daughter. The story of Dena McKain, the pretty, but shy daughter of a famous movie star, and her experiences in a new school when she discovers that her new friends are accepting her only because she has a famous father.

Cast: Dena McKain: Trini Alvarado; Hal McKain: Frank Converse; Barbara McKain: Marcia Rodd; Alison: Laura Dean; Geri: Alexa Kenin.

THE ABC AFTERSCHOOL SPECIAL—60 minutes—ABC—Premiered: October 4, 1972.

03 THE ABC MONDAY NIGHT SPECIAL

Specials. A weekly series of entertainment and news specials.

Included:

The Emperor's New Clothes. An animated version of the Hans Christian Anderson story about a vain emperor whose vanity gets the best of him.

Voices: Marmaduke: Danny Kaye; Princess: Imogene Coca; Emperor: Cyril Ritchard; Mufti: Allen Swift; Jasper: Robert McFadden.
Songs-Music: Maury Laws, Jules Bass.

The Monty Hall Smokin'-Stokin' Fire Brigade. A comedy salute to California happenings—from block parties to Mexican fiestas.

Host: Monty Hall.
Guests: Cass Elliot, Fred Smoot, Solomon Burke, The Mike Curb Congregation.
Cameos: Annette Funicello, Jim Backus, Johnny Brown, Fabian Forte, Rosey Grier.

Bill Bixby and Brandon Cruz At the Budapest Circus. A variety hour that highlights great moments from the Budapest Circus.

Hosts: Bill Bixby and Brandon Cruz.

The Perpetual People Puzzle. A variety hour of song, dance, drama and satire.

Hostess: Gwen Verdon.
Guests: Howard Cosell, Richie Havens, Jack Cassidy, Robert Klein, James Earl Jones.
Producer: Al Perlmatter.

THE MONDAY NIGHT SPECIAL—60 minutes—ABC—January 10, 1972–August 14, 1972.

04 THE ABC MOVIE OF THE WEEK / THE ABC TUESDAY MOVIE OF THE WEEK

Movies. Feature-length films produced especially for television.

Included:

The Girl Who Came Gift-Wrapped. The misadventures of a pretty country girl who journeys to the big city in search of a husband.

Cast: Sandy: Karen Valentine; Michael: Richard Long; Sylvia: Louise Sorel; Miss Marklin: Reta Shaw; Stanley: Dave Madden; Harold: Tom Bosley; Cindy: Patti Cubbison; Patty: Farrah Fawcett; Louise: Shelley Morrison.

Hit Lady. The story of Angela Villard, a beautiful and successful artist who works part time as a ruthless syndicate assassin.

Cast: Angela Villard: Yvette Mimieux; Doug: Dack Rambo; Jeff Baine: Joseph Campanella; Roarke: Clu Gulager; McCormack: Keenan Wynn; Hanson: Del Monroe.

Satan's School for Girls. A chilling tale about a posh girls' school plagued by supernatural occurrences.

Cast: Elizabeth: Pamela Franklin; Roberta: Kate Jackson; Jody: Cheryl Jean Stoppelmoor (Cheryl Ladd); Headmistress:

Jo Van Fleet; Dr. Clampett: Roy Thinnes; Debbie: Jamie Smith Jackson; Dr. Delacroix: Lloyd Bochner; Lucy Dembrow: Gwynne Gilford; Sheriff: Bing Russell.

A Summer Without Boys. A bittersweet love story, set during World War II, about a middle-aged woman suffering through the final moments of her dissolving marriage.

Cast: Ellen Hailey: Barbara Bain; Ruth Hailey: Kay Lenz; Abe Battle: Michael Moriarty; Lenore: Debralee Scott; Mrs. LaCava: Mildred Dunnock; Joe: Ric Carrott; Burt: Michael Lembeck; Mrs. Potter: Sue Taylor; Mrs. Margolis: Jan Burrell; Mrs. Denning: Diane Hill.

The Sex Symbol. The rise and fall of Kelly Williams, a beautiful, but neurotic Hollywood film star.

Cast: Kelly Williams: Connie Stevens; Agatha Murphy: Shelley Winters; Manny Foxe: Jack Carter; Grant O'Neal: Don Murray.

THE ABC MOVIE OF THE WEEK—90 minutes—ABC—September 23, 1969–September 2, 1975. Also titled: *The ABC Tuesday Movie of the Week.*

05   THE ABC MOVIE OF THE WEEKEND
THE ABC WEDNESDAY MOVIE OF THE WEEK

Movies. Feature-length films produced especially for television.

Included:

The Feminist and the Fuzz. The complications that ensue when a beautiful, liberated woman doctor agrees to share an apartment with a cop she considers to be a sexual bigot.

Cast: Dr. Jane Bowers: Barbara Eden; Officer Jerry Frazer: David Hartman; Kitty Murdock: Farrah Fawcett; Lilah McGuinnes: Julie Newmar; Debby Inglefinger: Jo Anne Worley; Wyatt Foley: Herb Edelman; Mr. Sorenson: John McGiver; Horace Bowers: Harry Morgan; Dr. Lassiter: Roger Perry.

All My Darling Daughters. The story of Charles Raleigh, a compassionate judge with four beautiful daughters — and numerous problems.

Cast: Judge Charles Raleigh: Robert Young; Susan Raleigh: Darleen Carr; Robin Raleigh: Judy Strangis; Jennifer Raleigh: Sharon Gless; Charlotte Raleigh: Fawne Harriman; Matthew Cunningham: Raymond Massey; Miss Freeling: Eve Arden.

Haunts of the Very Rich. Character studies of seven people who

are invited to fulfill their wildest fantasies at a mysterious hideaway.

Cast: Ellen Blunt: Cloris Leachman; Dave Woodbrough: Lloyd Bridges; Al Hunsicker: Edward Asner; Anette Larrier: Anne Francis; Laurie: Donna Mills; Mr. Fellows: Robert Reed; Lyle: Tony Bill.

The Crooked Hearts. The story of a pair of fortune hunting schemers who meet at a lonely hearts club — and secretly plan to steal each other's imagined wealth.

Cast: Laurita Dorsey: Rosalind Russell; Rex Willoughby: Douglas Fairbanks, Jr.; Daniel Shane: Ross Martin; Lillian Stanton: Maureen O'Sullivan; Frank Adamic: Michael Murphy.

The Last Child. A futuristic drama about a young couple who are expecting their first baby — and a population control law that dictates that the child must be killed.

Cast: Senator George: Van Heflin; Allen Miller: Michael Cole; Karen Miller: Janet Margolin; Howard Drumm: Harry Guardino; Barstow: Edward Asner; Iverson: Kent Smith.

THE ABC MOVIE OF THE WEEKEND—90 minutes—ABC—September 18, 1971–May 27, 1972.

THE ABC WEDNESDAY MOVIE OF THE WEEK—90 minutes—ABC—September 13, 1972–September 3, 1975.

THE ABC SHORT STORY SPECIAL

See title *The ABC Weekend Special.*

06   THE ABC SUSPENSE MOVIE

Movies. Suspense oriented, feature-length films produced especially for television.

Included:

Scream, Pretty Peggy. A mystery thriller about a rarely seen housekeeper in an unusual house run by a recluse mother and her son.

Cast: Mrs. Elliot: Bette Davis; Jeffrey Elliot: Ted Bessell; Peggy Johns: Sian Barbara Allen; George Thornton: Charles Drake; Agnes: Tovah Feldshuh; Dr. Saks: Allan Arbus.

The Devil and Miss Sarah. A Western thriller about a captured outlaw who plans to use his strange power over a woman to help him escape.

Cast: Rankin: Gene Barry; Sarah Turner: Janice Rule; Gil Turner: James Drury; Holmes: Logan Ramsey; Duncan: Charles McGraw; Stoney: Slim Pickens.

Maneater. A story of human intelligence vs. animal instinct as four vacationers attempt to escape two hungry tigers set on them by an insane animal trainer.

Cast: Brenner: Richard Basehart; Nick Baron: Ben Gazzara; Gloria Baron: Sheree North; Shep Sanders: Kip Niven; Polly: Laurette Spang; Paula Brenner: Claire Brennan.

You'll Never See Me Again. The story of a husband's frantic search to find his wife — who stormed out of the house after a violent argument and vowed never to return.

Cast: Ned Bliss: David Hartman; Mary Alden: Jane Wyatt; Will Alden: Ralph Meeker; Vicki Bliss: Jess Walton; Lt. John Stillman: Joseph Campanella; Bob Sellini: Colby Chester.

THE ABC SUSPENSE MOVIE—90 minutes—ABC—September 29, 1973–August 31, 1974.

07   ABC THEATRE

Anthology. Outstanding dramatic presentations.

Included:

Antony and Cleopatra. Shakespeare's romantic tragedy about Marc Antony, the brilliant Roman general whose infatuation with Cleopatra, Queen of the Nile, undermined his judgment and toppled his military empire.

Cast: Marc Antony: Richard Johnson; Cleopatra: Janet Suzman; Enobarbus: Patrick Stewart; Octavius Caesar: Corin Redgrave; Charmain: Rosemary McHale; Lepidus: Raymond Westwell; Octavia: Mary Rutherford.

Breaking Up. The story of a middle-aged housewife's attempts to cope with life after her marriage of 16 years ends in divorce.

Cast: JoAnn Hammil: Lee Remick; Tom Hammil: Granville Van Dusen; Amy: Vicky Dawson; T.C.: David Stambaugh; Tony: Fred Scollay; Edie: Cynthia Harris; Louise Crawford: Meg Mundy; Robert Crawford: Frank Latimore.

Eleanor and Franklin. A dramatization of the early life and personal crises of Eleanor and Franklin Roosevelt, distant cousins from socially prominent families, who married in 1905.

Cast: Eleanor Roosevelt: Jane Alexander; Franklin Roosevelt: Edward Herrmann; Sara Delano Roosevelt: Rosemary Murphy; Anna Hall: Pamela Franklin; Elliott Roosevelt, Sr.: David Huffman; Eleanor (age 14): Mackenzie Phillips; Theo-

dore Roosevelt: William Phipps; Laura Delano: Anna Lee.

The Women's Room. The story, which spans 19 years, depicts changing attitudes toward love and marriage as typified in the life of Mira Adams, a troubled divorcée seeking self-fulfillment.

Cast: Mira: Lee Remick; Lily: Patty Duke Astin; Val: Colleen Dewhurst; Ben: Gregory Harrison; Bliss: Kathryn Harrold; Iso: Tovah Feldshuh; Chris: Mare Winningham; Kyla: Lisa Pelikan.

ABC THEATRE—Varying Times (2 to 3 hours)—ABC—December 18, 1974–January 2, 1978. 12 programs.

08   THE ABC WEEKEND SPECIAL

Anthology. Varying presentations (comedy, drama, mystery) geared to children.

Music: Ray Ellis, John Cacavas, Tommy Leonetti, Dean Elliot.
Executive Producer: Allen Ducovny, Robert Chenault, Joe Ruby, Ken Spears.
Producer: William Beaudine, Jr., Tom Armistead, Jerry Isenberg.
Director: Hollingsworth Morse, Arthur H. Nadel, Ezra Stone, Larry Elikann.

Included:

The Girl With E.S.P. The story of Laura Hoffman, a pretty high school girl who feels overshadowed by her family until she discovers that she can predict the future.

Cast: Laura Hoffman: Rachel Longaker; Laura's mother: Barbara Sharma; Laura's father: Michael Griswold; Dennis Hoffman: Adam Starr; Beth: Lisa Alpert; Jill Hoffman: Tracy Bergman; Mr. Kane: Jonathan Harris.

The Winged Colt. The adventures of Coot, a former movie stuntman, and Charles, his greenhorn nephew, the owners of a mysterious colt born with wings.
Cast: Uncle Coot: Slim Pickens; Charles: Ike Eisenmann; Mrs. Minney: Jane Withers; Mr. Minney: Frank Cady; Hiram the Hermit: Keenan Wynn.

The Trouble With Miss Switch. An animated story about a student's attempts to save his teacher, a good witch, from banishment by other witches.

Voices: Janet Waldo, June Foray, Nancy McKeon, Eric Taslitz.

The Haunted Trailer. The story concerns Sharon Adams, a college coed, and her attempts, after purchasing a mobile home haunted by four elderly male ghosts, to find them a house to haunt.

Cast: Sharon Adams: Lauren Tewes; Mickey Adams, her sister: Monie Ellis; Clifford Tredwell, the ghost spokesman: Murray Matheson.

THE ABC WEEKEND SPECIAL— 30 minutes — ABC — September 10, 1977– May 27, 1978. Returned, Premiered: September 9, 1978. Also titled: *ABC Children's Novel for Television, The ABC Short Story Special,* and *The Out-Of-School Special.*

09 ABC WIDE WORLD OF ENTERTAINMENT

Anthology. A varying series of entertainment programs broadcast weeknights from 11:30 p.m. to 1 a.m. (EST).

Included:

A Little Bit Like Murder. A mystery thriller about a house, seemingly possessed by evil, that destroys its inhabitants.

Cast: Camilla: Elizabeth Hartman; Jeff: Roger Davis; Linda: Sharon Farrell; Nellie: Nina Foch; Mrs. Clay: Sharon Gless.

Bachelor of the Year. A spoof of beauty pageants wherein unmarried male celebrities vie for the title "Bachelor of the Year."

Hosts: Karen Valentine, Ken Berry.
Commentator: Pat Paulsen.

Sorority Kill. A suspense story about six young women held hostage by three fugitives in their sorority house.

Cast: Diane: JoAnna Cameron; Janice: Kathy Gackle; Mrs. Hiller: Martha Scott; Jim: Nicholas Hammond; Kirk: Tony Geary.

Marilyn Remembered. A documentary tracing the career of film star Marilyn Monroe.

Host: Peter Lawford.
Guest: Shelley Winters.
Film Clips Narrator: John Houston.

Hard Day at Blue Nose. A mystery thriller about a police investigation into the death of an attractive young woman.

Cast: Ad: Patty Duke Astin; Greenburg: John Astin; Claude: Mark Jenkins; Obie: Royal Dano; Pete: Jim Gannon; Leon: Erik Estrada.

Rock of the Sixties. Film-recorded performances by Rock personalities popular in the 1960s.

Host: Dick Clark.
Performers: The Rolling Stones, Chuck Berry, The Supremes,
James Brown, Smokey Robinson and the Miracles, Marvin Gaye, Jan and Dean, Gerry and the Pacemakers, Lesley Gore.

ABC WIDE WORLD OF ENTERTAINMENT— 90 minutes — ABC — January 8, 1973 – January 10, 1976.

10 THE ADAMS CHRONICLES

Biographical Drama. A profile of the Adamses, an historic American family that produced two U.S. Presidents and a Secretary of State.

CAST
John Quincy Adams	George Grizzard
	David Birney
	William Daniels
Abigail Adams, his wife	Kathryn Walker
	Tammy Heinz
	Leora Dana
Louisa Katherine Adams	Pamela Payton-Wright
Samuel Adams	W.B. Brydon
Thomas Adams	Asher Pergament
John Quincy Adams II	Steven Grover
	Mark Wentworth
	Nicholas Pryor
	Alan Carlsen
Minnie Adams	Patricia Elliott
Molly Adams	Julia Barr
Abigail Adams II	Lisa Lucas
	Katherine Houghton
	Nancy Coleman
Fanny Adams	Susan Bjurman
Charles Francis Adams II	J.C. Powell
	John Beal
	Philip Anglim
	Thomas A. Stewart
	Charles Siebert
Brook Adams	Charles Tenny
George Washington Adams	Donald Ellis
Thomas Adams	Tom V.V. Tommi
Justice Gridley	John Houseman
Mrs. Smith	Nancy Marchand
John Hancock	Curt Dawson
The Rev. Mr. Smith	Addison Powell
Jonathan Sewall	James Noble
Benjamin Franklin	Robert Symonds
Patrick Henry	William Shust
Count de Vergennes	Guy Sorel
Thomas Jefferson	Albert Stratton
Colonel Smith	Richard Cox
George III	John Tellinger
Jay Gould	Paul Hecht
Alexis de Toqueville	Jean-Pierre Stewart
Tappan	Jerome Dempsey
Cinque	Norman Bush
Abraham Lincoln	Stephen D. Newman
Lord Russell	Emery Battes
Czar Alexander I	Christopher Lloyd
Andrew Jackson	Wesley Addy
Henry Clay	Peter Brandon
	George Hearn
Pickering	Reid Shelton
Calhoun	Robert Phalen

Narrator: Michael Tolan.
Music: John Morris.
Producer: Virginia Kassel, Robert Costello, Paul Bogart, Jack Benza, George Bormis.
Director: Paul Bogart, Anthony Page.
Creator: Virginia Kassel.

THE ADAMS CHRONICLES — 60 minutes — PBS — January 20, 1976 – April 13, 1976. 13 episodes.

11 ADAMS OF EAGLE LAKE

Crime Drama. The story of Sam Adams, sheriff of Eagle Lake, a small, peaceful resort town, as he attempts to maintain law and order.

CAST
Sheriff Sam Adams	Andy Griffith
Margaret Kelly, his assistant	Abby Dalton
Officer Jerry Troy	Nick Nolte
Officer Jubal Hammond	Iggie Wolfington
Monty, a townsperson	Paul Winchell
Quinn, a townsperson	Sheldon Allman
Leonard, a townsperson	Eldon Quick
Lucas Pratt, a townsperson	William Mims

Sam's home address: 500 North Shore Road.
Music: Jerry Goldsmith, Harry Lojewski.
Executive Producer: Richard O. Linke.
Producer: Walter Grauman, Charles Stewart.
Writer: Charles Stewart, Jonathan Daly, Michael Hayes.
Director: Walter Grauman, Lawrence Dobkin.
Director of Photography: Robert B. Hauser.
Art Director: Stan Jolley.

ADAMS OF EAGLE LAKE — 60 minutes — ABC — August 23, 1975 – August 30, 1975. 2 episodes. See also "Winter Kill" in the pilot film section for information on the series pilot episode.

12 ADAM'S RIB

Comedy. The series, set in Los Angeles, focuses on the relationship between Adam Bonner, the assistant district attorney, and his wife Amanda, a lawyer with the firm of Kipple, Kipple and Smith, and the problems that arise when Amanda, as defense attorney, and Adam, as prosecuting attorney, are assigned to the same case. Adapted to television from the motion picture of the same title.

CAST
Adam Bonner (nickname "Pinky")	Ken Howard
Amanda Bonner (nickname "Pinkie")	Blythe Danner
Kip Kipple, Amanda's employer	Edward Winter
Grace Peterson, Amanda's secretary	Dena Dietrich
Roy Mendelsohn, Adam's partner	Ron Rifkin
Francis Donahue, the district attorney	Norman Bartold

Music: Perry Botkin, Jr.
Producer: William Froug.

ADAM'S RIB — 30 minutes — ABC — September 14, 1973 – December 28, 1973. 13 episodes.

13 ADAM-12

Crime Drama. The series, set in Los Angeles, realistically follows the day-to-day assignments of Pete Malloy and Jim Reed, police officers assigned to patrol car Adam-12.

CAST
Officer Pete Malloy	Martin Milner
Officer Jim Reed	Kent McCord
Sergeant MacDonald	William Boyett
Officer Ed Wells	Gary Crosby
Officer Woods	Fred Stromsoe
Officer Walters	William Stevens
Sgt. Jerry Miller	Jack Hogan
Jean Reed, Jim's wife	Mikki Jamison
Voice of the police radio dispatcher	Sharon Claridge
Captain Grant	Art Balinger
Lt. Tom Aston	Robert Dowdell
Sergeant Powers	Edward Faulkner
Detective Speer	Robert Patten
Detective Sanchez	Carlos Romero
Sergeant McCall	Chuck Bowman
Marilyn Wells, Pete's romantic interest; Ed's niece	Christina Sinatra
Paul Ryan, the district attorney	Robert Conrad
Mrs. O'Brien, Pete's landlady	Lillian Bronson
Betty Wells, Ed's wife	Barbara Baldavin
Officer Russo	Robert Rockwell
Lt. Val Wangsgard (early episodes)	Art Gilmore
Lieutenant Moore	Art Gilmore

Malloy's badge number: 2430.
Reed's badge number: 744.
Creator: Jack Webb.
Music: Frank Comstock.
Music Supervision: Stanley Wilson.
Executive Producer: Jack Webb, Herman S. Saunders.
Producer: Tom Williams, Jack Webb.
Director: Dennis Donnelly (most of the series), Leo Gordon, Ozzie Nelson, Jack Webb, Harry Morgan, Hollingsworth Morse, James Neilson, Stephen J. Cannell, Kenneth Johnson, Joseph Pevney, Alan Crosland, Jr., Lawrence Doheny, Harry Harris, Christian I. Nyby II.

ADAM-12 — 30 minutes — NBC — September 21, 1968 – August 26, 1975. Syndicated. 174 episodes.

14 THE ADDAMS FAMILY

Comedy. The story of the Addams family, the eccentric residents of a macabre house in an unnamed town on North Cemetery Ridge. Living in their own "real" world and believing themselves to be normal, they struggle to cope with the situations that foster their rejection by the outside world.

CAST
Morticia Addams, the mother	Carolyn Jones
Gomez Addams, the father	John Astin
Wednesday Addams, their daughter	Lisa Loring

Pugsley Addams,
    their son   Ken Weatherwax
Uncle Fester,
    Morticia's uncle   Jackie Coogan
Lurch, the zombie-like butler   Ted Cassidy
Grandmama Addams,
    Gomez's mother   Blossom Rock
Ophelia Frump,
    Morticia's sister   Carolyn Jones
Esther Frump,
    Ophelia's mother Margaret Hamilton
Cousin Itt, a family relative   Felix Silla
Mr. Briggs, the postman   Rolfe Sedan
Arthur J. Henson, the Addamses'
    insurance agent   Parley Baer
Horace Beesley, Henson's
    assistant   Eddie Quillan
Sam Hillard, the truant officer
    turned politician   Allyn Joslyn
Mother Lurch   Ellen Corby
Thing, the Addamses' servant,
    a human right hand   Itself*

Wednesday's doll: Marie Antoinette.
Addams Family pets: Kit Kat, a lion; Cleopatra, Morticia's man-eating African Strangler (a plant); Aristotle, Pugsley's octopus; and Homer, Wednesday's black widow spider.
The Addams address: 000 North Cemetery Lane.
Educational institute attended by Wednesday and Pugsley: The Sherwood School.
Creator: Charles Addams (developed for television by David Levy).
Music: Vic Mizzy.
Music Supervision: Dave Kahn.
Executive Producer: David Levy.
Producer: Nat Perrin.
Associate Producer: Harry Browar.
Director: Sidney Lanfield, Jean Yarbrough, Sidney Miller, Sidney Solkon, Jerry Hopper, Nat Perrin.
Art Director: Edwin Lilou.

THE ADDAMS FAMILY — 30 minutes — ABC — September 18, 1964 – September 2, 1966. Syndicated. 64 episodes.

*In an interview conducted on the series *Let's Go Go* in 1965, Ted Cassidy revealed that he played "Thing" in addition to his "Lurch" character.

15   THE ADDAMS FAMILY

Animated Cartoon. An updated version of the previous title. Stories relate the misadventures of the Addams family as they leave Cemetery Ridge and embark on a motor tour of America.

VOICES

Morticia Addams, the mother   Janet Waldo
Gomez Addams, the father   Lennie Weinrib
Wednesday Addams,
    their daughter   Cindy Henderson
Pugsley Addams, their son   Jodie Foster
Fester, Morticia's uncle   Jackie Coogan
Lurch, their butler   Ted Cassidy
Grandmama Addams,
    Gomez's mother   Janet Waldo

Additional Voices: Don Messick, Herb Vigran, Pat Harrington, Jr., Bob Holt, Howard Caine, John Stephenson.
Music: Hoyt Curtin.
Music Supervision: Paul DeKorte.
Executive Producer: William Hanna, Joseph Barbera.
Producer: Iwao Takamoto.
Director: Charles A. Nichols.

THE ADDAMS FAMILY — 30 minutes — NBC — September 8, 1973 – August 30, 1975.

16   THE ADDAMS FAMILY

Comedy. An extension episode of the original series in which the Addams family celebrate their favorite holiday: Halloween.

CAST

Morticia Addams,
    the mother   Carolyn Jones
Gomez Addams, her husband   John Astin
Wednesday Addams,
    their daughter   Lisa Loring
Pugsley Addams,
    their son   Ken Weatherwax
Fester, Morticia's uncle   Jackie Coogan
Lurch, their butler   Ted Cassidy
Grandmama Addams,
    Gomez's mother   Jane Rose
Ophelia Frump,
    Morticia's sister   Carolyn Jones
Cousin Itt, a relative   Felix Silla
Esther Frump,
    Ophelia's mother   Elvia Allman

Music: Vic Mizzy.
Executive Producer: Charles Fries.
Producer: David Levy.
Writer: George Tibbles.
Director: Dennis Steinmetz.

THE ADDAMS FAMILY — 90 minutes — NBC — Aired October 30, 1977. The episode, originally titled "Halloween with the Addams Family," has been syndicated as a movie.

17   THE ADVENTURER

Adventure. The story of Gene Bradley, a multimillionaire businessman turned U.S. government espionage agent. Episodes depict Bradley's exploits, posing as an international film star, as he attempts to carry out his assignments.

CAST

Agent Gene Bradley   Gene Barry
Mr. Parminter, his contact   Barry Morse
Diane Marsh, a contact   Catherine Schell
Gavin Jones, an agent posing
    as Bradley's accompanist,
    Wildman Jones   Garrick Hagon
Various roles   Stuart Damon

Music: John Barry.
Producer: Monty Berman.

THE ADVENTURER — 30 minutes — Syndicated in 1972. 26 episodes.

18   THE ADVENTURES OF BLACK BEAUTY

Adventure. While exploring the surroundings of their new home in Hartfordshire, England (1877), Victoria and Kevin Gordon, the teenage children of widower Dr. James Gordon, find an injured ebony stallion in the woods. While caring for the animal, Victoria develops a strong attachment for it, but is saddened to learn that its rightful owner, the elder Mr. Ryder, has claimed it. When fate intervenes and Dr. Gordon, with the aid of the horse's swiftness, saves Ryder's life, Ryder repays him by giving him the horse.

"I suppose he ought to have a name," Dr. Gordon comments after giving Victoria the horse. "Now let's see, Jet? Swift?" "No, they're not right," responds Victoria. "... Something that describes him. He's black, and he's very beautiful (pause) Black Beauty."

Stories depict the love, devotion and adventures shared by Victoria Gordon and her horse, Black Beauty. Based on the novel by Anna Sewell. Produced by London Weekend Television and Fremantle International.

CAST

Dr. James Gordon   William Lucas
Victoria Gordon, his daughter   Judi Bowker
Kevin Gordon, his son   Roderick Shaw
Amy Winthrop, their
    housekeeper   Charlotte Mitchell

Music: Dennis King.
Executive Producer: Paul Knight.
Producer: Sidney Cole.
Head Writer: Sir Ted Willis.
Writers: Richard Carpenter, Rosemary Sisson, Joy Thwaytes, Michael Watson.
Director: Charles Crichton, John Reardon.

THE ADVENTURES OF BLACK BEAUTY — 30 minutes — Syndicated 1972. 52 episodes.

19   THE ADVENTURES OF GULLIVER

Animated Cartoon. Adapted from Jonathan Swift's novel, *Gulliver's Travels*, which told of the voyages of Lemuel Gulliver. The series, set in the eighteenth century, follows the adventures of Lemuel's son Gary, who begins his own trek to find his missing father. His search begins on the island of Lilliput where, with the help of the six-inch tall Lilliputians, he seeks the clues necessary to end his quest.

VOICES

Gary Gulliver   Jerry Dexter
Flurtacia, a Lilliputian   Ginny Tyler
Eager, a Lilliputian   Jerry Dexter
Bunko, a Lilliputian   Allan Melvin
Edgar, a Lilliputian   Herb Vigran

King Pomp, the Lilliputian
    leader   John Stephenson
The Evil Captain Leech   John Stephenson
Tag, Gary's dog   Don Messick

Music Director: Ted Nichols.
Executive Producer: William Hanna, Joseph Barbera.
Producer: Charles A. Nichols.
Director: William Hanna, Joseph Barbera.

THE ADVENTURES OF GULLIVER — 30 minutes — ABC — September 14, 1969 – September 5, 1970. Syndicated.

20   THE ADVENTURES OF JONNY QUEST

Animated Cartoon. The global expeditions of Dr. Benton Quest and his young son, Jonny, as they search for answers to scientific mysteries.

VOICES

Dr. Benton Quest   John Stephenson
Jonny Quest, his son   Tim Matthieson
Roger "Race" Bannon, their
    bodyguard   Mike Road
Hadji, their traveling
    companion   Danny Bravo
Bandit, their dog   Don Messick

Music: Hoyt Curtin.
Music Director: Ted Nichols.
Executive Producer: William Hanna, Joseph Barbera.
Producer: Charles A. Nichols.
Writer: William Hanna, Joseph Barbera, Douglas Widley.
Director: William Hanna, Joseph Barbera.

THE ADVENTURES OF JONNY QUEST — 30 minutes. ABC: September 18, 1964 – September 9, 1965. CBS: September 9, 1967 – September 5, 1970. NBC: September 11, 1971 – September 2, 1972. Syndicated. 26 episodes.

21   THE ADVENTURES OF RIN TIN TIN

Adventure. Set in the 1880s. While on a routine patrol, the Fighting Blue Devils of the 101st Cavalry discover a young boy named Rusty and his dog Rin Tin Tin, the sole survivors of an Apache raid on a wagon train. The boy and his dog, brought to Fort Apache in Arizona, become the unofficial guardians of Lieutenant Rip Masters; Rusty is later made a corporal (to ensure his presence at the fort is within regulations) when he and Rin Tin Tin help foil an Indian plot to kill a visiting general.

The series focuses on the adventures of Corporal Rusty, his dog Rin Tin Tin, and their efforts to help the 101st Cavalry maintain the peace.

CAST

Corporal Rusty	Lee Aaker
Lt. Rip Masters	James L. Brown
Sgt. Biff O'Hara	Joe Sawyer
Corporal Randy Boone	Rand Brooks
Corporal Carson	Tommy Farrell
Corporal Clark	Hal Hopper
Major Swanson	William Forest
Colonel Barker	John Hoyt

Music: Hal Hopper.
Producer: Herbert B. Leonard, Fred Briskin.
Director: Robert G. Walker, Lew Landers, Charles Gould, Earl Bellamy, Douglas Heyes, Fred Jackman.
Rin Tin Tin Owned and Trained By: Lee Duncan.

THE ADVENTURES OF RIN TIN TIN—30 minutes. ABC: October 15, 1954–September 22, 1961. CBS: September 29, 1962–September 19, 1964. Syndicated. 164 episodes. In 1975, the original stories were resyndicated in sepia tint. New opening and closing segments, filmed in color in Utah, were added. James L. Brown, recreating his role of Lt. Rip Masters, appeared to relate stories of Rusty and his dog to a group of children visiting the fort.

22   A.E.S. HUDSON STREET

Comedy. A satirization of medical series as seen through the antics of the staff of a poorly equipped Adult Emergency Service (A.E.S.) hospital on Hudson Street on the lower East Side of Manhattan in New York City. (In the pilot film, A.E.S. is referred to as the Ambulance Emergency Service.)

CAST

Dr. Tony Menzies (pilot episode)	F. Murray Abraham
Dr. Tony Menzies (series)	Gregory Sierra
Nurse Rosa Santiago	Rosana Soto
Nurse Rhonda Todd	Julienne Wells
Foshko, the ambulance driver	Susan Peretz
Stawky, Foshko's assistant	Ralph Manza
Nurse Newton	Ray Stewart
Karbow, the hospital administrator (pilot episode)	Irwin C. Watson
Karbow (series)	Stefan Gierasch
Dr. Jerry Meckler	Bill Cort
Dr. Glick, the psychiatrist	Allan Miller
Dr. Sorrentino	Jane Marla Robbins
Dr. Friedman	Bob Dishy

Creator: Danny Arnold, Tony Sheenan, Chris Hayward.
Music: Jack Elliott, Allyn Ferguson.
Executive Producer: Danny Arnold.
Producer: Roland Kibbee.
Director: Noam Pitlik.

A.E.S. HUDSON STREET—30 minutes—ABC—March 16, 1978–April 20, 1978. 5 episodes. The pilot film aired on ABC on July 21, 1977.

23   AFTER BENNY, THAMES PRESENTS . . .

Comedy. Episodes from various Thames-produced television series that are broadcast in the United States after *The Benny Hill Show* under the umbrella title *After Benny, Thames Presents.* Series episodes, which begin with a short skit from *The Benny Hill Show,* then an announcer intoning "After Benny, Thames Presents," are comprised of adult oriented comedy sketches.

Included Series:
Cribbins.
Starring: Bernard Cribbins.
Regulars: Bob Todd, Sheila Steafel, Jerri Campbell, Carol Friday, Jan Butlin, Terence Brady, Ted Barrett.
Writer-Creator: Johnnie Mortimer, Brian Cooke.
Music: Ted Dicks, Ted Brennan, Geoffrey Love.
Producer-Director: Alan Tarrant.

The Tommy Cooper Show.
Starring: Tommy Cooper.
Creator-Writer: Johnnie Mortimer, Brian Cooke.
Music: Norman Stevens.
Producer-Director: Royston Moyoh.

What's On Next?
Starring: William Franklyn.
Regulars: Anna Dawson, Bob Todd, Ann Denere, Sanda Dickinson, Pam Ayres, Jim Davidson, Linda Lou Allen, Anne Bruzac, Barry Cryer.
Creator: Johnnie Mortimer, Brian Cooke.
Music Director: Sam Harding.
Writer: Barry Cryer, David Renwick, Bernie Sharp, John Junkin, Eddie Braben.
Producer-Director: Mark Stuart.

AFTER BENNY, THAMES PRESENTS . . .—30 minutes—Syndicated 1980.

24   AGAINST THE WIND

Drama. An Australian produced miniseries that follows the life of Mary Mulvane, a spirited Irishwoman. The story, which begins in Ireland, in 1796, explores the hardships that faced many poor Irishmen at the time: exploitive landlords, corrupt church agents, and oppressive British rule that denied the Irish their political freedom. To demonstrate the harsh realities, the series follows the plight of Mary Mulvane, the daughter of a poor family, who rebels against the system. Her ill-fated efforts cause her to be sentenced to seven years of penal service in Australia. Mary's life in the Australian colony of New South Wales, as she fights for freedom and dignity, is dramatized.

CAST

Mary Mulvane	Mary Larkin
Michael Connor, her friend	Bryan Brown
Mrs. Mulvane, Mary's mother	Roz de Winter
Francis Mulvane, Mary's father	Peter Gwynne
Polly McNamara, Mary's friend	Kerry McGuire
Jonathan Garrett, Mary's husband	Jon English
Will Price, the innkeeper	Frank Gallacher
Lt. Morris Grenville	Warwick Sims
Charles Wiltshire, Garrett's employer	Fred Parslow
Louisa Wiltshire, Charles' wife	Lynn Rainbow
Captain Dennott	Tim Elliott
Dinny O'Byrne, Garrett's friend	Gerald Kennedy
Dinny's wife	Justine Saunders

Creator: Ian Jones, Bronwyn Binns.
Music: Jon English, Mario Millo.
Executive Producer: Ian Jones, Bronwyn Binns.
Producer: Henry Crawford.
Writer: Tom Hegerty, Ian Jones, Bronwyn Binns.
Director: Simon Winger, George Miller.
Art Director: Tracy Watt, Clive Jones.

AGAINST THE WIND—2 hours—Syndicated—August 26, 1979–September 1, 1979 (dates on which it was broadcast nationally over Metromedia stations). 6 episodes. The first major Australian TV production to be broadcast in the United States.

25   ALIAS SMITH AND JONES

Western. The series, set in Kansas during the 1890s, follows the misadventures of Jed "Kid" Curry and Hannibal Heyes, leaders of the infamous Devil Hole Gang and two of the West's most wanted outlaws, as they attempt to end their lives of crime and go straight.

Unable to crack newly developed safes and hoping to begin a new life, Curry and Heyes approach the governor and are granted a provisional amnesty, which will become a full pardon if, within twelve months, they can prove themselves worthy. Leaving the Devil Hole Gang, Curry and Heyes adopt the aliases Thaddeus Jones (Curry) and Joshua Smith (Heyes). Episodes depict their misadventures as they roam the Kansas Territory trying to keep clear of troublesome situations that could endanger their pardons.

CAST

Jed "Kid" Curry / Thaddeus Jones	Ben Murphy
Hannibal Heyes / Joshua Smith	Peter Deul
	Roger Davis
Sheriff Lom Trevors, their friend	James Drury
	Mike Road
Harry Briscoe, the Batterman detective seeking Curry and Heyes	J.D. Cannon
The Devil Hole Gang:	
Wheat	Earl Holliman
Lobo	Read Morgan
Kyle	Dennis Fimple
Recurring Roles (friends of Curry and Heyes):	
Clementine Hale	Sally Field
Big Mac McCreedy, a rancher	Burl Ives
Silky O'Sullivan	Walter Brennan
Blackjack Jenny, the card shark	Ann Sothern
Georgette Sinclair	Michele Lee
Winford Fletcher, the real estate broker	Rudy Vallee

Opening Theme Narration: Roger Davis.
Creator: Glen A. Larson.
Music: Bob Prince, Billy Goldenberg.
Executive Producer: Roy Huggins.
Producer: Glen A. Larson.
Director: Barry Shear, Bruce Kessler, Edward Abroms, Alexander Singer, David Moessinger, Arnold Laven, Douglas Heyes, Jeff Corey, Fernando Lamas, Leslie H. Martinson, Jeannot Szwarc, Vincent Sherman, Jack Arnold, Richard L. Bare, Gene Levitt, Richard Benedict, Harry Falk, Russ Mayberry, Mel Ferber.

ALIAS SMITH AND JONES—60 minutes—ABC—January 21, 1971–January 13, 1973. 48 episodes. Syndicated. The 90-minute pilot film aired on ABC on January 5, 1971.

26   ALICE

Comedy. The story of Alice Hyatt, aspiring singer and widowed mother, and her attempts to provide a decent life for herself and her 12-year-old son, Tommy. Her misadventures, working as a waitress at Mel's Diner, a less than fashionable café in Phoenix, Arizona, are depicted. Based on the film *Alice Doesn't Live Here Anymore.*

CAST

Alice Hyatt	Linda Lavin
Tommy Hyatt, her son (pilot film)	Alfred Lutter
Tommy Hyatt (series)	Philip McKeon
Florence Jean Castleberry (Flo), the sexy, loud-mouthed waitress	Polly Holliday
Mel Sharples, the owner of the diner	Vic Tayback
Vera Louise Gorman, the shy, clumsy waitress	Beth Howland
Belle, the waitress who replaced Flo*	Diane Ladd
Andy, a diner customer	Pat Cranshaw
Travis, a diner customer	Tom Mahoney
Earl Hicks, Flo's friend	Dave Madden
Marie Massey, Mel's girlfriend	Victoria Carroll

Carrie Sharples, Mel's
 mother   Martha Raye
Robbie Mitchell, Carrie's fiancé,
 later husband   Howard Witt
Henry, a diner customer Marvin Kaplan
Debbie, Tommy's
 girlfriend   Annrae Walterhouse

Creator: Robert Getchell.
Music: David Shire.
Theme: "There's a New Girl in
 Town" by Alan and Marilyn
 Bergman (lyrics) and David
 Shire (music).
Theme Vocal: Linda Lavin.
Executive Producer: David
 Susskind, William P. D'Angelo,
 Ray Allen, Harvey Bullock,
 Thomas Kuhn.
Producer: Bruce Johnson, Made-
 lyn Davis, Bob Carroll, Jr.
Associate Producer: Jerry Mad-
 den.
Director: Bill Hobin, Bill Persky,
 Jim Drake, James Sheldon,
 Norman Abbott, William P.
 D'Angelo, Marc, Daniels, Lee
 Lochhead, Gary Shimokawa,
 Linda Lavin, William Asher, Kim
 Friedman, Paul Bogart.

ALICE — 30 minutes — CBS —
Premiered: September 29, 1976.
The pilot episode aired on CBS
on August 31, 1976. Spin-off series: *Flo.*

*The character "Flo" left the series on
 February 24, 1980 for a waitress job
 in Houston. The spin-off series, *Flo*
 then evolved.

27   ALL ABOUT FACES

Game. Two teams, composed of
two celebrity members, compete.
A film, which involves unsuspecting people in a prearranged situation, is stopped prior to its
conclusion. Based on the facial
expressions and mannerisms of
the people involved, the teams
have to predict the outcome —
whether or not the individual
went along with the situation.
Teams begin with fifty dollars and
bet money as they wish. After the
bets, the film is played to reveal
the outcome. Money is awarded
or deducted accordingly. Winning teams (highest scorers) do-
nate their earnings to charity.

Host: Richard Hayes.
Candid Film Sequences Cast:
 Glenna Jones, Ken Deas, Andy
 Kunkel.
Music: John Michael Hill, Gordon
 Fleming.
Executive Producer: Dan Enright.
Producer: David B. Fein.
Studio Portions Director: Bill
 Burrows.
Film Portions Director: Dan
 Enright.

ALL ABOUT FACES — 30
minutes — Syndicated 1971. 130
programs.

28   ALL IN THE FAMILY

Comedy. The story of the Bunkers, a white middle-class Anglo-
Saxon American family: Archie, a
dock foreman for the Prendergast
Tool and Dye Company (in later
episodes, the owner of a bar
called "Archie Bunker's Place"), a
prejudiced, uncouth, loud-
mouthed, hardhat conservative
who is unable to accept a changing America; Edith, his dim-
witted, sensitive and totally honest wife; Gloria, their married
daughter, beautiful and independent; and Mike Stivic, Gloria's
husband, an unemployed, idealistic college student (in later episodes, a college instructor).
Through the events that befall
and test the reactions of the
Bunker and Stivic families,
American television comedy was
led out of infancy and into maturity. The series, which reveals the
little traces of Archie Bunker that
are within everyone, allows the
viewer to laugh at his own flaws
as it presents life as it is: rampant
with bigotry and racism.

CAST
Archie Bunker   Carroll O'Connor
Edith Bunker ("Dingbat") Jean Stapleton
Gloria Stivic   Sally Struthers
Mike Stivic ("Meathead")   Rob Reiner
Joey Stivic, Gloria and
 Mike's son   Corey Miller
                       Jason Drager
Barney Hefner, Archie's friend Allan Melvin
George Jefferson, their
 neighbor   Sherman Hemsley
Louise Jefferson,
 George's wife   Isabel Sanford
Lionel Jefferson, their son   Mike Evans
Henry Jefferson, Lionel's uncle Mel Stewart
Irene Lorenzo, Archie's
 neighbor   Betty Garrett
Frank Lorenzo, Irene's
 husband   Vincent Gardenia
Bert Munson, Archie's friend,
 the cab driver   Billy Halop
Tommy Kelsey, Archie's
 friend, the owner of
 Kelsey's Bar   Brendon Dillon
                      Bob Hastings
                      Frank Maxwell
Jerome "Stretch" Cunningham,
 Archie's co-worker James Cromwell
Teresa Betancourt, the
 Bunker's boarder   Liz Torres
Mildred "Boom Boom" Turner,
 Archie's waitress   Gloria LeRoy
Harry Snowden, Archie's
 bartender   Jason Wingreen
Stephanie Mills, the daughter of
 Edith's cousin Floyd; now
 being cared for by
 the Bunkers   Danielle Brisebois
Blanche Heffner, Barney's
 wife   Estelle Parsons
Justin Quigley, a friend of
 Edith's   Burt Mustin
Jo Nelson, Justin's girlfriend Ruth McDevitt
Maude Findlay, Edith's
 cousin   Beatrice Arthur
Carol, Maude's daughter   Marcia Rodd
Walter Findlay, Maude's husband Bill Macy

The Bunkers' address: 704
Houser Street, Queens, New
York.
Archie's lodge: The Kings of
Queens.
Announcer: John Rich, Rob
 Reiner.
Music: Roger Kellaway.
Opening Theme: "Those Were the
 Days" by Charles Strouse
 (music) and Lee Adams
 (lyrics).
Closing Theme: "Remembering
 You" by Roger Kellaway
 (music) and Carroll O'Connor
 (lyrics).
Executive Producer: Norman
 Lear, Woody Kling, Hal Kanter,
 Mort Lachman, Don Nicholl.
Producer: Lou Derman, Brigit
 Jensen, John Rich, Milt
 Josefsberg, Michael Ross, Ber-
 nie West, Bill Danoff.
Director: Paul Bogart, John Rich,
 H. Wesley Kenney.
Art Director: Don Roberts.

ALL IN THE FAMILY — 30
minutes — CBS — January 12,
1971 — September 16, 1979. Syndicated. 207 episodes. Spin-off
series: *Archie Bunker's Place, The
Jeffersons,* and *Maude.* See also
Till Death Us Do Part for information on the British series on
which *All in the Family* is based.

29   ALL MY CHILDREN

Serial. The dramatic story of the
Tyler family, residents of the
community of Pine Valley. Episodes depict the conflicts and
tensions that arise from the interactions of the characters.

CAST
Phoebe Tyler   Ruth Warrick
Amy Tyler   Rosemary Prinz
Ann Tyler   Diana de Vegh
                     Beverley Owen
                     Judith Barcroft
Paul Martin   Ken Rabat
                     Bill Mooney
Mary Kennicott   Susan Blanchard
Kate Martin   Kay Campbell
                     Christine Thomas
Ruth Brent   Mary Fickett
Jeff Martin   Christopher Wines
                     Charles Frank
                     Robert Perault
                     James O'Sullivan
Dr. Charles Tyler   Hugh Franklin
Tara Martin   Karen Gorney
                     Stephanie Braxton
                     Nancy Frangione
Lois Sloane   Hilda Haynes
Mona Kane   Frances Heflin
Nick Davis   Larry Keith
Erica Kane   Susan Lucci
Dr. Joseph Martin   Ray MacDonnell
Lincoln Tyler   Paul DuMont
                     Nicholas Pryor
                     Peter White
Sydney Scott   Deborah Soloman
Kitty Shea   Francesca James

Jason Maxwell   Tom Rosqui
Edie Hoffman   Marilyn Chris
Bill Hoffman   Michael Shannon
Margo Flax   Eileen Letchworth
Clyde Wheeler   Kevin Conway
Philip Brent   Richard Hatch
                     Nicholas Benedict
Dr. Hoffman   Peter Simon
Franklin Grant   John Danelle
Ted Brent   Mark Dawson
Bobby Martin   Mike Bersell
Nancy Grant   Avis MacArthur
                     Lisa Wilkinson
Hal Short   Dan Hamilton
Little Philip Tyler   Ian Miller Washam
                     Brian Lima
Dr. Marcus Polk   Norman Rose
Mark Dalton   Mark LaMura
Myrtle Lum   Eileen Herlie
David Thornton   Paul Gleason
Maureen Teller   Rosemary Murphy
Ellen Shepherd   Kathleen Noone
Danny Kennicott   Daren Kelly
Donna Beck   Francesca Poston
                     Candice Earley
Brooke English   Elissa Leeds
                      Julia Barr
Dr. Christina Karras   Robin Strasser
Carolyn Murphy   Pat Dixon
Benny Sago   Larry Fleischman
Edna Thornton   Sandy Gabriel
Tom Cudahy   Richard Shoberg
Tad Gardner Martin   Matthew Anton
                     John E. Dunn
Charles Tyler II   Jack Stauffer
                     Chris Hubbell
                     Richard Van Vleet
Dr. Cliff Warner   Peter Bergman
Father Tierney   Mel Boudrot
Dottie Thornton   Dawn Marie Boyle
Betsy Kennicott   Carla Oragoni
Langley Wallingford   Louis Edmonds
Wally McFadden   Jack Magee
Nina Cortlandt   Taylor Miller
Palmer Cortlandt   James Mitchell
Freddie   Fred Porcell
Devon McFadden   Tricia Pursley
Littie Jean   Judith Roberts
Nancy Blair   Lisa Wilkinson
Donna Tyler   Candice Manera
Mel Jacobi   Chris Wallace
Adrian Shepherd   Bob Hover
Eddie Dorrance   Warren Burton
Billy Clyde Tuggle   Matthew Cowles
Estelle Tuggle   Kathleen Dezina
Harlan Tucker   William Griffis
Devon Shepherd   Tricia Pursley Hawkins
Kelly Cole   Francesca James
Claudette Montgomery Paulette Breen
                     Susan Plantt-Winston

Musical Director: James Reichert.
Creator: Agnes Nixon.
Producer: John Winther, Bud
 Kloss, Felicia Behr.
Writer: Agnes Nixon, Wisner
 Washam, Jack Wood, Mary K.
 Wells, Ken Harvey, Cathy
 Chicos, Anita Jaffe, William
 Delligan.
Director: Del Hughes, Henry Kap-
 lan, Jack Coffy, Sherrell
 Hoffman, Jean Dadario, Diana
 Wenman.

ALL MY CHILDREN — 30 min-
utes — ABC — January 5, 1970 —
April 22, 1977. 60 minutes: Premiered: April 25, 1977.

ABC Tuesday Movie of the Week: The Sex Symbol. Connie Stevens.

ABC Theatre: Antony and Cleopatra. Janet Suzman and Richard Johnson. Courtesy of the Independent Television Corporation.

All's Fair. Richard Crenna and Bernadette Peters.

The American Girls. From left, Debra Clinger, David Spielberg and Priscilla Barnes.

30   THE ALL-NEW POPEYE HOUR

Animated Cartoon. The overall title for two series: *Popeye the Sailor* and *Dinky Dog*.

Popeye the Sailor. A television adaptation of the 1930s and 40s theatrical cartoon hero. The series continues to follow the exploits of Popeye, the sailor who, with the aid of the incredible strength he derives from spinach, protects the good against evil.

VOICES

Popeye the Sailor	Jack Mercer
Olive Oyl, his girlfriend	Marilyn Schreffler
Bluto, their nemesis	Allan Melvin
Wimpy, Popeye's friend	Daws Butler
The Evil Sea Hag	Marilyn Schreffler

Dinky Dog. The story of a family that is plagued by the antics of a very large and mischievous dog.

VOICES

Uncle Dudley, the unfortunate owner of Dinky	Frank Nelson
Sandy, his niece	Jackie Joseph
Monica, his niece	Jean VanderPyl
Dinky Dog	Daws Butler

Additional Voices: Roger Behr, Julie Bennett, Ross Martin, Hal Smith, Pat Parris, William Schallert, Joan Gerber, John Stephenson, Ted Cassidy.
Music: Hoyt Curtin.
Executive Producer: William Hanna, Joseph Barbera.
Producer: Alex Lovy.
Creative Producer: Iwao Takamoto.
Writer: Glenn Leopold, Dalton Sandefer, Jack Hanrahan, Tom Dagenais.
Director: Ray Patterson, Carl Urbano.

THE ALL-NEW POPEYE HOUR — 55 minutes — CBS — Premiered: September 9, 1978.

31   ALL'S FAIR

Comedy. A political satire set in Washington, D.C., focuses on the unlikely relationship between Richard Barrington III, a 49-year-old conservative newspaper columnist, and Charlotte "Charlie" Drake, a beautiful 23-year-old free-lance photographer.

CAST

Richard Barrington III	Richard Crenna
Charlotte "Charlie" Drake	Bernadette Peters
Al Brooks, Richard's assistant	J.A. Preston
Ginger Livingston, Charlie's roommate	Judy Kahan
Lucy Daniels, a CBS-TV newswriter; later Al's wife	Lee Chamberlain
Senator Wayne Joplin, Richard's adversary	Jack Dodson
Barbara Murray, Richard's agent	Salome Jens
Lenny Wolf, President Carter's joke writer; Ginger's romantic interest	Michael Keaton

Music: Jeff Barry.
Executive Producer: Rod Parker.
Producer: Bob Weiskopf, Bob Schiller, Michael Elias.
Director: Hal Cooper, Bob Claver.

ALL'S FAIR — 30 minutes — CBS — September 20, 1976 – August 15, 1977. 22 episodes.

32   ALL STAR ANYTHING GOES

Game. Two three- (or four-) member teams, each composed of celebrities from the entertainment world, compete in various outlandish games — just for the fun of it.

Host: Bill Boggs.
Play-by-play Description: Jim Healy.
Score Girl: Judy Abercrombie.
Executive Producer: Bob Banner.
Producer: Sam Riddle.
Director: Louis J. Horvitz.

ALL STAR ANYTHING GOES — 30 minutes — Syndicated September 1977.

33   ALL STAR SECRETS

Game. One of three competing contestants pushes a button and establishes a money score from a series of flashing numbers. A true secret regarding one of four (of five guest) celebrities is read. The one celebrity to whom the secret will not refer seeks to help the contestants by predicting the celebrity to whom the secret does pertain. Each contestant locks in the name of the celebrity he believes is the subject of the secret (a personal happening from the star's past). The celebrity to whom the secret refers is revealed and the previously established money is scored accordingly: split three ways if each contestant is correct; divided in half if two are correct; or awarded entirely to the player with the only correct response. Winners, who receive the money they've won, are the highest scorers.

Host: Bob Eubanks.
Announcer: Charlie O'Donnell.
Music: Lee Ringuette.
Executive Producer: Bob Eubanks, Michael Hill.
Supervising Producer: Walt Case.
Producer: Earl Durham.
Director: Bill Carruthers, Chris Darley.
Creator: Michael Hill.

ALL STAR SECRETS — 30 minutes — NBC — January 8, 1979 – August 10, 1979. 150 episodes.

34   ALL THAT GLITTERS

Comedy Drama. An off-beat series that reverses the male-female role to focus on a society wherein the women are the workers and the men the housekeepers and secretaries. Serial-type episodes relate the harried existences of the female executives of the Globatron Corporation, a large conglomerate.

CAST

Christina Stockwood, a Globatron executive	Lois Nettleton
Nancy Langston, same as Christina	Anita Gillette
L.W. Carruthers, the head of Globatron	Barbara Baxley
Andrea Martin, a lawyer	Louise Shaffer
Bert Stockwood, Christina's husband	Chuck McCann
Linda Murkland, a model	Linda Gray
Glenn Langston, Nancy's husband	Wes Parker
Michael McFarland, Andrea's romantic interest	David Haskell
Grace Smith "Smitty," a Globatron executive	Marte Boyle Slout
Dan Kincaid, a Globatron secretary	Gary Sandy
Peggy Horner, a Globatron executive	Vanessa Brown
Joan Hamlyn, a theatrical agent	Jessica Walter
Jeremy Stockwood, Christina's son	Jim Greenleaf
Ma Packer, the kidnapper	Eileen Brennan
Sonny Packer, her son	Tim Thomserson

Also: Greg Evigan.

Music: Alan and Marilyn Bergman.
Theme Vocal: Kenny Rankin.
Instrumentals: Shelly Mann, Ray Brown.
Executive Producer: Stephanie Sills.
Producer: Viva Knight.
Director: Herbert Kenwith, Jim Frawley.
Developed by: Norman Lear.

ALL THAT GLITTERS — 30 minutes — Syndicated 1977.

35   ALMOST ANYTHING GOES

Game. Three teams, each composed of six members and representing towns with a population of less than 15,000, compete. The players, all of whom are amateurs, compete in a series of stunt contests. The team that acquires the highest score at the end of a seventh game is the winner and receives the opportunity to compete in the national finals, which pit three of the highest scoring teams against each other. A trophy is awarded to the team that proves itself superior in the playoffs.

Hosts: Charlie Jones, Lynn Shakelford, Sam Riddle.
Field Interviewers: Dick Wittington, Regis Philbin.
Executive Producer: Bob Banner, Beryl Vertue.
Producer: Jeff Harris, Robert Stigwood, Camilla Dunn.
Director: Mark Hemion, Kip Walton.

ALMOST ANYTHING GOES — 60 minutes — ABC — July 31, 1975 – August 28, 1975; January 24, 1976 – May 9, 1976.

36   ALVIN AND THE CHIPMUNKS

Animated Cartoon. The misadventures of Dave Seville, a songwriter and manager of the Chipmunks (Alvin, Theodore and Simon), a group of singing animals. Stories revolve around Seville's reluctant involvement in the Chipmunks' unpredictable antics.

VOICES

Dave Seville	Ross Bagdasarian
Alvin, Theodore, and Simon	Ross Bagdasarian

Music: Ross Bagdasarian.
Producer: Herbert Klynn.
Director: Rudy Lariva, Osmond Evans.

ALVIN AND THE CHIPMUNKS — 30 minutes — NBC — April 10, 1979 – September 1, 1979. Originally broadcast on CBS as *The Alvin Show* from October 14, 1961 to September 12, 1962.

37   A.M. AMERICA

Variety. News and information coupled with celebrity interviews. Broadcast from 7-9 a.m. (EST).

East Coast Hosts: Bill Beutel, Stephanie Edwards.
West Coast Hosts: Ralph Story, Melanie Noble.
Guest Hostesses: Jessica Walter, Barbara Feldon, Lynn Redgrave, Rene Carpenter, Candice Bergan, Barbara Howar.
Newscaster: Peter Jennings.
Regulars: Roger Caras, Dr. Sonya Friedman, Dr. Tim Johnson.
Producer: Jules Power.

A.M. AMERICA — 2 hours — ABC — January 6, 1975 – October 31, 1975. Revised as *Good Morning, America.*

38   THE AMATEUR'S GUIDE TO LOVE

Game. A taped, prearranged romantic situation, which involves unsuspecting individuals, is played and stopped prior to its conclusion. Two of the subjects involved in the situation appear opposite a panel of three guest celebrities, "The Guidebook Experts." The celebrities first advise as to what the outcome of the situation should be, then predict the subjects' answers — whether or not they actively involved themselves in it. The tape is played to reveal the answers. The subject receives $200 if the celebrities predicted correctly; $100 if they were wrong.

Host: Gene Rayburn.
Announcer: Kenny Williams.
Candid Sequences Performer: Barbara Crosby.
Executive Producer: Merrill Heatter, Bob Quigley.
Producer: Robert Noah.
Studio Director: Jerome Shaw.
Location Director: Don Stern.

THE AMATEUR'S GUIDE TO LOVE — 30 minutes — CBS — March 27, 1972 – June 23, 1972. 65 tapes.

39   THE AMAZING CHAN AND THE CHAN CLAN

Animated Cartoon. The investigations of Charlie Chan, a Chinese detective who specializes in solving baffling crimes. Plots concern the intervention of his ten children and their meaningful, but disastrous efforts to assist him.

VOICES

Charlie Chan	Keye Luke
His Children:	
Henry Chan	Robert Ito
Stanley Chan	Stephen Wong
	Lennie Weinrib
Suzie Chan	Virginia Ann Lee
	Cherylene Lee
Alan Chan	Brian Tochi
Anne Chan	Leslie Kumamota
	Jodie Foster
Tom Chan	Michael Takamoto
	John Gunn
Flip Chan	Jay Jay Jue
	Gene Andrusco
Nancy Chan	Debbie Jue
	Beverly Kushida
Mimi Chan	Leslie Kawai
	Cherylene Lee
Scooter Chan	Robin Toma
	Michael Morgan
Also:	
Chu Chu, the clan dog	Don Messick

Additional Voices: Lisa Gerritsen, Hazel Shermit, Janet Waldo, Len Wood.
Music: Hoyt Curtin.
Executive Producer: William Hanna, Joseph Barbera.
Producer: Alex Lovy.
Director: William Hanna, Joseph Barbera.
Animation Director: Charles A. Nichols.

THE AMAZING CHAN AND THE CHAN CLAN — 30 minutes — CBS — September 9, 1972 – September 22, 1974. Syndicated.

40   THE AMAZING SPIDER-MAN

Adventure. Following a demonstration on radioactivity, Peter Parker, a graduate student at Empire State University, is bitten by a spider that had been exposed to the deadly effects of the demonstration. Shortly after, Peter realizes that the spider's venom has become part of his bloodstream and he has absorbed the proportionate power and ability of a living spider. Hoping to use his new abilities to battle evil, Parker develops a special costume to conceal his true identity and, to be able to learn of crimes immediately, he acquires a position as a part-time photographer for the *New York Daily Bugle.* The series depicts Parker's battle against crime as the mysterious Spider-Man.

CAST

Peter Parker / Spider-Man	Nicholas Hammond
Spider-Man (stunt sequences)	Fred Waugh
J. Jonah Jameson, editor of the *Bugle* (pilot episode)	David White
J. Jonah Jameson (series)	Robert F. Simon
Police Captain Barbera	Michael Pataki
Rita Conway, Jonah's secretary	Chip Fields
Julie Masters, a rival freelance photographer	Ellen Bry

Music: Stu Phillips, Dana Kaproff.
Executive Producer: Charles Fries, Daniel R. Goodman.
Producer: Robert Janes, Ron Satlof, Lionel E. Siegel.
Director: Ron Satlof, Fernando Lamas, Dennis Donnelly, Cliff Bole, Larry Stewart, Tom Blank, Joseph Manduke.

THE AMAZING SPIDER-MAN — 60 minutes — CBS. April 5, 1978 – May 3, 1978. September 5, 1978 – September 12, 1978. Additional episodes aired on the following dates: November 25, 1978; December 30, 1978; February 7, 1979; February 21, 1979; and July 6, 1979. 12 episodes total. The 90-minute pilot film aired on CBS on September 14, 1977.

41   AMERICA

History. A thirteen-episode "personal history" of the United States. The country is explored through historical paintings and commentary from its founding to the twentieth century. Filmed by the BBC.

Host-Narrator: Alistair Cooke.
Music: Charles Chilton, William Davies.
Executive Producer: Michael Gill.
Producer-Director: Ann Turner.

AMERICA — 60 minutes — NBC — November 14, 1972 – May 15, 1973. Syndicated. 13 episodes.

42   AMERICA ALIVE!

Variety. A daily series of interviews, music and news reports.

Host: Jack Linkletter.
Co-hosts: Janet Langhart, Bruce Jenner, Pat Mitchell.
Regulars: David Horowitz, Virginia Graham, David Sheehan.
Music Theme: Don Costa.
Music: Elliot Lawrence.
Executive Producer: Woody Fraser.
Producer: Susan Winston, Kenny Price, Marty Berman, Joan Auritt.
Senior Director: Don King, Bob Coudin.

AMERICA ALIVE! — 60 minutes — NBC — July 24, 1978 – January 5, 1979. 104 programs.

43   AMERICA 2-NIGHT

Satire. A spin-off from *Fernwood Tonight,* which see. Unable to raise the necessary funds to continue his local talk show in Ohio, Barth Gimble relocates to fictional Alta Coma, California, "the unfinished furniture capitol of the world," where he becomes the host of "America 2-Night" over the U.B.S. (United Broadcasting System) Network ("The Network that puts U before the B.S."). The series, which spoofs talk-variety programs, presents interviews with well-known celebrities as well as the most grotesque people imaginable.

Host: Martin Mull as the conceited Barth Gimble.
Announcer: Fred Willard as the dim-witted Jerry Hubbard.
Music: Frank DeVol (as Happy Kyne) and his Orchestra (the Mirth Makers).
Regulars: Michelle and Tanya Della Fave (singers-dancers), Kenneth Mars (as William W.B. "Bud" Prize, the talent scout), Jim Varney (as Virgil Simms, the mobile home daredevil; he uses a mobile home, instead of a motorcycle to perform daring feats), Bill Kirchenbauer (as Tony Roletti, the lounge singer).
Producer: Alan Thicke.
Writer: Jeremy Stevens, Tom Moore, Tom Boni, Norman Stiles, Tom Dunsmuir, Don Wilcox, Robert Illes, James Stein, Alan Thicke.
Director: Jim Drake, Jerry Leshay, Marvin Kupfer, Randy Winburn, James Field, Dick Weinberg.
Creator: Norman Lear.

AMERICA 2-NIGHT — 30 minutes — Syndicated 1978. 65 programs.

44   AMERICAN BANDSTAND

Variety. Music and entertainment geared to teenagers.

Host: Dick Clark.
Original Hosts: Ron Joseph, Lee Stewart (1952-1956; Dick Clark became the host in August 1956).
Announcers: Charlie O'Donnell, Dick Clark.
Original Theme: "The Bandstand Boogie," composed by Charles Albertine; performed by the Les Elgart Orchestra.
Current Theme: Opening performed by Joe Porter; closing vocal by Barry Manilow.
Creator: Bob Horn, Lee Stewart.
Executive Producer: Dick Clark.
Producer: Judy Price.
Director: Barry Glazer.

AMERICAN BANDSTAND — 60 minutes — ABC — Premiered: October 7, 1957. Original premiere: WFIL-TV, Ch. 6 (Philadelphia): October 1952.

45   THE AMERICAN DOCUMENTS

Documentary. The series explores the foundations and development of America through newsreel footage. photographs and film clips.

Narrators: Guests, including Lowell Thomas and Jean Stapleton.
Music: From the Syracuse University Audio Archives; recorded by Walter L. Welch.
Additional Music: Ralph Berlinker, Walter Welch.
Executive Producer: David Shepard.
Producer: Ray Hubbard, Charles Horich.
Director: Larry Ward.

THE AMERICAN DOCUMENTS — 60 minutes — Syndicated 1975.

46   THE AMERICAN GIRLS

Drama. The story of Rebecca Tompkins and Amy Waddell, two beautiful roving reporter-researchers for "The American Report," a television newsmagazine series.

CAST

Rebecca Tompkins	Priscilla Barnes
Amy Waddell	Debra Clinger
Francis X. Casey, their producer	David Spielberg
Jason Cook, the host of "The American Report"	William Prince

Creator: Lane Slate, Mike Lloyd Ross, Lee Philips.
Music: Jerrold Immel.
Executive Producer: Harve Bennett, Harris Katleman.
Producer: Simon Muntner, George Lehr.
Director: Rod Holcomb, Alvin Ganzer, James D. Parriott, John Peyser, Lee Philips.

THE AMERICAN GIRLS — 60 minutes — CBS — September 23, 1978 – November 10, 1978. 6 episodes.

47   THE AMERICAN SHORT STORY

Anthology. Dramatizations based on short stories by American authors.

Host: Coleen Dewhurst, Henry Fonda.
Music: Ed Bogas, Elizabeth Swados, Dick Hyman.
Executive Producer: Robert Geller.
Producer: Paul Gurain, Dan McCann, Calvin Skaggs.
Director: Ralph Rosenbaum, Noel Black, Joan Micklin Silver.

Included:

Rappaccini's Daughter. An eerie tale that revolves around Beatrice Rappaccini, the beautiful and alluring daughter of a reclusive botanist — a girl who possesses the touch of death — and the complications that ensue when she falls in love with a student who takes up lodging next door. Based on the story by Nathaniel Hawthorne.

Cast: Beatrice Rappaccini: Kathleen Beller; Dr. Rappaccini, her father: Leonardo Cimino; Giovanni Gasconti, the student: Kristoffer Tabori; Baglioni: Michael Egan; Emma: Antonia Rey; Lisabetta: Madeline Willemsen.

The Greatest Man in the World. The story, set in the 1930s, follows the exploits of Jack Smurch, an intoxicated pilot who attempts the first solo flight across the world. Based on the story by James Thurber.

Cast: Jack Smurch: Brad Davis; His girlfriend: Caren Kane; Jack's mother: Sudi Bond; The editor: Howard da Silva; The reporter: John McMartin; The Secretary of State: William Prince.

Soldier's Home. The drama focuses on a troubled World War II veteran who is unable to readjust to his placid, rural hometown. Based on the story by Ernest Hemingway.

Cast: Harold Krebs: Richard Backus; Mrs. Krebs: Nancy Marchand; Roselle: Lane Binkley; Kenner: Mark LaMura.

THE AMERICAN SHORT STORY — 90 and 60 minutes (depending on the production) — PBS. April 5, 1977 – May 10, 1977. 9 episodes. February 4, 1980 – April 28, 1980. 13 episodes.

48   AMERICA'S TOP TEN

Music. A weekly series that spotlights the current top ten singles on *Billboard* magazine's pop chart.

Host: Casey Kasem.
Executive Producer: Syd Vinnedge, Tony Scotti.
Producer: George Ilos, Casey Kasem.
Director: Bill Rainbolt.
Art Director: Ed Flesh.

AMERICA'S TOP TEN — 30 minutes — Syndicated May 1980.

49   AMY PRENTISS

Crime Drama. The story of Amy Prentiss, a chief of detectives of the San Francisco Police Department, a beautiful woman with style and intelligence who often finds her investigations compounded by resentment from her male colleagues.

CAST

Amy Prentiss (a widow)	Jessica Walter
Jill Prentiss, her daughter	Helen Hunt
Sgt. Tony Russell	Steve Sandor
Detective Roy Pena	Art Metrano
Joan Carter, Amy's secretary	Gwenn Mitchell
Chief Demsey	M. Emmet Walsh

Music: John Cacavas, Don Costa.
Producer: Cy Chermak.
Director: Boris Sagal, Gordon Hessler, Noel Black, Lou Antonio.
AMY PRENTISS — 90 minutes — NBC — December 1. 1974 – July 6, 1975. Originally broadcast as part of *The NBC Mystery Movie.*

50   AN ENGLISHMAN'S CASTLE

Drama. A miniseries based on the premise that Britain lost World War II to Germany. Story focuses on the life of British playwright Peter Ingrim, his family, and the censorship problems he encounters with "An Englishman's Castle," a serial he writes for state-controlled television, that explores Britain's involvement in World War II and the situation that existed between the German and Jewish people at the time.

CAST

Peter Ingrim	Kenneth More
His wife	Kathleen Byron
Henry Ingrim, his son	David Myer
Mark Ingrim, his son	Nigel Havers
Jill, one of the serial stars	Isla Blair
Connie Worth, same as Jill	Noel Dyson
Fred Worth, Connie's husband	Rob Edwards
Harmer, the Controller (TV Censor)	Anthony Bate
Susan, Harmer's secretary	Fiona Gray
John Worth, Connie's son	Peter Hughes

Also:

Jimmy	Brian Peck
Theo	Jonathan Swift
Inspector	Philip Bond
Anja	Suzanne Roquette
Head Waiter	David Roy Paul
Soldier	Derek Holt
Soldier	Edward Kalinski
Soldier	Dyfed Thomas

Producer: Innes Lloyd, Peter Ingram.
Writer: Peter Mackie.
Director: Peter Ciapessoni.

AN ENGLISHMAN'S CASTLE — 60 minutes — PBS — September 2, 1979 – September 16, 1979. 3 episodes.

51   THE ANDROS TARGETS

Crime Drama. The exploits of Mike Andros, an investigative reporter for the *New York Forum,* a crusading newspaper.

CAST

Mike Andros	James Sutorius
Sandi Farrell, his assistant	Pamela Reed
Norman Kale, the city editor	Alan Mixon
Chet Reynolds, the managing editor	Roy Poole
The Metropolitan Editor	Jordan Charney
The National Editor	Ted Beniades
Judy, the *Forum* switchboard operator	Gwyn Gillis

Creator: Jerome Coopersmith.
Music: Bill Conti, Jerry Fielding, Morton Stevens, Patrick Williams.
Executive Producer: Bob Sweeney, Larry Rosen.
Producer: Edward H. Feldman.
Director: Bob Sweeney, Don Weis, Marc Danials, Harry Falk, Seymour Robbie, Edward H. Feldman, Irving J. Moore.

THE ANDROS TARGETS — 60 minutes — CBS — January 31, 1977 – May 16, 1977.

52   THE ANDY GRIFFITH SHOW

Comedy. The story of Andy Taylor, the sheriff of Mayberry, a small town in North Carolina, as he attempts to maintain the peace in a virtually crime-free town.

CAST

Sheriff Andy Taylor (a widower)	Andy Griffith
Barney Fife, his deputy	Don Knotts
Opie Taylor, Andy's son	Ron Howard
Bee Taylor, Andy's aunt	Frances Bavier
Peggy McMillan, Andy's girlfriend	Joanna Moore
Ellie Walker, a druggist, Andy's girlfriend (later)	Elinor Donahue
Helen Crump, the school teacher; later Andy's wife	Aneta Corsaut
Mary Simpson, the county nurse	Sue Ane Langdon Julie Adams
Irene Fairchild, the county nurse (later episodes)	Nina Shipman
Thelma Lou, Barney's girlfriend	Betty Lynn
Otis Campbell, the town drunk	Hal Smith
Howard Sprague, the county clerk	Jack Dodson
Floyd Lawson, the barber	Howard McNear
Gomer Pyle, the gas station attendant at Wally's Filling Station	Jim Nabors
Goober Pyle, Gomer's cousin	George Lindsey
Warren Ferguson, the deputy who replaced Barney	Jack Burns
Ernest T. Bass, the trouble-making hillbilly	Howard Morris
Emma Brand, the hypochondriac	Cheerio Meredith
Clara Edwards, Bee's friend	Hope Summers
Sam Jones, the councilman	Ken Berry
Millie Swanson, Sam's girlfriend	Arlene Golonka
Mike Jones, Sam's son	Buddy Foster
Emmet Clark, the Fix-it-Shop owner	Paul Hartman
Martha Clark, Emmet's wife	Mary Lansing
Leon, the boy with the peanut butter sandwich	Clint Howard
Johnny Paul, Opie's friend	Richard Keith
Briscoe Darling, a hillbilly	Denver Pyle
Charlene Darling, his daughter	Margaret Ann Peterson
Briscoe Darling's Boys	The Dillard Brothers
Malcolm Meriweather, Andy's friend	Bernard Fox
Mayor Pike (early episodes)	Dick Elliott
Mayor Stoner (later episodes)	Parley Baer
Captain Barker, the State Police Chief	Ken Lynch
Skippy, the fun-loving girl sweet on Andy	Joyce Jameson
Daphne, her girlfriend, sweet on Barney	Jean Carson
Jim Lindsey, Andy's friend	James Best
Mrs. Sprague, Howard's mother	Mabel Albertson

Andy's home address: 14 Maple Street.
Music: Earle Hagen.
Executive Producer: Sheldon Leonard (in association with Danny Thomas Enterprises)
Producer: Aaron Ruben, Richard O. Linke, Bob Ross.
Director: Alan Rafkin, Theodore J. Flicker, Coby Ruskin, Earl Bellamy, Bob Sweeney, Lee Philips, Richard Crenna.

THE ANDY GRIFFITH SHOW — 30 minutes — CBS — October 3, 1960 – September 16, 1968. Syndicated. 249 episodes. Spin-off series: *Gomer Pyle, USMC, Mayberry, R.F.D., The New Andy Griffith Show,* and *Goober* (pilot film section).

53   THE ANDY WILLIAMS SHOW

Variety.

Host: Andy Williams.
Regulars: Janos Prohaska (as "The Cookie-Seeking Bear"), Irwin Corey, Charlie Callas, The Jaime Rogers Singers, The Earl Brown Dancers, The Archie Tayir Dancers.
Orchestra: Mike Post.
Executive Producer: Alan Bernard, Andy Williams.
Producer: Chris Bearde, Allan Blye.
Writer: Phil Hahn, Jack Hanrahan, Chris Bearde, Allan Blye, Mark Shekter, Bob Arnott, George Burditt, Brian Joseph.
Director: Norman Campbell.

THE ANDY WILLIAMS SHOW — 60 minutes — NBC — September 20, 1969 – July 17, 1971.

54   THE ANDY WILLIAMS SHOW

Variety.

Host: Andy Williams.
Regular: Wayland Flowers (a puppeteer).

Orchestra: George Wyle.
Executive Producer: Pierre Cosette.
Producer: Robert Scheerer.
Writer: Jeremy Stevens, Tom Moore.
Director: Robert Scheerer.

THE ANDY WILLIAMS SHOW— 30 minutes—Syndicated September 1976.

55   ANGIE

Comedy.

Original Format: The romantic story of Angie Falco, a poor Philadelphia waitress who marries Brad Benson, a wealthy pediatrician, and the ensuing misadventures as she tries to adjust to a new life style.

Second Format: While continuing to focus on the struggles of newlyweds, the series also depicts Angie's misadventures as she struggles to run The Liberty Coffee Shop, the restaurant in which she once worked and now, through Brad, owns.

Third Format: In the episode of January 21, 1980, Angie and her mother, Theresa, purchase Rose's House of Beauty, a salon, after Angie gives up the coffee shop and her mother sells her newsstand. The series ended with a focus on their struggles to run the beauty shop.

CAST

Angie Falco Benson	Donna Pescow
Dr. Brad Benson, her husband	Robert Hays
Marie Falco, Angie's sister	Debralee Scott
Theresa Falco, Angie's mother	Doris Roberts
Joyce Benson, Brad's sister	Sharon Spelman
Hillary Benson, Joyce's daughter	Tammy Lauren
Di Di Malloy, Angie's waitress	Diane Robin
Randall Benson, Brad's father	John Randolph
Phipps, Brad and Angie's butler	Emory Bass
Hector, the coffee shop chef	Richard Beauchamp
Julie, Brad's nurse	Aileen Fitzpatrick
Petey Fortunato, Angie's cousin	Carlo Imperato
Mary Katherine, the nun, Angie's friend	Nancy Lane
Mary Mary, Angie's friend	Valri Bromfield
Mary Grace Moroni, Angie's friend	Susan Duvall
Doug Moroni, Mary Grace's husband	Michael McManus
Bev, a coffee shop waitress	Kit McDonough
Gianni, Theresa's assistant at the beauty shop	Tim Thomerson
Connie, the shop beautician	Tessa Richards
Ceil, a regular at the beauty shop	Florence Halop
Vincent Tortelli, Mary Katherine's brother, a priest	Marty Ferraro

Angie's home address: 4221 Vermont Street.

Commercial Break Announcer: Donna Pescow, Robert Hays.
Music: Dan Foliart, Howard Pearl.
Theme Vocal: "Different Worlds" by Maureen McGovern.
Executive Producer: Bob Ellison, Dale McRaven, Robert Boyett, Edward Milkis, Garry K. Marshall, Leonora Thuna.
Supervising Producer: Thomas L. Miller, Edward K. Milkis, Robert L. Boyett.
Producer: Harry Cauley, Gloria Banta, Bruce Johnson, Alan Einstein, Larry Mintz.
Director: Howard Storm, Jeff Chambers, Tony Mordente, Lowell Ganz, Harvey Medlinsky, Robert Drivas, Norman Abbott, John Tracy.
Creator: Garry K. Marshall, Dale McRaven.

ANGIE—30 minutes—ABC. February 8, 1979–July 12, 1979. September 11, 1979–February 18, 1980. April 12, 1980–April 26, 1980. July 31, 1980–October 23, 1980. 37 episodes.

ANIMAL DOCTOR

See title *Woobinda—Animal Doctor* in the regular program section.

56   ANIMALS, ANIMALS, ANIMALS

Children. A magazine type of series that attempts to explain the relationship of animals to man in history, art, music, mythology and literature.

Host: Hal Linden.
Cartoon Segment Voices: Estelle Parsons, Mason Adams.
Vocalist: Lynn Kellogg.
Executive Producer: Lester Cooper.
Producer: Peter Weinberger.

ANIMALS, ANIMALS, ANIMALS— 25 minutes—ABC—Premiered: September 12, 1976.

57   ANNA AND THE KING

Comedy-Drama. The story, set in Siam in 1862, follows the adventures of Anna Owens, an American school teacher hired by the King to educate and introduce Western culture to his royal children. Based on the motion picture of the same title.

CAST

The King of Siam	Yul Brynner
Anna Owens	Samantha Eggar
Louis Owens, Anna's son	Eric Shea
Prince Kralahome	Keye Luke
The Crown Prince Chulolongkorn	Brian Tochi
Lady Thiang, the King's head wife	Lisa Lu
Princess Serana, the King's eldest daughter	Rosalind Chao
Child (unnamed), the King's daughter	Wendy Tochi
Kai-Lee Ling, the King's daughter	Tracy Lee

Music: Richard Shores.
Executive Producer: Gene Reynolds.
Producer: Bill Idelson, Harvey Miller.

ANNA AND THE KING—30 minutes—CBS—September 17, 1972–December 31, 1972. 13 episodes.

58   ANOTHER DAY

Comedy. The series, set in Los Angeles, focuses on the lives of Don and Ginny Gardner, a married couple whose lives are complicated by their jobs, their children and Don's outspoken mother.

CAST

Don Gardner	David Groh
Ginny Gardner, his wife	Joan Hackett
Kelly Gardner, their daughter	Lisa Lindgren
Mark Gardner, their son	Al Eisenmann
Olive Gardner, Don's mother	Hope Summers

Music: Paul Williams.
Executive Producer: James Komack.
Producer: Paul Mason, George Kirgo.
Director: James Komack, Gary Shimokawa, Nick Havinga, Burt Brinkerhoff.
Creator: James Komack.

ANOTHER DAY—30 minutes— CBS—April 8, 1978–April 29, 1978. 4 episodes.

59   ANOTHER WORLD

Serial. The dramatic story of two families, the Randolphs and the Matthews, residents of the town of Bay City. Episodes relate the conflicts and tensions that arise from the interactions of the characters.

CAST

Jim Matthews	John Beal
	Leon Janney
	Shepperd Strudwick
	Hugh Marlowe
Mary Matthews	Virginia Dwyer
Grandma Matthews	Vera Allen
Alice Matthews	Jacqueline Courtney
Patricia Matthews	Susan Trustman
	Beverly Penberthy
Russ Matthews	Joe Trent
	Sam Groom
	Robert Hover
	David Bailey
Janet Matthews	Liza Chapman
Liz Matthews	Sara Cunningham
	Audra Lindley
	Nancy Wickwire
	Irene Dailey
Bill Matthews	Joe Gallison
Melissa Palmer	Carol Roux
Ken Baxter	William Prince
Tom Baxter	Nicholas Pryor
Walter Matthews	Gerald Davis
Helen Moore	Muriel Williams
Dr. John Bradford	John Crawford
Susan Matthews	Fran Sharon
	Lisa Cameron
John Randolph	Michael Ryan
Lee Randolph	Gaye Huston
	Barbara Rodell
Danny Fargo	Anthony Ponzini
Michael Dru	Geoffrey Lumb
Wayne Addison	Robert Milli
Walter Curtin	Val Dufour
Cindy Clark	Leonie Norton
Ted Clark	Steve Bolster
Michael Bauer	Garry Pillar
Alex Gregory	James Congdon
Karen Gregory	Ellen Watson
Dr. Ernest Gregory	Mark Lenard
Peggy Harris	Micki Grant
Mrs. Hastings	Mona Burns
Flo Murray	Marcella Martin
Hope Bauer	Elissa Leeds
Cathryn Corniny	Ann Sheridan
The Assistant D.A.	Billy Dee Williams
	Alex Wipf
Lenore Moore	Judith Barcroft
	Susan Sullivan
Luella Watson	Dorothy Blackburn
David Thornton	Joseph Ponazecki
	Colgate Salisbury
Ellen	Irene Biendie
	Gail Dixon
Andy Cummings	Jim Secrest
Bernice Addison	Janis Young
Chris Tyler	Steve Harmon
Fred Douglas	Charles Baxter
Ernie Downs	Harry Bellaver
Dan Shearer	John Cunningham
Barbara Shearer	Christine Cameron
Jane Overstreet	Frances Sternhagen
Belle Clark	Janet Ward
Marianne Randolph	Tracy Brown
	Ariane Munker
Michael Randolph	Christopher J. Brown
	Christopher Corwin
	Lionel Johnston
Rachel Davis	Robin Strasser
	Margaret Impert
	Victoria Wyndham
Mark Venable	Andrew Jarkowsky
Philip Lessner	Ed Bryce
Mrs. McCrea	Nancy Marchand
Raymond Scott	James Preston
Dr. Philbin	Charles Siebert
Jamie Matthews	Aidan McNulty
Robert Delaney	Nick Coster
Zack Richards	Terry Alexander
Gil McGowen	Dolph Sweet
Linda Metcalf	Vera Moore
Gloria Metcalf	Rosetta LeNoire
Ada Downs	Constance Ford
Eliot Carrington	James Douglas
Iris Carrington	Beverlee McKinsey
Louise Goddard	Anne Meacham
Lahoma Vane	Ann Wedgeworth
Dr. Paula McCrea	Beverley Owen
Stephen Frame	George Reinholt
Frank Chadwick	Robert Kya-Hill
Tom Albini	Pierrino Mascorino
Gil McGowen	Charles Durning
Madge Murphy	Doris Belack
Lefty Burns	Larry Keith
Walter Curtin, Jr.	Scott Firestone
	Denis McKiernan
	Jason Gladstone
Tim McGowen	Christopher Allport
MacKenzie Corey	Robert Emhardt
	Douglas Watson
Sam Lucas	Jordan Charney
Dr. Curt Landis	Donald Madden
Olga Bellin	Ann Fuller
Carole Lamont	Jeanne Lange
David Gilchrist	John Aprea
	David Ackroyd

Vic Hastings	John Considine
Neil Johnson	John Getz
Angela Perrini	Toni Kalem
	Maeve Kinkead
Sally Spencer	Cathy Greene
Beatrice Gordon	Jacqueline Brookes
Chris Pierson	Stephen Yates
Clarice Hobson	Gail Brown
Loretta Simpson	Elaine Kerr
Pam Sloane	Karen Wolfe
Scott Bradley	Michael Goodwin
Alice Frame	Susan Harney
Roy Gordon	Ted Shackelford
	Gary Carpenter
Brian Bancroft	Paul Stevens
Daryll Stevens	Richard Dunne
Donna Beck	Francesca Poston
Sharlene Matthews	Laura Heineman
Burt McGowan	William Russ
Sven Peterson	Robert Blossom
Quentin Ames	Peter Ratray
Helga Lindstrom	Helen Stenborg
Regine Lindeman	Barbara eda Young
Jeff Stone	Dan Hamilton
Theresa Lamont	Nancy Marchand
Tracy DeWitt	Caroline McWilliams
Ken Palmer	Kelly Monaghan
	William Lyman
Barbara Weaver	Kathryn Walker
Willis Frame	John Fitzpatrick
	Leon Russom
Keith Morrison	Fred Beir
Rocky Olsen	John Braden
Evan Webster	Barry Jenner
Olive Gordon	Jennifer Leak
Gwen Parrish	Dorothy Lyman
Molly Ordway	Rolonda Mendels
Rose Perrini	Kathleen Widdoes
Vivian	Gretchen Oehler
Emma Ordway	Tresa Hughes
Ted Bancroft	Eric Roberts
	Richard Backus
Dino Amati	John DeVries
Sharon Amati	Kaiulani Lee
Dennis	Mike Hammett
Brooks	Joseph Maher
	John Horton
	John Tillinger
Laura Burtram	Karen Campbell
Jamie Frame	Bobby Doran
	William McMillan
	Richard Bekins
Ben Campbell	David Butler
Rita Connelly	Camilla Carr
Charles Hobson	Fred J. Scollay
Rudy	Joel Simon
Morgan Simpson	Gary Tomlin
Scott Bradley	Paul Tulley
Blaine Ewing	Laura Malone
Bill Simpson	Ben Hammer
Dennis Carrington	Jim Poyner
	Mike Hammett
Joey Perrini	Ray Liotta
Kirk Laverty	Charles Cioffi
June Laverty	Geraldine Court
Phil Higley	McLin Crowell
Sylvie Kosloff	Leora Dana
Eileen Simpson	Vicky Dawson
Fred Ewing	Barton Heyman
Paul Connelly	Stephen Joyce
Cecile DePoulignac	Susan Keith
Janice Frame	Victoria Thompson
	Christine Jones
Linda Metcalf	Vera Moore
Alice Gordon	Wesley Pfenning
Sally Frame	Julie Phillips
Elena	Christina Pickles
Cory McGowan	Carmine Rizzo

Announcer: Bill Wolff.
Music: Chet Kingsbury.
Executive Producer: Paul Rauch.
Producer: Mary S. Bonner, Joseph Rothenberger.
Writer: Harding Lemay, Douglas Marland, Mel Brez, Ethel Brez.
Director: Ira Cirker, Melvin Bernhardt, Paul Lammers.
Program Open:
Announcer: We do not live in this world alone, but in a thousand other worlds. The events of our own lives represent only the surface, and in our minds and feelings we live in many other worlds.

ANOTHER WORLD — 30 minutes — NBC — May 4, 1964 – January 3, 1975. 60 minutes — January 6, 1975 – March 2, 1979. 90 minutes — March 5, 1979 – August 1, 1980. 60 minutes — Premiered: August 4, 1980.

60 ANYTHING YOU CAN DO

Game. Two three-member teams, the male vs. the female, compete in a series of contests wherein each team has to perform specified stunts within a specific time period (usually 90 seconds). The team that accumulates the least amount of overall time is the winner and receives an assortment of merchandise prizes.

Host: Gene Wood, Don Harron.
Announcer: Bill Luxton.
Executive Producer: Don Reid.
Producer: Lorne Freed.
Music: Score Productions.
ANYTHING YOU CAN DO — 30 minutes — Syndicated 1971. 156 programs.

61 APPLE PIE

Comedy. The series, set in Kansas City, Kansas, in 1933, concerns itself with the antics of the Hollyhocks, strangers who became a family through the efforts of Ginger-Nell Hollyhock, a lonely woman who acquired her family by placing ads in the local newspaper.

CAST

Ginger-Nell Hollyhock, the mother	Rue McClanahan
"Fast" Eddie Barnes, the father	Dabney Coleman
Grandpa Hollyhock	Jack Gilford
Anna Marie Hollyhock, the daughter	Caitlin O'Heaney
Junior Hollyhock, the son	Derrel Maury

Music: Theme only, a recorded, by not credited version of "Happy Days Are Here Again."
Producer: Charlie Hauck.
Associate Producer: Rita Dillon.
Director: Peter Bonerz.
Program Open:
Ginger-Nell: March the fourth, nineteen and thirty-three. Mercy, what times these are. Nobody in this whole country

has enough money to buy dirt. Luckily though, we live here in Kansas City, Kansas where there is plenty of dirt for free. Just everything else we can't afford.
APPLE PIE — 30 minutes — ABC — September 23, 1978 – October 7, 1978. 7 episodes were produced but only 3 aired.

62 APPLE'S WAY

Drama. The dreams, frustrations and ambitions of the Apple family, residents of the small town of Appleton, Iowa. Stories depict the attempts of George, the father, to recapture for himself and his family the treasured memories of his childhood: "the wonders of streams and woods ... the mystery of growing crops and days filled with adventure ... with participation in good and comforting things."

CAST

George Apple, the father	Ronny Cox
Barbara Apple, his wife	Frances Lee McCain
Paul Apple, their son	Vincent Van Patten
Patricia Apple, their daughter	Franny Michel / Kristy McNichol
Cathy Apple, their daughter	Patti Cohoon
Steven Apple, their son	Eric Olsen
Aldon Apple, George's father	Malcolm Atterbury

Apple family pets: Muffin, Sam and Bijou (dogs); and Ruby, a snake.
Music: Morton Stevens, Sandy Courage.
Executive Producer: Lee Rich, Earl Hamner.
Producer: John Furia, Jr.
Writer: John T. Dugan, Joseph Bonaduce, David Moessinger, Don Appell, William Best, Hindi Brooks, Jim McGinn, John McGreevey, John Furia, Jr., Gene Thompson, Irma Kalish, Austin Kalish, Richard Fielder, Calvin Clements, Jr.
Director: Hal Cooper, Marc Daniels, David Moessinger, James Sheldon, Alexander Singer, Jack Shea, Ivan Dixon, Edward Abroms, Richard Bennett.
APPLE'S WAY — 60 minutes — CBS — February 10, 1974 – January 12, 1975. 24 episodes.

63 ARCHER

Crime Drama. The exploits of Lew Archer, a private detective working out of Melrose, California. Based on the character created by Ross Macdonald.

CAST

Lew Archer	Brian Keith
Lt. Barney Brighton	John P. Ryan

Music: Jerry Goldsmith.
Executive Producer: David Carp.
Producer: Jack Miller, Leonard B. Kaufman.

ARCHER — 60 minutes — NBC — January 30, 1975 – March 14, 1975. 7 episodes. See also "The Underground Man" in the pilot film section.

64 ARCHIE BUNKER'S PLACE

Comedy. A spin-off from *All in the Family.* The revised format follows the misadventures of Archie Bunker, the prejudiced, loud-mouthed conservative, now co-owner of Archie Bunker's Place, a restaurant-bar, and his Jewish partner, Murray Klein, whose political opinions provide a basis for continual bickering between the two.

CAST

Archie Bunker	Carroll O'Connor
Murray Klein	Martin Balsam
Barney Hefner, Archie's friend	Allan Melvin
Stephanie Mills, Archie's ward	Danielle Brisebois
Edith Bunker, Archie's wife (occasional appearances)	Jean Stapleton
Mr. Van Ranseleer, a bar customer	Bill Quinn
Harry Snowden, the bartender	Jason Wingreen
Veronica Rooney, the cook	Anne Meara
Dotty Worth, the waitress	Sheree North
Fred, the waiter	Dino Scofield
Jose Perez, a bar employee	Abraham Alvarez
Hank, a regular customer	Danny Dayton
Linda, the waitress	Heidi Hagman (Larry Hagman's daughter)
Ellen Canby, Archie's housekeeper	Barbara Meek
Polly Swanson	Janet MacLachlan
Ed Swanson, Polly's husband	Mel Bryant

Music: Ray Conniff.
Opening Theme: "Those Were the Days" by Charles Strouse and Lee Adams.
Closing Theme: "Remembering You" by Roger Kellaway and Carroll O'Connor.
Executive Producer: Mort Lachman.
Producer: Milt Josefsberg.
Associate Producer: Joe Gannon.
Writer: Pat Shea, Harriet Weiss, Milt Josefsberg, Jerry Rose, Bob Schiller, Bob Weiskopf.
Director: Paul Bogart, Bob LaHendro, Carroll O'Connor, Lila Garrett, Dick Martin, John Sharp, Peter Bonerz.
Art Director: Don Roberts.

ARCHIE BUNKER'S PLACE — 30 minutes — CBS — Premiered: September 23, 1979.

65 THE ARCHIE COMEDY HOUR

Animated Cartoon. The misadventures of Archie Andrews and his friends Betty Cooper, Veronica Lodge, Jughead Jones and Reggie Mantle, high school students in the mythical town of Riverdale. Based on the comic *Archie* by Bob Montana.

Angie. Clustered around Donna Pescow and Tammy Lauren, are, from left, Debralee Scott, Doris Roberts, Robert Hays, Sharon Spelman and Diane Robin.

Apple Pie. Rue McClanahan, at left, and Dabney Coleman.

The Avengers. Diana Rigg and Patrick Macnee.

The Avengers. Linda Thorson.

VOICES

Archie Andrews	Dallas McKennon
Betty Cooper	Jane Webb
Veronica Lodge	Jane Webb
Jughead Jones	Howard Morris
Reggie Mantle	Dallas McKennon

Music: George Blais, Jeff Michael.
Music Supervision: Don Kirshner.
Producer: Norm Prescott, Lou Scheimer.
Director: Hal Sutherland.

THE ARCHIE COMEDY HOUR— 60 minutes — CBS — September 13, 1969 – September 5, 1970. As *Archie's Funhouse:* 30 minutes — CBS — September 12, 1970 – September 4, 1971.

THE ARCHIES

The syndicated title for *The Archie Comedy Hour, Archie's Funhouse, Everything's Archie* and *The U.S. of Archie.* See individual titles for information.

ARCHIE'S FUNHOUSE

See *The Archie Comedy Hour.*

66   ARCHIE'S TV FUNNIES

Animated Cartoon. Adaptations of eight comic strips ("Dick Tracy," "The Captain and the Kids," "Moon Mullins," "Smokey Stover," "Nancy and Sluggo," "Here Come the Dropouts," "Broom Hilda," and "Emmy Lou") which are presented as the programs of a television station operated by the Archie gang (Archie Andrews, Jughead Jones, Betty Cooper, Veronica Lodge, Reggie Mantle and Hot Dog, the gang pet).

Voices: Jane Webb, Howard Morris, Dallas McKennon.
Music: George Blais, Jeff Michael.
Music Supervision: Don Kirshner.
Producer: Norm Prescott, Lou Scheimer.
Director: Hal Sutherland.

ARCHIE'S TV FUNNIES — 30 minutes — CBS — September 11, 1971 – September 1, 1973.

67   ARK II

Science Fiction Adventure. Once fertile and rich for millions of years, the Earth suddenly falls into ruin as pollution and waste take their toll. It is the year A.D. 2476 and conventional civilization no longer exists; and only a handful of scientists remain to rebuild what man has destroyed. Their one major achievement is *Ark II,* a mobile storehouse of scientific knowledge manned by three young scientists: Jonah, Ruth and Samuel. Stories relate their experiences as they set out "to bring the hope of the new future to mankind."

CAST

Jonah	Terry Lester
Ruth	Jean Marie Hon
Samuel	Jose Flores
Adam, their chimpanzee assistant	Himself

Music: Yvette Blais, Jeff Michael; The Horta-Mahana Corporation.
Executive Producer: Norm Prescott, Lou Scheimer.
Producer: Dick Rosenbloom.
Director: Ted Post.

ARK II — 25 minutes — CBS — September 11, 1976 – August 25, 1979.

68   ARNIE

Comedy. The story of Arnie Nuvo, a dock foreman for Continental Flange, Inc., a Los Angeles-based company, who is suddenly promoted to the position of New Head of Product Improvement. Episodes concern his attempts to adjust to the responsibilities of an executive position.

CAST

Arnie Nuvo	Herschel Bernardi
Lillian Nuvo, Arnie's wife	Sue Ane Langdon
Andrea Nuvo, their daughter	Stephanie Steele
Richard Nuvo, their son	Del Russell
Hamilton Majors, Jr., the company president	Roger Bowen
Julius, Arnie's friend	Tom Pedi
Neil Ogilvie, the plant supervisor	Herbert Voland
Fred Springer, the advertising head	Olan Soule
Felicia Farfas, Arnie's secretary	Elaine Shore
Randy Robinson, Arnie's neighbor, TV's "The Giddyap Gourmet"	Charles Nelson Reilly

Creator: David Swift.
Music: Harry Geller.
Music Supervision: Lionel Newman.
Producer: Duke Vincent, Bruce Johnson, David Swift, Rick Mittleman.
Writer: Art Baer, Ben Joelson, Jack Elinson, Norman Paul, Barry Blitzer.
Director: Don Richardson, David Swift.

ARNIE — 30 minutes — CBS — September 19, 1970 – September 9, 1972. 48 episodes.

69   AROUND THE WORLD IN 80 DAYS

Animated Cartoon. When Phineas Fogg and Belinda Maze may not marry because her uncle, Lord Maze, objects, Fogg accepts Lord Maze's challenge to travel around the world in eighty days to prove himself worthy of the girl. Believing him incapable of the feat, Lord Maze wagers twenty thousand pounds (about $42,000) against him and hires, unbe-

knownst to Fogg, the evil Mister Fix to foil the attempt and ensure his winning the bet.

Later, Fogg and his aide, Jean Passepartout, depart England (the series is set in 1877) in a hot-air balloon. Episodes depict their attempts to overcome the foul deeds of Mr. Fix and complete their journey within the allotted time. Based on the novel by Jules Verne.

VOICES

Phineas Fogg	Alastair Duncan
Jean Passepartout	Ross Higgins
Mister Fix	Max Obestein

Music: John Sangster.
Producer: Walter Hucker.
Director: Richard Slapezynski.

AROUND THE WORLD IN 80 DAYS — 30 minutes — NBC — September 9, 1972 – September 1, 1973. 16 episodes. Syndicated.

70   ASPEN

Drama. A miniseries, set in Aspen, Colorado, that follows the trial of Lee Bishop, an accused rapist-murderer.

CAST

Tom Keating	Sam Elliott
Gloria Osborne	Michelle Phillips
Lee Bishop	Perry King
Carl Osborne	Gene Barry
Kit Pepe	Jessica Harper
Alex Budde	Anthony Franciosa
Max Kendrick	Roger Davis
Owen Keating	John McIntire
Jon Osborne	Douglas Heyes, Jr.
Angela Morelli	Debi Richter
Budd Townsend	Bo Hopkins
Joseph Drummond	John Houseman
Horton Paine	Joseph Cotten
Jude Kendrick	William Prince
Abe Singer	George DiCenzo
Joan Carolinian	Martine Beswick

Music: Tom Scott, Michael Melvoin.
Executive Producer: Michael Klein.
Producer: Jo Swerling, Jr.
Director: Douglas Heyes.

ASPEN — 2 hours — NBC — November 5, 1977 – November 7, 1977. 3 episodes. Rebroadcast as "The Innocent and the Damned" on NBC from May 31, 1979 – June 14, 1979.

71   ASSIGNMENT: VIENNA

Adventure. The series, set in Vienna, Austria, follows the exploits of Jake Webster, a United States government agent who poses as the owner of Jake's Bar and Grill.

CAST

Jake Webster	Robert Conrad
Major Bernard Caldwell, his contact	Charles Cioffi
Inspector Hoffman	Anton Diffring

Music: Dave Grusin, John Parker.
Executive Producer: Robert H. Justman.

Producer: Jerry Ludwig, Eric Berovich.

ASSIGNMENT: VIENNA — 60 minutes — ABC — September 28, 1972 – June 9, 1973. 6 episodes. See also "Assignment: Munich" in the pilot film section.

72   THE ASSOCIATES

Comedy. The series, set in New York City, follows the misadventures of the legal staff of the Bass and Marshall Law Offices, a prestigious Wall Street firm.

CAST

Emerson Marshall, the senior partner	Wilfred Hyde-White
Sara James, a lawyer	Shelley Smith
Leslie Dunn, a lawyer	Alley Mills
Tucker Kerwin, a lawyer	Martin Short
Eliot Streeter, a lawyer	Joe Regalbuto
Johnny Danko, the mailboy	Tim Thomerson
Ginger, a secretary	Adrienne Hampton
Susan Warren, the mother of Danko's illegitimate child	Francine Tacker

Last Commercial Break Vocalist ("We'll be right back"): B.B. King.
Creator: James L. Brooks. Stan Daniels, Charlie Hauck, Ed Weinberger.
Music: A. Brooks.
Theme Vocal: B.B. King.
Executive Producer: James L. Brooks, Stan Daniels, Ed Weinberger.
Producer: Michael Leeson.
Writer: Michael Leeson, Charlie Hauck, David Lloyd, John Owen.
Director: James Burrows, Tony Mordente.

THE ASSOCIATES — 30 minutes — ABC. September 23, 1979 – October 28, 1979. 5 episodes. March 27, 1980 – April 17, 1980. 4 episodes.

73   AS THE WORLD TURNS

Serial. Events in the day-to-day lives of three closely related families, the Hughes, Lowells and Stewarts, residents of the town of Oakdale, U.S.A.

CAST

William Hughes	Santos Ortega
Chris Hughes	Don McLaughlin
Nancy Hughes	Helen Wagner
Penny Hughes	Rosemary Prinz
	Phoebe Dorin
Lisa Miller Colman	Eileen Fulton
Tom Hughes	Peter Link
	Peter Galman
	Paul O'Keefe
	David Colson
Hank Barton	Gary Sandy
Dr. Douglas Cassen	Nat Polen
Alma Miller	Ethel Rainey
Judge Lowell	William Johnstone
Dr. John Dixon	Larry Bryggman
Julia Burke	Fran Carlon
Dan Stewart	John Reilly
	John Colenbeck

Jennifer Ryan	Geraldine Court	Edith Hughes	Ruth Warrick
	Gillian Spencer	Jim Lowell	Les Damon
Dawn Stewart	Jean Mazza	Dr. Tim Cole	William Redfield
Carol Ann Stewart	Ariane Munker	Betty Stewart	Pat Benoit
	Barbara Jean Ehrhardt	Natalie Bannon	Judith Chapman
Betsy Stewart	Tiberia Mitri	Kim Dickson	Patricia McCormack
	Susan Davids	Holly Bauer	Ellen Barber
	Simone Schacter	Ralph Mitchell	Keith Charles
	Suzanne Davidson	Pat Holland	Melinda Peterson
Dr. Rick Ryan	Con Roche	Ellen Stewart	Pat Bruder
Paul Stewart	Dean Santoro	Ted Ellison	Joseph Christopher
	Stephen Mines	Anne Stewart	Martina Deignam
	Michael Hawkins	Laurie Keaton	Laurel Delmar
Charles Shea	Pip Sarser	Beau Spencer	Wayne Hudgins
Sara Fuller	Gloria DeHaven	Valerie Conway	Judith McConnell
Jack Davis	Martin Sheen	Mary Ellison	Kelly Wood
Barbara Ryan	Donna Wandry	Dana Woodward	Deborah Hobart
Grant Coleman	Konrad Matthaei	Matt	John Tripp
	James Douglas	Steve Farrell	Phil Peters
Jay Stallings	Dennis Cooney	Douglas Campbell	Dennis Romer
Kim Reynolds	Kathryn Hays	Brian Ellison	Bob Hover
Marty	Don Scardino	Amy (baby)	Claire Doyle
Amy Hughes	Yah-Ling Sun	Mark Lewis	Biff Warren
Carol Demming	Rita McLaughlin	Dr. Alexander Deith	Jon Cypher
Peggy Reagan	Lisa Cameron	Alma Miller	Ethel Remy
Dr. Flynn	Sidney Walker	Ellie	Swoosie Kurtz
Simon Gilbey	Jerry Lacy	Emmy Stewart	Jenny Harris
Meredith Harcourt	Nina Hart		Marissa Morell
Claire Shea	Anne Burr	Bennett Hadley	Doug Higgins
	Nancy Wickwire	Kate	Rachel Kelly
	Barbara Berjer	Douglas Campbell	Dennis Romer
David Stewart	Henderson Forsythe	Ian McFarland	Peter Simon
Dr. Michael Shea	Roy Schumann		
Martha Wilson	Anna Minot		
Carl Wilson	Martin Ruby		
Dick Martin	Edward Kemmer		
Roy McGuire	Konrad Matthaei		
Ellen Stewart	Wendy Drew		
	Patricia Bruder		
Nick Andropolous	Michael Forest		
Donald Hughes	Peter Brandon		
	Martin West		
	Conrad Fowkes		
James Stenbeck	Anthony Herrera		
Sheila Winston	Martha Lambert		
Bob Hughes	Robert Alford		
	Don Hastings		
Dr. Jeff Ward	Robert Lipton		
Melinda Gary	Ariane Munker		
Franny Hughes	Maura Gilligan		
	Tracy O'Neill		
Eric Hollister	Peter Reckell		
Annie Spencer	Julie Ridley		
Joyce Hughes	Barbara Rodell		
Stavaros Andropolous	Frank Runyeon		
Dee Stewart	Marcia McClain		
	Jacqueline Schultz		
Tom Hughes	Tom Tammi		
Carol Stallings	Rita M. Walter		
Barbara Ryan	Coleen Zenk		
Susan Stewart	Jada Rowland		
	Marie Masters		
	Judith Barcroft*		
Dana Woodward	Deborah Hobart		
Jimmy McGuire	Michael Cody		
Karen Adams	Doe Lang		
Mrs. Brando	Ethel Everett		
Alice	Jean McClintock		
Sandy McGuire	Dagne Crane		
	Barbara Rucker		
Sally Graham	Kathleen Cody		
Dr. Jerry Turner	James Earl Jones		
Neil Wade	Michael Lipton		
Franny Brennan	Toni Darnay		
	Kelly Campbell		
Wally Matthews	Charles Siebert		
Jeff Baker	Mark Rydell		
Bruce Elliott	James Prichett		
Elizabeth Talbot	Jane House		

Announcer: Dan McCullough.
Music: Charles Paul, Mi-Voix.
Producer: Ted Corday, Allen Potter, Charles Fisher, William Howell, Fred Bartholomew, Joe Willmore, Arthur Richards, Susan Bedson.
Writer: Jerome Dobson, Bridget Dobson, Chuck DiZenzo, Patti DiZenzo, Nancy Ford, Jean Rouverol, Robert White, Phyllis White.
Director: Leonard Valenta, John Litvack, Robert Myhram, Allen Fristoe, Heather Hill, Bruce Barry.
Creator: Irna Phillips, Ted Corday.

AS THE WORLD TURNS — 30 minutes — CBS — April 2, 1956 — November 28, 1975. 60 minutes: Premiered: December 1, 1975.

*Temporary replacement for Marie Masters.

74   THE AVENGERS

Adventure. The original concept of the British-produced series, from 1961 to 1962, depicts the crime-fighting exploits of two men: the mysterious John Steed, a dilettante man about town and a purveyor of old-world courtesy, and David Keel, a doctor who first joins Steed to avenge the murder of his fiancée by drug pushers, and remains with him for one season until an actors' strike ended the series.

In 1962 the series returned to depict the exploits of two British Government Ministry Agents: the dashing and debonair John Steed and his glamorous female assistant, Catherine Gale. When Catherine resigns (1965), Steed befriends the "lovely and delectable" Emma Peel, widow of a test pilot. Emancipated and independently wealthy, Peel teams with Steed for the sheer love of adventure. Stories depict their investigations as they attempt to solve baffling crimes.

When Emma's husband, Peter Peel, believed to have been killed in an airplane crash in the Amazon, is found alive, Emma returns to him (1968) and Steed is teamed with Tara King, a beautiful and shapely brunette (to 1969). Stories relate their attempts to avenge bizarre crimes perpetrated against the British government.

CAST

John Steed	Patrick Macnee
David Keel	Ian Hendry
Catherine Gale	Honor Blackman
Emma Peel	Diana Rigg
Tara King	Linda Thorson
Mother (a man), Steed's invalid superior (1968–1969)	Patrick Newell

Also: Rhonda, Mother's beautiful aide (a nonspeaking part for which credit is not given).
Steed's address: Number Three Stable Mews, City of London.
Tara's address: Number Nine Primrose Crescent, City of London.
Music: Johnny Dankworth, Laurie Johnson, Howard Blake.
Producer: Leonard White, John Bryce, Julian Wintle, Brian Clemens, Albert Fennell.
Director: Charles Crichton, Don Leaver, Richmond Harding, Roger Jenkins, Cliff Owen, Peter Sykes, Bill Bain, Gerry O'Hara, Quentin Lawrence, John Hough, Robert Day, Robert Fuest, Peter Graham Scott, James Hill, Don Sharp, Leslie Norman, Ray Austin, John Moxey, Robert Asher, Peter DuFell, Roy Baker, Cyril Frankel, Sidney Hayers, Gordon Flemyng.

Program Open:
Announcer: Extraordinary crimes against the people and the state had to be avenged by agents extraordinary. Two such people are John Steed, top professional, and his partner, Emma Peel, talented amateur, otherwise known as the Avengers.

THE AVENGERS — 60 minutes — ABC — March 28, 1966 — September 1, 1966; January 20, 1967 — September 1, 1967; January 10, 1968 — September 15, 1969. 83 episodes. Syndicated. CBS (rebroadcasts) — 70 minutes (ten extra minutes for commercials) — December 21, 1979 —

April 14, 1980; May 10, 1980 — September 5, 1980. 25 selected episodes starring Patrick Macnee, Diana Rigg and Linda Thorson. Spin-off series, *The New Avengers.* The episodes produced from 1961 to 1965 were not telecast in the United States.

75   THE AWAKENING LAND

Drama. A three-part miniseries, set in the community of Moonshine in the Ohio Territory from 1790 throug 1817, that follows the life of Sayward Luckett and her triumphant struggles over the hardships of pioneer life. Based on the novels by Conrad Richter.

CAST

Sayward Luckett	Elizabeth Montgomery
Genny Luckett, her sister	Jane Seymour
Achsa Luckett, her sister	Derin Altay
Sulie Luckett, her sister	Michelle Stacy
Worth Luckett, Sayward's father	Tony Mockus
Jary Luckett, Sayward's mother	Louise Latham
Portius Wheeler, the lawyer; later Sayward's husband	Hal Holbrook
Resolve Wheeler, their son	Sean Frye
Resolve Wheeler (adult)	Martin Scanlan
Little Sulie Wheeler, their daughter	Theresa Landreth
Huldah Wheeler, their daughter	Pia Romans
Huldah Wheeler (adult)	Devon Ericson
Kinzie Wheeler, their son	Johnny Timko
Kinzie Wheeler (adult)	Paul Swanson
Chancey Wheeler, their son	Dennis Dimster
Also:	
Will Beagle	W.H. Macy
Jake Tench	Steven Keats
Louie Scurrah	Barney McFadden
Granny	Jeanette Nolan
Angus Witherspoon	James O'Reilly
Mistress Bartram	Dorrie Kavanaugh
Isaac Barker	Bert Remsen
Cora Barker	Sandra Wheeler
Rosa Tench	Katy Kurtzman
Aunt Cornelia Wheeler	Joan Tompkins
Minister	Charles Tyner
Mathias Tull	Bernie Kubie
Idie Tull	Jane Alderman
Zeplin Brown	Louis Plante
Moses	Olesley Cole
Lady peddler	Julie Briggs
Alan Hamilton	Charles Golin
Fiddle player	Bill Neal

Narrator: Elizabeth Montgomery.
Music: Fred Karlin.
Executive Producer: Harry Bernstein, Tom Kuhn.
Producer: Robert E. Relyea.
Writer: James Lee Barrett.
Director: Boris Sagal.
Director of Photography: Michel Hugo.

THE AWAKENING LAND — 7 hours total (2 two-hour episodes; one three-hour episode) — NBC — February 19, 1978 — February 21, 1978. 3 episodes. Rebroadcasts: NBC — July 20, 1980 — July 22, 1980.

B

BAA BAA BLACK SHEEP

See title *The Black Sheep Squadron*.

76   BABY, I'M BACK!

Comedy. Unable to cope with the responsibilities of raising a family, Ray Ellis departs, leaving his wife Olivia and children Angie and Jordan to fend for themselves. The series, set in Washington, D.C., follows Ray's misadventures when, returning after seven years, he tries to win back his wife's affections and prove that he can be a good husband.

CAST

Ray Ellis, the father	Demond Wilson
Olivia Ellis, his wife	Denise Nicholas
Angie Ellis, their daughter	Kim Fields
Jordan Ellis, their son	Tony Holmes
Luzelle Carter, Olivia's mother	Helen Martin
Col. Wallace Dickey, Olivia's boss at the Pentagon	Ed Hall

Music: Jeff Berry.
Executive Producer: Charles Fries, Sandy Krinski.
Producer: Lila Garrett.
Director: Dick Harwood, Nick Havinga, Asaad Kelada, Mark Warren.
Creator: Lila Garrett, Mort Lachman.

BABY, I'M BACK!—30 minutes—CBS—January 30, 1978–August 12, 1978. 12 episodes.

77   BACKSTAIRS AT THE WHITE HOUSE

Drama. A four-part miniseries that reveals the private lives of eight First Families, from the Tafts (1909) to the Eisenhowers (1963), as seen through the eyes of White House maids Maggie Rogers and her daughter Lillian Rogers Parks. Based on the book *My Thirty Years At the White House* by Lillian Rogers Parks and Frances Spatz Leighton.

CAST

The White House Staff:

Maggie Rogers, a maid	Olivia Cole
Lillian Rogers Parks, a maid	Leslie Uggams
Levi Mercer, the houseman	Louis Gossett, Jr.
John Mays, the doorman	Robert Hooks
Ike Hoover, the chief usher	Leslie Nielsen
Butler Coates	Harry Rhodes
Doorman Jackson	Bill Overton
Mrs. Jaffrey, the housekeeper	Cloris Leachman
Mrs. Nesbitt, the housekeeper	Louise Latham
Mrs. Long, the housekeeper	Diane Shalet
Miss Walker, the housekeeper	Marged Wakeley
Chief Usher Howell Krimm	Richard Roat
Head Maid Annie Gilhooley	Helena Carroll
Third Butler Dickson	David Downing
Houseman James Frazier	James A. Watson, Jr.
Houseman Michaels	Joe Lowry
Butler Roch	Tom Scott
Moira, a maid	Kathleen Doyle
Vietta, a maid	Betty Bridges
Maureen, a maid	Anna Mathias
Sevilla, a maid	Bee Bee Drake Hooks
Butler Luke Henry	Stymie Beard

The First Families:

Pres. William Howard Taft	Victor Buono
Mrs. Helen Nellie Taft	Julie Harris
Pres. Woodrow Wilson	Robert Vaughn
Mrs. Ellen Wilson (Woodrow's first wife)	Kim Hunter
Mrs. Edith Galt Wilson (his second wife)	Claire Bloom
Pres. Warren G. Harding	George Kennedy
Mrs. Florence Harding	Celeste Holm
Pres. Calvin Coolidge	Ed Flanders
Mrs. Grace Coolidge	Lee Grant
Pres. Herbert Hoover	Larry Gates
Mrs. Lou Hoover	Jan Sterling
Pres. Franklin Delano Roosevelt	John Anderson
Mrs. Eleanor Roosevelt	Eileen Heckart
Pres. Harry S. Truman	Harry Morgan
Mrs. Bess Truman	Estelle Parsons
Pres. Dwight D. Eisenhower	Andrew Duggan
Mrs. Mamie Eisenhower	Barbara Barrie

Also:

Emmett Rogers, Jr., Maggie's son	Kevin Hooks
Lillian Rogers, as a girl	Tania Johnson
Emmett Rogers, as a boy	Murphy Robinson
Emmett Rogers, Sr., Maggie's husband	Paul Winfield
Wheatley Parks, Lillian's husband	Harrison Page
Charlie Taft, William's son	Gary Borden
Calvin Coolidge, Jr., Calvin's son	Carson Spies
Margaret Leland, Roosevelt's secretary	Bibi Besch
Presidential Secretary	Lee Kessler
Alexander Wolcott, the writer	Tom Clancy
Margaret Truman, Harry's daughter	Nancy Morgan
Ellen Truman, Harry's mother	Ann Doran
Mrs. Wallace, Bess's mother	Heather Angel
Attorney General Harry Daugherty	Barry Sullivan
Judge Jessie Smith	Harry Townes
Charles Kramer, the lawyer	Noble Willingham

Narrator: Leslie Nielsen.
Music: Morton Stevens.
Executive Producer: Ed Friendly.
Producer: Ed Friendly, Michael O'Herlihy.
Writer: Gwen Bagni, Paul Dubov.
Director: Michael O'Herlihy.
Art Director: Richard Haman.
Director of Photography: Robert L. Morrison.

BACKSTAIRS AT THE WHITE HOUSE—9 hours (total)—NBC—January 29, 1979–February 19, 1979. 4 episodes (three two-hour episodes; one three-hour episode). Rebroadcasts (NBC): August 24, 1980–August 28, 1980.

78   B.A.D. CATS

Crime Drama. The exploits of Ocee James and Nick Donovan, stock car racers, and Samantha Jensen, a beautiful back-up cop, members of B.A.D., the Burglary Auto Detail of the Los Angeles Police Department.

CAST

Ocee James	Steven Hanks
"Sunshine" Samantha Jensen	Michelle Pfeiffer
Nick Donovan	Asher Brauner
Captain Skip Nathan, their superior	Vic Morrow
Rodney Washington, their informant, the owner of a car repossession agency	Jimmie Walker
Ma, the owner of Ma's Place, a bar-restaurant	LaWanda Page
Mike Cole, the police garage mechanic	Morris Buchanan
Mrs. Bernardi, Nick and Ocee's landlady	Peggy Santon

Music: Barry DeVorzon, Mundell Lowe, Andrew Kulberg.
Music Supervision: Rocky Moriana, J.J. Johnson.
Supervising Producer: E. Duke Vincent.
Executive Producer: Aaron Spelling, Douglas S. Cramer.
Producer: Everett Chambers.
Writer: Al Martinez, David Harmon, Shorty Rogers.
Director: Bernard L. Kowalski, Ted Post, Sutton Roley.

B.A.D. CATS—60 minutes—ABC—January 4, 1980–February 8, 1980. 6 episodes.

79   THE BAD NEWS BEARS

Comedy. The series, set in Santa Barbara, California, follows the hectic misadventures of Morris Buttermaker, a pool cleaner who volunteers to become coach for the W. Wendell Weever School Bears, an undisciplined Little League baseball team, rather than spend a year's jail term for driving a client's car into a swimming pool (In the final episode of the first season, the Weever Bears win the championship and the title is explained: it's going to be "Bad News" for any team they now play.)

CAST

Morris Buttermaker	Jack Warden
Dr. Emily Rappant, the principal	Catherine Hicks

The Weever Bears:

Amanda Wurlitzer	Tricia Cast
Ogilvie	Sparky Marcus
Tanner Boyle	Meeno Peluce
Rudi Stein	Billy Jacoby
Regi	Corey Feldman
Timothy Lupus	Shane Butterworth
Ahmad Abdual Rahim	Christoff St. John
Mike Engelberg	J. Brennan Smith
Kelly Leak	Gregg Forrest
Josh Matthews	Rad Daly

Also:

Roy Turner, manager of the Lions baseball team	Philip R. Allen
Alice Wurlitzer, Amanda's mother	Joyce Bulifant

Address of the Weever School: 1647 Lorraine Court.
Based on Characters Created by Bill Lancaster. (Developed for television by Bob Brunner and Arthur Silver.)
Music: David Frank.
Executive Producer: Arthur Silver, Bob Brunner.
Producer: John Boni, Norman Stiles, Jeffrey Ganz, Ron Leavitt, Brian Levant.
Director: Bruce Bilson, William Asher, Norman Abbott, Gene Nelson, Alan Myerson, Lowell Ganz, Jeffrey Ganz.

THE BAD NEWS BEARS—30 minutes—CBS—March 24, 1979–October 6, 1979. 16 episodes. June 7, 1980–July 26, 1980. 7 episodes.

80   BAFFLE

Game. Two teams, each composed of a celebrity captain and a noncelebrity contestant, compete. One member of each team is placed in a sound/proof booth and the sound is turned off in one of the cubicles. The outside player of the other team places, at six-second intervals, large plastic letters on a wall rack that will eventually spell out a phrase. The object is for the booth player to identify the phrase as quickly as possible. When the phrase is identified, the other team competes in the same manner with the same phrase. The team that scores the least amount of overall time is the winner and the contestant receives merchandise prizes. A later format, titled "All Star Baffle," involves four celebrities playing the exact same game for selected studio audience members.

Host: Dick Enberg.
Announcer: Kenny Williams.
Music: Mort Garson.

BAFFLE—30 minutes—NBC—March 26, 1973–October 5, 1973. 130 programs.

ALL STAR BAFFLE—30 minutes—NBC—October 8, 1973–March 29, 1974. 115 programs.

81   BAGGY PANTS AND THE NITWITS

Animated Cartoon.

Segments:
Baggy Pants. The misadventures of a nonspeaking hobo cat that is reminiscent of Charlie Chaplin's famous tramp.

NBC

The Awakening Land. Hal Holbrook and Elizabeth Montgomery.

ABC

B.A.D. Cats. From left, Steven Hanks, Michelle Pfeiffer and Asher Brauner.

ABC

Barefoot in the Park. Scoey Mitchlll, at left, with Tracy Reed.

CBS

Barnaby Jones. Buddy Ebsen and Lee Meriwether.

The Nitwits. The misadventures of Tyrone, a retired super hero who forsakes retirement to assist the world in its battle against crime.

VOICES

Tyrone	Arte Johnson
Gladys, his wife	Ruth Buzzi

Music: Doug Goodwin, Steve DePatie.
Producer: David DePatie, Friz Freleng.
Director: Bob McKimson, Sid Marcus, Spencer Peel, Brad Case.

BAGGY PANTS AND THE NIT-WITS—30 minutes—NBC—September 10, 1977–October 28, 1978.

82   BAILEY'S COMETS

Animated Cartoon. The saga of a global skating race and of the seventeen competing roller derby teams who are seeking the million-dollar first prize. Clues to the prize are presented through an endless trail of poetic rhymes; and episodes depict the attempts of one team, Bailey's Comets, to overcome the diabolical schemes of the other teams as they attempt to eliminate them from the competition.

Teams: Bailey's Comets; The Broomer Girls; The Roller Bears; The Doctor Jekyll/Hydes; The Hairy Madden Red Eyes; The Duster Busters; The Yo Ho Ho's; The Mystery Mob; The Rambling Rivits; The Cosmic Rays; The Roller Coasters; The Texas Flycats; The Stone Rollers; The Gusta Pastas; The Rock 'N' Rollers; The Black Hats; The Gargantuan Giants.
Bailey's Comets Team Members: Barnaby, Dee Dee, Bunny, Wheelie, Pudge, and Sarge.
Helicopter Reporters: Dooter Roo, the pilot; and Gabby, the race commentator.
Voices: Don Messick, Sarah Kennedy, Daws Butler, Jim Brigg, Karen Smith, Robert Holt, Kathi Gori, Frank Welker.
Music: Doug Goodwin, Eric Rogers.
Producer: Friz Freleng, David DePatie.
Director: Brad Case, Sid Marcus, Bob McKimson, Spencer Peel.

BAILEY'S COMETS—30 minutes—CBS—September 8, 1973–January 26, 1974. 16 episodes.

83   BALL FOUR

Comedy. A satire about major league baseball as seen through the off-field antics of the Washington Americans, a disorganized baseball team. Based on the book, *Ball Four* by Jim Bouton.

CAST

Jim Barton, the relief pitcher	Jim Bouton
Rayford Plunkett, the pitcher	Marco St. John
Benjamin "Rhino" Rhinelander, the catcher	Ben Davidson
C.B. Travis, the outfielder	Sam Wright
Orlando Walter Lopez, the utility man	Jaime Tirelli
Harold "Pinky" Pinkney, the coach	Bill McCutcheon
Cappy, the manager	Jack Somack
Bill Westlake, the rookie	David-James Carroll
Lenny "Birdman" Siegel, the troublemaker	Lenny Schultz

Music: Harry Chapin.
Producer: Don Segall.
Director: Jay Sandrich, Nick Havinga, Peter Lewis.

BALL FOUR—30 minutes—CBS—September 22, 1976–October 27, 1976. 4 episodes.

84   BANACEK

Crime Drama. The investigations of Thomas Banacek, a Boston-based, self-employed insurance company detective who recovers stolen merchandise for ten percent of its value.

CAST

Thomas Banacek	George Peppard
Felix Mulholland, his information man	Murray Matheson
Jay Drury, his chauffeur	Ralph Manza
Carlie Kirkland, an agent for the Boston Insurance Company	Christine Belford

Music: Billy Goldenberg, Jack Elliott, Allyn Ferguson.
Executive Producer: George Eckstein.
Producer: Howie Horowitz
Writer: David Moessinger, Mort Fine, Del Reisman, Stanley Ralph Ross, Theodore J. Flicker, Stanley Roberts, Jimmy Sangster, Robert Van Scoyk, Robert Presnell, Jr., Stephen Kandel, Jack Turley, Stephen Lord, Lee Stanley, Paul Playdon, Harold Livingston.
Director: Richard T. Heffron, Bernard L. Kowalski, George McCowan, Bernard McEveety, Andrew McLaglen, Herschel Daugherty, Daryl Duke, Lou Antonio, Jack Smight, Theodore J. Flicker, Jimmy Sangster.

BANACEK—90 minutes—NBC—September 13, 1972–November 21, 1973 (as part of *The NBC Wednesday Mystery Movie*); January 15, 1974–September 3, 1974 (as part of *The NBC Tuesday Mystery Movie*). The two-hour pilot film aired on NBC on March 20, 1972.

BANANA SPLITS AND FRIENDS

The syndicated title for *The Banana Splits Adventure Hour.*

85   THE BANANA SPLITS ADVENTURE HOUR

Children. A series of cartoons and live-action segments hosted by the Banana Splits, four animals: Fleegle, the dog; Drooper, the lion; Bingo, the gorilla; and Snorky, the runt elephant.

VOICES

Fleegle	Paul Winchell
Bingo	Daws Butler
Drooper	Allan Melvin
Snorky	Don Messick

Cartoon Segments:
The Three Musketeers.
Voices: D'Artagnan: Bruce Watson; Porthos: Barney Phillips; Aramis: Don Messick; Athos: Jonathan Harris; Tooly: Ted Eccles; The Queen: Julie Bennett; Constance: Julie Bennett.

The Arabian Knights.
Voices: Bez: Henry Corden; Evil Vangore: Paul Frees; Raseem: Frank Gerstle; Princess Nidor: Shari Lewis; Turban: Jay North; Fariik: John Stephenson.

The Hillbilly Bears.
Voices: Paw Rugg: Henry Corden; Maw Rugg: Jean VanderPyl; Flora Rugg: Jean VanderPyl; Shagg Rugg: Don Messick.

Film Segments:
The Micro Venture. Life in the world of microscopic creatures.
Voices: Professor Carter: Don Messick; Jill Carter: Patsy Garrett; Mike Carter: Tommy Cook.

Danger Island. The adventures of Professor Irwin Hayden, an archeologist-explorer.
Cast: Irwin Hayden: Frank Aletter; Leslie Hayden, his daughter: Ronne Troup; Link Simmons, his assistant: Jan Michael Vincent; Morgan, the castaway: Rockne Tarkington.
Music: Hoyt Curtin, Jack Eskew.
Producer: William Hanna, Joseph Barbera.

THE BANANA SPLITS ADVENTURE HOUR—60 minutes—NBC—September 7, 1968–September 5, 1970. Syndicated title: *Banana Splits and Friends.*

86   THE BANG-SHANG LALAPALOOZA SHOW

Animated Cartoon. The adventures of Archie Andrews, Betty Cooper, Veronica Lodge, Jughead Jones and Reggie Mantle, high school students in the town of Riverdale.

VOICES

Archie Andrews	Dallas McKennon
Betty Cooper	Jane Webb
Veronica Lodge	Jane Webb
Jughead Jones	Howard Morris
Reggie Mantle	John Erwin
Carlos, their friend	Jose Flores
Hot Dog, the gang pet	Don Messick
Sabrina, the teenage witch	Jane Webb

Music: Yvette Blais, Jeff Michael.
Executive Producer: Norm Prescott, Lou Scheimer.
Producer: Don Christensen.

THE BANG-SHANG LALAPALOOZA SHOW—30 minutes—NBC—November 19, 1977–January 28, 1978. 11 episodes.

87   BANYON

Crime Drama. The series, set in Los Angeles in 1937, follows the exploits of Miles C. Banyon, a private detective.

CAST

Miles C. Banyon	Robert Forster
Sgt. Peter McNeil	Richard Jaeckel
Peggy Revere, Banyon's friend, the owner of the Revere Secretarial School	Joan Blondell
Abby Graham, Banyon's friend, a singer	Julie Gregg
The Revere Secretaries:	
Mabel	Teri Garr
Lottie	Virginia Ann Lee
Helena	Char Fontane
Alma	Sarah Fankboner
Tina	Victoria Perry
	Barbara George
Vera	Elaine Giftos
Doris	Sherry Lansing
Dee Dee	Melanie Roba
Brenda	Pamela McMyler

Music: Leonard Rosenthal.
Executive Producer: Richard Alan Simmons, Quinn Martin.
Producer: Ed Adamson.
Director: Robert Day, Ralph Senensky, Reza S. Badiyi, Daniel Haller, Theodore J. Flicker, Charles S. Dubin.

BANYON—60 minutes—NBC—September 15, 1972–January 12, 1973. 13 episodes.

88   THE BARBARA WALTERS SPECIAL

Interview. A series of specials in which prominent people are interviewed.

Hostess: Barbara Walters.
Executive Producer: Don Mischer.
Producer: Lucy Jarvis, Daniel Wilson, Joann Goldberg.
Director: John Desmond, Don Mischer.

The Series:
Program 1: Dec. 14, 1976. Guests: President Gerald Ford, President-elect Jimmy Carter, Barbra Streisand, Jon Peters.
Program 2: April 6, 1977. Guests: Elizabeth Taylor and her husband John Warner, the Shah and Empress of Iran.
Program 3: May 31, 1977. Guests: Bob Hope, Bing Crosby, Redd Foxx.
Program 4: Dec. 6, 1977. Guests: Dolly Parton, Henry Winkler, Lucille Ball.
Program 5: Nov. 29, 1978. Guests: Alan Alda, Diana Ross, Steve

Martin, King Hussein and Queen Noor of Jordan.

Program 6: Dec. 14, 1978. Guests: President Jimmy Carter and his wife Rosalyn.

Program 7: March 13, 1979. Guests: John Wayne, Carroll and Nancy O'Connor, Jane Fonda.

Program 8: Dec. 5, 1979. Guests: Suzanne Somers, Sylvester Stallone, Stevie Wonder.

Program 9: April 1, 1980. Guests: Farrah Fawcett, Cheryl Ladd, Bo Derek, Bette Midler.

THE BARBARA WALTERS SPECIAL — 60 minutes — ABC — Premiered: December 14, 1976.

89   THE BARBARY COAST

Adventure. The story of Jeff Cable, an undercover agent for the governor of California, and Cash Canover, his partner, the owner of Cash Canover's Golden Gate Casino. Episodes relate their attempts to apprehend lawbreakers on the San Francisco's notorious Barbary Coast of the 1880s.

CAST

Jeff Cable	William Shatner
Cash Canover (pilot film)	Dennis Cole
Cash Canover (series)	Doug McClure
Moose Moran, works for Canover	Richard Kiel
Thumbs, works for Canover	Dave Turner
Brandy, a dance hall girl	Francine York
Rusty, a dance hall girl	Brooke Mills
Flame, a dance hall girl	Bobbi Jordan
Sam, the bartender	John Dennis
	Eddie Fontaine
The Casino Waiter	Jason Wingreen

Creator: Douglas Heyes.
Music: George Tipton, John Andrew Tartaglia.
Executive Producer: Cy Chermak.
Producer: Douglas Heyes.
Director: Winrich Kolbe, Bill Bixby, Alex Grasshoff, Herb Wallerstein, John Florea, Don McDougall.

THE BARBARY COAST — 60 minutes — ABC — September 8, 1975 – January 9, 1976. 13 episodes. The two-hour pilot film aired on ABC on May 4, 1975.

90   BAREFOOT IN THE PARK

Comedy. The story of Paul and Corie Bratter, newlyweds struggling to survive the difficult first years of marriage in New York City. Based on the play by Neil Simon.

CAST

Paul Bratter, a lawyer with the firm of Kendricks, Kein and Klein	Scoey Mitchlll
Corie Bratter, his wife	Tracy Reed
Honey Robinson, their friend, the owner of "Honey's Pool Hall"	Nipsey Russell
Mabel Bates, Corie's mother	Thelma Carpenter

Arthur Kendricks, Paul's employer — Harry Holcombe

The Bratters' address: 49 West 10th Street, Apt. 5-B.
Music: J.J. Johnson, Charles Fox.
Music Supervision: Kenyon Hopkins.
Executive Producer: William P. D'Angelo.
Producer: Robert Williams.
Writer: Jerry Belson, Garry Marshall, Bill Idelson, Harvey Miller.
Director: Jerry Paris, Bruce Bilson, Charles R. Rondeau.

BAREFOOT IN THE PARK — 30 minutes — ABC — September 24, 1970 – January 14, 1971. 12 episodes.

91   BARETTA

Crime Drama. The exploits of Tony Baretta, an undercover police detective with the 53rd Precinct (in an unidentified city) who has little respect for standard police procedures.

CAST

Tony Baretta	Robert Blake
Billy Truman, his friend, the house detective at the King Edward Hotel	Tom Ewell
Inspector Schiller	Dana Elcar
Lt. Hal Brubaker	Edward Glover
Rooster, Tony's informant	Michael D. Roberts
Mimi Ames, Tony's girlfriend	Sharon Cintron
Detective Foley	John Ward
Fats, the overweight detective	Chino Williams
Little Moe, Tony's informant	Angelo Rosetti
Detective Palanski	Art Metrano
Fred, Tony's pet cockatoo	Lala

Music: Dave Grusin, Tom Scott.
Theme: "Keep Your Eye on the Sparrow."
Vocal: Sammy Davis Jr.
Executive Producer: Bernard L. Kowalski, Anthony Spinner.
Producer: Charles E. Dismukes, Howie Horwitz, Jo Swerling, Jr., Robert Lewis, Robert Harris.
Director: Don Medford, Reza S. Badiyi, Vincent Sherman, Bernard L. Kowalski, John Ward, Chris Robinson, Bruce Kessler, Robert Douglas, Robert Blake, Douglas Heyes, Burt Brinkerhoff, Sutton Roley, Ted Post, Paul Stanley, Michael Schultz, Russ Mayberry, Charles R. Rondeau.
Creator: Stephen J. Cannell.

BARETTA — 60 minutes — ABC — January 17, 1975 – June 1, 1978. Syndicated.

92   THE BARKLEYS

Animated Cartoon. The main characters are dogs who are patterned after the characters in *All in the Family*. Episodes relate the life of Arnie Barkley, an outspoken, opinionated and loud-mouthed bus driver as he attempts to cope with life, understand his progressive children, and bridge the generation gap that exists between them.

VOICES

Arnie Barkley, the father	Henry Corden
Agnes Barkley, his wife	Joan Gerber
Terri Barkley, their daughter	Julie McWhirter
Chester Barkley, their son	Steve Lewis
Roger Barkley, their son	Gene Andrusco

Additional Voices: Frank Welker, Robert Holt, Don Messick, Bob Frank, Michael Bell.
Music: Doug Goodwin, Eric Rogers.
Producer: Friz Freleng, David DePatie.
Director: Bob McKimson, Spencer Peel, Sid Marcus, Brad Case.

THE BARKLEYS — 30 minutes — NBC — September 9, 1972 – September 1, 1973. 13 episodes.

93   BARNABY JONES

Crime Drama. The investigations of Barnaby Jones, a private detective working out of Los Angeles.

CAST

Barnaby Jones	Buddy Ebsen
Betty Jones, his daughter-in-law and assistant	Lee Meriwether
Jedidiah (J.R.) Jones, Barnaby's cousin and legman	Mark Shera
Lt. John Biddle, L.A.P.D.	John Carter

Music: Bruce Broughton, Frank Comstock, John Elizalde, Duane Tatro, Jerry Fielding, Jeff Alexander, George Romanis, Jerry Goldsmith, Lance Rubin.
Executive Producer: Quinn Martin, Philip Saltzman.
Producer: Philip Saltzman, Robert Sherman.
Director: Kenneth Gilbert, Ernest Pintoff, Walter Grauman, Michael Caffey, Seymour Robbie, Bruce Kessler, Winrich Kolbe, Graeme Clifford, Lewis Teague, Michael Preece, Leslie H. Martinson, Leo Penn, William Hale, Dick Lowry, Ron Satlof, Mel Damski, Allen Reisner, Larry Elikann, Allen Baron, Robert Day.

BARNABY JONES — 60 minutes — CBS — January 28, 1973 – April 3, 1980; May 1, 1980 – September 4, 1980. Syndicated.

94   BARNEY MILLER

Comedy. The trials and tribulations of Captain Barney Miller, the chief of detectives of the 12th Precinct on 6th Avenue in New York City's Greenwich Village.

CAST

Capt. Barney Miller	Hal Linden
Elizabeth Miller, his wife (pilot film)	Abby Dalton
Elizabeth Miller (series)	Barbara Barrie
Rachel Miller, their daughter	Anne Wyndham
David Miller, their son	Michael Tessier
Sgt. Phil Fish	Abe Vigoda
Bernice Fish, Phil's wife	Florence Stanley
Sgt. Stan Wojehowicz	Max Gail
Det. Chano Amengual	Gregory Sierra
Sgt. Nick Yemana	Jack Soo
Det. Ron Harris	Ron Glass
Frank Luger, the police inspector	James Gregory
Det. Janet Wentworth	Linda Lavin
Detective Battista	June Gable
Sgt. Arthur Dietrich	Steve Landesberg
Det. Mike Lovaetti	Art Metrano
Officer Kogan	Milt Kogan
Officer Carl Levitt	Ron Carey
Arnold Ripner, the lawyer	Alex Henteloff

Music: Jack Elliott, Allyn Ferguson.
Executive Producer: Danny Arnold, Theodore J. Flicker.
Producer: Chris Hayward, Tony Sheehan, Reinhold Weege, Noam Pitlik.
Director: Alex March, Danny Arnold, Noam Pitlik, Dennis Steinmetz, David Swift, Max Gail, Bruce Bilson, Theodore J. Flicker.
Creator: Danny Arnold. Theodore J. Flicker.

BARNEY MILLER — 30 minutes — ABC — Premiered: January 23, 1975. The 30-minute pilot film, "The Life and Times of Captain Barney Miller," aired on ABC on August 22, 1974. Spin-off series: *Fish*.

95   THE BASTARD/KENT FAMILY CHRONICLES

Drama. A miniseries based on John Jake's multi-volume saga of the Kents, a fictional American family. *The Bastard,* based on the first novel, begins in France in 1771 and tells the story of Phillipe Charboneau, the illegitimate son of the dying Duke of Kentland and heir to half of the British nobleman's estate. The series also focuses on the early years of the American Revolution as the colonists begin the overthrow of British rule.

CAST

Phillipe Charboneau/ Philip Kent	Andrew Stevens
Dan O'Brien	Noah Beery
Girard	Peter Bonerz
Benjamin Franklin	Tom Bosley
Anne Ware	Kim Cattrall
Lord North	John Colicos
Samuel Adams	William Daniels
Benjamin Edes	Buddy Ebsen
Bishop Francis	Lorne Greene
Will Campbell	James Gregory
Alicia	Olivia Hussey
Lucas	Herbert Jefferson, Jr.
Captain Plummer	Cameron Mitchell
Captain Caleb	Harry Morgan
Marie Charboneau	Patricia Neal
Lady Amberly	Eleanor Parker
Solomon Sholto	Donald Pleasence

Paul Revere	William Shatner
Johnny Malcolm	Keenan Wynn
Doctor Warren	Jim Antonio
British Officer	William Bassett
Landlord	Roger Bowen
Hosea Sholto	Robert Burke
Seadog	George Chandler
Major	Sam Chew, Jr.
Lt. Stark	John De Lancie
Jeremy Thaxter	Johnny Doran
Gil	Ike Eisenman
General	Peter Elbling
George Lumden	Charles Haid
Henry Knox	Alex Henteloff
Col. James Barrett	Russell Johnson
Fat Man	Claude Earl Jones
Turly	Monte Landis
Dr. Bleeker	Alan Napier
Roger Amberly	Mark Neely
Emma Sholto	Elizabeth Shepherd
Dr. Prescott	John Mark Robinson
Daisy O'Brien	Carol Tru Foster
Esau Sholto	James Whitmore, Jr.
British Sergeant	Michael Alldredge
Charlotte	Beege Barkette
Valet	Albert Carrier
Auguste Du Pleis	Damon Douglas
Bertrand	Stephen Furst
Beggar	James Garrett
Shopkeeper	Phil Hall
Coachman	Keith McConnell
Captain Rotch	Richard Peel
Woman	Peggy Rea
Mister Dawes	Clint Ritchie
Innkeeper	Banjamin Stewart
Polly	Pamela White

Narrator: Raymond Burr.
Music: John Addison.
Executive Producer: John Wilder.
Producer: Joe Byrne.
Writer: Guerdon Trueblood.
Director: Lee H. Katzin.
Art Director: Loyd S. Papez.
Director of Photography: Michel Hugo.
Costumes: Vincent Dee and Jean Pierre Dorleac.
Associate Producer: Susan Lichtwardt.

THE BASTARD/KENT FAMILY CHRONICLES — 2 hours — Operation Prime Time — May 1978. 2 episodes.

96 BATTLE OF THE NETWORK STARS

Game. A twice yearly event in which stars from ABC, CBS and NBC compete against each other in a series of athletic events to determine which network is best in the athletic field. First-place team members each receive $20,000; $15,000 is awarded to each member of the second-place team; and members of the third-place team receive $10,000 apiece.

Executive Producer: Roone Arledge.
Producer: Don Ohlmeyer, Doug Wilson.
Director: Roger Goodman, Jim Jennette.

Program 1: Nov. 13, 1976:

Host: Howard Cosell.
Team Captains: Gabriel Kaplan (ABC), Telly Savalas (CBS), Robert Conrad (NBC).
ABC Team: Darleen Carr, Lynda Carter, Richard Hatch, Robert Hegyes, Ron Howard, Hal Linden, Farrah Fawcett, Penny Marshall, John Schuck.
CBS Team: Adrienne Barbeau, Gary Burghoff, Kevin Dobson, Pat Harrington, Bill Macy, Lee Meriwether, Mackenzie Phillips, Loretta Swit, Jimmie Walker.
NBC Team: Melissa Sue Anderson, Karen Grassle, Tim Matheson, Ben Murphy, Barbara Parkins, Joanna Pettet, Kevin Tighe, Bobby Troup, Demond Wilson.

Program 2: Feb. 28, 1977:

Host: Howard Cosell.
Team Captains: Gabriel Kaplan (ABC), Telly Savalas (CBS), Robert Conrad (NBC).
ABC Team: LeVar Burton, Darleen Carr, Richard Hatch, Ron Howard, Lawrence Hilton Jacobs, Hal Linden, Penny Marshall, Kristy McNichol, Jaclyn Smith.
CBS Team: Sonny Bono, Kevin Dobson, Mike Farrell, David Groh, Linda Lavin, Lee Meriwether, Rob Reiner, Loretta Swit, Marcia Wallace.
NBC Team: Elizabeth Allen, Carl Franklin, Lynda Day George, Karen Grassle, Dan Haggerty, Art Hindle, Kurt Russell, Jane Seymour, W. K. Stratton.

Program 3: Nov. 4, 1977:

Hosts: Howard Cosell, Telly Savalas.
Team Captains: Gabriel Kaplan (ABC), Jimmie Walker (CBS), Dan Haggerty (NBC).
ABC Team: Fred Berry, Billy Crystal, Chris DeRose, Victor French, Cheryl Ladd, Penny Marshall, Kristy McNichol, Suzanne Somers, Parker Stevenson.
CBS Team: Adrienne Barbeau, Valerie Bertinelli, Kevin Dobson, Jamie Farr, Caren Kaye, James MacArthur, Jimmy McNichol, Loretta Swit, Lyle Waggoner.
NBC Team: Robert Conrad, Elinor Donahue, Patrick Duffy, Peter Isacksen, Lance Kerwin, Donna Mills, Belinda J. Montgomery, Michelle Phillips, Larry Wilcox.

Program 4: May 7, 1978:

Hosts: Suzanne Somers, Howard Cosell, Bruce Jenner.
Team Captains: Gabriel Kaplan (ABC), Tony Randall (CBS), Richard Benjamin (NBC).

ABC Team: Cheryl Tiegs, Debby Boone, Daryl Dragon, Toni Tennille, Parker Stevenson, Kene Holliday, Steve Landesberg.
CBS Team: Kevin Dobson, James MacArthur, Denise Nicholas, Mackenzie Phillips, Victoria Principal, Bo Svenson, Jimmie Walker.
NBC Team: Dan Haggerty, Rhonda Bates, Dennis Dugan, Melissa Gilbert, Arte Johnson, Lance Kerwin, Larry Wilcox, Jane Curtin.

Program 5: Nov. 18, 1978:

Hosts: Howard Cosell, Frank Gilford.
Team Captains: Gabriel Kaplan (ABC), McLean Stevenson (CBS), Robert Conrad (NBC).
ABC Team: Debby Boone, Billy Crystal, Joyce DeWitt, Richard Hatch, Maren Jensen, Robert Urich, Robin Williams.
CBS Team: Valerie Bertinelli, LeVar Burton, Lou Ferrigno, Pat Klous, David Letterman, Tim Reid, Charlene Tilton.
NBC Team: Joseph Bottoms, William Devane, Pamela Hensley, Brianne Leary, Wendy Rastatter, William Shatner, Caskey Swaim.

Program 6: May 7, 1979:

Host: Howard Cosell.
Team Captains: Dick Van Patten (ABC), Jamie Farr (CBS), Robert Conrad (NBC).
ABC Team: Scott Baio, Billy Crystal, Richard Hatch, Donna Pescow. Susan Richardson, Toni Tennille, Robert Urich.
CBS Team: Catherine Bach, Valerie Bertinelli, Patrick Duffy, Jamie Farr, Lou Ferrigno, Leif Garrett, Victoria Principal, Gary Sandy.
NBC Team: Todd Bridges, Mary Crosby, Jane Curtin, William Devane, Greg Evigan, Brianne Leary, Larry Wilcox.

Program 7: Nov. 2, 1979:

Hosts: Howard Cosell, Billy Crystal.
Team Captains: Dick Van Patten (ABC), Edward Asner (CBS), Robert Conrad (NBC).
ABC Team: Willie Aames, Diana Canova, Joanna Cassidy, Max Gail, Robert Hays, Kristy McNichol, Shelley Smith.
CBS Team: Valerie Bertinelli, Gregory Harrison, Howard Hesseman, Kathryn Leigh Scott, Jan Smithers, Judy Norton-Taylor, Allen Williams.
NBC Team: Greg Evigan, Gil Gerard, Melissa Gilbert, Erin Gray, Randi Oakes, Sarah Purcell, Patrick Wayne.

Program 8: May 4, 1980:

Hosts: Joyce DeWitt, Howard Cosell.

Team Captains: Cathy Lee Crosby (ABC), Chad Everett (CBS), William Devane (NBC).
ABC Team: Scott Baio, Robyn Douglass, Robert Hays, Grant Goodeve, Kent McCord, Caroline McWilliams, Joan Prather.
CBS Team: Jonelle Allen, Catherine Bach, Gregory Harrison, Sherman Hemsley, Gary Sandy, Charlene Tilton, Joan Van Ark.
NBC Team: Gil Gerard, Karen Grassle, Pamela Hensley, Brian Kerwin, Randi Oakes, Sarah Purcell, Larry Wilcox.

BATTLE OF THE NETWORK STARS — 2 hours — ABC — Premiered: November 13, 1976.

97 BATTLE OF THE PLANETS

Animated Cartoon. The series, set in the year 2020, depicts the exploits of Center Neptune's G-Force (an Earth-based defense organization established beneath the sea) as it battles Zoltar, leader of the planet Spectre, and his power-mad attempts to destroy Earth.

VOICES

7-Zark-7, the head of Center Neptune	Alan Young
Zoltar	Keye Luke
G-Force:	
Mark	Casey Kasem
Princess	Janet Waldo
Keop	Ronnie Schell
Jason	Ronnie Schell
Tiny	Alan Dinehart

Music: Hoyt Curtin.
Executive Producer: Jameson Brewer.
Producer: David Hanson.
Director: David Hanson.

BATTLE OF THE PLANETS — 30 minutes — Syndicated 1978. 85 episodes.

98 BATTLESTAR GALACTICA

Science Fiction Adventure. In the seventh millenium of time, in a galaxy far beyond that of our own, a thousand-year-old war rages: that of mankind versus the Cylons, a mechanical race of beings bent on destroying the human race because they pose a threat to their existence. When a last-ditch effort on the part of mankind to effect peace fails, and their twelve-colony planets are destroyed, the surviving members, representing every known colony in the galaxy, band together (in spaceships) and follow the *Galactica,* a gigantic battlestar spaceship, in an attempt to rebuild their lives on their thirteenth colony — a distant and unknown planet called Earth. The series follows their perilous

Battlestar Galactica. Maren Jensen in foreground. Behind her, from left, Dirk Benedict, Richard Hatch and Lorne Greene.

The Baxters. Anita Gillette and Larry Keith.

Bewitched. Clockwise, Agnes Moorehead, Dick Sargent, Erin Murphy, Elizabeth Montgomery and Maurice Evans.

The Bionic Woman. Lindsay Wagner.

journey—warding off alien creatures and battling the Cylon robots who are now determined to thwart their plans—as they seek the planet Earth.

CAST

Members of Galactica:

Commander Adama	Lorne Greene
Captain Apollo, his son	Richard Hatch
Athena, his daughter	Maren Jensen
Lt. Starbuck	Dirk Benedict
Lt. Boomer	Herb Jefferson, Jr.
Colonel Tigh	Terry Carter
Flight Sgt. Jolly	Tony Swartz
Boxey, Apollo's son	Noah Hathaway
Cassiopea	Laurette Spang
Sheba	Anne Lockhart
Regal	Sarah Rush
Flight Sgt. Greenbean	Ed Begley, Jr.
Girl Warrior	Jennifer Joseph
Girl Warrior	Leann Hunley
Girl Warrior	Millicent Crisp
Voice of Cora, the computer	Cathy Pine
Lt. Zac	Rick Springfield
Woman Galactican	Randi Oakes
Bridge Officer Omega	David Greenan
Operative	David Matthau
Dr. Salik	George Murdock
Dietra	Sheila De Windt
Brie	Janet Louise Johnson
Sorrell	Janet Lyn Curtis
Giles	Larry Manetti

Cylons:

Count Balter, the leader	John Colicos
Cylon Warrior	Chip Johnson
Cylon Warrior	Geoffrey Binney
Cylon Pilot	Paul Coufas
Cylon Deck Hand	Bruce Wright

Creator: Glen A. Larson.
Theme Song: "Galactica" by Glen A. Larson and Stu Phillips.
Music: Stu Phillips.
Music Played By: The Los Angeles Symphonic Orchestra.
Executive Producer: Glen A. Larson.
Supervising Producer: Leslie Stevens.
Associate Producer: Winrich Kolbe, David Phinney.
Producer: John Dykstra, Don Bellisario, Paul Playdon, David J. O'Connell.
Director: Richard Colla, Christian I. Nyby II, Rod Holcomb, Vince Edwards, Daniel Haller, Don Bellisario.
Special Effects: John Dykstra.
Program Open:
Announcer: There are those that believe that life here began out there, far across the universe with tribes of humans who may have been the forefathers of the Egyptians or the Toltecs or the Mayans. Some believe there may yet be brothers of man who even now fight to survive, somewhere beyond the heavens (theme plays).

BATTLESTAR GALACTICA—60 minutes—ABC—September 17, 1978–April 29, 1979. 20 episodes. Repeats: June 2, 1979–August 4, 1979. Syndicated. See also *Galactica 1980,* the spin-off series.

99   THE BAXTERS

Drama. A half-hour series that is divided into two parts: the first half dramatizes events in the lives of the Baxters: parents Nancy and Fred, and their children Naomi (age 19), Jonah (15), and Rachele (11), a middle-class St. Louis family struggling to cope with the important problems faced by everyone in today's world. In each episode approximately eleven minutes is devoted to a problem faced by the family. The telecast is then turned over to each local station on which the program is airing. In part two, a local host then conducts a debate with an audience about the context of the first half.

CAST

Nancy Baxter, the mother	Anita Gillette
Fred Baxter, the father	Larry Keith
Naomi Baxter, their daughter	Derin Altay
Jonah Baxter, their son	Chris Petersen
Rachele Baxter, their daughter	Terri Lynn Wood

National Credits:
Host (first episode only): Norman Lear.
Music: Marvin Laird.
Executive Producer: Norman Lear.
Producer: Fern Field.
Associate Producer: Robert J. Clayman.
Writer: Jon Surgal, Harry Cauley, Sandra Shepherd, John Owen.
Director: John Bowab, Jim Drake.

THE BAXTERS—30 minutes—Syndicated 1979.

100   THE BAXTERS

Drama. A revised version of the previous title, using the same format.

CAST

Jim Baxter, the father	Sean McCann
Suzie Baxter, the mother	Terry Tweed
Alison Baxter, their daughter	Marianne McIsaac
Greg Baxter, their son	Sammy Snyders
Lucy Baxter, their daughter	Megan Follows

Executive Producer: Chet Collier.
Producer: Wendell Wilks.
Writer: Jerry Rannow, Jewel Jaffe, Martin Ross.
Director: Ray Arsenault.

THE BAXTERS—30 minutes—Syndicated 1980.

101   THE BAY CITY ROLLERS SHOW

Variety. Music, songs and comedy sketches geared to children.

Hosts: The Bay City Rollers Rock Group.
Regulars: Billy Hayes, Jay Robinson, Billy Barty, Paul Gale, Sharon Baird, Patty Maloney, Louise Duart, Micky McMeel, Van Snowden.
Music: Tommy Oliver.

Executive Producer: Alvin J. Tenzer.
Producer: Jack Regas, Sid and Marty Krofft.
Director: Jack Regas.

THE BAY CITY ROLLERS SHOW—30 minutes—ABC—November 4, 1978–January 27, 1979. Originally broadcast under the title *The Krofft Superstar Hour* for 60 minutes on ABC from September 9, 1978 through October 28, 1978.

102   THE BEACHCOMBER

Adventure. Pressured by society, John Lackland, a wealthy merchandising executive, leaves San Francisco and retreats to Amura, an island paradise in the South Pacific. Adopting the lifestyle of a beachcomber, he searches for the true meaning of life. Stories relate his struggles as he encounters and assists people in distress.

CAST

John Lackland	Cameron Mitchell
Captain Huckabee, his friend	Don Megowan
Andrew Crippen, the commissioner (series)	Sebastian Cabot
Andrew Crippen (first episode)	Edmond Mills
Tarmu, Crippen's houseboy	Jerry Summers
Kallea, John's friend	Stan Josol
Reverend Snow, the island priest	George Mitchell
Alfy, the bartender, John's friend	Bill Hess

Narrator: Cameron Mitchell.
Theme: Elmer Bernstein.
Music: Marlin Skiles, Elmer Bernstein, Raoul Krashaaur, Joseph Hooven.
Executive Producer: Robert Stambler.
Producer: Nat Perrin.
Director: Bud Townsend, Tay Garnett, James P. Yarbrough.
Creator: Walter Brown Newman.

THE BEACHCOMBER—30 minutes—First Syndicated in 1961. Resyndicated in 1979 under the title *Mystery Adventure: The Beachcomber.* 39 episodes.

103   BEACON HILL

Serial. The series, set in Boston during the 1920s, depicts dramatic incidents in the lives of the Lassiters, a rich, powerful Irish-American family; and their servants, Irish immigrants, who live "below stairs" in the fashionable home on Louisburgh Square.

CAST

The Lassiter Family:

Benjamin Lassiter, an attorney	Stephen Elliott
Mary Lassiter, his wife	Nancy Marchand
Emily Bullock, their married daughter	DeAnn Mears
Trevor Bullock, Emily's husband	Roy Cooper
Betsy Bullock, their daughter	Linda Purl
Maude Palmer, Ben and Mary's married daughter	Maeve McGuire
Richard Palmer, Maude's husband	Edward Herrmann
Rosamond Lassiter, Ben and Mary's daughter	Kitty Winn
Robert Lassiter, Ben and Mary's son	David Dukes
Fawn Lassiter, Ben and Mary's daughter	Kathryn Walker

The Servants:

Mr. Hacker, the head butler	George Rose
Emmaline Hacker, his wife	Beatrice Straight
William Piper, the cook	Richard Ward
Brian Mallory, the chauffeur	Paul Rudd
Terence O'Hara, Hacker's assistant	David Rounds
Eleanor, a maid	Sydney Swire
Maureen, a maid	Susan Blanchard
Kate, a maid	Lisa Pelikan

Also:

John Broderick, the mayor	Joseph Mahen
Harry Emmit	Barry S. Snider
Marilyn Gardner	Harlan Taylor
Hortense, the brothel owner	Marlene Warfield
Georgio Belloni, Fawn's voice coach	Michael Nouri

Music: Marvin Hamlisch.
Executive Producer: Beryl Vertue.
Producer: Jacqueline Babbin.
Director: Fielder Cook, Peter Lewis, Jay Sandrich, Mel Ferber.

BEACON HILL—60 minutes—CBS—August 25, 1975–November 4, 1975. 13 episodes. Based on the British series, *Upstairs, Downstairs.*

104   BEARCATS!

Adventure. The series, set in the turbulent Southwest of 1914, features Hank Brackett and Johnny Reach, two free-lance troubleshooters who undertake the cases of people in trouble, but who are unable to turn to police for help.

CAST

Hank Brackett	Rod Taylor
Johnny Reach	Dennis Cole

Music: Dave Kahn.
Executive Producer: Douglas Heyes.
Producer: David Friedkin, Morton Fine.

BEARCATS!—60 minutes—CBS—September 16, 1971–December 30, 1971. 13 episodes. The pilot film "Powderkeg," aired on CBS on April 16, 1971.

105   BEAT THE CLOCK

Game.* Four contestants, divided into two teams of two, perform various stunts with the object being to beat the amount of time established on a ticking second clock. The winners of each round receive points, and the highest overall scorers at the end of the game are awarded merchandise prizes. A later format (after 35 programs) involves four celebrity guests who play for members of the studio audience.

Host: Monty Hall.
Announcer: Jack Narz.
Music: Score Productions.
Music Conductor: Arthur B. Rubinstein.
Models (assistants, as identified): Autumn, Lisa, Cindy.
Executive Producer: Frank Wayne.
Producer: Paul Alter.
Associate Producer: Jack Narz.
Director: Paul Alter.

BEAT THE CLOCK — 30 minutes — CBS — September 17, 1979 – October 2, 1979. 35 programs. Revised, celebrity format: November 5, 1979 – February 1, 1980. 55 programs.

*Two prior versions of the series appeared. The first, on CBS (March 23, 1950 – Febuary 16, 1958) with Clayton "Bud" Collyer as host and Dolores Rosedale ("Roxanne") as his assistant; and the second via syndication (1969) with Jack Narz as host and Gail Sheldon, Betsy Hirst, Ellen Singer, Linda Somer and Diane Mead as his assistants.

106   BEDTIME STORIES

Game. First, two married couples are interviewed in their bedrooms and candidly discuss their secrets for a successful relationship; later, the couples appear in the studio and compete in a game wherein they have to predict the highest scoring answers based on questions asked of one-hundred people. Each correct prediction scores $500 and three such questions are played. The winners, highest scorers, use their earnings to purchase merchandise from "The Bedtime Stories Gift Book."

After 10 programs, the format became that of a contest between two married couples to answer questions regarding each other's love life. With both couples on stage, a segment from a recorded bedroom interview is played and a question is asked — but the tape is stopped before the answer is given. The couple not involved in the interview must predict how the other couple responded to the question. The tape is played to reveal the answer and a correct response scores the team $500; an incorrect response awards the money to the other team. Round No. 2 reverses the couples situation for play and the highest scoring team is the winner.

Host: Al Lohman, Roger Barkley ("The Bedroom Ambassadors").
Announcer: Kenny Williams, Johnny Gilbert.
Music: Stan Worth.
Supervising Producer: Merrill Heatter, Bob Quigley.
Executive Producer: Jerry Readick.
Producer: Robert Noah.
Director: Bob Loudin.

BEDTIME STORIES — 30 minutes — Syndicated June 1979. 40 programs.

107   BEGGARMAN, THIEF

Drama. A miniseries that begins where the novels and prior miniseries "Rich Man, Poor Man," left off. "Beggarman, Thief," based on the novel by Irwin Shaw, is set in the late 1960s and revolves around three central characters: Gretchen Jordache Burke, a soul searching, guilt-ridden widow battling to make a career for herself as a Hollywood director; Billy Abbott, a ne'er-do-well army sergeant who is swept into black-market dealings and a dangerous romance in West Berlin; and Wesley Jordache, Billy's cousin, a hot-tempered, strong-willed youth seeking revenge in France for the murder of his father.

CAST
Gretchen Jordache Burke	Jean Simmons
Billy Abbott	Andrew Stevens
Wesley Jordache	Tom Nolan
David Donnelly	Glenn Ford
Kate Jordache	Lynn Redgrave
Monika Wolner	Tovah Feldshuh
Bunny Dwyer	Bo Hopkins
Jean Delacroix	Jean-Pierre Aumont
Dr. Moira O'Dell	Dr. Joyce Brothers
Evans Kinsella	Alex Cord
Teresa Kraler	Anne Francis
Sartene	Michael Gazzo
Honor Day	Anne Jeffreys
Ida Cohen	Susan Strasberg
Colonel Day	Robert Sterling
Inspector Charboneau	Christian Marquand
The Magistrate	Marcel Hillaire
Kraler	Frank Marth
U.S. intelligence agent	Walter Brooke
German intelligence agent	Stefan Gierasch

Also: Joe Maross, Chip Johnson, Cliff Osmond, Norman Lloyd, Ben Hamer, Kenneth O'Brien, Timothy O'Hagen, Robert Cameron.
Music: Eddie Sauter.
Producer: Jack Laird.
Writer: Art Eisenson, Mary Agnes Donahue.
Director: Lawrence Doheny.
Art Director: Loyd S. Papez.

BEGGARMAN, THIEF — 2 hours — NBC — November 26, 1979 – November 27, 1979. 2 episodes.

108   THE BENNY HILL SHOW

Comedy. Adult oriented comedy sketches (sexually provocative language and women in various stages of undress). Produced by Thames TV of London.

Host: Benny Hill.
Hill's Straight Man: Jackie Wright.
Regulars: Sue Bond, Patricia Hayes, Verne Morgan, Helli Louise, Chai-Lee, Henry McGee, Bob Todd, Diane Davey, Samantha Stevens, Lee Gibson, Nicholas Parsons, Ronnie Brody, The Ladybirds (Vocal trio), Carol Mills, Kay Frazer, Eira Heath, Yvonne Paul, Nina Martin, Rita Webb, Connie Georges, Andrea Melly, Bella Emberg, Debbie Greenwood, Stella Moray, Mia Martin, Lesley Goldie, Sue Bishop, Jimmy Thompson, Two's Company, Dan Jackson, Cheryl Gilham, Monica Ringwald, Sue Young, Patrick Newell, Earl Adair, Anne Bruzac, Eddie Buchanan, Claire Russell, Terry Day, Brian Nolan, Jenny Lee-Wright, Los Zafrios, Dan Jackson, Jan Butlin, Carmen Bene, The Love Machine, Jennie Lee Rich, John John Keefe, Yvonne Deerman, Helen Horton, Pat Ashton, Sue Lipton, Roger Finch, Erica Lindley, Hill's Angels (singers and dancers), Sharon Haywoode, Samantha Spencer Lane, Cheryl Cross, Ken Sedd.
Musical Director: Ronnie Aldrich, Jackie Grimsley.
Music Associate: Syd Lucas, Ted Taylor.
Original Songs: Benny Hill.
Executive Producer: Denis Spencer.
Producer: Keith Beckett, Mark Stuart, David Bell, John Robins, Peter Frazer-Jones, Dennis Kirkland.
Director: Keith Beckett, David Bell, John Robins, Peter Frazer-Jones, Dennis Kirkland.
Choreographer: Linda Finch, John Greenland, Arlene Phillips, Russ Hutchinson.

THE BENNY HILL SHOW — 30 minutes — Syndicated (to the U.S.) in 1979.

109   BENSON

Comedy. A spin-off from *Soap* wherein Benson, the Tate family butler, agrees to help Jessica's cousin, Gene Gatling, the governor of an unidentified Eastern state, organize his household. Learning that the governor is a paper mill industrialist who has entered politics reluctantly (to give the people an honest government) and actually is incapable of running the state, Benson soon becomes indespensible when his suggestions help the governor solve a controversial problem. The series follows Benson's adventures as the governor's butler — and the man responsible for keeping the state afloat.

CAST
Benson	Robert Guillaume
Governor Gene Gatling, a widower	James Noble
Marcie Hill, the governor's secretary	Caroline McWilliams
Gretchen Kraus, the housekeeper	Inga Swenson
John Taylor, the governor's aide	David Hedison Lewis J. Stadlen
Katie Gatling, Gene's daughter	Missy Gold
Clayton, the governor's aide	Rene Auberjonois
Pete, the press agent	Ethan Phillips

Last Commercial Break Announcer: James Noble.
Music: George Tipton.
Executive Producer: Tony Thomas, Paul Junger Witt, John Rich.
Producer: Susan Harris, Tom Reeder, Don Richetta, Tom Whedon.
Writer: Susan Harris, Tom Reeder, Bob Colleary, Paul Wayne, Paul Raley.
Director: Jay Sandrich, Peter Baldwin, John Bowab, Tony Mordente, Don Barnhart.
Creator: Susan Harris.

BENSON — 30 minutes — ABC — Premiered: September 13, 1979.

110   BEN VAREEN . . . COMIN' AT YA

Variety. Music, songs, dances and comedy sketches.

Host: Ben Vareen.
Regulars: Arte Johnson, Avery Schreiber, Liz Torres, The Louis DaPron Dancers.
Ben's Dancing Partner: Lee Lund.
Orchestra: Jack Elliott, Allyn Ferguson.
Special Musical Material: Ray Charles.
Choreography: Jerry Grimes.
Dance Numbers Staged by: Louis DaPron.
Producer: Jaime Rogers, Jean McAvoy.
Writer: Buz Kohan.
Director: Peter Calabrese.
Art Director: Tony Marchesi.

BEN VAREEN . . . COMIN' AT YA — 60 minutes — NBC — August 7, 1975 – August 28, 1975. 4 programs.

111   BERT D'ANGELO/ SUPERSTAR

Crime Drama. The story of Bert D'Angelo, a tough, unorthodox Los Angeles police detective who constantly defies rules and regulations in an attempt to get his job done. Because of his impressive record of arrests and convictions, he has earned the nickname "Superstar."

CAST

Bert D'Angelo	Paul Sorvino
Det. Larry Lorenzo, his partner	Robert Pine
Capt. Jack Breen, their superior	Dennis Patrick

Music: Duane Tatro, Patrick Williams, John Elizalde.
Executive Producer: Quinn Martin.
Producer: Mort Fine.
Director: David Friedkin, Virgil W. Vogel, Michael Caffey, Harry Falk, Bill Bixby, William Wiard.

BERT D'ANGELO/SUPERSTAR— 60 minutes—ABC—February 21, 1976–April 10, 1976; May 29, 1976–July 10, 1976.

THE BEST OF DONNY AND MARIE

Repeats of selected programs from the ABC network series, *Donny and Marie.*

112   THE BEST OF THE JACKIE GLEASON SHOW

Comedy. A series of excerpts compiled from Jackie Gleason's former CBS network series, *The American Scene Magazine* (1962-1966).

Host: Jackie Gleason.
Regulars: Phil Bruns, Frank Fontaine, Helen Curtis, Stormy Berg, Dave Ballard, Jerry Berger, Stan Ross, Jan Crockett, Frank Marth, Barbara Heller, Pat Dahl, Barney Martin, Lucille Patton, Rip Taylor, Alice Ghostley, Charley Bolender, The June Taylor Dancers.
Regulars in "It Pays to be Ignorant" Skit: Jayne Mansfield, Irwin Corey, Frank Fontaine.
Announcer: Johnny Olsen.
Orchestra: Sammy Spear.
Producer: Jack Philbin.
Writer: Sid Stone, Marvin Marx, Mel Diamond, Keith Fowler, Fred Freeman, Harry Harris, Sid Kuller, Ron Clark, J. Franklin Jones.
Director: Seymour Robbie, Frank Bunetta.
Choreography: June Taylor.

THE BEST OF THE JACKIE GLEASON SHOW—30 minutes—Syndicated 1979.

113   THE BEST OF EVERYTHING

Serial. The story, set in New York City, follows the experiences of April Morrison, Linda Warren and Kim Jordan, secretaries at Key Publishing, as they struggle to fulfill their lives.

CAST

April Morrison	Julie Mannix
Linda Warren	Patricia McCormack
Kim Jordan	Kathy Glass
Violet Jordan	Geraldine Fitzgerald
Amanda Key	Gale Sondegaard
Ed Peronne	Vice Arnold
Ken Lamont	Barry Ford
Johnny Lomart	Stephen Grover
Randy Wilson	Ted La Platt

Also: M'el Dowd, Terry O'Sullivan, Jill Melody, Jane Alice Brandon.

THE BEST OF EVERYTHING—30 minutes—ABC—March 30, 1970–September 24, 1970. 115 episodes.

114   THE BEST OF ERNIE KOVACS

Comedy. A ten-part series that spotlights the genius of Ernie Kovacs through film and videotape clips from his various network series.

Narration Host: Jack Lemmon.
Starring: Ernie Kovacs.
Regulars: Jolene Brand, Edie Adams, Maggi Brown, Bobby Leuher, Joe Mikalos, Leonard Allstar, Alice Novice, Francis McHale, Bob Warren, Kenny Delmar, Harry Lacoe, Al Keith, Peter Hanley.
Music: Eddie Hatrak, Harry Geller.
Executive Producer: Ernie Kovacs.
Producer: Milt Hoffman.
Director: Ernie Kovacs, Maury Orr, Ken Herman.
Producer-Director (of "The Best of Ernie Kovacs"): Dave Erdman.

THE BEST OF ERNIE KOVACS— 30 minutes—PBS—April 14, 1977–June 16, 1977. 10 episodes.

115   THE BEST OF SATURDAY NIGHT LIVE

Edited, prime time (10 p.m.– 11 p.m., EST) repeats (60 minutes—NBC—October 24, 1979 –April 11, 1980) of selected episodes of *Saturday Night Live.* 19 episodes.

116   BEST SELLERS

Anthology. The overall title for four miniseries: *The Captains and the Kings, Once An Eagle, The Rhinemann Exchange,* and *Seventh Avenue.* See individual titles for information.

Best Sellers Theme: Elmer Bernstein.

BEST SELLERS—NBC—September 30, 1976–March 21, 1977.

117   THE BETTER SEX

Game. Two teams of men versus women, each composed of six members, compete. A player from one team (determined by a flip of a coin) appears at the verbal attack post. A question is read by the host (or hostess, depending on which team is at the post) and a card, which contains two answers (one correct, the other a bluff) is given to the player. He or she then chooses an answer and states it. It is up to the opposing team to determine whether the answer is correct or incorrect. Each of the players is asked his (or her) opinion—to agree or disagree. When two opinions match, the correct answer is given. If the attack player fooled the opponents, his (or her) team wins that round and two opposing players are defeated. If, however, the attack player failed to fool the opposing team, he, or she, as well as one other member of his or her team is defeated. The game continues in this manner until one team defeats the other by knocking out all its members. One-thousand dollars is divided between the winning team members.

Host: Bill Anderson.
Hostess: Sarah Purcell.
Announcer: Gene Wood.
Music: Score Productions.
Executive Producer: Mark Goodson, Bill Todman.
Producer: Robert Sherman.
Director: Paul Alter.

THE BETTER SEX—30 minutes—ABC—July 18, 1977–January 13, 1978. 120 programs.

118   THE BETTY WHITE SHOW

Comedy. A satirization of television series as seen through the experiences of Joyce Whitman, a struggling, mediocre actress who stars in "Undercover Woman," a second-rate series directed by her estranged husband John Elliott. The recurring story line concerns Joyce's attempts to reconcile with John even though he insists they cannot live together.

CAST

Joyce Whitman	Betty White
John Elliott, her estranged husband	John Hillerman
Mitzi Maloney, Joyce's roommate	Georgia Engel
Fletcher Huff, the police chief in "Undercover Woman"	Barney Phillips
Hugo Muncy, Joyce's double	Charles Cyphers
Doug Porterfield, the CBS liaison for "Undercover Woman"	Alex Henteloff
Tracy Garrett, an actress on "Undercover Woman"	Caren Kaye
Lisa Vincent, same as Tracy	Carla Borelli

Music: Dick De Benedictis.
Executive Producer: Ed Weinberger, Stan Daniels.
Producer: Bob Ellison, Dale McRaven.
Director: Bill Persky, Doug Rogers, James Burrows, Naom Pitlik.

Creator: Ed Weinberger, Stan Daniels.

THE BETTY WHITE SHOW—30 minutes—CBS—September 12, 1977–January 9, 1978. 13 episodes.

119   BETWEEN THE WARS

Documentary. An historical retrospective that traces, through film clips and photos, America's diplomacy from Versailles to Pearl Harbor.

Host-Narrator: Eric Sevareid.
Music: William Loose, Jack Tillar.
Executive Producer: Alan Landsburgh.
Producer: Anthony Potter.
Sponsor: The Mobil Oil Corporation.

BETWEEN THE WARS—30 minutes—Syndicated 1978. 16 episodes.

120   BEULAH LAND

Drama. A three-part miniseries, set in Richmond County, Georgia, from 1827 to the post Civil War Reconstruction (1870s), that depicts events in the lives of two families: the Kendricks, owners of the Beulah Land Plantation, and the Davises, the owners of the nearby Oaks Plantation. Based on the novels *Beulah Land* and *Look Away, Beulah Land* by Lonnie Coleman.

CAST

Sarah Pennington Kendrick, the mistress of Beulah Land	Lesley Ann Warren
Lauretta Pennington, Sarah's sister	Meredith Baxter Birney
Leon Kendrick, Sarah's husband	Paul Rudd
Deborah Kendrick, Leon's mother	Hope Lange
Selma Kendrick, Leon's sister	Madeline Stowe
Penelope Kendrick, Leon's aunt	Martha Scott
Felix Kendrick, Leon's uncle	Eddie Albert
Nell Kendrick, Felix's wife	Bibi Osterwald
Edna Davis, the owner of Oaks Plantation	Allyn Ann McLerie
Bonard Davis, Edna's son	Don Johnson
Annabelle Davis, Edna's daughter	Ilene Graff
Bruce Davis, Edna's son	Robert Walker, Jr.
Rachel Kendrick, Leon's child by Lauretta	Laurie Prange
Roscoe Corlay, the overseer of Beulah Land	Paul Shenar
Lizzie Corlay, Roscoe's wife	Jenny Agutter
Casey Troy, the artist	Michael Sarrazin
Floyd, a slave	Dorian Harewood
Lovey, Floyd's mother	Clarice Taylor
Ezra, Lovey's husband	James McEachin
Roman, a slave	Franklyn Seales
Jubal, a slave	Peter DeAnda
Adam Davis, Leon's nephew	Jonathan Frakes
Doreen Davis, Bruce's daughter	Betsy Slade

Benjamin Davis, Rachel's
son — James Naughton
Dorothy, a slave — Elizabeth Robertson
Pauline, a slave, Selma's
friend — Jean Renee Foster
Priscilla, Benjamin's romantic
interest — Ruth Cox
Alonzo, a slave — Michael G. Stewart
Roscoe Corlay, Jr.,
Roscoe's son — Stewart Mabray
Abraham, Floyd's son — Deveraux White
Sarah, as a girl — Kyle Richards
Leon, as a boy — Todd Lookinland
Lauretta, as a girl — Tanya Punn
Bruce, as a boy — Ken Brill
Roman, as a boy — Christoff St. John
Benjamin, as a boy — K.C. Martel
Sheriff Baines — Kevin Hagen
Sergeant Smede — Taylor Lacher

NBC Announcer: Peggy Taylor, Donald Rickles.
Music: Allyn Ferguson.
Executive Producer: David Gerber.
Producer: Christopher Morgan.
Writer: Jacques Meunier (pseudonym for JP Miller).
Director: Virgil W. Vogel, Harry Falk.
Director of Photography: Andrew Jackson.

BEULAH LAND — 2 hours (6 hours total) — NBC — October 7, 1980 – October 9, 1980. 3 episodes.

121 THE BEVERLY HILLBILLIES

Comedy. The story of Jed Clampett, a widowed, simple backwoods mountaineer who becomes a millionaire when oil is discovered on his property in Sibly (an Ozark community). Episodes relate his misadventures when he and his family move to Beverly Hills, California, and struggle to adjust to the fast, sophisticated, modern life of the big city.

CAST

Jed Clampett — Buddy Ebsen
Daisy Moses ("Granny"), Jed's
mother-in-law — Irene Ryan
Elly May Clampett,
Jed's daughter — Donna Douglas
Jethro Bodine, Jed's
not-too-bright nephew — Max Baer
Milburn Drysdale, president of the
Commerce Bank, which houses
Jed's money — Raymond Bailey
Margaret Drysdale, Milburn's
wife — Harriet MacGibbon
Jane Hathaway, Milburn's
secretary — Nancy Kulp
Pearl Bodine, Jethro's
mother — Bea Benaderet
Jethrene Bodine, Jethro's sister — Max Baer
Jethrene Bodine (voiced
by) — Linda Kaye Henning
John Brewster, head of the O.K.
Oil Company — Frank Wilcox
Isabel Brewster, John's wife — Lisa Seagram
Lester Flatt, Jed's friend — Himself
Earl Scruggs, Jed's friend — Himself
Gladys Flatt, Lester's wife — Joi Lansing

Louise Scruggs, Earl's wife — Midge Ware
Homer Winch, Pearl's romantic
interest — Paul Winchell
Jasper DePew, Jethrene's
boyfriend — Phil Gordon
Ravenscott, the Drysdale's
butler — Arthur Gould Porter
Marie, the Drysdale's maid — Shirry Steffin
Dash Riprock (Homer Noodleman), a
movie star, Elly May's
boyfriend — Larry Pennell
Mark Templeton, Elly May's beau
(later episodes) — Roger Torrey
Homer Cratchit, the bank
bookkeeper — Percy Helton
Sonny Drysdale, Milburn's son — Louis Nye
Janet Trego, a bank secretary — Sharon Tate
Dr. Roy Clyburn, Granny's
nemesis (objects to Granny
practicing her unlicensed
mountain doctoring) — Fred Clark
Harry Chapman, a movie producer
at Mammoth Studios
(Jed's company) — Milton Frome
The Psychiatrist — Richard Deacon

The Clampetts' address: 518 Crestview Drive.
The Clampetts' dog: Duke, a bloodhound.
Announcer: Bill Baldwin.
Music; Perry Botkin, Curt Massey.
Theme: "The Ballad of Jed Clampett" by Lester Flatt and Earl Scruggs.
Theme Vocal: Jerry Scoggins.
Executive Producer: Al Simon.
Producer: Paul Henning, Joseph DePew, Mark Tuttle.
Director: Joseph DePew, Robert Leeds.

THE BEVERLY HILLBILLIES — 30 minutes — CBS — September 26, 1962 – September 7, 1971. Syndicated.

122 BEWITCHED

Comedy. The series, set in West Port, Connecticut, follows the life of Samantha, a beautiful witch who marries a mortal named Darrin Stevens, an account executive with the Manhattan advertising firm of McMahon and Tate. Episodes relate the misadventures that befall the Stevenses as Samantha attempts to adjust to life as a mortal.

CAST

Samantha Stevens — Elizabeth Montgomery
Darrin Stevens — Dick York
Dick Sargent
Endora, Samantha's
mother — Agnes Moorehead
Maurice, Samantha's
father — Maurice Evans
Larry Tate, Darrin's employer — David White
Louise Tate, his wife — Irene Vernon
Kasey Rogers
Gladys Kravitz, the Stevens'
nosey neighbor — Alice Pearce
Sandra Gould
Abner Kravitz, Gladys's
husband — George Tobias
Harriet Kravitz, Abner's
sister — Mary Grace Canfield

Frank Stevens, Darrin's
father — Robert F. Simon
Roy Roberts
Phyllis Stevens, Darrin's
mother — Mabel Albertson
Tabitha Stevens, Samantha and
Darrin's daughter — Erin Murphy
Diane Murphy
Adam Stevens, Samantha and
Darrin's son — David Lawrence
Greg Lawrence
Clara, Samantha's aunt, a bumbling
and aging witch — Marion Lorne
Arthur, a warlock,
Samantha's uncle — Paul Lynde
Dr. Bombay, Samantha's
family physician — Bernard Fox
Esmeralda, the shy witch — Alice Ghostley
Hagatha, Samantha's
aunt — Ysabel MacClosky
Reta Shaw
The drunk Darrin meets
at the bar — Dick Wilson
Serena, Samantha's fun-loving
cousin — Elizabeth Montgomery
Betty, Darrin's secretary — Marcia Wallace
Samantha Scott
Jean Blake
Samantha Hathaway
Howard McMahon, Larry's
partner — Leon Ames
Gilbert Roland
Margaret McMahon, Howard's
wife — Louise Sorel
The Apoticary, the old
warlock — Bernie Kopell
Various clients of Darrin's — Charles Lane

The Stevens's address: 1164 Morning Glory Circle.
Music: Warren Barker, Jimmie Haskell.
Theme: "Bewitched" by Howard Greenfield and Jack Keller.
Executive Producer: Harry Ackerman.
Producer: William Froug, Danny Arnold, Jerry Davis.
Writer: Howard Leeds, Ruth Brooks Flippen, Paul Wayne, Ed Jurist, Barbara Avedon, David Robison, Rick Mittilman, Robert Riley Crutcher, James Henerson, Ron Friedman, Jerry Mayer, Paul Friedman, Jerry Myer, Michael Morris, Tom August, Helen August, John Greene.
Director: Ernest Losso, Richard Kinon, William Asher, Richard Michaels, Robert Rosenbaum, Jerry Davis, E. W. Swackhamer, Seymour Robbie.
Creator: Sol Saks.

BEWITCHED — 30 minutes — ABC — September 17, 1964 – July 1, 1972. 306 episodes. Syndicated. Spin-off series: *Tabitha*.

123 BEYOND WESTWORLD

Adventure. Westworld, a futuristic playground in which adults act out their wildest fantasies with human-like robots, is built by the Delos Corporation. Simon Quaid, creator of the robots, then destroys Westworld because he

feels Delos has used his robots for purposes other than his dream of a harmonious society. But then Quaid goes "Beyond Westworld" in a rampage of revenge and destruction. The series follows Quaid, bitter and disillusioned, as he launches his virtually indestructible robots on missions that endanger the world; and the Delos Corporation's battle to end his reign of terror.

CAST

Simon Quaid — James Wainwright
John Moore, Delos's chief
agent — Jim McMullan
Pamela Williams, Moore's
assistant — Connie Sellecca
Joseph Oppenheimer, a
Delos scientist — William Jordan
Laura Garvey, a Delos
agent — Judith Chapman
Roberta, Oppenheimer's
assistant — Ann McCurry
Jan, a Delos agent — Mo Lauren
Foley, Quaid's aide — Stewart Moss
Severn Darden
The Gunfighter (in program
open) — Alex Kubick
The Gunfighter's Opponent
(program open) — Edward Coch, Jr.
Dance Hall Girl (program
open) — Cassandra Peterson

Music: George Romanis.
Executive Producer: Lou Shaw.
Supervising Producer: Leonard B. Kaufman.
Producer: John Meredyth Lucas, Fred Freiberger.
Writer: Lou Shaw, Martin Roth.
Director: Ted Post, Rod Holcomb, Paul Stanley.

BEYOND WESTWORLD — 60 minutes — CBS — March 5, 1980 – March 19. 1980. 3 episodes.

124 BICENTENNIAL MINUTES

History. A series of 732 sixty-second programs celebrating the birth of America. Celebrities relate bits of American history — obscure or well-known incidents that occurred two hundred years prior to that particular evening's broadcast.

Appearing: Bernadette Peters, Walter Matthau, Pat Harrington, Jr., Darren McGavin, Celeste Holm, Annette Funicello, Nancy Malone, Vikki Carr, Pat O'Brien, Jason Evers ,Neil Sedaka, Raymond Massey, Richard Deacon, Ann B. Davis, Theodore Bikel, Rex Reed, Norman Fell, Paul Newman, Roger Moore, Red Buttons, Milton Berle, Bethel Leslie, Raymond Burr.
Executive Producer: Bob Markell, Lewis Freedman.
Producer: Gareth Davis, William Kayden, Paul Waigner.
Director: Sam Sherman.
Creator: Louis Freedman.

BICENTENNIAL MINUTES — 01 minute each (12 hours total) — CBS — July 4, 1974 – July 4, 1976. 732 episodes. On July 5, 1976, CBS decided to continue the series and began airing one-minute programs dealing with historic U.S. events which occurred two hundred years prior to that evening's broadcast. After 180 more such minutes, the series ended its run on December 31, 1976.

125   BIG CITY COMEDY

Comedy. Various comedy sketches that satirize life in the big city.

Host: John Candy.
Regulars: Dino Ansonia, Tim Casarinski, Donald Mont. Audrey Neenan, Patty Oakley.
Announcer: John Candy.
Music: Ian Bernard.
Executive Producer: Toby Martin.
Producer: Carolyn Raskin.
Writer: Jim Fisher, Jim Staahl, John Candy, Michael Short.
Director: Mark Warren.
Art Director: Alfred Benson.

BIG CITY COMEDY — 30 minutes — Syndicated 1980.

126   BIG EDDIE

Comedy. The misadventures of "Big" Eddie Smith, a former gambler turned legitimate entrepreneur as the owner of the Big E Sports Arena in New York City.

CAST

"Big" Eddie Smith	Sheldon Leonard
Honey Smith, his wife	Sheree North
Ginger Smith, his granddaughter	Quinn Cummings
Monty "Bang Bang" Valentine, his cook	Billy Sands
Jessie Smith, Eddie's brother	Alan Oppenheimer
Eddie's Confederates:	
Raymond McKay	Ralph Wilcox
Too Late	Lonnie Shorr
The Goniff	Milton Parsons
No Marbles	Cliff Pellow

Creator: Bill Persky and Sam Denoff.
Music: Jack Elliott, Allyn Ferguson, Earle Hagen.
Executive Producer: Bill Persky, Sam Denoff.
Producer: Hy Averback.
Writer: Bill Persky, Sam Denoff, Jerry Davis.
Director: Hy Averback.
Art Director: Al Heshcong.

BIG EDDIE — 30 minutes — CBS — August 23, 1975 – November 7, 1975. The thirty-minute pilot film aired on CBS on May 2, 1975.

127   BIG FOOT AND WILD BOY

Adventure. The series, set in the Northwestern United States, concerns itself with the crime fighting exploits of the legendary man-beast, Big Foot, and his foundling, Wild Boy, a child who was lost in the wilderness and reared by Big Foot.

CAST

Big Foot	Ray Young
Wild Boy	Joseph Butcher
Cindy, their friend	Wonne Regalado
Suzie, their friend	Monika Ramirez

Music: Michael Melvoin, Tom Hensley, John Madara, Gino Cunico.
Supervising Producer: Arthur McLaird.
Executive Producer: Sid and Marty Krofft.
Producer: Donald R. Boyle.
Writer: Donald R. Boyle.
Director: Charles R. Rondeau, Donald R. Boyle, Leslie H. Martinson, Gordon Wiles.
Creator: Joe Ruby and Ken Spears.

BIG FOOT AND WILD BOY — 30 minutes — ABC — June 2, 1979 – August 11, 1979. 11 episodes. Originally broadcast as a segment of *The Krofft Supershow II* on ABC from September 10, 1977 to September 2, 1978.

128   BIG HAWAII

Drama. The series, set on the Paradise Ranch in Ohana, Hawaii, focuses on the lives of Barrett Fears, a wealthy rancher, and his son, Mitch, a determined, rebellious youth.

CAST

Barrett Fears, the father	John Dehner
Mitch Fears, his son	Cliff Potts
Karen "Kete" Fears, Barrett's niece	Lucia Stralser
Oscar Kalahani, the ranch foreman	Bill Lucking
Anita Kalahani, Oscar's wife	Josie Oliver
Lulu, the Fears's housekeeper	Elizabeth Smith
Garfield, a ranch hand	Moe Keale
Kimo, Garfield's son	Remi Abellira

Music: Jack Elliott, Allyn Ferguson.
Executive Producer: Perry Lafferty.
Producer: William Wood, William Finnegan.
Director: Lawrence Doheny, Seymour Robbie, Marvin Chomsky, Harry Falk, Richard Michaels, Robert Douglas, Noel Black.
Creator: William Wood.

BIG HAWAII — 60 minutes — NBC — September 21, 1977 – November 30, 1977. 7 episodes. Originally titled "The New Hawaiians," then "Big Island," "Danger in Paradise," and finally "Big Hawaii." The two-hour pilot film, "Danger in Paradise," aired on NBC on May 12, 1977.

129   BIG JOHN, LITTLE JOHN

Comedy. While vacationing in Florida, John Martin, science teacher at Madison Junior High School, and his family visit the Ponce De Leon National Park. Straying from his family, John finds a small spring — the mythical Fountain of Youth sought by De Leon — and drinks from it. Some weeks later, the effects of the water become evident. The middle-aged Big John reverts unpredictably to the 12-year-old Little John, and vice-versa. Stories depict Martin's struggles to cope with the situations that occur as a result of the changes, and his attempts to discover an antidote for the rejuvenation process.

CAST

Big John Martin	Herb Edelman
Little John Martin	Robbie Rist
Marjorie Martin, John's wife	Joyce Bulifant
Ricky Martin, John's son	Mike Darnell
Bertha Bottomly, the principal	Olive Dunbar
Big John's Students:	
Valerie	Cari Anne Warder
Homer	Christoff St. John
Stanley	Stephen Cassidy

Music: Richard La Salle.
Executive Producer: William P. D'Angelo, Harvey Bullock, Ray Allen, Sherwood Schwartz.
Producer: Lloyd J. Schwartz.
Director: Gordon Wiles, Wes Kenny, Ross Bowan.

BIG JOHN, LITTLE JOHN — 30 minutes — NBC — September 11, 1976 – September 3, 1977.

130   BIG SHAMUS, LITTLE SHAMUS

Drama. The series, set in the Ansonia Hotel in Atlantic City, New Jersey, follows the activities of Arnie Sutter, the hotel's veteran house detective (the "Big Shamus of the title") and his thirteen-year-old son, Max ("Little Shamus"), a budding gumshoe. Episodes depict their attempts to protect the hotel guests from slick con artists who have come to the gambling capital of the East seeking easy money.

CAST

Arnie Sutter	Brian Dennehy
Max Sutter, his son	Doug McKeon
George Korman, the security chief	George Wyner
Stephanie Marsh, the assistant manager	Kathryn Leigh Scott
Jingles Lodestar, the computer operator	Cynthia Sikes
Jerry Wilson, the desk clerk	Ty Henderson
Police Lt. Tom Grainger	Dennis Cole

Music: Mike Post, Pete Carpenter, James Di Pasquale.
Executive Producer: Sam H. Rolfe, Lee Rich.
Producer: Fred Freiberger.
Associate Producer: Tim King.

Writer: Dick Robbins, Norman Katkov, Don Heckman.
Director: Leslie H. Martinson, Rod Holcomb.
Art Director: Bob Jillson.
Director of Photography: Ken Lamkin.
Creator: Tracy Hotchner.

BIG SHAMUS, LITTLE SHAMUS — 60 minutes — CBS — September 29, 1979 – October 6, 1979. 2 of 3 scheduled episodes aired.

131   THE BIG SHOW

Variety. A weekly showcase that spotlights top talent from around the world.

Hosts: Steve Allen, Gary Coleman (first show); Marie Osmond, Gavin MacLeod (second show); Mariette Hartley, Dean Martin (third show); Tony Randall, Herve Villechaize (fourth show); Steve Lawrence, Don Rickles (fifth show); Loretta Swit, Victor Borge (sixth show); Steve Allen, Sarah Purcell (seventh show); Barbara Eden, Dennis Weaver (eighth show); Gene Kelly, Nancy Walker (ninth show); Shirley Jones, Steve Allen (tenth show); Sarah Purcell, Flip Wilson (eleventh show).
Regulars: Mimi Kennedy, Graham Chapman, Charlie Hill, Owen Sullivan, Adolfo Quinones, Joe Baker, Paul Grimm, Edie McClurg, Pamela Myers, Shabba-Doo (a dance troupe), The Dick Williams Singers, The David Winters Dancers.
Orchestra: Nick Perito.
Special Musical Material: Norman Martin.
Producer: Nick Vanoff.
Head Writers: George Bloom, David Axelrod.
Director: Walter C. Miller, Steve Binder, Tony Charmoli.
Choral Director: Dick Williams.
Ice Choreography: Cathy Steele.
Shabba-Doo Choreography: David Winters.

THE BIG SHOW — 90 minutes — NBC — March 4, 1980 – May 27, 1980. 11 programs.

132   THE BIG SHOWDOWN

Game. Three contestants compete in a game wherein they answer questions, valued at from one to six points, seeking to score the exact playoff-point value that is established at the beginning of each round. The first player to score the exact playoff-point value in each round receives a money prize ranging from $25 to $500. The highest scoring player at the end of several rounds earns the opportunity to play the "Big Showdown." In this segment, he uses oversize dice and tries to roll the word Showdown ("Show" is printed on one side of one die; "Down" is printed on one side of the other die) in one try for $10,000. If he fails, the player has a second chance to win a possible $5,000 if he can roll "Showdown" within 30 seconds.

Host: Jim Peck.
Assistant: Heather Cunningham.
Announcer: Dan Daniels.
Music: Score Productions.
Executive Producer: Don Lipp, Ron Greenberg.
Producer: Shelley Dobbins.
Director: Dick Scheinder.

THE BIG SHOWDOWN — 30 minutes — ABC — December 23, 1974 – July 4, 1975. 130 programs.

133   THE BILL COSBY SHOW

Comedy. The trials and tribulations of Chet Kincaid, a physical education instructor and athletic coach for the mythical Richard Allen Holmes High School in Los Angeles.

CAST

Chet Kincaid	Bill Cosby
Marsha Patterson, the guidance counselor	Joyce Bulifant
Brian Kincaid, Chet's brother	Lee Weaver
Verna Kincaid, Brian's wife	Olga James
	Dee Dee Young
Roger Kincaid, Brian's son	Donald Livingston
Rose Kincaid, Chet's mother	Lillian Randolph
	Beah Richards
Chet's father	Fred Pinkard
Tom Bennett, the coach	Robert Rockwell

Music: Quincy Jones.
Executive Producer: William H. Cosby, Jr.
Producer: Marvin Miller.
Director: Bill Cosby, Ivan Dixon, Eliot Lewis, Jay Sandrich, Seymour Robbie, Luther James, Coby Ruskin.
Creator: William H. Cosby, Jr., Ed Weinberger, Michael Zager.

THE BILL COSBY SHOW — 30 minutes — NBC — September 14, 1969 – August 31, 1971. 52 episodes. Syndicated.

134   BILLBOARD'S DISCO PARTY

Disco Music.

Hostess: Donna Summer.
Executive Producer: Sheldon Riss.
Producer: John H. Davis.
Director: Vincent Scariza.

BILLBOARD'S DISCO PARTY — 60 minutes — Syndicated 1978.

135   BILLY

Comedy. The series, set in Pennsylvania, focuses on the experiences of Billy Fisher, a 19-year-old who prefers his colorful fantasies to life's realities.

CAST

Billy Fisher	Steve Guttenberg
Alice Fisher, his mother	Peggy Pope
George Fisher, his father	James Gallery
Billy's grandmother	Paula Trueman
Arthur Milikan, Billy's friend	Bruce Talkington
Mr. Shadrock, Billy's employer at Shadrock and Shadrock, a mortuary	Michael Alaimo

Music: Earle Hagen.
Music Supervision: Lionel Newman.
Theme Vocal: Ray Kennedy.
Producer: John Rich.
Director: John Rich.

BILLY — 30 minutes — CBS — February 26, 1979 – April 28, 1979. 7 episodes.

136   THE BIONIC WOMAN

Adventure. When Jaime Sommers, the beautiful girlfriend of Steve Austin ("The Six Million Dollar Man"), is critically injured during a sky-diving accident, Oscar Goldman of the O.S.I. (Office of Scientific Intelligence) authorizes Dr. Rudy Wells to perform a bionic operation in an attempt to save her life. Jaime's body, however, rejects the artificial replacements (both legs, her right arm and right ear), causing extreme pain and finally death.

Having experimented with cyrogenic surgery and believing that he can bring Jaime back to life, Dr. Michael Marchetti (a member of Rudy's bionic surgery team) performs the extremely delicate and complicated surgery that restores Jaime's life and her body's acceptance of the bionic limbs.

Relinquishing her career as a tennis pro, and taking up residence in the home of her foster parents in Ojai, California, Jaime works as a schoolteacher at the Ventura Air Force Base — her cover as an agent for the O.S.I. Stories depict Jaime's assignments on behalf of O.S.I. A spin-off from *The Six Million Dollar Man.*

CAST

Jaime Sommers	Lindsay Wagner
Oscar Goldman, her superior	Richard Anderson
Dr. Rudy Wells	Martin E. Brooks
Jim Elgin, Jaime's foster father	Ford Rainey
Helen Elgin, Jaime's foster mother	Martha Scott
Janet Callahan (a.k.a. Peggy Callahan), Oscar's secretary	Jennifer Darling
Mark Russell (Russ), Oscar's aide	Sam Chew, Jr.
Chris Williams, an O.S.I. agent	Christopher Stone
Dr. Michael Marchetti	Richard Lenz
Pam, one of Jaime's students	Robin Harlan
Stacy, same as Pam	Stacy O'Brien
Andrew, same as Pam	Robbie Rist
Mark, same as Pam	Robbie Wolcott
Steve Austin (guest roles)	Lee Majors

Also: Max, the bionic dog.
Jaime's telephone number: 311-555-2368.
Bionic Woman Theme: Jerry Fielding.
Music: Jerry Fielding, Joe Harnell, Charles Albertine, Bobby Bryant, J.J. Johnson.
Executive Producer: Kenneth Johnson.
Producer: Harve Bennett, Nancy Malone, Arthur Rowe, Ralph Sariego, Craig Schiller, James D. Parriott.
Director: Don McDougall, Kenneth Gilbert, Ernest Pintoff, Michael Preece, Larry Stewart, Alan J. Levi, Phil Bondelli, Leo Penn, Alan Crosland.
Director of Photography: Enzo A. Martinelli, Allen M. Davey, Gene Talvin.

THE BIONIC WOMAN — 60 minutes. ABC — January 14, 1976 – May 4, 1977. NBC — September 10, 1977 – September 2, 1978. Syndicated.

137   B.J. AND THE BEAR

Adventure. The story of B.J. McKay, a former Vietnam "chopper" pilot turned independent trucker who, with his pet chimpanzee named Bear,* will haul anything anywhere for $1.50 a mile (as long as it is legal).

CAST

B.J. (Billie Joe) McKay	Greg Evigan
Elroy S. Lobo, the corrupt Orly County sheriff with a grudge against B.J.†	Claude Akins
Deputy Perkins, Lobo's bumbling assistant	Mills Watson
Birdwell "Birdie" Hawkins, Lobo's honest deputy	Brian Kerwin
Stilts (Florence), the girl who involved B.J. with Lobo (see second footnote)	Penny Peyser
Barbara Sue McAllister, B.J.'s friend in Orly	Kitty Ruth
	Jo Ann Harris
Harry Cunningham, the bank owner (Orly)	Dennis Burkley
Lillian Polovich (Pogo Lil), B.J.'s friend	Anne Lockhart
Sheriff Masters, law officer of Winslow County	Richard Deacon
Beauregard Wiley, the lustful deputy sheriff of Winslow	Slim Pickens
Wilhelmina "The Fox" Johnson, Wiley's corrupt deputy	Conchata Ferrell
Tommie, a girl trucker friend of B.J.'s (also the girl seen in the program open)	Janet Louise Johnson
Snow White, the girl trucker who involved B.J. with Wiley‡	Laurette Spang
Bullits, the manager of the Country Comfort Trucker's Stop in Bowlin county	Joshua Shelley
Captain John Sebastian Cain, the righteous sheriff of Bishop County	Ed Lauter
Deputy Higgins, Cain's assistant	Otto Felix
Jack "The Hammer" Benedict, a trucker	Charles Napier
Dixie, the Country Comfort waitress	Liberty Godshall
Manny, a trucker friend of B.J.'s	Bert Rosario
J.P. Pierson, the head of the High Ballers, the organized truckers who are opposed to the independents	M.P. Murphy
Bear	Sam

The Pistin' Packin' Mamas (see footnote ‡): Laurette Spang, Janet Louise Johnson, Julie Gregg, Carlene Watkins, Spray Rosso, Daryle Ann Lindley, Angela Aames, Sonia Manzano.
B.J.'s Red Kenworth-Semi License Plate Number: 806 536 (later: 635 608).
Music: Dick Halligan, William Broughton, John Cacavas, Peter Ives, Stu Philips, Dave Fisher.
Theme: "B.J. and the Bear" written by Glen A. Larson.
Theme Vocal: Greg Evigan.
Supervising Producer: Christopher Crowe, Richard Lindheim, John Peyser.
Executive Producer: Glen A. Larson, Michael Sloan, John Peyser.
Producer: Joe Boston, Lester Berke, Richard Lindheim, Robert F. O'Neil.
Director: Christian I. Nyby II, Bruce Bilson, Ray Austin, Cliff Bole, Rod Holcomb, Michael Caffey, Bernard McEveety, Charles R. Rondeau, Vince Edwards, Bruce Kessler, Michael Preece, Gil Bettman, Keith Atkinson.
Creator: Glen A. Larson, Michael Sloan.

B.J. AND THE BEAR — 60 minutes — NBC — February 10, 1979 – June 30, 1979. 11 episodes; September 29, 1979 – September 13, 1980. 19 episodes. The pilot film aired on NBC on October 4, 1978. Spin-off series: *The Misadventures of Sheriff Lobo.* See also Program No. 1876.

*Named after Bear Bryant, whom B.J. considers to be the greatest football coach (University of Alabama).
†With the help of a beautiful girl named Stilts, B.J. broke up Lobo's white slavery ring (the pilot episode). Lobo now seeks to discredit B.J. and even the score.
‡Snow White, an independent trucker assisted by B.J., forms with other girl truckers, "The Pistin' Packin' Mamas," an all-female group of truckers who operate out of Winslow County — and against Wiley's wishes.

NBC

B.J. and the Bear. Foreground, from left, Julie Gregg, Laurette Spang and Carlene Watkins. Center row, from left, Spray Rosso, Daryle Ann Lindley, Janet Louise Johnson, Angela Aames and Sonia Manzano, all of The Pistin' Packin' Mamas. Standing on the running board, Greg Evigan.

ABC

The Brady Bunch. Bottom, from left, Ann B. Davis, Florence Henderson, Michael Lookinland, Maureen McCormick. Top, from left, Eve Plumb, Barry Williams, Susan Olsen, Robert Reed and Christopher Knight.

CBS

The Bob Newhart Show. From left, Marcia Wallace, Bob Newhart, Peter Bonerz, Suzanne Pleshette and Bill Daily.

Buck Rogers in the 25th Century. Erin Gray and Gil Gerard.

138 BLACK BEAUTY

Drama. A miniseries based on the novel by Anna Sewell. The basic storyline follows a thirteen-year period (1880-1893) in the life of a roving colt named Black Beauty. The saga begins on a Maryland farm owned by Tom Gray, his wife Annie, and their son Luke, where the foal named Black Beauty is born and raised. When Tom is paralyzed by a stroke, Annie sells the farm and the horse. Though he has to give up his beloved colt, Luke vows to one day return for it. Black Beauty's adventures, passing from owner to owner, and Luke's attempts to regain possession of the horse, are depicted.

CAST

Tom Gray	Martin Milner
Annie Gray	Eileen Brennan
Luke Gray (as a boy)	Ike Eisenman
Luke Gray (older)	Kristoffer Tabori
Squire Henry Gordon	Cameron Mitchell
Amelia Gordon	Diane Ladd
John Manly	William Devane
James Howard	Daniel Tamm
Ruth Manly	Jenny O'Hara
Charmichael	Brock Peters
Dr. Trumbull	Stuart Silbar
Dr. Halvorson	Peter Breck
Enos Sutton	Farley Granger
Anne Sutton	Simone Griffith
Elizabeth Sutton	Diana Muldaur
Peter Blantyre	Christopher Stone
Reuben Smith	Clu Gulager
York	Forrest Tucker
Lewis Barry	Edward Albert
Phyllis Carpenter	Glynnis O'Connor
Jonas McBride	Jack Elam
Jerry Baker	Warren Oates
Polly Baker	Zohra Lampert
Jennifer Charles	Jane Actman
Dinah Brown	Lee Ann Fahey
Martin Tremaine	Don DeFore
Nicholas Skinner	Mel Ferrer
Horace Tompkins	Van Johnson

Narrator: David Wayne.
Music: John Addison.
Executive Producer: Peter S. Fischer.
Producer: Benjamin Bishop.
Director: Daniel Haller.

BLACK BEAUTY—5 hours (total)—NBC—January 31, 1978—February 4, 1978. 5 episodes.

139 THE BLACK SHEEP SQUADRON

Adventure. The series, set on the island of Bella La Cava in the South Pacific during World War II, follows the exploits of Major Gregory ''Pappy'' Boyington, a daring air ace. Boyington commands the VMF 214 Black Sheep, a group of misfits who, once awaiting court-martial, were fashioned by Boyington into an often decorated, but seldom disciplined fighter squadron.

CAST

Major Gregory ''Pappy'' Boyington	Robert Conrad
General Thomas Moore	Simon Oakland
Colonel Carl Lard	Dana Elcar

The Black Sheep Squadron:

Capt. James W. Gutterman	James Whitmore, Jr.
Lt. Joseph E. Wiley (T.J.)	Robert Ginty
Lt. Jerry Bragg	Dirk Blocker
Capt. Lawrence Casey	W.K. Stratton
Lt. Robert Anderson	John Larroquette
Lt. Robert Boyle	Jake Mitchell
	Larry Manetti
Lt. Donald French	Jeff MacKay
Lieutenant Hutch	Joey Aresco
Lt. Jeb Pruitt	Jeb Adams
Sgt. Andy Micklin, the mechanic	Red West
Pvt. Stan Richards, Andy's assistant	Steve Richmond

The Fighting Angels (Nurses):

Nancy Gilmore	Nancy Conrad
Samantha Greene	Denise DuBarry
Capt. Dottie Dickson	Katherine Cannon
Ellie Farrell	Kathy McCullem
Sue Webster	Brianne Leary
Anne Wilson	Leslie Charleson
Cheryl	Sharon Ullrick

Also:

Capt. T. Harachi, the Japanese squadron commander	Byron Chung
Meatball, Pappy's dog	True Grit

Narrator: Robert Conrad.
Music: Mike Post and Pete Carpenter.
Supervising Producer: Philip DeGuere, Alex Beaton.
Executive Producer: Stephen J. Cannell.
Producer: Russ Mayberry, Alex Beaton, Philip DeGuere, Donald Bellisario, Chuck Bowman.
Director: Jackie Cooper, Philip DeGuere, Jeannot Szwarc, Barry Shear, John Peyser, Russ Mayberry, Lawrence Doheny, Ivan Dixon, Edward Dein, Robert Conrad, Dana Elcar, William Wiard.
Creator: Stephen J. Cannell.

THE BLACK SHEEP SQUADRON—60 minutes—NBC—December 14, 1977—September 1, 1978. As *Baa Baa Black Sheep*—September 21, 1976—August 30, 1977.

140 BLANK CHECK

Game. Of the six players who compete, one is designated as the check writer and the other five are the challengers. The check writer pulls a lever that reveals five numbers and secretly selects one. A question is read to the challengers and the first player to correctly answer it receives the opportunity to guess the number chosen by the check writer. If he does not guess it, the number chosen by the check writer appears in the fourth digit of a four-digit blank check. The check writer then selects another number and another question is asked to acquire another challenger. If the challenger fails to guess the number, it appears in the third digit. The object is for the check writer to fill in a four-digit blank check. However, should the challenger guess the number, he defeats the check writer (who in turn loses the money) and becomes the new check writer. The six players compete for five days and the player who writes the single largest check is the grand winner and receives, in addition to the money, a new car.

Host: Art James.
Assistant: Judy Rich.
Announcer: Johnny Jacobs.
Music: Score Productions.
Executive Producer: Jack Barry.
Producer: Mike Metzger.
Director: Marty Pasetta, Richard S. Kline.

BLANK CHECK—25 minutes—NBC—January 6, 1975—July 4, 1975. 120 programs.

141 BLANKETY BLANKS

Game. Four contestants compete. A subject category board is revealed along with six numbered but concealed clues to its identity. The host selects a computer type card from a revolving wheel and places it in an electronic machine that pinpoints one of the players and reveals an amount of money, ranging from ten to one-hundred dollars. The player selects a clue, which is then revealed, and receives a chance to identify the subject. If he does, he wins the money; if not, another player is selected in the same manner (each player has an equal amount of cards). Once a subject is identified, the contestant at play receives the opportunity to double his winnings by answering the ''Blankety Blank''—a nonsense riddle (e.g., ''The hurricane that hit the pretzel factory was a real . . .''). If he can supply the missing word, (''twister'') he wins the money. The first player to score $2,000 is the winner.

Host: Bill Cullen.
Announcer: Bob Stewart.
Music: Score Productions.
Executive Producer: Bob Stewart.
Producer: Donald Epstein.
Director: Mike Gargiulo.

BLANKETY BLANKS—30 minutes—ABC—April 21, 1975—June 27, 1975. 45 programs.

142 BLANSKY'S BEAUTIES

Comedy. The series, set in the Oasis Hotel in Las Vegas follows the trials and tribulations of Nancy Blansky, seamstress, producer and den mother to ten beautiful showgirls.

CAST

Nancy Blansky	Nancy Walker
Joey Delucca, her nephew	Eddie Mekka
Anthony Delucca, Joey's brother	Scott Baio
Horace ''Studs'' Wilmington, manager of the hotel for Major Putnam, its never-seen owner	George Pentecost
Arnold Takahashi, the owner of the coffee shop	Pat Morita

The Showgirls:

Bambi Benton	Caren Kaye
Ethel ''Sunshine'' Akalino	Lynda Goodfriend
Hillary Prentiss	Taaffe O'Connell
Misty Knight	Jill Owens
Arkansas Baits	Rhonda Bates
Bridget Muldoon	Elaine Bolton
Sylvia Silver	Antonette Yuskis
Jackie Outlaw	Gerri Reddick
Gladys ''Cochise'' Littlefeathers	Shirley Kirkes
Lovey Carson	Bond Gideon

Nancy's dog: Blackjack.
Music: Charles Fox.
Theme Vocal: ''I Want It All'' by Cyndi Grecco.
Executive Producer: Garry K. Marshall, Edward Milkis, Thomas Miller.
Producer: Bruce Johnson, Nick Abdo, Tony Marshall.
Director: Garry Marshall, Jerry Paris, Alan Rafkin.

BLANSKY'S BEAUTIES—30 minutes—ABC—February 12, 1977—April 30, 1977. Returned with two additional episodes which aired on June 6, and June 27, 1977.

143 BLESS THIS HOUSE

Comedy. Events in the hectic lives of the Abbotts, a family of four residing at 2 Howard Road in London, England.

CAST

Sid Abbott, the father	Sidney James
Jean Abbott, the mother	Diana Coupland
Sally Abbott, their daughter	Sally Geeson
Mike Abbott, their son	Robin Stewart
Betty, their neighbor	Patsy Rowlands
Trevor, Betty's husband	Anthony Jackson

Music: Geoff Love.
Producer-Director: William Stewart.

BLESS THIS HOUSE—30 minutes—Syndicated (to U.S.) 1977. Produced in England.

144 BLIND AMBITION

Drama. A miniseries that reconstructs the incidents that brought about the Watergate coverup. Based on the books, *Blind Ambition* by John Dean and *Mo* by Maureen Dean.

CAST

John Dean	Martin Sheen
Pres. Richard Nixon	Rip Torn
H.R. Haldeman	Lawrence Pressman
Maureen Dean	Theresa Russell
Gordon Liddy	William Daniels
John Ehrlichman	Graham Jarvis
John Mitchell	John Randolph
Caulfield	Gerald S. O'Loughlin
Charles Shaffer	Ed Flanders
Fielding	Clifford David
Colson	Michael Callan
Magruder	Christopher Guest
Mardian	Peter Mark Richman
Richard Kleindienst	William Windom
Hoover	Logan Ramsey
Kalmbach	William Schallert
Donald Segretti	Fred Grandy
L. Patrick Gray	Lonny Chapman
Henry Peterson	Edward Mallory
Ron Ziegler	James Sloyan
Judge Sirica	Al Checco

Music: Fred Karlin.
Executive Producer: David Susskind.
Producer: George Schaefer, Renee Valante.
Director: George Schaefer.

BLIND AMBITION — 2 hours — CBS — May 20, 1979 – May 23, 1979. 4 episodes.

145   THE BLUE KNIGHT

Crime Drama. A miniseries that follows four days in the life of William "Bumper" Morgan, a tough Los Angeles cop. Based on the novel by Joseph Wambaugh.

CAST

William "Bumper" Morgan	William Holden
Cassie Walters, his girlfriend	Lee Remick
Sgt. Cruz Segovia	Joe Santos
Det. Charles Bronski	Sam Elliott
Officer Grogan	Vic Tayback

Music: Nelson Riddle.
Executive Producer: Lee Rich.
Producer: Walter Coblenz.
Writer: E. Jack Neuman.
Director: Robert Butler.

THE BLUE KNIGHT — 60 minutes — NBC — November 13, 1973 – November 16, 1973. 4 episodes. Syndicated as a two-hour movie.

146   THE BLUE KNIGHT

Crime Drama. The exploits of William "Bumper" Morgan, a veteran Los Angeles cop-on-the-beat. Stories realistically detail the life of a policeman "whose beat is his world and whose people are his people." Based on the novel by Joseph Wambaugh.

CAST

William "Bumper" Morgan	George Kennedy
Carrie Williamson, his girlfriend	Barbara Rhoades
Sgt. Newman, his superior	Philip Pine
Vera, his friend, the owner of a pawnshop	Aneta Corsaut
Wimpy, his informant	John Steadman
Toby, his informant	Billy Benedict

Also: Leo, a seemingly stray dog who plagues Bumper.
Music: Pete Rugolo, Henry Mancini, Robert Prince.
Executive Producer: Lee Rich.
Director: Gordon Hessler, Charles S. Dubin, Don Mc-Dougall, Paul Krasny, Daniel Haller, Alvin Ganzer, Robert Scheerer.

THE BLUE KNIGHT — 60 minutes — CBS — December 17, 1975 – July 28, 1976; September 22, 1976 – October 20, 1976. The 90-minute pilot film, which is syndicated as a movie titled *The Blue Knight*, aired on CBS on May 9, 1975.

147   BOB & CAROL & TED & ALICE

Comedy. The story, set in Los Angeles, follows the lives of two families: The Sanders, a young, progressive couple in their late twenties; and their neighbors, the Hendersons, an older, conservative couple in their thirties. Episodes relate the incidents and situations that test their reactions, their values and their marriages. Based on the motion picture of the same title.

CAST

Bob Sanders, a film director	Robert Urich
Carol Sanders, his wife	Anne Archer
Ted Henderson, a lawyer	David Spielberg
Alice Henderson, Ted's wife	Anita Gillette
Elizabeth Henderson, Ted and Alice's daughter	Jodie Foster
Sean Sanders, Bob and Carol's son	Bradley Savage

Music: Artie Butler.
Executive Producer: M.J. Frankovich.
Producer: Jim Henerson.

BOB & CAROL & TED & ALICE — 30 minutes — ABC — September 26, 1973 – November 7, 1973. 7 episodes.

148   BOBBIE GENTRY'S HAPPINESS HOUR

Variety. Music, songs, dances and comedy sketches.

Hostess: Bobbie Gentry.
Regulars: Valri Bromfield, Michael Greer, Earl Pomerantz.
Orchestra: Jack Elliott, Allyn Ferguson.
Producer: Frank Peppiatt.
Writer: Arnold Kane, Gordon Farr, Marc London.
Director: Bill Davis.
Choreographer: Don Bradburn.

BOBBIE GENTRY'S HAPPINESS HOUR — 60 minutes — CBS — June 5, 1974 – June 26, 1974. 4 programs.

149   THE BOBBY DARIN AMUSEMENT COMPANY

Variety. Music, songs, dances and comedy sketches.

Host: Bobby Darin.
Regulars: Dick Bakalyan, Geoff Edwards, Tony Amato, Steve Landesberg, Charlene Wong, Rip Taylor, Kathy Cahill, Sarah Frankboner, Dorrie Thompson, The Jimmy Joyce Singers.
Announcer: Roger Carroll.
Orchestra: Eddie Karam.
Producer: Saul Ilson, Ernest Chambers.
Writer: Charles Isaacs, Howard Albrecht, Sol Weinstein, Jack Hanrahan, Don Sherman, Alan Thicke, Bryan Joseph, Tom Dagenais, Sidney Miller, Saul Ilson, Ernest Chambers, Neal Marshall.
Director: Gordon Wiles, Gary Lockwood.

THE BOBBY DARIN AMUSEMENT COMPANY — 60 minutes — NBC — July 27, 1972 – September 7, 1972. As *The Bobby Darin Show* — 60 minutes — NBC — January 19, 1973 – April 27, 1973.

150   THE BOBBY GOLDSBORO SHOW

Musical Variety.

Host: Bobby Goldsboro.
Regular: Peter Cullen (as the voice for Calvin Calaveris, a frog muppet; and Jonathan Rebel, the dog muppet).
Announcer: Peter Cullen.
Musical Director: Robert Montgomery, Timmy Tappan.
Executive Producer: Bill Graham.
Producer: Bill Hobin, Jane Dowden, Reginald Dunlap.
Writer: Ed Hinder.
Director: Bill Hobin.

THE BOBBY GOLDSBORO SHOW — 30 minutes — Syndicated 1973.

151   THE BOBBY VINTON SHOW

Variety. Music, songs and comedy sketches.

Host: Bobby Vinton.
Regulars: Billy Van, Arte Johnson, Freeman King, Jack Duffy.
Orchestra: Jimmy Dale.
Vinton's Vocal Backing: The Peaches.
Executive Producer: Allan Blye, Chris Bearde.
Producer: Alan Thicke, Bud Granoff.
Director: Michael Steele.

THE BOBBY VINTON SHOW — 30 minutes — Syndicated 1975. Produced in Canada.

152   THE BOB CRANE SHOW

Comedy. The series, set in Los Angeles, follows the experiences of Bob Wilcox, a 42-year-old executive who quits his job as an insurance salesman to pursue a medical career.

CAST

Bob Wilcox	Bob Crane
Ellie Wilcox, his wife, a real estate broker	Trisha Hart
Pam Wilcox, their daughter	Erica Petal
Ernest Busso, their landlord	Ronny Graham
Lyle Ingersoll, the dean of the City Medical School of University Hospital	Jack Fletcher
Marvin Sussman, a medical student	Todd Susman
Jerry Mallory, a medical student	James Sutorius

Music: Mike Post and Pete Carpenter.
Producer: Martin Cohen, Norman S. Powell.
Director: Norman S. Powell, Buddy Tyne.

THE BOB CRANE SHOW — 30 minutes — NBC — March 6, 1975 – June 19, 1975. 13 episodes.

153   THE BOB HOPE SPECIAL

Variety. A series of music and comedy specials broadcast on an irregular basis each year.

Host: Bob Hope.
Orchestra: Les Brown.
Supervising Producer: Linda Hope.
Executive Producer: Bob Hope.
Producer: Linda Hope, Sheldon Keller, Malcolm Leo, Andrew Solt, Bob Wynn.
Director: Kip Walton, Sid Smith, Bob Wynn.

THE BOB HOPE SPECIAL — Varying times — NBC — Premiered: April 9, 1950.

154   THE BOB NEWHART SHOW

Comedy. The home and working life of Robert Hartley, a Chicago-based psychologist.

CAST

Robert (Bob) Hartley	Bob Newhart
Emily Hartley, his wife	Suzanne Pleshette
Howard Borden, their neighbor	Bill Daily
Jerry Robinson, their friend, an orthodontist	Peter Bonerz
Carol Kester, Bob and Jerry's secretary	Marcia Wallace
Margaret Hoover, Emily's friend	Patricia Smith
Dr. Bernie Tupperman, Bob's friend	Larry Gelman
Ellen Hartley, Bob's sister	Pat Finley
Howard Borden, Jr., Howard's son	Moosie Drier
Herb Hartley, Bob's father	Barnard Hughes
Martha Hartley, Bob's mother	Martha Scott
Corneilius "Junior" Harrison, Emily's father	John Randolph
Aggie Harrison, Emily's mother	Ann Rutherford

Cliff Murdock, Bob's friend   Tom Poston
Larry Bondaurant, Carol's boyfriend;
    later husband   Will MacKenzie
Bob's Patients:
Elliott Carlin   Jack Riley
Lillian Bakerman   Florida Friebus
Michelle Nardo   Renne Lippin
Emile Peterson   John Fiedler
Victor Gianelli   Noam Pitlik
Edgar Vickers   Lucien Scott

Music: Pat Williams.
Executive Producer: Jay Tarsas, Tom Patchett, Michael Zinberg.
Producer: Glen Charles, Les Charles, Gordon Farr, Lynne Farr.
Director: Alan Myerson, John C. Chauley, Alan Rafkin, Michael Zinberg, Peter Bonerz, Dick Martin, Jeff Corey.
Note: In early episodes Emily is a third-grade teacher at Gorman Elementary School. In later episodes she is vice principal at Tracey Grammar School.
    Bob's office is located in the Rampo Medical Arts Building; and Howard is an airline navigator.

THE BOB NEWHART SHOW — 30 minutes — CBS — September 16, 1972 – April 1, 1978; June 3, 1978 – September 2, 1978. Syndicated.

155   THE BOLD ONES

Drama. The overall title for four rotating series: *The Doctors, The Law Enforcers, The Lawyers,* and *The Senator.* See individual titles for information.

Series Open:
Announcer: The Bold Ones! Burl Ives . . . Joseph Campanella . . . James Farentino — lawyers defending justice in the nation's courtrooms. Leslie Nielsen . . . Hari Rhodes — public servants enforcing the laws of a challenging society. E.G. Marshall . . . John Saxon and David Hartman — doctors expanding the horizons of medicine — The Bold Ones!

THE BOLD ONES — 60 minutes — NBC — September 14, 1969 – January 9, 1973. 85 episodes.

156   BONANZA

Western. Set in the mid-1800s. Possessing a dream to travel west and settle in California, but lacking the necessary resources, Ben Cartwright, a first mate, marries his long-time fiancée, Elizabeth Stoddard, and settles in New England, where he begins a ship chandler's business.
    A year later, after giving birth to a son they name Adam, Elizabeth dies. Motivated by Elizabeth's desire for him to seek his dream, Ben sells his business, journeys

west, and settles in St. Joseph, Missouri, where, eight years later, he marries a Swedish girl named Inger.
    With Inger's help and understanding, Ben organizes a wagon train and begins his journey west. During the hazardous trek through Nevada, Inger gives birth to a son she and Ben name Eric Hoss. Shortly thereafter, during an Indian attack, Inger is killed. Abandoning his dream forever, Ben settles in Virginia City, Nevada and establishes the Ponderosa Ranch in the Comstock Lode Country.
    The birth of Little Joe, Ben's third son, evolves from a complex story in which Ben journeys to New Orleans to personally fulfill the last request of a ranch hand who died while saving his life. Love develops as a result of his meeting with Marie DeMarné, the widow of the ranch hand, and a marriage ultimately results. Shortly after the birth of their son, Little Joe, Marie is thrown by her horse and dies.
    Stories relate the struggles of the Cartwright family as they attempt to maintain and operate their one-thousand-square-mile timberland ranch, the Ponderosa, in an era of violence and lawlessness.

CAST
Ben Cartwright, the father   Lorne Greene
Adam Cartwright, his son   Pernell Roberts
Hoss (Eric) Cartwright, his son   Dan Blocker
(Little) Joe Cartwright, his son   Michael Landon
Jamie Cartwright, Ben's adopted son   Mitch Vogel
Hop Sing, their houseboy   Victor Sen Yung
Sheriff Roy Coffee   Ray Teal
Deputy Clem Poster   Bing Russell
Mr. Canaday (Candy), the ranch foreman   David Canary
Griff King, a ranch hand   Tim Matheson
Dusty Rhodes, a ranch hand   Lou Frizzell
Elizabeth Stoddard (flashback episode, "Elizabeth, My Love")   Geraldine Brooks
Inger (flashback episode, "Inger, My Love")   Inga Swenson
Marie (flashback episode, "Marie, My Love")   Felicia Farr
Laura Dayton, Adam's fiancée   Kathie Brown

Music: David Rose, Harry Sukman, Raoul Kraushaar.
Theme: "Bonanza" by Jay Livingston and Ray Evans.
Producer: Richard Collins, David Dortort, Robert Blees.
Director: Don Richardson, Lee H. Katzin, Marc Daniels, Tay Garnett, Don McDougall, Paul Landers, William F. Claxton, Arthur Lubin, John Florea, Gerd Oswald, Herbert Stark, R.G. Springstein, Christian Nyby, Jacques Tourneur, Michael Landon, William Witney, Leon

Benson, Alan Crosland, Jr., James Clark, Irving J. Moore, Lewis Allen, Charles R. Rondeau, Virgil W. Vogel, William Wiard, Paul Henried.
Creator: David Dortort.

BONANZA — 60 minutes — NBC — September 12, 1959 – January 16, 1973. 440 episodes. Syndicated. Selected episodes were rebroadcast on NBC as *Ponderosa* from May 12, 1972 – August 29, 1972.

157   BONKERS!

Variety. Music, songs and outlandish comedy.

Hosts: Bill, Mark and Brett Hudson.
Regulars: Bob Monkhouse, Jack Burns, Linda Cunningham, The Bonkettes Chorus.
Orchestra: Jack Parnell.
Executive Producer: Thomas M. Battista.
Producer: Jack Burns.
Director: Peter Harris.
Choreographer: Norman Maen.

BONKERS! — 30 minutes — Syndicated 1978. 26 episodes.

158   BORN FREE

Adventure. The series, set in Kenya, East Africa, follows the experiences of George Adamson, a game warden, and his wife and assistant, Joy. Derived from and continuing the films "Born Free" and "Living Free" ended. A story of man-animal relationship as depicted through the Adamsons' raising, conditioning (to face the rigorous life of her native habitat) and releasing of Elsa, a young lioness. Emphasis is placed upon game conservation in contemporary Africa.

CAST
George Adamson   Gary Collins
Joy Adamson, his wife   Diana Muldaur
Makedde, their senior scout   Hal Frederick
Nuru, a servant   Peter Lukoye
Kanini, a servant   Joseph de Graft

Music: Dick De Benedictis, Richard Shores.
Executive Producer: David Gerber.
Producer: Paul Radin.
Creator: Carl Furman.

BORN FREE — 60 minutes — NBC — September 9, 1974 – December 30, 1974. 13 episodes.

159   BOWLING FOR DOLLARS

Game. The format, which is syndicated, varies slightly from market to market. Basically, it encompasses non-professional bowlers who strive to acquire two strikes in a row and break a jackpot for its cash award. De-

pending on the local station's financial resources, the jackpot also varies. In New York, for example, it begins at $500 and increases by $20 with each bowler's failure to break it.
    Unlike the format, talent (host) and technical staff are provided by each station in which the program airs. Radio personality Larry Kenney, for example, hosts the New York edition, while former "Dating Game" emcee Jim Lange hosts in Los Angeles.

BOWLING FOR DOLLARS — 30 minutes — Syndicated 1971.

160   BRACKEN'S WORLD

Drama. A behind-the-scenes look at the world of film producing as seen through the eyes of John Bracken, the head of Century Studios in Hollywood. Filmed at 20th Century-Fox Studios.

CAST
John Bracken   Leslie Nielsen
Sylvia Caldwell, his secretary   Eleanor Parker
Anne Frazer, John's secretary in later episodes   Bettye Ackerman
Kevin Grant, a producer   Peter Haskell
Marjorie Grant, Kevin's alcoholic wife   Madlyn Rhue
Laura Deane, the head of the New Studio Talent School   Elizabeth Allen
Davey Evans, a student   Dennis Cole
Rachel Holt, a student   Karen Jensen
Paulette Douglas, a student   Linda Harrison
Diane Waring, a student   Laraine Stephens
Tom Hutson, a student   Stephen Oliver
Mark Grant, Kevin's son   Gary Dubin
Bobby Jason, Kevin's assistant   William Tyler
Sally, the script girl   Marie Windsor
Mitch, Kevin's secretary   Kathleen Hughes
Grace Douglas, Paulette's mother   Jeanne Cooper
Millie, Sylvia's secretary   Sue Englund
Jim Carter, the studio gate guard   Lee Amber
Bernie, Kevin's assistant   Fred Sardoff
The Sound Mixer   Edward G. Robinson, Jr.
Pat, the screening room projectionist   Billy Halop

Music: David Rose, Jack Elliott, Robert Drasnin, Harry Geller, Lionel Newman, Warren Barker.
Theme: "Worlds" by Alan and Marilyn Bergman.
Theme Vocal: The Lettermen.
Executive Producer: Del Reisman.
Producer: George M. Lehr, Stanley Rubin, Robert Lewin.
Director: Gerald Mayer, Jack Erman, Herschel Daugherty, Paul Henried, Charles S. Dubin, Lee Philips, Gary Nelson, James Neilson, Allen Reisner, Robert Day.
Creator: Dorothy Kingsley.

BRACKEN'S WORLD — 60 minutes — NBC — September 19, 1969 – January 1, 1971. 41 episodes. Syndicated.

161 THE BRADY BUNCH

Comedy. The story of Mike Brady, a widower with three sons, and Carol Martin, a widow with three daughters, who marry and set up housekeeping in a four-bedroom home on Clinton Avenue in Los Angeles. Episodes depict their attempts to cope with the problems and chaos that exist in trying to raise six children.

CAST

Mike Brady, the father, an architect	Robert Reed
Carol Brady, his wife	Florence Henderson
Alice Nelson, their housekeeper	Ann B. Davis

The Brady Children:

Marcia Brady	Maureen McCormick
Jan Brady	Eve Plumb
Cindy Brady	Susan Olsen
Greg Brady	Barry Williams
Peter Brady	Christopher Knight
Bobby Brady	Michael Lookinland

Also:

Sam, a butcher, Alice's boyfriend	Allan Melvin
Oliver, Carol's nephew	Robbie Rist

Brady family dog: Tiger.
Educational institution attended by Marcia and Greg: Westdale High School.

Music: Frank DeVol.
Theme: "The Brady Bunch" by Frank DeVol and Sherwood Schwartz.
Executive Producer: Sherwood Schwartz.
Producer: Lloyd Schwartz, Howard Leeds.
Director: Leslie H. Martinson, Peter Baldwin, Bernard Wiesman, John Rich, Robert Reed, George Cahan, Hal Cooper, Jack Donahue, Lloyd Schwartz, Bruce Bilson, Richard Michaels, Russ Mayberry, Oscar Rudolph, Jack Arnold, George Tyne, Jerry London.

THE BRADY BUNCH—30 minutes—ABC—September 26, 1969–August 30, 1974. 117 episodes. Syndicated. Spin-off series: *The Brady Bunch Hour* and *The Brady Kids.*

162 THE BRADY BUNCH HOUR

Variety. The format features the fictional Brady family (see *The Brady Bunch*) in songs, dances and comedy sketches set against the background of a beach house in Southern California.

CAST

Carol Brady, the mother	Florence Henderson
Mike Brady, the father	Robert Reed
Marcia Brady, their daughter	Maureen McCormick
Greg Brady, their son	Barry Williams
Jan Brady, their daughter	Geri Reischl
Peter Brady, their son	Christopher Knight
Cindy Brady, their daughter	Susan Olsen
Bobby Brady, their son	Michael Lookinland
Alice Nelson, their housekeeper	Ann B. Davis

Regulars: The Krofft Dancers, The Water Follies.
Orchestra: George Wyle.
Musical Arrangements: Sid Feller, Van Alexander.
Executive Producer: Sid and Marty Krofft.
Producer: Lee Miller.
Director: Jack Regas.
Choreographer: Joe Cassini.

THE BRADY BUNCH HOUR—60 minutes—ABC—January 23, 1977–May 24, 1977.

163 THE BRADY KIDS

Animated Cartoon. A spin-off from *The Brady Bunch*. The story of the Brady children, Marcia, Jan, Cindy, Greg, Peter and Bobby, and their misadventures as they attempt to independently solve problems without help from the adult world.

VOICES

Marcia Brady	Maureen McCormick
Jan Brady	Eve Plumb
Cindy Brady	Susan Olsen
Greg Brady	Barry Williams
Peter Brady	Christopher Knight
Bobby Brady	Michael Lookinland
Moptop, their dog	Larry Storch
Marlon, the magic bird	Larry Storch
Ping and Pong, the Panda Bears	Jane Webb

Music: Yvette Blais, Jeff Michael.
Executive Producer: Sherwood Schwartz.
Producer: Lou Scheimer, Norm Prescott.
Director: Hal Sutherland.

THE BRADY KIDS—30 minutes—ABC—September 9, 1972–August 31, 1974. Syndicated.

164 BREAK THE BANK

Game. Two contestants compete. Nine celebrity guests appear, each of whom are seated on the left side and top of a large board that contains twenty numbered boxes. Nine boxes contain three money amounts (three $100, three $200 and three $500), five are blank, one is a wild card, and five contain money bags. One contestant selects a box and the content is revealed. If it is other than a blank (which costs a player his turn) or a money bag, two celebrities, represented by that particular box, are asked a question by the host. One celebrity gives the correct response, the other fibs. If the contestant chooses the correct answer, he wins that box and continues to play. The object is to win by acquiring three boxes with the same money amounts. If the contestant chooses the incorrect answer, the opponent receives the box and a turn at play. If three money bags are picked, the player breaks the bank, which begins at $5,000 and increases by $500 after each game until it is broken.

Host: Tom Kennedy.
Announcer: Johnny Jacobs, Ernie Anderson.
Music: Stu Levin.
Executive Producer: Jack Barry, Dan Enright.
Director: Richard S. Kline.

BREAK THE BANK—30 minutes—ABC—April 12, 1976–July 23, 1976. 70 programs.

165 BREAK THE BANK

Game. A revised version of the previous title, which see. The game is played in the same manner using larger money boxes ($100, $300 and $500) and a $10,000 bank that is broken when a contestant acquires three money bags.

Host: Jack Barry.
Announcer: Ernie Anderson, Jack Barry.
Music: Stuart Zachary.
Executive Producer: Jack Barry, Dan Enright.
Director: Richard S. Kline.

BREAK THE BANK—30 minutes—Syndicated 1976.

THE BRIAN KEITH SHOW

See title *The Little People.*

166 BRIDGET LOVES BERNIE

Comedy. Bridget Fitzgerald, a Catholic, an elementary school teacher in New York, and Bernie Steinberg, Jewish, a struggling writer and cabdriver, marry. Religious and social differences are dramatized.

Bridget's parents, Walter and Amy Fitzgerald, are wealthy socialites. Walter is a staunch Irish-Catholic; Amy, pleasant and rather naive; and their son Michael is a liberal, realistic priest.

Bernie's parents, Sam and Sophie Steinberg, own a Jewish delicatessen in lower Manhattan, where they live over the store, as do Bridget and Bernie. They are simple, unpretentious and unsophisticated.

The series depicts the efforts of Bridget and Bernie to overcome family opposition and bridge the ethnic gap that exists in their lives.

CAST

Bridget Fitzgerald Steinberg	Meredith Baxter
Bernie Steinberg	David Birney
Walter Fitzgerald, Bridget's father	David Boyle
Amy Fitzgerald, Walter's wife	Audra Lindley
Sam Steinberg, Bernie's father	Harold J. Stone
Sophie Steinberg, Sam's wife	Bibi Osterwald
Moe Plotnic, Sophie's brother	Ned Glass
Father Michael Fitzgerald, Bridget's brother	Robert Sampson
Charles, the Fitzgerald's butler	Ivor Barry

Music: Jerry Fielding.
Producer: William Frye.

BRIDGET LOVES BERNIE—30 minutes—CBS—September 16, 1972–September 8, 1973. 24 episodes.

167 BRIGHT PROMISE

Serial. The story of Professor Thomas Boswell, the president of Bancroft, a college community beset by contemporary crises. Episodes depict incidents in the lives of the faculty members, their families and the students of Bancroft College.

CAST

Thomas Boswell	Dana Andrews
Sylvia Bancroft	Regina Gleason
	Anne Jeffreys
William Ferguson	Paul Lukather
Ann Boyd Jones	Coleen Gray
	Gail Kobe
Jennifer	Nancy Stevens
Chet	Gary Pillar
Red Wilson	Richard Eastham
Gypsy	Annette O'Toole
Bob Cocharan	Philip Carey
Jody Harper	Sherry Alberoni
Martha Ferguson	Susan Brown
Dr. Tracy Graham	Dabney Coleman
Dr. Brian Walsh	John Considine
Charles Diedrich	Anthony Eisley
David Lockhart	Tony Geary
Henry Pierce	David Lewis
Samantha Pudding	Cheryl Miller
Howard Jones	Mark Miller
Sandra Jones Pierce	Pamela Murphy
Stuart Pierce	Peter Ratray
Amanda Winninger	June Vincent
Isabel Jones	Lesley Woods
Clara	Ruth McDevitt
Sandy	Susan Darrow
Dean Pierce	Tod Andrews
Professor Townley	Nigal McKeard
Bert	Peter Hobbs
Alice	Synda Scott
Fay	Kimetha Laurie

Executive Producer: Frank Hursley, Doris Hursley.
Producer: Jerry Layton, Richard Dunn.
Writer: Frank Hursley, Doris Hursley.
Director: Gloria Monty, Dick Franchot.

BRIGHT PROMISE—30 minutes—NBC—September 29, 1969–March 31, 1972. 605 episodes.

168   BRITT EKLAND'S JUKE BOX

Music. Performances by top-name Rock performers.

Hostess: Britt Ekland.
Theme: "Juke Box" performed by Hollywood and Vine.
Executive Producer: Bruce Gowers.
Producer: Paul Flattery.
Director: Bruce Gowers.

BRITT EKLAND'S JUKE BOX—30 minutes—Syndicated 1979. See also *Twiggy's Juke Box* for the original version of the series.

169   BRONK

Crime Drama. The story of Alex "Bronk" Bronkov, a police lieutenant operating under special assignment to the mayor of Ocean City, California.

CAST

Lt. Alex Bronkov	Jack Palance
Ellen Bronkov, his daughter	Dina Ousley
Pete Santori, the mayor	Joseph Mascolo
Sgt. John Webster, Alex's partner	Tony King
Harry Mark, Alex's friend*	Henry Beckman
Marci, Pete's secretary	March Lafferty
Mrs. Moury, Ellen's nurse†	Peggy Rea
Policewoman Harley	Sally Kirkland

Bronk's Badge Number: 25.
Music: Lalo Schifrin, George Romanis, Robert Drasnin.
Executive Producer: Carroll O'Connor, Bruce Geller.
Producer: Leigh Vance.
Director: Stuart Hagmann, Richard Donner, John Peyser, Sutton Roley, Russ Mayberry, Corey Allen, Paul Krasny, Reza S. Badiyi, Allen Baron.
Creator: Carroll O'Connor.

*In early episodes Harry is a former cop who operates the M & B Junk Yard and is also Alex's information man. In later episodes, he is a police sergeant.
†Cares for Ellen who was crippled in a car crash that killed her mother.

BRONK—60 minutes—CBS—September 21, 1975—July 18, 1976. The 90-minute pilot film aired on CBS on April 17, 1975.

170   BROTHERS AND SISTERS

Comedy. The series, set at the Larry Krandall College, focuses on the madcap high jinks between the Pi Nu Fraternity and its sister sorority, Gamma Delta Iota.

CAST

Larry Krandall, the dean	William Windom

The Pi Nu Fraternity:

Checko Sabolick	Chris Lemmon
Stanley Zipper	Jon Cutler
Ronald Holmes	Randy Brooks
Harlan Ramsey	Larry Anderson
Seymour	Roy Teicher

The Gamma Delta Iota Sorority:

Suzi Cooper	Mary Frances Crosby
Mary Lee	Amy Johnston
Isabel	Susan Gotton
Margie	Jan Hill
Yoko	Marilyn Tokuda

Also:

Hattie, the Pi Nu Housemother	LaWanda Page

Music: Mark Snow.
Executive Producer: Arthur Silver, Bob Brunner.
Producer: Nick Abdo, Jerry Mayer, Hy Averback.
Director: Lowell Ganz, Buddy Tyne, Dick Martin, Tony Mordente, Dennis Steinmetz, John Bowab, Will MacKenzie, Nick Abdo.

BROTHERS AND SISTERS—30 minutes—NBC—January 21, 1979–April 6, 1979. 12 episodes.

171   BUCK ROGERS IN THE 25th CENTURY

Science Fiction Adventure. In the year 1987, NASA launches the Ranger III, the last of its deep space probes. A freak accident, however, knocks the Ranger III out of its trajectory and into an orbit which freezes the vital life support systems of its pilot, Captain William "Buck" Rogers. After 504 years, he awakens and returns to Earth, and America's capital, New Chicago, in the year 2491. There he becomes part of the Earth Federation, an organization established to protect the Earth from sinister, alien forces. The series, which is based on the 1929 comic strip, follows Buck's adventures in the 25th century.

CAST

Capt. William "Buck" Rogers	Gil Gerard
Col. Wilma Deering, commander of the Third Force of the Earth Directory	Erin Gray
Dr. Huer, the Earth scientist	Tim O'Connor
Twiki, Buck's robot aide	Patty Maloney Felix Silla
Twiki (voiced by)	Mel Blanc
Dr. Theopolis, the computer housed in Twiki (voiced by)	Eric Server
Princess Ardala, the seductive Draconian villainess	Pamela Hensley
Kane, Ardala's aide	Michael Ansara

Narrator: William Conrad.
Music: Stu Phillips, Les Baxter, Johnny Harris, J.J. Johnson, John Cacavas, Robert Prince.
Theme Music: Glen A. Larson.
Supervising Producer: Leslie Stevens, Bruce Landsbury.
Executive Producer: Glen A. Larson.
Producer: Richard Caffey, John Gaynor, David J. O'Connell.
Writer: Glen A. Larson, Leslie Stevens, Steven Greenberg, Anne Collins, Alan Brennert, David Carren, Bill Taylor, Michael Richards, Kathleen Barnes, Michael Bryant, Guy Magar.
Director: Daniel Haller, Michael Caffey, Sigmund Neufeld, Jr., Dick Lowry, Philip Leacock, Leslie H. Martinson, David Moessinger, Larry Stewart, David Phinney.

BUCK ROGERS IN THE 25th CENTURY—60 minutes—NBC—September 27, 1979–September 13, 1980. 22 episodes. The pilot film, "The Awakening," aired on NBC on September 20, 1979. See also Program No. 1881.

172   BUFORD AND THE GHOST

Animated Cartoon.

Segments:

Buford. The exploits of a crime solving bloodhound named Buford and his two human assistants, Cindy Mae and Woody.

The Galloping Ghost. The story of Nugget Nose, the ghost of an old West prospector who haunts a dude ranch in modern times.

Additional characters: Fenwick Fuddy, the owner of the ranch; and Wendy and Rita, his assistants.
Voices: Pat Parris, Don Messick, Hal Peary, John Stephenson, Hal Smith, Jim MacGeorge, Virginia Gregg, Ronnie Schell, Henry Corden, Bob Hastings.
Music: Hoyt Curtin.
Executive Producer: William Hanna, Joseph Barbera.
Producer: Art Scott.
Director: Ray Patterson.

BUFORD AND THE GHOST—30 minutes—NBC—February 3, 1979–September 1, 1979.

173   THE BUGALOOS

Comedy. The story of the Bugaloos, Harmony, Joy, Courage and I.Q., human-formed singing insects and protectors of Tranquility Forest. Episodes concern the evil Benita Bizarre's disastrous attempts to destroy their "disgusting goodness."

CAST

Benita Bizarre	Martha Raye
Joy	Caroline Ellis
Harmony	Wayne Laryea
Courage	John Philpott
I.Q.	John Mcindoe
Sparky, the firefly	Billy Barty
Tweeter, Benita's aide	Van Snowden
Woofer, Benita's aide	Joy Campbell
Flunky Rat, Benita's chauffeur	Sharon Baird

Voices: Joan Gerber, Walker Edmiston.
Music: Charles Fox.
Executive Producer: Si Rose.
Producer: Sid and Marty Krofft.
Director: Tony Charmoli.

THE BUGALOOS—30 minutes—NBC—September 12, 1970–September 2, 1972. 26 episodes. Syndicated.

174   THE BUGS BUNNY SHOW

Animated Cartoon. The antics of Bugs Bunny, a rabbit who excels in causing misery to others. Often depicted are the attempts of Elmer Fudd and Yosemite Sam to shoot that "darned wabbit" and end his relentless pranks.

Additional Segments:

The Road Runner. A hungry coyote's determined efforts to catch a decent meal—the Road Runner, an out-foxing bird.

Sylvester the Cat. The efforts of a hungry cat to catch himself a decent meal—Tweety Pie, a canary.

Voice Characterizations: Mel Blanc.
Music: William Lava, Carl Stalling, Milt Franklin, John Celly.
Producer: Leon Schlesinger.
Director: Charles Jones, I. Freleng.

Versions:

THE BUGS BUNNY SHOW—30 minutes—ABC—October 11, 1960–September 25, 1962; September 8, 1973–August 30, 1975.

THE BUGS BUNNY–ROAD RUNNER HOUR—60 minutes—CBS—September 14, 1968–September 4, 1971. Returned and premiered on CBS on September 6, 1975 (current at time of publication).

THE BUGS BUNNY SHOW—30 minutes—CBS—September 11, 1971–September 1, 1973 (Saturday mornings); April 27, 1976–June 1, 1976 (Prime time).

175   BULLSEYE

Game. Of the two players that compete, one pushes a button that stops three spinning wheels. The first two wheels reveal a category topic and a money amount; the third wheel reveals a number (1 through 5). The player chooses one of the two categories and must answer the number of questions dictated by the third wheel. Each correct response scores the player the specified money amount. When a contract has been completed (all the questions answered) a new round begins and the opponent receives his turn at play. The first player to score $1,000 is the winner and keeps what money he has accumulated.

Host: Jim Lange.
Announcer: Jay Stewart.
Music: Hal Hidey.
Executive Producer: Ron Greenberg.
Producer: Jack Barry, Dan Enright.

Associate Producer: Mark Phillips, Kathy Phillips.
Director: Richard S. Kline.
Art Director: John C. Mula.

BULLSEYE — 30 minutes — Syndicated 1980.

176   THE BURNS AND SCHREIBER COMEDY HOUR

Variety. Low-key, physical comedy that spoofs everyday life.

Hosts: Jack Burns and Avery Schreiber.
Regulars: Teri Garr, Fred Willard, Gloria Mills, Pat Proft, Jacque Colton, True Boardman, Frank Welker, Frank Link, Robert Ito, Fred Willard, Charles Guardino.
Orchestra: Jack Elliott, Allyn Ferguson.
Executive Producer: Bernice Brillstein.
Producer: Bob Ellison.
Writer: Bob Ellison, George Yanok, Bob Garland, Jack Burns, Norman Barasch, Carroll Moore, Avery Schreiber.
Director: John Moffitt.

THE BURNS AND SCHREIBER COMEDY HOUR — 60 minutes — ABC — June 30, 1973 — September 1, 1973.

177   BUSTING LOOSE

Comedy. The series, set in New York City, follows the life of Lenny Markowitz, a 24-year-old who decides to cut the apron strings. Stories concern his attempts to search for a career and independence while constantly finding his life hampered by his domineering parents.

CAST
Lenny Markowitz	Adam Arkin
Sam Markowitz, Lenny's father	Jack Kruschen
Pearl Markowitz, Sam's wife	Pat Carroll
Melody Feebeck, Lenny's neighbor	Barbara Rhoades
Vinnie Mordabito, Lenny's friend	Greg Antonacci
Allan Simmonds, Lenny's friend	Stephen Nathan
Woody Warshaw, Lenny's friend	Paul Sylvan
Ralph Kabell, Lenny's employer, the owner of the Wear-Well Shoe Store	Paul B. Price
Raymond St. Williams, Ralph's salesman	Ralph Wilcox
Lester Bellman, Lenny's friend	Danny Goldman

Music: Jack Elliott, Allyn Ferguson.
Executive Producer: Lowell Ganz, Mark Rothman.
Producer: Lawrence Kasha, John Thomas Lenox.
Director: Howard Storm, James Burrows, Tony Mordente, Mel Ferber, John Thomas Lenox.

BUSTING LOOSE — 30 minutes — CBS — January 17, 1977 — May 9, 1977; July 27, 1977 — November 16, 1977.

178   BUTCH CASSIDY AND THE SUNDANCE KIDS

Animated Cartoon. The global investigations of Butch Cassidy and the Sundance Kids (Stephanie, Marilee, Wally and Freddy), U.S. government agents who pose as a Rock group under contract with the World Wide Talent Agency, a front for an international spy ring.

The Gang Dog: Elvis.
Voices: Ross Martin, Hans Conried, Ronnie Schell, Mickey Dolenz, Cameron Arthur Clark, Alan Oppenheimer, Virginia Gregg, Pamela Peters, Frank Maxwell, Henry Corden, John Stephenson.
Music: Hoyt Curtin.
Executive Producer: William Hanna, Joseph Barbera.
Producer: Alex Lovy.
Director: William Hanna, Joseph Barbera

BUTCH CASSIDY AND THE SUNDANCE KIDS — 30 minutes — NBC — September 8, 1973 — August 31, 1974, 13 episodes.

C

179   CADE'S COUNTY

Modern Western. The story of Sam Cade, the sheriff of Madrid County, a Southwestern community, and his attempts to maintain law and order in an area easily able to become a lawless wasteland. The series emphasizes relations with and acceptance of the Indian.

CAST
Sheriff Sam Cade	Glenn Ford
Deputy J.J. Jackson	Edgar Buchanan
Deputy Arlo Pritchard	Taylor Lacher
Deputy Rudy Davillo	Victor Campos
Pete, a deputy	Peter Ford
Kitty Ann Sundown, the radio dispatcher	Sandra Ego
	Betty Ann Carr

Music: Henry Mancini.
Executive Producer: David Gerber.
Producer: Charles Larson.
Creator: Anthony Wilson, Rick Huskey.

CADE'S COUNTY — 60 minutes — CBS — September 19, 1971 — September 4, 1972. 24 episodes.

180   CALIFORNIA FEVER

Comedy-Drama. The series, set at Sunset Beach in Southern California, follows the day-to-day activities of a group of teenagers.

CAST
The Teenagers:	
Vince Butler	Jimmy McNichol
Laurie	Michele Tobin
Ross Whitman	Marc McClure
Rick, the owner of Rick's Place, the local hangout	Lorenzo Lamas
Vicki	Ruth Cox
Cathy	Jane Milmore
Bobby	Cosie Costa
Sue	Lisa Cori
Pattie	Heidi Bohay
Lucille	April Clough
Marv	Jay Kerr
Robbie	Rene Lamart
Also:	
Mary Butler, Vince's mother	Barbara Tarbuck

Other friends of the teenagers (character names are not given): Matthew Dunn, Tammy Taylor, Becca Edwards.
Ross's car: The *Grossmobile.*
Creator: Dan Polier, Jr.
Music: Dick Halligan, Harry Betts, Artie Butler, Don Peake.
Theme Vocal: "California Fever" by Jimmy McNichol.
Supervising Producer: Mel Swope.
Executive Producer: Paul R. Picard.
Producer: Joseph Bonaduce, Harvey Frand, Lee Sheldon.
Writer: Stephen Kandel, Joseph Bonaduce, Janet Meyers, Tom Sawyer, Ray Parker, Lee Sheldon, Sandra Siegel.
Director: Claudio Guzman, Bob Claver, Alan Myerson, Charles R. Rondeau, Noman Abbott, Dennis Donnelly, Bruce Kessler.
Art Director: Patricia Van Ryker.

CALIFORNIA FEVER — 60 minutes — CBS — September 25, 1979 — December 11, 1979. 9 episodes.

181   CALL IT MACARONI

Children. Various aspects of the adult world are explained to children through films prepared especially for the program.

Music: David Lucas.
Producer: Gail Frank.
Producer for KDKA-TV: Jim Powell.
Associate Producer: Donald Roland.
Director: Gail Frank.

CALL IT MACARONI — 30 minutes — Syndicated 1974.

182   CALLAN

Crime Drama. The exploits of David Callan, a British intelligence agent. Produced in England by Thames TV.

Starring: Edward Woodward as David Callan.
Producer: Reginald Collin.

CALLAN — 60 minutes — Syndicated (to the U.S.) in 1976.

183   CALUCCI'S DEPARTMENT

Comedy. The series depicts the harassed life of Joe Calucci, a soft-hearted New York State Unemployment Office supervisor who constantly finds himself at odds with his position of authority as he attempts to curtail the antics of his staff of seven rude and raucous bureaucrats.

CAST
Joe Calucci	James Coco
Shirley Balukis, his girlfriend, a secretary	Candice Azzara
Ramon Gonzales, Joe's assistant	Jose Perez
Oscar Cosgrove, the claims adjuster	Jack Fletcher
Elaine P. Fusco, a secretary	Peggy Pope
Jack Woods, an employee	Bill Lazarus
Mitzi Gordon, the telephone operator	Rosetta Lenore
Walter Frohler, an employee	Bernard Wexler
Mrs. Clairmont, a claimant	Judith Lowry
Mrs. Calucci, Joe's mother	Vera Lockwood
The Priest	Philip Stirling

Music: Marvin Hamlisch.
Executive Producer: Robert H. Precht.
Producer: Howard Gottfried.
Director: Burt Brinkerhoff.

CALUCCI'S DEPARTMENT — 30 minutes — CBS — September 14, 1973 — December 28, 1973. 13 episodes.

184   CAMOUFLAGE

Game. Two players compete in a game wherein they must trace the outlines of specific items that are contained in a photograph, but concealed by a number of camouflaged overlays. The first player to correctly answer a general knowledge question wins $50 and the opportunity to trace the concealed object (which is stated at the beginning of the game). A portion of the camouflage is removed after each correct response to a question. A player can elect to relinquish his turn if he so desires (fearing to give his opponent a free chance at play if he should fail to trace the outline). The first player to successfully find the camouflaged object (three are played per show) wins the game and what money he has acquired to that point.

Host: Tom Campbell.
Announcer: Johnny Jacobs.
Music: Milton DeLugg.
Executive Producer: Chuck Barris.
Producer: Steve Friedman, Mike Metzger.
Writer: Mike Metzger.
Director: John Dorsey.

CAMOUFLAGE — 30 minutes — Syndicated February 1980. A

prior version of the series appeared on ABC (from January 9, 1961–November 16, 1962) with Don Morrow as the host.

185 CANDID CAMERA

Comedy. Ordinary people, suddenly confronted with prearranged, ludicrous situations are filmed by hidden cameras and caught in the act of being themselves.

Version 1:

Host: Allen Funt.
Regular: Jerry Lester.
Announcer: Ken Roberts
Producer: Allen Funt.

CANDID CAMERA—30 minutes. ABC—December 5, 1948–August 15, 1949; CBS—September 12, 1949–August 19, 1951; ABC—August 27, 1951–August 22, 1956.

Version 2:

Host: Allen Funt.
Co-Hosts: Arthur Godfrey (1960–61), Durward Kirby (1961–66), Bess Myerson (1966–67).
Regulars: Marilyn Van De Bur ("The Candid Camera Girl"), Al Kelly, Dorothy Collins, Joey Faye, Betsy Palmer, Marge Green, Tom O'Malley, Thelma Pellmige, Fannie Flagg.
Announcer: Frank Simms.
Music: Sid Ramin, Henri Rene.
Producer: Allen Funt, Bob Banner, Julio Di Bendetto.
Director: John Peyser, Mel Ferber.

CANDID CAMERA—30 minutes—CBS—October 2, 1960–September 3, 1967.

Version 3:

Host: Allen Funt.
Co-Hosts: John Bartholomew Tucker (1974–75), Phyllis George (1975–76), Jo Ann Pflug (1976–77), Betsy Palmer (1977–79).
Regulars: Sheila Burnett, Fannie Flagg.
Announcer: T. Tommy Catria.
Music: Frank Grant.
Executive Producer: Allen Funt.
Producer: Richard Birglia.
Director: Herb Gardner, Bob Schwartz.

THE NEW CANDID CAMERA—30 minutes—Syndicated 1974–1979.

186 CANNON

Crime Drama. The exploits of Frank Cannon, a highly paid and overweight private detective working out of Los Angeles.

CAST

Frank Cannon	William Conrad
Lt. Ed Misner	Andy Romano
Lt. Rea Eiler	Kathryn Reynolds
Lt. Lloyd Daggett	Dabney Coleman
Lieutenant Coxon	Larry Ward

Music: George Romanis, Duane Tatro, John Parker, John Cannon.
Supervising Producer: Russell Stoneman.
Executive Producer: Quinn Martin.
Producer: Anthony Spinner, Alan A. Armer.
Director: Paul Stanley, Chris Robinson, Lawrence Dobkin, Lewis Allen, Jimmy Sangster, George McCowan, Edward Abroms, John Badham, Harry Falk, Leo Penn, William Wiard, Richard Donner, Don Medford, Corey Allen, Leslie H. Martinson, Alf Kjellin, Allen Reisner, Kenneth Gilbert, Michael Caffey, David Whorf, Gene Nelson, Seymour Robbie, Charles S. Dubin, Herschel Daugherty, Robert Douglas.

CANNON—60 minutes—CBS—September 14, 1971–September 19, 1976. 96 episodes. Syndicated.

187 THE CAPTAIN AND TENNILLE

Variety. Music, songs, dances and comedy sketches.

Hosts: The Captain and Tennille (Toni Tennille and her husband, Daryl Dragon, the Captain).
Regulars: Dave Shelley, Damian London, Billy Barty, Melissa Tennille (Toni's sister), Jerry Trent, Joan Lawrence, Milton Frome, and Broderick and Elizabeth, Toni's bulldogs.
Orchestra: Lenny Stack.
Dance Music: Al Mello.
Choreographer: Bob Thompson.
Executive Producer: Alan Bernard, Dick Clark, Mace Neufeld.
Producer: Bob Henry.
Writer: Stephen Spears, Thad Mumford, John Boni, Norman Stiles, Ray Jessel, Tom Dunsmuir, Ed Hider, Lennie Ripps, Robert Sand, Robert Illes, James Stein, April Kelly, George Geiger.
Director: Tony Charmoli, Bob Henry.
Art Director: Romain Johnston.

THE CAPTAIN AND TENNILLE—60 minutes—ABC—September 20, 1976–March 14, 1977. The 60-minute pilot episode aired on ABC on August 17, 1976.

188 CAPTAIN CAVEMAN AND THE TEEN ANGELS

Animated Cartoon. While exploring a cave, Taffy Dare, Brenda Chance and Dee Dee Sykes, three girls known as the Teen Angels, release and befriend a prehistoric caveman they find frozen in a block of ice. The series depicts their adventures as they team to battle crime.

VOICES

Captain Caveman	Mel Blanc
Taffy Dare	Laurel Page
Brenda Chance	Marilyn Schraffler
Dee Dee Sykes	Vernee Watson

Additional Voices: Julie Bennett, Michael Bell, Pat Foster, Robert Holt, Jim Fletcher, Bill Woodman, Lennie Weinrib, George Goode, Casey Kasem, Virginia Gregg, Henry Corden, Ronnie Schell, Vic Perrin.
Music: Hoyt Curtin, Paul DeKorte.
Executive Producer: William Hanna, Joseph Barbera.
Producer: Alex Lovy.
Director: Charles A. Nichols.

CAPTAIN CAVEMAN AND THE TEEN ANGELS—25 minutes—ABC—March 8, 1980–June 21, 1980.

189 CAPTAIN KANGAROO

Children. Various aspects of the adult world are explained to children through cartoons, stories, songs and sketches.

CAST

Captain Kangaroo (host)	Bob Keeshan
Mr. Green Jeans, his assistant	Lumpy Brannum
Debbie, a regular	Debbie Weems
Cosmo, a regular	Cosmo Allegretti
Mr. Baxter, a regular	James E. Wall
Banana Man, a regular	A. Robbins

Viewer Participation Segment Host: Bill Cosby.
Additional Regulars: Ann Leonardo, Bennye Gatteys, Dr. Joyce Brothers.
Music: John Myer.
Vocalists: The Kangaroos (Beverly Hanshaw, Holly Mershon, Phil Casnoff, Terrence Emanuel).
Puppeteer: Cosmo Allegretti.
Characters: Mr. Moose, Bunny Rabbit, Dancing Bear, Grandfather Clock.
Producer: Peter Birch, Jon Stone, Robert Myhreim, Bob Claver, Dave Connell, Sam Gibbon, Al Hyslop, Jack Miller, Jim Hirschfield.
Director: Peter Birch.

CAPTAIN KANGAROO—60 minutes—CBS—Premiered: October 3, 1955.

190 CAPTAINS AND THE KINGS

Drama. A nine-part miniseries, based on the novel by Taylor Caldwell, that depicts incidents in the life of Joseph Armagh, a strong-willed Irish immigrant, as he struggles for wealth.

CAST

Joseph Armagh	Richard Jordan
Bernadette	Patty Duke Astin
Rory Armagh	Perry King
Mr. Squibbs	Ray Bolger
Elizabeth Healey	Blair Brown
Father Hale	John Carradine
Moira Armagh	Katherine Crawford
Ed Healey	Charles Durning
Sen. Enfield Bassett	Henry Fonda
Sister Angela	Celeste Holm
Judge Newell Chisholm	John Houseman
Sean Armagh	David Huffman
Old Syrup	Burl Ives
Haroun Zeff	Harvey Jason
Tom Hennessey	Vic Morrow
Martinique	Barbara Parkins
Katherine Hennessey	Joanna Pettet
Marjorie Armagh	Jane Seymour
Mrs. Finch	Ann Sothern
Charles Desmond	Robert Vaughn
Miss Emmy	Beverly D'Angelo
Strickland	Joe Kapp
Sean Armagh (as a child)	Johnny Doran
Mary Armagh	Missy Gold
Bernadette (as a child)	Elizabeth Cheshire
Clair Montrose	Peter Donat
O'Herlihy	Neville Brand
Sean Armagh (as a pre-teen)	Kristopher Marquis
Shannon	James O'Connell
Ryan	George Berkeley
Boland	Sean McClory
Mrs. Whyte	Barbara Morrison
Dr. Gill	William Gordon
Peg	Linda Kelsey
Sister Teresa	June Whitley Taylor
Father Corish	Woody Skaggs
Braithwaite	Pernell Roberts
Mrs. Calvin	Roberta Storm
Mr. Calvin	Charles H. Gray
Honora Armagh	Jenny Sullivan
Claudia Desmond Armagh	Cynthia Sikes
Courtney Wickersham	Terry Kiser
Kevin Armagh	Douglas Heyes, Jr.
President Garfield	Richard Matheson
Abraham Lincoln	Ford Rainey
Governor Skerritt	Clifton James
Anne-Marie	Anne Dusenberry
Brian Armagh	Cliff DeYoung
Pearl Gray	Connie Kreski

Music: Elmer Bernstein.
Executive Producer: Roy Huggins.
Producer: Jo Swerling, Jr.
Writer: Douglas Heyes.
Director: Douglas Heyes, Allan Reisner.
Art Director: John W. Curso.

CAPTAINS AND THE KINGS—60 minutes—NBC—September 23, 1976–November 11, 1976. 9 episodes.

191 CARD SHARKS

Game. A question, based on a survey of one-hundred people, is asked of two contestants that compete. Each player responds by predicting how many people said "yes" to the question. The player whose response is closest to the actual answer wins the round and a chance to play high-low card. Each player has a line of five concealed playing cards. When the first card is revealed, the player has to predict what the next card will be—higher or lower than the exposed card. The round continues in this manner until one player correctly reveals his line of five cards, which earns him the championship and a cash prize. (An incorrect prediction at any point ends the round and new questions are asked until a line of five cards is correctly revealed.)

Host: Jim Perry.
Hostesses: Becky Price, Linda Hocks.
Announcer: Gene Wood.
Music: Score Productions.
Executive Producer: Jonathan Goodson.
Producer: Chester Feldman.
Director: Marc Breslow.

CARD SHARKS — 30 minutes — NBC — Premiered: April 22, 1978.

192   CARIBE

Crime Drama. The cases of Ben Logan and Mark Walters, Miami-based police agents who handle special assignments fighting crime in the Caribbean.

CAST

Lt. Ben Logan	Stacy Keach
Sgt. Mark Walters	Carl Franklin
Captain Rawlings	Robert Mandan

Music: John Elizalde, Nelson Riddle.
Executive Producer: Quinn Martin.
Producer: Anthony Spinner.
Director: Virgil W. Vogel, William Hale, Barry Crane, Harry Falk.
Creator: Charles Peck, Jr.

CARIBE — 60 minutes — ABC — February 17, 1975 – August 11, 1975. 18 episodes.

193   CAROL BURNETT AND COMPANY

Variety. Music, songs and comedy sketches.

Hostess: Carol Burnett.
Regulars: Tim Conway, Vicki Lawrence, Kenneth Mars, Craig Richard Nelson.
Orchestra: Peter Matz.
Special Musical Material: Billy Barnes, Artie Malvin.
Producer: Joe Hamilton.
Director: Roger Beatty.

CAROL BURNETT AND COMPANY — 60 minutes — ABC — August 18, 1979 – September 8, 1979. 4 programs.

194   CAROL BURNETT AND FRIENDS

Comedy. A series of half-hour programs culled from *The Carol Burnett Show,* which see for information.

CAROL BURNETT AND FRIENDS — 30 minutes — Syndicated 1977.

195   THE CAROL BURNETT SHOW

Variety. Music, songs, dances and comedy sketches.

Hostess: Carol Burnett.
Regulars: Harvey Korman, Vicki Lawrence, Tim Conway, Dick Van Dyke, Shirley Kirkes, April Nevins, Vivian Bonnell, Don Crichton, Lyle Waggoner, The Ernest Flatt Dancers.
Announcer: Lyle Waggoner.
Orchestra: Harry Zimmerman, Peter Matz.
Special Musical Material: Artie Malvin, Ken and Mitzie Welch, Nat Farber.
Choral Arrangements: Ronnell Bright, David Black.
Executive Producer: Joe Hamilton.
Producer: Ed Simmons, Arnold Rosen.
Director: Dave Powers.

THE CAROL BURNETT SHOW — 60 minutes — CBS — September 11, 1967 – March 29, 1978; June 14, 1978 – August 9, 1978. Syndicated as *Carol Burnett and Friends.*

196   THE CAROL MANN CELEBRITY GOLF CHALLENGE

Game. The format pits golf pro Carol Mann against a celebrity guest. A nine-hole match is played, but due to time restrictions, only the highlights are seen. The celebrity receives a check for $5,000 for participating.

Hostess: Carol Mann.
Announcer-Assistant: Bruce Roberts.
Producer-Director: Roger Blaemiere.

THE CAROL MANN CELEBRITY GOLF CHALLENGE — 30 minutes — Syndicated 1975.

197   CARRY ON LAUGHING

Comedy. A series of satiric anthologies that parody famous stories and movies. Produced in England by Thames TV.

Starring: Sid James, Barbara Windsor, Jack Douglas, Joan Sims, Diane Langton, Kenneth Connor, Ronnie Brady, Peter Butterworth, David Lodge.
Music: John Marshall, Max Harris, Richard Tattersall.
Executive Producer: Peter Rogers.
Producer: Gerald Thomas.
Director: Alan Tarrant.
Animation: Len Lewis.

Included:
The Prisoner of Splendor. The story, set in 1900, finds the enemies of Prince Rupert of Pluritana (Sid James) attempting to abduct him before he can ascend the throne.

The Case of the Coughing Parrot. Two inept detectives (Jack Douglas, Peter Butterworth) attempt to discover the whereabouts of a missing ruby from two seemingly unrelated clues: an Egyptian mummy with a curse and a coughing parrot.

And in My Lady's Chambers. The story revolves around Sir Henry, a retired and confused general (Kenneth Clark) and the complications that ensue when he attempts to rekindle his affair with Lottie Van Titsenhausen (Barbara Windsor), a voluptuous, five-times widowed baroness.

CARRY ON LAUGHING — 30 minutes — Syndicated (to the U.S.) in 1980.

198   CARTER COUNTRY

Comedy. The series, set in Clinton Corners, Georgia, focuses on the bickering relationship between Roy Mobey, a white, old-fashioned police chief, and Curtis Baker, an urbane, black New York City trained police officer, as his sergeant. (The series derives its title from the fact that Clinton Corners is just a "hoot 'n' a holler" from Plains, Georgia, the home of former President Jimmy Carter.)

CAST

Chief Roy Mobey	Victor French
Sgt. Curtis Baker	Kene Holliday
Mayor Teddy Burnside	Richard Paul
Officer Jasper De Witt, Jr.	Harvey Vernon
Officer Cloris Phebus	Barbara Cason
Officer Harley Puckett	Guich Koock
Lucille Banks, the mayor's secretary	Vernee Watson
Tracy Davenport, the police reporter	Melanie Griffith
Julia Mobey, Roy's mother	Amzie Strickland

Music: Pete Rugolo.
Executive Producer: Bud Yorkin, Saul Turteltaub, Bernie Orenstein, Austin and Irma Kalish.
Producer: Douglas Arango, Phillip Doran.
Director: Bud Yorkin, Peter Baldwin.

CARTER COUNTRY — 30 minutes — ABC. September 15, 1977 – March 9, 1978. 20 episodes. May 2, 1978 – January 13, 1979. 11 episodes. March 29, 1979 – August 23, 1979. 12 episodes.

199   CASPER AND THE ANGELS

Animated Cartoon. The series, set in the year 2179, follows the exploits of Casper, the Friendly Ghost, as the Guardian Ghost to Minnie and Maxie, two misadventure-prone Space Patrol Women, as they seek to dispense justice in space.

VOICES

Casper, the Friendly Ghost	Julie McWhirter
Harry Scary, his assistant	John Stephenson
Space Patrol Officer Minnie	Laurel Page
Space Patrol Officer Maxie	Diana McCannon

Additional Voices: Rick Dees, Dick Bels, Ronnie Schell, Hal Smith, Frank Welker, Paul Winchell.
Music: Hoyt Curtin.
Music Supervision: Paul DeKorte.
Executive Producer: William Hanna, Joseph Barbera.
Producer: Art Scott, Alex Lovy.
Director: Ray Patterson, George Gordon, Carl Urbano.

CASPER AND THE ANGELS — 30 minutes — NBC — September 22, 1979 – September 20, 1980.

THE CASTAWAYS ON GILLIGAN'S ISLAND

See title: *Gilligan's Island.*

200   THE CATTANOOGA CATS

Animated Cartoon.

Segments:
The Cattanooga Cats. The misadventures of Chessie, Kitty Jo, Scootz, Groovey and Country, a feline Rock group who are known as The Cattanooga Cats.

VOICES

Chessie	Julie Bennett
Kitty Jo	Julie Bennett
Groovey	Casey Kasem
Scootz	Jim Begg
Country	Bill Calloway

It's the Wolf. The story of Mildew, a hungry wolf who is determined to catch himself a decent meal: Lambsy, the poor defenseless lamb. Savior of the lamb is Bristol Hound — "Bristol Hound's my name and saving sheep's my game."

VOICES

Mildew Wolf	Paul Lynde
Lambsy	Daws Butler
Bristol Hound	Allan Melvin

Around the World in 79 Days. The adventures of Phineas Fogg, Jr., as he attempts to travel around the world in 79 days. His aides: Jenny Trent and Happy; his enemies, who plot to thwart his efforts: Crumdon and Bumbler.

VOICES

Phineas Fogg, Jr.	Bruce Watson
Jenny Trent	Janet Waldo
Happy	Don Messick
Crumdon	Daws Butler
Bumbler	Allan Melvin

Auto Cat and Motor Mouse. The story of a cat who is determined to beat a mouse in an automobile race.

VOICES

Motor Mouse	Dick Curtis
Auto Cat	Marty Ingels

Series Credits:
Music: Hoyt Curtin.

Executive Producer: William Hanna, Joseph Barbera.
Producer: Charles Nichols.
Director: William Hanna, Joseph Barbera.

THE CATTANOOGA CATS—60 minutes—ABC—September 6, 1969—September 5, 1970. 30 minutes—ABC—September 13, 1970—September 4, 1971. Spin-off series: *Motor Mouse.*

201   THE C.B. BEARS

Animated Cartoon. A series of cartoons hosted by the C.B. Bears (Hustle, Boogie and Bum), three crime-fighting, trouble-prone bears who receive their orders from a female named Charlie via a C.B. radio. A take-off on *Charlie's Angels.*

Additional Segments:

Blast-off Buzzard and Crazy Legs. Set in a desert, the cartoon focuses on the attempts of a hungry buzzard to catch himself a decent meal: an out-foxing snake named Crazy Legs. A take-off on *The Road Runner.*

Heyyyy, It's the King. The misadventures of the King, a 1950s type, hip-talking lion, and his friends Big H, the hippo; Clyde, the ape; Yukey Yuka, the mole, and Skids, the alligator. A take-off on *Happy Days.*

Posse Impossible. The exploits of an old West sheriff and his three bumbling deputies as they attempt to maintain the peace in the town of Saddle Sore.

Shake, Rattle and Roll. The misadventures of Shake, Rattle and Roll, three ghosts who run the Haunted Inn, a hotel for the unearthly.

Undercover Elephant. The cases of Undercover Elephant, a fumbling U.S. government agent, and his assistant Loud Mouse.

Voices: Sheldon Allman, Daws Butler, Henry Corden, Joe E. Ross, Paul Winchell, Joan Gerber, Vic Perrin, Lennie Weinrib, William Woodson, Pat Parris, Susan Silo.
Music: Hoyt Curtin, Paul DeKorte.
Executive Producer: William Hanna, Joseph Barbera.
Producer: Iwao Takamoto.
Director: Charles A. Nichols.

THE C.B. BEARS—60 minutes—NBC—September 10, 1977—January 28, 1978.

202   THE CBS AFTERNOON PLAYHOUSE

Anthology. A series of dramatic specials geared to children.

Music: Jimmie Haskell, Glenn Paxton, Bob Rozario.
Executive Producer: Daniel Wilson, William P. D'Angelo, Lawrence Jacobson.

Producer: Fran Sears, Joseph M. Taritero, Lawrence Jacobson, Dennis Johnson.
Writer: Richard Landau, Stephen Gyllenhaal, Dennis Kane, Barney Cohen, Paul Elliott, Fred Freiberger.
Director: Larry Elikann, Gerald Mayer, Stephen Gyllenhaal, Dennis Kane.
Art Director: Fred R. Price, Lilly Kilvert, Doug Johnson.

Included:

Joey and Redhawk. The story of an Ohio Youth (Joey) and a runaway Apache (Redhawk) and their adventures in the Colorado Rockies.

Cast: Joey: Chris Petersen; Redhawk: Guillermo San Juan; Sukie: Danny Bonaduce.

One Last Ride. The story of Tracy Gibbs, a rodeo champion who is suddenly confronted with the prospect of raising a ten-year-old son he once deserted.

Cast: Tracy Gibbs: Ronny Cox; Ben Gibbs, his son: David Hollander; Big Ed Morgan: Andrew Duggan; Mrs. Martinez: Carmen Zapata; Ellen: Cathey Paine.

Lost in Death Valley. A struggle of survival as seen through the experiences of five high school students who are stranded in the searing heat of Death Valley after a plane crash.

Cast: Darlene: Leslie Winston; Bob: Bennet Liss; Jeremy: Paul Kent; Maggie: Grace Zabriskie; Barbara: Teri Lyn Taylor; Marion Boyd: Barbara Tarbuck.

THE CBS AFTERNOON PLAYHOUSE—30 minutes—CBS—Premiered: November 23, 1978.

203   THE CBS LIBRARY

Anthology. Dramatizations of various stories, classic and contemporary.

Music: Charles Alexander, Larry Wolff.
Executive Producer: Diane Asselin.
Producer: Paul Asselin, Nick Bosustow, Diane Asselin.
Writer: Kimmer Ringwald, George Arthur Bloom.
Director: Paul Asselin, Sam Weiss, Seth Pinsker, Nell Cox.
Director of Photography: Erik Daarstad, Robert Elswit, David Sanderson.
Art Director: Jeremy Railton.

Included:
The Ghost Belonged to Me. Richard Peck's story about the ghost of a young woman who, having drowned at sea, appears to a teenage boy to warn him of a pending accident in which many people will drown.

Cast: Episode host: Vincent Price; The Ghost: Alexandria Johnson; Alexander Armsworth, the teenager: Christian Berrigan; Blossom: Jessica Lynn Pennington; Bus Driver: Wayne Heffler.

The House with a Clock in Its Walls. John Bellairs story about a modern-day wizard and his nephew and their attempts to find a time bomb, hidden by a ghost, that is capable of destroying the world.

Cast: Episode host: Vincent Price; Jonathan, the wizard: Severn Darden; Lewis, his nephew: Michael Brick; Selena, the ghost: Mary Betten.

Flight of the White Wolf. The story of Russ, a teenager who raises a white wolf from a pup only to find his full-grown pet the target of a deadly hunt.

Cast: Episode host: Anthony Newley; Russ: Lance Kerwin; Mathewson: John Quade; Judge: Hugh Gillin.

THE CBS LIBRARY—60 minutes—CBS—Premiered: October 21, 1979.

204   THE CBS NEWCOMERS

Variety. Performances by new and promising performers in the fields of music, song, dance and comedy.

Host: Dave Garroway.
Regulars: Cynthia Clawson, Peggy Sears, Rex Allen, Jr., Rodney Winfield, Joey Garya, David Arlen, Paul Perez, Gay Perkins, The Good Humor Company, The Californians.
Orchestra: Nelson Riddle.
Producer: Bill Hobin.
Writer: Charles Isaacs, Artie Phillips, Fred Fox, Seaman Jacobs, Ed Haas, Ed Hinder.
Director: Bill Hobin.

THE CBS NEWCOMERS—60 minutes—CBS—July 12, 1971—September 6, 1971. 13 programs.

205   CELEBRITY BOWLING

Game. Four celebrities, divided into teams of two, bowl a ten-frame game. The highest scoring team wins an assortment of prizes for the studio audience members they represent.

Host: Jed Allan.
Assistants: Bill Buneta, Bobby Cooper, Dave Davis.
Announcer: Jed Allan.
Producer: Joe Siegman, Don Gregory.
Director: Don Buccola.

CELEBRITY BOWLING—30 minutes—Syndicated 1971.

206   CELEBRITY CHALLENGE OF THE SEXES

Game. Male and female TV personalities are pitted against one another in various athletic contests.

Host: Tom Brookshire.
Female Team Coach: Barbara Rhoades.
Male Team Coach: McLean Stevenson.
Judge: Jim Tunney.
Music: Peter Matz.
Executive Producer: Howard Katz.
Producer: Mel Ferber.
Director: Bernie Hoffman.

CELEBRITY CHALLENGE OF THE SEXES—30 minutes—CBS—January 31, 1978—February 28, 1978. 5 episodes.

207   CELEBRITY CHALLENGE OF THE SEXES

Game. A twice yearly series of specials in which motion picture and television personalities engage in various athletic contests to determine which is the better sex.

Executive Producer: Howard Katz.
Producer: Rudy Tellez, Ken Weinstock.
Director: Bill Hobin, Stan Harris.

Program 1: April 17, 1977
Host: Vin Scully, Phyllis George.
Female Team Captain: Penny Marshall.
Male Team Captain: Rob Reiner.
Female Team: Farrah Fawcett, Roz Kelly, Brenda Vaccaro, Susan Howard, Stefanie Powers, Lola Falana, Cindy Williams, Phyllis George, Connie Stevens, Kathy Crosby, Kristy McNichol.
Male Team: Bill Cosby, Redd Foxx, Elliott Gould, Gabriel Kaplan, Tony Randall, Edward Asner, Lloyd Bridges, Robert Conrad, O.J. Simpson, Flip Wilson, McLean Stevenson, Dan Haggerty.

Program 2: Nov. 20, 1977
Host: Flip Wilson, Brent Musburger.
Female Team Coach: Valerie Perrine.
Male Team Coach: McLean Stevenson.
Female Team: Farrah Fawcett, Kristy McNichol, Elke Sommer, Phyllis George, Susan Saint James. Linda Blair, Suzanne Somers, Lola Falana, Leslie Uggams.
Male Team: Dick Van Patten, Bruce Jenner, Gabriel Kaplan, Robert Conrad, Steve Garvey, David Cassidy, Tab Hunter, James Farentino, Jack Klugman, LeVar Burton, James Franciscus.

Program 3: Feb. 25, 1979
Host: Buddy Hackett, Tom Brookshire.
Female Team Captain: Carol Wayne.
Male Team Captain: Ted Knight.
Female Team: Suzanne Somers, Valerie Bertinelli, Jayne Kennedy, Connie Stevens, Quinn Cummings, Tanya Tucker, Brianne Leary, Joyce DeWitt, Donna Pescow, Susan Richardson, The Boone Sisters.
Male Team: Sammy Davis, Jr., Lou Ferrigno, Scott Baio, Carl Reiner, Gary Coleman, Dan Haggerty, Patrick Duffy, Dirk Benedict, Gavin MacLeod, Erik Estrada, The Hudson Brothers.

Program 4: Oct. 20, 1979
Host: Tom Brookshire.
Female Team Coach: Phyllis George.
Male Team Coach: Bill Cosby.
Female Team: Catherine Bach, Barbi Benton, Charo, Toni Tennille, Joan Rivers, Martina Navratilova, Elaine Joyce, Lola Falana, The Dallas Cowboys Cheerleaders.
Male Team: Michael Douglas, Leif Garrett, Redd Foxx, Charley Pride, Howard Hesseman, LeVar Burton, Bill Cosby, Richard Dawson, Gallagher, The Temptations.

Program 5: April 19, 1980
Host: Tom Brookshire.
Female Team Coach: Victoria Principal.
Male Team Coach: Robert Conrad.
Female Team: Cathy Lee Crosby, Judy Norton-Taylor, Joan Van Ark, Melissa Gilbert, Erin Gray, Jayne Kennedy, Catherine Bach, Laurie Walters, Connie Needham, Lani O'Grady, Susan Richardson, Brooke Shields, Sarah Purcell, Connie Sellecca.
Male Team: Leif Garrett, Jay Johnson, Vic Tayback, Andy Gibb, Tom Wopat, Steve Kanaly, Ken Michaelman, Kevin Hooks, Ira Angustain, Scott Baio, Jamie Farr, Gil Gerard.

CELEBRITY CHALLENGE OF THE SEXES — 2 hours — CBS — Premiered: April 17, 1977.

208 CELEBRITY CHARADES

Game. Two four-member teams of celebrities compete. Each celebrity performs a charade (to his own team) with the object being to have it guessed in the least amount of time. The team with the lowest time total (eight charades are played, each with a 75-second time limit) is the winner and receives a check for $500 (which is donated to charity).
Host: Jay Johnson (with his puppet Squeaky).

Regularly Appearing: Judy Landers, Lani O'Grady, Vernee Watson, Jamie Farr, Robert Mandan, Jon "Bowzer" Bauman, Judy Norton-Taylor.
Announcer: Dick Patterson.
Music: Score Productions.
Executive Producer: David B. Fein, Allan Schwartz.
Producer: Don Segall.
Director: Ron Kantor.

CELEBRITY CHARADES — 30 minutes — Syndicated 1979.

209 CELEBRITY CONCERTS

Variety. Solo performances by celebrity guests.

Appearing: Vikki Carr, Paul Williams, Tom Jones, Anne Murray, Jack Jones.
Music: The Edmonton Orchestra, conducted by Lawrence Holloway, and Johnnie Spencer.
Additional Orchestrations: Jimmie Haskell, Sid Feller, Bob Frank.
Executive Producer: Wendell Wilkes.
Producer: Gary Jones, Tommy Banks.
Director: Stanley Dorfman.

CELEBRITY CONCERTS — 60 minutes — Syndicated 1976.

210 CELEBRITY COOKS

Variety. Guest celebrities are first interviewed then prepare their own recipes.

Host: Bruno Gerussi.
Music: Jim Walchuk.
Theme: Kevin Gillis.
Executive Producer: Derek Smith.
Producer: Frank Andreoli, Trevor Evans.
Director: Frank Andreoli.

CELEBRITY COOKS — 30 minutes — Syndicated 1978. Produced in Canada.

211 CELEBRITY REVUE

Variety. A daily series that features interviews with and performances by celebrities.

Hostess: Carole Taylor.
Host: Tommy Banks.
Orchestra: Tommy Banks.
Executive Producer: Jack Rhodes.
Producer: Tommy Banks, Gary Jones.
Director: Stanley Dorfman, Geoff Theobald.

CELEBRITY REVUE — 60 minutes — Syndicated 1976.

212 CELEBRITY SWEEPSTAKES

Game. A general-knowledge question is asked of six celebrity

guests. Each member of the studio audience votes for the celebrity he feels has the correct answer. Once the audience votes and the odds are established (number of people who chose a specific celebrity), each of the two competing players chooses a celebrity he feels has the correct answer and bets a specific amount of money ($2, $5, $10 or $20). The celebrities' answers, which are written on cards, are revealed. If a player chose a celebrity with a correct answer, his money is increased by the displayed odds; if he chose incorrectly, the bet amount is deducted from his score. Several varying, but similar rounds are played and the contestant with the highest overall money score is the winner.
Host: Jim McKrell.
Announcer: Bill Armstrong.
Regular Panelists: Carol Wayne, Joey Bishop, Buddy Hackett.
Music: Stan Worth, Alan Thicke.
Executive Producer: Ralph Andrews, Burt Sugarman.
Producer: Tom Cole, Neil Marshall.
Director: Dick McDonough.

CELEBRITY SWEEPSTAKES — 30 minutes — NBC — April 1, 1974 – October 10, 1976. Syndicated first run.

213 CENTENNIAL

Drama. The series, based on the novel by James Michener, chronicles the growth of Colorado from 1756 to 1978 beginning with the Plains Indians, and continuing through the first settlers, the growth of the fictional town of Centennial, and modern times from the Depression to the present.

CAST

Pasquinel, the fur trapper	Robert Conrad
Alexander McKeag	Richard Chamberlain
Lise Bockweiss	Sally Kellerman
Henry Bockweiss	Raymond Burr
Clay Basket	Barbara Carrera
Joe Bean	Clint Walker
Col. Frank Skimmerhorn	Richard Crenna
Maxwell Mercy	Chad Everett
Hans Brumbaugh	Alex Karras
Dr. Richard Butler	Robert Walden
The Arapaho Leader	Michael Ansara
Blue Leaf	Maria Potts
Rude Water	Robert Tessier
Gray Wolf	Ivan Naranjo
Levi Zendt	Gregory Harrison
Lucinda Zendt	Cristina Raines
Marcel Pasquinel	Kario Salem
Lisette Mercy	Karen Carlson
John McIntosh	Mark Harmon
General Asher	Pernell Roberts
Spade Larkin	James Sloyan
John Skimmerhorn	Cliff De Young
Oliver Secombe	Timothy Dalton
Sindy Enderman	Sharon Gless
Prof. Lewis Venor	Andy Griffith
Cisco Calendar	Merle Haggard
R.J. Poteet	Dennis Weaver
Maude Wendell	Lois Nettleton
Paul Garrett	David Janssen
Sheriff Axel Dumire	Brian Keith
Samuel Purchase	Donald Pleasence
Charlotte Buckland	Lynn Redgrave
Morgan Wendell	Robert Vaughn
Mervin Wendell	Anthony Zerbe
Old Sioux	Chief Dan George
Alvarez	Henry Darrow
Jim Bridger	Reb Brown
Elly Zendt	Stephanie Zimbalist
Mother Zendt	Irene Tedrow
Rebecca Stolfitz	Debi Richter
Abel Tanner	Barney McFadden
Nate Person	Glynn Turman
Jacques Pasquinel	Stephen McHattie
	Vincent Roberts
Oliver Seecombe	Timothy Dalton
Young Lame Beaver	Ray Tracey
Laura Lou Booker	Leslie Winston
General Wade	Morgan Woodward
Gompert	Robby Weaver
Amos Calendar	Jesse Vint
Bufe Coker	Les Lannom
Mule Canby	Greg Mullavey
Emma Lloyd	Jay W. MacIntosh
Claude Richards	Robert Douglas
Clemma Zendt	Adrienne LaRusso
Martin Zendt	Mark Neely
Muerice	Art Metrano
Finlay Perkin	Clive Revill
Mr. Norris	Lou Frizzell
Alice Grebe	Julie Sommars
Vesta Volkema	Lynn Borden
Magnes Volkema	Bo Brundin
Judge Hart	Dana Elcar
Aunt Agusta	Gale Sondergaard
Hank Garvey	James Best
Major Sibley	Robert Easton
Donald McPherson	Gordon Steele
Lost Eagle	Nick Ramus
Reverend	James Kisicki
Pvt. Clark	Steve Burns
Capt. Ketchum	Burt Douglas
Sergeant	Robert Sommers
Major O'Neil	Barry Cahill
Keefe	Christopher Lowell
Stringer	Gene Otis
William Savage	Damon Douglas
Buck	Dennis Fimple
Mrs. Brumbaugh	Gloria McMillan
Tom Ragland	Ralph Lewis
Nacho	Rafael Campos
Tranquilino	A. Martinez
Serafina	Silvava Galendo
Earl Grebe	Claude Jarman
Sheriff Bogardus	Geoffrey Lewis
Colonel Salcedo	Joaquin Martinez
William Bellamy	William Bogert
Holmes	Royce Applegate
Truinfador Marquez	Alex Colon
Sgt. Lykes	Richard Jaeckel

Narrator: David Janssen.
Introduced By: James Michener.
Music: John Addison.
Supervising Producer: Richard Caffey.
Executive Producer: John Wilder.
Producer: Howard Alston, Malcolm Harding, George E. Crosby.
Writer: John Wilder, Jerry Ziegman, Charles Larson.
Director: Paul Krasny, Virgil W. Vogel, Harry Falk, Bernard McEveety.
Art Director: Seymour Klate, Mark

CBS

California Fever. Foreground, Jimmy McNichol. Behind him, from left, Lorenzo Lamas, Michele Tobin and Marc McClure.

ABC

Charlie's Angels. The first team, from left, Jaclyn Smith, Farrah Fawcett and Kate Jackson.

ABC

Charlie's Angels. The second team, from left, Kate Jackson, Cheryl Ladd and Jaclyn Smith.

ABC

Charlie's Angels. The third team, from left, Jaclyn Smith, Shelley Hack and Cheryl Ladd.

Mansbridge, Sherman Loudermilk, Lou Montejano, Jack Senter, John Bruce, John Corso, Loyd S. Papez.

CENTENNIAL — 26 hours (total) — NBC — October 1, 1978 – February 4, 1979. 12 chapters.

214 CHAIN REACTION

Game. Two teams compete, each composed of two celebrities and one non-celebrity challenger. A chain reaction board, which contains eight boxes, is revealed. The first and last boxes each contain a visible word and the remaining six boxes each conceal a word that relates to the others to form a chain reaction. The game begins when one player asks for a letter below or above one of the visible words. If the player guesses the word from the letter that appears, he scores one point per letter that the word contains for his team. If he fails to guess it, his opponents receive their chance to ask for a letter. Players continue rotating turns until all the chain reaction words are guessed. The first team to score fifty points is the winner and receives $250.

Host: Bill Cullen.
Substitute Host: Geoff Edwards.
Announcer: Johnny Gilbert.
Music: Bob Cobert.
Semi-Regular Panelists: Lois Nettleton, Soupy Sales, Nipsey Russell, Debralee Scott, Joanna Gleason.
Executive producer: Bob Stewart.
Producer: Sande Stewart.
Director: Bruce Burmester.

CHAIN REACTION — 30 minutes — NBC — January 14, 1980 – June 20, 1980. 110 programs.

215 CHALLENGE OF THE SUPER FRIENDS

Animated Cartoon. A spin-off from *The Super Friends.* The revised format pits the Super Friends (Wonder Woman, Superman, Batman and Robin, Aquaman, and the Space Twins, Zan and Jana) against the Legion of Doom, thirteen sinister villains who have united to wreak havoc on the universe. Each episode finds the Justice League of America (the organization formed by the Super Friends to combat evil) facing a challenge from the Legion of Doom.

Voices: Wonder Woman: Shannon Farnon; Superman: Danny Dark; Aquaman: Bill Callaway; Batman: Olan Soule; Robin: Casey Kasem; Zan: Mike Bell; Jana: Louise Williams.
Music: Paul DeKorte, Hoyt Curtin.
Executive Producer: William Hanna, Joseph Barbera.
Producer: Iwao Takamoto.

Director: William Hanna, Joseph Barbera.

CHALLENGE OF THE SUPER FRIENDS — 55 minutes — ABC — September 9, 1978 – September 15, 1979. As *The World's Greatest Super Heroes* — 55 minutes — ABC — Premiered: September 22, 1979.

216 CHARLIE'S ANGELS

Crime Drama. The exploits of Sabrina Duncan, Jill Munroe and Kelly Garrett, three beautiful private detectives employed by Charles Townsend, the never-seen owner of the Los Angeles based Townsend Investigations.

CAST
Sabrina Duncan*	Kate Jackson
Jill Munroe†	Farrah Fawcett
Kelly Garrett	Jaclyn Smith
Kris Munroe, Jill's sister†	Cheryl Ladd
Tiffany Welles, replaced Sabrina*	Shelley Hack
Julie Rogers, replaced Tiffany*	Tanya Roberts
John Bosley, Charlie's representative for the girls	David Doyle
Voice of Charles Townsend	John Forsythe
Linda, the Townsend Agency receptionist	Kim Basinger Linda Oliver
Bill Duncan, Sabrina's ex-husband	Michael Bell
The Townsend Agency Linen Service Girl (not named)	Judy Landers
Lt. Mike Torres, Oahu Police Department	Soon-Teck Oh

The Townsend Agency phone number: 213 555-0267.
Creator: Ivan Goff, Ben Roberts.
Music: Jack Elliott, Allyn Ferguson.
Executive Producer: Aaron Spelling, Leonard Goldberg.
Producer: Rick Huskey, David Levinson, Barney Rosenzweig, Ronald Austin, James David Buchanan, Edward J. Lakso, Robert Janes, Elaine Rich.
Writer: Sue Milburn, David Levinson, Edward J. Lakso, John D.F. Black, Kathryn Powers, Rick Huskey, B.W. Sandefur, Pat Fielder, Jeff Myrow, Lee Sheldon, Laurie Lakso.
Director: Richard Benedict, George McCowan, Daniel Haller, George Brooks, Robert Kelljan, Cliff Bole, Georg Stanford Brown, Lawrence Doheny, John Moxey, Richard Lang, Allen Baron, Phil Bondelli, Charles S. Dubin, Paul Stanley, George W. Brooks, Lawrence Dobkin, Don Chaffey, Dennis Donnelly, Les Carter, Kim Manners, Ronald Austin, Leon Carrere, Curtis Harrington, Don Weis, Bernard McEveety, Harry Falk, Sutton Roley, Larry Stewart.

CHARLIE'S ANGELS — 60 minutes — ABC — Premiered: September 22, 1976. The 90-minute pilot film aired on ABC on March 21, 1976.

*The character of Sabrina, who remained with the series for three years, left at the end of the 1978 – 79 season to marry and raise a family. For the 1979 – 80 season Charlie hired Tiffany Welles, the daughter of his friend, a chief of detectives in Boston. When the new character failed to instill viewer interest in the series, Tiffany was dropped and replaced by Julie Rogers, a street-wise New Yorker who moves to California to join the Townsend Agency (1980 – 81).

†The character of Jill remained for one season, 1976 – 77, and left to pursue her racing career in Europe. Though she returned throughout the remainder of the series in a guest-star status, her younger sister, Kris, replaced her.

217 CHASE

Crime Drama. The series follows the exploits of Chase, a secret corps of undercover police agents that tackles the cases left unsolved by the homicide, robbery and burglary divisions of the Los Angeles Police Department.

CAST
Capt. Chase Reddick	Mitchell Ryan
Sgt. Sam MacCray	Wayne Maunder
Officer Steve Baker	Michael Richardson
Officer Fred Sing	Brian Fong
Inspector Frank Dawson	Albert Reed
Officer Ed Rice	Gary Crosby
Officer Tom Wilson	Graig Gardner

Creator: Stephen J. Cannell.
Music: Oliver Nelson.
Executive Producer: Robert A. Cinader.
Producer: William Stark, David Friedkin, Jack Webb.
Director: Jack Webb, Stephen J. Cannell, Alan Crosland, Jr., Christian Nyby, Christian I. Nyby II, William Wiard.

CHASE — 60 minutes — NBC — September 11, 1973 – September 4, 1974. 24 episodes. The 90-minute pilot film aired on NBC on March 24, 1973.

218 THE CHEAP SHOW

Game. Two contestants appear with their loved ones (a friend or relative) and one member of each team is placed in the punishment pit. A question, based on a ridiculous category (e.g., "Underwear Nostalgia"), is read to two guest celebrities (one answers truthfully; the other fibs). By a flip of the coin, one of the two outside-the-pit players chooses the celebrity he feels has the right answer. If he is correct, he wins a cheap prize (articles valued under $16) and his opponent's loved one is punished (hit with harmless foods).If the player chooses the wrong celebrity, the prize is awarded to his opponent and his own loved one is punished. Two such rounds are played, each worth one point. Round two consists of one twenty-point question, played in the same manner, which determines the winner.

The two members of the winning team then play "The Super Colossal Prize Sweepstakes Finale." A large spinning wheel board with twelve holes is displayed. Oscar the Wonder Rodent (a white rat) is brought out and placed on the board. Oscar runs briefly about the board and into one of the holes. The team wins a prize corresponding with the numbered hole Oscar enters. A decent and expensive merchandise prize is awarded to the players.

Host: Dick Martin.
Wanda, the Hostess: Janelle Price.
Polly, the Prize Lady: Shirl Bernheim.
Oscar, the Wonder Rodent: Himself.
Roger, Oscar's Security Guard: Roger Chapline.
The Purveyors of Punishment: Joe Baker, Billy Beck.
Announcer: Charlie O'Donnell.
Music: John Phillips.
Executive Producer: Chris Bearde, Bob Wood.
Producer: Terry Kyne, Kathy Connolly.
Director: Terry Kyne.

THE CHEAP SHOW — 30 minutes — Syndicated 1978.

219 CHER

Variety. Music, songs, dances and comedy sketches.

Hostess: Cher.
Regulars: The Tony Charmoli Dancers.
Orchestra: Jimmy Dale.
Additional Orchestrations: Jack Eskew.
Special Musical Material: Earl Brown, Billy Barnes.
Choreographer: Anita Mann, Tony Charmoli.
Executive Producer: George Schlatter.
Producer: Lee Miller, Alan Katz, Don Reo.
Director: Bill Davis, Art Fisher.

CHER — 60 minutes — CBS — February 16, 1975 – January 4, 1976.

220 THE CHICAGO TEDDY BEARS

Comedy. The series, set in Chicago during the 1920s, depicts the clash that exists between rival night club owners Linc McCray and his cousin "Big" Nick Marr, a mobster who plots to gain control of Linc's legit club and add it to his list of illegal speakeasies.

CAST

Linc McCray	Dean Jones
"Big" Nick Marr	Art Metrano
Uncle Latzi, Linc's partner	John Banner
Marvin, Linc's accountant	Marvin Kaplan
Nick's Mob:	
Duke	Mickey Shaughnessy
Dutch	Huntz Hall
Lefty	Jamie Farr
Julius	Mike Mazurki

Music: Jerry Fielding.
Producer: Jerry Thorpe.
Director: Norman Tokar.

THE CHICAGO TEDDY BEARS — 30 minutes — CBS — September 17, 1971 – December 17, 1971. 13 episodes.

221   CHICO AND THE MAN

Comedy. The story of two men: Ed Brown, an honest but cynical one-pump garage owner in Los Angeles, and his partner, Chico Rodriquez, a cheerful young Mexican-American who fast-talked Ed into hiring him and letting him live in an old truck that is parked in the garage. Episodes depict their continual bickering, as they, representing different cultures and the generation gap, struggle to survive inflation in the seventies.

CAST

Ed Brown	Jack Albertson
Chico Rodriquez	Freddie Prinze
Louie Wilson, Ed's friend	Scatman Crothers
Della Rogers, Ed's landlady	Della Reese
Reverend Bemis, Ed's friend	Ronny Graham
Rudy, Ed's friend	Rodolfo Hoyos
Mabel, the letter carrier	Bonnie Boland
Mondo, Chico's friend	Isaac Ruiz
Raul, the Mexican boy Ed adopts	Gabriel Melgar
Monica, the aspiring actress	Julie Hill
Margie, Monica's friend	Teri Payne
Lynn, Monica's friend	Hilary Thompson
Susie, Monica's friend	Patch Mackenzie
Barbara, Monica's friend	Danuta

Music: José Feliciano.
Chico and the Man Theme Vocal: José Feliciano.
Executive Producer: James Komack.
Producer: Hal Kanter, Michael Morris, Alan Sacks, Ed Scharlach.
Director: Peter Baldwin, James Komack, Jack Donohue.
Creator: James Komack.

CHICO AND THE MAN — 30 minutes — NBC — September 13, 1974 – January 27, 1978; June 2, 1978 – July 28, 1978. Syndicated.

222   CHIPS

Crime Drama. The exploits of Jon Baker and Francis "Ponch"

Poncherello, members of Chips, the California Highway Patrol.

CAST

Officer Jon Baker	Larry Wilcox
Officer Francis Poncherello	Erik Estrada
Sgt. Joe Getraer	Robert Pine
Officer Sindy Cahill	Brianne Leary
Officer Bonnie Clark	Randi Oakes
Officer Arthur Grossman	Paul Linke
Officer Baricza	Brodie Greer
Officer Fritz	Lew Sanders
Officer Turner	Michael Dorn
Harlan, the mechanic	Lou Wagner

Creator: Rick Rosner.
Music: Billy May, John Parker, Mike Post, Pete Carpenter, Alan Silvestri.
Music Theme: John Parker.
Music Supervision: Harry Lojewski.
Executive Producer: Cy Chermak.
Producer: Rick Rosner, Ric Randall.
Director: Paul Krasny, Christian I. Nyby II, Michael Caffey, Edward Abroms, Georg Fenady, John Florea, Don Chaffey, Phil Bondelli, Larry Wilcox, Don Weis, Barry Crane, Gordon Hessler.

CHIPS — 60 minutes — NBC — Premiered: September 15, 1977.

223   THE CHISHOLMS

Western. The miniseries, which spans two years, 1842–1844, follows the hardships and perils of the Chisholm family, Virginia farmers who lost their land in a legal dispute, as they travel west seeking to build a new life in the untamed Oregon Territory.

CAST

Hadley Chisholm, the father	Robert Preston
Minerva Chisholm, the mother	Rosemary Harris
Will Chisholm, their son	Ben Murphy
Bonnie Sue Chisholm, their daughter	Stacey Nelkin
Annabelle Chisholm, their daughter	Susan Swift
Bo Chisholm, their son	James Van Patten
Gideon Chisholm, their son	Brian Kerwin
Elizabeth Chisholm, Will's wife (first episode)	Glynnis O'Connor
Kewedinok Chisholm, Will's Indian wife (later)	Sandra Griego
Lester Heckett, their guide	Charles Frank
Also:	
Timothy Oates	David Hayward
Jimmy Jackson	Anthony Zerbe
Andrew Blake	Brian Keith
Fiddler Ephraim	Doug Kershaw
Harlow Cooper	Tom Taylor
Brian Cassidy	Gavin Troster
Luke Cassidy	James D. O'Reilly
Jeremy Stokes	Dean Hill
Squire Bailey	David Allen
Benjamin Lowery	Dennis Kennedy
Doc Simpson	James Harrell
Millie Bain	Maureen Steindler
Jonah Comyns	Jerry Hardin
Sarah Comyns	Katie Hantlley
Judge Wilson	Charles L. Campbell
Bartender	Mike Genovese

Ferocious Storm	Geno Silva
Otaktay	Ron Godines
Teetonkah	Billy Drago
Enapay	Don Shanks
Howahkan	Joe Garcia
Ambrose Miller	Jack Wallace
Franz Schwarzenbacher	Christopher Allport
Major Duggan	Roger Frazier
Captain Kelsey	Richard L. Jamison

Music: Elmer Bernstein.
Music Based On: Aaron Copland's themes from "Billy the Kid," "Rodeo," and "Appalachian Spring."
Executive Producer: Alan Landsburg, David Dortort.
Producer: Paul Freeman.
Writer: Evan Hunter.
Director: Mel Stuart.
Art Director: Fred Price.
Director of Photography: Jacques Marquette.

THE CHISHOLMS — 12 hours (total) — CBS — March 29, 1979 – April 19, 1979. 4 episodes.

224   THE CHISHOLMS

Western. The saga of the Chisholms, a pioneering Virginian family, as they travel by wagon train from Wyoming (where the miniseries, previous title, left off) to seek a new life in California. The hardships endured by the family is the focal point of the series, which is set in 1844.

CAST

Hadley Chisholm, the father	Robert Preston
Minerva Chisholm, the mother	Rosemary Harris
Will Chisholm, their son	Ben Murphy
Bo Chisholm, their son	James Van Patten
Bonnie Sue Chisholm, their daughter	Delta Burke
Gideon Chisholm, their son	Brett Cullen
Kewedinok Chisholm, Will's wife	Victoria Racimo
Cooper Hawkins, the wagon master	Mitchell Ryan
Mercy Hopwell, the young girl traveling with the Chisholms	Susan Swift*
Lester Hackett, the gambler engaged to Bonnie Sue	Reid Smith
Betsy O'Neal, a member of the wagon train	Devon Ericson
Frank O'Neal, Betsy's brother	Guich Koock
Jeremy O'Neal, Betsy's brother	Les Lannom
Enos, a member of the wagon train	Donald Moffat

Creator: Evan Hunter.
Music: Gerald Fried, William Kraft.
Executive Producer: Alan Landsburg.
Producer: Paul Freeman.
Writer: Paul Savage, Corey Blechman, Harold Swanton.
Director: Mel Stuart, Nicholas Webster, Edward Abroms, Sigmund Neufeld, Jr.

THE CHISHOLMS — 60 minutes — CBS — January 19, 1980 – March 15, 1980. 9 episodes.

*Originally, in the miniseries, Annabelle Chisholm, who "died" of injuries suffered during an Indian attack.

225   CHOPPER ONE

Crime Drama. The exploits of Officers Gil Foley and Don Burdick, West California Police Department helicopter pilots (of Chopper One) as they assist patrol car officers.

CAST

Officer Gil Foley	Dirk Benedict
Officer Don Burdick	Jim McMullan
Capt. Ted McKeegan, their superior	Ted Hartley
Mitch, the helicopter mechanic	Lou Frizzell

Music: Dominic Frontiere.
Executive Producer: Aaron Spelling, Leonard Goldberg.
Producer: Ronald Austin, James David Buchanan.

CHOPPER ONE — 30 minutes — ABC — January 17, 1974 – July 11, 1974. 13 episodes.

226   CHUCK ASHMAN'S AMERICAN FREEWAY

Variety. Music and songs coupled with celebrity interviews.

Host: Chuck Ashman.
Showgirls: Jean Carol Lopez and Sue Darty (from the Casino de Paris Club in Las Vegas).
Announcer: Jay Stewart.
Orchestra: Earl Green.

CHUCK ASHMAN'S AMERICAN FREEWAY — 90 minutes — Syndicated 1975.

227   THE CHUCK BARRIS RAH-RAH SHOW

Variety. Performances by professional and amateur talent acts.

Host: Chuck Barris.
Regulars: Jaye P. Morgan, The Unknown Comic, Gene Gene, the Dancing Machine.
Announcer: Johnny Jacobs.
Orchestra: Milton DeLugg.
Executive Producer: Chuck Barris.
Producer: Gene Banks.
Director: John Dorsey.

THE CHUCK BARRIS RAH-RAH SHOW — 60 minutes — NBC — February 28, 1978 – April 11, 1978. 6 episodes.

228   CIMARRON STRIP

Western. The series, set in Cimarron City, Oklahoma, during the 1880s, follows the exploits of U.S. Marshal Jim Crown as he attempts to settle the question of the Cimarron Strip — land over which a range war is pending between settlers and cattlemen.

CAST

Marshal Jim Crown	Stuart Whitman
Dulcey Coopersmith, the operator of the hotel's coffee shop	Jill Townsend
Francis Wilde, Jim's friend, a photographer	Randy Boone
MacGregor, Jim's deputy	Percy Herbert
Judge Gilroy	Leonard Stone

Music: Maurice Jarre, Morton Stevens.
Supervising Producer: Christopher Knopf.
Executive Producer: Philip Leacock.
Producer: Bernard McEveety.
Director: Sam Wanamaker, Robert Butler, Charles R. Rondeau, Don Medford, Alvin Ganzer, Lamont Johnson, Boris Sagal, Richard Sarafian, Bernard McEveety, Herschel Daugherty, Vincent McEveety, Gerald Mayer, Charles R. Rondeau.

CIMARRON STRIP — 90 · minutes — CBS — September 7, 1967 – September 19, 1968. Rebroadcasts: July 20, 1971 – September 7, 1971. 26 episodes.

229   CIRCLE OF FEAR

Anthology. Tales of the supernatural. A spin-off from *Ghost Story.*

Music: Billy Goldenberg, Robert Prince.
Executive Producer: William Castle.
Producer: Joel Rogosin.
Director: James Neilson, John Llewellyn Moxey, Robert Day, Leo Penn, David Lowell Rich, Arnold Laven, Alexander Singer, Richard Donner, Jimmy Sangster, Daryl Duke.

Included:

Doorway to Death. A weird story about a bargain apartment and a strange figure, visible only to children, who haunts it.

Cast: Peggy: Susan Dey; Jim: Barry Nelson; Jane: Dawn Lyn; Robert: Leif Garrett; Truthers: Henry Jones; Man Upstairs: Scott Thomas; Woman Upstairs: Carolyn Stellar.

Dark Vengeance. The story of a woman and her attempts to escape from a series of terrifying events that are directed at her by a child's toy horse.

Cast: Cindy: Kim Darby; Frank: Martin Sheen; Art: Shelly Novack.

Bad Connection. A chilling tale of a bride-to-be who receives phoned death warnings from her former husband — who was killed in action.

Cast: Barbara Shepherd: Karen Black; Keith Norton: Michael

Tolan; Angie: Sandra Deel; Appleton: James A. Watson, Jr.; Phil Briggs: Kaz Garas; Steve: Skip Homeier.

The Ghost of Potter's Field. The story of a magazine writer who is plagued by a ghost seeking to possess him so it can live again.

Cast: Bob Herrick: Tab Hunter; Nisa King: Louise Sorel; John Walsh: Gary Conway; Mark Riceman: Pat Harrington; Ted Murray: Robert Mandan; Dolf Ellis: Philip Pine; Carlson: Paul Winchell.

The Phantom of Herald Square. A drama about a man who fears growing old.

Cast: Old Man: Victor Jory; James Barlow: David Soul; Old Woman: Meg Wyllie; Holly Brown: Sheila Larken; Art Student: Dennis Lee Smith.

CIRCLE OF FEAR — 60 minutes — NBC — January 5, 1973 – June 22, 1973.

230   CIRCUS

Variety. The series spotlights various European circus variety acts.

Host-Narrator: Bert Parks.
Producer: Joe Cates.
Director: Gil Cates.

CIRCUS — 30 minutes — Syndicated 1971. 52 episodes.

231   CIRCUS OF THE STARS

Variety. An irregular series of specials in which show business personalities perform circus acts.

Music: Harper McKay, Nick Carras.
Executive Producer: Bob Stivers.
Producer: Bill Waters, Don Kibbee, Dominique Perrin, Bob Finkel.
Director: Sid Smith, Tony Charmoli.

Program 1: Jan. 10, 1977
Host: John Forsythe.
Ringmasters: Jean-Pierre Aumont, George Hamilton, Bernadette Peters, Jack Cassidy.
Stars: Marty Allen, Valerie Perrine, David Doyle, Rue McClanahan, Mary Ann Mobley, Jean Stapleton, Deborah Raffin, Edward Asner, Claudia Cardinale, Peter Fonda, Peter Marshall, Joey Heatherton, Bobby Van, Janet Leigh, David Nelson, Anny Duperey, Lilliane Montvecchi, Abe Vigoda, Rosey Grier, Pat Morita, Billy Barty, Jo Anne Worley, David Janssen, Lynda Carter, Wayne Rogers, Karen Black, Gary Collins.

Program 2: Dec. 5, 1977
Ringmasters: Lucille Ball, Telly Savalas, Cindy Williams, Michael York.

Stars: Peter Fonda, Penny Marshall, Richard Roundtree, George Burns, Lynda Carter, Lola Falana, Earl Holliman, Jack Klugman, Valerie Perrine, Mackenzie Phillips, Susan Saint James, Abe Vigoda, Paul Williams, Kristy and Jimmy McNichol, Lee Meriwether, Betty White, Marty Allen, Tony LoBianco, Lucie Arnaz, Robert Conrad, Gary Collins, Richard Hatch, David Nelson, Deborah Raffin, Tom Sullivan, Mary Ann Mobley.

Program 3: June 20, 1979
Ringmasters: Lauren Bacall, Sammy Davis, Jr., Jerry Lewis, Anthony Newley, Bernadette Peters.
Stars: Marty Allen, Dirk Blocker, Foster Brooks, Charlie Callas, Gary Collins, Cathy Lee Crosby, Jamie Lee Curtis, Jamie Farr, Buddy Hackett, Tony LoBianco, Carol Lynley, Eddie Mekka, Lee Meriwether, Mary Ann Mobley, David Nelson, Ken Norton, Valerie Perrine, Michelle Phillips, Bob Seagren, Martin Sheen, Betty White.

Program 4: Dec. 16, 1979
Ringmasters: Erik Estrada, Douglas Fairbanks, Jr., Lola Falana, Mariette Hartley, Loretta Swit.
Stars: Lesley Aletter, Marty Allen, Loni Anderson, Bob Barker, Barbi Benton, Candy Clark, Cary Collins, Cathy Lee Crosby, Quinn Cummings, Christy Curtis, Vince Edwards, Jamie Farr, Christine Gordon, Marjoe Gortner, Richard Hatch, Richard Kiel, Lee Meriwether, Mary Ann Mobley, David Nelson, John Schneider, Bob Seagren, Brooke Shields, Elke Sommer, Trish Stewart, Vic Tayback, Rip Taylor, Charlene Tilton.

CIRCUS OF THE STARS — 2 hours — CBS — Premiered: January 10, 1977.

232   CIRCUS OF THE 21st CENTURY

Variety. A presentation of unusual and sometimes dangerous circus acts.

Hosts: Sherisse Laurence, Cal Dodd.
Music: Russ Little.
Executive Producer: Arthur Weinthal, Ed Richardson.
Producer: Bill Hartley.
Director: Jack Sampson.
Choreographer: Ken Atkinson.

CIRCUS OF THE 21st CENTURY — 30 minutes — Syndicated 1979. Produced in Canada.

233   CITY OF ANGELS

Crime Drama. The series, set in Los Angeles during the 1930s, details the exploits of Jake Axminster, a hard-boiled private de-

tective. (The title is derived from the fact that at the time L.A. was one of the least corrupt cities.)

CAST

Jake Axminster	Wayne Rogers
Marsha, his friend, who operates an answering service for call girls	Elaine Joyce
Lieutenant Quint	Clifton James
Lester, Jake's informant	Timmie Rogers
Michael Brimm, Jake's attorney	Philip Sterling
Marsha's Girls:	
Darla	Janice Heiden
Thelma	Veronica Hamel

Music: Nelson Riddle, Hal Mooney.
Executive Producer: Jo Swerling, Jr.
Producer: Roy Huggins.
Director: Don Medford, Sigmund Neufeld, Jr., Douglas Heyes, Robert Douglas, Barry Shear, Ralph Senensky.
Creator: Stephen J. Cannell, Roy Huggins.

CITY OF ANGELS — 60 minutes — NBC — February 3, 1976 – August 24, 1976. 13 episodes.

234   CLIFFHANGERS

Serial. The overall title for three adventure serials: *The Curse of Dracula, The Secret Empire,* and *Stop Susan Williams.* See individual titles for information.

CLIFFHANGERS — 60 minutes — NBC — February 27, 1979 – May 1, 1979.

235   THE CLIFFWOOD AVENUE KIDS

Comedy. The misadventures of a group of pre-teen children, members of the Cliffwood Avenue Club, as they stumble upon and seek to solve crimes.

CAST

The Cliffwood Avenue Kids:	
Poindexter	Himself
Samwich	J. Brennan Smith
	Kevin "King" Cooper
Melora	Melora Hardin
Tara	Tara Talboy
Jeremy	Jeremy Lawrence
Sheldon	Kristopher Marquis
Andre	Andre Broadin
Also:	
Sgt. Pat O'Dennis, their friend	Dennis Patrick

Music: Larry Taylor.
Producer-Director: Win Opie.

THE CLIFFWOOD AVENUE KIDS — 30 minutes — Syndicated 1977. 6 episodes.

236   THE CLUE CLUB

Animated Cartoon. The investigations of Pepper, Larry, Dotty and D.D., four professional teenage detectives who comprise the Clue Club. Assisted by Woofer and Wimper, two cowardly, talking bloodhounds, they strive to solve baffling crimes.

VOICES

Pepper	Patricia Stich
Larry	David Jolliffe
D.D.	Bob Hastings
Dotty	Tara Talboy
Woffer	Paul Winchell
Wimper	Paul Winchell
Sheriff Bagley	John Stephenson

Additional Voices: Joan Gerber, Julie McWhirter, Janet Waldo, Vic Perrin, Virginia Gregg.
Music: Hoyt Curtin.
Executive Producer: William Hanna, Joseph Barbera.
Producer: Iwao Takamoto.
Director: Charles A. Nichols.

THE CLUE CLUB—25 minutes—CBS—August 14, 1976–September 3, 1977; September 10, 1978–September 2, 1979.

237   CODE R

Adventure. The series, set on Channel Island, a small coastal community off Southern California, focuses on the work of the Emergency Services, a specialized organization that combines police, fire and ocean rescue departments into the Code R rescue forces.

CAST

Walt Robinson, the police chief	Tom Simcox
Rick Wilson, the fire chief	James Houghton
George Baker, chief lifeguard	Martin Kove
Suzy, the Emergency Services secretary	Susanne Reed
Ted Milbank, the deputy	Ben Davidson
Harry, the owner of the Lighthouse Bar	W.T. Zacha
Bobby Robinson, Walt's son	Robbie Rundle
Barbara Robinson, Walt's wife	Joan Freeman
Dr. Southerland	Tom Williams

Music: Lee Holdridge.
Producer: Edwin Self.
Director: Richard Benedict, Bruce Kessler, Georg Fenady, Andrew McLaglen, Phil Bondelli, Leslie H. Martinson, Alf Kjellin.
Creator: Edwin Self.

CODE R—60 minutes—CBS—January 21, 1977–June 10, 1977. 13 episodes.

238 · CO-ED FEVER

Comedy. The series, set at Baxter University in Connecticut, focuses on the misadventures that occur when the posh Eastern girls' school becomes a co-educational institution.

CAST

The Brewster House Students:

Melba, the luscious coed	Jillian Kesner
Sandi, the alluring coed	Heather Thomas
Hope, the independent coed	Tacey Phillips
Elizabeth, the girl next door type of coed	Cathryn O'Neil
Maria (Mousie), the bright coed	Alexa Kenin
Tucker Davis, the romantic but shy student	David Keith
Doug, the sophisticated student	Christopher S. Nelson
Gobo, the wacky student	Michael Pasternak

Also:

Mrs. Selby, the housemother	Jane Rose

Music: Henry Mancini.
Theme: "Dear Mom and Dad" by Alan and Marilyn Bergman (lyrics) and Henry Mancini (Music).
Executive Producer: Martin Ransohoff.
Producer: Frank Shaw.
Writer: Michael Elias, Frank Shaw.
Director: Marc Daniels.
Art Director: John C. Mula.

CO-ED FEVER—30 minutes—CBS—Premiered/Ended: February 4, 1979. 1 episode.

239   COLUMBO

Crime Drama. The exploits of Lieutenant (no first name) Columbo, an underpaid and untidy detective with the Central Homicide Division of the Los Angeles Police Department.

CAST

Lieutenant Columbo	Peter Falk
Captain Sampson	Bill Zuckert

Music: Robert Prince, Henry Mancini, Bernard Segal, Jeff Alexander, Oliver Nelson, Dick De Benedictis, Billy Goldenberg.
Executive Producer: Richard Levinson, William Link, Dean Hargrove, Roland Kibbee, Leonard B. Stern.
Producer: Everett Chambers, Dean Hargrove, Roland Kibbee, Richard Alan Simmons.
Director: Jack Smight, Steven Spielberg, Patrick McGoohan, Bernard L. Kowalski, Robert Douglas, Harvey Hart, Edward Abroms, Robert Butler, Jeremy Kagan, Stephen J. Cannell, Roland Kibbee, Ted Post, Jeannot Szwarc, James Frawley, Hy Averback, Norman Lloyd, Alf Kjellin, Sam Wanamaker, Peter Falk, Richard Quine, Nicholas Colasanto.
Columbo's badge number: 436.

COLUMBO—90 minutes to two hours—NBC. September 15, 1971–September 6, 1972 (as part of *The NBC Wednesday Mystery Movie*); September 17, 1972–September 4, 1977 (as part of *The NBC Sunday Mystery Movie*); November 21, 1977–September 1, 1978. The two-hour pilot film, "Ransom for a Dead Man," aired on NBC on March 1, 1971.

240   COMEBACK

Documentary. Dramatic profiles of people who, after reaching the zenith of their careers, fell from those heights and then fought their way back again to the top.

Host: James Whitmore.
Executive Producer: Lawrence Jacobson.
Producer: Richard Arlett.
Director: Steven North.
Creator: Roy Baxter, Lawrence Jacobson.
Art Director: Michael Hollyfield.
Director of Photography: Verne Carlson.

COMEBACK—30 minutes—Syndicated 1979.

241   THE COMEDY SHOP

Comedy. Performances by guest comics—name celebrities and new and upcoming performers.

Host: Norm Crosby.
Music: Jack Elliott, Allyn Ferguson.
Executive Producer: Paul Roth.
Producer: Joe Siegman, Perry Rosemond.
Director: Perry Rosemond.

THE COMEDY SHOP—30 minutes—Syndicated 1978. Titled *Norm Crosby's Comedy Show* in 1980.

242   COMEDY TONIGHT

Comedy. Various sketches that satirize everyday life.

Host: Robert Klein.
Regulars: Lin Lipton, Jerry Lacy, Barbara Cason, Marty Barris, Peter Boyle, Bonnie Enten, Judy Graubart, Laura Greene, Madeline Kahn, Macintyre Dixon.
Orchestra: Jack Elliott, Allyn Ferguson.
Producer: Joe Cates.
Writer: Gary Belkin, Tom Meehan, Barry Sand, Norman Steinberg, Tony Geiss.
Director: Walter C. Miller.

COMEDY TONIGHT—60 minutes—CBS—July 5, 1970–August 23, 1970.

243   THE COMMANDERS

Documentary. The series profiles World War II's military geniuses via rare photos and never-before-seen combat footage. Produced by the BBC.

Narrator: Frank Gillard.
Producer: Harry Hastings.
Director: Maurice Kanareck.

THE COMMANDERS—60 minutes—Syndicated 1975.

244   CONCENTRATION

Game. Displayed on stage is a large electronic board which contains thirty numbered, three-sided wedges. One of two competing players chooses two numbers. The wedges rotate and reveal prizes. If they match, the wedges rotate again and reveal two puzzle parts. The player then attempts to guess what the puzzle will show (slogan, name, or place). If he is unable to solve the puzzle, he picks two more numbers. If two different prizes appear, the wedges revert to numbers and his opponent receives a chance to play. The first player to identify the puzzle is the winner and receives the prizes he has accumulated on his side of the board.

Host, Network Version: Hugh Downs, Jack Barry, Art James, Bill Mazer, Ed McMahon, Bob Clayton.
Host, Syndicated Version: Jack Barry.
Announcer, Network Version: Wayne Howell, Art James, Bob Clayton.
Announcer, Syndicated Version: Johnny Olsen.
Music, Network Version: Milton DeLugg, Dick Hyman, Milton Kaye, Tony Columbia.
Music, Syndicated Version: Ed Kalehoff.

CONCENTRATION—30 minutes—NBC—August 25, 1958–March 23, 1973. Syndicated, first run, 1973.

245   THE CONTENDER

Drama. The story of Johnny Captor, an amateur boxer from Coos Bay, Oregon, who forsakes his college studies for a chance at fame in the ring. Guided by George Beifus, his trainer, a former prize fighter who believes Johnny will be the next "great white hope," the series follows Johnny's struggles to become a world champion.

CAST

Johnny Captor	Marc Singer
George Beifus, his trainer	Moses Gunn
Jill Cyndon, Johnny's girlfriend	Katherine Cannon
Brian Captor, Johnny's brother	Alan Stock
Alma Captor, Johnny's mother	Louise Latham
Missy Dinwittie, the sister of a fighter who helps Johnny	Tina Andrews
Lou Waverly, the sportswriter	Susan Walden
Mike Captor, Johnny's father	Art Lund
"Killer" Dinwittie, Missy's brother	Albert Myles
Thomas Waverly, Lou's father	Linwood McCarthy
Harry, the man who owns Johnny's contract	Don Gordon
Andy, Harry's assistant	William Watson

Creator: Robert Dozier, Herman Groves.
Music: James Di Pasquale.
Executive Producer: Jon Epstein.
Producer: Tony Kiser, Howard Berk, Richard Collins.

Oregon Sequences Produced by: Robert Dozier.
Writer: Herman Groves, Robert Dozier, Robert Hamilton, Howard Berk, Richard Collins.
Director: Harry Falk, Sutton Roley, Richard Costalano, James Sheldon.
Director of Oregon Sequences: Lou Antonio.
Director of Photography: Enzo A. Martinelli.

THE CONTENDER — 60 minutes — CBS — April 3, 1980 — May 1, 1980. 5 episodes.

246   COOL MILLION

Crime Drama. The investigations of Jefferson Keyes, a former U.S. government agent turned confidential private detective who charges one million dollars and guarantees results or refunds the money. Impatient with busy signals, he establishes a base in Lincoln, Nebraska (where telephone lines are always open), in the home of a woman named Elena. When his special telephone number, 30-30100 is dialed, Elena, the only person who is able to contact him, relays the message to him.

CAST
Jefferson Keyes	James Farentino
Tony Baylor, the pilot of his private jet	Ed Bernard
Elena, the girl who contacts Keyes	Adele Mara

Music: Billy Goldenberg.
Executive Producer: Roy Huggins.
Producer: Jo Swerling, Jr.
Director: Gene Levitt, Daryl Duke, John Badham, Barry Shear, Charles S. Dubin.

COOL MILLION — 90 minutes — NBC — October 25, 1972 — July 11, 1973 (as a segment of *The NBC Wednesday Mystery Movie*). The two-hour pilot film aired on NBC on October 16, 1972.

247   THE COP AND THE KID

Comedy. The misadventures of Frank Murphy, a tough bachelor police officer with the 6th Division of the Los Angeles Police Department, and the guardian of Lucas Adams, a streetwise youth.

CAST
Officer Frank Murphy	Charles Durning
Lucas Adams, his ward	Tierre Turner
Mary Goodhew, the social worker	Sharon Spelman
Brigid Murphy, Frank's mother	Patsy Kelly
Sgt. Zimmerman, Frank's superior	William Preston
Mouse, Lucas's friend	Eric Laneuville
Shortstuff, Lucas's friend	Curtiz Willis
Killer, Lucas's dog	Shadrock

Music: Jerry Fielding, Joe Reisman.
Executive Producer: Jerry Davis.
Producer: Ben Joelson, Art Baer.
Director: Alexander March, Gary Nelson.
Creator: Jerry Davis.

THE COP AND THE KID — 30 minutes — NBC — December 4, 1975 — March 4, 1976.

248   THE CORAL JUNGLE

Documentary. Filmed studies of the world beneath the sea.

Host-Narrator: Leonard Nimoy.
Music: Tom Anthony.
Executive Producer: Jack Reilly.
Producer: Richard Perin.
Writer: Richard Schickel.
Director: Ben Cropp.

THE CORAL JUNGLE — 60 minutes — Syndicated 1976. 8 episodes.

249   THE CORNER BAR

Comedy. The story of Harry Grant, owner of Grant's Toomb, a restaurant-bar in Manhattan, as he becomes involved with and struggles to solve staff and clientele problems.

CAST
Harry Grant	Gabriel Dell
Meyer Shapiro, the waiter	Shimen Ruskin
Mary Ann, the waitress	Langhorne Scruggs
Phil Bracken, the henpecked Wall Street executive	Bill Fiore
Peter Panama, the male fashion designer	Vincent Schiavelli
Fred Costello, the cab driver	J.J. Barry
Joe, the restaurant cook	Joe Keyes

Address of Grant's Toomb: 137 Amsterdam Avenue in New York City.
Music: Norman Paris.
Executive Producer: Alan King.
Producer: Howard Morris.
Director: Rick Edelstein.

THE CORNER BAR — 30 minutes — ABC — June 21, 1972 — August 23, 1972.

250   THE CORNER BAR

Comedy. A revised version of the previous title. The story of Mae and Frank, co-owners of the The Corner Bar, a restaurant-bar in Manhattan, as they struggle to run it amid numerous staff and clientele problems.

CAST
Mae, co-owner of the bar	Anne Meara
Frank Flynn, her partner	Eugene Roche
Meyer Shapiro, the waiter	Shimen Ruskin
Fred Costello, the cab driver	J.J. Barry
Phil Bracken, the Wall Street executive	Bill Fiore
Donald Hooten, the actor	Ron Carey

Address of The Corner Bar: 137 Amsterdam Avenue in New York City.

Music: Norman Paris.
Executive Producer: Alan King.
Producer: Howard Morris.
Director: Dave Wilson.

THE CORNER BAR — 30 minutes — ABC — August 3, 1973 — September 7, 1973.

251   CORONATION STREET

Serial. Stories dramatize the lives and problems of the working class Britons who inhabit the Rovers Bar, at Number Eleven Coronation Street in Weatherfield, England.

CAST
Ena Sharples	Violet Carson
Annie Walker	Doris Speed
Len Fairclough	Peter Adamson
Ray Langton	Neville Buswell
Rita Fairclough	Barbara Knox
Ken Barlow	William Roache
Suzie Birchall	Cheryl Murray
Gail Potter	Helen Worth
Steve Fisher	Laurence Mullin
Eddie Yeats	Geoffrey Hughes
Emily Bishop	Eileen Derbyshire
Marvis Riley	Thelma Barlow
Bert Lynch	Julie Goodyear
Fred Gee	Fred Feast
Albert Tatlock	Jack Howarth
Alf Roberts	Bryan Mosley
Billy Walker	Kenneth Farrington
Richard Cresswell	Timothy Carlton
Deirdre Langton	Anne Kirkbride
Stan Ogden	Bernard Youens
Mrs. Harbottle	Penny Gowling
Lorry Driver	Ted Carroll
Freda Loftus	Poppy Lane
Hilda Ogden	Jean Alexander
Sonia Forrester	Sylvia Coleridge
Barry Goodwin	Christopher Coll
Minni Caldwell	Margot Bryant
Elsie Howard	Patricia Phoenix
George Greenwood	Arthur Penlow
Peter Bromley	Jonathan Adams
Arnold Sheppard	Julian Somers
Frank Bradley	Alan Browning
Tommy Deacon	Paddy Joyce
Dirty Dick	Talfryn Thomas
Francois Dubois	Francois Pacal
Jerry Booth	Graham Haberfield
Ernest Bishop	Stephen Hancock
Dave Robbins	Jon Rollason
Yvonne Chappell	Alexandra Marshall
Maggie Clegy	Irene Sutcliffe
Vera Hopkins	Kathy Staff
Idris Hopkins	Kathy Jones
Rita Littlewood	Barbara Mullaney
Norma Ford	Diana Davies
Megan Hopkins	Jessie Evan

Music: Eric Spear.
Producer: Bill Podmore.
Writer: Julian Roach, Leslie Duxbury, John Stevenson, Kay McManus.
Stories: Esther Rose, Peter Tonkinson.
Designer: Eric Deakins.
Director: Ken Grieve, Charles Sturridge.

CORONATION STREET — 30 minutes — Syndicated (to the U.S.) in 1972. Produced in England by Granada TV.

252   COS

Variety. Monologues, music, songs and comedy sketches.

Host: Bill Cosby.
Regulars: Marion Ramsey, Jeff Altman, Timothy Thomerson, Pat Delaney, Willie Bobo, Maurice Jorrin, Buzzy Linhart.
Announcer: John Wilson.
Orchestra: Stu Gardner.
Producer: Chris Bearde.
Writer: Larry Markes, Tony Geiss, Tom Meehan, June Reisner.
Director: Jeff Margolis.
Choreographer: Kevin Carlisle, Alan Johnson.
Animation: John Wilson.
Art Director: Charles Lisanby, Ed La Porta.

COS — 60 minutes — ABC — September 19, 1976 — October 31, 1976.

253   COUNTRY MATTERS

Anthology. Four dramas, based on short stories by A.E. Coppardo, that depict various aspects of life in England during the 1920s.

Producer: Derek Granger.

The Stories:
The Higgler. The story of a produce peddler who is down on his luck until he discovers a small farm run by a widow and her daughter.

Cast: Harvey: Keith Drinkel; Mrs. Sadgrove: Sheila Ruskin; Mary Sadgrove: Rosalie Crutchley.

The Watercress Girl. The story recounts a crime of passion: a woman who threw acid in the face of her former boyfriend's fiancée.

Cast: Mary: Susan Fleetwood; Frank: Gareth Thomas; Father: John Welsh; Elizabeth: Susan Tebbs.

The Black Dog. The story, set at the Black Dog Inn, shows a meeting between two couples and the tragic results: the innkeeper and his young mistress; and the man's calculating daughter who has come home with a well-to-do admirer.

Cast: Orianda: Jane Lapotaire; Gerald: Stephen Chase; Crabbe: Glyn Houston; Lizzie: June Watson.

The Mill. The story of a naive 17-year-old girl who, employed by a bedridden old woman suddenly finds herself the object of the taciturn husband's lust.

Cast: Alice: Rosalind Ayres; Holland: Ray Smith; Albert: Tom Chadborn; Hartop: Robert Keegan.

COUNTRY MATTERS — 60 minutes — PBS — February 2, 1975 – February 24, 1975. 4 episodes.

254 COUNTRY MUSIC CARAVAN

Musical Variety. A series of film clips from various country and western programs of the 1950s.

Rotating Hosts: Marty Robbins, Ernest Tubb, Jimmy Dickins, Carl Smith, Ray Price, Grandpa Jones.
Regulars: Faron Young, Johnny and Jack, The Tunesmiths, Minnie Pearl, The Carter Family, Moon Mulligan, The George Morgan Square Dancers, The Tennessee Mountain Boys, Stringbean, The Country Square Dancers, Kitty Wells, Ruby Wright, The Carter Sisters, Rod Brasfield, The Grand Ole Opry Square Dancers, June Carter, Rita Faye, The Jordanaires, The North Carolina Square Dancers, Gordon Terry, The College Kids Square Dancers, Ferlin Husky, The Carolina Cloggers, Ray Price, Red Savin.
Producer-Director: Albert Gannaway.

COUNTRY MUSIC CARAVAN — 60 minutes – Syndicated 1974.

255 THE COURTSHIP OF EDDIE'S FATHER

Comedy Drama. The series, set in Los Angeles, depicts the relationship between widower Tom Corbett, editor of *Tomorrow* magazine, and his six-year-old son, Eddie.

CAST
Tom Corbett	Bill Bixby
Eddie Corbett, his son	Brandon Cruz
Mrs. Livingston, their housekeeper	Miyoshi Umeki
Cissy Drummond, the magazine editor	Tippi Hedren
Norman Tinker, the art editor	James Komack
Etta, Tom's secretary, early episodes	Karen Wolfe
Tina Rickles, Tom's secretary, later episodes	Kristina Holland
Joey Kelley, Eddie's friend	Jodie Foster

Music: George Tipton.
Theme Vocal: Nilsson.
Executive Producer: James Komack.
Producer: Ralph Riskin.
Director: Alan Rafkin, Bob Sweeney, Ralph Senensky, Harry Falk, Hal Cooper, Randal Hood, Bill Bixby, James Komack, Luther James.

THE COURTSHIP OF EDDIE'S FATHER — 30 minutes — ABC — September 17, 1969 – June 14, 1972. 78 episodes. Syndicated.

256 THE COWBOYS

Western. The series, set on the Longhorn Ranch in Spanish Wells, New Mexico, during the 1870s, follows the exploits of seven children*, aged nine to fifteen, a range cook (Mr. Nightlinger) and the widowed ranch owner (Kate Andersen), as they struggle to maintain a cattle ranch in a turbulent era.

CAST
Mr. Nightlinger, the range cook and guardian of the children	Moses Gunn
Kate Andersen, the ranch owner	Diana Douglas
Bill Winter, the marshal	Jim Davis
The Children:	
Cimarron	A Martinez
Slim	Robert Carradine
Homer	Kerry MacLane
Steve	Clint Howard
Weedy	Clay O'Brien
Jim	Sean Kelly
Hardy	Mitch Brown

Music: Johnny Williams, Harry Sukman.
Executive Producer: David Dortort.
Producer: John Hawkins.

THE COWBOYS — 30 minutes — ABC — February 6, 1974 – August 14, 1974. 13 episodes.

*Originally hired by the ranch owner, Will Andersen (John Wayne in the feature film on which the series is based) to help him drive a herd of 1,500 cattle to Dodge City. When Will is killed by rustlers, the boys stay on as ranch hands to help Kate run the ranch.

257 C.P.O. SHARKEY

Comedy. The series, set at a navy recruit training center in San Diego, presents a satirical look at naval life as seen through the experiences of C.P.O. (Chief Petty Officer) Steve Sharkey, an acid-tongued, twenty-four-year veteran who has waged his own private war against the changes that constitute the new navy

CAST
C.P.O. Steve Sharkey	Don Rickles
C.P.O. Robinson	Harrison Page
Captain Quinlan	Elizabeth Allen
Captain Buck Buckner	Richard X. Slattery
Lieutenant Wipple	Jonathan Daly
Drill Sgt. Pruitt	Peter Isacksen
Recruit Leon Sholnick	David Landsberg
Recruit Kowalski	Tom Ruben
Recruit Shimokawa	Evan Kim
Recruit Mignone	Barry Pearl
Recruit Rodriquez	Richard Beauchamp
Recruit Daniels	Jeff Hollis
Recruit Apocuda	Philip Sims

Music: Peter Matz.
Executive Producer: Aaron Ruben.
Producer: Gene Marcione.
Director: Peter Baldwin, Mel Ferber.
Creator: Aaron Ruben.

C.P.O. SHARKEY — 30 minutes — NBC — December 1, 1976 – August 30, 1977; October 21, 1977 – April 28, 1978; May 26, 1978 – July 28, 1978.

258 CRIMES OF PASSION

Anthology. Dramatizations based on the files of the French criminal records of *crimes passionels* (crimes of passion). Stories begin with a crime being committed in an emotional moment of passion. A courtroom trial follows, and through the use of flashbacks as witnesses testify, the program attempts to determine whether or not the crime was premeditated.

CAST
The President of the Courts (Judge)	Anthony Newlands
Maitre Saval, the defense attorney	Daniel Moynihan
Maitre Lacan, the prosecuting attorney	John Phillips
Maitre DuBois, the prosecuting attorney (several episodes)	Bernard Archard

Music: Derek Scott.
Producer: Ian Fordyce, Robert Cardona.
Director: Peter Moffatt, Peter Jeffries, Valerie Hanson, Robert Cardona, Gareth Davies.

CRIMES OF PASSION — 60 minutes — Syndicated 1976.

259 THE CROSS WITS

Game. Two three-member teams compete, each composed of two celebrities and one noncelebrity captain. A large crossword board, which contains the names of persons, places or things, is revealed. The captain selects a position (e.g., one across; nine down) for which the host reads a corresponding clue and which one of the celebrities must answer. If the correct answer is given, the word appears on the board and the team scores ten points for each filled space. Failure to figure out a clue ends that team's turn at play; the opponents then receive their chance. The team that is first to identify the puzzle is the winner and the noncelebrity player receives merchandise prizes.

Host: Jack Clark.
Announcer: John Harlan, Jerry Bishop, Jay Stewart.
Assistant: Jerri Fiala.
Substitute for Jerri: Kitty Hilton.
Music: Ron Kaye, Buddy Kaye, Philip Springer.

Executive Producer: Ralph Edwards.
Producer: Roy Horl, Bruce Belland.
Director: Richard Gottlieb, Jerry Payne.

THE CROSS WITS — 30 minutes — Syndicated 1975.

260 CURIOSITY SHOP

Children. Various aspects of the adult world are explained to children via sketches, cartoons and films.

CAST
Gittel the Witch	Barbara Minkus
The Children:	
Pam	Pamelyn Ferdin
Gerard	John Levin
Ralph	Kerry MacLane
Cindy	Jerelyn Fields

Featured: The Bob Baker Marionettes.
Voices (for animated segments): Mel Blanc, June Foray, Chuck Jones, Robert Holt.
Music: Dick Elliott.
Theme: Henry Mancini.
Producer: Chuck Jones.
Animation Producer: Herbert Klynn, Abe Levitow.
Writer: Gene Moss, Jim Thurmar.

CURIOSITY SHOP — 60 minutes — ABC — September 11, 1971 – September 9, 1973.

261 THE CURSE OF DRACULA

Serial. The story, set in present-day San Francisco, focuses on the attempts of Kurt von Helsing and Mary Gibbons to destroy Count Dracula, a 512-year-old vampire they believe is alive and living in California — and posing as a professor of East European History at Southbay College.

CAST
Count Dracula	Michael Nouri
Kurt von Helsing	Stephen Johnson
Mary Gibbons	Carol Baxter
Amanda Gibbons, Mary's mother, a vampire	Louise Sorel
Antoinette, a student controlled by Dracula	Antoinette Stella
Christine, same as Antoinette	Bever Leigh Banfield

Narrator: Brad Crandall.
Music: Joe Harnell, Charles R. Casey, Les Baxter.
Theme Music: Joe Harnell.
Executive Producer: Kenneth Johnson.
Supervising Producer: B. W. Sandefur.
Producer: Richard Milton, Paul Samuelson.
Director: Kenneth Johnson, Jeffrey Hayden, Richard Milton.
Creator: Kenneth Johnson.

THE CURSE OF DRACULA — 20 minutes — NBC — February 27, 1979 – May 1, 1979 (as a segment of *Cliffhangers*). 10 chapters. Also titled *Dracula '79.*

D

262   THE D. A.

Crime Drama. The story of Paul Ryan, a Los Angeles County District Attorney who functions as both a detective and a prosecutor.

CAST

D. A. Paul Ryan	Robert Conrad
H. M. "Staff" Stafford, the chief deputy	Harry Morgan
Katy Benson, the deputy public defender	Julie Cobb
Bob Ramerez, Ryan's chief investigator	Ned Romero
Charlotte, Ryan's secretary	Sonja Dunson
Judge Simmons	Victor Izay
Lieutenant Vaughn	Ron Foster
Captain Langham	Russ Conway

Music: Frank Comstock.
Executive Producer: Jack Webb.
Producer: Robert H. Forward.
Director: Harry Harris, Jack Webb, Harry Morgan, Dennis Donnelly, Ozzie Nelson, Alan Crosland, Jr., Paul Krasny, Hollingsworth Morse.

THE D. A. — 30 minutes — NBC — September 17, 1971 — January 7, 1972. 13 episodes.

263   DAD'S ARMY

Comedy. A British-produced series, set at the time when Hitler threatened to invade England, that focuses on the antics of a Home Guard unit at Walmington on the south coast as they train to repel the enemy.

CAST

Captain Mainwaring	Arthur Lowe
Sergeant Wilson	John Le Mesurier
Lance Corporal Jone	Clive Dunn
Private Frazer	John Laurie
Private Walker	James Beck
Private Godfrey	Arnold Ridley
Private Pike	Ian Lavender
ARP Warden Hodges	Bill Pertwee

DAD'S ARMY — 30 minutes — Syndicated (to the U.S.) in 1976. Originally broadcast in England on the BBC from 1967 – 1977.

264   THE DAFFY DUCK SHOW

Animated Cartoon. The misadventures of an easily irritated, wacky mallard named Daffy Duck.

Voice Characterizations: Mel Blanc.
Music: Carl Stalling, William Lava, Steve DePatie, Milt Franklin.
Executive Director: Hal Geer.
Director: Friz Freleng, Robert McKimson, Bill Perez, Chuck Jones.

THE DAFFY DUCK SHOW — 30 minutes — NBC — November 4, 1978 — September 1, 1979. 60 minutes — September 8, 1979 —

September 15, 1979. 30 minutes — Premiered: September 22, 1979.

265   THE DAIN CURSE

Mystery. A three-part miniseries based on Dashiell Hammett's 1929 mystery. Private detective Hamilton Nash attempts to crack a two-bit diamond heist, a case that brings him in contact with Gabrielle Leggett, a strange, confused and frightened girl who believes she has inherited from her mother the Dain family curse, by which anyone involved with her dies.

CAST

Hamilton Nash	James Coburn
Owen Fitztephan	Jason Miller
Gabrielle Leggett	Nancy Addison
Ben Feeney	Hector Elizondo
Aaronia Haldorn	Jean Simmons
Dickerson, the old man	Paul Stewart
Alice Dain Leggett	Beatrice Straight
Sgt. O'Gar	Tom Bower
Jack Santos	David Canary
Marshall Cotton	Beeson Carroll
Eric Collinson	Martin Cassidy
Tom Vernon	Brian Davies
Daisy Cotton	Roni Dengel
Foley	Clarence Felder
Edgar Leggett	Paul Harding
Maria Grosso	Karen Ludwig
Mickey Lenihan	Malachy McCourt
Tom Fink	Brent Spiner
Judge Cochran	Ron Weyand
Minnie Hershey	Hattie Winston
Hubert Collinson	Roland Winters
Joseph Haldron	Ellie Rabb

Music: Charles Gross.
Executive Producer: Bob Markell.
Producer: Martin Poll.
Associate Producer: William C. Gerrity, William Craver, Sonny Grosso.
Director: E. W. Swackhamer.
Director of Photography: Andrew Laszlo.

THE DAIN CURSE — 2 hours — CBS — May 22, 1978 – May 24, 1978. 3 episodes.

266   DALLAS

Drama. The series, set in Dallas, concerns itself with a feud that exists between the Ewing and Barnes families. It started when John "Jock" Ewing, an oil and cattle baron, supposedly cheated his now neighbor, Willard "Digger" Barnes, in earlier days when they were partners drilling for oil. In later episodes, the series depicts incidents in the lives of the individual members of the Ewing family, in particular those of brothers J. R. and Bobby, executives with the Ewing Oil Company.

At the close of the 1980 season, when it was tentative Larry Hagman would return to the series, his "J. R." character was shot and viewers were left in suspense as to who pulled the trigger and

whether he survived. This shooting, as it turned out, became the producers' way of keeping Hagman in line: if he demanded too much money to continue in the role, J. R. would die.

The producers agreed to Hagman's terms to continue playing J. R., but found it a bargain when "who shot J. R.?" became the talk of the nation and ratings began to soar. The episode of Nov. 21, 1980, which revealed that it was Kristen who shot the evil J. R. (ending seven months of viewer speculation) set a Nielsen rating record. The program received a 53.3 rating and a 76% audience share. A conservative estimate is that 83 million people watched that particular episode.

It is also interesting to note that in England, where *Dallas* is seen one day later than in the U.S., regular programming was interrupted when it was learned who shot J. R. Announcers warned viewers to lower the sound if they did not want to know the culprit in advance. Telecommunication between England and the U.S. was also chaotic when eager fans attempted to call American friends and overloaded lines for hours.

CAST

John "Jock" Ewing, Sr., the owner of the Southfork Ranch in Braddock, Texas	Jim Davis
Eleanor Ewing, his wife	Barbara Bel Geddes
J. R. (John Ross) Ewing, Jr., their eldest son	Larry Hagman
Bobby Ewing, their youngest son	Patrick Duffy
Sue Ellen Ewing, J. R.'s wife	Linda Gray
Pamela Barnes Ewing, Bobby's wife	Victoria Principal
Lucy Ewing, Jock's granddaughter	Charlene Tilton
Willard "Digger" Barnes, Pamela's father	David Wayne Keenan Wynn
Cliff Barnes, Digger's son	Ken Kercheval
Ray Krebbs, the Southfork ranch foreman	Steve Kanaly
Valene Ewing, Lucy's mother	Joan Van Ark
Gary Ewing, Valene's husband	Ted Shackelford
Julie Gray, J. R.'s secretary	Tina Louise
Kristin Shepard, Sue Ellen's sister	Mary Crosby
Alan Beam, J. R.'s lawyer	Randolph Powell
Mrs. Shepard, Kristin's mother	Martha Scott
Harve Smithfield, Jock's lawyer	George Petrie
Rudy Millington, Kristin's boyfriend	Terry Lester
Chip Totsin, the Ewing Oil Company representative	Joseph Hacker
Dusty Farlow, Sue Ellen's extramarital affair	Jared Martin
Donna Culver, Ray's romantic interest	Susan Howard
Liz Craig, Pam's employer at "The Store," a fashion boutique	Barbara Babcock
Harrison Page, "The Store" owner in later episodes	Mel Ferrer
Jenna Wade, Bobby's ex-girlfriend	Francine Tacker
Betty Lou Barker, Alan's ex-girlfriend	Laura Johnson
Connie, a Ewing Oil Company secretary	Jenna Michaels
John Ross Ewing III, J. R.'s son	Tyler Banks
Mitch Cooper, Lucy's romantic interest	Leigh McCloskey
Ewing Oil Company secretary	Meg Gallagher
Raul, the Ewing butler	Paco Vela
Arliss, Mitch's mother	Anne Francis
Afton, Mitch's sister	Audrey Landers
Dr. Elby, Sue Ellen's psychiatrist	Jeff Cooper
Leslie Stewart, P.R. lady for J. R.	Susan Flannery

Music: Jerrold Immel, John Parker, Michael Warren, Richard Lewis Warren, Bruce Broughton.
Dallas Theme: Jerrold Immel.
Executive Producer: Philip Capice, Lee Rich.
Producer: Leonard Katzman.
Director: Robert Day, Irving J. Moore, Alex March, Barry Crane, Vincent McEveety, Don McDougall, Leonard Katzman, Leslie H. Martinson, Dennis Donnelly, Gunnar Hellstrom, Larry Hagman, Harry Harris, Alexander Singer.
Creator: David Jacobs.

DALLAS — 60 minutes — CBS — April 2, 1978 – April 30, 1978. 5 episodes. Returned: CBS — Premiered: September 23, 1978. Spin-off series: *Knots Landing*.

267   DAN AUGUST

Crime Drama. The series, set in Santa Luisa, California, a small, fictitious coastal community, follows the life of Dan August, a detective police lieutenant caught between the hatreds of the establishment and his duty to protect.

CAST

Det. Lt. Dan August	Burt Reynolds
Sgt. Charles Wilentz	Norman Fell
Police Chief George Untermeyer	Richard Anderson
Sgt. John Rivera	Ned Romero
Katy Grant, the secretary	Ena Hartman

Music: Dave Grusin.
Executive Producer: Quinn Martin.
Producer: Anthony Spinner.
Director: George McCowan, Harvey Hart, Robert Collins, Michael Caffey, Lewis Allen, Walter Grauman, Richard Benedict, Ralph Senensky, Gerald Mayer, Seymour Robbie, Robert Totten, Robert Douglas, Virgil W. Vogel.

DAN AUGUST — 60 minutes — ABC — September 23, 1970 — September 9, 1971. 26 episodes. CBS rebroadcasts: April 23, 1973 – October 17, 1973; April 16, 1975 – June 25, 1975.

268   DANCE FEVER

Variety. Music, songs and dance contests (which are judged by three guest celebrities).

Host: Deney Terrio.
Regulars: Freeman King, The Motions.
Theme: "Dance Fever" performed by The Triple Connection.
Producer: Paul Abeyta, Stan Harris.
Associate Producer: Michael Gara.
Writer: Tony Garofalo.
Director: Jack Regas, Stan Harris.
Assistant Director: Rick Locke.
Choreographer: Joanne DiVito, Tad Tadlock.
Art Director: Bob Rang.
Creator: Merv Griffin.

DANCE FEVER — 30 minutes — Syndicated 1979.

269   DANIEL BOONE

Adventure. The series, set in Boonesborough, Kentucky, during the latter half of the eighteenth century, details the exploits of Daniel Boone, the legendary frontiersman-pioneer.

CAST

Daniel Boone	Fess Parker
Rebecca Boone, his wife	Patricia Blair
Jemima Boone, their daughter	Veronica Cartwright
Israel Boone, their son	Darby Hinton
Yadkin, Daniel's sidekick	Albert Salmi
Mingo, Daniel's Oxford educated friend, a Cherokee Indian	Ed Ames
Cincinnatus, Daniel's friend	Dallas McKennon
Josh Clements, Daniel's friend	Jimmy Dean
Gabe Cooper, Daniel's friend	Roosevelt Grier
Gideon, Daniel's friend	Don Pedro Colley
Cully, Daniel's friend	James Wainwright
Prater Beasley, the teller of tall tales	Burl Ives
Gabriel, Daniel's friend	Armando Silvestre

Boonesborough Citizens:

Little Dan'l	Ezekiel Williams
Mary	Claire Wilcox
Sam	Joel Davison
Ethan	Kevin Tate
Gordon	Lee J. Lambert
Storekeeper	Jack Gainer
Judge	Ian Wolfe
Bryant	Richard Webb
Tom Stoneman	William Keller
Governor Carleton	Robert Cornthwaite
Tavern Keeper	I. Stanford Jolley
John	Joey Coons
Whitmore	Booth Coleman
Bartender	Sean McClory
Colonel Hamilton	Ivor Barry
	Peter Bromilow
Ben	Warren Vanders

Music: Alexander Courage, Lyn Murray, Irving Getz, Joseph Mullendore, Leigh Harline, Lionel Newman, Harry Sukman, Herman Stein, Leith Stevens, Fred Steiner.
Theme Vocal: The Imperials.

Executive Producer: Aaron Rosenberg, Aaron Spelling.
Producer: George Sherman, Barney Rosenzweig, Joseph Silver, Ted Schliz.
Director: Nathan Juran, William Wiard, George Marshall, John Newland, Gerd Oswald, Alex Nicol, Tony Leader, Earl Bellamy, John Florea, Barry Shear, Fess Parker, William Witney.

DANIEL BOONE — 60 minutes — NBC — September 24, 1964 – September 10, 1970. 165 episodes. Syndicated.

270   DARK SHADOWS

Serial. The series, set in Collinsport, a small fishing village in Maine, follows the experiences of Victoria Winters, a young woman who is hired as governess for ten-year-old David Collins, and her involvement in the supernatural experiences of the Collins family.

CAST

Victoria Winters	Alexandra Moltke
Elizabeth Collins Stoddard	Joan Bennett
Flora Collins	Joan Bennett
Barnabas Collins	Jonathan Frid
Barnabas Collins-Bramwell	Jonathan Frid
Carolyn Stoddard	Nancy Barrett
Charity	Nancy Barrett
Letitia Faye	Nancy Barrett
Roger Collins	Louis Edmonds
Edward Collins	Louis Edmonds
Daniel Collins	Louis Edmonds
Dr. Julia Hoffman	Grayson Hall
Magda Ricosa	Grayson Hall
Julia Collins	Grayson Hall
Maggie Evans	Kathryn Leigh Scott
Angelique	Lara Parker
Cassandra	Lara Parker
Valerie Collins	Lara Parker
Joe Haskell	Joel Crothers
Quentin Collins	David Selby
Willie Loomis	John Karlen
Desmond Collins	John Karlen
David Collins	David Henesy
Tad Collins	David Henesy
Peter Bradford	Roger Davis
Sarah Collins	Sharon Smyth
Sam Evans	David Ford
Mrs. Johnson	Clarice Blackburn
Harry Johnson	Craig Slocum
Cyrus Longworth	Chris Pennock
Jeb Hawks	Chris Pennock
Burke Devlin	Anthony George
Daphne Harridge	Kate Jackson
Bruno	Michael Stroka
Amy	Denise Nickerson
Sabrina Stuart	Lisa Richards
Mrs. Collins	Diana Millay
Adam	Robert Rodan
Eve	Marie Wallace
Beth	Terry Crawford
Edith Collins	Terry Crawford
King Johnny Romano	Paul Richard
Hallie Stokes	Kathy Cody
Carrie Stokes	Kathy Cody
Prof. Elliot Stokes	Thayer David
Count Petofi	Thayer David
Mordecai Grimes	Thayer David
Reverend Trask	Jerry Lacy
Balberith, Prince of Darkness	Humbert A. Astredo
Charles Dawson	Humbert A. Astredo
Rondell Drew	Gene Lindsey
Amanda Harris	Donna McKechnie
Olivia Corey	Donna McKechnie
Michael	Michael Maitland
Philip Todd	Christopher Bernau
Gabriel Collins	Chris Pennock
Samantha Collins	Virginia Vestoff
Morgan Collins	Keith Prentice
Gerald Stiles	James Storm
Laszlo	Michael Stroka
Roxane Drew	Donna Wandrey
The Werewolf	Alex Stevens

Also: Gregory Frank, Mitchell Ryan, Don Briscoe, Alan Feinstein, Conrad Fowkes, Alan Yorke.
Music: Robert Cobert.
Producer: Dan Curtis, Robert E. Costello.

DARK SHADOWS — 30 minutes — ABC — June 27, 1966 – April 2, 1971. 1,000 episodes. Syndicated.

271   DASTARDLY AND MUTTLEY IN THEIR FLYING MACHINES

Animated Cartoon. The program, set during World War I, follows the misguided efforts of the evil Dick Dastardly as he attempts to intercept the vital messages of Yankee Doodle Pigeon, the American courier, and win the war for his unnamed country.

VOICES

Dick Dastardly	Paul Winchell
Muttley, his snickering aide	Don Messick
The General, his superior	Paul Winchell
Klunk, one of Dick's aides	Don Messick
Zilly, same as Klunk	Don Messick

Music: Hoyt Curtin.
Music Director: Ted Nichols.
Executive Producer: William Hanna, Joseph Barbera.
Producer: Charles Nichols.
Director: William Hanna, Joseph Barbera.

DASTARDLY AND MUTTLEY IN THEIR FLYING MACHINES — 30 minutes — CBS — September 13, 1969 – September 3, 1971. 17 episodes. Syndicated.

272   THE DATING GAME

Game. A young woman appears on stage and is seated opposite three bachelors who are hidden from her view by a wall. Based on the men's answers to a series of specially prepared questions, she selects the one she would most like to have as a date. The couple is united and receives an all-expenses paid romantic date. (Also played in reverse: one bachelor; three bachelorettes).

Host: Jim Lange.
Announcer: Johnny Jacobs.
Model: Kathy McCullem.
Music: Frank Jaffe.

Executive Producer: Chuck Barris.
Producer: Mike Metzger.
Director: John Dorsey.

THE DATING GAME — 30 minutes — ABC — October 6, 1966 – July 6, 1973. Syndicated first run in 1978.

273   DAVE ALLEN AT LARGE

Comedy. Various sketches and blackouts that satirize everyday life.

Host: Dave Allen.
Regulars: Susan Baker, Jacqueline Clarke, Robert East, Paul MacDowell, Ralph Watson, Chris Serle, Ivan Buford, Ronnie Brody, Michael Sharwell-Martin.
Writer: Dave Allen, Austin Steele, Peter Vincent.
Producer-Director: Peter Whitmore.

DAVE ALLEN AT LARGE — 30 minutes — Syndicated (to the U.S.) in 1975. Produced in England.

274   DAVID CASSIDY — MAN UNDERCOVER

Crime Drama. The exploits of Dan Shay, an undercover agent for the Los Angeles Police Department.

CAST

Officer Dan Shay	David Cassidy
Joanne Shay, his wife	Wendy Rastatter
Cindy Shay, their daughter	Elizabeth Reddin
Sgt. Walt Abrams, Dan's superior	Simon Oakland
Paul Sanchez, an undercover agent	Michael A. Saleido
T. J., an undercover agent	Ray Vitte

Music: Harold Betts.
Theme Vocal: David Cassidy.
Theme Arranged and Produced By: Ken Mansfield.
Executive Producer: David Gerber.
Producer: Mark Rodgers, Mel Swope.
Director: Bernard McEveety, Vincent Edwards, Sam Wanamaker, Alvin Ganzer, Alexander Singer, Don Medford, Edward Abroms, Alf Kjellin, Virgil W. Vogel.
Creator: Richard Fielder.

DAVID CASSIDY — MAN UNDERCOVER — 60 minutes — NBC — November 2, 1978 – January 18, 1979. 9 episodes. Returned: July 5, 1979 – August 2, 1979. 1 new episode.

275   THE DAVID FROST REVUE

Satire. Sketches and blackouts based on various topical issues (e.g., inflation, politics, health care, etc.).

Host: David Frost.

Regulars: Marcia Rodd, Jack Gilford, Cleavon Little, Lynne Lipton, George Irving, Larry Moss, Jim Catusi.
Music: Billy Taylor.
Executive Producer: David Frost, Marc Merson.
Producer: Allan Manings, Mike Gargiulo.
Director: Mike Gargiulo.

THE DAVID FROST REVUE—30 minutes—Syndicated 1971. 26 programs.

276   THE DAVID LETTERMAN SHOW

Variety. A daily series of music, comedy and celebrity interviews.

Host: David Letterman.
Regulars: Edie McClurg, Valri Bromfield, Bob Sarlatte, Wil Shriner, Edwin Newman (newscaster), Paul Raley.
Announcer: Bill Wendell.
Model: Kim Carney.
Music: The Frank Owens Band.
Theme Music: Michael McDonald.
Executive Producer: Jack Rollins.
Producer: Edyth Chan, Barry Sand.
Writer: Merrill Markoe, Valri Bromfield, Rich Hall, Gary Jacobs, Edie McClurg, Paul Rally, Ron Richards, David Letterman.
Director: Bruce Burmester, Hal Gurnee.

THE DAVID LETTERMAN SHOW—90 minutes—NBC—June 23, 1980–August 1, 1980. 30 programs. 60 minutes—NBC—August 4, 1980–October 24, 1980. 60 programs.

277   DAVID NIVEN'S WORLD

Adventure. Documentary-style presentations that showcase the adventurous activities of ordinary people.

Host-Narrator: David Niven.
Executive Producer: John Fleming Hall.
Producer: Marianne Lamour, Jim DeKay.
Director: Jim DeKay, Geoffrey Weaver.

DAVID NIVEN'S WORLD—30 minutes—Syndicated 1976.

278   THE DAVID STEINBERG SHOW

Variety. Various comedy sketches and blackouts that are designed to satirize the world and its problems.

Host: David Steinberg.
Announcer: Bill Thompson.
Orchestra: Artie Butler.
Producer: Bob Booker, George Foster.
Director: Bill Hobin.

THE DAVID STEINBERG SHOW—60 minutes—CBS—July 19, 1972–August 16, 1972. 4 programs.

279   DAYS OF OUR LIVES

Serial. The dramatic story of Dr. Thomas Horton, a professor of medicine at the University Hospital in Salem, Massachusetts. Episodes depict the conflicts and tensions that arise from the interactions of characters.

CAST

Dr. Thomas Horton	Macdonald Carey
Alice Horton	Frances Reid
Dr. Laura Spencer	Susan Flannery
	Kate Woodville
	Susan Oliver
	Rosemary Forsyth
Mickey Horton	John Clarke
Sandy Horton	Heather North
Dr. Thomas Horton, Jr.	John Lupton
Michael Horton	Alan Decker
	John Amour
	Dick DeCort
	Wesley Eure
Dr. William Horton	Edward Mallory
Craig Merritt	David McLean
John Martin	Robert Brubaker
Helen Martin	K.T. Stevens
Susan Martin	Denise Alexander
Addie Olson	Patricia Huston
	Patricia Barry
Greg Peters	Peter Brown
Kim Douglas	Helen Funai
Doug Williams	Bill Hayes
Jim Phillips	Victor Holchak
Cliff Patterson	John Howard
Scott Banning	Robert Hogan
	Ryan MacDonald
	Mike Farrell
Linda Peterson	Margaret Mason
Julie Olson	Charla Doherty
	Kathy Dunn
	Cathy Ferrar
Julie Olson Williams (above character, married)	Susan Seaforth Hayes
Rick	Myron Natwick
Phyllis Anderson	Nancy Wickwire
	Corinne Conley
Eric Peters	Stanley Kamel
Anne Peters	Jeanne Bates
Phil Peters	Herb Nelson
Wilbur Austin	Arlund Schubert
Diane Hunter	Coleen Gray
Richard Hunter	Terry O'Sullivan
Susan Peters	Bennye Gatteys
Jean Barton	Jocelyn Somers
Detective	Robert J. Stevenson
Stephanie Woodruff	Eileen Barnett
Donna Craig	Tracy Bergman
Amanda Peters	Mary Frann
David Banning	Jeffrey Williams
	Richard Guthrie
Mimi	Gail Johnson
Melissa Phillips	Debbie Lytton
Dr. Jordan Barr	George McDaniel
Doug LaClair	Mikey Martin
Jennifer Horton	Jennifer Peterson
Dr. Kate Winograd	Elaine Princi
Rosie Carlson	Fran Ryan
Hope Williams	Natasha Ryan
Marie Horton	Marie Cheatham
	Lanna Saunders
Bob Anderson	Mark Tapscott
Mary Anderson	Brigid Bazlen
	Karen Wolfe
	Carla Borelli
	Barbara Stanger
Chris Kositchek	Josh Taylor
Margo Horton	Suzanne Zenor
Don Craig	Jed Allan
Meg Hansen	Suzanne Rogers
Hank	Frederick Downs
Dr. Neil Curtis	Joe Gallison
Ben Olson	Robert Knapp
Steve Olson	Flip Mark
Jim Fisk	Burt Douglas
Tony Merritt	Dick Colla
	Ron Husmann
Letty Lowell	Ivy Bethune
Jeri Clayton	Kaye Stevens
Mrs. Jackson	Pauline Myers
Betty Worth	Jenny Sherman
Brooke Hamilton	Adrianne LaRussa
Karl DuVal	Alejando Rey
Cathy Craig	Dorrie Kavanough
	Jennifer Harmon
Trish Clayton	Patty Weaver
Robert LeClair	Robert Clary
Helen Grant	Ketty Lester
Maggie Horton	Suzanne Rogers
Danny Grant	Hassan Shaheed
Sharon DuVal	Sally Stark
Rebecca LeClair	Brooke Bundy
Valerie Grant	Tina Andrews
Paul Grant	Lawrence Cook
Samantha Evans	Andrea Hall Lovell
Marlena Evans	Diana Douglas
	Deidre Hall
Theresa Harper	Elizabeth Brooks
Steve Olson	Flip Mark
	Stephen Schnetzer
Toni	Chip Fields
Fred Barton	John Lombardo
Wendy	Maria Grimm
Dr. Shapiro (later Dr. Speer)	Martin Shaker
Lee Carmichael	Brenda Benet
Ben	Ben Ditosti
Max	Hal Riddle

Music: Tommy Boyce, Bobby Hart, Barry Mann, Charles Albertine.
Executive Producer: Betty Corday, H. Wesley Kenney.
Producer: Jack Herzberg, Al Rabin.
Director: Joe Behar, Frank Pacelli, Richard Sandwick, Alan Puitz, Al Ravin.

DAYS OF OUR LIVES—30 minutes—NBC—Premiered: November 8, 1965.

280   DAYTIME

Celebrity Interview.

Hostess: Penny DuPont.
Special Events Correspondent: Brian Lamb.
Film Reviewer: Joan O'Neill.
Music: Ed Kalehoff.
Producer: Sunni Davis, Ernest Sauer.
Director: Ernest Sauer.

DAYTIME—60 minutes—Syndicated 1976.

281   DEALER'S CHOICE

Game. Three contestants compete in a series of various games based on gambling. Players, who each begin with one hundred chips, are permitted to wager up to twenty-five chips in round one, fifty chips in round two, and unlimited wagering in round three. The winner, the player with the highest chip total, trades in his chips for merchandise prizes.

Host: Bob Hastings, Jack Clark.
Assistant: Jane Nelson.
Announcer: Jim Thompson.
Music: Richard La Salle.
Executive Producer: Ralph Edwards.
Producer: Ed Fishman, Randall Freer.
Director: Dan Smith.

DEALER'S CHOICE—30 minutes—Syndicated 1974.

282   DEAN MARTIN PRESENTS MUSIC COUNTRY, U.S.A.

Variety. Newcomers and established singers perform against the background of various Tennessee locales.

Regularly Appearing: Donna Fargo, Loretta Lynn, Mac Davis, Jerry Reed, Lynn Anderson, Tom T. Hall, Kris Kristofferson, Marty Robbins, Ray Stevens, Tammy Wynette, Doug Kershaw, Doug Dillard.
Music: Jonathan Lucas.
Music Supervision: Doug Gilmore.
Music Arranger: Ed Hubbard.
Executive Producer: Greg Garrison.
Producer: Rich Eustis, Al Rogers.
Director: Perry Rosemond.

DEAN MARTIN PRESENTS MUSIC COUNTRY, U.S.A.—60 minutes—NBC—July 26, 1973–September 6, 1973.

283   DEAN MARTIN'S CELEBRITY ROAST

Comedy. Celebrities from various aspects of the entertainment world are honored via a comical roast. Presented as a series of specials.

Roastmaster (Host): Dean Martin.
Regulars: Nipsey Russell, Foster Brooks, Ruth Buzzi, Milton Berle, Orson Welles, LaWanda Page, Rich Little, Charlie Callas, Red Buttons, Don Rickles, Georgia Engel.
Roasted: Bobby Riggs, Michael Landon, Telly Savalas, Redd Foxx, Joe Namath, Peter Marshall, Dan Haggerty, Betty White, Don Rickles, Angie Dickinson, George Burns, Sammy Davis, Jr., Jack Klugman, Dennis Weaver, Suzanne Somers, Jackie Gleason, Muhammad Ali, Danny Thomas, Ted Knight, Gabriel Kaplan, Frank Sinatra, Joe Garagiola, Evel Knievel, Bob Hope.

The Courtship of Eddie's Father. From left, Bill Bixby, Brandon Cruz and Miyoshi Umeki.

Dark Shadows. Lara Parker as the beautiful, but evil Angelique.

Department S. From left, Peter Wyngarde, Joel Fabiani and Rosemary Nicols. Courtesy of the Independent Television Corporation.

Diana. Diana Rigg.

Orchestra: Les Brown.
Executive Producer: Greg Garrison.
Producer: Lee Hale.
Director: Greg Garrison.

DEAN MARTIN'S CELEBRITY ROAST—Varying times (60 minutes to 2 hours)—NBC—February 8, 1974–January 19, 1979. 28 programs.

284 DEAN MARTIN'S COMEDY WORLD

Variety. Performances by new comedy talent. Taped at various locations throughout the United States and England.

Host: Jackie Cooper.
Locational Hosts: Barbara Feldon, Nipsey Russell.
Regularly Appearing: Eric Morecambe, Ernie Wise, Lonnie Shorr, Rich Little, Jud Strunk, Don Rickles, Phyllis Diller, Jack Benny, Ruth Buzzi, The Committee.
Music: Les Brown.
Producer: Greg Garrison.
Director: John Moffitt.

DEAN MARTIN'S COMEDY WORLD—60 minutes—NBC—June 6, 1974–August 8, 1974.

285 THE DEAN MARTIN SHOW

Variety. Music, songs, dances, monologues, blackouts and comedy sketches.

Host: Dean Martin.
Regulars: Ken Lane, Marian Mercer, Kay Medford, Lou Jacoby, Tom Bosley, Inga Nielson, Dom DeLuise, Nipsey Russell, Rodney Dangerfield, The Golddiggers, The Krofft Marionettes, The Ding-a-Ling Sisters (Lynn Lathem, Tara Leigh, Helen Funai, Jayne Kennedy).
Announcer: Frank Barton. ·
Orchestra: Les Brown.
Musical Arrangements: Van Alexander.
Music Consultant: Ken Lane.
Music Coordinator: Mack Gray.
Special Musical Material: Norman Hopps.
Music Routines: Geoffrey Clarkson.
Producer: Greg Garrison.
Writer: Harry Crane, Stan Daniels, Tom Tenowich, Norm Liebmann, Rod Parker, George Bloom, Jay Burton, Jack Wohl, Jonathan Lucas, Ed Scharlach, Jay Burton, Bernie Rothman.
Director: Greg Garrison.
Choreographer: Jonathan Lucas.
Choral Director: Jack Halroran.
Art Director: Spencer Davis.

THE DEAN MARTIN SHOW—60 minutes—NBC—September 16, 1965–May 24, 1974. 26 selected episodes are syndicated (1980).

286 DEAR ALEX AND ANNIE

Advice. Teen-agers Alex and Annie answer child-related problems, submitted by viewers, through specially written songs.

CAST
Alex	Bing Bingham
Annie	Donna Drake

Music and Songs: Lyn Aherns.
Producer: Lyn Aherns.
Director: Larry Einhorn.
Creator: Marilyn Olin, Lyn Aherns.

DEAR ALEX AND ANNIE—05 minutes—ABC—Premiered: September 22, 1979.

287 DEAR DETECTIVE

Crime Drama. The story of Detective Sergeant Kate Hudson, a beautiful undercover officer with the Los Angeles Police Department who is also a single parent (divorced) struggling to raise a young daughter.

CAST
Det. Sgt. Kate Hudson	Brenda Vaccaro
Lisa Hudson, her daughter	Jet Yardum
Richard Weyland, Kate's romantic interest, a professor of Greek literature	Arlen Dean Snyder
Det. Chuck Morris, Kate's associate	Jack Ging
Det. Sgt. Harry Brock	Michael MacRae
Sergeant Schwartz	Ron Silver
Mrs. Hudson, Kate's mother	Lesley Woods
Captain Mike Gorcey, Kate's superior	M. Emmet Walsh
Sergeant Clay	John Dennis Johnston
Vern, Kate's aunt	Corinne Conley

Music: Dick and Dean De Benedictis.
Producer: Roland Kibbe, Dean Hargrove.
Director: Dean Hargrove, Paul Stanley, Alan Cooke.

DEAR DETECTIVE—60 minutes—CBS—March 28, 1979–April 18, 1979. 4 episodes.

288 THE DEBBIE REYNOLDS SHOW

Comedy. Events in the lives of the Thompsons: Jim, a sportswriter for the *Los Angeles Sun,* and his beautiful and unpredictable wife, Debbie, who yearns for a career as a newspaper feature writer. Reluctant to have two newspaper writers in the family, Jim wants her to remain as she is: "a loving and beautiful housewife devoting herself to making her lord and master happy." Stories depict Debbie's attempts to prove her abilities and achieve her goal; and Jim's struggles to discourage her.

CAST
Debbie Thompson	Debbie Reynolds
Jim Thompson, her husband	Don Chastain
Charlotte Landers, Debbie's sister	Patricia Smith
Bob Landers, Charlotte's husband	Tom Bosley
Bruce Landers, their son	Bobby Riha
Mr. Crawford, Jim's employer	Herbert Rudley

The Thompsons' address: 804 Devon Lane, Los Angeles, California.
Music: Tony Romeo, Jack Marshall.
Theme Vocal: Debbie Reynolds.
Producer: Jess Oppenheimer.
Creator: Jess Oppenheimer.

THE DEBBIE REYNOLDS SHOW—30 minutes—NBC—September 16, 1969–September 8, 1970. 17 episodes.

289 THE DELPHI BUREAU

Crime Drama. The exploits of Glenn Garth Gregory, an investigator for the Delphi Bureau, a top secret intelligence agency that is responsible only to the President of the United States and whose sole function is to protect national security.

CAST
Glenn Garth Gregory	Laurence Luckinbill
Sybil Van Loween, his contact (pilot film)	Celeste Holm
Sybil Van Loween (series)	Anne Jeffreys

Music: Frank DeVol, Harper McKay.
Producer: Sam Rolfe.

THE DELPHI BUREAU—60 minutes—ABC—October 5, 1972–September 1, 1973 (as a segment of *The Men*). 8 episodes. The two-hour pilot film aired on ABC on March 6, 1972.

290 DELTA HOUSE

Comedy. The series, based on the film "National Lampoon's Animal House," follows the outrageous antics of the students (animals) who comprise the Delta House Fraternity of Faber College in 1962.

CAST
The Animals of Delta House:
Jim "Blotto" Blutarski	Josh Mostel
Kent "Flounder" Dorfman	Stephen Furst
Robert Hoover	James Widdoes
Eric "Otter" Stratton	Peter Fox
Larry "Pinto" Kruger	Richard Seer
Daniel Simpson Day ("D-Day")	Bruce McGill

Also:
Vernon Wormer, the dean	John R. Vernon
Doug Niedermeyer, a member of the Omega House Fraternity	Gary Cookson
Muffy Jones, Pinto's girlfriend	Wendy Goldman
Bombshell, a beautiful, shapely blonde; "Delta's secret weapon"	Michelle Pfeiffer
Miss Leonard, Wormer's secretary	Patricia Luris
Mr. Jennings, a teacher at Faber	Peter Kastner
Greg Marmalade, a member of Omega House	Brian Patrick Clarke
Marion Wormer, Vernon's wife	Gloria De Haven
Mandy Pepridge, a student at Faber	Susanna Dalton
Tamara Torton, a student at Faber	Karrie Emerson

Music: Elmer Bernstein, David Spear, Dick De Benedictis, Vic Mizzy.
Supervising Producer: Edward J. Montagne.
Executive Producer: Matty Simmons, Ivan Reitman.
Producer: Edward J. Montagne, Elias Davis, David Pollock.
Director: Alan Myerson, Don Weis, Carl Gottlieb, Hollingsworth Morse, Joshua White, Nicholas Sgarro.

DELTA HOUSE—30 minutes—ABC—January 18, 1979–April 28, 1979. 13 episodes.

291 DELVECCHIO

Crime Drama. The story of police Detective Dominick Delvecchio, a law school graduate whose legal ambitions are hindered by the demands and pressures of his job. (Delvecchio, whose badge number is 425, works out of the Washington Heights division of the Los Angeles Police Department).

CAST
Sgt. Dominick Delvecchio	Judd Hirsch
Det. Paul Shonski, his partner	Charles Haid
Lieutenant Macavan, their superior	Michael Conrad
Thomas Delvecchio, Dom's father	Mario Gallo
Assistant D.A. Dorfman	George Wyner

Music: Billy Goldenberg, Richard Clements.
Executive Producer: William Sackheim.
Producer: Michael Rhodes.
Director: Jerry London, Lou Antonio, Ivan Nagy, Arnold Laven, Walter Doniger.

DELVECCHIO—60 minutes—CBS—September 9, 1976–July 17, 1977.

292 DEPARTMENT S

Mystery. The investigations of Jason King, a successful author of Mark Cain mystery novels; Annabell Hurst, a pretty scientific minded young woman, and Stewart Sullivan, the American member of the British team. As top operatives of Department S, a special investigative branch of Interpol (headquartered in Paris, France), the trio undertakes the task of resolving the baffling crimes of any law enforcement organization in the world.

CAST

Jason King — Peter Wyngarde
Annabell Hurst — Rosemary Nicols
Stewart Sullivan — Joel Fabiani
Sir Curtis Seretse, the director of
Department S — Dennis Alaba Peters

Music: Edwin Astley.
Producer: Monty Berman.
Director: John Gilling, Gil Taylor, Leslie Norman, Cyril Frankel, Ray Baker, Ray Austin, Paul Dickson.
Creator: Monty Berman, Dennis Spooner.

DEPARTMENT S — 60 minutes — Syndicated 1971. 28 episodes.

293 THE DES O'CONNOR SHOW

Variety. Music, songs, dances and comedy sketches. Videotaped in England.

Host: Des O'Connor.
Regulars: Connie Stevens, Charlie Callas, Joe Baker, Jack Douglas, The Bonnie Birds Plus Two, The New Faces, The Paddy Stone Dancers, The Mike Sammes Singers.
Announcer: Paul Griffith (from London), Ed Herlihy (for the sponsor — Kraft foods).
Orchestra: Jack Parnell.

THE DES O'CONNOR SHOW — 60 minutes — NBC — June 21, 1971 – September 1, 1971.

294 DETECTIVE SCHOOL

Comedy. The series, set in Los Angeles, follows the escapades of a group of aspiring gumshoes, students of the Hannigan Detective School and Agency, which is run by Nick Hannigan, a supposedly world-famous investigator.

CAST

Nick Hannigan, the owner
of the school — James Gregory
The Students:
Eddie Dawkins, a shoe
salesman — Randolph Mantooth
Teresa Cleary, a secretary — Jo Ann Harris
Maggie Ferguson, a model
for the La Fleke Lingerie
Company — Melinda Naud
Robert Redford, an elderly
gentleman — Douglas V. Fowley
Charlene Jenkins, a
housewife — LaWanda Page
Leo Frack, a door-to-door
salesman — Pat Proft
Silvio DaSalvo, a mailroom
clerk — Taylor Negron
Also:
Walter Jenkins, Charlene's
husband — Arnold Jackson

Address of the Hannigan School: 1407 East Figaroa.
Music: Peter Matz.
Supervising Producer: Caryn Sneider.

Executive Producer: Bernie Kukoff, Jeff Harris, Caryn Sneider.
Producer: Hank Bradford.
Writer: Bernie Kukoff, Jeff Harris, Pat Proft.
Director: Bernie Kukoff, Jeff Harris, Ralph Levy, Walter C. Miller, Bob LaHendro.
Art Director: Don Roberts.

DETECTIVE SCHOOL — 30 minutes — ABC — July 31, 1979 – August 14, 1979. 3 of 4 taped episodes aired (the original last episode, scheduled for August 21, 1979, was canceled for a one-hour episode of *Happy Days*). Returned: ABC — 30 minutes — September 15, 1979 – November 24, 1979. 10 episodes. Originally titled *Detective School — One Flight Up.*

DETECTIVE SCHOOL — ONE FLIGHT UP

See *Detective School.*

295 DEVLIN

Animated Cartoon. The story of Ernie, Todd and Sandy Devlin, three orphans, and their struggles to support themselves by performing as a motorcycle stunt team.

VOICES

Ernie Devlin — Michael Bell
Todd Devlin — Mickey Dolenz
Sandy Devlin — Michele Robinson
Hank, their friend — Norman Alden

Additional Voices: Philip Clarke, Don Diamond, Sarina Grant, Bob Hastings, Stan Livingston, Derrell Maury, Barney Phillips, Fran Ryan, John Stephenson, John Tuell, Ginny Tyler, Jesse White, Don Weiss, Robie Lester.
Music: Hoyt Curtin.
Executive Producer: William Hanna, Joseph Barbera.
Producer: Iwao Takamoto.
Director: Charles A. Nichols.

DEVLIN — 30 minutes — ABC — September 7, 1974 – February 15, 1976.

296 THE DIAHANN CARROLL SHOW

Variety. Music, songs, dances and comedy sketches.

Hostess: Diahann Carroll.
Orchestra: H.B. Barnum.
Special Musical Material: Earl Brown.
Choreographer: Carl Jablonski.
Executive Producer: Robert DeLeon, Max Youngstein.
Producer: Ray Aghayan, Dick DeLeon.
Director: Mike Warren.

THE DIAHANN CARROLL SHOW — 60 minutes — CBS — August 14, 1976 – September 4, 1976. 4 programs.

297 THE DIAMOND HEAD GAME

Game. Eight players compete, two at a time. The first four rounds involve players in a question and answer session wherein the four highest scoring players are the winners. In the fifth round, the four players are situated at the bottom of a three-step climb. A category topic is stated (e.g., "Types of Birds") and a pertinent list of names is read. Players, who have to rely on their memories after hearing the names only once, each have to relate one of the subjects. Failure to mention one that is on the list or repeating one that has already been said defeats that player. The three remaining players then move up one step and a new round begins. The game continues until only one player remains.

The champion is escorted to Diamond Head, a glass room that contains thousands of U.S. currency bills and slips of paper containing merchandise prizes. An air machine is activated (which blows the bills and paper about the room) and the player has fifteen seconds to gather the bills. Whatever bills and/or gift certificates the player has managed to snag (there is a limit of ten) are his prizes.

Host: Bob Eubanks.
Assistant: Jane Nelson.
Announcer: Jim Thompson.
Music: Alan Thicke.
Producer: Randall Freer, Ed Fishman.
Director: Terry Kyne.

THE DIAMOND HEAD GAME — 30 minutes — Syndicated 1975. Videotaped in Hawaii.

298 DIANA

Comedy. The trials and tribulations of Diana Smythe, a beautiful young divorcée newly arrived in New York City from London.

Stories depict her home life at 4 Sutton Place, Apartment 11-B, a bachelor flat that is owned by her brother, Roger, an anthropologist who is presently in Equador; her work as a fashion illustrator at Buckley's Department Store; and her attempts to reclaim the numerous keys that were given out by her brother to his friends, acquaintances and drinking companions — people who are unaware of his absence and seek to use his apartment at all hours.

CAST

Diana Smythe — Diana Rigg
Norman Brodnik, the president
of Buckley's Department
Store — David Sheiner
Norma Brodnik, his wife, the
merchandising department
head — Barbara Barrie

Howard Tolbrook, the
copywriter — Richard B. Shull
Marshall Tyler, the
window dresser — Robert Moore
Holly Green, Diana's friend,
a model — Carol Androsky
Jeff Harmon, Diana's friend,
a writer — Richard Mulligan
Smitty, the Sutton Place
Bellboy — Liam Dunn

Roger's Great Dane: Gulliver.
Music: Jerry Fielding.
Producer-Director: Leonard B. Stern.

DIANA — 30 minutes — NBC — September 10, 1973 – January 7, 1974. 15 episodes.

299 THE DICK CAVETT SHOW

Discussion-Variety.

Host: Dick Cavett.
Announcer: Fred Foy.
Orchestra: Bobby Rosengarden.
Producer: Tony Converse.
Director: David Barnhizer.

THE DICK CAVETT SHOW — 90 minutes — ABC — December 12, 1969 – January 1, 1975.

300 THE DICK CAVETT SHOW

Talk-Variety.

Host: Dick Cavett.
Regulars: Leigh French, Imogene Coca, Marshall Efron.
Orchestra: Stephen Lawrence.
Producer: Carole Hart, Bruce Hart.
Writer: Dick Cavett, Carole Hart, Bruce Hart, Marshall Efron, Tom Meehan, Tony Geiss, Clark Gessner.
Director: Alan Myerson, Clark Jones.

THE DICK CAVETT SHOW — 60 minutes — CBS — August 16, 1975 – September 6, 1975. 4 programs.

301 THE DICK CAVETT SHOW

Discussion.

Host: Dick Cavett.
Music: Bobby Rosengarden.
Producer: Christopher Porterfield, Robin Breed.
Director: Gordon Rigsby, Richard Romagnola.

THE DICK CAVETT SHOW — 30 minutes — PBS — Premiered: October 10, 1977.

302 DICK CLARK PRESENTS THE ROCK AND ROLL YEARS

Variety. A nostalgic backward glance into the music and personalities of the fifties, sixties and seventies via live appearances, videotape, film and newsreel footage.

Host: Dick Clark.
Orchestra: Billy Strange.
Executive Producer: Dick Clark.
Producer: Bill Lee.
Director: Mark Warren.

DICK CLARK PRESENTS THE ROCK AND ROLL YEARS—30 minutes—ABC—November 28, 1973—January 9, 1974.

303   DICK CLARK'S LIVE WEDNESDAY

Variety. A live Wednesday evening variety hour (8 p.m., EST) that features top showbusiness performers, reunions and tributes to screen idols (a pre-recorded segment).

Host: Dick Clark.
Announcer: Jerry Bishop.
Orchestra: Lenny Stack.
Executive Producer: Dick Clark.
Producer: Bill Lee.
Director: John Moffitt.
Locations Producer-Director: Perry Rosemond.

DICK CLARK'S LIVE WEDNESDAY—60 minutes—NBC—September 20, 1978—December 27, 1978. 13 programs.

304   THE DICK VAN DYKE SHOW

Comedy. The series, set in New Rochelle, New York, depicts comical incidents in the lives of the Petrie family: Rob, the head writer for the fictitious "Alan Brady Show"; his beautiful wife, Laura, and their son, Richie.

CAST

Rob Petrie	Dick Van Dyke
Laura Petrie, his wife	Mary Tyler Moore
Richie Petrie, their son	Larry Matthews
Buddy Sorrell, Rob's co-worker	Morey Amsterdam
Sally Rogers, Rob's co-worker	Rose Marie
Jerry Helper, the Petrie's neighbor, a dentist	Jerry Paris
Millie Helper, Jerry's wife	Ann Morgan Guilbert
Mel Cooley, the producer of the "Brady" show	Richard Deacon
Alan Brady, the neurotic star	Carl Reiner
Feona "Pickles" Sorrell, Buddy's wife	Barbara Perry / Joan Shawlee
Freddie Helper, Millie and Jerry's son	Peter Oliphant / David Fresco
Herman Glimcher, Sally's mother-dominated boyfriend	Bill Idelson
Mrs. Glimcher, Herman's mother	Elvia Allman
Sol Pomeroy, Rob's army buddy	Marty Ingels / Allan Melvin
Sam Petrie, Rob's father	Will Wright / Tom Tully / J. Pat O'Malley
Clara Petrie, Rob's mother	Carol Veazie / Isabel Randolph
Ben Meehan, Laura's father	Carl Benton Reid
Mrs. Meehan, Ben's wife	Geraldine Wall
Stacy Petrie, Rob's brother	Jerry Van Dyke
Edward Petrie, Rob's grandfather	Cyril Delevanti

The Petrie Address: 148 Bonnie Meadow Road.
Sally's Cat: Mr. Henderson.
Music: Earle Hagen.
Executive Producer: Carl Reiner, Sheldon Leonard.
Producer: Ronald Jacobs.
Director: Jerry Paris, Sheldon Leonard, Hal Cooper, Theodore J. Flicker, Lee Philips, John Rich, Howard Morris, Claudio Guzman, James Niver, Stanley Z. Cherry, Robert Butler, James Komack, Peter Baldwin.

THE DICK VAN DYKE SHOW—30 minutes—CBS—October 3, 1961—September 7, 1966. 158 episodes. Syndicated. See also *The New Dick Van Dyke Show.*

305   DIFF'RENT STROKES

Comedy. The story of Phillip Drummond, a Park Avenue (New York) millionaire who adopts two Harlem orphans, Arnold and Willis Jackson, the sons of his late housekeeper.

CAST

Phillip Drummond	Conrad Bain
Edna Garrett, his housekeeper	Charlotte Rae
Kimberly Drummond, his daughter	Dana Plato
Arnold Jackson, his adopted son	Gary Coleman
Willis Jackson, his adopted son	Todd Bridges
Adelaide Brubaker, Phillip's housekeeper in later episodes	Nedra Volz

Music: Alan Thicke, Al Burton, Gloria Loring.
Executive Producer: Budd Grossman, Howard Leeds.
Producer: Howard Leeds, Herbert Kenwith, John Maxwell Anderson, Ben Starr, Martin Cohan.
Director: Herbert Kenwith, Doug Rogers, Garren Keith.
Creator: Bernie Kukoff, Jeff Harris, Herbert Kenwith.

DIFF'RENT STROKES—30 minutes—NBC—November 3, 1978—September 10, 1980. 45 episodes. Returned, premiered: November 19, 1980. Spin-off series, *The Facts of Life.*

306   DINAH!

Talk-Variety.

Hostess: Dinah Shore.
Music: The John Rodby Group.
Executive Producer: Henry Jaffe, Carolyn Raskin.
Producer: Fred Tatashore.
Director: Glen Swanson.

DINAH!—60- and 90-minute versions (depending on local stations)—Syndicated 1974—1979.

307   DINAH AND FRIENDS

Talk-Variety. Basically the same as *Dinah!* with the addition of several rotating co-hosts (friends).

Hostess: Dinah Shore.
Co-Hosts: Don Meredith, Paul Williams, Charles Nelson Reilly, Fernando Lamas.
Announcer: Johnny Jacobs.
Music: The John Rodby Group.
Executive Producer: Henry Jaffe.
Producer: Fred Tatashore.
Director: Glen Swanson.
Art Director: Bill Morris.

DINAH AND FRIENDS—60- and 90-minute versions (depending on local stations)—Syndicated 1979.

308   DINAH AND HER NEW BEST FRIENDS

Variety. Music, songs, dances and comedy sketches.

Hostess: Dinah Shore.
Regulars: Diana Canova. Leland Palmer, Mike Neun, Gary Mule Deer, Bruce Kimmel, Michael Preminger, Avie Falana, Dee Dee Rescher.
Orchestra: Ian Bernard.
Executive Producer: Henry Jaffe.
Producer: Carolyn Raskin, Rita Scott.
Director: Jeff Margolis.
Choreographer: Hugh Lambert.

DINAH AND HER NEW BEST FRIENDS—60 minutes—CBS—June 5, 1976—July 31, 1976.

309   DINAH'S PLACE

Variety. Talk, interview, fashion, cooking, songs, decorating ideas, health and beauty tips.

Hostess: Dinah Shore.
Regulars: Jerry Baker, Carol Board, Mary Ann Ryan, David Horowitz, Bill Toomey, Merle Ellis.
Frequent Guests: Karen Valentine, Lyle Waggoner.
Music: The John Rodby Group.
Executive Producer: Henry Jaffe.
Producer: Robert Stivers.
Director: Ernie Sherry.

DINAH'S PLACE—30 minutes—NBC—August 3, 1970—July 26, 1974.

310   DIRTY SALLY

Western Comedy. Sally Fergus, a ragged, tough, gray-haired, red-eye drinkin', tobacco chewin' collector of prairie junk, and Cyrus Pike, an ornery young outlaw and a former ex-gunfighter whom she regards as the son she never had, join forces and become traveling companions destined for the gold fields of California. Stories, set in the 1880s, relate one aspect of their journey—their attempts to aid people they find in distress.

CAST

Sally Fergus	Jeanette Nolan
Cyrus Pike	Dack Rambo

Sally's Mule: Worthless.
Music: John Parker.
Executive Producer: John Mantley.
Producer: Leonard Katzman.

DIRTY SALLY—30 minutes—CBS—January 11, 1974—July 19, 1974. 13 episodes.

311   DISCO '77

Music. Performances by current recording personalities.

Announcer: Ron St. John.
Producer-Director: Steve Marcus.

DISCO '77—30 minutes—Syndicated 1977.

312   DOC

Comedy. The trials and tribulations of Dr. Joe Bogert, a general practitioner who lives in a run-down neighborhood in New York City and strives to treat his patients like human beings.

CAST

Dr. Joe Bogert	Barnard Hughes
Annie Bogert, his wife	Elizabeth Wilson
Beatrice Tully, his nurse	Mary Wickes
Laurie Fenner, Joe's daughter	Judy Kahan
Fred Fenner, Laurie's husband	John Harkins
Happy Miller, Joe's friend	Irwin Corey
Ben Goldman, a patient of Joe's	Herbie Faye
Michael Fenner, Laurie's son	Moosie Drier

Music: Pat Williams.
Executive Producer: Ed Weinberger, Stan Daniels.
Producer: Paul Wayne.
Director: Joan Darling, Bob Claver.
Creator: Ed Weinberger, Stan Daniels.

DOC—30 minutes—CBS—September 13, 1975—August 14, 1976.

313   DOC

Comedy. A revised and updated version of the previous title. Events in the life of Dr. Joe Bogert, the medical director of the hectic and free New York Westside Community Clinic.

CAST

Dr. Joe Bogert	Barnard Hughes
Janet Scott (Scotty), his nurse	Audra Lindley
Teresa Ortega, the receptionist	Lisa Mordente
Stanley Moss, the director of the clinic	David Ogden Stiers
Woody Henderson, a doctor	Ray Vitte

Music: Dick De Benedictis.
Theme: Stan Daniels.
Executive Producer: Ed Weinberger, Stan Daniels.
Producer: Lawrence Marks.
Director: Howard Storm.

Creator: Ed Weinberger, Stan Daniels.

DOC — 30 minutes — CBS — September 25, 1976 – October 30, 1976. 6 episodes.

314   DOC ELLIOT

Drama. The story of Benjamin R. Elliot, a former New York staff doctor at Bellevue Hospital, who resigns his position and retreats to the Alora Valley in the backwoods of Southern Colorado. There, as the only available physician, he seeks to help people — with care and involvement — something he yearns for, but was unable to achieve in New York.

CAST

Dr. Benjamin Elliot	James Franciscus
Barney Weeks, the owner of the general store	Noah Beery, Jr.
Margaret "Mags" Brimble, Ben's landlady	Neva Patterson
Eldred McCoy, a bush pilot who aids Ben	Bo Hopkins

Music: Earle Hagen.
Executive Producer: Lee Rich.
Producer: Sander Stern.
Director: Robert Totten, Edward Abroms, James Sheldon, Harry Harris.

DOC ELLIOT — 60 minutes — ABC — October 10, 1973 – August 14, 1974. 15 episodes.

315   DOCTOR DOLITTLE

Animated Cartoon. The world travels of Dr. John Dolittle, a veterinarian who possesses the ability to talk to and understand animals. Stories relate his attempts to overcome the evils of Sam Scurvy, a fiend bent on learning his secret to control animals for purposes of world dominance. Based on the stories by Hugh Lofting.

VOICES

Dr. John Dolittle	Robert Holt
Sam Scurvy, the villain	Lennie Weinrib
Tommy Stubbins, John's aid	Hal Smith
Animal Voices	Don Messick
	Barbara Towers
The Grasshoppers (Vocalists)	Ronnie Fallon
	Colin Julian
	Annabell

Music: Arthur Leonardi, Doug Goodwin, Eric Rogers.
Producer: David DePatie, Friz Freleng.

DOCTOR DOLITTLE — 30 minutes — NBC — September 12, 1970 – September 2, 1972. 17 episodes. Syndicated.

316   DOCTOR IN THE HOUSE

Comedy. The series, set at the Saint Swithin's Teaching Hospital in London, England, follows the struggles and misadventures of seven young medical students. Later episodes focus on the young doctors seeking to establish a practice. Based on the *Doctor* books by Richard Gordon.

CAST

The Interns:

Michael Upton	Barry Evans
Duncan Waring	Robin Nedwell
Paul Collier	George Layton
Huw Evans	Martin Shaw
Dick Stuart-Clark	Geoffrey Davies
Danny Wholey	Jonathan Lynn
Dave Briddock	Simon Cuff

Also:

Sir Geoffrey Loftus, the professor of surgery	Ernest Clark
The Dean	Ralph Michael
Helga, Dave's girlfriend	Yvette Stengaard
Mrs. Loftus, Geoffrey's wife	Joan Benham
Valerie Loftus, Geoffrey's daughter	Lynn Dalby
Mr. Upton, Michael's father	Peter Barthurst

Producer: Humphrey Barclay, David Askey.
Writer: John Cleese, Graham Chapman.
Director: David Askey, Bryan Izzard.
Designers: David Catley, Colin Monk.

DOCTOR IN THE HOUSE — 30 minutes — Syndicated (to the U.S.) in 1971. 52 episodes. Also titled, in England, *Doctor On the Go.*

317   DOCTOR KILDARE

Drama. The experiences, struggles, defeats and victories of James Kildare, a young intern (later resident physician) at Blair General Hospital.

CAST

Dr. James Kildare	Richard Chamberlain
Dr. Leonard Gillespie, his mentor	Raymond Massey
Nurse Zoe Lawton	Lee Kurtz
Dr. Thomas Gerson	Jud Taylor
Dr. Simon Agurski	Eddie Ryder
Dr. Lowry	Steven Bell
Dr. Kapish	Ken Berry
Nurse Conant	Jo Helton

Music: Jerry Goldsmith, Pete Rugolo, Harry Sukman.
Producer: David Victor, Calvin Clements, Norman Felton, Herbert Hirschmann.
Director: Alf Kjellin, Don Medford, Ralph Senensky, Lawrence Dobkin, Michael Ritchie, James Goldstone, Richard Sarafian.

DOCTOR KILDARE — 60 minutes — NBC — September 27, 1961 – September 9, 1965. 132 episodes. 30 minutes — NBC — September 13, 1965 – August 29, 1966. 58 episodes. Spin-off series: *Young Dr. Kildare.*

318   THE DOCTORS

Drama. The series, set in the Benjamin Craig Institute, a medical research center in Los Angeles, follows the career of Dr. Benjamin Craig, its founder, a neurosurgeon, and the work of his protégés, Drs. Ted Stuart, Paul Hunter and Martin Cohen.

CAST

Dr. Benjamin Craig	E.G. Marshall
Dr. Ted Stuart	John Saxon
Dr. Paul Hunter	David Hartman
Dr. Martin Cohen	Robert Walden
Nurse Robbins	Sally Kemp
Dr. Lee Williams	Michael Baseleon
Nurse Tate	Pat Anderson
Admitting Nurse	Lyvonne Walder
Emergency Room Nurse	Fran Ryan
Nurse	Peggy Lowles
Nurse	Penelope Gillette
Anesthetist	Peter Morrow

Music: Richard Clements.
Executive Producer: Cy Chermak, Herbert Hirschman.
Producer: Joel Rogosin, Robert Scheerer.
Director: Robert Collins, Marvin Chomsky, Daryl Duke, Jerry Lewis, Jeremy Kagan, Jud Taylor, John Badham, Richard Benedict, Abner Biberman, Alf Kjellin, Michael Caffey, Frank Pierson.
Creator: Richard Landau, Paul Mason, Steve Bochco.

THE DOCTORS — 60 minutes — NBC — September 14, 1969 – January 9, 1973; May 4, 1973 – June 22, 1973 (as part of *The Bold Ones*).

319   THE DOCTORS

Serial. Dramatic incidents in the working and personal lives of the doctors and nurses attached to Hope Memorial Hospital.

CAST

Dr. Matt Powers	James Pritchett
Brock Hayden	Adam Kennedy
Nora Hansen	Joan Alexander
Dr. Maggie Fielding	Bethel Leslie
	Kathleen Murray
	Ann Williams
	Lydia Bruce
Jackie	Louise Lasser
Mr. Fielding	Fred Stewart
Steve	Craig Huebing
Dr. Althea Davis	Elizabeth Hubbard
	Virginia Vestoff
	Joselyn Somers
Willard	Court Benson
Peter Bonds	Gerald S. O'Loughlin
Gloria	Nancy Berg
Nurse Kathy Ryker	Nancy Barrett
	Holly Peters
Dr. Hank Iverson	Palmer Deane
Dr. Nick Bellini	Gerald Gordon
Martha Allen	Sally Gracie
Dr. John Morrison	Patrick Horgan
Dr. Vito McCray	Paul Itkin
Dr. Karen Werner	Laryssa Lauret
Dr. Steve Aldrich	David O'Brien
Ginny	Greta Rae
Emma Simpson	Katherine Squire
Toni Ferra	Anna Stuart
Dr. John Rice	Terry Kiser
Dr. Bill Winters	James Noble
Carolee Aldrich	Carolee Campbell
	Jada Rowland
Billy Aldrich	Bobby Henesy
	David Elliott
Sara Dancy	Antoinette Panneck
	Dorothy Fielding
Dr. Michael Powers	Peter Burnell
	Armand Assante
	John Shearin
	James Storm
Colin Wakefield	Philip English
Mrs. Winters	Ann Whiteside
Kate Harris	Denise Nickerson
Dr. Ann Latimer	Geraldine Court
Margo Stewart	Mary Denham
Dr. Alan Stewart	Gil Gerard
Lauri James	Marie Thomas
Dr. Gil Lawford	Dale Robinette
Nurse	Susan Adams
Kurt Van Olsen	Byron Sanders
Simon Gross	Luis Van Rooten
Nurse Brown	Dorothy Blackburn
Keith Wilson	Morgan Sterne
Penny Davis	Julia Duffy
Anna Ford	Zaida Coles
Ed Stark	Conrad Roberts
Dr. Simon Harris	Mel Winkler
Mr. Stark	Clarissa Gaylor
Ma Thatcher	Madeleine Sherwood
Pa Thatcher	John Cullum
Dr. George Mitchell	Staats Cotsworth
Nora Harper	Muriel Kirkland
Margaret Liggett	Jean Sullivan
Mrs. Murtrie	Ruth McDevitt
Judy Stratton	Joanna Pettet
Dr. Johnny McGill	Scott Graham
Dr. DeSales	Thomas Connolloy
Shana Golan	Marta Heflin
Jody Lee Brown	C.C. Courtney
Dr. Nancy Bennett	Nancy Donahue
Mona Aldrich	Meg Mundy
Liz Wilson	Pamela Toll
Theodora Rostand	Clarice Blackburn
Stacy Sommers	Leslie Ann Ray
Paul Sommers	Paul Carr
Toni Powers	Anna Stuart
Jason Aldrich	Glenn Corbett
M.J. Carroll	Kathy Glass
Bettina Chambers	Patricia Hayling
Lee Ann	Robin Holzman
Paul Powers	Rex Thompson
	Harry Packwood
	Robert La Tourne
	Peter Burnell
	John Downes
Hank Chambers	Count Stovall
Laurie Lynn	Brooke Taylor
Rico Bellini	Chandler Hill Harben
Dr. McIntire	Dino Narizzano
Dr. Tom Barrett	Anthony Cannon
Dawn Eddington	Roni Dengel
Andy Anderson	Lloyd Bremseth
Mary Jane March	Lauren White
William Berenson	R. Mack Miller
Dr. Kate Bartock	Ellen McRae
Wayne Spaulding	Tom Sminkley
Darren Match	Arthur Brooks
Virginia Dancy	Elizabeth Lawrence
Det. Ernie Cadman	George Smith
Luke Dancy	Frank Telfer
Greta Powers	Jennifer Houlton
	Jennifer Reilly
	Eileen Kearney
Jessie Rawlings	Patricia Paley
Dr. Cummings	John Newton
Kim	Jane Fleiss
Ted Kingston	Philip Krauss
Kyle Wilson	Wayne Tippit
	Gene Lindsey

Erich Aldrich	Keith Blanchard
Stephanie Aldrich	Thor Fields
	Bridget Breen
Billie Aldrich	Shawn Campbell
Sweeney	Peggy Cass
Missy Roberts	Dorian Lopinto
Mona Croft	Meg Mundy
Barney Dancy	Larry Weber
Nola Dancy	Kathryn Harrold
Eleanor Conrad	Lois Smith
Wendy Conrad	Fannie Speiss
	Kathleen Eckles
Dave Davis	Karl Light
Faith Collins	Katherine Meskill
Joan Dancy	Peggy Whilton
Jerry Dancy	Jonathan Hogan

Music: John Geller.
Producer: Chuck Weiss, Joseph Stuart.
Director: Hugh McPhillips, Norman Hall, Joseph Stuart, Gary Bowen, Ivan Cury.
Creator: Orin Tourov.

THE DOCTORS — 30 minutes — NBC — Premiered: April 1, 1963.

320 DOCTORS HOSPITAL

Drama. Life in the neurological wing of Lowell Memorial Hospital as seen through the eyes of Jake Goodwin, the chief neurosurgeon.

CAST

Dr. Jake Goodwin	George Peppard
Dr. Norah Purcell	Zohra Lampert
Dr. Felipe Ortega	Victor Campos
Nurse Connie Kimbrough	Elisabeth Brooks
Dr. Janos Varga	Albert Paulsen
Heather Stanton, the admissions nurse	Adrian Ricard
Dr. Anson Brooks	James Almanzar
Dr. Paul Herman	John Larroquette
The circulating nurse	Susan Franklin
Nurse Forester	Barbara Darrow
Nurse Wilson	Elaine Church

Music: Don Ellis.
Executive Producer: Matthew Rapf.
Producer: Jack Laird.
Director: David Friedkin, Edward Abrams, Leo Penn, Vincent Sherman, Robert Abrams, Lawrence Doheny.
Creator: James E. Mosher.

DOCTORS HOSPITAL — 60 minutes — NBC — September 10, 1975 – January 14, 1976. The two-hour pilot film, "One Of Our Own," aired on NBC on May 5, 1975.

321 DOCTOR SHRINKER

Comedy. Three teenagers are captured by Dr. Shrinker, a mad scientist, after their plane crashes on a remote island where the doctor makes his headquarters. The teens, B.J., Brad and Gordie, are held prisoner and used as guinea pigs for Shrinker's diabolical invention: a machine that is capable of reducing the size of objects. When reduced to a height of six inches, B.J., Brad and Gordie manage to escape from the doctor's lab and later establish a base of safety in the woods. Stories concern Dr. Shrinker's efforts to recapture his escaped prisoners ("the shrinkees") and the attempts of B.J., Brad and Gordie to regain their normal height and escape from the island.

CAST

Dr. Shrinker	Jay Robinson
Hugo, his assistant	Billy Barty
B.J.	Susan Lawrence
Brad	Ted Eccles
Gordie	Jeff McKay

Music: Jimmie Haskell.
Executive Producer: Sid and Marty Krofft.
Producer: Jack Regas.
Director: Jack Regas, Bill Hobin, Bob Lally.

DOCTOR SHRINKER — 15 minutes — ABC — September 11, 1976 – September 3, 1977 (as a segment of *The Krofft Super Show*).

322 DOCTOR SIMON LOCKE

Drama. The series, set in Dixon Mills, Canada, follows the experiences of Drs. Andrew Sellers and Simon Locke as they struggle to help the people of a poor community.

CAST

Dr. Simon Locke	Sam Groom
Dr. Andrew Sellers	Jack Albertson
Nurse Louise Wynn	Nuala Fitzgerald
Dan Palmer, the police chief	Len Birman

Music: Score Productions.
Executive Producer: Wilton Schiller.
Producer: Chester Krumholz.
Writer: Wilton Schiller, Chester Krumholz.
Director: Richard Gilbert.

DOCTOR SIMON LOCKE — 30 minutes — Syndicated 1971. 39 episodes. Spin-off series: *Police Surgeon*.

323 DOCTORS' PRIVATE LIVES

Drama. The professional and private lives of the doctors in the cardiovascular unit of City Hospital in California.

CAST

Dr. Jeffrey Latimer, head of the unit	John Gavin
Dr. Michael Wise, his chief surgeon	Ed Nelson
Dr. Rick Calder	Randolph Powell
Dr. Sheila Castle	Gwen Humble
Nurse Diane Curtis	Eddie Benton
Mona Wise, Michael's wife	Elinor Donahue
Kenny Wise, Michael's son (pilot episode)	Leigh McCloskey
Kenny Wise (series)	Phil Levien
Frances Latimer, Jeff's wife	Barbara Anderson
Dr. Trilling	William Smithers

Music: Richard Markowitz, John Cacavas.

Executive Producer: David Gerber.
Producer: Matthew Rapf.
Director: Marc Daniels, Edward Abrams, Richard Benedict.

DOCTORS' PRIVATE LIVES — 60 minutes — ABC — March 5, 1979 – April 26, 1979. 4 episodes. The two-hour pilot film aired on ABC on March 20, 1978.

324 DOCTOR WHO

Science Fiction Adventure. The adventures of Dr. Who, a scientist and inventor of Tardis (Time and Relative Dimension In Space), a time machine that is capable of transporting him to any time or to any planet in the endless heavens. Episodes relate his battle against the sinister forces of evil.

CAST

Dr. Who	William Hartnell
	Peter Cushing
	Jon Pertwee
Jo Grant, his assistant	Katy Manning
Liz Shaw, his assistant	Caroline John
Barbara, his niece	Jennie Linden
Susan, his niece	Roberta Tovey
Louise, his niece	Jill Curzon
Ian, his bumbling aid	Roy Castle
Tom Campbell, his aid	Bernard Cribbins
The Master, his nemesis	Roger Delgado

Music: Bill McGiffie.
Musical Director: Malcolm Lockyer.
Electronic Music: Barry Gray.
Executive Producer: Joe Vegoda.
Producer: Max J. Rosenberg, Milton Subotsky.
Director: Gordon Flemyng, Anthony Waye.

DOCTOR WHO — 30 minutes — Syndicated (to the U.S.) in 1973. 117 episodes. Produced in England.

325 DOCTOR WHO

Science Fiction Adventure. A revised version of the previous title. The story of a Time Lord, a being from the planet Gallifrey who is referred to as "The Doctor," as he travels via his Tardis* to the past, present or futures of various planets. Episodes relate his attempts to protect their beings from the sinister forces that seek to destroy.

CAST

Dr. Who	Tom Baker
Sarah Jane Smith, his aid, a beautiful Earth girl	Elisabeth Sladen
Lt. Harry Sullivan, an Earthling, his occasional assistant	Ian Marter
Leela, the beautiful alien huntress, his partner in later episodes	Louise Jameson
K-9, the Doctor's mechanical dog (voice)	John Leeson
	David Brierly
Brigadier Alistair Stewart, Harry's C.O.	Nicholas Courtney

The Doctor's favorite candy: Jelly Babies.
Narrator: Howard Da Silva.

Theme Music: Ron Grainer.
Incidental Music: Dudley Simpson, the BBC Radiophonic Orchestra.
Music: Geoffrey Burgon.
Producer: Graham Williams, Barry Letts.
Director: Pennant Roberts, Christopher Barry, Douglas Camfield, Paddy Russell, David Maloney, Derrick Goodwin, Lennie Mayne, George Spenton Foster, Rodney Bennett, Norman Stewart, Gerald Blake.
Special Effects: Dave Havard.
Creator: Terry Nation.

DOCTOR WHO — 30 minutes — Syndicated (to the U.S.) in 1978. 96 episodes. Produced in England.

*A time machine that resembles a British police telephone booth.

326 DOG AND CAT

Crime Drama. The exploits of J.Z. Kane, "The Cat," and her partner, Jack Ramsey, "The Dog," undercover police officers with the 42nd Division of the Los Angeles Police Department. (The title refers to precinct slang for male and female police teams.)

CAST

Officer J.Z. Kane	Kim Basinger
Sgt. Jack Ramsey	Lou Antonio
Lt. Art Kipling, their superior	Matt Clark

Music: Barry De Vorzon.
Executive Producer: Lawrence Gordon.
Producer: Robert Singer.
Director: Michael Preece, Stephen Stern, Paul Stanley, Robert Davis, Arnold Laven.
Creator: Walter Hill.

DOG AND CAT — 60 minutes — ABC — March 5, 1977 – May 14, 1977.

327 THE $1.98 BEAUTY SHOW

Contest. A spoof of beauty pageants wherein six females compete in contests of beauty, poise, talent and swimwear, for title of "The $1.98 Beauty of the Week" and the top prize — a $1.98 in cash. A comical search to find the most beautiful girl in the world.

Host: Rip Taylor.
Announcer: Johnny Jacobs.
Assistant: Larry Spencer (as the annoying page who brings Rip the envelope with the winner's name).
Music: Milton DeLugg.
Executive Producer: Chuck Barris.
Producer: Gene Banks, Diana Fell, Linda Howard, Ruth Goldberg.
Writer: Larry Spencer.
Director: John Dorsey.
Creator: Chuck Barris.
First $1.98 Winner: Annie Peck.

THE $1.98 BEAUTY SHOW — 30 minutes — Syndicated 1978.

328 DOLLY

Musical Variety.

Hostess: Dolly Parton.
Orchestra: Jerry Whitehurst.
Producer: Bill Graham, Reg Dunlap.
Writer: Bill Graham, Paul Elliott.
Director: Bill Turner.

DOLLY—30 minutes—Syndicated 1976. 52 episodes.

329 THE DON ADAMS SCREEN TEST

Game. Two contestants, chosen from six finalists, re-enact a different scene from a famous movie with a guest celebrity. The player whose screen test is judged to be best by a guest producer or director receives a part in a motion picture or a television series.

Host: Don Adams.
Announcer: Dick Tufeld.
Music: Hal Mooney.
Executive Producer: Don Adams.
Producer: Marty Pasetta.
Director: Marty Pasetta.
Screen Tests Director: Don Adams.
Creator: Don Adams.

THE DON ADAMS SCREEN TEST—30 minutes—Syndicated 1975.

330 THE DON HO SHOW

Musical Variety.

Host: Don Ho.
Regulars: Sam Kapu, Jr., Pat Swalli, Angel Pablo, Tokyo Joe.
Orchestra: Johnny Todd.
Executive Producer: Bob Banner.
Producer: Brad Lachman.
Director: Jack Regas, Jeff Margolis.

THE DON HO SHOW—30 minutes—ABC—October 25, 1976—March 4, 1977. 90 programs. Taped in Hawaii.

331 DON KIRSHNER'S ROCK CONCERT

Variety. Performances by Rock personalities.

Series Host: Don Kirshner.
New Talent Segment Host: Budd Friedman.
Executive Producer: Don Kirshner.
Producer: David Yarnell.
Director: Steve Binder.

DON KIRSHNER'S ROCK CONCERT—90 minutes—Syndicated 1973.

332 THE DON KNOTTS SHOW

Variety. Music, songs and comedy sketches.

Host: Don Knotts.
Regulars: Elaine Joyce, John Dehner, Gary Burghoff, Eddy Carroll, Kenneth Mars, Mickey Deems, Frank Welker, Bob Williams and his dog Louis.
Announcer: Dick Tufeld.
Orchestra: Nick Perito.
Executive Producer: Nick Vanoff.
Producer: William O. Harbach.
Writer: George Balzar, Sam Perrin, Elias Davis, David Pollock, Sid Green, Dick Hollis, Roger Price, Chuck Stewart, Ken Hecht.
Director: Norman Abbott.

THE DON KNOTTS SHOW—60 minutes—NBC—September 15, 1970—July 6, 1971. 24 programs.

333 THE DON LANE SHOW

Variety. Music, songs and celebrity interviews. The program, produced in Australia, features that country's most popular star, Bronx-born Don Lane, and interviews and performances by celebrities from around the world.

Host: Don Lane.
Announcer-Assistant: Burt Newton.
Orchestra: Graeme Lyall.
Musical Director: Alan Deak.
Executive Producer: Peter Faiman.
Producer: Kate Holliday.
Writer: Tim Evans, Trevor Jones.
Director: Peter Faiman.
Choreographer: Tony Bartuccio.
Art Director: Geoff Howben.

THE DON LANE SHOW—60 minutes—Syndicated (to the U.S.) in 1980.

334 THE DON RICKLES SHOW

Comedy. The series, set in Great Neck, Long Island, New York, follows the misadventures of Don Robinson, an account executive with the advertising firm of Kingston, Cohen and Vanderpool, as he struggles to survive the red tape and mechanizations of a computerized society.

CAST

Don Robinson	Don Rickles
Barbara Robinson, his wife	Louise Sorel
Janie Robinson, their daughter	Erin Moran
Tyler Benedict, their neighbor	Robert Hogan
Jean Benedict, Tyler's wife	Joyce Van Patten
Audrey, Don's secretary	Judy Cassmore
Conrad Musk, Don's associate	Barry Gordon
Arthur Kingston, Don's employer	Edward Andrews, M. Emmet Walsh
Mr. Vanderpool, Don's employer	Parley Baer

Music: Earle Hagen.
Executive Producer: Sheldon Leonard, Joseph Scandore.
Producer: Hy Averback.
Director: Hy Averback.

THE DON RICKLES SHOW—30 minutes—CBS—January 14, 1972—May 26, 1972.

335 THE DONNA FARGO SHOW

Variety. Comedy skits coupled with performances by country and western artists.

Hostess: Donna Fargo.
Regular: Tom Biener.
Announcer: Harrison Henderson.
Orchestra: Bob Rozario.
Executive Producer: The Osmond Brothers.
Producer: Tom Biener.
Director: Rick Bennewitz.
Choreographer: Marilyn Magness.

THE DONNA FARGO SHOW—30 minutes—Syndicated 1978.

336 DONNY AND MARIE

Variety. Music, songs, dances and comedy sketches.

Hosts: Donny and Marie Osmond.
Regulars: Paul Lynde, Sharon Baird, Jim Connell, Patty Maloney, Van Snowden, Jimmy Osmond, The Osmond Brothers, The Ice Vanities.
Announcer: George Fenneman, George Benedict, Wayne Osmond.
Orchestra: Bob Rozario, Tommy Oliver.
Special Musical Material: Earl Brown.
Executive Producer: Raymond Katz, Wayne, Merrill, Alan and Jay Osmond.
Producer: Sid and Marty Krofft, Art Fisher.
Writer: Shelly Zellman, Bill Larkin, Sandy Krinski, Chet Dowling, Audrey Tabman.
Director: Art Fisher, Perry Rosemond.
Choreographer: Ron Poindexter.
Creator: Sid and Marty Krofft.

DONNY AND MARIE—60 minutes—ABC—January 23, 1976—May 26, 1978; September 22, 1978—January 19, 1979. Syndicated as *The Best of Donny and Marie.* Spin-off series: *The Osmond Family Show.*

337 THE DORIS DAY SHOW

Comedy. Dissatisfied with the congestion of the big city, Doris Martin, a beautiful widow and mother of two children, relinquishes her career as a singer and returns home to her father's ranch in Mill Valley, California. Her attempts to raise her children—and her involvement in local community affairs—are comically depicted (from September 24, 1968 through September 16, 1969).

Feeling the need to assist with the growing expenses on the ranch, Doris acquires a job in San Francisco as the executive secretary to Michael Nicholson, the editor of *Today's World Magazine.* Stories, from September 22, 1969 through September 7, 1970, relate her home and working life.

With occasional reporting assignments and difficulty commuting from the country to the city, Doris relocates to San Francisco and rents Apartment 207, over Pallucci's Italian Restaurant, at 965 North Parkway. Episodes, broadcast from September 14, 1970 through September 6, 1971, depict Doris's misadventures, both at home and at work.

Beginning with the episode of September 13, 1971, the series' format changed to depict the working and romantic life of Doris Martin, a beautiful bachelorette and a general news reporter for *Today's World Magazine.* The revised format, set in San Francisco, ran until September 3, 1973.

CAST

Doris Martin	Doris Day
Buck Webb, her father	Denver Pyle
Billy Martin, her son	Philip Brown
Toby Martin, her son	Todd Starke
Leroy B. Simpson, Buck's handyman	James Hampton
Aggie Thompson, Buck's housekeeper (early episodes)	Fran Ryan
Juanita, Buck's housekeeper (later episodes)	Naomi Stevens
Michael Nicholson, the editor of *Today's World*	McLean Stevenson
Cyril Bennett, the magazine editor in later episodes	John Dehner
Myrna Gibbons, Michael's secretary	Rose Marie
Jackie Parker, Cyril's secretary	Jackie Joseph
Ron Harvey, the associate editor (Nicholson episodes)	Paul Smith
Willard Jarvis, Doris's neighbor	Billy DeWolfe
Angie Pallucci, Doris's landlady	Kaye Ballard
Louie Pallucci, Angie's husband	Bernie Kopell
Colonel Fairburn, the publisher of *Today's World*	Edward Andrews
Ethel, Billy and Toby's babysitter	Carol Worthington
Duke Farentino, Doris's friend, a boxer	Larry Storch
Dr. Peter Lawrence, Doris's romantic interest	Peter Lawford
Jonathan Rusk, Doris's romantic interest, a foreign correspondent	Patrick O'Neal
Detective Broder, San Francisco Police Department	Ken Lynch

Martin family sheep dog: Lord Nelson.
Music: Jimmie Haskell.
Theme: "Que Sera, Sera" by Jay Livingston and Ray Evans.
Theme Scoring: Bob Mersey.
Theme Vocal: Doris Day.
Executive Producer: Terry Melcher, Doris Day, Don Genson.
Producer: Jack Elinson, Norman Paul, Edward H. Feldman, George Turpin, Bob Sweeney, Richard Dorso.

Dolly. Dolly Parton.

Donny and Marie. Marie and Donny Osmond.

The Doris Day Show. Doris Day.

Eight Is Enough. Foreground, Willie Aames, at left, and Adam Rich. Back row, from left, Laurie Walters, Susan Richardson, Dick Van Patten, Grant Goodeve, Betty Buckley, Dianne Kay, Lani O'Grady and Connie Newton.

Director: Bob Sweeney, Coby Ruskin, Paul Smith, Norman Tokar, Marc Daniels, Denver Pyle, Reza S. Badiyi, William Wiard.
Creator: James Fritzell.

THE DORIS DAY SHOW — 30 minutes — CBS — September 24, 1968 – September 3, 1973. 128 episodes. Syndicated.

338   DOROTHY

Comedy. The story of Dorothy Banks, a former Broadway trouper turned music and drama teacher at the Hannah Huntley School for Girls in Connecticut.

CAST

Dorothy Banks	Dorothy Loudon
Burton Foley, the headmaster	Russell Nype
Lorna Cathcart, the French teacher	Priscilla Morill
T. Jack Landis, the biology teacher	Kenneth Gilman
Hannah Huntley Foley, Burton's mother, the school's chairman of the board	Irene Tedrow

The Students:

Meredith	Susan Brecht
Frankie Sumpter	Linda Manz
Cissy	Elissa Leeds
Margo	Michele Greene

Music: Billy Goldenberg
Music Theme: Billy Goldenberg, Bill Dyer.
Theme Vocal: Dorothy Loudon.
Executive Producer: Madelyn Davis, Bob Carroll, Jr., Frank Konigsberg.
Producer: Jerry Madden.
Writer: Liz Sage, Rick Hawkins, Madelyn Davis, Bob Carroll, Jr.
Director: John Rich.
Creator: Nick Arnold, Bob Carroll, Jr., Madelyn Davis.
Art Director: Tom John.

DOROTHY — 30 minutes — CBS — August 8, 1979 – August 29, 1979. 4 episodes.

339   THE DRAK PACK

Animated Cartoon. The story of Drak, Jr., Frankie and Howler, the teenage descendants of movie monsters Dracula, Frankenstein and the Wolfman, and their attempts to atone for the sins of their ancestors by battling the sinister forces of evil. Possessed of unique powers, Drak, Frankie and Howler form a do-gooders group called The Drak Pack. Episodes relate their battle against the diabolical Dr. Dred, his assistants Vampira, Mummy Man, Toad and Fly, and his evil organization O.G.R.E. (the Organization of Generally Rotten Enterprises).

Voices: Hans Conried (as Dr. Dred), Chuck McCann, Jerry Dexter, Julie McWhirter, Don Messick, Alan Oppenheimer, Marian Zajac.
Music: Paul DeKorte, Hoyt Curtin.
Executive Producer: William Hanna, Joseph Barbera.

Producer: Art Scott.
Director: Chris Cuddington.

THE DRAK PACK — 25 minutes — CBS — Premiered: September 6, 1980.

340   DRAGNET

Crime Drama. A realistic approach to crime prevention as seen through the cases of Joe Friday, a sergeant with the Los Angeles Police Department.

CAST

Sgt. Joe Friday	Jack Webb
Officer Bill Gannon, his partner	Harry Morgan
Captain Brown	Art Ballinger
Captain Nelson	Clark Howat
	Len Wayland
Captain Mack	Byron Morrow
Captain Al Trembly (later Capt. Brooks)	Clark Howat
Sgt. Andy Blakeley	Ed Deemer
Sgt. Tom Benson	Morris Erby
Sgt. Bill Pailing (later Sgt. Sam Hunter)	William Boyett
Sgt. Dick Reed	Don Ross
Officer Earl McNevin	Marc Hannibal
Officer Keefer	John McCook
Officer Lathrop	Charles Brewer
Also, various roles	Chanin Hale

Music: Frank Comstock, Lyn Murray, Stanley Wilson.
Narrator: Jack Webb.
Announcer: George Fenneman.
Producer-Director: Jack Webb.
Program Open:
Sgt. Friday: This is the city, Los Angeles, California. I work here, I carry a badge.
Music: Dum De Dum Dum.
Announcer: Ladies and gentlemen, the story you are about to see is true, the names have been changed to protect the innocent.

ORIGINAL SERIES CAST
(1951 – 1959)

Sgt. Joe Friday	Jack Webb
Sgt. Ben Romero	Barton Yarborough
Sgt. Jacobs	Barney Phillips
Officer Frank Smith	Ben Alexander
Ann Baker, Joe's fiancée	Dorothy Abbott

Announcer: Hal Gibney, George Fenneman.
Music: Frank Comstock, Lyn Murray, Nathan S. Scott, Walter Schumann.
Producer: Jack Webb.

DRAGNET — 30 minutes — NBC — January 12, 1967 – September 10, 1970. Syndicated. Original version: 30 minutes — NBC — December 16, 1951 – September 6, 1959. Syndicated as *Badge 714* (which is Joe's badge number).

341   THE DREAM MERCHANTS

Drama. A miniseries, based on Harold Robbins' novel about the early years of Hollywood. The story focuses on the power struggle among visionary film pioneers, glamorous film stars and financial manipulators from the turn-of-the-century nickelodeons to the beginning of talkies in the late 1920s.

CAST

Johnny Edge	Mark Harmon
Peter Kessler	Vincent Gardenia
Dulcie Warren	Morgan Fairchild
Doris Kessler	Brianne Leary
Mark Kessler	Robert Picardo
Coralee	Eve Arden
Esther Kessler	Kaye Ballard
Astrid James	Morgan Brittany
Bruce Benson	Red Buttons
Henry Farnum	Robert Culp
Charles Slade	Howard Duff
George Pappas	Jose Ferrer
Craig Warren	Robert Goulet
Rocco Salvatore	David Groh
Vera	Carolyn Jones
Conrad Stillman	Fernando Lamas
Lawrence Radford	Ray Milland
Murray Tucker	Jan Murray
Zack Larsen	Chris Robinson
Captain Casey	Don "Red" Barry
Harriet Farnum	Lola Mason
Fraser	George Petrie
Bobby Edge	Seth Wagerman
Humber	Fred Wayne
Thelma Benson	Lauren White
Hansen	Raymond Young

Music: George Duning.
Executive Producer: Milton Sperling.
Producer: Hugh Benson.
Writer: Chester Krumholz, Richard DeRoy.
Director: Vincent Sherman.
Art Director: Ross Bellah, John Beckman.
Choreography: Tad Tadlock.

THE DREAM MERCHANTS — 2 hours — Operation Prime Time — May 1980. 2 episodes.

342   THE DUCHESS OF DUKE STREET

Drama. The story of Louisa Trotter, a scullery maid who becomes proprietor of the exclusive Bentinck Hotel in London — and a confidante of the rich and famous. Based on the real life of Edwardian hostess Rosa Lewis.

CAST

Louisa Trotter	Gemma Jones
Lottie Trotter, her daughter	Lalla Ward
Arthur Trotter, her brother	Martin Shaw
Mary, a maid	Victoria Plucknett
Merriman, a waiter	John Welsh
Starr, the porter	John Cater
Violet, a maid	Holly de Jong

Also:

Major Smith — Barton	Richard Vernon
Gaspard	John Moreno
Appleby	Jeremy Clyde
Brewster	Alan Gifford
Bartlett	Derek Farr
Sir Martin Mallory	T.P. McKenna
Charlie	Christopher Cazenove
Mr. Leighton	John Rapley
Mrs. Leighton	June Brown
Miss Applegate	Anna Calder-Marshall
Nick	Jeremy Nichols
Margaret	Joanna David
Tommy	Patrick Newell
Daphne	Sue Nicholls
Pearl	Pauline Quirke
Ethel	Sammie Winmill
Clive	Paul Aston
Brian	Simon Chandler
Mason	William Hoyland
Horsfield	Richard Pearson
Howard	Richard Morant

Starr's dog: Fred.
Producer: John Hawkesworth.
Director: Bill Bain.

THE DUCHESS OF DUKE STREET — 60 minutes — PBS — December 16, 1979 – April 6, 1980. 16 episodes. Produced by the BBC.

343   THE DUDLEY DO-RIGHT SHOW

Animated Cartoon.

Segments:

Dudley Do-Right. The story, set in Alberta, Canada, follows the exploits of Dudley Do-Right, a simple-minded, dim-witted, naive Mountie as he attempts to apprehend Snidley Whiplash, the most diabolical of fiends.

VOICES

Dudley Do-Right	Bill Scott
Inspector Ray K. Fenwick, Dudley's superior	Paul Frees
Nell Fenwick, Ray's daughter	June Foray
Snidley Whiplash, the villain	Hans Conried

Narrator: Paul Frees.

The Hunter. The exploits of a Beagle detective as he attempts to apprehend the villainous Fox.

Tutor the Turtle. The story of Tutor, a turtle who becomes what he wishes through the magic of Mr. Wizard, the lizard.

The World of Commander McBragg. The tall tales of a retired naval officer.

Voices (above segments): Bill Conrad, Walter Tetley, Skip Craig, Barbara Baldwin.
Music: Sheldon Allman, Stan Worth.
Producer: Jay Ward, Bill Scott.

THE DUDLEY DO-RIGHT SHOW — 30 minutes — ABC — April 27, 1969 – September 6, 1970. Syndicated.

344   THE DUKE

Crime Drama. The story of Oscar "Duke" Ramsey, an over-the-hill boxer turned two-fisted private detective working out of Chicago.

CAST

Oscar "Duke" Ramsey	Robert Conrad
Joe Cadillac, his friend, a bookie	Larry Manetti
Sgt. Mick O'Brien (with the 11th Precinct of the C.P.D.)	Red West
Dedra, Ramsey's girlfriend	Patricia Conwell
Eddie, the bartender at "Duke and Benny's Corner," the tavern Ramsey owns	Ed O'Bradovich

Music: Mike Post, Pete Carpenter.
Supervising Producer: Alex Beaton.
Executive Producer: Stephen J. Cannell.
Producer: Don Carlos Dunaway, J. Rickley Dumm.
Director: Lawrence Doheny, Tony Lobianca, Dana Elcar, Robert Conrad.

THE DUKE — 60 minutes — NBC — March 5, 1979 – May 18, 1979. 5 episodes.

345   THE DUKES OF HAZZARD

Comedy Drama. The series, set in Hazzard County, Georgia, follows the lives of the Duke Cousins — Luke, Bo and Daisy — and their exploits in a corrupt community as they attempt to ferret out evil.

CAST

Luke Duke	Tom Wopat
Bo Duke	John Schneider
Daisy Duke	Catherine Bach
Jesse Duke, their uncle	Denver Pyle
Jefferson Davis Hogg (Boss Hogg), the corrupt "Boss" of Hazzard County	Sorrell Booke
Roscoe Coltrane, Hogg's corrupt sheriff	James Best
Cooter Davenport, the garage mechanic	Ben Jones
Enos Strate, Roscoe's deputy	Sonny Shroyer
B.B. Davenport, Cooter's cousin	Mickey Jones
Sheriff Grady Byrd, replaced Roscoe for a short time	Dick Sargent
The Balladeer	Waylon Jennings
Reserve Deputy Cletus Hogg	Rick Hurst
Sheriff Buster Moon	James Hampton
Mabel, telephone operator	Ginny Parker
	Lindsay Bloom

Music Performed By: The Waylors.
Music Composed and Sung By: Waylon Jennings.
Music Producer: Richie Albright.
Additional Music: Fred Werner.
Supervising Producer: Hy Averback, Rod Amateau.
Executive Producer: Joseph Gantman, Hy Averback, Paul R. Picard.
Producer: Gy Waldron, Bill Kelley, Ralph Riskin, Myles Wilder.
Director: Rod Amateau, Bob Kelljan, Don McDougall, Hy Averback, Bob Claver, William Asher, Gy Waldron, Hollingsworth Morse, Richard Moder, Jack Starrett, Ernest Pintoff, Paul Baxley, Allen Baron, Jack Whitman, Arthur Marks.

THE DUKES OF HAZZARD — 60 minutes — CBS — Premiered: January 26, 1979.

346   THE DUMPLINGS

Comedy. The trials and tribulations of Joe and Angela Dumpling, married, overweight proprietors of Dumplings Luncheonette, a sandwich bar on the ground floor of the Bristol Oil Company, a New York office building.

CAST

Joe Dumpling	James Coco
Angela Dumpling, Joe's wife	Geraldine Brooks
Stephanie, Angela's sister	Marcia Rodd
Frederick Steele, Joe's landlord	George Furth
Charles Sweetzer, the V.P. of Bristol Oil	George S. Irving
Norah McKenna, Sweetzer's secretary	Jane Connell
Cully, Joe's cashier	Mort Marshall
The Prud	Will Albert

Music: Billy Goldenberg.
Theme Vocal: Steve Lawrence.
Executive Producer: Don Nicholl, Michael Ross, Bernie West.
Producer: George Sunga.
Writer: Don Nicholl, Michael Ross, Bernie West.
Director: Paul Bogart, Hal Cooper, Dennis Steinberg.
Creator: Don Nicholl, Michael Ross, Bernie West.

THE DUMPLINGS — 30 minutes — NBC — January 28, 1976 – March 24, 1976.

347   DUSTY'S TRAIL

Western Comedy. Set in the 1880s. A wagon train, destined for California, begins its long, hazardous journey. Through the efforts of a dim-witted scout, a stage and wagon are separated from the main body and lost. Stories relate the wagon master's efforts to safely deliver his passengers to the Promised Land.

CAST

Mr. Callahan, the wagon master	Forrest Tucker
Dusty, the trail scout	Bob Denver
Lulu, a beautiful dancehall girl seeking to open a saloon in California	Jeannine Riley
Betsy, a beautiful teacher seeking to begin a school in California	Lori Saunders
Carter Brookhaven, a wealthy banker	Ivor Francis
Daphne Brookhaven, Carter's wife	Lynn Wood
Andy, the resourceful pioneer	Bill Cort

Callahan's horse: Blarney.
Dusty's horse: Freckles.
Music: Frank DeVol, Jack Plees.
Theme: Sherwood Schwartz.
Executive Producer: Sherwood Schwartz.
Producer: Elroy Schwartz.

DUSTY'S TRAIL — 30 minutes — Syndicated 1973. 13 episodes.

348   DUSTY'S TREEHOUSE

Children. Various aspects of the adult world are related to children via films, puppets, songs and stories.

Host: Stu Rosen (as Dusty).
Puppet Characters: Maxine the Crow, Stanley Spider, Scooter Squirrel.
Puppet Movement and Voices: Tony Urbano and Company.
Music: Barbara Rottman.
Producer: Don Hall.
Director: Jim Johnson.

DUSTY'S TREEHOUSE — 30 minutes — Syndicated 1973.

E

349   THE EDDIE CAPRA MYSTERIES

Mystery. The story of Eddie Capra, an attorney with the Los Angeles firm of Devlin, Linkman and O'Brien, who has an uncanny knack for solving complex crimes.

CAST

Eddie Capra	Vincent Baggetta
Lacey Brown, his secretary	Wendy Phillips
J.J. Devlin, Capra's employer	Ken Swofford
Harvey Mitchell, Capra's legman	Michael Horton
Jennie Brown, Lacey's daughter	Seven Ann McDonald
Devlin's secretary	Lynn Topping

Music: John Addison, John Cacavas.
Executive Producer: Peter S. Fischer.
Producer: James McAdams.
Director: James Frawley, Ron Satlof, James Benson, Nicholas Sgarro, Edward Abroms, Sigmund Neufeld, Jr., William Wiard.
Creator: Peter S. Fischer.

THE EDDIE CAPRA MYSTERIES — 60 minutes — NBC — September 22, 1978 – January 12, 1979. 13 episodes. Repeats (NBC): June 8, 1979 – September 7, 1979. The series was "sneak previewed" on September 8, 1978 (NBC) with a two-hour episode entitled "Who Killed Charles Pendragon?"

350   THE EDGE OF NIGHT

Serial. The series, set in the turbulent Midwestern city of Monticello, follows the lives of ordinary people who are driven by intense feeling and difficult circumstances. Emphasis is placed on crime detection methods and courtroom proceedings.

CAST

Mike Karr	John Larkin
	Lawrence Hugo
	Forrest Compton
Sarah Lane	Teal Ames
Grace O'Leary	Maxine Stuart
Jackie Lane	Don Hastings
Adam Drake	Donald May
Dr. Kevin Reed	Stanley Grover
Cookie Christopher	Fran Sharon
Winston Grimsley	Walter Greza
Ed Gibson	Larry Hagman
Ron Christopher	Burt Douglas
Kate Sloane	Jan Farrand
Elly Jo Jamison	Dorothy Lyman
Raven Alexander	Juanin Clay
Raven Jamison, above character, married	Sharon Gabet
Philip Caprice	Ray MacDonnell
	Robert Webber
Ken Emerson	Alan Manson
Joe Pollock	Allen Nourse
	John Gibson
Tango	Lynn Ann Redgrave
Steve Prentiss	Conrad Fowkes
Dr. Katherine Lovell	Mary Fickett
Ruth Tuttle	Barbara Hayes
Ernie	George Hall
Bart Fletcher	James Ray
Harry Constable	Dolph Sweet
Dr. Jim Fields	Alan Feinstein
Liz Hillyer	Alberta Grant
Frank Sloane	Sam Grey
Martha Marceau	Teri Keane
Bill Marceau	Alan Feinstein
	Carl Frank
	Mandel Kramer
Orin Hillyer	Lester Rawlins
Simon Jessep	Hugh Riley
Vic Lamont	Ted Tinling
Nurse Hubbell	Frances Beers
Trudy	Mary Hayden
Lobo Haines	Fred J. Scollay
Fred Burns	William Kiehl
Celia Burns	Carol Teitel
Corky	Joy Claussen
Doug Hastings	Hal Studer
Angela Morgan	Valerie French
Jack Berman	Ward Costello
Dr. Warner	Richard Buck
Jessica Webster	Rita Lloyd
Jason Everett	Barry Ford
Phoebe Smith	Renne Jarrett
	Johanna Leister
	Hedi Vaughn
Pamela Stuart	Irene Dailey
Cliff Nelson	Ernie Townsend
Rev. Elliot Dorn	Lee Godart
Dr. Miles Cavanaugh	Joel Crothers
Laura Hillyer	Millette Alexander
Julie (Laura's twin)	Millette Alexander
Johnny Dallas	John LaGioia
Ansel Scott	Patrick Horgan
April Cavanaugh	Terry Davis
Dean	Gordon Rigsby
Bartender	Dan Ziskie
Geraldine Whitney	Lois Kibbee
Senator Colin Whitney	Anthony Call
Tiffany Whitney	Lucy Martin
Dr. Charles Weldon	David Hooks
Keith Whitney	Bruce Martin
Rose Pollock	Kay Campbell
	Virginia Kaye
Tracy Carroll	Kendall March
Laurie Anne Karr	Kathy Cody
Louise Caprice	Mary K. Wells
	Lisa Howard
Eric Morgan	John Lehve
Lennie Small	Mike Minor
Lee Pollock	Tony Roberts
Kevin Jamison	Dick Schoberg
	John Driver
Laurie Lamont	Jeanne Ruskin
Lt. Luke Chandler	Herb Davis
D.A. Peter Quinn	George Petrie
Mr. Lamarti	James Gallery
Kaye Reynolds	Elizabeth Farley
Babs	Leslie Ray
Dr. Lacy	Brooks Rogers
Sam English	Edward Moore
Floyd	James Ray
Ben Travis	Cec Linder
Mr. LePage	William Post, Jr.
Danny	Lou Criscuolo
Betty Jean Lane	Mary Moor

The Detective Sergeant	Ian Martin
The Police Dept. secretary	Maxine Stuart
Mattie Lane	Betty Garde
Harry Lane	Lauren Gilbert
Harry's wife	Sarah Burton
Harry's secretary	Mary Alice Moore
Andre Lazor	Val Dufour
Malcolm Thomas	Edward Kemmer
John Barnes	Barry Newman
Rick Oliver	Keith Charles
Gerry McGrath	Millee Taggart
Nicole Travis	Maeve McGuire
Nicole Drake, above character, married	Jayne Bentzen
Daisy	Karen Weeden
Nola Madison	Kim Hunter
Carole Barclay	Polly Adams
Winter Austin	Lori Cardille
Joni Collier	Eileen Finley
Deborah Saxon	Frances Fisher
Cody Patrick	David Garrison
Wade Meecham	Dan Hamilton
Calvin Stoner	Irving Lee
Dr. Gus Norwood	Wyman Pendleton
Mrs. Thatcher	Billie Lou Watt
Laurie Dallas	Emily Prager
	Jeanne Ruskin
	Linda Cook
Mark Farraday	Bernie McInerney
Ada Chandler	Billie Allen
Brandy Henderson	Dixie Carter
Noel Douglas	Dick Latessa
Tracy Dallas	Patricia Conwell
Quentin Henderson	Michael Stroka
Gerald Kincaid	Allen Mixon
Beau Richardson	David Gale
Josie and Serena Farraday	Louise Shaffer
Draper Scott	Tony Craig
Clay Jordan	Niles McMaster
Steve Guthrie	Denny Albee
Nadine Alexander	Dorothy Stinnette
Timmy Farraday	Doug McKenon
Tony Saxon	Louis Turenne
Claude Revenant	Scott McKay
Molly O'Connor	Helena Carroll
Logan Swift	Joe Lambie
Diana Selkirk	Susan Yusen
Margo Huntington	Ann Williams
Nicky Dials	Vasili Bogazianos
Paige Madison	Margaret Colin
April Scott	Terry Davis
Sarah	Jenny Lyons
Brian Madison	Stephen McNaughton
Cliff Nelson	Ernie Townsend
Star Wilson	Yahee

Also: Barbara Sharma, Janet Margolin, Ruby Dee, Jan Miner, Audra Lindley, Charles Baxter, David Ford, Kathleen Cody, Eva Marie Saint, Wesley Addy, Nancy Wickwire, Karen Thorsell, Ruth Mattheson, Peter Kastner, Priscilla Gillette, Jeremy Slate, Sam Groom, Diana Van derVlis, Nancy Pinkerton.

Announcer: Herbert Duncan, Harry Kramer, Hal Simms.
Music: Paul Taubman, Elliott Lawrence.
Musical Coordinator: Barbara Miller.
Producer: Charles Fisher, Charles Pollachek, Don Wallace, Gail Kobe, Erwin W. Nicholson, Bud Gowen.
Director: Allen Fristoe, John Sedwick, Richard Pepperman, Andrew Weyman.

THE EDGE OF NIGHT — 30 minutes — CBS — April 2, 1956 — November 28, 1975. ABC — 30 minutes — Premiered: December 1, 1975.

351 THE ED SULLIVAN SHOW

Variety. Performances by top-rated entertainment acts.

Host: Ed Sullivan.
Regulars: Jim Henson's Muppets, The Toastettes Chorus Line, The Hugh Lambert Dancers.
Commercial Spokeswoman: Julia Meade.
Announcer: Ralph Paul.
Orchestra: Ray Bloch.
Producer: Jack Meegan, Ed Sullivan, Bob Precht, Jack McGeehan, Marlo Lewis, Stu Erwin, Jr., Ken Campbell, John Wray, John Moffitt, Jacques Andre.
Director: John Wray, Tim Kily, John Moffitt.

THE ED SULLIVAN SHOW — 60 minutes — CBS — September 25, 1955 — June 6, 1971. Broadcast as *Toast of the Town* on CBS from June 10, 1948 through September 18, 1955.

352 EDWARD AND MRS. SIMPSON

Drama. The miniseries, based on the novel by Frances Donalson, explores the century's best-known love story: Edward, the Prince of Wales, the charming heir apparent to the British throne, and Mrs. Wallis Warfield Simpson, the Baltimore-born divorcée for whom Edward relinquishes his crown to marry. Covering the period from 1928 to 1936, the program chronicles the events that led to Edward's abdication.

CAST
Edward	Edward Fox
Wallis Simpson	Cynthia Harris
Freda Dudley	Kika Markham
Thelma	Cherie Lunghi
Ernest Simpson	Charles Keating
King George V	Marius Goring
Queen Mary	Peggy Ashcroft
Angie	Caroline Embling
Sir Percy Watkins	John Kidd
Duke of York	Andrew Ray
Duchess of York	Amanda Reiss

Host: Robert MacNeil.
Music: Ron Grainer.
Violinist: Jennie Wren.
Producer: Andrew Brown.
Director: Waris Hussin.
Sponsor: Mobil Oil Corporation.

EDWARD AND MRS. SIMPSON — 60 minutes — Syndicated 1980. 6 episodes.

353 EDWARD THE KING

Biography. The life of England's Edward VII (1841 – 1910), the eldest son of Queen Victoria, who is remembered as the Peacemaker King — but not forgotten as the Playboy Prince.

CAST
Edward the King	Charles Sturridge
	Timothy West
Edward (as a boy)	Simon Kent
Queen Victoria	Annette Crosbie
Prince Albert	Robert Hardy
Viscount Melbourne	Joseph O'Connor
Duke of Wellington	John Welsh
Vicky	Felicity Kendal
Alix	Deborah Grant
Alice	Shirley Steedman
Alfred	Ian Gelder
Alexandra	Helen Ryan
Benjamin Disraeli	Sir John Gielgud
Sir Robert Peel	Michael Barrington
Baroness Lehzen	Patience Collier
Baron Stockmar	Noel Willman

Host: Robert MacNeil.
Music: Cyril Ornadel.
Producer: Cecil Clarke.
Associate Producer: Lorna Mason.
Director: John Gorrie.
Choreographer: Geraldine Stephenson.

EDWARD THE KING — 60 minutes — Syndicated 1979. 13 episodes.

354 EIGHT IS ENOUGH

Comedy Drama. Events in the day-to-day lives of the Bradfords, a ten-member family living in Sacramento, California.

CAST
Tom Bradford, the father, a columnist for the *Sacramento Register*	Dick Van Patten
Joan Bradford, his first wife	Diana Hyland
Abby Abbott, Tom's fiancé, then wife (November 9, 1977) after Joan's death	Betty Buckley

The Bradford Children:
Mary Bradford	Lani O'Grady
David Bradford	Mark Hamill
	Grant Goodeve
Joanie Bradford	Laurie Walters
Nancy Bradford	Kimberly Beck
	Dianne Kay
Elizabeth Bradford	Connie Newton Needham
Susan Bradford	Susan Richardson
Tommy Bradford	Chris English
	Willie Aames
Nicholas Bradford	Adam Rich

Also:
Donna, Tom's secretary	Jennifer Darling
Dr. Greg Maxwell, Tom's friend	Michael Thoma
Daisy Maxwell, Greg's wife	Virginia Vincent
Janet McCarther, David's girlfriend, later his wife	Joan Prather
Merle "The Pearl" Stockwell, a pitcher for the Cyclones Baseball team; married Susan	Brian Patrick Clarke
Ernie Fields, Tommy's friend	Michael Goodrow
Tammi, Ernie's girlfriend	Cyndi Bain
Jill, Tommy's girlfriend	Michele Green
Elliott Randolph, Tom's publisher	James Karen
Jeffrey Trout, Joanie's employer at KTNS, Channel 8, where she works as a newscaster	Nicholas Pryor
Joe Simons, Nicholas's friend, a retired con artist	Jack Elam
Ms. Chovick, Nancy's employer at the stock brokerage firm	Kate Woodville
Marvin Harris, Nicholas's friend	K.C. Martel
Vivian (Auntie V), Tom's sister	Janis Paige
Vincent, Nicholas's friend	Keith Mitchell
Linda Mae Stockwell, Merle's sister	Sondra West
Irving Moore, Nicholas's friend	Jeff Cotler
Receptionist at Goodman, Saxon and Twitty, the law firm for which Janet works	Elizabeth Dorman
Jeremy Andreddi, Abby's nephew	Ralph Macchio

The Bradford's address: 1436 Oak Street.
Based on the Book by: Thomas Braden; developed for TV by William Blinn.
Music: Fred Werner, Earle Hagen.
Theme Vocal: Grant Goodeve.
Executive Producer: Lee Rich, Philip Capice, Lee Mendelson.
Supervising Producer: Gary Adelson.
Producer: Robert L. Jacks, Gary Adelson, Greg Strangis, Phil Fehrle.
Director: E.W. Swackhamer, David Moessinger, Reza S. Badiyi, Vincent McEveety, Harvey Laidman, Harry Harris, Bernard McEveety, Leslie H. Martinson, Stan Lathan, Arnold Laven, Carl Kugel, Jack Bender, Irving J. Moore, Marc Daniels, Philip Leacock, Jack B. Hively.

EIGHT IS ENOUGH — 60 minutes — ABC — March 15, 1977 — May 3, 1977.
Returned: Premiered: August 10, 1977.

355 EISCHIED

Crime Drama. The story of Earl Eischied (pronounced Eye-shyed), the New York Police Department's chief of detectives and an abrasive cop who puts crime solving above everything — including his own life and department policy. Based on the novel *To Kill a Cop,* which became a 1978 TV Movie and served as the basis for the series. (Eischied is attached to the 23rd Precinct.)

CAST
Earl Eischied	Joe Don Baker
Edward Parks, the Internal Affairs chief	Eddie Egan
Det. Rick Alessi	Vincent Bufano
Det. Carol Wright	Suzanne Lederer
Capt. John Finnerty	Alan Oppenheimer
Irene Stefan, Earl's girlfriend	Laraine Stephens
The Police Commissioner (not named; pilot episode)	Patrick O'Neal
Howard Knight, the police commissioner (series)	Raymond Burr
Sgt. Jim Kimbrough, the deputy commissioner	Alan Fudge

Detective Dietrich   Jonathan Goldsmith
Detective Chason   Roger Robinson
Louie Shifflen, Earl's chauffeur
   (pilot)   David Toma
Louie Shifflen (series)   Mallory Jones
Ruth Finnerty, John's wife   Sunja Svenson
Detective Malfitano   Joe Cirillo

Earl's cat: P.C. (Police Commissioner).
Music: John Cacavas.
Supervising Producer: Matthew Rapf.
Executive Producer: David Gerber.
Producer: Jay Daniel.
Director: Robert Kelljan, Harvey Laidman, Larry Elikann, Nicholas Sgarro, Gene Kearney, Leo Penn, Jack Starrett.

EISCHIED — 60 minutes — NBC — September 21, 1979 – December 30, 1979. 11 episodes. Returned with two final episodes on NBC on January 20, 1980 and July 29, 1980. Original title: *The Force.* The series is broadcast in England as *Chief of Detectives.*

356 ELECTRA WOMAN AND DYNA GIRL

Adventure. The exploits of Laurie and Judy, reporters for *Newsmaker Magazine*, who, through the electronic abilities of Crimescope, an amazing computer complex, become Electra Woman and Dyna Girl, daring crime fighters. Stories detail their battle against diabolical villains.

CAST
Laurie/Electra Woman   Deidre Hall
Judy/Dyna Girl   Judy Strangis
Frank Heflin, the head of
   Crimescope   Norman Alden
The Villains:
The Pharoah   Peter Mark Richman
The Spider Lady   Tiffany Bolling
The Sorcerer   Michael Constantine
The Empress of Evil   Claudette Nevins
Lucriza   Jacqueline Hyde
Ali Baba   Malachi Throne
Cleopatra   Jane Elliot

Narrator: Marvin Miller.
Music: Jimmie Haskell.
Executive Producer: Sid and Marty Krofft.
Producer: Walter C. Miller.
Director: Walter C. Miller.

ELECTRA WOMAN AND DYNA GIRL — 15 minutes — ABC — September 11, 1976 – September 3, 1977 (as part of *The Krofft Supershow*).

357 THE ELECTRIC COMPANY

Children. The series, aimed at second through fourth graders, attempts to help slow readers increase their speed through cartoons, sketches and musical numbers that present the specifics of whole words and complete sentences.

Regulars: Judy Graubart, Skip Hinnant, Rita Moreno, Bill Cosby, Jimmy Boyd, Lee Chamberlain, Morgan Freeman, Hattie Winston, Luis Avalos.
The Short Circus (singers and dancers): Byan Johnson, June Angela, Todd Graff, Rodney Lewis, Janina Matthews, Greg Burge, Rejane Magloire.
Announcer: Ken Roberts.
Original Music Composed and Conducted By: Joe Raposo.
Musical Director: Gary William Friedman, Dave Connar.
Musical Coordinator: Danny Epstein.
Choreographer: Patricia Birch, Liz Thompson.
Producer: Andrew B. Ferguson, Jr.
Director: Henry Behar.

THE ELECTRIC COMPANY — 30 minutes — PBS — Premiered: October 25, 1971.

358 ELLERY QUEEN

Mystery. The series, set in New York City in 1947, details the work of Ellery Queen, a gentleman detective and writer, and his father, Richard Queen, a police inspector with the 3rd Division of the Center Street Precinct in Manhattan. Based on the characters created by Frederic Dannay and Manfred B. Lee, the format allows the viewer to match wits with Ellery Queen. The viewer sees the murder committed, is told who the suspects are, and is presented with all the clues — none are withheld from him and nothing extra is given to Ellery. Before the last commercial break, Ellery faces the camera and asks viewers to identify the murderer. After the commercial break, Ellery reconstructs the crime and reveals the guilty party.

CAST
Ellery Queen   Jim Hutton
Inspector Richard Queen   David Wayne
Sergeant Velie, Richard's aide   Tom Reese
Frank Flannigan, a reporter for the
   New York Gazette   Ken Swofford
Simon Brimmer, a criminologist and
   radio broadcaster   John Hillerman
Grace, Richard's secretary   Nina Roman
Vera, Frank's secretary   Maggie Nelson
Director of Simon's radio
   programs   John H. Lowler
Actor for Simon's programs   Jimmy Lydon

Ellery's home address: 212-A West 87th Street.
Simon's radio series: "The Casebook of Simon Brimmer."
Music: Elmer Bernstein, Hal Mooney, Dana Kaproff.
Theme: "Ellery Queen" by Elmer Bernstein.
Executive Producer: Richard Levinson, William Link.
Producer: Peter S. Fischer, Michael Rhodes.

Director: David Greene, Charles S. Dubin, Peter H. Hunt, Jack Arnold, James Sheldon, Seymour Robbie.
Note: Two prior versions of *Ellery Queen* have appeared. The first, which ran on the DuMont Network from 1950–55, featured Richard Hart (1950), Lee Bowman (1951–54) and Hugh Marlowe (1954–55) as Ellery Queen. Florenz Ames played his father, Inspector Richard Queen, and Charlotte Keane, his secretary, Nikki Porter. The second version, titled *The Further Adventures of Ellery Queen,* ran on NBC (1958–59) with George Nader (1958) and Lee Philips (1959) as Ellery Queen.

ELLERY QUEEN — 60 minutes — NBC — September 11, 1975 – September 19, 1976. The two-hour pilot film aired on NBC on March 23, 1975.

359 EMERGENCY!

Drama. The series details the work of the paramedics from Squad 51 of the Los Angeles County Fire Department, Rescue Division, and the doctors and nurses of Rampart Hospital.

CAST
Dr. Kelly Brackett   Robert Fuller
Dr. Joe Early   Bobby Troup
Nurse Dixie McCall   Julie London
Fireman Roy DeSoto   Kevin Tighe
Fireman John Gage   Randolph Mantooth
Fire Captain Henderson   Dick Hammer
Fire Captain Stanley   Michael Norell
Batallion Chief   Art Ballinger
Fireman Marco Lopez   Marco Lopez
Fireman Chet Kelly   Tim Donnelly
Fireman Mike Woiski   Jack Kruschen
Fireman Stoker   Mike Stoker
Nurse Carol Williams   Lillian Lehman
Dr. Morton   Ron Pincard
Nurse   Deidre Hall
Dr. Frye   Jack Manning
Nurse   Ginny Golden

Music: Nelson Riddle, Billy May.
Executive Producer: Jack Webb, R. A. Cinader.
Producer: Edwin Self, R. A. Cinader.
Director: Cliff Bole, Dennis Donnelly, Joseph Pevney, Alan Crosland, Jr., Herschel Daugherty, Christian Nyby, Don Richardson, Lawrence Dobkin, Randolph Mantooth, Christian I Nyby, II, Joel Olinsky, Kevin Tighe, Jack Webb, Richard Newton.
Creator: Harold J. Bloom, R. A. Cinader.

EMERGENCY! — 60 minutes — NBC — January 22, 1972 – September 3, 1977. Syndicated. Also titled, for syndication purposes, *Emergency One.* Four two-hour episodes also aired on NBC on January 7, 1978, February 25, 1978, March 4, 1978, and December 31, 1978.

360 EMERGENCY!

Drama. A revised version of the previous title which focuses on the work of John Gage and Roy DeSoto, as visiting paramedics with the 87th Rescue Unit of the San Francisco Fire Department.

CAST
Fireman John Gage   Randolph Mantooth
Fireman Roy DeSoto   Kevin Tighe
Paramedic Laurie
   Campbell   Deirdre Lenihan
Paramedic Gail Warren   Patricia McCormack
Fire Captain Peter Delaney   Paul Sylvan
Paramedic Joe Marshall   Jordan Suffin
Nurse Ellen Ankers   Zacki Murphy
Dr. DeRoy, of the Harbor Emergency
   Hospital   John De Lancie

Music: Gerald Fried.
Executive Producer: R. A. Cinader.
Producer: Hannah L. Shearer, Gian Grimaldi.
Director: Georg Fenady.

EMERGENCY! — 2 hours — NBC — June 26, 1979 – July 3, 1979. 2 episodes.

361 EMERGENCY PLUS FOUR

Animated Cartoon. A spin-off from *Emergency!* Assisted by four youngsters, Sally, Matt, Jason and Randy (the "Plus Four"), John Gage and Roy DeSoto, paramedics with the Squad 51 Rescue Division of the Los Angeles County Fire Department, continue their work, rescuing people trapped in life-and-death situations.

VOICES
Roy DeSoto   Kevin Tighe
John Gage   Randolph Mantooth
Sally   Sarah Kennedy
Carol (later replaced Sally)   Carol Harper
Matt   David Jolliffee
   Matthew Harper
Jason   Donald Fullilove
   Jason Phillips
Randy   Peter Haas
   Randy Alrich

Music: The Soundtrack Music Company.
Producer: Fred Calvert, Michael Caffey.
Director: Fred Calvert.

EMERGENCY PLUS FOUR — 30 minutes — NBC — September 8, 1973 – September 4, 1976.

EMERGENCY ONE

The syndicated (1976) title for *Emergency!*

362 THE ENGELBERT HUMPERDINCK SHOW

Musical Variety.

Host: Engelbert Humperdinck (Arnold Dorsey).
Regulars: The Irving Davies Dancers.
Orchestra: Jack Parnell.
Producer: Colin Clews.

Writer: Sheldon Keller, Bryan Blackburn, Tony Hawes.
Director: Ian Fordyce.

THE ENGELBERT HUMPER-DINCK SHOW — 60 minutes — ABC — January 21, 1970 — September 19, 1970. 13 programs. Syndicated.

363 THE ERROL FLYNN THEATRE

Anthology. Varying presentations, both comedic and dramatic.

Host: Errol Flynn.
Executive Producer: Marcel Leduc.
Producer: Norman Williams.
Director: John Lemont.

THE ERROL FLYNN THEATRE — 30 minutes — Resyndicated in 1979 as *Mystery Adventure: The Errol Flynn Theatre*. Originally broadcast on the DuMont Network in 1957–1958.

364 ESCAPE

Anthology. True stories of people caught in life-and-death situations.

Narrator: Jack Webb.
Music: Frank Comstock.
Executive Producer: R. A. Cinader.
Producer: Jerome H. Stanley.

The Series:
(Episode Untitled). The story, set during the Korean War, follows one day in the life of Brian Collyer, a congressional investigator who is blinded in a helicopter crash and saved from capture by the enemy through the efforts of a courageous Korean girl who finds him and guides him to safety.

Cast: Brian Collyer: John Ericson; Korean Girl: Charlene Wong; General Trebner: James Gregory; Sergeant: James McEachin.

(Episode Untitled). The story focuses on the efforts of a team of rescuers to find two children lost in dangerous mountain lion country.

Cast: Larry McGowan: Glenn Corbett; Fran McGowan: Marion Ross; Kate McGowan: Dana Laurita; Matthew McGowan: Lee H. Montgomery.

(Episode Untitled). The story, set during World War II, focuses on the efforts of a U.S. submarine captain to evade a Japanese destroyer.

Cast: Capt. Frank Wyatt: Ed Nelson; Mike Coles: Ron Hayes; Murphy: Dennis Rucker; Kurczak: Kip Niven.

(Episode Untitled). The story of a has-been demolitions expert as he attempts to regain his reputation by finding and defusing a bomb hidden in the Los Angeles Harbor.

Cast: Devlon: Bernie Hamilton; Valero: Scott Walker; Nieman: Leo Gordon; Diel: Norman Fell.

ESCAPE — 30 minutes — NBC — February 11, 1973 – April 1, 1973. 4 episodes. Rebroadcasts (NBC): August 19, 1973 – September 9, 1973.

365 EVENING IN BYZANTIUM

Drama. The story of Jesse Craig, a movie producer whose attempts to make a film about a terrorist plot become reality when terrorists invade the Cannes Film Festival in France and hold its audience hostage, demanding the release of comrades from Paris jails. Based on the novel by Irwin Shaw.

CAST

Jesse Craig	Glenn Ford
Brian Murphy	Eddie Albert
Bret Easton	Vince Edwards
Ian Waldeigh	Patrick Macnee
Fabricio	Gregory Sierra
Jerry Olson	Harry Guardino
Danny	Michael Cole
Walter Klein	Simon Oakland
Sonia Murphy	Gloria De Haven
Inspector Le Dioux	Marcel Hillaire
Constance Dobson	Shirley Jones
Gail McKinnon	Erin Gray
Inspector DuBois	Christian Marquand
Monsieur Carroll	Lee Bergere
Leonardo	Len Birman
Jack Conrad	James Booth
Roger Tory	George Lazenby
Penny Craig	Cynthia Ford
John Macklin	Anthony Costello
Senator Kennedy	Nick Dyrenforth
Sybil	Carol Baxter
William Bast	William Dozier
Michael Ruddy	Chris Winfield
Asted	Sid Haig
Sine	Ben Frommer
Moustapha Kamel	George Skaff
Angie	Larry Rings
Bellman	Andre Landcatt
Reporter	Michael Quinn
Reporter	Marine Kelley
Reporter	Ken Del Conte
Rent-A-Girl	Stephanie Page Saunders
Stewardess	Susan Woolen
Pilot	Geoffrey Beeny
Pilot	Doug Hale
Pilot	Randy Kirby
Flight Captain	Duncan Gamble
Controller	Larry Watson
Controller	Walt Davis
Blonde	Katie Zerbe
Girl at Palais	Janice Lynde

Music: Stu Phillips.
Executive Producer: Glen A. Larson.
Supervising Producer: Michael Sloan.
Producer: Robert F. O'Neill.
Writer: Glen A. Larson, Michael Sloan.
Director: Jerry London.

Art Director: Loyd S. Papez.
Director of Photography: Michael Margulies.

EVENING IN BYZANTIUM — 4 hours (total) — Operation Prime Time — August 1978. 2 two-hour episodes.

366 THE EVERLY BROTHERS SHOW

Musical Variety.

Hosts: Phil Everly, Don Everly.
Regulars: Ruth McDevitt (as Aunt Hattie), Joe Higgins, Dick Clair, Jenna McMahon.
Announcer: Mike Lawrence.
Orchestra: Jack Elliott and Allyn Ferguson.
Executive Producer: Harold D. Cohen, Joe Bryne.
Producer: Bernie Kukoff, Jeff Harris.
Writer: David Pollock, Elias Davis, Mike Settle, Bernie Kukoff, Jeff Harris.
Director: Marty Pasetta.

THE EVERLY BROTHERS SHOW — 60 minutes — ABC — July 8, 1970 – September 16, 1970. 13 programs. Official title: *Johnny Cash Presents The Everly Brothers Show*.

367 EVERYDAY

Variety. A daily series of music, comedy and song.

Hosts: Stephanie Edwards, John Bennett Perry.
Regulars: Tom Chapin, Murray Langston, Anne Bloom, Judy Gibson, Robert Corff, Emily Levine.
Executive Producer: David Salzman.
Producer: Viva Knight.
Director: Louis J. Horvitz.

EVERYDAY — 60 minutes — Syndicated 1978.

368 EVERYTHING'S ARCHIE

Animated Cartoon. The misadventures of the Archie Gang (Archie Andrews, Jughead Jones, Betty Cooper, Veronica Lodge, Reggie Mantle and Hot Dog, the gang pet), high school students in the fictional town of Riverdale.

VOICES

Archie Andrews	Dallas McKennon
Betty Cooper	Jane Webb
Veronica Lodge	Jane Webb
Jughead Jones	Howard Morris
Reggie Mantle	Dallas McKennon

Music: George Blais, Jeff Michael.
Music Supervision: Don Kirshner.
Producer: Norm Prescott, Lou Scheimer.
Director: Hal Sutherland.

EVERYTHING'S ARCHIE — 30 minutes — CBS — September 8, 1973 – January 26, 1974.

369 THE EVIL TOUCH

Anthology. Stories of people who are driven to evil through frustration. The series, which is filmed in Australia, features American personalities and Australian supporting actors.

Host: Anthony Quayle.
Music: Laurie Lewis.
Producer: Mende Brown.

Included:
Seeing Is Believing. The story of a movie producer whose horror film turns out to be just that — when a real monster visits the set.

Cast: Archie MacGauffin: Robert Lansing; Charlie: John Derum; Inspector Williams: Alfred Sandor.

Dear Cora, I'm Going to Kill You. The story of a woman who plots the almost-perfect murder of her husband.

Cast: Cora Blake: Carol Lynley; Harry Winston: Charles McCallum; Lt. Brennan: Dennis Clinton.

The Upper Hand. The story of Roger Carlyle, a wormlike husband who contrives the accidental death of his wife — then finds himself being blackmailed by his wife's maid, who witnessed the act.

Cast: Jenny, the maid: Julie Harris; Roger Carlyle: Peter Gwynne; Louise Carlyle: June Salter.

Marci. A woman attempts to prevent her hostile stepchild from destroying her life.

Cast: Elizabeth: Susan Strasberg; Marci: Elizabeth Crosby; John: Peter Gwynne.

THE EVIL TOUCH — 30 minutes — Syndicated 1973. 26 episodes.

370 EXECUTIVE SUITE

Drama. A behind-the-scenes look at the problems that befall members of the fictitious Cardway Corporation, a large industrial conglomerate in California.

CAST

Don Walling, the president of Cardway	Mitchell Ryan
Helen Walling, his wife	Sharon Acker
Brian Walling, their son	Leigh McCloskey
Stacey Walling, their daughter	Wendy Phillips
Howell Rutledge, the vice president	Stephen Elliott
Mark Desmond, the consumer relations head	Richard Cox
Yvonne Holland, Mark's mistress	Trisha Noble
Astrid Rutledge, Howell's wife	Gwyda DonHowe
Tom Dalessio, the plant manager	Paul Lambert
Glory Dalessio, Tom's daughter	Joan Prather

Summer Johnson, Brian's
  girlfriend   Brenda Sykes
Hilary Madison, the advertising
  head   Madelyn Rhue
Anderson Galt, a board
  member   William Smithers
Harry Ragin, the labor
  manager   Carl Weintraub
Malcolm Gibson, a board
  member   Percy Rodrigues
Pearce Newberry, a board
  member   Byron Morrow
Maggie, Don's secretary   Marged Wakeley
Leona Galt, Anderson's wife   Patricia Smith
Marge Newberry, Pearce's
  wife   Maxine Stuart
Katie, Hilary's secretary   Abbe Kanter
Elly Gibson, Malcolm's wife   Paulene Myers
    Kim Hamilton
Sharon Cody, the head of
  Capricorn International,
  a rival corp.   Joanna Barnes
Nick Kaslow, an industrial
  spy   Scott Marlowe
B. J. Kaslow, Nick's son   Moosie Drier
Julie Solkin, Leona's
  friend   Geraldine Brooks
Bernie Solkin, Julie's husband   Norman Fell
Sy Bookerman, the lawyer   John Randolph
David Valerio, Helen's drama
  coach   Ricardo Montalban
Walter Johnson, Summer's
  brother   Nat Jones
Bessy Johnson, Summer's
  grandmother   Hilda Haynes
Also:
Helga   Kathleen Hughes
Lois   Nancy Stephens
Rick   Tom Harper
David   Dennis Redfield
Karen   Alba Francesca
Guenther   Sander Johnson
Davis   Burt Douglas
Carter   James Karen

Music: Billy Goldenberg, John Parker, Nelson Riddle, Bill Conti, Gerald Fried, Gil Mellé.
Executive Producer: Norman Felton, Stanley Rubin, Rita Lakin.
Producer: Don Brinkley, Buck Houghton.
Director: Joseph Hardy, Charles S. Dubin, Joseph Pevney, Vincent Sherman, John Newland, Corey Allen.
Based on the novel Executive Suite *by:* Cameron Hawley.
Art Director: Marvin Summerfield, Edward C. Carfango.

EXECUTIVE SUITE — 60 minutes — CBS — September 20, 1976 – February 11, 1977.

371   THE EXPERT

Crime Drama. The exploits of Dr. John Hardy, a forensic scientist who works with police in Warwickshire, England. The series is inspired by the work of John Glaister, a former professor of forensic medicine at Glasgow University.

CAST
Dr. John Hardy   Marius Goring
Dr. Jo Harding, his wife   Ann Morrish
Susan Bartlett, John's
  assistant   Virginia Stride

Chief Detective Inspector
  Fleming   Victor Windling
Dr. Worsley   Noel Johnson

THE EXPERT — 60 minutes — Syndicated (to the U.S.) in 1970. Produced in England from 1970 through 1976.

F

372   THE FABULOUS FUNNIES

Animated Cartoon. Through the use of cartoon characters adapted from the Sunday Funnies, the series attempts to explain various aspects of the adult world to children.

Voices: June Foray, Robert Holt, Jayne Hamil, Alan Oppenheimer.
Music: Yvette Blais, Jeff Michael, David Jeffrey, Mark Jeffrey.
Executive Producer: Norm Prescott, Lou Scheimer.
Producer: Don Christensen.
Director: K. Wright, Ed Friedman, Gwen Weltzler, Marsh Lamore, Lou Zukor.

THE FABULOUS FUNNIES — 30 minutes — NBC — September 9, 1978 – September 1, 1979.

373   FACE THE MUSIC

Game. The first two rounds involve three players in a game wherein they have to identify persons, places or things from song titles. The orchestra plays a musical selection; the first player to identify it receives the opportunity to guess the subject to which it refers. The two highest scoring players are the winners and proceed to round three, where the determining game is played (same format as the previous rounds).

The highest scoring player is the winner and competes in the championship round where, with the previous champion, he attempts to identify a mystery celebrity. A board with six blank spaces is revealed. Behind each blank is a picture of a celebrity, ranging from childhood (box 1) to maturity (box 6). As the first picture is revealed, the orchestra plays a song associated with the mystery celebrity. The first player to identify the song receives the first opportunity to identify the celebrity. The first player to identify the celebrity is the winner and receives prizes according to the box on which the identification was made ($10,000 on Box 1 down to $1,000 on box 6).

The champion competes (with the winner of the next game) until defeated or until he reaches the limit of ten games when he wins a trip around the world.

Host: Ron Ely.
Announcer: Dave Williams, Art James, John Harlan.
Vocalist: Lisa Donovan.
Orchestra: Tommy Oliver.
Model: Jane Nelson, Lisa Donovan.
Executive Producer: David Levy, Bruno Ziarto.
Producer: Roy Horl, Peggy Touchstone.
Director: Lou Tedesco.
Art Director: John C. Mula.
First Champion to Win 10 Straight Games: Sarabeth Rothfield.

FACE THE MUSIC — 30 minutes — Syndicated January 1980.

374   THE FACTS OF LIFE

Comedy. A spin-off from *Diff'rent Strokes.* The series, set at the Eastland School for Girls, follows the experiences of Edna Garrett, the former Drummond housekeeper, as she takes a leave of absence to become the housemother to a group of teenage girls who are just learning the "facts of life."

CAST
Edna Garrett   Charlotte Rae
Steven Bradley, the
  headmaster   John Lawlor
Emily Mahoney, a teacher   Jenny O'Hara
The Girls:
Blair Warner   Lisa Whelchel
Cindy Webster   Julie Ann Haddock
Sue Anne Weaver   Julie Piekarski
Nancy Moore   Felice Schacter
Molly Parker   Molly Ringwald
Natalie Greene   Mindy Cohn
Tootie Ramsey   Kim Fields
Also:
Steve, the delivery boy   Greg Bradford
Monica Warner, Blair's
  mother   Pamela Huntington
Jeff Parker, Molly's father   William Bogert
Jason Ramsey, Tootie's
  father   Duane La Dage

Blair's horse: Chestnut.
Tootie's rabbits: Romeo and Juliet.
Music: Alan Thicke, Gloria Loring, Al Burton.
Producer: Jerry Mayer.
Associate Producer: Sue Nevens, John Maxwell Anderson.
Writer: Brad Ryder, Jerry Mayer, Martin A. Ragaway, Warren Murray.
Director: Nick Havinga, Jim Drake, John Bowab, Asaad Kelada.
Creator: Dick Clair, Jenna McMahon.
Art Director: C. Murawski.

THE FACTS OF LIFE — 30 minutes — NBC — August 24, 1979 – September 14, 1979. 4 episodes. March 12, 1980 – May 2, 1980; June 4, 1980 – October 3, 1980. 9 episodes. See also program No. 1887.

375   THE FALL AND RISE OF REGINALD PERRIN

Comedy. Events in the dreary day-to-day life of Reginald Perrin, an executive with Sunshine Desserts in England. His fall: dismissal from Sunshine. His rise: starting his own business, Perrin Products, Ltd., a company that sells "gifts for people you hate" (e.g. round dice, square footballs, foul tasting wine).

CAST
Reginald Perrin   Leonard Rossiter
Elizabeth Perrin, his wife   Pauline Yates
Joan Greengross, his sexy secretary;
  the woman with whom he
  fantasizes about having
  an affair   Sue Nicholls
C.J., Reginald's employer   John Barron
Linda, Reginald's married
  daughter   Sally-Jane Spencer
Tom, Linda's husband   Tim Preece
Mark Perrin, Reginald's
  son   David Warwick
Doc Morrisey, Reginald's
  friend   John Horsley
Peter Cartwright, the man
  Reginald meets on the
  train to work   Terence Conoley
Mrs. C.J., C.J.'s wife   Dorothy Frere
Jimmy Anderson, Elizabeth's
  brother   Geoggrey Palmer
Tony Webster, works for
  Sunshine   Trevor Adams
David Harris-Jones, same as
  Tony   Bruce Bould

Reginald's cat: Poncenbee.
Music: Ronnie Hazelhurst.
Producer: Gareth Gwenlan.

THE FALL AND RISE OF REGINALD PERRIN — 30 minutes — Syndicated (to PBS) in 1978. 14 episodes.

376   FAMILY

Drama. Incidents in the complex day-to-day lives of the Lawrences, a middle-income family of six living in Pasadena, California.

CAST
Doug Lawrence, the father,
  a lawyer   James Broderick
Kate Lawrence, his wife   Sada Thompson
Nancy Maitland, their married
  daughter, a lawyer
  also   Elayne Heilveil
    Meredith Baxter Birney
Lititia "Buddy" Lawrence,
  their daughter   Kristy McNichol
Willie Lawrence, their son   Gary Frank
Annie Cooper-Lawrence, their
  adopted daughter   Quinn Cummings
Jeff Maitland, Nancy's
  husband   John Rubinstein
Mrs. Canfield, the Lawrences'
  housekeeper   Mary Grace Canfield
Salina Magee, Willie's
  girlfriend   Season Hubley
Elaine Hogan, Kate's
  friend   Priscilla Morrill
    Louise Latham
Fred Hogan, Elaine's
  husband   William Putch
Claire Hopkins, Kate's
  friend   Claudette Nevins

The Facts of Life. Foreground, kneeling from left, Mindy Cohn, Molly Ringwald, Julie Piekarski and Kim Fields. Standing, from left, Julie Ann Haddock, Lisa Whelchel, Charlotte Rae, John Lawlor and Felice Schachter.

Family. From left, Meredith Baxter Birney, Gary Frank, James Broderick, Sada Thompson and Kristy McNichol. Courtesy of the *Call-Chronical Newspapers,* Allentown, Pa.

Family Affair. Bottom, from left, Kathy Garver and Anissa Jones. Top, from left, Sebastian Cabot, Johnnie Whitaker and Brian Keith.

Fantasy Island. From left, guest star Tom Ewell, Ricardo Montalban, Herve Villechaize, guest Foster Brooks, guest Ray Bolger, and guest Phil Foster in a scene from "The Over-the-Hill Caper" episode. Courtesy of the *Call-Chronicle Newspapers,* Allentown, Pa.

Timmy Maitland, Nancy's
  son   Michael David Shackleford
Linda, Buddy's girlfriend   Cynthia Grover
Audrey Pfeiffer, Buddy's
  friend   Louise Foley
Deborah Greenfield, Timmy's
  nursery school teacher   Nancy Locke
Clara, Nancy's secretary   Deborah White
Debbie, Annie's friend   Dana Plato

The Lawrences' address: 1230
Holland Street.
Music: John Rubinstein, Pete
  Rugolo, Mark Snow.
Music Supervision: Rocky
  Moriano.
Executive Producer: Aaron Spel-
  ling, Leonard Goldberg, Mike
  Nichols.
Producer: Edward Zwick, Carroll
  Newman, Nigel McKeand,
  Carol McKeand.
Director: Mark Rydell, Glenn Jor-
  dan, Rendil Kleiser, John Er-
  man, Richard Kinon, Gwen
  Arner, Marshall Lerskovitz,
  Joanne Woodward, Edward
  Parone, James Broderick.

FAMILY — 60 minutes — ABC.
March 9, 1976 – April 13, 1976;
September 28, 1976 – May 17,
1979; December 24, 1979 – March
17, 1980; June 4, 1980 – June 25,
1980. Syndicated.

377   FAMILY AFFAIR

Comedy Drama. When his brother and sister-in-law are killed in
an automobile accident, Bill
Davis, the president of the Davis
and Gaynor Construction Company in New York City, agrees to
raise his brother's children rather
than split them up among rela-
tives who do not want them. Assisted by his gentleman's gentleman, Giles French, Davis attempts to provide love and security to the teenager (Catherine
known as Cissy) and two lonely
and disillusioned children (twins
Buffy and Jody).

Realistically presenting children's needs and feelings, and
showing that adults are capable
of making mistakes, "Family Affair" distinguishes itself from
other family comedies by its
heartwarming, sentimental and at
times, sad stories.

CAST

Bill Davis   Brian Keith
Giles French, gentleman's
  gentleman   Sebastian Cabot
Catherine "Cissy" Davis,
  Bill's niece   Kathy Garver
Jody Davis, Bill's nephew Johnnie Whitaker
Buffy Davis, Bill's niece   Anissa Jones
Miss Faversham, Giles's
  friend   Heather Angel
Nigel French, Giles's
  brother   John Williams
Gregg Bartlett, Cissy's
  boyfriend   Gregg Fedderson
Sharon James, Cissy's
  girlfriend   Sherry Alberoni
Emily Turner, Bill's maid   Nancy Walker
Ted Gaynor, Bill's partner   Philip Ober
                   John Hubbard

Miss Lee, Bill's secretary   Betty Lynn
Miss Cummings, the twin's
  teacher   Joan Vohs
Scotty, the doorman   Karl Lucas

Buffy's doll: Mrs. Beasley.
Music: Frank DeVol, Jeff Alexan-
  der, Gerald Fried, Nathan Scott.
Music Supervision: Edwin T.
  Luckey.
Executive Producer: Don Fed-
  derson.
Producer: Edmund Hartmann,
  Edmund Beloin, Henry Gar-
  son, Fred Henry.
Director: William D. Russell,
  Charles Barton, James Sheldon.
The Davis Address: 600 East 32nd
  Street, Apt. 27-A.

FAMILY AFFAIR — 30 minutes —
CBS — September 12, 1966 –
September 9, 1971. 114 episodes.
Syndicated.

378   A FAMILY AT WAR

Drama. Events in the lives of the
Ashtons, a family of seven living
in Liverpool, England, during
World War II. The series covers
the period from 1938 to 1945.

CAST

Edwin Ashton, the father   Colin Douglas
Jean Ashton, the mother   Stelagh Fraser
Margaret Ashton, their
  daughter   Lesley Nunnerly
Freida Ashton, their
  daughter   Barbara Flynn
Philip Ashton, their son   Keith Drinkel
David Ashton, their son   Colin Campbell
Sheila Ashton, their
  daughter-in-law   Coral Atkins
John Porter, their friend   Ian Thompson
Ceila Porter, John's wife   Margery Mason
Harry Porter, their son   Patrick Troughton

Hostess: Thalassa Cruso.
Producer: Richard Doubleday.

A FAMILY AT WAR — 60 min-
utes — PBS — October   10,
1974 – October 9, 1975.

379   FAMILY FEUD

Game. Two five-member families
compete. The heads of each family are involved first. A board,
with various blank spaces is revealed. A question, previously
answered in a survey of one-
hundred people, is read. The first
player to sound a buzzer receives
a chance to answer. If the answer
was among survey responses, it
appears on the board in its
appropriate ranking. Its cash
amount, based on the number of
people who responded that way,
is revealed and placed in the
bank. If the contestant's answer is
incorrect, or not the No. 1 response, the opponent receives a
chance to answer. Whichever
team's player picked the highest
answer receives the option to
either pass or play the category. If
they play (or pass) the object is
for that team to build up the bank
account by filling in the remain-

ing blank spaces. If they are successful they keep the money;
however, if after three strikes
(wrong answers) the family fails
to fill in a blank, the opposing
family can steal the money by
correctly filling in the blank. Four
such rounds are played, each involving different members of the
families. The family that is first to
score two hundred dollars is the
winner.

Host: Richard Dawson.
Announcer: Gene Wood.
Music: Score Production.
Executive Producer: Mark Good-
  son, Bill Todman.
Producer: Howard Flesher.
Director: Paul Alter.

FAMILY FEUD — 30 minutes —
ABC — Premiered: July 12, 1976.

380   FAMILY
          FEUD — P.M.

Game. An evening version of the
afternoon game show, *Family
Feud*, which can be seen for format, cast and credits.

FAMILY FEUD — P.M. — 30 minutes — Syndicated 1977.

381   THE FAMILY
          HOLVAK

Drama. The story of Tom Holvak,
a minister in the small town of
Bensfield, Tennessee, in 1933, as
he struggles to feed his family
and maintain the faith of his congregation during the Depression.
Based on the novel *Ramey* by
Jack Farris.

CAST

Rev. Tom Holvak   Glenn Ford
Elizabeth Holvak, his wife   Julie Harris
Ramey Holvak, their son   Lance Kerwin
Julie Mae Holvak, their
  daughter   Elizabeth Cheshire
Jim Shanks, the
  deputy   William McKinney
Chester Purdle, the general
  store owner   Ted Gehring
Ida, Chester's assistant   Cynthia Hayward
Mr. Skinner, the owner of
  the Skinner Lumber
  Company   Henry Beckman
Ellen Baldwin, Ramey's
  school teacher   Cristina Raines

Music: Dick De Benedictis, Lee
  Holdridge.
Music Supervision: Hal Mooney.
Theme: "Look How Far We've
  Come."
Theme Vocal: Denny Brooks.
Executive Producer: Roland Kib-
  bee, Dean Hargrove.
Producer: Richard Collins.
Director: Alf Kjellin, Ralph Se-
  nensky, John Newland, Corey
  Allen, Vincent Sherman.

THE FAMILY HOLVAK — 60 minutes — NBC — September 7,
1975 – October 27, 1975. 6 episodes. The pilot film, "The
Greatest Gift," aired on NBC on
November 4, 1974.

382   FAMOUS CLASSIC
          TALES

Animated Cartoon. Adaptations of
literary classics. Produced in
Australia.

Included:

Gulliver's Travels. Jonathan
Swift's story about the travels of
Lemuel Gulliver and his adventures,
first on an island of small
people, then in a world of giants.
Voices: Ross Martin (as Gulliver),
  Hal Smith, John Stephenson,
  Don Messick, Rage Cordi, Julie
  Bennett, Janet Waldo.
Credits: Music: Angelo Revello;
  Executive Producer: Neil Bal-
  naves; Producer: William Han-
  na, Joseph Barbera; Writer:
  Kimmer Ringwald; Director:
  Chris Cuddington.

The Three Muskateers. The story,
based on the novel by Alexandre
Dumas, tells how D'Artagnan, a
Gascon, came to join Athos,
Aramis and Porthos, the King's
Musketeers.
Voices: James Condon, Barbara
  Frawley, Neil Fitzpatrick, Ron
  Haddrick, Jane Harders, John
  Martin, Richard Meickle.
Credits: Music: Bob Young, Hoyt
  Curtin; Producer: William
  Hanna, Joseph Barbera; Direc-
  tor: Peter Luschwitz.

Five Weeks in a Balloon. The
story, based on the novel by Jules
Verne, follows the adventures of
Samuel Ferguson, his nephew
Buck, and Irumu, Samuel's servant, as they travel across nineteenth century Africa seeking a
fabulous diamond that sits on an
altar atop an active volcano.
Voices: Brooker Bradshaw, Loren
  Lester, Gene Whittington, Cathleen Cordell, Laurie Mann,
  Johnny Hayner, John Stephenson.
Credits: Executive Producer: Neil
  Balnaves; Producer: Doug Patterson; Writer: Kimmer Ringwald; Director: Chris Cuddington.

FAMOUS CLASSIC TALES — 60
minutes — CBS — Premiered: September 23, 1973. Broadcast as a
series of specials on an irregular
basis.

383   FANG FACE

Animated Cartoon. The misadventures of Sherman "Fang"
Fangsworth, a teenager who
changes into a werewolf under
the moon and reverts to normal at sunup. Together with
his friends Kim, Biff and Pugsey,
Fang fights the forces of evil —
more often than not as a werewolf. (Every four hundred years a
baby werewolf is born into the
Fangsworth family. When the
moon's rays first shone on little
Sherman, it was discovered that
he had inherited the family
curse.)

Voices: Frank Welker, Susan Blue, John Stephenson, Allan Melvin, Bart Braverman, Jerry Dexter, Joan Gerber, Hattie Lynne Hurtes, Lewis Bailey, Ted Cassidy, Michael Rye, Larry D. Mann.
Music: Dean Elliott.
Executive Producer: Joe Ruby, Ken Spears.
Producer: Jerry Eisenberg.
Director: Rudy Larriva.

FANG FACE — 25 minutes — ABC — September 9, 1978 — September 8, 1979. Became a segment of "The Plastic Man Comedy Adventure Show," on September 22, 1979.

384 THE FANTASTIC FOUR

Animated Cartoon. When their rocket ship penetrates a strange radioactive belt that is encircling the Earth, four people acquire fantastic powers. Scientist Reed Richards acquires the ability to stretch like taffy; Sue Richards, his wife, possesses the ability to become invisible at will; Benn Grimm, a scientist, becomes "The Thing," a beast with the strength of a thousand men; and Johnny Storm, who acquires the ability to turn to fire, becomes "The Human Torch." Stories relate their battle against the sinister forces of evil.

VOICES

Reed Richards	Gerald Mohr
Sue Richards	Jo Ann Pflug
Ben Grimm	Paul Frees
Johnny Storm	Jack Flounders

Music: Hoyt Curtin.
Executive Producer: William Hanna, Joseph Barbera.
Producer: Alex Lovy.
Director: William Hanna, Joseph Barbera.

THE FANTASTIC FOUR — 30 minutes — ABC — September 9, 1967 — March 15, 1970. 26 episodes. Syndicated.

385 THE FANTASTIC FOUR

Animated Cartoon. A new version of the previous title. While testing a new rocket, three people are bombarded by strange cosmic rays emanating from outer space — rays that mysteriously affect their DNA structures. Reed Richards, a scientist, becomes the plastic-skinned "Mr. Fantastic"; Sue Richards, his wife, becomes "The Invisible Girl"; and Ben Grimm, their assistant, becomes the powerful "Thing." Stories depict their adventures, assisted by Herbie the Robot, as they battle the sinister forces of evil.

VOICES

Reed Richards	Mike Road
Sue Richards	Ginny Tyler
Ben Grimm	Ted Cassidy
Herbie the Robot	Frank Welker

Music: Dean Elliott.
Conductor: Eric Rogers.
Producer: David DePatie, Friz Freleng.
Director: Brad Case.
Creator: Stan Lee.

THE FANTASTIC FOUR — 30 minutes — NBC — September 9, 1978 — September 1, 1979.

386 THE FANTASTIC JOURNEY

Science Fiction Adventure. Hoping to further man's knowledge of the sea, a scientific party charters the ship *Yonda* and embarks on an expedition for the Caribbean. Shortly after leaving Coral Cove, Florida, the ship passes through the Bermuda Triangle and is engulfed by a billowing green cloud that leaves them shipwrecked on a mysterious, uncharted island.

Several days later, after exploring the island, the survivors (Paul Jordan, Eve Costigan, Fred Walters, Jill Sands and Scott Jordan) meet and ally themselves to Varian, a man from the twenty-third century who tells them that they have passed through a time warp and are in a seemingly endless land where the past, present and future coexist. They also learn that other people from other times also exist on the island — people who pose a threat to their safety. Stories depict their adventures as they encounter the various life forms that exist on the island.

CAST

Varian, the man from the twenty third century	Jared Martin
Dr. Fred Walters	Carl Franklin
Jonathan Willaway, an ally, a rebel scientist from the 1960s	Roddy McDowall
Liana, an ally, an alien from the galaxy Aros	Katie Saylor
Dr. Paul Jordan	Scott Thomas
Scott Jordan, Paul's son	Ike Eisenmann
Dr. Eve Costigan	Susan Howard
Dr. Jill Sands	Karen Sommerville

Liana's cat: Selel.
Main Title Narration: Mike Road.
Music: Robert Prince, Dick De Benedictis.
Executive Producer: Bruce Lansbury.
Producer: Leonard Katzman.
Director: Andrew McLaglen, Vincent McEveety, Barry Crane, Irving J. Moore, Virgil W. Vogel, Art Fisher, David Moessinger.
Program Open:
Narrator: Lost in the Devil's Triangle, trapped in a dimension with beings from the future and from other worlds, a party of adventurers journeys through zones of time back to their own time. Varian, a man from the twenty-third century, possessing awesome powers; from 1977, Fred, a young doctor just out of medical school;

Scott Jordan, the thirteen-year-old son of a famous scientist; Liana, daughter of an Atlantian father and an extraterrestial mother; and Jonathan Willaway, a rebel scientist from the 1960s. Together they face the frightening unknown on The Fantastic Journey.

THE FANTASTIC JOURNEY — 60 minutes — NBC — February 3, 1977 — April 21, 1977. Returned with one last episode on June 17, 1977.

387 FANTASTIC VOYAGE

Animated Cartoon. The story of Jonathan Kidd, Erica Stone, Cosby Birdwell and The Guru, four people who, through the Combined Miniature Defense Force, a secret U.S. government organization, are reduced to microscopic size. Episodes depict their exploits as they battle the unseen, unsuspecting enemies of the free world (criminal and germinal matter).

VOICES

Commander Jonathan Kidd	Ted Knight
Biologist Erica Stone	Jane Webb
Scientist Cosby Birdwell	Ted Knight
The Guru, "The Master of Mysterious Powers"	Marvin Miller

Music: Gordon Zahler.
Producer: Lou Scheimer, Norm Prescott.
Director: Hal Sutherland.

FANTASTIC VOYAGE — 30 minutes — ABC — September 14, 1968 — September 5, 1970. 26 episodes. Syndicated.

388 FANTASY ISLAND

Anthology. A series of interwoven vignettes set against the background of Fantasy Island, a mysterious tropical resort where, for an unspecified price, dreams are granted. Stories open with guests arriving on the island, followed by their meeting with Mr. Roarke, the man who arranges for people to act out their wildest fantasies. The individual's fantasy is then dramatized with the program showing how that person's life changes as a result of the experience.

CAST

Mr. Roarke*	Ricardo Montalban
Tattoo, his assistant	Herve Villechaize
Cindy, his assistant (several episodes)	Kimberly Beck
Helena Marsh, the fashion designer†	Samantha Eggar
Jamie Marsh, Helena's son	Paul John Balson
Harillia, one of the native girls	Ingrid Wong
Princess Nia, the Mermaid (recurring role)	Michelle Phillips

Various Roles: Carol Lynley, Mary Ann Mobley, Lynda Day

George, Toni Tennille, Melinda Naud, Fred Grandy, Ken Berry, Maureen McCormick.
Also: Chester, Tattoo's pet chimpanzee.
Music: Elliot Kaplan, Laurence Rosenthal, Charles Albertine, Lance Rubin, Shorty Rogers, Ken Harrison.
Music Theme: Laurence Rosenthal.
Supervising Producer: Arthur Rowe.
Executive Producer: Aaron Spelling, Leonard Goldberg.
Producer: Michael Fisher, Arthur Rowe, Skip Webster, Don Ingalls.
Director: Don Weis, Cliff Bole, John Newland, Phil Bondelli, Gene Nelson, George McCowan, Mike Vejar, Earl Bellamy, Lawrence Dobkin, Rod Holcomb.
Creator: Gene Levitt.

Included:
Charlie's Cherubs. The story of Amber Ainsley, Ginny Winthrop, and Claudia Ames, three beautiful secretaries who come to the island to be like their heroines — TV's "Charlie's Angels." With Tattoo acting as "Bosley," the girls attempt to solve the theft of a half-million dollars in jewels.

Cast: Amber Ainsley: Melinda Naud; Ginny Winthrop: Brenda Benet; Claudia Ames: Bond Gideon; Lizzie Clark, the girl who hires the Cherubs: Nita Talbot.

Class of '69. The story of Brenda Richards, an overweight woman who comes to Fantasy Island to become a knockout at her ten-year high school reunion.

Cast: Brenda Richards: Adrienne Barbeau; Lance Reynolds: Tim Thomerson; Bernie: Fred Gandy.

My Fair Pharoah. The story of Lucy Atwill, a stunningly beautiful woman whose fantasy takes her back to Egypt in 49 B.C. — as Cleopatra — where she immediately becomes involved in a power struggle to overthrow the throne.

Cast: Lucy Atwill: Joan Collins; Marc Antony: Ron Ely; Ptolemy: Michael Ansara.

Lady of the Evening. The story of Belinda Greene, a high-priced call girl who comes to the island to be Renee Lansing, an ordinary girl, so she can enjoy a vacation where nobody will recognize her for what she really is.

Cast: Belinda Greene: Carol Lynley; Bill Fredericks: Paul Burke.

FANTASY ISLAND — 60 minutes — ABC — Premiered: January 28, 1978. The first pilot film, titled "Fantasy Island," aired on ABC on January 14, 1977. The second pilot film, "Return to Fantasy Island," aired on ABC on November 20, 1977.

*According to episode 54, "Elizabeth," written by Steve Fisher and broadcast on January 12, 1980, the mysterious Mr. Roarke is more than 300 years old. Through Marge Corday (guest Tina Louise) who has come to the island to end a recurring nightmare about a castle and a spirit, it is learned that the spirit seeks to possess Marge to live again and kill Roarke whom she once loved—more than 300 years ago.

†Character began in a recurring role and eventually love developed between her and Roarke. A marriage resulted in the November 3, 1979 episode, but unfortunately, Helena "died" due to an inoperable brain tumor.

389   FARADAY AND COMPANY

Crime Drama. Frank Faraday, escaping from a Caribbean prison after twenty-eight years of internment on false charges, returns to the U.S. After exposing and apprehending the man responsible for his plight in 1945, Faraday assumes his former position as a private detective with his now-grown son, Steve, a security consultant for industry in Los Angeles. Stories relate the investigations of a 1940s-style private detective and the dated techniques he uses to apprehend criminals in the 1970s.

CAST

Frank Faraday	Dan Dailey
Steve Faraday, his son	James Naughton
Louise "Lou" Carson, Frank's former secretary and Steve's mother	Geraldine Brooks
Holly Barrett, Steve's secretary	Sharon Gless
Police Captain Brinkley	Andrew Duggan

Music: Jerry Fielding.
Executive Producer: Leonard B. Stern.
Producer: Stanely Kallis.
Director: Gary Nelson, Reza S. Badiyi, Leonard J. Horn, Jimmy Sangster, Richard L. Bare.

FARADAY AND COMPANY—90 minutes—NBC—September 26, 1973—January 9, 1974 (as part of *The NBC Wednesday Mystery Movie*); April 30, 1974—August 30, 1974 (as part of *The NBC Tuesday Mystery Movie*). 6 episodes.

390   FAR OUT SPACE NUTS

Comedy. While loading food aboard a moon rocket at a NASA space center, ground crewmen Junior and Barney accidentally launch the ship and are propelled into the vast regions of outer space. Stories relate their misadventures on unknown planets and their attempts to return to Earth.

CAST

Junior	Bob Denver
Barney	Chuck McCann
Honk, their pet space creature	Patty Maloney
Lantana, their alien friend	Eve Bruce
Crakor, Lantana's robot servant	Stan Jensen

Also, various roles: Leo Gordon, Joan Gerber, Richard Kennedy, Mickey Morton, Robert Dunlap.
Junior and Barney's Space Ship: PXL 1236.
Music: Michael Lloyd, Reg Powell.
Executive Producer: Sid and Marty Krofft.
Producer: Al Schwartz.
Director: Claudio Guzman, Wes Kenney.
Creator: Sid and Marty Krofft, Chuck McCann.

FAR OUT SPACE NUTS—25 minutes—CBS—September 6, 1975—September 4, 1977. Syndicated.

391   FAT ALBERT AND THE COSBY KIDS

Animated Cartoon. Bill Cosby's recollections of his northern Philadelphia buddies: Fat Albert, Rudy, Weird Harold, Edward, Mush Mouth, Donald, Bucky and Russell (Bill's brother). Characters and situations are designed, through their activities, to educate and entertain children as to the meanings of topics in everyday life.

VOICES

Fat Albert	Bill Cosby
Mush Mouth	Bill Cosby
Dumb Donald	Bill Cosby
Weird Harold	Bill Cosby
Bill Cosby	Himself

Additional Voices: Keith Allen, Pepe Brown, Erika Carroll, Jan Crawford, Gerald Edwards, Lane Vaux.
Host: Bill Cosby.
Music: The Horta-Mahana Corporation.
Executive Producer: William H. (Bill) Cosby, Jr.
Producer: Norm Prescott, Lou Scheimer.
Director: Hal Sutherland, Don Towsley, Lou Zukor.

FAT ALBERT AND THE COSBY KIDS—30 minutes—CBS—Premiered: September 9, 1972.

392   FATHER DEAR FATHER

Comedy. The chaotic misadventures of Patrick Glover, a divorced British thriller writer, as he attempts to understand and cope with his ex-wife, Barbara, his beautiful teenage daughters, Anna and Karen, and his well-meaning housekeeper, Matilda Harris.

CAST

Patrick Glover	Patrick Cargill
Anna Glover, his elder daughter	Natasha Pyne
Karen Glover, his younger daughter	Ann Holloway
Matilda Harris (Nanny), his housekeeper	Noel Dyson
Barbara Mossman, Patrick's ex-wife	Urusla Howells
Bill Mossman, Barbara's husband	Tony Britton Patrick Holt
Georgie Thompson, Patrick's agent	Sally Bazely Dawn Addams
Mrs. Glover, Patrick's mother	Joyce Carey
Philip Glover, Patrick's brother	Donald Sinden
Ian Smythe, Patrick's publisher	Michael Segal
Norah Smythe, Ian's wife	Diana King
Timothy Tanner, Anna's husband, later episodes	Jeremy Child

Patrick's dog: H.G. Wells.
Patrick's address: 121 Hillsdown Avenue (early episodes); 21 Ingrim Avenue (later episodes), both in England.
Music: Gordon Franks.
Writer-Creator: Johnnie Mortimer, Brian Cooke.
Producer-Director: William Stewart.

FATHER DEAR FATHER—30 minutes—Syndicated (to the U.S.) in 1977. 39 episodes. Produced by Thames TV of London in 1969.

393   FATHER KNOWS BEST

Comedy. The dreams, ambitions and frustrations of the Anderson family: Jim, manager of the General Insurance Company; his wife Margaret, and their children, Betty, Bud and Kathy. Stories tenderly mirror their lives.

CAST

Jim Anderson, the father	Robert Young
Margaret Anderson, his wife	Jane Wyatt
Betty Anderson (Princess), their daughter	Elinor Donahue
James "Bud" Anderson, Jr., their son	Billy Gray
Kathy Anderson (Kitten), their daughter	Lauren Chapin
Miss Thomas, Jim's secretary	Sarah Selby
Claude Messner, Bud's friend	Jimmy Bates
Kippy Watkins, Bud's friend	Paul Wallace
Joyce Kendall, Bud's girlfriend	Roberta Shore
Ralph Little, Betty's boyfriend	Robert Chapman
Ed Davis, Jim's neighbor	Robert Foulk
Myrtle Davis, Ed's wife	Vivi Jannis
Dottie Snow, Betty's friend	Yvonne Lime
Patty Davis, Kathy's friend	Tina Thompson Reba Waters
April Adams, Bud's girlfriend	Sue George
Burgess Vale, Kathy's boyfriend (early episodes)	Richard Eyer
Grover Adams, April's brother, Kathy's boyfriend (later episodes)	Richard Eyer
Emily Vale, Margaret's friend	Lenore Kingston
Joe Phillips, Bud's friend	Peter Heisser
Hubert Armstead, the high school principal	Sam Flint

The Andersons' address: 607 South Maple Street in the town of Springfield.
Music: Irving Friedman.
Announcer: Carl Caruso.
Producer: Eugene B. Rodney, Robert Young.
Director: William D. Russell, Peter Tewksbury.

FATHER KNOWS BEST—30 minutes. CBS—October 3, 1954—March 27, 1955. NBC—August 31, 1955—September 17, 1958. CBS—September 22, 1958—September 17, 1962. ABC (rebroadcasts)—September 30 1962—February 3, 1967. 203 episodes. Syndicated. See the following title for information on the two extension episodes of *Father Knows Best.*

394   FATHER KNOWS BEST: EXTENSION EPISODES

Comedy-Drama. Storylines, casts and credits for the two extension episodes that were broadcast based on the original *Father Knows Best* series (see previous title).

The Father Knows Best Reunion. The first extension episode in which the Anderson children, Betty, Bud, and Kathy, return to their original home to celebrate the thirty-fifth wedding anniversary of their parents, Jim and Margaret. (Betty, the eldest daughter, is a widow with two children; Bud, the son, is a motorcycle racer, married, and the father of a son; and Kathy, the youngest child, is single, but engaged to a man ten years her senior.)

Father Knows Best: Home for Christmas. The second extension episode in which Betty, Bud and Kathy join their parents, Jim and Margaret Anderson, for a Christmas celebration—a celebration that is saddened by the prospect of Jim and Margaret selling their home, which is so rich in memories. (To make the way for a possible third episode, the story ended with Bud buying his parent's home, and Jim and Margaret using part of the money to purchase a motor home and tour America.)

CAST

Jim Anderson, the father	Robert Young
Margaret Anderson, the mother	Jane Wyatt
Betty, their daughter	Elinor Donahue
Bud Anderson, their son	Billy Gray
Kathy Anderson, their daughter	Lauren Chapin
Jean Anderson, Bud's wife	Susan Adams
Robby Anderson, Bud's son	Christopher Gardner
Jenny, Betty's daughter	Cari Anne Warder

Ellen, Betty's daughter   Kyle Richards
Dr. Jason Harper, Kathy's
fiance   Hal England
Frank Carlson, Betty's romantic
interest   Jim McMullan

Music: George Duning.
Producer: Eugene B. Rodney
(first episode); Hugh Benson
(second episode).
Director: Marc Daniels (first episode); Norman Abbott (second
episode).

THE FATHER KNOWS BEST RE-
UNION — 90 minutes — NBC —
May 15, 1977.
FATHER KNOWS BEST: HOME
FOR CHRISTMAS — 90 min-
utes — NBC — December 18,
1977.

395   FAWLTY TOWERS

Comedy. The chaotic misadventures of Basil Fawlty, the rude and
totally incompetent innkeeper of
the Fawlty Towers, a hotel on 16
Elwood Avenue in England.

CAST

Basil Fawlty, the innkeeper   John Cleese
Sybil Fawlty, his wife   Prunella Scales
Polly Sherman, the waitress   Connie Booth
Manuel, the bellboy   Andrew Sachs
Terry, the cook   Brian Hall
Major Gowen, a regular hotel
guest   Ballard Berkeley
Miss Tibbs, a regular guest   Gilly Flower
Miss Gatsby, a regular guest   Renee Roberts

Music: Dennis Wilson.
Producer: Douglas Argent, John
Davies.
Writer-Creator: John Cleese,
Connie Booth.
Director: Bob Spiers.

FAWLTY TOWERS — 30 min-
utes — Syndicated to PBS in 1977.
12 episodes. Produced by BBC-2
in England.

396   FAY

Comedy. The joys, sorrows and
romantic misadventures of Fay
Stuart, a middle-aged divorcée
living in San Francisco.

CAST

Fay Stuart, a legal secretary   Lee Grant
Jack Stuart, her philandering
ex-husband   Joe Silver
Linda Baines, Fay's married
daughter   Margaret Willock
Dr. Elliott Baines, Linda's
husband   Stewart Moss
Lillian, Fay's neighbor   Audra Lindley
Danny Messina, Fay's employer   Bill Gerber
Al Cassidy, Danny's partner   Norman Alden
Letty Gilmore, Al's secretary   Lillian Lehman

Music: George Tipton.
Theme Vocal: Jaye P. Morgan.
Executive Producer: Paul Junger
Witt.
Producer: Jerry Mayer, Tony
Thomas.
Director: Richard Kinon, James
Burrows, Alan Arkin.
Creator: Susan Harris.

FAY — 30 minutes — NBC —
September 4, 1975 — October 23,

1975; May 19, 1976 – June 2, 1976.
8 episodes.

397   THE F.B.I.

Crime Drama. Case dramatizations based on the actual files of
the Federal Bureau of Investigation.

CAST

Inspector Lewis Erskine   Efrem Zimbalist, Jr.
Arthur Ward, the assistant
director   Philip Abbott
Jim Rhodes, Erskine's
assistant   Stephen Brooks
Barbara Erskine, Lewis's
daughter   Lynn Loring
Agent Tom Colby   William Reynolds
Agent Chris Daniels   Shelly Novack
Agent Chet Randolph   Anthony Eisley

Narrator: Marvin Miller.
Music: Richard Markowitz, John
Elizalde, Bronislau Kaper, Sid-
ney Cutner, Dominic Fron-
tiere, Duane Tatro.
F.B.I. Theme: Bronislau Kaper.
Executive Producer: Quinn
Martin.
Producer: Philip Saltzman,
Charles Lawton, Charles
Lawson.
Director: Charles Larson, Virgil W.
Vogel, Paul Wendkos, Seymour
Robbie, Richard Donner, Jesse
Hibbs, Don Medford, Ralph
Senensky, Christian Nyby, Wil-
liam Hale, Robert Day, Robert
Douglas.

THE F.B.I. — 60 minutes —
ABC — September 19, 1965 —
September 1, 1974. 208 episodes.
Syndicated.

398   THE FEATHER
AND FATHER GANG

Crime Drama. The cases of Toni
"Feather" Danton, a beautiful attorney with the Los Angeles firm
of Huffaker, Danton and Binkwell, and her father, Harry Danton, her assistant, and ex-
confidence man who incorpo-
rates his knowledge of the con
game to outwit and apprehend
criminals.

CAST

Toni Danton   Stefanie Powers
Harry Danton, her father   Harold Gould
Lou, Harry's aide   Lewis Charles
Margo, Harry's aide   Joan Shawlee
Enzo, Harry's aide   Frank Delfino
Michael, Harry's aide   Monte Landis
Murphy, Harry's aide   Dick O'Neill
J.C. Hadley, the
Deputy D.A.   Edward Winter
Jesse, Toni's secretary   Jessica Rains
"Huff" Huffaker, Toni's
partner   William H. Bassett
Binkwell, Toni's partner   Allen Williams

Music: George Romanis, Bert
Gold
Feather and Father Gang Theme:
George Romanis.
Executive Producer: Larry White.
Producer: Robert Mintz, Bill
Driskill, Buzz Kulick.
Director: Seymour Robbie, Ernest

Pintoff, Bruce Bilson, Jackie
Cooper, Jerry London, Barry
Shear, Buzz Kulick, Edward
Abroms.
Creator: Bill Driskill.

THE FEATHER AND FATHER
GANG — 60 minutes — ABC —
March 7, 1977 – April 4, 1977; May
21, 1977 – August 6, 1977. The
pilot film, titled "Feather and Father," aired on ABC on December
6, 1976.

399   FEELING GOOD

Educational. Tips on staying
healthy are presented through
the health problems and behavior of a group of people who
inhabit Mac's Place, a luncheonette.

CAST

Mac, the proprietor   Rex Everhart
Rita, the waitress   Priscilla Lopez
Mrs. Stebbins, the
gossip monger   Ethel Shutta
Jason, a doctor   Joe Morton
Melba, Jason's wife   Marjorie Barnes
Hank, the sporting-goods
store owner   Ben Slack

Host: Dick Cavett.
Regular: Bill Cosby.
Orchestra: Stephen Lawrence
Executive Producer: Robert Ben-
edict, Bill Kobin.
Producer: Albert Waller.
Director: John Desmond.

FEELING GOOD — 60 min-
utes — PBS — November 20,
1974 – January 29, 1975.

400   FERNWOOD
2-NIGHT

Satire. An intentionally appalling
series that satirizes the television
talk show. Produced by fictional
Channel 6 in imaginary Fernwood, Ohio, the home of "Mary
Hartman," the program literally
presents the most grotesque
people imaginable to be interviewed by an obnoxious, conceited host, and his dim-witted
announcer. The summer re-
placement for *Mary Hartman,
Mary Hartman.*

Host: Martin Mull as Barth
Gimble.
Announcer: Fred Willard as Jerry
Hubbard.
Music: Frank Devol (as Happy
Kyne) and his Orchestra (the
Mirth Makers).
Executive Producer: Louis J.
Horvitz.
Producer: Alan Thicke.
Writer: Tom Moore, Jimmy Ste-
vens, Alan Thicke.
Director: Howard Storm, Tony
Csiki, Jim Drake, Louis J.
Horvitz.
Creator: Norman Lear.

FERNWOOD 2-NIGHT — 30
minutes — Syndicated 1977. 65
episodes. Spin-off series: *America
2-Night.*

401   50 GRAND SLAM

Game. Two players, knowledgeable in the same field, compete.
Each is tested separately and the
player who scores the highest
wins and reaches the first plateau
of $200. Seven additional pla-
teaus remain, worth $500, $1,000,
$2,000, $5,000, $10,000, $20,000
and $50,000 each. The player's
decision to quit or continue playing after achieving various pla-
teaus determines his winnings.
However, should he risk taking a
certain plateau and fail to complete it, he is defeated and loses
everything he has earned to that
point.

Host: Tom Kennedy.
Announcer: John Harlan.
Music: Score Productions.
Producer: Ralph Andrews.
Director: Marty Pasetta.

50 GRAND SLAM — 30 min-
utes — NBC — October 4, 1976 –
December 31, 1976. 60 programs.

402   FIREHOUSE

Drama. The work of the men of
Engine Company Number 23 of
the Los Angeles County Fire Department.

CAST

Capt. Spike Ryerson   James Drury
Fireman Hank Myers   Richard Jaeckel
Fireman Sonny Capito   Mike Delano
Fireman Cal Dakin   Bill Overton
Fireman Scotty Smith   Scott Smith
Fireman Billy DelZel   Brad David

Music: Billy Goldenberg.
Executive Producer: Leonard
Goldberg, Aaron Spelling, Dick
Berg.
Producer: Ron Austin, James
David Buchanan, Joe Manduke.

FIREHOUSE — 30 minutes — ABC
— January 17, 1974 – August 1,
1974. 13 episodes. See also "Firehouse" in the pilot film section.

403   FISH

Comedy. On a leave of absence
after thirty-eight years with the
New York Police Department, Detective Phil Fish reluctantly
abides by his wife's decision to
care for five children — five
streetwise delinquents assigned
to him by the Social Services Center in Brooklyn. Stories relate his
attempts to cope with a new life-
style and supervise his newly acquired family. A spin-off from
Barney Miller.

CAST

Phil Fish   Abe Vigoda
Bernice Fish, his wife   Florence Stanley
Charlie Harrison, the associate
host parent (to help care
for the kids)   Barry Gordon
The Children:
Diane Palanski   Sarah Natoli
Jilly   Denise Miller
Mike   Lenny Bari
Victor Croitson   John Cassisi

Loomis	Todd Bridges
Manuel (brought on later)	David Yanez

Music: Jack Elliott, Allyn Ferguson.
Executive Producer: Danny Arnold.
Producer: Norman Barasch, Roy Kammerman, Steve Pretzker.
Director: Lee Bernardhi, Mike Warren, Dennis Steinmetz, Gary Shimokawa.

FISH — 30 minutes — ABC — February 5, 1977 – March 30, 1978; May 4, 1978 – June 8, 1978. 35 episodes. Syndicated.

404   THE FITZPATRICKS

Drama. Events in the lives of the Fitzpatricks, an Irish-Catholic family of six living in Flint, Michigan.

CAST

Mike Fitzpatrick, the father, a steelworker	Bert Kramer
Maggie Fitzpatrick, his wife	Mariclare Costello
Jack Fitzpatrick, their son	James Vincent McNichol
Maureen "Mo" Fitzpatrick, their daughter	Michele Tobin
Max Fitzpatrick, their son	Sean Marshall
Sean Fitzpatrick, their son	Clark Brandon
Kerry Gerardi, Jack's friend	Helen Hunt
R. J., Max's friend	Derek Wells

The Fitzpatrick's dog: Detroit.
Music: John Rubinstein, Fred Werner.
Executive Producer: Philip Mandelker.
Producer: John Cutts.
Director: Gene Reynolds, Harvey S. Laidman, Marc Daniels, John Young, Harry Harris, Peter Tewksbury, Stuart Margolin, Lawrence Dobkin, Robert Totten, Joe Manduke.
Creator: John Young.

THE FITZPATRICKS — 60 minutes — CBS — September 5, 1977 – January 10, 1978. 13 episodes.

405   FLAMBARDS

Drama. The series, set in England during World War I, follows the life of Christina Russell, a teenage orphan who comes to live with her crippled and tyrannical uncle at Flambards, his dreary and decaying estate. Adapted from the books by K.M. Pyton.

CAST

Christina Russell	Christine McKenna
Mr. Russell, her uncle	Edward Judd
Mark Russell, his eldest son	Steven Grives
William Russell, his youngest son	Alan Parnaby
Mary, a maid	Rosalie Williams
Violet, a maid	Gillian Davey
Dick, the stableman	Sebastian Abineri
Dorothy, Christina's friend	Carol Leader
Christina's Cousin Jessica	Gwynne Gray
Christina's Aunt Grace	Olive Pendleton
Dr. Porter	Michael MacCowan
The Vicar	Arthur Fortune

Narrator: Joan Friedman.
Music: David Fanshane.
Executive Producer: David Cunliffe.
Producer: Leonard Lewis.
Writer: Alan Plater.
Director: Michael Ferguson, Lawrence Gordon Clarke, Leonard Lewis.
Designer: Roger Andrews, Mike Long.

FLAMBARDS — 60 minutes — PBS — July 8, 1980 – September 23, 1980. 12 episodes.

406   FLASH GORDON

Animated Cartoon. The series, set in the twenty-first century, details the exploits of Flash Gordon, the son of a famous scientist, as he struggles to protect the universe from the evils of Ming the Merciless, diabolical ruler of the planet Mongo. Based on the comic strip by Alex Raymond.

VOICES

Flash Gordon	Robert Ridgely
Dale Arden, his girlfriend	Melendy Britt
Dr. Hans Zarkov, a scientist, Flash's assistant	Alan Oppenheimer
Ming the Merciless	Alan Oppenheimer
Princess Aura, Ming's daughter	Diane Pershing
Thun, the leader of the Lion People	Allan Melvin
Prince Baron, the ruler of the planet Aboria	Robert Ridgely
Queen Fria, Queen of the planet Fridgia	Diane Pershing
Vultan, King of the Hawk Men	Allan Melvin

Music: Yvette Blais, Jeff Michael, George Mahana.
Executive Producer: Norm Prescott, Lou Scheimer.
Producer: Don Christensen.
Director: Hal Sutherland, Don Towsley, Lou Zukor.

FLASH GORDON — 30 minutes — NBC — September 8, 1979 – December 1, 1979.

407   FLATBUSH

Comedy. The series, set in Flatbush in Brooklyn, New York, focuses on the unlikely misadventures of the Fungos, a wild, unpredictable, close-knit street gang.

CAST

The Fungos:

Presto Prestopolos	Joseph Cali
Socks Palermo	Adrian Zmed
Turtle Romero	Vincent Bufano
Joey Dee	Randy Stumpf
Figgy Figueroa	Sandy Helberg

Also:

Mrs. Fortunato, the cantankerous old woman	Helen Verbit
Mr. Esposito, the store owner	Anthony Ponzini

Music: Mark Snow.
Supervising Producer: George Yanok.
Executive Producer: Philip Capice, Gary Adelson.
Producer: Norman S. Powell.
Director: William Asher, Mel Ferber, Tony Mordente.

FLATBUSH — 30 minutes — CBS — February 26, 1979 – March 12, 1979. 3 episodes.

408   THE FLINTSTONES

Animated Cartoon. The series, set in the town of Bedrock, in 1,000,040 B.C., follows events in the lives of Fred and Wilma Flintstone, and their neighbors Betty and Barney Rubble.

VOICES

Fred Flintstone, a dino operator for the Slaterock Gravel Company	Alan Reed
Wilma Flintstone, his wife	Jean VanderPyl
Barney Rubble, Fred's co-worker	Mel Blanc
Betty Rubble, Barney's wife	Bea Benaderet
	Gerry Johnson
Dino, Fred's pet dinosaur	Don Messick
Pebbles Flintstone, Fred's daughter	Jean VanderPyl
Bamm Bamm Rubble, Barney's son	Don Messick
Hoppy, Barney's pet dinosaur	Don Messick
George Slate (a.k.a. George Slaterock), Fred's employer	John Stephenson
Arnold, the newspaper boy	Don Messick
The Great Gazeoo, a space creature	Harvey Korman
Mrs. Flaghoople, Wilma's mother	Jean VanderPyl

The Flintstones' Address: 345 Stove Cave Road.
Construction companies for which Fred works: The Slaterock Gravel Company; The Bedrock Gravel Company; and The Rockhead Quarry Cave Construction Company.
Music: Hoyt Curtin, Ted Nichols.
Producer: William Hanna, Joseph Barbera.
Director: William Hanna, Joseph Barbera, Charles A. Nichols.

THE FLINTSTONES — 30 minutes — ABC — September 30, 1960 – September 2, 1966. NBC — September 2, 1967 – September 5, 1970. Syndicated. Spin-offs: *The Flintstones Comedy Hour, Fred and Barney Meet the Thing, The New Fred and Barney Show,* and *Pebbles and Bamm Bamm.*

409   THE FLINTSTONES COMEDY HOUR

Animated Cartoon. Continued events in the lives of the Flint-

stone and Rubble families. A spin-off from *The Flintstones*.

VOICES

Fred Flintstone, the father	Alan Reed
Wilma Flintstone, his wife	Jean VanderPyl
Pebbles Flintstone, their daughter	Mickey Stevens
Barney Rubble, their neighbor	Mel Blanc
Betty Rubble, Barney's wife	Gay Hartwig
Bamm Bamm Rubble, Barney and Betty's son	Jay North

Friends of Pebbles and Bamm Bamm:

Moonrock	Lennie Weinrib
Fabian	Carl Esser
Penny	Mitzi McCall
Schleprock	Don Messick
Wiggy	Gay Hartwig
Bronto	Lennie Weinrib
Zonk	Mel Blanc
Noodles	John Stephenson
Stub	Mel Blanc

Also:

George Slate, Fred's employer	John Stephenson

Music: Hoyt Curtin.
Executive Producer: William Hanna, Joseph Barbera.
Producer: Charles Nichols.
Director: William Hanna, Joseph Barbera.

THE FLINTSTONES COMEDY HOUR — 60 minutes — CBS — September 9, 1972 – September 1, 1973. As *The Flintstones Show* — 30 minutes — CBS — September 8, 1973 – January 26, 1974.

410   THE FLIP WILSON SHOW

Variety. Music, songs and comedy sketches.

Host: Flip Wilson.
Dancers: The Flipettes: Maguerite DeLain, Ka Ron Brown, Jaki Morrison, Edwetta Little, Bhetty Waldron, Mary Vivian.
Orchestra: George Wyle.
Additional Music: Sid Feller.
Producer: Bob Henry.
Associate Producer: Patricia Rickey.
Writer: Bob Schiller, Winston Moss, Bob Weiskopf, Jack Burns, Hal Goodman, Larry Klein, Herbert Baker, Flip Wilson.
Director: Tim Kiley, Bob Henry.
Choreographer: Jack Regas.
Art Director: Romain Johnston.

THE FLIP WILSON SHOW — 60 minutes — NBC — September 17, 1970 – June 27, 1974. Syndicated.

411   FLO

Comedy. A spin-off from *Alice*. Promised a hostess job in Houston, Florence Jean Castleberry leaves Arizona and Mel's Diner and heads for greener pastures in Texas. Enroute, however, she stops off at her hometown, Cowtown, Texas, and on a dare* buys a rundown roadhouse which she renames "Flo's Golden Rose." The series follows her misadventures as she attempts to run the bar.

CAST

Florence Jean Castleberry	Polly Holliday
Earl Tucker, the bartender	Geoffrey Lewis
Miriam, the waitress	Joyce Bulifant
Fran Castleberry, Flo's sister	Lucy Lee Flippen
Velma "Mama" Castleberry, Flo's mother	Sudie Bond
Les Kincaid, the piano player	Stephen Keep
Farley Waters, the banker	Jim B. Baker
Wendell Tubbs, Fran's fiancé	Terry Wills
Randy, the mechanic	Leo Burmester
Betty, Velma's friend	Amzie Strickland
Inez, Velma's friend	Georgia Schmidt
Chester, a diner customer	Mickey Jones

Music: Fred Werner.
Theme: "Flo's Golden Rose" by Suzie Glickman (lyrics) and Fred Werner (music).
Theme Vocal: Hoyt Axton.
Supervising Producer: Ron Landry, George Geiger, Tom Biener.
Executive Producer: Jim Mulligan.
Producer: Robert Illes, James Stein, Ron Landry, George Geiger, Tom Biener.
Writer: Stephen Miller, Ron Landry, George Geiger, Tom Biener, Dick Clair, Jenna McMahon, Robert Illes, Rick Orloff.
Director: Marc Daniels.
Art Director: Lynn Griffin.

FLO — 30 minutes — CBS. March 24, 1980 – April 28, 1980. 6 episodes. Rebroadcasts: July 21, 1980 – September 1, 1980. Returned, Premiered: October 27, 1980.

*That she can run a bar — as a woman, better than any man.

412   FLYING HIGH

Comedy-Drama. The story of Pam Bellagio, Marcy Bower and Lisa Benton, three beautiful stewardesses for Sun West Airlines, which is based in Los Angeles.

CAST

Stewardess Pam Bellagio	Kathryn Witt
Stewardess Marcy Bower	Pat Klous
Stewardess Lisa Benton	Connie Sellecca
Captain Douglas Robert March, a pilot	Howard Platt
Raymond Strickman, the passenger relations agent (series)	Ken Olfson
Burt Stahl, the passenger relations agent (pilot film)	David Hayward

Music: Robert Prince, Arthur Rubinstein.
Music Theme: "Flying High" by David Shire.
Executive Producer: Mark Carliner.
Producer: Robert Van Scoyk, Marty Cohan.

Director: Peter H. Hunt, Nicholas Sgarro, Alan Myerson, William Jurgenson, James Sheldon, Alan Bergman, Dennis Donnelly, Sigmund Neufeld, Jr.

FLYING HIGH — 60 minutes — CBS — September 29, 1978 – January 23, 1979. 14 episodes. The series was "sneak-previewed" with its two-hour pilot film on CBS on August 28, 1978.

413   FOREVER FERNWOOD

Serial. The revised series title for *Mary Hartman, Mary Hartman* without star Louise Lasser ("Mary"*). The series depicts events in the sometimes hectic lives of the people of the fictional town of Fernwood, Ohio.

CAST

Tom Hartman, Mary's husband	Greg Mullavey
Heather Hartman, Tom's daughter	Claudia Lamb
Loretta Haggers, Tom's neighbor	Mary Kay Place
Charlie Haggers, Loretta's husband	Graham Jarvis
Martha Schumway, Tom's mother-in-law	Dody Goodman
George Schumway, Martha's husband	Tab Hunter† Phil Bruns†
Cathy Schumway, Martha's daughter	Debralee Scott
Merle Jeeter, Tom's friend	Dabney Coleman
Wanda Jeeter, Merle's wife	Marian Mercer
Raymond Larkin, Martha's father	Victor Kilian
Eleanor Major, the woman who attaches herself to Tom	Shelley Fabares
Penny Major, Eleanor's sister	Judy Kahan
Mac Slattery, the truck driver	Dennis Burkley
Harmon Farinella, Loretta's admirer	Richard Hatch
Reverend Brim	Orson Bean
Jerry Hubbard, Loretta's manager	Fred Willard
Bob Truss, the loan shark	Ben Piazza
Elke Sommer, the actress	Herself
Sal DiVito, Bob's assistant	Joe Penny
Mickey Mo Jeeter, Merle's brother	Tony Palmer
Dr. Popesco, the balloonist	Severn Darden
Jeffrey DiVito, Sal's brother	Randall Carver
Mel Beach, Martha's lover of 30 years ago	Shelly Berman
Annabelle Kearns, the psycho who believes she is Mary Hartman	Renee Taylor
Nat Dearden, the lawyer	Lou Frizzell
Eva, the marriage counselor	Nancy Malone
Piersall, the government agent	Ronnie Schell

Music: Bobby Knight.
Executive Producer: Norman Lear.
Producer: Eugenie Ross-Leming, Brad Buckner.
Director: Jim Drake, Dennis

Klein, Randy Winburn, Alejandro Rey.
Creator: Gail Parent, Ann Marcus, Jerry Adelman, Daniel Gregory Browne.

FOREVER FERNWOOD — 30 minutes — Syndicated 1977.

*The closing episode of *Mary Hartman* found Mary leaving her husband Tom to run off with her lover, Police Sgt. Dennis Foley.

†George, an auto plant assembly line worker, fell asleep on a conveyor belt and was dumped into a vat of Rustoleum. Extensive plastic surgery changed the original George (Phil Bruns) into the new George (Tab Hunter). Several months later, after being severely burned in an auto accident, surgery was again performed and the old George (Phil Bruns) emerged again.

414   FORMBY'S ANTIQUE WORKSHOP

Advice. Hints concerning the repair and care of furniture.

Host: Homer Formby.
Hostess-Announcer-Assistant: Marge Thrasher.
Producer: Bob Honoroe.
Director: John Wulf.

FORMBY'S ANTIQUE WORKSHOP — 30 minutes — Syndicated 1975.

415   FOR RICHER, FOR POORER

Serial. Dramatic incidents in the lives of two families, the Saxtons and the Cushings, residents of the town of Point Claire near Boston. A revamped and updated version of *Lovers and Friends*.

CAST

Bentley Saxton	David Abbott
Bill Saxton	Tom Harper
Austin Cushing	Rod Arrants
Megan Cushing	Darlene Parks
Tessa Saxton	Breon Gorman
Edith Cushing	Laurinda Barrett
Viola Brewster	Patricia Barry
Eleanor Kimball	Flora Plumb
Connie Ferguson	Cynthia Bostick
Geroge Kimball	Stephen Joyce
Rachel Corey	Victoria Wyndham
Amy Gifford	Christine Jones
Laurie Hamilton	Julia MacKenzie
Lester Saxton	Albert Stratton
Jason	Richard Backus
Roger Hamilton	Charles Bateman
Dean Ferguson	Robert Burton
Paco	Chu Chu Malone
Corinne Griffin	Nancy Snyder
Barbara Manners	Lynne MacLaren
Dr. Roy White	Dennis Romer

Music: Score Productions.
Executive Producer: Paul Rauch.
Producer: Harriet Goldstein, John Wendall.
Director: Jack Hofsiss, Barnet Kellman.
Creator: Harding Lemay.

FOR RICHER, FOR POORER — 30 minutes — NBC — December 6, 1977 – September 29, 1978. 200 episodes.

416   FOR THE LOVE OF ADA

Comedy. The British series on which America's *A Touch of Grace* is based. The series, which has not been telecast in the United States, focuses on the romantic misadventures of two old-age pensioners (senior citizens): Ada Cresswell and Walter Bingley.

CAST

Ada Cresswell	Irene Handl
Walter Bingley	Wilfred Pickles
Ruth Pollitt, Ada's overbearing daughter	Barbara Mitchell
Leslie Pollitt, Ruth's hen-pecked husband	Jack Smethurst

Creator: Vince Powell, Harry Driver.

FOR THE LOVE OF ADA — 30 minutes. Produced and telecast in England on Thames TV from 1970-1972.

417   FOUR-IN-ONE

Drama. The overall title for four rotating series: *McCloud, Night Gallery, The Psychiatrist,* and *San Francisco International Airport.* See individual titles for information.

FOUR-IN-ONE — 60 minutes — NBC — September 16, 1970 – September 8, 1971.

418   FRED AND BARNEY MEET THE THING

Animated Cartoon.

Segments:

Fred and Barney. Newly animated adventures in the lives of Fred and Wilma Flintstone and their friends Barney and Betty Rubble.

VOICES

Fred Flintstone	Henry Corden
Wilma Flintstone, Fred's wife	Jean VanderPyl
Barney Rubble, their neighbor	Mel Blanc
Betty Rubble, Barney's wife	Janet Waldo

The Thing. The story of Benji Grimm, a high school student who, when the need arises, changes himself into the Thing, an orange hulk he uses to help good defeat evil. (By placing two halves of a ring together, and speaking the words "Thing ring do your thing," Benji becomes the Thing; by again touching the ring halves, which he wears one on each hand, he returns to normal.)

VOICES

Thing	Joe Baker
Benjy	Wayne Morton
Benjy's friend Kelly	Noelle North
Benjy's friend Betty	Marilyn Schreffler
Spike, the bully	Art Metrano
Ronald, the rich kid	John Erwin
Miss Twilly, the teacher	Marilyn Schreffler

Series Credits:
Music: Hoyt Curtin.
Executive Producer: William Hanna, Joseph Barbera.
Producer: Alex Lovy.
Director: Ray Patterson, George Gordon, Carl Urbano.

FRED AND BARNEY MEET THE THING — 55 minutes — NBC — September 22, 1979 – December 1, 1979. As *Fred and Barney Meet the Shmoo* — 90 minutes — NBC — Premiered: December 8, 1979. For information on *The Shmoo* see *The New Shmoo*, the series that was broadcast before it combined with *Fred and Barney*.

419 FRED FLINTSTONE AND FRIENDS

Animated Cartoon. The series features excerpts from the Hanna-Barbera produced series originally broadcast by the various networks on Saturday mornings: *The Flintstones Comedy Hour, Goober and the Ghost Chasers, Jeannie, Partridge Family: 2200 A.D.* (retitled *The Partridge Family in Space*), *Pebbles and Bamm Bamm,* and *Yogi's Gang.* See individual titles for information.

Program Host: Fred Flintstone (voiced first by Alan Reed, then Henry Corden).
Executive Producer: William Hanna, Joseph Barbera.
Producer: Iwao Takamoto.
Director: Charles A. Nichols.

FRED FLINTSTONE AND FRIENDS — 30 minutes — Syndicated 1977.

420 FREE COUNTRY

Comedy. The series, set in Manhattan (New York), focuses on the lives of Joseph and Anna Bresner, Lithuanian immigrants, from 1909 to 1978. The program opens with Joseph at 89 as he talks about his life. Flashback sequences are used to highlight the events of both his and Anna's arrival and struggles in a new land.

CAST

Joseph Bresner	Rob Reiner
Anna Bresner, his wife	Judy Kahan
Ida Gewertzman, their friend	Renee Lippin
Sidney Gewertzman, Ida's husband	Fred McCarren
Leo Gold, their friend	Larry Gelman
Louie Peschi, their friend	Joe Pantoliano
Willie Bresner, Joe's cousin	Larry Hankin

Music: Jack Elliott, Allyn Ferguson.

Executive Producer: Rob Reiner, Phil Mishkin.
Producer: Gareth Davies.
Director: Hal Cooper, James Burrows.
Creator: Rob Reiner, Phil Mishkin.

FREE COUNTRY — 30 minutes — ABC — June 24, 1978 – July 22, 1978. 5 episodes.

421 THE FRENCH ATLANTIC AFFAIR

Drama. A three-part miniseries, based on the novel by Ernest Lehman, that details the hijacking of a luxury liner by religious cultists who demand $70 million in ransom.

CAST

Harold Columbine	Chad Everett
Father Craig Dunleavy	Telly Savalas
Jennie	Michelle Phillips
Capt. Charles Girodt	Louis Jourdan
Helen Wabash	Shelley Winters
Julian	Richard Jordan
Dr. Chabot	Horst Bucholz
Louise	Stella Stevens
Lisa	Marie-France Pisier
Maggie Joy	Dana Hill
Sauvinage	James Coco
Billy	Dennis Dimster
Herb	John Rubinstein
Don Crawford	Bill Lucking
Dechambre	Donald Pleasence
Raffin	Jean Pierre Aumont
President Broussard	Jose Ferrer
Terrence Crown	Richard Anderson
Clemens	John Houseman
Admiral Knox	Dane Clark
Harriet	Rebecca Balding
Brother Abe	Dan O'Brien
Brother Paul	Martin Costi
Wendell Cornin	Mark Gorman
Betty	Deborah Benson
Claude	Paul Verdier
Bobo	Peter Schrum
Jerry Dunphy	Himself
Plessier	Harvey Jason
Mrs. Joy	Melissa Converse
Brother David	John Sheren
Tony	Frank McCarthy
Tony's wife	Ellen Blake
Earl	James Jeeter
Brian Joy	Dennis Howard
Mme. Grilley	Jacqueline Beer
Fleschmann	Duane Grey
Brother Thomas	Michael Carr
Barney	Kenneth White
Barney's wife	Gwen Van Dane
Lanner	Peter Mamakos
Plainclothes Detective	Eric Holland
Controller	John Parks
Keegan	Lee DeBraux

Music: John Addison.
Supervising Producer: E. Duke Vincent.
Executive Producer: Aaron Spelling, Douglas S. Cramer.
Producer: Robert Mintz.
Writer: Douglas Heyes.
Director: Douglas Heyes.

THE FRENCH ATLANTIC AFFAIR — 2 hours (6 hrs. total) — ABC — November 15, 1979 – November 18, 1979. 3 episodes.

422 FRIDAYS

Comedy. A satiric and humorous look at the foibles of modern society. Broadcast live from Los Angeles on Friday evenings from 11:30 p.m. to 12:40 a.m. (seen live in the East; on videotape on the West Coast).

Cast: Mark Blankfield, Maryedith Burrell, Melanie Chartoff, Larry David, Darrow Igus, Michael Richards, Brandis Kemp, Bruce Mahler, John Roarke, Kenny Loggins.

Announcer: Jack Burns.
Orchestra: Fred Thaler.
Executive Producer: Bill Lee, John Moffitt.
Producer: Vic Kaplan.
Director: John Moffitt.

FRIDAYS — 70 minutes — ABC — Premiered: April 11, 1980.

423 FRIENDS

Comedy-Drama. A seriocomic look at growing pains as seen through the eyes and experiences of Pete Richards, Nancy Wilks and Randy Summerfield, three eleven-year-olds who live in Westerby, California.

CAST

Pete Richards	Charles Aiken
Nancy Wilks	Jill Whelan
Randy Summerfield	Jarrod Johnson
Frank Richards, Pete's father	Andy Romano
Pamela Richards, Pete's mother	Karen Morrow
Cynthia Richards, Pete's sister	Alicia Fleer
Warren Summerfield, Randy's father	Roger Robinson
Jane Summerfield, Randy's mother	Janet MacLachlan
Tug Summerfield, Warren's father	Charles Lampkin
Charlie Wilks, Nancy's father	Dennis Redfield
Bill, the school bus driver	Lew Horn

Music: Fred Karlin.
Supervising Producer: E. Duke Vincent.
Executive Producer: Aaron Spelling, Douglas S. Cramer.
Producer: Bob Sand, Bo Kaprall, Cindy Levin, Glenn Jordan.
Director: Arnold Laven, Glenn Jordan, Buddy Tyne, Roger Duchowny.

FRIENDS — 60 minutes — ABC — March 25, 1979 – April 22, 1979. 5 episodes.

FRIENDS AND LOVERS

See title *Paul Sand in Friends and Lovers.*

424 FROM A BIRD'S EYE VIEW

Comedy. The series, set in London, follows the misadventures of two International Airline stewardesses: Millie Grover, British, meddlesome and scatterbrained; and Maggie Ralston, her partner, a level-headed American on loan from the U.S. to International's European division.

CAST

Stewardess Millie Grover	Millicent Martin
Stewardess Maggie Ralston	Pat Finley
Clyde Beachamp, the personnel director	Peter Jones
Bert Grover, Millie's uncle	Robert Cawdron
Miss Fosdyke, Clyde's secretary	Noel Hood

Music: Frank Barber.
Producer: Ralph Levy.

FROM A BIRD'S EYE VIEW — 30 minutes — NBC — March 29, 1971 – August 16, 1971. 18 episodes.

425 FROM HERE TO ETERNITY

Drama. A three-part miniseries, based on the novel by James Jones. Set in Hawaii in 1941, the story focuses on military life on the eve of the attack on Pearl Harbor (December 7).

CAST

Karen Holmes	Natalie Wood
Sgt. Milt Warden	William Devane
Pvt. Robert E. Lee Pruitt	Steve Railsback
Capt. Dana Holmes	Roy Thinnes
Pvt. Angelo Maggio	Joe Pantoliano
Lorene Rogers	Kim Basinger
Cpl. Cheney (later Sgt.)	Will Sampson
Pfc. Hanson	Rick Hurst
Gert Kipfer	Salome Jens
Pfc. Stack	Andrew Robinson
General Slater	Andy Griffith
Sgt. James "Fatso" Hudson	Peter Boyle
Lt. David Ross	David Spielberg
Col. Jake Delgant	Richard Venture
Sgt. Doehm	Richard Bright
Cpl. Leva	Wynn Irwin
Violet	Morgan Kester
Sgt. McKay	Ron Max
Cpl. Lewis	Christopher Murney
Della	Dea St. Lamount
Cpl. Kowalski	Gene Scherer
Cpl. Herbert	Gary Swanson
Sgt. Preem	Kenneth White
Suzie	Sally Kim
Raven	Bebe Louie
Sam the Cabbie	Clem Low
Tawny	Karin Mani
Colleen	Victoria Perry
China	Julia Sabre
Zola	Mariko Tse
Chip Holmes	Jonathan B. Woodward
Doctor	Allan G. Wood

Music: Walter Scharf.
Big Band Music: Shorty Rogers.
Vocals: Helen O'Connell, The Modernaires.
Executive Producer: Harve Bennett, Harris Katleman.
Producer: Buzz Kulik.
Writer: Don McGuire.
Director: Buzz Kulik.
Art Director: Ross Bellah, Robert Peterson.
Director of Photography: Gerald Perry Finnerman.

FROM HERE TO ETERNITY — 2 hours (6 hours total) — NBC — February 14, 1979 – February 28, 1979. 3 episodes.

426 FROM HERE TO ETERNITY

Drama. A continuation of the miniseries of the same title. The series, set in Hawaii in the aftermath of the attack on Pearl Harbor during World War II, accents the personal crises of the military personnel (of G Company, 24th Infantry Division) and the civilians with whom they come in contact during wartime. Based on the novel by James Jones; adapted for television by Harold Gast.

CAST

Sgt. Milt Warden — William Devane
Major Dana Holmes — Roy Thinnes
Karen Holmes, Dana's unfaithful wife — Barbara Hershey
Lorene Rogers, the prostitute — Kim Basinger
Gert Kipfer, the madam — Salome Jens
Jeff Pruitt, Robert's brother; from miniseries; killed in action — Don Johnson
Emily Austin, the society girl — Lacey Neuhaus
Lt. David Ross — David Spielberg
Spencer Austin, Karen's father — Richard Roat
Amelia Austin, Karen's mother — Priscilla Pointer
Lt. Ken Barrett — John Calvin
Pfc. Ignacio Carmona — Rocky Echevarria
Sgt. Cheney — Will Sampson
Lt. George Bennington — Colby Chester
Pfc. Moss — Gino Ardito
Colonel Harry Thompson — John Crawford
Lt. Rosemary Clark — Joan Goodfellow
Joan Driscoll
Private Ridgely — Michael Jeter
Dr. Miyamoto — Ted Hamaguchi
Curt Von Nordland, the book shop owner — Richard Erdman
Dr. Anne Brewster — Claire Malis
Private Dazovik — Robert Phillips
Della, the maid in the New Congress Hotel (a brothel) — Dea St. Lamount
Raven, a prostitute — Bebe Louie
Suzie, a prostitute — Sally Kim
Rose, a prostitute — Janet Wood
The Holmes's butler — Larry Cook
Aimee, Carmona's girlfriend — JoAnn Gordon
Nurse — Deirdre Lenihan
Nurse — Wendy Oakes
Sgt. James "Fatso" Hudson* — Claude Jones
Pvt. Robert Pruitt* — Gary Swanson

Story Line Recap Narration: William Devane.
Music: Walter Scharf, Richard Clements.
Supervising Producer: Lionel E. Siegel.
Executive Producer: Harve Bennett, Harris Katleman.
Producer: Carl Pingitore.
Writer: Rudy Day, Tony Palmer, James D. Parriott, R. A. Ruso, Allen Williams.
Director: Ron Satlof, Rick Hauser, James D. Parriott, Ray Austin, Harry Mastrogeorge, Jeffrey Hayden.
Art Director: Ross Bellah, Robert Purcell.

FROM HERE TO ETERNITY—60 minutes—NBC—March 10, 1980—April 9, 1980. 5 episodes. 2 hours—NBC—August 3, 1980—August 5, 1980 (actually six one-hour episodes that were re-edited into three two-hour episodes). The final episode, "Hello, Goodbye, and Farewell," aired for 60 minutes on NBC on August 16, 1980 (an unscheduled presentation that preempted *The 6 O'Clock Follies* and *Good Time Harry* on that date).

*First episode only to show how, in the miniseries, Pruitt killed Fatso and was later killed himself; and to introduce Jeff, who seeks to learn the fate of his brother.

427 THE FUN FACTORY

Variety. Music, comedy, songs and various game contests wherein studio audience members vie for cash and merchandise prizes.

Host: Bobby Van.
Regulars: Betty Thomas (as the housewife), Jane Nelson, Doug Steckler, Dick Blasucci, Deborah Harmon.
Model: Jane Nelson.
Announcer: Jim Thompson.
Orchestra: Stan Worth.
Executive Producer: Ed Fishman, Randall Freer.
Producer: Doug Fishman.
Director: Walter C. Miller, Tom Trbovichi.

THE FUN FACTORY—30 minutes—NBC—June 14, 1976—October 1, 1976. 75 programs.

428 THE FUNKY PHANTOM

Animated Cartoon. The exploits of Jonathan "Musty" Muddlemore, a spirit,* and his friends April, Skip and Augie, as they battle the sinister forces of evil.

VOICES

Jonathan Muddlemore — Daws Butler
April Stewart — Kristina Holland
Skip — Mickey Dolenz
Augie — Tommy Cook

The Gang dog: Elmo.
Musty's cat: Boo.

Additional Voices: Julie Bennett, Jerry Dexter.
Music: John Sangster.
Executive Producer: William Hanna, Joseph Barbera.
Producer: Charles Nichols.
Director: William Hanna, Joseph Barbera.

THE FUNKY PHANTOM—30 minutes—ABC—September 11, 1971—September 1, 1972. Syndicated.

*In 1776, Muddlemore ran into a deserted mansion and hid in a large grandfather clock to escape the British soldiers who were pursuing him. Unfortunately, the clock door locked from the outside and trapped him. Almost 200 years later his spirit is released and befriended by April, Skip and Augie when they find the deserted mansion and set the clock to its correct time.

429 FUNNY FACE

Comedy. The series, set in Los Angeles, follows the life of Sandy Stockton, a student teacher enrolled at U.C.L.A., and a part-time actress employed by the Prescott Advertising Agency.

CAST

Sandy Stockton — Sandy Duncan
Alice MacRaven, her friend — Valorie Armstrong
Pat Harwell, her landlord — Henry Beckman
Kate Harwell, Pat's wife — Kathleen Freeman
Maggie Prescott, Sandy's employer — Nita Talbot

Music: Patrick Williams.
Executive Producer: Jerry Davis.
Producer: Carl Kleinschmitt.
Director: Hal Cooper.

FUNNY FACE—30 minutes—CBS—September 18, 1971—December 11, 1971. 13 episodes. See also *The Sandy Duncan Show.*

430 THE FUNNY SIDE

Satire. The funny side of everyday life as seen through the eyes of five couples.

The Couples: The Blue Collar Couple: Warren Berlinger, Pat Finley. The Sophisticated Couple: Dick Clair, Jenna McMahon. The Young Couple: Michael Lembeck, Cindy Williams. The Middle-Class Black Couple: John Amos, Teresa Graves. The Senior Citizen Couple: Burt Mustin, Queenie Smith.

Host: Gene Kelly.
Orchestra: Jack Elliott, Allyn Ferguson.
Special Musical Material: Ray Charles.
Additional Music: David Fishberg.
Producer: Bill Persky, Sam Denoff.
Writer: Norman Barasch, Michael Elias, Arnold Kane, Pat McCormick, Mickey Rose, Sanford Sheldon, Bill Persky, Sam Denoff, Bob Garland, Carroll Moore, Gordon Farr, Arnie Koger.
Director: Clark Jones.

THE FUNNY SIDE—60 minutes—NBC—September 14, 1971—December 28, 1971. 13 programs.

431 FUTURE COP

Crime Drama. The cases of Joe Cleaver, Bill Bundy and John "Kid" Haven, officers with the Los Angeles Police Department. Unknown to Bundy, Haven is an android rookie programmed to be the perfect cop, and has been secretly assigned to Cleaver for training in the field.

CAST

Officer Joe Cleaver — Ernest Borgnine
Officer Bill Bundy — John Amos
Officer John Haven — Michael Shannon
Captain Skaggs, their superior — Herbert Nelson
Dr. Tingley, Haven's creator — Irene Tsu
Peggy, the waitress at Hennessey's, the café frequented by Joe and Bill — Angela May

Music: J. J. Johnson.
Executive Producer: Anthony Wilson, Gary Damsker.
Producer: Everett Chambers.
Director: Robert Douglas, Earl Bellamy, Vincent McEveety.

FUTURE COP—60 minutes—ABC—March 5, 1977—April 22, 1977. Returned with an additional episode on August 6, 1977. The 90-minute pilot film aired on ABC on May 1, 1976. On March 28, 1978, NBC aired "The Cops and Robin," an unsold 90-minute pilot attempt to revive the *Future Cop* series with Ernest Borgnine, John Amos and Michael Shannon reviving their roles.

G

432 GALACTICA 1980

Science Fiction Adventure. A continuation of the series, *Battlestar Galactica,* which see for background information. After many years in space, the starship *Galactica* reaches Earth in the year 1980. The Galacticans, however, are unable to land on the planet, fearing they will bring with them their enemies, the waring Cylons and destruction.* The series focuses on the Galacticans' attempts to advance Earth's technology to a point where it can fend off aliens; and on Galacticans Troy and Dillon and a group of Galactican children who are sent to Earth as scouts to pave the way for the remainder of the alien population to settle on our planet.

CAST

Commander Adama, the Galactican leader — Lorne Greene
Captain Troy, a Galactican — Kent McCord
Lieutenant Dillon, a Galactican — Barry Van Dyke
Dr. Zee, the Galactican's scientific genius — Robbie Rist
Patrick Stuart
Jamie Hamilton, the Earth girl who helps Troy and Dillon; a United Broadcasting Company TV reporter — Robyn Douglass
Colonel Boomer, a Galactican — Herbert Jefferson, Jr.

Mr. Brooks, Jamie's
employer   Fred Holliday
Xavier, the renegade Galactican
who escapes into
time to change
Earth's past   Richard Lynch
Colonel Sydell, the U.S.
Air Force agent seeking
Troy and Dillon   Allan Miller
Anne, Mr. Brooks's secretary Sharon Acker
Dr. Donald Mortinson, the Earth
scientist who befriends
Troy and Dillon   Robert Reed
Miss Carlyle, Donald's
secretary   Pamela Shoop

The Galactican Children: Lindsay Kennedy, Michael Brick, Jeff Cotler, Mark Everett, Nicholas Davis, Ronnie Densford, Tracy Justrich, David Larson, Eric Larson, Georgi Irene, Eric Taslitz, Jerry Supiran, Michele Larson.

Theme Narration: Lorne Greene.
Music: Stu Phillips, Glen A. Larson.
Theme: "Galactica Song" by John Andrew Tartiglia.
Supervising Producer: David J. O'Connell.
Executive Producer: Glen A. Larson.
Producer: Gary B. Winter, Jeff Freilich, Ben Kadish, Frank Lupo, David Zanetos.
Director: Sidney Hayers, Vince Edwards, Barry Crane, Sigmund Neufeld, Jr., Daniel Haller, Ron Satlof.

GALACTICA 1980 — 60 minutes — ABC — January 27, 1980 — February 10, 1980. 3 episodes. March 16, 1980 — May 4, 1980. 6 episodes. Rebroadcasts: June 29, 1980 — August 17, 1980.

*The Cylons, a robot society, seek to destroy humans because they fear they present a threat to their existence.

433   THE GALAXY GOOFUPS

Animated Cartoon. The antics of Officers Yogi Bear and Huckleberry Hound, members of the Galaxy Goofups, a futuristic, celestial police force.

VOICES
Officer Yogi Bear   Daws Butler
Officer Huckleberry Hound Daws Butler
The General, their
superior   John Stephenson

Additional Characters: Officer Quack Up, Officer Scare Bear and Captain Snurdly, the general's aide.

Additional Voices: Richard Behr, Joe Besser, Ted Cassidy, Don Messick, Janet Waldo, Henry Corden, Joan Gerber, Lennie Weinrib, Jim MacGeorge.

Music: Hoyt Curtin.
Executive Producer: William Hanna, Joseph Barbera.

Producer: Art Scott.
Director: Ray Patterson.

THE GALAXY GOOFUPS — 30 minutes — NBC — November 4, 1978 — March 3, 1979.

434   GAMBIT

Game. Two married couples compete in a game based on blackjack (21). An oversized deck of fifty-two playing cards is opened and the first card is revealed. A general-knowledge question is read and the first team to correctly answer it receives the option of either keeping or passing the exposed card. Questions (and cards) continue with each team seeking to score as close as possible to twenty-one without going over. Winning couples receive $100 per game and compete until defeated.

Host: Wink Martindale.
Dealer: Elaine Stewart.
Announcer: Kenny Williams.
Music: Mort Garson.
Executive Producer: Merrill Heatter, Bob Quigley.
Producer: Robert Noah.
Director: Jerome Shaw.

GAMBIT — 30 minutes — CBS — September 4, 1972 — December 10, 1976. 910 programs.

435   GAMES PEOPLE PLAY

Human Interest. A review of sporting games and contests in which average people compete. See also *The Sunday Games* in the pilot film section.

Host: Bryant Gumbel.
Co-Hosts: Donna de Varona, Cyndy Garvey, Johnny Bench, Mike Adamle, Ian Wooldridge.
Announcer: Gary Owens.
Music: Roger Nichols.
Executive Producer: Don Ohlmeyer.
Producer: Howard Katz.
Co-Producer: Jim Cross.
Writer: Norman Bleichman, Dennis Snee, Howard Katz, Don Ohlmeyer.
Director: Jim Cross.
Senior Staff Producer: Chris Pye.
Coordinating Producer: Don Azares.
Art Director: Bob Keene.

GAMES PEOPLE PLAY — 60 minutes — NBC — August 21, 1980 — December 25, 1980.

436   THE GEMINI MAN

Science Fiction Adventure. While attempting to recover a space capsule from the ocean, Intersect Agent Sam Casey is caught in an underwater explosion that, due to heavy radiation, effects his DNA molecular field structure and causes invisibility. By incorporating a sophisticated subminiature DNA stabilizer in a nuclear

powered digital wristwatch, Dr. Abby Lawrence finds a means by which to control Casey's invisibility: when the three gold contacts on the base of the watch touch his skin, he remains visible; however, by pressing the stem of the watch, Sam can change the frequency and revert to invisibility for a limit of fifteen minutes a day; any longer and he will disintegrate. Stories depict Sam's assignments on behalf of Intersect (International Security Technics), a U.S. government research organization.

CAST
Sam Casey   Ben Murphy
Dr. Abby Lawrence   Katherine Crawford
Leonard Driscoll, their superior
(pilot film)   Richard A. Dysart
Leonard Driscoll (series) William Sylvester

Music: Lee Holdridge, Mark Snow.
Executive Producer: Harve Bennett.
Producer: Leslie Stevens, Frank Telford.
Director: Alan J. Levi, Michael Caffey, Charles R. Rondeau.

THE GEMINI MAN — 60 minutes — NBC — September 23, 1976 — October 28, 1976. 5 episodes. The two-hour pilot film aired on NBC on May 10, 1976.

437   GENERAL HOSPITAL

Serial. Intimate glimpses into the personal and professional lives of the doctors and nurses attached to the Internal Medicine Division, seventh floor, of General Hospital.

CAST
Dr. Steve Hardy	John Beradino
Audrey March	Rachel Ames
Nurse Iris Fairchild	Peggy McCay
Brooke Clinton	Indus Arthur
Al Weeks	Tom Brown
Sharon Pinkham	Sharon DeBord
Carol Murray	Nancy Pinkard
Howie Dawson	Ray Girardin
Lee Baldwin	Peter Hansen
Jane Dawson	Shelby Hiatt
Mrs. Dawson	Phyllis Hill
Dr. Peter Taylor	Craig Huebing
Diana Taylor	Valerie Starrett
	Davey Davison
	Brooke Bundy
Pat Lambert	Laura Campbell
Nurse Jesse Brewer	Lois Kibbee
	Emily McLaughlin
	Aneta Corsaut
Lisa	Janice Heiden
Dorrie Fleming	Angela Cheyne
Heather Grant	Mary O'Brien
David Hamilton	Jerry Ayres
Dr. Monica Webber	Patsy Ryan
	Iris Garrison
	Leslie Carleson
Laura Vining	Stacey Baldwin
	Genie Francis
Eddie Weeks	Craig Curtis
	Doug Lambert

Dr. Jeff Webber	Richard Dean Anderson
	Scott Mulhern
	Rick Anderson
Mrs. Grant	Camilla Ashland
	Lieux Dressler
Lamont Corbin	George E. Carey
	William Bryant
Dr. Mark Dante	Michael DeLano
	Gerald Gordon
	Vincent Baggetta
Tracy Quartermaine	Jane Elliot
Bryan Phillips	Todd Davis
Maria Schuller	Maria Perschy
Herbert Behrman	Richard Venture
Dr. Rick Webber	Michael Gregory
	Chris Robinson
Dr. Henry Pinkham	Peter Kilman
Nurse Kendell Jones	Joan Tompkins
Dr. Thomas Baldwin	Paul Savior
Nurse Lucille March	Lucille Wall
Peggy Mercer	K.T. Stevens
Angie Costello	Jana Taylor
Dr. Phil Brewer	Roy Thinnes
	Martin West
	Robert Hogan
Dr. Lyons	Martin Blaini
Randy	Mark Miller
Dr. Leslie Williams	Denise Alexander
Meg Bentley	Patricia Breslin
Mary Briggs	Anne Helm
Clampett	Robin Blake
Scotty	Tony Campo
Beverly Cleveland	Sue Bernard
Mrs. Nelson	Ann Morrison
The District Attorney	Ivan Bonar
Lieutenant Adams	Don Hammer
Denise Wilson	Julie Adams
Mrs. Bailey	Florence Lindstrom
Polly Prentice	Jennifer Billingsley
Nurse Linda Cooper	Linda Cooper
Augusta McLeod	Judith McConnell
Dr. James Hobart	James Sikking
Gordon Gray	Eric Server
Florence Grey	Ann Collings
Mr. Chamberlain	Ed Platt
Marge	Mae Clark
Johnny	Butch Patrick
Dr. Miller	Ed Platt
Secretary	Iris Fairchild
Janie Dawson	Shelly Hiatt
Ling Wang	George Chiang
Mailin	Virginia Ann Lee
Ann Coheen	Virginia Grey
Dr. Joel Stratton	Rod McCarey
Owen Stratton	Joel Mareden
Kira Faulkner	Victoria Shaw
Wallace Baxter	Len Wayland
Heather Grant	Georganne LaPiere
Sally Grimes	Jenny Sherman
Cameron Faulkner	Don Matheson
Chase Murdock	Ivan Bonner
Martha Taylor	Jennifer Peters
Dr. Adam Streeter	Brett Halsey
Teri Arnett	Bobbi Jordan
Mary Ellen Dante	Lee Warick
Barbara Vining	Judy Lewis
Dr. Eric Lombard	Ivor Francis
Spence	Dan Travanti
Larry Joe Baker	Hunter Von Leer
Tommy	Bradley Greene
Stephen Lars	Robert Beitzel
Gina	Donna Bacalla
Gloria Roberts	Kate Carlson
Barbara Spencer	Jackie Zeman
Kent Murray	Mark Hamill
Carol Murray	Anne Wyndham
Teddy Holmes	John Gabriel
Darren Blythe	Bill Schreiner
Edna Hadley	Leslie Wood

Flying High. From left, Kathryn Witt, guest star George
Gobel and Connie Sellecca.

George and Mildred. Brian Murphy and Yootha Joyce.
Courtesy of Kevin Schluter, *TV Times* magazine, Sydney,
Australia.

The Ghost and Mrs. Muir. At left, Kellie Flanagan (bottom)
and Charles Nelson Reilly. At right, from bottom, Harlen
Carraher, Hope Lange and Edward Mulhare.

The Ghost Busters. From left, Forrest Tucker, Larry Storch
and Tracy (portrayed by Bob Burns).

Tom Baldwin	Don Chastain
Beth Maynard	Michele Conway
Margaret Colson	Betty Ann Rees
Mrs. Chandler	Augusta Dabney
Roy Lansing	Robert Clarke
Cynthia Allison	Carolyn Craig
Philip Mercer	Neil Hamilton
Priscilla Longworth	Allison Hayes
Mrs. Weeks	Lenore Kingston
Mike Costello	Ralph Manza
Dr. Ken Martin	Hunt Powers
Roy DeLucca	Asher Brauner
Dr. Gail Baldwin	Susan Brown
Thelma	Helena Carroll
Miss O'Neal	Carol Cook
Dr. Alan Quartermaine	Stuart Damon
Claudia	Bianca Ferguson
Maggie	Nancy Fox
Luke Spencer	Anthony Geary
Tom Baldwin, Jr.	Bradley Green
Lila Quartermaine	Anna Lee
Edward Quartermaine	David Lewis
Dr. Todd Levine	Craig Littler
Dan Rooney	Frank Maxwell
Chris	Christopher Nelson
Heather Webber	Mary O'Brien
Ann Logan	Susan O'Hanlon
Mitch Williams	Chris Pennock
Susan Moore	Gail Rae
Howard	Richard Sarradet
Joe Kelly	Doug Sheehan
Scotty Baldwin	Kin Shriner
Jeremy Hewitt	Philip Tanzini
Bobbi	Jackie Zeman-Kaufman

Musical Director: George Wright.
Executive Producer: Gerald Jaskulski.
Producer: James Young, Gene Banks, Lucy Ferri, Tom Donovan, Gloria Monty.
Director: Marlena Laird, Alan Pultz, Phil Sogard.

GENERAL HOSPITAL — 30 minutes — ABC — April 1, 1963 – July 23, 1976. 45 minutes — ABC — July 26, 1976 – January 13, 1978. 60 minutes — ABC — Premiered: January 16, 1978.

438   GEORGE AND MILDRED

Comedy. The British series on which America's *The Ropers* is based. The series, which has not been broadcast in the United States, is a spin-off from *Man About the House* (which see) and follows the misadventures of George and Mildred Roper, a bickering married couple, as they move to a better class neighborhood — a neighborhood George feels is full of "toffee-nosed snobs." (Their address: 46 Peacock Crescent, Hampton Wick, Middlesex, England.)

CAST

George Roper	Brian Murphy
Mildred Roper, his wife	Yootha Joyce
Jeffrey Fourmile, their snobbish neighbor	Norman Eshley
Anne Fourmile, Jeffrey's wife	Sheila Fearn
Tristram Fourmile, their son	Nicholas Bond-Owen
Ethel, Mildred's sister	Avril Elgar
Humphrey, Ethel's husband	Reginald Marsh
Hilda, Mildred's sister	Jean Marlow
Mildred's mother	Gretchen Franklin

Producer: Peter Frazer-Jones.
Designer: Michael Minas.
Director: Peter Frazer-Jones.
Creator: Johnnie Mortimer, Brian Cooke.

GEORGE AND MILDRED — 30 minutes. Produced and telecast in England on Thames TV from 1976 – 1979.

439   GEORGE OF THE JUNGLE

Animated Cartoon.

Segments:

George of the Jungle. The story, set in the Imgwee Gwee Valley in Africa, follows the exploits of George, the king of the jungle, a tree-crashing, simple-minded klutz who aids people in distress.

Additional Characters: Bella and Ursula, his native girlfriends; Ape, his overgrown gorilla; Shep, his elephant; Seymour, the man-eating plant; Wiggy, the rhino; and Tiger and Weavel, his enemies, who seek to foil his good deeds.

Super Chicken. The story of Henry Cabot Henhouse III, a mild-mannered scientist who discovers Super Sauce, a drink that transforms him into the daring crime fighter Super Chicken. Episodes relate his battle against the forces of evil. His assistant: Fred, the lion.

Tom Slick. The misadventures of Tom Slick, a simple-minded racing car driver. His aide: Marigold; his car: *The Thunderbolt Grease Slapper.*

Voices: Bill Scott (as George of the Jungle), June Foray, Paul Frees, Bill Conrad, Walter Tetley, Skip Craig, Barbara Baldwin.
Music: Sheldon Allman, Stan Worth.
Producer: Jay Ward, Bill Scott.

GEORGE OF THE JUNGLE — 30 minutes — ABC — September 9, 1967 – September 6, 1970. Syndicated.

440   GET CHRISTIE LOVE!

Crime Drama. The investigations of Christie Love, an undercover agent with the Los Angeles Police Department who encompasses beauty, charm, wit and an understanding of human nature as her weapons. The series is based in part on the real-life experiences of Olga Ford, a New York City Police Woman.

CAST

Christie Love	Teresa Graves
Lt. Matthew Reardon	Charles Cioffi
Captain Arthur P. Ryan	Jack Kelly
Lt. Steve Belmont	Dennis Rucker
Lt. Joe Caruso	Andy Romano
Officer Pete Gallagher	Michael Pataki
Detective Valencia	Scott Peters
Lt. Casey Reardon (pilot episode character for Matthew Reardon)	Harry Guardino

Christie's badge number: 7332.
Music: Jack Elliott, Allyn Ferguson, Luchi de Jesus.
Executive Producer: David L. Wolper, Laurence Turman.
Producer: Paul Mason, Peter Nelson, Glen A. Larson, Ron Satlof.
Director: William Graham, Glen A. Larson, Ron Satlof, Bruce Kessler, Phil Bondelli, Alex Grasshoff, Ivan Dixon, Gene Nelson.
Developed for Television by: Peter Nelson, George Kirgo.

GET CHRISTIE LOVE! — 60 minutes — ABC — September 11, 1974 – July 18, 1975. 22 episodes. The 90-minute pilot film aired on ABC on January 22, 1974.

441   GET SMART

Comedy. The exploits of Maxwell Smart, Secret Agent 86, a bumbling klutz, and his beautiful, level-headed female partner, Agent 99, the top operatives of C.O.N.T.R.O.L., an international spy organization dedicated to destroying the diabolical objectives of K.A.O.S., an international organization of evil. (To protect their identities in the presence of 99's mother, Max and The Chief, the head of the Washington branch of C.O.N.T.R.O.L., adopt the aliases of Maxwell Smart, a salesman for the Pontiac Greeting Card Company, and the Chief, Howard Clark, his employer. Unaware of her activities as a spy, 99's mother believes her daughter is Howard's secretary.)

CAST

Maxwell Smart, Agent 86	Don Adams
Agent 99 (real name not revealed)	Barbara Feldon
Thaddeus, The Chief	Edward Platt
Conrad Siegfried, the head of K.A.O.S.	Bernie Kopell
Starker, Siegfried's aide	King Moody
99's mother	Jane Dulo
Harry Hoo, the Oriental detective who assists Maxwell Smart	Joey Forman
C.O.N.T.R.O.L. Personnel:	
Agent Larrabee	Robert Karvelas
Hymie, the robot	Dick Gautier
Agent 13	David Ketchum
Agent 44	Victor French
Dr. Steele, the head of the crime lab	Ellen Weston
Professor Windish, a scientist	Robert Cornthwaite
Professor Carlson, a scientist	Stacy Keach
Dr. Bascomb, a scientist	George Ives
Charlie Watkins, a beautiful agent, supposedly a man in disguise	Angelique
Admiral Harold Harmon Hargrade, the former chief	William Schallert

C.O.N.T.R.O.L.'s dog agent: Fang (Agent K-13).
C.O.N.T.R.O.L.'s address: 123 Main Street, Washington, D.C.
Music: Irving Szathmary.
Executive Producer: Leonard B. Stern.
Producer: Jess Oppenheimer, Jay Sandrich, Bert Nodella, Arnie Rosen.
Director: James Komack, Tony Leader, David Alexander, Norman Abbott, Sidney Miller, Reza S. Badiyi, Bruce Bilson, Paul Bogart, Gary Nelson, Richard Donner, Earl Bellamy, Murray Golden, Joshua Shelley, Frank McDonald.
Creator: Mel Brooks, Buck Henry.

GET SMART — 30 minutes — NBC — September 18, 1965 – September 13, 1969. CBS — September 26, 1969 – September 11, 1970. 138 episodes. Syndicated.

442   GETTING READY

Children. Music, songs, puppet antics, arts and crafts, and related entertainment geared to children.

Hostess: Renee Sweeney.
Featured: The Ronn Bohn Puppets.
Music: Renee Sweeney.
Producer: Irene Berner.
Director: Paul Marquez.

GETTING READY — 30 minutes — Syndicated 1978.

443   GETTING TOGETHER

Comedy. The misadventures of Bobby Conway, a composer, and Lionel Poindexter, a tone-deaf lyricist, two unknown songwriters living in Los Angeles and anxiously awaiting success.

CAST

Bobby Conway	Bobby Sherman
Lionel Poindexter	Wes Stern
Jenny Conway, Bobby's sister	Susan Neher
Rita Simon, their landlady	Pat Carroll
Rudy Colcheck, Rita's boyfriend	Jack Burns

Music: George Duning, Hugo Montenegro, David Shire.
Songs Producer: Ward Sylvester.
Executive Producer: Bob Claver.
Producer: Paul Junger Witt.
Creator: Bernard Slade.

GETTING TOGETHER — 30 minutes — ABC — September 18, 1971 – January 8, 1972. 15 episodes.

444   THE GHOST AND MRS. MUIR

Comedy. Determined to rebuild her life after the death of her husband, Carolyn Muir, a freelance magazine writer, moves to

Schooner Bay, New England, and into Gull Cottage, which is haunted by the spirit of its nineteenth-century owner, Captain Daniel Gregg. The ghost, having passed away before he was able to complete his plans for the cottage's development, is determined to maintain his privacy and continue with his original goal. Stories relate Carolyn's efforts to make Gull Cottage her home despite the protests of the Captain.

CAST

Carolyn Muir	Hope Lange
Captain Daniel Gregg	Edward Mulhare
Jonathan Muir, Carolyn's son	Harlen Carraher
Candy Muir, Carolyn's daughter	Kellie Flanagan
Martha Grant, their housekeeper	Reta Shaw
Claymore Gregg, the Captain's nephew	Charles Nelson Reilly
Ed Peevey, Martha's boyfriend	Guy Raymond
Noorie Coolidge, the owner of the town lobster house restaurant	Dabbs Greer
Ed's friend	Gil Lamb

Muir family dog: Scruffy.
Music: Dave Grusin, Warren Barker, George Greeley.
Executive Producer: David Gerber.
Producer: Howard Leeds, Gene Reynolds, Stanley Rubin.
Director: Lee Philips, Gene Reynolds, John Erman, David Alexander, Ida Lupino, Hollingsworth Morse, Oscar Rudolph, Sherman Marks, Gary Nelson, Jay Sandrich, Carl Shain, Bruce Bilson.

THE GHOST AND MRS. MUIR—30 minutes. NBC—September 21, 1968–September 6, 1969. ABC—September 18, 1969–September 18, 1970. 50 episodes. Syndicated.

445   THE GHOST BUSTERS

Comedy. The comic escapades of Kong and Spencer, Ghost Busters, and their assistant, Tracy, a gorilla, as they battle and attempt to dematerialize the ghosts of legendary fiends.

CAST

Kong, the head of Ghost Busters, Inc.	Forrest Tucker
Eddie Spencer, his assistant	Larry Storch
Tracy, the gorilla	Bob Burns

Music: Yvette Blais, Jeff Michael.
Producer: Norman Abbott.
Director: Norman Abbott, Larry Preece.

THE GHOST BUSTERS—25 minutes—CBS—September 6, 1975–September 4, 1976.

446   GHOST STORY

Anthology. Suspense dramas relating the plight of people who are suddenly confronted with supernatural occurences.

Host: Sebastian Cabot (as Winston Essex, a mysterious psychic gentleman who introduces stories).
Music: Billy Goldenberg.
Executive Producer: William Castle.
Producer: Joel Rogosin.
Director: Paul Stanley, Robert Day, John Llewellyn Moxey, David Lowell Rich, Alexander Singer, Arnold Laven, Don McDougall, Jimmy Sangster, Leslie H. Martinson, Daryl Duke, Richard Donner.

Included:

Half a Death. The story of a ghost who beseeches her twin sister to join her in death.

Cast: Christina/Lisa: Pamela Franklin; Paula: Eleanor Parker; Ethan: Stephen Brooks; Jeremy: Andrew Duggan; Mrs. Eliscu: Signe Hasso; Charlie: Taylor Lacher.

House of Evil. The story of an old man, who possesses voodoo powers, and his chilling plan for revenge on his former son-in-law.

Cast: Grandpa: Melvyn Douglas; Tom: Richard Mulligan; Fran: Joan Hotchkis; Judy: Jodie Foster; Kevin: Brad Savage; Mrs. Rule: Mildred Dunnock; Dr. Parker: Alan Fudge.

Elegy for a Vampire. The story of David Wells, a college professor with an unquenchable thirst for human blood.

Cast: Prof. David Wells: Hal Linden; Owen Huston: Arthur O'Connell; Laura Benton: Marlyn Mason; Frank Simmons: Mike Farrell; Marne Simmons: Sheila Larken; Fern: Susan Foster; Dana: Heather North; Detective Thorpe: John Milford.

She Cries. The pilot episode about a young wife who is terrorized by the spirit of a hanging victim who refuses to be evicted from the home she loved when she was alive.

Cast: Eileen: Barbara Parkins; John: David Birney; Mrs. Ramsey: Jeanette Nolan; DeWitt: Sam Jaffe; Also: Allyn Ann McLerie, Caitlin Wyles, Ivor Francis, John Crawford.

GHOST STORY—60 minutes—NBC—September 15, 1972–December 29, 1972. The 60-minute pilot film aired on NBC on July 24, 1972. Spin-off series: *Circle of Fear.*

447   GIBBSVILLE

Drama. The series, set in Gibbsville, a Pennsylvania mining town during the 1940s, depicts events in the lives of its citizens as seen through the eyes of Ray Whitehead, reporter for the *Gibbsville Courier,* the town newspaper, a one-time prestigious foreign correspondent whose career and reputation have been destroyed by alcohol. Based on the short stories by John O'Hara.

CAST

Ray Whitehead	Gig Young
Jim Malloy, Ray's friend, a reporter	John Savage
Dr. Michael Malloy, Jim's father	Biff McGuire
Mrs. Malloy, Jim's mother	Peggy McCay
Pell, the city editor	Bert Remsen
Lefty Lintzie, the bartender	Frank Campanella

Music: Leonard Rosenman, Jack Elliott, Allyn Ferguson.
Executive Producer: David Gerber.
Producer: John Furia, Jr.
Director: Alexander Singer, Harry Harris, Alf Kjellin, Gene Levitt, Marc Daniels.

Program Open:
Ray: When I walk through the streets of Gibbsville, I see a small but growing town, a busy town with its roots deep in the coal-mined earth. But behind the closed doors and drawn curtains are the secret lives of its people. The lives of the wealthy and the poor, filled with ambition and need, love and hate, sorrow and private wars, and the dreams that make men go on. Behind the closed doors of Gibbsville lies the truth about this town, about any town. The real stories waiting to be told.

GIBBSVILLE—60 minutes—NBC—November 11, 1976–December 30, 1976. 8 episodes. The 90-minute pilot film, titled "John O'Hara's Gibbsville," aired on NBC on April 12, 1975.

448   GILLIGAN'S ISLAND

Comedy. The series, set on an uncharted island in the South Pacific, follows the misadventures of the seven members of the shipwrecked S.S. *Minnow,* a sight-seeing charter boat that was caught in and destroyed by a tropical storm at sea, as they struggle for survival and seek a way off the island.

CAST

Jonas Grumby, the skipper	Alan Hale, Jr.
Gilligan, the first-mate	Bob Denver
Ginger Grant, a beautiful movie actress	Tina Louise
Thurston Howell III, a millionaire	Jim Backus
Lovey Howell, Thurston's wife	Natalie Schafer
Mary Ann Summers, a pretty clerk from Kansas	Dawn Wells
Roy Hinkley, the professor, a brilliant scientist	Russell Johnson
Wrong Way Feldman, the pilot (an occasional visitor of the island; his plane: *Spirit of the Bronx*)	Hans Conried
Dr. Boris Balinkoff, the mad scientist from a nearby island	Vito Scotti

Music: Sherwood Schwartz, Johnny Williams, Herschel Burk Gilbert, Lyn Murray, Gerald Fried, Morton Stevens.
Theme: "The Ballad of Gilligan's Isle" by George Wyle and Sherwood Schwartz.
Theme Vocal: The Wellingtons.
Executive Producer: William Froug, Sherwood Schwartz.
Producer: Jack Arnold, Robert L. Rosen.
Director: Stanley Z. Cherry, Charles Norton, William D'Arcy, Ida Lupino, George M. Cahan, Jack Arnold, Jerry Hopper, John Rich, Tony Leader, David McDearmon, Hal Cooper, John Murray, Leslie Goodwins.
Creator: Sherwood Schwartz.

GILLIGAN'S ISLAND—30 minutes—CBS—September 26, 1964–September 3, 1967. 98 episodes. Syndicated. Spin-off series, which see *The New Adventures of Gilligan.*

449   GILLIGAN'S ISLAND: EXTENSION EPISODES

Comedy. Storylines, casts, and credits for the two extension episodes broadcast in 1978 and 1979, based on the original 1964–67 series.

Rescue From Gilligan's Island. The first extension episode, which takes place fifteen years later, finds the castaways escaping from the island, when, as a title wave approaches, they lash their huts together and form a large, odd-looking raft. Several days later they are rescued by the Coast Guard and brought to Hawaii where, after readjusting to civilization, each goes his separate way. Several months later, the former castaways reunite for a reunion cruise on the Skipper's new ship, the *Minnow II.* During the cruise, the ship is caught in a tropical storm and the seven castaways are again shipwrecked—on the same island on which they had spent the last fifteen years.

The Castaways On Gilligan's Island. The second extension episode continues the story from where "Rescue from Gilligan's Island" leaves off. Shortly after the shipwreck, Gilligan, the first-mate, finds the remains of two non-working World War II airplanes and through the efforts of the professor to combine parts from the two to make one plane, the castaways again depart from the island—and are again rescued by the Coast Guard when their craft malfunctions. When they are brought to Hawaii, Thurston Howell, the millionaire, decides to turn (Gilligan's) Island into a tropical resort. The story follows the misadventures of "The Shipwrecked Seven," now all partners in the resort, as they attempt to operate "The Castaways" resort island.

CAST

Jonas Grumby, the skipper	Alan Hale, Jr.
Gilligan, the first-mate	Bob Denver
Ginger Grant, the actress	Judith Baldwin
Thurston Howell III, the millionaire	Jim Backus
Lovey Howell, Thurston's wife	Natalie Schafer
Mary Ann Summers, the clerk from Kansas	Dawn Wells
Roy Hinkley, the professor	Russell Johnson

Music: Gerald Fried.
Executive Producer: Sherwood Schwartz.
Producer: Lloyd J. Schwartz.
Director: Leslie H. Martinson (first episode); Earl Bellamy (second episode).

RESCUE FROM GILLIGAN'S ISLAND—60 minutes—NBC—October 14, 1978 and October 21, 1978. 2 episodes. Repeated as a two-hour movie on August 5, 1979.

THE CASTAWAYS ON GILLIGAN'S ISLAND—90 minutes—NBC—May 3, 1979.

450   GIGGLESNORT HOTEL

Children. The series, set against the background of the Gigglesnort Hotel, attempts to explain various aspects of the world to children through the antics of the people (puppets) who inhabit the establishment.

Starring: Bill Jackson as B. J., the hotel manager.
Puppeteers-Voices: Ian Harris, Nancy Wettler.
Music: A recorded opening and closing theme.
Producer-Writer: Bill Jackson.
Associate Producer: Stephanie Hyman.
Director: Carl Tubbs.
Puppets: Dirty Dragon, the maintenance engineer; Weird, the bellboy; Mother and Father Plumtree, hotel guests; the Blob, the changeable clay figure that lives in the hotel; and Mr. Gigglesnort, the hotel owner.

GIGGLESNORT HOTEL—30 minutes—Syndicated 1979.

451   THE GIRL IN MY LIFE

Testimonial. Recognition of that "special girl in everyone's life" who has been kind, unselfish and undemanding. The format unites or reunites the recipient of the good deed with the woman who performed it. Various merchandise gifts are presented to that special girl.

Host: Fred Holliday.
Announcer: John Harlan.
Music: Ed Kalehoff.
Executive Producer: William Carruthers, Tom Naud, Steve Freedman.
Producer: Bob Henry, Brad Lackman, Warren Williamson, Bill Yagerman.
Director: Tony Charmoli, Chris Darley.

THE GIRL IN MY LIFE—30 minutes—ABC—July 9, 1973–December 20, 1974. 110 programs.

THE GIRL, THE GOLD WATCH, AND EVERYTHING

See title: "Operation Prime Time: The Girl, The Gold Watch, and Everything."

452   THE GIRL WITH SOMETHING EXTRA

Comedy. The trials and tribulations of young marrieds: John Burton, an attorney with the Los Angeles firm of Metcalf, Klein and Associates, and his wife, Sally, who possesses E.S.P. and can perceive his every thought. Stories relate John's attempts to cope with the situations that develop when Sally inadvertently meddles into his private thoughts.

CAST

Sally Burton	Sally Field
John Burton	John Davidson
Jerry Burton, John's brother	Jack Sheldon
Anne, Sally's friend, who operates "The Store," a variety shop	Zohra Lampert
Owen Metcalfe, John's employer	Henry Jones
Angela, John's secretary	Stephanie Edwards
Stewart Klein, Owen's partner	William Windom

Music: Dave Grusin.
Executive Producer: Bob Claver.
Producer: Mel Swope.
Program Open:
John: . . . let me get this straight, you can read everybody's mind?
Sally: Of course not. Just some people.
John: What people?
Sally: Well, some people none of the time, and then some people some of the time, and a very few people most of the time.
John: What category do I fall into?

Sally: The last one.
John: Most of the time?
Sally: (softly) Yea . . . (the theme music then plays).

THE GIRL WITH SOMETHING EXTRA—30 minutes—NBC—September 14, 1973–May 24, 1974. 22 episodes.

453   GIVE-N-TAKE

Game. Four female contestants, seated in a circle surrounding a large electronic spinning arrow, each receive an expensive merchandise gift, the value of which is not stated. Another prize is revealed and a question is read. The first player to correctly answer the question presses a button that slowly stops the arrow. If it pinpoints her, she receives the prize; if the arrow chooses another player, that player receives it. The player who is selected by the arrow can either keep or pass the prize. The object is for players not to exceed $5,000 in merchandise cash value, but come as close as possible to that amount to win. Players are not made aware of their cash totals and work blindly on keeping or passing items. Six prizes are played per game and the player who comes the closest to the game's limit is the winner and receives the prizes she has accumulated.

Host: Jim Lange.
Models: Jane Nelson, Judy Rich.
Announcer: Johnny Jacobs.
Music: Stan Worth.
Executive Producer: William Carruthers.
Producer: Joel Stein.
Director: John Dorsey.
First Champion: Sharon Burr.

GIVE-N-TAKE—30 minutes—CBS—September 8, 1975–December 10, 1976. 370 programs.

454   GLADYS KNIGHT AND THE PIPS

Variety. Music, songs, dances and comedy sketches.

Hostess: Gladys Knight.
Co-Hosts: The Pips, her backup trio: Edward Patten, William Guest and Merald "Bubba" Knight (Gladys' brother).
Orchestra: George Wyle.
Additional Orchestrations: Sid Feller.
Choreographer: Tony Charmoli.
Producer: Bob Henry.
Director: Tony Charmoli.

GLADYS KNIGHT AND THE PIPS—60 minutes—NBC—July 10, 1975–July 31, 1975. 4 programs.

455   THE GLEN CAMPBELL GOODTIME HOUR

Variety. Music, songs and comedy sketches set against a Country and Western atmosphere.

Host: Glen Campbell.
Regulars: Jerry Reed, Eddie Mayehoff, Larry McNeely, R. G. Brown, John Hartford, Pat Paulsen, Mel Tillis, The Mike Curb Congregation.
Announcer: Roger Carroll.
Orchestra: Marty Paich.
Executive Producer: Nick Sevane.
Producer: Jack Shea, Rich Eustis, Al Rogers, Cecil Tuck.
Writer: John Bradford, Sandy Kirinski, Ray Jessel, Coslough Johnson, Frank Shaw, Michael Elias.
Director: Jack Shea.

THE GLEN CAMPBELL GOODTIME HOUR—60 minutes—CBS—June 23, 1968–September 8, 1968; January 22, 1969–June 13, 1972.

456   THE GLITTERING PRIZES

Drama. The series, which is set in England, depicts the lives of Cambridge University students during and after college.

CAST

Joyce Bradley	Angela Down
Jim Bradley	Malcolm Stoddard
Tim March	Tim Preece
Nigel Harvis	Dennis Pearce
Rex Deacon	John Williams
Kevin	Chris Leonard
Bill Bourne	Clive Merrison
Joann	Suzanne Stone
Gavin	Dinsdale Landen
Austin Denny	Ray Smith
Jeanne Dent	Carolle Rousseau
Tim Dent	Tim Piggot-Smith
Ronald	Roger Hammond
Ursula	Peggy Ann Wodd
Sarah Porter	Denise Scott
Alice Knight	Jenny Anderson
Dan	Malcolm Stoddard
Alan	John Gregg
Mike Clode	Mark Wing-Davey
Barbara	Anna Carteret
Adam Morris	Tom Conti
Anna Cunningham	Emily Richard
Barbara (different than above)	Barbara Kellermann
Derek Morris	Kim Fortune
Tom Morris	Luke Crampton
Christine	Rynagh O'Grady
Carol	Prunella Gae

Producer: Mark Shibas.
Director: Wuris Hussien, Robert Knights.

THE GLITTERING PRIZES—90 minutes—Syndicated (to the U.S. and shown on PBS) in 1978. 6 episodes. Produced in England.

457   THE GODZILLA POWER HOUR

Animated Cartoon.

Segments:
Godzilla. The program brings to life Godzilla, the "star" of many Japanese science fiction films, in a new series of American adven-

ABC

Galactica 1980. From left: Robyn Douglass, Kent McCord, Lorne Greene, and Barry Van Dyke.

NBC

The Girl With Something Extra. Sally Field.

NBC

Gilligan's Island. From left, Russell Johnson, Jim Backus, Natalie Schafer, Alan Hale, Bob Denver, Judith Baldwin and Dawn Wells.

tures. Originally destroyed in the 1956 film, *Godzilla, King of the Monsters,* then resurrected in the 1960s and '70s as both an evil and kind monster, the series presents Godzilla as a thirty-story tall, fire-breathing dragon and "friend" to Captain Carl Rogers, a scientist who roams the seas on his boat the *Calico*. Godzilla's exploits, as he and Captain Rogers battle evil is the focal point of the program. (Details as to how Capt. Rogers found Godzilla are not related. It is only revealed that he can summon Godzilla by a special control device on his belt.)

Additional Characters: Quinn, Rogers aide (a pretty scientist); Pete, the young boy; Brock, Pete's friend; and Godzuki, the fumbling monster.

Jana of the Jungle. A boat, traveling down the Great River in Africa, strikes a rock and sinks. One of the passengers, a young girl named Jana, is rescued by Montaro, a warrior from a lost civilization of people and she is raised by Montaro and the animals. As the years pass, Jana becomes a legend — the protector of the jungle and all its creatures. The series depicts her adventures as she battles unscrupulous characters.

Additional Characters: Ghost, Jana's white Jaguar, and Tico, a pack-rat possum.

VOICES

Godzilla	Ted Cassidy
Godzuki	Don Messick
Carl	Jeff David
Quinn	Brenda Thompson
Brock	Hilly Hicks
Pete	Al Eisenman
Jana	B. J. Ward
Montaro	Ted Cassidy

Music: Hoyt Curtin.
Executive Producer: William Hanna, Joseph Barbera.
Producer: Doug Wildey.
Creative Producer: Iwao Takamoto.
Director: Arny Patterson.

THE GODZILLA POWER HOUR — 60 minutes — NBC — September 9, 1978 – October 28, 1978. 90 minutes (as *The Godzilla Super 90*) — NBC — November 4, 1978 – September 1, 1979. 30 minutes (as *Godzilla*) — NBC — Premiered: September 8, 1979.

458   THE GOLDDIGGERS

Variety. Music, songs, dances and comedy sketches that feature the Golddiggers, a group of beautiful and talented young ladies between eighteen and twenty-two years of age.

The Golddiggers: Michelle and Tanya Della Fave, Rosetta Cox, Lucy Codham, Paula Cinko, Peggy Hansen, Nancy Bonetti, Susan Lund, Barbara Sanders, Patricia Mickey, Francie Mendenhall, Loyita Chapel, Lee Crawford, Jimmie Cannon, Nancy Reichert, Janice Whitby, Jackie Chidsey, Liz Kelley, Karen Cavenaugh, Rebecca Jones.

Regulars: Larry Storch, Alice Ghostley, Charles Nelson Reilly, Jackie Vernon, Lonnie Shorr, Barbara Heller, Don Rice, Jennifer Buriner.

Orchestra: Van Alexander.
Producer: Greg Garrison.
Writer: Dick Hollis, Sid Green, Tom Tenowich, Norm Liebman.
Director: Jonathan Lucas, Tim Kiley.

THE GOLDDIGGERS — 30 minutes — Syndicated 1971.

459   THE GOLDDIGGERS IN LONDON

Variety. Music, songs and comedy sketches set against the background of London.

The Golddiggers: Michelle and Tanya Della Fave, Rosetta Cox, Rebecca Jones, Janice Whitby, Lucy Codham, Peggy Hansen, Nancy Bonetti, Susan Lund, Barbara Sanders, Patricia Mickey, Francie Mendenhall, Loyita Chapel, Lee Crawford, Jimmie Cannon, Nancy Reichert, Janice Chidsey, Liz Kelley.

Regulars: Marty Feldman, Tommy Tune, Julian Chagrin.
Orchestra: Jack Parnell.
Executive Producer: Greg Garrison.
Producer: Norman Campbell.
Writer: Stan Daniels, Tom Tenowich, David Mayer, Bill Lynn, Jerry Rose.
Director: Norman Campbell.

THE GOLDDIGGERS IN LONDON — 60 minutes — NBC — July 16, 1970 – September 10, 1970.

460   GOMER PYLE, U.S.M.C.

Comedy. The life of Gomer Pyle, a simple-minded and naive private with the Second Platoon, B Company of Camp Henderson, a Marine base in Los Angeles. Stories depict the chaos that ensues when he unconsciously deviates from the rules and complicates matters. A spin-off from *The Andy Griffith Show,* wherein Gomer Pyle was depicted as a gas-station attendant before he decided to join the Marines.

CAST

Pvt. Gomer Pyle	Jim Nabors
Sgt. Vincent Carter	Frank Sutton
Pvt. Duke Slattery	Ronnie Schell
Pvt. Frankie Lombardi	Ted Bessell
Bunny Olsen, Carter's girlfriend	Barbara Stuart
Sgt. Charles Hacker	Allan Melvin
Cpl. Charles Boyle, Carter's aide	Roy Stuart
Lou Anne Poovie, Gomer's friend, a singer at the Blue Bird Café	Elizabeth MacRae
Col. Edward Gray, the C.O.	Forrest Compton
Pvt. Hummel	William Christopher

Music: Earle Hagen.
Executive Producer: Sheldon Leonard, Aaron Ruben, Ronald Jacobs.
Producer: E. Duke Vincent, Bruce Johnson.
Director: Coby Ruskin (most of the series), Gary Nelson, John Rich.
Creator: Aaron Ruben.

GOMER PYLE, U.S.M.C. — 30 minutes — CBS — September 25, 1964 – September 19, 1969. Rebroadcasts: CBS — September 8, 1969 – March 22, 1972. 230 episodes. Syndicated.

461   THE GONG SHOW

Variety. Three celebrity judges rate the performances of undiscovered professional talent. If, after forty-five seconds, a judge feels that an act is not worthy of continuing, he hits a large gong and the act is discontinued. Acts that are permitted to complete a performance are rated by the judges on a scale from one to ten. The highest scoring act is the winner and receives a trophy and a check for $516.32.

Host: Chuck Barris.
Original Host (of five episodes that were never aired): John Barbour.
Assistant: Siv Aberg.
Substitutes for Ms. Aberg: Carol Connor, Stella Barris, Marlana Clark, Julie McCray, Jill Freeman.
Regular Panelists: Jaye P. Morgan, Arte Johnson, Jamie Farr.
Announcer: Johnny Jacobs.
Music: Milton DeLugg ("and his band with a thug").
Executive Producer: Chuck Barris, Chris Bearde, Gene Banks.
Producer: Diana Fell, Linda Howard.
Director: John Dorsey, Terry Kyne.

THE GONG SHOW — 25, then 30 minutes — NBC — June 14, 1976 – July 21, 1978. Syndicated.

462   THE GONG SHOW

Variety. A syndicated, first-run version of the previous title. Same format is used but the prize money increases to $712.05.

Host: Gary Owens, Chuck Barris.
Assistant: Siv Aberg.
Announcer: Johnny Jacobs.
Orchestra: Milton DeLugg.
Producer: Chuck Barris, Chris Bearde.
Director: John Dorsey.

THE GONG SHOW — 30 minutes — Syndicated 1976.

463   GOOBER AND THE GHOST CHASERS

Animated Cartoon. The investigations of Ted, Tina and Gillie, the staff members of *Ghost Chasers* magazine. Assisted by Goober, a dog who is able to become invisible when he is scared, they incorporate scientific evaluation in their attempt to expose the frauds who perpetrate ghostly occurrences.

VOICES

Goober	Paul Winchell
Ted	Jerry Dexter
Tina	Jo Ann Harris
Gillie	Ronnie Schell

Music: Hoyt Curtin.
Executive Producer: William Hanna, Joseph Barbera.
Producer: Iwao Takamoto.
Director: Charles A. Nichols.

GOOBER AND THE GHOST CHASERS — 30 minutes — ABC — September 8, 1973 – August 31, 1975. 17 episodes.

464   GOOD DAY!

Talk-Interview. Produced in Boston.

Hostess: Janet Langhart.
Host: John Willis.
Music: Dave Witney.

GOOD DAY! — 30 minutes — Syndicated 1976.

465   THE GOOD GUYS

Comedy. Seeking to better their lives, Bert Gramus and Rufus Butterworth, life-long friends, pool their resources and purchase a diner in Los Angeles. Assisted by Claudia, Bert's wife, they struggle to run "Bert's Place" and live the good life.

CAST

Rufus Butterworth	Bob Denver
Bert Gramus	Herb Edelman
Claudia Gramus	Joyce Van Patten
Big Tom, Rufus' friend	Alan Hale, Jr.
Gertie, Tom's girlfriend	Toni Gilman
Hal, a diner customer	George Furth
Andy, a diner customer	Ron Masak
Arlene, the waitress	Joan Delaney
Henry Arsdale, Claudia's father	Jim Backus
Harry, the mailman	Oscar Lane
D. W. Watson, the owner of the "Mother Watson" diner chain, Bert's competition	Liam Dunn
Gertie's brother	George Wilburn

Music: Jerry Fielding.
Executive Producer: Jerry Davis, Leonard B. Stern.

Producer: Bob Schiller, Bob Weiskopf, Jack Rose.
Director: Alan Rafkin, Reza S. Badiyi, Gary Nelson.
Creator: Jack Rose.

THE GOOD GUYS — 30 minutes — CBS — September 25, 1968 – January 23, 1970. 42 episodes.

466   GOOD HEAVENS

Anthology. The series, which presents a different comedy story and cast each week, features Mr. Angel, a celestial messenger whose function on Earth is to fulfill fantasies by granting deserving people one wish.

Starring: Carl Reiner as Mr. Angel.
Music: Patrick Williams.
Executive Producer: Carl Reiner.
Producer: Mel Swope, Austin and Irma Kalish.
Director: Carl Reiner, John Erman, Peter Bonerz, Mel Swope, James Sheldon.
Creator: Bernard Slade.

Included:

Good Neighbor Maxine. When a recently widowed mother helps a stranger complete a telephone call, she is approached by Mr. Angel and granted her wish: to have more excitement in her life.

Cast: Maxine: Loretta Swit; Jim Pearson: Clu Gulager; Buck: Ron Masak; Barney: Huntz Hall.

Superscoop. When Henry Clyde, a struggling reporter, performs an act of generosity, Mr. Angel grants him his wish: to scoop the world on a big story.

Cast: Henry Clyde: Paul Williams; Mr. Clay: Don Ameche; Beautiful woman on the plane: Julie Newmar; Mr. Pyle: Stuart Nisbet; L. Bruce Jones: John Zaremba; Emily Hardy: Liberty Williams.

See Jane Run. When the owner of an exclusive boutique refers a customer of limited resources to a less expensive dress shop, Mr. Angel rewards her kind deed by granting her wish: to find her long-lost twin sister.

Cast: Julia and Jane Grey: Florence Henderson; Dick: Edward Winter; Gary Lawrence: George Maharis.

GOOD HEAVENS — 30 minutes — ABC — February 29, 1976 – June 24, 1976.

467   THE GOODIES

Comedy. The chaotic misadventures of the Goodies, three British men who will do anything at anytime as they attempt to succeed in the business world.

Starring: The Goodies (Graeme Garden, Tim Brooke-Taylor, Bill Oddie).

Regulars: Patricia Hayes, Michael Aspel, Milton Reid, Julie Desmond.
Music: Bill Oddie, Michael Gibbs.
Producer: John Howard Davis.
Director: Jim Franklin.

THE GOODIES — 30 minutes — Syndicated (to the U.S.) in 1976. Produced in England.

468   THE GOOD LIFE

Comedy. The story of Albert and Jane Miller, a married couple who pose as a butler and cook to escape life's endless problems and expenses. They acquire a position with Charles Dutton, the wealthy head of Dutton Industries. The series relates their misadventures as they struggle to keep secret their charade, run the Dutton mansion — and enjoy the good life.

CAST

Albert Miller	Larry Hagman
Jane Miller, his wife	Donna Mills
Charles Dutton, their employer	David Wayne
Grace Dutton, Charles's sister (pilot film)	Kate Reed
Grace Dutton (series)	Hermione Baddeley
Nick Dutton, Charles's son	Danny Goldman

Music: Sacha Distel, Jack Elliott, Allyn Ferguson.
Executive Producer: Lee Rich.
Producer-Director: Claudio Guzman.

THE GOOD LIFE — 30 minutes — NBC — September 18, 1971 – January 8, 1972. 15 episodes. The thirty-minute pilot film aired on NBC on August 23, 1971.

469   GOOD MORNING, AMERICA

Variety. News, information and celebrity interviews. A spin-off from *A.M. America.* Broadcast from 7 to 9 a.m. EST.

Hosts: David Hartman, Nancy Dussault, Sandra Hill, Joan Lunden.
Regulars: Rona Barrett, Jonathan Winters, John Lindsay, Geraldo Rivera, Jack Anderson, Erma Bombeck, Nena and George O'Neil, Joan Lunden, Bill Beutel, Peter Jennings, Cheryl Tiegs, Howard Cosell, Pat Collins, Paul Harvey, Steve Bell, Margaret Osmer.
Music Theme: Marvin Hamlisch.
Executive Producer: Mel Ferber, Woody Fraser.
Producer: George Merlis, Bob Lissit.
Director: Jan Rifkinson.

GOOD MORNING, AMERICA — 2 hours — ABC — Premiered: November 11, 1975.

470   GOODTIME GIRLS

Comedy. The series, set in Washington, D.C., in 1942, follows the experiences of Camille Rittenhouse, Edith Beatlemeyer, Betty Crandall and Loretta Smoot, four working girls sharing an apartment and enduring the home-front hardships of World War II — including rationing and the man shortage.

CAST

Camille Rittenhouse, a photographer	Francine Tacker
Edith Beatlemeyer, a war department secretary	Annie Potts
Betty Crandall, a U.S.O. show hostess	Lorna Patterson
Loretta Smoot, a defense plant worker	Georgia Engel
Frankie Molardo, their friend, a cab driver	Adrian Zmed
Irma Coolidge, their landlady	Marcia Lewis
George Coolidge, Irma's husband	Merwin Goldsmith
Skeeter Coolidge, Irma's son	Sparky Marcus
Benny Lohman, Frankie's friend	Peter Scolari

Commercial Break Announcer: Annie Potts, Francine Tacker, Georgia Engel, Lorna Patterson.
Opening Theme Narration: Annie Potts.
Music: Charles Fox, Ben Lanzarone, John Beal.
Supervising Producer: Leonora Thuna.
Executive Producer: Thomas L. Miller, Edward K. Milkis, Robert I. Boyett.
Producer: Paula A. Roth, Judy Pioli.
Writer: Ken Estin, Michael Warren, William Bickley, Roy Teicher.
Director: Joel Zwick, Howard Storm, Tony Mordente.

Program Open:
Edith: When I arrived in Washington in 1942 I didn't have a place to live. Then, quite by chance, I met Betty Crandall; she'd come all the way from Iowa to help the war effort. Our cab driver, Frankie Molardo, became our first friend in Washington — and quite a life saver. He brought us to Coolidge House, the place that turned out to be our new home. George and Irma Coolidge were the landlords, and thanks to Loretta Smoot, one of the sweetest of my new-found friends, we were soon sharing her room in the attic. Oh, then there was Camille Rittenhouse; she sweet-talked Mr. Coolidge into letting her stay in the attic too. ... Coolidge House was crowded, but we all became good friends — and although there were hard times, there

were plenty of good times too (the theme lyric then plays).

GOODTIME GIRLS — 30 minutes — ABC — January 22, 1980 – February 12, 1980; April 12, 1980 – April 26, 1980; August 1, 1980 – August 29, 1980. 11 episodes.

471   GOOD TIME HARRY

Comedy. The misadventures of Harry Jenkins, ace sportswriter for the *San Francisco Sentinel,* and an accomplished womanizer who often confuses sport and play. (In later episodes Harry works for the *San Francisco Journal.*)

CAST

Harry Jenkins	Ted Bessell
Jimmy Hughes, the sports editor	Eugene Roche
Carol Younger, a sportswriter	Marcia Strassman
Billie Howard, Harry's girlfriend	Jesse Welles
Sally, Jimmy's secretary	Ruth Manning
Lenny, the bartender at Danny's, Harry's hangout	Richard Karron
Stan, Harry's neighbor	Barry Gordon
Martin Springer, the copy boy	Steve Peterman
Sid, Harry's friend	Phil Leeds
Debbie Howard, Billie's daughter	Kyle Richards
Carmine Howard, Billie's ex-husband	Dan Hedaya
Bertram, the drunk	Neil Flanagan

Music: Peter Matz.
Theme Vocal: "Wild About Harry" by Norman Brooks.
Supervising Producer: Steve Gordon.
Executive Producer: Charles H. Joffe, Larry Brezner.
Producer: Gareth Davies.
Writer: Steve Gordon, Mickey Rose, Glen Gordon Caron.
Director: Jeff Chambers, James Burrows, Steve Gordon, Mark Gordon.
Creator: Steve Gordon.

GOOD TIME HARRY — 30 minutes — NBC — July 19, 1980 – September 13, 1980. 5 episodes.

472   GOOD TIMES

Comedy. The story, set in Chicago, follows the struggles of the Evanses, a poor black family in rough times when jobs are scarce and money is tight. A spin-off from *Maude.*

CAST

James Evans, the husband	John Amos
Florida Evans, the wife	Esther Rolle
James Evans, Jr. (J.J.), their son	Jimmie Walker
Thelma Evans, their daughter	BernNadette Stanis
Michael Evans, their son	Ralph Carter
Willona Woods, their neighbor	Ja'net Dubois
Penny Gordon, the battered child Willona adopts	Janet Jackson

Nathan Bookman, the
  janitor   Johnny Brown
Violet Bookman, Nathan's
  wife   Marilyn Coleman
Keith Anderson, Thelma's boyfriend;
  later husband   Ben Powers
Carl Dickson, Florida's romantic
  interest; later husband (after
  James's "death")   Moses Gunn
Mr. Harris, J.J.'s employer (J.J. works
  in the drafting department of
  an ad agency)   J. Jay Saunders
Valerie Harris, Harris's
  daughter   Tanya L. Boyd
Monty, a friend of the Evans
  family   Stymie Beard
Henry Evans, James's father Richard Ward
Lena Anderson, Henry's
  fiancée   Paulene Myers

The Evans' address: 763 North Gilbert, Apt. 17-C of the Cabrini Housing Project (address is also given as 963 North Gilbert).

Music: Marilyn Bergman, Alan Bergman, Dave Grusin.
Announcer: Jimmie Walker.
Executive Producer: Norman Lear, Allan Manings, Austin and Irma Kalish, Norman Paul.
Producer: Gordon Mitchell, Lloyd Turner, Sid Dorfman, George Sunga, Bernie West, Don Nicholl, Austin and Irma Kalish.
Director: Herbert Kenwith, Jack Shea, Gerren Keith.
Art Director: Don Roberts.
Creator: Eric Monte, Mike Evans.

GOOD TIMES — 30 minutes — CBS — February 8, 1974 – August 1, 1979. Syndicated

THE GOSSIP COLUMNIST

See title: *Operation Prime Time: The Gossip Columnist.*

473   GO — U.S.A.

Anthology. Dramatizations based on legendary folk heroes and heroines.

Music: Robert Maxwell.
Producer: George Heinemann, Chris Schwartz, Langbourne Rust.
Director: J. Phillip Miller.
Included:

Oregon Bound. An Old West story that follows the hazardous trek of a Missouri family as they journey to Oregon seeking a new life.

Cast: Pa: Bill Jordan; Ma: Aubri Martin; John: Tony Markes; Catherine: Julie Markes.

Gordon. The story of an escaped slave who sacrifices his freedom to help the Continental Army fight the British.

Cast: Gordon: Northern J. Calloway; Isaac: Richard Ward.

Go Away Kid, You Bother Me. The story of a carnival pitchman who undertakes the task of taking an orphan to his new foster parents.

Cast: Joseph: David Brooks; Marion: Andrew Ian MacMillan; Dunston: Ron Faber.

GO — U.S.A. — 30 minutes — NBC — September 6, 1975 – September 4, 1976.

474   THE GOVERNOR AND J.J.

Comedy. The series, set in an unidentified Midwestern state, depicts incidents in the life of its governor, William Drinkwater, and his 23-year-old daughter, J.J. (Jennifer Jo), the curator of the local children's zoo.

CAST
Gov. William Drinkwater, a
  widower   Dan Dailey
Jennifer Jo Drinkwater, his
  daughter   Julie Sommars
George Callison, his press
  secretary   James Callahan
Maggie McCloud, William's
  secretary   Neva Patterson
Sara, the housekeeper   Nora Marlowe

Music: Jerry Fielding.
Executive Producer: Leonard B. Stern.
Producer: Arne Sultan.
Director: Alan Rafkin, Reza S. Badiyi, Arne Sultan, Leonard B. Stern.

THE GOVERNOR AND J.J. — 30 minutes — CBS. September 23, 1969 – January 6, 1971; June 1, 1972 – August 11, 1972. 39 episodes.

475   GRADY

Comedy. A spin-off from *Sanford and Son.* The story of Grady Wilson, and the misadventures that occur when he moves in with his daughter, Ellie, her husband, Hal, and their two children.

CAST
Grady Wilson   Whitman Mayo
Ellie Marshall, his daughter   Carol Cole
Hal Marshall, Ellie's husband Joe Morton
Laurie Marshall, Ellie's
  daughter   Rosanne Katon
Haywood Marshall, Ellie's
  son   Haywood Nelson
Mr. Pratt, their landlord   Jack Fletcher
Rose, their neighbor   Alix Elias

The Marshalls' address: 636 Carlisle Street, Santa Monica, California.

Music: John Addison.
Executive Producer: Saul Turteltaub, Bernie Orenstein.
Producer: Jerry Ross, Howard Leeds.
Director: Gerren Keith.

GRADY — 30 minutes — NBC December 4, 1975 – March 4, 1976.

476   GRANDPA GOES TO WASHINGTON

Comedy-Drama. Forced to retire at age 66, Joe Kelley, an honest and outspoken professor of political science in California, is persuaded to run for the U.S. Senate in the wake of a political scandal. Winning the election, Joe, now a U.S. senator, moves to Washington, D.C., where his adventures, as he tries to practice what he taught — honest government — are dramatized.

CAST
Senator Joe Kelley   Jack Albertson
Gen. Kevin Kelley, his son   Larry Linville
Rose Kelley, Kevin's wife   Sue Ane Langdon
Cathleen Kelley, Kevin's
  daughter   Michele Tobin
Kevin Kelley, Jr.,
  Kevin's son   Sparky Marcus
Madge, Joe's secretary   Madge Sinclair
Tony DuVall, Joe's adviser   Tom Mason
The President of the U.S.   Richard Eastham

Music: Artie Butler.
Executive Producer: Richard P. Rosetti, Leonora Thuna.
Producer: Robert Stambler.
Director: Richard Crenna, Michael Caffey, Herbert Kenwith, Larry Elikann, Paul Stanley, George Tyne, Allen Baron, Joseph Pevney.
Creator: Richard P. Rosetti, Len Slate, Noel Baldwin.

GRANDPA GOES TO WASHINGTON — 60 minutes — NBC — September 20, 1978 – January 16, 1979. 11 episodes. The series was "sneak previewed" on September 7, 1978.

477   THE GREAT AMERICAN DREAM MACHINE

Satire. A television magazine format designed "to make significant statements about the good and bad trends in our society." A satirization of everyday life — from true love to baking an apple pie.

Semi-regulars: Marshall Efron, Ken Shapiro, Chevy Chase, Lee Meredith, Nicholas Van Hoffman, Andrew Rooney, Robert Townsend.

Producer: Al Perlmatter.

THE GREAT AMERICAN DREAM MACHINE — 60 minutes — PBS — October 6, 1971 – February 9, 1972.

478   THE GREAT GRAPE APE SHOW

Animated Cartoon. The misadventures of a forty-foot purple gorilla (Grape Ape) and his friend Beegle Beagle, the fast-talking dog.

VOICES
Grape Ape   Bob Holt
Beegle Beagle   Marty Ingels

Music: Hoyt Curtin, Paul DeKorte.
Executive Producer: William Hanna, Joseph Barbera.
Producer: Iwao Takamoto.
Director: Charles A. Nichols.

THE GREAT GRAPE APE SHOW — 30 minutes — ABC — September 11, 1977 – September 3, 1978.

479   THE GREAT MOVIE COWBOYS

Movies. A television revival of rarely broadcast Western theatrical films of the 1930s and '40s.

Host: Roy Rogers.
Producer: Tele Scene, Inc.
Director (of Roy Rogers Segment): Bruce Fox.

THE GREAT MOVIE COWBOYS — 60 minutes — Syndicated 1977. Originally titled *Cowboy Classics.*

480   GREATEST HEADLINES OF THE CENTURY

Documentary. Events of world history are recalled through film clips. Because of its relatively short length (three minutes), the program is often seen as a filler (e.g., when a movie runs short and a station needs something to fill time) and therefore is generally not listed as a series.

Narrator: Tom Hudson.
Producer: Sherm Grinberg.

GREATEST HEADLINES OF THE CENTURY — 03 minutes — Syndicated 1970.

481   GREATEST HEROES OF THE BIBLE

Anthology. A miniseries of dramatizations based on stories from the Old Testament.

Announcer: Brad Crandall.
Music: Bob Summers.
Music Supervision: Don Perry.
Supervising Producer: James L. Conway.
Executive Producer: Charles E. Sellier, Jr.
Producer: Jim Simmons.
Director: James L. Conway.
Developed for TV by: Charles E. Sellier, Jr., James L. Conway.

CASTS AND STORIES
The Story of David and Goliath
David   Roger Kern
Goliath   Ted Cassidy
Abner   Hugh O'Brian
Saul   Jeff Corey
Debunkar   John Dehner

The Story of Samson and Delilah
Samson   John Beck
Delilah   Ann Turkel
Polah   James Olson
Horaz   Victor Jory
Jair   John Schuck
Nizra   Ann Doran

Goodtime Girls. From left, Georgia Engel, Annie Potts, Adrian Zmed, Lorna Patterson and Francine Tacker.

The Governor and J.J. Julie Sommars and Dan Dailey.

The Guiding Light. Nancy Addison.

Hart to Hart. Robert Wagner and Stefanie Powers.

The Story of Noah

Noah	Lew Ayres
Xantha	Rita Gam
Ham	Jay Hammer
Lilla	Eve Plumb
Ularat	Ed Lauter
Japheth	William Adler
Shem	Sam Weisman

The Story of Joshua and the Battle of Jericho

Joshua	Robert Culp
Assurabi	Cameron Mitchell
King Agadiz	Sydney Lassick
Reuben	John Doucette
Rahab	Sondra Carrie
Gad	Royal Dano
Queen	Julie Adams

The Story of Moses in Egypt

Moses	John Marley
Pharoah	Joseph Campanella
Ocran	Frank Gorshin
Zipporah	Anne Francis
Beseleel	Ron Rifkin
Voice of God	Peter Mark Richman

The Story of Moses and the Ten Commandments

Moses	John Marley
Pharoah	Joseph Campanella
Vizier	Robert Alda
Ocran	Frank Gorshin
Aaron	Al Ruscio
Queen	Julie Adams
Imhotep	Lloyd Bochner

The Story of Daniel in the Lion's Den

Daniel	David Birney
Darius	Robert Vaughn
Malimar	Nehemiah Persoff
Hissar	Dean Stockwell
Joanna	Sherry Jackson

The Story of Solomon and Bathsheba

Solomon	Tom Hallick
Bathsheba	Carol Lawrence
King David	John Carradine
Adonijah	John Saxon
Jaob	Kevin Dobson

The Story of Joseph and His Brothers

Joseph	Sam Bottoms
Potiphar	Bernie Kopell
Pharoah	Barry Nelson
Har-Gatep	Albert Salmi
Nairubi	Carol Rossen
Reuben	Harvey Jason

GREATEST HEROES OF THE BIBLE — 8 hours, 30 minutes (total) — NBC — November 19, 1978 – November 22, 1978. 3 two-hour programs; one 2-hour, 30-minute program.

482   GREATEST HEROES OF THE BIBLE

Anthology. Dramatizations based on stories from the Old Testament. A continuation of the miniseries of the same title.

Narrator: Victor Jory.
Announcer: Brad Crandall.
Music: Bob Summers.
Music Supervision: Don Perry.
Supervising Producer: James L. Conway.
Executive Producer: Charles E. Sellier, Jr.

Producer: Biff Johnson.
Director: Jack B. Hively, Charles Davis.

CASTS AND STORIES

The Story of the Ten Commandments

Moses	John Marley
Aaron	Richard Mulligan
Eleazar	Kristoffer Tabori
Nabar	Anson Williams
Sira	Lorrie Mahaffey
Joshua	Granville Van Dusen

The Story of the Tower of Babel

Amathar	Vince Edwards
Joktan	Richard Basehart
Tova	Erin Moran
Ranol	Dana Elcar
Hevet	Ron Palillo
Mardon	Cliff Emmich

The Story of Abraham

Abraham	Gene Barry
King Phagon	Peter Mark Richman
Darghir	Rick Jason
Nagar	Dorothy Malone
Hasdrugar	David Opatoshu
Shebelah	Julie Parrish
Lot	Ed Ames

GREATEST HEROES OF THE BIBLE — 60 minutes — NBC — May 8, 1979 – May 22, 1979. 3 episodes.

483   GREEN ACRES

Comedy. Oliver Wendell Douglas, an attorney who yearns to be a farmer, purchases, sight unseen the 160-acre Haney farm in Hotterville. Despite the objections of his glamorous and sophisticated wife, Lisa, they relinquish their life of luxury in New York City and retreat to a shabby, broken-down, unfurnished nightmare — Oliver's Green Acres dream. The series follows their misadventures in coping with the numerous trials and tribulations of farming and country living.

CAST

Oliver Douglas	Eddie Albert
Lisa Douglas, his wife	Eva Gabor
Eb Dawson, their handyman	Tom Lester
Mr. Haney, the coniving salesman	Pat Buttram
Hank Kimball, the agricultural representative	Alvy Moore
Fred Ziffel, the pig farmer	Hank Patterson
Doris Ziffel, Fred's wife	Fran Ryan
	Barbara Pepper
Sam Druker, the general store owner	Frank Cady
Newt Kiley, a farmer	Kay E. Kuter
Alf Monroe, the repairman	Sid Melton
Ralph Monroe, Alf's sister	Mary Grace Canfield
Joe Carson, the manager of the Shady Rest Hotel	Edgar Buchanan
Eunice Douglas, Oliver's mother	Eleanor Audley
Darlene Wheeler, Eb's girlfriend	Judy McConnell
Mr. Wheeler, Darlene's father	Robert Foulk
Brian Williams, Oliver's law partner	Rick Lenz

Roy Trendell, a farmer	Robert Foulk
Lori Baker, the Douglases' house guest	Victoria Meyerink
Sarah, the telephone operator	Merie Earle

Also: Arnold, Fred and Doris' pet pig.

Music: Vic Mizzy.
Music Supervision: Dave Kahn.
Theme Vocal: Eddie Albert, Eva Gabor.
Executive Producer: Paul Henning.
Producer: Jay Sommers.
Director: Richard L. Bare (the entire series, except for one episode that was directed by Ralph Levy).
Creator: Jay Sommers.

GREEN ACRES — 30 minutes — CBS — September 15, 1965 – September 7, 1971. 170 episodes. Syndicated.

484   GRIFF

Crime Drama. The investigations of Wade "Griff" Griffin, a former police captain turned private detective who works out of Los Angeles.

CAST

Wade Griffin	Lorne Greene
Mike Murdoch, his partner	Ben Murphy
Grace Newcombe, their secretary	Patricia Stich
Police Captain Barney Marcus	Vic Tayback

Music: Elliot Kaplan, Mike Post, Pete Carpenter.
Executive Producer: David Victor.
Producer: Steve Bocho.
Director: Allen Baron, Edward Abroms, Lou Antonio, Boris Sagal, Arnold Laven.

GRIFF — 60 minutes — ABC — September 29, 1973 – January 4, 1974. 12 episodes.

485   THE GROOVIE GOOLIES

Animated Cartoon. The antics of the Groovie Goolies, a group of musically inclined practical jokers who resemble various celluloid monsters of the 1930s and '40s.

Voices: Larry Storch, Don Messick, Howard Morris, Jane Webb, Dallas McKennon, John Erwin.
Music: George Mahana.
Producer: Norm Prescott, Lou Scheimer.
Director: Don Christensen.

THE GROOVIE GOOLIES — 30 minutes. CBS — September 12, 1971 – September 17, 1972. ABC — October 25, 1975 – September 5, 1976.

486   THE GROOVIE GOOLIES AND FRIENDS

Animated Cartoon. The overall title for rebroadcasts in excerpt form of several series that were originally broadcast by the net-

works on Saturday mornings: *The Groovie Goolies, Lassie's Rescue Rangers, The New Adventures of Gilligan, My Favorite Martians* and *The Secret Lives of Waldo Kitty.* See individual titles for information.

THE GROOVIE GOOLIES AND FRIENDS — 30 minutes — Syndicated 1978.

487   THE GUIDING LIGHT

Serial. The dramatic story of the Bauer family, residents of the town of Springfield, U.S.A. Episodes relate the conflicts and tensions that arise from the interactions of the characters.

CAST

Papa Bauer	Theo Goetz
Dr. Edward Bauer	Robert Gentry
	Mart Hulswit
Christina Bauer	Cheryl Lynn Brown
Michael Bauer	Glenn Walker
	Michael Allen
	Garry Pillar
	Paul Prokop
	Bob Pickering
	Don Stewart
Bertha Bauer	Charita Bauer
Hillary Bauer	Marsha Clark
Rita Bauer	Lenore Kasdorf
Hope Bauer	Elissa Leeds
	Robin Matson
	Elvera Roussel
Mark Holden	Whitfield Connor
Anne Benedict	Joan Gray
Dr. Paul Fletcher	Bernard Grant
Susan Carver	Judy Lewis
Leslie Jackson	Barbara Rodell
	Lynne Adams
Don Peters	Paul Gallantyne
Kathy Grant	Susan Douglas
Joe Roberts	Herb Nelson
George Hayes	Philip Sterling
Jane Hayes	Chase Crosley
Tracy Delmar	Victoria Wyndham
Dianah Buckley	Courtney Sherman
Kit Vested	Nancy Addison
Dr. Sara McIntyre	Millette Alexander
	Patricia Roe
Barbara Norris	Barbara Berjer
Deborah Mehren	Olivia Cole
Holly Norris	Lynn Deerfield
	Maureen Garrett
Peter Wexler	Michael Durrell
Charlotte Waring	Melinda Fee
David Vested	Dan Hamilton
Marion Conway	Kate Harrington
Janet Mason	Caroline McWilliams
Peggy Fletcher	Fran Myers
Ken Norris	Roger Newman
Linell Conway	Christine Pickles
Stanley Norris	William Smithers
Dr. Stephen Jackson	Stefan Schnabel
Karen Martin	Tudi Wiggins
Roger Thorpe	Michael Zaslow
Dr. Joe Werner	Ed Zimmerman
	Anthony Call
Ellen Mason	Jeanne Arnold
Gil Mehren	David Pendleton
Flip Malone	Paul Carpinelli
Mrs. Herbert	Rosetta LeNoire
Fred Fletcher	Albert Zungalo III
Billy Fletcher	James Long
Adam Thorpe	Robert Milli

Marie Wallace Grant	Lynne Rogers
Dr. John Fletcher	Don Scardino
	Erik Howell
Betty Eiler	Madeline Sherwood
Charles Eiler	Graham Jarvis
Capt. Jim Swanson	Lee Richardson
Maeve Kincaid	Vanessa Chamberlain
Dr. Bruce Banning	Barnard Hughes
	Les Damon
	Sidney Walker
	Bill Roerick
Bill Bauer	Lyle Sudrow
	Ed Bryce
Dr. Jim Frazier	James Earl Jones
Martha Frazier	Cecily Tyson
	Ruby Dee
Claudia Dillman	Grace Matthews
Ann Fletcher	Elizabeth Hubbard
Alex Bowden	Ernest Graves
	Tom Klunis
Helene Benedict	Kay Campbell
Sir Clayton Olds	Myles Easton
Karl	Richard Morse
Victoria Ballinger	Carol Teitel
Lincoln Yates	Peter MacLean
Trudy Bauer	Actress unknown
Dr. Wilson Frost	Jack Bels
Robin Holden	Zina Bethune
	Gillian Spencer
Tom Baldwin	Don Chastain
Viola Stapleton	Sudie Bond
	Kate Wilkinson
Pam Chandler	Maureen Silliman
Billie Fletcher	Shane Nickerson
Dr. Tim Ryan	Jordan Clarke
T. J. Werner	T. J. Hargrave
Andrew Norris	Barney McFadden
Chad Richards	Everett McGill
Justin Marlen	Tom O'Rourke
Rita Stapleton	Lenore Kasdorf
Elizabeth Spaulding	Lezlie Dalton
Maureen Mooney	Ann Jeffers
Hillary Kincaid	Linda McCullough
Brandy Shellooe	Jobeth Williams
Dr. Peter Chapman	Curt Dawson
Stuart Kennicott	Jack Stauffer
Meta Banning	Jone Allison
	Ellen Demming
Alan Spaulding	Christopher Bernau
Jennifer Richards	Geraldine Court
Amanda McFarren	Kathleen Cullen
Laine Marler	Kathleen Kellaigh
Diane Ballard	Sofia Landon
Lucille Wexler	Rita Lloyd
Floyd Parker	Tom Nielsen
Katie Parker	Denise Pence
Jackie Spaulding	Cindy Pickett
Phillip Spaulding	Jarrod Ross
Kelly Nelson	John Wesley Shipp
Ross Marler	Jerry ver Dorn
Morgan Richards	Kristen Vigard
Dr. Mark Hamilton	Burton Cooper
Gordon Middleton	Marcus Smythe
Eve McFarren	Janey Grey
Freddie Bauer	Robbie Berridge
Dr. Richard Grant	James Lipton
Laura Grant	Alice Yourman
Nick	Robert Lowry
Max Chapman	Ben Hammer

Also: Sandy Dennis, Willard Waterman, Joseph Campanella, Diana Hyland, Ethel Everett, Kathryn Hays, Betty Lou Gerson.

Announcer: Hal Simms.
Music: Charles Paul, Mi-Viox.
Executive Producer: Allan M. Potter.

Producer: Leslie Kwartin, Joe Willmore.
Associate Producer: Susan Bedsow.
Director: Harry Eggart, Len Valenta, Michael Gilona, Bruce Barry, Ted Corday, Jeff Bleckner.
Creator: Irna Phillips.

THE GUIDING LIGHT—30 minutes—CBS—June 30, 1952–November 4, 1977. 60 minutes—Premiered: November 7, 1977.

488 THE GUINNESS GAME

Game. Players bet on whether an ordinary person can beat or establish a Guinness Book world's record. Three players receive one-thousand dollars apiece which they use to wager on the outcome of the three feats that are performed on each show. The player with the highest cash score at the end of the third round is the winner and receives what money he has accumulated.

Host: Don Galloway.
Assisting Contestants: Donny Evans, Toby Hoffman.
Announcer: Charlie O'Donnell, Tony McClay.
Music: Lee Ringuette.
Executive Producer: Marvin Minoff.
Producer: Walt Case.
Writer: Peter Berlin.
Director: Ron Kantor.
Art Director: Ed Flesh.

THE GUINNESS GAME—30 minutes—Syndicated 1979.

489 GUNSMOKE

Western. Set in Dodge City, Kansas, during the 1880s, the series focuses on the lives and experiences of five people: Matt Dillon, fearless United States marshal; Kitty Russell, proprietor of the Longbranch Saloon, a woman with a heart of gold and eyes for Matt; Galen "Doc" Adams, the kindly and dedicated physician; Chester Goode, Matt's deputy, a man who walks with a limp and "brews a mean pot of coffee" (half-hour episodes); and Festus Haggen, the comic relief, Matt's unkempt, hillbilly deputy (hour episodes).

CAST

Marshal Matt Dillon	James Arness
Kitty Russell	Amanda Blake
Dr. Galen Adams (Doc)	Milburn Stone
Chester Goode	Dennis Weaver
Festus Haggen	Ken Curtis
Newly O'Brien, the gunsmith	Buck Taylor
Sam, the Longbranch bartender	Glenn Strange
	Robert Brubaker
Quint Asper, the blacksmith	Burt Reynolds
Nathan Burke, the freight agent	Ted Jordan
Hank Patterson, the stableman	Hank Patterson
Thad Greenwood, a townsperson	Roger Ewing
Mr. Jones, the general store owner	Dabbs Greer
Barney, the telegraph operator	Charles Seel
Ma Smalley, the owner of the boarding house	Sarah Selby
Mr. Bodkin, the banker	Roy Roberts
Howie, the hotel clerk	Howard Culver
Percy Crump, the undertaker	John Harper
Lathrop, the storekeeper	Woody Chambliss
Halligan, a townsperson	Charles Wagenheim
Ed O'Connor, a rancher	Tod Brown
Louis Pheeters, the town drunk	James Nusser
Dr. John Chapman (temporary replacement for Doc Adams)	Pat Hingle
Miss Hannah, the saloon owner after Kitty	Fran Ryan

Announcer: George Walsh.
Music: Rex Koury, Jerrold Immel, Richard Shores, John Parker.
Executive Producer: Charles Warren, John Mantley, Philip Leacock.
Producer: Norman MacDonnell, Philip Leacock, John Mantley, Edgar Peterson, Joseph Dackow, Leonard Katzman.
Director: Victor French, Robert Butler, Leo Penn, Bernard McEveety, Clyde Ware, William Conrad, Arnold Laven, Charles Warren, Andrew V. McLaglen, Ted Post, Richard Sarafian, Joseph Sargent, Tay Garnett, Gunnar Hellstrom, Philip Leacock, R. G. Springstein, Marc Daniels, Vincent McEveety, Herschel Daughtery, Harry Harris, Sobey Martin, Irving J. Moore, Michael O'Herlihy, Herb Wallerstein, Christian Nyby, Robert Totten, Mark Rydell, Paul Stanley, Harry Horner.

GUNSMOKE—30- and 60-minute versions—CBS—September 10, 1955–September 1, 1975. Syndicated. 233 half-hour episodes; 400 hour episodes. Half-hour episodes are also syndicated as *Marshal Dillon*.

H

490 HAGEN

Crime Drama. The exploits of Paul Hagen, a trapper and hunter who leaves the backwoods of Idaho and journeys to San Francisco where his battles against big city crooks and rip-off artists are dramatized.

CAST

Paul Hagen, a legman for Carl Palmer and Associates, a law firm	Chad Everett
Carl Palmer, Paul's employer	Arthur Hill
Mrs. Chavez, Carl's housekeeper	Carmen Zapata
Captain Hagstrom, S.F.P.D.	Paul Larson
Jody, Carl's secretary	Aldine King
Dr. Dorman	Ray Strickland

Carl Palmer & Associates telephone number: 555-7382.

Music: George Romanis.
Music Supervision: Lionel Newman.
Executive Producer: Frank Glicksman.
Producer: Jack Sowards.
Writer: Charles Larson, Jack Sowards, Simon Wincelberg.
Director: Vincent Sherman, Michael Caffey, Paul Wendkos, Joseph Pevney, Alex March, Seymour Robbie.
Creator: Charles Larson, Frank Glicksman.

HAGEN—60 minutes—CBS—March 1, 1980–April 24, 1980. 9 episodes.

491 HALF THE GEORGE KIRBY COMEDY HOUR

Variety. Sketches coupled with music and songs.

Host: George Kirby.
Regulars: Connie Martin, Jack Duffy, Julie Amato, Steve Martin, Joey Hollingsworth, The Walter Painter Dancers.
Orchestra: Hank Marr.
Executive Producer: Burt Rosen, David Winters, Murray Chercover.
Producer: Bernard Rothman, Jack Wohl.
Writer: Bernard Rothman, Jack Wohl.
Director: Michael Steele.

HALF THE GEORGE KIRBY COMEDY HOUR—30 minutes—Syndicated 1972.

492 HAL ROACH PRESENTS

Anthology. A series of half-hour programs originally produced by the Hal Roach Studios and seen on various series throughout the 1950s.

Included:

It's Always Sunday. An unsold pilot film that revolves around Charles Parker, a soft-touch minister whose kind reputation constantly causes trouble.

Cast: Rev. Charles Parker: Dennis O'Keefe; George: Sheldon Leonard; Eddie: Chick Chandler.

Arroya. A western drama about a self-appointed judge and his attempts to uphold the law in the ruthless town of Arroya.

Cast: Lamar Kendell: Jack Carson; Hattie Warren: Lynn Bari; Hank: Lloyd Corrigan; The Lawyer: William Schallert; Deputy Dodd: Bob Steele; Bart Craddick: Neville Brand.

The Silent Partner. The story focuses on the plight of a once famous, but now forgotten silent movie star.

Cast: Kelsey Dutton: Buster Keaton; Arthur Vail: Joe E. Brown; Selma: Zasu Pitts; Bob Hope: himself; Mr. Shanks: Jack Elam.

HAL ROACH PRESENTS — 30 minutes — Syndicated 1978.

493   THE HALLMARK HALL OF FAME

Anthology. Classical and serious dramas, period plays, and musical adaptations.

Hostess-Performer-Narrator (early years): Sarah Churchill.
Frequently Cast: Julie Harris, Dame Judith Anderson, Maurice Evans.
Announcer: Lee Vines.
Producer: Duane C. Bogie, Gary Smith, Dwight Hemion, John Houseman, Philip Barry, Martin Starger, Walt DeFaria, Warren L. Lockhart, Harry Hirschman, John LeVien, Andre Osborn, Gary Smith, David Susskind, George Schaefer, Frank O'Connor, Norman Rosemont, George Lefferts.

Included:

Stubby Pringle's Christmas (Dec. 17, 1978). The story, set in Montana in 1910, concerns itself with Stubby Pringle, a young cowboy who's eagerly bound for a Christmas Eve dance — until he encounters impoverished homesteaders badly in need of holiday cheer.

Cast: Stubby Pringle: Beau Bridges; Mrs. Henderson: Julie Harris; Red: Edward Binns; Mrs. Harper: Kim Hunter; Hollander: Strother Martin; Janitor: Chill Wills.

Lisa, Bright and Dark (Nov. 28, 1973). An unusual drama about Lisa Schilling, a pretty, bright and outgoing teenage girl who suddenly becomes depressed, withdrawn and subject to outbursts of strange behavior. The tender drama, which offers no simple cure for Lisa's illness, depicts her struggles to cope with a problem no one seems to take seriously.

Cast: Lisa Schilling: Kay Lenz; Margaret Schilling: Anne Baxter; William Schilling: John Forsythe; Mary Nell: Debralee Scott; Betsy: Jamie Smith Jackson; Elizabeth: Anne Lockhart; Brian: Anson Williams.

Peter Pan (Dec. 12, 1976). J. M. Barrie's classic story about Peter Pan, the perennial youth, and his adventures with the Darling children in Never-Never Land, where children never grow up.

Cast: Peter Pan: Mia Farrow; Captain Hook: Danny Kaye; Mrs. Darling: Virginia McKenna; Tiger Lily: Paula Kelly; Wendy Darling: Briony McRoberts; John Darling: Ian Sharrock;

Michael Darling: Adam Stafford; Smee: Tony Sympson; Narrator: John Gielgud.

The Snow Goose (Nov. 15, 1971). The story set on the marshes of England's Essex coast, follows the relationship between Philip Rhayader, a deformed artist, and an orphaned teenage girl named Frith, who are brought together by an injured snow goose.

Cast: Philip: Richard Harris; Frith: Jenny Agutter; Jane: Ludmilla Crowden; Postmistress: Freda Bamford; Recruiting Officer: Graham Crowden; Captain: Noel Johnson.

THE HALLMARK HALL OF FAME — Various Times — NBC — December 24, 1951 – December 17, 1978. 131 programs. CBS — Premiered: November 14, 1979.

494   HANGING IN

Comedy. The story of Louis Harper, a former football hero who, after assisting in politically oriented educational programs, becomes the president of Braddock University. His struggles, as he attempts to adjust to the responsibilities of the position, are the focal point of the series. Originally intended as a new series idea for the departing *Maude*, star Beatrice Arthur bowed out at the last minute and the idea was scratched. It was later turned into "Onward and Upward," a series about a black athlete turned businessman who wins a seat in Congress. John Amos, chosen as the star, quit soon after over a format dispute when the title was changed to "Mr. Dooley." Cleavon Little was brought in to replace him and several episodes were videotaped under the title *Mr. Dugan*, but due to the unfavorable portrayal of blacks, the series never actually aired. Information concerning the story, cast and credits can be found by seeing the title *Mr. Dugan*.

CAST

Louis Harper, the college president	Bill Macy
Maggie Gallagher, the dean of faculty	Barbara Rhoades
Sam Dickey, the director of development	Dennis Burkley
Pinky Nolan, Lou's housekeeper	Nedra Volz
Rita Zepperette, Lou's student helper	Darian Mathias

Commercial Break Announcer: Barbara Rhoades.
Music: Bill Byers.
Executive Producer: Sy Rosen.
Producer: Ken Stump.
Writer: Charlie Hauck, Arthur Julian, William Davenport, Sy Rosen.
Director: Alan Rafkin, Walter C. Miller.
Art Director: C. Murswaki.
Creator: Arthur Julian, Charlie

Hauck, Rod Parker, William Davenport.

HANGING IN — 30 minutes — CBS — August 8, 1979 – August 29, 1979. 4 episodes.

495   THE HANNA-BARBERA HAPPY HOUR

Variety. Songs, dances, music and comedy sketches.

Hosts: Honey and Sis (two life-sized puppets).
Honey and Sis Voices: Udana Power, Wendy McKenzie.
Musical Director: Billy Byers.
Musical Material: Mitzie Welch, Ken Welch.
Executive Producer: Joseph Barbera.
Producer: Ken Welch, Joe Layton, Mitzie Welch.
Director: Jim Washburn, Joe Layton.
Choreographer: Joe Layton.
Puppeteers: Jerry Vogel, J. Paul Higgins, Greg Dendler.
Honey and Sis Segment Director: Bob Mackie.

THE HANNA-BARBERA HAPPY HOUR — 60 minutes — NBC — April 13, 1978 – May 4, 1978. 4 programs.

496   HAPPY DAYS

Variety. The music, dance, song and comedy of the 1930s.

Host: Louis Nye.
Regulars: Chuck McCann, Laara Lacey, Julie McWhirter, Clive Clerk, Bob Elliott and Ray Goulding (Bob and Ray), Alan Copeland, Bill Overland, Jerry Dexter, Jim MacGeorge, The Happy Days Singers, The Wisa D'Orso Dancers.
Orchestra: Jack Elliott, Allyn Ferguson.
Producer: Jack Burns, George Yanok.

Program Open:
Announcer: From television city in Hollywood ... (in echo effect) 39, 38, 37, 36, 35, 34, 33, 32, 31, 30, 30, 30 ...
Louis Nye: I am the thirties and welcome to those Happy Days.
Announcer: Yes, it's time for those Happy Days, with Bob and Ray, Chuck McCann, Laara Lacey, Julie McWhirter, Alan Copeland, Bill Overland, Jerry Dexter, Jim MacGeorge, The Happy Days Band with Jack Elliott and Allyn Ferguson, The Wisa D'Orso Dancers, The Happy Days Singers, and our own silver-tongued host of Happy Days, Louis Nye.
Louis Nye: Good evening ladies and gentlemen. From the fabulous Happy Days Ballroom in downtown Hollywood, California, just a hoot 'n' a holler from the shores of the blue Pacific, the Columbia

Broadcasting System is bringing your way the music and the manner of this wonderful decade, the 1930s.

HAPPY DAYS — 60 minutes — CBS — June 25, 1970 – September 10, 1970. 13 programs.

497   HAPPY DAYS

Comedy. The series, set in Milwaukee, Wisconsin, in the latter 1950s, presents a nostalgic backward glance into the Eisenhower era as seen through the eyes of Richie Cunningham, a shy, naive teenager, and his friend, the wordly wise Warren "Potsie" Webber, both Jefferson High School students.

CAST

Richie Cunningham	Ron Howard
Howard Cunningham, Richie's father (pilot film)	Harold Gould
Howard Cunningham (series)	Tom Bosley
Marion Cunningham, Richie's mother	Marion Ross
Joanie Cunningham, Richie's sister (pilot film)	Susan Neher
Joanie Cunningham (series)	Erin Moran
Chuck Cunningham, Richie's brother (pilot film)	Ric Carrott
Chuck Cunningham (series)	Gavan O'Herlihy Randolph Roberts
Warren "Potsie" Webber, Richie's friend	Anson Williams
Arthur Fonzarelli (Fonzie), Richie's friend, the cool, know-it-all garage mechanic	Henry Winkler
Ralph Malph, Richie's friend	Donny Most
Arnold, the owner of Arnold's, the after-school hangout	Pat Morita
Al Delvecchio, the owner of Arnold's in later episodes	Al Molinaro
Spike, Fonzie's delinquent nephew	Danny Butch
Charles "Chachi" Arcola, Fonzie's cousin	Scott Baio
Lori Beth Allen, Richie's girlfriend	Lynda Goodfriend
Wendy, Potsie's girlfriend	Wendy Hoffman
Arlene, Richie's girlfriend (before Lori)	Tannis Montgomery
Gloria, Richie's girlfriend (after Arlene)	Linda Purl
Marsha Simms, a waitress at Arnold's	Beatrice Colen
Trudy, a friend of the regulars	Tita Bell
Wendy, a waitress at Arnold's (different from previous Wendy)	Misty Rowe
Moose, a friend of Richie's	Ralph Greenberg
Bag, a friend of Richie's	Neil J. Schwartz
Bill "Sticks" Downey, Jr., a friend of Fonzie's	John Anthony Bailey
Pinky Tuscadero, Fonzie's love interest, a singer	Roz Kelly
Lola, one of Pinky's Pinkettes (a singer)	Kelly Sanders
Tina, same as Lola	Doris Hess
Mickey Malph, Ralph's father	Alan Oppenheimer Jack Dodson
Kat Mandu, "the mysterious woman" who helps Fonzie on occasion	Deborah Pratt

Leather Tuscadero, Pinky's kid
  sister, a singer also   Suzy Quatro
Laverne DeFazio, Fonzie's
  friend   Penny Marshall
Shirley Feeney, Laverne's
  friend   Cindy Williams
Harold Cunningham, Richie's
  uncle   Jackie Cooper
Bessie Cunningham,
  Richie's aunt   Peggy Rea
Jenny Piccalo, Joanie's friend Cathy Silvers
Roger Phillips, the basketball coach
  at Jefferson High   Ted McGinley

Address of Arnold's Drive In:
  2815 Lake Avenue.
Garages for which Fonzie works:
  Otto's Auto Orphanage; Herb's
  Auto Repairs; and finally,
  Bronko's Auto Repairing.
Richie's Fraternity (from fall 1977
  when he begins college): Delta
  Gamma.
Howard's Lodge: The Leopard
  Lodge of which he is a Leop-
  ard, first class; later he is made
  the Grand Puba.

Music: Pete King, Frank Com-
  stock, Jack Hays.
Supervising Producer: Lowell
  Ganz.
Executive Producer: Garry Mar-
  shall, Thomas L. Miller, Edward
  K. Milkis.
Producer: Tony Marshall, Jerry
  Paris, William S. Bickley, Gary
  Menteer, Walter Kempley.
Director: Jerry Paris (most of the
  series), Mel Ferber, Frank Bux-
  ton, James Tayne, Don Weis,
  Herb Wallerstein, Art Fisher.

HAPPY DAYS — 30 minutes —
ABC — Premiered: January 15,
1974. The 30-minute pilot film
aired on ABC on February 25,
1972. Spin-off series: *Laverne
and Shirley.*

HAPPY DAYS
AGAIN

The syndicated (1979) title for
"Happy Days" reruns while the
program remains in first run on
the ABC network.

498   THE HARDY BOYS

Animated Cartoon. The global
adventures of the Hardy Boys, a
Rock and Roll group who often
help people in need. Based on
the stories by Franklin W. Dixon.

Characters: Frank and Joe Hardy
  (brothers), Wanda Kay Breck-
  enridge, Pete and Chubby, the
  other members of the group.
Voices: Dallas McKennon, Jane
  Webb, Byron Kane.
Vocals: The real-life Rock group,
  the Hardy Boys.
Music: Gordon Zahler.
Producer: Norm Prescott, Lou
  Scheimer.

THE   HARDY   BOYS — 30
minutes — ABC — September 6,
1969 — September 4, 1970. 26 episodes. Syndicated.

THE HARDY
BOYS/NANCY DREW
MYSTERIES

See individual titles: *The Hardy
Boys Mysteries* and *The Nancy
Drew Mysteries.*

499   THE HARDY BOYS
MYSTERIES

Mystery. The series, set in the
town of Bayport, follows the investigations of juvenile detectives
Frank and Joe Hardy, the sometimes mischievous sons of world
famous private detective Fenton
Hardy. Based on the stories by
Franklin W. Dixon.

CAST

Frank Hardy   Parker Stevenson
Joe Hardy   Shaun Cassidy
Fenton Hardy   Edmund Gilbert
Gertrude Hardy, Fenton's
  sister   Edith Atwater
Calley Shaw, Fenton's
  secretary   Lisa Eilbacher
Harry Morton, the head of the U.S.
  Justice Department, for which
  Frank and Joe work in
  later episodes   Jack Kelly

Music: Stu Phillips.
Theme: Glen A. Larson.
Supervising Producer: Michael
  Sloan.
Executive Producer: Glen A.
  Larson.
Producer: Joyce Brotman, B. W.
  Sandefur, Christopher Crowe,
  Ben Kadish, Joe Boston.
Director: Fernando Lamas, Stuart
  Margolin, Ron Satlof, Vincent
  Edwards, Sidney Hayers, Don
  McDougall, Edward Abroms,
  Richard Benedict, Joseph Pev-
  ney, Dennis Donnelly, Daniel
  Haller.

THE HARDY BOYS MYSTERIES —
60 minutes — ABC — January
30, 1977 — January 21, 1979; June
24, 1979 — August 26, 1979.

500   THE HARLEM
GLOBETROTTERS

Animated Cartoon. The comedy
adventures of the Harlem Globetrotters, basketball magicians
who use their talents both on the
court and off to help good defeat
evil.

VOICES

The Globetrotters:
Meadowlark Lemon   Scatman Crothers
Freddie "Curly" Neal   Stu Gilliam
Gip   Richard Elkins
Bobby Joe Mason   Eddie Anderson
Geese   Johnny Williams
Pablo   Robert Do Qui

Music: Hoyt Curtin.
Executive Producer: William
  Hanna, Joseph Barbera.
Producer: Charles Nichols, Iwao
  Takamoto.
Director: William Hanna, Joseph
  Barbera.

THE HARLEM GLOBETROT-
TERS — 30 minutes — CBS — September 12, 1970 – May 13, 1973.
26 episodes.

501   THE HARLEM
GLOBETROTTERS POPCORN
MACHINE

Children. Varied musical numbers and comedy sketches that
are designed to relate social messages (e.g., good behavior, good
manners) to children.

Starring: The Harlem Globetrot-
  ters (Geese Ausbie, Nate
  Branch, Tex Harrison, Marques
  Haynes, Theodis Lee, Mead-
  owlark Lemon, Bobby Joe Ma-
  son, Curley Neal, John Smith).
Regulars: Avery Schreiber (as Mr.
  Evil), Rodney Allen Rippy.
Orchestra: Jack Elliott, Allyn
  Ferguson.
Executive Producer: Frank Pep-
  piatt, John Aylesworth.
Producer: Norman Baer.
Director: Tony Mordente.

THE HARLEM GLOBETROT-
TERS POPCORN MACHINE — 25
minutes — CBS — September 7,
1974 – August 30, 1975.

502   HARRIS AND
COMPANY

Drama. A realistic approach to
the problems facing a poor black
family as seen through the experiences of Mike Harris, a widowed Los Angeles mechanic and
the father of five children.

CAST

Mike Harris   Bernie Casey
Juanita "J.P."Harris, his
  daughter   Lia Jackson
Liz Harris, his daughter   Renee Brown
David Harris, his son   David Hubbard
Tommy Harris, his son   Eddie Singleton
Richard Allen Harris, his son   Dain Turner
Charlie Adams, Mike's cousin   Stu Gilliam
Harry Foreman, Mike's partner in the
  Foreman-Harris Garage   James Luisi
Louise Foreman, Harry's wife   Lois Walden
Angie Adams, Charlie's
  wife   C. Tillery Banks

The Harris family dog: Richard
Allen, Jr.

Music: J. J. Johnson.
Executive Producer: Stanley G.
  Robertson.
Producer: Arnold Turner.
Director: Tom Blank, Ivan Dixon.

HARRIS AND COMPANY — 60
minutes — NBC — March 15,
1979 – April 5, 1979. 4 episodes.

503   HARRY O

Crime Drama. The series, first set
in San Diego, then in Los Angeles,
follows the investigations of
Harry Orwell, an ex-cop turned
private detective. (During the investigation of a drug store robbery, Orwell is shot in the back
and disabled, and rather than face

a forced retirement, he decides
to become a detective.)

CAST

Harry Orwell   David Janssen
Det. Lt. Manuel ("Manny")
  Quinn, S.D.P.D.   Henry Darrow
Lt. K.C. Trench, L.A.P.D.   Anthony Zerbe
Detective Don Roberts   Paul Tully
Sue Ingrim, Harry's neighbor,
  a stewardess   Farrah Fawcett
Lindsay, Sue's roommate   Loni Anderson
Betsy, Harry's
  neighbor   Katherine Baumann
Lester Hodges, the
  criminologist   Les Lannom

Music: Kim Richmond, Billy Gol-
  denberg.
Executive Producer: Jerry
  Thorpe.
Producer: Robert E. Thompson,
  Robert   Dozier,   Buck
  Houghton, Alex Beaton.
Director: Richard Lang, Jerry
  Thorpe, Joe Manduke, Jerry
  London, Harry Falk, Don Weis,
  Russ Mayberry.
Creator: Howard Rodman.

HARRY O — 60 minutes — ABC —
September 12, 1974 – August 12,
1976. Syndicated. The first pilot
film, "Harry O" aired on ABC (60
minutes) on March 11, 1973. The
second pilot film, which sold the
series, "Smile Jenny, You're
Dead," aired on ABC (2 hours) on
February 3, 1974.

504   HART TO HART

Crime Drama. The story of
Jonathan Hart, the wealthy head
of Hart Industries, and Jennifer
Hart, his beautiful wife, an au-
thoress. They form a perfectly
matched couple with time,
money and a shared hobby —
helping people in trouble.

CAST

Jonathan Hart   Robert Wagner
Jennifer Hart   Stefanie Powers
Max, their Man Friday   Lionel Stander
Deanne, Jonathan's
  secretary   Mimi Maynard
Marcus Wheeler, Jonathan's office
  aide (pilot film)   Eugene Roche
Marcus Wheeler (series)   Alex Dreier
Stanley Frieson, works for
  Jonathan   Lee Wilkof
Police Lieutenant Moss   Michael Lerner

The Harts's address: 3100 Willow
  Pond Road, Los Angeles.
Hart Industries address: 112
  North La Palmas, Los Angeles.
The Harts's dog: Freeway.

Commercial Break Announcer:
  Lionel Stander.
Music: Mark Snow.
Theme: "Hart To Hart" by Roger
  Nichols.
Executive Producer: Aaron Spel-
  ling, Leonard Goldberg.
Producer: David Levinson, Mart
  Crowley.
Writer: Laurence Richards, David
  Solomon, Edward Martino,

Richard DeRoy, David Levinson, Allyn Freeman, Jeff and Donna Myrow, Bob Shayne, Donald Ross, Bill and Jo Lamond.

Director: Ray Austin, Earl Bellamy, Tom Mankiewicz, Sam Wanamaker, Leo Penn, Seymour Robbie, Ralph Senensky, Alan Cooke, George E. Brooks, Alex March.

Creator: Sidney Sheldon.

Program Open:

Max (over scenes of Jonathan and Jennifer driving): This is my boss, Jonathan Hart, a self-made millionaire, he's quite a guy. This is Mrs. H., she's gorgeous, what a terrific lady. By the way, my name is Max, I take care of them, which ain't easy—'cause their hobby is murder!

HART TO HART—60 minutes—ABC—Premiered: September 22, 1979. The two-hour pilot film aired on ABC on August 25, 1979.

505   THE HARVEY KORMAN SHOW

Comedy. The series, set in Hollywood, follows the misadventures of Harvey Kavanaugh, an aging actor with a small career, as he attempts to find work in a world that he feels is bypassing him.

CAST

Harvey A. Kavanaugh	Harvey Korman
Maggie Kavanaugh, his daughter (pilot film)	Susan Lawrence
Maggie Kavanaugh (series)	Christine Lahti
Jake, his agent	Milton Selzer
Stuart Stafford, Maggie's boyfriend	Barry Van Dyke
Bernie, Harvey's friend	Harry Gold

Music: Peter Matz.

Executive Producer: Hal Dresner.

Producer: Don Van Atta.

Director: Alan Myerson, Jeff Bleckner.

Creator: Hal Dresner.

THE HARVEY KORMAN SHOW—30 minutes—ABC—March 4, 1978–April 18, 1978; July 15, 1978–August 4, 1978. 6 episodes. The pilot episode aired on ABC on January 31, 1978.

HAVING BABIES

See titles *Julie Farr, M.D.,* in the regular program section, and "Having Babies I," "Having Babies II" and "Having Babies III," in the pilot film section.

506   HAWAII FIVE-O

Crime Drama. The cases of Steve McGarrett, a plainclothes detective with Hawaii Five-O, a special computerized branch of the Hawaiian Police Department (based in Honolulu in the Lolani Palace, the fictitious headquarters of the Hawaiian government).

CAST

Det. Steve McGarrett	Jack Lord
Det. Danny Williams	James MacArthur
Det. Chin Ho Kelly	Kam Fong
Det. Kono	Zulu
Det. Ben Kokua	Al Harrington
Det. Lori Wilson	Sharon Farrell
Det. James "Kimo" Carew	William Smith
Officer Moe "Truck" Kealoha	Moe Keale
Det. Che Fong	Harry Endo
Doc Bergman, the medical examiner	Al Eben
The governor	Richard Denning
John Manicote, the attorney general	Morgan White Glenn Cannon
Wo Fat, McGarrett's nemesis, the criminal	Khigh Dhiegh
Tony Alika, the underworld boss	Ross Martin
Det. Duke Mikila	Herman Wedemeyer
Edna, an H.P.D. secretary	Barbara Luna
Jenny, an H.P.D. secretary	Peggy Ryan Patricia Barne
May, an H.P.D. secretary	Maggi Parker
Dr. Judith Patrick	Linda Ryan

Music: Morton Stevens, Pete Rugolo, Bruce Broughton, Don B. Ray, Richard Clements, James Di Pasquale, Duane Tatro.

Supervising Producer: Gene Levitt, Fredric Baum, Franklin Barton.

Executive Producer: Philip Leacock, Bob Sweeney, Gene Levitt, Fred Baum, Leonard Freeman.

Producer: Andrew Gottlieb, William Phillips, Bob Sweeney, Bill Finnegan, Douglas Greene, Richard Newton, Stanley Kallis, William O'Brien, Leonard B. Kaufman, Leonard Katzman, Jim Heinz.

Director: Barry Crane, Don Weis, Robert Morrison, Edward Abroms, Reza S. Badiyi, Harry Hogan, Ralph Levy, John Peyser, Ernest Pintoff, Philip Leacock, Jack Lord, Joe Manduke, Bruce Bilson, Michael O'Herlihy, Douglas Greene, Paul Stanley, Beau Van den Ecker, Robert Butler, Marvin Chomsky, William Hale, Gary Nelson, Leo Penn, Sutton Roley, Barry Shear, David Friedkin, Richard Benedict, Abner Biberman, Michael Caffey, Charles S. Dubin, Robert Gist, Alf Kjellin, Robert Scheerer, Allen Reisner, Tony Leader.

Creator: Leonard Freeman.

HAWAII FIVE-O—60 minutes—CBS—September 26, 1968–April 5, 1980. 284 episodes. Syndicated.

507   HAWK

Crime Drama. The story of John Hawk, a detective with the Manhattan (New York) district attorney's special detective squad, an elite team of plainclothes operatives that is designed to corrupt

the inner workings of the underworld. Part Iroquois Indian and a prowler of the night, Hawk excels in solving crimes perpetrated by those whose specialty is working by dark.

CAST

Det. John Hawk	Burt Reynolds
Det. Dan Carter, his assistant	Wayne Grice
Sam Crown, Hawk's informant	John Marley
Murray Slacken, the assistant D.A.	Bruce Glover
Ed Gorten, Hawk's superior	Leon Janney

Music: Nelson Riddle, Kenyon Hopkins.

Music Consultant: Don Kirshner.

Music Supervision: Ed Forsythe.

Executive Producer: Hubbell Robinson.

Producer: Paul Bogart.

Director: Paul Henried, Burt Reynolds, Leonard J. Horn, Richard Benedict, Sam Wanamaker, Tom Donovan.

Creator: Allan Sloane.

HAWK—60 minutes—ABC—September 15, 1966–December 29, 1966. NBC Rebroadcasts: April 21, 1976–August 11, 1976. 17 episodes.

508   HAWKINS

Crime Drama. The cases and courtroom defenses of Billy Jim Hawkins, a shrewd, common-sense criminal attorney working out of West Virginia.

CAST

Billy Jim Hawkins	James Stewart
R. J. Hawkins, his cousin and assistant	Strother Martin
D.A. Harrelson	David Huddleston
Judge	Ivan Bonar

Music: George Romanis, Jerry Goldsmith.

Executive Producer: Norman Felton.

Producer: David Karp.

Director: Jeff Corey (six episodes), Jud Taylor (one episode).

HAWKINS—90 minutes—CBS—October 2, 1973–September 3, 1974. 7 episodes. The 90-minute pilot film, "Hawkins on Murder," aired on CBS on March 13, 1973.

509   HEADLINERS WITH DAVID FROST

Interview. Live and videotaped interviews with "people who are making the news."

Host: David Frost.

Regulars: Liz Smith, Kelly Garrett.

Music: Elliott Lawrence.

Executive Producer: David Frost.

Producer: John Gilroy.

Director: Bruce Gowers.

HEADLINERS WITH DAVID FROST—60 minutes—NBC—May 31, 1978–July 5, 1978. 6 programs.

510   HEADMASTER

Comedy Drama. A tender portrayal of student-teacher relationships and their problems, both scholastic and personal, as seen through the eyes of Andy Thompson, the headmaster of Concord, a small, private coeducational high school in California.

CAST

Andy Thompson	Andy Griffith
Margaret Thompson, his wife	Claudette Nevins
Jerry Brownell, the athletic coach	Jerry Van Dyke
Mr. Purdy, the school custodian	Parker Fennelly
Judy, Andy's student helper	Lani O'Grady

Music: Patrick Williams.

Theme: "He's Only a Man" by Dick Williams.

Theme Vocal: Linda Ronstadt.

Executive Producer: Richard O. Linke.

Producer: Aaron Ruben.

Creator: Aaron Ruben.

HEADMASTER—30 minutes—CBS—September 18, 1970–January 1, 1971. Rebroadcasts (CBS): June 25, 1971–September 10, 1971. 13 episodes.

511   HE AND SHE

Comedy. The series, set in New York City, follows the trials and tribulations of the Hollisters: Dick, a cartoonist, the creator of the comic-strip-turned-television series, "Jetman," and his wife, Paula, a beautiful, but scatter-brained traveler's-company aide.

CAST

Richard Hollister	Richard Benjamin
Paula Hollister, his wife	Paula Prentiss
Oscar North, the egotistical star of "Jetman"	Jack Cassidy
Andrew Hummel, the apartment building's not-so-handyman	Hamilton Camp
Harry, Richard's friend, the fireman	Kenneth Mars
Norman Nugent, Richard's employer	Harold Gould
Murray Mouse, Richard's accountant	Alan Oppenheimer

Music: Jerry Fielding.

Executive Producer: Leonard B. Stern.

Producer: Don Melnick, Arne Sultan.

Director: Leonard B. Stern, Jay Sandrich.

Creator: Leonard B. Stern.

HE AND SHE—30 minutes—CBS—September 6, 1967–September 18, 1968. CBS Rebroadcasts: June 26, 1970–September 11, 1970.

512   THE HEATHCLIFF AND DINGBAT SHOW

Animated Cartoon.

Segments:

Heathcliff. The antics of Heath-

CBS

Hawaii Five-O. From left, Jack Lord, Sharon Farrell,
William Smith, Herman Wedemeyer and Moe Keale.

NBC

Hello, Larry. Gary Coleman, at left, with Conrad Bain of
Diff'rent Strokes. At right, McLean Stevenson with Kim
Richards of *Hello, Larry.* Courtesy of the *Call-Chronicle
Newspapers,* Allentown, Pa.

CBS

The Honeymooners. From left, Jackie Gleason, Audrey
Meadows, Art Carney and Joyce Randolph.

cliff, a very mischievous cat who delights in annoying others.

Dingbat and the Creeps. The misadventures of Dingbat, a vampire dog, Bone Head (a skeleton), and Nobody (a pumpkin), as they attempt to help people in distress.

Voices: Mel Blanc (as Heathcliff), Julie McWhirter, Marilyn Schreffler, Michael Bell, Melendy Britt, Rachel Blake, Henry Corden, Joan Van Ark, Joe Baker, Alan Oppenheimer, Shep Menkin.
Music: Dean Elliott.
Executive Producer: Joe Ruby, Ken Spears.
Producer: Jerry Eisenberg.
Director: Rudy Larriva, Charles A. Nichols, John Kimball.

THE HEATHCLIFF AND DINGBAT SHOW—30 minutes—ABC— Premiered: October 4, 1980.

513   HEC RAMSEY

Western. The series, set in New Prospect, Oklahoma, in 1901, details the exploits of Deputy Hector "Hec" Ramsey, an ex-gunfighter turned law enforcer who attempts to solve crimes by means of scientific evaluation and deduction.

CAST

Deputy Hec Ramsey	Richard Boone
Sheriff Oliver B. Stamp	Richard Lenz
Amos B. Coogan, the town barber	Harry Morgan
Norma Muldoon, Hec's romantic interest	Sharon Acker
Andy Muldoon, Norma's son	Brian Dewey

Narrator: Harry Morgan.
Music: Fred Steiner, Lee Holdridge.
Producer: Douglas Benton, Harold Jack Bloom.
Writer: Richard Fiedler, Harold Swanton, Brad Radnitz, John Meston, Mann Rubin, Simon Wincelberg, Harold Jack Bloom, Douglas Benton, S. Bar-David, William R. Cox, Joseph Michael Calvelli.
Director: Harry Morgan, Richard Quine, Herschel Daughtery, George Marshall, Andrew V. McLaglen, Douglas Benton, Nicholas Colasanto, Alex March, Daniel Petrie.

HEC RAMSEY—90- and 120-minute versions—NBC—October 8, 1972–August 25, 1974 (as a segment of *The NBC Sunday Mystery Movie*). The first episode and pilot film, "The Century Turns," is syndicated as a two-hour movie.

514   HEE HAW

Variety. Performances by Country and Western artists coupled with short skits and running gags played against the Nashville Sound.

Hosts: Buck Owens, Roy Clark.
Regulars: Barbi Benton, Linda Thompson, Kathie Lee Johnson, Gailard Sartain, Misty Rowe, Gunilla Hutton, Cathy Baker, Roni Stoneman, Louis Marshall (Grandpa Jones), Don Harron, John Henry Faulk, Buck Trent, Archie Campbell, Sheb Wooley, The Hagers, Gordie Tapp, Jeannine Riley, Susan Raye, Jennifer Bishop, Lulu Roman, Minnie Pearl, Zella Lehr, Alvin "Junior" Samples, Claude Phelps, Jimmy Riddle, Don Rich, Ann Randall, Mary Ann Gordon, Kenny Price, Don Gibson, George Lindsey, Jimmy Little, The Hagers, The Buckaroos, The Inspiration, The Nashville Addition, and Beauregard the Wonder Dog.

Musical Director: George Richey, Charlie McCoy.
Executive Producer: Frank Peppiatt.
Producer: Sam Lovullo, Bill Davis.
Writer: Gordie Tapp, Don Harron, Archie Campbell, Bud Wingard.
Director: Bob Boatman, Bill Davis.

HEE HAW—60 minutes—CBS— June 15, 1969–July 13, 1971. Syndicated first run in September 1971.

515   THE HEE HAW HONEYS

Comedy-Variety. The story of the Honey family, the owner-operators of a Country music nightclub in Nashville, Tennessee. The series, which is actually an extension of *Hee Haw*, presents music and songs by guests.

CAST

Kenny Honey, the father	Kenny Price
Lulu Honey, his wife	Lulu Roman
Kathie Lee Honey, their daughter	Kathie Lee Johnson
Misty Honey, their daughter	Misty Rowe
Willy Billy Honey, their son	Gailard Sartain

Music: Charlie McCoy.
Executive Producer: Sam Louvello.
Producer: Barry Adelman.
Director: Bob Boatman.

THE HEE HAW HONEYS—30 minutes—Syndicated 1978. See also *The Hee Haw Honeys* in the pilot film section for information on the original concept of the series.

516   THE HELEN REDDY SHOW

Musical Variety.

Hostess: Helen Reddy.
Regulars: The Jaime Rogers Dancers.
Orchestra: Nelson Riddle.

Executive Producer: Monte Kay, Flip Wilson.
Producer: Carolyn Ruskin.
Writer: Gene Perret, Ray Taylor, Lila Garrett, Lynn Roth.
Director: Tim Kiley.

THE HELEN REDDY SHOW—60 minutes—NBC—June 28, 1973– August 16, 1973.

517   HELLO, LARRY

Comedy. The story of Larry Adler (later changed to Alder), the host of "Hello, Larry" (later, "The Larry Alder Show"), a radio phone-in program in Portland, Oregon, and the divorced father of two pretty teenage daughters, Ruthie and Diane. Episodes relate his misadventures as he struggles to raise his daughters and cope with the situations that arise from being a single parent. (Larry works for station KLOW, the phone number of which is 555-3567.)

CAST

Larry Adler (Alder)	McLean Stevenson
Ruthie Adler (Alder), his daughter	Kim Richards
Diane Adler (Alder), his daughter	Donna Wilkes
	Krista Errickson
Morgan Winslow, Larry's producer	Joanna Gleason
Earl, Larry's engineer	George Memmoli
Leona Wilson, Larry's neighbor	Ruth Brown
Meadowlark Lemon, the sporting goods store owner; Larry's friend	Himself
Henry Alder, Larry's father	Fred Stuthman
Marion Alder, Larry's ex-wife	Shelley Fabares
Scott Taylor, Marion's boyfriend	Don Chastain
Tommy Roscini, the Alder's neighbor	John Femia
Marie Roscini, Tommy's mother	Rita Taggert
Wendell, the drunk, Larry's fan club president	Will Hunt
Lionel Barton I, the owner of KLOW	Parley Baer
Lionel Barton III, Barton's grandson	David Landesberg

Larry's home phone number: 555-4521.
Morgan's potted plant: Fern.
Off-Camera Voices (Telephone callers for Larry's show): Judith Hurst, Kip King, John Myhers, Johnny Silver, F. William Parker, Sheryl Ford.
Music: John La Salle, Tom Smith.
Executive Producer: Perry Grant, Dick Bensfield, George Tibbles.
Producer: Patricia Fass Palmer, George Tibbles, Rita Dillon, Woody Kling.
Director: Doug Rogers.
Art Director: Don Roberts.
Creator: Doug Rogers.

HELLO, LARRY—30 minutes— NBC. January 26, 1979–August 10, 1979. 11 episodes (includes

one episode broadcast as "Diff'rent Strokes/Hello, Larry"). October 12, 1979–April 30, 1980. 22 episodes.

518   HELP! IT'S THE HAIR BEAR BUNCH

Animated Cartoon. The misadventures of the Hair Bear Bunch (Hair, Square and Bubi), three bears who live in Cave Block Number 9 of the Wonderland Zoo, as they struggle to improve their living conditions.

VOICES

Hair Bear	Daws Butler
Bubi Bear	Paul Winchell
Square Bear	Bill Calloway
Mr. Peevley, the zoo keeper	John Stephenson
Botch, Peevley's assistant	Joe E. Ross

Additional Voices: Hal Smith, Jeannine Brown, Joan Gerber, Janet Waldo, Lennie Weinrib.
Music: Hoyt Curtin.
Executive Producer: William Hanna, Joseph Barbera.
Producer: Charles Nichols.
Director: William Hanna, Joseph Barbera.

HELP! IT'S THE HAIR BEAR BUNCH—30 minutes—CBS— September 11, 1971–September 2, 1972.

519   HERE COME THE BRIDES

Adventure. The series, set in Seattle, Washington, in 1870, follows the adventures of Jason, Joshua and Jeremy Bolt, three brothers who run a logging camp. Episodes during the first season also depict the Bolts' efforts to keep in Seattle for one year a hundred marriageable women, mostly war widows Jason transported from Massachusetts to satisfy his woman-starved loggers. Failure to do so awards to Aaron Stemple, the sawmill owner who financed Jason's trip and saved the camp, Bridal Veil Mountain, the legacy left to the Bolts by their parents.

CAST

Jason Bolt	Robert Brown
Joshua Bolt	David Soul
Jeremy Bolt	Bobby Sherman
Lottie Hatfield, the saloon owner	Joan Blondell
Candy Puritt, Jeremy's romantic interest	Bridget Hanley
Aaron Stemple, the sawmill owner	Mark Lenard
Fred R. Clancy, the ship captain	Henry Beckman
Corky Sam McGee, the camp foreman	Bo Svenson
Biddie Gloom, one of the brides	Susan Tolsky
Miss Essie, the school teacher	Mitzi Hoag
Ben Jenkins, a logger	Hoke Howell
Molly Pruitt, Candy's sister	Patti Cohoon
Christopher Pruitt, Candy's brother	Eric Chase

Reverend Mr. Gaddings	William Schallert
Reverend (later	
episodes)	Lindsay Workman
Amanda, one of	
the brides	Kristina Holland
Peggy, one of the brides	Mary Jo Kennedy
Lulu, one of the brides	Stefani Warren
Ann, one of the brides	Cynthia Hull
Franny, one of the brides	Carole Shelyne
Maude, one of the brides	Myra de Groot
Polly, one of the brides	Loretta Leversee
Beth, one of the brides	Susannah Darrow

Music: Warren Barker, Hugo Montenegro.
Executive Producer: Bob Claver.
Producer: Stan Schwimmer, Paul Junger Witt.

HERE COME THE BRIDES—60 minutes—ABC—September 25, 1968–September 18, 1970. 52 episodes. Syndicated.

520   HERE COME THE DOUBLE DECKERS

Comedy. The misadventures of Scooper, Spring, Billie, Brains, Doughnut, Sticks and Tiger, seven children, as they attempt to solve problems without help from the adult world. (The title is derived from the children's club house, a double-decker bus that is parked in a London junkyard.)

CAST

Scooper	Peter Firth
Spring	Brinsley Forde
Billie	Gillian Bailey
Brains	Michael Auderson
Doughnut	Douglas Simmonds
Sticks	Bruce Clark
Tiger	Debbie Russ
Albert, their adult friend	Melvyn Hayes

HERE COME THE DOUBLE DECKERS—30 minutes—ABC—September 12, 1970–September 3, 1972. 17 episodes. Produced in England.

521   HERE'S BOOMER

Adventure. The story of Boomer, a homeless shaggy dog, who roams the country and helps people in distress.

Starring: Boomer (owned and trained by Ray Berwick, Bryan Refreno).
Music: David Frank.
Theme: "Here's Boomer" by Zoey Wilson, Edward Leonetti.
Supervising Producer: Daniel Wilson.
Executive Producer: Daniel Wilson, A. C. Lyles.
Producer: Fran Sears.
Director: Larry Elikann, Michael Caffey, Claudio Guzman, Paul Leaf, Victor Lobl, Sigmund Neufeld, Jr.

Included:

Molly. The premiere episode in which Boomer seeks to help a young girl named Molly, who is actually hard of hearing, but believed by her parents to be retarded.

Cast: Molly: Natasha Ryan; Alice, her mother: Dee Wallace; Ken, her father: Guy Boyd.

Tell 'Em Boomer Sent You. Boomer's misadventures when he is chosen to represent a new dog food's advertising campaign—and how he reunites a father, an executive with the ad agency, with his son, whom he neglects.

Cast: Matt, the father: John Reilly; Jackie, his son: Michael J. Fox; Liz: Doris Roberts; Bonnie: Marie Masters.

Private Eye. Boomer's attempts to help a typical out-of-the movies type of private eye guard a wealthy family's jewels.

Cast: Kolodny, the private eye: Ron Silver; Samantha Caldwell: Janet Julian; Thelma Caldwell: Rue McClanahan; Eugene: Stephen Pearlman; Philip Osborne: Jonathan Franks.

HERE'S BOOMER—30 minutes—NBC—March 14, 1980–August 29, 1980. 10 episodes. See also "A Christmas for Boomer" in the pilot film section.

522   HERE'S LUCY

Comedy. The misadventures of Lucille Carter, the nosey, overzealous secretary to Harrison Otis Carter, her brother-in-law, the owner of the Unique Employment Agency ("Unusual Jobs for Unusual People").

CAST

Lucille Carter, a widow	Lucille Ball
Harrison Otis Carter,	
her employer	Gale Gordon
Kim Carter, her daughter	Lucie Arnaz
Craig Carter, her son	Desi Arnaz, Jr.
Mary Jane Lewis, Lucille's	
friend	Mary Jane Croft

The Carters' address: 4863 Valley Lawn Drive, Los Angeles.
Music: Marl Young.
Executive Producer: Gary Morton.
Producer: Cleo Smith.
Director: Jerry Paris, Herbert Kenwith, Danny Dayton, Ross Martin, Jack Donohue, Jack Baker, Jack Carter, Coby Ruskin, George Marshall.

HERE'S LUCY—30 minutes—CBS—September 23, 1968–September 2, 1974. 144 episodes.

523   HERE WE GO AGAIN

Comedy. The series, set in Encino, California, is a story of love, divorce and remarriage.

Richard Evans, an easy-going architect, and his bossy and formidably efficient wife, Judy, the editor of *Screen World* magazine, terminate their relationship after seventeen years. They have one son, Jeff.

Jerry Standish, a philandering ex-quarterback for the Los Angeles Rams, now the owner of the Polynesia Paradise Café, and his wife Susan, end their marriage of ten years due to his endless romantic involvements. They have two children, Cindy and Jan.

Seeking information concerning the development of a research center for underprivileged children, Susan and Richard meet, fall in love, marry and establish housekeeping in the Standish home. Jerry Standish maintains a bachelor apartment one block away; and Judy Evans lives one-half mile away.

Episodes relate the struggles of the newlyweds to find serenity in a neighborhood where they are plagued by the constant intrusion of their former spouses.

CAST
(Character relationships are stated in the story line)

Richard Evans	Larry Hagman
Susan Evans (Standish)	Diane Baker
Judy Evans	Nita Talbot
Jerry Standish	Dick Gautier
Jan Evans (Standish)	Kim Richards
Cindy Evans (Standish)	Leslie Graves
Jeff Evans	Chris Beaumont

Music: Al DeLory.
Theme: "Here We Go Again" vocal by Carol Sagar and Peter Allen.
Executive Producer: Charles Fries.
Producer: Robert Kaufman, Stan Schwimmer.
Writer: Charlotte Brown, Ray Brenner, Pamela Herbert Chais, Gordon Farr, Jack Guss, Bernie Kahn, Austin and Irma Kalish, Arnold Kane, Bob Kaufman, Jerry Mayer, Steve Pritzker, Milt Rosen, Gene Thompson.
Director: Marc Daniels, Theodore J. Flicker, Jerry London, Russ Mayberry, Bill Persky, Alan Rafkin, Oscar Rudolph, Jay Sandrich, Mel Stuart.
Director of Photography: Robert C. Moreno, Meredith M. Nicholson, Leonard Smith.
Art Director: Paul Sylos.

HERE WE GO AGAIN—30 minutes—ABC—January 20, 1973–June 23, 1973. 13 episodes.

524   THE HIGH CHAPARRAL

Western. The series, set in Tucson, Arizona, during the 1870s, follows the saga of the Cannon family as they struggle to maintain and operate the High Chaparral Ranch in an era of violence and lawlessness.

CAST

John Cannon, the ranch	
owner	Leif Erickson
Buck Cannon, his	
brother	Cameron Mitchell
Victoria de Montoya Cannon,	
John's wife	Linda Cristal
Billy Blue Cannon, John's son, by a	
former marriage	Mark Slade
Don Sebastian de Montoya,	
the owner of the	
Montoya Ranch	Frank Silvera
Manolito de Montoya, Don	
Sebastian's son	Henry Darrow
Sam, the ranch foreman	Don Collier
Ira, a wrangler	Jerry Summers
Soldado, a ranch hand	James Almonza
Ted Reno, a ranch hand	Ted Markland
Pedro, a ranch hand	Roberto Contreras
Wind, a ranch hand	Rudy Ramos
Joe, a ranch hand	Bob Hoy
Vaquero, a ranch hand	Rodolfo Acosta

Music: Harry Sukman, David Rose.
Executive Producer: David Dortort.
Producer: William F. Claxton, James Schmerer.
Director: Leon Benson, William F. Claxton, Harry Harris, Joseph Pevney, Allen Reisner, Don Richardson, Seymour Robbie, Richard Sarafian, Ralph Senensky, Paul Stanley, William Wiard, William Witney.
Creator: David Dortort.

THE HIGH CHAPARRAL—60 minutes—NBC—September 10, 1967–September 10, 1971. 96 episodes. Syndicated.

525   HIGHCLIFFE MANOR

Comedy. A gothic farce about the eccentric residents of the Blacke Foundation, a scientific research institute located in Highcliffe Manor on a desolate island.

CAST

Helen Blacke, the owner of	
the foundation	Shelley Fabares
Frances Cascan, a	
scientist	Eugenie Ross-Leming
Wendy Sparks, a secretary	Audrey Landers
Rebecca, the housekeeper	Jenny O'Hara
Bram Shelley, the bionic man Frances	
is building	Christian Marlowe
Dr. Felix Morger, the man who seeks	
to seduce Helen	Gerald Gordon
The Rev. Mr. Ian	
Glenville	Stephen McHattie
Smythe, Glenville's valet	Ernie Hudson
Cheng, Frances' assistant	Harold Sakata
Dr. Sanchez	Luis Avalos
Dr. Koontz	Marty Zagon

Narrator: Peter Lawford.
Theme: "Highcliffe Manor" by Frank DeVol.
Music: Robert Alberti.
Producer: Brad Buckner, Eugenie Ross-Leming.
Associate Producer: Patricia Fass Palmer.
Director: Nick Havinga.

HIGHCLIFFE MANOR—30 minutes—NBC—April 12, 1979–May 3, 1979. 4 episodes. The series ended one week earlier than scheduled (May 10, 1979) due to the rush-on premiere of *Hizzoner*.

526 HIGH HOPES

Serial. The dramatic story of Dr. Neal Chapman, a family counselor in the fictional town of Cambridge, Canada.

CAST

Dr. Neal Chapman	Bruce Gray
Jessie Chapman	Miranne McIsaac
Paula Myles	Nuala Fitzgerald
Trudy Bowen	Barbara Kyle
Walter Telford	Colin Fox
Meg Chapman	Doris Petrie
Amy Sperry	Gena Dick
Louise Bates	Jayne Eastwood
Michael Stewart, Sr.	Michael Tait
Michael Stewart, Jr.	Gordon Thompson
Georgia Morgan	Gerry Salsberg
Carol Tauss	Dorothy Malone
Victor Tauss	Nehemiah Persoff
Dr. Dan Gerard	Jan Muszynski

Music: Aeolus Productions.
Music Supervision: Teri Smith.
Producer: Dick Cox.
Director: Patrick Corbett, Barry Cranston, Bruce Minnix.

HIGH HOPES — 30 minutes — Syndicated 1978. 65 episodes.

527 HIGH ROLLERS

Game. A general-knowledge question is read and the first of two players to answer receives control of two large dice, the roll of which he may either keep or pass to his opponent.

The dice are rolled, and according to the numbers that appear, the player is permitted to select any combination of numbers from a large board that equal the rolled numbers. Each number contains a concealed merchandise prize and once selected, that number becomes inactive for the round. The game continues in this manner until one player is disqualified by rolling a number that cannot be duplicated on the board. The winner receives the prizes he has accumulated on his side of the board.

Host: Alex Trebek.
Dice Roller: Ruta Lee.
Substitute Dice Roller: Linda Kaye Henning, Suzanne Somers, Dawn Wells, Nanette Fabray, Leslie Uggams.
Announcer: Kenny Williams.
Music: Stan Worth.
Executive Producer: Merrill Heatter, Bob Quigley.
Producer: Robert Noah.
Director: Jerome Shaw.

HIGH ROLLERS — 30 minutes — NBC — July 1, 1974 – June 11, 1976. 465 programs.

528 HIGH ROLLERS

Game. A syndicated version of the previous title, which see for format.

Host: Alex Trebek.
Dice Roller: Elaine Stewart.
Announcer: Kenny Williams.
Music: Stan Worth.
Executive Producer: Merrill Heatter, Bob Quigley.
Producer: Robert Noah.
Director: Jerome Shaw.

HIGH ROLLERS — 30 minutes — Syndicated 1975.

529 HIGH ROLLERS

Game. An updated version of the NBC series which encompasses the same format, but with much more valuable prizes. See the first *High Rollers* title for format.

Host: Alex Trebek.
Announcer: Kenny Williams.
Music: Stan Worth.
Executive Producer: Merrill Heatter, Bob Quigley.
Producer: Robert Noah.
Director: Jerome Shaw.

HIGH ROLLERS — 30 minutes — NBC — April 22, 1978 – June 10, 1980. 520 programs.

530 THE HILARIOUS HOUSE OF FRIGHTENSTEIN

Children. The series, which is set in the castle of Frightenstein in Transylvania, is composed of comedy sketches, songs, blackouts and music that revolve around Count Frightenstein, his servant Igor and their attempts to bring to life Bruce, an "out of order" Frankenstein-style monster.

CAST

Count Frightenstein	Billy Van
Igor, his assistant	Rais Fishka
Dr. Pet Vet	Billy Van
The Librarian	Billy Van
Gruselda, the cook	Billy Van

Host: Vincent Price.
Regulars: Professor Julius Sumner Miller, Joe Torby, Guy Big.
Executive Producer-Director-Creator-Writer: Rif Markowitz.

THE HILARIOUS HOUSE OF FRIGHTENSTEIN — 30 minutes — Syndicated 1975.

531 HIZZONER

Comedy. The life and times of Michael Cooper, the kind-hearted mayor of an unidentified Midwestern city.

CAST

Mayor Michael Cooper	David Huddleston
Ginny Linden, his assistant	Diana Muldaur
Annie Cooper, his daughter	Kathy Cronkite
Nails Doyle, Michael's butler	Mickey Deems
Melanie, Ginny's secretary	Gina Hecht
Timmons, the mayor's chief of staff	Don Galloway
James Cooper, the mayor's son	Will Seltzer

Music: Bob Alberti.
Theme Vocal: David Huddleston.

Executive Producer: David Huddleston.
Producer: Sheldon Keller, Leonard Friedlander.
Director: Joan Darling, Will MacKenzie, Howard Storm.
Creator: David Huddleston, Sheldon Keller.

HIZZONER — 30 minutes — NBC — May 10, 1979 – June 24, 1979. 5 episodes. The series premiered one week earlier than originally scheduled, thus canceling the last episode of *Highcliffe Manor.*

532 HOGAN'S HEROES

Comedy. The series, set in Stalag 13, a German prisoner-of-war camp during World War II, follows the exploits of Robert Hogan, a U.S. Air Corps colonel, as he manipulates the camp to aid the Allies (operating under the code name "Papa Bear") and obtain top secret German information for his superiors.

CAST

Col. Robert Hogan	Bob Crane
Col. Wilhelm Klink, the commandant of Stalag 13	Werner Klemperer
Sgt. Hans Schultz, Klink's bumbling assistant	John Banner
Helga, Klink's secretary (early episodes)	Cynthia Lynn
Hilda, Klink's secretary (later episodes)	Sigrid Valdis
Colonel Crittendon, the commandant of Stalag 16	Bernard Fox
Major Hockstedder, the Gestapo commander	Howard Caine
Marya, the beautiful Russian spy	Nita Talbot
Gen. Alfred Burkhalter, the Luftwaffe officer in charge of prison camps	Leon Askin
Gertrude Linkmier, Alfred's sister*	Kathleen Freeman
The Prisoners of War:	
Louis LeBeau, the French corporal	Robert Clary
Peter Newkirk, the English corporal	Richard Dawson
Andrew Carter, the American sergeant	Larry Hovis
Richard Baker, the American sergeant	Kenneth Washington
James Kinchloe, the American corporal	Ivan Dixon

Music: Jerry Fielding, Fred Steiner.
Music Supervision: Richard Berres.
Producer: Edward H. Feldman.
Director: Robert Butler, Irving J. Moore, Ivan Dixon, Gene Reynolds, Howard Morris.

HOGAN'S HEROES — 30 minutes — CBS — September 17, 1965 – July 4, 1971. 168 episodes. Syndicated.

*Her husband, Otto, is reported to be missing in Russia. Alfred is thus trying to marry her off to Klink.

533 HOLLYWOOD

Documentary. A British-produced series that traces the history of the Hollywood silent film via film clips and interviews with guests from the golden era.

Narrator: James Mason.
Music: Carl Davis.
Executive Producer: Mike Wooler.
Producer-Writer-Director: Kevin Browlow, David Gill.

HOLLYWOOD — 60 minutes — Syndicated April 1980. 13 episodes.

534 THE HOLLYWOOD CONNECTION

Game. Six guest celebrities appear, divided into two three-member teams. A question is read that involves three of the celebrities in a hypothetical situation. One of the two competing players chooses one team and has to predict how each member answered the question. Each correct prediction awards the player one point. The remaining player competes in the same manner with the remaining celebrities (although a different question is used). Rounds two and three follow the same basic format with points doubled, then tripled. The player with the highest score is the winner and receives merchandise prizes.

Host: Jim Lange.
Announcer: Jay Stewart.
Music: Score Productions.
Producer: Jack Barry, Dan Enright.
Director: Richard S. Kline.

THE HOLLYWOOD CONNECTION — 30 minutes — Syndicated 1977.

535 THE HOLLYWOOD PALACE

Variety. Performances by top name entertainers.

Regulars: Raquel Welch (The Hollywood Palace Card Holder), The Ray Charles Singers, The Buddy Schwab Dancers.
Announcer: Dick Tufeld.
Orchestra: Mitchell Ayres.
Choreographer: Tom Hanson.
Executive Producer: William O. Harbach, Nick Vanoff.
Writer: Joe Bigelow, Bernie Orenstein, Jay Burton.
Producer: William O. Harbach.
Director: Gary Lockwood, Marc Breaux.

THE HOLLYWOOD PALACE — 60 minutes — ABC — January 4, 1964 – February 7, 1970.

536 THE HOLLYWOOD SQUARES

Game. A game of tic-tac-toe that involves two players and nine celebrity guests, who each occupy one square in a large board. One player begins by choosing a celebrity, who is then asked a question by the host. The player has to determine whether the answer given by the celebrity is true or false. If the player chooses correctly, his "X" or "O" is placed in the box; if he is wrong, his opponent receives the box. The game continues in this manner until one player wins by acquiring three squares in a row, up and down or diagonally (for which he receives $200). Players compete until they are defeated or until they reach $2,000.

Host: Peter Marshall.
Announcer: Kenny Williams.
Regulars: Wally Cox, Cliff Arquette (as Charlie Weaver), Paul Lynde, Rose Marie, Karen Valentine, George Gobel.
Executive Producer: Merrill Heatter, Bob Quigley.
Producer: Jay Redack.
Director: Jerome Shaw.

THE HOLLYWOOD SQUARES — 30 minutes — NBC — October 17, 1966 – June 20, 1980.

537   THE HOLLYWOOD SQUARES

Game. A syndicated version of the previous title, which is played in the exact same manner; the only change being larger cash awards ($250 per game).

Host: Peter Marshall.
Announcer: Kenny Williams.
Regulars: Paul Lynde, George Gobel, Vincent Price.
Executive Producer: Merrill Heatter, Bob Quigley.
Producer: Jay Redack.
Director: Jerome Shaw.

THE HOLLYWOOD SQUARES — 30 minutes — Syndicated 1976.

538   HOLLYWOOD'S TALKING

Game. A videotape is played and celebrity guests are seen expressing their opinions about people, places or things. The object is for one of three players to determine what they are talking about. Money is awarded to the player who correctly identifies the subject. Awards vary ($150, $100 and $50) depending on where in the videotape the identification was made. The first player to score $250 is the winner.

Host: Geoff Edwards.
Announcer: Johnny Jacobs.
Music: Score Productions.

HOLLYWOOD'S TALKING — 30 minutes — CBS — March 26, 1973 – June 23, 1973. 60 programs.

539   HOLLYWOOD TEEN

Variety. Interviews with and performances by young Hollywood personalities.

Host: Jimmy McNichol.
Executive Producer: Jerry Harrison.
Producer: Sam Riddle.
Director: Arthur Forrest.

HOLLYWOOD TEEN — 30 minutes — Syndicated 1978.

540   HOLLYWOOD TELEVISION THEATRE

Anthology. Original dramatic productions written especially for television; and adaptations of well-known stories.

Included:

The Ashes of Mrs. Reasoner. The story of an attractive widow who brings back her husband from the dead (through a séance) to find out if he had an affair with another woman while he was alive.

Cast: Sylvia Reasoner: Cara Williams; The Bellhop: E. J. Andre; Muriel Fenton: Barbara Colby; Arthur Fenton: Charles Durning; Richard Reasoner: Herb Edelman.

The Fatal Weakness. A look at love and marriage as seen through the eyes of Ollie Espenshade, an incurable romantic.

Cast: Ollie: Eva Marie Saint; Paul: John McMartin.

Invitation to a March. A modern adaptation of the Sleeping Beauty fable. The story of Norma Brown, a socialite bride-to-be who is bored to slumber by her ho-hum conformist social circle, and Aaron Jablonski, a free spirit beachcomber who shows her a different side of life.

Cast: Norma Brown: Blythe Danner; Aaron Jablonski: Cliff Potts; Camilla Jablonski: Pat Quinn; Lily Brown: Louise Latham; Deedee Grogan: Rosemary Murphy; Tucker Grogan: Gordon Pinsent.

Winesburg, Ohio. A view of small town life as seen through the eyes of Elizabeth Willard, a chronically ill matron resigned to a dreary existence.

Cast: Elizabeth Willard: Jean Peters; Dr. Reefy: William Windom; George Willard: Joseph Bottoms; Tom Willard: Albert Salmi; Helen White: Laurette Spang; Old Pete: Norman Foster.

HOLLYWOOD TELEVISION THEATRE — Various times (60 minutes to 3 hours) — PBS — October 7, 1971 – February 21, 1978.

541   HOLMES AND YOYO

Comedy. The exploits of Alexander Holmes, a not-too-bright Los Angeles police officer, and his partner Gregory "Yoyo" Yoyonovich, a not-yet-perfect computer robot designed to combat evil.

CAST

Sgt. Alexander Holmes	Richard B. Shull
Sgt. Gregory Yoyonovich	John Schuck
Captain Harry Sedford, their superior	Bruce Kirby
Police Woman Maxine Moon	Andrea Howard
Chief Dwight Buchanan, Harry's superior	Ben Hammer
Dr. Babcock, Yoyo's creator	Larry Hovis
Mrs. Buchanan, Dwight's wife	Fritzi Burr
The Police Commissioner	G. Wood

Music: Leonard Rosenman, Dick Halligan.
Executive Producer: Leonard B. Stern.
Producer: Arne Sultan.
Director: Reza S. Badiyi, John Astin, Noam Pitlik, Leonard B. Stern, Richard Kinon.
Creator: Jack Sher, Lee Hewitt.

HOLMES AND YOYO — 30 minutes — ABC — September 25, 1976 – December 11, 1976. Returned with one episode on August 1, 1977.

542   HOLOCAUST

Drama. A four-part miniseries, based on the novel by Gerald Green, that details a fictionalized account of the Nazi persecution of Jews during World War II.

CAST

Dr. Josef Weiss	Fritz Weaver
Berta Weiss	Rosemary Harris
Rudi Weiss	Joseph Bottoms
Anna Weiss	Blanche Baker
Erik Dorf	Michael Moriarty
Marta Dorf	Deborah Norton
Inga Helms Weiss	Meryl Streep
Reinhard Heydrich	David Warner
Helena Slomova	Tovah Feldshuh
Karl Weiss	James Woods
Moses Weiss	Sam Wanamaker
Uncle Sasha	Lee Montague
Emil Frey	Peter Vogel
Kurt Dorf	Robert Stephens
Hans Frank	John Bailey
Hans Helms	Michael Beck
Frau Lowy	Kate Jaenicke
Dr. Kohn	Charles Korvin
Herr Helms	Werner Kreindl
Frau Palitz	Nora Minor
Maria Kalova	Irene Prador
Rabbi Samuel	Gabor Vernon
Peter Dorf, age 9	Jim Anbach
Peter Dorf, age 15	Edward Gilkrist
Dr. Heintzen	Hubert Berger
Nadya	Vera Borek
Rabbi Karsh	Martin Brandt
Sederman	Peter Capell
Laura Dorf	Courtney Hill
Sara the nurse	Kathina Kaiser
Sofia Alatri	Hanna Mahler
Sgt. Foltz	Stefan Paryla
Kapo Melnick	Bruno Thost

Music: Morton Gould.
Executive Producer: Herbert Brodkin.
Producer: Robert Berger.
Director: Marvin Chomsky.

HOLOCAUST — 9 hrs. 30 min. (total) — NBC — April 16, 1978 – April 19, 1978. 4 episodes. Rebroadcasts (NBC): September 9, 1979 – September 13, 1979.

543   THE HONEYMOONERS

Comedy. The series, set in Brooklyn, New York, follows the misadventures of two neighboring families: Alice and Ralph Kramden and Trixie and Ed Norton. Ralph is a bus driver on the Madison Avenue line with the Gotham Bus Company. Ed is a sewer worker with the Department of Sanitation. The series, which is now a classic, tenderly details their struggles to better their lives.

CAST

Ralph Kramden	Jackie Gleason
Alice Kramden, his wife	Audrey Meadows
Ed Norton, Ralph's friend	Art Carney
Trixie Norton, Ed's wife	Joyce Randolph

Also, Various Roles: Frank Marth, George Petrie.
The Kramdens' address: 328 (later 728) Chauncey Street in Bensonhurst.
Announcer: Jack Lescoulie.
Orchestra: Sammy Spear.
Theme: "You're My Greatest Love" by Jackie Gleason (music) and Bill Templeton (lyrics).
Executive Producer: Jack Philbin.
Producer: Jack Hurdle.
Director: Frank Satenstein.

THE HONEYMOONERS — 30 minutes — CBS — October 1, 1955 – September 22, 1956. 39 episodes. Syndicated.

544   THE HONEYMOONERS

Comedy. An updated version of the old series (see previous title) which continues to depict events in the lives of the Kramdens and the Nortons.

CAST

Ralph Kramden, a bus driver	Jackie Gleason
Alice Kramden, his wife	Sheila MacRae
Ed Norton, their friend, a sewer worker	Art Carney
Trixie Norton, Ed's wife	Jane Kean

Regulars: The June Taylor Dancers.
Announcer: Johnny Olsen.
Orchestra: Sammy Spear.
Executive Producer: Jack Philbin.
Producer: Ronald Wayne.
Director: Frank Bunetta.

THE HONEYMOONERS — 60 minutes — Syndicated 1977. 13 episodes. Compiled from segments broadcast on *The Jackie Gleason Show* on CBS from 1966 through 1970.

545 THE HONEYMOONERS: EXTENSION EPISODES

Storylines, casts and credits for the four extension episodes, broadcast between 1976 and 1978, based on the original 1955–56 series, *The Honeymooners*.

The Honeymooners Second Honeymoon. The first extension episode wherein the Kramdens and Nortons are reunited to celebrate the 25th wedding anniversary of Ralph and Alice.

The Honeymooners Christmas. The second extension episode wherein Ralph takes on the task of directing a stage play of *A Christmas Carol* for his fraternity, the Raccoon Lodge.

The Honeymooners Valentine Special. In this third extension episode, Ralph believes Alice is having an affair with another man and planning to kill him when he overhears a conversation and, as usual, jumps to the wrong conclusion. With the help of Ed Norton, Ralph goes "undercover" and learns the awful truth: Alice had been planning to surprise him with a new suit for Valentine's Day.

The Honeymooners Christmas Special. The last of the four extension episodes finds Ralph attempting one of his famous get-rich-quick schemes: gambling his and Ed's life savings on lottery tickets—to win one million dollars.

CAST
Ralph Kramden, a
  bus driver   Jackie Gleason
Alice Kramden, his wife   Audrey Meadows
Ed Norton, their friend   Art Carney
Trixie Norton, Ed's wife   Jane Kean
Alice's mother   Eileen Heckart
   Templeton Fox

Announcer: Johnny Olsen.
Music Composed and Conducted By: Jackie Gleason.
Musical Arrangements: George Williams.
Executive Producer: Jack Philbin.
Producer: Ed Waglin.
Director: Jackie Gleason.

THE HONEYMOONERS: EXTENSION EPISODES—60 minutes—ABC. "The Honeymooners Second Honeymoon" aired on February 2, 1976; "The Honeymooners Christmas," November 28, 1977; "The Honeymooners Valentine Special," February 13, 1978; and "The Honeymooners Christmas Special," December 10, 1978.

546 HONG KONG PHOOEY

Animated Cartoon. The story of Henry, a meek police station janitor who can transform himself into the disaster-prone Hong Kong Phooey, "America's secret weapon against crime." Episodes relate his fumbling attempts to solve baffling acts of injustice.

VOICES
Henry/Hong Kong
  Phooey   Scatman Crothers
Police Sgt. Flint   Joe E. Ross
Rosemary, the telephone
  operator   Jean VanderPyl
   Kathi Gori
Spot, Henry's cat   Don Messick

Additional Voices: Richard Dawson, Ron Feinberg, Casey Kasem, Jay Lawrence, Peter Leeds, Allan Melvin, Lee Vines, Frank Welker, Janet Waldo, Paul Winchell, Lennie Weinrib.
Hong Kong's car: The *Phooeymobile*.
Music: Hoyt Curtin.
Theme Vocal: Scatman Crothers.
Executive Producer: William Hanna, Joseph Barbera.
Producer: Iwao Takamoto.
Director: Charles A. Nichols.

HONG KONG PHOOEY—30 minutes. ABC—September 7, 1974–September 4, 1976; NBC—February 4, 1978–September 2, 1978.

547 HOT CITY DISCO

Music. Performances by Disco personalities.

Host: Shadoe Stevens, David Jones.
Regulars: The Jeff Kutect Dancers.
Music Theme: Vernee White, Robert Wright, Gary Goetzman.
Executive Producer: Marc Robertson, Ed Warren.
Producer: Kip Walton.
Director: Kip Walton.

HOT CITY DISCO—60 minutes—Syndicated 1978.

548 HOT DOG

Educational. Films exploring the technical mysteries that surround the making of everyday items (e.g., pencils, blue jeans, baseballs, rope, ties).

Regulars: Woody Allen, Jonathan Winters, Jo Anne Worley.
Music: The Youngbloods.

HOT DOG—30 minutes—NBC—September 12, 1970–September 4, 1971. 26 episodes.

549 HOT FUDGE

Children. Sketches geared to teach children various aspects of the adult world.

The Hot Fudge Gang: Yolando Williams. Marilyn O'Connor, Bob Taylor, Ron Loden.

Music: Larry Santos, Dan Ressin.
Producer: Barry Hurd, Bob Elnicky.
Director: Bob Lipson.

HOT FUDGE—30 minutes—Syndicated 1976.

550 HOT HERO SANDWICH

Children. A potpourri of celebrity interviews, music and comedy aimed at young people.

Regulars: Vicky Dawson, Paul O'Keefe, Matt McCoy, Denny Dillon, Nan-Lynn Nelson, Jarrett Smithwrick, L. Michael Craig.
Also: Claudette Sutherland, Andy Beckman, Adam Ross, Frankie Faison.
Rock Group: Hot Hero.
Musical Director: Felix Pappalardi.
Executive Producer: Carol Hart, Bruce Hart.
Producer: Howard Malley.
Director: Tom Trbovichi.

HOT HERO SANDWICH—60 minutes—NBC—November 10, 1979–April 5, 1980.

551 HOT L BALTIMORE

Comedy. Life in the seedy Hotel Baltimore (the E in the neon sign has burned out) as seen through the activities of the eleven people who live like a family in the decaying Maryland establishment. Based on the Broadway play of the same title.

CAST
Bill Lewis, the desk clerk   James Cromwell
Clifford Ainsley, the hotel
  manager   Richard Masur
Suzy Madaraket, a
  prostitute   Jeannie Linero
April Green, a prostitute   Conchata Ferrell
Winthrop Morse, the cantankerous
  old man   Stan Gottlieb
Charles Bingham, the young
  philosopher   Al Freeman, Jr.
Jackie, a young, unemployed
  woman   Robin Wilson
Millie, the waitress   Gloria LeRoy
Esmee Belotti, the mother of the
  never-seen psychotic youngster,
  Moose   Charlotte Rae
George, a homosexual   Lee Bergere
Gordon, a homosexual   Henry Calvert

Music: Marvin Hamlisch.
Executive Producer: Rod Parker.
Producer: Norman Lear.
Director: Bob LaHendro.

HOT L BALTIMORE—30 minutes—ABC—January 24, 1975–June 13, 1975. 13 episodes.

552 HOT SEAT

Game. Two husband-and-wife teams play, but compete one at a time. One member is placed in the Hot Seat, a skin-response machine that measures emotional reactions when two electrodes are attached to the fingers. The sound is turned off in the booth and the outside member is asked a question (e.g., What does [name of wife] think of herself as a woman? Does she think she is healthy and wholesome or sexy and seductive?). In this case, the husband chooses the response he feels will register highest on the machine. The sound is turned on in the booth and the wife is asked to respond negatively (e.g., "No, I'm not like that") to the question she will hear. Each response is registered, and if the higher score matches the response her husband selected, they receive $100 (in round two, $200, and in round three, $400). The other couple competes in the same manner and the winners are the highest scorers.

Host: Jim Peck.
Announcer: Kenny Williams.
Music: Stan Worth.
Executive Producer: Merrill Heatter, Bob Quigley.
Producer: Bob Synes.
Director: Jerome Shaw.

HOT SEAT—30 minutes—ABC—July 12, 1976–October 22, 1976. 70 programs.

553 THE HOUNDCATS

Animated Cartoon. The investigations of the Houndcats, a group of bumbling U.S. government dog and cat agents organized to combat evil. A take-off on *Mission: Impossible*.

VOICES
Studs, the leader   Daws Butler
Muscle Mutt, the strong dog   Aldo Ray
Rhubarb, the inventor   Arte Johnson
Puddy Puss, the cat of a thousand
  faces   Joe Besser
Ding Dog, the daredevil   Stu Gilliam

Their car: Sparkplug.
Music: Doug Goodwin.
Producer: Friz Freleng, David DePatie.
Director: Sid Marcus, Bob McKimson, Spencer Peel, Brad Case.

THE HOUNDCATS—30 minutes—NBC—September 9, 1972–September 1, 1973. 26 episodes.

554 HOUSE CALLS

Comedy. The escapades of the staff of fictional Kensington General Hospital in Los Angeles. Based on the motion picture of the same title.

CAST
Dr. Charley Michaels, the playboy
  surgeon   Wayne Rogers
Ann Anderson, the
  administrator   Lynn Redgrave
Dr. Amos Weatherby, the
  senile surgeon   David Wayne

Dr. Norman Solomon,
   the mother-dominated
   obstetrician   Ray Buktenica
Head Nurse Bradley   Aneta Corsaut
The Admissions Nurse   Sharon DeBord
Louella Grady, Charley's
   girlfriend   Candice Azzara
Mrs. Phipps, a hospital
   volunteer   Deedy Peters
Conrad Peckler, Ann's
   supervisor   Mark L. Taylor
The Anesthesiologist   Vincent Howard
Dr. Albert   Richard Stahl
Nurse   Peggy Frees
Nurse   Terri Berland
Nurse   Georgia Jeffries
Nurse's aide   Linda Dangcil
Orderly   Bob Larkin
Orderly   Christopher Blanc

Music: Jack Elliott, Allyn Ferguson, Michael Lang.
Executive Producer: Jerry Davis.
Supervising Producer: Kathy Greer, Bill Greer.
Producer: Sheldon Keller.
Writer: Kathy Greer, Bill Greer, Sheldon Keller, Bryan Blackburn, Jeffrey Davis, Lee Aronsohn.
Director: Alex March, Nick Havinga, Mel Ferber, Bob Claver.
Creator: Max Shulman, Julius Epstein.

HOUSE CALLS — 30 minutes — CBS — December 17, 1979 – March 17, 1980. 12 episodes. Rebroadcasts: May 19, 1980 – September 1, 1980. Returned, Premiered: November 17, 1980.

555   HOWDY DOODY

Children. On December 27, 1941, in the town of Doodyville, Texas, twin boys were born to the wife of a ranch hand named Doody. The boys, named Howdy and Double, grew quickly and enjoyed life on the ranch where their parents earned a living by performing chores for the owner. The boys, at age six, learn that their rich Uncle Doody has died and bequeathed them a small parcel of land in New York City (that would later turn out to be 30 Rockefeller Plaza). When NBC offered to purchase the land to construct a television studio, Mr. Doody arranged it so that Howdy, who yearned to run a circus, could have his dream come true. NBC built a circus grounds, surrounded it with cameras, and appointed Buffalo Bob Smith as Howdy's guardian.

Set against the background of Doodyville, and surrounded by the "Peanut Gallery" (children), the program depicts the efforts of a circus troupe to perform against the wishes of Phineas T. Bluster, an old man who is opposed to people having fun.

CAST
Buffalo Bob Smith, the host   Bob Smith
Clarabell Hornblow,
   the clown   Bob Keeshan
                                  Bob Nicholson
                                  Lew Anderson
The Story Princess   Arlene Dalton
Tim Tremble, Bob's friend   Don Knotts
Chief Thunderthud, Phineas'
   friend   Bill Lecornec
Princess Summer-Fall-
   Winter-Spring   Judy Tyler
Lowell Thomas, Jr., the
   traveling lecturer   Himself
VOICES
Howdy Doody, Buffalo Bob's
   assistant   Bob Smith
Phineas T. Bluster, the
   old man   Dayton Allen
Double Doody, Howdy's brother Bob Smith

Additonal Characters (Puppets): Dr. Jose Bluster, Phineas' brother; Heidi Doody, Howdy's cousin; Ugly Sam, the wrestler; Lanky Lou, the cowboy; Trigger Happy, the bad man; Spin Platter, the D.J.; the Flubadub, the main circus attraction; Inspector John, the police chief; Dilly Dally, Howdy's friend; Sandy McTavish, the Scotsman; Doc Ditto, the toymaker; Sandra, the witch; and the Bloop, an invisible, sometimes visible creature.

Additional Voices: Allen Swift, Herb Vigran.
Puppeteers: Rhoda Mann, Lee Carney.
Music: Edward Kean.
Narrator of the Silent Film Segment: Dayton Allen.
Producer: Martin Stone, Roger Muir.

HOWDY DOODY — 60- and 30-minute versions — NBC — December 27, 1947 – September 24, 1960. 2,543 programs. Spin-off series: *The New Howdy Doody Show.*

556   HOW THE WEST WAS WON

Western. The saga of the Macahans, a Virginia homesteading family, as they attempt to establish a new life on the Great Plains during the mid-1860s.

CAST
Zeb Macahan, the mountain
   man   James Arness
Kate Macahan, his widowed
   sister-in-law   Eva Marie Saint
Luke Macahan,
   Kate's son   Bruce Boxleitner
Laura Macahan, Kate's
   daughter   Kathryn Holcomb
Jessie Macahan, Kate's
   daughter   Vicki Schreck
Josh Macahan, Kate's
   son   William Kirby Cullen
Molly Culhane, a relative
   who cares for the Macahan
   children after Kate's
   "death"   Fionnuala Flanagan

Jim Anderson, Kate's romantic
   interest   Don Murray
Martin Grey, the bounty hunter
   seeking Luke (an army
   deserter)   Anthony Zerbe
Timothy Macahan, Kate's husband
   (killed in the Civil War;
   flashbacks)   Richard Kiley
Elam Hanks, the Simonite
   (religious sect)   Royal Dano
Erica Hanks, Elam's daughter   Brit Lind
Joshua Hanks,
   Elam's son   Todd Lookinland
Bishop Benjamin, a Simonite   John Dehner
Cully Madigan, Zeb's friend   Jack Elam
Henry Coe, the ruthless
   land baron   Morgan Woodward
Shoshine Chief Claw   Richard Angarola
Arapaho Chief   Woody Strode
Jeremiah Taylor, the Mormon   John Reilly

Narrator: William Conrad.
Music: Jerrold Immel, Bruce Broughton, John Parker.
Music Supervision: Harry Lojewski.
Executive Producer: John Mantley.
Producer: Jeffrey Hayden, John G. Stevens.
Writer: Jim Byrnes, William Kelley, John Mantley, Earl Wallace, Ron Bishop.
Director: Burt Kennedy, Daniel Mann, Vincent McEveety, Bernard McEveety, Alf Kjellin.

HOW THE WEST WAS WON — 2 hours — ABC — February 6, 1977 – February 14, 1977. 3 episodes. February 12, 1978 – May 21, 1978. 12 episodes. January 15, 1979 – April 23, 1979. 11 episodes. 21 of the 26 produced episodes are syndicated. The pilot film, "The Macahans," aired on ABC on January 19, 1976.

557   HOW TO SURVIVE A MARRIAGE

Serial. The series, which is aimed primarily at young marrieds and divorcées, dramatizes the problems of marriage, divorce, separation and readjustment.

CAST
Dr. Julie Franklin   Rosemary Prinz
Monica Courtland   Joan Copeland
Sandra Henderson   Lynn Lowry
Maria McGhee   Lauren White
Chris Kirby   Jennifer Harmon
Rachel Bachman   Elissa Leeds
David Bachman   Allan Miller
Fran Bachman   Fran Brill
Joan Willis   Tricia O'Neil
Lori Ann Kirby   Suzanne Davidson
                             Cathy Greene
                             Lori Lowe
Terry Courtland   Peter Brandon
Dr. Max Cooper   James Shannon
Dr. Tony DeAngelo   George Webles
Neil Abbott   George Shannon
Dr. Brady   Don Keyes
Larry Kirby   Michael Landrum
Dr. Charles Maynard   Paul Vincent
Jerry Nelson   Dino Narizzano
Joshua Browne   F. Murray Abraham
Johnny McGhee   Armand Assante
Dr. Robert Monday   Gene Bua

Susan Pritchett   Veleka Gray
Peter Willis   Steve Elmore
                             Berkeley Harris
Moe Bachman   Albert Ottenheimer
Greg Bachman   Richie Schectman
Lt. Bowling   Al Fann

Music: Score Productions.
Music Supervision: Sybil Weinberger.
Orchestrations: William Goldstein.
Executive Producer: Peter Engel.
Producer: Peter Andrews.
Director: Richard McCue, Robert Myhrum.

HOW TO SURVIVE A MARRIAGE — 30 minutes — NBC — January 7, 1974 – April 17, 1975. 305 episodes.

558   H.R. PUFNSTUF

Adventure. While playing near the edge of a river, Jimmy and his talking gold flute, Freddie, board a boat that beckons to them. As it drifts out to sea, the evil Miss Witchiepoo, seeking Freddie for her collection, casts a spell and makes the boat vanish. Swimming to the shore of Living Island, Jimmy is rescued by its mayor, H.R. Pufnstuf who, in an attempt to help them get back home, takes them to the secret escape path. But Miss Witchiepoo follows and makes the path vanish when Jimmy refuses to give up Freddie. The story follows the efforts of Jimmy and Freddie to escape from the island; and the efforts of Miss Witchiepoo to acquire Freddie (the world's only talking flute) for her collection.

CAST
Jimmy   Jack Wild
Miss Witchiepoo   Billie Hayes

Also (portraying life-size puppets): Joan Gerber, Felix Silla, Jerry Landon, John Linton, Angelo Rosetti, Hommy Stewart, Buddy Douglas.
Characters (The Sid and Mary Krofft Puppets): H.R. Pufnstuf, the mayor; Dr. Blinkey; Cling and Clang, H.R.'s friends; Dumb, Stupid, Orville and Seymour, the Witch's aides.

Orchestra: Glen Paige, Jr.
Vocals: The Pufnstuf.
Producer: Sid and Marty Krofft.
Director: Hollingsworth Morse.

H.R. PUFNSTUF — 30 minutes — NBC — September 6, 1969 – September 4, 1971. ABC — September 9, 1972 – September 1, 1973. 17 episodes. Syndicated.

559   THE HUDSON BROTHERS RAZZLE DAZZLE SHOW

Variety. Music, songs and sketches that are designed to convey value-related messages to children.

Hosts: Bill, Brett, and Mark Hudson.
Regulars: Billy Van, Peter Cullen, Ted Zeigler, Murray Langston, Rod Hull, Scott Fisher.
Announcer: Peter Cullen.
Orchestra: Jimmy Dale.
Executive Producer: Allan Blye, Chris Bearde.
Producer: Coslough Johnson, Stan Jacobson.
Director: Art Fisher.

THE HUDSON BROTHERS RAZZLE DAZZLE SHOW—25 minutes—CBS—September 7, 1974 –April 17, 1977.

560   THE HUDSON BROTHERS SHOW

Variety. Musical numbers, sketches and blackouts.

Hosts: Bill, Brett, and Mark Hudson.
Regulars: Katie McClure, Stephanie Edwards, Ronny Graham, Gary Owens, Rod Hull, The Jaime Rogers Dancers.
Announcer: Gary Owens.
Orchestra: Jack Eskew.
Special Musical Material: Earl Brown.
Choreographer: Jaime Rogers.
Executive Producer: Allan Blye, Chris Bearde.
Producer: Coslough Johnson, Stan Jacobson, Bob Arnott.
Writer: George Burditt, Bob Einstein, David Panich, Ronny Graham, Chris Bearde, Allan Blye.
Director: Art Fisher.

THE HUDSON BROTHERS SHOW—60 minutes—CBS—July 31, 1974–August 28, 1974.

561   HUNTER

Adventure. The cases of James Hunter and his beautiful assistant Marty Shaw, U.S. Government Special Intelligence agents who cover the world of contemporary espionage. (In his free time, Hunter operates a book shop in Santa Barbara; Marty is a model.)

CAST

James Hunter	James Franciscus
Marty Shaw	Linda Evans
Harold Baker, their superior	Ralph Bellamy

Music: Richard Shores.
Executive Producer: Lee Rich, Philip Capice.
Producer: Christopher Morgan.
Director: Gerald Mayer, Bruce Bilson, Harry Harris, Barry Crane, Gary Nelson.
Creator: William Blinn.

HUNTER—60 minutes—CBS—February 18, 1977–March 22, 1977. One additional episode aired on May 27, 1977.

562   HUSBANDS, WIVES, AND LOVERS

Comedy. The series, set in the San Fernando Valley in California, focuses on the hassles, foibles and frivolities of five suburban couples, each with diverse backgrounds.

CAST

Murray Zuckerman, a salesman	Alex Rocco
Paula Zuckerman, Murray's wife	Cynthia Harris
Harry Bellini (Harry Bell in the pilot episode), a garbage tycoon	Ed Barth
Joy Bellini, Harry's wife (pilot film)	Suzanne Zenor
Joy Bellini (series)	Lynne Marie Stewart
Lennie Bellini, Harry's brother, co-owner of a boutique shop	Mark Lonow
Rita DeLatorre, Lennie's partner; the girl with whom he lives*	Randee Heller
Ron Willis (Ron Cutler in the pilot film), a dentist	Ron Rifkin
Helene Willis, Ron's wife (pilot)	Linda Miller
Helene Willis (series)	Jesse Welles
Dixon Fielding, a lawyer	Charles Siebert
Courtney Fielding, Dixon's wife	Claudette Nevins

Music: Jack Elliott, Allyn Ferguson.
Music Supervision: Lionel Newman.
Theme: "Husband, Wives, and Lovers" by Ken and Mitzie Welch.
Executive Producer: Hal Dresner, Edgar Rosenberg.
Producer: Don Van Atta.
Director: Marc Daniels, Bill Persky, Alan Myerson, James Burrows.
Creator: Joan Rivers, Hal Dresner.
Art Director: Jack Stewart.

HUSBANDS, WIVES, AND LOVERS—60 minutes—CBS—March 10, 1978–June 30, 1978. 9 episodes. The pilot episode, titled "Husbands and Wives," aired on CBS (60 minutes) July 18, 1977.

*Rita Bell in the pilot film, and married to Lennie.

I

563   I AM THE GREATEST: THE ADVENTURES OF MUHAMMAD ALI

Animated Cartoon. The exploits of heavyweight boxing champion Muhammad Ali, who, as a modern-day Robin Hood, helps good defeat evil.

VOICES

Muhammad Ali	Himself

Music: Charles Blaker.
Executive Producer: Fred Calvert.

Producer: Janis Diamond.
Director: Fred Calvert.

I AM THE GREATEST: THE ADVENTURES OF MUHAMMAD ALI—30 minutes—NBC—September 10, 1977–September 2, 1978.

564   THE IAN TYSON SHOW

Variety. Performances by U.S. and Canadian Country and Western entertainers.

Host: Ian Tyson.
Regular: Sylvia Tyson.
Music: The Great Speckled Bird.

THE IAN TYSON SHOW—30 minutes—Syndicated 1970. 90 programs. Also known as *Nashville Now.*

565   THE ICE PALACE

Variety. Entertainment acts set against the background of a mythical Ice Palace.

Hosts: Guests (for its eight program run): Vikki Carr, Dean Jones, The Lennon Sisters, Roger Miller, Leslie Uggams, Jack Jones, Johnny Mathis, John Davidson.
Regulars (Skating Personalities): Tim Wood, Linda Carbonetto, Billy Chappell, Gisela Head, Don Knight, Tim Noyers, Roy Powers, Sandy Parker, The Bob Turk Ice Dancers.
Orchestra: Alan Copeland.
Executive Producer: Peter Engel.
Producer: Perry Cross.
Director: John Moffitt.

THE ICE PALACE—60 minutes—CBS—May 23, 1971–July 25, 1971. 8 programs.

566   I CLAUDIUS

Drama. The story of the early Roman Empire, from 24 B.C. to 54 A.D., as seen through the eyes of the eventual emperor, Tiberius Claudius. Based on the novels, *I Claudius* and *Claudius the God* by Robert Graves and produced by the BBC.

CAST

Claudius	Derek Jacobi
Augustus	Brian Blessed
Livia	Sian Phillips
Agrippa	John Paul
Marcellus	Christopher Guard
Julia	Frances White
Tiberius	George Baker
Octavia	Angela Morant
Drusus	Ian Ogilvy
Claudius, as a boy	Ashely Knight
Postumus	John Castle
Livilla	Patricia Quinn
Germanicus	David Robb
Pios	Stratford Johns
Piancina	Irene Hamilton
Agrippina	Fiona Walker
Young Caligula	Robert Morgan
Caligula (older)	John Hurt
Sejanus	Patrick Stewart
Antonia	Margaret Tyzak
Helene	Karin Foley
Drusilla	Beth Morris
Herod	James Faulkner
Marco	John Rhys-Davies
Senator	Lockwood West
Gemulius	Douglas Melbourne
Lentulus	Jon Laurimore
Briseis	Anne Dyson
Calpurnia	Jo Rowbottom
Cassius	Sam Dastor
Messalina	Sheila White
Marcus	Norman Eshley
Silanus	Lyndon Brook
Herod	James Faulkner
Domitia	Moira Redmond
Pallas	Bernard Hepton
Mnester	Nicholas Amer
Silas	Stewart Wilson
Agrippinilla	Barbara Young
Nero	Christopher Biggins

Music: Wilfred Josephs.
Producer: Martin Liesmore.
Director: Herbert Wise.

I CLAUDIUS—60 minutes—PBS—June 10, 1979–September 2, 1979. 13 episodes.

567   I DREAM OF JEANNIE

Comedy. During the test flight of a NASA rocket, a third stage misfires, causing it to crash-land on a deserted island in the South Pacific. Its astronaut, U.S. Air Force Captain Tony Nelson escapes unharmed. As he begins to make an S.O.S. signal from debris, he finds a strange green bottle, which he opens—and there emerges a pink smoke that materializes into a beautiful girl dressed as a harem dancer—a genie.

"Thou may ask anything of thy slave, Master," she informs him; and with her hands crossed over her chest and a blink of her eyes, she proceeds to provide a rescue helicopter for him. Realizing the problems her presence and powers will cause him at NASA, he sets her free, despite her desire to remain with him. Blinking herself back into smoke, and into her bottle, she places herself in Tony's survival kit without his knowledge.

When Tony returns to his home in Cocoa Beach, Florida, and discovers Jeannie, he learns of her fate* and permits her to remain with him—provided she curtail her powers and grant him no special treasures. Though reluctant, Jeannie agrees, but secretly vows to always ensure his safety.

Stories depict the attempts of the jealous and zealous genie to protect her master from harm and from the influx of feminine admirers; and a master's efforts to control and conceal the presence of a beautiful, fun-loving genie.

Hunter. Linda Evans and James Franciscus.

Images of Indians. Will Sampson.

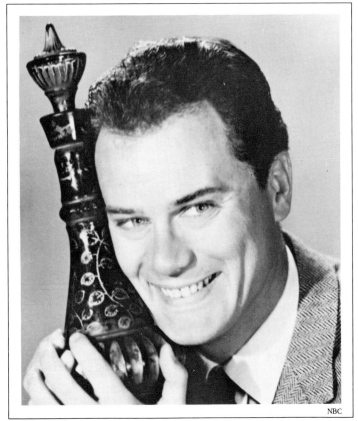

I Dream of Jeannie. Larry Hagman and Barbara Eden.

CAST

Jeannie	Barbara Eden
Jeannie II, her sister, a genie also	Barbara Eden
Captain (later Major) Anthony Nelson (Tony)	Larry Hagman
Captain (later Major) Roger Healey, Tony's friend	Bill Daily
Dr. Alfred Bellows, the Air Force psychiatrist plagued by Jeannie's antics	Hayden Rorke
Amanda Bellows, Alfred's wife	Emmaline Henry
Gen. Martin Peterson, Tony's superior	Barton MacLane
General Winfield Schaffer, Tony's superior	Vinton Hayworth
Hadji, the master of all genies	Abraham Sofaer
Habib, Jeannie's sister's master	Ted Cassidy
Jeannie's mother	Florence Sundstrom
	Lurene Tuttle
	Barbara Eden
Jeannie's father	Henry Corden
Various roles, including the Blue Djin, the most powerful and most feared of genies	Michael Ansara

Jeannie's Genie Dog: Gin Gin.
Addresses used for Tony's home: 1137 Oak Grove Street; 811 Pine Street; and 1020 Palm Drive.
Theme Narration: Paul Frees.
Music: Hugo Montenegro, Richard Wess, Buddy Kaye.
Music Supervision: Ed Forsythe.
Producer: Sidney Sheldon, Claudio Guzman.
Director: E. W. Swackhamer, Bruce Kessler, Gene Nelson, Hal Cooper, Claudio Guzman, Alan Rafkin, Joseph Goodson, Michael Ansara.
Creator: Sidney Sheldon.

I DREAM OF JEANNIE—30 minutes—NBC—September 18, 1965–September 8, 1970. 139 episodes. Syndicated. Spin-off series: *Jeannie.*

*When as a young girl in Bagdad over 2,000 years ago, Jeannie refused the marriage proposal of the Blue Djin, the most powerful and the most feared of all genies. In punishment she was turned into a genie, placed in a bottle and sentenced to a life of loneliness on a deserted island.

568   IKE

Drama. A three-part miniseries that follows the World War II career of Dwight D. Eisenhower, the general who led the mightiest invasion force in history, conquered a continent and became a beloved American hero in the 1940s and '50s.

CAST

Dwight D. Eisenhower	Robert Duvall
Kay Summersby	Lee Remick
Gen. George Marshall	Dana Andrews
Gen. Walter Bedell Smith	J.D. Cannon
Capt. Ernest Lee	Paul Gleason
Maj. Richard Arnold	Laurence Luckinbill
Gen. George S. Patton	Darren McGavin

Winston Churchill	Wensley Pithey
Sir Bernard Montgomery	Ian Richardson
Franklin Delano Roosevelt	Steven Roberts
Gen. Mark Clark	William Schallert
Alfred Jodl	Wolfgang Preiss
Mamie Eisenhower	Bonnie Bartlett
Gen. Lucian Truscott	Charles H. Gray
Gen. Charles de Gaulle	Vernon Dobtcheff
Gen. Omar Bradley	Richard T. Herd
Mrs. Westerfield	K Callan
Gen. Arthur Tedder	Terrence Alexander
Noel Coward	Francis Matthews
Gertrude Lawrence	Patricia Michael
Mickey McKeogh	Vincent Marzello
Lowell Thomas	Himself

Narrator: Lowell Thomas.
Music: Fred Karlin.
Executive Producer: Melville Shavelson.
Producer: Bill McCutchen.
Writer: Melville Shavelson.
Director: Melville Shavelson (United States and North African sequences); Boris Sagal (European sequences).
Director of Photography: Arch Dalzell (U.S.), Freddie Young (U.K.).
Art Director: Ward Preston (U.S.), Peter Murton (U.K.).
Choreographer: Miriam Nelson (U.S.), Marge Champion (U.K.).

IKE—2 hours (6 hours total)—ABC—May 3, 1979–May 6, 1979. 3 episodes.

569   IMAGES OF INDIANS

Documentary. A five-part series that traces the stereotyped image of the American Indian as depicted in motion pictures. Film clips and interviews with producers, writers, directors and actors are featured.

Host-Narrator: Will Sampson.
Music: Mark Hoover.
Producer-Writer-Director: Phil Lucas, Robert Hagopian.

IMAGES OF INDIANS—30 minutes—PBS—August 7, 1980–September 4, 1980. 5 episodes.

570   THE IMMIGRANTS

Drama. A two-part miniseries, based on the novel by Howard Fast, that chronicles the rise and fall of Daniel Lavetta, a shipping magnate and the son of Italian immigrants who settled in San Francisco at the turn of the century.

CAST

Daniel Lavetta	Stephen Macht
Jean Seldon Lavetta	Sharon Gless
May Ling	Aimee Eccles
Thomas Seldon	Richard Anderson
Maria Cassala	Ina Balin
Chris Noel	Lloyd Bochner
Pete Lomas	Kevin Dobson
Calvin Braderman	Michael Durrell
Mark Levy	Roddy McDowall
Mary Seldon	Kathleen Nolan
Anthony Cassala	Pernell Roberts
Alan Brocker	John Saxon

Feng Wo	Yuki Shimoda
Sarah Levy	Susan Strasberg
Grant Whittier	Barry Sullivan
Joseph Lavetta	Aharon Ipale
Anna Lavetta	Michele Marsh
Tony	Paul Sylvan
Gregory Pastore	Joe Bennett
Mrs. Whittier	Monica Lewis
So-Toy	Beulah Quo
Joseph (as a boy)	Shane Sinutko
Dan Lavetta (as a boy)	Ari Macht
Barbara	Cynthia Eilbacher
Doctor	Don Keefer

Music: Gerald Fried.
Executive Producer: Robert A. Cinader.
Producer: Gino R. Grimaldi, Hannah L. Shearer.
Writer: Richard Collins.
Director: Alan J. Levi.
Art Director: George Renne.
Director of Photography: Frank Thackery.
Costumes: Burton Miller, Lorry Richter.

THE IMMIGRANTS—2 hours (4 hours total)—Operation Prime Time—November 1978. 2 episodes.

571   THE IMMORTAL

Adventure. Seriously injured when his plane passes through an electrical turbulence area, aged and dying billionaire Jordan Braddock, the owner of Braddock Industries, is given a transfusion of Type O blood donated earlier by Ben Richards, an employee in the automotive division. Shortly after, Braddock miraculously recovers, looking and feeling younger.

Matthew Pearce, Braddock's doctor, conducts tests and discovers that Richards is immortal, possessing a rare blood type that makes him immune to old age and disease. Further tests reveal that Braddock's rejuvenation is only temporary; and that to sustain it, periodic transfusions are necessary. To insure the supply of life-saving blood, Braddock imprisons Ben, then begins a search to find Jason Richards, Ben's long-lost brother (separated as infants), who may also possess the same blood antibodies. Braddock's plan is thwarted, however, when Ben escapes and begins his own search to find Jason. The series depicts Ben's attempt to find Jason and warn him of Braddock's diabolical plan.

CAST

Ben Richards	Christopher George
Jordan Braddock	Barry Sullivan
Fletcher, Braddock's assistant	Don Knight
Jason Richards, Ben's brother	Michael Strong
Sylvia Cartwright, Ben's fiancée	Carol Lynley
Janet Braddock, Jordan's wife	Jessica Walter
Matthew Pearce, Jordan's doctor	Ralph Bellamy

Music: Dominic Frontiere, Leith Stevens.
Executive Producer: Anthony Wilson.
Producer: Lou Morheim, Howie Horwitz.

THE IMMORTAL—60 minutes—ABC—September 24, 1970–September 8, 1971. 13 episodes. The 90-minute pilot film aired on ABC on September 30, 1969.

572   INCH HIGH, PRIVATE EYE

Animated Cartoon. The exploits of Inch High, the world's smallest man, a master detective employed by the Finkerton Organization.

VOICES

Inch High	Lennie Weinrib
Laurie, his niece	Kathi Gori
Braveheart, his coward dog	Don Messick
Mr. Finkerton, his employer	John Stephenson
Mrs. Finkerton	Jean VanderPyl

Additional Voices: Ted Knight, Jamie Farr, Alan Oppenheimer, Vic Perrin, Janet Waldo.
Music: Hoyt Curtin.
Executive Producer: William Hanna, Joseph Barbera.
Producer: Iwao Takamoto.
Director: Charles A. Nichols.

INCH HIGH, PRIVATE EYE—30 minutes—NBC—September 8, 1973–August 31, 1974. 13 episodes.

573   THE INCREDIBLE HULK

Adventure. Scientist David Banner and his assistant, Elaina Marks, undertake a research program to determine how certain people are able to tap hidden resources of strength when under stress. During an experiment, Banner is exposed to an extreme overdose of gamma radiation, which causes a change in his body's DNA chemistry. Whenever he becomes angry or enraged, a startling metamorphosis takes place: the mild Banner is transformed into the green Hulk, a creature of incredible strength.

During a fit of rage, the Hulk destroys Banner's car. Intrigued by the enormous footprints found at the scene, Jack McGee, a reporter for the *National Register,* traces the creature to the lab where Banner and Elaina (who previously witnessed the transformation and has agreed to help David find a cure) are planning an experiment. While speaking with David outside, a leaking chemical solution triggers an explosion in the lab. McGee and Banner are knocked down by its force. David, still conscious, becomes enraged when flames prevent him from entering the building to help Elaina. David is transformed into the Hulk and rescues Elaina, who dies shortly after. Regaining his senses, McGee sees the Hulk with Elaina and assumes that he killed her. Unable to find Banner, McGee theorizes that he perished in the fire he mistakenly believes was caused by the Hulk.

Believed to be dead, Banner wanders across the country, seeking a way to control the creature and find a means by which to reverse the process. However, his efforts are hindered by McGee, who has vowed to bring the Hulk to justice. (Though the creature is innocent, David can't prove it — he has little or no recollection of his actions as the Hulk, so he keeps moving until he can stop the occurrences.)

CAST

Dr. David Banner	Bill Bixby
The Hulk	Lou Ferrigno
Jack McGee, the reporter	Jack Colvin
The Demi Hulk*	Ric Drasin
Elaina Marks (first pilot film)	Susan Sullivan

Music: Joseph Harnell, Charles R. Cassey.
Theme: "The Incredible Hulk" (closing piano solo) by Joseph Harnell.
Supervising Producer: Nicholas Corea.
Executive Producer: Kenneth Johnson.
Producer: James D. Parriott, Chuck Bowman, Nicholas Corea, James G. Hirsch, Robert Steinhauer, Karen Harris, Jill Sherman.
Director: Alan J. Levi, Kenneth Gilbert, Larry Stewart, Sigmund Neufeld, Jr., Jeffrey Hayden, Harvey Laidman, Reza S. Badiyi, Frank Orsatti, Joseph Pevney, Ray Danton, Chuck Bowman, John McPherson, Barry Crane, Richard Milton.

THE INCREDIBLE HULK — 60 minutes — CBS — Premiered: March 10, 1978. The first pilot film, "The Incredible Hulk," aired on CBS on November 4, 1977. The second pilot, "The Incredible Hulk Part II," aired on CBS on November 28, 1977.

*Shown in the transition stage from Hulk to human.

574   INNER SPACE

Documentary. Films that explore the undersea world.

Narrator: William Shatner.
Music: Sven Liback.
Director: Robert Walker.
Underwater Photography: Ron and Valerie Taylor.

INNER SPACE — 30 minutes — Syndicated 1975.

THE INNOCENT AND THE DAMNED

See *Aspen,* the original title, for information.

575   IN SEARCH OF . . .

Documentary. A series that attempts to explain and provide answers for some of the mysteries that surround us in our everyday lives (e.g., ghosts, U.F.O.s and myths).

Host-Narrator: Leonard Nimoy.
Music: Laurin Rinder, Michael Lewis.
Executive Producer: Alan Landsburg.
Producer Robert Lang, Deborah Blum, Alex Pomansanof, William Kirnick, Jeffrey Pill, Seth Hill, Barbara Wegher.
Director: H. G. Stark.
Program Open:
Announcer: This series presents information, based in part on theory and conjecture. The producers' purpose is to suggest some possible explanations, but not necessarily the only ones to the mysteries we will examine.

IN SEARCH OF . . . — 30 minutes — Syndicated 1976.

576   THE INTERNATIONAL ANIMATION FESTIVAL

Animated Cartoon. A series of award-winning cartoons from around the world.

Hostess: Jean Marsh.
Music: Gerig McRitchie.
Executive Producer: Zev Putterman.
Producer: Sheldon Renan.
Miss Marsh's Segment Director: James Scalem.

THE INTERNATIONAL ANIMATION FESTIVAL — 30 minutes — PBS — April 7, 1975 – June 30, 1975. 13 episodes.

577   THE INTERNS

Drama. The personal and professional lives of Greg Pettit, Lydia Thorpe, Pooch Hardin, Sam Marsh and Cal Barrin, interns at New North Hospital in Los Angeles.

CAST

Dr. Peter Goldstone, the interns' supervisor	Broderick Crawford
Dr. Pooch Hardin	Christopher Stone
Dr. Lydia Thorpe	Sandra Smith
Dr. Sam Marsh	Mike Farrell
Dr. Greg Pettit	Stephen Brooks
Dr. Cal Barrin	Hal Frederick
Bobbie Marsh, Sam's wife	Elaine Giftos
Dr. Jacoby	Skip Homeier
Dr. Lansing	Edward Faulkner
Nurse	Jenny Blackton
Dr. Cherry	David Sachs

Music: Shorty Rogers.

Executive Producer: Bob Claver.
Producer: Charles Larson.

THE INTERNS — 60 minutes — CBS — September 18, 1970 — September 10, 1971. 24 episodes.

578   IN THE BEGINNING

Comedy. The story of Father Dan Cleary, an uptight, conservative priest, and Sister Agnes, a free-spirited, street-wise nun, and the bickering that ensues when the two join forces and open a mission at 122 15th Street amid hookers, drunks, runaways and teenage gangs. Their inability to agree on issues concerning the welfare of the mission and its people is the focal point of the series.

CAST

Father Dan Cleary	McLean Stevenson
Sister Agnes	Priscilla Lopez
Sister Lillian, Agnes' superior	Priscilla Morrill
Monsignor Frank Barlow, Dan's superior	Jack Dodson
Willie, one of the neighborhood kids	Olivia Barash
Jerome Rockefeller, same as Willie	Bobby Ellerbee
Tony, same as Willie	Cosie Costa
Bad Lincoln, same as Willie	Michael Anthony
Frank, same as Willie	Fred Lehne

Music: Barry DeVorzon.
Executive Producer: Mort Lachman, Norman Steinberg.
Producer: Jim Mulligan, Rita Dillon.
Director: Jack Shea, Doug Rogers, Randy Winburn.
Creator: Jack Shea, Jim Mulligan; developed by Norman Lear.

IN THE BEGINNING — 30 minutes — CBS — September 20, 1978 – November 1, 1978. 6 episodes.

579   THE INVISIBLE MAN

Adventure. While working on a formula to transfer matter from one place to another through the use of laser beams, Daniel Weston, a scientist employed by the KLAE Corporation, injects himself with a newly developed serum that renders him invisible. When he discovers that his serum is to be used for military purposes, he destroys the process and his only means by which to again become visible. By wearing a special plastic face mask and hands developed by a friend, Weston appears as he did before the experiment. Stories detail Weston's investigations on highly dangerous national and international assignments for the KLAE Corporation, a Los Angeles-based research center that undertakes government contracts.

CAST

Daniel Weston	David McCallum
Kate Weston, his wife	Melinda Fee
Walter Carlson, his superior (pilot film)	Jackie Cooper
Walter Carlson (series)	Craig Stevens
Nick Maggio, the doctor who developed Weston's special mask	Henry Darrow
The gate guard for KLAE	Ted Gehring
KLAE Security Chief	Paul Kent

Music: Henry Mancini, Pete Rugolo, Richard Clements.
Music Supervision: Hal Mooney.
Executive Producer: Harve Bennett.
Producer: Leslie Stevens, Steve Bochco, Robert F. O'Neil.
Director: Robert Michael Lewis, Alan J. Levi, Sugmund Neufeld, Jr., Leslie Stevens.

THE INVISIBLE MAN — 60 minutes — NBC — September 8, 1975 – January 9, 1976. 13 episodes. The 90-minute pilot film aired on NBC on May 6, 1975.

580   IRONSIDE

Crime Drama. While on vacation, Robert T. Ironside, chief of detectives of the San Francisco Police Department, is shot by an assassin and crippled when the bullet shatters his spinal nerve column. Determined to continue his crusade against crime, he is appointed special consultant to the S.F.P.D. and is assigned a staff of crime fighters: Detective Sergeant Ed Brown and Police Woman Eve Whitfield (later replaced by Police Woman Fran Belding); and Mark Sanger, an ex-con who serves as Ironside's "legs" and general helper before becoming a lawyer. The series depicts their investigations.

CAST

Chief Robert Ironside	Raymond Burr
Sgt. Eve Whitfield	Barbara Anderson
Sgt. Ed. Brown	Don Galloway
Mark Sanger, Ironside's helper	Don Mitchell
Sgt. Fran Belding	Elizabeth Baur
Diana Sanger, Mark's wife	Jane Pringle
Police Commissioner Randall	Gene Lyons

Music: Marty Paich, Oliver Nelson.
Executive Producer: Joel Rogosin, Frank Price, Cy Chermak.
Producer: Albert Aley, Norman Jolley, Paul Mason, Cy Chermak, Douglas Benton, Frank Price.
Director: William Graham, Bruce Kessler, Leo Penn, Barry Shear, David Lowell Rich, David Friedkin, Jimmy Sangster, Jerry Jameson, Jeannot Szwarc, Charles S. Dubin, Leonard Horn, Alf Kjellin, Tony Leader, James Neilson, Christian I. Nyby II, Allen Reisner, Robert Scheerer, James Sheldon, Daniel Petrie, John Florea, Ralph Senensky, Dick Colla, Don Weis, Boris Sagal, Russ

Mayberry, Abner Biberman, Don McDougall, Daniel Haller. *Creator:* Collier Young.

IRONSIDE—60 minutes—NBC —September 14, 1967–January 16, 1975. Syndicated. 120 episodes. Also titled for syndication while still first-run on the network, *The Raymond Burr Show*.

581   ISIS

Adventure. The series, set in Larkspur, a small town in California, follows the exploits of Andrea Thomas, a beautiful high school science teacher who, through the powers of a magic amulet she found in Egypt* becomes Isis, a "dedicated foe of evil, a defender of the weak, and a champion of truth and justice." (When Andrea holds the amulet, which she wears as a necklace, and speaks the words "Oh mighty Isis," she becomes Isis.)

CAST

Andrea Thomas/Isis   JoAnna Cameron
Rick Mason, Andrea's friend,
    a teacher   Brian Cutler
Cindy Lee, Andrea's friend,
    a student   Joanna Pang
Renee Carroll, Andrea's friend,
    a student   Ronalda Douglas
Dr. Barnes, the head of the
    science department   Albert Reed

Andrea's pet crow: Tut.
Music: Yvette Blais, Jeff Michael.
Executive Producer: Lou Scheimer, Norm Prescott, Dick Rosenbloom.
Producer: Arthur H. Nadel.
Director: Hollingsworth Morse, Arnold Laven, Earl Bellamy, Arthur H. Nadel.

ISIS—25 minutes—CBS—September 6, 1975–September 2, 1978. Also titled, for a short time, *The Secrets of Isis*.

*In ancient Egypt, the Royal Sorcerer presented his queen with a magic amulet that endowed her and her descendants with the power of the goddess Isis; the ability to soar, the power of the animals and control over the elements of earth, sea and sky. Three thousand years later, while on an expedition in Egypt, Andrea finds the amulet and inherits the powers of Isis.

582   IT'S ANYBODY'S
GUESS

Game. Two contestants compete and appear opposite a panel of five studio audience members. A question is read to the panel and an answer, chosen by the producers of the program, appears on a screen that is visible to everyone except the panelists. One contestant, chosen by a flip of a coin, has to predict whether or not the panel will come up with the same response. Each panelist then answers the ques-

tion. Depending on the results, one point is scored: in favor of contestant if he predicted correctly or for his opponent if the player predicted incorrectly. Contestants alternate turns and the first player to score five points is the winner.

Host: Monty Hall.
Announcer: Jay Stewart.
Music: Score Productions.
Executive Producer: Stefan Hatos, Monty Hall, Stu Billet.
Producer: Steve Feke.
Director: Joe Behar.

IT'S ANYBODY'S GUESS—30 minutes—NBC—June 13, 1977 –September 30, 1977. 80 programs.

583   IT TAKES A THIEF

Adventure. Through an arrangement with S.I.A. Chief Noah Bain, Alexander Mundy, a sophisticated and cunning cat burglar, is granted a pardon when he agrees to become a spy for the United States. Posing as an international playboy, he attempts to perform necessary, but highly dangerous feats of thievery through the use of his unique skills.

CAST

Alexander Mundy   Robert Wagner
Noah Bain, his superior   Malachi Throne
Alister Mundy, Alex's father, a
    master thief   Fred Astaire
S.I.A. Agent Dover   John Russell
Wally Powers, Mundy's superior
    in later episodes   Edward Binns
Charlotte "Chuck" Brown, the
    beautiful, but kooky thief
    who complicates Mundy's
    assignments   Susan Saint James

Music: Benny Golson, Ralph Ferraro.
Executive Producer: Frank Price, Gordon Oliver, Jack Arnold.
Producer: Winston Miller, Paul Mason, Gene L. Coon, Mort Zarcoff.
Director: Don Weis, Jack Arnold, Gerd Oswald, Roland Kibbee, Michael Caffey, Barry Shear, Lee H. Katzin, Tony Leader.

IT TAKES A THIEF—60 minutes—ABC—January 9, 1968– September 14, 1970. 65 episodes. Syndicated.

584   IT TAKES TWO

Game. A question, that has to be answered with a number, is read to three guest celebrity couples. The team totals are calculated and a contestant is chosen from the studio audience. The player chooses the couple he feels has come closest to the correct answer. When the host reveals the answer, the contestant receives an expensive merchandise prize if he chose the correct couple or a much less expensive gift if he chose incorrectly.

Host: Vince Scully.
Announcer: John Harlan.

IT TAKES TWO—30 minutes— NBC—March 31, 1969–August 1, 1970. 320 programs.

585   IT WAS A VERY
GOOD YEAR

Variety. The music, fads, sports, politics and the sensational and tragic moments of the years 1918 through 1968 are recalled through film clips.

Host-Narrator: Mel Tormé.
Theme Vocal/Piano Music: Mel Tormé.
Executive Producer: Alan Landsburg.
Producer: Mel Torme, Draper Lewis.
Director: Allan Angus.

IT WAS A VERY GOOD YEAR— 30 minutes—ABC—May 10, 1971–August 30, 1971. 13 programs.

586   IVAN THE
TERRIBLE

Comedy. The trials and tribulations of Ivan Petrovsky, headwaiter at the Hotel Metropole in Moscow, Russia, and head of a family of nine living in a three-and-one-half-room apartment. Stories stress his attempts to solve family problems.

CAST

Ivan Petrovsky   Lou Jacobi
Olga Petrovsky,
    Ivan's wife   Maria Karnilova
Vladimir, Olga's ex-husband   Phil Leeds
Tationa, Olga's mother   Despo
Sonia Petrovsky, Ivan's
    daughter   Caroline Kava
Sascha Petrovsky,
    Ivan's son   Matthew Barry
Nikolai Petrovsky,
    Ivan's son   Alan Cauldwell
Sventlana Petrovsky,
    Nikolai's wife   Nana Tucker
Raoul Sanchez, the Cuban exchange
    student   Manuel Martinez
Federov, the government
    official   Christopher Hewell
Mr. Yoshanka, Ivan's
    employer   Joseph Leon

Petrovsky family dog: Rasputan.
Music: Joe Raposo.
Executive Producer: Alan King.
Producer: Rupert Hitzig.
Director: Peter H. Hunt.
Creator: Peter Slone, Herb Sargeant.

IVAN THE TERRIBLE—30 minutes—CBS—August 21, 1976–September 18, 1976.

587   I'VE GOT A
SECRET

Game. The object calls for three celebrity panelists to guess the secret of a guest contestant through a series of question-

and-answer rounds. Contestants receive both cash and merchandise prizes for participating.

Version 1:

Host: Garry Moore, Steve Allen.
Regular Panelists: Jayne Meadows, Bill Cullen, Henry Morgan, Betsy Palmer, Faye Emerson, Steve Allen.
Announcer: John Cannon, Johnny Olsen.
Music: The Irving Fields Trio.
Producer: Chester Feldman, Mark Goodson, Bill Todman, Gil Fates.

I'VE GOT A SECRET—30 minutes—CBS—June 26, 1952– September 3, 1967.

Version 2:

Host: Steve Allen.
Regular Panelists: Pat Carroll, Richard Dawson, Nanette Fabray, Gene Rayburn, Anita Gillette, Henry Morgan, Jayne Meadows.
Announcer: Johnny Olsen.
Music: Score Productions.
Executive Producer: Gil Fates.
Producer: Ira Skutch.

I'VE GOT A SECRET—30 minutes—Syndicated 1972.

Version 3:

Host: Bill Cullen.
Panelists: Henry Morgan, Elaine Joyce, Phyllis George, Richard Dawson, Pat Collins.
Announcer: Johnny Olsen.
Music: Norman Paris.
Executive Producer: Mark Goodson, Bill Todman, Gil Fates.
Producer: Chester Feldman.
Director: Lloyd Gross.

I'VE GOT A SECRET—30 minutes—CBS—June 15, 1976– July 6, 1976.

J

588   JABBERJAW

Animated Cartoon. The series, set in a futuristic undersea world, follows the adventures of Biff, Shelley, Bubbles and Clam Head, the teenage members of the Neptunes Rock Group. Assisted by Jabberjaw, a fifteen-foot pet white shark who plays drums, they attempt to solve bizarre underwater crimes—the deeds of fiends who seek to control the ocean floor.

VOICES

Jabberjaw   Frank Welker
Bubbles   Julie McWhirter
Shelley   Pat Parris
Biff   Tommy Cook
Clam Head   Barry Gordon

Music: Hoyt Curtin, Paul DeKorte.

In the Beginning. Priscilla Lopez and McLean Stevenson.

Isis. JoAnna Cameron.

Joe and Valerie. Paul Regina and Char Fontane from "The Wedding" episode. Courtesy of the *Call-Chronicle Newspapers,* Allentown, Pa.

Karen. Karen Valentine.

Executive Producer: William Hanna, Joseph Barbera.
Producer: Iwao Takamoto.
Director: Charles A. Nichols.

JABBERJAW—25 minutes—ABC—September 11, 1976—September 3, 1978.

589   JABBERWOCKY

Variety. Sketches, music and songs geared to children.

Regulars: Joanna Sopko, Peter Johnson, Carl Thomas, Bob Porsky, Bob Fromy, Joseph Williams.
Music: David Lucas.
Piano: Andy Gaus.
Producer: Gail Frank.
Assistant Producer: Michele Connors.
Vocalists: Tucker Smallwood, Sam Bealieu.
Director: Don Kolshrud.
Animation Director: Tom Jurkoski.

JABBERWOCKY—30 minutes—Syndicated 1974.

590   THE JACKIE GLEASON SHOW

Variety. Music, songs, dances and comedy sketches, including a revival of "The Honeymooners," a sketch that revolves around the lives of Ralph and Alice Kramden and their friends Ed and Trixie Norton. For more information on the series, see *The Honeymooners* title.

Host: Jackie Gleason.
Regulars: Lanita Kent, Jami Henderson, Andrea Duda, Carlos Bas, The Glea Girls, The June Taylor Dancers.
Honeymooners Cast: Jackie Gleason as Ralph Kramden, Sheila MacRae as Alice Kramden, Art Carney as Ed Norton, and Jane Kean as Trixie Norton.
Announcer: Johnny Olsen.
Orchestra: Sammy Spear.
Executive Producer: Jack Philbin.
Producer: Ronald Wayne.
Director: Frank Bunetta.

THE JACKIE GLEASON SHOW—60 minutes—CBS—September 17, 1966—September 12, 1970. See also *The Best of the Jackie Gleason Show*.

591   JACK PAAR TONIGHT

Variety.

Host: Jack Paar.
Co-Host: Peggy Cass.
Announcer: Peggy Cass.
Orchestra: Charles Randolph Green.
Producer: Bob Carman.
Writer: David Lloyd, Jim Mulholland, Jack Douglas, Bob Howard.
Director: Hal Gurnee.

JACK PAAR TONIGHT—90 minutes—ABC—January 8, 1973–November 16, 1973.

592   JACKPOT

Game. Of the sixteen players that compete, one is designated as the expert and he pushes a button to establish a money amount (from $3,000 to $10,000). The fifteen remaining players, who each possess a riddle of varying cash value, are called on one at a time by the expert. When called, a player states the cash value of his riddle (which is calculated on a board) then reads it. If the expert solves it, he keeps his place and calls on another player; if he fails to solve it, he trades places with the person who stumped him. Each riddle that is solved increases the money on the board and it can only be won by the expert (at the time of play) when enough riddles have been answered to equal or surpass a previously established amount.

The sixteen players compete for five days, and although each player is permitted to keep the monies he has earned, the highest overall cash scorer receives the added bonus of varied merchandise gifts.

Host: Geoff Edwards.
Announcer: Don Pardo.
Music: Score Productions.
Executive Producer: Bob Stewart.
Producer: Bruce Burmester.

JACKPOT—30 minutes—NBC—January 7, 1974–September 26, 1975. 420 programs.

593   THE JACKSON FIVE

Animated Cartoon. The misadventures of the Jackson Five, a Motown rock group.

Voices: The Jackson Five, Paul Frees, Edmund Silvers, Joe Cooper.
Music: The Jackson Five, Maury Laws.
Producer: Arthur Rankin, Jr., Jules Bass.
Director: Robert Balser.

THE JACKSON FIVE—30 minutes—ABC—September 11, 1971–September 1, 1973.

594   THE JACKSONS

Variety. Music, songs, dances and comedy sketches.

Host: The Jackson Five (brothers Michael, Marlon, Randy, Jackie and Tito).
Regulars: The Jackson Sisters (Rebie, LaToya, and Janet), Jim Samuels, Marty Cohen.
Orchestra: Rick Wilkins.
Choreographer: Anita Mann.
Executive Producer: Joe Jackson, Richard Arons.

Producer: Bill Davis, Arnie Hogen, Bonnie Burns, Ray Jessel.
Writer: Jim Mulligan, Wayne Kline, Biff Maynard, David Smilow, James Tisdale.
Director: Bill Davis.
Art Director: Bill Camden.

THE JACKSONS—30 minutes—CBS—June 16, 1976–July 7, 1976; January 26, 1977–March 9, 1977.

595   JACK THE RIPPER

Mystery. A six-part series that recreates three terrifying months in British history—August 31, 1888, to November 9, 1888—a time when five women met death in Whitechapel, London, at the hands of the famed, but still mysterious, Jack the Ripper. Through the modern-day investigations of Scotland Yard detectives Barlow and Watt, new evidence is presented in an attempt to uncover the identity of history's most notorious criminal.

CAST

Detective Jack Barlow	Alan Stratford-Johns
Detective Watt	Frank Windsor

Host: Sebastian Cabot.
Music: Bill Southgate.

JACK THE RIPPER—60 minutes—Syndicated 1974. 6 episodes.

596   JAMES AT 15

Drama. A realistic approach to the problems faced by today's teenagers as depicted in the experiences of James Hunter, a student at Bunker Hill High School in Boston.

CAST

James Hunter	Lance Kerwin
Paul Hunter, his father	Linden Chiles
Joan Hunter, his mother	Lynn Carlin
Sandy Hunter, his younger sister	Kim Richards
Kathy Hunter, his older sister	Deirdre Berthrong
Marlene Mahoney, James's friend	Susan Myers
Ludwig "Sly" Hazeltine, James's friend	David Hubbard

Music: Jimmie Haskell, J.A.C. Redford, Miles Goodman.
Music Supervision: Lionel Newman.
Theme Vocal ("James"): Lee Montgomery.
Executive Producer: Martin Manulis, Joseph Hardy.
Producer: Ernest Losso, Ronald Rubin.
Director: Joseph Hardy, James Sheldon, Ernest Losso, Ernest Pintoff, Peter Levin, Marc Daniels, George Tyne.
Creator: Dan Wakefield.

JAMES AT 15—60 minutes—NBC—October 27, 1977–January 26, 1978. 10 episodes. As

"James at 16"—60 minutes—NBC—February 9, 1978–March 16, 1978; June 1, 1978–July 27, 1978. 11 episodes. The two-hour pilot film, "James at 15," aired on NBC on September 5, 1977.

JAMES AT 16

See title *James at 15*.

597   JASON OF STAR COMMAND

Science Fiction Adventure. The exploits of Jason, a pilot with the futuristic Star Command, space-age interplanetary police station, as he battles Dragos, the most sinister being in the universe who seeks to control the galaxy. Originally broadcast as a segment of *Tarzan and the Super Seven*, which see for original cast information.

CAST

Jason	Craig Littler
Commander Stone, the head of Star Command	John Russell
Prof. E.J. Parsafoot, the chief science officer	Charlie Dell
Samantha, the alien ally	Tamara Dobson
The Evil Dragos	Sid Haig

Jason's ship: The *Starfire*.
The Star Command Robot: Peepo.
Music: Yvette Blais, Jeff Michael.
Executive Producer: Lou Scheimer, Norm Prescott.
Producer: Arthur H. Nadel.
Director: Arthur H. Nadel.

JASON OF STAR COMMAND—30 minutes—CBS—Premiered: September 15, 1979.

598   JEANNIE

Animated Cartoon. While surfing, Corey Anders, a high school student in the town of Center City, is overcome by a wave that washes him ashore and uncovers a bottle that had been buried in the sand. Upon opening it, a beautiful young genie, named Jeannie, and her friend Babu, an inept apprentice genie, emerge and become his slaves. Stories depict Corey's attempts to conceal their presence and live the normal life of a teenager; and Jeannie's efforts—hindered by Babu—to adjust to life in the 1970s and protect Corey from the wiles of other girls. A spin-off from *I Dream of Jeannie* and unlike Barbara Eden's portrayal of a genie, whose powers are evoked by crossing her hands over her chest and blinking her eyes, the animated genie's powers are contained in her hair, which she wears as a pony tail.

VOICES

Jeannie	Julie McWhirter
Corey Anders	Marc Hammil
Henry Glopp, Corey's friend	Bob Hastings
Babu, the apprentice genie	Joe Besser

Additional Voices: Tommy Cook, Don Messick, Ginny Tyler, Julie Bennett, Sherry Alberoni.
Corey's address: 636 North Beach Street.
Music: Hoyt Curtin, Paul DeKorte.
Executive Producer: William Hanna, Joseph Barbera.
Producer: Iwao Takamoto.
Director: Charles A. Nichols.

JEANNIE—30 minutes—CBS—September 8, 1973–August 30, 1975.

599 JEAN SHEPHERD'S AMERICA

Documentary. Perspectives on American life as seen through the eyes of humorist Jean Shepherd.

Narrator: Jean Shepherd.
Producer: Olivia Tappar, Fred Barzyk.
Writer-Creator: Jean Shepherd.
Director: Fred Barzyk.

JEAN SHEPHERD'S AMERICA—30 minutes—PBS—1971–1972; 1975–1976. 13 episodes. In 1977, Jean Shepherd was the host of *Shepherd's Pie*, a local New Jersey series wherein he viewed, in the same humoristic light as his *America*, various aspects of the Garden State.

600 THE JEFFERSONS

Comedy. The trials and tribulations of the Jefferson family: George, the snobbish, pompous and wealthy owner of several dry cleaning establishments; Louise, his tolerant, long-suffering wife; and Lionel, their twenty-two-year-old son. A spin-off from *All in the Family*.

CAST

George Jefferson	Sherman Hemsley
Louise Jefferson, his wife	Isabel Sanford
Lionel Jefferson, their son	Mike Evans
	Damon Evans
	Mike Evans
Tom Willis, their neighbor	Franklin Cover
Helen Willis, Tom's wife	Roxie Roker
Jenny Willis, Tom's daughter and later Lionel's wife	Berlinda Tolbert
Harry Bentley, George's neighbor	Paul Benedict
Olivia Jefferson, George's mother	Zara Cully
Florence Johnston, the Jeffersons' maid	Marla Gibbs
Ralph, the apartment building doorman	Ned Wertimer
Buzz Thatcher, Florence's boyfriend	Larry McCormick

Music: Jeff Berry, Ja'net Dubois.
Executive Producer: George Sunga, Jay Moriarty, Mike Mulligan, Don Nicholl, Michael Ross, Bernie West.
Producer: Sy Rosen, Mike Mulligan, Don Nicholl, Michael Ross, Bernie West, Jack Shea, Ron Leavitt, David W. Duclon.
Director: Jack Shea, Bob Lally.

THE JEFFERSONS—30 minutes—CBS—Premiered: January 17, 1975.

601 JENNIE: LADY RANDOLPH CHURCHILL

Biography. A seven-part series that dramatizes the life of Lady Randolph Churchill (nee Jennie Jerome, 1845-1921), the American-born mother of England's Sir Winston Churchill.

CAST

Lady Randolph Churchill	Lee Remick
Lord Randolph Churchill	Ronald Pickup
Mr. Jerome	Dan O'Herlihy
Mrs. Jerome	Helen Horton
Leonie	Barbara Parkins
Clara	Linda Lilies
Duke of Marlborough	Rachel Kempson
Prince of Wales	Thorley Walters
Montie Porch	Charles Kay
Sir Henry James	John Barley
George Cornwallis-West	Christopher Cazenove
Bertha	Barbara Laurenson

Music: Tom McCall.
Music Theme: Andre Previn.
Executive Producer: Stella Richman.
Producer: Andrew Brown.
Writer: Julian Mitchell.
Director: James Cellan Jones.
Art Director: Mike Hall, Fred Pusey.

JENNIE: LADY RANDOLPH CHURCHILL—60 minutes—PBS—October 8, 1975–November 19, 1975. 7 episodes.

602 JEOPARDY

Game. Three players compete in a game wherein they must supply answers to questions. A category board containing six subjects, each with five concealed answers and each worth a varying amount of money, is revealed. A player selects a subject and a money amount and must supply the question for the answer that is asked. If he gives a correct question, he wins the money and continues to play. When he fails to supply a correct answer the value of that particular question is deducted from his score, and of the remaining two players, the one who can supply the correct question is next in control of the board. The game continues in this manner with the highest scoring player being declared the winner.

Host: Art Fleming.
Announcer: Don Pardo, John Harlan.
Music: Score Productions.
Producer: Bob Rubin.
Director: Jeff Goldstein.

JEOPARDY—30 minutes—NBC—April 30, 1964–January 3, 1975.

603 THE JERRY REED WHEN YOU'RE HOT, YOU'RE HOT HOUR

Variety. Music, songs and comedy sketches set against a Country and Western background.

Host: Jerry Reed.
Regulars: Cal Wilson, Spencer Quinn, Merie Earle, John Twomey, Norman Alexander, The Lou Regas Dancers.
Announcer: Bill Thompson.
Orchestra: George Wyle.
Executive Producer: Rich Eustis, Al Rogers.
Producer: Jerry McPhie.
Writer: Frank Shaw, Ray Jessel, Coslough Johnson, Mark Shekter, Pat Buttram, Rich Eustis, Al Rogers.
Director: Jack Regas.

THE JERRY REED WHEN YOU'RE HOT, YOU'RE HOT HOUR—60 minutes—CBS—June 20, 1972–July 25, 1972.

604 JERRY VISITS

Interview. Hollywood celebrities open their homes to television cameras and reveal their dreams, ambitions and aspects of their private and public lives.

Host: Jerry Dunphy.
Music: Joseph Byrd Productions.
Producer: Jerry Dunphy.
Director: Ervin Zavada.

JERRY VISITS—30 minutes—Syndicated 1971.

605 THE JETSONS

Animated Cartoon. The misadventures of the Jetsons, an Earth family in the twenty-first century: George, an employee of Spacely Space Sprockets; his wife Jane; and their children, Judy and Elroy.

VOICES

George Jetson, the father	George O'Hanlon
Jane Jetson, his wife	Penny Singleton
Judy Jetson, their daughter	Janet Waldo
Elroy Jetson, their son	Daws Butler
Astro, their dog	Don Messick
Rosie, their electronic maid	Jean VanderPyl
Cosmo G. Spacely, George's employer	Mel Blanc
Henry Orbit, the apartment building janitor	Howard Morris
Cogswell, the owner of the rival firm, Cogswell Cogs	Daws Butler

Music: Hoyt Curtin.
Executive Producer: William Hanna, Joseph Barbera.
Writer: Warren Foster, Mike Maltese, Harvey Bullock, Larry Markes, Tony Benedict.
Director: William Hanna, Joseph Barbera.

THE JETSONS—30 minutes. ABC—September 1962–September 1964. CBS—September 4, 1965–September 3, 1966. NBC—September 10, 1966–September 2, 1967. CBS—September 13, 1969–September 5, 1970. NBC—September 11, 1971–August 30, 1975. NBC—October 25, 1975–September 4, 1976. 24 episodes. Syndicated.

606 JIGSAW

Crime Drama. The exploits of Frank Dain, a detective lieutenant with the Sacramento State Bureau of Missing Persons, a man who possesses a genius for solving complicated, clueless mysteries.

CAST

Lt. Frank Dain	James Wainwright

Music: Harper McKay, Robert Drasnin.
Producer: Stanley Kallis, Harry Tatelman.
Writer: Walter Doniger, David Friedkin, Charles Thomas, Thomas Drake, Herb Bermann, Jerrold Freedman, Bo May.
Director: Calvin Clements, Mark Rodgers, Barry Shear, Stephen J. Cannell, Marc Daniels, Walter Graham.

JIGSAW—60 minutes—ABC—October 12, 1972–August 11, 1973 (as a segment of *The Men*). 6 episodes. The two-hour pilot film, "Man on the Move," aired on ABC on March 26, 1972.

607 JIGSAW JOHN

Crime Drama. The cases of John St. John, nicknamed "Jigsaw John" by his colleagues, a Los Angeles Police Department homicide detective whose best weapon is his talent for figuring people and solving complex crimes.

CAST

Det. John St. John	Jack Warden
Maggi Hearn, his girlfriend	Pippa Scott
Det. Sam Donner, John's partner	Alan Feinstein

Music: Pete Rugolo, Harry Lejowski.
Producer: Ronald Austin, James David Buchanan.
Director: Harry Falk, Reza S. Badiyi, Charles S. Dubin, Paul Krasny, Charles R. Rondeau.
Creator: Al Martinez.

JIGSAW JOHN—60 minutes—NBC—February 2, 1976–April 13, 1976; May 31, 1976–September 13, 1976.

608 THE JIMMY DEAN SHOW

Variety. Performances by Country and Western entertainers.

Host: Jimmy Dean.
Vocalists: The Imperials.

THE JIMMY DEAN SHOW—30 minutes—Syndicated 1974.

609   JIMMY DURANTE PRESENTS THE LENNON SISTERS HOUR

Variety. Music, songs, dances and comedy sketches.

Host: Jimmy Durante.
Hostesses: Dianne, Peggy, Kathy and Janet Lennon.
Regulars: Edna O'Dell, Bernie Kukoff.
Announcer: Charlie O'Donnell, Jay Stewart.
Orchestra: George Wyle.
Executive Producer: Harold Cohen.
Producer: Bernie Kukoff, Jeff Harris.
Writer: Hugh Wedlock, Jr., Bill Bux, Don Reo, Bernie Kukoff, Jeff Harris.
Director: Bill Davis.

JIMMY DURANTE PRESENTS THE LENNON SISTERS HOUR—60 minutes—ABC—September 26, 1969—July 4, 1970. 26 programs.

JIM ROCKFORD, PRIVATE INVESTIGATOR

See title *The Rockford Files.*

610   THE JIMMY STEWART SHOW

Comedy. The series, set in Easy Valley, California, follows the trials and tribulations of James K. Howard, an anthropology professor at Josiah Kessel College.

CAST

James K. Howard	Jimmy Stewart
Martha Howard, his wife	Julie Adams
P.J. Howard, their son	Jonathan Daly
Wendy Howard, P.J.'s wife	Ellen Geer
Teddy Howard, James and Martha's son	Dennis Larson
Jake Howard, P.J. and Wendy's son	Kirby Furlong
Luther Quince, the chemistry professor	John McGiver

The Howards' Address: 35 Hillview Drive.
Music: Van Alexander.
Producer-Director: Hal Kanter.

THE JIMMY STEWART SHOW—30 minutes—NBC—September 19, 1971—September 3, 1972. 26 episodes.

611   THE JIM NABORS HOUR

Variety. Music, songs, dances and comedy sketches.

Host: Jim Nabors.
Regulars: Frank Sutton, Ronnie Schell, Karen Morrow, The Tony Mordente Dancers, The Nabors Kids.
Orchestra: Paul Weston.
Producer: E. Duke Vincent, Bruce Johnson.
Writer: Ben Joelson, Art Baer, Buddy Atkinson, Arnie Kogen, Jack Mendleson, Arnold Kane, Hal Goodman, Al Gordon.
Director: Jack Donohue.

THE JIM NABORS HOUR—60 minutes—CBS—September 25, 1969—.May 20, 1971. 52 programs.

612   THE JIM NABORS SHOW

Variety. Music, interviews and comedy sketches.

Host: Jim Nabors.
Regulars: Susan Ford, Ronnie Schell.
Orchestra: Fred Werner.
Special Musical Material: Ed Scott.
Executive Producer: Carol Raskin.
Producer: Ken Harris.
Director: Barry Glazer.

THE JIM NABORS SHOW—60 minutes—Syndicated 1978.

613   THE JIM STAFFORD SHOW

Variety. Music, songs, dances and comedy sketches.

Host: Jim Stafford.
Regulars: Valerie Curtin, Richard Stahl, Phil MacKenzie, Deborah Allen, Jeannie Sheffield, Tom Biener, Gallagher, Lyndi Wood.
Announcer: Dick Tufeld, Bill Thompson.
Dancers: The Carl Jablonski Dancers.
Orchestra: Eddie Karam.
Executive Producer: Phil Gernhard, Tony Scotti.
Producer: Al Rogers, Rich Eustis.
Writer: Rich Eustis, Al Rogers, Jim Stafford, Rod Warren, April Kelly, Bo Kaprall, Pat Proft, George Tricker, Stuart Birnbaum, Matt Neuman.
Director: Lee Bernhardi.
Choreographer: Carl Jablonski.

THE JIM STAFFORD SHOW—60 minutes—ABC—July 30, 1975—September 3, 1975.

614   JOANNE CARSON'S V.I.P.'S

Celebrity Interviews.

Hostess: Joanne Carson.
Announcer: Hugh Douger.
Music: A recorded opening and closing theme.

JOANNE CARSON'S V.I.P.'S—30 minutes—Syndicated 1972.

615   JOE AND SONS

Comedy. The trials and tribulations of Joe Vitale, a widowed sheet metal worker living in Hoboken, New Jersey, as he struggles to raise his teenage sons, Mark and Nick.

CAST

Joe Vitale	Richard Castellano
Mark Vitale, his son	Barry Miller
Nick Vitale, his son (pilot episode)	Mitch Brown
Nick Vitale (series)	Jimmy Baio
Estelle, Joe's neighbor (pilot episode)	Maureen Arthur
Estelle (series)	Bobbi Jordan
Josephine Molonaire, Joe's married sister	Florence Stanley
Gus Duesic, Joe's friend	Jerry Stiller

Music: David Shire.
Executive Producer: Douglas S. Cramer.
Producer: Bernie Kukoff, Jeff Harris.
Director: Peter Baldwin.
Creator: Robert Illes, James Stein.
Art Director: Bill Bohnert.

JOE AND SONS—30 minutes—CBS—September 9, 1975—January 13, 1976.

616   JOE AND VALERIE

Comedy. The series, set in Brooklyn, follows the romantic misadventures of Joe Pizo, an apprentice plumber, and Valerie Sweetzer, a cosmetics salesgirl.

CAST

Joe Pizo	Paul Regina
Valerie Sweetzer	Char Fontane
Frank Berganski, Joe's friend who works in a health spa	Bill Beyers
Paulie Barone, Joe's friend who drives a hearse	David Elliott
Stella Sweetzer, Valerie's mother	Pat Benson
Thelma Medina, Valerie's friend	Donna Ponterotto
Vincent Pizo, Joe's father, a plumber	Robert Costanzo

Music: Jack Elliott, Allyn Ferguson.
Theme Vocal: Char Fontane, Randy Winburn.
Executive Producer: Linda Hope.
Producer: Bernie Kahn.
Director: Bill Persky, Bob Claver.
Creator: Bernie Kahn, Ronald Rubin.
Choreographer: Anita Mann.

JOE AND VALERIE—30 minutes—NBC—April 24, 1978—May 10, 1978. 4 episodes.

617   JOE AND VALERIE

Comedy. Basically the same format as the original version (previous title) with stories centering on the courtship and marriage of Joe Pizo, a plumber, and Valerie Sweetzer, a clothing salesgirl.

CAST

Joe Pizo	Paul Regina
Valerie Sweetzer, married Joe on Jan. 12, 1979	Char Fontane
Frank Berganski, Joe's friend	Lloyd Alann
Paulie Barone, Joe's friend	David Elliott
Stella Sweetzer, Valerie's mother	Arlene Golonka
Rita, Valerie's friend	Donna Ponterotto
Vince Pizo, Joe's father	Robert Costanzo
Ed Sweetzer, Stella's ex-husband	Jack Riley

Music: Joe Raposo, Pattie Brooks.
Theme Vocal: Patti Brooks, Jean Raposo.

Supervising Producer: Hal Dresner.
Executive Producer: Linda Hope.
Producer: Frank Badami.
Director: Bob Claver.
Creator: Bernie Kahn, Ronald Rubin.

JOE AND VALERIE—30 minutes—NBC—January 5, 1979—January 19, 1979. 3 episodes.

618   JOE FORRESTER

Crime Drama. A realistic portrayal of police work in action as seen through the experiences of Joe Forrester, a veteran policeman who rejects a desk job to walk his old beat as a uniformed cop.

CAST

Officer Joe Forrester (Badge 147)	Lloyd Bridges
Sgt. Bernie Vincent, his superior	Eddie Egan
Georgia Cameron, Joe's girlfriend	Patricia Crowley
Jolene Jackson, Joe's informant	Dwan Smith
Detective Marshall	Mike Warren
Sergeant Storm	Lynn Redding
Assistant D.A. Johnson	Andra Akers
Polygraph Operator	Dale Tarter

Music: Richard Markowitz, Robert Drasnin.
Executive Producer: David Gerber.
Producer: Mark Rodgers, James H. Brown.
Director: Reza S. Badiyi, Alf Kjellin, Alexander Singer, Jerry London, Barry Shear, Alex March, Alvin Ganzer.
Creator: Mark Rodgers.

JOE FORRESTER—60 minutes—NBC—September 9, 1975—August 30, 1976.

619   THE JOE FRANKLIN SHOW

Variety. Celebrity interviews and performances by established and new entertainment acts. Nostalgic, rarely shown films from Hollywood's golden era also are featured.

Host: Joe Franklin.
Music: A recorded version of "12th Street Rag" is used as the theme.
Director: Bob Diamond.

THE JOE FRANKLIN SHOW—60 minutes—Syndicated (via cable systems) in 1979. Originally broadcast as a local New York program, beginning in 1954.

620   JOE'S WORLD

Comedy. The home and working life of Joe Wabash, a union painter living in Detroit.

CAST

Joe Wabash	Ramon Bieri
Katie Wabash, his wife	K Callan
Steve Wabash, their son	Christopher Knight

Maggie Wabash, their
daughter — Melissa Sherman
Jimmy Wabash, their son — Michael Sharrett
Linda Wabash, their
daughter — Missy Francis
Rick Wabash, their son — Ari Zeltzer
Judy Wilson, a member of
Joe's crew — Misty Rowe
Brad Hopkins, also a crew
member — Russ Banham
Andy, a crew member — Frank Coppola
Tessie, the owner of the
Hangout Bar — Joan Shawlee

Wabash address: 623 Eucaliptus
Avenue.
Linda's doll: Jennifer.
Music: Alan Thicke.
Executive Producer: Mel Tolkin,
Larry Rhine, Jack Elinson,
Chuck Stewart.
Producer: Herbert Kenwith.
Associate Producer: Sue Nevens.
Writer: Mel Tolkin, Larry Rhine,
Bert and Adell Styler, Al
Schwartz, Ray Singer, Jeremy
Stevens, Tom Moore, Gordon
Mitchell, Chuck Stewart, Jack
Elinson, Joseph Bonaduce, Phil
Sharp.
Director: Herbert Kenwith, John
Bowab, Jim Drake.
Art Director: Don Roberts.
Creator: Mel Tolkin, Larry Rhine.

JOE'S WORLD — 30 minutes —
NBC — December 28, 1979 —
January 2, 1980. 3 episodes. May
10, 1980 — July 26, 1980. 7 episodes.

621   JOEY AND DAD

Variety. Music, songs, dances and
comedy sketches.

Hostess: Joey Heatherton.
Host: Ray Heatherton (Joey's
father).
Regulars: Henny Youngman, Pat
Paulsen, Pat Proft, Bob Ein-
stein, Nick Nicholas, Dorothy
Meyers, Gene Taylor.
Announcer: Peter Cullen, Roger
Carroll.
Orchestra: Lex de Azevedo.
Special Musical Material: David
Black.
Choreographer: Joe Tremaine.
Executive Producer: Allan Blye,
Bob Einstein.
Producer: Bob Arnott, Coslough
Johnson, Stan Jacobson.
Writer: George Burditt, Robert
Illes, Jim Stein, Harvey
Weitzman, Allan Blye, Bob
Einstein.
Director: Mark Warren.

JOEY AND DAD — 60 minutes —
CBS — July 6, 1975 — July 27, 1975.
4 programs.

622   THE JOHN BYNER
COMEDY HOUR

Variety. Music, songs and comedy
sketches.

Host: John Byner.
Regulars: Patty Deutsch, Linda
Sublette, R. G. Brown, Gary Mil-
ler, Dennis Flannigan, The Lori
Regas Dancers.
Announcer: Bill Thompson.
Orchestra: Ray Charles.
Executive Producer: Nick Sevano,
Rich Eustis, Al Rogers.
Producer: Jerry McPhie.
Writer: Rudy DeLucca, Barry
Levinson, Craig Nelson, Ed
Haas, Coslough Johnson, Harry
Lee Scott, Bob Comfort, John
Byner, Rich Eustis, Al Rogers.
Director: Jack Regas.

THE JOHN BYNER COMEDY
HOUR — 60 minutes — CBS — August 1, 1972 — August 29, 1972. 4
programs.

623   THE JOHN
DAVIDSON SHOW

Variety. Music, songs and comedy
skits.

Host: John Davidson.
Regular: Pete Barbutti.
Announcer: Pete Barbutti.
Orchestra: Lenny Stack.
Choreographer: Ron Poindexter.
Executive Producer: Dick Clark,
Oliver Bernard.
Producer: Bill Lee.
Director: Barry Glazer.

THE JOHN DAVIDSON SHOW —
60 minutes — NBC — May 24,
1976 — June 14, 1976. 4 programs.

624   THE JOHN
DAVIDSON SHOW

Talk-Variety.

Host: John Davidson.
Music: John Toben.
Executive Producer: Frank R.
Miller.
Producer: Vince Calandra.
Director: Terry Kyne.
Art Director: John McAdam.

THE JOHN DAVIDSON SHOW —
90 minutes — Syndicated June
1980.

625   JOHNNY CASH
AND FRIENDS

Variety. Performances by Country
and Western personalities.

Host: Johnny Cash.
Regulars: June Carter Cash, Steve
Martin, Jim Varney, Howard
Mann, The B.C. and M. Choir.
Orchestra: Bill Walker.
Executive Producer: Joseph
Cates.
Producer: Chet Hagen, Walter C.
Miller.
Director: Walter C. Miller.

JOHNNY CASH AND FRIENDS —
60 minutes — CBS — August 29,
1976 — September 19, 1976. 4
programs.

626   THE JOHNNY
CASH SHOW

Variety. Performances by Country
and Western entertainers.

Host: Johnny Cash.
Regulars: June Carter, The Carter
Family, Carl Perkins, The Stat-
ler Brothers, The Tennessee
Three.
Announcer: Mike Lawrence.
Orchestra: Bill Walker.
Executive Producer: Harold D.
Cohen, Joe Byrne.
Producer: Stan Jacobson.
Writer: Stan Jacobson, Aubrey
Todman, Gary Ferrier, Red
Lane, Bill Walker.
Director: Allan Angus.

THE JOHNNY CASH SHOW — 60
minutes — ABC — June 7, 1969 —
September 6, 1969; January 21,
1970 — May 21, 1971. 39
programs.

627   JOHNNY MANN'S
STAND UP AND CHEER

Variety. The series presents
America in a musical revue.

Host: Johnny Mann.
The Johnny Mann Singers: Marty
McCall, Diane Bellis, Richard
Brettiger, Thurl Ravenscroft,
Mike Redman, Merry Vernon,
Sharalee Beard, Errol Horne,
Rob Stevens, Lyn Dolin, Steve
Sweetland, Barbara Harris, Pat
Corbett, Cathy Cahill, Tony
Quinn, Freeman Clemente, Er-
roll Rorigwynne, Ken Prymus,
Marcia Darcangelo.
Orchestra: Johnny Mann.
Musical Coordinator: Paul Suter.
Musical Conductor: Dave Pell.
Executive Producer: Pierre Cos-
sette, Burt Sugarman.
Producer-Director: Dean Whit-
more.

JOHNNY MANN'S STAND UP AND
CHEER — 30 minutes — Syndicated 1971.

628   JOKER! JOKER!!
JOKER!!!

Game. A children's version of *The
Joker's Wild.* Game is played in
the same manner, however
prizes are $500 savings bonds in-
stead of cash.

Host: Jack Barry.
Announcer: Jay Stewart.
Music: Score Productions.
Executive Producer: Jack Barry,
Dan Enright.
Producer: Ron Greenberg.
Director: Richard S. Kline.

JOKER! JOKER!! JOKER!!! — 30
minutes — Syndicated January
1980.

629   THE JOKER'S
WILD

Game. One of two contestants
pulls a lever to activate a large
slot machine-like mechanism that
contains five category topics.
When the machine stops, it pinpoints three question categories,
one of which is chosen by the
player. If the contestant answers
correctly, he wins money and
continues to play; if he is wrong,
he loses his turn and his opponent receives the opportunity to
win money. The winner is the
first player to score $500.

Contained within the categories are jokers, as in a deck of
playing cards, which sometimes
appear with a subject and allow a
player to double his money (if
one appears with two identical
categories) or triple his money
(if two jokers appear with one
category). If three jokers appear
during one spin, the player automatically wins the game and $500.

Host: Jack Barry.
Announcer: Johnny Jacobs, Jay
Stewart.
Music: Score Productions.
Executive Producer: Dan Enright.
Producer: Burt Sugarman, Jack
Barry, Dan Enright, Justin
Edgerton, Ron Greenberg.
Director: Richard S. Kline.

THE JOKER'S WILD — 30
minutes — CBS — September 4,
1972 — October 31, 1975. Syndicated first run.

630   JOSIE AND THE
PUSSYCATS

Animated Cartoon. The global
adventures of Josie and the Pussycats, an all-girl Rock group.

VOICES
Josie, group leader (speaking
voice) — Janet Waldo
Josie (singing voice) — Cathy Douglas
Melody, the drummer (speaking
voice) — Jackie Joseph
Melody (singing voice) — Cheryl Ladd
Valerie, the guitarist (speaking
voice) — Barbara Pariot
Valerie (singing voice) — Patricia Holloway
Alan, the group manager — Jerry Dexter
Alexander, Alan's assistant — Casey Kasem
Alexandra, Alexander's
sister — Sherry Alberoni
Sebastian, their pet cat — Don Messick

Music: Hoyt Curtin.
Vocals: Josie and the Pussycats.
Executive Producer: William
Hanna, Joseph Barbera.
Producer: Alex Lovy.
Director: William Hanna, Joseph
Barbera.
Animation Director: Charles A.
Nichols.
Creator: John Goldwater, Richard
Goldwater.

JOSIE AND THE PUSSYCATS — 30
minutes — CBS — September 12,
1970 — September 2, 1972.
NBC — September 6, 1975 —
September 4, 1976. 26 episodes.
Syndicated.

631   JOSIE AND THE
PUSSYCATS IN OUTER SPACE

Animated Cartoon. A Rock group,
Josie and the Pussycats, is posing
for publicity pictures near a
spaceship at NASA when Alex-

andra, a member of the group, moves forward and accidentally knocks the others off balance. As they fall backward into the open capsule hatch, Alexandra's arm hits and activates the blast-off mechanism, sending the craft and its passengers into the far reaches of outer space. The series details the group's adventures as they try to return to Earth.

VOICES

Josie, group leader (speaking voice)   Janet Waldo
Josie (singing voice)   Cathy Douglas
Melody, the drummer (speaking voice)   Jackie Joseph
Melody (singing voice)   Cheryl Ladd
Valerie, the guitarist (speaking voice)   Barbara Pariot
Valerie (singing voice)   Patricia Holloway
Alan, the group's manager   Jerry Dexter
Alexander, Alan's assistant   Casey Kasem
Alexandra, Alexander's sister   Sherry Alberoni
Sebastian, the group's pet cat   Don Messick
Bleep, the space creature Melody befriends on the planet Zelcor   Don Messick

Music: Hoyt Curtin.
Vocals: Josie and the Pussycats.
Executive Producer: William Hanna, Joseph Barbera.
Producer: Alex Lovy.
Director: William Hanna, Joseph Barbera, Charles A. Nichols.
Creator: John and Richard Goldwater.

JOSIE AND THE PUSSYCATS IN OUTER SPACE — 30 minutes — CBS — September 9, 1972 — January 26, 1974. 26 episodes. Syndicated.

632   THE JOYCE DAVIDSON SHOW

Celebrity Interviews.

Hostess: Joyce Davidson.
Music: A recorded opening and closing theme.
Producer: Sandra Faire.

THE JOYCE DAVIDSON SHOW — 30 minutes — Syndicated 1975.

633   THE JOYCE JILLSON SHOW

Variety. Astrology coupled with celebrity interviews.

Hostess: Joyce Jillson.
Theme Music: Al Kasha, Joel Hirschhorn.
Announcer: Charlie Tuna.
Producer: Steve Syatt.

THE JOYCE JILLSON SHOW — 30 minutes — Syndicated 1978.

JUKE BOX

See titles *Britt Ekland's Juke Box* and *Twiggy's Juke Box* in the regular program section.

634   JULIA

Comedy. The story of Julia Baker, a registered nurse with the Inner Aero-Space Center, an industrial health office in Los Angeles. Episodes relate her struggles as she attempts to adjust after the death of her husband (an Air Force captain killed in Vietnam) and raise her young son, Corey.

CAST

Nurse Julia Baker   Diahann Carroll
Dr. Morton Chegley, Julia's employer   Lloyd Nolan
Corey Baker, Julia's son   Marc Copage
Earl J. Waggedorn, Corey's friend   Michael Link
Marie Waggedorn, Earl's mother   Betty Beaird
Len Waggedorn, Marie's husband   Hank Brandt
Hannah Yarby, the head nurse   Lurene Tuttle
Carol Deering, Julia's part-time mother's helper   Alison Mills
Sol Cooper, Julia's landlord   Ned Glass
Mrs. Deering, Carol's mother   Virginia Capers
Ted Neumann, Julia's boyfriend   Don Marshall
Paul Carter, Julia's boyfriend   Chuck Wood
Paul Winfield
Steve Bruce, Julia's boyfriend, a student lawyer   Fred Williamson
Roberta, Corey's baby-sitter   Jenear Hines
Lou, Julia's uncle   Eugene Jackson
Melba Chegley, Morton's wife   Mary Wickes
Mrs. Bennett, a tenant in Julia's building   Jeff Donnell

Music: Van Alexander, Elmer Bernstein.
Producer: Hal Kanter.
Associate Producer: Harold Stone.
Director: Hal Kanter, Coby Ruskin, Bernard Wiesen, Barry Shear.
Creator: Hal Kanter.

JULIA — 30 minutes — NBC — September 17, 1968 — May 25, 1971. 86 episodes. Syndicated.

635   THE JULIE ANDREWS HOUR

Variety. Music, songs, dances and comedy sketches.

Hostess: Julie Andrews.
Regulars: Rich Little, Alice Ghostley, The Tony Charmoli Dancers, The Dick Williams Singers.
Announcer: Dick Tufeld.
Orchestra: Nelson Riddle.
Special Musical Material: Dick Williams.
Music Associate: Ian Frazier.
Choreographer: Tony Charmoli.
Producer: Nick Vanoff, William Hardach.
Writer: John Aylesworth, Jay Burton, George Bloom, Bob Ellison, Hal Goodman, Larry Klein, Lila Garrett.

Director: Bill Davis.
Art Director: Jim Tompkins.

THE JULIE ANDREWS HOUR — 60 minutes — ABC — September 13, 1972 — April 28, 1973.

636   JULIE FARR, M.D.

Drama. The story of Julie Farr, an obstetrician at City Memorial Hospital in Los Angeles. Originally titled *Having Babies*, the series deals with the joys and traumas of childbirth.

CAST

Dr. Julie Farr   Susan Sullivan
Dr. Blake Simmons   Mitchell Ryan
Kelly Williams, Julie's receptionist   Beverly Todd
Intern Rod Daniels (later Dr. Rod Danvers)   Dennis Howard
Nurse   Deborah Green

Music: Lee Holdridge, George Tipton.
Theme: "There Will Be Love" by Alan and Marilyn Bergman.
Theme Vocal: Marilyn McCoo.
Executive Producer: B. W. Sandefur, Gerald I. Isenberg, Gerald Abrams.
Producer: James Heinz, Joel Rogosin.
Director: Mel Damski, Edward Parone, Bob Kelljan, Jeffrey Hayden, Gerald I. Isenberg.
Creator: Peggy Elliott, Ann Marcus.

JULIE FARR, M.D. — 60 minutes — ABC — March 28, 1978 — April 18, 1978. 2 episodes. June 12, 1979 — June 26, 1979. 3 episodes. As *Having Babies* — 60 minutes — ABC — March 7, 1978 — March 21, 1978. 3 episodes. See also "Having Babies I," "Having Babies II" and "Having Babies III" in the pilot film section.

637   JUNIOR ALMOST ANYTHING GOES

Game. A children's version of *Almost Anything Goes,* which features three four-member teams competing in outrageous outdoor games for prizes.

Host: Soupy Sales.
Commentator: Eddie Alexander.
Music: The Junior High School Band.
Executive Producer: Bob Banner, Beryl Vertue.
Producer: Kip Walton.
Director: Kip Walton.

JUNIOR ALMOST ANYTHING GOES — 25 minutes — ABC — September 11, 1976 — September 4, 1977.

JUST FRIENDS

See title *Stockard Channing in Just Friends.*

K

638   THE KALLIKAKS

Comedy. The story of the Kallikaks, a family from Appalachia transplanted to California as owner-operators of a gas station, in their struggle for a better life.

CAST

Jasper T. Kallikak, Sr., the father   David Huddleston
Venus Kallikak, his wife   Edie McClurg
Bobbi Lou Kallikak, their daughter   Bonnie Ebsen
Jasper T. Kallikak, Jr., their son   Patrick J. Petersen
Oscar Heinz, Jasper's mechanic   Peter Palmer

Music: Tom Wells.
Theme Vocal ("Beat the System"): Roy Clark.
Executive Producer: Stanley Ralph Ross.
Producer: George Yanok.
Director: Dennis Steinmetz, Bob LaHendro, Ron Kantor.
Creator: Roger Price, Stanley Ralph Ross.

THE KALLIKAKS — 30 minutes — NBC — August 3, 1977 — August 31, 1977. 5 episodes.

639   KAREN

Comedy. The trials and tribulations of Karen Angelo, a young, idealistic staff worker for Open America, a Capitol Hill citizens' lobby in Washington, D.C.

CAST

Karen Angelo   Karen Valentine
Dale W. Bush, the founder of Open America   Denver Pyle
Charles Lane
Dena Madison, a staff worker at Open America   Dena Dietrich
Cissy Peterson, Karen's roommate   Aldine King
Adam Cooperman, same as Dena   Will Seltzer
Jerry Siegel, a tenant in Karen's rooming house   Oliver Clark
Cheryl Siegel, Jerry's wife   Alix Elias
Senator Bob Hartford, Karen's friend   Edward Winter
Ernie, Karen's friend   Joseph Stone

Karen's address: 1460 Cambridge Street in Jamestown, Washington, D.C.

Music: Benny Golson.
Executive Producer: Gene Reynolds.
Producer: Burt Metcalfe.
Director: Gene Reynolds.
Creator: Gene Reynolds, Carl Kleinschmidt, Larry Gelbart.

KAREN — 30 minutes — ABC — January 30, 1975 — June 19, 1975. 13 episodes.

THE KAREN VALENTINE SHOW

See title *Karen.*

640 KATE LOVES A MYSTERY

Mystery. A retitled and revamped version of *Mrs. Columbo,* which see. The story of Kate Callahan, the former wife of famed police Lieutenant Columbo (now divorced, Kate has reassumed her maiden name), a newspaper reporter for the *Valley Advocate* in San Fernando, California. Episodes detail her attempts to solve baffling crimes.

CAST

Kate Callahan	Kate Mulgrew
Jenny Callahan, her daughter	Lili Haydn
Josh Alden, Kate's publisher	Henry Jones
Sgt. Mike Varrick, Kate's friend, with the Valley Municipal Police Department	Don Stroud
Stuart, the paper's copy boy	Robert Hardy
Mrs. Barish, Kate's baby-sitter	Ceil Cabot

Kate's license plate number: 304 MGD.

Music: John Cacavas, Charles R. Cassey.
Supervising Producer: James McAdams.
Executive Producer: Bill Driskill.
Producer: Merwin Gerard, Stuart Cohen.
Writer: Lawrence Hertzog, Merwin Gerard, Simon Muntner, E. Arthur Kean, Robert McKee, Mary Ann Kascia.
Director: Don Medford, Leo Penn, Reza S. Badiyi, Sigmund Neufeld, Jr., Philip Leacock, Sam Wanamaker, Seymour Robbie.

KATE LOVES A MYSTERY — 60 minutes — NBC — October 18, 1979 – December 6, 1979. 7 episodes. Originally scheduled as *Kate Columbo,* then *Kate the Detective* and finally *Kate Loves a Mystery.*

641 KATE McSHANE

Drama. The cases and courtroom defenses of Kate McShane, an uninhibited and unorthodox Irish-American lawyer working in Los Angeles.

CAST

Kate McShane	Anne Meara
Pat McShane, her father and investigator	Sean McClory
Ed McShane, her brother, a Jesuit priest	Charles Haid
Julie, Kate's secretary	Rachel Malkin

Music: Charles Bernstein.
Executive Producer: E. Jack Neuman.
Producer: Robert Foster, Robert Stampler.
Director: Marvin Chomsky, Robert Scheerer, Jack Shea, David Friedkin, Corey Allen, John Peyser, Bill Bixby.
Creator: E. Jack Neuman.

KATE McSHANE — 60 minutes — CBS — September 10, 1975 – November 12, 1975. The 90-minute pilot film aired on CBS on April 11, 1975.

KATE THE DETECTIVE

See title *Kate Loves a Mystery.*

642 KAZ

Crime Drama. The story of Martin "Kaz" Kazinski, an ex-con turned attorney who studied for the bar while serving a six-year prison term for auto theft. The series follows Kazinski's cases, working with the Los Angeles firm of Bennett, Reinhart and Colcourt, as he helps people in deep trouble.

CAST

Martin Kazinski	Ron Leibman
Samuel Bennett, the senior partner in the law firm	Patrick O'Neal
Mary Parnell, the owner of the Starting Gate Nightclub over which Kaz lives	Gloria LeRoy
Malloy, the club owner, later episodes	Dick O'Neill
Irv, the bartender	Floyd Levine
Katie McKenna, Kaz's girlfriend, the court reporter for the *Herald*	Linda Carlson
Peter Colcourt, Bennett's junior partner	Mark Withers
Illsa Fogel, Bennett's secretary	Edith Atwater
Frank Revko, the district attorney	George Wyner

Music: Fred Karlin.
Executive Producer: Lee Rich, Marc Merson.
Producer: Peter Katz, Sam Rolfe.
Director: Russ Mayberry, Bob Kelljan, Bernard McEveety, David Moessinger, Don Medford, Tony LoBianco, Mel Damski, Peter Levin, Ken Lamkin, Leo Penn.

KAZ — 60 minutes — CBS — September 24, 1978 – April 18, 1979; July 29, 1979 – August 19, 1979. 22 episodes. The series was "sneak previewed" on September 10, 1978.

643 KEAN

Comedy. A two-part miniseries that chronicles the life of Edmund Kean (1787-1833), an English actor of the nineteenth century who suffered deeply from society's attitude toward actors (an actor was not considered man enough to fight a duel with a nobleman). Kean carried on shamelessly with women, and, dissatisfied with life, drowned his frustrations in alcohol. Based on Jean-Paul Sartre's 1953 play.

CAST

Edmund Kean	Anthony Hopkins
Countess de Koefeld, the woman with whom Kean imagines he is in love	Sara Kestelman
Count de Koefeld, her husband	Barrie Ingham
The Prince of Wales	Robert Stephens
Anna, the would-be actress	Cherie Lunghi

Producer: David Jones.
Director: James Cellan Jones.

KEAN — 60 minutes — PBS — September 9, 1979 – September 16, 1979. 2 episodes.

644 THE KEANE BROTHERS SHOW

Variety. Music, songs and dances.

Hosts: John and Tom Keane.
Regulars: Jimmy Caesar, The Anita Mann Dancers.
Orchestra: Alan Copeland.
Executive Producer: Pierre Cossette.
Producer: Buz Kohan.
Director: Tony Charmoli.
Choreographer: Anita Mann.

THE KEANE BROTHERS SHOW — 30 minutes — CBS — August 12, 1977 – September 2, 1977. 4 programs.

645 KEEP ON TRUCKIN'

Comedy. A potpourri of broad comedy sketches and freewheeling spoofs and blackouts.

Starring: Fred Travalena, Larry Ragland, Richard Lee Sung, Rhonda Bates, Marion Ramsey, Gailard Sartain, Franklyn Ajaye, Rilo, Welland Flowers, Jack Riley, Dee Dee Kahn, Jeannine Burnier, Kathryn Bauman, Charles Fleischer.
Musical Director: Marvin Larlaird.
Producer: Frank Peppiatt, John Aylesworth.
Director: Tony Mordente.
Choreographer: Charlene Painter.

KEEP ON TRUCKIN' — 60 minutes — ABC — July 12, 1975 – August 2, 1975. 4 programs.

646 THE KELLY MONTEITH SHOW

Variety. Music, songs and comedy sketches.

Host: Kelly Monteith.
Regulars: Nellie Bellflower, Henry Corden.
Orchestra: Dick De Benedictis.
Producer: Ed Simmons, Robert Wright.
Writer: Ed Simmons, Gene Perrett, Bill Richmond, Rick Hawkins, Liz Sage.
Director: Dave Powers.

THE KELLY MONTEITH SHOW — 30 minutes — CBS — June 16, 1976 – July 7, 1976. 4 programs.

647 THE KEN BERRY WOW SHOW

Variety. A nostalgic look at the 1930s-1960s through music, dance, song and comedy.

Host: Ken Berry.
Regulars: Cheryl Ladd, Steve Martin, Billy Van, Carl Gotlieb, Teri Garr, Barbara Joyce, Don Ray, The New Seekers, The Jaime Rogers Dancers.
Orchestra: Jimmy Dale.
Producer: Allan Blye, Chris Beard.
Writer: Paul Wayne, George Burditt, Bob Einstein, Phil Hahn, Jim Mulligan, Steve Martin, Allan Blye, Chris Bearde.
Director: Perry Rosemond.
Animation: John Wilson.
Musical Material: Jaime Rogers.
Musical Conductor: Denny Vaughn.

THE KEN BERRY WOW SHOW — 60 minutes — ABC — July 15, 1972 – August 12, 1972.

648 KHAN!

Crime Drama. The exploits of Khan, a Chinese private detective working out of San Francisco's Chinatown. (Khan lives above the Canton Bazaar.)

CAST

Detective Khan	Khigh Dhiegh
Ann Khan, his daughter	Irene Yah-Ling Sun
Kim Khan, his son	Evan Kim
Police Lt. Gubbins	Vic Tayback

Music: Morton Stevens, Bruce Broughton.
Producer: Laurence Heath, Joseph Henry.
Director: Ivan Dixon, Bill Derwin.
Creator: Chet Gould.

Note: *Khan!* is the only television series in which the star refused billing.

KHAN! — 60 minutes — CBS — February 7, 1975 – February 28, 1975. 4 episodes.

649 KICKS

Music. Performances by Disco personalities.

Host: Jeff Kutash.
Music Theme: A recorded open and close.
Executive Producer: Jamie Kellner.
Producer: Kip Walton.
Director: Kip Walton.
Choreographer: Jeff Kutash.

KICKS — 60 minutes — Syndicated 1979.

650 KID POWER

Animated Cartoon. The story of a group of children, all members of the Rainbow Club, who are struggling to save the environment and improve the world. The object of the program is to show kids of different ethnic backgrounds sharing thoughts on prejudice, teamwork and responsibility.

The Children: Connie, Diz, Wellington, Oliver, Nipper, Sybil, Ralph, Jerry and Albert. Also: Polly, Wellington's parrot; General Lee, Nipper's dog; and Tom, Ralph's cat.
Voices: Michele Johnson, Allan Melvin, Jeff Thomas, Jay Silverheels, Jr., Joan Gardner, Charles Kennedy, Jr., Carey Wong, Gregg Thomas, Gary Shiparo.
Music: Perry Botkin, Jr.

KID POWER — 30 minutes — ABC — September 16, 1972 – September 1, 1974.

651   KIDS ARE PEOPLE TOO

Children. Celebrity interviews, music, information, cartoons and related entertainment geared to show that kids are people too.

Host: Bob McAllister, Michael Young.
Traveling Correspondent: Ellie Dylan.
Executive Producer: Lawrence Einhorn.
Producer: Laura Schrock.
Director: Lawrence Einhorn.

KIDS ARE PEOPLE TOO — 90 minutes — ABC — September 10, 1978 – August 31, 1980. 60 minutes: Premiered: September 7, 1980.

652   THE KIDS FROM C.A.P.E.R.

Comedy. The series, set in the town of Northeast Southwestern, follows the escapades of P. T., Bugs, Doomsday and Doc, four teenage boys who comprise the Kids from C.A.P.E.R. (The Civilian Authority for the Protection of Everybody, Regardless), a special crime-fighting unit of the local 927th police precinct.

CAST

P. T.	Steve Bonino
Bugs	Cosie Costa
Doomsday	Biff Warren
Doc	John Lansing
Sergeant Vinton, their superior	Robert Emhardt
Mr. Clintsinger, the reporter	Robert Lussier

Music: Wally Gold, Jay Siegel.
Music Supervision: Don Kirshner.
Executive Producer: Alan Landsburg, Don Kirshner.
Producer: Stanley Z. Cherry.
Director: Roger Duchowny, Stanley Z. Cherry.

THE KIDS FROM C.A.P.E.R. — 30 minutes — NBC — September 11, 1976 – November 20, 1976; April 16, 1977 – September 3, 1977.

653   KID TALK

Discussion. Two guest celebrities discuss topical issues with four children.

Host: Bill Adler.
Panelists: Mona Tera (age seven), Andy Yamamoto (ten), Nellie Henderson (twelve), Alan Winston (twelve).
Announcer: Johnny Olsen.
Music: A recorded opening and closing theme.

KID TALK — 30 minutes — Syndicated 1972.

654   KING OF KENSINGTON

Comedy. Events in the lives of the Kings, a family of three living in the city of Kensington near Toronto, Canada.

CAST

Larry King, the owner of King's Variety Store	Al Waxman
Cathy King, his wife	Fiona Reid
Gladys King, Larry's mother	Helene Winston
Nestor Best, Larry's friend	Ardon Bess
Duke Zaro, Larry's friend	Bob Vinci
Max, Larry's friend	John J. Dee
Rosa Zaro, Duke's wife	Vivian Reis

Max's dog: Mary Theresa.

Music: Bob McMillin.
Theme Vocal ("King of Kensington"): Bob Francis.
Executive Producer: Perry Rosemond.
Producer: Jack Humphrey, Louis Del Grande.
Director: Herb Roland, Garry Plaxton, Stan Jacobson, Sheldon Larry.

KING OF KENSINGTON — 30 minutes — Syndicated 1977.

655   KINGSTON: CONFIDENTIAL

Crime Drama. The story of R. B. Kingston, chief reporter and editor-in-chief of the Frazier News Group, an influential organization of newspapers and TV stations in California.

CAST

R. B. Kingston	Raymond Burr
Beth Kelly, a reporter	Pamela Hensley
Tony Marino, a reporter (series)	Art Hindle
Tony Kolsky, a reporter (pilot film)	James Conway
Jessica Frazier, the head of Frazier (series)	Nancy Olson
Laura Frazier (same as Jessica, but in the pilot film)	Lenka Peterson
Lieutenant Vokeman	Milt Kogan

Music: Pete Rugolo, Henry Mancini, Richard Shores.
Executive Producer: David Victor.
Producer: James Hirsch, Don Ingalls, Joe L. Cramer, Don Nicholl.
Director: Robert Day, Christian I. Nyby II, Richard Moder, Harvey Laidman, Michael Caffey, Don Weis, Don McDougall.

KINGSTON: CONFIDENTIAL — 60 minutes — NBC — March 23, 1977 – August 10, 1977. The two-hour pilot film, "Kingston: The Power Play," aired on NBC on September 15, 1976.

656   KNOCKOUT

Game. Three contestants compete in a game wherein they have to spell the word Knockout. Four items (e.g., peach, apple, mustard and pizza) appear on a board and the first player to identify the out-of-place item (mustard in this example) wins one letter of the word Knockout. The player can win a second letter by identifying the common denominator for all three items (pies in this instance). The first player to spell the word Knockout is the winner and receives merchandise prizes.

Host: Arte Johnson.
Announcer: Jay Stewart.
Music: Score Productions.
Executive Producer: Ralph Edwards.
Producer: Bruce Belland.
Director: Arthur Forrest.

KNOCKOUT — 30 minutes — NBC — October 3, 1977 – April 21, 1978. 135 programs.

657   KNOTS LANDING

Drama. A spin-off from *Dallas*. The series, set in fictional Knots Landing, California, focuses on the lives of Valene and Gary Ewing, outcast members of the Ewing family, as they attempt to begin a new life. The focal point is their struggle to survive the pressures of the past and the temptations of the future. The program also stresses the emotional turmoil faced by their friends and neighbors.

CAST

Gary Ewing, works as a car salesman for Knots Landing Motors	Ted Schackelford
Valene Ewing, his wife	Joan Van Ark
Karen Fairgate, their neighbor	Michele Lee
Sid Fairgate, Karen's husband and Gary's employer	Don Murray
Ginger Ward, their neighbor	Kim Lankford
Kenny Ward, Ginger's husband, a record company executive	James Houghton
Laura Avery, their neighbor	Constance McCashin
Richard Avery, Laura's husband, an attorney	John Pleshette
Annie Fairgate, Sid's rebellious daughter (from a previous marriage)	Karen Allen
Diana Fairgate, Karen and Sid's daughter	Claudia Lonow
Michael Fairgate, Karen and Sid's son	Pat Petersen
Eric Fairgate, Karen and Sid's son	Steve Shaw
Jason Avery, Laura and Richard's son	Justin Dana
Susan Philby, Sid's ex-wife	Claudette Nevins
Abby Cunningham, Sid's younger sister	Donna Mills
Olivia Cunningham, Abby's daughter	Tonya Crowe
Brian Cunningham, Abby's son	Bobby Jacoby

Music: Jerrold Immel, Ron Grant.
Executive Producer: Lee Rich, Michael Filerman.
Producer: Joseph B. Wallenstein, David Jacobs.
Writer: David Jacobs, Elizabeth Pizer, William Carlisle Hopkins, Rena Down.
Director: Peter Levin, James Sheldon, Henry Levin, Edward Parone, David Moessinger, Kim Friedman, Nicholas Sgarro, Roger Young.

KNOTS LANDING — 60 minutes — CBS — December 27, 1979 – March 27, 1980. 13 episodes. Rebroadcasts: June 12, 1980 – September 4, 1980. Returned, Premiered: November 20, 1980.

658   KODIAK

Crime Drama. The exploits of Cal "Kodiak" McKay, a member of the Alaska State Police Patrol. (McKay has been nicknamed "Kodiak" by the natives for a great bear that roams the area.)

CAST

Cal "Kodiak" McKay	Clint Walker
Abraham Lincoln Imhook, his assistant	Abner Biberman
Mandy, the radio dispatcher	Maggie Blye

Music: Morton Stevens.
Producer: Stan Shpetner.
Director: William Witney.

KODIAK — 30 minutes — ABC — September 13, 1974 – October 11, 1974. 4 episodes.

659   KOJAK

Crime Drama. The investigations of Lieutenant Theo Kojak, a plainclothes detective with the Manhattan South Precinct in New York City. One of the more realistic police dramas dealing with current and sometimes controversial topics and crimes.

CAST

Lt. Theo Kojak	Telly Savalas
Chief of Detectives Frank McNeil	Dan Frazer
Lt. Bobby Crocker	Kevin Dobson
Detective Stavros	George Savalas
Detective Rizzo	Vince Conti
Detective Saperstein	Mark Russell
Marie Stella, the owner of Stella's, the restaurant frequented by Kojak	Carole Cook
Detective Agajanian	Darrell Zivering
Detective Prince	Borah Silver

Music: Billy Goldenberg, Kim Richmond, John Cacavas, Jerry Fielding.
Supervising Producer: James MacAdams.
Executive Producer: Matthew Rapf.

ABC

The Krofft Supershow. From left, Debby Clinger, Michael Lembeck, Louise Duart and Micky McMeel.

NBC

Land of the Lost. Spencer Milligan and Kathy Coleman.

ABC

Laverne and Shirley. Bottom, from left, Michael McKean and David L. Lander. Center, from left, Carol Ita White, Penny Marshall and Cindy Williams. Back row, from left, Phil Foster, Eddie Mekka and Betty Garrett.

CBS

Logan's Run. From left, Randy Powell, Heather Menzies, Donald Moffat and Gregory Harrison.

Producer: James MacAdams, Jack Laird, Chester Krumholz.
Director: Sigmund Neufeld, Jr., David Friedkin, Jerry London, Daniel Haller, Richard Donner, Paul Stanley, Allen Reisner, Charles S. Dubin, Ernest Pintoff, Telly Savalas, Russ Mayberry, Joel Olinsky, Edward Abroms, Christian Nyby, Jerrold Freedman, Nicholas Sgarra, Paul Stanley.
Creator: Abby Mann.

KOJAK — 60 minutes — CBS — October 24, 1973 – April 1, 1978. Syndicated.

KOLCHAK: THE NIGHT STALKER

See title *The Night Stalker.*

660   THE KOPYKATS

Variety. Songs, dances and comedy sketches that feature impersonations of show-business personalities.

The Kopykats: Rich Little, Marilyn Michaels, Frank Gorshin, George Kirby, Charlie Callas, Joe Baker, Fred Travalena.
Featured: The Norman Maen Dancers.
Orchestra: Jack Parnell.
Producer: Dwight Hemion, Gary Smith.
Writer: Frank Peppiatt, Jay Burton, Jack Burns, John Aylesworth, Bryan Blackburn, Tony Hawes.
Director: Dwight Hemion.

THE KOPYKATS — 60 minutes — ABC — June 21, 1972 – August 10, 1972. Syndicated.

661   KORG: 70,000 B.C.

Adventure. The series, set in the year 70,000 B.C., depicts the struggle for survival of a Neanderthal family. Based on assumptions and theories drawn from artifacts.

CAST

Korg	Jim Malinda
Bok	Bill Ewing
Mara	Naomi Pollack
Tane	Christopher Man
Tor	Charles Morted
Ree	Janelle Pransky

Narrator: Burgess Meredith.
Music: Hoyt Curtin.
Executive Producer: William Hanna, Joseph Barbera.
Producer: Richard L. O'Connor, Fred Freiberger.
Director: Irving J. Moore, Christian Nyby.

KORG: 70,000 B.C. — 30 minutes — ABC — September 7, 1974 – August 31, 1975. 24 episodes.

662   THE KRAFT MUSIC HALL

Variety. The format, which varies weekly, is tailored to the talents of guest hosts.

Hosts: Mitzi Gaynor, Jack Jones, Roy Rogers and Dale Evans, Don Rickles, Wayne Newton, Debbie Reynolds, Alan King, Eddie Arnold, Rock Hudson, Mike Douglas.
Regulars: The Peter Gennaro Dancers, The Michael Bennett Dancers.
Announcer: Ed Herlihy.
Orchestra: Peter Matz.
Producer: Gary Smith, Dwight Hemion.
Director: Dwight Hemion.
Sponsor: Kraft Dairy Products.

THE KRAFT MUSIC HALL — 60 minutes — NBC — September 13, 1967 – September 8, 1971.

663   THE KROFFT SUPERSHOW

Children. The overall title for three series: *Dr. Shrinker, Electra Woman and Dyna Girl,* and *Wonderbug.* See individual titles for information.

Segment Hosts: Kaptain Kool and The Kongs, a Rock group.
Executive Producer: Sid and Marty Krofft.
Director: Art Fisher.

CAST

Kaptain Kool, the group leader	Michael Lembeck
Superchick, a group member	Debby Clinger
Nashville, a group member	Louise Duart
Turkey, a group member	Micky McMeel

THE KROFFT SUPERSHOW — 55 minutes — ABC — September 11, 1976 – September 3, 1977.

664   THE KROFFT SUPERSHOW II

Children. The overall title for three series: *Big Foot and Wild Boy, Magic Mongo,* and *Wonderbug.* See individual titles for information.

Segment Hosts: Kaptain Kool and the Kongs, a Rock group.
Executive Producer: Sid and Marty Krofft.
Director: Jack Regas.

CAST

Kaptain Kool, the group leader	Michael Lembeck
Superchick, a group member	Debby Clinger
Nashville, a group member	Louise Duart
Turkey, a group member	Micky McMeel

THE KROFFT SUPERSHOW II — 55 minutes — ABC — September 10, 1977 – September 2, 1978.

THE KROFFT SUPERSTAR HOUR

See title *The Bay City Rollers Show.*

665   THE KROFFT SUPERSTARS

Children. The syndicated title for several Sid and Marty Krofft-produced series: *The Bugaloos, Far Out Space Nuts, Land of the Lost, The Lost Saucer, H. R. Pufnstuf,* and *Sigmund and the Sea Monsters.* See individual titles for information.

THE KROFFT SUPERSTARS — 30 minutes — Syndicated 1978.

666   KUKLA, FRAN, AND OLLIE

Children. The antics of the Kuklapolitans, a group of puppets: Kukla, the bald-headed, round nosed little man; Ollie, the dragon; Beulah, the witch; Madame Ooglepuss; Mrs. Cow; Hubert the skunk; and Fletcher Rabbit.

Hostess: Fran Allison.
Puppeteer/Voices: Burr Tillstrom.
Producer: Burr Tillstrom, Martin Tahse.
Creator: Burr Tillstrom.
Prior Versions: Kukla, Fran, and Ollie first appeared on station WBKB in Chicago on October 13, 1947. On November 29, 1948, it premiered on the Midwest network and became a network attraction on NBC in 1949 (Nov. 12 1949 to June 13, 1954). ABC then aired the series from September 6, 1954 to August 30, 1957. After an absence of four years, NBC revived it for a short time in 1961. PBS aired it next, from 1969 through 1971, and it made its most recent appearance in syndication in 1975.

KUKLA, FRAN, AND OLLIE — 30 minutes — Syndicated 1975.

667   KUNG FU

Drama. In China during the 1850s, an orphan named Kwai Chang Caine (born of an American father and a Chinese mother), is accepted into the Temple of Shaolin to study the art of Kung Fu, the medieval Chinese science of disciplined combat developed by Taoist and Buddhist monks.

While still a boy, Caine befriends Po, the blind Master who nicknames him "Grasshopper," and learns of his great ambition to make a pilgrimage to the Forbidden City.

Caine completes his training in his twenties and leaves the temple with the final words of Master Teh: "Remember. The wise man walks always with his head bowed, humble, like the dust."

Recalling Master Po's dream, and desiring to help him achieve it, Caine meets the old man on the road to the Temple of Heaven. As they journey, the body guards of the Royal Nephew pass, pushing people aside. One is tripped by Master Po. A ruckus ensues and Master Po is shot. At the request of his mentor, Caine picks up a spear and kills the Royal Nephew. Before he dies, Master Po warns his favorite pupil to leave China and begin life elsewhere.

Caine leaves China for the American frontier, where the series is set during the 1870s. The Emperor dispatches men to seek Caine, and the Chinese Legation circulates posters calling for his apprehension.

Episodes depict the exploits of Kwai Chang Caine as a Shaolin priest, wandering through the frontier during the early days of social injustice and discrimination in search of an unknown brother. The program also recalls his days of training (seen via flashbacks) while a student in China. Situations he encounters parallel those of the past; and through the use of flashbacks, the viewer learns of Caine's strict training and of the wisdom of his Masters as he disciplines himself to face circumstances as a respected Shaolin priest.

Unique in its approach, the photography adds power to the drama, and through slow motion, heightens and enhances the strength and discipline of the young priest.

CAST

Kwai Chang Caine	David Carradine
Danny Caine, Kwai's half brother	Tim McIntire
Master Po (flashbacks)	Keye Luke
Master Kan (flashbacks)	Philip Ahn
Master Teh (flashbacks)	John Leoning
Caine (flashbacks, age 6)	Stephen Manley
Caine (flashbacks, older)	Radames Pera

Also, various roles: Beulah Quo, James Hong, Benson Fong, Victor Sen Yung, David Chow.
Music: Jim Helms.
Executive Producer: Jerry Thorpe.
Producer: John Furia, Jr., Jerry Thorpe, Herman Miller, Alex Beaton.
Writer: Gene L. Coon, Ron Bishop, Herman Miller, John Dugan, George Johnson, Gustave Field, Robert Specht, Simon Muntner.
Director: Robert Butler, Richard Lang, Jerry Thorpe, John Moxey, David Carradine, Robert Totten, Charles S. Dubin, Barry Crane, Robert Michael Lewis, Harry Harris, Gordon Hessler.
Kung Fu Adviser: Kam Yuen.
Creator: Ed Spielman.

KUNG FU — 60 minutes — ABC — October 14, 1972 – June 27, 1975. 72 episodes. Syndicated. The 90-minute pilot film aired on ABC on February 22, 1972.

L

668   LANCELOT LINK, SECRET CHIMP

Comedy. The investigations of Lancelot Link, a fumbling counter-espionage agent for A.P.E., the Agency to Prevent Evil, an international organization dedicated to fighting C.H.U.M.P. (Criminal Headquarters For Underground Master Plan) and its goal of world domination. Characters are enacted by chimpanzees with voice-over dubbing.

Characters: Lancelot Link, an A.P.E. agent; Commander Darwin, the head of A.P.E.; Marta Hari, Link's assistant; Baron Von Butcher, the commander of C.H.U.M.P.; Creator, Butcher's assistant.
Producer: Allan Sandler, Stan Burns, Mike Marmer.

LANCELOT LINK, SECRET CHIMP — 60 minutes — ABC — September 12, 1970 – September 4, 1971. 30 minutes — ABC — September 11, 1971 – September 2, 1972. 26 episodes.

669   LANCER

Western. The series, set on the Lancer Ranch in California's San Joaquin Valley during the 1870s, follows the story of three men: Murdoch Lancer, widowed ranch owner, and his two sons, born of different mothers, Scott Lancer (son of an Irish lass), and Johnny Madrid Lancer (son of a Mexican wench). Episodes depict their attempts to maintain a 100,000-acre cattle and timberland ranch in an era of lawlessness.

CAST

Murdoch Lancer, the father	Andrew Duggan
Scott Lancer, his son	Wayne Maunder
Johnny Madrid Lancer, his son	James Stacy
Teresa O'Brien, Murdoch's ward	Elizabeth Baur
Jelly Hoskins, the ranch foreman	Paul Brinegar

Music: Joseph Mullendore, Hugo Friedhofer.
Music Supervision: Lionel Newman.
Music Theme: Jerome Moross.
Producer: Sam Wanamaker, Alan A. Armer.
Director: Leo Penn, Alexander Singer, Michael Caffey, Sam Wanamaker, Don McDougall, Sobey Martin, Don Medford, Christian Nyby, Allen Reisner, Don Richardson, Gene Nelson.
Creator: Samuel A. Peeples.

LANCER — 60 minutes — CBS — September 24, 1968 – September 8, 1970; May 27, 1971 – September 9, 1971. 51 episodes. Syndicated.

670   LAND OF THE GIANTS

Science Fiction. Enroute from New York to London, the *Spindthrift*, suborbital flight 612, passes through a mysterious atmospheric disturbance that alters the flight plan and badly damages the craft. The inoperable plane crash-lands in a dense forest and becomes the base for its crew and passengers when they discover they are marooned in an unknown world of human giants.

As their presence becomes known, they are branded fugitives, "The Little People," and a reward is offered for their capture. Death is the penalty for assisting them.

Stories depict the humans' struggle for survival, and their attempts to secure the precious metals they need to repair their craft and try to return to Earth.

CAST

Steve Burton, the pilot	Gary Conway
Dan Erickson, the copilot	Don Marshall
Betty Hamilton, the stewardess	Heather Young
Valerie Scott, a passenger, an heiress	Deanna Lund
Alexander Fitzhugh, a passenger, a master thief	Kurt Kasznar
Mark Wilson, a passenger, a tycoon	Don Matheson
Barry Lockridge, a passenger, an orphan	Stefan Arngrim
S.I.B. Inspector Kobic, the giant seeking the little people	Kevin Hagen

Barry's dog: Chipper.
Music: Johnny Williams, Lionel Newman.
Producer: Irwin Allen.
Director: Irwin Allen, Harry Harris, Sobey Martin. (Harris and Martin directed most of the episodes).

LAND OF THE GIANTS — 60 minutes — ABC — September 22, 1968 – September 6, 1970. 51 episodes. Syndicated.

671   LAND OF THE LOST

Science Fiction Adventure. While exploring the Colorado River on a raft, forest ranger Rick Marshall and his children, Will and Holly, are caught in a time vortex and transported to a mysterious, forbidding world called the Land of the Lost — a world of prehistoric creatures.

Stories, during the first season, depict the Marshall family's struggle for survival and their attempts to find the secret of the way back to their time. During its second season, with the introduction of the character Enik, a Sleestak (a tall lizard-like creature who fell through a time doorway and is now in his future), it is learned that the Land of the Lost was built by Enik's ancestors — a once peaceful people who are now savages. Desperate to return to his own time and prevent his people from becoming the savages, he discovers that the Land of the Lost is a closed universe and that the only way to escape is through a time doorway contained in the Pylon — a mysterious, magical device. With this added knowledge, both the Marshalls and Enik seek to unravel the mystery of the Pylon. (Although Enik is a friend of the Marshalls, the other Sleestak are not and pose a constant danger to their survival.)

The third season brought additional changes: while experimenting with a Pylon, Rick Marshall activates a time doorway and is swept back into his own time. However, since the Land of the Lost is a closed universe, when one being leaves, another must take his place.

While searching for his missing brother Rick, Jack Marshall is suddenly caught in a mysterious time vortex and, as Rick is freed, Jack is transported to the Land of the Lost. He meets Will and Holly and learns what has happened. Stories concern the Marshall family's continuing attempts to escape from the Land of the Lost.

CAST

Rick Marshall	Spencer Milligan
Holly Marshall, his daughter	Kathy Coleman
Will Marshall, his son	Wesley Eure
Jack Marshall, Rick's brother	Ron Harper
Enik, the Sleestak leader	Walker Edmiston
Chaka, the monkey-boy, a member of the Palcus tribe	Philip Paley
Sa, the monkey-girl	Sharon Baird
Ta, the Palcus leader	Scott Fullerton
Malak, an enemy of the Marshalls	Richard Kiel
Zarn, a creature of glowing light also lost in time (portrayed by)	Van Snowden
Zarn (voiced by)	Marvin Miller
The Sleestak Leader (before Enik)	Jon Locke

Sleestak: Jack Tingley, Joe Giamalva, Scotty McKay, Mike Weston, Bill Boyd, Cleveland Porter.
Music: Jimmie Haskell, Linda Laurie, Michael Lloyd.
Executive Producer: Sid and Marty Krofft.
Producer: Jon Kubichan.
Director: Bob Lally, Joe Scanlon, Rich Bennewitz, Dennis Steinmetz, Gordon Wiles.

LAND OF THE LOST — 30 minutes — NBC — September 7, 1974 – September 3, 1977. Syndicated.

672   LANIGAN'S RABBI

Crime Drama. The series, set in Cameron, California, depicts the work of Paul Lanigan, the police chief, and his friend and sometimes assistant, David Small, rabbi of the Temple Beth Halell Synagogue.

CAST

Chief Paul Lanigan	Art Carney
Kate Lanigan, his wife	Janis Paige
Rabbi David Small (pilot film)	Stuart Margolin
Rabbi David Small (series)	Bruce Solomon
Miriam Small, David's wife	Janet Margolin
Police Lieutenant Osgood	Robert Doyle
Bobbi Whittaker, the reporter	Barbara Carney
Hannah Prince, one of the temple members	Reva Rose

Music: Don Costa.
Supervising Producer: Don Mankiewicz, Gordon Cotler.
Executive Producer: Leonard B. Stern.
Producer: David J. O'Connell.
Director: Leonard B. Stern, Joseph Pevney, Noel Black, Lou Antonio.

LANIGAN'S RABBI — 90 minutes — NBC — January 30, 1977 – July 3, 1977 (as part of *The NBC Sunday Mystery Movie*). The two-hour pilot film aired on NBC on June 17, 1976.

673   LASSIE

Adventure. The series featured eight formats in the course of its run.

Format 1:

Jeff's Collie (Syndicated title) — 30 minutes — CBS — September 1954 – September 1957.

The series, set on the Miller farm in Calverton, follows the adventures of Jeff Martin and his collie Lassie, whom he inherited from a neighbor.

CAST

Jeff Miller	Tommy Rettig
Ellen Miller, his mother, a widow	Jan Clayton
George Miller (Gramps), Jeff's grandfather	George Cleveland
Sylvester "Porky" Brockway, Jeff's friend	Donald Keeler
Sheriff Clay Horton	Richard Garland
Dr. Peter Wilson, the vet (early episodes)	Arthur Space
Dr. Frank Weaver, the vet (later shows)	Arthur Space
Dr. Stuart, the Miller's physician	Dayton Loomis
Matt Brockway, Porky's father	Paul Maxey
Jenny, the telephone operator	Florence Lake

Porky's dog: Pokey.
Music: Raoul Kraushaar.
Executive Producer: Jack Wrather.
Producer: Sheldon Leonard, Robert Maxwell, Dusty Bruce.
Director: Philip Ford, Lesley Selander, Sheldon Leonard.

Format 2:

Timmy and Lassie (Syndicated title) — 30 minutes — CBS — September 1957 — September 1964.

Shortly after the death of Gramps, a seven-year-old boy named Timmy runs away from an orphanage. Found by Lassie, he is taken to the Miller farm and given a temporary home. Ellen, who is alone and unable to run the farm, sells it to Paul and Ruth Martin, a childless couple who later adopt Timmy. Lassie is left with a new master, Timmy. Stories depict the adventures shared by a boy and his dog.

CAST

Timmy Martin	Jon Provost
Ruth Martin, his mother	Cloris Leachman
	June Lockhart
Paul Martin, Timmy's father	Jon Shepodd
	Hugh Reilly
Petrie Martin, Timmy's uncle	George Chandler
Boomer Bates, Timmy's friend	Todd Ferrell
Dr. Frank Weaver, the vet	Arthur Space
Sheriff Harry Miller	Robert Foulk
Cully Wilson, Timmy's friend	Andy Clyde
Scott, Timmy's friend	Ricky Allen

Boomer's dog: Mike.
Cully's dog: Silky.
Music: Sid Sidney, Nathan Scott.
Executive Producer: Jack Wrather.
Producer: Robert Golden, Bonita Granville Wrather, William Beaudine, Jr., Rudy Abel.
Director: William Beaudine, Jr., Christian Nyby, Dick Moder, James B. Clark, Robert Sparr, Jack B. Hively, Paul Nichol.

Format 3:

Lassie — 30 minutes — CBS — September 1964 — September 1968.

The need for American farmers overseas prompts Paul to sell the farm and move to Australia. Unable to take Lassie because of quarantine laws, she is left with Timmy's friend, the elderly Cully Wilson. Shortly after, Cully is saved after a serious heart attack when Lassie brings to his aid Corey Stuart, a forest ranger. Recovering, but unable to properly care for Lassie, Cully gives her to Corey. Her adventures, as she protects the forests, are dramatized.

CAST

Ranger Corey Stuart	Robert Bray
Ranger Scott Turner	Jed Allan
Ranger Bob Erickson	Jack DeMave
Kirby Newman, Corey's assistant	John Archer

Music: Nathan Scott.
Executive Producer: Jack Wrather.
Producer: Bonita Granville Wrather, Robert Golden, William Beaudine, Jr.
Director: Dick Moder, William Beaudine, Jr., Robert Sparr, Jack B. Hively, James B. Clark, Ray English, Christian Nyby, Paul Nickell.

Format 4:

Lassie — 30 minutes — CBS — September 1968 — September 1971.

No longer bound to a human master, Lassie roams and assists those she finds in distress, both human and animal.

Starring: Lassie.
Music: Nathan Scott.
Executive Producer: Jack Wrather.
Producer: Bonita Granville Wrather.

Format 5:

Lassie — 30 minutes — Syndicated 1971. The story and cast are the same as the fourth format.

Format 6:

Lassie — 30 minutes — Syndicated 1972.

Though still something of a wanderer, Lassie finds a temporary home at the California ranch of Keith Holden where her adventures in and around the ranch are dramatized.

CAST

Keith Holden, the ranch owner	Larry Pennell
Dale Mitchell, his assistant	Larry Wilcox
Ron Holden, Keith's son	Skip Burton
Mike Holden, Keith's son	Joshua Albee
Lucy Baker, their neighbor	Pamelyn Ferdin
Sue Lampbert, the vet	Sherry Boucher

Music: Nathan Scott.
Executive Producer: Jack Wrather.
Producer: Bonita Granville Wrather.

Format 7:

Lassie's Rescue Rangers — Animated Cartoon — 30 minutes — ABC — September 8, 1973 — August 30, 1975.

The series, set in the Rocky Mountains, follows the exploits of Lassie as the commander of the Rescue Force, the animal assistants of the Turner family rescue team.

VOICES

Ben Turner, the father	Ted Knight
Laura Turner, his wife	Jane Webb
Jackie Turner, their son	Lane Scheimer
Susan Turner, their daughter	Erica Scheimer
Ranger Jean Fox	Ted Knight

Animals: Lassie; Toothless, the mountain lion; Robbie, the raccoon; and Musty, the skunk.
Music: Yvette Blais, Jeff Michael.
Producer: Norm Prescott, Lou Scheimer.
Director: Hal Sutherland.

Format 8:

Lassie: The New Beginning. See title in the pilot film section.

LASSIE'S RESCUE RANGERS

See title *Lassie.*

674   THE LAST CONVERTIBLE

Drama. A three-part miniseries that chronicles the lives of George Virdon, Russ Currier, Jean des Barres, Terry Garrigan and Ron Dalrymple, five close-knit Harvard classmates, from 1940 to 1969. Based on the novel by Anton Myrer. The title is inspired by a 1939 Packard, which, over the years, passes through the hands of each of the classmates, who called themselves "The Five Fusiliers of F Entry" (F Entry refers to their dormitory entrance).

CAST

George Virdon	Bruce Boxleitner
Russ Currier	Perry King
Jean des Barres	Michael Nouri
Terry Garrigan	John Shea
Ron Dalrymple	Edward Albert
Chris Farris	Deborah Raffin
Kay Haddon	Sharon Gless
Ann Rowan	Kim Darby
Denise	Jeanna Michaels
Nancy	Caroline Smith
Sheila Garrigan	Stacey Nelkin
Mel	Sam Weisman
Liz	Tracy Brooks Swope
Paul McCreed	Fred McCarren
Colonel Elkart	Stuart Whitman
Chief Lonborg	Vic Morrow
Sgt. Drabic	Martin Milner
Major Goodman	Pat Harrington
Rosamond Ardely	Lisa Pelikan
Dr. Wetherell	John Houseman
Bobby Dalrymple	Shawn Stevens
Peggy Virdon	Peggy Foster

Music: Pete Rugolo.
Executive Producer: Jo Swerling, Jr.
Producer: Robert F. O'Neill.
Writer: Philip DeGuere, Stephen McPherson, Clyde Ware.
Director: Sidney Hayers, Jo Swerling, Jr., Gus Trikonis.
Art Director: Howard E. Johnson, Sherman Laudermilk.
Director of Photography: Thomas Del Ruth.

THE LAST CONVERTIBLE — 2 hours — NBC — September 24, 1979 — September 26, 1979. 3 episodes.

675   THE LAST RESORT

Comedy. The misadventures of Michael Lerner, Duane Kaminski, Zach Comstock and Jeffrey Barron, four college students who turn a genteel mountain hotel into a madhouse while working for the summer as waiters.

CAST

Michael Lerner, a waiter	Larry Breeding
Gail Collins, the pastry chef	Stephanie Faracy
Duane Kaminski, a waiter	Zane Lasky
Zach Comstock, a waiter	Walter Olkewicz
Jeffrey Barron, a waiter	Ray Underwood
Kevin, the Japanese cook	John Fujioka
Murray, the maitre d'	Robert Costanzo
Mrs. Trilling, the overbearing hotel guest	Dorothy Konrad

Commercial Break Announcer: Stephanie Faracy.
Music: Patrick Williams.
Producer: Gary David Goldberg.
Writer: Gary David Goldberg, Patricia Jones, Marty Nadler, Donald Reiker, Lloyd Garver, Rich Reinhart.
Director: Asaad Kelada.
Creator: Gary David Goldberg.
Art Director: Ken Reid, Jacqueline Webber.

THE LAST RESORT — 30 minutes — CBS — September 19, 1979 — October 3, 1979. 4 episodes (a fifth scheduled episode never aired); December 17, 1979 — March 17, 1980. 11 episodes.

676   THE LATE FALL, EARLY SUMMER BERT CONVY SHOW

Variety. Music, songs, dances and comedy sketches.

Host: Bert Convy.
Regulars: Sallie Janes, Donna Ponterotto, Henry Polic II, Marty Barris, Lennie Schultz (as "The Bionic Chicken"), The Tyvana Light Opera and Pottery Company.
Bert's Girls (dancers): Susie Guest, Shirley Kirkes, Judy Pierce, Darcell Wynne.
Announcer: Donna Ponterotto.
Orchestra: Perry Botkin, Jr.
Executive Producer: Sam Denoff, Howard Hinderstein.
Producer: Sam Bobrick.
Writer: Jim Mulligan, Jay Grossman, Sam Bobrick, Sam Denoff.
Director: Bill Hobin.
Choreographer: Dee Dee Wood.

THE LATE FALL, EARLY SUMMER BERT CONVY SHOW — 30 minutes — CBS — August 25, 1976 — September 15, 1976. 4 programs.

L.A.T.E.R.

See title *The Life and Times of Eddie Roberts.*

677   LAUGH-IN

Variety. A satirization of the contemporary scene through music, song, dance and comedy sketches.

Hosts: Dan Rowan and Dick Martin.
Regulars: Goldie Hawn, Judy Carne, Pamela Rodgers, Teresa Graves, Arte Johnson, Byron Gilliam, Jeremy Lloyd, Dennis Allen, Eileen Brennan, Roddy Maude-Roxby, Barbara Sharma, Ann Elder, Harvey Jason, Richard Dawson, Jo Anne Worley, Alan Sues, Henry Gibson, Betty Ann Carr, Patty Deutsch, Sarah Kennedy, Brian Bressler, Donna Jean Young, Jud Strunk, Dave Madden, Ruth Buzzi, Lily Tomlin, Chelsea Brown, Johnny Brown, Larry Hovis,

Nancy Phillips, Pigmeat Markham, Charlie Brill, Mitzie McCall, Willie Tyler, Todd Bass, Dick Wittington, Muriel Landers, Elaine Beckett, Moosie Drier, and the Beautiful Downtown Beauties (Janice Whitby, Rosetta Cox, Adele Yoshioka, Kyra Carlton, Joy Robiero and Meredith Bernhardt).

Announcer: Gary Owens.
Musical Director: Ian Bernard.
Executive Producer: George Schlatter.
Producer: Paul W. Keyes.
Writer: Paul Keyes, Bill Richmond, Gene Perrett, Jack Wohl, Jim Mulligan, Gene Farmer, John Rappaport, Stephen Spears, Chet Dowling, Larry Siegel, Don Reo, Jack Margolis, Allan Katz.
Director: Mark Warren.

LAUGH-IN — 60 minutes — NBC — January 22, 1968– May 7, 1973. 124 programs. Also known as *Rowan and Martin's Laugh-In.*

678   LAUGH-IN

Variety. A revised version of the previous title that features a cast of virtual unknowns in comedic nonsense satirizing everyday life.

Starring: Nancy Bleiwess, Ed Bluestone, Kim Braden, Claire Faulkonbridge, Antoinette Attell, Robin Williams, Wayland Flowers, June Gable, Jim Giovanni, Ben Powers, Bill Rafferty, Michael Sklar, Lennie Schultz, April Tatro, Hack Harrell.
Orchestra: Tommy Oliver.
Special Musical Material: Billy Barnes.
Producer: George Schlatter.
Writer: Digby Wolfe.
Director: Don Mischer.
Choreographer: Dee Dee Wood.

LAUGH-IN — 60 minutes — NBC — September 5, 1977– February 8, 1978. 6 programs.

679   LAUREL AND HARDY LAUGHTOONS

Comedy. Edited versions of silent Laurel and Hardy shorts of the 1920s.

Starring: Stan Laurel and Oliver Hardy.
Music: George Korngold.
Original Film Producer: Hal Roach.
TV Executive Producer: Hal Dennis.
TV Producer: Richard Feiner.

LAUREL AND HARDY LAUGHTOONS — 30 minutes — Syndicated 1979.

680   LAVERNE AND SHIRLEY

Comedy. The chaotic misadventures of Laverne DeFazio, a

realist, and Shirley Feeney, a romantic, two pretty working girls who room together and work in the capping division of the Shotz Brewery in Milwaukee, Wisconsin, in 1959. A spin-off from *Happy Days.*

CAST
Laverne DeFazio	Penny Marshall
Shirley Feeney	Cindy Williams
Lenny Kosnoski, their friend	Michael McKean
Andrew "Squiggy" Squigman, their friend	David L. Lander
Carmine Ruguso, "The Big Ragu," their friend	Eddie Mekka
Frank DeFazio, Laverne's father, the owner of the Pizza Bowl, a combination pizzeria and bowling alley	Phil Foster
Edna Babbish, Laverne's landlady; married Frank on Nov. 1, 1979	Betty Garrett
Rosie Greenbaum, Laverne's nemesis	Carole Ita White
Mary, the Pizza Bowl waitress	Frances Peach
Norman Hughes, Laverne's romantic interest (briefly)	Bo Kaprall

Lenny and Squiggy's lodge: The Fraternal Order of the Bass.
Music: Charles Fox, Richard Clements, John Beal.
Theme Vocal: Cyndi Grecco.
Supervising Producer: Tony Marshall, Gary Menteer, Phil Mishkin.
Executive Producer: Thomas L. Miller, Edward K. Milkis, Garry K. Marshall.
Producer: Mark Rothman, Lowell Ganz, Thomas L. Miller, Tony Marshall, Monica Johnson, Eric Cohen, Edward K. Milkis, Garry K. Marshall, Chris Thompson, Marc Sotkin, David W. Dulcon, Jeff Franklin.
Director: Michael Kidd, Dennis Klein, Howard Storm, John Thomas Lennox, James Burrows, Joel Zwick, Garry K. Marshall, Alan Myerson, Jay Sandrich, Maurice Bar-David, Ray DeVally, Jr., Linda McMurray, Frank Alesia.
Creator: Garry K. Marshall.

LAVERNE AND SHIRLEY — 30 minutes — ABC — Premiered: January 27, 1976.

681   THE LAW

Crime Drama. A three-part miniseries, based on the television movie of the same title (October 22, 1974), that follows the exploits of Murray Stone, a criminal attorney working out of Los Angeles. The series portrays American justice as it is usually practiced — replete with red tape, plea bargaining and deals.

CAST
Murray Stone	Judd Hirsch
Michael	Fiona Guinness
Van Lorn	Alex Nicol
Hiller	Gerald McRaney

Abby	Susan Gay Powell
Caroline	Annazette Chase
Ginger	Dori Brenner
Masterson	Howard Platt
Dr. Burdick	Alex Henteloff
Judge Richter	George Gaynes
Wilson	Michael Bell
Mary Ellen	Tyne Daly
Meston	Michael McGuire
Berkley	Robert Hogan
Keefer	Ben Piazza
Burgholzer	Ben Hammer
Monk Liu Chen Nu	Grayland R. Gleason
Shopkeeper	M. Emmet Walsh
Judge Marker	Dick O'Neill
Piper	George Wyner
Tracy	Carol Larson
Matt Lee	Ron Masak
Judge Longello	Nicholas Colasanto
Mincher	Eugene Roche
Starnes	Jim Antonio
Ouspensky	Val Avery
Sean	Joe Clarke
Pratt	Quinn Redeker
Linda	Caryn Matchinga
Mrs. Simpson	Royce Wallace

Producer: William Sackheim.
Director: John Badham, Joel Oliansky.

THE LAW — 60 minutes (3 hours total) — NBC — March 19, 1975– April 3, 1975. 3 episodes.

682   THE LAW ENFORCERS

Crime Drama. The story of the relationship between two men: Sam Danforth, a deputy police chief, and William Washburn, the district attorney, as they attempt to maintain law and order in a city (unnamed California locale) beset by urban crises.

CAST
Sam Danforth	Leslie Nielsen
William Washburn	Hari Rhodes

Executive Producer: Jack Laird.
Producer: Jerrold Freedman.
Director: Daryl Duke, Fernando Lamas.

THE LAW ENFORCERS — 60 minutes — NBC — September 28, 1969– September 6, 1970 (as part of *The Bold Ones*).

683   THE LAWRENCE WELK SHOW

Variety. Music, songs and dances presented in "Champagne-style."

Host: Lawrence Welk.
Regulars: Ava Barber, Bobby Burgess, Henry Cuesta, Dick Dale, Ken Delo, Arthur Duncan, Gail Farrell, Myron Floren, Sandi Griffiths, Charlotte Harris, Clay Hart, Larry Hooper, Guy Hovis, Radna Netherton, Bob Ralston, Jim Roberts, Tanya Welk, Norma Zimmer, The Otwell Twins, The Six Semonski Sisters, Anacani, Joe Feeney.
Announcer: Bob Orrin.
Orchestra: Lawrence Welk.

Musical Director: George Cates.
Executive Producer: Sam J. Lutz.
Producer: James Hobson.
Director: James Hobson.

THE LAWRENCE WELK SHOW — 60 minutes — Syndicated 1971. The series was also broadcast on ABC from July 2, 1955 through September 3, 1971.

684   THE LAWYERS

Crime Drama. The cases of Walter Nichols, a Los Angeles attorney, and his protégés Brian and Neil Darrell, brothers.

CAST
Walter Nichols	Burl Ives
Brian Darrell	Joseph Campanella
Neil Darrell	James Farentino
Lt. Paul Hewitt	John Milford
Deputy D.A. Jeff Skinner	Todd Martin
Walter's secretary	Marcelle Fortier
D.A. Braddock	George Murdock
D.A. Dekker	Charles Brewer
Judge Howe	Walter Brooke

Executive Producer: Roy Huggins.
Producer: Steve Hellpern, Jo Swerling, Jr.
Director: Leonard Horn, Richard Heffron, David Moessinger, Roy Huggins, Gene Levitt, Richard Benedict, Daniel Petrie, Fernando Lamas, Vincent Sherman.

THE LAWYERS — 60 minutes — NBC — September 21, 1969– September 10, 1972 (as a segment of *The Bold Ones*).

685   THE LAZARUS SYNDROME

Drama. The story of MacArthur St. Clair, a thirty-seven-year-old, nononsense cardiologist whose dedication to his work often takes its toll on his personal life. The series also chronicles the unusual relationship between St. Clair and Joe Hamill, a tough investigative reporter (later the administrator of Webster Memorial Hospital*) and their fight to run a hospital that is in business to save lives, not just make money. The title, *The Lazarus Syndrome,* refers to a situation where a patient believes a doctor is a godlike miracle worker — a view Hamill holds of St. Clair.

CAST
Dr. MacArthur St. Clair	Louis Gossett, Jr.
Joe Hamill	Ronald Hunter
Gloria St. Clair, Mac's wife	Sheila Frazier
Stacy, Joe's assistant	Peggy McCay
Virginia Hamill, Joe's ex-wife	Peggy Walton Walker
The Admissions Nurse	Christina Alvila

Music: John Rubinstein, Billy Goldenberg.
Supervising Producer: Robert Schlitt.

Executive Producer: Jerry Thorpe, William Blinn.
Producer: Mark A. Hoey.
Director: Jerry Thorpe, Barry Crane, Harvey Laidman, Georg Stanford Brown.
Creator: William Blinn.

THE LAZARUS SYNDROME — 60 minutes — ABC — September 11, 1979 – October 9, 1979. 6 episodes. The 90-minute pilot aired on ABC on September 4, 1979. The series was actually scheduled to end after five episodes on October 2, 1979; a rainout cancellation of the first game of the 1979 World Series forced ABC to schedule regular programming, which included, on October 9, 1979, a sixth episode of *The Lazarus Syndrome.*

*When St. Clair proves the hospital administrator, Dr. Mendel (played by E.G. Marshall) is incompetent, Hamill, a heart-attack patient whose life St. Clair has saved, takes over the job to help Mac fight the bureaucracy.

686   LET'S MAKE A DEAL

Game. Ten of forty previously selected audience members vie for the opportunity to trade their homemade articles for cash and/or valuable merchandise prizes. The host selects a player and offers him his first deal — an unknown amount of cash or merchandise for what he has. After a deal is made, the player is asked to trade what he's just won for a chance at something better — usually what is behind a curtain on stage. If the player is undecided, the host tempts him by offering him money if he will trade. Usually the outcome of this trade determines what the player will receive — anything from $5,000 in cash to a color television set or a zonk (a nonsense prize). Although trades vary greatly in presentation, the basic format is the offer, the counteroffer and the final offer — all designed to measure greed.

Host: Monty Hall.
Announcer-Assistant: Jay Stewart.
Model: Carol Merrill.
Music: Ivan Ditmars.
Substitute Host: Tom Kelly.
Executive Producer: Stefan Hatos.
Producer: Stefan Hatos, Monty Hall, Joe Behar.
Director: Joe Behar.

LET'S MAKE A DEAL — 30 minutes — NBC — December 30, 1964 – December 27, 1968; ABC — December 30, 1968 – July 9, 1976 (daytime run); February 7, 1969 – August 30, 1971 (ABC evening run). Syndicated first run in 1976.

687   LET'S MAKE A DEAL

Game. A new syndicated version of the previous title, same format. Produced in Canada and made specifically for the United States and Canada.

Host: Monty Hall.
Executive Producer: Stefan Hatos.
Producer: Monty Hall, Ian MacLennan.
Director: Daryl Regan, Geoff Theobald.
Art Director: Donald J. Halton.

LET'S MAKE A DEAL — 30 minutes — Syndicated 1980.

688   LETTERS TO LAUGH-IN

Comedy Game. A spin-off from *Laugh-In.* Four joke tellers (guest celebrities) relate jokes submitted to *Laugh-In* by home viewers. Jokes are rated by a panel of ten selected studio audience members on a scale ranging from plus one hundred to a minus one hundred. The winner of the week's highest scoring joke receives merchandise prizes. The lowest scoring joke wins its sender "seven action-packed days in beautiful downtown Burbank."

Host: Gary Owens.
Announcer: Gary Owens.
Producer: Alan Newman.
Writer: Hal Collins, Jack Kaplan, Harry Morton, Paul Freedman, Edward Morganstern, Stan Dreben.
Director: Alan J. Levi.

LETTERS TO LAUGH-IN — 30 minutes — NBC — September 29, 1969 – March 3, 1970. 110 programs.

689   THE LIAR'S CLUB

Game. Two players compete. A panel of four liars (guest celebrities) describes in detail the purpose of a real, but unusual item. Three explanations are false; one relates the truth. The players must determine which celebrity told the truth. Each correct guess awards the player one point and the player with the highest score at the end of the game is the winner and receives $100.

Host: Rod Serling.
Resident Liar: Betty White.
Announcer: Jim Isaics.

THE LIAR'S CLUB — 30 minutes — Syndicated 1969.

690   THE LIAR'S CLUB

Game. Four players compete. Each of four celebrity guests who appear describe an unusual, but real item. Three explanations are false; one tells the truth. Players, who each receive one hundred

dollars, bet any part of it they wish on the celebrity whom they feel is telling the truth. Incorrect guesses cost the player as his bet is deducted from his score; correct guesses add the money in accord with the established odds which vary from round to round. Winners are the highest scoring players.

Host: Bill Armstrong, Allen Ludden.
Resident Liar: Larry Hovis.
Frequent Guest Liars: Joey Bishop, Dick Gautier, Betty White.
Announcer: Joe Sider, Bill Beary.
Executive Producer: Larry Hovis.
Producer: Bill Yageman.
Director: Dick McDonoughe, Chris Darley.

THE LIAR'S CLUB — 30 minutes — Syndicated 1976.

691   LIDSVILLE

Adventure. Intrigued by a magician's performance and the wonders he draws from his hat, a young boy named Mark remains behind as the theater empties. Alone, he picks up the magician's hat, which is on stage. The hat suddenly begins to grow larger. Unable to hold it any longer, Mark places it on the floor, where it keeps growing to an enormous size. Climbing on the brim, and attempting to look inside, he loses his balance, falls in, and reappears in Lidsville, the land of living hats.

First spotted by the hats of Whoo Doo, an evil magician, Mark is captured and imprisoned because Whoo Doo believes he is a spy for the good hats. In his cell, Mark meets Weenie, a genie who is also a prisoner and Whoo Doo's slave because he possesses her magic ring. Offering to help her escape from Whoo Doo, and promising to take her back to America with him, Mark convinces Weenie to use her power to set him free. Spotting the magic ring on a table, Mark grabs it and now, in control of Weenie, commands her to take them to safety. Instantly they are transported to the village of the good hats.

Gaining the assistance of the good hats, Mark and Weenie struggle to find the secret of the way back to his world. They are opposed by Whoo Doo who seeks to regain his prisoner, his genie and the magic ring.

CAST
Mark	Butch Patrick
Whoo Doo	Charles Nelson Reilly
Weenie the Genie	Billie Hayes

Also, portraying life-size Sid and Marty Krofft puppets: Sharon Baird, Joy Campbell, Jerry Marling, Angelo Rosetti, Van

Snowden, Hommy Stewart, Felix Silla, Buddy Douglas, The Hermine Midgets.
Voices: Lennie Weinrib, Joan Gerber, Walker Edmiston.
Orchestra: Charles Fox.
Theme: "Lidsville" by Les Szarvas.
Producer: Sid and Marty Krofft.
Director: Tony Charmoli.
Art Director: William Smith.

LIDSVILLE — 30 minutes — ABC — September 11, 1971 – September 1, 1973; NBC — September 8, 1973 – August 31, 1974. 17 episodes.

692   THE LIFE AND TIMES OF EDDIE ROBERTS

Serial. The story of Eddie Roberts, an anthropology professor at Cranepool College (in Anaheim, California), who desperately wants to be granted tenure.

CAST
Eddie Roberts	Renny Temple
Dolores Roberts, his wife, who yearns to be a big league baseball player	Udana Power
Chrissy Roberts, their daughter	Allison Balson
Harold Knitzer, the college dean	Allen Case
Dr. Zindell, the college medical genius, inventor of the drug T.S.U.	Anne O'Donnell
Cynthia Lombocker, a student	Wendy Schaal
Vivian Blankett, Dr. Zindell's assistant	Loyita Chapel
Professor Boggs, the elderly instructor	John Lormer
Prof. Tony Cranepool, the head of student activities	Stephen Parr
Turner LaQuatro, Eddie's friend	Daryl Roach
Chiquita Zamora, a teacher at Cranepool	Maria O'Brien
Gertrude McQuillan, Dolores's friend	Victoria Carroll
	Lenore Nemetez
Lydia Knitzer, Harold's wife	Joan Hotchkis
William Billy, the detective	Billy Barty
Senator Lombocker, Cynthia's father	William Wintersole

Also: Keone Young, Martin Brooks.
Music: Harry Betts.
Executive Producer: Anne and Ellis Marcus.
Producer: Marc Daniels, Leonard Frielander.
Director: Marc Daniels, Jim Drake, Bob Nigro.

THE LIFE AND TIMES OF EDDIE ROBERTS — 30 minutes — Syndicated on a national basis — January 7, 1980 – March 28, 1980. 60 episodes. Also known as *L.A.T.E.R.*

693   THE LIFE AND TIMES OF GRIZZLY ADAMS

Adventure. Falsely accused of a crime* he did not commit, James Adams flees to the wilderness where as mountain man Grizzly Adams, he becomes a friend to all living creatures. Stories concern his adventures in the wilderness of the 1850s. Based on the motion picture of the same title.

CAST

James "Grizzly" Adams	Dan Haggerty
Mad Jack, his friend, a mountain man	Denver Pyle
Nakuma, Grizzly's Indian blood brother	Don Shanks

Grizzly's Bear: Ben (played by Bozo).
Mad Jack's Mule: Number 7.
Narrator: Denver Pyle.
Music: Bob Summers.
Music Supervision: Don Perry.
Theme Vocal: Thom Pace.
Executive Producer: Charles E. Sellier, Jr.
Producer: Art Stolnitz.
Director: James L. Conway, Sharron Miller, Jack B. Hively, Irving J. Moore, Richard Frieberg.
Creator: Charles E. Sellier, Jr.

THE LIFE AND TIMES OF GRIZZLY ADAMS — 60 minutes — NBC — February 9, 1977 – July 26, 1978. Returned with one last episode on December 19, 1978. Syndicated.

*According to the film, a murder occurred near his home, but he is innocent.

694   THE LIFE OF RILEY

Comedy. The series, set in Los Angeles, follows the misadventures of Chester A. Riley, a riveter with Stevenson Aircraft and Associates.

CAST

Chester A. Riley, the father	Jackie Gleason
Peggy Riley, his wife	Rosemary DeCamp
Barbara "Babs" Riley, their daughter	Gloria Winters
Chester Riley, Jr., their son	Lanny Rees
Jim Gillis, Chester's neighbor	Sid Tomack
Olive "Honeybee" Gillis, Jim's wife	Maxine Semon
Egbert Gillis, Jim's son	George McDonald
Digby "Digger" O'Dell, the mortician	John Brown
Waldo Binny, Chester's friend	Bob Jellison
Carl Stevenson, Chester's employer	Bill Green Emory Parnell
Millie, Carl's secretary	Mary Treen
Simon Vanderhopper, Babs's boyfriend	Jimmy Lydon

The Rileys' address: 1313 Blue View Terrace.
Announcer: James Wallington.
Music: Lou Kosloff (when originally broadcast; the syndicated version is without music).
Producer: Irving Brecher.
Writer: Reuben Shipp, Alan Lipscott, Irving Brecher, Ashmead Scott, Sid Dorfman.
Director: Leslie Goodwins, Herbert I. Leeds.

THE LIFE OF RILEY — 30 minutes — Syndicated 1977. Originally broadcast on the DuMont Network from October 4, 1949 – March 28, 1950. 26 episodes.

695   THE LIFE OF RILEY

Comedy. The misadventures of Chester A. Riley, a riveter for Cunningham Aircraft. A revised version of the previous title.

CAST

Chester A. Riley	William Bendix
Peggy Riley, his wife	Marjorie Reynolds
Barbara "Babs" Riley, their daughter	Lugene Sanders
Chester Riley, Jr., their son	Wesley Morgan
Jim Gillis, their neighbor	Tom D'Andrea
Olive "Honeybee" Gillis, Jim's wife	Veda Ann Borg Gloria Blondell
Egbert Gillis, Jim's son	Gregory Marshall
Don Marshall, Babs's boyfriend; later husband	Martin Milner
Babs and Don's baby	Melodie Chaney
Waldo Binny, Chester's friend	Sterling Holloway
Millicent, Waldo's girlfriend	Stanja Lowe
Otto Schmidlap, Chester's friend	Henry Kulky
Calvin Dudley, the Riley's neighbor	George O'Hanlon
Belle Dudley, Calvin's wife	Florence Sundstrom
Cissy Riley, Chester's sister	Mary Jane Croft
Anne Riley, Chester's sister	Larraine Bendix
Pa Riley, Chester's father	James Gavin
Ma Riley, Chester's mother	Sarah Pudden
Mr. Cunningham, Chester's employer	Douglas Dumbrille
Hank Hawkins, the plant foreman	Emory Parnell
Cunningham's secretary	Tamar Cooper
Moose, Junior's friend	Denny Miller
Alvin Winkley, the Riley's landlord	Arthur Shields
Arnold Willis, the paper boy	Joe Conley

The Rileys' address (early episodes): 1313 Blue View Terrace, Los Angeles.
The Rileys' address (later episodes): 5412 Drone Ave., Del Mar Vista, California.
Babs and Don's address: 1451 Blue View Terrace.
Music: Jerry Fielding.
Producer: Tom McKnight.
Director: Abby Berlin, Jean Yarbrough.

THE LIFE OF RILEY — 30 minutes — Resyndicated 1977. Originally broadcast on NBC from January 2, 1953 – August 22, 1958, then syndicated. 91 episodes.

696   LIFELINE

Profile. An unusual television series that, using no actors or scripts, follows the actual day-to-day lives of various doctors on and off the job.

Narrator: Jackson Beck.
Music: Theo Mocero.

Executive Producer: Thomas W. Moore.
Producer: Nancy Smith, E. Fuisz, M.D.
Director: Alfred Kelman, Robert Elfstrom.

LIFELINE — 60 minutes — NBC — October 8, 1978 – December 30, 1978. 10 episodes. Three additional, first-run episodes also aired on NBC: August 13, 1979 (2 episodes back-to-back) and one on September 6, 1979. The series was "sneak previewed" on September 7, 1978.

697   LITTLE HOUSE ON THE PRAIRIE

Drama. The series, set in the town of Walnut Grove in Plumb Creek, Minnesota, during the 1870s, follows the struggles of the pioneering Ingalls family: Charles, the father; his wife Caroline; and their children, Laura, Mary and Carrie. Their experiences as homesteaders in the vastly unsettled regions of the Southwestern frontier are viewed through the sentimental eyes of Laura, the second-born daughter. Based on the *Little House* books by Laura Ingalls Wilder.

CAST

Charles Ingalls, the father	Michael Landon
Caroline Ingalls, his wife	Karen Grassle
Laura Ingalls, their daughter	Melissa Gilbert
Mary Ingalls, their daughter	Melissa Sue Anderson
Carrie Ingalls, their daughter	Lindsay Greenbush Sidney Greenbush
Grace Ingalls, their daughter	Wendi Turnbaugh Brenda Turnbaugh
Adam Kendall, married Mary	Linwood Boomer
Albert, the street urchin Charles adopts	Matthew Laborteaux
Nels Oleson, the general store owner	Richard Bull
Harriet Oleson, Nels's wife	Katherine MacGregor
Nellie Oleson, their daughter	Alison Arngrim
Willie Oleson, their son	Jonathan Gilbert
Lars Hanson, the lumber mill owner	Karl Swenson
The Rev. Mr. Alden	Dabbs Greer
Isaiah Edwards, Charles's friend	Victor French
Grace Edwards, Isaiah's wife	Bonnie Bartlett
John Edwards, Isaiah's adopted son	Radames Pera
Carl Edwards, Isaiah's adopted son	Brian Part
Aliscia Edwards, Isaiah's adopted daughter	Kyle Richards
Jonathan Garvey, a farmer	Merlin Olsen
Alice Garvey, Jonathan's wife	Hersha Parady
Andy Garvey, Jonathan's son	Patrick Laborteaux
Grace Beadle, the school teacher	Charlotte Stewart
Eliza Jane Wilder, the school teacher (later)	Lucy Lee Flippen
Almanzo Wilder, Eliza's brother	Dean Butler
Ebenezer Sprague, the banker	Ted Gehring
Dr. Baker	Kevin Hagen
Christy Kennedy, Laura's friend	Tracie Savage
Sandy Kennedy, Laura's friend	Robert Hoffman
Percival Dalton, married Nellie (May 12, 1980)	Steve Tracy
Mr. Toms, the hotel supervisor	Frederic Downs
Anna Craig, married Mr. Alden (October 22, 1979)	Iris Korn
Harve Miller, Eliza's boyfriend	James Cromwell

Ingalls' family dog: Jack (early episodes); Bandit (later).
Music: David Rose.
Executive Producer: Michael Landon, Ed Friendly.
Producer: John Hawkings, B. F. Sandefur, Winston Miller, Kent McCray.
Director: Michael Landon, William F. Claxton, Victor French, Alf Kjellin, Leo Penn, Lewis Allen, Maury Dexter.
Storyline Note: In the show of September 11, 1978, the Ingalls family leaves Walnut Grove (due to hard times) and begins a new life in Winoka City, Dakota. There, Charles becomes a hotel manager and Caroline a cook. Mary, who loses her sight, acquires a job teaching blind children and later marries a teacher, Adam Kendall. In the episode of October 16, 1978, the Ingalls move back to Walnut Grove because they were discontent with life in the city.

LITTLE HOUSE ON THE PRAIRIE — 60 minutes — NBC — Premiered: September 11, 1974. The two-hour pilot film aired on NBC on March 30, 1974.

698   THE LITTLE PEOPLE

Comedy. The trials and tribulations of doctors Sean Jamison and his daughter, Anne Jamison, pediatricians with a clinic in Kahala, Hawaii.

CAST

Dr. Sean Jamison	Brian Keith
Dr. Anne Jamison	Shelley Fabares
Puni, their nurse	Victoria Young
Ronnie Collins, their general helper	Michael Gray
Alfred Landis, a patient of Sean's	Stephen Hague
Moe O'Shaughnessy, Puni's cousin	Moe Keale
Stewart, Alfred's friend	Sean Tyler Hill
Dr. Spencer Chaffey, the allergist	Roger Bowen
Millar Gruber, Sean's landlady	Nancy Kulp

Sean's parrot: Sam.
Music: Jerry Fielding, Artie Butler.

*Executive Producer:*Jerry Thorpe, Garry Marshall.
Producer: Bruce Johnson, E. Duke Vincent.

THE LITTLE PEOPLE — 30 minutes — NBC — September 15, 1972 – September 7, 1973. As *The Brian Keith Show* — September 21, 1973 – August 30, 1974. 48 episodes.

699   THE LITTLEST HOBO

Adventure. The adventures of London, an unowned, roving German shepherd dog who aids people in distress.

Starring: London (trained by Charles P. Eisenmann).
Music: Jacques Urbont.
Theme Vocal: "Maybe Tomorrow" by Terry Bush.
Supervising Producer: Peter Miller.
Executive Producer: Ed Richardson, Seymour Berns.
Producer: Simon Christopher Dew.
Director: Allan Eastman, Stan Olsen.
Art Director: Barbara Matis.
Director of Photography: Paul Vander Linden.

THE LITTLEST HOBO — 30 minutes — Syndicated 1980.

700   LITTLE VIC

Drama. A six-part miniseries that depicts incidents in the life of Gillie Walker, a 14-year-old orphan who becomes a jockey. (Little Vic is the horse he trains and later rides in the Santa Anita Derby.)

CAST

Gillie Walker	Joey Green
Clara Scott, Gillie's friend	Carol Ann Seflinger
Julie Sayer, Gillie's friend	Doney Oatman
Richie Miller, the track bully	David Levy
Mr. Hammer, Little Vic's first owner	Del Hinkley
Mr. Lawson, Little Vic's second owner	Charles Stewart
George Gordon, the owner of the Spring Dale Horse Farm	Ned Flory
Mr. Simpson, the owner of the horse Sunfox	Patrick Burke
Dr. Freeman	J. Jay Saunders
Fred Amble, the stable owner	Myron Natwick

Music: Tom Scott.
Music Supervision: George Craig.
Executive Producer: Daniel Wilson.
Producer: Linda Marmelstein.
Writer: Art Wallace.
Director: Harvey Herman.
Director of Photography: Bob Stedman.

LITTLE VIC — 30 minutes — Syndicated 1978. 6 episodes.

701   LITTLE WOMEN

Serial. The story, set in New England in the 1860s, follows the joys and sorrows of Jo, Meg, Amy and Beth March, four close-knit sisters. Based on the novel by Louisa May Alcott and produced in England by the BBC.

CAST

Josephine "Jo" March, the aspiring writer	Angela Down
Margaret "Meg" March, the social butterfly	Jo Rowbottom
Amy March, the flirtatious sister	Janina Faye
Beth March, the frail and sickly sister	Sarah Craze
Margaret "Marmee" March, their mother	Stephanie Bidmead
Jonathan March, their father	Patrick Troughton
Aunt Katherine March	Jean Anderson
Theodore "Laurie" Lawrence, Amy's romantic interest	Stephen Turner
Prof. Friedrich Bhaer, Jo's romantic interest	Frederick Jaeger
Hannah, the March's maid	Pat Nye
James Lawrence, Laurie's grandfather	John Welsh
Rogers, James's butler	Philip Raye
John Brooke, Laurie's tutor	Martin Jarvis

Music: Patrick Harvey.
Producer: John McRae.
Writer: Denis Constanduros, Alistair Bell.
Director: Paddy Russell.
Art Director: Stewart Walker.

LITTLE WOMEN — 30 minutes — Syndicated 1971. 9 episodes.

702   LITTLE WOMEN

Drama. The series, set in Concord, Massachusetts, during the late 1860s, follows the dreams, frustrations and ambitions of sisters Jo, Meg and Amy March. As seen through the sentimental eyes of Jo, an aspiring writer, stories of Victorian manners and mores unfold. Based on the novel by Louisa May Alcott.

CAST

Josephine "Jo" March, the second-born sister, the aspiring writer (pilot film)	Susan Dey
Josephine "Jo" March (series)	Jessica Harper
Margaret "Meg" March, the oldest sister, a social butterfly (pilot film)	Meredith Baxter Birney
Margaret "Meg" March (series)	Susan Walden
Amy March, the third-born sister, coy, mischievous and resolute	Ann Dusenberry
Beth March, the youngest sister*	Eve Plumb
Melissa Jane Darnell, their cousin*	Eve Plumb
Margaret "Marmee" March, Jo, Meg, Amy and Beth's mother	Dorothy McGuire
Rev. Jonathan March, Margaret's husband	William Schallert
John Brooke, Meg's husband	Cliff Potts
Theodore "Laurie" Lawrence, Amy's husband	Richard Gilliland
Prof. Friedrich Bhaer, Jo's fiancé (pilot film)	William Shatner
Prof. Friedrich Bhaer (series)	David Ackroyd
James Lawrence, Laurie's grandfather	Robert Young
Aunt Kathryn March (pilot film)	Greer Garson
Aunt Kathryn March (series)	Mildred Natwick
Hannah, the March's cook	Virginia Gregg
Amanda, James's housekeeper	Maggie Malooly

Music: Elmer Bernstein.
Executive Producer: David Victor.
Producer: Richard Collins.
Director: Leo Penn, Gordon Hessler, John Newland, Philip Leacock.
Costumes: Edith Head.
Art Director: Howard E. Johnson.

LITTLE WOMEN — 60 minutes — NBC — February 8, 1979 – March 8, 1979. 4 episodes. The four-hour, two-episode pilot film ran on NBC on October 1, 1978 and October 2, 1978 (repeated June 16, 1979 and June 17, 1979).

*In the second episode of the four-hour combined TV movie-pilot film, Beth, the gentle, shy and frail sister, dies after scarlet fever; she is replaced by Melissa, her cousin — and identical lookalike.

703   LIVING EASY

Variety. Music, guests, interviews, cooking, decorating tips and other entertainment geared to housewives.

Hostess: Dr. Joyce Brothers.
Announcer: Mike Darrow.
Orchestra: Bernie Green.

LIVING EASY — 30 minutes — Syndicated 1973.

704   LOGAN'S RUN

Science Fiction Adventure. Following an atomic holocaust in the year 2319, the surviving segment of civilization establishes itself in the City of Domes. In this programmed society, no one over the age of thirty is permitted to live. At precisely that age, individuals go willingly into a carousel for the ceremony of the Great Sleep, where it is believed that life is renewed. In reality, each person is exterminated because the city cannot support a large population. Those who challenge and attempt to evade the ceremony are labeled "Runners" and become the prey of Sandmen, whose duty is to pursue and destroy them. Runners are seeking Sanctuary, a supposed haven where all are permitted to live beyond thirty.

Logan, a Sandman, begins to question the ceremony (having never seen anyone reborn) and when he meets Jessica, a Runner he is pursuing, he learns the truth and joins her in a search for Sanctuary.

The series follows the adventures of Logan and Jessica, and the attempts of Francis, a Sandman, to capture them. They are to be used to show would-be Runners that Sanctuary does not exist.

CAST

Logan 5	Gregory Harrison
Jessica 6	Heather Menzies
Francis 7	Randy Powell
Rem, the Android*	Donald Moffat
Morgan, a leader in the City of Domes	Morgan Woodward
Jonathan, same as Morgan	Wright King
Martin, same as Morgan	E. J. Andre
Benjamin, Francis' assistant	Stan Stratton

Music: Laurence Rosenthal, Jerrold Immel.
Music Supervision: Harry Lojewski.
Executive Producer: Ivan Goff, Ben Roberts.
Producer: Leonard Katzman.
Director: Robert Day, Alexander Singer, Irving J. Moore, Michael Preece, Steven Stern, Gerald Mayer, Paul Krasny, Michael O'Herlihy.

LOGAN'S RUN — 60 minutes — CBS — September 16, 1977 – January 16, 1978. 11 episodes.

*An android with human-like qualities who abandons his robot city to join forces with Logan and Jessica.

705   LONGSTREET

Crime Drama. The series, set in New Orleans, follows the investigations of Michael Longstreet, a blind* investigator for the Great Pacific Casualty Insurance Company, as he uses his other highly developed senses to apprehend people who defraud insurance companies.

CAST

Michael Longstreet	James Franciscus
Nikki Bell, his braille teacher (pilot film)	Martine Beswick
Nikki Bell (series)	Marlyn Mason
Duke Paige, his employer (pilot film)	Bradford Dillman
Duke Paige (series)	Peter Mark Richman
Li Tsung, Mike's self-defense instructor	Bruce Lee
Mrs. Kingston, Mike's housekeeper	Ann Doran
Ingrid Longstreet, Mike's wife (flashbacks)	Judy Jones

Mike's seeing eye dog: Pax.
Mike's address: 835 Charters Street.
Music: Billy Goldenberg, Robert Drasnin, Oliver Nelson.
Executive Producer: Stirling Silliphant.
Producer: Joel Rogosin.

LONGSTREET — 60 minutes — ABC — September 16, 1971 – August 10, 1972. 24 episodes. The 90-minute pilot film aired on ABC on September 9, 1971.

*An explosion intended to kill him took the life of his wife, Ingrid, and blinded Longstreet. After enrolling in a clinic for the blind, and with the aid of Pax, his seeing eye dog, Mike apprehends Ingrid's killers: members of a jewel gang who, having read about Mike's skill in solving crimes, decided to eliminate him before their next caper.

706 LOOSE CHANGE

Drama. A three-part miniseries, based on the novel by Sara Davidson, that explores the lives of three women during the 1960s: Kate Evans, a journalist, Tanya Berenson, an artist, and Jenny Reston, an activist.

CAST

Kate Evans	Cristina Raines
Tanya Berenson	Season Hubley
Jenny Reston	Laurie Heineman
Joe Norman	Ben Masters
Mark Stewart	Michael Tolan
Peter Lane	Stephen Macht
Irene Evans	June Lockhart
Tom Pfeiffer	Theodore Bikel
Dr. Moe Sinden	David Wayne
Rob Kagan	Guy Boyd
Hank Okun	Gregg Henry
John Campbell	John Getz
Roxanne	Paula Wagner
Sasha Berenson	Judy Strangis
Timmy Reston	Richard Stanley
Mrs. Berenson	Peggy McCay
Mike	Jon Lormer
Hilda	Kate Reid
George Worley	Gary Swanson
Marita Kagan	Maria Elena Cordero
Rosemary	Alice Hirson
Dave Goodwin	Robert Symonds

Music: Don Costa.
Executive Producer: Jules Irving.
Producer: Michael Rhodes.
Writer: Corinne Jacker, Charles E. Israel, Jennifer Miller.
Director: Jules Irving.
Art Director: William Campbell.
Director of Photography: John Elsenbach, Harry Wolf.

LOOSE CHANGE—2 hours (6 hours total)—NBC—February 26, 1978–February 28, 1978. Rebroadcast as *The Restless Years* on NBC from July 8, 1979–July 15, 1979.

707 THE LORENZO AND HENRIETTA MUSIC SHOW

Variety. Music, interviews, songs and comedy sketches.

Hosts: Lorenzo and Henrietta Music.
Regulars: Samantha Harper, Dave Willock, Bob Gibson, Erick Darling, Bella Bruck, Sandy Hellberg, Murphy Dunne.
Announcer: Dave Willock.
Orchestra: Jack Eskew.

Executive Producer: Lorenzo Music, Lewis Arquette.
Producer: Albert J. Simon.
Writer: Lorenzo Music, John Gibbons, Sandy Hellberg, Richard Philip Lewis, Ira Miller, Dennis Reagan, Lewis Arquette.
Director: Bob Lally.

THE LORENZO AND HENRIETTA MUSIC SHOW—60 minutes—Syndicated 1976.

708 LORNE GREENE'S LAST OF THE WILD

Documentary. Wildlife films depicting the animal struggle for survival.

Host-Narrator: Lorne Greene.
Music: Bill Loose, Jack Tillar.
Executive Producer: Skip Steloff.
Producer: Julian Ludwig.
Writer: Ivan Tors, Anthony Jay.

LORNE GREENE'S LAST OF THE WILD—30 minutes—Syndicated 1974. 78 episodes.

709 THE LOST SAUCER

Comedy. While exploring the universe in the year 2369, androids Fi and Fum, from the planet ZR-3, penetrate a time warp and land on present-day Earth. Anxious to make friends, they invite two earthlings, a young boy named Jerry and his baby sitter, Alice, aboard their space ship (shaped like a saucer). Suddenly, as curious people begin to crowd around the alien craft, Fum is alarmed and activates the launch mechanism, sending the ship back into space, where they become lost in time. Stories concern their adventures in strange, futuristic worlds, and Fi and Fum's attempts to return their unwilling passengers to Earth in the year 1975.

CAST

Fi	Ruth Buzzi
Fum	Jim Nabors
Alice	Alice Playten
Jerry	Jarrod Johnson
The Dorse, Fi and Fum's pet (half dog, half horse)	Larry Larson

Also, various roles: Richard Deacon, Jane Dulo, Joe E. Ross, Marvin Kaplan.

Music: Michael Lloyd.
Producer: Sid and Marty Krofft.
Director: Jack Regas, Dick Darley.

THE LOST SAUCER—30 minutes—ABC—September 6, 1975–September 4, 1976.

710 LOTSA LUCK

Comedy. The trials and tribulations of Stanley Belmont, a clerk in the lost and found department of the New York City Bus Lines.

CAST

Stanley Belmont	Dom DeLuise
Iris Belmont, his mother	Kathleen Freeman
Olive Swann, his married sister	Beverly Sanders
Arthur Swann, Olive's unkempt and unemployed husband	Wynn Irwin
Bummy Fitzer, Stanley's neighbor, a bus driver	Jack Knight

Music: Jack Elliott, Allyn Ferguson.
Executive Producer: Bill Persky, Sam Denoff.
Producer: Norman Barasch, Carroll Moore, Don Van Atta.

LOTSA LUCK—30 minutes—NBC—September 10, 1973–May 24, 1974. See also *On the Buses*, the British series on which *Lotsa Luck* is based.

711 LOU GRANT

Drama. The story of Lou Grant, city editor of the *Los Angeles Tribune*, the second largest newspaper in the city. The series, which gives viewers a look at the working lives of newspaper people, can be considered a spin-off from *The Mary Tyler Moore Show* inasmuch as the title character evolved from it. Following his dismissal from the Minneapolis TV station, Lou relocates to Los Angeles where, after looking up an old newspaper friend, he acquires the job of city editor. (Originally, the paper had been called the *City Tribune*.)

CAST

Lou Grant, the city editor	Edward Asner
Joe Rossi, a reporter	Robert Walden
Billie Newman, a reporter	Linda Kelsey
Charlie Hume, the managing editor	Mason Adams
Margaret Pynchon, the publisher	Nancy Marchand
Art Donovan, Lou's assistant	Jack Bannon
Dennis "Animal" Price, the photographer	Daryl Anderson
Carla Mardigian, a reporter	Rebecca Balding
Adam Wilson, the financial editor	Allen Williams
Marion Hume, Charlie's wife	Peggy McCay
The Foreign Editor	Laurence Haddon
The National Editor	Emilio Delgado
Heidi, works for the paper	Cassandra Foster

Margaret's dog: Barney (later Max).

Music: Patrick Williams, Michael Melvoin.
Executive Producer: Allan Burns, James L. Brooks, Gene Reynolds.
Producer: Gene Reynolds, Gary David Goldberg, Seth Freeman.
Director: Richard Crenna, Jackie Cooper, Gene Reynolds, Charles S. Dubin, Jay Sandrich, Alexander Singer, Jud Taylor, Mel Damski, James Burrows, Michael Zinberg, Paul Leaf, Burt Brinkerhoff, Roger Young, Peter Levin, Ralph Senensky, Gerald Mayer.
Creator: Allan Burns, James L. Brooks, Gene Reynolds.

LOU GRANT—60 minutes—CBS—Premiered: September 20, 1977.

712 LOVE, AMERICAN STYLE

Anthology. Comedy vignettes that tackle the world's oldest subject: love. Segments are interspersed with blackouts.

Blackout Regulars: Phyllis Elizabeth Davis, Bernie Kopell, Stuart Margolin, Tracy Reed, James Hampton, Buzz Cooper, Mary Grover, Bill Callaway, Barbara Minkus, Lynne Marta, Jaki DeMar, Richard Williams.
Music: Charles Fox.
Music Supervision: Kenyon Hopkins.
Theme Vocal: "Love, American Style" by the Charles Fox Singers.
Executive Producer: Ray Allen, Harvey Bullock, Jim Parker, Arnold Margolin.
Producer: Bill Idelson, Harvey Miller, Bruce Bilson, Alan Rafkin, William P. D'Angelo, Charles B. Fitzsimons, Stuart Margolin, Donald Boyle.
Director: Bruce Bilson, Ross Martin, Arnold Margolin, Howard Morris, Ken Johnson, William F. Claxton, Leslie Martinson, Jack Arnold, Richard Michaels, Charles R. Rondeau, Coby Ruskin, Oscar Rudolph, Allen Baron, Herb Kenwith, Gary Nelson, Harry Harris, Jerry London, Stan Strangis, Frank Buxton.

Included:
Love and the Love Potion. The complications that ensue when a girl gives her not-too-affectionate boyfriend a love potion.

Cast: Polly: Tammy Grimes; Freddy: Dick Sargent; Asho: Pat Morita.

Love and the First Kiss. The story, set in prehistoric times, revolves around the circumstances that brought about the first kiss.

Cast: Gork: Allen Garfield; Fisik: Claude Akins; Gornoka: Ahna Capri; Termaila: Deanna Lund.

Love and the Impressionist. The story concerns a night club impressionist who finds it difficult to be himself with his fiancée.

Cast: Jackie Kane: Rich Little; his fiancée: Michele Carey.

Love and the Plumber. The story of a pretty girl who goes to elaborate lengths to romance her plumber.

Cast: Agatha Mullavey: Louise Lasser; Plumber: Howard Morris.

Love and the Tuba. The story of a newlywed couple who manage to get stuck in a tuba on their wedding night.

Cast: Millie: Annette Funicello; Henry: Frankie Avalon; Bellboy: Gary Crosby; Manfried the Great: Hans Conried.

LOVE, AMERICAN STYLE—60 and 30 minute versions—ABC—September 22, 1969–January 11, 1974. 65 episodes. Syndicated.

713   THE LOVE BOAT

Comedy. The series, set on the *Pacific Princess,* a luxury liner nicknamed "The Love Boat" by her crew, depicts incidents in the lives of the people who board the ship seeking romance.

CAST

Merrill Stubing, the captain	Gavin MacLeod
Julie McCoy, the cruise director	Lauren Tewes
Adam Bricker, the physician	Bernie Kopell
Burl "Gopher" Smith, the yeoman purser	Fred Grandy
Isaac Washington, the bartender	Ted Lange
Vicki Stubing, Merrill's daughter	Jill Whelan
April Lopez, the entertainer (recurring role)	Charo
Nurse Temple, Adam's assistant	Mary Farrell

Music: Charles Fox, Artie Kane, George Tipton, Duane Tatro, John Parker.
Theme Vocal: "The Love Boat" by Jack Jones.
Supervising Producer: Gordon Farr.
Executive Producer: Aaron Spelling, Douglas S. Cramer.
Producer: Henry Colman, Gordon Farr, Lynne Farr, Ben Joelson, Art Baer, Harvey Bullock.
Director: Richard Kinon, Stuart Margolin, Alan Rafkin, Allen Baron, James Sheldon, Jack Arnold, George McCowan, Bud Tyne, Roger Duchowny, George Tyne, Bob Claver, Gordon Farr.

THE LOVE BOAT—60 minutes—ABC—Premiered: September 29, 1977. Three pilot films aired: "The Love Boat I," "The Love Boat II" and "The Love Boat III." See titles in pilot film section.

714   THE LOVE EXPERTS

Advice. A panel of four celebrities offers advice to real people with problems of living and loving in today's world.

Host: Bill Cullen.
Regular Panelist: Geoff Edwards (plus three guests).
Announcer: Jack Clark.

Executive Producer: Bob Stewart.
Producer: Anne Marie Schmitt.
Director: Bruce Burmester.

THE LOVE EXPERTS—30 minutes—Syndicated 1978.

715   LOVE FOR LYDIA

Drama. The series, set in Depression-era England (1929), follows the life, romances and tragedies of Lydia Aspen, a woman who comes to live with her two elderly aunts after her father's death. Based on the novel, *Love for Lydia* by H. E. Bates.

CAST

Lydia Aspen	Mel Martin
Edward Richardson, her romantic interest	Christopher Blake
Bertie Aspen, her aunt	Beatrix Lehmann
Juliana Aspen, her aunt	Rachel Kempson
Lily, the maid	Ruby Head

Music: Harry Rabinowitz.
Producer: Tony Wharmby.
Writer: Julian Bond.
Director: Tony Wharmby.

LOVE FOR LYDIA—60 minutes—PBS—September 23, 1979–December 9, 1979. 12 episodes.

716   LOVE IS A MANY SPLENDORED THING

Serial. The series, set in San Francisco, dramatizes incidents in the lives of three families: the Chernaks, the Donnellys and the Garrisons.

CAST

Betsy Chernak	Andrea Marcovicci
Mark Elliot	David Birney
	Michael Hawkins
	Vincent Cannon
	Tom Fuccello
Laura Elliott	Donna Mills
	Veleka Gray
	Barbara Stanger
Iris Garrison	Leslie Charleson
	Bibi Besch
Sara Hanley	Sasha von Scherler
	Martha Greenhouse
Dr. Peter Chernak	Vincent Baggetta
Ricky Donnelly	Shawn Campbell
Lily Chernak	Diana Douglas
Senator Al Preston	Don Gantry
Helen Donnelly	Gloria Hoye
Celia	Abigail Kellogg
Will Donnelly	Judson Laire
Doug Preston	Sean Lindsey
Spence Garrison	Edward Power
Joe Taylor	Leon Russom
Angel Chernak	Suzie Kay Stone
Tom Donnelly	Albert Stratton
Marion Hiller	Constance Towers
Mrs. Taylor	Betty Miller
Nichole Chernak	Andrea Grossman
Dr. Hiller	Stephen Joyce
	Peter White
Maria	Judy Safran
Dr. Chernak	Paul Michael Glaser
Andy Hurley	Russ Thacker
Rusty Jackson	Greg Brown
Judd Washington	Thurman Scott
Rocco Fiore	Carmine Stipo
Jean	Jane Manning
Audrey Hurley	Salome Jens
Tommy Hale	Christopher Papes
Dr. Ellis	Robert Drew
Roger	David Jay
Mia	Nancy Hsuek
Amos Crump	Jack Somack
Donna Patrick	Barbara Stanger

Announcer: Lee Jordan, Harry Falk.
Music: Eddie Layton.

LOVE IS A MANY SPLENDORED THING—30 minutes—CBS—September 18, 1967–March 23, 1973.

717   LOVE OF LIFE

Serial. The original story line, 1951-1961, set in Barrowsville, Anywhere, U.S.A., follows the dramatic story of two sisters, Vanessa Dale and Meg Dale Harper. Episodes contrast their life-styles and moral outlooks. The revised story line, which began in 1961, and which is set in Rosehill, New York, depicts dramatic incidents in the lives of marrieds Vanessa and Bruce Sterling.

CAST

Vanessa Dale Sterling	Peggy McCay
	Bonnie Bartlett
	Audrey Peters
Meg Dale Harper	Jean McBride
	Tudi Wiggins
Bruce Sterling	Ron Tomme
Charles Harper	Paul Potter
Beanie Harper	Dennis Parnell
	Christopher Reeve
Paul Raven	Richard Coogan
	Robert Burr
Ellie Hughes	Hildy Parks
Mrs. Rivers	Marie Kennery
Bill Prentiss	Gene Bua
Judith Cole	Marsha Mason
	Virginia Robinson
Sandy Porter	Bonnie Bedelea
Arden Dellacorte	Geraldine Brooks
Candy Lowe	Susan Hubly
	Nancy MacKay
Dr. Leader	Shelley Blanc
Stacy Corby	Cindy Grover
Sarah Dale	Jane Rose
	Joanna Roos
Alex Caldwell	Charles White
Barbara Latimer	Zina Bethune
Hank Latimer	David Stambaugh
Vivian Carlson	Helen Dumas
Henry Carlson	Jack Stamberger
Diana Lamont	Diane Rousseau
Tess Krakauer	Toni Bull Bua
Jamie Rollins	Ray Wise
Sally Rollins	Catherine Bacon
Dan Phillips	Drew Snyder
Kate Swanson	Sally Stark
Link Morrison	John Gabriel
Todd	Rod Gibbons
Josh Bendarik	Brian Brownlee
Helen Hunt	Polly Rowles
Mrs. Swanson	Jane Hoffman
Gerry Brayley	Julia Duffy
Dr. Joseph Corelli	Tony LoBianco
	Paul Michael Glaser
Jason Ferris	Robert Alda
John Prentiss	John O'Hare
	Andrew Tolan
	Trip Randall
Mrs. Bendarik	Lois Smith
Mr. Bendarik	Edward Grover
Link Porter	Gene Pellegrini
Tammy Porter	Ann Loring
Linda Crawford	Romola Robb Allrud
Carrie Lovell	Peg Murray
Baby Johnny	Oren Jay
	Raymond Cass
Miguel	Raul Julia
Josh	Rick Losey
Baby Debbie	Mary Elizabeth Haring
Charles Lamont	John W. Moore
	Stan Watt
Alan Sterling	Dennis Cooney
Rick Latimer	Jerry Lacy
	Edward Moore
	Paul Savior
Mrs. Phillips	Nancy Marchand
	Beatrice Straight
Beatrice Swanson	Jane Hoffman
Jeff Hart	Charles Baxter
Caroline Aleata	Deborah Courtney
	Roxanne Gregory
Betsy Crawford	Elizabeth Kemp
Paul Waterman	Michael Fairman
Howie Howells	Ed Crowley
Dr. Ted Chandler	Keith Charles
David Hart	Brian Farrell
Mrs. Porter	Joan Copeland
Evans Baker	Ronald Long
Sharon Ferris	Eileen Letchworth
	Margo Flax
John Randolph	Byron Sanders
Tom Craythrone	Lauren Gilbert
Link Morrison	John Gabriel
Sarah Sprague	Zoe Connell
Julie Morano	Jessica Walter
Bob Mackey	Richard Cox
Walter Morgan	Richard McKensie
Jack Andrews	Donald Symington
Sally Bridgeman	Cathy Bacon
Clair Bridgeman	Renee Rory
Richard Rollins	Larry Weber
Dr. Kreisinger	Leon B. Stevens
Will Dale	Ed Jerome
Hal Craig	Steven Gethers
Ben Harper	Christopher Reeve
	Chandeler Hill Harben
Ian Russell	Michael Allinson
Betty Harper	Elizabeth Kemp
Edouard Aleata	John Aniston
James Crawford	Kenneth McMillan
David Hart	Brian Farrell
Felicia Fleming	Pamela Lincoln
Vivian Carlson	Helene Dumas
Mia Marriott	Veleka Gray
Will Dale	Ed Jerome
Sarah Dale	Jane Rose
Dr. Joe Cusack	Peter Brouwer
Charles Lamont	Jonathan Moore
Zachary Bly	Jake Turner
Paul Graham	Gary Giem
Cherie Manning	Elizabeth Stack
Betsy Crawford	Margo McKenna
Suzanne Crawford	Tamara Hummel
Dory Patton	Sherry Rooney
Lynn Henderson	Amy Gibson
Tony Alphonso	Peter Gatto
Mary Owens	Corinne Neuchateau
Kate Swanson	Sally Stark
Andrew Marriott	Richard Higgs
	Christian Marlowe
	Ron Harper
Ray Slater	Lloyd Battista
Sarah Caldwell	Valerie Cossart
Elliott Hampton Lang	Ted LePlatt
Mama Gaspero	Vera Lockwood
Bambi Brewster	Ann McCarthy
Gina Gaspero	Amy Niles

Prof. Timothy McCauley	Sheppard Strudwick
Arlene Lovett Slater	Birgitta Tolksdorf
Tom Crawford	Richard K. Weber
Amy Russell	Dana Delany
Kin SooLing	Irene Yah-Ling Sun
Suzanne Harper	Heather Bicknell
Wesley Osborne III	Woody Brown
Steve Harbach	Paul Craggs
Liane Wilson	Mary Ann Johnson
Tom Crawford	Mark Pinter
Arlene Slater	Gitanna Tolksdorf

Also: Warren Beatty, Carl Betz, Peter Falk, Anne Jackson, Roy Scheider, Bert Convy, Jan Miner, David Ford, Clarice Blackburn, Conrad Fowkes, Alfred Markim, Joe Allen, Jr.

Narrator: Charles Mountain.
Announcer: Don Hancock, Herbert Duncan, Ken Roberts.
Organist: John Gart.
Music: Carey Gold.
Theme: "Love of Life" by Haygood Hardy.
Executive Producer: Jean Arley, Darryl Hickman.
Producer: Roy Windsor, Ernest Ricca, Joseph Hardy, Cathy Abbi, Paul Sladkus, Jean Arley.
Director: Larry Auerbach, Heather Hill, Jerry Evans.

LOVE OF LIFE—15 minutes—CBS—September 24, 1951–April 11, 1958. 30 minutes—April 14, 1958–February 1, 1980. 7,316 episodes.

718   LOVE ON A ROOFTOP

Comedy. The story of Dave Willis, an apprentice architect, and his wife Julie, the pampered daughter of a wealthy car salesman, and their struggles to survive the difficult first years of marriage.

CAST

Julie Willis	Judy Carne
Dave Willis	Peter Deuel
Stan Parker, their neighbor	Rich Little
Carol Parker, Stan's wife	Barbara Bostock
Fred Hammond, Julie's father	Herbert Voland
Phyllis Hammond, Fred's wife	Edith Atwater
Jim Lucas, Dave's co-worker	Sandy Kenyon

Dave and Julie's address: 1400 McDoogal Street in San Francisco, California (where they live in a rooftop apartment).

Music: Warren Barker, Mundell Lowe.
Executive Producer: Harry Ackerman.
Producer: E. W. Swackhamer.
Associate Producer: Stan Schwimmer.
Creator: Bernard Slade, Harry Ackerman.

LOVE ON A ROOFTOP—30 minutes—ABC—September 6, 1966–January 6, 1967; May 19, 1971–August 8, 1971.

719   LOVERS AND FRIENDS

Serial. The series, set in Point Clare, a Chicago suburb, follows the dramatic story of two families: the affluent Cushings, and their middle-class neighbors, the Saxtons.

CAST

Peter Cushing	Ron Rondell
Edith Cushing	Nancy Marchand
Eleanor Kimball	Flora Plumb
Connie Ferguson	Susan Foster
Megan Cushing	Patricia Estrin
Barbara Manners	Karen Phillipp
Amy Gifford	Christine Jones
Marlow	Daniel Heyes
Josie Saxton	Patricia Englund
Rhett Saxton	Bob Purvey
	David Ramsey
George Kimball	Stephen Joyce
Jason Saxton	Richard Backus
Sophia Slocum	Margaret Barker
Tessa Saxton	Vicky Dawson
Austin Cushing	Rod Arrants
Lester Saxton	John Hefferman
Bentley Saxton	David Abbott
Laurie Brewster	Dianne Harper

Music: Score Productions.
Executive Producer: Paul Rauch.
Producer: John Wendell, Harriet Goldstein.
Director: Peter Levin, Jack Hofsiss, Kevin Kelly.
Creator: Harding Lemay.

LOVERS AND FRIENDS—30 minutes—NBC—January 3, 1977–May 6, 1977. 105 episodes.

720   LOVES ME, LOVES ME NOT

Comedy. The romantic escapades of Jane Benson, a beautiful, but indecisive grammar school teacher, and Dick Phillips, a klutz newspaper reporter, who meet, fall in love and struggle to make it through the travails of a latter 1970s romance in California.

CAST

Jane Benson	Susan Dey
Dick Phillips	Kenneth Gilman
Sue, Jane's friend	Udana Power
	Phyllis Glick
Tom, Dick's friend	Art Metrano

Music: George Tipton.
Music Supervision: Lionel Newman.
Executive Producer: Paul Junger Witt, Tony Thomas.
Producer: Susan Harris, Ernest Losso.
Director: Jay Sandrich, Richard Kinon, Noam Pitlik.

LOVES ME, LOVES ME NOT—30 minutes—CBS—March 20, 1977–April 27, 1977. 6 episodes.

721   LOVE STORY

Anthology. Adult and contemporary variations on the theme of love.

Music: Peter Matz, David Shire.
Theme: "Love Story" by Francis Lai.
Producer: George Schaefer.

Included:

When the Girls Come Out to Play. The story of Jimmy Lewin, a singles-apartment Romeo accustomed to shallow affairs without commitment. He suddenly finds it difficult to handle his emotions when he really falls in love.

Cast: Jimmy Lewin: Frank Langella; Karen: Victoria Principal; Marlene: Valerie Perrine; Jimmy's father: Booth Colman; Jimmy's mother: Claudia Bryar.

The Youngest Lovers. The story of an innocent summertime romance between Ellie Madison and Sam Burnett, two twelve-year-olds from broken homes.

Cast: Ellie Madison: Jodie Foster; Sam Burnett: Michael-James Wixted; Dick Madison: Larry Hagman; Angie Burnett: Diane Baker; Virginia Madison: Susan Oliver.

The Soft Kind Brush. The story of David Coryell and Miriam Fannon, two college sweethearts now married to other people, who still find they love each other when they attend a class reunion.

Cast: David Coryell: James Farentino; Miriam Fannon: Trish Van Devere; Peggy Gallagher: Lynnette Mettey; Fern: Mary Ann Gibson; Stan: Phillip Pine; Nora: Ellen Clark.

The Cardboard House. The story of the relationship between Ruth Wilson, a secretary with a penchant for neatness and organization, and Dave Walters, a devil-may-care charmer who lives for the moment.

Cast: Ruth Wilson: Samantha Eggar; Dave Walters: Vic Morrow; Dr. Mac Merrill: Robert Emhardt; Al Perrin: Bill Zuckert; Jean Merrill: Priscilla Morrill.

LOVE STORY—60 minutes—NBC—October 3, 1973–January 2, 1974.

722   LOVE THY NEIGHBOR

Comedy. The series, set at the Sherwood Forest Estates in San Fernando, California, follows the lives of a middle-class white couple, Charlie Wilson, a shop steward at Turner Electronics, and his wife Peggy; and a black couple in the formerly all-white neighborhood, Ferguson Bruce, the efficiency expert at Turner Electronics, and his wife Jackie. Dramatizing racial prejudices, stories depict the attempts of neighbors to adjust to each other.

CAST

Peggy Wilson	Joyce Bulifant
Charlie Wilson, her husband	Ron Masak
Jackie Bronson, their neighbor	Janet MacLachlan
Ferguson Bruce, Jackie's husband	Harrison Page
Murray Bronson, Charlie's friend	Milt Kamen
Louie Gordon, Charlie's friend	Louis Gus

The Wilsons' address: 327 North Robin Hood Road (the Bruces live next door).

Music: Pete Rugolo.
Theme: "Love Thy Neighbor" by Arthur Julian.
Theme Vocal: Soloman Burke.
Executive Producer: Ted Bergman, Norman Rush.
Producer-Writer: Arthur Julian.
Director: Hal Cooper.

LOVE THY NEIGHBOR—30 minutes—ABC—June 15, 1973–September 19, 1973. 12 episodes. See also *Love Thy Neighbour*, next title, for information on the British version of the series.

723   LOVE THY NEIGHBOUR

Comedy. The British series on which America's *Love Thy Neighbor* (previous title) is based. The program, which has not been broadcast in the United States, follows events in the lives of Eddie and Joan Booth, a middle-class white couple, and their neighbors Bill and Barbie Reynolds, a black couple who made the radical move into a white neighborhood.

CAST

Eddie Booth	Jack Smethurst
Joan Booth, his wife	Kate Williams
Bill Reynolds, their neighbour	Rudolph Walker
Barbie Reynolds, Bill's wife	Nina Baden-Semper
Arthur, Eddie's friend	Tommy Godfrey
Jocko, Eddie's friend	Keith Marsh
Terry, Eddie's friend	Leslie Meadows

Producer-Director: Stuart Allen, Ronnie Baxter.

LOVE THY NEIGHBOUR—30 minutes. Produced by Thames TV of London from 1972 to 1976.

724   LOWELL THOMAS REMEMBERS

Documentary. Events of the past, based on newsreel footage from Fox-Movietone between 1919 to 1963, are recalled by Lowell Thomas.

Host-Narrator: Lowell Thomas.
Music: Jack Shindlin.
Producer: James W. Jackson.
Director: Larry Lancit.

LOWELL THOMAS REMEMBERS—30 minutes—PBS—1975–1976.

ABC

The Love Boat. Front, from left: Lauren Tewes, Gavin MacLeod, Jill Whelan. Back, from left: Fred Grandy, Ted Lange, Bernie Kopell.

NBC

Lovers and Friends. Patricia Estrin.

CBS

Loves Me, Loves Me Not. Susan Dey.

ABC

The MacKenzies of Paradise Cove. Foreground, from left, Randi Kiger and Lory Walsh. Behind them, from left, Sean Marshall, Keith Mitchell and Shawn Stevens. Courtesy of the *Call-Chronicle Newspapers,* Allentown, Pa.

725 LUCAN

Drama. Original story line: While stalking game in northern Minnesota during the summer of 1967, a group of hunters stumbles upon a strange creature—a ten-year-old boy who eats, sleeps, howls and hunts like a wolf. The boy is captured by scientists and named Lucan. Attempts fail to discover how he came to be there or who his parents are. Brought to a research center and taught the ways of modern man, the boy survives and adapts. Now, ten years later, educated and free, he roams the country searching for his natural parents. His adventures on this quest and the people in distress he helps along the way are dramatized.

In the three-month interval between telecasting the first and second episodes, a drastic change occurred: instead of being set free by the university research center to search for his parents, the revised story line finds Lucan escaping from the authorities who tried to keep him captive, fearing he would revert back to wolf. Stories still depict Lucan's search for his parents—a search that is hindered by Prentiss, a bounty hunter hired by the university to capture Lucan.

After another short absence, the series returned with a slightly revised story line: one night, while in the university lab, Lucan comes across two men trying to steal drugs. As he attempts to stop them, one is killed in a fire and Lucan is unjustly blamed. Innocent, but unable to prove it, Lucan escapes, and as he seeks to prove his innocence, he is relentlessly pursued by a police lieutenant named Prentiss. Stories depict his adventures as a fugitive.

CAST

Lucan	Kevin Brophy
Don Hoagland, Lucan's friend, the doctor who educated him	John Randolph
Prentiss, the bounty hunter (later Lt. Prentiss)	Don Gordon

Music: J. J. Johnson.
Theme Narration: John Randolph.
Executive Producer: Barry Lowen.
Producer: David Greene, Lew Gallo, Harold Gast, Everett Chambers.
Director: David Greene, Georg Stanford Brown, Joseph Pevney, Hollingsworth Morse, Peter H. Hunt, Robert Day, Sutton Roley, Barry Shear, Curtis Harrington.
Creator: Michael Zagor.

LUCAN — 60 minutes — ABC — September 12, 1977 – January 16, 1978. 5 episodes. March 13, 1978 – March 20, 1978. 2 episodes. November 13, 1978 – December 4, 1978. 4 episodes. The 90-minute pilot film aired on ABC on May 22, 1977.

726 LUCAS TANNER

Drama. A realistic portrayal of student-teacher relationships as seen through the eyes of Lucas Tanner, an English instructor at Harry S. Truman Memorial High School in Webster Groves, Missouri.

CAST

Lucas Tanner	David Hartman
Margaret Blumenthal, the principal	Rosemary Murphy
John Hamilton, the principal (later episodes)	John Randolph
Glendon Farrell, Tanner's neighbor	Robbie Rist
Jaytee Druman, the school D.J.	Alan Abelew
Cindy Damin, a student	Trish Soodik
Terry, a student	Kimberly Beck
Wally, a student	Michael Dwight-Smith
Grace Baden, Glendon's grandmother (with whom he lives)	June Dayton

Tanner's dog: Bridget (originally O'Casey).

Music: David Shire, Richard Clements.
Executive Producer: David Victor.
Producer: Charles S. Dubin, Jay Benson.
Director: Alexander Singer, Jay Benson, Leo Penn, Randal Kleiser, Richard Donner, Allen Baron, Richard Benedict, Charles S. Dubin, Paul Krasny, Jerry London.
Creator: Jerry McNuley.

LUCAS TANNER — 60 minutes — NBC — September 11, 1974 – August 20, 1975. 24 episodes. The 90-minute pilot film aired on NBC on May 8, 1974.

M

727 McCLOUD

Crime Drama. The investigations of Sam McCloud, a deputy marshal from Taos, New Mexico, who is assigned to the Manhattan 27th Precinct in New York City to study crime-detection methods.

CAST

Deputy Sam McCloud	Dennis Weaver
Police Chief Peter B. Clifford	J. D. Cannon
Sgt. Joe Broadhurst	Terry Carter
Chris Coughlin, Sam's romantic interest	Diana Muldaur
Sgt. Maggie Clinger	Sharon Gless Nancy Fox
Detective Grover	Ken Lynch

Music: Billy Goldenberg, Richard Clements, Stu Phillips, David Shire.
Executive Producer: Leslie Stevens, Glen A. Larson.
Producer: Ron Satlof, Michael Gleason, Dean Hargrove, Glen A. Larson.
Director: Alex March, Bruce Kessler, Jack Smight, Douglas Heyes, Hy Averback, Russ Mayberry, Robert Day, Boris Sagal, Glen A. Larson, Jimmy Sangster, Richard A. Colla, Jerry Jameson, Jack Arnold, E.W. Swackhamer, Lou Antonio, Noel Black.
Creator: Herman Miller.

McCLOUD — 60-, 90- and 120-minute versions — NBC — September 16, 1970 – August 28, 1977 (as part of both *Four-in-One* and *The NBC Sunday Mystery Movie*). The pilot film, "McCloud: Who Killed Miss U.S.A.?" aired on NBC on February 17, 1970.

728 McCOY

Crime Drama. The exploits of McCoy, an engaging con artist who, to pay off his gambling debts, first undertakes a criminal case, then, by incorporating his unique skills, seeks to solve the crime.

CAST

McCoy	Tony Curtis
Gideon Gibbs, his assistant	Roscoe Lee Browne
Lucy, the owner of the diner frequented by McCoy	Lucille Meredith

Music: Billy Goldenberg, Dick De Benedictis.
Producer: Roland Kibbee.
Director: Richard Quine, Stanley Dragoti.

McCOY — 2 hours — NBC — October 5, 1975 – September 12, 1976 (as part of *The NBC Sunday Mystery Movie*).

729 THE MAC DAVIS SHOW

Musical Variety.

Host: Mac Davis.
Regulars: Kay Dingle, Bo Kaprell, The Tony Mordente Dancers.
Orchestra: Mike Post.
Special Musical Material: Billy Barnes, Earl Brown.
Additional Orchestrations: Sid Feller.
Executive Producer: Sandy Gallin.
Producer: Arnie Rosen, Bob Ellison.
Writer: Stan Burns, Don Hinckley, Arthur Julian, Mike Marmer.
Director: Tim Kiley.

THE MAC DAVIS SHOW — 60 minutes — NBC — July 11, 1974 – August 29, 1974; December 19, 1974 – May 22, 1975.

730 THE MAC DAVIS SHOW

Musical Variety.

Host: Mac Davis.
Regulars: Shields and Yarnell, Ron Silver, The Strutts.
Orchestra: Tom Bahler, Mike Post.
Choreographer: Jim Bates.
Executive Producer: Gary Smith, Dwight Hemion.
Producer: Mike Post, Steve Binder, Nancy Henson.
Director: Steve Binder, Jim Cox.

THE MAC DAVIS SHOW — 60 minutes — NBC — March 18, 1976 – June 17, 1976.

731 McDUFF, THE TALKING DOG

Comedy. The comic misadventures of Calvin Campbell, a young, trouble-prone veterinarian in the town of Peach Blossom. His escapades are helped and hindered by McDuff, the ghost of a sheep dog who appears and speaks only to him.

CAST

Dr. Calvin Campbell	Walter Willson
Amos Ferguson, his neighbor	Gordon Jump
Squeaky, Amos' nephew	Johnnie Collins III
Mrs. Osgood, Calvin's housekeeper	Monty Margetts
Kimmy Campbell, Calvin's sister	Michelle Stacy
McDuff's Voice	Jack Lester

Music: Richard LaSalle.
Executive Producer: William P. D'Angelo, Ray Allen, Harvey Bullock.
Producer: Victor Paul.
Director: Gordon Wiles, James Sheldon, William P. D'Angelo.

McDUFF, THE TALKING DOG — 30 minutes — NBC — September 11, 1976 – November 20, 1976.

732 THE MacKENZIES OF PARADISE COVE

Drama. The series, set in Honolulu, follows the adventures of Bridget, Kevin, Celia, Michael and Timothy MacKenzie, five orphaned children who, in an attempt to remain a family after their parent's death in a sailing accident, adopt Cuda Webber, a reluctant seagoing fisherman as their substitute "uncle" so that authorities won't split them up.

CAST

Cuda Webber, runs a charter boat service	Clu Gulager
Bridget MacKenzie, the eldest daughter	Lory Walsh
Kevin MacKenzie, the eldest son (pilot film)	Sean Roche
Kevin MacKenzie (series)	Shawn Stevens
Celia MacKenzie, the youngest daughter	Randi Kiger
Michael MacKenzie, the fourth-born child	Sean Marshall
Timothy MacKenzie, the youngest child	Keith Mitchell
"Big" Ben Kalakeeni, Cuda's friend	Moe Keale

"Little" Ben Kalakeeni,
Ben's son   Sean Tyler Hall
Mrs. Kalakeeni, Ben's wife   Lelanna Heine
Barney, Cuda's friend   Harry Chang

Cuda's boat: The *Viking.*

Music: Fred Werner, John Rubinstein.
Producer: Jerry Thorpe, William Blinn.
Director: Jerry Thorpe, Harry Harris.
Creator: William Blinn, Jerry Thorpe.

THE MacKENZIES OF PARADISE COVE — 60 minutes — ABC — March 27, 1979 – April 11, 1979. 3 episodes. April 27, 1979 – May 18, 1979. 3 episodes. Original title: *Wonderland Cove.* The 90-minute pilot film, "Stickin' Together," aired on ABC on April 14, 1978.

733   THE McLEAN STEVENSON SHOW

Comedy. The series, set in Evanston, Illinois, follows the misadventures of Mac Ferguson, a hardware store owner, as he struggles to cope with life, both at home and at work.

CAST

Mac Ferguson   McLean Stevenson
Peggy Ferguson, his wife   Barbara Stuart
Janet, their divorced daughter Ayn Ruymen
Chris Ferguson, their son   Steve Nevil
Muriel, Peggy's mother   Madge West
David, Janet's son   David Hollander
Jason, Janet's son   Jason Whitney

Music: Paul Williams.
Executive Producer: Monty Hall.
Producer: Arnold Margolin, Don Van Atta.
Director: Alan Myerson, Bill Hobin.

THE McLEAN STEVENSON SHOW — 30 minutes — NBC — December 1, 1976 – March 9, 1977. 13 episodes.

734   McMILLAN

Crime Drama. The cases of Stewart "Mac" McMillan, the San Francisco police commissioner. A spin-off from *McMillan and Wife,* which see (next title), without series co-star Susan Saint James (Sally, the character portrayed by Susan, "died" in an airplane crash).

CAST

Stewart McMillan   Rock Hudson
Agatha Thornton, his
housekeeper   Martha Raye
Lt. Charles Enright   John Schuck
Sergeant Di'Maggio   Richard Gilliland
Maggie, Stewart's secretary   Gloria Stroock
Police Chief Paulson   Bill Quinn

Music: Jerry Fielding.
Executive Producer: Leonard B. Stern.
Producer: Jon Epstein.
Director: Jackie Cooper, John Astin, James Sheldon, Lou Antonio.

McMILLAN — 2 hours — NBC — December 15, 1976 – August 21, 1977 (as a segment of *The NBC Sunday Mystery Movie*).

735   McMILLAN AND WIFE

Crime Drama. The saga of Sally McMillan, the pretty, but trouble-prone wife of San Francisco Police Commissioner Stewart "Mac" McMillan. Stories depict their investigations into crimes into which Sally accidentally stumbles and involves Mac.

CAST

Stewart McMillan   Rock Hudson
Sally McMillan, his wife   Susan Saint James
Sgt. Charles Enright   John Schuck
Mildred, the McMillan's
housekeeper   Nancy Walker
Maggie, Mac's secretary   Gloria Stroock
Police Chief Paulson   Bill Quinn

Music: Jerry Fielding.
Executive Producer: Leonard B. Stern.
Producer: Jon Epstein, Paul Mason.
Director: Lou Antonio, Edward Abroms, Harry Falk, Bob Finkel, Lee H. Katzin, James Sheldon, Robert Michael Lewis, Daniel Petrie Gary Nelson, Barry Shear, John Astin, Mel Ferber, Hy Averback, Leonard J. Horn, Alf Kjellin, E. W. Swackhamer.

McMILLAN AND WIFE — 90-minute and 2-hour versions — NBC — September 29, 1971 – September 12, 1976 (as a segment of *The NBC Sunday Mystery Movie*).

736   McNAUGHTON'S DAUGHTER

Crime Drama. The cases and courtroom prosecutions of Laurel McNaughton, a trial lawyer and the deputy district attorney of Los Angeles County.

CAST

Laurel McNaughton   Susan Clark
Lou Farragut, her
investigator   James Callahan
Charles Quintero, the D.A.
                  Ricardo Montalban
Ed Hughes, Laurel's assistant   John Elerick

Music: George Romanis.
Music Supervision: Hal Mooney.
Executive Producer: David Victor.
Producer: Harold Gast.
Director: Gene Nelson, Jack Arnold, Daniel Haller.

McNAUGHTON'S DAUGHTER — 60 minutes — NBC — March 24, 1976 – April 7, 1976. 3 episodes. The two-hour pilot film aired on NBC on March 4, 1976.

737   THE MADHOUSE BRIGADE

Comedy. A series of blackouts and sketches that satirize politics and culture.

Starring: J. J. Lewis, Karen Rushmore, Alexander Marshall, Frank Nastasi, Joe Piscopo, Dan Resin, Carlos Carrasco, Rocket Ryan, Nola Fairbanks.

Music: Tony Monte.
Executive Producer: Jim Larkin.
Producer: Dale Keidel, Alexander Marshall.
Director: Dale Keidel.

THE MADHOUSE BRIGADE — 30 minutes — Syndicated 1978.

738   MADIGAN

Crime Drama. The exploits of Sergeant Dan Madigan, an embittered plainclothes detective attached to the Manhattan 10th Precinct in New York City.

CAST

Sgt. Dan Madigan   Richard Widmark

Music: Jerry Fielding.
Producer: Roland Kibbee.
Writer: Roland Kibbee, William McGovern, Dean Hargrove, Peter Allan Fields, David Freeman, Bernard Schoenfeld, Stanford Whitmore.
Director: Alex March, Jack Smight, Boris Sagal.

MADIGAN — 90 minutes — NBC — September 20, 1972 – August 22, 1973 (as a segment of *The NBC Wednesday Mystery Movie*). 6 episodes.

739   THE MAGIC GARDEN

Children. Setting: The Magic Garden, a small, forest-like area where make-believe becomes real. With hostesses Carole and Paula, and through the antics of puppets Sherlock Squirrel and Flap the bird, stories, songs and related entertainment for children, are charmingly and amusingly presented.

CAST

Carole   Carole Demas
Paula   Paula Janis
Sherlock   Cary Antebi
Flap   Cary Antebi

Music: Alton Alexander, George Kayatta, Alexander Demas.
Theme Vocal: Carole Demas, Paula Janis.
Themes: "Magic Window" (opening theme) and "See Ya" (closing theme) by George Kayatta.
Producer: Irv Jarvis, Joseph L. Hall, Virginia Martin.
Associate Producer: Ray J. Hoesten.
Writer: Virginia Martin, Alton Alexander.
Director: Irv Jarvis, Joseph L. Hall.

THE MAGIC GARDEN — 30 minutes — Syndicated 1974. 48 episodes.

740   THE MAGICIAN

Adventure. The series, set in Hollywood, follows the exploits of Anthony Blake, the world's greatest magician. Using the wizardry of his craft, he attempts to assist people in distress — people who are seeking escape, but who are unable to turn to police for help.

CAST

Anthony Blake (Anthony Dorian
in the pilot film)   Bill Bixby
Max Pomeroy, his contact   Keene Curtis
Jerry Anderson, his pilot   Jim Watkins
Dennis Pomeroy, Max's son   Tod Crespi
Dominick, the owner of the
Magic Castle Club   Joseph Sirola

Blake's address: 315 Vinewood.
Blake's plane: The *Spirit,* a Boeing 737.
Announcer: Bill Baldwin.
Music: Patrick Williams.
Executive Producer: Laurence Heath.
Producer: Barry Crane.
Director: Marvin Chomsky, Alexander Singer, Barry Crane.

THE MAGICIAN — 60 minutes — NBC — October 2, 1973 – May 20, 1974. 24 episodes. The pilot film aired on NBC on March 17, 1973.

741   MAGIC MONGO

Comedy. The series concerns itself with the misadventures of three teenagers, Laraine, Christy and Donald, and their mischievous genie, Magic Mongo, whom Donald found on a beach trapped in a bottle and released.

CAST

Magic Mongo   Lennie Weinrib
Laraine   Helaine Lembeck
Christy   Robin Dearden
Donald Connelly   Paul Hinckley
Ace, the hood-like beach
bully   Bart Braverman
Duncey, Ace's cohort   Larry Larsen
Huli, the owner of the
beach cafe   Sab Shimondo

Music: Michael Melvoin.
Executive Producer: Sid and Marty Krofft.
Producer: Jack Regas.
Director: Bill Foster, Jack Regas, Rick Locke.
Creator: Joe Ruby, Ken Spears.

MAGIC MONGO — 15 minutes — ABC — September 10, 1977 – September 2, 1978 (as a segment of *The Krofft Supershow II*).

742   THE MAGIC OF MARK WILSON

Variety. A half-hour series that spotlights the talents of magician Mark Wilson.

Host: Mark Wilson.
Regulars: Nani Dranell, Greg Wilson.
Music: Frank Ortega.
Producer-Director: Herb Waterson.

THE MAGIC OF MARK WILSON — 30 minutes — Syndicated 1977.

743   THE MAGNIFICENT MARBLE MACHINE

Game. Two teams, composed of one celebrity and one non-celebrity contestant, compete. The team that scores highest during a series of question and answer rounds wins and plays the bonus round: the Magnificent Marble Machine, which is a large, electronic pinball machine. The team receives two minutes at play and each time a bumper is hit by the large ball, five hundred points are scored and a prize is won.

If the player reaches a goal of 15,000 points, he receives the opportunity to play the gold money ball. Within one minute of play, each bumper that is hit earns him $500. Players compete until defeated.

Host: Art James.
Frequent Celebrity Guests: Pat Harrington, Jr., Lee Meriwether, Florence Henderson, Adrienne Barbeau, Anson Williams, Karen Valentine, Arte Johnson, Earl Holliman, Leslie Uggams.
Announcer: Johnny Gilbert.
Music: Mort Garson.
Executive Producer: Merrill Heatter, Bob Quigley.
Producer: Robert Noah.

THE MAGNIFICENT MARBLE MACHINE—30 minutes—NBC—July 7, 1975–June 11, 1976.

744   THE MAGNIFICENT SIX AND A HALF

Comedy. The series, set in England, follows the adventures of six boys (Steve, Whizz, Dumbo, Toby, Stodger and Pee Wee)—the Magnificent Six—and a young girl, Liz, the Half.

CAST
Steve	Len James
Whizz	Michael Auderson
Dumbo	Ian Ellis
Toby	Brinsley Forde
Stodger	Lionel Hawkes
Pee Wee	Kim Tallmadge
Liz	Suzanne Togni

THE MAGNIFICENT SIX AND A HALF—18 minutes—Syndicated (to the U.S.) in 1970. 12 episodes.

745   MAKE A WISH

Children. Through animation, films, songs and sketches, the difference between fantasy and the real world is explained to children.

Host: Tom Chapin.
Orchestra: Bernie Green.
Producer: Tom Bywaters.
Field Producer: Patricia Sides, Terry Howard, Phyllis Gura, Don Belth.
Writer: Chester Cooper.
Director: Arthur J. Ornitz.

Field Director: Barbara Miller, Al Niggemeyer.

MAKE A WISH—30 minutes—ABC—September 12, 1971–September 3, 1977.

746   MAKE ME LAUGH

Game. A contestant appears and sits opposite a panel of three guest comedians. At sixty-second intervals, the comedians approach the contestant and attempt to make him laugh. For each second that the contestant remains straight-faced he wins one dollar up to a limit of $360. If a contestant does laugh before the three minutes are up, he receives money calculated by the amount of time used before he laughed.

Host: Bobby Van.
Announcer: Bill Beary.
Music: Artie Butler.
Producer: George Foster.
Director: Glen Swanson.

MAKE ME LAUGH—30 minutes—Syndicated 1979.

747   MAKE ROOM FOR DADDY

Comedy. The series, set in New York City, follows events in the life of Danny Williams, a nightclub comedian (at the Copa Club), whose career leaves him little time to spend with his family.

CAST
Danny Williams	Danny Thomas
Margaret Williams, his wife (1953-1957)	Jean Hagen
Kathy Williams, his wife (1957-1964)*	Marjorie Lord
Teresa (Terry) Williams, Danny's daughter (by Margaret)	Sherry Jackson
Russell (Rusty) Williams, Danny's son (by Margaret)	Rusty Hamer
Linda Williams, Kathy's daughter	Angela Cartwright
Patty Williams, Kathy's daughter*	Lelani Sorenson
Louise, their maid	Louise Beavers
	Amanda Randolph
Charlie Helper, the owner of the Copa Club	Sid Melton
Bunny Helper, Charlie's wife	Pat Carroll
Jesse Leeds, Danny's first agent	Jesse White
Phil Arnold, Danny's second agent	Horace McMahon
	Sheldon Leonard
Elizabeth Margaret O'Neal, Danny's press agent	Mary Wickes
Ben Lessy, Danny's piano player	Himself
Frank Jenks, Danny's tailor	Himself
Uncle Tonoose, the head of the Williams family	Hans Conried
Pat Hannegan, Terry's boyfriend; later (1960) husband	Pat Harrington, Jr.
Harry Ruby, Danny's songwriter	Himself
Gina Minelli, the Italian exchange student residing with the Williamses	Annette Funicello
Piccola Pupa, the Italian singer discovered by Danny	Herself
Buck, Gina's boyfriend	Richard Tyler
José Jiménez, the elevator operator	Bill Dana
Alfie, a Copa Club waiter	Bernard Fox
Mr. Heckendorn, Danny's building super	Gale Gordon
Mr. Daly, Kathy's father	William Demarest

The Williamses' address: 505 East 50th Street, Apt. 542.
The Williamses' dog: Laddie, a terrier.
Music: Herbert Spencer, Earle Hagen.
Executive Producer: Louis F. Edelman.
Producer: Charles Stewart, Sheldon Leonard, Jack Elinson, Ronald Jacobs.

MAKE ROOM FOR DADDY—30 minutes. ABC—September 29, 1953–July 17, 1957. CBS (as *The Danny Thomas Show*)—October 7, 1957–September 14, 1964. 336 episodes. Syndicated. Spin-off series, which see *Make Room for Granddaddy*.

*In 1957, after Margaret's "death," Danny married Kathleen O'Hara (later referred to as Kathleen Daly), a widowed nurse and the mother of a young daughter named Patty—the character's name was later changed to Linda.

748   MAKE ROOM FOR GRANDDADDY

Comedy. The series, which is a spin-off from *Make Room for Daddy*, continues to depict events in the lives of Danny Williams, now a grandfather, and his family.

CAST
Danny Williams, a nightclub entertainer	Danny Thomas
Kathy Williams, his wife	Marjorie Lord
Linda Williams, their daughter	Angela Cartwright
Rusty Williams, their son	Rusty Hamer
Terry Johnson, their married daughter	Sherry Jackson
Michael Johnson, Danny's grandson	Michael Hughes
Susan Williams, Rusty's wife	Jana Taylor
Charlie Helper, the owner of the Copa Club	Sid Melton
Uncle Tonoose, the head of the Williams family	Hans Conried
Rosey Robbins, Danny's accompanist	Rosey Grier
Henry, the elevator operator	Stanley Myron Handleman

Music: Earle Hagen.
Executive Producer: Danny Thomas.
Producer: Richard Crenna.

MAKE ROOM FOR GRANDDADDY—30 minutes—ABC—September 23, 1970–September 2, 1971. 24 episodes.

749   MAKE YOUR OWN KIND OF MUSIC

Variety. Musical numbers are interspersed with comedy sketches.

Host: Karen and Richard Carpenter (brother and sister).
Regulars: Al Hirt, Mark Lindsay, The New Doodletown Pipers, Patchett and Tarses (comics).
Orchestra: Jack Elliott, Allyn Ferguson.
Producer: Arnold Kane, Gordon Farr, Ken Hecht.
Director: Stan Harris.

MAKE YOUR OWN KIND OF MUSIC—60 minutes—NBC—July 20, 1971–September 7, 1971. 8 programs.

750   MAKIN' IT

Comedy. The series, set in Passaic, New Jersey, follows the misadventures of Billy Manucci, an easygoing young man who lives at home with his parents—and in the shadow of a swinging older brother—while working his way through college to become a teacher. Stories are centered around a disco called The Inferno.

CAST
Billy Manucci	David Naughton
Joseph Manucci, his father	Lou Antonio
Dorothy Manucci, his mother	Ellen Travolta
Tina Manucci, Billy's sister	Denise Miller
Tony Manucci, Billy's older brother	Greg Antonacci
Corky, Billy's girlfriend	Rebecca Balding
Kingfish, Billy's friend	Ralph Seymour
Bernard, Billy's friend	Gary Prendergast

Music: Don Peake.
Disco Music: The Bee Gees.
Theme Vocal: "Makin' It": David Naughton.
Executive Producer: Thomas L. Miller, Edward K. Milkis, Lowell Ganz, Mark Rothman.
Producer: David W. Dulcon, Deborah Leschin, Jeffrey Ganz.
Director: Lowell Ganz, Joel Zwick, John Tracy.
Creator: Lowell Ganz, Garry K. Marshall.

MAKIN' IT—30 minutes—ABC—February 1, 1979–March 16, 1979. 8 episodes.

751   MAN ABOUT THE HOUSE

Comedy. The British series on which America's *Three's Company* is based. The program, which has not been broadcast in the United States, follows the misadventures of Jo and Chrissy, two girls who share a flat in England, and the problems that ensue when their landlord raises the rent and they sublet a room to Robin Tripp, a male cookery student.

CAST
Jo	Sally Thomsett
Chrissy	Paula Wilcox
Robin Tripp	Richard O'Sullivan
George Roper, their landlord	Brian Murphy
Mildred Roper, George's wife	Yootha Joyce

Producer-Director: Peter Jones.

MAN ABOUT THE HOUSE—30 minutes—Produced by Thames TV of London from 1973–1976. See also *George and Mildred* for the spin-off series. In 1977, Thames TV aired *Robin's Nest*, a series that updates the life of Robin Tripp: having completed his cookery exams, he is now a fully qualified, but unemployed chef.

752   THE MAN AND THE CITY

Drama. The series, set in an unidentified Southwestern metropolis, the fictional equivalent of Albuquerque, New Mexico, follows the life of Mayor Thomas Jefferson Alcala, a man who strays from the offices of city hall, mixes with the people and struggles to solve their problems.

CAST

Mayor Thomas Alcala	Anthony Quinn
Andy Hays, his assistant	Mike Farrell
Marian Crane, his secretary	Mala Powers
Josefina, his housekeeper	Carmen Zapata

Music: Alex North.
Executive Producer: David Victor.
Producer: Stanley Rubin.
Director: Daniel Petrie, Daniel Haller, Fernando Lamas, Lee Philips, Charles S. Dubin, Jeannot Szwarc, Robert Scheerer, Paul Henried.
Creator: Howard Rodman.

THE MAN AND THE CITY—60 minutes—ABC—September 15, 1971–January 5, 1972. 13 episodes.

753   A MAN CALLED INTREPID

Adventure. A three-part miniseries, based on the novel by William Stevenson, that details the formation of an allied espionage network during World War II. Focusing on the exploits of William Stephenson, a patriotic Canadian who is recruited by Winston Churchill to set up an espionage network, the series reveals the best-kept secret of World War II—President Roosevelt's attempts to bring America into the war in 1939—two years before Pearl Harbor. (The title is derived from the code name under which Stephenson operates: *Intrepid*.)

CAST

Sir William Stephenson	David Niven
Evan Michaelian	Michael York
Madelaine	Barbara Hershey
Col. Jurgen	Paul Harding
Sister Luke	Flora Robson
Gubbins	Peter Gilmore
Mrs. Wainwright	Renee Asherson
Winston Churchill	Nigel Stock
Alexander Korda	Ferdy Mayne
Anna	Shirley Steedman
Deidra	Belinda Mayne
Cynthia	Gayle Hunnicutt
Heisenberg	Chris Wiggins
Nils Bohr	Larry Reynolds
Einstein	Joseph Golland
J. Edgar Hoover	Ken James
Donovan	Dick O'Neill
Willoughby	Shayne Rimmer

Music: Robert Farnon.
Executive Producer: Harold Greenberg, Philip Capice, Lee Rich.
Producer: Peter Katz.
Writer: William Blinn.
Director: Peter Carter.

A MAN CALLED INTREPID—2 hours (6 hours total)—NBC—May 20, 1979–May 22, 1979. 3 episodes.

754   A MAN CALLED SLOANE

Adventure. The exploits of Thomas Remington Sloane III, Priority One Agent for UNIT, a select counterespionage team. Using a toy store, "The Toy Boutique," as a front, UNIT battles the evils of KARTEL, an enemy organization that seeks to destroy the world.

CAST

Thomas R. Sloane	Robert Conrad
Torque, his assistant	Ji-Tu Cumbuka
Mr. Director, the head of UNIT	Dan O'Herlihy
Kelly O'Neal, a UNIT agent	Karen Purcill
Effie, the sexy voiced EFI Series 3000 Computer—the "brains" behind UNIT	Michele Carey
Sara, Sloane's romantic interest	Diane Stilwell

Announcer: Michele Carey.
Music: Tom Scott, Patrick Williams, Don Bagley, Les Hooper, Bill Byers.
Music Supervision: John Elizalde.
Theme: "A Man Called Sloane" by Patrick Williams.
Executive Producer: Philip Saltzman.
Supervising Producer: Quinn Martin.
Producer: Gerald Sanford.
Writer: Peter Fields, Stephen Kandel, Dick Nelson, B.W. Sandefur, Jimmy Sangster, Gerald Sanford, Pat Dunlap, Rich Meyer, Jack Fogarty, Don Ingalls, Patrick Mathews.
Director: Alan J. Levi, Michael Preece, Elizabeth Gallagher, Winrich Kolbe, Ray Austin, Jimmy Sangster, Jack Starrett, Lewis Teague, Robert Conrad.

A MAN CALLED SLOANE—60 minutes—NBC—September 22, 1979–December 22, 1979. 12 episodes. Rebroadcasts: June 13, 1980–July 18, 1980; September 5, 1980–September 12, 1980.

755   THE MANCINI GENERATION

Musical Variety.
Host: Henry Mancini.

Music: The forty-piece Mancini Orchestra.
Additional Orchestrations: Alan Copeland.
Producer: Burt Sugarman.

THE MANCINI GENERATION—30 minutes—Syndicated 1972.

756   THE MAN FROM ATLANTIS

Adventure. A storm deep in the Pacific Ocean unearths the sole survivor of the fabled lost kingdom of Atlantis and brings him to shore. Elizabeth Merrill, a naval doctor with the Foundation for Oceanic Research in California, returns him to the sea and saves his life when he falls ill. Though the government permits the Atlantian, named Mark Harris by Elizabeth, to return to his former existence, Mark decides to remain with the foundation—to help further man's knowledge of the sea and gain his own knowledge about man. Stories detail Mark's work on behalf of the foundation.

CAST

Mark Harris, the Atlantian	Patrick Duffy
Dr. Elizabeth Merrill	Belinda J. Montgomery
Dr. Miller Simon, Elizabeth's associate	Kenneth Tigar
Ginny Mendoza, the receptionist at the foundation	Annette Cardona
C.W. Crawford, the head of the foundation	Alan Fudge
Mr. Schubert, the mad scientist	Victor Buono
Brent, Schubert's assistant	Robert Lussier

The Crew of the Foundation Submarine Citation:

Jane	Jean Marie Hon
Jimmy	J. Victor Lopez
Jumo	Anson Downs

Music: Fred Karlin.
Executive Producer: Herbert F. Solow.
Producer: Herman Miller, Robert Lewin.
Director: Virgil W. Vogel, Harvey Laidman, Richard Benedict, Barry Crane, Michael O'Herlihy, David Moessinger, Robert Douglas, Paul Krasny, Edward Abroms, Dennis Donnelly, Reza S. Badiyi, Marc Daniels, Lee H. Katzin, Charles S. Dubin.

THE MAN FROM ATLANTIS—60 minutes—NBC—September 22, 1977–January 10, 1978. 9 episodes. April 18, 1978–May 2, 1978. 3 episodes. June 6, 1978–July 25, 1978 (repeats). The two-hour pilot film aired on NBC on March 4, 1977.

757   THE MANHATTAN TRANSFER

Variety. A nostalgic series that recalls the music, song and dance of the 1930s and '40s.

Hosts: The Manhattan Transfer, a flashy vocal quartet comprised of Laurel Masse, Janis Seigel, Alan Paul and Tim Hauser.
Orchestra: Ira Newborn.
Executive Producer: Aaron Russo.
Producer: Bernard Rothman, Jack Wohl.
Director: Ron Field, Tom Trbovichi.
Choreographer: Ron Field.

THE MANHATTAN TRANSFER—60 minutes—CBS—August 10, 1975–August 31, 1975. 4 programs.

758   THE MANHUNTER

Crime Drama. The series, set in Cleary County, Idaho, during the "public enemy" days of the Depression (1934), details the exploits of Dave Barrett, an amateur crime fighter who assists law-enforcement officials by tracking down criminals to claim the rewards.

CAST

Dave Barrett	Ken Howard
Lizabeth Barrett, his sister	Hilary Thompson
James Barrett, his father	Ford Rainey
Mary Barrett, his mother	Claudia Bryar
Sheriff Paul Tate	Robert Hogan

Dave's dog: Beau.
Music: Duane Tatro.
Executive Producer: Quinn Martin.
Producer: Sam Rolfe.
Director: George McCowan, Leslie H. Martinson, Lawrence Dobkin, Allen Reisner, Michael Caffey, Seymour Robbie, Paul Stanley, Bernard McEveety, Walter Grauman.

THE MANHUNTER—60 minutes—CBS—September 11, 1974–April 10, 1975. 24 episodes. The 90-minute pilot film aired on CBS on February 26, 1974.

759   MANNIX

Crime Drama. The original format, set in Los Angeles, follows the exploits of Joe Mannix, an investigator for Intertect, a computerized private detective organization. After one year, the format changed to depict the investigations of Mannix as a private detective working independently out of his home at 17 Paseo Verde, Los Angeles.

CAST

Joe Mannix	Mike Connors
Lou Wickersham, his superior at Intertect	Joseph Campanella
Peggy Fair, Joe's secretary	Gail Fisher
Lt. Arthur Malcolm	Ward Wood
Lt. George Kramer	Lawrence Linville
Lt. Adam Tobias	Robert Reed
Lt. Daniel Ives	Jack Ging
Toby Fair, Peggy's son	Mark Stewart

Music: Lalo Schifrin, Kenyon Hopkins.

Producer: Ivan Goff, Ben Roberts.
Director: Sutton Roley, Gerald Mayer, Allen Reisner, Seymour Robbie, Fernando Lamas, Barry Crane, Don Taylor, Harry Harvey, Jr., Lee H. Katzin, Murray Golden, Arnold Laven, Paul Krasny, Reza S. Badiyi, Ralph Senensky, Paul Stanley, E.W. Swackhamer, Michael Caffey.

MANNIX — 60 minutes — CBS — September 7, 1967 – August 27, 1975. 194 episodes.

760   MANTRAP

Discussion. One male guest, selected to comment on a topic of current interest, appears and sits opposite a panel of three women. Both sides first state their opinions, then debate the issue.

Host: Al Hamel.
Regular Panelists: Meredith MacRae, Phyllis Kirk, Jaye P. Morgan, Carol Wayne, Selma Diamond.
Music: A recorded opening and closing theme.

MANTRAP — 30 minutes — Syndicated 1971.

761   MARCUS WELBY, M.D.

Drama. The series, set in Santa Monica, California, follows the experiences of doctors Marcus Welby, a general practitioner, and his assistant, Steven Kiley, as they attempt to treat people as individuals in an age of specialized medicine and uncaring physicians. (Welby and Kiley work part-time at Lang Memorial Hospital.)

CAST

Dr. Marcus Welby	Robert Young
Dr. Steven Kiley	James Brolin
Consuelo Lopez, their nurse	Elena Verdugo
Nurse Kathleen Faverty	Sharon Gless
Janet Blake, the hospital public relations woman; married Kiley on Oct. 21, 1975	Pamela Hensley
Myra Sherwood, Welby's romantic interest	Anne Baxter

Music: Leonard Rosenman.
Music Supervision: Hal Mooney.
Executive Producer: David Victor.
Producer: David J. O'Connell.
Director: Leo Penn, Jon Epstein, Hollingsworth Morse, Arnold Laven, Jerry London, David Alexander, Nicholas Cosalano, Bruce Kessler, Walter Doniger, Jeannot Szwarc, Robert Collins, Randal Kleiser, Daniel Petrie, David Lowell Rich, Philip Leacock, Joseph Pevney, Marc Daniels, Richard Benedict, Herschel Daughtery, Dennis Donnelly, Bernard McEveety, Russ Mayberry.

MARCUS WELBY, M.D. — 60 minutes — ABC — September 23,

1969 – May 11, 1976. 172 episodes. Syndicated. Also titled, for syndication purposes, *Robert Young, Family Doctor.*

762   MARIE CURIE

Biography. A five-part miniseries that traces the life of Marie Curie, a Polish-born scientist who would become the first woman to receive the Nobel Peace Prize for her work. Based on the book, *Marie Curie* by Robert Reid, and produced by the BBC.

CAST

Marie Curie	Jane Lapotaire
Pierre Curie	Nigel Hawthorne
Bronka	Adrienne Bryne
	Penelope Lee
Dr. Jean Curie	Maurice Denham
Irene Curie	Kellie Byrne
Henrietta Perrin	Sally Home
Jeannie	Madelyn Bellamy
Mary Rutherford	Anna Bentincle
Dean	Michael Poole
Kazimierz	Robin Holstead
Nikolai	Kenny Stoker
Sophie	Daphne Heard

Introduction: Dr. Rosalyn Yalow.
Music: Carl Davis.
Producer: Peter Goodchild.
Writer: Elaine Morgan.
Director: John Glenister.

MARIE CURIE — 60 minutes — Syndicated to PBS in 1979. 5 episodes.

763   THE MARILYN McCOO AND BILLY DAVIS, JR. SHOW

Variety. Music, songs and comedy sketches.

Hosts: Marilyn McCoo and Billy Davis, Jr.
Regulars: Lewis Arquette, Tim Reid, Jay Leno.
Orchestra: John Myles.
Special Musical Material: Phil Moore.
Executive Producer: Dick Broder.
Producer: Ann Elder, Ed Scharlach.
Director: Gerren Keith.
Choreographer: Ron Poindexter.

THE MARILYN McCOO AND BILLY DAVIS, JR. SHOW — 30 minutes — CBS — June 15, 1977 – July 20, 1977. 6 programs.

764   MARLO AND THE MAGIC MOVIE MACHINE

Children. The series, set in the sub-subbasement of the L. Dullo Computer Company in New York City, revolves around Marlo Higgins, a struggling computer operator who was banished to the basement by his employer, Leo Dullo. Here, by day, he continues working, making his dull job exciting by secretly perfecting the L. Dullo Computer. After working hours, he opens a secret doorway

and activates his invention — the Magic Movie Machine, a computer that can talk, tell jokes, relate funny stories and display a wide variety of film and videotape material. Acting as a disc jockey, Marlo and his Magic Movie Machine present films, stories, jokes and other related entertainment for children.

Starring: Laurie Faso as Marlo Higgins.
Voice of the Movie Machine: Mert Hoplin.
Music: Pete Dino; Score Productions.
Executive Producer: Sanford H. Fisher.
Producer: Ted Field.
Director: George Jason, Lynwood King.

MARLO AND THE MAGIC MOVIE MACHINE — 60- and 30-minute versions — CBS — Premiered: April 3, 1977.

765   MARRIED: THE FIRST YEAR

Drama. A chronicle of the courtship and marriage of teenage sweethearts Billy Baker (age 19) and Joanna Huffman (18), and their struggles to survive the difficult first year of marriage.

CAST

Billy Baker	Leigh McCloskey
Joanna Huffman Baker, his wife	Cindy Grover
Barbara Huffman, Joanna's mother	Claudette Nevins
Mike Huffman, Barbara's ex-husband	Joshua Bryant
Cheryl Huffman, Mike's wife	Constance McCashin
Jennifer Huffman, Joanna's half-sister	Tracy Justrich
Cathy Baker, Billy's mother	K Callan
Bert Baker, Billy's father	Stanley Grover
Millie Baker, Billy's sister	Jennifer McAllister
Donny Baker, Billy's brother	Stephen Manley
Emily Gorey, Cathy's sister	Christine Belford
Sharon Kelly, Joanna's friend	Stephanie Kramer
Cookie Levin, Joanna's friend	Gigi Vorgan
Tom Liberatore, Billy's friend	Gary Epp
Elizabeth Gorey, Cathy's mother	Martha Scott
Calvin Gorey, Cathy's father	Pitt Herbert

Music: Jerrold Immel.
Theme Vocal: Chuck Cochran.
Executive Producer: Lee Rich, Philip Capice.
Producer: David Jacobs.
Director: Robert Michael Lewis, Peter Levin.
Creator: David Jacobs.
Art Director: Ned Parsons.

MARRIED: THE FIRST YEAR — 60 minutes — CBS — February 28, 1979 – March 21, 1979. 4 episodes.

766   THE MARTIAN CHRONICLES

Science Fiction. A three-part miniseries, based on the novel by Ray Bradbury, about man's first look at the beauties, mysteries and terrors of Mars. Part one, set in January 1999, focuses on NATO'S plans to explore and eventually colonize the Red Planet. Earth's first two manned probes mysteriously disappear moments after touching down on the Martian surface. Colonel John Wilder organizes a third expedition to find some explanation for the previous disasters and to discover if there is life on Mars. The concluding two episodes depict man's colonization of Mars — and a cataclysmic war that destroys Earth and shows the surviving colonists attempting to preserve and repopulate their species.

CAST

Col. John Wilder	Rock Hudson
Ruth Wilder, his wife	Gayle Hunnicutt
Father Stone, the priest who fears the Martians	Roddy McDowall
Father Peregrine, the priest who accepts the Martians	Fritz Weaver
Capt. Arthur Black	Nicholas Hammond
Genevieve, "the sexiest woman on Mars"	Bernadette Peters
Capt. Jeff Spender	Bernie Casey
Capt. Sam Parkhill	Darren McGavin
Ylla, a Martian	Maggie Wright
Anna Lustig, a settler on Mars	Maria Schell
Capt. David Lustig	Michael Anderson, Jr.
Marilyn Becker, Arthur's girlfriend	Linda Lou Allen
Captain Briggs	John Cassidy
Captain Conover	Richard Heffer
Capt. Bill Wilder, John's brother	Burrell Tucker
Captain Hinkston	Vadim Glowna
Capt. Nathaniel York	Richard Oldfield
Lafe Lustig, Anna's husband	Wolfgang Reichmann
Elma Parkhill, Sam's wife	Joyce Van Patten
Ben Driscoll, a settler on Mars	Christopher Connelly
Peter Hathaway, a scientist	Barry Morse
Alice Hathaway, Peter's wife	Nyree Dawn Porter
Mr. K, the first Martian	James Faulkner

Narrator: Bill Brown.
Music: Stanley Myers.
Executive Producer: Charles Fries, Dick Berg.
Producer: Anthony Donally, Milton Subotsky.
Writer: Richard Matheson.
Director: Michael Anderson.
Special Effects: John Stears.

THE MARTIAN CHRONICLES — 2 hours — NBC — January 17, 1980 – January 29, 1980. 3 episodes.

767   THE MARTY FELDMAN COMEDY MACHINE

Comedy. A blend of contemporary humor with that of the Max Sennett era of slapstick comedy.

Starring: Marty Feldman.
Regulars: Barbara Feldon, Orson Welles, Spike Milligan, Fred Smoot, Lennie Schultz, Thelma Houston, Fred Roman.

THE MARTY FELDMAN COMEDY MACHINE — 30 minutes — ABC — April 12, 1972 – August 23, 1972.

768   THE MARTY ROBBINS SPOTLITE

Variety. The program pays tribute to Country and Western performers by spotlighting a guest and his music.

Host: Marty Robbins.
Executive Producer: Bill Graham.
Producer: Reg Dunlap, Ralph Emery.
Writer: Paul Elliott, Bill Graham.

THE MARTY ROBBINS SPOTLITE — 30 minutes — Syndicated 1978.

769   MARY

Variety. A comedy-accented series that spotlights the talents of Mary Tyler Moore as a comedienne, singer and dancer.

Hostess: Mary Tyler Moore.
Regulars: Dick Shawn, Judy Kahan, James Hampton, Swoosie Kurtz, Michael Keaton, David Letterman, Leonard Barr, Jack O'Leary.
Orchestra: Alf Clausen.
Producer: Tom Patchett, Jay Tarses.
Director: Rob Iscove.
Choreographer: Tony Stevens.

MARY — 60 minutes — CBS — September 24, 1978 – October 8, 1978. 11 episodes were produced but only 3 aired.

770   MARY HARTMAN, MARY HARTMAN

Serial. The series, set in the Woodland Hills section of fictional Fernwood, Ohio, is a satirization of life as seen through the endless frustrations of Mary Hartman, a pretty, typical middle-aged housewife and mother.

CAST

Mary Hartman	Louise Lasser
Tom Hartman, her husband, an auto plant assembly line worker	Greg Mullavey
Heather Hartman, her daughter	Claudia Lamb
Cathy Schumway, Mary's sister	Debralee Scott
George Schumway, Mary's father	Philip Bruns
Martha Schumway, Mary's mother	Dody Goodman
Loretta Haggers, Mary's neighbor	Mary Kay Place
Charlie Haggers, Loretta's husband	Graham Jarvis
Raymond Larkin, Mary's senile grandfather	Victor Kilian

Dennis Foley, the police sergeant who falls in love with Mary	Bruce Solomon
Blanche Fedders, Mary's neighbor	Reva Rose
Leroy Fedders, Blanche's husband	Norman Alden
Mae Olinski, the sexy auto plant bookkeeper	Salome Jens
Roberta Walashak, the social worker	Samantha Harper
Detective Mike Johnson (later Det. H.V. Johnson)	Ron Feinberg
Fanny Krovkshanke, Raymond's friend	Sudi Bond
Steve Fletcher, Cathy's boyfriend	Ed Begley, Jr.
Davy Jessup, the mass murderer of the Lombardi family, their two goats and eight chickens	Will Selzer
Police Lieutenant Trask	Billy Beck
Judge Earl Clifford Stanley	Ivor Francis
Clete Meizenheimer, the TV reporter for Channel 6	Michael Lembeck
Harold Clemens, the newspaper reporter	Archie Hahn
Dr. Ferman, Mary's physician	Oliver Clark
Mona McKenzie, the sexy sex therapist	Sallie Janes
Muriel Haggers, Charlie's hateful ex-wife	L.C. Downey
Tiny, the auto plant foreman	Hugh Gilian
Clyde Munsey, Loretta's record company manager	Harry Basch
Betty McCullough, Mary's neighbor	Vivian Blaine
Ed McCullough, Betty's son	Larry Haddon
Howard McCullough, Betty's son	Beeson Carroll
Jimmy Joe Jeeter, the eight-year-old minister	Sparky Marcus
Merle Jeeter, Jimmy's father	Dabney Coleman
The Help Line Lady	Beverly Sanders
Father Frank DeMarco	Vincent Baggetta
Billy Twelvetrees, Martha's real father (she was adopted)	John Verros
Annie "Tippytoes" Wylie, the lesbian friend of Tom's	Gloria De Haven
Gore Vidal, the author seeking to write a book on Mary's life	Himself
Patty Gimble, Mary's friend	Susan Browning
Garth Gimble, Patty's husband, a wife beater	Martin Mull
Barth Gimble, Garth's twin brother	Martin Mull
Garth Gimble, Jr., Patty's son	Eric Shea
Mac Slattery, the truck driver	Dennis Burkley
Cookie LaRue, Patty's cellmate (imprisoned for killing Garth with a Christmas tree)	Beverly Garland
Lila, Merle's maid	Marjorie Battles
Howie Freeze, Cathy's boyfriend, a reporter for WJGL radio	Sid Weisman
Tex, an employee at the auto plant	Sid Haig
Dewey Johnson, the auto plant janitor	Richard Ward
Vernon Bales, the auto plant manager	David Bird
The Capri Lounge bartender	Robert Stoneman
Big Foot's Child	Matthew Laborteaux

Brian Adams, the man who arranged for Cathy to father his baby	John Fink
Christine Adams, Brian's wife	Andra Akers
Dr. Andrew Ackerman, the head of the Fernwood Psychiatric Ward*	Howard Morton
Wanda Rittenhouse, a patient (later Merle's wife)	Marian Mercer
Chester Markham, a patient	John Heffernan
Mrs. Defarge, a patient	Nedra Volz
Ronald Drayton, a patient	Robert Snively
Stuart Danville, a patient	Barry Greenberg
Dr. Williams	Howard Hesseman
Dr. Fratkis	Geno Conforti
Voice in the opening calling "Mary Hartman, Mary Hartman"	Dody Goodman

Guests: Dr. Joyce Brothers, Dinah Shore, David Susskind, Merv Griffin.

Mary's address: 343 Bratner Avenue.

Martha's address: 4309 Bratner Avenue.

Loretta's goldfish: Conway and Twitty.

Music: Earle Hagen.
Music Supervision: Bobby Knight.
Executive Producer: Norman Lear.
Producer: Lew Gallo, Vivi Knight, Perry Krauss, Eugenie Ross-Leming, Brad Buckner.
Director: Joan Darling, Jim Drake, Mack Bing, Art Wolff, Bob Lally, Nessa Hyams, Giovanni Nigro, Harlene Kim Friedman, Jack Heller, Dennis Klein, Hal Alexander.
Creator: Gail Parent, Ann Marcus, Jerry Adelman, Daniel Gregory Browne.

MARY HARTMAN, MARY HARTMAN — 30 minutes — Syndicated 1976. 325 episodes.

*In the second season opener, Mary is committed to the psychiatric ward for observation after she has a nervous breakdown on *The David Susskind Show.*

771   THE MARY TYLER MOORE HOUR

Comedy-Variety. The series, which is sort of a show within a show, focuses on the on- and off-the-air life of Mary McKinnon, a television performer whose program, *The Mary McKinnon Show*, provides a vehicle for guests to perform; and whose off-camera life provides the backdrop for the comedy play and interactions of Mary's staff and friends.

CAST

Mary McKinnon	Mary Tyler Moore
Harry Sinclair, her producer	Michael Lombard
Iris Chapman, her secretary	Joyce Van Patten
Kenneth Christy, the usher	Michael Keaton
Artie Miller, the writer-director	Ron Rifkin

Crystal, Mary's housekeeper, first show	Doris Roberts
Ruby, Mary's housekeeper, series	Dody Goodman
Mort Zimmick, the head writer	Bob Ramsen

Music: Alf Clausen.
Theme: "Love Is All Around" by Sonny Curtis.
Special Musical Material: Stan Freeman.
Producer: Perry Lafferty.
Director: Robert Scheerer, Noam Pitlik.
Choreographer: Tony Stevens.

THE MARY TYLER MOORE HOUR — 60 minutes — CBS — March 4, 1979 – May 6, 1979. 10 episodes. Returned with one final episode on June 6, 1979.

772   THE MARY TYLER MOORE SHOW

Comedy. The series, set in Minneapolis, Minnesota, follows the misadventures, joys, sorrows and romantic heartaches of Mary Richards, a beautiful young bachelorette.

Stories depict: her home life (at 119 North Weatherly, Apartment D) with her friends, Rhoda Morgenstern, the upstairs tenant who is an interior decorator at Hempel's Department Store, and Phyllis Lindstrom, a busybody and the owner of the building; and her working life in the newsroom of WJM-TV, Channel 12, where, as the associate producer of *The Six O'Clock News* program, she struggles to function in the man's world of an irascible producer (Lou Grant), a soft-hearted newswriter (Murray Slaughter) and a narcissistic anchorman (Ted Baxter).

CAST

Mary Richards	Mary Tyler Moore
Rhoda Morgenstern, her friend	Valerie Harper
Lou Grant, the producer	Edward Asner
Murray Slaughter, the writer	Gavin MacLeod
Ted Baxter, the anchorman	Ted Knight
Phyllis Lindstrom, Mary's friend	Cloris Leachman
Bess Lindstrom, Phyllis' daughter	Lisa Gerritsen
Gordon Howard (Gordie), the station weatherman	John Amos
Ida Morgenstern, Rhoda's mother	Nancy Walker
Martin Morgenstern, Rhoda's father	Harold Gould
Debbie Morgenstern, Rhoda's sister	Liberty Williams
Georgette Franklin, Ted's romantic interest and later his wife	Georgia Engel
Sue Anne Nivens, the host of Channel 12's *Happy Homemaker Show*	Betty White
Dotty Richards, Mary's mother	Nanette Fabray

McMillan and Wife. Susan Saint James and Rock Hudson.

Make Room for Daddy. Danny Thomas and Marjorie Lord.

Mary. Mary Tyler Moore.

Mary Hartman, Mary Hartman. Front, from left, Philip Bruns and Debralee Scott. Standing, from left, Greg Mullavey, Claudia Lamb, Dody Goodman, Louise Lasser and Victor Kilian.

Walter Reed Richards,
    Mary's father   Bill Quinn
Marie Slaughter, Murray's
    wife   Joyce Bulifant
Edie Grant, Lou's ex-wife   Priscilla Morrill
Pete, a news staff
    member   Benjamin Chauley
Andy Rivers, Mary's
    occasional date   John Gabriel
Charlene McGuire, Lou's
    girlfriend   Sheree North
David Baxter, Ted and Georgette's
    adopted son   Robbie Rist
The bartender at the Happy
    Hour Bar   Peter Hobbs
Howard Gordon, Edie's second
    husband   Brad Trumbull
Janey Grant, Lou's daughter   Nora Heflin
Philly, Lou's friend   Dick Balduzzi
Tony, the bartender at the
    Ballantine Bar (where
    Charlene sings)   Chuck Bergansky
Joe Warner, Mary's boyfriend   Ted Bessell
Flo Meredith, Mary's aunt   Eileen Heckart
Chuckles the Clown, a performer
    on Channel 12   Mark Gordon
Paula Kovacs, Mary's neighbor
    (final season)   Penny Marshall
Mary's landlord (final
    season)   Claude Stroud
WJM-TV announcer   Lee Vines
Bonnie Slaughter, Murray's
    daughter   Sherry Hursey
Fred, Mary's apartment
    building super   Ted Lehman

Music: Patrick Williams.
Theme: "Love Is All Around" writ-
    ten and sung by Sonny Curtis.
Executive Producer: James L.
    Brooks, Allan Burns.
Producer: Stan Daniels, Ed Wein-
    berger.
Director: Jay Sandrich (most of
    the series), Marjorie Mullen,
    James Burrows, Harry Mas-
    trogeorge, Mel Ferber, Doug
    Rogers, Joan Darling.
*Title Visualization Sequences Di-
    rector:* Reza S. Badiyi.
Creator: James L. Brooks, Allan
    Burns.

THE MARY TYLER MOORE
SHOW — 30 minutes — CBS —
September 19, 1970 – September
3, 1977. 147 episodes. Syndicated.
Spin-off series: *Phyllis* and *Rhoda*.

773   M*A*S*H

Comedy Drama. The series, set in
Korea during the war in the early
1950s, follows the antics of the
medical staff of the 4077th
M*A*S*H (Mobile Army Surgical
Hospital).

CAST

Captain Benjamin Franklin
    Pierce (Hawkeye), the
    chief surgeon   Alan Alda
Captain John "Trapper John"
    McIntire, his friend   Wayne Rogers
Lt. Col. Henry Blake,
    the C.O.   McLean Stevenson
Major Margaret "Hot Lips" Houlihan,
    the head nurse   Loretta Swit
Col. Sherman Potter (replaced
    Blake)   Harry Morgan

Capt. B.J. Hunnicutt (replaced
    McIntire)   Mike Farrell
Major Frank Burns   Larry Linville
Major Charles Emerson Winchester
    III   David Ogden Stiers
Corporal Walter "Radar"
    O'Reilly   Gary Burghoff
Father John Francis
    Mulcahy   George Morgan
                      William Christopher
Nurse (Lt.) Maggie Dish   Karen Philipp
Dr. "Spearchucker" Jones   Timothy Brown
Nurse (Lt.) Ginger Ballis   Odessa Cleveland
Corporal Maxwell Klinger   Jamie Farr
Ho-Jon, Hawkeye's Korean
    houseboy   Patrick Adiarte
Ugly John, the anesthetist   John Orchard
Gen. Hamilton Hammond, the
    chief medical officer   G. Wood
Nurse (Lt.) Leslie Scorch   Linda Meiklejohn
Nurse (Lt.) Jones   Barbara Brownell
Nurse Louise Anderson   Kelly Jean Peters
Supply Sgt. Zale   Johnny Haymer
Pvt. Luther Rizzo   G.V. Bailey
Nurse Maggie Cutler   Marcia Strassman
                          Lynnette Mettey
Gen. Brandon Clayton   Herbert Voland
The company cook   Joseph Perry
Mr. Kwang, the bartender at
    the officers club   Leland Sung
Colonel Flagg, the hard-nosed
    C.I.A. agent   Edward Winter
Major Sidney Freedman,
    the compassionate
    psychiatrist   Allan Arbus
Nurse Bigelow   Enid Kent
Nurse Abel   Judy Farrell
Major Donald Penobscott (married
    Margaret on March 15,
    1977)   Beeson Carroll
Nurse Baker   Jean Powell
                       Lynne Marie Stewart
                          Linda Kelsey
Nurse Mary Jo Walsh   Mary Jo Catlett
Nurse Gaynor   Carol Locatell
Nurse Preston   Patricia Sturges
Nurse   Shari Saba
Nurse Mendenhal   Shelly Long
Nurse   Jennifer Davis
Nurse   Gwen Farrell
Nurse   Connie Izay
P.A. system voice   Sal Viscuso

Music: Johnny Mandel, Duane
    Tatro, Lionel Newman, Earle
    Hagen.
Executive Producer: Larry Gel-
    bart, Gene Reynolds, Burt Met-
    calfe.
Producer: Alan Katz, Don Reo,
    John Rappaport, Gene Reyn-
    olds, Jim Mulligan.
Director: Charles S. Dubin, Hy
    Averback, E.W. Swackhamer,
    James Sheldon, William Wiard,
    Jackie Cooper, Alan Alda, Gene
    Reynolds, Harry Morgan, Burt
    Metcalfe, Joan Darling, William
    Jurgenson, Larry Gelbart, Mike
    Farrell, Loretta Swit, Jamie Farr,
    George Tyne, Tony Mordente.

M*A*S*H — 30 minutes — CBS —
Premiered: September 17, 1972.

774   MASQUERADE
        PARTY

Game. Five celebrity panelists attempt to identify elaborately dis-

guised guest personalities. Each
panelist is permitted to ask five
questions of the guest. Each second of questioning scores one
dollar to a maximum of three
hundred dollars. At the end of
five-minute segments, or at any
time in between, panelists may
hazard a guess as to the identity
of the guest. Whether correct or
incorrect, the money that is established is donated to charity.

Host: Bud Collyer, Eddie Brack-
    en, Peter Donald, Bert Parks,
    Robert Q. Lewis, Douglas Ed-
    wards.
Panelists: Ilka Chase, Phil Silvers,
    Adele Jergens, Peter Donald,
    Madge Evans, Buff Cobb, John
    Young, Ogden Nash, Johnny
    Johnston, Betsy Palmer, Frank
    Palmer, Jonathan Winters, Jinx
    Falkenberg, Pat Carroll, Faye
    Emerson, Gloria De Haven,
    Audrey Meadows, Sam Levin-
    son, Lee Bowman.
Announcer: Don Morrow, Wil-
    liam T. Lazar.
Producer: Herb Wolf.

MASQUERADE PARTY — 30 minutes. NBC — July 14, 1952 –
August 25, 1952. CBS — June 22,
1953 – September 13, 1954.
ABC — September 29, 1954 – December 15, 1956. CBS — August
4, 1958 – September 15, 1958.
CBS — November 2, 1959 – January 18, 1960.

775   MASQUERADE
        PARTY

Game. Three celebrity panelists
attempt to identify an elaborately
disguised guest from a series of
indirect question and answer
rounds. Once the questioning is
completed, two contestants are
chosen from the studio audience
and asked who they think the
guest is. The identity of the guest
is revealed and contestants receive merchandise prizes if they
are correct.

Host: Richard Dawson.
Panelists: Bill Bixby, Lee Meri-
    wether, Nipsey Russell.
Announcer: Jay Stewart.
Music: Sheldon Allman.
Executive Producer: Stefan Hatos,
    Monty Hall.
Producer: Alan Gilbert.
Director: Lee Behar.

MASQUERADE PARTY — 30 minutes — Syndicated 1974.

776   MASTERPIECE
        THEATRE

Anthology. The American title for
a series of British-produced
serials.

Host: Alistair Cooke.

Included:
Madame Bovary. A four-part adaptation of Gustave Flaubert's

1857 novel about the adventures
of Emma Bovary, an adulterous
Frenchwoman.

CAST

Emma Bovary   Francesca Annis
Charles Bovary   Tom Conti
Rouault   Richard Beale
Mrs. Bovary   Kathleen Heleme
Felicite   Gabrielle Lloyd
Father Bournisien   David Walter
Leon   Brian Stirner
Homais   Ray Smith
Nastasie   Elizabeth Proud
Rodolphe   Denis Lill

Sunset Song. A six-part drama
based on Lewis Grassic Gibbon's
novel about an adolescent girl
coming of age in turn-of-the-
century Scotland.

CAST

Chris Guthrie   Vivien Heilborn
John Guthrie   Andrew Keir
Jean Guthrie   Edith Macarthur
Will Guthrie   Paul Young
Rob Guthrie   Derek Anders
Reverend Gibbon   Charles Kearney
Evan   James Grant
Mrs. Melon   Jean Taylor Smith

Poldark. A sixteen-part romantic
adventure, set in Europe during
the 1700s, that focuses on the life
of Ross Poldark, a dashing war
veteran in the period immediately following the American
revolution.

CAST

Ross Poldark   Robin Ellis
Elizabeth   Jill Townsend
Demelza   Angharad Rees
Verity   Norma Streader
Zacky   Forbes Collins
Jud   Paul Curran
Charles   Frank Middlemoss

Cakes and Ale. A three-part
adaptation of the Somerset
Maugham story about a promis-
cuous English barmaid and the
men in her life.

CAST

Rosie, the barmaid   Judy Cornwell
Willie   Michael Hordern
Driffield   Mike Pratt
Lord George Kemp   James Grout

Shoulder to Shoulder. A six-part
drama, produced by the BBC, that
shows how women fought for
and won the right to vote in England.

CAST

Pankhurst   Michael Gough
Emmeline   Sian Phillips
Christabell   Patricia Quinn
Sylvia   Angela Down
Kier Hardie   Fulton MacKay
Mrs. Lawrence   Sheila Allen

MASTERPIECE THEATRE — 60
minutes — PBS — Premiered: January 10, 1971.

777   THE MATCH GAME

Game. Two teams are composed
of one celebrity captain and two
noncelebrity contestants. An in-

complete sentence that contains a blank is read and the players each fill in the blank with the word or words each feels will best complete the thought. Answers are revealed and if two players match by using the same word, twenty-five points are scored. If the celebrity matches the two players, fifty points are scored. The team first to score one hundred points is the winner (their points are transferred into dollars and the money divided between the two contestants).

Host: Gene Rayburn.
Announcer: Johnny Olsen.
Producer: Mark Goodson, Bill Todman, Jean Kopelman.

THE MATCH GAME — 25 minutes — NBC — December 31, 1962 – September 20, 1969.

778   THE MATCH GAME

Game. A revised version of the previous title. An incomplete sentence, which contains a blank, is read to six celebrities who fill in the blank by writing the word or words each feels will best complete the thought. Of the two contestants that compete, one is asked to verbally give his response to the question. For each celebrity he matches (same word used) he scores one point. His opponent next receives a chance at play and the contestant with the highest score at the end of two rounds is the winner and receives $250.

Host: Gene Rayburn.
Announcer: Johnny Olsen.
Regular Panelists: Richard Dawson, Charles Nelson Reilly, Brett Somers.
Music: Score Productions.
Producer: Mark Goodson, Bill Todman.
Director: Marc Breslow.

THE MATCH GAME — 30 minutes — CBS — June 25, 1973 – April 20, 1979. Syndicated first run.

779   MATCH GAME P.M.

Game. A syndicated, prime-time version of the CBS series, *Match Game*, which see previous title for format.

Host: Gene Rayburn.
Regulars: Brett Somers, Charles Nelson Reilly.
Announcer: Johnny Olsen.
Music: Michael Malone.
Producer: Mark Goodson, Bill Todman.
Director: Marc Breslow.

MATCH GAME P.M. — 30 minutes — Syndicated 1975.

780   MATT HELM

Crime Drama. The investigations of Matt Helm, a dashing U.S. government intelligence agent turned private detective.

CAST
Matt Helm	Tony Franciosa
Claire Kronski, his lawyer and romantic interest	Laraine Stephens
Lieutenant Hanrahan, L.A.P.D.	Gene Evans
Ethel, Matt's telephone answering service girl	Jeff Donnell

Music: Morton Stevens, Jerrold Immel, John Parker.
Executive Producer: Irving Allen.
Producer: Buzz Kulick, Ken Pettus, Charles B. Fitzsimons.
Director: Earl Bellamy, Richard Benedict, Don Weis, John Newland, Buzz Kulick.

MATT HELM — 60 minutes — ABC — September 20, 1975 – November 3, 1975. The 90-minute pilot film aired on ABC on May 7, 1975.

781   MATT LINCOLN

Drama. The cases of Matt Lincoln, a Los Angeles psychiatrist who practices preventive psychiatry and struggles to assist people in the early stages of emotional distress to avoid further, more complicated treatment.

CAST
Matt Lincoln	Vince Edwards
Tag, his assistant	Chelsea Brown
Jimmy, his assistant	Felton Perry
Ann, his assistant	June Harding
Kevin, his assistant	Michael Larrain

Music: Oliver Nelson.
Executive Producer: Frank Pierce.
Producer: Irving Elman.

MATT LINCOLN — 60 minutes — ABC — September 24, 1970 – January 14, 1971. The pilot film, "Dial Hot Line," in which Vince Edwards portrayed David Leopold, aired on ABC on March 8, 1970.

782   MAUDE

Comedy. The series, set in Tuckahoe, New York, follows the life of Maude Findlay, an outspoken liberal married for the fourth time. Episodes relate her struggles to solve the incidents that creep in, disrupt and threaten to destroy her attempts to achieve a lasting relationship with her husband. A spin-off from *All in the Family.*

CAST
Maude Findlay	Beatrice Arthur
Walter Findlay, her husband, the owner of "Findlay's Friendly Appliance Store"	Bill Macy
Carol Trener, Maude's daughter (divorced)	Adrienne Barbeau
Philip Trener, Carol's son	Brian Morris Kraig Metzinger
Arthur Harmon, their neighbor, a doctor	Conrad Bain
Vivian Harmon, Arthur's wife	Rue McClanahan
Florida Evans, the Findlay's maid (early episodes)	Esther Rolle
Henry Evans, Florida's husband	John Amos
Nell Naugatuck, the Findlay's maid (later episodes)	Hermione Baddeley
Victoria Butterfield, the Findlay's maid (after Nell)	Marlene Warfield
Bert Beasley, married Nell (Nov. 22, 1976)	J. Pat O'Malley
Chris, Carol's romantic interest for a short time	Fred Grandy
Dr. Hubie Binder, Arthur's friend	Larry Gelman
Sam, the bartender	Jan Arvan
Fred, the bartender	Fred Zuckert

The Findlay's address: 39 Crenshaw Street (later: 271 Elm Street).

Music: Theme only, "And Then There's Maude" by Alan and Marilyn Bergman (lyrics) and Dave Grusin (music).
Theme Vocal: Donny Hathaway.
Executive Producer: Norman Lear, Rod Parker.
Producer: Rod Parker, Bob Weiskopf, Bob Schiller.
Director: Robert H. Livingston, Bill Hobin, Bud Yorkin, Hal Cooper.
Creator: Norman Lear.

MAUDE — 30 minutes — CBS — September 12, 1972 – August 29, 1978. Syndicated. Spin-off series: *Good Times.*

783   MAVERICK

Western. The exploits of brothers Bret and Bart Maverick, self-centered, unconventional and untrustworthy gentlemen gamblers. Seeking rich prey, they roam the West of the 1880s, and more often than not, assist people they find in distress.

Though considered a western adventure, *Maverick* is actually a spoof of westerns. The less-than-honorable intentions of the Mavericks are meant to satirize the square Western Code and square-headed lawmen.

CAST
Bret Maverick	James Garner
Bart Maverick	Jack Kelly
Beau Maverick, their British cousin	Roger Moore
Brent Maverick, their other brother	Robert Colbert
Samantha Crawford, a con-artist friend of Bret and Bart	Diane Brewster
Dandy Jim Buckley, a con-artist friend	Efrem Zimbalist, Jr.
Bauregard "Pappy" Maverick, Bret, Bart and Brent's father	James Garner
Gentleman Jack Darby, a con-artist friend	Richard Long

Music: David Buttolph.
Producer: Roy Huggins, William T. Orr, Howie Horwitz.
Director: Robert Altman, Stuart Heisler, Richard Sarafian, Budd Boetticher, James Garner, André De Toth, Paul Stewart, Paul Henried, Robert Douglas, Lawrence Dobkin, Virgil W. Vogel, Charles R. Rondeau, Michael O'Herlihy, Irving J. Moore, Leslie H. Martinson, Alan Crosland, Jr., William F. Claxton, Abner Biberman, Richard Benedict, Richard L. Bare, George WaGGner, Lee Sholem, Arthur Lubin, Paul Landers, Charles Haas, Douglas Heyes.
Creator: Roy Huggins.

MAVERICK — 60 minutes — ABC — September 22, 1957 – July 8, 1962. 124 episodes. Syndicated. Spin-off series: *Young Maverick.*

784   MAYBERRY R.F.D.

Comedy. The simple pleasures and trying times of Sam Jones, a full-time farmer and part-time city councilman in Mayberry, North Carolina. A spin-off from *The Andy Griffith Show.*

CAST
Sam Jones, a widower	Ken Berry
Mike Jones, his son	Buddy Foster
Millie Swanson, Sam's girlfriend	Arlene Golonka
Goober Pyle, the gas station attendant	George Lindsey
Bee Taylor, Sam's housekeeper	Frances Bavier
Howard Sprague, the county clerk	Jack Dodson
Emmet Clark, the fix-it shop owner	Paul Hartman
Martha Clark, Emmet's wife	Mary Lansing
Aunt Alice, Sam's housekeeper (later episodes)	Alice Ghostley
Ralph, Mike's friend	Richard Steele
Arnold, Mike's friend	Sheldon Collins

Music: Earle Hagen.
Executive Producer: Andy Griffith, Richard O. Linke.
Producer: Bob Ross.

MAYBERRY R.F.D. — 30 minutes — CBS — September 23, 1968 – September 6, 1971. 78 episodes. Syndicated.

785   ME AND MAXX

Comedy. The series, set in New York City, focuses on the relationship between Norman Davis, a divorced womanizer, and Maxx Davis, his seldom-seen,* precocious eleven-year-old daughter. The girl suddenly becomes his responsibility when his ex-wife unexpectedly appoints him as her guardian. Episodes focus on the disruption Maxx causes in Norman's life, and his attempts to change his life-style to accommodate her. (Norman heads Empire Tickets, a service that provides tickets for various events.)

CAST
Norman Davis	Joe Santos
Maxx Davis, his daughter	Melissa Michaelson

Barbara, Norman's business
  partner   Jenny Sullivan
Mitch Russell, Norman's friend Jim Weston
Gary, the elevator operator   Denny Evans

Music: Michael Lloyd.
Theme: "Is It Because of Love?"
  arranged by John D'Andrea.
Theme Vocal: Lenore O'Malley.
Supervising Producer: Don Van
  Atta.
Executive Producer: James
  Komack.
Producer: George Tricker, Neil
  Rosen, Stan Cutler.
Producer (New York Outdoor Se-
  quences): John E. Quill.
Associate Producer: Phyllis
  Nelson.
Writer: James Komack, George
  Tricker, Neil Rosen, Mike
  Marmer, Stan Cutler.
Director: Herbert Kenwith, James
  Komack, Don Van Atta.
Associate Director: Randy Win-
  burn.
Art Director: Ron Christopher.

ME AND MAXX—30 minutes—
NBC—March 22, 1980–April 5,
1980. 4 episodes. May 30, 1980–
July 25, 1980. 5 episodes. Re-
broadcasts: September 5, 1980–
September 12, 1980.

*Norman walked out on his wife
when Maxx was born because he felt
he couldn't handle the responsibility. He saw his daughter four times
in eleven years. Eleven years later,
Norman's ex-wife decides it's his
turn to care for Maxx.

786   ME AND THE CHIMP

Comedy. The series, set in San
Pascal, California, follows the
misadventures of Mike Reynolds,
a dentist, as he struggles to adjust
to Buttons, a chimpanzee his
children found in a park and
adopted. (The chimp is named
after his continual habit of pressing buttons and has escaped from
an Air Force test lab.)

CAST
Mike Reynolds, the father   Ted Bessell
Liz Reynolds, his wife   Anita Gillette
Kitty Reynolds, their daughter Kami Cotler
Scott Reynolds, their son   Scott Kolden
Buttons, the chimpanzee   Jackie

Music: Artie Butler, Jerry Fielding.
Executive Producer-Creator:
  Garry K. Marshall.
Producer-Director: Alan Rafkin.

ME AND THE CHIMP—30 min-
utes—CBS—January 13, 1972–
May 18, 1972. 13 episodes.

787   MEDICAL CENTER

Drama. The series, set at University Medical Center in Los
Angeles, follows the experiences
of two doctors: Paul Lochner,
administrative surgeon, and Joe
Gannon, professor of surgery.
Adult-oriented and technically

accurate, episodes depict the
problems that face doctors in a
large city hospital.

CAST
Dr. Paul Lochner   James Daly
Dr. Joe Gannon (pilot
  film)   Richard Bradford
Dr. Joe Gannon (series)   Chad Everett
Nurse Chambers   Jayne Meadows
Dr. Bartlett   Corinne Comacho
Nurse Holmby   Barbara Baldavin
Nurse Courtland   Chris Huston
Nurse Higby   Catherine Ferrar
Nurse Murphy   Jane Dulo
Nurse Wilcox   Audrey Totter
Nurse Crawford   Virginia Hawkins
Nurse Bascomb   Louise Fitch
Dr. Corelli   Robert Walden
Jenny Lochner, Paul's daughter Tyne Daly
Dr. Bolton   Jack Garner
Nurse Loring   Nancy Priddy
Dr. Weller   Eugene Peterson
Dr. Holmby   Paul Stewart
Anesthesiologist   Sheldon Coburn
                       Ron Masak
Dr. Barnes   Fred Holliday
Lieutenant Samuels,
  L.A.P.D.   Martin E. Brooks
Sergeant Boyce, L.A.P.D. Jonathan Lippe
Dr. Grover   Sidney Clute
Dr. Poens   Boyd Berlind
Dr. Faraday   Herb Armstrong
Resident   Doug Pence
Resident   Richard Stuart

Music: Lalo Schifrin, George
  Romanis, Philip Springer, John
  Parker.
Theme: "Medical Center" by Lalo
  Schifrin.
Executive Producer: Frank
  Glicksman, Al C. Ward.
Producer: Don Brinkley.
Director: Daniel Petrie, Boris
  Sagal, William Graham, Mi-
  chael Caffey, Vincent Sherman,
  Michael O'Herlihy, Christian I.
  Nyby II, Charles S. Dubin, E.W.
  Swackhamer, Chad Everett,
  Ralph Senensky, Jud Taylor.

MEDICAL CENTER—60 minutes
—CBS—September 24, 1969–
September 6, 1976. 144 episodes.
Syndicated. The two-hour pilot
film, titled "U.M.C.," aired on CBS
on April 17, 1969.

788   MEDICAL STORY

Anthology. Dramatizations that
stress an open, human approach
to the problems of medicine as
seen through the eyes of the doctor rather than the patient.

Music: Richard Shores, Jerry
  Goldsmith, Arthur Morton.
Executive Producer: David
  Gerber, Abby Mann.
Producer: Christopher Morgan.
Director: Gary Nelson, Robert
  Collins, Paul Wendkos, Richard
  Benedict, Ralph Senensky.
Creator: David Gerber, Abby
  Mann.

Included:
The God Syndrome. The story of
a brilliant surgeon and his attempts to deal with his patients as

human beings rather than just
medical challenges.
Cast: Dr. Paul Brandon: Tony
  Musante; Dr. Charles Galpin:
  Richard Basehart; Susan
  Stewart: Leslie Charleson; Joe
  Hudson: Broderick Crawford;
  Dr. Kendrick: Don Galloway.

Us Against the World. The story
focuses on the problems faced by
three female surgeons in a busy
hospital.
Cast: Sunny: Meredith Baxter
  Birney; Audrey: Donna Mills;
  Hope: Christine Belford; Kim:
  Linda Purl; Ted: Sam Groom;
  Peter: Michael LeClair; Dan-
  ziger: Theodore Bikel.

Million Dollar Baby. The story of
Alma Geary, a 22-year-old blind
woman who brings a million dollar malpractice suit against the
doctor who delivered her prema-
turely, claiming that his improper
use of pure oxygen caused her
loss of sight.
Cast: Dr. Amos Winkler: John Forsythe; Liz Winkler: Geraldine
  Brooks; Alma Geary: Catherine
  Burns; Raymond Steller: Farley
  Granger; Mrs. Taber: Whitney
  Blake; Daniel Codroy: David
  White.

MEDICAL STORY—60 minutes—
NBC—September 4, 1975–January 8, 1976.

789   MEL AND SUSAN TOGETHER

Musical Variety.

Hosts: Mel Tillis, Susan Anton.
Orchestra: Bob Rozario.
Executive Producer: The Os-
  mond Brothers.
Producer: Jerry McPhie, Toby
  Martin.
Director: Jack Regas.

MEL AND SUSAN TOGETHER—
30 minutes—ABC—April 22,
1978–May 13, 1978. 4 programs.

790   THE MELBA MOORE-CLIFTON DAVIS SHOW

Variety. Music, songs, dances and
comedy sketches set against the
background of a Manhattan
brownstone.

Hosts: Melba Moore, Clifton
  Davis.
Regulars: Ron Carey, Timmie Ro-
  gers, Dick Libertini, Liz Torres.
Announcer: Johnny Olsen.
Orchestra: Charles H. Coleman.
Producer: Stan Harris.
Writer: Jack Burns, Ken Friedman,
  Hal Goodman, Al Goodman,
  George Yanok.
Director: Stan Harris.
Choreographer: Tony Mordente.

THE MELBA MOORE-CLIFTON
DAVIS SHOW—60 minutes—
CBS—June 7, 1972–July 5, 1972.
5 programs.

791   THE MELTING POT

Cooking. Guest celebrities assist
in the preparation of various
forms of cooking.

Host: Orson Bean.
Music: Doug Dowdle.
Producer: Fred Rheinstein.
Director: Fred Rheinstein.

THE MELTING POT—30 min-
utes—Syndicated 1978.

792   THE MEMORY GAME

Game. Five women begin competition with fifty dollars. Each is
presented with a packet of five
questions and given twenty seconds to study them. At the end of
the time, the questions are taken
back and the host asks one player
a question. If she cannot answer
it, she is permitted to pass it to
any other player by calling her
number (1, 2, 3, 4 or 5). The
player who correctly answers it
scores five dollars; if a player fails
to correctly answer it, five dollars
is deducted from her total. The
player who was last to give a correct answer becomes the first
player to receive the next question. The player with the highest
cash score at the end of two
rounds is the winner and keeps
what she has earned.

Host: Joe Garagiola.
Announcer: Johnny Olsen.
Music: Score Productions.

THE MEMORY GAME—30 min-
utes—NBC—February 15, 1971–
July 30, 1971. 110 programs.

793   THE MEN

Mystery-Adventure. The overall
title for three rotating series: *Assignment: Vienna, The Delphi
Bureau* and *Jigsaw.* See individual titles for information.

THE MEN—60 minutes—ABC—
September 21, 1972–September
1, 1973. 24 episodes.

794   MEN AT LAW

Crime Drama. The cases and
courtroom defenses of David
Hansen, Deborah Sullivan and
Gabriel Kay, lawyers attached to
the Neighborhood Legal Services
Offices in Century City (in Los
Angeles), who defend indigent
clients. A spin-off from *The
Storefront Lawyers.*

CAST
Attorney David Hansen   Robert Foxworth
Attorney Deborah Sullivan   Sheila Larken
Attorney Gabriel Kay   David Arken
Devlin McNeil, their
  superior   Gerald S. O'Loughlin
Kathy, their secretary   Nancy Jeris

Music: Harper MacKay.
Executive Producer: Bob Stivers.
Producer: Bill Waters, Don Kib-
  bee, Dominique Perrin.

CBS

*M*A*S*H*. Seated, from left, Loretta Swit, Harry Morgan, Alan Alda and Mike Farrell. Standing, from left, William Christopher, Gary Burghoff, David Ogden Stiers and Jamie Farr.

CBS

Maude. From left, Adrienne Barbeau, Beatrice Arthur and Bill Macy.

NBC

Me and Maxx. Joe Santos and Melissa Michaelsen.

NBC

The Misadventures of Sheriff Lobo. From left, Mills Watson, Claude Akins and Brian Kerwin.

MEN AT LAW — 60 minutes — CBS — February 3, 1971 — September 1, 1971. 13 episodes.

795   THE MEN FROM SHILOH

Western. A spin-off from *The Virginian*. The series, set in Medicine Bow, Wyoming, during the 1890s, follows the exploits of four men: Colonel Alan MacKenzie, the owner of the Shiloh Ranch; The Virginian, the foreman; and hired hands Trampas and Roy Tate, as they attempt to maintain law and order.

CAST
The Virginian	James Drury
Col. Alan MacKenzie	Stewart Granger
Trampas	Doug McClure
Roy Tate	Lee Majors

Music: Leonard Rosenman.
Producer: Herbert Hirschman, Leslie Stevens.
Director: Murray Golden, Herbert Hirschman, Hollingsworth Morse, Harry Harris, Don McDougall, Abner Biberman, Marc Daniels, Gene L. Coon, Jeannot Szwarc, Jack Arnold, Philip Leacock, Richard Benedict.

THE MEN FROM SHILOH — 90 minutes — NBC — September 16, 1970 – September 8, 1971. 24 episodes.

796   THE MERV GRIFFIN SHOW

Talk-Variety.

Host: Merv Griffin.
Announcer: Arthur Treacher, Merv Griffin.
Orchestra: Mort Lindsey.
Executive Producer: Murray Schwartz.
Producer: Bob Murphy.
Director: Dick Carson.

THE MERV GRIFFIN SHOW — 90 minutes — Syndicated 1972.

797   THE MICKEY MOUSE CLUB

Children. Music, songs, dances, cartoons and adventure serials.

Host: Jimmie Dodd.
Co-Host: Roy Williams ("The Big Mooseketeer").
Assistant: Bob Amsberry.

CAST
(The Mouseketeers)
Annette	Annette Funicello
Darlene	Darlene Gillespie
Cubby	Carl O'Brien
Karen	Karen Pendleton
Bobby	Bobby Burgess
Tommy	Tommy Cole
Cheryl	Cheryl Holdridge
Lynn	Lynn Ready
Doreen	Doreen Tracy
Linda	Linda Hughes
Lonnie	Lonnie Burr
Bonni	Bonni Lynn Fields
Sharon	Sharon Baird
Ronnie	Ronnie Young
Jay Jay	Jay Jay Solari
Margene	Margene Storey
Nancy	Nancy Abbate
Billie Jean	Billie Jean Beanblossom
Mary	Mary Espinosa
Bonnie Lou	Bonnie Lou Kern
Mary Lou	Mary Lou Sartori
Bronson	Bronson Scott
Dennis	Dennis Day
Dickie	Dickie Dodd
Michael	Michael Smith
Ron	Ronald Steiner
Mark	Mark Sutherland
Don	Don Underhill
Sherry	Sherry Allen
Paul	Paul Petersen
Judy	Judy Harriett
John	John Lee Johnson
Eileen	Eileen Diamond
Charley	Charley Laney
Sherry	Sherry Alberoni
Mickey	Mickey Rooney, Jr.
Tim	Tim Rooney
Johnny	Johnny Crawford
Larry	Larry Larsen
Don	Don Agrati (a.k.a. Don Grady)

Professor Wonderful: Julius Sumner Miller.
Voice of the Animated Jiminy Cricket: Cliff Edwards.
Voice of Mickey Mouse: Jim Macdonald (for the TV series; Walt Disney's voice is heard as Mickey's voice in cartoons prior to 1949).
Narrator of the Newsreel: Hal Gibney.
Special News Correspondent: Dick Metzzi.
Music: The Disneyland Band, Joseph Dubin, Buddy Baker, William Lava, Joseph Mullendore, Franklin Marks.
Director of the Mouseketeers: Sid Miller, Clyde Geronimi.
Executive Producer: Walt Disney.
Producer: Bill Walsh, Dick Darley.
Director: Jonathan Lucas, William Beaudine, Charles Haas, Lee Clark.
Choreographer: Tom Mahoney.

THE MICKEY MOUSE CLUB — 60- and 30-minute versions — ABC — October 3, 1955 – September 25, 1959. Syndicated (then withdrawn and resyndicated in 1975). Spin-off series: *The New Mickey Mouse Club.*

798   MICKEY ROONEY'S SMALL WORLD

Discussion. Eight children, aged four to eight who vary from program to program, discuss various matters with celebrity guests.

Host: Mickey Rooney.
Music: Theme only; a recorded version of the Walt Disney song, "It's a Small World."
Producer: Mickey Rooney.

MICKEY ROONEY'S SMALL WORLD — 30 minutes — Syndicated 1975.

799   THE MIDNIGHT SPECIAL

Music. Performances by Rock, Pop, Soul and Country and Western entertainers.

Hostess: Helen Reddy (for a short time; weekly guests originally hosted and do so again).
Frequently Appearing: Carol Wayne.
Announcer: Wolfman Jack.
Executive Producer: Burt Sugarman.
Producer: Stan Harris.

THE MIDNIGHT SPECIAL — 90 minutes — NBC — Premiered: February 2, 1973.

800   THE MIKE DOUGLAS SHOW

Talk-Variety.

Host: Mike Douglas.
Announcer: Jay Stewart.
Music: The Ellie Frankel Quartet, The Joe Harnell Sextet, The Frank Hunter Band, The Joe Massimino Band.
Executive Producer: Jack Reilly.
Producer: Woody Fraser, E.V. Dismissa, Jr.
Director: Peter Calabrese, Ernie Sherry, Don King, Arthur Forrest.

THE MIKE DOUGLAS SHOW — 90 minutes — Syndicated 1966.

801   MINDREADERS

Game. Two teams of four players, men versus women, compete. Each team is comprised of one celebrity captain and three noncelebrity players. A question calling for a yes-or-no answer is read to one team and the noncelebrity players secretly answer by pressing a button. Their celebrity captain has to predict how each of his teammates responded. A correct prediction awards the team fifty dollars; an incorrect guess awards the opposing team the same amount of money. The opposing team then receives its turn at play. The first team to score three hundred dollars is the winner.

Host: Dick Martin.
Announcer: Johnny Olsen.
Music: Score Productions.
Supervising Producer: Mark Goodson, Bill Todman.
Producer: Mimi O'Brien Maturo.
Director: Ira Skutch.

MINDREADERS — 30 minutes — NBC — August 12, 1979 – January 11, 1980. 105 episodes.

802   THE MISADVENTURES OF SHERIFF LOBO

Comedy. The story of Elroy S. Lobo, the accident-prone, slightly dishonest sheriff of Orly County, Georgia, a man who dispenses his own brand of justice — for fun and profit. A spin-off from *B.J. and the Bear.*

CAST
Sheriff Elroy S. Lobo	Claude Akins
Deputy "Perky" Perkins, Elroy's bumbling assistant	Mills Watson
Deputy Birdwell "Birdie" Hawkins, Elroy's straight and narrow assistant	Brian Kerwin
Sarah Cumberland, the manager of the Orly Hot Springs Hotel	Leann Hunley
Rose Perkins, Perkins' wife	Cydney Crampton
Margaret Ellen Mercer, the waitress at Danny's restaurant	Janet Lyn Curtis
Oscar Gorley, the promoter	J.D. Cannon
Mayor Hawkins, Birdie's father	William Schallert
Mrs. Lobo, Elroy's mother	Rosemary DeCamp
The hotel waitress	Pamela Myers
The hotel bartender	Dick Winslow

Music: William Broughton, Jimmie Haskell, John Andrew Tartiglia.
Theme: "The Ballad of Sheriff Lobo" by Glen A. Larson.
Theme Vocal: Frankie Laine.
Supervising Producer: William P. D'Angelo, Edward J. Montagne, Mort Zarcoff.
Executive Producer: Glen A. Larson.
Producer: Joe Boston, Richard Bluel.
Director: Dick Harwood, James Sheldon, Charles R. Rondeau, Daniel Haller, Mel Ferber, Bruce Bilson, William P. D'Angelo, Leslie H. Martinson, Christian I. Nyby II, Jack Arnold.
Creator: Glen A. Larson.

THE MISADVENTURES OF SHERIFF LOBO — 60 minutes — NBC — September 18, 1979 – September 2, 1980. 22 episodes. *See also* program number 1900.

803   MISSION: IMPOSSIBLE

Adventure. The cases of the I.M.F. (Impossible Missions Force), a top secret U.S. government organization that handles dangerous and highly sensitive international assignments. Stories depict the step-by-step planning and final execution of very tense and complicated missions.

CAST
Jim Phelps, the head of the I.M.F.	Peter Graves
Dan Briggs, the original head of the I.M.F. (1966-67)	Steven Hill
Cinnamon Carter, an I.M.F. agent	Barbara Bain
Rollin Hand, an I.M.F. agent, a master of disguise	Martin Landau
Barney Collier, an I.M.F. agent, the electronics expert	Greg Morris

Mission: Impossible. Bottom, from left, Peter Lupus, Greg Morris and Martin Landau. Top, Barbara Bain and Peter Graves.

Miss Winslow and Son. From left, Roscoe Lee Browne, Darleen Carr, Elliott Reid and Sarah Marshall. Baby not identified.

Mork and Mindy. Pam Dawber and Robin Williams.

The Most Deadly Game. From left, George Maharis, Ralph Bellamy and Yvette Mimieux.

Willy Armitage, an I.M.F. agent, the strongman	Peter Lupus
Paris (replaced Rollin)	Leonard Nimoy
Dana (replaced Cinnamon)	Lesley Ann Warren
Casey (replaced Dana)	Lynda Day George
Mimi Davis, an I.M.F. agent	Barbara Anderson
Dr. Doug Lang, an I.M.F. agent	Sam Elliott
The recorded voice that gives Jim his assignment	Bob Johnson

Girls used in the interim between Barbara Bain and Lesley Ann Warren:

Tracey	Lee Meriwether
Lisa	Michele Carey
Beth	Sally Ann Howes
Monique	Julie Gregg
Nora	Antoinette Bower
Valerie	Jessica Walter

Also, various villainous roles: Sid Haig.

Music: Lalo Schifrin, Richard Markowitz, Gerald Fried, Richard Haig, Robert Drasnin, Jerry Fielding, Kenyon Hopkins, Benny Golson, Harry Geller, Robert Prince, Leith Stevens.

Theme: "Mission: Impossible" by Lalo Schifrin.

Executive Producer: Bruce Geller.

Producer: Stanley Kallis, Lee H. Katzin, Richard Benedict, Robert Thompson, John W. Rogers, Joseph Gantman, Robert F. O'Neil, Laurence Heath, Bruce Lansbury.

Director: Richard Benedict, Leonard J. Horn, Michael O'Herlihy, Alexander Singer, Stuart Hagmann, Bruce Kessler, Reza S. Badiyi, Marvin Chomsky, Barry Crane, Murray Golden, Georg Fenady, Robert Butler, Robert Gist, John Moxey, Paul Stanley, Alf Kjellin, Lewis Allen, Marc Daniels, Robert Totten, Don Richardson, Sutton Roley, John Florea, Virgil W. Vogel, David Lowell Rich, Paul Krasny, Seymour Robbie, Gerald Mayer, Terry Becker, Allan Greedy.

Creator: Bruce Geller.

MISSION: IMPOSSIBLE — 60 minutes — CBS — September 17, 1966 – September 8, 1973. 171 episodes. Syndicated.

804   MISSION MAGIC

Animated Cartoon. The story of Miss Tickle, a school teacher who possesses magical powers, which she uses for good over evil. With her students (Carol, Vinnie, Kim, Socks, Harvey and Franklin) and Rick Springfield, a troubleshooter, the group forms the Adventurers Club and travels to fantasy lands to help deserving underdogs.

VOICES

Rick Springfield	Himself
Miss Tickle, the teacher	Erica Scheimer
Carol, a student	Lola Fisher
Vinnie, a student	Lane Scheimer
Kim, a student	Lola Fisher
Harvey, a student	Howard Morris
Franklin, a student	Lane Scheimer
Socks, a student	Howard Morris

Additional Characters: Tomaly, Rick's owl; Mr. Samuels, the principal; and Tut Tut, Miss Tickle's magic cat.

Music: Yvette Blais, Jeff Michael.

Producer: Lou Scheimer, Norm Prescott.

Director: Don Christensen.

MISSION MAGIC — 30 minutes — ABC — September 8, 1973 – August 31, 1974. 13 episodes.

805   MISS JONES AND SON

Comedy. The British series on which America's *Miss Winslow and Son* is based. The program, which has not been broadcast in the United States, focuses on the complicated life of Elizabeth Jones, an unmarried mother, as she struggles to adjust to a new life-style.

CAST

Elizabeth Jones	Paula Wilcox
Geoffrey	Christopher Beeny
Elizabeth's mother	Charlotte Mitchell
Elizabeth's father	Norman Bird

Theme Music: Roger Webb.

Producer-Director: Peter Frazer-Jones.

Designer: Martyn Herbert.

MISS JONES AND SON — 30 minutes. Produced and broadcast by Thames TV from April 18, 1977 – May 19, 1977. 6 episodes.

806   MISS WINSLOW AND SON

Comedy. The series, set in Cincinnati, Ohio, follows the life of Susan Winslow, an unmarried mother, as she struggles to make a life for herself and her baby. A commercial artist, Susan has decided it would be better to be an unmarried mother rather than be unhappily married to the father of her child.

CAST

Susan Winslow	Darleen Carr
Harold Devore Neistader, her adverse-to-noise neighbor	Roscoe Lee Browne
Warren Winslow, Susan's father	Elliott Reid
Evelyn Winslow, Susan's mother	Sarah Marshall
Joseph X. Callahan, Susan's employer	William Bogert
Edmund Hillary Winslow, Susan's son	Benjamin Margolis
Rosa Vallone, Susan's friend	Ellen Sherman
Angelo Vallone, Rosa's husband	Joe Rassulo

Music: Pete Rugolo.

Supervising Producer: Alan J. Levitt.

Executive Producer: Ted Bergmann, Don Taffner.

Producer: Mimi Seawell, Don Van Atta.

Director: George Tyne, Jack Donohue.

Art Director: Ken Johnson.

MISS WINSLOW AND SON — 30 minutes — CBS — March 28, 1979 – May 2, 1979. 6 episodes. Based on the British series, *Miss Jones and Son.*

807   MOBILE ONE

Drama. The adventures of reporter Pete Campbell and cameraman Doug McKnight, newsmen employed by television station KONE, Channel 1, in Southern California. (Mobile One is the code name for their car.)

CAST

Pete Campbell, a reporter	Jackie Cooper
Doug McKnight, his cameraman	Mark Wheeler
Maggie Spencer, their assignment editor	Julie Gregg
Bruce Daniels, a station employee	Gary Crosby
Police Lt. Baker	Warren Stevens

Music: Nelson Riddle.

Music Supervision: Hal Mooney.

Executive Producer: Jack Webb.

Producer: William Bowers.

Director: David Moessinger, Don Taylor, Dennis Donnelly, Joseph Pevney, George Sherman, Paul Krasny, E.W. Swackhamer, Jackie Cooper.

MOBILE ONE — 60 minutes — ABC — September 12, 1975 – December 29, 1975. 13 episodes. The 90-minute pilot film, "Mobile Two," aired on ABC on September 2, 1975.

808   THE MOD SQUAD

Crime Drama. Pete Cochrane, Julie Barnes and Linc Hayes, young adults arrested on minor charges,* are recruited by Los Angeles Police Captain Adam Greer to form the Mod Squad: a special youth detail of undercover agents designed to infiltrate organizations that are impenetrable by police. Stories focus on the Mod Squad's investigations and Pete, Julie and Linc's attempts to work out their own identities.

CAST

Pete Cochrane	Michael Cole
Julie Barnes	Peggy Lipton
Linc Hayes	Clarence Williams III
Capt. Adam Greer	Tige Andrews
Barney Metcalf, Greer's superior	Simon Scott

Pete's Woodie: *Old Paint* (Woodie is surfer's slang for an old station wagon).

Music: Earle Hagen, Shorty Rogers, Billy May.

Executive Producer: Aaron Spelling, Danny Thomas.

Producer: Harve Bennett, Tony Barrett.

Director: Gary Nelson, Robert Michael Lewis, George McCowan, Don Taylor, Barry Shear, Seymour Robbie, Philip Leacock, Jerry Jameson, Richard Newton, Georg Olden, Earl Bellamy, Terry Becker, Lee H. Katzin, Michael Caffey, Gene Nelson.

THE MOD SQUAD — 60 minutes — ABC — September 24, 1968 – August 23, 1973. 124 episodes. Syndicated. See also *The Mod Squad: Extension Episode.*

*Pete, anti-establishment and the troubled child of a wealthy family, was arrested for taking a joy ride in a stolen car; Julie, a poor white girl who wants no part of her mother's life as a prostitute, was charged with having no visible means of support; and Linc, a tough ghetto black, was arrested during a raid in Watts.

809   THE MOD SQUAD: EXTENSION EPISODE

Crime Drama. An extension episode based on *The Mod Squad* series, titled *The Return of Mod Squad,* that reunites the original cast after seven years. Story finds the squad — Pete Cochrane, Julie Barnes and Linc Hayes — seeking a mysterious assailant who is threatening to kill their former captain, now Deputy Police Commissioner Adam Greer. Pete, who was anti-everything, has calmed down and moved home to Beverly Hills to take over his late father's business. Julie, who finally found happiness, married Dan Bennett and moved to a ranch in Northern California where she lives with her husband and daughter. Linc, who moved to New York City, completed his college education and acquired a job as a school teacher.

CAST

Pete Cochrane	Michael Cole
Julie Barnes	Peggy Lipton
Linc Hayes	Clarence Williams III
Adam Greer	Tige Andrews
Barney Metcalf, the police commissioner	Simon Scott

Also:

Dan Bennett, Julie's husband	Roy Thinnes
Jason Hayes, Linc's adopted son	Todd Bridges
Buck Prescott, the dope pusher	Ross Martin
Johnny Starr, the "reformed" criminal	Victor Buono
Richie Webber, Buck's runner	Mark Slade
Frank Webber, Richie's father	Tom Bosley

Music: Shorty Rogers, Mark Snow.

Supervising Producer: E. Duke Vincent.

Executive Producer: Danny Thomas, Aaron Spelling.

Producer: Lynn Loring.

Director: George McCowan.

THE RETURN OF MOD SQUAD —
2 hours — ABC — May 18, 1979.

810 MOLL FLANDERS

Drama. A four-part miniseries that follows the adventures of Moll Flanders, a seventeenth century woman who married five times, was twelve years a prostitute and twelve years a thief. A faithful adaptation of the novel by Daniel Defoe. The program, produced by the BBC in 1975, contains scenes of frontal nudity (waist up) and full rear nudity of Moll Flanders; hence, limited airing in the U.S.

Starring: Julia Foster as Moll Flanders.
Music: Martin Caithy.
Producer: Cedric Messina.
Director: Donald McWhinnie.

MOLL FLANDERS — 60 minutes — Syndicated to PBS (not all stations) in December 1979. 4 episodes.

811 THE MONEYCHANGERS

Drama. A four-part miniseries, based on the novel by Arthur Hailey, that presents a behind-the-scenes look at the world of banking — a world dominated by greed, corruption, sex and power.

CAST

Alex Vandervoort	Kirk Douglas
Roscoe Heyward	Christopher Plummer
Miles Eastin	Timothy Bottoms
Margot Bracken	Susan Flannery
Edwina Dorsey	Anne Baxter
Avril Devereaux	Joan Collins
Jerome Patterson	Ralph Bellamy
Nolan Wainright	Percy Rodrigues
Tony Bear	Robert Loggia
Beatrice Heyward	Jean Peters
Celia Vandervoort	Marisa Pavan
Lewis Dorsey	Hayden Rorke
Wizard Wong	James Shigeta
Juanita Nunez	Amy Tivell
Harold Austin	Patrick O'Neal
George Quartermain	Lorne Greene
Dr. McCartney	Helen Hayes
Fergus Gatwick	Roger Bowen
Danny Kerigan	Douglas V. Fowley
Stanley Inchbeck	Basil Huffman
Deanon Euphrates	Lincoln Kilpatrick
Jules LaRocca	Joseph Sicari
Mr. Tottenhoe	Woodrow Parfrey
Ben Rosselli	Leonardo Carmino
John Dinkerwell	Stan Shaw
Miss Callahan	Virginia Grey
Mr. Timberwell	Bing Russell

Music: Henry Mancini.
Producer: Ross Hunter, Jacque Mapes.
Writer: Dean Reisner, Stanford Whitmore.
Director: Boris Sagal.
Art Director: Jack DeShields.

THE MONEYCHANGERS — 6 hours, 30 minutes (total time) — NBC — December 4, 1976 — December 19, 1976.

812 THE MONEY MAZE

Game. Two married couples compete. One member of each team stands before a large maze that is contructed on stage level one. The other member of each team is situated on stage level two. A category topic is revealed along with two clues. One player, through a flip-of-coin decision, chooses one clue (e.g., in the category, "Girls in Movies," "My Friend . . .") and challenges his opponent to fill in the blank. For a correct answer ("Irma" in the example) his team receives one point. Eight clues are played per category with contestants alternating turns during several such rounds of play. (A wrong answer awards the opponent the point.) The player with the highest score is the winner and receives a chance to play the Money Maze. Five large boxes, which each contain one figure of 10,000 dollars, are lit. The player on stage level two directs his partner who has to run through the maze, enter each of the five boxes, press a button to activate a light, and return to the starting point to press a red button — all within one minute. Cash awards are determined by the number of boxes that are activated and whether or not the player made it back to the starting point before time expired.

Host: Nick Clooney.
Announcer: Alan Caulfield.
Music: Score Productions.
Producer: Don Lipp.

THE MONEY MAZE — 30 minutes — ABC — December 23, 1974 — July 4, 1975. 150 programs.

813 THE MONKEES

Comedy. The misadventures of The Monkees, a Rock and Roll quartet, as they romp through various comic escapades. Slapstick situations are played within nonrealistic frameworks and encompass speed photography and photographic nonsense.

CAST

The Monkees:

Davy Jones	Himself
Mike Nesmith	Himself
Mickey Dolenz	Himself
Peter Tork	Himself

Also:

Miss Purdy, their neighbor	Jesslyn Fax
Mr. Babbitt, their landlord	Henry Corden

Music: The Monkees.
Background Score: Stu Phillips.
Music Supervision: Don Kirshner.
Producer: Robert Rafelson, Ward Sylvester.
Director: Robert Rafelson, Bruce Kessler, Gerald Shepard, David Winters, Peter H. Torkleson, James Frawley, Bruce Kessler, Alexander Singer.

THE MONKEES — 30 minutes. NBC — September 12, 1966 — August 19, 1968. CBS — September 13, 1969 – September 2, 1972. ABC — September 9, 1972 – September 1, 1973. 58 episodes. Syndicated.

814 THE MONSTER SQUAD

Comedy. While working as a night watchman at Fred's Wax Museum, Walt, a criminology student, activates the crime computer he has invented, and, through its oscillating vibrations, brings to life three legendary monsters — Frankenstein, Dracula and the Werewolf. Hoping to make up for their past misgivings, they join Walt and work independently of police in attempting to solve crimes.

CAST

Walt	Fred Grandy
Dracula	Henry Polic II
Bruce W. Wolf (the Werewolf)	Buck Kartalian
Frank N. Stein	Michael Lane
Police Officer McMac Mac	Paul Smith

Music: Richard La Salle.
Executive Producer: William P. D'Angelo, Ray Allen, Harvey Bullock.
Producer: Michael McClean.
Director: Herman Hoffman, James Sheldon.

THE MONSTER SQUAD — 30 minutes — NBC — September 11, 1976 – September 2, 1977.

815 THE MONTE CARLO SHOW

Variety. Performances by American and European variety acts. Taped in Monte Carlo at the Sporting Club.

Host: Patrick Wayne.
Regulars: Les Girls (singers and dancers), Andre Cahoune (as Ploom, a puppet).
Orchestra: Dennis McCarthy.
Producer: Marty Pasetta.
Associate Producer: Michael Seligman.
Writer: Eddie Braden.
Director: Lee H. Bernardi.
Choreographer: Walter Painter.
Art Director: Ray Klausen.

THE MONTE CARLO SHOW — 60 minutes — Syndicated 1980.

816 THE MONTEFUSCOS

Comedy. The trials and tribulations of three generations of Montefuscos, a large Italian-American family living in New Canaan, Connecticut.

CAST

Tony Montefusco, the father, a painter	Joe Sirola
Rose Montefusco, his wife	Naomi Stevens
Frankie Montefusco, their son, a dentist	Ron Carey
Theresa Montefusco, Frankie's wife	Phoebe Dorin
Joseph Montefusco, Tony's son, a priest	John Aprea
Nunzio Montefusco, Tony's son, an actor	Sal Viscuso
Angelina Cooney, Tony's married daughter	Linda Dano
Jim Cooney, Angelina's husband	Bill Cort
Carmine Montefusco, Frankie's son	Jeffrey Palladini
Gina Montefusco, Frankie's daughter	Dominique Pinassi
Jerome Montefusco, Frankie's son	Robby Paris
Anthony Cooney, Angelina's son	Damon Raskin

Music: Jack Elliott, Allyn Ferguson.
Executive Producer: Bill Persky, Sam Denoff.
Producer: Tom Van Atta, Bill Idelson.
Director: Bill Persky, Don Richardson.
Creator: Bill Persky, Sam Denoff.

THE MONTEFUSCOS — 30 minutes — NBC — September 4, 1975 – October 23, 1975.

817 MONTY NASH

Adventure. The exploits of Monty Nash, a United States government special investigator who handles top-secret White House affairs. Based on the spy yarns of Richard Jessup.

CAST

Monty Nash	Harry Guardino

Music: The Good Stuff.
Theme Music: Michael Lloyd.
Executive Producer: Everett Chambers.
Producer: Richard M. Rosenbloom.
Creator: Richard Jessup.

MONTY NASH — 30 minutes — Syndicated 1971. 31 episodes.

818 MONTY PYTHON'S FLYING CIRCUS

Satire. An absolutely meaningless title for a program of tasteless, uneven and insane material: men in drag; glamorous women in various stages of undress; foul language; and sexually provocative animation — all of which is ingeniously interwoven into a highly intellectual and entertaining program.

The British Broadcasting Corporation produced the show, which first began airing in 1969 as an answer to America's *Laugh-In.* It was created by five men, all graduates of Oxford or Cambridge, who use live action and animation to achieve their comedic results. Whether enjoyable or not rests solely with the individual.

Starring: Graham Chapman, John Cleese, Eric Idle, Terry Gilliam, Terry Jones, Michael Palin.
Regulars: Carol Cleveland, Donna Reading, Katy Wayech, Dick Vosburgh, Rita Davis, Connie Booth, Niki Howorth, Sandra Richards, Ian Davidson, The Fred Tomalson Singers.
Music: John Gould.
Producer-Director: Ian MacNaughton, John Davies.
Animation: Terry Gilliam.

MONTY PYTHON'S FLYING CIRCUS — 30 minutes — Syndicated to PBS in 1974.

819 THE MOONMAN CONNECTION

Music. A Disco version of *American Bandstand*, wherein young adults dance to Disco music.

Host: Moonman-Bacote.
Co-Host: Alfie Williams.
Executive Producer: B.B. & R. Productions.
Producer: Willie Bacote.
Associate Producer: Randy Allen.
Director: Larry Jordan, Jackson Polk.
Choreographer: Larry Campbell, Kenneth Hale.

THE MOONMAN CONNECTION — 60 minutes — Syndicated 1979.

820 THE MORECAMBE AND WISE SHOW

Comedy. Burlesque-type comedy skits and blackouts.

Host: Eric Morecambe and Ernie Wise.
Regulars: Ann Hamilton, Kenny Ball and His Jazzmen.
Orchestra: Peter Knight.
Executive Producer: Madelyn Goldberg, Peter Hansen.
Producer: John Ammonds, Ernest Maxim.
Choreographer: Ernest Maxim.

THE MORECAMBE AND WISE SHOW — 30 minutes — Syndicated (to the U.S.) in 1980. 70 programs.

821 MORK AND MINDY

Comedy. Dispatched from the planet Ork to study life on primitive Earth, Mork lands in Boulder, Colorado, where he meets and befriends Mindy McConnell, a pretty 21-year-old girl who becomes taken aback by his peculiar manner. When Mork tells Mindy that he is an alien and has been assigned to study earthlings, she agrees to keep his secret and help him. The series focuses on Mork's attempts to adjust to life on Earth.

CAST
Mork	Robin Williams
Mindy McConnell	Pam Dawber

Frederick McConnell, Mindy's father, the owner of a music store	Conrad Janis
Cora Hudson, Mindy's grandmother	Elizabeth Kerr
Mr. Bickley, Mindy's neighbor	Tom Poston
Remo DaVinci, Mork's friend, the owner of the New York Delicatessen	Jay Thomas
Jeanie DaVinci, Remo's sister	Gina Hecht
Nelson Flavor, Mindy's cousin	Jim Staahl
Exidor, the religious fanatic befriended by Mork	Robert Donner
Orson, Mork's superior on Ork	Ralph James
Susan Taylor, Mindy's friend	Morgan Fairchild
Ambrosia Malspar, married Exidor on Dec. 16. 1979	Georgia Engel
Cathy McConnell, Mindy's stepmother	Shelley Fabares
Eugene, a friend of Mork's	Jeffrey Jacquet
Holly, a music student of Cora's	Tammy Lauren
Mindy, as a young girl (flashbacks)	Missy Francis
Glinda Comstock, Nelson's romantic interest	Crissy Wilzak
Miles Sternhagen, Mindy's employer at KTNS, Ch. 31 (where she works as a TV newscaster)	Foster Brooks
Mrs. Fowler, the head of the Pine Tree Day Care Center (where Mork works)	Priscilla Morrill
Lola, one of the day care center kids	Amy Tenowich
Stephanie, same as Lola	Stephanie Kona
Billy, same as Lola	Corey Feldman
Bebo, Mork's pet Orkin creature	Itself

Mindy's address: 1619 Pine Street.
Music: Perry Botkin, Jr.
Executive Producer: Garry K. Marshall, Tony Marshall.
Supervising Producer: Bruce Johnson, Dale McRaven.
Producer: Dale McRaven, Bruce Johnson, Tom Tenowich, Ed Scharlach.
Director: Howard Storm, Harvey Medlinsky, Joel Zwick, Jeff Chambers.

MORK AND MINDY — 30 minutes — ABC — Premiered: September 14, 1978.

822 MOSES THE LAWGIVER

Drama. The series, set in Egypt during the Thirteenth Century B.C. and drawn from the Book of Exodus, follows Moses as he defies the Egyptian empire to deliver the Jews from their enslavement and lead them to the promised land. Produced by England's Independent Television Corporation (I.T.C.) and Italy's RAI-TV.

CAST
Moses	Burt Lancaster
Moses, as a young man	Will Lancaster
Aaron	Anthony Quayle
Zipporah	Irene Papas
Miriam	Ingrid Thulin
Pharoah Mernephta	Laurent Terzieff
Dathan	Yousef Shiloah
Joshua	Aharon Ipale
Eliseba	Marina Berti
Pharoah's wife	Melba Englander
Caleb	Michele Placido
Koreb	Antonio Pivonelli
Jethro	Shmuel Rodensky
Egyptian Princess	Mariangela Melato
Cotbi	Simonetta Stefanelli
Ramses II	Mario Ferrari
Tutor	Paul Muller
Minister	Jose Quaglio
Minister	Umberto Raho
Magician	Jacques Herlin
Abihu	Renato Chiantoni
Gherson	Didi Lukof
Zimri	Fausto Di Bella

Narrator: Richard Johnson.
Music: Ennio Morricone.
Additional Music and Songs: Dov Seltzer.
Music Conductor: Bruno Nicolai.
Producer: Vincenzo Labella.
Writer: Anthony Burgess, Vittorio Bonicelli, Bernardino Zapponi, Gianfranco De Bosio.
Director: Gianfranco De Bosio.
Art Director: Pier Luigi Basile.
Costumes: Enrico Sabbatini.
Director of Photography: Marcello Gatti.

MOSES THE LAWGIVER — 60 minutes — CBS — June 21, 1975 – August 7, 1975; June 17, 1979 – June 22, 1979 (repeats). 6 episodes.

823 THE MOST DEADLY GAME

Crime Drama. The series, set in Los Angeles, follows the exploits of Ethan Arcane, a master criminologist, and Vanessa Smith and Jonathan Croft, his protégés, as they seek to solve crimes of the most deadly nature — murder.

CAST
Ethan Arcane	Ralph Bellamy
Vanessa Smith	Yvette Mimieux
Jonathan Croft	George Maharis

Music: George Duning.
Music Supervision: Lionel Newman.
Executive Producer: Aaron Spelling.
Producer: Joan Harrison.
Creator: Mort Fine, David Friedkin.

THE MOST DEADLY GAME — 60 minutes — ABC — October 10, 1970 – January 16, 1971. 13 episodes. Originally titled *Zig Zag* and intended to star Inger Stevens.

824 MOST WANTED

Crime Drama. The exploits of the Most Wanted Unit, an elite law enforcement division of the Los Angeles Police Department that is designed to apprehend criminals on the most-wanted list.

CAST
Captain Lincoln Evers	Robert Stack
Sgt. Charlie Nelson	Shelly Novack

Officer Kate Manners	Jo Ann Harris
The Mayor	Harry Rhodes

Music: Patrick Williams, Lalo Schifrin, Richard Markowitz.
Executive Producer: Quinn Martin, John Wilder, Paul King.
Producer: Harold Gast.
Director: Don Medford, Virgil W. Vogel, William Wiard, Corey Allen, Leslie H. Martinson, Walter Grauman.

MOST WANTED — 60 minutes — ABC — October 16, 1976 – April 4, 1977. The 90-minute pilot film aired on ABC on March 21, 1976.

825 MOTOR MOUSE

Animated Cartoon.

Segments:
Motor Mouse. The story of a cat (Auto Cat) and his endless, but fruitless attempts to beat a mouse (Motor Mouse) in a car race.

VOICES
Auto Cat	Marty Ingels
Motor Mouse	Dick Curtis

It's the Wolf. The story of Mildew Wolf and his attempts to acquire a decent meal — in the form of Lambsy, a poor defenseless lamb.

VOICES
Mildew Wolf	Paul Lynde
Lambsy	Marty Ingels
Bristol Hound, Lambsy's savior	Allan Melvin

Music: Hoyt Curtin.
Executive Producer: William Hanna, Joseph Barbera.
Producer: Alex Lovy.
Director: William Hanna, Joseph Barbera.

MOTOR MOUSE — 30 minutes — ABC — September 12, 1970 – September 4, 1971. 26 episodes. Syndicated.

826 THE MOUSE FACTORY

Variety. Guest celebrities appear and through the use of film clips from various Walt Disney-produced features, they attempt to explain various aspects of the world to children.

Guest Hosts: Annette Funicello, Jonathan Winters, Joe Flynn, Wally Cox, Jo Anne Worley, Pat Paulsen, Pat Buttram, Johnny Brown, John Astin.
Music: George Bruns.
Producer-Director: Ward Kimball.

THE MOUSE FACTORY — 30 minutes — Syndicated 1972. 17 episodes.

827 MOVIN' ON

Drama. The series, set in various areas between Oregon, Utah and Nevada, follows the experiences of two gypsy truck drivers: Sonny Pruitt, a tough, uneducated veteran; and Will Chandler, his part-

ner, a rebellious, college-edu-
cated youth, who is seeking to
discover how the other half lives.

CAST

Sonny Pruitt	Claude Akins
Will Chandler	Frank Converse
Myrna, Sonny's girlfriend	Janis Hansen
Betty, Will's girlfriend	Ann Coleman
Benjy, a gypsy truck driver	Rosey Grier
Moose, Benjy's partner	Art Metrano

Music: George Romanis, Earle
Hagen.
Theme Vocal: "Movin' On" by
Merle Haggard.
Executive Producer: Barry Whitz,
Philip D'Antoni.
Producer: Ernie Frankel.
Director: Corey Allen, Michael
Schultz, Robert Kelljan, Law-
rence Dobkin, Leo Penn, Alex
Grasshoff, Bernard L. Kowalski.
MOVIN' ON — 60 minutes —
NBC — September 12, 1974 –
April 20, 1976; June 1, 1976 –
September 14, 1976.

828   MOVIOLA: THIS YEAR'S BLONDE

Drama. The first episode of a
three-part miniseries, based on
Garson Kanin's novel featuring
three different, but related stories
about Hollywood. See also *Moviola: The Scarlett O'Hara War* and
Moviola: The Silent Lovers.

Part 1: This Year's Blonde.

The story recalls the early
Hollywood years of Marilyn Monroe, beginning in 1949 when,
after several screen appearances,
she meets Johnny Hyde, a powerful William Morris agent who begins her successful — and later
fatal — career. The story also
tensely recalls Marilyn's personal
and emotional turmoils, and
Hyde's stormy battles on her behalf against the studio tyrants.

CAST

Marilyn Monroe	Constance Forslund
Johnny Hyde	Lloyd Bridges
Harry Cohn	Vic Tayback
Jack Warner	Michael Lerner
Pat Toledo	Norman Fell
Joe Schenck	John Marley
Samuel Goldwyn	Lee Wallace
John Huston	William Frankfather
Mrs. Baker	Sondra Blake
Daryl Zanuck	Peter Maloney
Sol Silverman	Michael Strong
Margot Revere	Kathleen King
Dory Scharey	Stephen Keep
Eddie Mannix	Barney Martin
Patty	Lee Wilkof
Dr. Freed	Philip Stirling

NBC Announcer: Casey Kasem.
Music: Elmer Bernstein.
Executive Producer: David L.
Wolper.
Producer: Stan Marguiles.
Writer: James Lee.
Director: John Erman.
Art Director: Michael Baugh.
Director of Photography: Gayne
Rescher.

MOVIOLA: THIS YEAR'S BLONDE
— 2 hours — NBC — May 18, 1980.

829   MOVIOLA: THE SCARLETT O'HARA WAR

Drama. The second episode of a
three-part miniseries based on
the novel by Garson Kanin. See
also *Moviola: This Year's Blonde*
and *Moviola: The Silent Lovers.*

Part 2: The Scarlett O'Hara War.

The story recalls the excitement,
drama, tension and disappoint-
ment of Hollywood's greatest
casting call: the search to find an
actress to play Scarlett O'Hara in
Gone with the Wind (1939).

CAST

David O. Selznick	Tony Curtis
Myron Selznick	Bill Macy
Clark Cable	Edward Winter
Joan Crawford	Barrie Youngfellow
Carole Lombard	Sharon Gless
George Cukor	George Furth
Vivien Leigh	Morgan Brittany
Louis B. Mayer	Harold Gould
Tallulah Bankhead	Carrie Nye
Charlie Chaplin	Clive Revill
Paulette Goddard	Gwen Humble
Walter Winchell	Joey Forman
Louise Knight	Patricia Smith
Lucille Ball	Gypsie DeYoung
Laurie Lee	Melodie Thomas
Sidney Howard	Dan Caldwell
Louella Parsons	Jane Kean
Katharine Hepburn	Merleann Taylor
Jean Arthur	Vicki Delmonte
Miriam Hopkins	Sheila Wells
Russel Broadwell	William Bogert

NBC Announcer: Casey Kasem.
Music: Walter Scharf.
Executive Producer: David L.
Wolper.
Producer: Stan Marguiles.
Writer: William Hanley.
Director: John Erman.
Art Director: Michael Baugh.
Director of Photography: Gayne
Rescher.

MOVIOLA: THE SCARLETT
O'HARA WAR — 2 hours — NBC —
May 19, 1980.

830   MOVIOLA: THE SILENT LOVERS

Drama. The concluding episode
of a three-part miniseries based
on the novel by Garson Kanin.
See also *Moviola: This Year's
Blonde* and *Moviola: The Scarlett
O'Hara War.*

Part 3. The Silent Lovers.

The story recalls the fiery on-
and-off screen romance between
John Gilbert and Greta Garbo,
who were first teamed in 1927 for
Flesh and the Devil.

CAST

John Gilbert	Barry Bostwick
Greta Garbo	Kristina Wayborn
Louis B. Mayer	Harold Gould
Mauritz Stiller	Brian Keith
Irving Thalberg	John Rubinstein
Victor Seastrom	James Olson
King Vidor	Joseph Hacker
Laura Hope Crews	Audra Lindley
Lillian Gish	Mackenzie Phillips
Eddie Mannix	Barney Martin
Clarence Brown	Hank Garrett
Eleanor Boardman	Kerry McGrath
Antonio Moreno	Thaao Penghlis

NBC Announcer: Casey Kasem.
Music: Gerald Fried.
Executive Producer: David L.
Wolper.
Producer: Stan Marguiles.
Writer: William Hanley.
Director: John Erman.
Art Director: Michael Baugh.
Director of Photography: Gayne
Rescher.

MOVIOLA: THE SILENT LOV-
ERS — 2 hours — NBC — May 20,
1980.

831   MR. CHIPS

Home Repair and Advice.

Host-Announcer: Don Megowan.
Mr. Chips, "The do-it-yourselfer":
Bill Brown.
Executive Producer: Don Forsyth.
Producer-Director: Lou Albert.

MR. CHIPS — 30 minutes — Syndicated 1974.

832   MR. DUGAN

Comedy. The story of Matthew
Dugan, the owner of a successful
construction business and a former college football hero who
moves to Washington, D.C., to
succeed the late Pennsylvania
Congressman Hampton. The
fledgling black legislator arrives
in D.C. with his ideals about the
national legislative process still
intact. Episodes depict his misadventures when he is confronted
by the practical politics of the system and the self-assured attitude
of his inherited staff — a situation
that makes him unsure of his
congressional future.

Although "Mr. Dugan" never
aired, it is included here because
two of its episodes are listed, with
descriptions, in various TV programming guides. It is also a
unique series because outside
pressure killed it before it ever
got on the air. After a special
screening, a seventeen-member
caucus of black Congressmen declared *Mr. Dugan* to be offensive
to black elected officials and
threatened a nationwide switch-
off campaign if the series aired.
Norman Lear and his T.A.T. Communications Company, the producers, withdrew the program
with an explanation being "we
have not yet totally fulfilled our
intention for the series. . . ."

CAST

Matthew Dugan	Cleavon Little
Maggie Gallagher, his legislative assistant	Barbara Rhoades
Sam Dickey, his chief of staff	Dennis Burkley
Pinkie Nolan, his housekeeper	Nedra Volz
Aretha Balducci, his office press secretary	Sarina C. Grant

Executive Producer: Norman
Lear.
Producer: Charlie Hauck.
Associate Producer: Ken Stump.
Writer: Rod Parker.
Director: Jeff Bleckner.
Art Director: Chuck Murawski.

MR. DUGAN — 30 minutes — CBS.
Three episodes were produced
and were scheduled to air March
11-25, 1979. The series *Alice* filled
the *Mr. Dugan* spot on March 11;
and *One Day at a Time* aired on
the remaining Sundays. *Mr. Dugan,* which was originally titled
Mr. Dooley then *Onward and
Upward,* was to star John Amos,
then Lou Gossett, but both actors
rejected the role. See also *Han-
gin' In* for information on the series that evolved from the *Mr.
Dugan* plot.

833   MR. ROGERS' NEIGHBORHOOD

Children. The program concerns
the emotional development of
children from three to eight years
of age. Through actual demon-
strations and guests who discuss
topics, an attempt is made to help
children cope with or overcome
their problems.

CAST

Host (Mr. Rogers)	Fred Rogers
Lady Aberlin	Betty Aberlin
Handyman Negri	Joe Negri
Pilot Ito	Yoshi Ito
Chief Brockett	Don Brockett
Francois	Francois Clemmons
Elsie	Elsie Neal
Audrey Cleans Everything	Audrey Roth
Mrs. McFeely	Betsy Nadas

PUPPET VOICES

King Friday XIII	Fred Rogers
X The Owl	Fred Rogers
Queen Sara Saturday	Fred Rogers
Henrietta Pussycat	Fred Rogers
Daniel Tiger	Fred Rogers
Dr. Duckbill	William Barker
Henrietta Crow	Robert Trow
Donkey Hodie	Fred Rogers
Lady Elaine Fairchilde	Fred Rogers

Music: John Costa.
Executive Producer: Fred Rogers.
Producer: Bill Moates, Bob Walsh.
Director: David Fu-Yung Chen,
Bill Moates, Bob Walsh.

MR. ROGERS' NEIGHBORHOOD
— 30 minutes — PBS — October
1970 – June 1975. Syndicated to
PBS stations.

834   MR. T AND TINA

Comedy. The trials and tribulations of Taro Takahashi, a widowed Japanese businessman who
moves from Tokyo to Chicago
with his family, and the com-

plications that ensue when he hires Tina Kelly, a pretty, but dizzy young American woman, as governess for his children.

CAST

Taro Takahashi, the vice president of Moyati Industries	Pat Morita
Tina Kelly, his children's governess	Susan Blanchard
Sachi Takahashi, his daughter	June Angela
Aki Takahashi, his son	Gene Profanata
Matsu, his uncle	Jerry Hatsuo Fujikawa
Michi, his sister-in-law	Pat Suzuki
Miss Llewellyn, the apartment building manager	Miriam Byrd-Nethery
Harvard, the building's janitor	Ted Lange

Music: George Tipton.
Executive Producer: James Komack.
Producer: Madelyn Davis, Bob Carroll, Jr.
Director: James Sheldon, Rick Edelstein, James Komack, Dennis Steinmetz.

MR. T AND TINA — 30 minutes — ABC — September 26, 1976 – October 30, 1976. 5 episodes.

835   MR. WIZARD

Educational. The workings of various scientific experiments are explained to children.

Host: Don Herbert, as Mr. Wizard.
Producer (first series): James Pewolar.
Producer (revised series): Del Jack.
Director (first series): Larry Auerback.
Director (revised series): William McKee.
Music (revised series): Peter Jermyn.

MR. WIZARD — 30 minutes — NBC. First series: March 5, 1951 – September 5, 1965. Revised series: September 11, 1971 – September 2, 1972.

836   MRS. COLUMBO

Crime Drama. The series, set in San Fernando, California, follows the life of Kate Columbo, the pretty wife of TV's famed Lieutenant Columbo, as a journalist for the *Weekly Advertiser.* Episodes detail her attempts to solve baffling crimes.

CAST

Kate Columbo	Kate Mulgrew
Jenny Columbo, her daughter	Lili Haydn
Josh Alden, her publisher	Henry Jones

Kate's basset hound: White Fang.
Kate's license plate number: 044 A.P.D.

Music: John Cacavas.
Supervising Producer: Richard Alan Simmons.
Executive Producer: James MacAdams.
Producer: David Levinson.

Writer: Al Reynolds, Howard Berk, Gregory Dinallo.
Director: Boris Sagal, Don Medford, Edward Abroms, Sam Wanamaker.
Art Director: Richard Lewis.

MRS. COLUMBO — 60 minutes — NBC — February 26, 1979 – March 29, 1979; August 9, 1979 – September 6, 1979. 5 episodes. Revised title: *Kate Loves a Mystery,* which see.

837   MUGGSY

Drama. The series, set in an unidentified city, explores life in the inner city as seen through the eyes of Margaret "Muggsy" Malloy, a 13-year-old orphan, and her older half-brother and guardian, Nick Malloy, a taxicab driver. The program, though aimed at children, is realistic and penetrating. Taped in Bridgeport, Connecticut.

CAST

Margaret "Muggsy" Malloy	Sarah MacDonnell
Nick Malloy, her brother	Ben Masters
Gus Gardician, their friend, the owner of "Gus's Gas," an auto service station	Paul Michael
Clytemnestra, Muggsy's friend	Star-Shemah
T. P., Clytemnestra's brother	Danny Cooper

Address of Gus's Gas: 103 Brown Street.

Music Performed By: Blood, Sweat and Tears.
Musical Coordinator: Phebe Haas, Robert Gessinger.
Theme: David Collins, J. Philip Miller.
Producer: George A. Heineman.
Director: Bert Saltzman, J. Philip Miller, Sidney Smith.

MUGGSY — 30 minutes — NBC — September 11, 1976 – April 9, 1977.

838   MULLIGAN'S STEW

Comedy Drama. The series, set in Birchfield, California, follows the lives of the Mulligan family: Michael, a high school athletic coach; his wife, Jane, the school nurse; their three children, Mark, Melinda and Jimmy; and their four adopted children, Stevie, Adam, Polly and Kimmy. The cousins became part of the family after Mike's sister and husband perished in a plane crash. Stories focus on the attempts of the family members to accept and understand each other's differences.

CAST

Michael Mulligan, the father	Lawrence Pressman
Jane Mulligan, his wife	Elinor Donahue
Mark Mulligan, their son (pilot film)	Johnny Whitaker
Mark Mulligan (series)	Johnny Doran
Melinda Mulligan, their daughter	Julie Anne Haddock
Jimmy Mulligan, their son	K.C. Martel
Stevie Freeman Mulligan, their adopted daughter	Suzanne Crough
Adam "Moose" Freeman Mulligan, their adopted son	Christopher Ciampa
Polly Freeman Mulligan, their adopted daughter	Lory Kochheim
Kimmy Freeman Mulligan, their adopted Vietnamese daughter	Sunshine Lee

The Mulligan's address: 1202 Circle Drive.

Music: George Tipton, Morton Stevens.
Producer: Joanna Lee.
Director: Hollingsworth Morse, Leslie H. Martinson, Curtis Harrington, Herb Wallerstein.

MULLIGAN'S STEW — 60 minutes — NBC — October 25, 1977 – December 13, 1977. 5 episodes. The 90-minute pilot film aired on NBC on June 20, 1977.

839   THE MUPPET SHOW

Variety. An adult-oriented series wherein the Muppets (fanciful puppets created by Jim Henson) perform in sketches (with guests), sing and dance.

Host: Kermit the Frog (voiced by Jim Henson).
Voices: Frank Oz, Jim Henson, Jerry Nelson, Richard Hunt, Peter Friedman, Dave Goelz, John Loveday, Jane Henson.
Puppeteers: Jim Henson, Frank Oz, Jerry Nelson, Richard Hunt, Dave Goelz, John Loveday, Frank Brill.
Orchestra: Jack Parnell.
Musical Conductor: Derek Scott.
Musical Coordinator: Larry Grossman.
Executive Producer: Jim Henson.
Producer: Jack Burns, Jon Stone.
Director: Peter Harris.

THE MUPPET SHOW — 30 minutes — Syndicated 1976.

840   MUSICAL CHAIRS

Game. A song, either sung by the host or a guest, is stopped one line before its conclusion and three possible last lines of the lyric appear on a board. Four competing players press a button and lock in their choice for one of the lines. The answer from the first player to register a choice is revealed and if it is correct he scores money; if not, the answer from the second player is revealed (and so on to determine if the correct line has been chosen). In the first round three songs are played and each is worth $50. In the second round the three songs that are played are worth $75. Round three is the elimination round and at the end of each song, the player with the lowest score is defeated (songs

are worth $100). The winner is the highest scoring player.

Host: Adam Wade.
Announcer: Pat Hernan.
Music: The Musical Chairs Orchestra directed by Derek Smith.
Producer: Bill Chastain.
Director: Lynwood King.

MUSICAL CHAIRS — 30 minutes — CBS — June 16, 1975 – October 31, 1975. 90 programs.

841   MUSIC HALL AMERICA

Musical Variety.

Hosts: Guests.
Regulars: Dean Rutherford, Sadi Burnett, The Even Dozen.
Orchestra: Bill Walker.
Vocal Backgrounds: L'Adidas.
Executive Producer: Lee Miller.
Director: Lee Bernhardi.

MUSIC HALL AMERICA — 60 minutes — Syndicated 1976.

842   THE MUSIC PLACE

Variety. Performances by Country and Western entertainers.

Host: Stu Phillips.
Regulars: Bob and Pat Geary.
Producer: Gary Brockhurst.

THE MUSIC PLACE — 30 minutes — Syndicated 1975.

843   THE MUSIC SCENE

Variety. Performances by the top artists in various fields of music (Country and Western, Ballad, Rock, Folk and Blues). Musical numbers are interwoven with comedy sketches.

Host: David Steinberg.
Regulars: Paul Reid Roman, Lily Tomlin, Larry Hankin, Christopher Ross, Pat Williams.
Orchestra: Pat Williams.
Producer: Ken Fritz, Stan Harris.
Director: Stan Harris, Carl Gottlieb.
Art Director: Lewis Logan.

THE MUSIC SCENE — 45 minutes — ABC — September 22, 1969 – January 12, 1970. 13 episodes.

844   MY FAVORITE MARTIAN

Comedy. Enroute to the office, Tim O'Hara, a newspaper reporter for the *Los Angeles Sun,* witnesses the crash of a damaged U.F.O. Investigating, he discovers and befriends its passenger, a professor of anthropology from Mars whose specialty is the primitive planet Earth. Tim takes the marooned professor back to his apartment where the Martian adopts the guise of Martin O'Hara, an uncle staying with Tim after a long journey.

Hindered by the need for

items which are presently unknown on Earth, Martin struggles to repair his crippled craft, conceal his true identity and adjust to the discomforts of a primitive, backward planet.

CAST

Martin O'Hara (Uncle Martin)	Ray Walston
Tim O'Hara	Bill Bixby
Lorelei Brown, Tim's landlady	Pamela Britton
Detective Bill Brennan, Martin's rival for Lorelei's affections	Alan Hewitt
Mr. Burns, Tim's employer	J. Pat O'Malley
The police captain	Roy Engle

Music: George Greeley.
Producer: Jack Chertok.

MY FAVORITE MARTIAN — 30 minutes — CBS — September 15, 1963 – September 4, 1966. 107 episodes. Syndicated. Spin-off series: *My Favorite Martians.*

845 MY FAVORITE MARTIANS

Animated Cartoon. A spin-off from *My Favorite Martian.* A damaged alien spacecraft lands on Earth (in Los Angeles). Its occupants, Uncle Martin, his nephew Andy and their dog, Oakie Doakie, are befriended by the sole witnesses, newspaper reporter Tim O'Hara and his niece Katy.

Sheltering the stranded Martians, Tim arouses the suspicions of free-lance security officer Bill Brennan, who sets out to uncover Martin's true identity.

Plagued by the discomforts of primitive Earth, Martin struggles to maintain his false identity and repair his craft so he can return home.

VOICES

Uncle Martin	Jonathan Harris
Tim O'Hara	Lane Scheimer
Katy O'Hara, Tim's niece	Jane Webb
Lorelei Brown, Tim's landlady	Jane Webb
Bill Brennan	Lane Scheimer
Andy, Martin's nephew	Edward Morris
Brad Brennan, Bill's son	Edward Morris

Music: George Mahana.
Producer: Norm Prescott, Lou Scheimer.
Director: Hal Sutherland, Don Towsley, Rudy Larriva, Bill Reed, Lou Zukor, Ed Solomon.

MY FAVORITE MARTIANS — 25 minutes — CBS — September 8, 1973 – August 30, 1975. 16 episodes.

846 MY PARTNER THE GHOST

Crime Drama. While investigating a case, Marty Hopkirk, a British private detective, is killed. Returning as a ghost, he appears only to his former partner, Jeff Randall. Assisted by Jeff, he solves his own murder, but violates an ancient adage* and is cursed to remain on Earth for a hundred years. The series, set in England, follows the exploits of Jeff and his ghostly partner as they attempt to solve crimes.

CAST

Marty Hopkirk	Kenneth Cope
Jeff Randall	Mike Pratt
Jean Hopkirk, Marty's wife; working as Jeff's secretary	Annette Andre
Police Inspector Large	Ivor Dean

Music: Edwin Astley.
Producer: Monty Berman.
Director: Cyril Frankel, Jeremy Summers.
Creator: Dennis Spooner.

MY PARTNER THE GHOST — 60 minutes — Syndicated 1973. 26 episodes.

*"Before the sun shall rise on you, each ghost unto his grave must go. Cursed the ghost who dares to stay and face the awful light of day."

847 MY SON, MY SON

Drama. The story of two men, lifelong friends, and their dreams for their sons. Episodes follow the lives in England of William Essex, a novelist, and Dermot O'Riorden, a transplanted Irishman, from 1897 through the end of World War I. Title derives from Essex' attempts to forget his own impoverished boyhood by making life easy for his son; and O'Riorden's goal that his son should grow up to aid the Irish cause. Based on the novel by Howard Spring.

CAST

William Essex	Michael Williams
Dermot O'Riorden	Frank Grimes
Nellie Essex, William's wife	Sherrie Hewson
Oliver Essex, William's son	Patrick Ryecart
Rory O'Riorden, Dermot's son	Gerard Murphy
Maeve O'Riorden, Dermot's daughter	Prue Clarke
Livia Vaynol	Ciaran Madden
Wertheim	Georgoire Aslan
Sheila	Kate Binchy
Josie Wertheim	Joy Nichols
Poyson	Julian Fellows
Annie Southurst	Patsy Rowlands
Sir Charles Blatch	Alan MacNaughton
Roy	Gerard Murphy

Music: Kenyon Roberts.
Producer: Keith Williams.
Writer: Julian Bond.
Director: Peter Cregeen.

MY SON, MY SON — 60 minutes — PBS — April 13, 1980 – May 25, 1980. 7 episodes.

848 MYSTERY!

Anthology. A series of British-produced mystery plays.

Host: Gene Shalit.
Music: Mike Moran.
Executive Producer: David Cunliffe.

Producer: Joan Wilson, Jacky Stoller.
Director: Lawrence Gordon Clarke.
Mystery Theme Animation: Edward Gorey, Derek Lumb.

Included:

Odds Against. Based on Dick Francis' *The Racing Game.* The story of Sid Halley, a champion jockey turned private detective. Halley and his sidekick, Chico Barnes, attempt to solve a series of race course accidents.

Cast: Sid Halley: Mike Gwilym; Chico Barnes: Mick Ford; Howard Graves: Gerald Flood; Rowland: James Maxwell; Jenny: Susan Woolridge; Dora: Rachel Davies; Wendy: Holly DeJorg; Annabell: Alyson Rees.

Trackdown. A second adaptation of a Dick Francis story. The episode follows private detective Sid Halley's attempts to unravel a mystery involving a race owner whose stable's favorites keep losing.

Cast: Sid Halley: Mike Gwilym; Chico Barnes: Mick Ford; Tom Mansfield: Jeremy Clyde; Meg Appleby: Jeananne Crowley; Trish Latham: Carol Royle; Grindley: David Calder; Stable Owner: Leslie Sands; Peter: Daniel Webb.

Sergeant Cribb. Sergeant Cribb, the Scotland Yard detective created by Peter Lovesey, attempts to solve the mysterious murder of a man, a competitor in a walking race, who stopped dead in his tracks.

Cast: Sgt. Cribb: Alan Dobie; Thackeray: William Simons; Cora Darrell: Bobbie Brown; Herriot: Michael Elphick.

MYSTERY! — 60 minutes — PBS — February 5, 1980 – May 20, 1980. 15 episodes.

MYSTERY ADVENTURE: THE BEACHCOMBER

See *The Beachcomber.*

MYSTERY ADVENTURE: THE ERROL FLYNN THEATRE

See *The Errol Flynn Theatre.*

MYSTERY ADVENTURE: THE VEIL

See *The Veil.*

849 MY THREE SONS

Comedy. The series, set first in Bryant Park, then in North Hollywood, California, follows the trials and tribulations of the Douglas family.

CAST

Steve Douglas, a widowed aeronautical engineer	Fred MacMurray
Mike Douglas, his son	Tim Considine
Robbie Douglas, his son	Don Grady
Richard "Chip" Douglas, his son	Stanley Livingston
Ernie Douglas, his adopted son	Barry Livingston
Michael Francis "Bub" O'Casey, the housekeeper	William Frawley
Charles O'Casey, replaced "Bub"	William Demarest
Sally Ann Morrison, married Mike	Meredith MacRae
Katie Miller, married Robbie	Tina Cole
Barbara Harper, married Steve	Beverly Garland
Polly Thompson (a.k.a. in later episodes, Polly Williams), married Chip	Ronne Troup
Dodie Harper Douglas, Barbara's daughter	Dawn Lyn
Steve Douglas, Jr., Robbie's son	Joseph Todd
Charley Douglas, Robbie's son	Michael Todd
Robbie Douglas II, Robbie's son	Daniel Todd
Bob Walters, Steve's employer	Russ Conway John Gallaudet
Sylvia Walters, Bob's wife	Irene Hervey
Tom Williams, Polly's father	Norman Alden
Margaret Williams, Polly's mother	Doris Singleton
Fergus McBain Douglas, Steve's cousin (enacted by)	Fred MacMurray
Fergus McBain Douglas (voiced by)	Alan Caillou
Terri Dowling, married Fergus	Anne Francis
Priscilla, Dodie's friend	Jodie Foster
Margaret, Dodie's friend	Victoria Meyernik

The Douglas family dog: Tramp.

Music: Frank DeVol, Jeff Alexander, Gerald Fried, Nathan Scott.
Executive Producer: Don Fedderson.
Producer: Edmund Hartmann, Fred Henry, George Tibbles.
Director: Gene Reynolds, Fred de Cordova, James V. Kern, Earl Bellamy, Herschel Daugherty.

MY THREE SONS — 30 minutes — ABC — September 29, 1960 – September 9, 1965; CBS — September 16, 1965 – August 24, 1972. 369 episodes. Episodes broadcast from 1960 to 1965 are not syndicated; the syndicated series begins with the wedding of Mike and Sally and with the introduction of "Uncle" Charley O'Casey.

850 MY WORLD... AND WELCOME TO IT

Comedy. The series, set in Westport, Connecticut, depicts the real life and dream world of John Monroe, a cartoonist for *Manhattanite* magazine. Discontent with his job, suspicious of smart children and hostile animals, intimidated by his loving wife and his precocious daughter, and scared to death of life, he retreats to his secret world of imagination. His cartoons become real, life becomes tolerable and he is transformed into a person who is irresistible to women and a tower of strength in the eyes of men. Animation is combined with live action to present life as viewed by John Monroe. Based on the "drawings, stories, inspirational pieces and things that go bump in the night" of humorist James Thurber.

CAST

John Monroe	William Windom
Ellen Monroe, his wife	Joan Hotchkis
Lydia Monroe, his daughter	Lisa Gerritsen
Hamilton Greeley, John's employer	Harold J. Stone
Phil Jensen, John's friend	Henry Morgan
Ruth Jensen, Phil's wife	Olive Dunbar

Monroe family dogs: Irving and Christabel.

Music: Warren Barker, Danny Arnold.
Executive Producer: Sheldon Leonard.
Producer: Danny Arnold.
Animation: David DePatie, Friz Freleng.
Creator: Melville Shavelson.

MY WORLD ... AND WELCOME TO IT — 30 minutes — NBC — September 15, 1969 – September 7, 1970. CBS rebroadcasts: May 25, 1972 – September 7, 1972. 26 episodes.

N

851   NAKIA

Crime Drama. The series, set in Davis County, New Mexico, details the exploits of Deputy Nakia Parker, a Navajo Indian who sometimes finds his heritage and beliefs clashing with the law he is sworn to uphold.

CAST

Deputy Nakia Parker	Robert Forster
Sheriff Sam Jericho	Arthur Kennedy
Deputy Irene James	Gloria De Haven
Deputy Hubbel Martin	Taylor Lacher
Ben Redearth, an Indian	Victor Jory
Half Cub, an Indian (series)	John Tenorio, Jr.
Half Cub (pilot film)	Jed Horner, Jr.

Music: Leonard Rosenman.
Executive Producer: Quinn Martin, Charles Larson.
Producer: Ernest Losso, George Sunga.

NAKIA — 60 minutes — ABC — September 21, 1974 – December 28, 1974. 15 episodes. The 90-minute pilot film aired on ABC on April 17, 1974.

852   THE NAMEDROPPERS

Game. The game involves three guest celebrities who comprise the panel; twenty contestants selected from the studio audience and two Namedroppers, people who are in some way related to the celebrities. One Namedropper appears and briefly tells how he is related to one of the celebrities, but does not say who. Each celebrity relates a story concerning their relationship, but only one story is true. Of the twenty studio audience members, two compete at a time. The eighteen remaining players each press a button and select the celebrity they believe is related to the Namedropper. The stage players verbally divulge their choice and then the celebrity identifies the Namedropper. The studio audience votes are revealed and each incorrect vote awards the correct player ten dollars; if neither of the two players are correct, the Namedropper receives the money. Two such rounds are played per game, enabling all twenty contestants to compete during a five-day period.

Host: Al Lohman, Roger Barkley.
Announcer: Kenny Williams.
Music: Score Productions.
Producer: Art Alisi.
Director: Jerome Shaw.

THE NAMEDROPPERS — 30 minutes — NBC — October 2, 1969 – March 27, 1970. 120 programs.

853   THE NAME OF THE GAME

Crime Drama. The series, set in Los Angeles, follows the exploits of three men: Glenn Howard, the publisher of *Crime* magazine, a man who built the (then fictional) defunct *People* magazine into a multimillion dollar empire; Dan Farrell, the senior editor, a former F.B.I. agent who is conducting a personal battle against the underworld (which killed his wife and child); and Jeff Dillon, the editor of the *People* segment of *Crime*. Their individual attempts to uncover story material are depicted on a rotating basis.

CAST

Glenn Howard, the publisher	Gene Barry
Dan Farrell, an editor	Robert Stack
Jeff Dillon, an editor	Tony Franciosa
Peggy Maxwell, their girl Friday	Susan Saint James
Joe Sample, a reporter	Ben Murphy
Andy Hill, a reporter	Cliff Potter
Ross Craig, a reporter	Mark Miller

Music: Dave Grusin, Stanley Wilson, Dominic Frontiere.
Theme Music: Dave Grusin.
Executive Producer: Richard Irving.
Producer: Richard Levinson, Wil-

liam Link, Leslie Stevens, George Eckstein, Dean Hargrove.
Director: Marvin Chomsky, William Graham, Robert Day, Harvey Hart, Alvin Ganzer, John Llewellyn Moxey, Barry Shear, Alexander Singer, William Conrad, Don Taylor, Joseph Pevney, Seymour Robbie, Richard Irving, Don Taylor, Stuart Rosenberg, Ben Gazzara.

THE NAME OF THE GAME — 90 minutes — NBC — September 20, 1968 – September 10, 1972. Syndicated.

854   NAME THAT TUNE

Game. The basic format calls for contestants to identify songs after hearing a few bars played by an orchestra.

Version 1:

Host: Red Benson, Bill Cullen, George DeWitt.
Songstress: Vicki Mills.
Announcer: Johnny Olsen, Wayne Howell.
Orchestra: Harry Salter, Ted Rapf.
Producer: Al Singer, Art Stark, Harry Salter.

NAME THAT TUNE — 30 minutes. NBC — 1953 – 1957; CBS — 1957 – 1960.

Version 2:

Host: Dennis James.
Announcer: John Harlan.
Orchestra: Bob Alberti.
Executive Producer: Ralph Edwards.
Producer: Ray Horl.
Director: Richard Gottlieb.

NAME THAT TUNE — 30 minutes — NBC — July 29, 1974 – January 3, 1975.

Version 3:

Host: Tom Kennedy.
Announcer: John Harlan.
Orchestra: Bob Alberti.
Executive Producer: Ralph Edwards.
Director: John Dorsey.

NAME THAT TUNE — 30 minutes — Syndicated 1974.

Version 4:

Titled *The $100,000 Name That Tune*, the format has the added bonus of allowing a player to win $100,000 by correctly identifying a very difficult mystery tune.

Host: Tom Kennedy.
Model: Jerri Fiala.
Announcer: John Harlan.
Orchestra: Tommy Oliver, Stan Worth.
Vocalists: Steve March, Monica Buris.
Rock Group: Dan Younger and the Sound System.
$100,000 Pianist: Joe Harnell.
Producer: Ralph Edwards.
Director: John Dorsey.

THE $100,000 NAME THAT TUNE — 30 minutes — Syndicated 1976.

Version 5:

Host: Tom Kennedy.
Announcer: John Harlan.
Model: Jerri Fiala.
Vocalist: Kathie Lee Johnson.
Orchestra: Tommy Oliver, Harry Salter.
Executive Producer: Ralph Edwards.
Producer: Ray Horl.
Director: John Dorsey.

NAME THAT TUNE — 30 minutes — NBC — January 3, 1977 – September 4, 1977.

855   NANA

Drama. A four-part miniseries based on the novel by Emile Zola. Set in France in the nineteenth century, the story focuses on Nana, actress and prostitute, and the roles of pleasure and prostitution in French society at the time.

CAST

Nana	Katharine Schofield
Fontan	Alan Browning
Muffat	Freddie Jones
Rose	Sheila Brennan

Also: Hilda Fenemore, Alex Marshall, Eric Flynn, Donald Burton.

Music: Mark Lubrock.
Producer: David Conroy.
Writer: Robert Muller.
Director: John Davies.

NANA — 45 minutes — Syndicated to PBS in 1977. 4 episodes.

856   NANCY

Comedy. The series, set in Center City, Iowa, depicts the courtship and marriage of Adam Hudson, a veterinarian, and Nancy Smith, the daughter of the President of the United States. Episodes relate their struggles to adjust to a life that is more public than private.

CAST

Nancy Smith Hudson	Renne Jarrett
Adam Hudson	John Fink
Abby Townsend, Nancy's guardian	Celeste Holm
Everett Hudson, Adam's uncle	Robert F. Simon
Willie Wilson, Adam's friend	Eddie Applegate
Tom, Adam's friend	Frank Aletter
Secret Serviceman Turner	William H. Bassett
Secret Serviceman Rodriquez	Ernesto Macias

Music: Sid Ramin.
Executive Producer: Sidney Sheldon.
Producer: Jerome Courtland.
Creator: Sidney Sheldon.

NANCY — 30 minutes — NBC — September 17, 1970 – January 7, 1971. 13 episodes.

857   THE NANCY DREW MYSTERIES

Mystery. The series, set in River Heights, New England, follows the adventures of Nancy Drew, the pretty, proficient teenage daughter of criminal attorney Carson Drew. Stories concern her investigations as she attempts to help her father solve baffling crimes. Based on the stories by Carolyn Keene.

CAST

Nancy Drew   Pamela Sue Martin
                      Janet Louise Johnson
Carson Drew, her father   William Schallert
George Fayne, Nancy's
    girlfriend   Jean Rasey
                            Susan Buckner
Ned Nickerson, Carson's
    assistant   George O'Hanlon, Jr.
Ned Nickerson, an investigator
    for the Boston D.A.
    (later episodes)   Rick Springfield
Bess, Nancy's girlfriend   Ruth Cox
The Sheriff   Robert Karnes

Music: Stu Phillips, Glen A. Larson.
Executive Producer: Glen A. Larson.
Producer: Arlene Sidaris, B. W. Sandefur, Joe Boston.
Director: E. W. Swackhamer, Noel Black, Alvin Ganzer, Joseph Pevney, Michael Caffey, Jack Arnold, Andy Sidaris, Michael Pataki.

THE NANCY DREW MYSTERIES — 60 minutes — ABC — February 6, 1977 – July 30, 1978.

858   THE NANCY WALKER SHOW

Comedy. The misadventures of Nancy Kitteridge, a Hollywood theatrical agent whose troubles stem not only from her difficulties in handling clients, but in her inability to cope with her family.

CAST

Nancy Kitteridge   Nancy Walker
Kenneth Kitteridge, her
    husband   William Daniels
Lorraine, Nancy's married
    daughter   Beverly Archer
Glen, Lorraine's husband   James Cromwell
Terry Folsom, Nancy's assistant   Ken Olfson

Music: Marilyn Bergman, Alan Bergman, Nancy Hamlisch.
Theme Vocal: Nancy Walker.
Executive Producer: Norman Lear.
Producer: Rod Parker.
Director: Hal Cooper, Alan Rafkin.
Creator: Norman Lear, Rod Parker.

THE NANCY WALKER SHOW — 30 minutes — ABC — September 30, 1976 – December 23, 1976. Returned with a final first-run episode on July 11, 1977.

859   NANNY AND THE PROFESSOR

Comedy. The story of Phoebe Figalilly, the enchanting housekeeper of Professor Harold Everett and his children, who is neither a witch nor a magician, but possesses the ability to spread love and joy.

CAST

Phoebe Figalilly (Nanny)   Juliet Mills
Harold Everett, a widower and
    professor of math at
    Clinton College   Richard Long
Hal Everett, his son   David Doremus
Bentley (Butch) Everett,
    his son   Trent Lehman
Prudence Everett, his
    daughter   Kim Richards
Francine Fowler, Hal's
    girlfriend   Eileen Baral
Florence Fowler, Francine's
    mother   Patsy Garrett
Henrietta, Nanny's aunt   Elsa Lanchester
The college dean   Harry Hickox

The Everett address: 10327 Oak Street in Los Angeles.
Everett pets: Waldo, a dog; Merytl and Mike, guinea pigs; Sebastian, a rooster; and Jerome and Geraldine, baby goats.

Music: George Greeley, Charles Fox.
Executive Producer: David Gerber.
Producer: Wes McAffe, Charles B. Fitzsimons.
Director: Peter Tewksbury, David Alexander, Jerry Bernstein, Norman Abbott, Bruce Bilson, Jack Arnold.
Creator: Thomas L. Miller, A. J. Carothers.

NANNY AND THE PROFESSOR — 30 minutes — ABC — January 21, 1970 – December 27, 1971. 65 episodes. Syndicated.

860   NASHVILLE 99

Crime Drama. The exploits of Stonewall "Stoney" Huff, and Trace Mayne, his partner, police detectives attached to the Nashville Metropolitan Police Department in Tennessee. (The title refers to Stoney's badge number: Nashville 99.)

CAST

Det. Lt. Stoney Huff   Claude Akins
Det. Trace Mayne   Jerry Reed
Birdie Huff, Stoney's
    mother   Lucille Benson
R. B., a deputy   Charlie Pride

Music: Earle Hagen.
Music Supervision: Lionel Newman.
Executive Producer: Ernie Frankel.
Director: Don McDougall, Lawrence Dobkin, George Sherman.

NASHVILLE 99 — 60 minutes — CBS — April 1, 1977 – April 22, 1977. 3 episodes.

NASHVILLE NOW

See *The Ian Tyson Show*.

861   NBC ACTION PLAYHOUSE

Anthology. Rebroadcasts of dramas that were originally aired on *The Bob Hope Chrysler Theatre* (NBC, October 4, 1963 – September 6, 1967).

Host: Peter Marshall.

Included:

The Sojourner. The story focuses on John Ferris, a foreign correspondent, as he struggles to piece together the events that led to the breakup of his marriage.

Cast: John Ferris: Efrem Zimbalist, Jr.; Beth Ferris: Vera Miles; Lou: Howard Duff; McCarthy: Herschel Bernardi; Jesse: Warren Stevens.

The Enemy on the Beach. The story, set during World War II, follows a demolition team as it tries to disarm two newly developed German mines.

Cast: Lt. Nick Raino: Robert Wagner; Allison Lang: Sally Ann Howes; Cdr. John McAuliffe: James Donald; Commander Hastings: Torin Thatcher.

The Fatal Mistake. The story of a blackmail victim who plots to kill the extortionist.

Cast: Donald Hammond: Arthur Hill; Harry Carlin: Roddy McDowall; Nancy Hammond: Marge Redmond; Major Tucker: Michael Wilding; Gordon Knight: Laurence Naismith.

The Crime. The story of a vengeful prosecuting attorney who attempts to pin a murder on the woman who jilted him.

Cast: Abe Perez: Jack Lord; Sarah Rodman: Dana Wynter; D. A. Hightower: Pat O'Brien; Mary: Sheree North; Fran Perez: Karen Steele; Frank Busch: Walter Woolf King.

NBC ACTION PLAYHOUSE — 60 minutes — NBC — June 24, 1971 – September 7, 1971; May 23, 1972 – September 5, 1972.

862   NBC ADVENTURE THEATRE

Anthology. Rebroadcasts of dramas that were originally aired on *The Bob Hope Chrysler Theatre* (NBC, October 4, 1963 – September 6, 1967).

Host: Art Fleming, Ed McMahon.

Included:

The Highest Fall of All. The story of a stuntman, desperately in need of money, who agrees to make a 200-foot jump for $10,000.

Cast: Vic Strode: Stuart Whitman; John Perry: Gary Merrill; Doyle Ralston: Steve Ihnat; Diane Skates: Terry Moore; Lili Strode: Joan Hacket.

Four Kings. The story of four GI criminals who are sent to Germany during World War II to steal top-secret plans.

Cast: Bert Graumann: Peter Falk; Gabriella: Susan Strasberg; Dr. King: Paul Lukas; Harry: Vito Scotti; Leonard: Than Wyenn; Major Stern: Simon Oakland.

Double Jeopardy. The story revolves around police efforts to discover which twin sister, Amanda or Barbara, is guilty of murder.

Cast: Amanda/Barbara: Lauren Bacall; Fred Piper: Jack Kelly; Lt. Courtney: Tom Poston; Pilot: Zsa Zsa Gabor; Maid: Jean Hale; Show Girl: Diane McBain; Piper's Secretary: Lee Meriwether.

War of Nerves. A story about an American student in Paris who witnesses the assassination of an Algerian representative, then, fearing for his life, goes into hiding.

Cast: Robert MacKay; Stephen Boyd; Phillipe Tabor: Louis Jourdan; Simone Dumail: Monique Lemaire; Paul Favrel: Emile Genest.

NBC ADVENTURE PLAYHOUSE — 60 minutes — NBC — July 24, 1971 – September 4, 1971; June 15, 1972 – August 31, 1972.

NBC BEST SELLERS

See *Best Sellers*.

863   NBC COMEDY PLAYHOUSE

Anthology. Rebroadcasts of comedy episodes that were originally aired on *The Bob Hope Chrysler Theatre* (NBC, October 4, 1963 – September 6, 1967).

Host: Jack Kelly.

Included:

The Seven Little Foys. The story of a vaudeville headliner who hits the road with his seven children. In the episode, he decides to break up the act and send the kids to school.

Cast: Eddie Foy: Eddie Foy, Jr.; George M. Cohan: Mickey Rooney; Barney Green: George Tobias; Aunt Clara: Naomi Stevens; The Foy Children: The Osmond Brothers.

In Any Language. The story of an actress who, while in Rome to star in a new movie, decides to try to win back her husband from an Arabian Princess.

Cast: Hannah King: Nanette Fabray; Aldo Carmenelli: Ricardo Montalban; Charlie: John Forsythe; Valerie Guthrie: Mabel Albertson; Princess Fawzia: Jean Hale.

... And Baby Makes Five. The story of a Pulitzer Prize-winning writer who forsakes his career in New York to become the editor of a weekly country newspaper.

Cast: Will Nye: Cliff Robertson; Christina: Angie Dickinson; Dee: Nina Foch; Reynard Pitney: Walter Abel; James Eckert: Van Hewitt.

Wake Up, Darling. The story of Polly Emerson, a housewife who lands a role in a Broadway play, and the problems that ensue when her husband objects.

Cast: Polly Emerson: Janet Blair; Don Emerson: Barry Nelson; Deerfield: Roddy McDowall; Martha: Ann B. Davis; Gloria: Joyce Jameson; Prescott: Jack Albertson.

NBC COMEDY PLAYHOUSE—60 minutes—NBC—July 7, 1971—August 30, 1971; July 8, 1972—September 4, 1972

864   THE NBC FOLLIES

Variety. A revue based on the music, song, dance and comedy of vaudeville.

Host: Sammy Davis, Jr.
Regulars: Mickey Rooney, The Carl Jablonski Dancers.
Announcer: Colin Mayer, John Harlan.
Orchestra: Harper MacKay.
Executive Producer: Sy Marsh.
Producer: Bob Wynn.
Writer: Bob Becker, George Foster, Howard Albrecht, Sol Weinstein, Hal Goldman, Al Gordon, Jack Raymond, Milt Rosen.
Director: Bob Wynn.

THE NBC FOLLIES—60 minutes—NBC—September 13, 1973—December 27, 1973. 7 programs. The 60-minute pilot program (videotape) aired on NBC on February 8, 1973.

865   NBC MYSTERY MOVIE

NBC SUNDAY MYSTERY MOVIE

Crime Drama. The overall title for nine rotating series: *Amy Prentiss, Columbo, Hec Ramsey, Lanigan's Rabbi, McCloud, McCoy, McMillan, McMillan and Wife,* and *Quincy, M.E.* See individual titles for information.

NBC MYSTERY MOVIE—90 minutes—NBC—September 15, 1971—September 12, 1972. NBC SUNDAY MYSTERY MOVIE—2 hours—NBC—September 17, 1972—September 4, 1977.

NBC's SATURDAY NIGHT

See *Saturday Night Live*.

866   NBC THEATRE

Anthology. Dramatic presentations produced especially for television.

Announcer: Donald Rickles.

Included:
Summer of My German Soldier. The story, set in Georgia during one summer of World War II, follows the bittersweet romance between Patricia Bergen, a 13-year-old Jewish girl, and Anton Reicher, an escaped Nazi P.O.W. with whom she falls in love.

Cast: Patricia Bergen: Kristy McNichol; Anton Reicher: Bruce Davison; Ruth: Esther Rolle; Harry Bergen: Michael Constantine; Pearl Bergen: Barbara Barrie.
Credits: Music: Stanley Myers; Producer: Linda Gottlieb; Director: Michael Tuchner.

The Miracle Worker. The story of Annie Sullivan, a governess who comes to Alabama from Boston in 1886 to care for Helen Keller, an unruly, unspeaking child due to an early illness which left her deaf and blind. Annie's struggles to bring Helen into the real world are dramatized. The movie, adapted from William Gibson's novel for TV in 1957 (*Playhouse 90*, February 1957), then rewritten for Broadway in 1959 and for Hollywood in 1962, is unique for Patty Duke: in 1959 she portrayed Helen, in the 1979 version she portrays Annie.

Cast: Annie Sullivan: Patty Duke Astin; Helen Keller: Melissa Gilbert; Kate Keller: Diana Muldaur; Capt. Arthur Keller: Charles Siebert; James Keller: Stanley Wells; Aunt Ev: Anne Seymour; Viny: Hilda Haynes.
Credits: Music: Billy Goldenberg; Executive Producer: Raymond Katz, Sandy Gallin; Producer: Fred Coe; Director: Paul Aaron.

Too Far to Go. Based on the short stories by John Updike, the movie follows the decline and fall of a suburban couple's twenty-year marriage.

Cast: Joan Maple: Blythe Danner; Richard Maple: Michael Moriarty; Rebecca Quine: Glenn Close; Jack Dennis: Ken Kercheval; Marion Sales: Kathryn Walker; Henry Mills: Josef Sommer.
Credits: Executive Producer: Robert Geller; Producer: Chris Schultz; Director: Fielder Cook.

NBC THEATRE—2 hours—NBC—Premiered: October 30, 1978.

867   NBC WEDNESDAY MYSTERY MOVIE

NBC TUESDAY MYSTERY MOVIE

Crime Drama. The overall title for six rotating series: *Banacek, Cool Million, Faraday and Company, Madigan, The Snoop Sisters* and *Tenafly.* See individual titles for information.

NBC WEDNESDAY MYSTERY MOVIE—90 minutes—NBC—September 13, 1972—January 9, 1974.
NBC TUESDAY MYSTERY MOVIE—90 minutes—NBC—January 15, 1974—September 4, 1974.

868   NEAREST AND DEAREST

Comedy. The British series on which America's *Thicker Than Water* is based. The program, which has not been broadcast in the United States, follows the misadventures of Nellie Pledge and her brother Eli, the black sheep of the family, when they become heirs to a derelict pickle factory.

CAST
Nellie Pledge	Hylda Baker
Eli Pledge	Jimmy Jewel
Stan	Joe Gladwin
Lily	Madge Hindle
Walter	Edward Malin

NEAREST AND DEAREST—30 minutes—Produced by Granada Television from 1968 to 1972.

869   NEEDLES AND PINS

Comedy. Life in the aggravating world of the garment industry as seen through the experiences of Wendy Nelson, a struggling young apprentice fashion designer with Lorelei Fashions in New York City.

CAST
Wendy Nelson	Deirdre Lenihan
Nathan Davidson, in charge of manufacturing	Norman Fell
Harry Karp, Nathan's partner	Louis Nye
Charlie Miller, the salesman	Bernie Kopell
Sonia Baker, the bookkeeper	Sandra Deel
Max, the material cutter	Larry Gelman
Myron Russo, the pattern maker	Alex Henteloff
Julius Singer, owner of Singer Sophisticates, the competition	Milton Selzer
Elliott, waiter at the local restaurant	Joshua Shelley

Address of Lorelei Fashions: 463 7th Avenue.

Music: Mike Post and Pete Carpenter.
Executive Producer: David Gerber.
Producer-Director: Hy Averback.

NEEDLES AND PINS—30 minutes—NBC—September 21, 1973

—December 28, 1973. 14 episodes.

870   THE NEIGHBORS

Game. Five actual neighbors, all women, are involved. Two are selected as the players, the others comprise the panel. A question is read. Each player is asked to whom the question refers—herself or her neighbor. The answers are based on a survey of the panel, and if the player's choice agrees with the panel's, she receives twenty-five dollars. Four such questions are asked.

The second round concerns the players' abilities to pinpoint which neighbor said something about her. A statement, made by one of the panelists, about one of the players is read. If the player can tell which of her neighbors made the statement she scores one hundred dollars. Four such situations are played.

In the third round, the host reads a statement about one of the two players that all three panelists agree with. Players have to determine to whom the statement refers. Four such questions are played, worth $50, $100, $200 and $500. The player with the highest cash score is the winner.

Host: Regis Philbin.
Model: Jane Nelson, Sylvia Neils.
Announcer: Joe Sinan.
Music: Stan Worth.
Producer: Bill Carruthers.
Director: Bill Carruthers.

THE NEIGHBORS—30 minutes—ABC—December 29, 1975—April 9, 1976. 70 programs.

871   THE NEW ADVENTURES OF BATMAN

Animated Cartoon. An animated adaptation of the comic book character that details the exploits of Batman, alias multimillionaire Bruce Wayne, and Robin, alias Dick Grayson, his ward, as they battle crime in Gotham City.

VOICES
Batman	Adam West
Robin	Burt Ward
Batgirl	Melendy Britt
Batmite, the mouse	Lennie Weinrib

Music: Yvette Blais, Jeff Michael.
Executive Producer: Lou Scheimer, Norm Prescott.
Producer: Don Christensen.
Director: Hal Sutherland.

THE NEW ADVENTURES OF BATMAN—25 minutes—CBS—February 12, 1977—September 2, 1978.

872   THE NEW ADVENTURES OF GILLIGAN

Animated Cartoon. A spin-off from *Gilligan's Island.* Shipwrecked on an uncharted island in the South Pacific when their

NBC

Mulligan's Stew. Bottom, Suzanne Crough. Center row, from left, Sunshine Lee, Elinor Donahue, Lawrence Pressman and K.C. Martel. Top row, from left, Chris Ciampa, Lory Kochheim, Julie Ann Haddock and Johnny Doran.

ABC

The Nancy Drew Mysteries. At center, Pamela Sue Martin. From left, George O'Hanlon, Jr., William Schallert and Jean Rasey.

NBC

Needles and Pins. Deirdre Lenihan and Norman Fell.

CBS

The New Adventures of Wonder Woman. Lynda Carter.

charter ship, the S.S. *Minnow*, is damaged in a tropical storm, the five passengers and two crew members develop a community when all attempts to acquire help fail. Stories relate their struggle for survival, to understand nature and their fellow humans.

VOICES

Jonas Grumby, the skipper	Alan Hale
Gilligan, his bumbling first mate	Bob Denver
Ginger Grant, the movie actress	Jane Webb
Thurston Howell III, the millionaire	Jim Backus
Lovey Howell, Thurston's wife	Natalie Schafer
Roy Hinkley, the research scientist, the "Professor"	Russell Johnson
Mary Ann Summers, a clerk from Kansas	Jane Edwards

Gilligan's pet monkey: Stubby.

Music: Yvette Blais, Jeff Michael.
Executive Producer: Lou Scheimer, Norm Prescott.
Producer: Don Christensen.
Director: Don Towsley, Lou Zukor, Rudy Larriva, Bill Reed.

THE NEW ADVENTURES OF GILLIGAN — 30 minutes — ABC — September 7, 1974 – September 4, 1977.

873 THE NEW ADVENTURES OF HUCKLEBERRY FINN

Live Action-Animation Adventure. Adapted from the novel, *The Adventures of Huckleberry Finn*, by Mark Twain. Pursued by the vengeful Injun Joe, Huckleberry Finn, Becky Thatcher and Tom Sawyer run into a cave where they are engulfed by a raging river and transported to a strange fantasy land that is inhabited by cartoon characters. The series depicts their adventures as, pursued by Joe, they wander through various lands, help people in need and try to find the way home to Hannibal, Missouri, in 1845. Live action is played against superimposed animated backgrounds.

CAST

Huckleberry Finn	Michael Shea
Becky Thatcher, his friend	Lu Ann Haslam
Tom Sawyer, his friend	Kevin Schultz
Injun Joe, their enemy	Ted Cassidy
Aunt Polly, Tom's aunt	Anne Bellamy
Mrs. Thatcher, Becky's mother	Dorothy Tennant

Voices: Hal Smith, Ted de Corsia, Peggy Webber, Charles Lane, Vic Perrin, Julie Bennett, Paul Frees, Marvin Miller.
Music: Hoyt Curtin, Ted Nichols.
Producer: William Hanna, Joseph Barbera.
Live Action Director: Bruce Bilson, Byron Haskin, Walter Burr, Hollingsworth Morse.
Animation Director: Charles A. Nichols.

THE NEW ADVENTURES OF HUCKLEBERRY FINN — 30 minutes — NBC — September 15, 1968 – September 7, 1969. 20 episodes. Syndicated in 1975.

874 THE NEW ADVENTURES OF MIGHTY MOUSE AND HECKLE AND JECKLE

Animated Cartoon.

Segments:

Mighty Mouse. Newly animated adventures of the super mouse as he struggles against evil. Recurring story line depicts Mighty Mouse's efforts to protect his girlfriend, Pearl Pureheart, from the evil villain, Oilcan Harry. Original version of the series was titled *The Mighty Mouse Playhouse*, which ran on CBS from December 10, 1955 to September 2, 1967, and featured the voice of Tom Morrison as Mighty Mouse.

VOICES

Mighty Mouse	Alan Oppenheimer
Pearl Pureheart	Diane Pershing
Oilcan Harry	Alan Oppenheimer

Heckle and Jeckle. Newly animated adventures of the mischievous magpies Heckle and Jeckle. The original series, titled "Heckle and Jeckle," was first syndicated in 1955 and featured the voice of Paul Frees as both Heckle and Jeckle.

VOICES

Heckle	Frank Welker
Jeckle	Frank Welker

Music: George Mahana.
Executive Producer: Lou Scheimer, Norm Prescott.
Producer: Don Christensen.

THE NEW ADVENTURES OF MIGHTY MOUSE AND HECKLE AND JECKLE — 55 minutes — CBS — September 8, 1979 – August 30, 1980. 25 minutes — Premiered: September 6, 1980.

875 THE NEW ADVENTURES OF PERRY MASON

Crime Drama. The cases and courtroom defenses of Perry Mason, a brilliant criminal attorney working out of Los Angeles. Based on the character created by Erle Stanley Gardner. See also *Perry Mason* for information on the original series.

CAST

Perry Mason	Monte Markham
Della Street, his secretary	Sharon Acker
Hamilton Burger, the prosecuting attorney	Harry Guardino
Paul Drake, Mason's investigator	Albert Stratton
Police Lt. Arthur Tragg	Dane Clark
Gertie Lade, Mason's receptionist	Brett Somers

Music: Earle Hagen.
Music Supervision: Lionel Newman.
Executive Producer: Conwall Jackson.
Producer: Ernie Frankel, Art Seid.

THE NEW ADVENTURES OF PERRY MASON — 60 minutes — CBS — September 16, 1973 – January 27, 1974. 15 episodes.

876 THE NEW ADVENTURES OF WONDER WOMAN

Adventure. A spin-off from *Wonder Woman*, which see for background information. (Story line begins where the original leaves off.) Having successfully aided America in its fight against the Nazis, Diana Prince, alias Wonder Woman, returns to Paradise Island in 1945 following World War II.

Now, thirty-two years later (1977), as a plane carrying U.S. officials to a meeting in Latin America passes through the Bermuda Triangle, a saboteur releases a gas that renders the crew and passengers unconscious. The plane, caught in the magnetic field of the Triangle, comes under the control of the inhabitants of the uncharted Paradise Island — a race of super women called Amazons. Entering the downed craft, the Princess Diana is startled to see a man whom she believes is Major Steve Trevor, a mortal she helped in the 1940s. Later, Diana learns that the man is U.S. Government Security Agent Steve Trevor, Jr., son of the late Major General Steve Trevor.

Realizing that the world is still threatened by evil, Diana requests permission from her Queen Mother to become an emissary and assist the outside world in its battle for truth and justice. A special council meeting is held and Diana's request is granted. To protect her true identity as Wonder Woman, the Princess again adopts the guise of Diana Prince. Steve is then hypnotized and led to believe that Diana is his replacement assistant, whom he is to meet in Latin America.

From the Queen Mother, Diana receives special wrist bracelets, made of feminum, to reflect bullets; a magic lariat, which compels people to tell the truth; and magic tiara, which contains a special ruby that enables Diana to contact her mother whenever the need arises. Diana then chooses a revealing red, white and blue costume (see photo) to signify her allegiance to freedom and democracy.

The passengers and crew, still unconscious, are put back aboard the plane. Diana pilots it, then plays a special musical tune to awaken the crew. As they begin to regain their senses, Diana leaves and boards her invisible plane, which she uses to guide the jet safely to its destination.

At the scheduled meeting, Diana introduces herself to Steve and is accepted as his assistant. Later, in Washington, D.C., Diana gains access to the government's computerized personnel files and programs her own employment record — the final step to again re-create Diana Prince, assistant to Steve Trevor of the I.A.D.C. (Inter Agency Defense Command).

Stories depict Diana's exploits as she battles for freedom and democracy throughout the world as the mysterious Wonder Woman. (By performing a twirling striptease, the attractive Diana Prince emerges into the gorgeous Wonder Woman.) Based on the character created by Charles Moulton.

CAST

Diana Prince/ Wonder Woman	Lynda Carter
Steve Trevor, Jr.	Lyle Waggoner
Joe Atkinson, Steve's superior	Normann Burton
The Queen Mother	Beatrice Straight
Eve, Steve's secretary	Saundra Sharp
Dale Hawthorn, Diana's superior*	John Durren
Bryce Kandel (a.k.a. Brett Cassidy), Diana's assistant*	Bob Seagren
Voice of Ira, the I.A.D.C. computer	Tom Kratochzil

Music: Artie Kane, Robert Prince, Richard La Salle, Johnny Harris, Angela Morley.
Theme: "Wonder Woman" by Charles Fox and Norman Gimbel.
Executive Producer: Douglas S. Cramer, Wilfred Lloyd Baumes.
Producer: Charles B. Fitzsimons, Mark Rodgers.
Director: Alan Crosland, Bob Kelljan, Jack Arnold, Dick Moder, Leslie H. Martinson, Sigmund Neufeld, Jr., Gordon Hessler, Ivan Dixon, Don McDougall, Curtis Harrington, John Newland, Michael Caffey.
Animation: Phill Norman.

THE NEW ADVENTURES OF WONDER WOMAN — 60 minutes — CBS — September 16, 1977 – February 19, 1979. 39 episodes. March 10, 1979 – March 17, 1979. 2 episodes. May 28, 1979 – May 29, 1979. 2 episodes. August 28, 1979 – September 11, 1979. 3 episodes.

*In the episode of August 28, 1979, which found Diana moving from Washington to Los Angeles, these characters were introduced in what appeared to be a new version of the series that never sold.

877   THE NEW ANDY GRIFFITH SHOW

Comedy. The trials and tribulations of Andy Sawyer, the former sheriff and justice of the peace turned mayor of Greenwood, North Carolina.

CAST

Mayor Andy Sawyer	Andy Griffith
Lee Sawyer, his wife	Lee Meriwether
Lori Sawyer, their daughter	Lori Ann Rutherford
T. J. Sawyer, their son	Marty McCall
Nora, Lee's sister	Ann Morgan Guilbert
Buff MacKnight, the senior town councilman	Glen Ash
Mrs. Gossage	Ruth McDevitt

Music: Earle Hagen.
Executive Producer: Richard O. Linke.
Producer: Aaron Ruben.

THE NEW ANDY GRIFFITH SHOW — 30 minutes — CBS — January 8, 1972 – June 4, 1972. 13 episodes.

878   THE NEW ARCHIE/SABRINA HOUR

Animated Cartoon. Newly animated adventures of the Archie Gang — Archie Andrews, Veronica Lodge, Betty Cooper, Reggie Mantle, Jughead Jones, Hot Dog and Sabrina, the teenage Witch.

Voices: Dallas McKennon, Jane Webb, Don Messick, John Erwin, Jose Flores, Howard Morris.
Music: Yvette Blais, Jeff Michael.
Executive Producer: Norm Prescott, Lou Scheimer.
Producer: Don Christensen.

THE NEW ARCHIE/SABRINA HOUR — 60 minutes — NBC — September 10, 1977 – November 12, 1977. 10 episodes.

879   THE NEW AVENGERS

Adventure. A revised and updated version of *The Avengers,* which see for original story line information. The new version, set in England, continues to depict the exploits of John Steed, a debonair British Government Agent, and his new assistants, Purdy, a beautiful and courageous woman, and the daring Mike Gambit.

CAST

John Steed	Patrick Macnee
Purdy	Joanna Lumley
Mike Gambit	Gareth Hunt

Music: Laurie Johnson.
Producer: Albert Fennell, Brian Clemens.
Director: Desmond Davis, Ray Austin, Ernest Day, Graeme Clifford, James Hill, Don Thompson, John Hough, Sidney Hayers, Richard Gilbert, Claude Fournier.

THE NEW AVENGERS — 70 minutes — CBS — September 15, 1978 – March 23, 1979. 25 episodes.

880   THE NEW BILL COSBY SHOW

Variety. Various songs, dances and comedy sketches that depict the world as seen through the eyes of comedian Bill Cosby.

Host: Bill Cosby.
Regulars: Susan Tolsky, Lola Falana, Foster Brooks, Oscar De Grury, Erin Fleming, The Donald McKayle Dancers.
Announcer: Lola Falana.
Orchestra: Quincy Jones, Bobby Bryant.
Producer: George Schlatter.
Writer: Pat McCormick, Stanley Ralph Ross, Frank Shaw, Jerry Mayer, Gene Perrett, Ronnie Graham.
Director: Mark Warren.

THE NEW BILL COSBY SHOW — 60 minutes — CBS — September 11, 1972 – May 17, 1973.

THE NEW CANDID CAMERA

See *Candid Camera.*

881   THE NEW CBS FRIDAY NIGHT MOVIE

THE NEW CBS TUESDAY NIGHT MOVIE

Movies. Feature-length films produced especially for television.

Included:

Coffee, Tea, or Me? The story of a stewardess with two husbands — one at each end of the Los Angeles-to-London run.

Cast: Carol Burnham/Carol Byrnes: Karen Valentine; Dennis Burnham: John Davidson; Tommy Byrnes: Michael Anderson, Jr.; Susan Edmonds: Louise Lasser; Waiter: Lou Jacobi; Lisa Benton: Erica Hagen.

Terror on the Beach. The story of a family whose vacation at the beach turns out to be a weekend of terror when they are attacked by a group of cultists.

Cast: Neil Glynn: Dennis Weaver; Arlene Glynn: Estelle Parsons; DeeDee Glynn: Susan Dey; Steve Glynn: Kristoffer Tabori; Jerry: Scott Hylands; Frank: Henry Olek; Gail: Roberta Collins; Helen: Carole Ita White; Jenny: Betsy Slade.

Sandcastles. A love story that centers around a girl named Jenna, a violinist who is in love with a ghost.

Cast: Jenna: Bonnie Bedelia; Michael: Jan-Michael Vincent; Alexis: Herschel Bernardi; Sarah: Mariette Hartley; Frank Watson: Gary Crosby; Ruth Watson: Loretta Leversee; Paul Fiedler: Lloyd Gough.

Gargoyles. The story of half-human, half-reptile creatures who are planning to take over the Earth.

Cast: Mercer Boley: Cornel Wilde; Diana Boley: Jennifer Salt; Head Gargoyle: Bernie Casey; Uncle Willie: Woodrow Chambliss; Police Chief: William Stevens; Mrs. Parks: Grayson Hall; James Reeger: Scott Glenn; Jesse: John Gruber.

THE NEW CBS FRIDAY NIGHT MOVIE — 90 minutes — CBS — September 17, 1971 – September 8, 1972.

THE NEW CBS TUESDAY NIGHT MOVIE — 90 minutes — CBS — September 12, 1972 – September 3, 1974.

882   THE NEW DICK VAN DYKE SHOW

Comedy. The series, set in Carefree, Arizona, follows the trials and tribulations of Dick Preston, host of *The Dick Preston Show*, a ninety-minute talk-variety program produced by KXIU-TV, Channel 2, in Phoenix.

CAST

Dick Preston	Dick Van Dyke
Jenny Preston, his wife	Hope Lange
Bernie Davis, Dick's agent	Marty Brill
Carol Davis, Bernie's wife	Nancy Dussault
Michele "Mike" Preston, Dick's sister and secretary	Fannie Flagg
Annie Preston, Dick and Jenny's daughter	Angela Powell
Lucas Preston, Dick and Jenny's son	Michael Shea
Ted Atwater, Dick's employer, the president of the Compton Broadcasting Company	David Doyle

Music: Jack Elliott, Allyn Ferguson.
Executive Producer: Carl Reiner.
Producer: Bernie Orenstein, Saul Turteltaub.

THE NEW DICK VAN DYKE SHOW — 30 minutes — CBS — September 18, 1971 – September 3, 1973.

883   THE NEW DICK VAN DYKE SHOW

Comedy. A revised version of the previous title. The series, set in Tarzana, California, follows the home- and work-life of Dick Preston, an actor who portrays Dr. Brad Fairmont, a surgeon at Pleasant Valley Hospital, on the fictional daytime television soap opera, *Those Who Care.*

CAST

Dick Preston	Dick Van Dyke
Jenny Preston, his wife	Hope Lange
Annie Preston, his daughter	Angela Powell
Max Mathias, the producer	Dick Van Patten
Alex Montez, the director	Henry Darrow
Dennis Whitehead, the writer	Barry Gordon
Richard Richardson, Dick's neighbor, the star of the *Harrigan's Holligans* series	Richard Dawson
Connie Richardson, Richard's wife	Chita Rivera
Margot Brighton, the serial lead, playing Dr. Susan Allison	Barbara Rush

The Prestons' address: 747 Bonnie Vista Road.

Music: Jack Elliott, Allyn Ferguson.
Executive Producer: Byron Paul.
Producer: Bernie Orenstein, Saul Turteltaub.

THE NEW DICK VAN DYKE SHOW — 30 minutes — CBS — September 10, 1973 – September 2, 1974.

884   THE NEW FRED AND BARNEY SHOW

Animated Cartoon. A spin-off from *The Flintstones.* Continued events in the lives of Fred and Wilma Flintstone and their neighbors, Barney and Betty Rubble.

VOICES

Fred Flintstone	Henry Corden
Wilma Flintstone	Jean VanderPyl
Barney Rubble	Mel Blanc
Betty Rubble	Janet Waldo

Additional Voices: Jim McGeorge, Barney Phillips, John Stephenson.
Music: Hoyt Curtin.
Executive Producer: William Hanna, Joseph Barbera.
Producer: Art Scott.
Director: Ray Patterson, Charles Nichols, Carl Urbano.

THE NEW FRED AND BARNEY SHOW — 30 minutes — NBC — February 3, 1979 – September 15, 1979. Spin-off series: *Fred and Barney Meet the Thing.*

885   THE NEW HOWDY DOODY SHOW

Children. A spin-off from *Howdy Doody,* which see for original story line information. The updated version features puppets, guest performances and comedy sketches geared to children.

CAST

Buffalo Bob Smith, the host	Bob Smith
Clarabell Hornblow, the clown	Lew Anderson
Happy Harmony, the school teacher	Marilyn Patch
Fletcher the Sketcher	Milt Neil
Jackie Davis, the singer	Himself
Cornelius Cobb, the prop man	Nick Nicholson
Nicholson Muir, the producer	Bill LeCornec

PUPPET VOICES

Howdy Doody, the boy who runs the Doodyville Circus	Bob Smith

Phineas T. Bluster, the
mean old man   Dayton Allen

Additional Characters: Dilly Dally, a friend of Howdy's; The Flubadub, the main circus attraction; Outer Orbit, the flying saucer.
Music: The Doodyville Doodlers, conducted by Jackie Davis.
Executive Producer: Nick Nicholson, E. Roger Muir.
Producer: Ronald Wayne.
Writer: Willie Gilbert, Lydia Wilen, Nick Nicholson.
Director: Errol Falcon.

THE NEW HOWDY DOODY SHOW — 30 minutes — Syndicated 1976.

886 A NEW KIND OF FAMILY

Comedy. The story of two families, the Flanagans and the Stones (later dropped in favor of the Ashtons) and the problems that arise when both families agree to share the same rented house at 1836 Loma Linda Drive in Los Angeles.

CAST

Kit Flanagan, a widow	Eileen Brennan
Tony Flanagan, her son	Rob Lowe
Hilary Flanagan, her daughter	Lauri Hendler
Andy Flanagan, her son	David Hollander
Abby Stone, a divorcée; a law student	Gwynne Gilford
Jill Stone, Abby's daughter	Connie Hearn
Jessica Ashton, divorced, runs the "Elegant Eats" catering service	Telma Hopkins
JoJo Ashton, Jessica's daughter	Janet Jackson
Harold Zimmerman, their landlord, the host of *The Homemaker's Midday Matinee* TV show	Chuck McCann
Michael Jansen, Kit's romantic interest	Robert Hogan
Carl Ashton, Jessica's ex-husband	Scoey Mitchlll

The Flanagan's dog: Heinz.

Music: Dan Foliart, Howard Pearl.
Supervising Producer: Don Van Atta.
Executive Producer: Margie Gordon, Jane Eisner.
Producer: Nick Arnold, Dick Clair, Jenna McMahon.
Writer: Roy Kammerman, Nick Arnold, Dick Clair, Jenna McMahon, Robert Illes, James Stein.
Director: James Burrows, Alan Myerson, Jerimiah Morris, Tom Connell, Will MacKenzie, Herb Kenwith.
Creator: Margie Gordon, Jane Eisner.
Art Director: Ken Johnson.

A NEW KIND OF FAMILY — 30 minutes — ABC — September 16, 1979 – October 21, 1979. 5 episodes. December 15, 1979 – December 22, 1979. 2 episodes. December 29, 1979 – January 5, 1980. 1 new episode (one repeat).

887 THE NEW LAND

Drama. Set in Minnesota in 1858, the series follows the life and struggles of the Larsen family, Scandinavian immigrants attempting to share in the American dream.

CAST

Christian Larsen, the father	Scott Thomas
Ann Larsen, his wife	Bonnie Bedelia
Tuliff Larsen, their son	Todd Lookinland
Annaliase Larsen, their daughter	Debbie Lytton
Bo Larsen, Christian's brother	Kurt Russell
Mr. Lundstrom, their neighbor	Donald Moffat
Molly Lundstrom, his wife	Gwen Arner
Rhodie Lundstrom, their daughter	Stephanie Steele
Mr. Murdock, their neighbor	Lou Frizzell

Music: The Orphanage.
Executive Producer: William Blinn.
Producer: Philip Leacock.
Director: John Erman, Philip Leacock.
Creator: William Blinn.

THE NEW LAND — 60 minutes — ABC — September 14, 1974 – October 19, 1974. 4 episodes.

THE NEW MAVERICK

See *Young Maverick.*

888 THE NEW MICKEY MOUSE CLUB

Children. An updated version of the 1950s *Mickey Mouse Club* show (which see), featuring twelve new Mouseketeers in songs, dances and sketches, and an array of never-before televised Disney cartoons and films.

MOUSEKETEERS CAST

Kelly	Kelly Parsons
Lisa	Lisa Whelchel
Julie	Julie Piekarski
Mindy	Mindy Feldman
Nita	Nita (DiGiampaolo) Dee
Curtis	Curtis Wong
Shawnte	Shawnte Northcutte
Allison	Allison Fonte
Todd	Todd Turquand
Angel	Angel Florez
Pop	William Attmore
Scott	Scott Craig

Voice of Mickey Mouse: Wayne Allwine (Walt Disney's voice is heard in the cartoons prior to 1949.)
Voice of Jiminy Cricket: Cliff Edwards.
Music: Buddy Baer, Robert F. Brunner, William Schaefer.
Executive Producer: Ron Miller.
Producer: Ed Ropolo, Mike Wuergler.

Writer: Marc Ray, Ron Bastone, Tedd Anasti, David Tallisman.
Director: John Tracy, Dick Krown, Dick Amos, James Field.

THE NEW MICKEY MOUSE CLUB — 30 minutes — Syndicated 1977. 130 programs.

THE NEW NEWLYWED GAME

See *The Newlywed Game.*

889 THE NEW OPERATION PETTICOAT

Comedy. A revised and updated version of *Operation Petticoat,* which see for information. After most of the original crew of the *Sea Tiger* transfers off the pink submarine, the *Sea Tiger* is reassigned to duty as a seagoing ambulance and staffed with a new crew, including three beautiful nurses. The series follows the misadventures of the *Sea Tiger* as it roams the South Pacific during the early years of World War II (circa 1942).

CAST

Captain Sam Haller, the skipper	Robert Hogan
Lt. Michael Bender, executive officer	Randolph Mantooth
Lt. Dolores Crandall, a nurse	Melinda Naud
Lt. Catherine O'Hara, a nurse	Jo Ann Pflug
Lt. Betty Wheeler, a nurse	Hilary Thompson
Chief Stanley Dobritch, the mechanic	Warren Berlinger
Yeoman Alvin Hunkle	Richard Brestoff
Lt. Travis Kern	Sam Chew, Jr.
Seaman Broom	Jim Varney
Seaman Horner	Don Sparks
Seaman Doplos, the cook	Fred Kareman
Seaman Kostos	Peter Mamakos
Chief Manhiannini, the electrician	Martin Azarow

Music: Peter Matz.
Executive Producer: Jeff Harris, Bernie Kukoff.
Producer: Michael Rhodes, Caryn Sneider.
Director: Hollingsworth Morse, Gene Nelson, Bruce Shurley, Bernie Kukoff.

THE NEW OPERATION PETTICOAT — 30 minutes — ABC — September 25, 1978 – October 19, 1978. 4 episodes. June 1, 1979 – August 3, 1979. 5 episodes.

THE NEW, ORIGINAL WONDER WOMAN

See *The New Adventures of Wonder Woman* and *Wonder Woman.*

890 THE NEW PEOPLE

Drama. A small inter-island charter, enroute from Southeast Asia to the mainland, is caught in a fierce storm and damaged. The plane crash-lands on Buamo, a remote Pacific island once operated by the Atomic Energy Commission as a bombsite but abandoned due to contamination fears.

Of the 50 passengers on board, 40 American college students in a cultural exchange program survive. Stories relate their struggles to establish a society untouched by the destruction of modern man.

CAST

Susan Bradley	Tiffany Bolling
Robert Lee	Zooey Hall
Eugene "Bones" Washington	David Moses
George Potter	Peter Ratray
Errol "Bull" Wilson	Lee Jay Lambert
Dexter	Kevin Michaels
Brenda	Brenda Sykes
Gloria	Nancy DeCarol
Stanley	Dennis Olivieri
	Kevin O'Neal
Ginny	Jill Jaress
Laura	Elizabeth Berger
Jack	Clive Clerk
Wendy	Donna Baccala
Dan Stoner	Carl Reindel

Music: Earle Hagen.
Executive Producer: Aaron Spelling, Danny Thomas.
Producer: Robert Justman, Robert Sabanoff.
Creator: Rod Serling.

THE NEW PEOPLE — 45 minutes — ABC — September 22, 1969 – January 12, 1970.

891 THE NEW SHMOO

Animated Cartoon. The adventures of the Shmoo, an Al Capp comic strip character, and its three human friends, Anita, Bella and Billie Joe, as they investigate psychic phenomena.

Voices: Joe Baker, Daws Butler, Don Hastings, Don Messick, Chuck McCann, Jim McGeorge, Margaret McIntyre, Hal Smith, John Stephenson, Janet Waldo, Frank Welker, Bill Idelson, William Woodson.
Music: Hoyt Curtin.
Executive Producer: William Hanna, Joseph Barbera.
Producer: Art Scott, Alex Lovy.
Director: Ray Patterson, George Gordon.

THE NEW SHMOO — 30 minutes — NBC — September 22, 1979 – December 1, 1979.

892 THE NEW SOUPY SALES SHOW

Variety. Music, songs and outlandish comedy sketches.

Host: Soupy Sales.
Regulars: Clyde Adler, Marty Brill.
Executive Producer: Sheldon Brodsky.
Producer: Perry Cross.
Director: Lou Tedesco.

THE NEW SOUPY SALES SHOW — 30 minutes — Syndicated 1979.

893   THE NEW SUPER FRIENDS HOUR

Animated Cartoon. A spin-off from *The Super Friends,* the world's mightiest heroes, who battle injustice throughout the world.

VOICES (Super Friends)

Superman	Danny Dark
Wonder Woman	Shannon Farnon
Batman	Olan Soule
Robin	Casey Kasem
Aquaman	Norman Alden
Zan	Michael Bell
Jana	Liberty Williams
Computer Voice	Casey Kasem
Narrator	Bill Woodson
	Bob Lloyd

Music: Hoyt Curtin, Paul DeKorte.
Executive Producer: William Hanna, Joseph Barbera.
Producer: Iwao Takamoto.
Director: William Hanna, Joseph Barbera.

THE NEW SUPER FRIENDS HOUR — 55 minutes — ABC — September 10, 1977 – September 2, 1978. Spin-off series: *Challenge of the Super Friends.*

894   THE NEW TEMPERATURES RISING SHOW

Comedy. A satirization of medical series as seen through the antics of the staff of Capitol General Hospital in Washington, D.C. A spin-off from *Temperatures Rising.*

CAST

Dr. Paul Mercy, the administrator	Paul Lynde
Wendy Winchester, a nurse	Jennifer Darling
Miss Tillis, the admissions nurse	Barbara Cason
Dr. Jerry Noland	Cleavon Little
Dr. Charles Claver	John Dehner
Dr. Lloyd Axton	Jeff Morrow
Edwina Mercy, Paul's sister	Alice Ghostley
Agatha Mercy, Paul's mother	Sudie Bond
Nurse Kelly	Barbara Rucker
Haskell, the orderly	Jerry Houser

Music: Vic Mizzy.
Producer: E. Duke Vincent, Bruce Johnson.

THE NEW TEMPERATURES RISING SHOW — 30 minutes — ABC — September 25, 1973 – January 8, 1974; July 28, 1974 – August 30, 1974.

895   THE NEW TREASURE HUNT

Game. Three contestants, chosen from the studio audience, select one of three boxes. The contestant whose box contains a "Treasure Hunt" card receives the opportunity to seek $25,000 in cash.

The player chooses one of thirty boxes that are displayed on stage. Before being shown the contents, the player is offered another box, a cash amount varying from $200 to $2,000. If the player refuses the money, she receives the contents of the box she's chosen — cash, valuable merchandise prizes, or a clunk (inexpensive items). Two such rounds are played per program.

Host: Geoff Edwards.
Host (Original Version): Jan Murray.
Assistants: Jane Nelson, Siv Aberg, Joey Faye.
Assistant (Original Version): Marian Stafford.
Announcer: Johnny Jacobs.
Music: Frank Jaffe, Lee Ringuette.
Executive Producer: Chuck Barris.
Producer: Michael J. Metzger.
Director: John Dorsey.
Creator: Jan Murray.
Check Guard: Emil Autouri.

THE NEW TREASURE HUNT — 30 minutes — Syndicated 1973. Original version: *Treasure Hunt* — 30 minutes — ABC — September 17, 1956 – August 23, 1957; NBC — August 12, 1957 – December 4, 1959.

THE NEW TRUTH OR CONSEQUENCES

See *Truth Or Consequences.*

896   THE NEW ZOO REVUE

Children. The series, set in a zoo, describes various aspects of the world to children via songs, sketches, dances and stories.

CAST

Doug, the host	Doug Momary
Emmy Jo, the hostess	Emily Peden
Charlie, the owl (portrayed by)	Sharon Baird
Charlie (voiced by)	Bill Callaway
	Bob Holt
Freddie, the frog (portrayed by)	Yanco Inone
Freddie (voiced by)	Joni Robbins
Henrietta, the hippo (portrayed by)	Thomas Carri
	Larri Thomas
Henrietta (voiced by)	Hazel Shermit
Mr. Dingle, the store owner	Chuck Woolery
Miss Goodbody	Fran Ryan

Orchestra: Denny Vaughn, Milton Greene.
Producer: Gordon Wiles, Thomas A. Hill.
Choreography: Andre Tayir.
Creator: Barbara Atlas, Douglas Momary.
Art Director: George Smith, Jim Tompkins.

THE NEW ZOO REVUE — 30 minutes — Syndicated 1972.

897   THE NEWLYWED GAME

Game. Four husband-and-wife teams compete. The husbands appear before camera; the wives are isolated backstage in a soundproof room. The host asks each husband three five-point questions. The couples are reunited and the questions are restated. If the wife matches her husband's answer, they receive the points.

The second half is played in reverse as the wives are asked three ten-point questions and one twenty-five-point bonus question. The husbands must match their wives' answers. The couple with the highest score wins a specially selected merchandise prize.

Host: Bob Eubanks.
Announcer: Johnny Jacobs.
Music: Frank Jaffe, Lee Ringuette.
Executive Producer: Chuck Barris.
Producer: Mike Metzger.
Director: John Dorsey.
Creator: Roger Muir.

THE NEWLYWED GAME — 30 minutes — ABC — July 11, 1976 – December 20, 1974. Syndicated first run in 1977.

898   THE NEXT STEP BEYOND

Anthology. A revised and updated version of *One Step Beyond,* true stories of psychic happenings.

Host-Narrator: John Newland.
Theme Music: Mark Snow.
Music: Ron Ramin.
Executive Producer: Collier Young.
Producer: Alan Jay Factor.
Director: John Newland.
Creator: Merwin Gerard.

Program Open:
Host: The dramatization you are about to see is based on an actual investigated and documented case history of psychic phenomena — it is the Next Step Beyond.

Included:
Possessed. The story of a young bride who is possessed by the spirit of a dead girl — a spirit that is determined to prove her death was accidental and not her husband's doing.

Cast: Caroline Adams: Toni Bull Bua; Paul Adams: Gene Bua; Also: Sam Shaw, Biff Elliott, Bo Hopkins, Warren Smith.

Other Voices. The story of Walter Hastings, who, when returning to the home of his birth, envisions the murder of a woman by her drunken husband.

Cast: Walter Hastings: Robert Walker; Carrie Jaris: Susan Keller; Frank Jeris: H. M. Wynant; Elsie: Audrey Christie.

The Legacy. Centered around an elaborate model railroad belonging to the grandson of a dead railroad worker, the story depicts the efforts of the railroad worker's ghost to help police solve a series of disasters by forecasting the exact accidents on the HO layout.

Cast: Alan: Stephen A. Clark; Gus: Delos V. Smith, Jr.; Patty: Tasha Lee Zemrus.

THE NEXT STEP BEYOND — 30 minutes — Syndicated 1978.

899   NICHOLS

Western. The series, set in Nichols, Arizona, in 1914, follows the less-than-honorable exploits of Nichols, the town's former owner and now its reluctant sheriff.*

CAST

(No first name) Nichols	James Garner
Jim Nichols, his twin brother†	James Garner
Mitchell, the deputy	Stuart Margolin
Sara "Ma" Ketchum, the self-appointed law	Neva Patterson
Ruth, the barmaid	Margot Kidder
Ketchum, Ma's son	John Beck
Salter, the owner of the Salter House Bar	John Harding
Johnson, the con artist	Paul Hampton
Bertha, the saloon keeper	Alice Ghostley
Judge Thatcher	Richard Bull
Gabe, the general store owner	M. Emmett Walsh
Scully One, the owner of the town	John Quade
Scully Two, his brother	Jesse Wayne

Mitchell's dog: Slump.

Music: Bernardo Segall.
Executive Producer: Meta Rosenberg.
Producer Frank Pierson.
Director: Gerd Oswald (most of the series), Paul Bogart, Jeremy Kagar, Gerald Mayer, Ivan Dixon, Tony Leader.

NICHOLS — 60 minutes — NBC — September 16, 1971 – August 8, 1972. 29 episodes. Also known as *James Garner as Nichols.*

*When he returned home after an eighteen-year absence, Nichols discovered that the town had been homesteaded from his mother. Later, when he is involved in a barroom brawl and unable to pay for the damages, he is made the sheriff to repay the debt through his salary.

†In the last episode, Nichols is killed while trying to stop a barroom brawl. His twin brother, Jim, was introduced in an attempt to present a more forceful lead. However, the series was not renewed and only one potential new episode was produced.

900 NIGHT GALLERY

Anthology. Supernatural tales of the horrifying confrontation between nightmare and reality.

Host: Rod Serling, as a guide through a bizarre Night Gallery whose exhibits hold beneath their canvasses twisted tales of another dimension.
Music: Eddie Sauter.
Theme: Gil Mellé.
Producer: Jack Laird.
Director: John Badham, Gene Kearney, John Meredyth Lucas, Don Taylor, Daryl Duke, Edward Abroms, Jerrold Freedman, Boris Sagal, Douglas Heyes, Jack Laird, John Newland, Steven Spielberg, Jeannot Szwarc, Jeff Corey, Leonard Nimoy, Allen Reisner, Richard Benedict, John Astin, Theodore J. Flicker.

Included:
Lindemann's Catch. Rod Serling's story about a mermaid who is captured by a cold-hearted sea captain.
Cast: Captain Lindemann: Stuart Whitman; Mermaid: Anabel Garth; Doctor: Jack Aranson; Suggs: Harry Townes.

A Question of Fear. The story of an adventurer who accepts a $15,000 bet to stay overnight in a haunted house.
Cast: Denny: Leslie Nielsen; Mazi: Fritz Weaver.

Brenda. A love story that concerns itself with a friendless girl and a grassy glob.
Cast: Brenda: Laurie Prange; Thing: Fred Carson; Richard Allen: Glenn Corbett; Flora: Barbara Babcock; Frances: Pamelyn Ferdin; Elizabeth: Sue Taylor.

Keep in Touch—We'll Think of Something. The strange story of a man driven to find a very special woman.
Cast: Erik Sutton: Alex Cord; Claire Foster: Joanna Pettet; Sgt. Brice: Richard O'Brien.

NIGHT GALLERY—60 minutes—NBC—September 15, 1971–September 6, 1972 (as part of *Four-in-One*). 30 minutes—September 17, 1972–January 14, 1973; May 13, 1973–August 12, 1973. Syndicated. Also known as *Rod Serling's Night Gallery.*

901 THE NIGHT STALKER

Mystery. The exploits of Carl Kolchak, a reporter for the Chicago based *Independent News Service* (I.N.S.). Stories relate his attempts to solve baffling, bizarre and supernatural crimes.

CAST
Carl Kolchak	Darren McGavin
Tony Vincenzo, his editor	Simon Oakland
Ron Updyke, an I.N.S. reporter	Jack Grinnage
Monique Marmelstein, an I.N.S. reporter	Carol Ann Susi
Gordon Spangler (Gordy the Ghoul), the mortician	John Fiedler
Emily Cowles, the advice columnist	Ruth McDevitt

Narrator: Darren McGavin.
Music: Gil Mellé, Jerry Fielding, Craig McRitchie.
Music Supervision: Hal Mooney.
Executive Producer: Cy Chermak.
Producer: Paul Playdon.
Director: Don Weis, Robert Scheerer, Alex Grasshoff, Seymour Robbie, Allen Baron, Gordon Hessler, Michael Caffey, Vincent McEveety, Don McDougall.
Creator: Jeff Rice.

THE NIGHT STALKER—60 minutes—ABC—September 13, 1974–August 30, 1975. 20 episodes. CBS repeats (70 minutes)—May 25, 1979–July 13, 1979; September 14, 1979–December 7, 1979. Original title: *Kolchak: The Night Stalker.* The first pilot film, "The Night Stalker," aired on ABC on January 11, 1972; the second pilot, "The Night Strangler," aired on ABC on January 16, 1973.

902 NOBODY'S PERFECT

Comedy. The exploits of Roger Hart, a brilliant Scotland Yard Inspector attached to the San Francisco Police Department's 22nd Precinct, who suffers from one imperfection: he is calamity prone. Originally titled *Hart of San Francisco.*

CAST
Insp. Roger Hart	Ron Moody
Off. Jennifer Dempsey, his partner	Cassie Yates
Lt. Vince DeGennaro, their superior	Michael Durrell
Careful Eddie, Hart's informant	Danny Wells
Detective Jacobi	Victor Brandt
Detective Grauer	Tom Williams
Detective Ramsey	Renny Roker
Dreyfus, the lab technician	Greg Monaghan
Policewoman (not named)	Melody Rogers

Music: Jack Elliott, Allyn Ferguson, Hal Mooney.
Executive Producer: Norman Barasch.
Producer: Arne Sultan, Chris Hayward, Lew Gallo, Edward Montagne.
Writer: Arne Sultan, Chris Hayward, Ken Hecht, Mike Marmer, Peter Galley, Donald Harris.
Director: Robert Douglas, Norman Abbott, Tony Mordente.
Creator: Arne Sultan, Chris Hayward, Kathy Greer, Bill Greer.

NOBODY'S PERFECT—30 minutes—ABC—June 26, 1980–August 28, 1980. 8 episodes.

903 NO HOLDS BARRED

Comedy. A look at the crackpot side of contemporary American life via film and videotaped segments.

Host: Kelly Monteith.
Music: Tony Romeo.
Theme Music Performed By: Lou Christie.
Executive Producer: Alan Landsburg.
Producer: Herbert Banska.
Writer: Hank Bradford, Kelly Monteith.
Director: Arthur Forrest.

NO HOLDS BARRED—70 minutes—CBS—September 12, 1980–October 3, 1980. 4 programs.

904 NO—HONESTLY

Comedy. The series, set in England, follows the courtship and early married life of the Danbys: Charles, an actor, and his scatterbrained wife, Clara, author of *Ollie the Otter*, stories for children.

CAST
Charles Danby (C.D.)	John Addison
Clara Danby, his wife	Pauline Collins
Lord Burrell, Clara's absentminded father	James Berwick
Lady Burrell, Clara's mother	Franny Rowe
Royal, the Burrells' butler	Kenneth Benda

Music: Lynsey DePaul.
Producer: Humphrey Barclay.
Director: David Askey.

NO—HONESTLY—30 minutes—PBS—July 9, 1975–September 3, 1975. 13 episodes. Produced in England.

905 THE NOONDAY SHOW

Variety. Interviews, comedy skits, news, songs and guests.

Host: David Steinberg.
Regulars: Stan Cann, Jane Dulo, Gailard Sartaine, Caroline Grosky.
Orchestra: Marty Pasetta.
Producer: David Foster.
Director: Eric Lieber.

THE NOONDAY SHOW—NBC—December 15, 1975–December 19, 1975. 5 programs: three were 25 minutes each; two were 55 minutes each.

NORM CROSBY'S THE COMEDY SHOP

See *The Comedy Shop.*

906 THE NORMAN CONQUESTS

Comedy. The miniseries is set in a country home, the scene of a family gathering. It tells of the conflicts and confusions that arise when Norman, a philandering librarian whose conquests are women, plans to have an affair with his sister-in-law, but neglects to consider the obstacles he must overcome—a family that just won't leave him alone. Based on Alan Ayckbourn's comic trilogy: *Living Together, Table Manners,* and *Round the Garden.*

CAST
Norman	Tom Conti
Annie, his sister-in-law	Penelope Wilson
Tom, Annie's boyfriend	David Troughton
Sarah, Norman's sister	Penelope Keith
Ruth, Norman's wife	Fiona Walker
Reg, Sarah's husband	Richard Briers

Producer: David Susskind, Verity Lambert.
Director: Herbert Wise.

THE NORMAN CONQUESTS—2 hours—PBS—July 9, 1979–July 11, 1979. 3 episodes.

907 NORMAN CORWIN PRESENTS

Anthology. Original dramatic presentations.

Host: Norman Corwin.
Producer: Arthur Joel Katz.
Writer: Norman Corwin.
Director: Ted Post.

NORMAN CORWIN PRESENTS—30 minutes—Syndicated 1971.

908 NOT FOR WOMEN ONLY

Discussion. A panel of five guests discusses topical issues.

Hostess: Aline Saarinen, Barbara Walters, Polly Bergen, Lynn Redgrave.
Host: Hugh Downs, Frank Field.
Executive Producer: Laurence Johnson.
Producer: Madeline Amgott.
Director: Jay Miller, Paul Freeman.

NOT FOR WOMEN ONLY—30 minutes—Syndicated 1972.

909 THE NOW EXPLOSION

Variety. Prerecorded Rock music is coupled with an appearance by the performer. Visual and audio effects prevail in an attempt to televise a radio program. Local station personalities serve as hosts who, using the voice-over technique, conduct the show as if it were a radio program.

THE NOW EXPLOSION—7 hours, 30 minutes—Syndicated 1970.

910 NOW YOU SEE IT

Game. Two teams compete, each comprised of two members.

A board is displayed that contains four vertical lines of run-on letters. The four vertical lines, which are numbered 1 through 4, become the *line;* and the fourteen letters each line contains (numbered 1 through 14) become the *position.* A player sits with his back to the board. A question is read and his teammate must locate the answer on the board by calling a *line* (1, 2, 3 or 4). Assuming the player is correct, his partner then faces the board and has to call the *position* of the answer (1 through 14).

Points are awarded according to the line and position total (e.g., line 3, position 7 equals 10 points). The other team competes in the same manner. Pair with the highest score is the winner.

Host: Jack Narz.
Announcer: Johnny Olsen, Gene Wood.
Music: Michael Malone.
Executive Producer: Frank Wayne.
Producer: Buck D'Amore, Mark Goodson, Bill Todman.
Director: Marc Breslow.

NOW YOU SEE IT—30 minutes—CBS—April 1, 1974–June 13, 1975.

911 THE ODDBALL COUPLE

Animated Cartoon. The misadventures of two trouble-prone, free-lance magazine writers: Fleabag the dog, a natural-born slob, and Spiffy, a perfectionist cat. A take-off on *The Odd Couple.*

VOICES

Fleabag	Paul Winchell
Spiffy	Frank Nelson
Goldie, their secretary	Joan Gerber

Additional Voices: Frank Welker, Sarah Kennedy, Joe Besser, Don Messick, Bob Holt, Ginny Tyler.
Music: Doug Goodwin.
Producer: David H. DePatie, Friz Freleng.
Writer: Bob Ogle, Joel Kane, David Detiege, Earl Kress, John W. Dunn.
Supervising Director: Lewis Marshall.

THE ODDBALL COUPLE—30 minutes—ABC—September 6, 1975–September 3, 1977.

912 THE ODD COUPLE

Comedy. The series, set in New York City, follows the misadventures of two divorced men, Oscar Madison, sportswriter for the *New York Herald,* an irresponsible slob; and Felix Unger, a commercial photographer, an excessively neat perfectionist, as they struggle to live together (at 1049 Park Avenue, Apartment 1102).

CAST

Oscar Madison	Jack Klugman
Felix Unger	Tony Randall
Police Officer Murray Grechner, their friend	Al Molinaro
Myrna Turner, Oscar's secretary	Penny Marshall
Miriam Welby, Felix' romantic interest	Elinor Donahue
Dr. Nancy Cunningham, Oscar's romantic interest	Joan Hotchkis
Gloria Unger, Felix' ex-wife	Janis Hansen
Blanche Madison, Oscar's ex-wife	Brett Somers
Howard Cosell, the sportscaster (recurring role)	Himself
Cecily Pigeon, Felix and Oscar's neighbor	Monica Evans
Gwen Pigeon, Cecily's sister	Carole Shelley
Edna Unger, Felix' daughter	Pamelyn Ferdin Doney Oatman
Leonard Unger, Felix' son	Leif Garrett Willie Aames
Speed, Oscar's friend	Garry Walberg
Vinnie, Oscar's friend	Larry Gelman
Roy, Oscar's friend	Ryan MacDonald

Music: Neil Hefti, Kenyon Hopkins.
Music Supervision: Leith Stevens.
Executive Producer: Garry Marshall, Jerry Belson, Harvey Miller, Sheldon Keller.
Producer: Tony Marshall.
Director: Mel Ferber, Jerry Paris, Frank Buxton, Dan Dailey, Hal Cooper, Charles R. Rondeau, Jay Sandrich, Jack Winter, Garry Marshall, Jack Donohue, Harvey Miller, Jerry Belson.

Program Open:
Announcer: On November thirteenth Felix Unger was asked to remove himself from his place of residence. That request came from his wife. Deep down he knew she was right. But he also knew that someday he would return to her. With nowhere else to go, he appeared at the home of his childhood friend, Oscar Madison. Sometime earlier, Madison's wife had thrown him out, requesting that he never return. Can two divorced men share an apartment without driving each other crazy?

THE ODD COUPLE—30 minutes—ABC—September 24, 1970–July 4, 1975. Syndicated.

913 O'HARA, UNITED STATES TREASURY

Crime Drama. The exploits of James O'Hara, a United States Treasury Department agent, as he investigates crimes perpetrated against Customs, Secret Service and Internal Revenue.

CAST

James O'Hara	David Janssen
Inspector Ed Miller	Paul Picerni
Ben Hazzard, O'Hara's superior	Stacy Harris

Music: Ray Heindorf.
Executive Producer: Jack Webb.
Producer: Leonard B. Kaufman.
Director: Lawrence Dobkin, Paul Landers, Alan Crosland, Jr., Daniel Haller, Gerald Mayer, Allen Reisner, James Neilson.

O'HARA, UNITED STATES TREASURY—60 minutes—CBS—September 17, 1971–September 8, 1972. 22 episodes.

914 ONCE AN EAGLE

Drama. The miniseries, adapted from the novel by Anton Myrer, chronicles the lives of Sam Damon and Courtney Massengale, two American soldiers, from 1918 through World War II.

CAST

Sam Damon	Sam Elliott
Courtney Massengale	Cliff Potts
Major George Caldwell	Glenn Ford
Tommy Caldwell Damon	Darleen Carr
Emily Massengale	Amy Irving
General McElvey	Andrew Duggan
Marge Chrysler	Lynda Day George
Jack Devlin	Gary Grimes
Lt. Alvin Merrick	Clu Gulager
Ben Chrysler	Robert Hogan
Mrs. Damon	Kim Hunter
Karl Preis	David Huddleston
Joyce	Juliet Mills
Bert McComadin	Albert Salmi
Captain Townsend	John Saxon
Lin Tsu-Han	James Shigeta
General Bannerman	Barry Sullivan
Colonel Avery	Forrest Tucker
Gen. Duke Lane	William Windom
Dave Shifkin	Anthony Zerbe
Miriam Shifkin	Jane Merrow
Ryetower	Kip Niven
Jinny Massengale	Melanie Griffith
Donny Damon	Andrew Stevens
Joe Brand	Kario Salem
George Varney	John Anderson
Reb Rayburne	Andrew Robinson
Sam Damon, as a boy	Jeff Cotler

Music: Dana Kaproff.
Executive Producer: William Sackheim.
Producer: Peter Fischer.
Writer: Peter Fischer.
Director: E. W. Swackhamer, Richard Michaels.
Art Director: William Campbell.
Director of Photography: J. J. Jones.

ONCE AN EAGLE—9 hours total—NBC—December 2, 1976–January 13, 1977.

915 ONE DAY AT A TIME

Comedy. The series, set in Indianapolis, Indiana, follows the life of Ann Romano, a pretty 34-year-old divorcée whose transition from wife to working mother (as an account executive with the Connors and Davenport Advertising Agency) is complicated by her two headstrong teenage daughters, Julie and Barbara Cooper. (Ann retains her maiden name; Julie and Barbara carry their father's name.)

CAST

Ann Romano	Bonnie Franklin
Julie Cooper, her daughter	Mackenzie Phillips
Barbara Cooper, her daughter	Valerie Bertinelli
Dwayne Schneider, the apartment building super	Pat Harrington
David Kane, Ann's boyfriend, a lawyer	Richard Masur
Ginny Wrobliki, Ann's friend, a waitress at the Alibi Room Bar	Mary Louise Weller
Ed Cooper, Ann's ex-husband	Joseph Campanella
Max Horvath, an airline pilot; married Julie on Oct. 10, 1979	Michael Lembeck
Claude Connors (a.k.a. Al Connors), Ann's employer	John Hillerman
Jerry Davenport, Claude's partner	Charles Siebert
Kathryn Romano, Ann's mother	Nanette Fabray
Bob Morton, Barbara's friend	John Putch
Cliff Randall, Barbara's friend	Scott Colomby
Francine Webster, Ann's co-worker	Shelley Fabares
Chuck Butterfield, Julie's friend	William Cullen Kirby
Vicki Cooper, Ed's second wife	Fawne Harriman
Elliott Newcombe, Barbara's friend	Steven Anderson
Alice Butterfield, Chuck's mother	K Callan
Hal Butterfield, Chuck's father	Howard Morton
Nick Woodloon, Ann's romantic interest	Ron Rifkin

Ann's address: 1344 Hartford Drive, Apt. 402.
Schneider's lodge: The Secret Order of Beavers.

Music: Theme Only: "One Day At A Time" by Jeff and Nancy Barry.
Executive Producer: Norman Lear, Mort Lachman, Norman Paul, Jack Elinson, Alan Rafkin, Bud Wiseman, Dick Bensfield, Perry Grant.
Producer: Allan Manings, Patricia Fass Palmer, Dick Bensfield, Perry Grant, Bud Wiser.
Director: Hal Cooper, Don Richardson, Norman Campbell, John Robins, Herbert Kenwith, Howard Morris, Sandy Kenyon, Alan Rafkin, Gloria Monty, Noam Pitlik.
Creator: Whitney Blake, Allan Manings.
Art Director: Don Roberts.

ONE DAY AT A TIME—30 minutes—CBS—Premiered: December 16, 1975.

916 THE ONEDIN LINE

Drama. The series, set in Liverpool, England, during the 1860s, depicts the exploits of tradesman James Onedin, captain of the *Charlotte Rhodes*, a three-masted top-sail schooner, as he seeks to maintain a cargo transporting business.

CAST

Capt. James Onedin	Peter Gilmore
Anne Onedin, his wife	Anne Stallybrass
Robert Onedin, James's brother	Brian Rawlinson
Elizabeth Onedin, James's sister	Jessica Benton
Capt. Joshua Webster, Anne's father	James Hayter
Sara Onedin, Robert's wife	Mary Webster
Albert Frazer, Elizabeth's romantic interest	Philip Bond

Music: Anthony Isaac.
Producer: Peter Graham Scott.
Director: Roger Jenkins, John Erman.

THE ONEDIN LINE — 60 minutes — Syndicated 1976.

THE $100,000 NAME THAT TUNE

See *Name That Tune.*

917   THE $128,000 QUESTION

Game. Players, who possess knowledge in at least one specific field, compete. Each is asked a series of questions ranging from $64 doubled to $64,000. The contestant, who risks loss of everything if, at any time he should give an incorrect response, can either continue playing or quit after answering a question. His decision determines his earnings, if any. Once a player earns $64,000, he receives the opportunity to return at a later date and compete further with the object being to win another $64,000.

Host: Mike Darrow, Alex Trebek.
Models: Lauri Locks, Cindy Reynolds, Pattie Lee, Sylvie Garant.
Announcer: Alan Calter, Sandy Hoyt.
Music: Guido Basso.
Executive Producer: Steve Carlin.
Producer: Willie Stein, Greg Harper, Candi Cazau.
Director: Dick Schneider, George Chodeker.
Security Director: Michael O'Rourke.

THE $128,000 QUESTION — 30 minutes — Syndicated 1976.

918   ONE IN A MILLION

Comedy. The story of Shirley Simmons, a cab driver who inherits controlling interest in the $200,000,000 Grayson Enterprises at the death of its founder, Jonathan Grayson, a friend of Shirley's. The series, set in New York, focuses on Shirley's efforts to fulfill Grayson's wishes: to run his company as the chairman of the board.

CAST

Shirley Simmons	Shirley Hemphill
Roland Cushing, the vice president of Grayson Enterprises	Keene Curtis
Nancy Boyer, Shirley's secretary	Dorothy Fielding
Barton Stone, Cushing's attorney	Richard Paul
Raymond Simmons, Shirley's father	Mel Stewart
Edna Simmons, Shirley's mother	Ann Weldon
Max Kalamo, the diner owner	Carl Ballantine
Grace Cushing, Roland's wife	Louise Sorel
Michael Boyer, Nancy's son	Jimmy Heth
Duke, Shirley's friend	Ralph Wilcox

Music: Harry Betts.
Executive Producer: Saul Turteltaub, Bernie Orenstein.
Producer: Sid Dorfman, Arnold Kane.
Writer: Alan Livingston, Saul Turteltaub, Bernie Orenstein, Barry Meadow, Jerry Winnick.
Director: Peter Baldwin.
Art Director: Ross Bellah.
Creator: Alan W. Livingston.

ONE IN A MILLION — 30 minutes — ABC — January 8, 1980 – March 15, 1980. 9 episodes. June 2, 1980 – June 23, 1980. 4 episodes.

919   ONE LIFE TO LIVE

Serial. The dramatic story of two Philadelphia families, each from different sides of the tracks: the Woleks, first-generation Americans struggling for a position on top of the social ladder; and the Lords, an established family entrenched in the dominant social and economic milieu.

CAST

Cathy Craig Lord	Amey Levitt
	Dorrie Kavanaugh
	Jane Alice Brandon
	Jennifer Harmon
Dr. James Craig	Nat Polen
Victoria Lord	Erika Slezak
	Gillian Spencer
Anna Wolek	Doris Belack
Meredith Lord Wolek	Lynn Benesch
	Trish Van Devere
Dr. Mark Toland	Tom Lee Jones
Bert Skelly	Bernard Grant
Dr. Larry Wolek	Michael Storm
Joe Riley	Lee Patterson
Vince Wolek	Anthony Ponzini
	Jordan Charney
	Michael Ingram
Melinda Cramer	Patricia Pearcy
	Jane Badleo
Wanda Webb Wolek	Marilyn Chris
	Lee Lawson
Tony Lord	George Reinholt
	Philip McHale
Dr. Will Vernon	Farley Granger
	Bernie McInerney
	Anthony George
Dorian Cramer Lord	Nancy Pinkerton
	Claire Malis
	Robin Strasser
Brad Vernon	Jamison Parker
	Steve Fletcher

Eileen Riley	Patricia Roe
	Alice Hirson
Dave Siegal	Allan Miller
Julie Siegal	Lee Warrick
Carla Gary	Ellen Holly
Dr. Marcus Polk	Norman Rose
	Donald Moffat
Victor Lord	Ernest Graves
	Shepperd Strudwick
Dr. Joyce Brothers	Herself
Lt. Ed Hall	Al Freeman, Jr.
Sadie Gray	Lillian Hayman
Susan Barry	Lisa Richards
Jack Dawson	Jack Ryland
Joshua West	Laurence Fishburne
	Todd Davis
Rachel Wilson	Nancy Barrett
Karen Martin	Niki Flacks
Tom Edwards	Joe Gallison
Merry	Lynn Benish
Millie Parks	Millee Taggart
Dr. Price Trainor	Peter DeAnda
Jenny Siegal	Kathy Glass
Mario Dane	Gerald Anthony
Peggy Filmore	Valerie French
Timmie Siegal	Tom Berenger
Julie Toland	Leonie Norton
John Douglas	Donald Madden
Sheila Rafferty	Christine Jones
Peter Blair	Peter Brouwer
Michiko	Lani Gerrie Miyazaki
Lana McLain	Jackie Zeman
Chris Kositcheck	Josh Taylor
Beck Lee Hunt	Jill Voight
Tina Clayton	Andrea Evans
Elliott Hampton	Ted Leplat
Luke Johnson	Marshall Borden
Pamela Shepherd	Kathleen Devino
Alice Lovelace	Kathryn Squire
Clint Buckley	Bruce Detrick
Robin Crosley	Linda Watkins
Richard Abbott	David Reilly
Peter Janssen	Jeffrey David Pomerantz
Roger Landover	Stephen Bolster
Karen Wolek	Judith Light
Mario Dane	Gerald Anthony
Dr. Jack Scott	Arthur Burghardt
Gwendolyn Abbott	Joan Copeland
Pat Ashley	Jacqueline Courtney
Gretel Cummings	Linda Dano
Tina Clayton	Andrea Evans
Brad Vernon	Steve Fletcher
Paul Kendall	Tom Fuccello
Ina Hopkins	Sally Gracie
Greg Huddleston	Paul Joynt
Samantha Vernon	Susan Keith
Edwina Lewis	Margaret Klenck
Adam Brewster	John Mansfield
Kevin Riley	Morgan K. Melis
Jenny Vernon	Brynn Thayer
Dr. Ivan Kipling	Jack Betts
Herb Callison	Anthony Call
Katrina	Nancy Snyder
Samantha Vernon	Susan Keith
	Julie Montgomery
Danny Wolek	Eddie Moran

Music: Aeolus Productions.
Theme: George Reinholt.
Producer: Doris Quinlan, Joseph Stuart.
Director: David Pressman, Peter Minor, Norman Hall, Jack Sullivan.
Creator: Agnes Nixon.

ONE LIFE TO LIVE — 30 minutes — ABC — July 15, 1968 – July 23, 1976. 45 minutes — July 26, 1976 – January 13, 1978. 60 minutes — Premiered: January 16, 1978.

920   ONE STEP BEYOND

Anthology. Dramatizations based on true events that are strange, frightening and unexplainable in terms of normal human experience.

Host: John Newland.
Music: Harry Lubin.
Executive Producer: Larry Marcus.
Producer: Collier Young.

Program Open:
Host: Come, you'll witness things strange, unexpected, mysterious, but not to be denied. Join me now and take One Step Beyond.

ONE STEP BEYOND — 30 minutes — Syndicated 1962. Spin-off series: *The Next Step Beyond.*

921   ON OUR OWN

Comedy. The series, set in New York City, follows the misadventures of two women in the creative department of the Bedford Advertising Agency: Julia Peters, a copywriter, and Maria Bonino, an art director.

CAST

Julia Peters	Bess Armstrong
Maria Teresa Bonino	Lynnie Greene
Toni McBain, the head of the agency	Gretchyn Wyler
April Baxter, a copywriter	Dixie Carter
Phil Goldstein, an associate	Michael Tucci
Eddie Barnes, the TV commercials producer	John Christopher Jones
Craig Boatwright, the agency salesman	Dan Resin
Mrs. Oblenski, Julia's landlady	Sasha von Scherler

Music: Bob Israel.
Executive Producer: David Susskind.
Producer: Sam Denoff.
Director: James Burrows, Doug Rogers, Noam Pitlik, Mel Shapiro.
Creator: Bob Randall.

ON OUR OWN — 30 minutes — CBS — October 9, 1977 – August 27, 1978. 22 episodes.

922   ON THE BUSES

Comedy. The British series on which America's *Lotsa Luck* is based. The program, which has not been broadcast in the United States, follows the misadventures of Stan Butler and Jack Carter, the crew on the Luxton Bus Company's Number 11 bus to Cemetery Gates.

CAST

Stan Butler, the driver	Reg Varney
Jack Carter, the conductor	Bob Grant
Mum, Stan's over-devoted mother	Cicely Courtneidge
	Doris Hare

CBS

The New Andy Griffith Show. Bottom, from left, Lori Rutherford and Lee Meriwether. Top, from left, Andy Griffith and Marty McCall.

CBS

The New Avengers. From left, Patrick Macnee, Joanna Lumley and Gareth Hunt.

ABC

A New Kind of Family. Front, from left, O.J. (as the family dog Heinz), Rob Lowe and David Hollander. Top, from left, Lauri Hendler, Gwynne Gilford, Eileen Brennan and Connie Ann Hearn.

CBS

One Day at a Time. From left, Pat Harrington, Valerie Bertinelli, Bonnie Franklin and Mackenzie Phillips.

Olive, his hypochondriac
sister — Anna Karen
Arthur, Olive's lazy, unemployed
husband — Michael Robbins
Bus Inspector Blake — Stephen Lewis

Producer: Ronald Wolfe, Ronald
Chesney.
Director: Harry Booth.

ON THE BUSES—30 minutes—
Produced by London Weekend
Television from 1969 through
1973.

923   ON THE ROCKS

Comedy. Life in the Alamesa State
Minimum Security Prison as seen
through the eyes of convict Hector Fuentes, a streetwise and
wisecracking petty thief. Based
on the British series, *Porridge*.

CAST

Hector Fuentes, a convict	Jose Perez
Lester DeMott, a convict	Hal Williams
Cleaver, a convict	Rick Hurst
Nick Palik, a convict	Bobby Sandler
Gabby, a convict	Pat Cranshaw
Mr. Gibson, a correctional officer	Mel Stewart
Mr. Sullivan, same as Gibson	Tom Poston
Wilbur Poindexter, the warden	Logan Ramsey
Dorothy Burgess, Wilbur's secretary	Cynthia Harris

Music: Jerry Fielding.
Producer: John Rich, H. R. Poin-
dexter.
Director: John Rich, Dick
Clement.

ON THE ROCKS—30 min-
utes—ABC—September 11,
1975– May 17, 1976.

924   OPERATION PETTICOAT

Comedy. The series, set in the
South Pacific during World War
II, revolves around the misadventures of the officers and crew of
the jury-built Navy submarine
USS *Sea Tiger*—a pink* sub, cap-
tained by Matthew Sherman,
whose crew includes five sexy
Army nurses (Dolores Crandall,
Claire Reid, Barbara Duran, Ruth
Colfax, and Edna Hayward). Rescued from a Pacific island, they
are now trapped aboard the *Tiger*
as it roams the seas.

CAST

Lt. Cmdr. Matthew Sherman	John Astin
Lt. Nick Holden, the supply officer	Richard Gilliland
Major Edna Hayward	Yvonne Wilder
Lt. Dolores Crandall	Melinda Naud
Lt. Barbara Duran	Jamie Lee Curtis
Lt. Ruth Colfax	Dorrie Thompson
Lt. Claire Reid	Bond Gideon
Yeoman Alvin Hunkle	Richard Brestoff
Ensign Stovall	Christopher J. Brown
Seaman Dooley	Kraig Cassity
Chief Herbert Molumphrey	Wayne Long
Seaman Gossett	Michael Mazes
Chief Tostin	Jack Murdock
Seaman Horwich	Peter Schuck
Lieutenant Watson	Raymond Singer
Seaman Broom	Jim Varney

Seaman Williams	Richard Marion
Ramone Gallardo, the cook	Jesse Dizon
Col. Maurice Milgrim	James Ray

Narrator: John Astin.
Music: Artie Butler, Hal Mooney.
Executive Producer: Leonard B.
Stern.
Producer: David J. O'Connell, Si
Rose.
Director: John Astin, Norman Ab-
bott, William Asher, Alan
Bergman, Hollingsworth
Morse.

OPERATION PETTICOAT—30
minutes—ABC—September 17,
1977– August 25, 1978. 22 episodes. The two-hour pilot film
aired on ABC on September 4,
1977. Spin-off series: *The New
Operation Petticoat*.

*Only a shocking pink undercoat was
possible because an enemy plane
destroyed the sub's supply of gray
paint.

925   OPERATION PRIME TIME: THE GOSSIP COLUMNIST

Drama. The first episode in a series of independently produced
specials that are broadcast nationally by member stations of
Operation Prime Time, an organization through which independent stations pool their resources
and purchase top quality, first-
run miniseries and specials.

The story of Dina Moran, a gossip columnist for the Roper
Newspaper Syndicate, is told.

CAST

Dina Moran	Kim Cattrall
Marty Kaplan	Bobby Vinton
Georgia O'Hanlon	Martha Raye
Alma Lewellyn	Sylvia Sidney
Ivan Bock	Conrad Janis
Paul Cameron	Joe Penny
Alan Keyes	Dick Sargent
Buddy Herman	Bobby Sherman
Phil	Stanley Kammel
Stacy Stanton	Lynne Randall
Maitre d'	Ivor Barry
David Sheehan	Himself
Darlene Daniels	Catherine Campbell
Director	Richard Deacon
Stewardess	Catherine Daly

Guests: Steve Allen, Jim Backus,
Henny Backus, Jack Carter,
Allen Ludden, Jayne Meadows,
Rip Taylor, Betty White, Lyle
Waggoner.
Music: Allyn Ferguson.
Executive Producer: Jon Epstein.
Writer: Michael Gleason.
Director: James Sheldon.

OPERATION PRIME TIME: THE
GOSSIP COLUMNIST—2 hours
—Operation Prime Time—
March 1980.

926   OPERATION PRIME TIME: THE GIRL, THE GOLD WATCH, AND EVERYTHING

Comedy-Fantasy. The second in a
series of independently pro-

duced specials broadcast nationally by member stations of
Operation Prime Time.

Kirby Winter, the nephew of a
multimillionaire, receives only a
gold watch as his inheritance—a
gold watch, he later discovers,
that can stop time.* The story focuses on the problems Kirby encounters when he and Wilma
Farnum, his late Uncle Omar's
personal secretary, are accused of
embezzling seventy-five million
dollars from Krepps Enterprises.
Complicating Kirby's life, as he
tries to prove his innocence, are
Bonny Lee Beaumont, a beautiful
girl from Carolina, and Charla
O'Rourke, a seductress pursuing
him to learn the secret of his uncle's success.

CAST

Kirby Winter	Robert Hays
Bonny Lee Beaumont	Pam Dawber
Charla O'Rourke	Jill Ireland
Wilma Farnum	Zohra Lampert
Leroy Wintermore	Maurice Evans
Joseph Locordolos	Ed Nelson
Walton Grumby	Macdonald Carey
Hoover Hess	Burton Gilliam
Hilton Hibber	John O'Leary
Raoul	Peter Brown
Rene	Larry Hankin
Michele	Michelle Burtin
Policeman Harris	John Roselius

Music: Hod David Schudson.
Theme: "Two Hearts in Perfect
Time" by Hod David Schudson
(music) and Ayn Robbins
(lyrics).
Theme Vocal: Richie Havens.
Executive Producer: Terry Kee-
gan, Arthur Fellows.
Producer: Myril A. Schreibman.
Writer: George Zateslo.
Director: William Wiard.
Art Director: Charles Hughes.

OPERATION PRIME TIME: THE
GIRL, THE GOLD WATCH, AND
EVERYTHING—2 hours—Op-
eration Prime Time—May, June
1980.

*Kirby's uncle, an eccentric inventor,
developed the watch to control
time—for profit.

927   OPERATION PRIME TIME: TOURIST

Drama. The third in a series of
independently produced specials
broadcast nationally by member
stations of Operation Prime
Time.

The story depicts incidents in
the lives of six people, all mem-
bers of a European tour: Barbara
Huggins, Jim Huggins, Lulu
Flemington, Harry Flemington,
Terry Carroll and Steve Konay.

CAST

Pepe Virgil, the tour guide	John McCook
Roseanne Wicker, his assistant	Laurette Spang-McCook
Barbara Huggins	Adrienne Barbeau
Jim Huggins	David Groh
Lulu Flemington	Lee Meriwether

Harry Flemington	Bradford Dillman
Terry Carroll	Lois Nettleton
Steve Konay	James Stephens
Mandy Burke, the girl Steve befriends in Rome	Bonnie Bedelia
Joe Virgil, Pepe's father	John Ireland
Marian, Pepe's friend in Paris	Marisa Berenson

Music: Jack Smalley.
Executive Producer: David Law-
rence.
Producer: David Lawrence.
Writer: Norman Hudis.
Director: Jeremy Summers.
Co-Producer: Jim Rich Green.

OPERATION PRIME TIME: TOUR-
IST—2 hours—Operation Prime
Time—June, July 1980.

928   OPERATION: RUNAWAY

Drama. The story of David McKay,
a former vice squad officer now
in private practice as a psychiatrist who specializes in tracking
down runaways. (McKay also
teaches psychology at Westwood
University in Los Angeles.)

CAST

Dr. David McKay	Robert Reed
Karen Wingate, the dean of women at Westwood	Karen Machon
Mark Johnson, David's assistant	Michael Biehn
Susan, David's ward	Ruth Cox

Music: Richard Markowitz.
Executive Producer: William
Robert Yates (for Quinn Martin
Productions).
Producer: Mark Rodgers.
Director: William Wiard, Michael
Preece, Walter Grauman.
Creator: William Robert Yates.

OPERATION: RUNAWAY—60 min-
utes—NBC—April 27, 1978–
May 18, 1978. August 10, 1978–
August 31, 1978. 4 episodes.
Spin-off series: *The Runaways*.

929   THE OREGON TRAIL

Western. The series, set in the
1840s, follows the journey of a
group of pioneers traveling by
wagon train from Illinois to Oregon to begin new lives.

CAST

Evan Thorpe, a widower, the wagon master	Rod Taylor
Andrew Thorpe, his son	Andrew Stevens
Rachel Thorpe, his daughter	Gina Marie Smika
William Thorpe, his son	Tony Becker
Margaret Devlin, a young pioneer	Darleen Carr
Luther Sprague, the trail scout	Charles Napier
Mr. Cutler, the captain	Ken Swofford
Jessica Thorpe, Evan's wife (pilot film)	Blair Brown

Music: Dick De Benedictis.
Theme Vocal: Danny Darst.
Executive Producer: Michael
Gleason.

Producer: Richard Collins, Carl Vitale.
Director: Herb Wallerstein, Virgil W. Vogel, Hollingsworth Morse, Don Richardson, Bill Bixby.
Creator: Samuel A. Peeples, Michael Gleason.

THE OREGON TRAIL—60 minutes—NBC—September 21, 1977 – November 30, 1977. 6 episodes. The two-hour pilot film aired on NBC on January 10, 1976.

930   ORSON WELLES' GREAT MYSTERIES

Anthology. Mystery presentations.

Host: Orson Welles.
Music: John Barry.
Executive Producer: Alan P. Sloan.
Producer: John Wolf.

Included:

Farewell to the Faulkners. An unusual tale in which a murdered man turns up alive at a masquerade party—in the guise of his wife.

Cast: Philip Faulkner: Keith Baxter; Harriet Faulkner: Jane Baxter.

Death of an Old-fashioned Girl. The story of a spirit who possesses the wife of an artist, to whom she was once married, to seek revenge for his killing her.

Cast: Carol: Carol Lynley; Paul: Stephen Chase; Nicole: Francesca Annis; Sid: John LeMesurier; Janet: Anne Stallybrass.

Captain Rogers. The story of a reformed pirate whose household is tyrannized by an old shipmate threatening to expose his past.

Cast: Captain Rogers: Donald Pleasence; Mullet: Joseph O'Connor; Joan: Janey Key.

The Monkey's Paw. The story of a cursed charm with wish-granting powers that inflicts a grim lesson on a family attempting to misuse it.

Cast: Mr. White: Cyril Cusack; Mrs. White: Megs Jenkins; Herbert: Michael Kitchen.

ORSON WELLES' GREAT MYSTERIES—30 minutes—Syndicated 1973. 26 episodes.

931   THE OSMOND FAMILY SHOW

Variety. Basically, a revised version of *Donny and Marie,* wherein various members of the Osmond family share the spotlight.

Hosts: Donny and Marie Osmond.
Regulars: Johnny Dark, The Osmond Family, The Osmond Ice Angels.
Announcer: Wayne Osmond.
Orchestra: Bob Rozario.

Special Musical Material: Earl Brown.
Executive Producer: The Osmond Brothers.
Producer: Alan Osmond, Phil Hahn.
Associate Producer: Craig Martin.
Director: Walter C. Miller.
Choreographer: Carl Jablonski.
Coral Director: Denny Crawford.

THE OSMOND FAMILY SHOW—60 minutes—ABC—January 28, 1979 – March 18, 1979. 6 episodes. May 6, 1979 – May 27, 1979. 4 episodes.

932   THE OSMONDS

Animated Cartoon. Appointed as goodwill ambassadors by the United States Music Committee, the Osmond Brothers Rock group begins a round-the-world concert tour to promote understanding between nations. Stories depict their various adventures as they become involved in foreign intrigues.

VOICES

Allen Osmond	Himself
Jay Osmond	Himself
Donny Osmond	Himself
Merrill Osmond	Himself
Wayne Osmond	Himself
Jimmy Osmond	Himself
Fugi, their dog	Paul Frees

Music: The Osmond Brothers (songs); Maury Laws (background filler instrumentals).
Producer: Arthur Rankin, Jr., Jules Bass.

THE OSMONDS—30 minutes—ABC—September 9, 1972 – September 1, 1974.

933   OUR STREET

Serial. The story of the Robinsons, a poor black family, as they search for dignity and respect. The title refers to an any street in an any city where families are caught in the echoes of slow-dying prejudice.

CAST

Mae Robinson, the mother	Barbara Mealy
Bull Robinson, her husband	Gene Cole
	Clayton Corbin
Jet Robinson, their son	Curt Stewart
Slick Robinson, their son	Darryl F. Hill
	Howard Rollins
Tony Robinson, their son	Tyrone Jones
Kathy Robinson, their daughter	Sandra Sharp
J. T. Robinson, Mae's half-brother	Arthur French
Grandma Robinson	Alfredine Parham
Cynthia, a friend	Janet League
Emily, a friend	Frances Foster
Mrs. Ryder, Grandma's friend	Birdie Hale
Pearlina, Slick's girlfriend	Pat Picketts

Music: Don Schwartz.

OUR STREET—30 minutes—PBS—October 4, 1971 – October 10, 1974.

934   OUT OF THE BLUE

Comedy. The story of Random, an angel who is sent to Earth to watch over the five Richards children, orphaned by the deaths of their parents in a plane crash six months earlier. Random, who reveals his true identity only to the children, becomes their boarder and poses as a high school science teacher. The series focuses on Random's attempts to avoid interfering with human destiny while showing people that they can control their own lives.

CAST

Angel Random	James Brogan
Boss Angel, Random's superior in Heaven	Eileen Heckart
Marion MacNelmor, the Richards children's aunt	Dixie Carter
Gladys, the family housekeeper	Hannah Dean
Chris Richards, age 16	Clark Brandon
Laura Richards, age 13	Olivia Barash
Stacey Richards, age 10	Tammy Lauren
Jason Richards, age 8	Jason Keller
Shane Richards, age 8	Shane Keller

The Richards' address: 217 Southampton Street, Chicago, Illinois.

Music: Ben Lanzarone.
Supervising Producer: Thomas L. Miller, Edward K. Milkis, Robert L. Boyett.
Executive Producer: Austin and Irma Kalish.
Producer: William Bickley, Michael Warren.
Writer: Barry Kemp, Laurie Gelman, Howard Albrecht, William Bickley, Michael Warren.
Director: Peter Baldwin, Jeff Chambers, John Tracy.
Art Director: Ken Davis.

OUT OF THE BLUE—30 minutes—ABC—September 9, 1979 – October 21, 1979. 7 episodes. Returned with one additional episode on December 16, 1979.

935   OWEN MARSHALL: COUNSELOR AT LAW

Crime Drama. The cases and courtroom defenses of Owen Marshall, an attorney based in Santa Barbara, California.

CAST

Owen Marshall, a widower	Arthur Hill
Melissa Marshall, his daughter	Christine Matchett
Jess Brandon, his assistant	Lee Majors
Frieda Krause, Owen's secretary	Joan Darling
Danny Paterno, Owen's colleague	Reni Santoni
Ted Warrick, Owen's colleague	David Soul
District Attorney Grant	Russell Johnson
Assistant D.A. Charlie Giannetta	Pat Harrington
Sgt. Roy Kessler	Henry Beckman
Judge	Lindsay Workman
	Bill Quinn
	John Zaremba

Music: Elmer Bernstein, Richard Clements.
Executive Producer: David Victor.
Producer: Jon Epstein.
Director: Harry Falk, David Lowell Rich, Buzz Kulick, Leo Penn, Daniel Haller, John Badham, Leon Benson, Steven Spielberg, Marc Daniels, Charles S. Dubin, E. W. Swackhamer, Allen Reisner, James Sheldon, Lou Antonio.

OWEN MARSHALL: COUNSELOR AT LAW—60 minutes—ABC—September 16, 1971 – August 24, 1974. 69 episodes. Syndicated. The two-hour pilot film aired on ABC on September 12, 1971.

936   OZZIE'S GIRLS

Comedy. The series, set in the town of Hillsdale, follows the misadventures of Ozzie and Harriet Nelson, a retired couple, and their boarders, Susan Hamilton and Brenda MacKenzie, beautiful college coeds. The four struggle to coexist despite the generation gap.

CAST

Ozzie Nelson	Himself
Harriet Nelson	Herself
Susan Hamilton	Susan Sennett
Brenda MacKenzie (first introduced as Jennifer MacKenzie)	Brenda Sykes
Lenore Morrison, their neighbor	Lenore Stevens
Alice Morrison, Lenore's daughter	Joie Guerico
Professor McCutcheon, the girls' psychology instructor	David Doyle
The Mailman	Jim Begg

Also, portraying various friends of Susan and Brenda: Mike Wagner, Gaye Nelson, Tom Harmon.
Music: Frank McKelvey.
Executive Producer: Al Simon.
Producer: David Nelson.
Writer-Director: Ozzie Nelson.

OZZIE'S GIRLS—30 minutes—Syndicated 1973. 24 episodes. The 30-minute pilot film aired on NBC on September 10, 1972.

P

937   THE PALACE

Variety. Celebrity guests perform against the background of the Hamilton Palace in Toronto, Canada.

Host: Jack Jones.
Orchestra: Tommy Banks.
Executive Producer: R. David Close, J. Arnold Gordon.
Producer: Wendell Wilks.
Writer: Alex Barris, Kate and Ted Lonsdale.
Director: Larry Schnurr.
Choreographer: Judy Shaw.

THE PALACE — 60 minutes — Syndicated 1979.

938 THE PALLISERS

Drama. The series, set in Victorian England and based on the novels by Anthony Trollope, chronicles twenty-five years in the lives of Plantagenet Palliser, a respected member of Parliament, and his wife, Lady Glencora M'Clockie Palliser. Produced by the BBC.

CAST

Plantagenet Palliser	Philip Latham
Lady Glencora Palliser	Susan Hampshire
The Duke of Omnium	Roland Culver
Alice	Caroline Mortimer
George	Garry Watson
Lady Dumbello	Rachel Herbert
Countess Midlothian	Fabia Drake
Marchioness of Auld Reekie	Sonia Dresdel
John Gray	Bernard Brown
Burgo Fitzgerald	Barry Justice
Phineas Finn	Donal McCann
Duke of St. Bungay	Roger Liversey
Slide	Clifford Rose
Laura Kennedy	Anna Massey
Violet	Mel Martin
Lizzie Eustace	Sarah Badel
Lord Fawn	Derek Jacobi
Mme. Max Goesler	Barbara Murphy
Mrs. Carbuncle	Helen Lindsay
Lord George	Terence Alexander

Host: Sir John Gielgud.
Music: Herbert Chappel, Wilfred Joseph.
Music Played By: The New Philharmonic Orchestra.
Conductor: Marcus Dodds.
Producer: Martin Lisemore, Roland Wilson.
Director: Hugh David.

THE PALLISERS — 60 minutes — PBS — January 13, 1977 – June 20, 1977. 22 episodes.

939 PALMERSTOWN, U.S.A.

Drama. The series, set in Palmerstown, Tennessee, in 1935, presents a view of life in a small town, where whites and blacks coexist for economic survival, as seen through the eyes of two boys. Stories feature David Hall and Booker T. Freeman, two nine-year-old boys, one white (David) and the other black (Booker), and their struggle to remain friends in a world that doesn't approve.

CAST

W. D. Hall, the father of the white family; a grocer	Beeson Carroll
Luther Freeman, the father of the black family; a blacksmith	Bill Duke
Coralee Hall, W. D.'s wife	Janis St. John
Bessie Freeman, Luther's wife	Jonelle Allen
David Hall, W. D.'s son	Brian G. Wilson
Booker T. Freeman, Luther's son	Jermain H. Johnson
Willie Joe Hall, David's brother	Michael Fox
Diana Freeman, Booker's sister	Star-Shemah Bobatoon
Sheriff	Kenneth White
Townspeople:	
Auntie Calpurnia	Claudia McNeil
Mrs. Miller	Sarina Grant
Mailman Jackson	Morgan Freeman
Banker Hodges	John Carter
Widder Brown	Iris Korn
Major	Arthur Malet
Reverend Teasdale	Davis Roberts
Roscoe	John Hancock
Hattie Lou	Susan Battson
Jed	Kenneth White
Noah	Ted Gehring
Charlie	Vernon Weddle
Agnes Peterson	Miriam Byrd-Nethery
Deacon Shaw	Fred Pinkard
Deacon Lewis	Stack Pierce
Willy, the barber	Michael Greene

Music: Al Schackman.
Executive Producer: Norman Lear, Alex Haley.
Producer: Ronald Rubin.
Writer: Ronald Rubin, Robert Price, Alex Haley, Odie Hawkins.
Director: Peter Levin, Jeffrey Hayden, Gilbert Moses.
Creator: Norman Lear, Alex Haley.

PALMERSTOWN, U.S.A. — 60 minutes — CBS — March 20, 1980 – May 1, 1980. 7 episodes. Originally titled *King of the Hill*.

940 THE PAPER CHASE

Drama. The series, set at a prestigious Northeastern University, follows the joys and frustrations of first-year law students. Especially featured is James Hart, an earnest, likeable Minnesota farm boy on a paper chase (a quest for a diploma that says he graduated from law school). The program focuses also on the relationship between Hart and Professor Charles Kingsfield, Jr., a brilliant contract law instructor who, feared for his classroom tyranny, either makes or breaks students. Based on the movie of the same title.

CAST

Professor Charles Kingsfield, Jr.	John Houseman
James T. Hart, a student	James Stephens
Elizabeth Logan, a student	Francine Tacker
Franklin Ford, a student	Tom Fitzsimmons
Willis Bell, a student	James Keane
Jonathan Brooks, a student	Jonathan Segal
Thomas Anderson, a student	Robert Ginty
Linda O'Connor, a student	Katharine Dunfee
Asheley Brooks, Jonathan's wife	Deka Beaudine
Ernie, the owner of Ernie's Tavern, where Hart works	Charles Hallahan
Susu, the waitress at the tavern	Marilu Henner
Mrs. Nottingham, Kingsfield's secretary	Betty Harford
Dean Rutherford, the head of the college	Jack Manning
Carol, the tavern waitress (later)	Carole Goldman
Gregarian, a student	Stanley DeSantis

Music: Charles Fox, Stephen Seretan, Richard Shores.
Music Supervision: Lionel Newman.
Theme Vocal: "The First Year" by Seals and Crofts.
Executive Producer: Robert C. Thompson.
Producer: Robert Lewin, Albert Aley.
Director: Joseph Hardy, Philip Leacock, Gwen Arner, Harvey Laidman, Alex March, William Hale, Robert C. Thompson, Seymour Robbie, Peter Levin, Carl Kugel, Kenneth Gilbert, Marvan Kupfer, Larry Elikann, Jack Bender.

THE PAPER CHASE — 60 minutes — CBS — September 19, 1978 – July 17, 1979. 22 episodes. The series was "sneak previewed" on September 9, 1978.

941 PAPER MOON

Comedy. The series, set in the Midwest during the 1930s, follows the adventures of Moses "Moze" Pray, a con artist and fast-talking salesman for the Dixie Bible Company, and Addie, a precocious eleven-year-old girl who believes that because he looks like her, he is her father. Traveling in a 1931 roadster, they struggle to survive the Depression through imaginative swindles. Based on the motion picture of the same title.

CAST

Moses "Moze" Pray	Christopher Connelly
Addie Pray	Jodie Foster

Music: Harold Arlen.
Theme: "Paper Moon."
Executive Producer: Anthony Wilson.
Producer: Robert Stambler.

PAPER MOON — 30 minutes — ABC — September 12, 1974 – January 2, 1975. 13 episodes.

942 THE PARENT GAME

Game. Three married couples compete in a game that compares their ideas about raising children with those of a child psychologist.

The host reads a question relating to children and reveals four possible answers. Each couple chooses the answer it believes is correct. The correct answer is revealed and points are awarded accordingly (round one: five points per correct choice; round two: ten points; round three: fifteen points; round four: thirty points). The highest scorers win a specially selected prize.

Host: Clark Race.
Announcer: Johnny Jacobs.
Music: Frank Jaffe.
Executive Producer: Chuck Barris.
Producer: Gary Jenks.
Director: John Dorsey.

THE PARENT GAME — 30 minutes — Syndicated 1972.

943 PARIS

Crime Drama. The story of Woodrow "Woody" Paris, captain of the Metro Squad, a special detective unit of the Los Angeles Police Department (14th Precinct), and a college professor who teaches criminology on the side.

CAST

Capt. Woodrow Paris	James Earl Jones
Barbara Paris, his wife	Lee Chamberlain
Deputy Chief Jerome Bench	Hank Garrett
Sgt. Stacey Erickson	Cecilia Hart
Sgt. Charlie Bogart	Jake Mitchell
Sgt. Ernie Villas	Frank Ramirez
Sgt. Willie Miller	Michael Warren

Music: Fred Karlin.
Supervising Producer: Gregory Hoblit.
Executive Producer: Steven Bochco.
Producer: Gregory Hoblit, Edward DeBlasio, Burton Arbus.
Writer: Steven Bochco, Edward DeBlasio, Burton Arbus, Del Reisman, Irv Pearlberg, Larry Alexander, Jackson Gillis, David Solomon.
Director: Jackie Cooper, Alvin Ganzer, Georg Stanford Brown, Alex March, Jerry McNeely, Alf Kjellin, Jack Starrett, Alan Rachins, Victor Lobl.
Creator: Steven Bochco.

PARIS — 60 minutes — CBS — September 29, 1979 – October 27, 1979. 5 episodes. December 4, 1979 – January 15, 1980. 7 episodes (series ended two weeks earlier than scheduled due to poor ratings).

944 PARIS 7000

Mystery. The series, set in Paris, France, depicts the exploits of Jack Brennan, an American troubleshooter who helps distressed United States citizens. (Paris 7000: the telephone number of the U.S. Consulate.)

CAST

Jack Brennan	George Hamilton
Jules Maurois, the Sûreté chief	Jacques Aubuchon
Robert Stevens, Jack's assistant	Gene Raymond

Music: Stanley Wilson.
Theme: "Paris 7000" by Michel Colombier.
Music Supervision: Lionel Newman.
Executive Producer: Richard Caffey.

On Our Own. Bess Armstrong, at left, with
Lynnie Greene.

Operation Petticoat. Melinda Naud.

The Paper Chase. John Houseman, back, and James
Stephens. Courtesy the *Call-Chronicle Newspapers,*
Allentown, Pa.

The Partridge Family. Bottom, from left, Suzanne Crough,
Shirley Jones and Susan Dey. Back, from left, Brian
Forster, David Cassidy and Danny Bonaduce.

Producer: John Wilder, Michael Gleason.
Director: Marc Daniels, Michael Caffey, Don Weis, Jeannot Szwarc, James Neilson.

PARIS 7000—60 minutes—ABC—January 22, 1970–June 4, 1970. 10 episodes.

945 THE PARTNERS

Comedy. The exploits of inept Lennie Crooke and level-headed George Robinson, police sergeants and partners attached to the 33rd Precinct in Los Angeles.

CAST

Sgt. Lennie Crooke	Don Adams
Sgt. George Robinson	Rupert Crosse
Capt. Aaron William Andrews	John Doucette
Sgt. Nelson Higgenbottom	Dick Van Patten
Freddie Butler, the man who confesses to every crime	Robert Karvelas

Music: Lalo Schifrin.
Executive Producer: Don Adams.
Producer: Arne Sultan.
Director: Gary Nelson, Christian Nyby, Earl Bellamy, Richard Benedict, Don Adams.

THE PARTNERS—30 minutes—NBC—September 18, 1971–January 8, 1972. 13 episodes. Repeats: July 28, 1972–September 8, 1972.

946 THE PARTRIDGE FAMILY

Comedy. The home and work lives, the joys and sorrows, and romantic misadventures of the Partridge family. An ordinary family, the Partridges became prominent when, after being organized into a Rock group, the sale of a demonstration tape later led to a recording contract and fame.

CAST

Shirley Partridge, the mother, a widow	Shirley Jones
Keith Partridge, her son	David Cassidy
Laurie Partridge, her daughter	Susan Dey
Danny Partridge, her son	Danny Bonaduce
Tracy Partridge, her daughter	Suzanne Crough
Chris Partridge, her son	Jeremy Gelbwaks, Brian Forster
Reuben Kincaid, their manager	Dave Madden
Walter Renfrew, Shirley's father	Ray Bolger, Jackie Coogan
Amanda Renfrew, Shirley's mother	Rosemary DeCamp
Ricky Stevens, the Partridge's four-year-old neighbor	Ricky Segal
Doris Stevens, Ricky's mother	Nita Talbot
Donna Stevens, Ricky's sister	Ronne Troup
Richard Lawrence, Shirley's romantic interest	Bert Convy
Cathy Lawrence, Richard's daughter	Anne Carol Pearson
Julie Lawrence, Richard's daughter	Jodie Foster
Gloria Hickey, Danny's girlfriend	Patti Cohoon
Bonnie Kleinschmitt, Reuben's girlfriend	Elaine Giftos
Punky Lazaar, Danny's friend	Gary Dubin
The Partridge's recording engineer	Martin Speer
Bernie Applebaum, the doctor with eyes for Shirley	Gerald Hiken
Snake, the motorcyclist friend of the Partridges	Rob Reiner, Stuart Margolin
Gorgo, Snake's friend	Henry Olek
Cindy, a girlfriend of Keith's	Claire Wilcox
Molly, a girlfriend of Keith's	Maggi Wellman
Mrs. Kornage, Shirley's neighbor	Shelley Morrison
Various waitress roles	Yvonne Wilder

Also, various roles: Vic Tayback, Gordon Jump, Mitzi Hoag and Bruce Kimmel.
Partridge family dog: Simone.
Partridge family bus license plate number: NLX 590.
Partridge family addresses: 698 Sycamore Road, San Pueblo, California; also, later, the 700 block on Vasarrio Road.
Last Commercial Break Announcer: Shirley Jones.
Music: Hugo Montenegro, Shorty Rogers, George Duning, Benny Golson.
First Theme: "When We're Singing" by Wes Farrell and Diane Hilderbrand.
Second Theme: "Come On Get Happy" by Wes Farrell and Danny Janssen.
The Partridge Family Vocals: Shirley Jones, David Cassidy, John Bahler, Tom Bahler, Jackie Ward, Ron Hicklin.
Executive Producer: Bob Claver.
Producer: Mel Swope, William S. Bickley, Paul Junger Witt.
Associate Producer: Michael Warren.
Records Producer: Wes Farrell.
Writer: Coslough Johnson, Bob Rodgers, Howard Storm, James Henerson, Harry Winkler, Harry Dolan, Chuck Shyer, Alan Mandel, Peggy Chantler Dick, Dale McRaven, Skip Webster, Bernard Slade, Charlotte Brown, Bill Manhoff, Richard DeRoy, Dick Bensfield, Perry Grant, Gordon Mitchell, Lloyd Turner, Martin Ragaway, Steve Pritzker, Ron Friedman, Martin Cohan, Susan Harris.
Director: Ernest Losso, Ralph Senensky, Paul Junger Witt, Herb Kenwith, Ross Bowman, Herb Wallerstein, Jerry Paris, E.W. Swackhamer, Mel Swope, Charles R. Rondeau, Roger Duchowny, Bob Claver, Richard Kinon, Peter Baldwin, Harry Falk, Russ Mayberry.
Creator: Bernard Slade.
Art Director: Ross Bellah, John Beckman, Robert Peterson, Carl Braunger, Cary Odell, Seymour Klate.

THE PARTRIDGE FAMILY—30 minutes—ABC—September 25,

1970–September 7, 1974. 96 episodes. Syndicated. Spin-off series: *Partridge Family: 2200 A.D.*

947 PARTRIDGE FAMILY: 2200 A.D.

Animated Cartoon. The series, set in 2200 A.D., follows the misadventures of the Partridge Family, a show business Rock group, touring the planets.

VOICES

Shirley Partridge, the mother	Sherry Alberoni
Laurie Partridge, her daughter	Susan Dey
Keith Partridge, her son	Chuck McLennan
Danny Partridge, her son	Danny Bonaduce
Tracy Partridge, her daughter	Suzanne Crough
Chris Partridge, her son	Brian Forster
Reuben Kincaid, their manager	Dave Madden
Marion, Laurie's friend	Julie McWhirter
Beannie, Keith's friend	Allan Melvin

Additional Voices: Joan Gerber, Mike Road, Alan Oppenheimer, Hal Smith, John Stephenson, Lennie Weinrib, Frank Welker.
Music: Hoyt Curtin.
Executive Producer: William Hanna, Joseph Barbera.
Producer: Iwao Takamoto.
Writer: Barry Blitzer, Larz Bourne, Dick Conway, Buddy Atkinson, Jim Begg, Rance Howard, Jack Mendelshon, John Fenton Perry, Ray Parker, Bill Raynor.
Director: Charles A. Nichols.

PARTRIDGE FAMILY: 2200 A.D.—25 minutes—CBS—September 7, 1974–March 9, 1975. 16 episodes.

948 PASS THE BUCK

Game. A category topic is stated (e.g., "Something that is inflated") and each of four competing players must name an item that relates to the subject. Prize money starts at $100 and increases by $25 each time an acceptable answer is given. When a player gives an incorrect response, he is defeated and a new topic is played. The game continues in this manner until one player remains. This player becomes the champion and wins the pot.

Host: Bill Cullen.
Announcer: Bob Stewart.
Music: Score Productions.
Executive Producer: Bob Clayton.
Producer: Sande Stewart.
Director: Mike Gargiulo.

PASS THE BUCK—30 minutes—CBS—April 3, 1978–June 30, 1978. 58 programs.

949 PASSWORD

Game. In the basic format, two teams composed of celebrity captain and a noncelebrity contestant compete. A player receives a

password (e.g., "discover") and through one-word clues must convey its meaning to his partner. Word values begin at ten points and diminish by one point for each unsuccessful clue. The highest scoring team is the winner, and the noncelebrity player receives a cash prize.

Version 1:

Host: Allen Ludden.
Announcer: Jack Clark, John Harlan.
Producer: Frank Wayne, Bob Stewart.

PASSWORD—30 minutes—CBS—October 2, 1961–September 15, 1967.

Version 2:

Host: Allen Ludden.
Announcer: John Harlan.
Producer: Frank Wayne.
Director: Stuart W. Phelps.

PASSWORD—30 minutes—ABC—April 5, 1971–November 15, 1974.

Version 3:

Host: Allen Ludden.
Announcer: John Harlan.
Producer: Frank Wayne, Howard Felscher.
Director: Stuart W. Phelps.

PASSWORD ALL STARS—30 minutes—ABC—November 18, 1974–February 21, 1975.

Version 4:

Host: Allen Ludden.
Announcer: John Harlan.
Producer: Frank Wayne, Howard Felscher.
Director: Stuart W. Phelps.

PASSWORD—30 minutes—ABC—February 24, 1975–June 27, 1975

Version 5:

Host: Allen Ludden.
Substitute Host: Bill Cullen, Tom Kennedy.
Announcer: Gene Wood.
Music: Score Productions.
Executive Producer: Howard Felscher.
Producer: Robert Sherman.
Director: George Choderker.

PASSWORD PLUS—30 minutes—NBC—Premiered: January 8, 1979.

950 THE PATCHWORK FAMILY

Children. Songs, games, sketches and related entertainment geared to children.

Hostess: Carol Corbett.
Voice of Rags the Puppet: Cary Antebi.
Regulars: Joanna Pang, John Canemaker, Arlene Thomas, Elaine Lefkowits.
Executive Producer: Linda Allen.
Producer-Director: Bill Bryan.

THE PATCHWORK FAMILY — 60 minutes — CBS Owned and Operated Stations — Premiered: January 1, 1974.

951   PAT PAULSEN'S HALF A COMEDY HOUR

Comedy. A satire of the contemporary scene.

Host: Pat Paulsen.
Regulars: Jean Byron, Sherry Miles, Bob Einstein, Peppe Brown, Vanetta Rogers and Pedro Regas (as Mrs. Buffalo Running Schwartz, an 87-year-old Indian).
Announcer: Billy Sands.
Music: Denny Vaughn.
Producer: Bill Carruthers.
Writer: Steve Martin, Bob Arbogast, Paul Wayne, Michael Elias, Frank Shaw, Tom Koch, Larry Marks.
Director: Mark Goode.

PAT PAULSEN'S HALF A COMEDY HOUR — 30 minutes — ABC — January 22, 1970 – March 9, 1970. 13 programs.

952   PAUL BERNARD — PSYCHIATRIST

Drama. The program dramatizes sessions between a psychiatrist (Dr. Paul Bernard) and his patients. The patient relates her elements of distress; and in the final moments of the program, Dr. Bernard analyzes her seemingly uncomplicated and innocent thoughts. Produced with the cooperation of the Canadian Mental Health Association.

CAST

Dr. Paul Bernard	Chris Wiggins
His Regular Patients:	
Alice Talbot	Dawn Greenhalgh
Mrs. Howard	Tudi Wiggins
Mrs. Finley	Marcia Diamond
Miss Parker	Valerie-Jean Hume
Connie Walker	Phyllis Maxwell
Katie Conner	Nuala Fitzgerald
Mrs. Wilkins	Vivian Reis
Barbara Courtney	Sheley Sommers
Mrs. Bradshaw	Diane Polley
Mrs. Collins	Kay Hawtrey
Mrs. Donaldson	Gale Garnett
Mrs. Roberts	Paisley Maxwell
Mrs. Patterson	Josephine Barrington
Mrs. Johnson	Anna Commeron
Miss Michaels	Peggy Mahon
Karen Lampton	Barbara Kyle
Mrs. Brookfield	Carol Lazare
Jennifer Barlow	Micki Moore
Vickie Lombard	Arlene Meadows

Music: Milani Kymlicka.

PAUL BERNARD — PSYCHIATRIST — 30 minutes — Syndicated 1972. 195 programs.

953   THE PAUL DIXON SHOW

Variety. Music, songs and conversation geared to women.

Host: Paul Dixon.

Regulars: Bonnie Lou, Coleen Sharp.
Music: The Bruce Brownfield Band.
Producer: Jack Taylor.
Director: Lee Hornback.

THE PAUL DIXON SHOW — 30 minutes — Syndicated 1974.

954   THE PAUL LYNDE SHOW

Comedy. The series, set in Ocean Grove, California, follows the misadventures of Paul Simms, an attorney with the firm of McNish and Simms, as he struggles to cope with life, his job and his family. Based on the stage play *Howie.*

CAST

Paul Simms	Paul Lynde
Martha Simms, his wife	Elizabeth Allen
Barbara Dickerson, their married daughter	Jane Actman
Howie Dickerson, Barbara's husband	John Calvin
Sally Simms, Paul's daughter	Pamelyn Ferdin
J. J. McNish, Paul's business partner	Herb Voland
Barney Dickerson, Howie's father; a butcher in Eagle Rock, California	Jerry Stiller
Grace Dickerson, Howie's mother	Anne Meara
Alice, Paul's secretary	Allison McKay
Jimmy Fowler, Sally's boyfriend	Anson Williams
Jimmy Lyons, Sally's boyfriend	Stuart Getz

Music: Shorty Rogers.
Executive Producer: Harry Ackerman.
Producer-Director: William Asher.

THE PAUL LYNDE SHOW — 30 minutes — ABC — September 13, 1972 – September 8, 1973. 26 episodes.

955   PAUL SAND IN FRIENDS AND LOVERS

Comedy. The life, fantasies and romantic misadventures of Robert Dreyfuss, a young bachelor and a bass violinist with the Boston Symphony Orchestra.

CAST

Robert Dreyfuss	Paul Sand
Charlie Dreyfuss, his brother	Michael Pataki
Janis Dreyfuss, Charlie's wife	Penny Marshall
Fred Myerback, Robert's friend	Steve Landesberg
Jack Reardon, the orchestra manager	Dick Wesson
Mason Woodruff, the orchestra conductor	Craig Richard Nelson
Ben Dreyfuss, Robert's father	Jack Gilford
Marge Dreyfuss, Robert's mother	Jan Miner
Susan, Robert's girlfriend	Sharon Spelman
Estelle, a member of the orchestra	Dena Dietrich
Fred's wife	Karen Morrow

Music: Patrick Williams.
Executive Producer: James L. Brooks, Allan Burns.
Producer: Steve Pritzker.
Writer: Gordon Farr, Arnold Kane, Steve Pritzker, Phil Mishkin, Steve Gordon, Bud Wiser, Mark Rothman, Lowell Ganz, Monika and Andrew Johnson, Colman Mitchell, Goeffrey Neigher, Elias Davis, David Pollock.
Director: Robert Moore, Jay Sandrich, Bob Claver, Alan Rafkin, Peter Bonerz, Tim Kiley, James Burrows.
Creator: James L. Brooks, Allan Burns.

PAUL SAND IN FRIENDS AND LOVERS — 30 minutes — CBS — September 14, 1974 – January 4, 1975. 13 episodes.

956   PEANUTS

Animated Cartoon. The misadventures of the Peanuts gang: eight children (Charlie Brown, Linus, Lucy, Schroeder, Pig Pen, Frieda, Peppermint Patty and Sally), and one mischievous dog, Snoopy, who believes he is a World War I flying ace in battle with the Red Baron. Stories depict their attempts to solve problems without help from the adult world.

VOICES

Charlie Brown	Peter Robbins
	Todd Barbee
	Chad Webber
	Duncan Watson
	Liam Sullivan
	Arrin Skelley
Snoopy	Bill Melendez
Lucy	Sally Dryer
	Tracy Stratford
	Pamelyn Ferdin
	Robin Kohn
	Michelle Muller
	Melanie Kohn
Linus	Christopher Shea
	Stephen Shea
	Melanie Kohn
	Daniel Anderson
Pig Pen	Jeff Orstein
	Thomas Muller
Peppermint Patty	Gail DeFaria
	Kip DeFaria
	Maureen McCormick
	Donna Forman
	Patricia Patts
Schroeder	Glenn Mendelson
	Danny Hjelm
	Brian Kazanjian
	Greg Felton
Sally	Cathy Steinberg
	Hilary Momberger
	Lynn Mortensen
Frieda	Ann Altieri
Woodstock (whistling)	Jason Serinus
Marcie	James Ahrens
	Casey Carlson
Violet	Linda Ercoli

Music: Vince Guaraldi.
Orchestra: John Scott Trotter.
Executive Producer: Lee Mendelson.

Producer: Bill Melendez.
Writer: Charles Schulz.
Director: Phil Roman.
Creator: Charles Schulz.
Animation: Bill Melendez, Ed Levitt, Bernard Gruver, Frank Smith, Ruth Kissane, Dean Spille, Bill Littlejohn, Rudy Zamora, Bob Carlson, John Freeman, Beverly Robbins, Eleanor Warren, Faith Kovaleski, Flora Hastings.

The Series (thus far: December 9, 1965 – February 25, 1980):

A Charlie Brown Christmas. The story relates Charlie's unsuccessful efforts to relate his feelings about the commercialism of Christmas to his friends, who are eagerly awaiting the big day.

A Charlie Brown Thanksgiving. The story focuses on Charlie's well-intentioned efforts to organize a Thanksgiving feast for his friends.

Be My Valentine, Charlie Brown. The episode focuses on several characters: Sally, who thinks Linus' purchase of a box of candy is for her, when in reality it is for her homeroom teacher; Lucy, who seeks Schroeder's attention; and Charlie Brown, who begins a vigil by his mailbox, hoping for a valentine.

Charlie Brown's All Stars. With 999 straight losses and 3,000 runs given up by its pitcher, Charlie Brown, the All Stars baseball team (five boys, three girls and a dog) play and lose their one-thousandth game.

He's Your Dog, Charlie Brown. The story follows Charlie's efforts to curtail the antics of his mischievous dog, Snoopy.

It's a Mystery, Charlie Brown. Snoopy, donning the guise of Sherlock Holmes, attempts to solve the mystery of Woodstock's missing nest.

It's Arbor Day, Charlie Brown. The chaos that results when the students of the Birchwood School decide to observe Arbor Day and proceed to beautify the world.

It's the Easter Beagle, Charlie Brown. The story focuses on the Peanuts gang as they prepare for the Easter Beagle, a mythical dog who magically appears to hand out candy and decorate eggs on Easter morning.

It's Your First Kiss, Charlie Brown. The story centers on Charlie's anxieties when he is chosen to escort Heather, the little red-haired girl on whom he has a crush, to the annual Homecoming Queen Dance.

It Was a Short Summer, Charlie Brown. Charlie and the gang recall a summer at a camp where the boys were pitted against the girls in various sports events.

Play It Again, Charlie Brown. Through Lucy's meddling, Schroeder, the gifted pianist, is booked to play his toy piano for the P.T.A. The story focuses on his efforts to please an audience who is expecting a rock concert from a boy who is strictly a Beethoven fan.

She's a Good Skate, Charlie Brown. The story focuses on Peppermint Patty as she attempts to prepare for a figure skating competition under the eagle eye of her coach—Snoopy.

There's No Time for Love, Charlie Brown. A hectic day in the lives of the Peanuts gang is recalled through essay tests, Peppermint Patty's crush on Charlie, and a misguided field trip.

What a Nightmare, Charlie Brown. Snoopy, the pampered beagle, has a nightmare when, after a snowstorm, Charlie Brown attempts to make a sled dog out of him. The dream carries Snoopy to the Arctic where he is harnessed to a team of snarling huskies and driven across the Tundra. The remainder of the story depicts Snoopy's efforts to work up enough courage to face the huskies.

You're a Good Sport, Charlie Brown. The story focuses on a cross-country race with the Peanuts characters as the main competitors.

You're Not Elected, Charlie Brown. Charlie's disastrous campaign against Linus for the presidency of the sixth grade.

You're in Love, Charlie Brown. With only two days left before the end of the term, Charlie attempts to inspire the affection of the little red-haired girl who sits in front of him.

You're the Greatest, Charlie Brown. Charlie's attempts to win the most demanding event in the junior Olympics: the decathlon.

PEANUTS—30 minutes—CBS—Premiered: December 9, 1965. Broadcast as a series of specials.

957   PEARL

Drama. A three-part miniseries, set in Hawaii, that focuses on the lives of a diverse group of people during the three days before the December 7, 1941, attack by the Japanese.

CAST

Midge Forrest, the unfaithful wife of Col. Forrest	Angie Dickinson
Capt. Cal Lanford	Robert Wagner
Col. Jason Forrest, Midge's husband	Dennis Weaver
Dr. Karel Lang, Cal's girlfriend	Lesley Ann Warren
Lt. (j.g.) Doug North	Gregg Henry
Holly Nagata, the reporter	Tiana Alexandra
Sally Colton, Midge's friend, a madam	Katherine Helmond
Pvt. "Fickle" Finger	Christian Vance
Sgt. Otto Chain	Brian Dennehy
Sgt. Brad Walder	Max Gail
Cmdr. John North, Doug's father	Richard Anderson
Mary North, Doug's mother	Marion Ross
Patricia North, Doug's sister	Mary Frances Crosby
Pvt. John Zylowski	Adam Arkin
Shirley, one of Sally's girls	Char Fontane
Lieutenant Christopher	Chip Lucia
Gen. Chester Harrison	Allan Miller
Lily Harrison, Chester's wife	Audra Lindley
Looper	Les Lannom
Nurse	Marjorie Reynolds
Taxi driver	Moe Keale
Radio man	Tom Drewes

Narrator: Joseph Campanella.
Music: John Addison.
Executive Producer: Stirling Silliphant, Franklin Konigsberg.
Producer: Sam Manners.
Writer: Stirling Silliphant.
Director: Alexander Singer, Hy Averback.
Art Director: Stewart Campbell.
Director of Photography: Gayne Rescher.

PEARL—2 hours (6 hours total)—ABC—November 16, 1978 – November 19, 1978. 3 episodes. Rebroadcast on ABC on September 9, 1980 through September 12, 1980.

958   THE PEARL BAILEY SHOW

Musical Variety.

Hostess: Pearl Bailey.
Announcer: Roger Carroll.
Orchestra: Louis Bellson.
Producer: Bob Finkel.
Writer: Bill Angelos, Buz Kohan, Pearl Bailey.
Director: Dean Whitmore.

THE PEARL BAILEY SHOW—60 minutes—ABC—January 23, 1971 – May 5, 1971. 13 programs.

959   PEBBLES AND BAMM BAMM

Animated Cartoon. A spin-off from *The Flintstones.* The story of Pebbles Flintstone, the teenage daughter of Fred and Wilma Flintstone, and Bamm Bamm Rubble, the adopted son of Barney and Betty Rubble. Episodes, set in the prehistoric era, revolve around their activities while attending Bedrock High School.

VOICES

Pebbles Flintstone	Sally Struthers
Bamm Bamm Rubble	Jay North
Moonrock, their friend	Lennie Weinrib
Fabian, their friend	Carl Esser
Penny, their friend	Mitzi McCall
Cindy, their friend	Gay Hartwig
Wiggy, their friend	Gay Hartwig

Music: Hoyt Curtin, Ted Nichols.
Executive Producer: William Hanna, Joseph Barbera.
Producer: Iowa Takamoto.
Writer: Joel Kane, Woody Kling, Howard Morganstern, Joe Ruby, Ken Spears.
Director: Charles A. Nichols.

PEBBLES AND BAMM BAMM—30 minutes—CBS—September 11, 1971 – September 2, 1972.

960   PENNIES FROM HEAVEN

Fantasy. The series, set in England during the 1930s, combines dramatic action with period songs to chronicle the travels of Arthur Parker, a sheet music salesman.

CAST

Arthur Parker	Bob Hoskins
Janet Parker, his wife	Gemma Craven
Eileen, his mistress	Cheryl Campbell
The Accordian Man	Kenneth Colley

Music: 1930s recordings.
Producer: Kenith Trodd.
Director: Piers Haggard.
Choreography: Tudor Davies.

PENNIES FROM HEAVEN—75 minutes—Syndicated 1979. 6 episodes.

961   PEOPLE

Variety. An adaptation of *People* magazine to television: celebrity profiles and interviews.

Hostess: Phyllis George.
Music: Tony Romeo.
Executive Producer: David Susskind.
Producer: Charlotte Schiff Jones.
Segment Producers: Clay Cole, Dolores Danska, Sue Solomon.
Director: Merrill Mazuer.

PEOPLE—30 minutes—CBS—September 18, 1978 – November 6, 1978. 6 episodes.

962   THE PERILS OF PENELOPE PITSTOP

Animated Cartoon. Becoming the legal guardian of Penelope Pitstop, a young and vulnerable female car racer, Sylvester Sneekly dons the guise of the Hooded Claw and intends to acquire her wealth by killing her. Traveling around the world in her car, the "Compact Pussycat," Penelope and her protectors, the Ant Hill Mob, struggle to foil the Hooded Claw's sinister efforts.

VOICES

Penelope Pitstop	Janet Waldo
Sylvester Sneekly	Paul Lynde
The Ant Hill Mob:	
Clyde	Paul Winchell
Softly	Paul Winchell
Zippy	Don Messick
Pockets	Don Messick
Dum Dum	Don Messick
Snoozy	Don Messick

Narrator: Gary Owens.
Music: Hoyt Curtin, Ted Nichols.
Producer-Director: William Hanna, Joseph Barbera.

THE PERILS OF PENELOPE PITSTOP—30 minutes—CBS—September 13, 1969 – September 4, 1971. 26 episodes. Syndicated.

963   PERRY MASON

Crime Drama. The cases and courtroom defenses of Perry Mason, a brilliant criminal attorney working out of Los Angeles. Based on the character created by Erle Stanley Gardner.

CAST

Perry Mason	Raymond Burr
Della Street, his secretary	Barbara Hale
Paul Drake, his investigator	William Hopper
Lt. Arthur Tragg	Ray Collins
Hamilton Burger, the prosecuting attorney	William Talman
Lt. Steve Drumm	Richard Anderson
Gertie Lade, Perry's receptionist	Connie Cezon
Margo, Drake's secretary	Paula Courtland
Drake's operator	Lynn Guild
David Gideon, Mason's associate	Karl Heid
Sergeant Brice	Lee Miller

Music: Richard Shores, Fred Steiner.
Executive Producer: Gail Patrick Jackson, Arthur Marks.
Producer: Art Seid, Sam White, Ben Brady.
Director: Gilbert L. Kay, Earl Bellamy, Arthur Marks, Jerry Hopper, John Peyser, Christian Nyby, Gordon Webb, Francis D. Lyon, Anton Leader, Ted Post, Bernard L. Kowalski, Richard Donner, James Goldstone, Arthur Hiller, Andrew V. McLaglen, Jack Arnold, Lewis Allen, Laslo Benedek, Charles Haas, Jesse Hibbs, Gerd Oswald, Vincent McEveety, Irving J. Moore, Charles R. Rondeau, James Sheldon.

PERRY MASON—60 minutes—CBS—September 21, 1957 – September 4, 1966. 271 episodes. Syndicated (except for the last episode, which was filmed in color). Spin-off series: *The New Adventures of Perry Mason.*

964   THE PERSUADERS!

Adventure. The series, set in Europe, follows the hectic exploits of two handsome playboys: Brett Sinclair, a wealthy and debonair British peer, and Daniel Wilde, a self-made millionaire from the Bronx. Tricked into becoming justice-seeking partners by retired Judge Fulton, the two reluctant troubleshooters encounter beautiful women, adventure and trouble as they seek to uncover the facts behind the criminal cases that Judge Fulton feels warrant further investigation.

CAST

Lord Brett Sinclair	Roger Moore
Daniel Wilde	Tony Curtis
Judge Fulton	Laurence Naismith
Chivers, Brett's butler	George Merritt

Music: John Barry, Ken Thorne.
Producer: Robert S. Baker.
Director: Roy Ward Baker, Roger Moore, Basil Dearden, David Greene, Leslie Norman, Peter H. Hunt, Val Guest, Sidney Hayers, Gerald Mayer, Peter Medak.

THE PERSUADERS! — 60 minutes — ABC — September 18, 1971 – June 14, 1972. 24 episodes. Syndicated.

965   THE PETER MARSHALL VARIETY SHOW

Variety. Music, songs, interviews and comedy sketches.

Host: Peter Marshall.
Regulars: Rod Gist, Denny Evans, The Chapter 5.
Orchestra: Alan Copeland.
Choreographer: Kevin Carlisle.
Executive Producer: David Salzman.
Producer: Rocco Urbisci, Neil Marshall, Beth Uffner.
Writer: George Tricker, Ed Scharlach.
Director: Jeff Margolis.
Art Director: Rene Lagler.

THE PETER MARSHALL VARIETY SHOW — 90 minutes — Syndicated 1976.

966   PETROCELLI

Crime Drama. The cases and courtroom defenses of Tony Petrocelli, an Italian, Harvard-educated attorney working out of San Remo, a Southwestern cattle town.

CAST

Tony Petrocelli	Barry Newman
Maggie Petrocelli, his wife	Susan Howard
Pete Toley, his investigator	Albert Salmi
Frank Kaiser, the Assistant D.A.	Michael Bell
Lt. John Clifford	David Huddleston

Music: Lalo Schifrin.
Executive Producer: Thomas L. Miller, Edward K. Milkis.
Producer: Leonard Katzman.
Director: Jerry London, Herschel Daugherty, Bernard McEveety, Irving J. Moore, Paul Stanley, Vincent McEveety, James Sheldon.

PETROCELLI — 60 minutes — NBC — September 11, 1974 – March 2, 1976. 48 episodes.

967   THE PET SET

Discussion. Topics include pet care, ecology and wildlife preservation.

Hostess: Betty White.
Regulars: Ralph Helfer, Dare Miller.
Announcer: Allen Ludden.
Music: A recorded, but uncredited opening and closing theme.

THE PET SET — 30 minutes — Syndicated 1971. 39 programs.

968   PETTICOAT JUNCTION

Comedy. The original story line follows the activities of Kate Bradley, a widow and proprietor of the Shady Rest Hotel in Hooterville, a farm valley. Following the untimely death of Bea Benaderet (Kate) in 1968, the series format changed to focus on the antics of Joe Carson, the manager of the Shady Rest. The recurring story line depicts the efforts of Homer Bedloe, the vice president of the C.F. and W. Railroad, to scrap the Cannonball, an 1890s steam engine that services Hooterville. Despite Kate's objections, he schemes to achieve his goal in the hopes of becoming a company big shot.

CAST

Kate Bradley	Bea Benaderet
Joe Carson, the hotel manager	Edgar Buchanan
Billie Jo Bradley, Kate's daughter	Jeannine Riley
	Gunilla Hutton
	Meredith MacRae
Bobbie Jo Bradley, Kate's daughter	Pat Woodell
	Lori Saunders
Betty Jo Bradley, Kate's daughter	Linda Kaye Henning
Charley Pratt, the Cannonball engineer	Smiley Burnett
Floyd Smoot, the conductor	Rufe Davis
Sam Drucker, the general store owner	Frank Cady
Steve Elliott, Betty Jo's husband	Mike Minor
Homer Bedloe, the railroad v.p.	Charles Lane
Norman Curtis, the railroad president	Roy Roberts
Dr. Janet Craig	June Lockhart
Dr. Barton Stuart	Regis Toomey
Wendell Gibbs, the Cannonball engineer (later episodes)	Byron Foulger
Selma Plout, Kate's neighbor	Elvia Allman
Henrietta Plout, Selma's daughter	Lynnette Winter
Kathy Jo Elliott, Betty Jo's daughter	Elaine Daniele Hubbel
Herby Bates, a friend of the Bradley girls	Don Washbrook
Fred Ziffel, a farmer	Hank Patterson
Ben Miller, a farmer	Tom Fadden
Newt Kiley, a farmer	Kay E. Kuter
Cousin Mae*	Shirley Mitchell
Aunt Helen*	Rosemary DeCamp

Bradley family dog: Boy.

Music: Curt Massey.
Executive Producer: Charles Stewart.

Producer: Paul Henning, Dick Wesson.
Director: Charles Barton, Paul Henning, Elliott Lewis, Ralph Levy, Guy Scarpitta.

PETTICOAT JUNCTION — 30 minutes — CBS — September 24, 1963 – September 12, 1970. 148 episodes. Syndicated.

*Both actresses temporarily replaced Bea Benaderet during her illness.

969   PEYTON PLACE

Serial. Dramatic incidents in the lives of the people of Peyton Place, a small New England town.

CAST

Constance MacKenzie Carson, the owner of the bookstore	Dorothy Malone
	Lola Albright
Elliot Carson, her husband, publisher of the *Peyton Place Clarion*	Tim O'Connor
Michael Rossi, the doctor	Ed Nelson
Alison MacKenzie, Constance's daughter	Mia Farrow
Rodney Harrington, the nephew of Martin Peyton, the town's founder	Ryan O'Neal
Eli Carson, Elliot's father	Frank Ferguson
Norman Harrington, Rodney's brother	Christopher Connelly
Betty Anderson Harrington, Rodney's wife	Barbara Parkins
Rita Jacks Harrington, Norman's wife	Patricia Morrow
Leslie Harrington, Rodney's father	Paul Langton
Ada Jacks, Rita's mother	Evelyn Scott
Stephen Cord, the illegitimate son of Martin's daughter	James Douglas
Martin Peyton, the founder of the town	George Macready
Hannah Cord, Martin's mistress	Ruth Warrick

Additional Principal Cast:

Matthew Swain	Warner Anderson
Laura Brooks	Patricia Breslin
David Schuster	William Smithers
Doris Schuster	Gail Kobe
Claire Morton	Mariette Hartley
Dr. Bob Morton	Kent Smith
Julie Anderson	Kasey Rogers
George Anderson	Henry Beckman
Paul Hanley	Richard Evans
Kim Schuster	Kimberly Beck
Susan Winter	Diana Hyland
Dr. Miles	Percy Rodrigues
Marsha Russell	Barbara Rush
Lew Miles	Glynn Turmann
The Reverend Mr. Bedford	Ted Hartley
Alma Miles	Ruby Dee
Joanne Walker	Jeanne Buckley
Carolyn Russell	Elizabeth Walker
Jennifer Ivers	Myra Fahey
Stella Chernak	Lee Grant
Adrienne	Gena Rowlands
Rachel	Leigh Taylor-Young
Eddie	Dan Duryea
John Fawler	John Kerr
Gus Chernak	Bruce Gordon
Marian Fawler	Joan Blackman
Mrs. Dowell	Heather Angel
Joe Chernak	Don Quinn
Vincent Markham	Leslie Nielsen
Russ Gehring	David Canary
Phyllis Sloane	Bek Nelson
Judge Jessup	Curt Conway

Music: Arthur Morton, Cyril Mockridge, Lee Holdridge, Lionel Newman.
Music Supervision: Lionel Newman.
Theme: Franz Waxman.
Executive Producer: Paul Monash.
Producer: Everett Chambers, Richard Goldstone, Felix Feist, Richard DeRoy.
Director: Walter Doniger, Ted Post.

PEYTON PLACE — 30 minutes — ABC — September 15, 1964 – June 2, 1969. 514 episodes. Syndicated. Spin-off series: *Return to Peyton Place*.

970   THE PHIL DONAHUE SHOW

Discussion. Discussions on the contemporary issues that affect everyone in their daily lives.

Host: Phil Donahue.
Executive Producer: Dick Mincer.
Producer: Patricia McMillen.
Director: Ron Weiner.

THE PHIL DONAHUE SHOW — 60 minutes — Syndicated 1969.

971   PHYL AND MIKHY

Comedy. The series, set in Beverly Hills, follows the lives of Phyllis (Phyl) Wilson, a pretty American female track star, and Mikhail (Mikhy) Orlov, a Russian track star who has defected. They meet, fall in love, marry and set up housekeeping in the home of Max Wilson — Phyl's father and her coach at Pacific Western University. Episodes depict their struggles to make their marriage work under difficult circumstances, and Mikhy's attempts to adjust to the American way of life.

CAST

Phyllis Wilson Orlov	Murphy Cross
Mikhy Orlov	Rick Lohman
Max Wilson, Phyl's father; a widower	Larry Haines
Vladimir Gimenko, the Russian agent seeking to persuade Mikhy to return to the mother land	Michael Pataki
Edgar "Truck" Morley, Max's employer	Jack Dodson
Gwyn Bates, Max's girlfriend	Rae Allen
Connie, Phyl's friend	Deborah Pratt
Beth, Phyl's friend	Valerie Landsburg
Phyl's friend (no character name)	Karen Werner
Phyl's friend (no character name)	Debbie Kalman
TV Announcer (reporting track events)	Sammy Jones

Music and Theme: Rod Parker and Hal Cooper.
Executive Producer: Rod Parker, Hal Cooper.

Producer: Rita Dillon.
Writer: Tom Reeder, Rod Parker, Lan O'Kun, Madlyn Daley.
Director: Hal Cooper.
Creator: Buddy Arnold.
Art Director: Chuck Murawski.

PHYL AND MIKHY—30 minutes—CBS—May 26, 1980–June 30, 1980. 6 episodes.

972 PHYLLIS

Comedy. A spin-off from *The Mary Tyler Moore Show.*

First season story line: Following the death of her husband Lars, Phyllis Lindstrom, a self-satisfied woman, leaves Minneapolis and relocates to San Francisco. She acquires a job as assistant to Julie Erskine, the owner of Erskine's Commercial Photography Studio. Stories relate the misadventures of the glamorous widow as she struggles to begin a new life.

Second season story line: A cast change dropped the Julie Erskine role. Julie, who supposedly married, has closed the studio, leaving Phyllis unemployed. She finds employment as administrative assistant to Dan Valenti, a supervisor for the San Francisco Board of Supervision. Stories continue to relate her misadventures as she attempts to adjust to the business world.

CAST

Phyllis Lindstrom	Cloris Leachman
Bess Lindstrom, her daughter	Lisa Gerritsen
Julie Erskine, her employer	Barbara Colby Liz Torres
Leo Heatherton, Julie's photographer	Richard Schaal
Audrey Dexter, Phyllis' mother-in-law	Jane Rose
Jonathan Dexter, Audrey's husband	Henry Jones
Sally Dexter, Jonathan's mother	Judith Lowry
Dan Valenti, Phyllis' employer	Carmine Caridi
Leonard Marsh, Dan's associate	John Lawlor
Harriet Hastings, Leonard's assistant	Garn Stephens
Mark Valenti, Dan's nephew, married Bess on Feb. 27, 1977	Craig Wasson
Arthur Lanson, married Mother Dexter on Dec. 13, 1976	Burt Mustin
Van Horn, the park wino, Phyllis' confidante	Jack Elam

Phyllis' address: 4482 Bayview Drive.

Music: Dick De Benedictis.
Executive Producer: Ed Weinberger, Stan Daniels.
Director: Jay Sandrich, Joan Darling, James Burrows, Harry Mastrogeorge, Asaad Keleda.

PHYLLIS—30 minutes—CBS—September 8, 1975–August 30, 1977.

973 PINK LADY

Variety. Music, comedy and song from Pink Lady, Japan's top-rated singers, and Jeff Altman, an American comic.

Host: Jeff Altman.
Starring: Pink Lady (Mie and Kei).
Regulars: Jim Varney, Sherry Eiken, Anna Mathias, The Peacock Dancers.
Recurring Guest: Sid Caesar (as Mie and Kei's father in skits).
Orchestra: Matthew McCauley.
Executive Producer: Albert J. Tenzer.
Producer: Sid and Marty Krofft.
Director: Art Fisher.
Choreographer: Joe Corssini.

PINK LADY—60 minutes—NBC—March 1, 1980–April 4, 1980. 5 programs. Original title *Pink Lady—and Jeff.*

974 THE PINK PANTHER

Children. Live-action segments are intersperced with the cartoon misadventures of the Pink Panther, a nontalking and non-discouraging animal that evolved from the "The Pink Panther" theme by Henry Mancini.

Hosts: Lennie Schultz, The Ritts Puppets.
Puppeteers: Paul and Mark Ritts.
Voices: John Byner, Dave Barry, Paul Frees, Rich Little, Marvin Miller, Athena Forde, June Foray, Mel Blanc, Arte Johnson, Joan Gerber, Barry Mann, Pat Harrington, Jr., Paul Winchell, Hal Smith, Larry Storch, Frank Welker, Tom Holland.
Music: William Lava, Doug Goodwin, Walter Green.
Producer: David DePatie, Friz Freleng.
Director: Hawley Pratt, Gerry Chiniquy, Arthur Davis.

THE PINK PANTHER—30 minutes—NBC—September 6, 1969–September 4, 1976. 60 minutes—September 11, 1976–September 2, 1978. ABC—90 minutes (as *The Pink Panther Half and a Half, Hour and a Half Show*)—September 9, 1978–September 1, 1979.

975 PIXANNE

Children. The series, set in a magic forest, follows the adventures of Pixanne, a pretty fairy, as she relates songs, stories and educational information to children.

Starring: Jane Norman as Pixanne.
Regulars: The Addid Williams Puppets.
Executive Producer: Jane Norman.
Producer-Director: Alan J. Shalleck.

PIXANNE—30 minutes—Syndicated 1978.

976 PLANET OF THE APES

Science Fiction. A United States Air Force space capsule, launched in the year 1988, penetrates a radioactive turbulence area and passes through a time barrier that propels it to the year 3085.

The craft crash-lands and two of the survivors, astronauts Alan Virdon and Pete Burke, find themselves in an era ruled by intellectual apes. Humans, treated as a lesser species, serve as laborers. As they explore the area, they are captured and imprisoned due to a fear among the ape leaders that their presence may cause a revolt among the other humans.

Intrigued by the intelligence of the astronauts, Galen, an intellectual ape, befriends them, seeking to absorb their knowledge. However, distrustful of the astronauts, Veska, one of the ape leaders, plans to kill them. In an unsuccessful attempt to ambush them after unlocking their cell door, he is himself accidentally killed by Galen. Galen, Burke and Virdon, branded dangerous fugitives, are sought for murder.

Stories depict their struggle for survival and the astronauts' attempts, assisted by Galen, to return to the Earth of the 1980s. Adapted from the series of motion pictures of the same title.

CAST

Galen	Roddy McDowall
Alan Virdon	Ron Harper
Pete Burke	James Naughton
Zaius, the ape leader	Booth Colman
Urko, Zaius' assistant	Mark Lenard
Veska (first episode)	Woodrow Parfrey

Music: Lalo Schifrin, Lionel Newman.
Music Supervision: Lionel Newman.
Executive Producer: Herbert Hirschman.
Producer: Stan Hough.
Director: Don Weis, Don McDougall, Arnold Laven, Bernard McEveety, Jack Starrett, Alf Kjellin, Ralph Senensky, John Meredyth Lucas.

PLANET OF THE APES—60 minutes—CBS—September 13, 1974–December 27, 1974. 13 episodes.

977 THE PLASTICMAN COMEDY/ADVENTURE SHOW

Animated Cartoon.

Segments:

Plasticman. The exploits of Plasticman, who can stretch his body into any shape, as he battles the forces of evil. Additional characters: The Chief, his female superior; Penny, his girlfriend; and Hula Hula, his assistant.

Mightyman and Yukk. The exploits of Mightyman, the world's smallest super hero, and Yukk, the world's ugliest dog, as they battle the sinister forces of evil.

Rickety Rocket. The exploits of a space age group of detectives: Rickety Rocket, a talking space ship, and its human assistants, Cosgrove, Venus, Splashdown and Sunstroke.

Voices: Melendy Britt, Johnny Brown, John Stephenson, Frank Welker, Mariene Aragon, Keith Barbour, Daws Butler, Ruth Buzzi, Henry Corden, Danny Dark, Walker Edmiston, Sam Edwards, Ron Feinberg, Linda Gray, Shep Menkin, Chuck McCann, Julie McWhirter, Don Messick, Howard Morris, Gene Moss, Alan Oppenheimer, Stanley Ralph Ross, Michael Rye, Hal Smith, Joan Gerber, Jerry Housner, Ralph James, Stanley Jones, Casey Kasem, Keye Luke, Allan Melvin, John Stephenson, Harold J. Stone, Fred Travalena, Ginny Tyler, Herb Vigran, Janet Waldo, Lennie Weinrib, Nancy Wible, William Woodson, Alan Young.

Music: Dean Elliott.
Executive Producer: Joe Ruby, Ken Spears.
Producer: Jerry Eisenberg.
Director: Charles A. Nichols, Rudy Lavarra, Manny Perez.

THE PLASTICMAN COMEDY/ADVENTURE SHOW—2 hours—ABC—September 22, 1979–December 15, 1979. 90 minutes—Premiered: December 22, 1979.

978 PLAY THE PERCENTAGES

Game. Two teams of two (usually husband and wife) compete. A question, based on a survey of 300 people, is read to the players. One member of each team is asked to predict the percentage of people surveyed who were able to answer the question. The actual percentage is revealed and the player who comes closest wins the percentage value in points. The game continues in this manner and the first team to score three hundred points wins the game and $300.

Host: Geoff Edwards.
Announcer: Jay Stewart.
Music: Hal Hidley.
Executive Producer: Ron Greenberg.
Producer: Jack Barry, Dan Enright.
Director: Richard S. Kline.

PLAY THE PERCENTAGES—30 minutes—Syndicated 1980.

979   PLEASE STAND BY

Comedy. The series, set in De-Queen, New Mexico, follows the misadventures of Frank Lambert, as he struggles to run KRDA, Channel 4, a television station fraught with problems.

CAST

Frank Lambert, the father	Richard Schaal
Carol Lambert, his wife	Elinor Donahue
Susan Lambert, their daughter	Darian Mathias
David Lambert, their son	Stephen Michael Schwartz
Rocky Lambert, their son	Bryan Scott
Vicki Janes, works at the station	Marcie Barkin
Dennis "Crash" Lopez, works at the station	Danny Mora
Sam, the Lambert's friend	Gary Oakes

Music: Phil Cody.
Theme: "Please Stand By" arranged by Jack Eskew.
Theme Vocal: Stephen M. Schwartz.
Executive Producer: Bob Banner.
Producer: William Bickley, Michael Warren.
Director: Howard Storm, Alan Myerson, Jim Drake.
Creator: William Bickley, Michael Warren.
Art Director: John Keene.

PLEASE STAND BY—30 minutes—Syndicated 1978.

980   P.M. MAGAZINE

Human Interest. The program spotlights both the usual and unusual activities of people in everyday life.

Hosts: Mike Cerre, Danielle Folquet.
Assistants: Linda Harris, Susan Murphy, Judy Missitt, Lea Feldman, Judi Shepherd, Jerry Baker, Joan Embry, Chef Tell Erhardt.
Producer: Peter J. Restivo, Don Smith.
Field Producer: Steven Fairchild.
Director: Jim Shasky.

P.M. MAGAZINE—30 minutes—Syndicated 1980.

981   POLICE STORY

Anthology. Dramatizations depicting the day-to-day struggles of police officers. Based on the files of various law-enforcement agencies throughout the country.

Music: Jack Elliott, Allyn Ferguson, Jerry Goldsmith, Richard Markowitz, John Parker.
Executive Producer: Stanley Kallis, David Gerber.
Producer: Liam O'Brien, David Gerber, Christopher Morgan, Hugh Benson, Mel Swope, Larry Brody, Carl Pingitore.
Director: Corey Allen, Vince Edwards, Barry Shear, Gary Nelson, Seymour Robbie, Alex March, Lee H. Katzin, Arthur

Kean, John Badham, Edward Abroms, Jeff Corey, E.W. Swackhamer.
Creator: Joseph Wambaugh; developed for TV by E. Jack Neuman.

Included:

Losing Game. The story focuses on the difficulties faced by a police woman, married to another officer, when she is offered a permanent position as a narcotics agent.

Cast: Margaret Case: Stella Stevens; William Allen: Alex Cord; Vinnie: Scott Brady; Valenzuela: Cesare Danova; Johnny Case: Burr DeBenning.

Confessions of a Lady Cop. The story of a veteran police woman who begins to buckle under the stress of a demanding criminal investigation, which comes at a time when her affair with a married cop is falling apart.

Cast: Officer Evelyn Carter: Karen Black; Sgt. Jack Leland: Don Murray; Gloria Leland: Patricia Crowley; George Merrick: Donald May; Capt. Harrison: Eddie Egan.

Dangerous Games. The story of Charlie Czonka, a vice officer who poses as a producer to apprehend the leader of a prostitution racket.

Cast: Charlie Czonka: James Farentino; Jannette Jackson: Elizabeth Ashley; Marilyn: Janet Margolin; Lassiter: Michael Strong; Faye: Francine York.

The Wyatt Earp Syndrome. The story of Curt Nations, a police officer obsessed with tracking down a suspected rapist—a condition that is provoking his fellow officers—and threatening his marriage.

Cast: Curt Nations: Cliff Gorman; Barbara Nations: Kim Darby; DiMarco: Harry Guardino; Vinnie: Scott Brady; Melanie: Kim Richards; Debbie: Cari Anne Warder; Psychiatrist: Mel Ferrer.

POLICE STORY—60 minutes—NBC—October 2, 1973–August 23, 1977. 2 hours—NBC—November 9, 1977–April 28, 1980. The two-hour pilot film, "The Police Story," aired on NBC on March 20, 1973.

982   POLICE SURGEON

Crime Drama. The series, set in Toronto, Canada, details the exploits of Simon Locke, a surgeon with the Emergency Medical Unit of the Metropolitan Police Department, a "doctor with the mind of a detective." A spin-off from *Dr. Simon Locke.*

CAST

Dr. Simon Locke	Sam Groom
Lt. Dan Palmer	Len Birman
Lt. Jack Gordon	Larry Mann
Tony, Simon's driver	Marc Hebet
The Police Radio Dispatcher	Nerene Virgin

Music: Lewis Helkman.
Executive Producer: Wilton Schiller.
Producer: Chester Krumholz, Gerald Mayer.

POLICE SURGEON—30 minutes—Syndicated 1972. 76 episodes.

983   POLICE WOMAN

Crime Drama. The story of Sergeant Suzanne "Pepper" Anderson, a sensual, brassy, compassionate, sincere and beautiful undercover police woman with the Criminal Conspiracy Division of the Los Angeles Police Department.

CAST

Sgt. Suzanne "Pepper" Anderson*	Angie Dickinson
Sgt. William Crowley	Earl Holliman
Sgt. Pete Royster	Charles Dierkop
Sgt. Joe Styles	Ed Bernard
Lt. Paul Marsh	Val Bisoglio
Cheryl, Pepper's sister	Nichole Kallis
Harriet Styles, Joe's wife	Kandi Keith

Pepper's address: 102 Crestview Drive, Los Angeles.

Music: Jerry Goldsmith, Morton Stevens, George Romanis, Pete Rugolo, Jeff Alexander, Bruce Broughton, Gerald Fried.
Executive Producer: David Gerber.
Producer: Douglas Benton, Edward DeBlasio.
Director: Barry Shear, John Newland, Alf Kjellin, Corey Allen, Alvin Ganzer, Alexander Singer, Douglas Benton, Herschel Daugherty, Barry Crane, Robert Vaughn, David Moessinger, George Lehr, Virgil W. Vogel, E. Arthur Kean.
Creator: Robert Collins.

POLICE WOMAN—60 minutes—NBC—September 13, 1974–August 30, 1978. Syndicated.

*Pepper's first name, during the second season, is given as Lee Anne.

984   POP! GOES THE COUNTRY

Musical Variety. Performances by Country and Western entertainers.

Host: Ralph Emery.
Music: Jim Malloy, Jerry Whitehurst.
Theme Vocal: The Statler Brothers.
Executive Producer: Bill Graham.
Producer: Reg Dunlap.
Director: Bill Turner.

POP! GOES THE COUNTRY—30 minutes—Syndicated 1974.

985   POPPI

Comedy. The series, set in New York City, follows the misadventures of Abraham Rodriquez, the Puerto Rican father of two children, as he struggles to hold down several part-time jobs and raise his mischievous sons.

CAST

Abraham, Rodriquez, a widower	Hector Elizondo
Abraham Rodriquez, Jr., his son	Anthony Perez
Luis Rodriquez, his son	Dennis Vasquez
Lupe, Abraham's girlfriend	Edith Diaz
Angelo Maggio, Abraham's friend	Lou Criscuolo
Mr. Diaz, Abraham's employer	Frank Lugo

Music: George Del Barrio.
Executive Producer: Herbert B. Leonard, Arne Sultan.
Producer: Nick Anderson, A. J. Nelson.
Director: Hy Averback, Al Viola, E. W. Swackhamer.
Creator: Tina and Lester Pine.

POPPI—30 minutes—CBS—January 20, 1976–March 2, 1976; July 20, 1976–August 24, 1976.

986   PORRIDGE

Comedy. The British series on which America's *On the Rocks* is based. The program, which has not been broadcast in the United States, depicts incidents in the life of Stanley Fletcher, a British criminal serving a five-year sentence in Her Majesty's Prison Slade for stealing a truck. (The title, *Porridge,* refers to British criminal slang for a term spent in prison.)

CAST

Stanley Fletcher	Ronnie Barker
Barrowclough	Brian Wilde
Mackay	Fulton Mackay
Godber	Richard Beckinsale
Grout	Peter Vaughan
Prison Governor	Michael Barrington

PORRIDGE—30 minutes—Produced by the BBC from 1974 to 1977.

987   THE PRACTICE

Comedy. The series, set in New York City, depicts the running battle that exists between Jules Bedford, a gruff but lovable doctor who practices in and refuses to leave the Lower East Side, and his son, Dr. David Bedford, a Park Avenue physician. The son objects to his father's methods (free treatment when patients are unable to pay) and longs for him to join him in his practice on Park Avenue.

CAST

Dr. Jules Bedford	Danny Thomas
Dr. David Bedford	David Spielberg
Jenny Bedford, David's wife	Shelley Fabares
Molly Gibbons, Jules's nurse	Dena Dietrich
Helen, Jules's receptionist	Didi Conn
Paul Bedford, David's son	Allen Price

CBS

Petticoat Junction. From left, Pat Woodell, Jeannine Riley and Linda Kaye Henning.

VIACOM ENTERPRISES

Please Stand By. Seated, Richard Schaal and Elinor Donahue. Back, from left, Stephen Michael Schwartz, Bryan Scott and Darian Mathias.

NBC

Police Woman. Angie Dickinson.

NBC

The Practice. Front, from left, Allen Price, Danny Thomas and Damon Raskin. Back, from left, Didi Conn, David Spielberg, Shelley Fabares, Mike Evans and Dena Dietrich.

Tony Bedford, David's son   Damon Raskin
Nate, the hospital restaurant
  waiter   Sam Laws
Dr. Roland Caine, David's
  partner   John Byner
Dr. Byron Fisk   Barry Gordon
Lenny, an intern   Mike Evans

Music: David Shire, James Di-
Pasquale.
Supervising Producer: Tony
Thomas.
Executive Producer: Danny
Thomas, Paul Junger Witt.
Producer: Steve Gordon, Tony
Thomas.
Director: Lee Philips, Noam Pitlik,
Bill Persky, Tony Mordente,
George Tyne.
Creator: Steve Gordon.

THE PRACTICE — 30 minutes —
NBC — January 30, 1976 – August
6, 1976; October 13, 1976 – January 20, 1977.

988   PRESENTING SUSAN ANTON

Variety. Music, comedy, song and
dance — all designed to highlight
the many talents of Susan Anton.

Hostess: Susan Anton.
Regulars: Jack Fletcher, Terry
McGovern, Jimmy Martinas,
Donovan Scott, Marcie Vos-
burgh, Dick Wilson, Jack
Knight, Barbara Brownell,
Buddy Powell, The Walter
Painter Dancers.
Announcer: Jack Fletcher.
Orchestra: Ian Bernard, Larry
White.
*Special Musical Material for Su-
san:* Larry White.
Executive Producer: Jack Stein.
Producer: Ernest Chambers.
Director: Jeff Margolis.
Choreographer: Walter Painter.

PRESENTING SUSAN ANTON —
60 minutes — NBC — April 26,
1979 – May 17, 1979. 4 programs.

989   THE PRICE IS RIGHT

Game. The game varies greatly in
presentation, but the basic format
for each version and each segment is for contestants to guess
the manufacturer's suggested re-
tail price for various merchandise. Players who surpass the selling price forfeit their chance to
win that particular item; the contestant whose bid comes closest
to the selling price receives
the item.

Version 1:

Host: Bill Cullen, Jack Clark.
Assistants: Beverly Bently, Toni
Wallace, June Ferguson.
Producer: Beth Ferro, Bob
Stewart.
Director: Paul Alter, Don Bohl.

THE PRICE IS RIGHT — 30 minutes — NBC — September 15,
1956 – September 9, 1963.

ABC — September 18, 1963 – September 3, 1965.

Version 2:

Host: Bob Barker.
Announcer: Johnny Olsen.
Assistants: Nancy Myers, Pamela
Parker, Anitra Ford, Holly
Hallstrom, Janice Pennington,
Dian Parkinson.
Music: Ed Kalehoff, Bert Es-
kander.
Executive Producer: Frank
Wayne.
Producer: Barbara Hunter, Philip
Wayne.
Director: Marc Breslow.

THE NEW PRICE IS RIGHT — 30
minutes — CBS — September 4,
1972 – October 31, 1975. As *The
Price Is Right* — 60 minutes —
CBS — Premiered: November 3,
1975.

Version 3:

Host: Dennis James, Bob Barker.
Announcer: Johnny Olsen.
Assistants: Anitra Ford, Holly
Hallstrom, Janice Pennington,
Dian Parkinson.
Music: Ed Kalehoff, Bert Es-
kander.
Supervising Producer: Mark
Goodson, Bill Todman.
Executive Producer: Frank
Wayne.
Producer: Barbara Hunter, Philip
Wayne, Jay Wolpert.
Director: Marc Breslow.

THE PRICE IS RIGHT — 30 minutes — Syndicated 1972.

990   THE PRIME OF MISS JEAN BRODIE

Drama. The series, set in Edin-
burgh, Scotland, in 1930, revolves
around the experiences of Jean
Brodie, a vain and eccentric
teacher employed at the Marcia
Blaine School for Girls. Based on
the 1961 novel by Muriel Spark
and produced by Scottish TV.

CAST

Jean Brodie	Geraldine McEwan
Mrs. MacDonald, a teacher	Madeleine Christie
Miss Gaunt, a teacher	Georgine Anderson
Sandy Stranger, a student	Lynsey Baxter
Giulia Cibelli, a student	Romana Kaye
Jenny Gray, a student	Amanda Kirby
Rose Stanley, a student	Tracey Childs
Mary, a student	Jean McKinley
Mr. Lawson, the music teacher	George Cormack
Ted Lloyd, the art teacher	John Castle

Hostess: Julie Harris.
Music: Marvin Hamlisch.
Executive Producer: Beryl Vertue.
Producer: Richard Bates.
Director: John Bruce.
*Producer (of Miss Harris' Seg-
ment):* Lisa Seguin.
*Director (of Miss Harris' Seg-
ment):* David Gerber.

THE PRIME OF MISS JEAN BRO-
DIE — 60 minutes — PBS — May 7,
1979 – June 11, 1979. 6 episodes.

991   PRIMUS

Adventure. The exploits of oceanographer Carter Primus, a global
underwater troubleshooter
working out of Nassau.

CAST

Carter Primus	Robert Brown
Toni Hyden, his assistant	Eva Renzi
Charlie Kingman, his assistant	Will Kuluva

Carter's equipment: Big Kate, an
underwater robot; the *Pegasus*,
an exploratory vehicle; *Teg-
tight*, his operational base;
Dagat, the mother ship; and
the *Orka*, his patrol boat.

Music: Leonard Rosenman.
Narrator: Robert Brown.
Producer: Ivan Tors, Tim T.
Michael, Andy White.
Director: John Florea, Ricou
Browning.
Creator: Michael and Andy White.

PRIMUS — 30 minutes — Syndicated 1971. 26 episodes.

992   PRISONER: CELL BLOCK H

Serial. An adult-oriented drama
that details life in the Wentworth
Detention Centre, a woman's
prison in Melbourne, Australia.
Stories trace the circumstances
that have caused prison sentences to be handed down to the
women, and also focuses on the
lives of the prison staff, and the
away-from-jail private lives of
those associated with the prison.
Produced at the Channel 0
studios in Melbourne by the
Grundy Organization for the 0-10
Network.

CAST

Prisoners:

Lynnette Warner	Kerry Armstrong
Karen Travers	Peita Toppano
Frieda "Franky" Doyle	Carol Burns
Bea Smith	Val Lehman
Marilyn Anne Mason	Margaret Laurence
Doreen Anderson (alias Debbie Raye)	Colette Mann
Jeannie "Mum" Brooks	Mary Ward
Elizabeth "Lizzie" Birdsworth	Sheila Florance
Chrissy Latham	Amanda Muggleton
Barbara Davidson	Sally Cahill
Monica Ferguson	Lesley Baker
Kathleen Leach	Penny Stewart
Roslyn Colson	Sigrid Thornton
Sharon Gilmour	Margot Knight
Helen Masters	Louise Pajo
Catherine Roberts	Margaret McLennan
Susan Rice	Briony Behets
Anne Yates	Kristy Child
Noelene Burke	Jude Kuring
Clara Goddard	Betty Lucas
Melinda Cross	Lulu Pinkus
Joyce Martin	Judy Nunn
Edith Warden	Colleen Clifford
Denise Crabtree	Lydia Keane
Martha Ives	Kate Jason

Bella Abrecht	Liddy Clark
Toni McNally	Pat Bishop
Pat O'Connell	Monica Maughan
Janet Dominquez	Deirdre Rubinstein
Roise Hudson	Anne Maree McDonald
Caroline Simpson	Rosalind Speirs
Vivienne Williams	Bernadette Gibson

Prison Personnel:

Erica Davidson, the governor	Patsy King
Meg Jackson, the sympathetic warden	Elspeth Ballantyne
Vera Bennett, the sadistic warden	Fiona Spence
Greg Miller, the doctor	Barry Quinn
Jean Vernon, the welfare officer	Christine Amor
Jim Fletcher, the deputy governor	Gerald Maguire
Bill Jackson, the psychologist; Meg's husband	Don Baker
Paul Reed, the social worker	George Mallaby
Sally, the receptionist	Kate Turner

Also:

Eddie Cook, the electrician	Richard Moir
Judith Anne, Mum's granddaughter	Kim Deacon
Ted Warner, Lynn's father	Ben Gabriel
Doug Parker, Lynn's husband (briefly)	John Arnold
Gary Doyle, Franky's brother	Greg Stroud
Steve Wilson, the lawyer	Jim Smillie
Angela Jeffries, the lawyer	Jeannie Drynan
Leila Fletcher, Jim's wife	Penny Ramsey
George Lucana, Anne's underworld connection	Bill Hunter
Ken Roberts, Catherine's husband	Tim Elliott
Col Burke, Noelene's brother	Brian Granrott
Lee Anne Burke, Noelene's daughter	Tracy Jo-Riley
Peter Clements, the sociology professor interested in prison reform	Carrillo Gantner
David O'Connell, Pat's son	David Letch
Alex Frazier, the reporter	Geoff Collins
Alice Hemmings, Doreen's mother	Anne Haddy
Mrs. Devlin, Pat's mother	Dorothy Sturgess
Det. Sgt. Allen	Ken Goodlet
Tony Reed, Paul's son	John Higginson
Kevin Burns, Doreen's friend	Ian Gilmour
Judy Bryant, Sharon's lover	Betty Bobbitt

Music Played By: Allan Caswell.
Music Composed By: William
Motzing.
Music Supervision: Australian
Screen Music, Inc.
Theme Vocal: Lynn Hamilton.
Executive Producer: Reg Watson,
Godfrey Philipp.
Producer: Ian Bradley.
Writer: Dave Worthington, Ian
Bradley, Michael Brindley,
Sheila Sibley, Denise Morgan,
John Drew, Ron McLean, John
Hepworth, David Barrington,
John Upton, S. E. Unsworth,
John Wood, Ray Kolle, Mar-
garet McClosky, Ann Lucas,
Michael Harvey.
Director: Graeme Arthur, Rod
Hardy, Gary Conway, Brian
McDuffie, Godfrey Philipp,
Simon Wincer, William Fitzwa-
ter, Marcus Cole, Julian Pringle,
Peita Letchford, Leigh Spence,

Brian Faull, Leon Thau, Philip East, Simon Hellings, Rod Hardy, Ken Fogarty.

PRISONER: CELL BLOCK H—30- and 60-minute versions—Syndicated to the U.S. in January 1980. Premiered in Australia in February 1979. Episode numbers: Available as 130 one-hour episodes; or 260 half-hour segments.

993   PROJECT U.F.O.

Drama. Dramatizations of U.F.O. (Unidentified Flying Object) incidents as seen through the investigations of USAF Major Jake Gatlin and his assistant Harry Fitz. Based on the official records of the U.S. Air Force's Project Bluebook, the federal government's record of U.F.O. reports and investigations (made possible by the Freedom of Information Act; names and locations of sightings, however, are changed).

CAST

Major Jake Gatlin	William Jordan
Staff Sgt. Harry Fitz	Caskey Swaim
Libby, their secretary	Aldine King
Capt. Ben Ryan (replaced Gatlin)	Edward Winter

Narrator: Jack Webb.
Music: Nelson Riddle.
Executive Producer: Jack Webb, Gene Levitt.
Producer: Robert Leeds, Colonel W. Coleman, USAF, Ret., Gene Levitt, Robert Blees.
Director: Richard Quince, Robert Leeds, Dennis Donnelly, Sigmund Neufeld, Jr., John Patterson, Richard Moder, Richard Green, Robert Blees.

PROJECT U.F.O.—60 minutes—NBC—February 19, 1978–January 4, 1979. 23 episodes. July 5, 1979–August 30, 1979. 3 episodes.

994   THE PROTECTORS

Adventure. The exploits of Harry Rule (American), Contessa Caroline di Contini (British), and Paul Buchet (French), three private detectives who are members of the Protectors, an international organization of the world's finest investigators united in the battle against crime in the capitals of Europe.

CAST

Harry Rule	Robert Vaughn
Caroline di Contini	Nyree Dawn Porter
Paul Buchet	Tony Anholt
Suki, Harry's housekeeper in London	Yasuko Nagazumi
Chino, a Protector	Anthony Chinn

Harry's dog: Gus.

Music: John Cameron.
Theme Vocal: "Avenues and Alleyways": Tony Christie.
Executive Producer: Sherwood Price.

Producer: Gerry Anderson, Reg Hill.

THE PROTECTORS—30 minutes—Syndicated 1972. 52 episodes.

995   THE PSYCHIATRIST

Drama. The story of James Whitman, a young Los Angeles psychiatrist who practices the new but controversial techniques of modern medical therapy.

CAST

Dr. James Whitman	Roy Thinnes
Dr. Bernard Altman, his mentor	Luther Adler

Music: Gil Mellé.
Executive Producer: Norman Felton.
Producer: Jerrold Freedman, Harry Tatleman.
Director: Steven Spielberg, Jeff Corey, Douglas Stewart, Daryl Duke, Jerrold Freedman.
Creator: Richard Levinson, William Link.

THE PSYCHIATRIST—60 minutes—NBC—February 3, 1971–September 1, 1971 (as part of *Four-in-One*). 6 episodes.

996   PUBLIC DEFENDER

Drama. The cases and courtroom defenses of Bart Andrews, a public defender of indigent people.

CAST

Bart Matthews	Reed Hadley

Producer: Hal Roach, Jr., Carroll Case.
Associate Producer: Harve Foster.
Director: Budd Boetticher, Sobey Martin, Paul Guilfoyle, Harve Foster, Erle C. Kenton, James Tinling.
Creator: Mort Lewis, Sam Shaynon.
Original Program Open:
Matthews: A public defender is an attorney employed by the community and responsible for giving legal aid without cost to any person who seeks it and is financially unable to employ private council. It is his duty to defend those accused of a crime until the issue is decided in a court of law. The first public defender's office in the United States was opened in January 1913. Over the years other offices were opened and today that handful has grown to a network. A network of lawyers cooperating to protect the rights of our clients.

PUBLIC DEFENDER—30 minutes—CBS—March 11, 1954–June 23, 1955. 69 episodes. In 1978, *Public Defender* was resyndicated in a somewhat unusual manner: the opening theme is cut and the title of each episode is the title the viewer sees on the

screen; no visual matter identifies the program as ever being *Public Defender*.

Q

997   QUARK

Comedy. The series, set in the year 2226 A.D., depicts the voyages of an interplanetary garbage scow whose mission, on behalf of the UGSP (United Galaxy Sanitation Patrol), is to clean up the Milky Way. A take-off on *Star Trek*.

CAST

Adam Quark, the captain	Richard Benjamin
Betty I, the copilot	Tricia Barnstable
Betty II, her clone, the copilot	Cyb Barnstable
Gene/Jean, the transmute, the engineer	Tim Thomerson
Ficus Panderato, the Vegeton, a plant, the science officer	Richard Kelton
Andy, the cowardly robot	Bobby Porter
Otto Palindrome, the designer of Space Station Perma One, the base for UGSP	Conrad Janis
The Head, the head of UGSP	Alan Caillou

Music: Perry Botkin, Jr.
Executive Producer: David Gerber.
Producer: Mace Neufeld, Bruce Johnson.
Director: Hy Averback, Bruce Bilson, Peter H. Hunt.
Creator: Buck Henry.

QUARK—30 minutes—NBC—February 24, 1978–April 14, 1978. 8 episodes. The 30-minute pilot film aired on NBC on May 7, 1977.

998   THE QUEST

Western. Eight years after being captured and raised by Cheyenne Indians who attacked the wagon train on which he was traveling, Morgan "Two Persons" Baudine, is freed by the Army. He begins a search for his sister, Patricia, who is reputed to be living among the Cheyenne, and meets his long-lost brother, Quentin, a young medical student. Quentin, who was raised by an aunt in San Francisco, also has begun a search for Patricia. Reunited by a common goal, they begin a hazardous quest to find their sister. The series concerns their adventures as they travel throughout the rugged West of the last quarter of the nineteenth century.

CAST

Morgan "Two Persons" Baudine	Kurt Russell
Quentin Baudine	Tim Matheson

Music: Richard Shores.
Executive Producer: David Gerber.

Producer: Mark Rogers, James H. Brown.
Director: Michael O'Herlihy, Irving J. Moore, Earl Bellamy, Corey Allen, Bernard Mc-Eveety.
Program Open:
Announcer: The legend of the Baudine brothers has etched itself into frontier history in the last quarter of the nineteenth century. Morgan "Two Persons" Baudine, captured by the Cheyenne and freed eight years later by the Army. Quentin Baudine, a young doctor from San Francisco. Across thousands of miles from the Missouri banks to the Canadian rivers, from the Rockies to the High Plains, both join together in a search for their sister, Patricia, still a captive of the Cheyenne. The legend of the Baudine brothers—this is their story, this is the Quest!

THE QUEST—60 minutes—NBC—September 22, 1976–December 22, 1976. The two-hour pilot film aired on NBC on May 13, 1976.

999   QUINCY, M.E.

Crime Drama. The story of Dr. R. Quincy, a medical examiner (M.E.) for the Los Angeles coroner's office, a doctor who prefers to probe as a detective rather than just working in a lab.

CAST

Dr. R. Quincy	Jack Klugman
Lee Potter, his girlfriend	Lynnette Mettey
Dr. Robert Astin, his superior	John S. Ragin
Dr. Sam Fugiyama, Quincy's assistant	Robert Ito
Lt. Frank Monahan, the homicide detective	Garry Walberg
Danny Tarvo, Quincy's friend, the owner of Danny's Place, a bar	Val Bisoglio
Robin, Astin's secretary	Karen Philipp
Sergeant Brill, Frank's partner	Joseph S. Roman
Alice Ting, an assistant pathologist	Amie Eccles
Danny's Place bartender	Johnny Nolan
Danny's waitress	Diane Markoff
Marc, a pathologist	Marc Scott Taylor

Music: Stu Phillips, Vic Mizzy, Bruce Broughton, Bob Alcivar.
Quincy Theme: Glen A. Larson.
Executive Producer: Glen A. Larson, Jud Kinberg, Richard Irving, Donald Bellisario, R. A. Cinader, Hannah Shearer, David Moessinger.
Supervising Producer: William Cairncross, Lester Berke.
Producer: Christopher Morgan, Edward J. Montagne, Peter J. Thompson, William Cairncross, Charles Dismukes, J. Rickley Dumm, Lou Shaw, Robert F. O'Neill, Michael Star, Sam Egan.

Director: Vic Morrow, Raymond Damon, Gerald Mayer, Herb Wallerstein, Paul Krasny, Ray Danton, Ron Satlof, Peter J. Thompson, Harvey Laidman, Rod Holcomb, Georg Fenady, Jeffrey Hayden, Laurence Doheny, Jerimiah Morris, David Moessinger, Bruce Kessler, E. W. Swackhamer, Stephen Stern, Noel Black, Corey Allen, Jackie Cooper.

QUINCY, M.E.—2 hours—NBC—October 3, 1976–January 2, 1977 (as part of *The NBC Sunday Mystery Movie*). 60 minutes—NBC—Premiered: February 4, 1977.

1000   THE QUIZ KIDS

Panel. The basic format has a panel of five exceptionally intelligent children attempt to answer difficult questions in return for scholarship bonds.

Version One:

Host: Joe Kelly, Clifton Fadiman.
Producer: Louis G. Cowan, John LeWellen.
Director: Don Meler.

THE QUIZ KIDS—30 minutes—CBS—November 13, 1952–September 27, 1956.

Version Two:

Host: Jim McKrell.
Announcer: Mike Adams.
Music: Score Productions.
Executive Producer: Geoffrey Cowan, Seymour Berns.
Producer: Kay Bachman.
Writer: Marsha Stall, Alexander Small.
Director: Dick Schneider.

THE QUIZ KIDS—30 minutes—Syndicated 1980.

R

1001   RAFFERTY

Drama. The story of Sid Rafferty, M.D., a former army doctor turned brilliant diagnostician in private practice in Los Angeles. He is a doctor who, working part-time in City General Hospital, "believes in healing people, not in setting himself up in a fancy business just to make money."

CAST
Dr. Sid Rafferty	Patrick McGoohan
Dr. Daniel Gentry, his associate	John Getz
Vera Wales, his office nurse	Millie Slavin
Beryl Kaynes, the hospital admissions nurse	Joan Pringle

Music: Leonard Rosenman, Richard Clements.
Executive Producer: Jerry Thorpe.

Producer: James Lee, Norman S. Powell, Robert Van Scoyk.
Director: Jerry Thorpe, Barry Crane, Alexander Singer, Patrick McGoohan, Edward H. Feldman, Arnold Laven.
Creator: James Lee.

RAFFERTY—60 minutes—CBS—September 5, 1977–November 28, 1977. 10 episodes.

1002   THE RAY STEVENS SHOW

Variety. Music, songs and comedy sketches.

Host: Ray Stevens.
Regulars: Lulu, Dick Curtis, Steve Martin, Carol Robinson, Florian Carr, Billy Van, Max Elliott, Cass Elliot.
Orchestra: Jimmy Dale.
Producer: Allan Blye, Chris Bearde.
Writer: Jack Hanrahan, Phil Hahn.

THE RAY STEVENS SHOW—60 minutes—NBC—June 28, 1970–September 6, 1970. Original title: *Andy Williams Presents the Ray Stevens Show*.

1003   REAL PEOPLE

Human Interest. A live newsmagazine series that spotlights real but unusual and eccentric people.

Hosts: Sarah Purcell, Fred Willard, John Barbour, Jimmy Breslin, Skip Stevenson, Bill Rafferty, Mark Russell, Byron Allen.
Announcer: Jack Herrold.
Executive Producer: George Schlatter.
Producer: Robert Long, Gary Necessary, Bob Wynn, John Barbour, Jeff Simon, Jack Tellander.
Director: Merrill Mauzer, Dave Caldwell.
Art Director: Robert Keene.

REAL PEOPLE—60 minutes—NBC—April 18, 1979–May 23, 1979. 6 episodes. Repeats: July 25, 1979–August 31, 1979. Returned, Premiered: September 6, 1979.

1004   THE REAL TOM KENNEDY SHOW

Talk-Variety.

Host: Tom Kennedy.
Regulars: Kelly Garrett, John McCormick, Foster Brooks.
Announcer: Tom Kennedy.
Orchestra: Dave Pell.
Producer: Roger E. Ailes.

THE REAL TOM KENNEDY SHOW—60 minutes—Syndicated 1970. 45 programs.

1005   THE REBELS

Drama. A sequel to *The Bastard*, the first miniseries based on John Jakes's *Kent Family* novels. *The Rebels*, the second novel, is set

during the American Revolution and continues the story of Philip Kent, the illegitimate son of an English duke. It depicts his exploits with colonial revolutionaries as they seek democracy.

CAST
Philip Kent	Andrew Stevens
Judson Fletcher	Don Johnson
Eph Tait	Doug McClure
Henry Knox	John Chappell
Mrs. Brumple	Joan Blondell
Peggy McLean	Gwen Humble
Charlotte Waverly	Pamela Hensley
Rachel	Tanya Tucker
Seth McLean	Robert Vaughn
George Washington	Peter Graves
Benjamin Franklin	Tom Bosley
John Quincy Adams	William Daniels
Thomas Jefferson	Kevin Tighe
Anne Kent	Kim Cattrall
John Waverly	William Smith
Ambrose Waverly	Warren Stevens
Dr. Church	Macdonald Carey
Angus Fletcher	Forrest Tucker
Duke of Kentland	Richard Basehart
Von Steuben	Nehemiah Persoff
General Lafayette	Marc Vahanian
General Howe	Wilfred Hyde-White
Mrs. Harris	Anne Francis

Narrator: William Conrad.
Music: Gerald Fried
Producer: R. A. Cinader.
Writer: Sean Bain, Robert A. Cinader.
Director: Russ Mayberry.

THE REBELS—2 hours—Operation Prime Time—May 1979. 2 episodes.

1006   THE REDD FOXX COMEDY HOUR

Variety. Basically, a series of comedy sketches that spotlight the talents of comedian Redd Foxx.

Host: Redd Foxx.
Regulars: Murray Langston, Deborah Pratt, Hal Smith, Dick Owens, Walt Hanna, Andrew Johnson.
Announcer: Roger Carroll.
Orchestra: Gerald Wilson.
Producer: Allan Blye, Bob Einstein.
Director: Donald Davis.
Choreographer: Lester Wilson.
Art Director: Jack McAdams.

THE REDD FOXX COMEDY HOUR—60 minutes—ABC—September 15, 1977–January 26, 1978. 16 programs.

1007   THE RED HAND GANG

Children. The adventures of Frankie, J. R., Joannie, Lil Bill and Doc, five pre-teen city children, members of the Red Hand Gang club, as they stumble upon and seek to solve crimes.

CAST
Frankie	Matthew Laborteaux
J. R.	J. J. Miller
Joannie	Jolie Neman
Lil Bill	Johnny Brogna
Doc	James Bond III

Music: Score Productions.
Executive Producer: William P. D'Angelo, Ray Allen, Harvey Bullock.
Producer: William P. D'Angelo.
Director: William P. D'Angelo, Charles R. Rondeau.

THE RED HAND GANG—30 minutes—NBC—September 10, 1977–January 21, 1978. 21 episodes.

1008   THE RED SKELTON SHOW

Variety. Music, songs, dances and comedy sketches.

Host: Red Skelton.
Regulars (1951-1970): Stanley Adams, Mike Wagner, Dorothy Lowe, Peggy Rea, Lester Matthews, Kathryn Cord, Beverly Powers, Chanin Hale, Adam Kaufman, Ida Moe McKenzie, Lloyd Kino, Jan Davis, Helen Funai, Billy Barty, Bob Duggan, Stuart Lee, Linda Sue Risk, The Skeltones Dancers, The Tom Hanson Dancers, The Alan Copeland Singers.
Regulars (1970-1971): John Magruder, Jan Arvan, Chanin Hale, Brad Logan, Emmaline Henry, Peggy Rea, Jackson Bostwick, Yvonne Ewald, The Burgundy Street Singers.
Announcer (1951-1971): Art Gilmore.
Orchestra (1951-1971): David Rose.
Producer (1951-1970): Nat Perrin, Freeman Keyes, Ben Brady, Cecil Baker, Gerald Gardner, Bill Hobin.
Producer (1970-1971): Guy della Cioppa, Gerald Gardner, Dee Caruso.
Writer (1970-1971): Mort Greene, Pat McCormick, Jeff Baron, Lionel Buit, Red Skelton.
Director (1970-1971): Terry Kyne.

THE RED SKELTON SHOW—30 minutes—NBC—September 30, 1951–June 12, 1953; CBS (as both a 30- and 60-minute version)—September 22, 1953–June 15, 1970. NBC—30 minutes—September 14, 1970–August 29, 1971.

RESCUE FROM GILLIGAN'S ISLAND

See *Gilligan's Island: Extension Episode*.

THE RESTLESS YEARS

See *Loose Change*.

1009   THE RETURN OF CAPTAIN NEMO

Adventure. During routine war games, Tom Franklin and Jim Por-

The Protectors. From left, Robert Vaughn, Nyree Dawn Porter and Tony Anholt.

Ryan's Hope. From left: Bernard Barrow, Helen Gallagher, John Gabriel, Nancy Addison, and Michael Levin.

Return of the Saint. Left, Roger Moore as the original Simon Templar. Right, Ian Ogilvy as the new Simon Templar.

ter, U.S. naval underwater intelligence agents, find trapped in a coral reef beneath the sea the fabled submarine *Nautilus*. Upon boarding the ship, they meet its captain, Nemo, and learn what has happened: on March 16, 1877, while searching for Atlantis, the *Nautilus* wedged itself under a coral reef and stuck. After dispensing the crew, Nemo, in the hope that one day help would come, suspended himself in a crystalline cylinder, from which, due to the depth charges used in the war games, he has emerged. The constant barrage also sets the *Nautilus* free and brings Nemo in contact with Miller, the naval intelligence head, who agrees to repair the damaged sub in return for Nemo's help in performing certain hazardous missions for the government. The series depicts Nemo's adventures as he aids the U.S. government while seeking the fabled Lost Continent of Atlantis. Based on the story by Jules Verne.

CAST

Captain Nemo	Jose Ferrer
Cmdr. Tom Franklin	Tom Hallick
Lt. Jim Porter	Burr DeBenning
Dr. Kate Melton, Nemo's aide	Lynda Day George
Prof. Waldo Cunningham, the evil, modern-day scientist; Nemo's nemesis	Burgess Meredith
Mr. Miller, the head of naval intelligence	Warren Stevens

Prof. Cunningham's sub: the *Raven*.

Music: Richard La Salle.
Producer: Irwin Allen.
Writer: Norman Kartkov, Preston Wood, Robert Block, William Keys, Larry Alexander, Robert C. Dennis, Mann Rubin.
Director: Alex March.
Creator: Irwin Allen.

THE RETURN OF CAPTAIN NEMO — 60 minutes — CBS — March 8, 1978 – March 29, 1978. 3 episodes.

THE RETURN OF MOD SQUAD

See *The Mod Squad: Extension Episode*.

1010   THE RETURN OF THE SAINT

Adventure. The series, set in Europe, depicts the exploits of Simon Templar, alias the Saint, a dashing, daredevil, free-lance troubleshooter, who aids people in distress. An updated version of *The Saint*.

CAST

Simon Templar	Ian Ogilvy

Simon's license plate number: ST-1.

Music: John Scott.
New Saint Theme: Brian Dae.

Original Saint Theme: Leslie Charteris.
Executive Producer: Robert S. Baker.
Producer: Anthony Spinner.
Director: Tom Clegg, Les Norman, Peter Medak, Charles Crichton, Ray Austin, Peter Sasdy, Sam Wanamaker, Cyril Frankel.
Creator: Leslie Charteris.
Opening Narration: Ian Ogilvy.

THE RETURN OF THE SAINT — 70 minutes — CBS — December 21, 1979 – March 14, 1980. 13 episodes. May 10, 1980 – August 15, 1980. 12 episodes.

1011   RETURN TO PEYTON PLACE

Serial. A spin-off from *Peyton Place*. The series, set in Peyton Place, a small New England town, continues to depict events in the turmoil-ridden lives of its citizens.

CAST

Constance MacKenzie Carson, the bookstore owner	Bettye Ackerman
Elliot Carson, her husband, publisher of the *Peyton Place Clarion*	Warren Stevens
Alison MacKenzie, their illegitimate daughter	Kathy Glass
Eli Carson, Elliot's father	Frank Ferguson
Rodney Harrington, the nephew of the founder of Peyton Place	Yale Summers Lawrence Casey
Norman Harrington, Rodney's brother	Ron Russell
Betty Anderson Harrington, Rodney's wife	Julie Parrish Lynn Loring
Rita Jacks Harrington, Norman's wife	Patricia Morrow
Leslie Harrington, Rodney's father	Stacy Harris
Ada Jacks, Rita's mother	Evelyn Scott
Dr. Michael Rossi, the town physician	Guy Stockwell
Stephen Cord, the illegitimate son of Martin Peyton's daughter	Joe Gallison
Martin Peyton, the founder of the town	John Hoyt
Hannah Cord, Martin's one-time mistress	Mary K. Wells
Benny Tate, a menacing figure from Alison's past	Ben Andrews
Matthew Carson, Constance's son	John Levin
Dr. Wells	Alex Nicol
Lt. Ed Riker	Chuck Daniel
Judge Foster	Anne Seymour
Selena Cross	Margaret Mason
Monica Bell	Betty Ann Carr
The attorney	Rudy Solari

Music: Linda Line.
Producer: Don Wallace, George Paris.
Director: Allen Pultz, Frank Pacelli.

RETURN TO PEYTON PLACE — 30 minutes — NBC — April 3, 1972 – January 4, 1974.

1012   RETURN TO THE PLANET OF THE APES

Animated Cartoon. A spin-off from *Planet of the Apes*. Traveling aboard the NASA spacecraft *Venture*, three astronauts, Bill Hudson, Judy Franklin and Jeff Carter, penetrate a time vortex and are hurled from present-day Earth (1975) to Earth in the year A.D. 3979 — a world that is ruled by intellectual apes.* Stories follow the astronauts' adventures as they struggle for survival and seek a way to return to the Earth of their time.

VOICES

Astronaut Bill Hudson	Tom Williams Richard Blackburn
Astronaut Judy Franklyn	Claudette Nevins
Astronaut Jeff Carter	Austin Stoker
Dr. Cornelius, an ape doctor	Edwin Mills
Dr. Zira, Cornelius' assistant	Phillippa Harris
General Urko, an ape leader	Henry Corden
Dr. Zarus, an ape leader	Richard Blackburn
Nova, a human friend of the astronauts	Claudette Nevins

Music: Dean Elliott, Eric Rogers.
Producer: David H. DePatie, Friz Freleng.
Writer: Larry Spiegel, Jack Kaplan, John Barrett, Bruce Shelly, John Strong.
Director: Doug Wilder.

RETURN TO THE PLANET OF THE APES — 30 minutes — NBC — September 6, 1975 – September 4, 1976.

*Humanoid greed, folly and lust for power caused man to destroy his civilization in a cataclysmic war. From his ruins, the ape society emerged, and humans, treated as a lesser species, serve as pets, servants and sport for hunters.

1013   REX REED'S MOVIE GUIDE

Information. Film reviews and celebrity interviews.

Host: Rex Reed.
Executive Producer: Mort Zimmerman.
Producer: Larry Strichman.
Director: Don Horan.

REX REED'S MOVIE GUIDE — 30 minutes — Syndicated 1980.

1014   THE RHINEMANN EXCHANGE

Drama. A three-part miniseries based on the novel by Robert Ludlum. The story, set during World War II, follows David Spaulding, an American engineer working for U.S. Intelligence, as he attempts to exchange industrial diamonds for a German bombsite gyroscope.

CAST

David Spaulding	Stephen Collins
Leslie Hawkewood	Lauren Hutton
Walter Kendall	Claude Akins
General Swanson	Vince Edwards
Erich Rhinemann	Jose Ferrer
Col. Edmund Pace	Larry Hagman
Ambassador Granville	John Huston
Bobby Ballard	Roddy McDowall
Asher Feld	Len Birman
Geoffrey Moore	Jeremy Kemp
Altmuller	Werner Klemperer
Irene	Trish Noble
Alex Spaulding	William Prince
Dietrich	John Van Dreeland
Anna	Isela Vega
Heinrich Stoltz	Bo Brundin
Mrs. Cameron	Kate Woodville
Dr. Lyons	Rene Auberjonois
German Scientist	John Hoyt
Dr. Azevedo	Ben Wright
Daniel Mehan	Ramon Bieri

Also: Victoria Racimo, Gene Evans, Charles Siebert, Thayer David.
Music: Michel Colombier.
Executive Producer: George Eckstein.
Producer: Richard Collins.
Writer: Richard Collins.
Director: Burt Kennedy.
Art Director: William Tuntke.
Director of Photography: Alex Phillips, Jr.

THE RHINEMANN EXCHANGE — 5 hours (total) — NBC — March 10, 1977 – March 24, 1977. 3 episodes.

1015   RHODA

Comedy. A spin-off from *The Mary Tyler Moore Show*. The original format, set in New York City, depicts incidents in the lives of Rhoda Morgenstern, a window dresser (and owner of Windows By Rhoda), and her husband Joe Gerard, the head of the New York Wrecking Company. The revised format, which begins two years later, after Rhoda and Joe's divorce, follows the romantic misadventures of Rhoda Morgenstern, a designer with the Doyle Costume Company in Manhattan.

CAST

Rhoda Morgenstern (Gerard)	Valerie Harper
Brenda Morgenstern, her sister	Julie Kavner
Joe Gerard, Rhoda's husband	David Groh
Ida Morgenstern, Rhoda's mother	Nancy Walker
Martin Morgenstern, Rhoda's father	Harold Gould
Voice of Carlton, Rhoda's never-seen, intoxicated doorman	Lorenzo Music
Mae, Joe's bookkeeper	Cara Williams
Alice, Joe's bookkeeper	Candice Azzara
Justin Culp, Joe's partner	Scoey Mitchlll
Nolan Arthur, Joe's partner	Bill Zuckert
Sally Gallagher, Rhoda's friend	Anne Meara
Myrna Morgenstein, Rhoda's friend	Barbara Sharma
Nick Lobo, Brenda's friend	Richard Masur
Lenny Fielder, Brenda's friend	Wes Stern
Gary Levy, Brenda's friend	Ron Silver
Donny Gerard, Joe's son	Todd Turquand Shane Sinutko
Marian Gerard, Joe's ex-wife	Joan Van Ark

Doris, Marian's
housekeeper   Cynthia Towne
Jack Doyle, the owner of the
Doyle Costume Company
(where Rhoda works,
1977-1978)   Kenneth McMillan
Ramon Diaz, Jack's
assistant   Rafael Campos
Benny Goodwin, Brenda's
boyfriend   Ray Buktenica
Tina Molinari, Rhoda's friend   Nancy Lane
Johnny Venture, Rhoda's
friend   Michael DeLano
Mr. Pennick, Rhoda's landlord at
Windows By Rhoda   Will MacKenzie
Carlton's mother   Ruth Gordon

Rhoda's address: 332 West 64th
Street (Manhattan), Apt. 9E
(Brenda, who lives in the same
building, has Apt. 21).
Ida's address: 3517 Grand Concourse (Bronx), Apt. 4G.

Music: Billy Goldenberg, Richard
Warren Lewis, Les Hooper.
Executive Producer: James L.
Brooks, Allan Burns, Charlotte
Brown.
Producer: Charlotte Brown,
David Davis, Lorenzo Music,
Allan Katz, Don Reo, Bob
Ellison.
Director: Robert Moore, Tony
Mordente, Howard Storm, Jay
Sandrich, Alan Rafkin, Doug
Rogers.
Creator: James L. Brooks, Allan
Burns.

RHODA — 30 minutes — CBS —
September 9, 1974 – December 9,
1978. Syndicated.

1016   RHYME AND
REASON

Game. A rhyming phrase is read
(e.g., "I did a double take when I
first met Mae West . . .") and each
of the two contestants writes
down a word that rhymes with
the last word of the phrase. One
player selects a celebrity, from six
who appear, who must make up a
rhyme to complete the phrase. If
the celebrity uses the same word
as the contestant, the contestant
scores two points; if the celebrity
matches the opponent, the opponent scores one point. Three
points are played per game and
the first player to win two games
is the champion and receives
$500.

Host: Bob Eubanks.
Announcer: Johnny Jacobs, Jack
Clark.
Regular Panelist: Nipsey Russell.
Semiregular Panelists: Conny Van
Dyke, Jaye P. Morgan, Charlie
Brill, Mitzi McCall, Pat Harrington, Frank Gorshin, Jamie
Farr.
Music: Score Productions.
Executive Producer: Steven
Friedman.
Producer: Walt Case.
Director: John Dorsey.

RHYME AND REASON — 30 minutes — ABC — July 7, 1975 – July
9, 1976.

1017   THE RICHARD
PRYOR SHOW

Variety. Basically, a series of comedy sketches that spotlight the
talents of comedian Richard
Pryor.

Host: Richard Pryor.
Regulars: Paula Kelly, Jeff Corey,
Sam Laws, Juanita Moore,
Charles Fleischer, Jimmy Martinez, The Chuck Davis Dance
Company.
Orchestra: Johnny Pate.
Special Musical Material: Lenny
LaCrox.
Executive Producer: Burt Sugarman.
Producer: Rocco Urbisci.
Director: John Moffitt.
Choreographer: Chuck Davis.

THE RICHARD PRYOR SHOW —
60 minutes — NBC — September
13, 1977 – October 20, 1977.

1018   RICHIE
BROCKELMAN,
PRIVATE EYE

Crime Drama. The series, set in
Los Angeles, depicts the exploits
of Richie Brockelman, a 23 year
old who, despite scrapes with the
law, is determined to make his
way as a private detective.

CAST

Richie Brockelman   Dennis Dugan
Sharon Deterson, his
secretary   Barbara Bosson
Sergeant Coopersmith   Robert Hogan
Richie's mother   Helen Page Camp
Richie's father (pilot film)   Norman Fell
Richie's father (series)   John Randolph

Richie's home address: 8410
North Turtle Dove Drive.

Music: Mike Post and Pete Carpenter.
Theme: Stephen Geyes, Herb
Pederson.
Executive Producer: Stephen J.
Cannell, Steve Bochco.
Supervising Producer: Alex
Beaton.
Producer: Peter S. Fischer.
Director: Hy Averback, Arnold Laven.
Creator: Stephen J. Cannell, Steve
Bochco.

RICHIE BROCKELMAN, PRIVATE
EYE — 60 minutes — NBC —
March 17, 1978 – April 14, 1978;
August 10, 1978 – August 24, 1978.
5 episodes. The 90-minute pilot
film aired on NBC on October 27,
1976.

1019   THE RICH
LITTLE SHOW

Variety. Music, songs and comedy
sketches.

Host: Rich Little.
Regulars: Julie McWhirter, Charlotte Rae, Joe Baker, R. G.
Brown, Mel Bishop.
Orchestra: Robert E. Hughes.
Executive Producer: Jerry Goldstein.
Producer: Rich Eustis, Al Rogers.
Writer: Ron Clark, Barry Blitzer,
Rudy DeLucca, Ray Jessell, Jack
Kaplan, Barry Levinson.
Director: Lee Bernhardi, Walter C.
Miller.

THE RICH LITTLE SHOW — 60
minutes — NBC — February 2,
1976 – May 18, 1976.

1020   RICH MAN,
POOR MAN, BOOK I

Drama. A nine-part miniseries
that follows the lives of the Jordache brothers: Rudy, the straight
one who moves up the establishment ladder; and Tom, the troublemaker. The series also simultaneously covers the changes in
America from World War II
through the mid-1960s. Based on
the novel by Irwin Shaw.

CAST

Rudy Jordache   Peter Strauss
Tom Jordache   Nick Nolte
Julie Prescott   Susan Blakely
Axel Jordache   Edward Asner
Mary Jordache   Dorothy McGuire
Kate Jordache   Kay Lenz
Wesley Jordache   Willie Aames
          Michael Morgan
Sue Prescott   Gloria Grahame
Bill Falconetti   William Smith
Willie Abbott   Bill Bixby
Duncan Calderwood   Ray Milland
Virginia Calderwood   Kim Darby
Teddy Boylan   Robert Reed
Linda Quales   Lynda Day George
Brad Knight   Tim McIntire
Smitty   Norman Fell
Marsh Goodwin   Van Johnson
Irene Goodwin   Dorothy Malone
Rod Dwyer   Herbert Jefferson, Jr.
Sid Gossett   Murray Hamilton
Colonel Bainbridge   Andrew Duggan
Bayard Nichols   Steve Allen
Teresa Santoro   Talia Shire
Arnold Simms   Mike Evans
Joey Quales   George Maharis
Asher Berg   Craig Stevens
Mr. Tinker   Frank Aletter
Al Fanducci   Dick Butkus
Claude Tinker   Dennis Dugan
Clothilde   Fionnuala Flanagan
Harold Jordache   Bo Brundin
Augie   Julius Harris
Bill Denton   Lawrence Pressman
Gloria Bartley   Jo Ann Harris
Pete Tierney   Roy Jenson
Papadakis   Ed Barth
Pinky   Harvey Jason
Martha   Helen Craig
Phil McGee   Gavan O'Herlihy
Billy   Leigh McCloskey

Music: Alex North.
Music Supervision: Hal Mooney.
Executive Producer: Harve Bennett.

Producer: Jon Epstein.
Writer: Dean Reisner.
Director: David Greene, Boris
Sagal, Ted Post, Harry Falk,
Paul Stanley.
Art Director: John E. Childberg II.
Director of Photography: Howard
Schwartz.

RICH MAN, POOR MAN, BOOK
I — 12 hours (total) — ABC — February 1, 1976 – March 22, 1976;
May 10, 1977 – June 21, 1977. 9 episodes (3 two-hour episodes; 6
one-hour episodes). Syndicated.

1021   RICH MAN,
POOR MAN, BOOK II

Drama. A continuation of the
miniseries, *Rich Man, Poor Man,
Book I.* Continued events in the
life of Rudy Jordache, now a
United States Senator.

CAST

Rudy Jordache   Peter Strauss
Kate Jordache   Kay Lenz
Maggie Porter   Susan Sullivan
Ramona Scott   Penny Peyser
Wesley Jordache   Gregg Henry
Billy Abbott   James Carroll Jordan
Bill Falconetti   William Smith
Diane Porter   Kimberly Beck
Mr. Scott   John Anderson
Charles Estep   Peter Haskell
Rod Dwyer   Herbert Jefferson, Jr.
Claire Estep   Laraine Stephens
Marsh Goodwin   Van Johnson
Marie Falconetti   Dimitra Arliss
Phil Greenberg   Sorrell Booke
Annie Adams   Cassie Yates
Arthur Raymond   Peter Donat
Senator Dillon   G.D. Spradlin
Senator Paxton   Barry Sullivan
Al Barber   Ken Swofford
John Franklin   Phillip Abbott
Vickie St. John   Colleen Camp
Mrs. Rowe   Joan Tompkins
Jake Logan   Richard X. Slattery
Ernest Dettmer   Nehemiah Persoff

Music: Alex North, Michael Isaacson.
Music Supervision: Stanley Wilson.
Executive Producer: Michael
Gleason.
Director: Alex Segal, Bill Bixby,
Karen Arthur, Paul Stanley,
Joan Darling, Lou Antonio.

RICH MAN, POOR MAN, BOOK
II — 60 minutes — ABC — September 21, 1976 – March 8, 1977. 21
episodes. See also *Beggerman,
Thief,* which continues the *Rich
Man, Poor Man* story.

1022   THE RIGHTEOUS
APPLES

Comedy-Drama. The socialawareness series, set in Boston,
focuses on the activities of The
Righteous Apples (Big Neck, D.C.,
Glorette, Sandy and J. T.), five
Sherwin High School musicians
who, in today's troubled world,
seek to help others who are not
as fortunate as they.

CAST

Samuel "D.C." Rosencrantz	Joey Camen
Sandy Burns	Elizabeth Daily
J. T.	Bob Harcum
Glorette Carson	Kutee
Charles "Big Neck" McMorris	Mykel T. Williamson
Mrs. Kent, the high school principal	Mary Gregory
Mr. Shelbourne, a teacher	Rene LeVant

Music: Archer/Bahler Associates, Inc.
Producer: Topper Carew.
Director: Stan Latham, Marlena Laird, Bob LaHendro.
Art Director: Don Roberts, Christopher Idione.

THE RIGHTEOUS APPLES — 30 minutes — Syndicated to PBS in May 1980.

1023 RIPPING YARNS

Comedy. Outlandish updates of classic stories.

Ripping Yarns Cast: Michael Palin, Terry Jones, Ian Ogilvy, John Wentworth, Gwen Watford, Isabel Dean, Denholm Elliot, Barbara New, John Barrett, Anita Carey, Kenneth Colley, Anthony Smee, Peter Graham, Melanie Watson, Vanessa Furse, Bridget Armstrong, Judy Loe.
Producer-Director: Terry Hughes, Jim Franklin.

Included:

Tomkinson's Schooldays. A take-off on *Tom Brown's Schooldays.* An incorrigible young boy named Tomkinson achieves success when he rises to the respected position of school bully.

The Curse of the Claw. A gothic tale about a man's efforts to return a cursed claw to its rightful owners in an attempt to lift its curse of misfortune from his life.

Murder at Moorstones Manor. The story of a murderer who matches wits with the Chiddingfold Clan, an odd assemblage with few wits to match.

RIPPING YARNS — 30 minutes — Syndicated to PBS in 1979. 6 episodes.

1024 THE RIVALS OF SHERLOCK HOLMES

Anthology. Mystery presentations based on fictional detectives who were popular in Europe at the time of Sherlock Holmes. Produced in England.
Music: Robert Sharples.
Executive Producer: Kim Mills, Lloyd Shirley.
Producer: Jonathan Alwyn, Robert Lane, Reginald Collen.
Director: Reginald Collen, Bill Bain.

Included:

The Woman in the Big Hat. The story focuses on Lady Molly, a Scotland Yard investigator as she attempts to solve the murder of a man in a tea room.
Cast: Lady Molly: Elvi Hale; Mary Granard: Ann Beach; Inspector Saunders: Peter Bowles; Lady Irene: Frances White.

The Assyrian Rejuvenation. The story of an unscrupulous detective and his attempts to solve a case of medical fraud.
Cast: Detective Rommey Pringle: Donald Sinden; Col. Sandstream: Michael Bates; Suzie: Jo Rowbottom; Henry Jacobs: Derek Smith.

Cell 13. Believing that a maximum security prison is not what it claims to be, a professor arranges to have himself locked in Maximum Security Cell 13 and proceeds to prove that he can escape within one week.
Cast: Professor Van Dusen: Douglas Wilmer; Head of the prison: Michael Gough.

THE RIVALS OF SHERLOCK HOLMES — 60 minutes — Syndicated to PBS in 1975.

1025 R. J. AND COMPANY

Music. Borrowing its format from *American Bandstand*, the program features teenagers dancing to popular music.
Host: Ron Joseph (R. J.).
Announcer: Jim Bacon, Mark Anthony, Gene Arnold.
Musical Director: Marty Morley, Glen Rosewald.
Executive Producer: Ron Joseph.

R. J. AND COMPANY — 30 minutes — Syndicated 1976. Originally aired locally over WTAF-TV, Channel 29, in Philadelphia.

1026 THE ROAD RUNNER SHOW

Animated Cartoon. Set in a desert, stories follow the endless, but fruitless, attempts of Wile E. Coyote, a scavenger, to catch himself a decent meal — a foxy, outsmarting bird called the Road Runner. Comprised of both theatrical and made-for-TV cartoons.
Voice characterizations: Mel Blanc.
Music: William Lava, Carl Stalling, Milt Franklin, John Celly.
Producer: Leon Schlesinger.
Director: Chuck Jones, I. Freleng.

THE ROAD RUNNER SHOW — 30 minutes — ABC — September 11, 1971 — September 2, 1972.

1027 THE ROADS TO FREEDOM

Serial. The collapse of pre-World War II France is dramatized as it is seen through the eyes of three people: Mathieu, an intellectual college professor; Daniel, a homosexual; and Brunet, a Communist, three men who are unable to act or think definitively. Based on Jean Paul Sartre's *The Roads to Freedom* trilogy: *The Age of Reason, Loss of Innocence* and *The Awakening.* Produced by the BBC.

CAST

Mathieu De LaRue, the professor	Michael Byant
Marcelle, his mistress	Rosemary Leach
Daniel, the homosexual	Daniel Massey
Brunet, the Communist	Donald Burton
Lola Montero, the singer	Georgia Brown
Boris, Lola's romantic interest	Anthony Corlan
Ivich, Boris' sister	Alison Fiske
Jacques De LaRue, Mathieu's brother	Clifford Rose
Odette De LaRue, Jacques's wife	Anna Fox

Music: Theme only, "La Route Est Dure" arranged by Richard Holmes.
Theme Vocal (in French): Georgia Brown.
Writer: David Turner.

THE ROADS TO FREEDOM — 45 minutes — Syndicated to PBS in 1972.

1028 ROALD DAHL'S TALES OF THE UNEXPECTED

Anthology. Dramatizations that depict how certain, unexpected events can alter the destinies of people. Produced in England.
Host: Roald Dahl, John Houseman.
Music: Ron Grainer, Elizabeth Swader.
Theme Music: Ron Grainer.
Executive Producer: Sir Jon Woolf, John Fleming Ball.
Producer: John Rosenberg, Christopher Lewis, Norman Lloyd, Bert Saltzman, Chiz Schultz.
Director: Michael Tuchner, Herbert Wise, Christopher Lewis, Ray Danton, Bert Saltzman, John Peyser, Deszo Magyar.

Included:

A Glowing Future. The story of a girl who plots to get even with her lover of three years when he suddenly decides to leave her for another woman.
Cast: Betsy: Joanna Pettet; Jack: John Beck; Moving man: Billy LaVoie.

Scrimshaw. The story follows a lonely girl's search for love — and her unfortunate fate when she meets Eric, a scrimshawer (carves bones) who seduces her, then kills her for her young and firm bones.
Cast: Brenda, the girl: Joan Hackett; Eric: Christopher Kimbrough.

Neck. A bizarre comedy about an eccentric art collector who is faced with a serious problem when his wife puts her head through one of his far-out masterpieces and gets stuck: to destroy the art work and save his wife? Or to chop off his wife's head and save the art work?
Cast: Lady Natalia, the wife: Joan Collins; Sir Basil, the husband: Michael Alredge; Jelks, the butler: John Gielgud.

The Landlady. The story of a traveler who takes up residence in an old boarding house run by an eccentric lady who poisons her guests then stuffs them.
Cast: Landlady: Siobhan McKenna; William Weaver (the traveler): Leonard Preston.

Program Open:
Host: A wise man believes only in lies, trusts only in the absurd, and learns to expect the unexpected!

ROALD DAHL'S TALES OF THE UNEXPECTED — 30 minutes — Syndicated 1979. Also titled *Tales of the Unexpected.*

1029 THE ROCK FOLLIES

Musical Drama. A penetrating satire that follows the progress of "The Little Ladies," a three-girl British Rock group, as they struggle to succeed in the world of Pop music. Produced in England.

CAST

The Little Ladies:

Anna Wynd	Charlotte Cornwell
Devonia Dee Rhoades	Julie Covington
Nancy "Q" Cunard de Longchamps	Rula Lenska

Also:

Spike, Dee's romantic interest	Billy Murray
Derek Huggin, their manager	Emlyn Price
Jack, Anna's romantic interest	Stephen Moore
Gloria, a friend	Angela Bruce
Bob, a friend	Bob Stewart
Mrs. Wynd, Anna's mother	Vivienne Burgess

The Little Ladies Rock Band: Brian Chatton, Peter Hooke, Tony Stevens, Ray Russel.
Music: Andy Mackay.
Music Associate: Sam Harding.
Producer: Andrew Brown.
Writer: Howard Schuman.
Director: Jon Scoffield, Brian Farnham.
Choreographer: David Toguri.

THE ROCK FOLLIES — 60 minutes — PBS — March 5, 1977 — March 10, 1977. 6 episodes.

1030 THE ROCKFORD FILES

Crime Drama. The exploits of Jim Rockford, the chief operative of the Rockford Private Detective Agency, as he attempts to solve criminal cases that are considered unsolvable and labeled inactive by police.

CAST

Jim Rockford	James Garner
Joseph "Rocky" Rockford, his	
father (pilot film)	Robert Donley
Joseph Rockford (series)	Noah Beery
Beth Davenport, a lawyer	
friend of Jim's	Gretchen Corbett
Sgt. Dennis Becker, L.A.P.D.	Joe Santos
Angel Martin, Jim's friend	Stuart Margolin
Peggy Becker, Dennis' wife	Pat Finley
Megan Dougherty, Jim's blind girlfriend	
(recurring role)	Kathryn Harrold
Lance White, Jim's rich, galling rival	
(recurring role)	Tom Selleck
Rita Capkovic, the prostitute	
who seeks Jim's help	
(recurring role)	Rita Moreno
Lieutenant Chapman, L.A.P.D.	James Luisi
Richie Brockelman, the	
budding gumshoe	Dennis Dugan

Jim's address: The Paradise Cove Trailer Colony at 29 Palm Road in Malibu, California (also given: 29 Cove Road).
Jim's telephone number: 555-2368.

Music: Mike Post, Pete Carpenter, Artie Kane.
Supervising Producer: Stephen J. Cannell.
Executive Producer: Meta Rosenberg, Stephen J. Cannell.
Producer: Chas. Floyd Johnson, Juanita Bartlett, David Chase.
Director: Stephen J. Cannell, Jerry London, Alex Grasshoff, Russ Mayberry, John Patterson, Corey Allen, Ivan Dixon, James Coburn, Joseph Pevney, Reza S. Badiyi, Richard Heffron, Bernard L. Kowalski, Alexander Singer, Meta Rosenberg, Michael Schultz, William Wiard, Vincent McEveety, Jeannot Szwarc, Lawrence Doheny, Christian Nyby, Lou Antonio, James Garner.
Creator: Roy Huggins, Stephen J. Cannell.

THE ROCKFORD FILES — 60 minutes — NBC — September 13, 1974 – January 10, 1980; March 6, 1980 – July 25, 1980. Syndicated. Also titled, for syndication purposes, *Jim Rockford, Private Investigator.* The 90-minute pilot film aired on NBC on March 17, 1974.

ROD SERLING'S NIGHT GALLERY

See *Night Gallery.*

1031   THE ROLLERGIRLS

Comedy. The on-and-off the rink antics of the Pittsburgh Pitts, a five-woman roller derby team based in Pennsylvania.

CAST

Don Mitchell, the owner	
of the Pitts	Terry Kiser
The Pittsburgh Pitts:	
Selma "Books" Cassidy	Joanna Cassidy
Mongo Sue Lampert	Rhonda Bates
Honey Bee Novack	Marcy Hanson
Shana "Pipeline" Akira	Marilyn Tokuda
J. B. Johnson	Candy Ann Brown
Also:	
Howard Divine, the rink	
announcer	James Murtaugh

Music: Tony Asher, John Bahler, Kevin Clark.
Theme Vocal: Shari Saba.
Executive Producer: James Komack, Stan Cutler, George Tricker.
Producer: Tom Cherones.
Director: Burt Brinkerhoff, James Komack, Gary Shimokawa.
Creator: James Komack.

THE ROLLERGIRLS — 30 minutes — NBC — April 24, 1978 – May 10, 1978. 4 programs.

1032   ROLLIN' ON THE RIVER

Variety. Music, song and comedy set on the Mississippi River Boat, the *River Queen.*

Host: Kenny Rogers.
Regulars: The First Edition (Mary Arnold, Mickey Jones, Kin Vassey, Terry Williams).
Musical Direction: Larry Cansler.
Executive Producer: Burt Rosen, David Winters, Zev Buffman Chercover.
Producer: Jim Stanley.
Writer: Alex Barris, Cecil Tuck.
Director: Michael Steele.

ROLLIN' ON THE RIVER — 30 minutes — Syndicated 1971. 26 programs. Also known as *Rollin' with Kenny Rogers and the First Edition.*

1033   ROLL OF THUNDER, HEAR MY CRY

Drama. The miniseries, set in Mississippi in 1933, follows the lives of the Logans, a proudly independent black family. Based on the novels by Mildred Taylor.

CAST

Mary Logan	Janet MacLachlan
David Logan	Robert Christian
Big Mama	Claudia McNeil
Uncle Hammer	Morgan Freeman
Morrison	Rockne Tarkington
Cassie	Lark Ruffin
Stacey	Tony Ross
Jamison	John Cullum
Wallace	Charles Briggs
Jeremy	Mark Keith
Granger	Roy Poole
T. J.	Larry Scott
Miss Crocker	Joan Lewis
Kaleb Wallace	Charles Briggs

Music: Fred Karlin.
Executive Producer: Thomas W. Moore.
Producer: Jean Anne Moore.
Writer: Arthur Heinemann.
Director: Jack Smight.

ROLL OF THUNDER, HEAR MY CRY — 60 minutes — ABC — June 2, 1978 – June 4, 1978. 3 episodes.

1034   ROLL OUT!

Comedy. The series, set during World War II France (1944), follows the adventures of the men assigned to the 5050th Quartermaster Trucking Company of the U.S. Third Army's Red Ball Express. The mostly black-staffed American trucking company delivers supplies to the front lines, swings around and returns for more.

CAST

Cpl. Carter "Sweet" Williams	Stu Gilliam
Pfc. Jed Brooks	Hilly Hicks
Sgt. B. J. Bryant (series)	Mel Stewart
Sgt. B. J. Bryant (pilot film)	Richard Ward
Capt. Rocco Calvelli	Val Bisoglio
Lt. Robert Chapman	Ed Begley, Jr.
Other members of the trucking company	
(as credited and/or identified):	
Wheels Dawson	Garrett Morris
High Strung	Theodore Wilson
Jersey Hampton	Darrow Igus
Phone Booth	Rod Gist
Focus	Jeff Burton
Sgt. Grease, the cook	Sam Laws
Heinz	Robert Boon
Stick Ramsey	Harry Caesar
Giles	Thierry Lemoine
MP Lieutenant	Louie Elias
MP Sergeant	Jerry Summers
Also:	
Madame Delacourt, the restaurant	
owner (series)	Penny Santon
Madame Delacourt (pilot	
film)	Fifi D'Orsay
Dominique Delacourt, her	
daughter	Dana Brady

Music: Dave Grusin, Benny Golson.
Producer: Gene Reynolds, Larry Gelbart.
Director: Gene Reynolds, William Wiard.

ROLL OUT! — 30 minutes — CBS — October 5, 1973 – January 4, 1974. 13 episodes. The 30-minute pilot film aired on CBS on June 5, 1973.

1035   THE ROMAN HOLIDAYS

Animated Cartoon. Twentieth-century life is depicted in Ancient Rome (A.D. 63) where the series follows the misadventures of Gus Holiday, an engineer with the Forum Construction Company, as he struggles to cope with the endless problems of a changing world.

VOICES

Gus Holiday, the father	Dave Willock
Laurie Holiday, his wife	Shirley Mitchell
Precocia Holiday, their	
daughter	Pamelyn Ferdin
Happius (Happy) Holiday,	
their son	Stanley Livingston
Mr. Evictus, their landlord	Dom DeLuise
Mr. Tycoonius, Gus's employer	Hal Smith
Groovia, Happy's girlfriend	Judy Strangis
Herman, Gus's friend	Hal Peary
Henrietta, Herman's wife	Janet Waldo
Brutus, the Holiday's pet lion	Daws Butler

The Holidays' address: 4960 Terrace Drive (the Venus DiMillo Arms apartment house in Pastafasullo, Rome).

Music: Hoyt Curtin.
Executive Producer: William Hanna, Joseph Barbera.
Producer: Iwao Takamoto.
Director: Charles A. Nichols.

THE ROMAN HOLIDAYS — 30 minutes — NBC — September 9, 1972 – September 1, 1973.

1036   THE RONA BARRETT SPECIAL

Interview. A series of celebrity interviews.

Hostess: Rona Barrett.
Executive Producer: William Trowbridge.
Producer: Rona Barrett, Lawrence Einhorn.
Director: Lawrence Einhorn.

Program 1: May 28, 1975

Interviewed: Ann-Margret, Cher, Liza Minnelli, Raquel Welch.

Program 2: December 11, 1975

Interviewed: James Caan, Michael Caine, Elliott Gould, Burt Reynolds.

Program 3: March 29, 1976

Interviewed: Isabelle Adjani, Louise Fletcher, Glenda Jackson, Ann-Margret, Walter Matthau, Jack Nicholson, Al Pacino, Maximilian Schell, James Whitmore.

Program 4: October 27, 1976

Interviewed: Carol Burnett, Valerie Harper, Sally Struthers, Nancy Walker.

Program 5: April 14, 1977

Interviewed: Kate Jackson, Penny Marshall, Toni Tennille, Cindy Williams.

Program 6: May 9, 1980

Interviewed: Bo Derek, Larry Hagman, Kristy McNichol, Kenny Rogers.

THE RONA BARRETT SPECIAL — 60 minutes — ABC — Premiered: May 28, 1975

1037   THE ROOKIES

Crime Drama. The story of William Gillis, Terry Webster, Michael Danko and Chris Owens, rookies attached to Station Number 7 of the Southern California Police Department. Reluctant to use firearms, they represent the new breed of law enforcer and the nonviolent approach to crime control.

CAST

Lt. Edward Ryker	
(series)	Gerald S. O'Loughlin
Sgt. Edward Ryker (pilot	
film)	Darren McGavin

The Rookies. Bottom, from left, Kate Jackson and Gerald S.
O'Loughlin. Top, from left, Georg Stanford Brown,
Michael Ontkean and Sam Melville.

ABC

Officer William Gillis   Michael Ontkean
Officer Terry Webster   Georg Stanford Brown
Officer Michael Danko   Sam Melville
Jill Danko, Michael's wife, a nurse
    at Memorial Hospital   Kate Jackson
Officer Chris Owens   Bruce Fairbairn
The Police Radio
    Dispatcher   Darlyn Ann Lindley
Kim Owens, Chris's sister   Season Hubley

Music: Elmer Bernstein, Lawrence Rosenthal, Pete Rugolo, Jack Elliott, Allyn Ferguson.
Executive Producer: Aaron Spelling, Leonard Goldberg.
Producer: Rick Husky, Skip Webster, William Blinn, Paul Junger Witt, Hal Sitowitz.
Director: E. W. Swackhamer, Phil Bondelli, Alvin Ganzer, Leonard Horn, Lee Philips, Gene Nelson, Harry Falk, Gerald S. O'Loughlin, Ralph Senensky, Jerry Jamison, William F. Claxton, Michael Caffey, Ivan Dixon, Fernando Lamas, Alex Grasshoff, Georg Stanford Brown, Bruce Bilson, Richard Benedict.
Creator: Rita Lakin; developed by William Blinn.

THE ROOKIES — 60 minutes — ABC — September 11, 1972 – June 15, 1976. 68 episodes. Syndicated. The 90-minute pilot film aired on ABC on March 7, 1972.

1038   ROOM 222

Comedy-Drama. Life at integrated Walt Whitman High School in Los Angeles, as seen through the eyes of Pete Dixon, a black American history instructor whose classes are held in Room 222.

CAST

Pete Dixon, a teacher   Lloyd Haynes
Seymour Kaufman, the
    principal   Michael Constantine
Liz Macintyre, the guidance
    counselor   Denise Nicholas
Alice Johnson, a student
    teacher   Karen Valentine
Miss Evans, a teacher   Hollis Irving
Miss Hogarth, a teacher   Patsy Garrett
Miss Portnoy, a teacher   Carol Worthington
Kenneth Dragen, the English
    teacher   Ivor Francis
Richie Lane, a student   Howard Rice
Jason Allen, a student   Heshimu
Bonnie, a student   Jane Actman
Helen Loomis, a student   Judy Strangis
Pamela, a student   Ta Tanisha
Larry, a student   Eric Laneuville
Bernie, a student   David Jolliffe
Laura, a student   Pamela Peters

Music: Richard La Salle, Jerry Goldsmith, Lionel Newman, Benny Golson.
Music Supervision: Lionel Newman.
Executive Producer: William P. D'Angelo.
Producer: Gene Reynolds, Jon Kubichan, Ronald Rubin.
Director: Allen Baron, Seymour Robbie, Lee Philips, Hal

Cooper, Herman Hoffman, James Sheldon, Leslie H. Martinson, Richard Michael's, Charles R. Rondeau, William Wiard, Gene Reynolds.
Creator James L. Brooks.

ROOM 222 — 30 minutes — ABC — September 17, 1969 – January 11, 1974. 78 episodes. Syndicated.

1039   ROOTS

Drama. An eight-part adaptation of the novel by Alex Haley, which dramatizes a century in Haley's family history — from his ancestors' life in eighteenth-century tribal Africa to their emancipation in the post-Civil War South.

CAST

Kunta Kinte   LeVar Burton
    John Amos
Ninta   Cicely Tyson
Ormoro   Thalmus Rasulala
Capt. Thomas Davies   Edward Asner
Slater   Ralph Waite
Nyo Boto   Maya Angelou
Brima Cesay   Harry Rhodes
Fanta   Ren Woods
    Beverly Wodd
Kintango   Moses Gunn
Missy Anne Reynolds   Sandy Duncan
Wrestler   Ji-Tu Cumbuka
Gardener   William Watson
Kadi Touray   O.J. Simpson
Fiddler   Louis Gossett, Jr.
William Reynolds   Robert Reed
John Reynolds   Lorne Greene
Mrs. Reynolds   Lynda Day George
Ames   Vic Morrow
John Carrington   Paul Shenar
Bell   Marge Sinclair
Grill   Gary Collins
Trumbull   Lee Jones DeBroux
Jennova   Tanya L. Boyd
Harlan   Thayer David
Drummer   Raymond St. Jacques
Tom Moore   Chuck Connors
Noah   Lawrence Hilton-Jacobs
Ordell   John Schuck
Kizzy   Leslie Uggams
Melissa   Roxie Roker
Ada   Elma Jackson
Mrs. Moore   Carolyn Jones
Squire James   Macdonald Carey
Mingo   Scatman Crothers
Mathilda   Olivia Cole
Stephen Bennett   George Hamilton
Eric Russell   Ian McShane
Sister Sara   Lillian Randolph
Sam Bennett   Richard Roundtree
Chicken George   Ben Vereen
Reverend   Wally Taylor
Leonard   Davis Roberts
Evan Brent   Lloyd Bridges
Tom   Georg Stanford Brown
Ol' George Johnson   Brad Davis
Lewis   Hilly Hicks
Jemmy Brent   Doug McClure
Irene   Lynne Moody
Martha Johnson   Lane Binkley
Sam Harvey   Richard McKenzie
Virgil   Austin Stoker
Lila Harvey   Sally Kemp
Sen. Arthur Johnson   Burl Ives
Sheriff Charley Biggs   John Quade
Drake   Charles Cyphers
Bud   Todd Bridges

Music: Gerald Fried, Quincy Jones.
Executive Producer: David L. Wolper.
Producer: Stan Margulies.
Writer: William Blinn, Ernest Kinoy, James Lee, M. Charles Cohen.
Director: David Greene, John Erman, Gilbert Moses, Marvin Chomsky.
Director of Photography: Steven Larner, Joseph M. Wilcots.

ROOTS — 12 hours (total) — ABC — January 23, 1977 – January 30, 1977. 8 episodes. Syndicated as nine 90-minute episodes with Ben Vereen as host.

1040   ROOTS: THE NEXT GENERATIONS

Drama. A continuation of the miniseries, *Roots.* Beginning where the original series leaves off, *Roots: The Next Generations,* opens in Henning, Tennessee, in 1882 and follows 88 years in the history of Alex Haley's family; and ends with Haley himself tracing his *Roots.* Based on the books, *Roots* and *Search* with additional notes by Alex Haley and developed for television by Ernest Kinoy.

CAST

Tom Harvey   Georg Stanford Brown
Colonel Warner   Henry Fonda
Jim Warner   Richard Thomas
Elizabeth   Debbi Morgan
Irene Harvey   Lynne Moody
Mrs. Warner   Olivia deHavilland
Andy Warner   Marc Singer
Chicken George Moore   Avon Long
John Dolan   Brian Mitchell
Beeman Jones   Greg Morris
Earl Crowther   Paul Koslo
Cynthia Harvey Palmer   Cynthia Sye
    Bever-Leigh Banfield
    Beah Richards
Will Palmer   Stan Shaw
Lee Garnett   Roger E. Mosley
Bob Campbell   Harry Morgan
T. J. Calloway   John Carter
Simon Haley (Alex'
    father)   Dorian Harewood
Bertha Palmer   Irene Cara
Dad Jones   Ossie Davis
Queen Haley   Ruby Dee
Aleck Haley   Hal Williams
Alex Haley, as a boy   Christoff St. John
Alex Haley, older   Damon Evans
Alex Haley, grown   James Earl Jones
Nan Haley   Debbie Allen
Malcolm X   Al Freeman, Jr.
George Lincoln Rockwell   Marlon Brando
Odlie   Lee Chamberlain
Sister Will Ada   Claudia McNeil

Also: James Daly, Ossie Davis, Bernie Casey, Gerald S. O'Loughlin, John Rubinstein, Dina Merrill, Andy Griffith, Diahann Carroll, Michael Constantine, Brock Peters, Norman Fell, Paul Winfield.
Music: Gerald Fried.

Executive Producer: David L. Wolper.
Producer: Stan Margulies.
Director: John Erman, Charles S. Dubin, Georg Stanford Brown, Lloyd Richards.

ROOTS: THE NEXT GENERATIONS — 14 hours (total) — ABC — February 18, 1979 – February 15, 1979. 7 two-hour episodes.

1041   THE ROPERS

Comedy. The series, set at the Royal Dale Condominium Town House in Chevia Hills, California, follows the misadventures of Stanley and Helen Roper as they seek, but seldom find, a life of peace and quiet. A spin-off from *Three's Company,* but based on the British series *George and Mildred.*

CAST

Stanley Roper   Norman Fell
Helen Roper   Audra Lindley
Jeffrey P. Brookes III,
    their neighbor   Jeffrey Tambor
Anne Brookes, Jeffrey's
    wife   Patricia McCormack
David Brookes, their son   Evan Cohen
Debbie Hopper, a resident of
    Royal Dale   Lois Areno
Jenny Ballinger, the young
    girl who lives with the
    Ropers   Louise Vallance
Ethel Armbrewster, Helen's
    sister   Dena Dietrich
Hubert Armbrewster, Ethel's
    husband   Rod Colbin
Helen's mother   Lucille Benson
Hilda, Helen's younger
    sister   Dulcie Pullman
Louise Cooper, Hubert's
    secretary   Timothy Blake

The Ropers' address: 46 Peacock Drive.
The Ropers' dog: Muffin.

Commercial Break Announcer: Norman Fell.
Music: Joe Raposo.
Executive Producer: Don Nicholl, Bernie West, Michael Ross.
Producer: George Sunga.
Associate Producer: Wendy Blair.
Director: Dave Powers, Jack Shea.
Art Director: Don Roberts.

THE ROPERS — 30 minutes — ABC — March 13, 1979 – April 18, 1979; August 12, 1979 – March 15, 1980; April 26, 1980 – May 22, 1980. 28 episodes.

1042   ROSETTI AND RYAN

Crime Drama. The series, set in Los Angeles, follows the exploits of Joseph Rosetti and Frank Ryan, a playboy and an ex-cop, now freewheeling attorneys who incorporate unorthodox methods as they strive to seek justice for their clients.

ABC

Room 222. Bottom, Michael Constantine and Karen Valentine. Top, Lloyd Haynes and Denise Nicholas.

CAST

Joseph Rosetti	Tony Roberts
Frank Ryan	Squire Fridell
Jessica Hornesby, the assistant D.A.	Jane Elliot
Rocky (originally Georgia), Joe's secretary	Randi Oakes
Rosa Rosetti, Joe's mother	Penny Santon
Emma, Joe's receptionist	Ruth Manning
Judge Marcus T. Block	William Marshall
Judge Praetor Hardcastle	Dick O'Neill

Music: Peter Matz, Gordon Jenkins.
Executive Producer: Leonard B. Stern.
Producer: Jerry Davis.
Director: John Astin, Alex March, Daniel Haller, Harry Falk, Richard Crenna, Joshua Shelley.

ROSETTI AND RYAN — 60 minutes — NBC — September 22, 1977 – November 10, 1977. 6 episodes. The two-hour pilot film, "Rosetti and Ryan: Men Who Love Women," aired on NBC on May 23, 1977.

1043 ROUGHNECKS

Drama. A two-part miniseries that follows the experiences of a group of roughnecks for the Marshall Drilling Company as they search for geothermal energy on a Southwestern ranch. The job is complicated by Tracy Carter, a beautiful reporter who, along with the ranch owners, opposes them for the destruction the well will cause to the land.

CAST

Tracy Carter, the reporter	Cathy Lee Crosby
O'Dell Hartmen, a driller	Sam Melville
Paul Marshall, the owner of Marshall Drilling	Steve Forrest
Ida McBride, the ranch owner	Vera Miles
Carol McBride, Ida's daughter	Sarah Rush
Tom McBride, Ida's son	Kevin Geer
Roy Bethke, a driller	Stephen McHattie
Yolanda Saurez, O'Dell's friend	Ana Alicia
Plug Champion, a driller	Harry Morgan
Willie Clayton, the ranch foreman	Wilford Brimley
Sal Espinoza, a driller	A Martinez
Boone Maddox, Willie's assistant	Timothy Scott
Lenny Booker, a driller	Rockne Tarkington
George Harris	Andrew Robir
Linda Booker	Luise Heath
Marcia	Janice Carroll
Go-Girl	Diane Defendorf
Wendell Todd	Mike Wagner
Deputy	John Locke
Roughneck (driller)	Henry Wills
Roughneck	Wallace Britz
Hooker	Mina Martinez
Hooker	Janelle Romero

Music: Jerrold Immel.
Music Producer: Les Sheldon.
Theme Vocal: "A Piece of the Action": Juice Newton.
Songs (all vocals by Juice Newton): "Taking It as It Comes," "Del Rio," "Workin' Man," "Roughnecks Ain't Got No Place to Go But Down," "Tear It Up."

Executive Producer: Douglas Netter.
Producer: Richard E. Lyons.
Co-Producer: Michael Michaelian.
Writer: Michael Michaelian.
Director: Bernard McEveety.
Director of Photography: John Flinn.

ROUGHNECKS — 2 hours — Golden Circle — July 1980. 2 episodes.

1044 RUN, JOE, RUN

Adventure.
Original format: Falsely accused of attacking his master, Joe, a black and tan Army-trained German shepherd, escapes before being destroyed. Declared an Army fugitive, a $200 reward is posted for his capture. Able to prove his innocence, his master, Sergeant William Corey, begins a cross-country trek, and, against numerous obstacles, attempts to capture Joe and clear his name.
Revised format: Before he is able to prove Joe's innocence, Corey is ordered back to active duty. Still wandering, Joe meets and befriends Josh McCoy, a backpacker who is unaware of Joe's past. Stories depict their adventures as they travel across the country.

CAST

Sgt. William Corey	Arch Whiting
Josh McCoy	Chad States
Joe	Heinrich of Midvale

Music: Richard La Salle.
Executive Producer: William P. D'Angelo.
Producer: Norm Prescott, Lou Scheimer, Dick O'Connor.
Director: Charles R. Rondeau, Herman Hoffman.
Creator: Richard Landau.

RUN, JOE, RUN — 30 minutes — NBC — September 7, 1974 – September 4, 1976.

1045 RUNAROUND

Game. A question is read and three possible answers appear on stage. Each of the nine children who compete chooses one of the answers, which are located on three lanes, and stands on it. A light reveals the correct answer, and players standing on that particular answer each receive one token; other players are placed in a penalty box. The game continues in this manner until one player remains. He is awarded an additional token, the other players are removed from the box, and a new round begins. The child with the most tokens is the winner and receives merchandise gifts.

Host: Paul Winchell.
Assistants: His dummy friends: Jerry Mahoney and Knuckelhead Smith.

Announcer: Kenny Williams.
Music: Mort Garson.

RUNAROUND — 30 minutes — NBC — September 9, 1972 – September 1, 1973.

1046 THE RUNAWAYS

Drama. The story of Steve Arizzio, a Los Angeles psychologist who specializes in tracking down runaways. A revised version of *Operation: Runaway.*

CAST

Steve Arizzio	Alan Feinstein
Karen Wingate, his romantic interest	Karen Machon
Debbie Shaw, Steve's ward	Patti Cohoon
Mark Johnson, Steve's ward	Michael Biehn
Det. Sgt. Hal Grady	James Callahan

Music: Ralph Kessler, Duane Tatro, Richard Markowitz, Bruce Broughton, John Elizalde, Nelson Riddle, Robert Drasnin.
Executive Producer: William Robert Yates.
Supervising Producer: Quinn Martin.
Producer: Andy White.
Director: Kenneth Gilbert, Michael Preece, Jeffrey Hayden.
Creator: William Robert Yates.
Program Open:
Announcer: Right at this moment thousands of children are running from their homes, crying out for help, seeking escape from brutality, indifference. One man hears them well — Steve Arizzio, a former juvenile officer, now a clinical psychologist, has spent a lifetime answering such calls.

THE RUNAWAYS — 60 minutes — NBC — May 29, 1979 – September 4, 1979. 12 episodes.

1047 RYAN'S HOPE

Serial. The triumphs and tragedies of the Ryans, an Irish-American family living in New York City.

CAST

Jillian Coleridge	Nancy Addison
Maeve Ryan	Helen Gallagher
Johnny Ryan	Bernard Barrow
Mary Ryan	Kate Mulgrew
	Mary Carney
	Nicolette Goulet
Delia Ryan Coleridge	Ilene Kristen
	Randall Edwards
Dr. Pat Ryan	Malcolm Groome
	John Blazo
Jack Fenelli	Michael Levin
Frank Ryan	Michael Hawkins
	Frank Robinson
	Daniel Hugh-Kelly
Faith Coleridge	Faith Catlin
	Nancy Barrett
	Catherine Hicks
	Karen Morris-Gowdy
Rae Woodward	Louise Shaffer
Amy Morris	Kaye de Lancey
Barry Ryan	Richard Backus
Ken George Jones	Trent Jones
Lily Danell	Christine Ebersole
Ryan Fenelli	Kerry MacNamara
Kimberly Harris	Kelli Maroney
Michael Pavel	Michael Corbett
Little Johnny Ryan	Jardien Steele
Tom Desmond	Tom MacGreevy
Martha McGee	Dorrie Kavanaugh
Dr. Clem Moultrie	Hannibal Penney
Nell Beaulac	Diana van der Vlis
Marian George	Rosetta Le Noire
Adam Cohen	Stan Birnbaum
Ethel Green	Nell Carter
Siobhan Ryan	Sarah Felder
Joe Novak	Richard Nuenz
Wes Leonard	David Rasche
Nancy Feldman	Nan Tucker
Thatcher Ross	Patrick Horgan
Bob Reid	Earl Hindman
Dr. Roger Coleridge	Ron Hale
Alex Webster	Ed Evanke
Father Richards	Bernie McInerney
Alicia	Anita Oritz
Annie Burney	Jody Catlin
Seneca Beaulac	John Gabriel
Nick Szabo	Michael Fairman
Dr. Bucky Carter	Justin Deas
Dr. Edward Coleridge	Frank Latimore
Ramona Gonzales	Rosalinda Guerra

Music: Aelous Productions, Carey Gold.
Music Supervision: Cybil Weinberger.
Executive Producer: Paul Avila Mayer, Claire Labine.
Producer: Bob Costello, Monroe Carroll, Ellen Barrett.
Director: Lela Swift, Jerry Evans.

RYAN'S HOPE — 30 minutes — ABC — Premiered: July 7, 1975.

S

1048 SABRINA, THE TEENAGE WITCH

Animated Cartoon. The misadventures of Sabrina, a high school student in the town of Riverdale and an apprentice witch, who struggles to conceal the existence of her powers.

Voice of Sabrina: Jane Webb.
Music: George Blais, Jeff Michael.
Producer: Norm Prescott, Lou Scheimer.
Director: Hal Sutherland, Anatole Kirsanoff.

SABRINA, THE TEENAGE WITCH — 30 minutes — CBS — September 11, 1971 – September 1, 1973. 35 episodes.

1049 THE SAINT

Adventure. The global exploits of Simon Templar, alias the Saint, a dashing, daredevil, free-lance troubleshooter. Wealthy, young, handsome and sophisticated, he possesses rich and fancy tastes in wine and women. Cunning, ingenious and a master among thieves, although considered criminal by police, he assists them in his quest to aid people in distress.

CAST

Simon Templar	Roger Moore
Claude Eustace Teal, the Chief Inspector of Scotland Yard	Winsley Pithey Norman Pitt Ivor Dean
Hoppy, Simon's houseboy	Percy Herbert

Music: Edwin Astley.
The Saint Theme: Leslie Charteris.
Producer: Robert S. Baker.
Creator: Leslie Charteris.

THE SAINT — 60 minutes. Syndicated 1963–1966; NBC — May 21, 1967 – September 2, 1967; February 18, 1968 – September 14, 1968; April 11, 1969 – September 12, 1969. 114 episodes. Syndicated. CBS — 70 minutes — July 2, 1980 – October 6, 1980. Spin-off series: *The Return of the Saint.*

1050 SALE OF THE CENTURY

Game. A general-knowledge question is read. The first of three competitors who correctly answer it scores five dollars, which is added to the twenty-five dollars bidding money each player receives at the beginning of the game (an incorrect answer deducts five dollars from the score).

After several questions, an "Instant Bargain" (e.g., "For only $27.95 you can buy an $800 mink coat") appears. The first player to sound a buzzer receives the merchandise and the amount, rounded off to the nearest dollar is deducted from his score. Rounds two and three follow the same format with money added or deducted by ten dollars, then twenty-five dollars per question. The highest cash scorer is the winner and he receives the opportunity to purchase expensive items from what cash he has accumulated.

Host: Jack Kelly, Joe Garagiola.
Announcer: Bill Wendell.
Music: Al Howard, Irwin Bazelon.
Executive Producer: Al Howard.
Producer: Ron Greenberg.
Director: Mike Gargiulo.

SALE OF THE CENTURY — 30 minutes — NBC — September 29, 1969 – July 13, 1973. Syndicated first run during the 1973–74 season.

1051 SALTY

Adventure. When their parents are killed by a hurricane in the Bahamas, Taylor Reed and his brother, Tim, are unofficially adopted by Clancy Ames, their rescuer, a retired lawyer who owns the Cove Marina in Nassau. Stories depict the difficulties in operating a marina, and the adventures shared by Tim and his pet sea lion, Salty. Filmed in the Bahamas.

CAST

Clancy Ames	Julius Harris
Taylor Reed	Mark Slade
Tim Reed	Johnny Doran
Rod Porterfield, Tim's friend	Vincent Dale

Music: Samuel Matlovsky.
Executive Producer: Kobi Jaeger.
Producer: Monroe Carroll.

SALTY — 30 minutes — Syndicated 1974. 26 episodes.

1052 SALVAGE I

Adventure. The exploits of Harry Broderick, the owner of the Jettison Scrap and Salvage Company in California, and his partners, Melanie "Mel" Slozar, a beautiful explosives expert, and Addison "Skip" Carmichael, a "crazy" ex-astronaut. Episodes relate their attempts to recover the unrecoverable.

CAST

Harry Broderick	Andy Griffith
Melanie "Mel" Slozar, his partner	Trish Stewart
Addison "Skip" Carmichael, his partner	Joel Higgins
Mack, Harry's assistant	J. Jay Saunders
Jack Klinger, the F.B.I. agent assigned to keep tabs on Harry	Richard Jaeckel
Michele Ryan, the orphan Mel adopts	Heather McAdam

Harry's rocket: The *Vulture.*
Harry's license plate number: JFY 534.

Music: Walter Scharf, Richard Clements, Ken Harrison.
Supervising Producer: Mike Lloyd Ross.
Executive Producer: Harve Bennett, Harris Katleman.
Producer: Norman S. Powell, Ralph Sariego.
Director: Lee Philips, Gene Nelson, Leslie Green, Gerald Perry Finnerman, Edward Abroms, Ron Satlof, James Benson, Ray Austin.

SALVAGE I — 60 minutes — ABC — January 29, 1979 – August 5, 1979. 13 episodes; November 4, 1979 – November 11, 1979. 2 episodes. The pilot film, "Salvage," aired on ABC (2 hours) on January 20, 1979.

1053 SAM

Crime Drama. The series, set in Los Angeles, follows the exploits of Officer Mike Breen and his partner, Sam, a yellow labrador retriever trained for police work.

CAST

Officer Mike Breen	Mark Harmon
Capt. Tom Clagett	Len Wayland
Captain Gene Cody	Gary Crosby
Sam	Sam

Music: Billy May.
Executive Producer: Jack Webb, Paul Donnelly.
Producer: James Doherty, Leonard B. Kaufman.

Director: Jack Webb, Robert Leeds, Richard Moder, John Florea, Robert Wynn.
Creator: Jack Webb, Dan Noble.
Art Director: Walter Scott Herndon.

SAM — 30 minutes — CBS — March 14, 1978 – April 18, 1978. 6 episodes. The half-hour pilot film aired on CBS on May 24, 1977.

1054 SAMMY AND COMPANY

Musical Variety.

Host: Sammy Davis, Jr.
Regulars: Avery Schreiber, Johnny Brown, Joyce Jillson, Kay Dingle.
Announcer: William B. Williams.
Orchestra: George Rhodes.
Executive Producer: Pierre Cossette.
Producer: Eric Lieber.
Director: John Moffitt.

SAMMY AND COMPANY — 90 minutes — Syndicated 1975.

1055 SANDBURG'S LINCOLN

Drama. A six-part portrait of Abraham Lincoln, the sixteenth President of the United States, adapted from the Pulitzer Prize-winning biography by Carl Sandburg.

CAST

Abraham Lincoln	Hal Holbrook
Mary Todd Lincoln	Sada Thompson
Salmon Chase	Roy Poole
John Nicolay	Michael Christopher
Willie	Michael-James Wixted
Kate	Elizabeth Ashley
Gideon	Severn Darden
Sara Bush	Beulah Bondi
William Seward	Whit Bissell
Judge Davis	Richard Dysart
Simon Cameron	John Randolph
Robert Lincoln	James Carrol Jordan
John Stuart	Robert Foxworth
Stephen Douglas	Walter McGinn
Mary Owens	Catherine Burns
Truett	James Greene
Urquhart	Gerald Hiken
Kitty Cavan	Martine Bartlett
Judge Thomas	Paul Fix
Mary Todd (as a girl)	Michele Marsh
General McClellan	Ed Flanders
Ellsworth	David Huffman
Seward	Lloyd Nolan
General Grant	Normann Burton
General Scott	Robert Emhardt
General Weitzel	Frank Maxwell
Tad	John Levin

Executive Producer: David L. Wolper.
Producer: George Schaefer.
Writer: Jerry McNeely, Jerome Lawrence, Robert E. Lee, Philip Reisman, Loring Mandel, Emmet Lavery, Irene and Luis Kamp.
Director: George Schaefer.

SANDBURG'S LINCOLN — 60 minutes — NBC — July 6, 1974 – April 14, 1976. 6 episodes.

1056 THE SANDY DUNCAN SHOW

Comedy. The series, set in Los Angeles, follows the misadventures of Sandy Stockton, a student-teacher enrolled at U.C.L.A., and a part-time secretary employed by the Quinn and Cohen Advertising Agency, as she struggles to divide her time between work, school and studies. A spin-off from *Funny Face.*

CAST

Sandy Stockton	Sandy Duncan
Bert Quinn, her employer	Tom Bosley
Kay Fox, Sandy's neighbor	Marian Mercer
Hilary, the agency receptionist	Pamela Zarit
Alex Lambert, Sandy's neighbor	M. Emmet Walsh
Leonard Cohen, Bert's partner	Alfie Wise
Ben Hamilton, the building janitor	Eric Christmas

Sandy's address: 130 North Weatherly (The Royal Weatherly Hotel, Apt. 2-A).

Music: Patrick Williams.
Executive Producer: Arne Sultan.
Producer: Earl Barrett.

THE SANDY DUNCAN SHOW — 30 minutes — CBS — September 17, 1972 – December 31, 1972. 13 episodes.

1057 SANFORD

Comedy. A continuation of the series *Sanford and Son.* Fred Sanford, the irascible Watts junkman, resumes his business assisted by Cal Pettie, a not-too-bright friend of Lamont's he suckers into becoming his partner. Stories relate their misadventures as they struggle to live together — and operate a junk business together. (Lamont, Fred's son, has taken a job on the Alaska pipeline.)

CAST

Fred Sanford	Redd Foxx
Cal Pettie, his partner	Dennis Burkley
Evelyn Lewis, Fred's romantic interest	Marguerite Ray
Rollo Larson, Fred's helper	Nathaniel Taylor
Clara, Evelyn's maid	Cathy Cooper
Cissy Lewis, Evelyn's daughter	Suzanne Stone
Winston, Evelyn's brother	Percy Rodrigues
Esther Anderson, Fred's sister-in-law	LaWanda Page
Cliff Anderson, Esther's son	Clinton Derricks-Carroll
Police Officer Smith ("Smitty"), Fred's friend	Hal Williams
Police Officer Hoppy, Smith's partner	Howard Platt

Fred's address: 4707 South Central, Los Angeles, California (same house as in *Sanford and Son,* but a different address).
Evelyn's address: 77 Kantwell Drive, Beverly Hills, California.

Commercial Break Announcer: Redd Roxx.
Music: Quincy Jones.
Executive Producer: Mort Lachman.
Producer: Sy Rosen, Larry Rhine, Mel Tolkin.
Associate Producer: Gloria Vinson.
Director: Jim Drake.
Art Director: Don Roberts.

SANFORD — 30 minutes — NBC — March 15, 1980 – September 10, 1980. 10 episodes.

1058 SANFORD AND SON

Comedy. The story of the relationship between two men: Fred Sanford, a 65-year-old black junk dealer who refuses to retire, and his 34-year-old son and partner, Lamont, a bachelor who is dissatisfied with the business and seeks to better himself by beginning a new life on his own. Episodes depict their misadventures as they struggle to operate a junk business. Based on the British series, *Steptoe and Son.*

CAST

Fred Sanford, a widower	Redd Foxx
Lamont Sanford, his son	Demond Wilson
Grady Wilson, Fred's friend	Whitman Mayo
Esther Anderson, Fred's sister-in-law	LaWanda Page
Rollo Larson, Lamont's friend	Nathaniel Taylor
Julio Fuentas, Fred's neighbor	Gregory Sierra
Melvin, Fred's friend	Slappy White
Officer Swanhauser, Fred's friend	Norman Pitlik
Officer Smith (Smitty), Fred's friend	Hal Williams
Officer Hopkins (Hoppy), Fred's friend	Howard Platt
Bubba, Fred's friend	Don Bexley
Donna Harris, Fred's romantic interest	Lynn Hamilton
Leroy, Fred's friend	Leroy Daniels
May Hopkins, Hoppy's mother	Nancy Kulp
Woody Anderson, Esther's husband	Raymond Allen
Janet, Lamont's girlfriend; divorced	Marlene Clark
Roger, Janet's son	Edward Crawford
Frances Victor, Fred's sister	Mary Alice
Rodney Victor, Frances' husband	Allan Drake
Ah Chu, Lamont's friend	Pat Morita
Daniel Anderson, Esther's son	Eric Laneuville

Fred's address: 9114 South Central, Los Angeles.

Music: Quincy Jones.
Executive Producer: Norman Lear, Bud Yorkin.
Producer: Bernie Orenstein, Saul Turteltaub.
Director: Norman Abbott, Chick Liotta, Peter Baldwin, Russ Petranto, Mike Warren, Alan Rafkin.

SANFORD AND SON — 30 minutes — NBC — January 14, 1972 – September 2, 1977. Syndicated. Spin-off series: *Grady, Sanford* and *Sanford Arms.*

1059 SANFORD ARMS

Comedy. A spin-off from *Sanford and Son.* The story of Phil Wheeler, a widower and retired army man who purchases the Sanford and Son Junkyard and turns it into the Sanford Arms rooming house as an investment to enable him to remain at home and properly raise his two children. The series focuses on his attempts to cope with the numerous problems associated with running a rooming house.

CAST

Phil Wheeler	Theodore Wilson
Angie Wheeler, his daughter	Tina Andrews
Nat Wheeler, his son	John Earl
Esther Anderson, his landlady	LaWanda Page
Woody Anderson, Esther's husband	Raymond Allen
Jeannie, Phil's romantic interest	Bebe Drake-Hooks
Grady Wilson, a tenant	Whitman Mayo
Bubba, the handyman-bellboy	Don Bexley

The Sanford Arms address: 9114 South Central, Los Angeles.

Music: Henry Mancini.
Executive Producer: Bud Yorkin, Saul Turteltaub, Bernie Orenstein.
Producer: Woody Kling.

SANFORD ARMS — 30 minutes — NBC — September 16, 1977 – October 14, 1977. 4 episodes.

1060 SAN FRANCISCO INTERNATIONAL AIRPORT

Drama. The series, set at the San Francisco International Airport, presents a behind-the-scenes look at the problems that plague large airports.

CAST

Jim Conrad, the manager (series)	Lloyd Bridges
Jim Conrad (pilot film)	Pernell Roberts
Bob Hatten, the security chief	Clu Gulager
Suzie Conrad, Jim's daughter	Barbara Sigel
June, Jim's secretary	Barbara Werle

Music: Pat Williams.
Executive Producer: Richard Irving.
Producer: William Read Woodfield, Allan Balter.
Director: Richard Benedict, John Llewellyn Moxey, Daniel Petrie, Allen Reisner, Boris Sagal.

SAN FRANCISCO INTERNATIONAL AIRPORT — 60 minutes — NBC — October 28, 1970 – August 25, 1971 (as part of *Four-in-One*). 6 episodes. The two-hour pilot film aired on NBC on September 29, 1970.

1061 THE SAN PEDRO BEACH BUMS

Comedy. The misadventures of five knockabout young men (Buddy, Boychick, Dancer, Stuf and Moose), who live on the *Our Boat* (originally called the *Challenger*), an old fishing boat docked in the San Pedro, California, harbor.

CAST

Buddy Binder	Christopher Murney
Boychick (pilot film)	Jeff Druce
Boychick (series)	Christopher DeRose
Edward "Dancer" McClory	John Mark Robinson
Anthony "Stuf" Danelli	Stuart Pankin
Moose Maslosky	Darryl McCullough
Suzi Camelli, their friend, the operator of a sight-seeing boat	Susan Mullen
Louise, the waitress at Tiny Teena's, the beach café	Louise Hoven
Marge, the lifeguard	Lisa Reeves
Julie, a friend	Nancy Morgan
Ralphie Walker, a friend	Christoff St. John

Music: Pete Rugolo, Mark Snow.
Executive Producer: Aaron Spelling, Douglas S. Cramer.
Producer: E. Duke Vincent, Earl Barrett, Simon Muntner.
Director: Barry Shear, Allen Baron, Don Weis, Gene Nelson, Earl Bellamy, George Tyne, Jack Arnold.
Creator: E. Duke Vincent.

THE SAN PEDRO BEACH BUMS — 60 minutes — ABC — September 19, 1977 – December 19, 1977. 10 episodes. The 90-minute pilot film, "The San Pedro Bums," aired on ABC on April 1, 1977.

1062 SARA

Western. The series, set in Independence, Colorado, in 1870, follows the life of Sara Yarnell, a pretty school teacher who leaves what she considers to be a dull existence in Philadelphia to teach school in the West. Episodes revolve around her difficulties as she struggles to educate the town of Independence.

CAST

Sara Yarnell	Brenda Vaccaro
Emmett Ferguson, her friend, a rancher	Bert Kramer
Martin Pope, the publisher of the town newspaper, the *Bulletin*	Albert Stratton
Julia Bailey, Sara's friend	Mariclare Costello
George Bailey, Julia's husband	William Wintersole
Calude Barstow, the mayor	William Phipps
Martha Higgins, the owner of the boarding house	Louise Latham
Emma Higgins, Martha's daughter	Hallie Morgan
Deborah Higgins, Martha's daughter	Debbie Leyton
Samual Higgins, Martha's husband	Al Henderson
Georgie Bailey, Julia's son	Kraig Metzinger
Claranet, the Bailey's housekeeper	Silvia Soares
Frank Dixon, a rancher	Jerry Hardin
Jimmy Waggins, a student of Sara's	Stephen Manley

Music: Lee Holdridge.
Music Supervision: Hal Mooney.
Sara's Theme: Lee Holdridge.
Producer: George Eckstein.
Director: Stuart Margolin, Gordon Hessler, Jud Taylor, Alf Kjellin, William F. Claxton, Michael Preece, William Wiard, Daniel Haller.
Creator: Richard Collins.

SARA — 60 minutes — CBS — February 13, 1976 – July 30, 1976.

1063 SARGE

Drama. Shattered emotionally after his wife is killed by an assassin's bullet meant for him, veteran detective Sarge Swanson enters the priesthood. Three years later he is ordained as Father Samuel Patrick Cavanaugh and assigned to the Saint Aloysius Parish in San Diego, California. Still referred to as "Sarge," and using unorthodox methods, he attempts to solve the problems of his urban community.

CAST

Father Samuel Patrick Cavanaugh	George Kennedy
Valerie, his secretary	Sallie Shockley
Lt. Barney Verick	Ramon Bieri
Kenji Takichi, the parish athletic coach	Harold Sakata
Father Terrence	Stewart Moss
Bishop Andrade	Henry Wilcoxon

Music: David Shire.
Executive Producer: David Levy.
Producer: David Levinson.
Director: John Badham, Seymour Robbie, Richard A. Colla, Jeannot Szwarc.

SARGE — 60 minutes — NBC — September 21, 1971 – January 11, 1972. The two-hour pilot film, "Sarge: The Badge or the Cross," aired on NBC on February 22, 1971.

1064 SATURDAY NIGHT LIVE

Variety. Musical acts coupled with topical comedy. Broadcast live from New York City (11:30 p.m. to 1:00 a.m.).

Guest Hosts Include: Kate Jackson, Jodie Foster, Lily Tomlin, Buck Henry, Rob Reiner, Robert Klein, Paul Simon, Raquel Welch, Desi Arnaz, Ted Knight, Jill Clayburgh, Candice Bergen, Steve Martin, Hugh Hefner.
The Not Ready For Prime Time Regulars: Chevy Chase, Gilda Radner, Laraine Newman, Jane Curtin, John Belushi, Dan Ackroyd, Garrett Morris, Bill Murray.

Also: Jim Hanson and his Muppets, Albert Brooks, Gary Weis.
Announcer: Don Pardo.
Music: Howard Shore.
Producer: Lorne Michaels.
Director: Dave Wilson.

SATURDAY NIGHT LIVE — 90 minutes — NBC — October 11, 1975 – May 24, 1980 (date of last first-run episode). 106 episodes. *See also* program number 1907.

1065   SATURDAY NIGHT LIVE WITH HOWARD COSELL

Variety. Appearances and/or performances by major stars, front-page newsmakers and celebrities from every continent. Broadcast live from the Ed Sullivan Theatre in New York City.

Host: Howard Cosell.
Regulars: the Peter Gennaro Dancers.
Announcer: John Bartholomew Tucker.
Orchestra: Elliott Lawrence.
Executive Producer: Roone Arledge.
Producer: Rubert Hitzig.
Director: Don Mischer.

SATURDAY NIGHT LIVE WITH HOWARD COSELL — 60 minutes — ABC — September 20, 1975 – January 17, 1976.

1066   THE SCARLET LETTER

Drama. A four-part miniseries, set in Boston in the mid-1600s, that tells the passionate story of Hester Prynne, a seamstress who, convicted of adultery, must wear a scalet letter "A" — for adulteress — on her dress forever as a badge of shame. The series, based on Nathaniel Hawthorne's 1850 novel, tells also of Reverend Arthur Dimmsdale, the man who shared Hester's sin, but did not publicly confess, and is now tortured by agonizing guilt; and Roger Chillingworth, Hester's husband, who seeks to learn the identity of the man Hester refuses to divulge and gain revenge.

CAST

Hester Prynne	Meg Foster
Roger Chillingworth	Kevin Conway
Rev. Arthur Dimmsdale	John Heard
Pearl, the daughter that resulted from Hester's affair; as an infant	Alexandra Smets
Pearl, age 3	Danielle Hoebeke
Pearl, age 5	Jessica Ruth Olin
Pearl, age 7	Elisa Erali
Nathaniel Hawthorne, the author, who appears for the introduction and narration	Josef Sommer

Music: John Morris.
Executive Producer: Herbert Hirschman.
Producer: Rich Hauser, Jerry Ballew, Diane K. Miller.
Director: Rick Hauser.

THE SCARLET LETTER — 60 minutes — PBS — March 2, 1979 – March 5, 1979. 4 episodes.

1067   SCENE 70

Musical Variety. Performances by Rock personalities.

Host: Jay Reynolds.
Featured: The Scene 70 Action Dancers.
Music: Provided by guests.

SCENE 70 — 60 minutes — Syndicated 1970.

1068   SCENES FROM A MARRIAGE

Drama. A penetrating study of the incidents that break up and lead to a couple divorcing after ten years of marriage. Produced in Sweden.

CAST

Marianne, the wife	Liv Ullmann
Johan, the husband	Eriand Josephson

Hostess: Liv Ullmann.
Producer: Lars-Owe Carlberg.
Director: Ingmar Bergman.
English Version Producer: Paulette Rubinstein.
Director of Liv Ullmann's Segments: John Marden.
Series Producer: David Griffiths.

SCENES FROM A MARRIAGE — 60 minutes — PBS — March 9, 1977 – April 20, 1977. 6 episodes. Originally aired in Sweden in 1973.

1069   SCOOBY-DOO AND SCRAPPY-DOO

Animated Cartoon. A spin-off from *Scooby-Doo, Where Are You?* The format is the same as the previous title with the only change being the addition of Scrappy-Doo, Scooby-Doo's nephew.

Voices: Ginny Tyler, Pat Stevens, Lennie Weinrib, Heather North, Bob Holt, Bob Hastings, Casey Kasem, Jack Angel, Stanley Jones.
Music: Hoyt Curtin.
Executive Producer: William Hanna, Joseph Barbera.
Producer: Don Jorwich.
Director: George Gordon, Ray Patterson, Charles A. Nichols, Carl Urbano, Oscar Dufau.

SCOOBY-DOO AND SCRAPPY-DOO — 30 minutes — ABC — September 22, 1979 – December 15, 1979.

1070   THE SCOOBY-DOO/DYNOMUTT HOUR

Animated Cartoon. A spin-off from *Scooby-Doo, Where Are You?*

Segments:

Scooby-Doo. See title *Scooby-Doo, Where Are You?* for format and voices.

The Blue Falcon. The crime fighting adventures of the Blue Falcon and his assistant, Dynomutt, a mechanical dog.

VOICES

The Blue Falcon	Gary Owens
Dynomutt	Frank Welker
Narrator	Ron Feinberg

Music: Ted Nichols.
Executive Producer: William Hanna, Joseph Barbera.
Producer: Iwao Takamoto.
Director: William Hanna, Joseph Barbera, Charles A. Nichols.

THE SCOOBY-DOO/DYNOMUTT HOUR — 55 minutes — ABC — September 11, 1976 – September 3, 1977.

1071   SCOOBY-DOO, WHERE ARE YOU?

Animated Cartoon. The exploits of Freddy, Daphne, Velma and Shaggy, the teenage members of a crime club, and their Great Dane, Scooby-Doo, as they travel throughout the country to solve supernatural-based crimes.

VOICES

Scooby-Doo	Don Messick
Freddy	Frank Welker
Daphne	Heather North
Shaggy	Casey Kasem
Velma	Nichole Jaffe

Music: Hoyt Curtin, Paul DeKorte, Ted Nichols.
Executive Producer: William Hanna, Joseph Barbera.
Producer: Alex Lovy, Iwao Takamoto.
Director: William Hanna, Joseph Barbera, Charles A. Nichols.

SCOOBY-DOO, WHERE ARE YOU? — 30 minutes — CBS — September 13, 1969 – September 2, 1972. 60 minutes — CBS — September 9, 1972 – August 31, 1974. Syndicated.

1072   SCOOBY'S ALL STAR LAFF-A-LYMPICS

Animated Cartoon. A spin-off from *The Scooby-Doo/Dynomutt Hour.*

Segments:

Captain Caveman and the Teen Angels. See title *Captain Caveman and the Teen Angels* for information.

The Blue Falcon and Dynomutt. See title, *The Scooby-Doo/Dynomutt Hour, The Blue Falcon* segment for information.

Scooby-Doo. See title *Scooby-Doo, Where Are You?* for information.

The Laff-A-Lympics. Features three teams (The Yogi Yahooes, The Scooby-Dooies, and The Really Rottens) competing in wild olympic-like games throughout the world.

YOGI YAHOOES VOICES

Snagglepuss	Daws Butler
Mildew Wolf	John Stephenson
Doggy Daddy	John Stephenson
Yakky Doodle Duck	Frank Welker
Huckleberry Hound	Daws Butler
Hokie Wolf	Daws Butler
Wally Gator	Daws Butler
Yogi Bear	Daws Butler
Snooper	Daws Butler
Blabber	Daws Butler
Augie Doggie	Daws Butler
Quick Draw McGraw	Daws Butler
Boo Boo Bear	Don Messick
Pixie	Don Messick
Grape Ape	Bob Holt
Cindy Bear	Julie Bennett

REALLY ROTTENS VOICES

Daisy Mayhem	Marilyn Schreffler
Sooey Pig	Frank Welker
Orful Octopus	Bob Holt
Dinky	Bob Holt
Dread Baron	John Stephenson
Mumbly	Don Messick
Dalton Brothers	Don Messick, Daws Butler

SCOOBY-DOOIES VOICES

Scooby-Doo	Don Messick
Scooby-Dum	Daws Butler
Speed Buggy	Casey Kasem
Shaggy	Casey Kasem

Music: Hoyt Curtin, Paul DeKorte.
Executive Producer: William Hanna, Joseph Barbera.
Producer: Iwao Takamoto.
Director: Charles A. Nichols.

SCOOBY'S ALL STAR LAFF-A-LYMPICS — 2 hours — ABC — September 10, 1977 – September 2, 1978.

1073   SCRUPLES

Drama. The story of Billy Ikehorn, the beautiful and glamorous owner of an exclusive Beverly Hills fashion boutique called Scruples. The miniseries, based on the book by Judith Krantz, is actually a series of flashbacks that trace Billy's life, first as Wilhelmina Winthrop, a tall, slightly overweight teenager who is sent to Paris by a rich aunt to help her lose weight and learn the fashion business; then, in New York, slender and glamorous, as a secretary to Ellis Ikehorn, a wealthy, but elderly businessman, whom she later marries. After his death, Billy inherits his fortune and uses it, in part, to build Scruples, the fashion boutique around which the remainder of the story unfolds.

CAST

Wilhelmina "Billy" Winthrop Ikehorn	Lindsay Wagner
Ellis Ikehorn, her husband	Efrem Zimbalist, Jr.
Michael "Spider" Elliott, the fashion photographer	Barry Bostwick
Valentine O'Neil, the fashion designer	Marie-France Pisier
Maggie MacGregor, the TV gossip reporter	Connie Stevens
Josh Hillman, Billy's lawyer	Robert Reed

Curt Arvey, the film tycoon   Gavin MacLeod
Sue Arvey, Curt's wife   Sarah Marshall
Harriet Toppingham,
  the "queen bee" of the
  fashion world   Gene Tierney
Melanie Adams, the model
  turned actress   Kim Cattrall
Vito Orsini, the film director   Nick Mancuso
Jake Cassidy, the nurse   Gary Graham
Joanne Hillman, Josh's wife   Lelia Goldoni
Alan Wilton, the owner
  of Wilton Associates
  Fashions   Michael Callan
Mary Ann Evans, Billy's
  assistant   Louise Latham
Lilianne De Vertdulae, the
  woman who cared for
  Billy in Paris   Genevieve
Wilhelmina Winthrop,
  Billy's aunt   Anna Lee
Dolly Moon, the actress   Murphy Cross
Sid Ames, the script writer   Milton Selzer
Pat O'Byrnne, the production
  manager   Paul Carr
Lt. Tony Bakersmith   John Hancock
John Prince, a designer   George Gaynes
Dr. Jonathan Dorman   Walker Edmiston
Edouard, the aristocrat who jilted Billy
  in Paris   Francois-Marie Benard
Receptionist   Berry Berenson
Fay Bostick   Carol O'Leary
Hank Sanders   Bert Wood
Clint Fuery   Robert Clarke
La Comtesse   Eloise Hardt
Scruples Doorman   Lori Main
Sandy   Chuck Todd
Rosie   Gloria LeRoy
Mrs. Elliott   Jan Clayton
Judge Riddle   Bill Quinn
Crafts Service Man   Michael Greene
Jessica   Linda Costanzo

Music: Charles Bernstein.
Executive Producer: Ron Samuels.
Producer: Leonard B. Kaufman.
Writer: James Lee.
Director: Alan J. Levi.

SCRUPLES — 2 hours — CBS — February 25, 1980 — February 28, 1980. 3 episodes.

1074   SEALAB 2020

Animated Cartoon. The series, set in the year A.D. 2020, depicts the struggles of 250 men, women and children, pioneers, as they attempt to maintain Sealab 2020, a complex, scientific experimental city that is constructed beneath the ocean floor.

VOICES

Capt. Mike Murphy   John Stephenson
Dr. Paul Williams   Ross Martin
Salli Murphy, Mike's niece   Pamelyn Ferdin
Bobby Murphy, Mike's nephew   Josh Albee
Gail, a diver   Ann Jillian
Hal, a diver   Jerry Dexter
Ed, a diver   Ron Pinckard
Sparks, the radio dispatcher   Bill Callaway
Jamie, a member of Sealab   Gary Shapiro
Mrs. Thomas, a member of
  Sealab   Olga James

Gail's pet dolphin: Tuffy.

Music: Hoyt Curtin.
Executive Producer: William Hanna, Joseph Barbera.
Producer: Iwao Takamoto.
Director: Charles A. Nichols.

SEALAB 2020 — 30 minutes — NBC — September 9, 1972 — September 1, 1973. 24 episodes.

1075   SEARCH

Adventure. The exploits of Hugh Lockwood, Probe One; Nick Bianco, Omega Probe; and Christopher Grove, Standby Probe, three highly skilled investigators attached to Probe, a super-computerized detective agency that operates out of the World Securities Corporation in Washington, D.C.

CAST

Hugh Lockwood   Hugh O'Brian
Nick Bianco   Tony Franciosa
Christopher R. Grove   Doug McClure
B. C. Cameron, the head of
  Probe   Burgess Meredith
Dr. Barnett, the senior director   Ford Rainey
Probe Control Agents:
Gloria Harding   Angel Tompkins
Kuroda   Byron Chung
Miss Keach   Ginny Golden
Miss James   Pamela Jones
Harris   Tom Hallick
Anna Mulligan   Ann Prentiss
Carlos   Ron Costro
Ramos   Tony DeCosta
Griffin   Albert Popwell
Amy   Cheryl Stoppelmoor
  (Cheryl Ladd)

Music: Dominic Frontiere.
Executive Producer: Leslie Stevens.
Producer: Robert H. Justman.
Director: Russ Mayberry, Jerry Jameson, Barry Shear, William Wiard, Paul Stanley, Joseph Pevney, Michael Caffey, Marc Daniels, George McCowan.
Creator: Leslie Stevens.

SEARCH — 60 minutes — NBC — September 12, 1972 — August 29, 1973. 26 episodes. The two-hour pilot film, "Probe," aired on NBC on February 21, 1972.

1076   SEARCH AND RESCUE: THE ALPHA TEAM

Adventure. The series, set on the Alpha Ranch in Canada, depicts the exploits of the Ganelle family: Bob, a widower, and his two teenage children, Katie and Jim, as they train wild animals for difficult rescue missions.

CAST

Bob Ganelle   Michael J. Reynolds
Katie Ganelle   Donann Cavin
Jim Ganelle   Michael Tough

Music: Lew Lehman.
Executive Producer: Seymour Berns, Will Lorin.
Producer: Lew Lehman.
Director: Peter Carter.

SEARCH AND RESCUE: THE ALPHA TEAM — 30 minutes — NBC — September 10, 1977 — January 28, 1978

1077   SEARCH FOR THE NILE

Documentary. Through on-location filmings, old journals and letters, the 1857 explorations of Sir Richard Francis Butler and John Hanning Speke, members of the Royal Geographical Society, are recounted as they attempt to uncover the source of the Nile River — the mysterious life source for Africa.

CAST

Sir Richard Butler   Kenneth Haigh
John Speke   John Quentin
David Livingston   Michael Gough
Henry Stanley   Keith Buckley
Isabel   Barbara Leigh-Hunt
James Grant   Ian McCulloch
Mutesa   Oliver Litondo
Samuel Baker   Norman Rosington
Florence   Catherine Schell

Narrator: James Mason.
Music: Joseph Horowitz.
Producer: Christopher Ralling.
Writer: Michael Hastings.
Director: Christopher Ralling, Fred Burnley.

SEARCH FOR THE NILE — 60 minutes — NBC — January 25, 1972 — February 29, 1972. Syndicated.

1078   SEARCH FOR TOMORROW

Serial. The dramatic story of Joanne Barron Vincente, her family and friends, residents of the Midwestern city of Henderson, U.S.A.

CAST

Joanne Barron Vincente   Mary Stuart
Victor Barron   Cliff Hall
Keith Barron   John Sylvester
Patty Barron   Lynn Loring
  Abigail Kellogg
  Patricia Harty
  Trish Van Devere
  Gretchen Walther
  Melissa Murphy
  Melinda Plank
  Leigh Lassen
  Tina Sloan
Irene Barron   Bess Johnson
Marge Bergman   Melba Raye
Henri Cartier   John LaGioia
Grace Boulton   Jill Clayburgh
Arthur Tate   Terry O'Sullivan
Susan Carter   Sharon Smyth
Ida Weston   Vera Allen
Andrea Whiting   Virginia Gilmore
  Joan Copeland
Dr. Wade Collins   John Cunningham
Stu Bergman   Larry Haines
Doug Martin   Ken Harvey
Dr. Dan Walton   Martin Brooks
  Philip Abbot
  Ron Husmann
Dr. Bob Rogers   Carl Low
Dr. Len Whiting   Dino Narizzano
  Jeff Pomerantz
Gary Walton   Tom Nordon
  John Driver
Scott Phillips   Peter Simon
Jim McCarren   Michael Shannon

Kathy Parker   Courtney Sherman
Carl Devlin   David Ford
Marcy   Jeanne Carson
Eunice Gardiner   Marion Brash
  Ann Williams
Lauri Phillips   Kelly Wood
Eric Lawson   Chris Lowe
Emily Hunter   Kathryn Walker
Nick Hunter   Ken Kercheval
Helen   Sandy Duncan
Wilbur   Don Knotts
Dr. Murphy   Charles Siebert
Ross Cavanaugh   Keith Charles
Bruce Carson   Bobby Benson
  Garry Tomlin
Sam Reynolds   Robert Mandan
  George Gaynes
  Ray Shuman
Bill Lang   Tom Ewell
Dr. Tony Vincente   Anthony George
Chris   Daniel Leddy
Dr. Facciola   Conrad Bain
Rose Peabody   Lee Grant
  Constance Ford
  Nita Talbot
Dr. Wheeler   Roy Scheider
Dr. Joe Foster   Joe Morton
John Wyatt   Val Dufour
Stephanie Wilkins   Marie Cheatham
Dr. Walter Osmond   Byron Sanders
Miss Markham   Sharon Spelman
Ralph Hayward   James O'Sullivan
Harriet Kane   Chase Crosley
Monica Bergman   Barbara Baxley
Larry Carter   Hal Linden
Hazel   Mary Patton
Rex Twining   Laurence Hugo
Cathy Phillips   Nikki Goulet
Frank Gardiner   Eric Dressler
  Harry Holcombe
Mrs. Millie   Frieda Allman
The social worker   Margaret Draper
Agnes Lake   Ann Revere
Fred Metcalf   David O'Brien
Janet Bergman   Ellen Spencer
  Sandy Robinson
  Fran Sharon
  Marian Hailey
  Millee Taggert
Nathan Walsh   George Petrie
Ellie Harper   Billie Lou Watt
Brette Moore   Martin Brooks
Allison Simmons   Ann Pearson
Harriet Baxter   Vicki Vola
Budd Gardner   George Maharis
Kathy Merritt   Donna Theodore
Ed Minter   Richard Cox
Jennifer Phillips   Morgan Fairchild
Walter Pace   Tom Klunis
Gail Caldwell   Sherry Rooney
Greg Hartford   Robert Rockwell
Sam Hunter   Stephen Joyce
Dave Wilkins   Dale Robinette
Clay Collins   Brett Halsey
Liza Walton   Denise Nickerson
  Kathy Beller
  Meg Bennett
Kitty Styles   Diane Ladd
Tom Bergman   Peter Broderick
  Ray Bellaran
  John James
Danny Walton   Neil Billingsley
Marc D'Antoni   Chris Goutman
Wendy Wilkins   Andrea McArdle
  Lisa Peluso
Bobby Stuart   Tucker Smallwood
Bruce Carson   Joel Higgins
Amy Carson   Anne Wyndham
Fay Chandler   Kathleen Devine

Vicky Parker	Lisby Larsen
Arthur Benson	David Canary
Steve Kaslo	Michael Nouri
Kylie	Lisa Buck
Donna Davis	Leslie Ann Ray
McCrady	Robert Burr
Mr. Pace	Ed Grover
Hal Conrad	Vince O'Brien
Joey	Marco St. John
Martin Tourneur	John Aniston
David Sutton	Lewis Arlt
Travis Sentell	Rod Arrants
Cliff Webster	George Bamford
Laine Adamson	Megan Bagot
Dr. Gary Walton	Stephen Burleigh
Mignon Sentell	Anita Keal
Nick D'Antoni	Jerry Lanning
Buck Peterson	Christopher Loomis
Liza Kaslo	Sherry Mathis
Sunny McClure	Marcia McCabe
Carolyn Hanley	Marilyn McIntyre
Suzie Watt	Stacey Moran
Sharon Peterson	Verna Pierce
Don McKay	Biff McGuire
Cissy Mitchell	Patsy Pease
Renata Sutton	Sonia Petrovna
Lee Sentell	Douglas Stevenson
Wood Reed	Kevin Kline
Dr. Allen Ramsey	Conrad Fowkes

Also: Ross Martin, Margaret Hamilton, Louise Larabee, Lenka Peterson, House Jameson, Audra Lindley, Jan Miner, Ken Rabat, Robert Gentry.

Announcer: Dwight Weist.
Organist: Chet Kingsbury, Ashley Miller.
Music: Elliott Lawrence.
Music Coordinator: Carol Crawford.
Producer: Charles Irving, Myron Golden, Frank Dodge, Mary-Ellis Bunin, Robert Getz.
Director: Charles Irving, Ned Stark, Robert Schwarz.

SEARCH FOR TOMORROW—15- and 30-minute versions—CBS—Premiered: September 3, 1951.

1079 SECOND CHANCE

Game. A question is read and each of three contestants writes his answer on a card. Three possible answers to the question appear and players have a second chance to change their answers if they wish. The correct answer is revealed and points are scored accordingly: three points for an original correct answer; one point for a second-chance correct answer.

Three such questions are played and the number of points earned are used by players for spins on a large electronic prize board (which is divided into a series of small squares containing cash amounts, merchandise prizes and devils). The machine, which is characterized by flashing lights (to indicate individual boxes), is started. When a player pushes a button, the machine stops and the lights pinpoint one box. Cash or merchandise prizes are added to a player's score; a devil erases all earnings up to that point. The second half of the game is played in the same manner and the player who scores the highest cash value is the winner.

Host: Jim Peck.
Announcer: Joe Sider, Jay Stewart, Jack Clark.
Music: Score Productions.
Executive Producer: Bill Carruthers.
Producer: Joel Stein.
Director: Chris Darley.

SECOND CHANCE—30 minutes—ABC—March 7, 1977—July 15, 1977. 90 programs.

1080 SECOND CITY TELEVISION

Comedy. The program, set at the mythical Second City television station, Channel 109, in Mellonville, Canada, satirizes life at a "typical" station by spoofing, via sketches, the programs broadcast throughout the day.

Starring: John Candy, Eugene Levy, Joe Flaherty, Andrea Martin, Catherine O'Hara, Harold Ramis, Dave Thomas.
Producer: Bernard Shalins, Milad Bessada.
Director: Milad Bessada.

SECOND CITY TELEVISION—30 minutes—Syndicated 1977.

1081 SECOND CITY TELEVISION NETWORK

Comedy. A revised version of the previous title. Six people, fed up with the fare TV has to offer, decide to do something about it, and begin their own station, Channel 109, in Mellonville. Television is spoofed by the programs the group creates and broadcasts.

Version One:

Starring: Catherine O'Hara, Andrea Martin, Dave Thomas, Eugene Levy, John Candy, Joe Flaherty.
Executive Producer: Jack Rhodes.
Producer: Andrew Alexander, Bernard Shalins, Milad Bessada.
Writer: Catherine O'Hara, Andrea Martin, Dave Thomas, Eugene Levy, John Candy, Joe Flaherty.
Director: George Bloomfield.

SECOND CITY TELEVISION NETWORK—30 minutes—Syndicated 1978.

Version Two:

Starring: Andrea Martin, Robin Duke, Joe Flaherty, Eugene Levy, Dave Thomas, Rick Moranis, Tony Rosato.
Executive Producer: Jack Rhodes, Andrew Alexander, Doug Holtby, Len Stuart.
Producer: Patrick Whitley, Carol Henson, Pamela Roberts.
Writer: Andrea Martin, Robin Duke, Joe Flaherty, Eugene Levy, Dave Thomas, Rick Moranis, Tony Rosato, Mike Short.
Director: John Blanchard.

SCTV TELEVISION NETWORK—30 minutes—Syndicated 1980.

1082 THE SECRET EMPIRE

Adventure. The series, set in Wyoming in 1880, tells the story of Jim Donner, a U.S. marshal who, while investigating a series of gold shipment thefts from the Aurora Mining Company, discovers Chimera, a futuristic society of aliens who fled their world of oppression to live inside the Earth. Episodes depict his attempts to thwart the evil Thorval's plans to conquer the Earth with his war machines.

CAST

Marshal Jim Donner	Geoffrey Scott
Millie Thomas, his friend	Carlene Watkins
Billy, the orphan boy; Jim's friend	Tiger Williams
Princess Tara, the evil daughter of the ruler of Chimera	Diane Markoff
Princess Maya, Jim's aide, the daughter of the former ruler of Chimera	Pamela Brull
Thorval, the evil ruler of Chimera	Mark Lenard
Demeter, Maya's father	Jay Robinson
Yannuck, Thorval's assistant	Sean Garrison
Jess Keller, the gold shipper (gold is needed by the aliens to control their machines)	Peter Breck

Music: Joe Harnell, Charles R. Casey, Les Baxter.
Narrator: Brad Crandall.
Supervising Producer: B. W. Sandefur.
Executive Producer: Kenneth Johnson.
Producer: Richard Milton, Paul Samuelson.
Director: Kenneth Johnson, Joseph Pevney, Alan Crosland.
Creator: Kenneth Johnson.

THE SECRET EMPIRE—15 minutes—NBC—February 27, 1979—May 1, 1979 (as part of *Cliffhangers*). 10 episodes.

1083 THE SECRET LIVES OF WALDO KITTY

Comedy. The program begins by introducing three live-action animals: Waldo, a cat; Felicia, a cat, his girlfriend; and Tyrone, a mean bulldog. When Tyrone becomes a threat to Felicia's safety, Waldo, who is a coward at heart, imagines himself as her heroic savior. Animation takes over and each week features Waldo as a different hero struggling to protect Felicia from harm.

VOICES

Waldo Kitty	Howard Morris
Felicia	Jane Webb
Tyrone	Allan Melvin

Music: Yvette Blais, Jeff Michael.
Producer: Lou Scheimer, Norm Prescott.
Director: Don Christensen.

THE SECRET LIVES OF WALDO KITTY—30 minutes—NBC—September 6, 1975—September 4, 1976.

THE SECRETS OF ISIS

CBS's fall 1977 title for *Isis*.

1084 THE SECRET STORM

Serial. Dramatic incidents in the lives of the Ames family, residents of the town of Woodridge.

CAST

Peter Ames	Peter Hobbs
	Cec Linder
	Ward Costello
Amy Ames	Jada Rowland
	Lynn Adams
Susan Ames	Jean Mowry
	Judy Lewis
Jerry Ames	Warren Berlinger
	Wayne Tippett
Pauline Reynolds	Haila Stoddard
Mr. Tyrell	Russell Hicks
Hugh Clayborn	Peter MacLean
Dan Kincaid	Bernard Barrow
Mickey Potter	Larry Block
Valerie Northcote	Lori March
Jill Stevens	Barbara Rodell
Kevin Kincaid	David Ackroyd
Belle Clements	Marla Adams
Nancy Vallin	Iris Braun
Ursula Winthrope	Jacqueline Brooks
Paul Britton	Nick Coster
	Linden Chiles
Ken Stevens	Joel Crothers
Lisa Britton	Judy Safran
	Diane Dell
	Terri Falis
Kitty Styles	Diane Ladd
Jonathan Styles	Scott Mefford
Peter Dunbar	Donnie Melvin
Grace Tyrell	Marjorie Gateson
	Eleanor Phelps
Dr. Ian Northcote	Gordon Rigsby
	Alexander Scourby
Doug Winthrope	Bruce Sherwood
Tom Gregory	Richard Venture
Aggie Parsons	Jane Rose
Reilly	Joe Ponazecki
Laurie Stevens	Stephanie Braxton
Polly	Susan Oakes
Phil Forrestor	Patrick Fox
Mike	Devin Goldenberg
Alden	Cliff De Young
Martha Ann Ashley	Audre Johnson
Freddy	Roberta Royce
Charlotte	Susan Sudert
Mulholland	Mike Galloway
Andrea	Roberta Rickett
Keefer	Troy Donahue
Kip Ripdale	Don Galloway
Ann Wicker	Diana Muldaur
Bob Hill	Roy Scheider
Tim Brannigan	Anthony Herrera
	Nicholas Lewis

Assistant D.A.	Gary Campbell
Irene Simms	Jennifer Darling
Cecilia	Kathleen Cody
Herbie Vail	Noel Craig
Nola Hollister	Rosemary Murphy
	Mary K. Wells
Myra Lake	Joan Hotchkis
	June Graham
Alan Dunbar	Liam Sullivan
	James Vicary
Frank Carver	Jack Ryland
	Robert Loggia
	Laurence Luckinbill
Cassie	Mildred Clinton
Mark Reddin	David Gale
Dr. Brian Neeves	Jeff Pomerantz
	Keith Charles
Clay Stevens	Jamie Grover
Jason Ferris	Robert Alda
Robert Landers	Dan Hamilton
Monsignor Quinn	Sidney Walker
Joanna Morrison	Audrey Landers
	Ellen Barber

Also: Virginia Dwyer. Robin Strasser, Charles Baxter.
Announcer: Ken Roberts.
Music: Carey Gould.

THE SECRET STORM—30 minutes—CBS—February 1, 1954–February 15, 1974.

1085   THE SEEKERS

Drama. A two-part sequel to *The Bastard* and *The Rebels. The Seekers,* the third of John Jakes's Kent Family novels, continues the story of Philip Kent, a veteran of the American Revolution and now an established publisher in Boston. The focal point of the program, however, is on his sons, Abraham and Gilbert, and their families.

CAST

Philip Kent	Martin Milner
Abraham Kent	Randolph Mantooth
Gilbert Kent	George Deloy
Elizabeth Kent	Delta Burke
Peggy Kent	Barbara Rush
Supply Pleasant	Ross Martin
Harriet Kent	Harriet Karr
Daniel Clapper	Robert Reed
Edna Clapper	Julie Gregg
Pell	Vic Morrow
General Wayne	Allan Rich
Lieutenant Stovall	George Hamilton
Jarod Kent	Timothy P. Murphy
Amanda Kent	Sarah Rush
Elijah Weatherby	Brian Keith
Rev. Blackthorn	Stuart Whitman
Piggott	Hugh O'Brian
Captain Drew	Neville Brand
Amos Samuels	Roosevelt Grier
Flora Cato	Edie Adams
Avery Mills	John Carradine
Oliver Prouty	Alex Hyde-White
Plenty Coups	Donald Mantooth
Jarod, age 5	Jeremy Licht
The Kent maid	Quinn Larid
Lt. Lewis	Skip Riley

Music: Gerald Fried.
Executive Producer: R.A. Cinader.
Producer: Gian Grimaldi.
Writer: Steve Hayes.
Director: Sidney Hayers.

THE SEEKERS—2 hours—Operation Prime Time—November/December 1979. 2 episodes. The series originally played on Home Box Office, a cable system, during July 1979.

1086   SEMI TOUGH

Comedy. The misadventures of Billy Clyde Puckett and Marvin "Shake" Tiller, two womanizing pro football players for the New York Bulls, a seldom winning team.

CAST

Billy Clyde Puckett (pilot film)	Douglas Barr
Billy Clyde Puckett (series)	Bruce McGill
Marvin Tiller (pilot film)	Josh Taylor
Marvin Tiller (series)	David Hasselhoff
Barbara Jane Bookman, their roommate (pilot film)	Mary Louise Weller
Barbara Jane Bookman (series)	Markie Post
Big Ed Bookman, Barbara's father	Hugh Gillin
Big Barbara Bookman, Ed's wife	Mary Jo Catlett
Bert Turnbee, the team owner	Jim McKrell
Harry Cooper, the coach	Ed Peck
Story Time, a football player	Freeman King
Puddin, a football player	Bubba Smith
T. J., a football player	Carlos Brown
The Waitress (at the restaurant frequented by the team)	Michele Leon
Pearly, the booth sportscaster	Chuck McCann
Hal, Pearly's partner	Jim MacGeorge

Music: Doug Gilmore, Tom Wells.
Theme: Doug Gilmore, Randy Sharp.
Supervising Producer: Jerry Davis.
Executive Producer: David Merrick.
Producer: John Whitman, Ira Gerwitz.
Writer: Bud Wiser, Ron Greenberg, Wally Dalton, Shelley Zalman, Norman Barasch, John Owen, Richard Reinhart.
Director: Richard Benjamin, Bill Persky, Dick Martin.
Art Director: Mary Ann Biddle.
Director of Photography: Jeff Engel.

SEMI TOUGH—30 minutes—ABC—May 29, 1980–June 19, 1980. 4 episodes. The 30-minute pilot aired on ABC on January 6, 1980. Based on the motion picture of the same title.

1087   THE SENATOR

Drama. The story of Senator Hays Stowe, a progressive California politician who attempts to meet and understand the needs and desires of the people he represents.

CAST

Hays Stowe	Hal Holbrook
Ellen Stowe, his wife	Sharon Acker
Norma Stowe, their daughter	Cynthia Elibacher
Jordan Boyle, Hays's assistant	Michael Tolan
The Governor	John Randolph
The Mayor	John Marley

Executive Producer: William Sackheim.
Producer: David Levinson.
Director: Robert Day, James Goldstone, Daryl Duke, Jerrold Freedman, John Badham, Fernando Lamas.

THE SENATOR—60 minutes—NBC—September 13, 1970–August 22, 1971 (as part of *The Bold Ones*).

1088   SERPICO

Crime Drama. The exploits of Frank Serpico, a daring undercover patrolman with the 22nd Police Precinct in New York City.

CAST

Off. Frank Serpico (Badge No. 21049)	David Birney
Lt. Sullivan, his superior	Tom Atkins

Music: Robert Drasnin, Elmer Bernstein.
Executive Producer: Emmet G. Larvey, Jr.
Producer: Dan Ingalls, Barry Oringer.
Director: Reza S. Badiyi, Paul Stanley, Alex March, Michael Caffey, Art Fisher, Sigmund Neufeld, Jr., Robert Markowitz, Robert Collins.

SERPICO—60 minutes—NBC—September 24, 1976–January 28, 1977. 13 episodes.

1089   SESAME STREET

Children. Live action, cartoons, puppets, sketches and songs are presented to help children solve problems, reinforce their reading skills and assist them in learning the alphabet and counting from one to twenty.

Regulars: Jim Henson's Muppets, Bob McGrath, Matt Robinson, Loretta Long, Will Lee, Charlotte Rae, Elmo Delgado, Roscoe Orman, Alaina Reed, Clarice Taylor, Anne Revere, Paul B. Brice, Raul Julia, Larry Block, Northern J. Calloway, Buffy St. Marie, Linda Bove.
Muppet Voices: Frank Oz, Carroll Spinney, Jim Henson, Jerry Nelson, Richard Hunt, Donald Smith.
Music: Joe Raposo.
Musical Director: Sam Pottle.
Musical Coordinator: Danny Epstein.
Executive Producer: Jon Stone.
Producer: Dulcy Singer.
Director: Robert Myhrum.

SESAME STREET—60 minutes—NET—November 10, 1969–November 6, 1970. PBS—Premiered: November 9, 1970.

1090   SEVENTH AVENUE

Drama. A three-part miniseries based on the novel by Norman Bogner. The story of Jay Blackman, a poor young man from New York's Lower East Side who becomes a power in the garment industry.

CAST

Jay Blackman	Steven Keats
Rhoda Gold Blackman	Dori Brenner
Eva Meyers	Jane Seymour
Myrna Gold	Anne Archer
Al Blackman	Kristoffer Tabori
Joe Vitelli	Herschel Bernardi
Frank Topo	Richard Dimitri
Finkelstein	Jack Gilford
Morris Blackman	Michael Kellin
Harry Lee	Alan King
Douglas Fredericks	Ray Milland
Dave Shaw	Paul Sorvino
Gus Farber	Eli Wallach
John Meyers	William Windom
Marty Cass	John Pleshette
Paula Cass	Ellen Greene
Mrs. Gold	Leora Dana
Celia Blackman	Anna Berger
Howard Horton	Richard Kline
Edward Gold	Robert Symonds
Moll	Gloria Grahame
Police Sergeant	Brock Peters
Credan	Lou Cristolo
Ray Boone	Ron Max

Music: Nelson Riddle.
Executive Producer: Franklin Barton.
Producer: Richard Irving.
Writer: Laurence Heath.
Director: Richard Irving, Russ Mayberry.
Art Director: Loyd Papez.
Director of Photography: Jack Priestley.

SEVENTH AVENUE—2 hours—NBC—February 10, 1977–February 24, 1977. 3 episodes.

1091   79 PARK AVENUE

Drama. A three-part miniseries based on the novel by Harold Robbins. The story, which spans 13 years beginning in New York in August 1935, focuses on the life of Marja Fludjicki, a beautiful high-priced call girl, and the two men who love her: Ross Savitch, the rich son of a syndicate boss, and Mike Koshko, a poor, hardworking young man. (The title is derived from the address of a model agency that fronts for high-priced call girls.)

CAST

Marja Fludjicki	Lesley Ann Warren
Ross Savitch	Marc Singer
Mike Koshko	David Dukes
Kaati Fludjicki	Barbara Barrie
Ben Savitch	Michael Constantine
Myrna Savitch	Margaret Fairchild
Peter Markevitch	Albert Salmi
Paulie Fludjicki	Scott Jacoby
Vera Keppler	Polly Bergen
Harry Vito	John Saxon
Armand Perfido	Raymond Burr
Joker	Jack Weston

Brian Whitfield	Peter Marshall
Frank Millerson	Alex Rocco
Joel Rannis	Sandy Helberg
Martin Stevens	Lloyd Haynes
Laura Koshko	Veronica Hamel
Hal Roper	Andy Romano
DeWitt	Robert Webber

Music: Nelson Riddle.
Executive Producer: George Eckstein.
Producer: Paul Wendkos.
Writer: Richard DeRoy, Jack Guss, Lionel Siegel.
Director: Paul Wendkos.

79 PARK AVENUE—2 hours— NBC—October 16, 1977–October 18, 1977. 3 episodes. Repeats: August 12, 1979–August 26, 1979.

1092 SHAFT

Crime Drama. The exploits of John Shaft, a hip, black, New York private detective who strives to solve complex and baffling crimes. Based on the movie of the same title with sex and violence curtailed for television.

CAST

John Shaft	Richard Roundtree
Lt. Al Rossi, N.Y.P.D.	Ed Barth

Music: Johnny Pate.
Shaft Theme: Isaac Hayes.
Executive Producer: Allan Balter.
Producer: William Reed Woodfield.
Director: John Llewellyn Moxey, Alexander Singer, Ivan Dixon.

SHAFT—90 minutes—CBS— October 9, 1973–September 3, 1974. 8 episodes.

1093 SHA NA NA

Variety. Musical numbers, blackouts and comedy sketches set against the background of a city neighborhood in the 1950s.

Starring: Sha Na Na, a ten-member Rock group: Lennie Baker, Jon "Bowzer" Bauman, Johnny Contardo, Denny Greene, "Dirty" Dan McBride, John "Jocko" Marcellino, Scott "Santini" Powell, David "Chico" Ryan, "Scream'" Scott Simon, Donny York.
Regulars: Avery Schreiber, Kenneth Mars, Pamela Myers, Jane Dulo, Phil Roth, Jack Wohl, Michael Sklar, June Gable, Soupy Sales (as the police officer).
Announcer: Pamela Myers.
Musical Director: Ray Charles.
Musical Material: Ray Charles, Les Charles.
Special Musical Material: Ray Charles, Jon Charles.
Executive Producer: Pierre Cossette.
Producer: Bernard Rothman, Jack Wohl, Walter C. Miller.
Writer: Gary Belkin, Coslough Johnson, Peter Galley.

Director: Walter C. Miller.
Choreographer: Walter Painter, Kevin Carlisle, Carl Jablonski.
Additional Music and Choreography: Sha Na Na.
Art Director: Jack McAdam.

SHA NA NA—30 minutes—Syndicated 1977.

1094 THE SHARI LEWIS SHOW

Children. The series, set at the Bearly Broadcasting Company, a television station that is run by 25 animal puppets, features Shari Lewis as the human assistant station manager. Show deals with people and how they relate to one another; how they create problems and how they resolve them.

Starring: Shari Lewis.
Shari's Partner: Ron Martin.
Puppeteers: Shari Lewis, Mallory Tarcher.
Voices: Shari Lewis.
Musical Director: Bob Alberti.
Theme Vocal: Shari Lewis.
Executive Producer: Florence Small.
Producer: Florence Small.
Director: Tony Verdi.
Creator: Shari Lewis, Jeremy Tarcher.

THE SHARI LEWIS SHOW—30 minutes—Syndicated 1975.

1095 SHAZAM!

Adventure. Selected by the immortal elders—Solomon, Mercury, Zeus, Achilles and Atlas— Billy Batson, a radio station broadcaster, is endowed with the ability to transform himself into Captain Marvel, a daring crusader for justice.

Stories relate Billy's battle against evil as the mysterious crime fighter, Captain Marvel. (When Billy utters the word "Shazam!" he is transformed into Captain Marvel.) Based on the comic book character, "Shazam!"

CAST

Billy Batson	Michael Gray
Mentor, his assistant	Les Tremayne
Captain Marvel	Jackson Bostwick
	John Davey

Music: Yvette Blais, Jeff Michael.
Executive Producer: Norm Prescott, Lou Scheimer, Dick Rosenbloom.
Producer: Arthur H. Nadel, Robert Chenault.
Director: Hollingsworth Morse, Robert Chernault, Harry Lange, Jr., Arnold Laven, Arthur H. Nadel.

SHAZAM!—30 minutes—CBS— September 7, 1974–September 3, 1977.

THE SHAZAM!—ISIS HOUR

See *Shazam!* and *Isis.*

1096 SHIELDS AND YARNELL

Variety. Music, comedy, songs, dances, blackouts and mime.

Hosts: Robert Shields and Lorene Yarnell.
Regulars: Joanna Cassidy, Ted Zeigler, Philip Reade, Gailard Sartaine.
Orchestra: Norman Mamey.
Executive Producer: Steve Binder.
Producer: Frank Peppiatt.
Director: Steve Binder.
Choreographer: Ronald DuPree.
Music Coordinator: Steve Binder, Dennis Drake.

SHIELDS AND YARNELL—30 minutes—CBS—June 13, 1977– July 25, 1977; January 31, 1978– March 28, 1978. 12 programs.

1097 SHIRLEY

Comedy-Drama. The story of Shirley Miller, an attractive widow with four children who fulfills her late husband's dream by moving from the bustle of New York to the shores of Placer County, Lake Tahoe, Nevada, to begin a new life.

CAST

Shirley Miller	Shirley Jones
Debra Miller, her daughter	Rosanna Arquette
Bill Miller, her son	Peter Barton
Hemm Miller, her son	Bret Shryer
Michelle Miller, her daughter	Tracey Gold
Charlotte McHenry, their housekeeper	Ann Doran
Ethan "Dutch" McHenry, Charlotte's ex-husband	John McIntire
Lew Armitage, Shirley's romantic interest	Patrick Wayne
Tracy Armitage, Lew's sister	Cynthia Eilbacher
Jake Miller, Shirley's husband (flashbacks)	Peter Haskell

The Millers' dog: Oregano.
The Millers' address: 602 Kingsbeach Road.

Music: Ben Lanzarone, Arthur Rubinstein, Jr., Richard Clements.
Theme: Charles Fox (music) and Norman Gimbel (lyrics).
Theme Vocal: Shirley Jones.
Executive Producer: Greg Strangis, William Hogan.
Producer: Bob Birnbaum, Paul Dubov, Gwen Bagni.
Writer: Dusty King, Terry Hart, Greg Strangis, Pat Green, Chris Manheim, Dave Hackel.
Director: Stan Lathan, Gene Nelson, Gerald Mayer, Mel Ferber, William F. Claxton, Alan Myerson, Bob Birnbaum, Michael Preece.
Creator: Lance Madrid III.

SHIRLEY—60 minutes—NBC— October 26, 1979–January 25, 1980. 12 episodes.

THE SHIRLEY MacLAINE SHOW

See *Shirley's World.*

1098 SHIRLEY'S WORLD

Comedy. The assignments of Shirley Logan, a beautiful photo journalist with *World Illustrated* magazine, who possesses an insatiable curiosity and a warm-hearted nature that involves her in other people's problems.

CAST

Shirley Logan	Shirley MacLaine
Dennis Croft, her editor (in London)	John Gregson

Music: John Barry, Laurie Johnson.
Shirley's World Theme: John Barry.
Executive Producer: Sheldon Leonard, Ronald Rubin.
Producer: Barry Delmaine, Ray Austin.
Director: Ralph Levy, Ray Austin, Charles Crichton.

SHIRLEY'S WORLD—30 minutes —ABC—September 15, 1971– January 5, 1972. 17 episodes.

1099 SHŌGUN

Drama. A six-part miniseries that chronicles the adventures of John Blackthorne, a navigator and pilot of the *Erasmus*, a Dutch trader-warship captured near the village of Anjiro in the Japans in 1600. The story details Blackthorne's exploits, when renamed Anjin-san (Pilot, by his captors), as he finds romance, political intrigue and ambitious warlords striving to become Shōgun (Supreme Military Leader). The twenty million dollar miniseries, which was three years in the making, parallels two real-life figures: Tokugawa Ieyasu, a political leader who is portrayed as Toranaga, and Will Adams, the English sea pilot who is portrayed as John Blackthorne. Their relationship and how Blackthorne broke the Portugese monopoly on trade between Japan and China, is the focal point of the program. Based on the novel by James Clavell.

CAST

John Blackthorne (Anjin-san)	Richard Chamberlain
Omi	Yuki Meguro
Mariko	Yoko Shimada
Rodrigues	John Rhys-Davies
Father Alvito	Damien Thomas
Lord Yabu	Frankie Sakai
Father Sebastio	Leon Lissek
Father Dell-Aqua	Alan Badel
Friar Domingo	Michael Hordern
Lord Toranaga	Toshiro Mifune
Lord Ishido	Nobuo Kaneko
Captain Ferriera	Vladek Sheybal
Buntaro	Hideo Takamatsu
Fujiko	Hiromi Senno

Kiku	Mika Kitagawa
Urano	Takeshi Ohbayashi
Vinct	George Innes
Brother Michael	Masumi Okada
Naga	Shin Takumi
Ginsel	John Carney

Narrator: Orson Welles.
Story Line Recap Narration: Paul Frees.
Music: Maurice Jarre.
Song: "Blackthorne's Shanty" by Eric Bercovici.
Executive Producer: James Clavell.
Producer: Eric Bercovici.
Writer: Eric Bercovici.
Director: Jerry London.
Director of Photography: Andrew Laszlo.

SHŌGUN—12 hours (total)—NBC—September 15, 1980—September 19, 1980. 5 episodes (three two-hour episodes; two three-hour episodes).

1100   SHOOT FOR THE STARS

Game. Two teams compete, each composed of one celebrity and one noncelebrity contestant. One player selects one box from a large board that contains 24 numbered boxes and a phrase is revealed (e.g., "Clever as a lash"). The contestant has to unscramble the first half of the phrase by providing a synonym for the first word (e.g., "smart as" for "clever as") and the celebrity has to unravel the second half (e.g., a "whip" for a "lash"). Each phrase is worth money and when both halves are correctly solved, the money is added to a player's score. Turns alternate back and forth between the teams and the first team to score $1,500 is the winner.

Host: Geoff Edwards.
Announcer: Bob Clayton.
Music: Bob Cobert.
Executive Producer: Bob Stewart.
Producer: Bruce Burmester.
Director: Mike Gargiulo.

SHOOT FOR THE STARS—30 minutes—NBC—January 3, 1977 –September 30, 1977. 185 programs.

1101   SHOWOFFS

Game. Two teams compete, each composed of two celebrities and one noncelebrity contestant. One team is placed in a soundproof isolation booth while the other team is at play. One player is the guesser; the other two are the actors. The object is for the actors to pantomime as many words as possible during a sixty-second time limit. Each word that is identified by the guesser scores one point. At the end of the round the other team is brought out and the game is played in the same man-ner. The team with the highest score is the winner of the round. A two-out-of-three match competition is played (the roles of actor and guesser alternate) and the highest scorer receives a thousand dollars in merchandise prizes.

Host: Bobby Van.
Announcer: Gene Wood.
Music: Score Productions.
Executive Producer: Mark Goodson, Bill Todman.
Producer: Howard Felsher.
Director: Paul Alter.

SHOWOFFS—30 minutes—ABC —June 30, 1975—December 26, 1975. 120 programs.

1102   SIERRA

Drama. The series, set in the fictional Sierra National Park, depicts the rescue operations of the National Park Service Rangers—men and women who dedicate their lives to protecting people from nature and nature from people. (In the pilot film, the setting is the Yosemite National Park in California.)

CAST

Ranger Tim Cassidy	James Richardson
Ranger Julie Beck	Susan Foster
Ranger Matt Harper (pilot film)	Colby Chester
Ranger Matt Harper (series)	Ernest Thompson
Ranger P. J. Lewis	Mike Warren
Chief Ranger Jack Moore (pilot film)	Jim B. Smith
Chief Ranger Jack Moore (series)	Jack Hogan

Music: Lee Holdridge.
Executive Producer: Robert A. Cinader.
Producer: Bruce Johnson, Edwin Self.

SIERRA—60 minutes—NBC—September 12, 1974–December 12, 1974. 13 episodes. The 90-minute pilot film, "The Rangers," aired on NBC on December 24, 1974.

1103   SIGMUND AND THE SEA MONSTERS

Comedy. The series, set in Cyprus Beach, California, follows the misadventures of brothers Johnny and Scott Stuart, and their pet sea monster, Sigmund. Disowned by his family for his inability to scare humans, Sigmund was found and befriended by Johnny and Scott, taken home, and concealed in their club house. Stories depict Johnny and Scott's attempts to hide Sigmund and protect him from the devious efforts of his family, who seek to retrieve him when emergencies arise that require his presence at home (a cave at Dead Man's Point).

CAST

Sigmund Ooz	Billy Barty
Johnny Stuart	Johnny Whitaker
Scott Stuart	Scott Kolden
Zelda Marshall, the Stuarts' housekeeper	Mary Wickes
Sheriff Chuck Bevins, Zelda's boyfriend	Joe Higgins
Sheldon, the Sea Genie	Rip Taylor
Miss Eddels, the Stuart's nosey neighbor	Margaret Hamilton
Shelby, Sheldon's nephew	Sparky Marcus
Gertrude Gouch, the housekeeper, later episodes	Fran Ryan

Also: Sharon Baird, Van Snowden, Paul Gale, Walter Edmonds, Larry Larson.
Additional Characters (not given screen credit): Big Daddy, Sigmund's father; Sweet Mama, Sigmund's mother; Blurp and Slurp Ooz, Sigmund's brothers; Great Uncle Siggy, Sigmund's namesake.

The Stuarts' address: 1730 (later 730) Ocean Drive.
Ooz family pet: Prince (a barking lobster).

Music: Jimmy Haskell, Wes Farrell, Michael Lloyd.
Producer: Sid and Marty Krofft.
Director: Dick Darley, Murray Golden.

SIGMUND AND THE SEA MONSTERS—30 minutes—NBC—September 8, 1973–October 18, 1975. Syndicated.

1104   THE SILENT FORCE

Crime Drama. The series, set in Washington, D.C., depicts the exploits of Amelia Cole, Jason Hart and Ward Fuller, undercover agents for the federal government who comprise the Silent Force, a secret organization designed to corrupt the inner workings of organized crime.

CAST

Amelia Cole	Lynda Day
Jason Hart	Percy Rodrigues
Ward Fuller	Ed Nelson

Music: George Duning.
Executive Producer: Walter Grauman.
Producer: Philip Barry.
Creator: Luther Davis.

THE SILENT FORCE—30 minutes—ABC—September 21, 1970 –January 11, 1971. 13 episodes.

1105   SIROTA'S COURT

Comedy. A comical look at life in a night court as seen through the hectic experiences of Matthew J. Sirota, a compassionate judge.

CAST

Judge Matthew Sirota	Michael Constantine
Maureen O'Connor, the court clerk	Cynthia Harris
Gail Goodman, the public defender	Kathleen Miller
Sawyer Dabney, the private attorney	Ted Ross
H.R. Bud Nugent, the assistant D.A.	Fred Willard
John Belson, the U.S. marshal	Owen Bush

Music: David Shire.
Theme Vocal: Ted Ross.
Producer: Harvey Miller, Peter Engel.
Director: Mel Ferber, Tom Trbovichi.

Program Open:
Announcer: This is the city. It could be your city.
Woman's voice: Luckily for you it's not. What a jungle!
Announcer: Yes, this city like many others is a victim of rising crime.
Man's voice: Tell me. I live with bars on my windows while the crooks are out on the streets!
Woman's voice: I bought one of those doberman dogs; they beat him up.
Announcer: And where does the average citizen find justice?
Man's voice: Not here buddy!
Woman's voice: Ooh, could we use Superman now!
Man's voice: Aah, nobody cares.
Announcer: Nobody? What about the honorable Matthew J. Sirota of Night Court?
Man's voice: Oh, he's the one who's tough but fair.
Woman's voice: Oh yea, he's a nice man.
(A song follows that tells of Judge Sirota, "the best defense against the rising tide of crime.")

SIROTA'S COURT—30 minutes—NBC—December 1, 1976–January 26, 1977.

1106   THE SIX MILLION DOLLAR MAN

Adventure. Seriously injured after crashing in an Air Force research jet that malfunctioned, civilian astronaut Steve Austin becomes the immediate concern of the Office of Strategic Operations (later the Office of Scientific Intelligence), a U.S. government organization that requires an extraordinary agent and spends six million dollars to reconstruct Steve Austin to their specifications.

Through bionic and cybernetic surgery, both of Austin's legs, one arm, and one eye are replaced with synthetic, nuclear-powered mechanisms that produce superhuman abilities and make him something that has never before existed: a cyborg (cybernetic organism), part human and part machine.

Stories detail Austin's attempts, on behalf of the O.S.I., to resolve situations that pose a threat to humanity.

Rhoda. From left, Julie Kavner, Ray Buktenica and Valerie Harper.

The Ropers. From left, Jeffrey Tambor, Patricia McCormack, Evan Cohen, Audra Lindley and Norman Fell.

Salvage 1. Center, Andy Griffith. From left, Joel Higgins, Trish Stewart and J. Jay Saunders. Courtesy of the *Call-Chronicle Newspapers,* Allentown, Pa.

Sara. Brenda Vaccaro.

CAST

Steve Austin	Lee Majors
Oscar Goldman, his superior	Richard Anderson
Dr. Rudy Wells, the aeromedical surgeon	Alan Oppenheimer Martin E. Brooks
Janet Callahan (a.k.a. Margaret Callahan), Oscar's secretary	Jennifer Darling
Miss Johnson, Oscar's secretary	Susan Keller

Recurring Roles:

Jaime Sommers, the Bionic Woman	Lindsay Wagner
Major Kelly Wood, Steve's girlfriend	Farrah Fawcett
Victoria Webster, a KNUZ-TV reporter (one episode)	Farrah Fawcett
Shalon, the alien Steve befriends, a deep space explorer marooned on Earth	Stefanie Powers
Gillian, same as Shalon	Sandy Duncan
Aploy, same as Shalon	Severn Darden
Big Foot, the creature created by Shalon	Andre the Circus Giant Ted Cassidy
Barney Hillyer, the first experimental bionic man	Monte Markham
Kuroda, the Japanese soldier Steve found in the jungle	John Fujioka

Music: Stu Phillips, Gil Melle, J. J. Johnson, Richard Clements.
Theme Vocal: "The Six Million Dollar Man" by Dusty Springfield.
Executive Producer: Harve Bennett, Allan Balter.
Producer: Kenneth Johnson, Lionel E. Siegel, Richard Landau, Fred Freiberger, Sam Strangis, Donald R. Boyle, Richard Irving.
Director: Tom Connors III, Rod Holcomb, Alf Kjellin, Richard Moder, Jerry London, Alan Crosland, Barry Crane, Richard Doner, John Meredyth Lucas, Cliff Bole, Phil Bondelli, James Lydon, Arnold Laven, Lawrence Doheny, Edward Abroms, Reza S. Badiyi, Richard Irving, Glen A. Larson, Jerry Jameson, Jeannot Szwarc.

THE SIX MILLION DOLLAR MAN —90- and 60-minute versions— ABC—October 20, 1973–February 27, 1978. Syndicated. Spin-off series: *The Bionic Woman.* The 90-minute pilot film aired on ABC on March 7, 1973.

1107   THE SIX O'CLOCK FOLLIES

Comedy. The series, set at the Armed Forces Vietnam Network (AFVN) television station in wartime Saigon (1967), follows the antics of the staff who produce *The AFVN News and Sports*, a six o'clock news program that is irreverently known as "The Follies."

CAST

Col. Harvey Marvin, the C.O.	Joby Baker
Candi LeRoy, the sexy weather girl	Aarika Wells
Specialist Sam Paige, the newscaster	A. C. Weary
Cpl. Don "Robby" Robinson, the newscaster	Larry Fishburne
Lt. Vaughn Beuhler, Marvin's aide	Randall Carver
Specialist Midas Metcovitch, the TV director — and con artist	Philip Charles MacKenzie
Ho, the Vietnamese station janitor	George Kee Cheung
Specialist Percy Wiggins, the technician	David Hubbard
Lou Roskoe, the Associated Press reporter	Howard Witt
Voice of President Lyndon B. Johnson	Fred Travalena
Marcel Valjean, the local, scheming businessman	Byron Webster

Music: Artie Butler, Harry Betts.
Theme Vocal: "Home" by Joe Crocker.
Producer: Marvin Kupfer, Norman Steinberg.
Writer: Marvin Kupfer, Norman Steinberg, John Steven Owen.
Director: Robert Sweeney, Don Weis.
Creator: Marvin Kupfer, Norman Steinberg.

THE SIX O'CLOCK FOLLIES—30 minutes—NBC—April 24, 1980– April 26, 1980. 2 episodes. Two additional episodes aired on NBC on August 2, 1980 and September 13, 1980.

1108   THE SIXTH SENSE

Drama. The investigations of Michael Rhodes, a professor of parapsychology at the University School in Los Angeles, as he attempts to aid people threatened by "ghosts" and solve crimes that are linked to supernatural occurrences.

CAST

Michael Rhodes	Gary Collins
Nancy Murphy, his assistant	Catherine Farrar

Music: Billy Goldenberg.
Producer: Stan Sheptner.
Director: Alf Kjellin, Daniel Haller, Barry Shear, Robert Day, Bernard Girard, John Newland, John Badham, Jeff Corey, Earl Bellamy, Allen Baron.
Creator: Anthony Lawrence.

THE SIXTH SENSE—60 minutes—ABC—January 15, 1972– December 30, 1972. 25 episodes. The series is edited and syndicated as part of *Night Gallery.* The 90-minute pilot film, "Sweet, Sweet Rachel," aired on ABC on October 2, 1971.

1109   THE SIX WIVES OF HENRY VIII

Historical Drama. The series chronicles the life and six marriages of Henry VIII (1491-1547), the ruler of England during the fifteenth century.

CAST

Henry VIII	Keith Michell
Catherine of Aragon, his first wife	Annette Crosbie
Anne Boleyn, his second wife	Dorothy Tutin
Jane Seymour, his third wife	Anne Stallybrass
Anne of Cleves, his fourth wife	Elvi Hale
Catherine Howard, his fifth wife	Angela Pleasance
Catherine Parr, his sixth wife	Rosalie Crutchley
The Duke of Norfolk	Patrick Troughton
Princess Mary	Verina Greenlaw
Thomas Seymour	John Ronane
Lady Rochford	Sheila Burrell
Archbishop Crammer	Bernard Hepton
Mark Smeaton	Michael Osborne
Bishop Gardner	Basil Dignam
Lord Hertford	Daniel Moynihan
Thomas Wriothesley	Patrick Godfrey
Francis Dereham	Simon Prebble

Narrator: Anthony Quayle.
Music: David Munrow.

THE SIX WIVES OF HENRY VIII —90 minutes—CBS—August 1, 1971–September 5, 1971. Syndicated. Produced by the BBC.

1110   SKAG

Drama. The story of Peter Skagska (called "Skag" by his friends), a 56-year-old, hard-working steel mill foreman (for East Pittsburgh Steel, Local 1602 in Pennsylvania), a loving husband and father of four troubled children. Stories, which are adult, realistic and penetrating, focus on family relationships and problems at work.

CAST

Peter "Skag" Skagska	Karl Malden
Jo Skagska, his wife	Piper Laurie
Patricia Skagska, their daughter	Kathryn Holcomb
Barbara Skagska, their daughter	Leslie Ackerman
David Skagska, Peter's son by an earlier marriage	Craig Wasson
John Skagska, Peter and Jo's son	Peter Gallagher
Petar Skagska, Peter's father	George Voskovec
Audrey, John's girlfriend	Gwen Humble
Jim Whalen, the mill supervisor	Powers Boothe
Zanski, a steel mill worker	R.G. Armstrong
Paczka, a steel mill worker	Frank Campanella
Dotti Jessup, the bartender at The Fat Lady's Bar, the hangout	Sally Prager
Madman Mesissik, a steel mill worker	Richard Bright

Music: Billy Goldenberg, Morton Stevens, Bruce Broughton.
Supervising Producer: Brad Dexter.
Executive Producer: Abby Mann, Lee Rich.
Producer: Brad Dexter.
Director: Frank Perry, Edward Parone, Virgil W. Vogel, Allen Reisner, Bruce Bilson.
Creator: Abby Mann.

SKAG—60 minutes—NBC—January 6, 1980–February 21, 1980. 6 episodes.

1111   THE SKATEBIRDS

Children. A series of cartoons hosted by three roller skating birds—Sach, Knock Knock and Scooter.

Animated Segments:
The Robonic Stooges. A take-off on the 1940s "Three Stooges" in which a space age Moe, Larry and Curley, robots constructed from the finest parts available, battle evil throughout the universe.

Wonder Wheels. The story of Wheelie, the owner of a decrepit motorcycle, which, when the need arises, he transforms into Wonder Wheels to battle evil. His girlfriend: Doolie.

Woofer and Wimper. The misadventures of detective dogs Woofer and Wimper and their human masters, the teenage members of the Clue Club, a professional investigative organization. See *The Clue Club* for further information.

Voices: Scatman Crothers, Susan Davis, Mickey Dolenz, Ron Feinberg, Bob Holt, Ralph James, Allan Melvin, Don Messick, Alan Oppenheimer, Robert Ridgely, Ronnie Schell, Hal Smith, John Stephenson, Lennie Weinrib.
Music: Hoyt Curtin.
Executive Producer: William Hanna, Joseph Barbera.
Animation Director: Charles A. Nichols.
Skatebirds Director: Sidney Miller.

Live Action Segment:
Mystery Island. Retreating to an uncharted island, the evil Dr. Strenge establishes a base where he constructs his diabolical machines to control the world. His device, however, is incomplete, and needs the aide of P.O.P.S., a sophisticated computer robot to fully activate it. Discovering that the robot is being transported by air, Dr. Strenge forces the plane carrying it to crash-land on his island, marooning scientists Chuck Kelly, Sue Corwin, her brother Sandy — and P.O.P.S. Stories concern Chuck, Sue and Sandy's attempts to safeguard P.O.P.S. from Dr. Strenge and escape from the island.

CAST

Chuck Kelly	Stephen Parr
Sue Corwin	Lynne Marie Johnston
Sandy Corwin	Larry Vouk
Dr. Strenge	Michael Kermotan
Voice of P.O.P.S.	Frank Welker

Music: Hoyt Curtin.
Executive Producer: William Hanna, Joseph Barbera.

Producer: Terry Morse, Jr.
Director: Hollingsworth Morse, Sidney Miller.

THE SKATEBIRDS—55 minutes—CBS—September 10, 1977—January 21, 1978. 21 episodes.

1112   THE SKIPPER CHUCK SHOW

Children. Music, songs, skits and game contests geared to children.

Host: Skipper Chuck (as identified and credited).
Announcer: Marc Carpona, Diane Harris.
Music: Tommy Gannon.
Producer: Doris Bernhardt.
Director: Tom Estrada.

THE SKIPPER CHUCK SHOW—30 minutes—Syndicated 1978.

1113   SKYHAWKS

Animated Cartoon. The assignments of Skyhawks, Incorporated, a daredevil air transport and rescue service owned and operated by the Wilson family.

Characters: Mike Wilson, the chief operator; Steve and Carolyn Wilson, his children; Red Hughes and Little Cindy, his foster children; and Patty Wilson, his father.
Voices: Bob Arbogast, Al Brooks, Melinda Casey, Dick Curtis, Susan Davis, Joan Gerber, Casey Kasem, Nora Marlowe, Michael Rye.
Music: Jack Fascinato.
Executive Producer: Ken Snyder.
Producer: Jeanne Lindsay, Charles Phalen, Dick Reed, Paul Shirley.
Supervising Director: Fred Crippen.
Director: Joe Bruno, George Singer, Irv Spector.

SKYHAWKS—30 minutes—ABC—September 6, 1969–September 2, 1971.

1114   THE SMITH FAMILY

Comedy-Drama. The series, set in Los Angeles, depicts events in the day-to-day lives of the Smith family: Chad, the father, a 25-year veteran detective sergeant with the L.A.P.D., his wife Betty, and their children Cindy, Bob and Brian.

CAST
Det. Sgt. Chad Smith	Henry Fonda
Betty Smith, his wife	Janet Blair
Cindy Smith, their daughter	Darleen Carr
Bob Smith, their son	Ron Howard
Brian Smith, their son	Michael-James Wixted
Ray Martin, Chad's partner	John Carter
Captain Hughes, Chad's superior	Charles McGraw

The Smiths's address: 219 Primrose Lane.

Music: Frank DeVol.
Theme Vocal: "Primrose Lane" by Mike Minor.
Executive Producer: Don Fedderson.
Producer: Edmund Hartmann.
Creator: Edmund Hartmann.

THE SMITH FAMILY—30 minutes—ABC—January 20, 1971–September 8, 1971; April 12, 1972–June 14, 1972. 39 episodes.

1115   THE SMOTHERS BROTHERS COMEDY HOUR

Variety. Controversial humor, satire, songs and topical sketches.

Verson 1:

Host: Tom and Dick Smothers.
Regulars: Pat Paulsen, John Hartford, Jennifer Warren, Murray Romas, Leigh French, Mason Williams, Bob Einstein (as Officer Judy), Don Wyatt, Carl Gottlieb, Cathy Cahill, Jessica Myerson, The Jimmy Joyce Singers, The Anita Kerr Singers, The Ron Poindexter Dancers, The Louis DaPron Dancers.
Announcer: Roger Carroll.
Orchestra: Nelson Riddle.

THE SMOTHERS BROTHERS COMEDY HOUR—60 minutes—CBS—February 5, 1967–June 8, 1969.

Version 2:

Host: Tom and Dick Smothers
Regulars: Sally Struthers, Spencer Quinn.
Announcer: Roger Carroll.
Orchestra: Denny Vaughn.
Producer-Director: Norman Stedawie.

THE SMOTHERS BROTHERS COMEDY HOUR—60 minutes—ABC—July 15, 1970–September 16, 1970.

1116   THE SMOTHERS BROTHERS SHOW

Variety. Music, songs and comedy sketches.

Host: Tom and Dick Smothers.
Regulars: Pat Paulsen, Don Novello, Leigh French, Pete Smith, Betty Aberlain, Evelyn Russell.
Orchestra: Marty Paich.
Executive Producer: Joe Hamilton.
Producer: Gail Parent, Kenny Solms.
Director: Mack Bing, Bill Foster.

THE SMOTHERS BROTHERS SHOW—60 minutes—ABC—January 3, 1975–May 26, 1975.

1117   THE SMOTHERS ORGANIC PRIME TIME SPACE RIDE

Variety. Offbeat, controversial comedy coupled with performances by new talent discoveries (the "Space Ride").

Host: Tom Smothers.
Occasional Co-Host: Dick Smothers.
Executive Producer: John Barrett.
Producer: Norman Sedawie.
Director: Norman Sedawie.

THE SMOTHERS ORGANIC PRIME TIME SPACE RIDE—30 minutes—Syndicated, 1971.

1118   THE SNOOP SISTERS

Crime Drama. The series, set in New York City, follows the investigations of sisters Ernestine and Gwendolyn Snoop, eccentric mystery story writers who become involved with and solve crimes while seeking book material.

CAST
Ernestine Snoop	Helen Hayes
Gwendolyn Snoop	Mildred Natwick
Lt. Steve Ostrowski, their nephew	Bert Convy
Barney, the ex-con Steve hires to watch over his aunts (pilot film)	Art Carney
Barney (series)	Lou Antonio

Music: Jerry Fielding.
Executive Producer: Leonard B. Stern.
Producer: Tony Barrett.
Director: Boris Sagal, Leonard B. Stern, David Friedkin, Leonard J. Horn.

THE SNOOP SISTERS—90 minutes—NBC—January 29, 1974–August 26, 1974 (as part of *The NBC Tuesday Mystery Movie*). One episode aired on December 19, 1973, as a segment of *The NBC Wednesday Mystery Movie*. The two-hour pilot film aired on NBC on December 18, 1972.

1119   SOAP

Satire. A spoof of afternoon soap operas in which the lives of two sisters are chronicled: the wealthy Jessica Tate, and the not-so-rich Mary Campbell. The series also focuses on the outlandish activities of their families, residents of the town of Dunns River, Connecticut.

CAST
Jessica Tate	Cathryn Damon
Mary Campbell	Katherine Helmond
Chester Tate, Jessica's husband	Robert Mandan
Burt Campbell, Mary's second husband	Richard Mulligan
Corinne Tate, Jessica's daughter	Diana Canova
Eunice Tate, Jessica's daughter	Jennifer Salt
Danny Dallas, Mary's son (from a first marriage)	Ted Wass
Jodie Dallas, Mary's son (from a first marriage)	Billy Crystal
Billy Tate, Jessica's son	Jimmy Baio
Benson, the Tates's butler	Robert Guillaume
Saunders, the Tates's butler, later episodes	Roscoe Lee Browne
The Major, Jessica's crazed father (believes he is living World War II)	Arthur Peterson
Chuck Campbell, Burt's son, a ventriloquist	Jay Johnson
Bob, Chuck's dummy (whom Chuck believes is alive)	Jay Johnson
Tim Flotski, the ex-priest who marries Corinne	Sal Viscuso
Peter Campbell, Burt's son	Robert Urich
Godfather, the head of the Mafia in which Danny is involved	Richard Libertini
Claire, Chester's secretary	Kathryn Reynolds
Carol Darwin, the nurse	Udana Power
Walter McCallam, Eunice's boyfriend	Edward Winter
Marilyn McCallam, Walter's wife	Judith Marie Bergan
Ingrid Svenson, Corinne's real mother	Inga Swenson
Randolph Svenson, Ingrid's husband	Bernard Fox
E. Ronald Mallu, Jessica's lawyer	Eugene Roche
Mr. Lefkowitz, the Mafia leader (later)	Sorrell Booke
Elaine Lefkowitz, his daughter, married Danny	Dinah Manoff
Sheila Fyne, Jessica's friend	Nita Talbot
Carol David, Mallu's assistant, married Jodie	Rebecca Balding
Sheriff Tinkler	Gordon Jump
George Donehue, the detective	John Byner
Dutch Lightner, the convict who resides with the Tates	Donnelly Rhodes
Polly Dawson, Danny's romantic interest (after Elaine)	Lynne Moody
Eddie Dawson, Polly's brother	Kene Holliday
Rose Dawson, Polly's mother	Royce Wallace
Walter Dawson, Polly's father	Mel Stewart
Saul, the earthling who helped Burt escape from the aliens	Jack Gilford
Lorelene David, Carol's mother	Peggy Pope
Millie, Danny's romantic interest (prior to Polly)	Candice Azzara
Leslie Walker, Billy's school teacher	Marla Pennington
Dennis Phillips, the quarterback	Bob Seagren
Dr. Alan Posner, Jessica's psychiatrist	Allan Miller
Devil's Voice (the devil possessed Corinne's baby)	Tim McIntire
Mrs. Flotski, Tim's mother	Doris Roberts
Sally, Burt's secretary (Burt owns a construction company)	Caroline McWilliams
Alice, the lesbian befriended by Jodie, a gay	Randee Heller
Dr. Hill, Jessica's physician	Granville Van Dusen
Maggie Chandler, the detective	Barbara Rhoades
Annie Selig, Eunice's friend	Nancy Dolman
Carlos El Puerco Valdez, the revolutionary who occupies Jessica's home	Gregory Sierra
Gwen, Danny's romantic interest (1981)	Jesse Welles

Announcer: Rod Roddy.
Music: George Tipton.
Supervising Producer: J.D. Lobue.

ABC

The Silent Force. From left, Ed Nelson, Percy Rodrigues and Lynda Day.

ABC

The Six Million Dollar Man. From left, Richard Anderson and Lee Majors.

ABC

Soap. Seated, from left, Billy Crystal, Katherine Helmond, Cathryn Damon and Jennifer Salt. Standing, from left, Robert Urich, Ted Wass, Richard Mulligan, Robert Guillaume, Robert Mandan, Jimmy Baio, Diana Canova and Arthur Peterson.

Executive Producer: Paul Junger Witt, Tony Thomas.
Producer: Susan Harris.
Writer: Susan Harris, Stu Silver.
Director: Jay Sandrich, J.D. Lobue.
Creator: Susan Harris.

SOAP—30 minutes—ABC—September 13, 1977–March 28, 1978. 26 episodes. September 14, 1978–March 15, 1979. 22 episodes. September 13, 1979–March 27, 1980. 22 episodes. Returned, premiered: October 29, 1980.

1120 SOAP FACTORY DISCO

Music. An *American Bandstand* type of program that features young adults dancing on stage to Disco music. (The title is taken from the name of a disco in Palisades Park, New Jersey, where the series is videotaped.)

Host: Paul Harriss.
Musical Director: Bobby Dj, Gutt Adero.
Music Theme: Lou Hensley.
Executive Producer: David Bergman.
Producer: Andrew Babbish.
Director: Joe Lo-Re, Steve Kahn.

SOAP FACTORY DISCO—30 minutes—Syndicated 1978. 39 programs.

1121 SOLID GOLD

Musical Variety. Performances by top recording artists.

Hostess: Dionne Warwick.
Regulars: Steve Allen, The Solid Gold Dancers.
Announcer: Robert W. Morgan.
Musical Director: Michael Miller.
Theme: "Solid Gold" by Michael Morgan and Dean Pitchford.
Executive Producer: Bob Banner.
Producer: Brad Lachman.
Writer: Jeffrey Barron, Irene Mecchi, Brad Lachman.
Director: Louis J. Horvitz.
Choreographer: Kevin Carlisle.
Art Director: Rene Lagler.

SOLID GOLD—60 minutes—Operation Prime Time Syndication (in association with Paramount Television)—1980.

1122 SOMERSET

Serial. A spin-off from *Another World.* The dramatic story of three families: the Lucases, the Grants and the Delaneys, residents of the town of Somerset.

CAST

Sam Lucas	Jordan Charney
Lahoma Lucas	Ann Wedgeworth
Missy Lucas	Carol Roux
Robert Delaney	Nicholas Coster
Laura Cooper	Dorothy Stinnette
Randy Buchanan	Gary Sandy
Ben Grant	Ed Kemmer
Jill Grant	Susan McDonald
David Grant	Ron Martin
Peter Delaney	Len Gochman
Marsha Davis	Alice Hirson
Ellen Grant	Georgann Johnson
Gerald Davis	Walter Matthews
Jessica Buchanan	Wynn Miller
India Delaney	Marie Wallace
Rex Cooper	Paul Sparer
Tom Cooper	Ernest Thompson
Chuck Hillman	Edward Winter
Dr. Stan Kurtz	Michael Lipton
Ginger Kurtz	Meg Winter
	Fawne Harriman
	Renne Jarrett
Leo Kurtz	Gene Fanning
Eve Lawrence	Bibi Besch
Julian Cannel	Joel Crothers
Dr. Terri Martin	Gloria Hoy
Frieda Lang	Polly Rowles
Becky Winkle	Jane Rose
Doris Hiller	Gretchen Wyler
Mark Mercer	Stanley Grover
Edith Mercer	Judy Searle
Tony Cooper	Barry Jenner
	Doug Chapin
Mrs. Benson	Eleanor Phelps
Greg Mercer	Gary Swanson
Pamela Davis	Pamela Toll
Crystal Ames	Diahn Williams
Danny Catsworth	Melinda Plank
Mitch Farmer	Dick Shoberg
Bill Greeley	Bill Hunt
Andrea Moore	Harriet Hall
Emily Moore	Lois Kibbee
Phil	Bob Gabriel
Kenny	Ed Bryce
Philip Matson	Frank Scofield
Dana Morton	Chris Pennock
Karen MacMillan	Nancy Pinkerton
Jasper Delaney	Ralph Clanton
Zoe Cannel	Lois Smith
Rafe Carter	Philip Sterling
Carter Matson	Jay Gregory
Virgil Paris	Marc Alaimo
Heather Lawrence	Audrey Landers
Luke MacKenzie	Robert Burr
Lai Ling	Helen Funai
Bobby Hanson	Matthew Greene
Joey Cooper	Sean Wood
Buffy	Roxanne Gregory
Carrie Wheeler	Jobeth Williams
Chip Williams	Roger Rathburn
Kate Cannell	Tina Sloan
Jerry Kane	James O'Sullivan
Lena Andrews	Abby Lewis
Victoria Paisley	Veleka Gray
Jack Wheeler	Bill Joyce
Jill Farmer	Susan MacDonald

Music: Chet Kingsbury, Charles Paul.
Announcer: Bill Wolff.
Executive Producer: Lyle B. Hill.
Producer: Sid Sirulnuck.
Director: Joseph K. Chomyn, Jack Coffy, Bruce Minnix.

SOMERSET—30 minutes—NBC—March 30, 1970–December 31, 1976. Originally titled *Another World in Somerset.*

1123 SONG BY SONG

Variety. A musical salute to American lyricists. The program, videotaped in London, highlights the careers of Alan Jay Lerner, Frederick Loewe, E. Y. Harburg, Lorenz Hart, Dorothy Fields, Howard Dietz, Oscar Hammerstein, and Sheldon Harnick.

Host: Ned Sherin.
Regulars: Millicent Martin, David Kernan, Gemma Craven, Linda Lewis, Polly James, Elaine Stritch.
Orchestra: Peter Knight.
Music Associate: Richard Holmes.
Music Adaptation: Peter Greenwald.
Producer: Ned Sherin.
Associate Producer: Deke Arlon.
Director: Vernon Lawrence.

SONG BY SONG—60 minutes—PBS—October 22, 1979–April 28, 1980. 7 programs.

1124 THE SONNY AND CHER SHOW

Variety. Music, songs, dances and comedy sketches.

Hosts: Sonny and Cher (Salvatore Bono and his wife Cher—Cheryl La Piere).
Regulars: Chastity Bono (their daughter), Peter Cullen, Clive Clerk, Murray Riff, Ted Zeigler, Teri Garr, Freeman King, Steve Parker, Ted Bickle, Tom Filari, Ralph Morrow, Billy Van, Murray Langston, The Jaime Rogers Dancers, The Tony Mordente Dancers, The Earl Brown Singers.
Announcer: Peter Cullen.
Orchestra: Jimmy Dale, Marty Paich.
Producer: Allan Blye, Chris Bearde.
Writer: Phil Hahn, Paul Wayne, George Burditt, Coslough Johnson, Bob Arnott, Bob Einstein, Allan Blye, Chris Bearde, Earl Brown.
Director: Jorn Winther, Art Fisher.

THE SONNY AND CHER SHOW—60 minutes—CBS—August 1, 1971–September 5, 1971; December 27, 1971–May 29, 1974. Also titled *The Sonny and Cher Comedy Hour.*

1125 THE SONNY AND CHER SHOW

Variety. Music, songs, dances and comedy sketches.

Hosts: Sonny and Cher.
Regulars: Ted Zeigler, Billy Van, Peter Cullen, Jack Harnell, Richard Lewis, Felix Silla.
Orchestra: Harold Battiste.
Special Musical Material: Billy Barnes, Earl Brown.
Producer: Nick Vanoff.
Director: Tim Kiley.
Choreographer: Jaime Rogers.

THE SONNY AND CHER SHOW—60 minutes—CBS—February 1, 1976–March 18, 1977.

1126 THE SONNY COMEDY REVUE

Variety. Music, songs, dances and comedy sketches.

Host: Sonny Bono.

Regulars: Teri Garr, Freeman King, Ted Zeigler, Peter Cullen, Billy Van, Murray Langston.
Announcer: Peter Cullen.
Orchestra: Lex DeAzevedo.
Producer: Allan Blye, Chris Bearde.
Writer: George Burditt, Coslough Johnson, Bob Arnott, David Panich, Ronny Graham, Chris Bearde, Allan Blye, Bob Einstein.
Director: Art Fisher.
Choreographer: Jaime Rogers.

THE SONNY COMEDY REVUE—60 minutes—ABC—September 22, 1974–December 29, 1974.

1127 SONS AND DAUGHTERS

Drama. A depiction of the last innocence of American youth as seen through the eyes of Anita Cramer and Jeff Reed, seniors at Southwest High School in Stockton, California, during the 1950s.

CAST

Anita Cramer	Glynnis O'Connor
Jeff Reed	Gary Frank
Ruth Cramer, Anita's mother	Jan Shutan
Walter Cramer, Anita's father	John S. Ragin
Lucille Reed, Jeff's mother (a widower)	Jay W. McIntosh
Danny Reed, Jeff's brother	Michael Morgan
Jeff and Anita's friends:	
Evie Martinson	Debralee Scott
Murray "Moose" Kerner	Barry Livingston
Mary Anne	Laura Siegel
Stash	Scott Colomby
Charlie	Lionel Johnston
Lisa	Chris Nelson
Tina	Randi Kallan
Marylou	Teresa Medaris
Dana	Cheryl Linde
Angie	Bonnie Van Dyke

Music: James Di Pasquale.
Executive Producer: David Levinson.
Producer: Michael Gleason.

SONS AND DAUGHTERS—60 minutes—CBS—September 12, 1974–November 6, 1974. "Senior Year," the 90-minute pilot film, aired on CBS on March 22, 1974.

1128 SOUL TRAIN

Musical Variety. Performances by Soul personalities.

Host: Don Cornelius.
Regulars: The Soul Train Dancers.
Announcer: Sid McCoy, Joe Cobb.
Theme Music: Don Cornelius, Dick Griffy.
Producer: Don Cornelius.
Director: Sid McCoy, J. D. Lobue.

SOUL TRAIN—60 minutes—Syndicated 1971.

1129 SPACE ACADEMY

Science Fiction. The series, set in the year A.D. 3732, depicts the exploits of the Nova Blue Team, a group of young cadets assigned for training to the man-made planetoid Space Academy. Their experiences, as they patrol, protect and explore the universe, are dramatized.

CAST

Commander Gampu	Jonathan Harris
Cadet Laura Gentry	Pamelyn Ferdin
Captain Chris Gentry	Ric Carrott
Cadet Adrian	Maggie Cooper
Lt. Paul Jerome	Ty Henderson
Cadet Tee Gar	Brian Tochi
Loki, the alien ally	Eric Greene

The Robot: Peepo.

Music: Yvette Blais, Jeff Michael.
Executive Producer: Norm Prescott, Lou Scheimer.
Producer: Arthur H. Nadel.
Director: Jeffrey Hayden, Ezra Stone, Arthur H. Nadel.
Creator: Allen Ducovny.

SPACE ACADEMY — 25 minutes — CBS — September 10, 1977 – September 8, 1979.

1130   SPACE: 1999

Science Fiction. In the year 1999, shortly after an early warning system is established on the moon to repel alien invaders, a radioactive chain reaction blasts the moon out of its Earth orbit. Three hundred men and women are marooned as the moon slowly begins to drift in space, seeking a new planet to which to affix itself. Considered the invaders by the inhabitants of other planets, the marooned earthlings struggle to combat the life forms of distant worlds, the elements of outer space, and sustain life on their new world in its odyssey across the universe.

CAST

Commander John Koenig	Martin Landau
Dr. Helena Russell	Barbara Bain
Prof. Victor Bergman	Barry Morse
Maya, the beautiful alien ally	Catherine Schell
Tony Verdeschi, the security officer	Tony Anholt
Captain Alan Carter	Nick Tate
Sandra Benes, the communications officer (a.k.a. San)	Zienia Merton
Yasko, a communications officer	Yasuko Negazumi
Dr. Bob Mathias	Anton Phillips
Dr. Ben Vincent	Jeffrey Kisson
Bill Fraser, a member of Moonbase Alpha	John Hug
Peter Irving, same as Bill	Michael Culver
Dr. Ed Spencer	Sam Destor
Nurse	Hazel McBride
David Kano, a member of Moonbase Alpha	Prentis Hancock
Commissioner Simmonds	Roy Dotrice

Opening Narration: Barbara Bain.
Music: Barry Gray, Vic Elms, Derek Wadsworth.
Executive Producer: Gerry Anderson.

Producer: Sylvia Anderson, F. Sherwin Greene, Fred Freiberger.
Director: Lee H. Katzin, Val Guest, Robert Lynn, Kevin Connor, Tom Clegg, Bob Brooks, Peter Medak, David Tomblin, Ray Austin, Bob Kellett, Charles Crichton.

SPACE: 1999 — 60 minutes — Syndicated 1975.

THE SPACE SENTINELS

See *The Young Sentinels.*

1131   SPEAK UP AMERICA

Human Interest. People speak directly into the camera and reveal their thoughts concerning issues that vitally affect their lives.

Moderators: Marjoe Gortner, Jayne Kennedy, Rhonda Bates, Herb Brooks, Felicia Jeter, Magic Johnson.
Artist: Sergio Aragonés.
Music: Billy Barnes.
Theme Vocal: Jim Kirk and the TM Singers.
Supervising Producer: John Barbour, Bob Wynn.
Executive Producer: George Schlatter.
Producer: Lloyd Thaxton, Andy Friendly.
Field Producer: Peter Brown.
Associate Producer: Gary Necessary.
Writer: David Panich, Gene Farmer, John Barbour, Bill Dana, George Schlatter.
Director: Dave Caldwell.
Art Director: Robert Keene.

SPEAK UP AMERICA — 60 minutes — NBC — April 22, 1980 – April 29, 1980. 2 episodes. August 1, 1980 – October 10, 1980. 9 episodes.

1132 SPECIAL BRANCH

Crime Drama. The series, set in England, depicts the exploits of the Special Branch, an elite team of Scotland Yard undercover agents. Produced in London by Thames TV.

CAST

Chief Inspector Craven	George Sewall
Chief Inspector Tom Haggerty	Patrick Mower
Chief Inspector Strand	Paul Eddington
Commander Fletcher	Frederick Jaeger

Music: Robert Earley.
Executive Producer: George Taylor.
Producer: Ted Childs.

SPECIAL BRANCH — 60 minutes — Syndicated (to the U.S.) in 1976.

1133 SPECIAL EDITION

Documentary. Filmed versions of magazine stories.

Hostess: Barbara Feldon.
Music: Richard La Salle.
Producer: Alan Sloan.
Director: Steve Kattin.

SPECIAL EDITION — 30 minutes — Syndicated 1977.

1134 SPECIAL TREAT

Anthology. A series of specials featuring comedy, drama, music and song geared to children.

Executive Producer: Daniel Wilson, Linda Gottlieb.
Producer: Fran Spears, Phyllis Minoff.
Animation Producers: Norm Prescott, Lou Scheimer.
Animation Director: Hal Sutherland.

Included:

Rodeo Red and the Runaway. The story of Stacy Winslow, a 13-year-old runaway who learns about compassion and understanding from a rugged farm woman who takes her in.

Cast: Ella McCune: Geraldine Fitzgerald; Stacy Wilson: Marta Kober; Chet: Gil Rogers; Barbara: Marlena Lustik.

Big Henry and the Polka Dot Kid. The story of the relationship between a 10-year-old boy and a blind dog.

Cast: Luke Baldwin: Chris Barnes; Uncle Henry: Ned Beatty; Edwina: Estelle Parsons; Stokey: Barry Corbin.

Treasure Island. An animated version of the Robert Louis Stevenson story about Long John Silver's search for Captain Flint's buried treasure.

Hostess: Melissa Sue Anderson.
Voices: Long John Silver: Richard Dawson; Capt. Flint: Larry Storch; Jim Hawkins: Davy Jones; Squire Trelawney: Larry D. Mann; Parrot: Dallas McKennon; Mother: Jane Webb.

Blizzard. A struggle for survival as seen through the experiences of two teenagers who are stranded by a blizzard in a mountainous area.

Cast: Cindy Reichart: Lisa Jane Persky; Tony: Michael Mullins.

SPECIAL TREAT — 60 minutes — NBC — Premiered: October 21, 1975.

1135   SPEED BUGGY

Animated Cartoon. The exploits of teenagers Debbie, Tinker and Mark, and their car, *Speed Buggy*, which possesses a Saint Bernard-like personality, as they travel throughout the country to help people in trouble.

Voice of Speed Buggy: Mel Blanc.
Voices: Chris Allen, Arlene Golonka, Phil Luther, Jr., Hal

Smith, Michele Road, Sid Miller, Ron Feinberg, Virginia Gregg, John Stephenson, Ira Paran.
Music: Hoyt Curtin, Paul DeKorte.
Executive Producer: William Hanna, Joseph Barbera.
Producer: Iwao Takamoto.
Director: Charles A. Nichols.

SPEED BUGGY — 30 minutes — CBS — September 8, 1973 – August 31, 1974; ABC — September 6, 1975 – September 4, 1976; CBS — January 28, 1978 – September 2, 1978.

1136   SPENCER'S PILOTS

Adventure. The exploits of Cass Garrett and Stan Lewis, charter pilots for Spencer Aviation, a California-based organization that undertakes hazardous assignments.

CAST

Cass Garrett	Christopher Stone
Stan Lewis	Todd Susman
Spencer Parish, their employer	Gene Evans
Linda Dann, Spencer's secretary	Margaret Impert
Mickey "Wig" Wiggins, the mechanic	Britt Leach

Music: Bruce Broughton, Jerrold Immel, Morton Stevens.
Executive Producer: Bob Sweeney, Edward H. Feldman.
Producer: Larry Rosen.
Director: Bill Bixby, Marc Daniels, Don Weis, Ernest Pintoff, Bruce Bilson, Gordon Hessler.

SPENCER'S PILOTS — 60 minutes — CBS — September 17, 1976 – November 19, 1976.

1137   SPIDER-MAN

Animated Cartoon. Completing his notes following a demonstration on radioactivity, New York Central High School student Peter Parker is bitten by a spider that has been exposed to the deadly effects of the demonstration.

Returning home, he realizes that the spider's venom has become part of his bloodstream and that he has absorbed the proportionate power and ability of a living spider.

Developing a special costume to conceal his true identity, and acquiring a position as a reporter for the *New York Daily Bugle* (to learn of trouble immediately), he institutes a battle against crime, dispensing justice as the mysterious Spider-Man.

VOICES

Peter Parker/ Spider-Man	Bernard Cowan Peter Soles
Betty Brandt, a reporter	Peg Dixon
J. Jonah Jameson, the editor	Paul Kligman

Music: Ray Ellis.

Theme: "Your Friendly Neighborhood Spider-Man" by Bob Harris and Paul Francis Webster.
Executive Producer: Robert L. Lawrence, Ralph Bakshi.
Producer: Ray Patterson.
Director: Ralph Bakshi, Ray Patterson, Grant Simmons, Sid Marcus, Clyde Geronimi.
Creator: Stan Lee.

SPIDER-MAN—30 minutes—ABC—September 9, 1972–August 30, 1969; March 22, 1970–September 6, 1970. 52 episodes. Syndicated. See also: *The Amazing Spider-Man*, in the regular program section.

1138 SPIDER-WOMAN

Animated Cartoon. While in her father's lab, Jessica Drew, the young daughter of a famous scientist, is bitten by a poisonous spider. With only one hope of saving his daughter's life, Dr. Drew injects her with an experimental spider serum—a serum that not only saves her life, but endows her with extraordinary powers. Stories depict Jessica's exploits, as editor-publisher of *Justice Magazine*, to battle evil. (By doing a twirling striptease, much in the same manner as does Diana Prince to become Wonder Woman, Jessica becomes the mysterious, costumed Spider-Woman.)

Additional Characters: Jeff Hunt, Jessica's photographer; and Billy Drew, Jessica's nephew.
Voice of Jessica Drew / Spider-Woman: Joan Van Ark.
Voices: Bryan Scott, Vic Perrin, Karen Machon, Larry Carroll, Tony Young, John Milford, Lou Krugman, John Mayer, Ilene Latter.
Announcer: Dick Tufeld.
Music: Eric Rodgers.
Executive Producer: David DePatie, Friz Freleng.
Producer: Lee Gunther.
Director: Bob Richardson.
Creator: Stan Lee.

SPIDER-WOMAN—25 minutes—ABC—September 22, 1979–March 1, 1980.

1139 SPIN-OFF

Game. Placed before each of two husband-and-wife teams are five wheels that have been marked with numbers (1 to 6) and spin at the rate of 17 numbers per second. A question is read and the team that correctly answers it receives a chance to play the spinning wheels. One player activates the wheels by pressing a green plunger. The other player pushes a red plunger that automatically stops the spinning wheel and reveals a number. Since scoring follows the rules of poker, they can either keep it or spin it off and try for a different number (only three spins are permitted per wheel). Once the decision is made, another question is asked and the game follows in the same manner (five questions are played per game). The team that scores the highest number values (as in cards) wins the game and the money associated with the numbers (1 pair: $50; 2 pair: $75; 3 of a kind: $100; straight: $125; full house: $150; 5 of a kind: $200).

Host: Jim Lange.
Music: Score Productions.
Executive Producer: Nick Nicholson, E. Roger Muir.
Producer: Willie Stein.
Director: Bob Schwarz.

SPIN-OFF—30 minutes—CBS—June 16, 1975–September 5, 1975. 55 programs.

1140 SPLIT SECOND

Game. Three players compete. Three topics are displayed (e.g., *Mad* magazine, *Playboy* magazine and *World* magazine) and a question is read that refers to them ("Pick one of these current magazines and tell me did it begin publishing before or after 1960"). Players sound a bell and receive a chance to answer as they are recognized. Each player chooses one of three topics and states his answer. If all three players choose the same topic and answer correctly, each receives five dollars; if two choose the same topic and answer correctly, those two players each receive ten dollars; if only one player is correct, he scores twenty-five dollars. (Answers: *Mad* and *Playboy* before 1960; *World* after 1960.) Several such rounds are played and the contestant with the highest cash score is the winner.

Host: Tom Kennedy.
Announcer: Jack Clark.
Music: Score Productions.
Producer: Stu Billet.
Director: Bob Synes.

SPLIT SECOND—30 minutes—ABC—March 20, 1972–June 27, 1975.

1141 STAR BLAZERS

Animated Cartoon. In the year A.D. 2199, Earth faces its greatest challenge when it is suddenly attacked by the evil beings of the planet Gamalon. Because of Earth's refusal to surrender, the Gamalons begin bombarding it with Planet Bombs, which release deadly radioactive poisons. In defense, the population has been forced to construct cities beneath the ground. The continual bombardment, which has destroyed the Earth's surface, is now seaping into the ground and threatening to destroy what is left of life on the planet. Still not willing to surrender, and with scientists predicting that the planet will only survive another year, the Earth Defense Fleet launches its last hope to save the world—Earth Flag Ship 225. The series depicts Earth's last-ditch battle against the Gamalons and their attempts to reach the planet Iscandar where hope of ridding the Earth of radiation lies.* Produced in Japan and dubbed in English. Voice credits are not translated into English (nor are American voices credited). Original title (translated from Japanese): *Star Cruiser Yamato.*

Characters: Captain Avatar; Cadets Derek and Alex Wildstar; Cadet Mark Venture; Nova, the medical center nurse; Dr. Saine, the head of the medical center; the Gamalon leader.

Music: Hiroshi Miyagawa.
Producer (Japanese): Yoshinobu Nishizaki.
Producer (English): Theodore Page (for Claster Television Productions and Sunwagon Productions, Inc.).
Director (Japanese): Reiji Matsumoto.
English Theme Lyrics: Ginny Redington.

STAR BLAZERS—30 minutes—Syndicated 1979. 60 episodes.

*A spaceship crash-lands on Mars where a message is found from Queen Starsha of the Planet Iscandar offering to help Earth. Starsha possesses Cosmo D.N.A., a device that will rid the Earth of radioactivity and save it from destruction. Iscandar, however, is 148,000 light years away from Earth—a situation that poses a serious problem. Queen Starsha does not have the proper means by which to transport Cosmo D.N.A., and man, having never traveled such a distance, must reach Iscandar—and return within one year to save the planet Earth. To accomplish this feat, the Star Force Fleet is organized and an ancient, but once (and still) great battleship, the *Arko*, is now Earth's only hope for survival.

1142 STAR CHART

Music. The program, set in Music Central, charts the progress of music stars (who also perform live) based on surveys in *Record World, Billboard* and *Cash Box* magazines.

Host: Terry David Mulligan.
Assistants: Donna Marie and Louise (as identified).
Music Consultant: Richard Mack.
Executive Producer: Doug Hutton.
Producer: Ken Gibson.
Director: Michael Watt.

Choreographer: James Hubbard.
Art Director: Danny Chan.

STAR CHART—30 minutes—Syndicated 1980.

1143 THE STARLAND VOCAL BAND

Variety. Music, songs, dances and comedy sketches.

Starring: The Starland Vocal Band: Bill Danoff, Taffy Danoff, Margot Chapman, Jon Carroll.
Regulars: Mark Russell, David Letterman, Jeff Altman, Peter Bergman.
Announcer: David Letterman.
Musical Conductor: Eddie Karam.
Musical Director: Milt Okin.
Executive Producer: Jerry Weintraub.
Producer: Al Rogers.
Writer: April Kelly, George Geiger, David Letterman, Phil Proctor, Peter Bergman.
Director: Rick Bennewitz.
Art Director: Ken Johnson.

THE STARLAND VOCAL BAND—30 minutes—CBS—July 31, 1977–September 2, 1977. 6 programs.

1144 THE STARLOST

Science Fiction. Setting: Earth in the year A.D. 2790. Unable to marry Rachel because he is the son of a poor farmer and not considered worthy of her, Devon defies the law and speaks in protest. Deemed unsuitable by the elders, he is sentenced to death for his actions. Escaping his bonds and seeking a place of shelter, Devon enters a forbidden cave in which the Earth Ship Ark lies. As he explores the ship, he touches a control panel that activates a computer, and from its host, Mulander 165, he learns of the fate of Earth: "In the year A.D. 2285, a catastrophe ... threatened all Earth life with extinction ... so the Committee of Scientists ... set about selecting desirable elements of Earth life to seed other planets ... to do this, the committee ... had to build Earth Ship Ark ... an organic cluster of environmental domes called biospheres, looped to each other through tubular corridors for life support power and communication. In the biospheres we have representative segments of Earth's population, three million souls in all. Whole, separate ecologies sealed from each other and isolated to preserve their characteristics. ... Earth Ship Ark was launched to seek out and find a solar system of class six star ... Earth Ship Ark traveled for one hundred years before ... there was an accident. Earth Ship Ark locked in collision course with class G solar star, an unidentified sun ... no further data recorded."

Returning to his home in Cypress Corners, Devon seeks out Rachel and they return to the ship. They are followed by Garth, the man who is pledged to marry her. Unable to persuade Rachel to return with him, Garth remains, determined to protect Rachel from Devon.

The series depicts the adventures of Devon, Rachel and Garth, as they explore the various biospheres searching for someone or something to explain the mystery of the great catastrophe and save the remains of Earth life by locating a class six star—the Starlost. Produced in Canada.

CAST

Devon	Keir Dullea
Rachel	Gay Rowan
Garth	Robin Ward
Mulander 165, the computer host	William Osler

Music: Score Productions.
Executive Producer: Doug Trumbull, Jerry Zeitman.
Producer: Bill Davidson.

THE STARLOST—60 minutes—Syndicated 1973. 16 episodes.

1145   STAR MAIDENS

Science Fiction. Far away in the solar system Proxsema Centauri there exists the planet Medusa, a world of advanced, humanlike life in which women are the rulers and men subservient. For one thousand orbits the populace enjoyed a life of peace and serenity. Then suddenly, the great comet Dionesis, with its awesome force, passed over the planet; Medusa's orbit was altered and the planet slowly dragged toward the frozen regions of outer space. Before its final destination—a planet of ice—the Medusians plan and construct a new world beneath the surface.

Now, frozen, and having drifted for generations, the planet locks itself on to a solar system in which another life-supporting planet—Earth—is discovered. The Earth, however, contradicts the Medusians' programmed society and is declared out of bounds to all its citizens.

As with all laws, this, too, is violated when two Medusian men, Adam and Shem, escape to Earth and thus open the doorway for the inhabitants of the two worlds. The series depicts incidents in the lives of the Earthlings and Medusians as they meet and interact for the first time.

CAST

Fulvia, a Medusian leader	Judy Geeson
Octavia, a Medusian leader	Christiane Kruger
Dr. Liz Becker, an Earth scientist	Lisa Harrow
Adam, Fulvia's servant	Pierre Brice
Shem, Adam's friend	Gareth Thomas

The Medusian P.A.

Announcer	Penelope Horner
Professor Evans, an Earth scientist	Derek Farr
Kate Moss, an earthling	Jenny Morgan
Dr. Rudi Schmitt, an Earth scientist	Christian Quadflieg
Octavia's assistant	Ann Maj Britt
Clara, the head of the Supreme Council of Medusa	Dawn Addams
Andrea, a Medusian	Uschi Mellin

Incidental Music: Friedel Berlipp.
Star Maidens Music Theme: Patrick Aulton.
Producer: James Gatward.
Director: James Gatward. Wolfgang Storch, Freddie Francis.
Creator: Eric Paice.

STAR MAIDENS—30 minutes—Syndicated 1977. Produced in England.

1146   STARSKY AND HUTCH

Crime Drama. The exploits of Dave Starsky and Ken "Hutch" Hutchinson, plainclothes detectives with the Metropolitan Division of the Los Angeles Police Department.

CAST

Det. Dave Starsky	Paul Michael Glaser
Det. Ken Hutchinson	David Soul
Capt. Harold Dobey, their superior (pilot film)	Richard Ward
Capt. Harold Dobey (series)	Bernie Hamilton
Huggy Bear, their informant	Antonio Fargas
Fat Rollo, their informant	Michael Lerner

Music: Lalo Schifrin, Tom Scott, Jack Elliott, Allyn Ferguson, Shorty Rogers.
Starsky and Hutch Theme: Tom Scott.
Executive Producer: Aaron Spelling, Leonard Goldberg.
Producer: Joseph T. Naar.
Director: George McCowan, Bob Kelljan, Don Weis, Earl Bellamy, David Soul, Fernando Lamas, Randal Kleiser, Claude Starrett, Jr., Sutton Roley, Paul Michael Glaser, Barry Shear, Ivan Dixon, Dick Moder.
Creator: William Blinn.

STARSKY AND HUTCH—60 minutes—ABC—September 10, 1975–August 28, 1979. Syndicated. The 90-minute pilot film aired on ABC on April 30, 1975.

1147   STAR TREK

Science Fiction. The series, set in the twenty-second century (later, the twenty-third century) follows the voyages of the starship U.S.S. *Enterprise*, representing the United Federation of Planets, as it explores the endless universe, seeking new life, new worlds and new civilizations.

CAST

Capt. James Kirk	William Shatner
Mr. Spock, the science officer; half earthling, half Vulcan	Leonard Nimoy
Dr. Leonard "Bones" McCoy, the chief medical officer	DeForest Kelley
Lieutenant Uhura, the communications officer	Nichelle Nichols
Lt. Montgomery "Scotty" Scott, the chief engineer	James Doohan
Yeoman Janice Rand	Grace Lee Whitney
Nurse Christine Chapel	Majel Barrett
Ensign Paval Chekov, a navigator	Walter Koenig
Mr. Sulu, the security chief	George Takei

Semi-Regular Crew Members:

Kevin Riley	Bruce Hyde
Lieutenant Starnes	James Wellman
Lt. John Farrell	Jim Goodwin
Angela	Barbara Baldavin
Lt. Kelowitz	Grant Woods
Lt. Hanson	Hagan Beggs
Transporter Chief Kyle	John Winston
Mr. DePaul	Sean Kenny
Lt. Palmer	Elizabeth Rogers
Lt. Leslie	Eddie Paskey
Robert Fox, the Ambassador of the United Federation of Planets	Gene Lyons

Enterprise identification number: NCC 1701.

Narrator: William Shatner.
Music: Alexander Courage, Fred Steiner, Gerald Fried, Wilbur Hatch, George Duning, Sol Kaplan.
Executive Producer Gene Roddenberry.
Producer: John Meredyth Lucas, Gene L. Coon, Fred Freiberger.
Associate Producer: John D. F. Black, Robert H. Justman.
Writer: George Clayton Johnson, Dorothy Fotana, Gene Roddenberry, Samuel A. Peeples, John D. F. Black, Richard Matheson, Stephen Kandel, Robert Bloch, Adrian Spies, Simon Wincelberg, Barry Trivers, Paul Schneider, Oliver Crawford, Fredric Brown, Gene L. Coon, Boris Sobelman, Stephen Carabatsos, Carel Wilber, Robert Hamner, Nathan Butler, Don Ingalls, Theodore Sturgeon, Gilber Ralston, Jerome Bixby, Max Ehrlich, Norman Spinrad, D. C. Fontana, David P. Harmon, Art Wallace, David Gerrold, Judd Crucis, John Kingsbridge, Lawrence Wolfe, Lee Cronin, Margaret Armen, Jean Lisette Aroests, Rick Vollaerts, Judy Barnes, Chet Richards, Meyer Dolinsky, Arthur Heineman, Joyce Muskat, John Meredyth Lucas, Lee Erwin, Jerry Sohl, Stanley Adams, Shari Lewis, Jeremy Tarcher, Michael Richards.
Director: Marc Daniels, Herschel Daugherty, Ralph Senensky, Harvey Hart, James Komack, John Meredyth Lucas, John

Newland, Joseph Pevney, Jud Taylor, Robert Sparr, Michael O'Herlihy, Herb Wallerstein, Murray Golden, David Alexander, Marvin Chomsky, Joseph Sargent, Herbert Kenwith, Don McDougall, Gerd Oswald, Robert Gist, James Goldstone, Vincent McEveety, Tony Leader, Lawrence Dobkin, Leo Penn.
Creator: Gene Roddenberry.

STAR TREK—60 minutes—NBC—September 8, 1966–April 4, 1969; June 3, 1969–September 9, 1969. 78 episodes. Syndicated.

1148   STAR TREK

Animated Cartoon. The series details the further explorations of the starship *Enterprise*. A continuation of the previous title.

VOICES

Captain James Kirk	William Shatner
Mr. Spock, the science officer	Leonard Nimoy
Dr. Leonard McCoy	DeForest Kelley
Lieutenant Uhura	Nichelle Nichols
Lt. Montgomery Scott	James Doohan
Mr. Sulu, the security officer	George Takei
Ensign Paval Chekov	James Doohan
Nurse Christine Chapel	Majel Barrett

Music: Yvette Blais, Jeff Michael.
Producer: Norm Prescott, Lou Scheimer.
Director: Hal Sutherland.

STAR TREK—30 minutes—NBC—September 8, 1973–August 30, 1975. Syndicated.

1149   STEPTOE AND SON

Comedy. The British series on which America's *Sanford and Son* is based. The program, which has not been broadcast in the United States, details the humorous adventures of a father and son team of rag and bone men (junk dealers).

CAST

Albert Ladysmith Steptoe, the father	Wilfrid Brambell
Harold Kitchener Steptoe, his son	Harry H. Corbett

Their cart-horse: Hercules (later, Delilah).

STEPTOE AND SON—30 minutes—Produced by the BBC from 1963 to 1973.

1150   STEVE ALLEN'S LAUGH-BACK

Comedy. Highlights of Steve Allen's television career are shown via film clips from his various series during the 1950s and 1960s.

Host: Steve Allen.
Regulars: Jayne Meadows, Louis Nye, Bill Dana, Martha Raye, Don Knotts, Skitch Henderson, Pat Harrington.

Music: The Terry Gibbs Sextet.
Executive Producer: Jerry Harrison.
Producer: Roger Ailes.
Director: John Rumbaugh, Anthony Carl.

STEVE ALLEN'S LAUGH-BACK — 90 minutes — Syndicated 1976.

1151   STOCKARD CHANNING IN JUST FRIENDS

Comedy. The story of Susan Hughes, a girl on the rebound from a broken marriage, and her experiences as the assistant manager at the Beverly Hills Fountain of Youth Health Spa.

CAST

Susan Hughes	Stockard Channing
Victoria Chasen, Susan's married sister	Mimi Kennedy
Milt DeAngelo, Susan's employer	Lou Criscuolo
Angelo DeAngelo, Milt's son	Albert Insinnia
Leonard Scribner, Susan's neighbor	Gerrit Graham
Coral, the waitress at the health spa juice bar	Sydney Goldsmith
Miranda DeAngelo, Milt's wife	Liz Torres
Mrs. Fisher, a spa customer	Joan Toletino

Music: Doug Gilmore.
Theme: Delaney Bramlett.
Supervising Producer: Peter Locke, Al Rogers.
Executive Producer: David Debin.
Producer: Al Rogers, Nick Arnold, George Bloom.
Director: Robert Drivas, Rick Bennewitz, Joan Darling, Bob LaHendro, Jay Sandrich, J. D. Lobue, Will MacKenzie.
Creator: Nick Arnold

STOCKARD CHANNING IN JUST FRIENDS — 30 minutes — CBS — March 4, 1979 – May 6, 1979; June 10, 1979 – August 11, 1979. 13 episodes.

1152   THE STOCKARD CHANNING SHOW

Comedy. A revised version of the previous title. The adventures of Susan Goodenow, a pretty divorcée who acquires a job as assistant to Brad Gabriel, a TV consumer advocate and host of *The Big Rip-off* on KXLA-TV in West Hollywood. The series follows Susan's antics as she dons various disguises in an attempt to expose the conmen and rip-off artists.

CAST

Susan Goodenow	Stockard Channing
Brad Gabriel, her employer	Ron Silver
Earline Cunningham, Susan's friend	Sydney Goldsmith
Gus Clyde, the owner of the station	Max Showalter
Mr. Cramer, Susan's landlord	Jack Somack
Alf, the not-too-bright station security officer	Bruce Baum
Lisa Cartwright, Susan's neighbor	Maureen Arthur

Barton Blair, the head of programming and demographics	Marty Cohen
Gus's wife	Valorie Armstrong
Bonnie, the sandwich girl	Marcie Barkin
Wendy Simon, Susan's assistant	Wendie Jo Sperber

Music: Doug Gilmore.
Theme Vocal: Delaney Bramlett.
Executive Producer: Aaron Ruben.
Producer: George Yanok.
Writer: Aaron Ruben, George Yanok, John Boni, Mickey Rose, Mitzi McCall, Ann Convy.
Director: Jeff Bleckner, Jay Sandrich, Will MacKenzie, James Burrows.
Creator: Nick Arnold, Eric Cohen.
Art Director: Ken Johnson.

THE STOCKARD CHANNING SHOW — 30 minutes — CBS — March 24, 1980 – April 28, 1980; June 7, 1980 – June 28, 1980. 11 episodes.

1153   STONE

Crime Drama. The story of Dan Stone, a tough homicide detective with the Metropolitan Division of the Los Angeles Police Department, and a sudden, best selling novelist. The situation causes a conflict with what he loves most: his family and his job.

CAST

Sgt. Dan Stone	Dennis Weaver
Gene Paulton, the police chief	Pat Hingle
Diane Stone, Dan's wife (pilot film)	Mariette Hartley
Diane Stone (series)	Beth Brickell
Officer Buck Rogers, Dan's assistant	Robby Weaver
Jill Stone, Dan's daughter	Nancy McKeon
Britte Martin, Dan's friend, a clinical psychologist	Barbara Rhoades
Murray, Dan's agent	Joby Baker

Dan's publisher: Burton House Publishing.

Music: Mike Post and Pete Carpenter.
Theme: "Stone" by Dennis Weaver and Nancy Adams.
Supervising Producer: Alex Beaton.
Executive Producer: Stephen J. Cannell, Donald Bellisario.
Producer: J. Rickley Dumm, Juanita Bartlett.
Director: Corey Allen, Winrich Kolbe, Stephen J. Cannell, Paul Stanley, Harry Winer.

STONE — 60 minutes — ABC — January 14, 1980 – March 17, 1980. 8 episodes. The two-hour pilot film aired on ABC on August 26, 1979.

1154   STOP SUSAN WILLIAMS

Drama. The series, which details the exploits of Susan Williams, a beautiful photographer for the *New York Dispatch*, follows her attempts to solve the murder of her brother and expose a group of conspirators who are planning a mission that could start a third world war.

CAST

Susan Williams	Susan Anton
Bob Richard, the managing editor of the paper	Ray Walston
Jennifer, the owner of the paper	Marj Dusay
Jack Schoengarth, Susan's aide	Michael Swan
Anthony Korf, the head of the conspiracy group	Albert Paulsen

Narrator: Brad Crandall.
Music: Joe Harnell, Charles R. Casey, Les Baxter.
Supervising Producer: B.W. Sandefur.
Executive Producer: Kenneth Johnson.
Producer: Richard Milton, Paul Samuelson.
Director: Kenneth Johnson, Reza S. Badiyi, Richard S. Harwood.
Creator: Kenneth Johnson.

STOP SUSAN WILLIAMS — 20 minutes — NBC — February 27, 1979 – May 1, 1979 (as a segment of *Cliffhangers*). 10 episodes.

1155   THE STOREFRONT LAWYERS

Crime Drama. The cases and courtroom defenses of David Hansen, Deborah Sullivan and Gabriel Kay, attorneys associated with the Neighborhood Legal Services (N.L.S.) in Century City, Los Angeles.

CAST

Attorney David Hansen	Robert Foxworth
Attorney Deborah Sullivan	Sheila Larken
Attorney Gabriel Kay	David Arkin
Attorney Roberto Barelli	A Martinez
Mr. Thatcher, the defense attorney	Gerald S. O'Loughlin
Rachel, the legal services secretary	Royce Wallace

Music: Harper MacKay, Morton Stevens.
Executive Producer: Bob Stivers.
Producer: Bill Waters, Ronald Kibbee, Dominique Perrin, Harold Gast.

THE STOREFRONT LAWYERS — 60 minutes — CBS — September 16, 1970 – January 13, 1971. Spin-off series: *Men at Law*.

1156   STORY THEATRE

Fables. Stories, based on tales by Aesop and the Brothers Grimm, are performed against the background of an improvisational theater with performers speaking their lines in narration, as if reading from a book, and providing their own narration.

Starring: Paul Sills Broadway Repertoire Company: Bob Dishy, Mina Kolb, Peter Bonerz, Judy Graubart, Richard Liber-

tini, Melinda Dillon, Paul Sand, Hamid Hamilton Camp, Ann Sweeny, Severn Darden, Dick Schall, Eugene Troabnick, Mickey LaGare, Jeff Brownstein.

Executive Producer: Burt Rosen.
Producer: David Winters.
Writer: Paul Sills.
Director: Jorn Winther.

STORY THEATRE — 30 minutes — Syndicated 1971. 26 episodes.

1157   STRANGE PLACES

Documentary. Films exploring various remote regions of the world. Produced by the BBC.

Host-Narrator: Peter Graves.
Music: Gerherd Trede.
Producer-Director: Ruben Brandern.

STRANGE PLACES — 30 minutes — Syndicated 1973. Also known as *Other People, Other Places*.

1158   THE STRANGE REPORT

Mystery. The series, set in London, England, follows the investigations of Adam Strange, a criminologist who intervenes in domestic and international crises to help police solve ingenious criminal acts of injustice.

CAST

Adam Strange	Anthony Quayle
Evelyn McLane, his assistant	Anneke Wells
Ham Gynt, his assistant	Kaz Garas

Music: Edwin Astley, Roger Webb.
Executive Producer: Norman Felton.
Producer: Buzz Berger.
Director: Peter Medak, Charles Crichton, Ray Austin, Sidney Hayers, David Greene, Roy Ward Baker.

THE STRANGE REPORT — 60 minutes — NBC — January 8, 1971 – September 12, 1971. 16 episodes.

1159   THE STRAUSS FAMILY

Biography. A seven-part dramatization depicting the lives of composers Johann Strauss and his son, Johann Strauss, Jr., the "Waltz Kings of the nineteenth century."

CAST

Johann Strauss	Eric Woolfe
Anna Strauss, his wife	Anne Stallybrass
Johann Strauss, Jr.	Stuart Wilson
Josef Lanner	Derek Jacobi
Emilie Trampusch	Barbara Ferris
Olga	Ania Marson
Madamee Smirnitska	Jill Balcon
Hirsh	David de Keyser
Dommayer	Christopher Benjamin
Lucari	Sonia Dresdel
Hetti	Margaret Whiting
Edi	Tony Anholt
Josef Strauss	Nikolas Simmonds

Star Trek. Front, from left, DeForest Kelley, William
Shatner and Leonard Nimoy. Back, from left, James
Doohan, Walter Koenig, Majel Barrett, Nichelle Nichols
and George Takei.

Space: 1999. At left, Martin Landau and Barbara Bain. At
right, Catherine Schell.

Lilli	Georgia Hale
Annele	Hilary Hardiman
Thereas	Amanda Walker
Max Steiner	William Dexter
Adele	Lynn Farleigh

Music: The London Symphony Orchestra.
Conductor: Cyril Ornadel.
Executive Producer: Cecil Clarke.
Producer: David Reid.
Writer: David Reid, David Butler, Anthony Skene.
Director: David Giles, David Reid, Peter Potter.

THE STRAUSS FAMILY — 60 minutes — ABC — May 5, 1973 – June 16, 1973.

1160   THE STREETS OF SAN FRANCISCO

Crime Drama. The series, set in San Francisco, depicts the investigations of Lieutenant Mike Stone, a street-smart homicide detective, and Steve Keller, his impulsive, college-trained partner.

CAST

Lt. Mike Stone	Karl Malden
Det. Steve Keller	Michael Douglas
Lt. Lessing	Lee Harris
Officer Haseejian	Vic Tayback
Jean Stone, Mike's daughter	Darleen Carr
Inspector Dan Robbins	Richard Hatch
Sgt. Sekulovich	Art Passarella

Music: Patrick Williams, John Elizalde.
Executive Producer: Quinn Martin.
Supervising Producer: Russell Stoneman.
Producer: John Wilder, Cliff Gould, William Robert Yates, Adrian Samish, Arthur Fellows.
Director: Virgil W. Vogel, Walter Grauman, William Wiard, Barry Crane, Robert Day, John Badham, Paul Stanley, Harry Falk, George McCowan, Kenneth Gilbert, William Hale, Bernard L. Kowalski, Barry Shear, Richard Donner, Theodore J. Flicker, Michael Preece, Michael O'Herlihy, Richard Lang, Dennis Donnelly, Don Medford, Seymour Robbie.

THE STREETS OF SAN FRANCISCO — 60 minutes — ABC — September 16, 1972 – June 23, 1977. Syndicated.

1161   STRUCK BY LIGHTNING

Comedy. Shortly after inheriting the Brightwater Inn, a decrepit Victorian Lodge in Maine, Ted Stein, a science teacher and descendant of the famous Dr. Frankenstein, discovers that Frank, the caretaker, is the 230-year-old creation of his great-great-grandfather. After much difficulty, Frank convinces Ted not to sell the inn, but to stay and try to re-create Dr. Frankenstein's

lost formula so he can remain alive. The series, which is an update of the Frankenstein legend, follows Ted's efforts to run the inn and save Frank by developing the special serum he needs every 50 years to maintain life.

CAST

Frank	Jack Elam
Ted Stein	Jeffrey Kramer
Nora, the manager of the inn	Millie Slavin
Glenn Hillman, a long-time boarder	Bill Erwin
Brian, Nora's son	Jeff Cotler
Walt, Nora's husband	Richard Stahl

Music Thomas Talbert.
Theme: "You Are So Beautiful."
Executive Producer: Arthur Fellows, Terry Keegan.
Producer: John Thomas Lenox, Bob Ellison, Steve Pritzker, Marvin Miller.
Writer: Fred Freeman, Lawrence J. Cohen, Bryan Joseph, Michael Russinow.
Director: Joel Zwick.
Art Director: Arch Bacon.

STRUCK BY LIGHTNING — 30 minutes — CBS — September 19, 1979 – October 3, 1979. 3 episodes. (Four episodes were scheduled to air, but, due to poor ratings, the fourth episode was never shown.)

1162   STUDS LONIGAN

Drama. A three-part miniseries based on the once-banned trilogy by James T. Farrell. The story, which is set in Chicago and spans fifteen years (1916 – 1931), follows the life of Studs Lonigan, an aimless, two-fisted young Irishman, and his personal and desperate quest for value — a quest that leads him to despair.

CAST

Studs Lonigan	Harry Hamlin
Mary Lonigan, his mother	Colleen Dewhurst
Paddy Lonigan, his father	Charles Durning
Loretta Lonigan, his sister	Jessica Harper
Fran Lonigan, his sister	Devon Ericson
Danny O'Neill	Brad Dourif
Catherine	Diana Scarwid
Father Gilhooley	Dolph Sweet
Davey Cohen	Sam Weisman
Weary Riley	David Wilson
Lucy Scanlon	Lisa Pelikan
Studs, as a boy	Dan Shor
Weary, as a boy	Fredric Lehne
Danny, as a boy	Kevin O'Brien
Davey, as a boy	Corey Pepper
Moxey	James Callahan
Helen Borax	Leslie Ackerman
Sally	Nora Heflin
Phil Rolfe	Jed Cooper
Eileen	Laurie Heinemann
Carroll	Bob Neill

Also: Anne Seymour, Jay W. McIntosh, Betty Cole, Shelley Juttner, James Canning, Bob Hastings, Pamela Hayden.
Music: Ken Lauber.

Executive Producer: Lee Rich, Philip Capice.
Producer: Harry Sherman.
Writer: Reginald Rose.
Director: James Goldstone.
Art Director: Jan Scott.
Costumes: Bill Jobe.

STUDS LONIGAN — 2 hours — NBC — March 7, 1979 – March 21, 1979. 3 episodes.

1163   STUMPERS

Game. Two teams, composed of one celebrity captain and one noncelebrity contestant, compete. A stumper, which contains three clues to the identity of a person, place or thing, is revealed to one member of one team. That player relates one of the clues to a member of the opposing team. If the player identifies the stumper he scores 15 points. If, within five seconds, he is stumped, a second clue is given (worth ten points), and finally a third clue (worth five points). If he is still stumped, the team at play is given a chance to solve it and win 15 points. Each player receives two turns at giving and guessing stumpers per round. Two such rounds are played, the second being the double-up round (points are 30, 15 and 10) and the team that scores the highest is the winner.

Host: Allen Ludden.
Music: Alan Thicke.
Executive Producer: Lin Bolen.
Producer: Walt Case, Noreen Colen.
Director: Marty Pasetta, Jeff Goldstein.

STUMPERS — 30 minutes — NBC — October 4, 1976 – December 31, 1976. 30 programs.

1164   SUGAR TIME

Comedy. The series, set in Los Angeles, follows the heartaches, loves, struggles and misadventures of Maxx Douglas, Diane Zukerman, and Maggie Barton, three starry-eyed Rock singers who comprise the act "Sugar" and hope to make the big time.

CAST

Maxx Douglas	Barbi Benton
Diane Zukerman	Didi Carr
Maggie Barton	Marianne Black
Al Marks, the owner of the Tryout Room Night Club	Wynn Irwin
Lightning Jack Rappaport, a performer at the Tryout Room	Charles Fleischer
Paul Landson, Diane's boyfriend	Mark Winkworth

Musical Director: David Garland.
Musical Supervision: Paul Williams.
Theme Vocal: "Girls, Girls, Girls" by Barbi Benton, Didi Carr and Marianne Black.

Executive Producer: James Komack.
Producer: Hank Bradford, Martin Cohan, Gary Belkin.
Director: Bill Hobin, Howard Storm, Bill Foster.
Choreographer: Helen Funai.
Creator: James Komack.

SUGAR TIME — 30 minutes — ABC — August 13, 1977 – September 3, 1977. 4 episodes. April 10, 1978 – May 29, 1978. 7 episodes.

1165   THE SULLIVANS

Serial. The series, set in suburban Melbourne, Australia, during World War II, chronicles the lives of the Sullivan family: parents Dave and Grace, and their children John, Tom, Terry and Kitty. The underlying theme is the focus on the changes in family relationships and the effect the war has on Australia. Produced in Australia by Crawford Productions.

CAST

Dave Sullivan	Paul Cronin
Grace Sullivan	Lorraine Bayly
Tom Sullivan	Steven Tandy
John Sullivan	Andrew McFarlane
Terry Sullivan	Richard Morgan
Kitty Sullivan	Susan Hannaford
Hans Kauffman	Leon Lissek
Lottie Kauffman	Marcella Burgoyne
Anna Kauffman	Ingrid Mason
Uncle Harry	Michael Caton
Aunty Rose	Maggie Dence
Norm Baker	Norman Yemm
Mrs. Jessup	Vivean Gray
Bert Duggan	Peter Hehir
Lill Duggan	Noni Hazlehurst
Maggie Hawyard	Vikki Hammond
Jack Fletcher	Reg Gorman
Mr. Jarvis	Fred Parslow

Producer: Henry Crawford, Jock Blair.
Director: Ian Jones.

THE SULLIVANS — 30 minutes — Syndicated (to the U.S.) in 1980. Produced in Australia in 1976.

1166   SUNSHINE

Comedy-Drama. The series, set in Vancouver, B.C., Canada, follows the life of Sam Hayden, a happy-go-lucky musician who is left in charge of his young daughter, Jill, after the death of his wife.

CAST

Sam Hayden	Cliff De Young
Jill Hayden, his daughter (pilot film)	Lindsay Greenbush Sidney Greenbush
Jill Hayden (series)	Elizabeth Cheshire
Nora, Sam's girlfriend	Meg Foster
Billy Weaver, Sam's friend	Bill Mumy
Cory Givits, Sam's friend	Corey Fischer
Ms. Cox, Jill's teacher	Barbara Bosson
Kate Hayden, Sam's wife (pilot film)	Cristina Raines

Music: Hal Mooney.
Theme: "Sunshine" by John Denver, Dick Kniss, Mike Taylor.

Producer: George Eckstein.

Director: Leon Benson, John Badham, Robert Day, Bernard L. Kowalski, Daniel Haller (most of the series).

Program Open:

Sam (over scene of him singing the theme, "Sunshine"):
That's me, Sam Hayden, my wife died a couple of years ago . . . so now there's just me and Jill, that's my little girl. What do I do? Well, I wash dishes, drive cabs, walk dogs, anything— anything to make a buck . . . I've got a kid to raise, right? Or I don't know, sometimes I think we're really raising each other. Anyhow, my friends Weaver and Givits and me, we have this trio, and I think we'll really make it someday, but meanwhile Jill and I are hanging in there and it's working out pretty good, well, most of the time.

SUNSHINE—30 minutes—NBC —March 6, 1975–June 19, 1975. 13 episodes. The two-hour, 30-minute pilot film aired on NBC on November 9, 1973. On December 12, 1977, NBC aired a special called "Sunshine Christmas," which reunited the original cast in a story that found Sam returning home to celebrate Christmas with his family.

1167   THE SUPER

Comedy. The trials and tribulations of Joe Girelli, the Italian-American superintendant of a less-than-fashionable apartment building in New York City. Plagued by tenant complaints, building condemnation threats and a family "which ain't got no respect," he struggles to solve problems, survive the daily tensions of city living and enjoy what simple pleasures life affords him.

CAST

Joe Girelli	Richard S. Castellano
Francesca Girelli, his wife	Ardell Sheridan
Joanne Girelli, their daughter	Margaret E. Castellano
Anthony Girelli, their son	Bruce Kirby, Jr.
Frankie Girelli, Joe's brother	Phil Mishkin
Officer Clark, a tenant	Ed Peck
Dottie Clark, his wife	Virginia Vincent
Sylvia Stein, a tenant	Janet Brandt
Janice Stein, Sylvia's daughter	Penny Marshall
Pizuti, Joe's friend	Vic Tayback
Fritz, Joe's friend	John Lawrence
Herbie, Joe's friend	Wynn Irwin
Louie, Joe's friend	Louis Basile

Music: Larry Grossman.
Executive Producer: Gerald I. Isenberg.
Producer: Alan Rafkin.
Writer: Rob Reiner, Phil Mishkin.
Director: Alan Rafkin.

THE SUPER—30 minutes—ABC —June 21, 1972–August 23, 1972. 13 episodes.

1168   SUPER FRIENDS

Animated Cartoon. The exploits of Aquaman, Batman and Robin, Superman, Wonder Woman, and Marvin, Wendy and Wonder Dog, indestructible crusaders who have united to form the Justice League of America. Stories depict their battles against the sinister forces of evil.

Voices: Superman: Danny Dark; Wonder Woman: Shannon Farnon; Batman: Olan Soule; Robin: Casey Kasem; Aquaman: Norman Alden; Narrator: Ted Knight.
Music: Hoyt Curtin, Paul DeKorte.
Executive producer: William Hanna, Joseph Barbera.
Producer: Iwao Takamoto.
Director: Charles A. Nichols.

SUPER FRIENDS—55 minutes— ABC—September 8, 1973–August 30, 1975. Spin-off series: *Challenge of the Super Friends* and *The New Super Friends Hour.*

1169   THE SUPER GLOBETROTTERS

Animated Cartoon. The exploits of the Harlem Globetrotters, a basketball team, as super crime fighters dispensing justice throughout the world.

Voices: Curley Neal: Stu Gilliam; Geese Ausbie: John Williams; Sweet Lou Dunbar: Adam Wade; Nate Branch: Scatman Crothers; Twiggy Sander: Buster Jones; Crime Globe: Frank Welker; Announcer: Michael Rye.
Music: Hoyt Curtin.
Executive Producer: William Hanna, Joseph Barbera.
Producer: Art Scott, Alex Lovy.
Director: Ray Patterson, George Gordon, Carl Urbano.

THE SUPER GLOBETROTTERS— 30 minutes—NBC—September 22, 1979–December 1, 1979.

1170   SUPERSONIC

Music. Performances by Rock personalities. The program does not include a host, announcer, regulars, or a studio orchestra (guests provide their own music). Produced in England.

Producer-Director: Mike Mansfield.

SUPERSONIC—30 minutes— Syndicated 1976.

1171   SUPERTRAIN

Anthology. Varying stories (adventure, comedy, drama) that follow brief incidents in the lives of passengers on the Supertrain— an ultramodern, atom-powered steam turbine streamlined train. Designed by the Trans-Allied Corporation to improve passenger service, the train can travel from New York to Los Angeles in thirty-six hours (at a speed of 200 mph).

CAST

Harry Flood, the engineer	Edward Andrews
Dave Noonan, the passenger relations officer	Patrick Collins
Dr. Dan Lewis, the physician	Robert Alda
Rose Casey, the nurse	Nita Talbot
George Boone, the chief porter	Harrison Page
Gilda, works in the health spa	Aarika Wells
Robert, works in the beauty salon	Charlie Brill
Wally, works in the health spa	William Nuckols
Lou Atkins, the bartender	Michael DeLano
Sharon, the gift shop salesgirl	Valorie Armstrong
The Maitre d'	Fritz Freed

Music: Bob Cobert.
Supervising Producer: Robert Stambler.
Executive Producer: Dan Curtis.
Producer: Anthony Spinner, Rod Amateau.
Director: Dan Curtis, Charles S. Dubin, Barry Crane, David Moessinger, Rod Amateau.
Creator: Donald E. Westlake.

SUPERTRAIN—60 minutes— NBC—February 7, 1979–March 14, 1979; June 2, 1979–June 30, 1979. 5 episodes.

1172   SUPERTRAIN

Anthology. A revised version of the previous title, with emphasis placed on character development and mystery-suspense stories.

CAST

Harry Flood, the engineer	Edward Andrews
George Boone, the passenger relations officer	Harrison Page
Dr. Dan Lewis, the physician	Robert Alda
Penny Whitaker, the social director	Ilene Graff
Wayne Randall, Harry's assistant	Joey Aresco
Tex, the assistant engineer	Ted Gehring
Supertrain Hostess	Rhonda Foxx

Music: Bob Cobert.
Executive Producer: Robert Stambler.
Producer: Donald Gold, Norman Siegel.
Director: Barry Crane, Dennis Donnelly.

SUPERTRAIN—60 minutes— NBC—April 7, 1979–May 5, 1979; July 14, 1979–July 28, 1979. 4 episodes.

1173   SUPER WITCH

Animated Cartoon. The series, set in the town of Riverdale, follows the misadventures of Sabrina, a beautiful, but mischievous teenage witch.

Additional Characters: The Archie Gang (Archie, Veronica, Betty, Reggi, Jughead, Carlos and Hot Dog) and The Groovie Goolies.
Voice of Sabrina: Jane Webb.
Voices: Dallas McKennon, Don Messick, John Erwin, Jose Flores, Howard Morris.
Music: Yvette Blais, Jeff Michael.
Executive Producer: Lou Scheimer, Norm Prescott.
Producer: Don Christensen.

SUPER WITCH—30 minutes— NBC—November 19, 1977–January 28, 1978. 11 episodes. See also *Sabrina, the Teenage Witch.*

1174   THE SURVIVORS

Serial. The struggles and emotional problems of the rich as seen through the activities of the wealthy Carlyle family, the owners of a Wall Street banking empire in New York City.

CAST

Baylor Carlyle, the head of the empire	Ralph Bellamy
Tracy Carlyle Hastings, his daughter	Lana Turner
Philip Hastings, her greedy husband	Kevin McCarthy
Duncan Carlyle, Baylor's son	George Hamilton
Jeffrey Carlyle, Tracy's illegitimate son	Jan-Michael Vincent
Jean Vale, Philip's mistress	Louise Sorel
Jonathan	Louis Hayward
Belle	Diana Muldaur
Riakos	Rossano Brazzi
Miguel Santerra	Robert Viharo
Marguerita	Donna Baccalor
Sheila	Kathy Cannon
Tom	Robert Lipton
Rosemary	Pamela Tiffin
Corbett	Michael Bell

Executive Producer: Walter Doniger.
Producer: Richard Caffey.
Director: Walter Doniger, Michael Caffey, Lee Philips, Harvey Hart, John Newland, Lewis Allen, Don Weis, Marc Daniels.
Creator: Harold Robbins.

THE SURVIVORS—60 minutes— ABC—September 22, 1969–September 17, 1970. 15 episodes.

1175   S.W.A.T.

Crime Drama. The cases of the Special Weapons and Tactics Unit (S.W.A.T.) of the West California Police Department, a group of five men who assist policemen who are in trouble.

CAST

Lt. Hondo Harrelson	Steve Forrest
Sgt. Deacon Kay	Rod Perry
Officer James Street	Robert Urich
Officer T. J. McCabe	James Coleman
Officer Dominic Luca	Mark Shera

Music: Barry De Vorzon, John Parker.
Executive Producer: Aaron Spelling, Leonard Goldberg.
Producer: Robert Hamner, Barry Shear, Gene Levitt.

Stockard Channing in Just Friends. From center, then clockwise from left, Lawrence Pressman, Stockard Channing (seated), Lou Criscuolo, Mimi Kennedy, Gerrit Graham, Sydney Goldsmith and Albert Insinnia.

Sugar Time. From left, Marianne Black, Barbi Benton and Didi Carr.

Supertrain. Top left, Supertrain Hostess Rhonda Foxx stands next to the actual model for Supertrain. Two miniature versions of Supertrain built to 1-1/2-inch scale (top right) and 3/4-inch scale (lower left) were used for exterior shots. The photo at lower right shows a depiction of the New York City train yards and illustrates the size and detail of the miniatures used for the series.

Director: George McCowan, Richard Benedict, Earl Bellamy, William Crane, Bruce Bilson, Harry Falk, Dick Moder, Reza S. Badiyi.
Creator: Robert Hamner.

S.W.A.T. — 60 minutes — ABC — February 24, 1975 – June 26, 1976; September 24, 1976 – April 15, 1977.

1176   SWEEPSTAKES

Anthology. Comedy-dramas that predict incidents in the lives of million-dollar lottery finalists (three per show). Characters are followed from entry through the sweepstakes drawing to see how each copes with the prospect of winning or losing.

CAST

Gregg Harris, the M.C. of the
    KBEX-TV Channel 6 show (in
    Hollywood) on which the final
    drawing is held   Edd Byrnes
Cindy, his assistant   Sally Kim
                            Wendy Raebeck
                            Jo McDonnell
                            Blake Harris
                            Robin Evans
                            Katherine Greko

Music: George Tipton, Fred Werner.
Theme Vocal: Ron Dante.
Supervising Producer: John Furia, Jr.
Executive Producer: Robert Dozier.
Producer: Ben Kadish.
Director: Philip Leacock, David Moessinger, Ernest Pintoff, E.W. Swackhamer, David Swift, Irving J. Moore, James Sheldon.
Creator: Thomas L. Miller, Robert Dozier.

SWEEPSTAKES — 60 minutes — NBC — January 26, 1979 – March 30, 1979. 9 episodes.

1177   THE SWEENEY

Crime Drama. The series, set in London, follows the exploits of the Flying Squad, an elite team of specially trained Scotland Yard police detectives.

CAST

Inspector Jack Regan   John Thaw
Sergeant Carter   Dennis Waterman
Chief Inspector Haskins Garfield Morgan

Music: Harry South.
Executive Producer: Lloyd Shirley, George Tayler.
Producer: Ted Childs.

THE SWEENEY — 60 minutes — Syndicated 1976.

1178   SWISS FAMILY ROBINSON

Adventure. The series, set during the nineteenth century, follows the adventures of the Robinson family, shipwrecked on an almost deserted tropical island after a storm at sea, as they struggle for survival and seek a way to escape. Based on the story by Johann Wyss.

CAST

Karl Robinson, the father   Martin Milner
Lotte Robinson, his wife   Pat Delany
Fred Robinson, their son (pilot
    film)   Michael-James Wixted
Fred Robinson (series)   Willie Aames
Ernie Robinson, their son   Eric Olson
Jeremiah Worth, a marooned
    sea dog   Cameron Mitchell
Helga Wagner, the Robinson's
    adopted daughter   Helen Hunt

The Robinsons' parrot: Mozart.

Music: Lionel Newman, Richard La Salle, Arthur Morton.
Executive Producer: Irwin Allen.
Producer: Arthur Weiss.
Director: Harry Harris, Georg Fenady, Leslie H. Martinson.

SWISS FAMILY ROBINSON — 60 minutes — ABC — September 14, 1975 – April 11, 1976. The two-hour pilot film aired on ABC on April 15, 1975.

1179 THE SWISS FAMILY ROBINSON

Adventure. The series, set on an uncharted island in the year 1881, follows the adventures of the Robinsons, a Swiss family who were shipwrecked on a deserted island, which they name New Switzerland, after their ship was destroyed in a tropical storm. Episodes depict their struggles for survival and attempts to escape from the island. Closely follows the novel by Johann Wyss; more so than the previous title. Produced in Canada.

CAST

Johann Robinson, the father Chris Wiggins
Elizabeth Robinson,
    his wife   Diana Leblanc
Marie Robinson, their
    daughter   Heather Graham
Franz Robinson, their son   Micky O'Neill
Ernest Robinson, their son Michael Duhig

Narrator: Chris Wiggins.
Music: Score Productions.
Music Supervision: Lewis Lehman.
Producer: Gerald Mayer.
Director: Peter Carter, Gerald Mayer, Don Haldane.

THE SWISS FAMILY ROBINSON — 30 minutes — Syndicated 1976.

1180   SWITCH

Crime Drama. The exploits of Frank MacBride, a retired bunco cop, and Pete Ryan, an ex-con, partners in the Ryan-MacBride Private Detective Organization. Stories relate their investigations as they attempt to beat swindlers at their own game.

CAST

Frank MacBride   Eddie Albert
Pete Ryan   Robert Wagner
Maggie Philbin, their
    secretary   Sharon Gless

Malcolm Argos, their assistant, the owner
    of the Bouziki Bar   Charlie Callas
Revel, the bar waitress   Mindi Miller
Wang, the cook   James Hong
Lieutenant Schiller   William Bryant

Music: Stu Phillips, Glen A. Larson, Ed Sauter, James Di Pasquale, Don Vincent, Dick Halligan.
Supervising Producer: Joe L. Cramer.
Executive Producer: Glen A. Larson, Matthew Rapf.
Producer: Leigh Vance, Jack Laird, John Guss, Paul Playdon, John Peyser, Gene Kearney.
Director: Noel Black, Bruce Kessler, John Peyser, Sutton Roley, Leo Penn, Sigmund Neufeld, Jr., Bruce Evans, Glen A. Larson, E. W. Swackhamer, Walter Doniger, Edward Abroms, Paul Krasny, Phil Bondelli, Bruce Kessler, David Friedkin, John Newland, Alf Kjellin, Douglas Heyes, Jerry London, David Impastata.

SWITCH — 60 minutes — CBS — September 9, 1975 – January 16, 1978; June 25, 1978 – September 3, 1978. Syndicated. The 90-minute pilot film aired on CBS on March 21, 1975.

1181   SWORD OF JUSTICE

Adventure. Jack Cole, a wealthy playboy, is framed and imprisoned for a crime he did not commit (embezzling $2.5 million from his father's company). Bitter at the wrong done him, Jack vows to get even with the crooks who framed him and begins by learning the tricks of the criminals' trade from his fellow prisoners. Released from prison two years short of his five-year sentence for good behavior, Jack teams with his cellmate, Hector Ramirez, and together they reveal the people responsible for the frame. Instilled with a goal to seek justice, Jack continues in his dual capacity: a New York playboy by day and an anonymous crime fighter by night, helping the federal authorities get the goods on white collar thieves.

Jack's trademark is a playing card — the three of spades — the three to represent the three years he spent in prison, the spade to indicate his task has been completed. These words are written on the card: "The spade is the Sword of Justice. It's rapier marks the end."

CAST

Jack Cole   Dack Rambo
Hector Ramirez   Bert Rosario
Arthur Woods, the federal
    agent Jack anonymously
    helps   Alex Courtney

Music: John Tartaglia.
Executive Producer: Glen A. Larson.

Supervising Producer: Michael Sloan.
Producer: Joe Boston, Herman Groves.
Director: Daniel Haller. Curtis Harrington, Ray Austin, Michael Caffey, Christian I. Nyby, II, Joseph Pevney, Winrich Kolbe, Larry Stewart.
Creator: Glen A. Larson, Michael Gleason.

SWORD OF JUSTICE — 60 minutes — NBC — October 7, 1978 – October 26, 1978; December 17, 1978 – December 31, 1978; July 11, 1979 – August 11, 1979. 10 episodes. The series was "sneak previewed" on September 10, 1978.

1182   SYLVESTER AND TWEETY

Animated Cartoon. The series, comprised of Warner Brothers theatrical cartoons, focuses on the attempts of Sylvester the cat to catch himself a decent meal — Tweety, the foxy canary.

Voice Characterizations: Mel Blanc.
Music: William Lava, Milt Franklin, John Seely, Carl Stalling.
Director: Robert McKimson, Friz Freling, Chuck Jones.

SYLVESTER AND TWEETY — 30 minutes — CBS — September 11, 1976 – September 3, 1977.

1183   SZYSZNYK

Comedy. The story of Nick Szysznyk (pronounced Ziznik), an ex-Marine Sergeant turned playground supervisor, as he attempts to salvage the financially troubled Northeast Community Center in Washington, D.C.

CAST

Nick Szysznyk   Ned Beatty
Ms. Harrison, the district
    supervisor   Olivia Cole
Sandi Chandler, Nick's
    assistant   Susan Lanier
Leonard Kreigler, the assistant
    to the director   Leonard Barr
Ray Gun, one of the teenagers
    at the center   Thomas Carter
Ralph, same as Ray   Jarrod Johnson
Tony, same as Ray   Scott Colomby
Bernard Fortwengler, same
    as Ray   Barry Miller

Music: Doug Gilmore.
Theme Vocal: Sonny Curtis.
Executive Producer: Jerry Weintraub.
Producer: Rich Eustis, Michael Elias.
Director: Peter Bonerz, James Burrows.
Creator: Jim Mulligan, Ron Landry.

SZYSZNYK — 30 minutes — CBS — August 1, 1977 – August 29, 1977. 5 episodes. December 7, 1977 – January 27, 1978. 5 episodes.

T

1184 TABITHA

Comedy. A spin-off from *Bewitched*. Events in the life of Tabitha Stevens, a beautiful witch (the daughter of Samantha and Darrin Stevens) who is employed as a production assistant at KXLA-TV in Los Angeles, and a young woman who frequently resorts to bits of conjured magic to achieve her goals.

CAST

Tabitha Stevens (pilot film)	Liberty Williams
Tabitha Stevens (series)	Lisa Hartman
Adam Stevens, her brother (pilot film)	Bruce Kimmel
Adam Stevens (series)	David Ankrum
Paul Thurston, a TV host at KXLA	Robert Urich
Marvin Decker, the producer of Paul's show	Mel Stewart
Minerva, Tabitha's aunt, a witch	Karen Morrow
Dr. Bombay, the warlock doctor	Bernard Fox

Music: Dick De Benedictis, Shorty Rogers.
Theme Vocal: "It's Magic" by Lisa Hartman.
Executive Producer: Jerry Mayer.
Producer: George Yanok.
Director: Charles S. Dubin, Charles R. Rondeau, Murray Golden, Herb Wallerstein, George Tyne.
Creator: Jerry Mayer.

TABITHA—30 minutes—ABC—September 10, 1977—January 14, 1978. 11 episodes. The thirty-minute pilot film aired on ABC on April 24, 1976.

1185 TAKE A GOOD LOOK

Game. A cast performs a dramatic sketch that relates clues to the identity of a mystery guest. The first celebrity panelist (of three who appear) to identify the guest receives one point. Winners are the highest scorers and prizes are awarded to the home viewers who are represented by the panelists.

Host: Ernie Kovacs.
Announcer: Johnny Jacobs.
Regular Panelists: Edie Adams, Cesar Romero, Carl Reiner.
Dramatic Cast: Ernie Kovacs, Peggy Connelly, Bob Lauher.
Executive Producer: Irving Mansfield, Peter Arnell.
Producer: Joe Landis, Milt Hoffman.
Director: Barry Shear, George Behar.

TAKE A GOOD LOOK—30 minutes—Syndicated 1978. 20 episodes (which were originally broadcast on ABC from October 22, 1959 through July 21, 1960).

1186 TAKE FIVE WITH STILLER AND MEARA

Comedy. A series of humorous blackouts satirizing various aspects of everyday life.

Starring: Jerry Stiller and Anne Meara.
Music: Score Productions.
Executive Producer: John Davis.
Producer: William Watts.
Director: Ivan Cury.

TAKE FIVE WITH STILLER AND MEARA—05 minutes—Syndicated 1977.

1187 TAKE KERR

Cooking. Cooking tips and advice.

Host: Graham Kerr.
Producer: Treena Kerr.

TAKE KERR—05 minutes—Syndicated 1975.

1188 TAKE MY ADVICE

Discussion. Four celebrity guests discuss and suggest answers to problems submitted by viewers.

Hostess: Kelly Lange.
Announcer: Bill Armstrong.
Music: Score Productions.
Executive Producer: Burt Sugarman.
Producer: Mark Massari, Ken Salter.
Director: Hank Behar.
Creator: Armand Grant.

TAKE MY ADVICE—25 minutes—NBC—January 5, 1976—June 11, 1976. 105 programs.

1189 TALES OF THE UNEXPECTED

Anthology. Suspense and mystery presentations.

Host-Narrator: William Conrad.
Music: Richard Markowitz, David Shire.
Theme: David Shire.
Executive Producer: Quinn Martin.
Producer: John Wilder, William Robert Yates.
Director: Allen Reisner, Walter Grauman, Harry Falk, Richard Lang.

Included:

Devil Pack. The story of a small, isolated community that is terrorized by fierce wild dogs.

Cast: Jerry Colby: Ronny Cox; Ann Colby: Christine Belford; Sheriff: Van Johnson.

The Mark of Adonis. The story concerns an aging producer who relies on the mysterious rejuvenation process of a doctor to maintain the appearance of a young man.

Cast: Alexander Cole: Robert Foxworth; Viviana: Marlyn Mason; Gerry: Linda Kelsey; Davidion: Victor Jory.

The Final Chapter. The story of Frank Harris, a crusading newspaper reporter who has himself placed on death row in an attempt to write a story about capital punishment. The unexpected occurs when he is scheduled for execution and cannot convince anyone of his masquerade.

Cast: Frank Harris: Roy Thinnes; Warden Greer: Ramon Bieri; Chaplain: Brendon Dillon.

TALES OF THE UNEXPECTED—60 minutes—NBC—February 2, 1977—March 9, 1977.

1190 THE TARZAN AND LONE RANGER ADVENTURE HOUR

Animated Cartoon.

Segments:

Tarzan. New adventures in the life of Tarzan, the protector of the jungle and its inhabitants. See *Tarzan: Lord of the Jungle* for information.

The Lone Ranger. The exploits of the Lone Ranger, a mysterious masked man (the lone survivor of a group of six slain Texas Rangers) and his Indian friend, Tonto, as they strive to help people in trouble in the turbulent days of the Old West.

VOICES

The Lone Ranger	William Conrad
Tonto	Ivan Naranjo

Narrator: William Conrad.
Series Credits:
Music: Yvette Blais, Jeff Michael.
Executive Producer: Norm Prescott, Lou Scheimer.
Producer: Don Christensen.
Art Director: Bob Kline.

THE TARZAN AND LONE RANGER ADVENTURE HOUR—55 minutes—CBS—Premiered: September 6, 1980.

1191 TARZAN AND THE SUPER SEVEN

Animated Cartoon.

Segments:

Batman. See *The New Adventures of Batman* for information.

Isis and the Freedom Force. The exploits of the Freedom Force: Isis, Goddess of the Elements; Hercules, Master of Strength; Merlin, the Master of Magic; Sinbad, Master of the Seven Seas; and Super Samurai, Giant of Justice.

Manta and Moray. The exploits of two super underwater crime fighters: Manta, the last living member of an ancient water-breathing civilization; and Moray, a female human who was rescued by a great whale after a shipwreck, and now joins forces with Manta to battle evil.

Micro Woman and Super Stretch. The exploits of Christy, a young girl who can change herself into Micro Woman, a microscopic sized crime fighter, and her husband, who is actually Super Stretch, a man who can stretch himself into any form.

Tarzan. See *Tarzan, Lord of the Jungle* for information.

Web Woman. When Kelly Webster risks her life to save a strange insect creature from drowning, she is endowed by alien creatures with the power of all insects, a power she uses to battle evil.

Voices: (for "Isis and the Freedom Force," "Manta and Moray," "Micro Woman and Super Stretch," and Web Woman"): Michael Bell, Lennie Weinrib, Linda Gray, Alan Oppenheimer, Bob Holt, Howard Morris, Diane Pershing, Kim Hamilton, Ty Henderson, Joan Van Ark, Joe Stern, Bob Denison.

Live Action Segment:

Jason of Star Command. The exploits of Jason, a space-age soldier of fortune and a member of Star Command, an interplanetary police station. Episodes depict his battle against Dragos, the most sinister element in the universe.

CAST

Jason	Craig Littler
Commander Carnarvin	James Doohan
Cadet Nichole	Susan O'Hanlon
Professor E. J. Parasfoot	Charlie Dell
The Evil Dragos	Sid Haig

Series Credits:
Music: Yvette Blais, Jeff Michael.
Executive Producer: Norm Prescott, Lou Scheimer.
Animated Segments Producer: Don Christensen.
Live Action Segment Producer: Arthur H. Nadel.
Animation Director: K. Wright, Ed Friedman, Gwen Wetzler, Marsh Lamore, Lou Zukor.
Live Action Director: Arthur H. Nadel.

TARZAN AND THE SUPER SEVEN—90 minutes—CBS—September 9, 1978—September 1, 1979. 60 minutes—CBS—September 15, 1979—August 31, 1980.

1192 TARZAN: LORD OF THE JUNGLE

Animated Cartoon. The series, set in Africa, details the exploits of Tarzan, the Lord of the Jungle, as he battles the evils of man and beast. Based on the character created by Edgar Rice Burroughs.

Tarzan's assistant: Nakima, a monkey.

Voice of Tarzan: Robert Ridgely.
Voices: Linda Gray, Joan Gerber,

Ted Cassidy, Barry Gordon, Alan Oppenheimer, Jane Webb.
Music: Yvette Blais, Jeff Michael.
Producer: Norm Prescott, Lou Scheimer.
Director: Don Christensen.
Program Open:
Tarzan: The Jungle; here I was born, and here my parents died when I was an infant. I would have soon perished too if I were not found by a kindly she-ape named Kahla who adopted me as her own and taught me the ways of the wild. I learned quickly and grew stronger each day. And now I share the friendship and trust of all jungle animals. The jungle is filled with beauty and danger, and lost cities filled with good and evil. This is my domain and I protect those who come here, for I am Tarzan, Lord of the Jungle!

TARZAN: LORD OF THE JUNGLE — 25 minutes — CBS — September 11, 1976 – September 2, 1978.

1193   TATTLETALES

Game. Three celebrity couples compete, each representing one third of the studio audience.

In round one, the wives appear on stage, while their husbands are isolated backstage in a soundproof room. A question is read (e.g., "It happened on vacation") and the first player to sound her buzzer signal relates a situation that concerns her marriage and a one- or two-word clue that summarizes the answer. The host presses a button and the husbands appear on television monitors that are placed before each of their mates. The question is restated and the clue is given. The husband who believes it is his wife's response sounds a bell and must relate a similar story. If he is correct, $100 is scored. Round two reverses round one and winners are the highest scoring teams. One thousand dollars is added to the total and it is divided among the studio audience members who are represented by that celebrity couple.

Host: Bert Convy.
Announcer: Jack Clark.
Music: Score Productions.
Executive Producer: Ira Skutch.
Producer: Paul Alter.
Director: Paul Alter.

TATTLETALES — 30 minutes — CBS — February 18, 1974 – March 31, 1978.

1194   TAXI

Comedy. The series, set in New York City, focuses on the antics of the drivers and garage crew of the Sunshine Cab Company.

CAST
Alex Reiger, a cabbie	Judd Hirsch
Elaine Nardo, a cabbie	Marilu Henner
Bobby Wheeler, a cabbie	Jeff Conaway
Tony Banta, a cabbie	Tony Danza
Louie De Palmer, the nasty dispatcher	Danny DeVito
Latka Gravas, the mechanic	Andy Kaufman
John Burns, a cabbie	Randall Carver
Suzanne Burns, John's wife	Ellen Regan
Reverend Jim Ignatowski, a cabbie, a refugee from the 1960s who hasn't quite put his life back together	Christopher Lloyd
Jeff, Louie's assistant	Jeff Thomas
Tommy, the waiter at Mario's, the restaurant hangout	T. J. Castronova
Zena, Louie's girlfriend	Rhea Perlman

Music: Bob James.
Executive Producer: James L. Brooks, Stan Daniels, Ed Weinberger, David Davis.
Producer: Glen Charles, Les Charles.
Director: Ed Weinberger (one episode), James Burrows (series).
Creator: James L. Brooks, Stan Daniels, Ed Weinberger, David Davis.

TAXI — 30 minutes — ABC — Premiered: September 12, 1978.

1195 THE TED KNIGHT SHOW

Comedy. The misadventures of Roger Dennis, the owner of the Mr. Dennis Escort Service in New York City.

CAST
Roger Dennis	Ted Knight
Dottie, his obnoxious secretary	Iris Adrian
Bert Dennis, Roger's brother	Normann Burton
Winston Dennis, Roger's son	Thomas Leopold
The Escort Service Girls:	
Graziella	Cissy Colpitts
Honey	Fawne Harriman
Irma	Ellen Regan
Cheryl	Janice Kent
Phil	Tanya Boyd
Joy	Debbie Harmon

Music: Michael Leonard.
Executive Producer: Mark Rothman, Lowell Ganz.
Producer: Martin Cohan, David W. Dulcon.
Director: Joel Zwick, Howard Storm, Martin Cohan.
Creator: Mark Rothman, Lowell Ganz.

THE TED KNIGHT SHOW — 30 minutes — CBS — April 8, 1978 – May 13. 1978.

1196   TEMPERATURES RISING

Comedy. A comical portrait of life in a hospital as seen through the eyes and antics of Jerry Noland, a doctor assigned to Capitol General Hospital in Washington, D.C. The gambling-inclined intern, with his cohorts, Nurses Ann Carlisle, Mildred MacInerney and Ellen Turner, struggles to aid patients who are in need of financial assistance.

CAST
Dr. Vincent Campanelli, the chief of surgery	James Whitmore
Dr. Jerry Noland	Cleavon Little
Nurse Ann Carlisle	Joan Van Ark
Nurse Mildred MacInerney	Reva Rose
Nurse Ellen Turner	Nancy Fox
Miss Llewellen, Campanelli's secretary	Olive Dunbar

Music: Shorty Rogers.
Executive Producer: Harry Ackerman.
Producer-Director: William Asher.

TEMPERATURES RISING — 30 minutes — ABC — September 12, 1972 – September 4, 1973. Spin-off series, *The New Temperatures Rising Show.*

1197   TENAFLY

Crime Drama. The cases of Harry Tenafly, a private detective employed by Hightower Investigations, Incorporated, in Los Angeles.

CAST
Harry Tenafly	James McEachin
Ruth Tenafly, his wife	Lillian Lehman
Lorrie, his secretary	Rosanna Huffman
Lt. Sam Church	David Huddleston
Herb Tenafly, Harry's son	Paul Jackson
Mrs. Church, Sam's wife	Mary Ann Gibson
Police Chief Vernon	Ford Rainey

Music: Gil Mellé.
Producer: Richard Link, William Levinson.
Director: Robert Day, Richard A. Colla, Bernard L. Kowalski, Jud Taylor, Gene Levitt.
Creator: Richard Levinson, William Link.

TENAFLY — 90 minutes — NBC — October 2, 1973 – January 2, 1974 (as part of *The NBC Wednesday Mystery Movie*); April 30, 1974 – August 26, 1974 (as part of *The NBC Tuesday Mystery Movie*).

1198   TENSPEED AND BROWN SHOE

Adventure. The story of an unlikely pair of private detectives: E. L. "Tenspeed" Turner, a streetwise con artist, and Lionel Whitney, a demure stockbroker whom Turner calls a "brown shoe—a guy in a three-piece suit with brown shoes; a square; a Dow Jones." The series follows their case assignments after they team and form Lionel Whitney Investigations in Los Angeles. A con by Tenspeed to heist gangland money found Lionel becoming his pawn; discovering adventure he could once only get from reading detective stories, Lionel teams with Tenspeed and together incorporate their unique skills to solve their cases. (Lionel's favorite reading matter: *A Mark Savage Mystery* by Stephen J. Cannell, who is the series producer.)

CAST
E. L. "Tenspeed" Turner	Ben Vereen
Lionel Whitney, "Brown Shoe"	Jeff Goldblum
Mike "Scoop" Magill, E.L.'s friend	James Sloyan
Sam Athena, Lionel's landlord	James Beach
Tommy Tedesco, the mobster who brought E. L. and Whitney together	Richard Romanus
The TV newscaster (female), usually at the end of each episode	Tawny Little
John Dalem, E. L.'s parole officer	Nicholas Coster
Bernice Coitney, Dalem's secretary	Candice Azzara
William Whitney, Lionel's father	John Hillerman
Harriet Whitney, Lionel's mother	Dana Wynter

Music: Mike Post and Pete Carpenter.
Supervising Producer: Alex Beaton.
Executive Producer: Stephen J. Cannell.
Producer: Charles Bowman, Juanita Bartlett.
Director: E. W. Swackhamer, Arnold Laven, John Patterson, Reza S. Badiyi, Georg Stanford Brown, Ivan Dixon, Rod Holcomb, Stephen J. Cannell, Harry Winer, Charles Bowman.

TENSPEED AND BROWN SHOE — 60 minutes — ABC — January 27, 1980 – March 30, 1980. 8 episodes. May 30, 1980 – July 11, 1980. 4 episodes.

THE $10,000 PYRAMID

See *The $20,000 Pyramid.*

1199 TEN WHO DARED

Documentary. A ten-episode series that re-creates the explorations of ten famous explorers. Produced in England by the BBC.

CAST
Christopher Columbus	Carlos Ballesteros
Francisco Pizarro	Francisco Cordova
James Cook	Dennis Burgess
Alexander von Humboldt	Matthias Fuchs
Jedediah Smith	Richard Clark
Robert Burke	Martin Shaw
William Wells (Burke's partner)	John Bell
Henry Morton Stanley	Sean Lynch
Charles Doughty	Paul Chapman
Mary Kingsley	Penelope Lee
Roald Amundsen	Per Theodor Hqugen

Host-Narrator: Anthony Quinn.
Producer: Michael Latham.
European Title: *The Explorers,* which is narrated by David Attenborough.

TEN WHO DARED — 60 minutes — Syndicated 1977.

1200 TESTIMONY OF TWO MEN

Drama. A three-part miniseries based on the novel by Taylor Caldwell. The story, which begins with the end of the Civil War and ends at the turn of the century, focuses on the lives of the Ferrier brothers: Jonathan, a crusading physician, and Harald, who seeks an easy life and ready money. *Testimony of Two Men,* produced during a 54-day shooting schedule, is the most lavishly produced and expensively mounted program created expressly for syndication, involving 21 stars, 180 speaking parts, 700 extras, 2,006 costumes, 110 sets and 20 locations. It is also the first series to be produced by Operation Prime Time, a project that allows independent stations to pool their resources and purchase excellent quality, first-run programs.

CAST

Jonathan Matthew Ferrier	David Birney
Harald Joseph Ferrier	David Huffman
Mavis Eaton Ferrier	Linda Purl
Marjorie Farmington Ferrier	Barbara Parkins
Hilda Eaton	Barbara Parkins
Dr. Martin Eaton	Steve Forrest
Adrian Ferrier	William Shatner
Flora Bumstead Eaton	Margaret O'Brien
Dr. Louis Hedler	Tom Bosley
Jenny Heger	Laurie Prange
Kenton Campion	J. D. Cannon
Howard Best	Barry Brown
Father Frank McNulty	Randolph Mantooth
Francis Campion	Kario Salem
Jonas Witherby	Ray Milland
Jeremiah Hadley	Cameron Mitchell
Peter Hagler	Theodore Bikel
Mr. Madden	Dan Dailey
Priscilla Madden	Trisha Noble
Mertyl Hager	Kathleen Nolan
Amelia Forster	Inga Swenson
Mrs. Zachary Robson	Joan Van Ark
Jerome Eaton	John de Lancie
Mavis Eaton (as a girl)	Missy Gold
Dr. Jim Spaulding	Ralph Bellamy
David Paxton	Leonard Frey
Priscilla Madden	Devon Ericson
Elizabeth Best	Lynn Tufeld
Jason Fowler	Jordan Rhodes
Dr. Collins	Jordan Clark
Dr. Abroms	Joel Parks
Jim	Hal Bowker
Anna	Anna O'Neil
Elizabeth (different from above)	Debi Richter
Mrs. Temple	Eve McVegh
Mr. Temple	Larry Watson
Amos	Robert Foulk
Station Master	Herb Vigran
Henrietta Campion	DeAnn Mears
William Simpson	Jeff Corey
Emil Schaefer	Logan Ramsey
Moe Abrams	Joel Parks
Albert Brians	Derek Murcott
Sarah	Lorna Day
Jonathan Ferrier (age 10)	Paul David
Carla	Christine Schneider
Mary Snowden	Geraldine Barron
Union Man	James O'Connell
Steward	Lou Fant
George Foster	Frank Bowline

Narrator: Tom Bosley.
Music: Gerald Fried.
Theme: Michel Colombier.
Producer: Jack Laird.
Writer: James M. Miller, William Hanley, Jennifer Miller.
Director: Larry Yust, Leo Penn.
Art Director: William H. Tuntke, John E. Chilberg II.
Director of Photography: Jim Dickson, Isodore Mankofsky.

TESTIMONY OF TWO MEN — 2 hours (6 hours total) — Operation Prime Time — 1977. 3 episodes.

1201 TEXAS

Serial. The story, set in Houston, Texas, depicts events in the lives of the Cookes, Dekkers and Marshalls, three oil business families. A spin-off from *Another World*.

CAST

Iris Bancroft	Beverlee McKinsey
Ginny Marshall	Barbara Rucker
Paige Marshall	Lisby Larson
Dennis Carrington	Jim Poyner
Victoria Bellman	Elizabeth Allen
Alex Wheeler	Bert Kramer
Reena Cooke	Carla Borelli
Justin Marshall	Jerry Lanning
Dr. Kevin Cooke	Lee Patterson
Clipper Blake	Scott Stevenson
Dr. Courtney Marshall	Catherine Hickland
Dawn Marshall	Dana Kimmell
Colonel Hassin	Maher Boutros
Ryan Connor	Philip Clark
Dr. Bart Walker	Joel Colodner
Princess Jasmin	Donna Cyrus
Striker Bellman	Robert Gerringer
Nita Wright	Ellen Maxted
Samantha Walker	Ann McCarthy
Kate Marshall	Josephine Nichols
Vivian	Gretchen Oehler
Sheik Cehdi	Mitch Gred
Rikki Dekker	Randy Hamilton
Max Dekker	Chandler Hill Harben
Billy Joe Wright	John McCafferty
Mike Marshall	Stephen D. Newman
Terry Dekker	Shanna Reed
Elena Dekker	Caryn Richmond
Maggie Dekker	Shirley Slater

Music: Score Productions.
Executive Producer: Paul Rauch.
Producer: Bud Kloss, Judy Lewis.
Senior Producer: Mary S. Bonner.
Director: Kevin Kelly, John Pasquin.
Remote Sequences Director: Andrew Weyman.
Art Director: Robert Franklin.
Creator: John William Corrington, Joyce Corrington, Paul Rauch.

TEXAS — 60 minutes — NBC — Premiered: August 4, 1980.

1202 THE TEXAS WHEELERS

Comedy. Deserting his family after the death of his wife, Zack Wheeler, a lazy good for nothing, returns to his children in Lamont, Texas, eight months later, intent on sponging off them. Disliked by his elder offspring, Truckie, 24, a general contractor, and Doobie, 17; and loved by the younger, Boo, 12, and T. J., 10, he struggles to revert to his previous, shiftless life, and solve the problems that ensue from four independent children who can't wait to grow up.

CAST

Zack Wheeler, the father	Jack Elam
Truckie Wheeler, his son	Gary Busey
Doobie Wheeler, his son	Mark Hamill
Boo Wheeler, his daughter	Karen Oberdiear
T. J. Wheeler, his son	Tony Becker
The Sheriff	Noble Willingham
Bud, Truckie's friend	Dennis Burkley
Sally, Doobie's girlfriend	Lisa Eilbacher
Bud, a friend	Bill Burton

Music: Mike Post, Pete Carpenter, John Andrew Tartiglia.
Executive Producer: Dale McRaven.
Producer: Chris Hayward.
Director: Jackie Cooper, Bob Claver.
Creator: Dale McRaven.

THE TEXAS WHEELERS — 30 minutes — ABC — September 13, 1974 – October 4, 1974; June 26, 1975 – July 24, 1975.

1203 THAT GIRL

Comedy. The series, set in New York City, tenderly depicts the joys and sorrows of Ann Marie, a would-be actress. She struggles to further her career, support herself by taking various part-time jobs, cope with parents who don't understand her, and share the interests of her boyfriend, Don Hollinger, a reporter for *Newsview* magazine.

CAST

Ann Marie	Marlo Thomas
Don Hollinger, her boyfriend	Ted Bessell
Lou Marie, Ann's father, the owner of the Le Parisienne Restaurant in Brewster, New York	Lew Parker
Helen Marie, Ann's mother	Rosemary DeCamp
Jules Benedict, Ann's drama coach	Bille De Wolfe
Judy Bessimer, Ann's neighbor	Bonnie Scott
Leon Bessimer, Judy's husband	Dabney Coleman
Jerry Myer, Don's co-worker (early episodes)	Bernie Kopell
Jerry Bauman, Don's co-worker (later episodes)	Bernie Kopell
Margie Myer, Jerry's wife (early episodes)	Arlene Golonka
Ruth Bauman, Jerry's wife (later episodes)	Carolyn Daniels
	Alice Borden
Marcy, Ann's friend	Reva Rose
Pete, Ann's friend	Ruth Buzzi
Gloria, Ann's telephone answering service girl	Bobo Lewis
Jonathan Adams, the publisher of *Newsview* magazine	Forrest Compton
	James Gregory
Agnes Adams, Jonathan's wife	Phyllis Hill
Bert Hollinger, Don's father	Frank Faylen
Mildred Hollinger, Bert's wife	Mabel Albertson
Nino, the owner of the Italian restaurant frequented by Ann and Don	Gino Conforti
Mr. Brantano, Ann's landlord	Frank Puglia
Mrs. Brantano, his wife	Renata Vanni

Ann's Agents: The Gilliam and Norris Theatrical Agency:

Seymour Schwimmer	Don Penny
Harvey Peck	Ronnie Schell
Sandy Stone	Morty Gunty
George Lester	George Carlin

Ann's address: 344 West 78th Street (later: 627 East 54th Street).

Music: Walter Scharf, Earle Hagen, Warren Barker, Harry Geller.
Executive Producer: Bill Persky, Sam Denoff.
Producer: Bernie Orenstein, Saul Turteltaub, Jerry Davis.
Director: Jay Sandrich, Homer Powell, James Sheldon, Danny Arnold, Alan Rafkin, Bob Sweeney, Sidney Miller, David MacDearmon, Jeff Hayden, Ted Bessell, John Rich, Bill Persky, Saul Turteltaub, Russ Mayberry, Hal Cooper, Harry Falk, John Erman, James Frawley, Jerry Davis.
Creator: Bill Persky, Sam Denoff.

THAT GIRL — 30 minutes — ABC — September 8, 1966 – September 10, 1971. 136 episodes. Syndicated.

1204 THAT GOOD OLD NASHVILLE MUSIC

Musical Variety. Performances by Country and Western entertainers.

Host: Jim Ed Brown.
Regulars: Marcy and Margie Cates, The Sound Seventy Singers, John Gimble, Ralph Sloan, The Tennessee Travelers.
Music: Jerry Weintraub.
Vocalists: The Dottie Lee Singers.
Executive Producer: Elmer Alley, Bill Fisher.
Producer: Elmer Alley.
Director: Byron Brinkley.
Art Director: Jim Stanley.

THAT GOOD OLD NASHVILLE MUSIC — 30 minutes — Syndicated 1974.

1205 THAT'S CAT

Children. A mixture of music, song and comedy that attempts to explain various aspects of the world to children.

CAST

Alice	Alice Playten
Me	Frank Cala

Music Composed and Performed By: John B. Sebastian.
Executive Producer: Giovani Nigro-Chacon.

ABC

Swiss Family Robinson. Front, from left, Eric Olsen, Pat Delaney and Willie Aames. Back, Helen Hunt and Martin Milner.

CBS

Switch. From left, Eddie Albert, Robert Wagner and Sharon Gless.

ABC

The Texas Wheelers. From lower left, Tony Becker, Mark Hamill, Jack Elam, Karen Oberdiear and Gary Busey.

ABC

That Girl. Marlo Thomas and Ted Bessell.

Producer: Susan Cuscuna.
Director: Joshua White.

THAT'S CAT — 30 minutes — Syndicated 1977.

1206   THAT'S HOLLYWOOD

Documentary. Various aspects of films produced by 20th Century-Fox — from leading ladies, to disaster epics, to westerns — are showcased with on-camera performances and behind-the-scenes preparations.

Narrator: Tom Bosley.
Music: Rudy Raksin.
Supervising Producer: Phillip Savenick.
Executive Producer: Jack Haley, Jr.
Producer: Lawrence Einhorn, Phillip Savenick, Draper Lewis, David Lawrence, David Fein, Bonnie Peterson, Susan Walker, Fletcher Markle, Eytan Keller.

THAT'S HOLLYWOOD — 30 minutes — Syndicated 1977.

1207   THAT'S INCREDIBLE!

Human Interest. Profiles of unusual people and strange phenomena.

Hosts: Cathy Lee Crosby, John Davidson, Fran Tarkenton.
Musical Supervision: Roy Prendergast.
Supervising Producer: Woody Fraser, Alex Pomansanoff.
Executive Producer: Alan Landsburg, Merrill Grant.
Producer: David Yarnell, Deborah Blum, Barbara Shotel, Karen Winters.
Director: Arthur Forrest, Jan S. Rafinkson, Chris Pechin, Mary Hardwick.

THAT'S INCREDIBLE! — 60 minutes — ABC — March 3, 1980 — May 26, 1980. Returned, Premiered: July 21, 1980.

1208   THAT'S MY LINE

Human Interest. The program spotlights the unusual occupations of ordinary people.

Host: Bob Barker.
Assistants: Tiiu Leek, Suzanne Childs.
Announcer: Johnny Olsen.
Music: Bob Cobert.
Executive Producer: Mark Goodson, Bill Todman.
Producer: Mike Gargiulo.
Co-Producer: Jonathan Goodson.
Director: Mike Gargiulo.

THAT'S MY LINE — 60 minutes — CBS — August 9, 1980 — August 23, 1980. 3 episodes.

1209   THAT'S MY MAMA

Comedy. Events in the lives of the Curtis family, residents of Washington, D.C., as seen through the eyes of Clifton Curtis, a 25-year-old bachelor who, while attempting to run his late father's business (Oscar's Barber Shop) and live his own life, constantly finds his life being run by his meddling, well-meaning mother, Eloise.

CAST

Clifton Curtis	Clifton Davis
Eloise "Mama" Curtis	Theresa Merritt
Tracy Taylor, Clifton's sister	Lynne Moody
	Joan Pringle
Leonard Taylor, Tracy's husband, a C.P.A. for Bancock, Schaefer and Fenton	Illunga Adell
Earl Chambers, the postman	Ed Bernard
	Theodore Wilson
Wildcat, Clifton's friend	Jester Hairston
Junior, Clifton's friend	Ted Lange
Josh, Clifton's friend	DeForest Covan
Laura, Eloise's friend	Helen Martin

Address of Oscar's Barber Shop: 14th and Grant Streets.

Music: Jack Eskew, Lamont Dozier.
Executive Producer: Allan Blye, Chris Bearde.
Producer: Walter N. Bien, Gene Farmer, David Pollock.
Director: Herbert Kenwith, Mort Lachman, Arnold Margolin.

THAT'S MY MAMA — 30 minutes — ABC — September 4, 1974 — December 24, 1975.

1210   THEN CAME BRONSON

Drama. Disillusioned after his friend commits suicide, Jim Bronson, a newspaper reporter, resigns. Inheriting his friend's motorcycle, he begins his travels across the United States to discover the meaning of life. Stories depict his involvement with the people he meets.

CAST

Jim Bronson	Michael Parks

Music: George Duning, Richard Shores.
Music Supervision: Harry Lojewski.
Executive Producer: Herbert F. Solow.
Producer: Robert H. Justman, Robert Sabaroff.
Director: Marvin Chomsky (most of the series), William F. Claxton, William Graham.

THEN CAME BRONSON — 60 minutes — NBC — September 17, 1969 — September 9, 1970. 26 episodes. Syndicated.

1211   THESE ARE THE DAYS

Animated Cartoon. Life in America at the turn of the century as seen through the experiences of the Day family, residents of the small town of Elmsville.

VOICES

Martha Day, the mother, a widow	June Lockhart
Cathy Day, her daughter	Pamelyn Ferdin
Danny Day, her son	Jackie Haley
Ben Day, her son	Andrew Parks
Jeff Day, the children's grandfather	Henry Jones
Homer, Jeff's friend	Frank Cady

Music: Hoyt Curtin.
Executive Producer: William Hanna, Joseph Barbera.
Producer: Iwao Takamoto.
Writer: Bernard Kahn, Gene Thompson, Dick Wesson, Sam Locke, Milton Pascal, Leo Rifkin.
Director: Charles A. Nichols.

THESE ARE THE DAYS — 30 minutes — ABC — September 7, 1974 — September 5, 1976.

1212   THICKER THAN WATER

Comedy. Aging and chronically ill for ten years, Jonas Paine, the founder of Paine's Pure Pickles, stipulates that for his children (Nellie, a 40-year-old spinster, and Ernie, a 34-year-old penniless playboy, who dislike each other) to receive an inheritance, they must live in the family residence for five years and operate the family pickle factory.

Stories depict the impatient wait for two feuding siblings as they struggle to live together, operate the business and care for a father who just won't kick the bucket. Based on the British series, *Nearest and Dearest*.

CAST

Nellie Paine, the daughter	Julie Harris
Ernie Paine, the son	Richard Long
Jonas Paine, the father	Malcolm Atterbury
Lily Paine, a cousin	Jessica Myerson
Walter Paine, Lily's husband	Lou Fant
Bert Taylor, the pickle factory foreman	Pat Cranshaw
Lyle Woodstock, Jonas' lawyer	Jim Connell
Agnes Dorsell, a factory employee	Dolores Albin

Music: Michael Melvoin.
Executive Producer: Bob Banner.
Producer: Tom Egan.
Director: Jerry Paris.

THICKER THAN WATER — 30 minutes — ABC — June 13, 1973 — August 8, 1973. 13 episodes.

1213   13 QUEENS BLVD.

Comedy. The series, centered around the lives of Felicia and Steven Winters, who reside at 13 Queens Boulevard in Queens, New York, follows their marital misadventures and the misadventures that befall their friends and neighbors — people who take an interest in each other's lives.

CAST

Felicia Winters	Eileen Brennan
Steven Winters	Jerry Van Dyke
Elaine Dowling, their neighbor	Marcia Rodd
Annie Dowling, Elaine's sister	Susan Elliott
Jill Kepestro, their neighbor	Louise Williams
Millie Kepestro, Jill's mother	Helen Page Camp
Lois Sherman, their neighbor	Frances Lee McCain
Camile, their neighbor	Karen Rushmore
Laurie, Camile's daughter	Rachel Jacobs
Donny Sherman, Lois' son	Nicky Barton

Commercial Break Announcer: Eileen Brennan.
Music: Barry De Vorzon.
Producer: Bud Yorkin, Bernie Orenstein, Saul Turteltaub.
Director: Kim Friedman, Nancy Walker, Will MacKenzie, Peter Baldwin.
Creator: Richard Baer.

13 QUEENS BLVD. — 30 minutes — ABC — March 20, 1979 — April 18, 1979; July 3, 1979 — July 24, 1979. 8 episodes. Originally titled *Queen's Court*.

1214   THIS IS TOM JONES

Musical Variety.

Host: Tom Jones.
Regulars: Big Jim Sullivan, The Mike Sammes Singers, The Norman Maen Dancers.
Orchestra: Jack Parnell, Johnnie Spence.
Producer-Director: Jon Scoffield.

THIS IS TOM JONES — 60 minutes — ABC — February 7, 1969 — January 7, 1971. 27 programs. Syndicated.

1215   THIS IS YOUR LIFE

Variety-Interview. A semidocumentary presentation in which the lives of show business personalities, who appear as guests, are relived through the testimony of friends and family.

Version 1:

Host: Ralph Edwards.
Announcer: Bob Warren.
Orchestra: Von Dexter.
Producer: Ralph Edwards, Axel Gruenberg.

THIS IS YOUR LIFE — 30 minutes — NBC — October 2, 1952 — September 10, 1961.

Version 2:

Host: Ralph Edwards.
Announcer: Bob Warren.
Orchestra: Nelson Riddle.
Executive Producer: Richard Gottlieb.
Producer: Bill Carruthers.
Writer: Warren Douglas, Terry Shenk.
Director: Bill Carruthers.

THIS IS YOUR LIFE — 30 minutes — Syndicated 1971.

1216 THOSE AMAZING ANIMALS

Human Interest. A fascinating look at the world of animals — and the amazing things they do.

Host: Burgess Meredith, Priscilla Presley, Jim Stafford.
Regulars: Jacques Cousteau, Joan Embery.
Music: Roy Prendergast.
Supervising Producer: Alan Landsburg, Woody Fraser, Merrill Grant.
Executive Producer: Mel Stuart.
Producer: Draper Lewis, Carol Fleischer.
Studio Producer: David Yarnell.
Director: Martin Morris, Mary Hardwick, Karen Howard, David Vasir.
Art Director: Gene McAvoy.

THOSE AMAZING ANIMALS — 60 minutes — ABC — Premiered: August 24, 1980.

1217 THREE FOR THE MONEY

Game. Two three-member teams, each composed of one celebrity captain and two noncelebrity contestants, compete for five days, Monday through Friday.

Three categories, each containing three questions, are revealed. One team, as determined by a flip of a coin, receives a chance at play. The captain either selects himself or his teammates to compete against the opposing team. If he chooses to match one player from his team against one opponent, the question is worth $100; should he choose to play one against two, the question value is $200; if one player is pitted against three, the question is worth $300 for the team at play.

A question chosen from one of the categories is read, and clues appear on an electronic board. The player who is first to sound a buzzer signal stops the clues from progressing and receives a chance to answer. If a correct response is given by the member of the team at play, the money is scored accordingly; however, should the opposing team respond first, or supply a correct answer for an incorrect response on the part of the team at play, they score $100. The remaining categories, as well as the game, are played in the same manner. The team whose cumulative five day score is the highest is the winner and the contestants divide the money between them.

Host: Dick Enberg.
Announcer: Jack Clark.
Model: Jane Nelson.
Music: Score Productions.
Executive Producer: Stefan Hatos, Monty Hall.
Producer: Stu Billett.
Director: Hank Behar.

THREE FOR THE MONEY — 25 minutes — NBC — September 29, 1975 — November 28, 1975. 45 programs.

1218 THREE FOR THE ROAD

Drama. The story of Pete Karras, a photographer who roams throughout the United States in his motor home, the *Zebec*, with his sons John and Endy.

CAST
Pete Karras, a widower   Alex Rocco
John Karras, his son   Vincent Van Patten
Endy Karras, his son   Leif Garrett

Music: James Di Pasquale, David Shire.
Executive Producer: Jerry McNelly.
Producer: John G. Stephens, William F. Phillips.
Writer: Dick Bensfield, Perry Grant, Jerry McNelly, William Kelley, Sid Dorfman, Jack Turley, Arnold and Lois Peyser, Jack Miller, Michael Kozoll, Dick Nelson, Nina Caemmle.
Director: Boris Sagal, Barry Crane, Bernard McEveety, Claudio Guzman, Hy Averback, Ralph Senensky, Herschel Daugherty, Lou Antonio.
Creator: Jerry McNelly.

THREE FOR THE ROAD — 60 minutes — CBS — September 14, 1975 — November 30, 1975. The 90-minute pilot film aired on CBS on September 4, 1975.

1219 THREE GIRLS THREE

Variety. A musical comedy series that spotlights the talents of three unknown "but terribly talented girls doing a variety series about three unknown but terribly talented girls."

Starring: Debbie Allen, Ellen Foley, Mimi Kennedy.
Regulars: Warren Burton, Richard Byrd, Oliver Clark.
Orchestra: Marvin Laird.
Executive Producer: Gary Smith, Dwight Hemion.
Producer: Kenny Solms, Gail Parent.
Director: Tony Mordente, Tim Kiley.
Choreographer: Alan Johnson.

THREE GIRLS THREE — 60 minutes — NBC — June 15, 1977 — June 29, 1977. One episode aired on March 30, 1977. 3 programs.

1220 THREE ON A MATCH

Game. Each of the three players who compete presses a button and locks in the number of questions he wishes to answer (one to four) about one of three category topics that are revealed. Each player's choice is revealed and each bet scores ten dollars, which becomes the money that is available for that round.

True-or-false questions are asked of the players, beginning with the highest bidder, and a player can only win money by correctly answering his wagered amount of questions.

When a player scores at least $150, he is permitted to play "Three On a Match." A large, twelve-square game board is displayed that is composed of three vertical rows of money amounts ($20, $30 or $40) and four horizontal rows of colors (red, green, yellow or blue). The player purchases a square by naming a color and an amount. A merchandise prize or a cash amount is revealed. If the player is able to match the first square with two identical squares, he receives the prize that is represented, becomes the champion and faces two new challengers. If he is unsuccessful, the game continues and follows the previous format until one player matches three squares (the prizes change position with each player's gamble).

Host: Bill Cullen.
Announcer: Roger Tuttle, Don Pardo.
Music: Bob Cobert.

THREE ON A MATCH — 30 minutes — NBC — August 2, 1971 — June 28, 1974.

1221 THE THREE ROBONIC STOOGES

Animated Cartoon. An updated version of the 1940s theatrical series, *The Three Stooges*. The exploits of a space-age Moe, Larry and Curly, robots constructed from the finest parts available, as they battle the sinister forces for evil.

Voices: Moe: Paul Winchell; Larry: Joe Baker; Curly: Frank Welker; Triple O, their superior: Ross Martin.
Music: Paul DeKorte.
Producer: William Hanna, Joseph Barbera.
Director: Charles A. Nichols.

THE THREE ROBONIC STOOGES — 25 minutes — CBS — January 28, 1978 — September 2, 1978; September 9, 1979 — December 30, 1979.

1222 THREE'S A CROWD

Game. The basis of the program is to determine who knows a husband best — his wife or his secretary? Three husbands appear on stage and are asked three personal questions relating to either his wife or his secretary. Following a commercial break, the secretaries appear with their employers and are asked the same questions. Each response

on the part of the secretary that matches her employer scores her one point. Following another commercial break, the wives appear with their husbands and their secretaries. Each wife is asked the same three questions — but in order to score points, she must match both her husband and his secretary. The team (secretary or wife) that scores the highest splits $1,000.

Host: Jim Peck.
Announcer: Johnny Jacobs.
Music: Lee Ringuette.
Executive Producer: Chuck Barris.
Producer: Mike Metzger.
Director: John Dorsey.

THREE'S A CROWD — 30 minutes — Syndicated 1979.

1223 THREE'S COMPANY

Comedy. Finding that the high cost of apartment living in Santa Monica, California, is preventing them from living comfortably, Janet Wood and Chrissy Snow resolve their problem by taking in a male roommate — Jack Tripper, a culinary student whom they find sleeping in their bathtub after a wild party. The series focuses on the misadventures that could occur in such a situation as Janet, Chrissy and Jack struggle to live their own lives while attempting to maintain a strictly platonic relationship. Based on the British series, *Man About the House*.

CAST
Janet Wood, runs the Arcade
    Florist Shop   Joyce DeWitt
Christmas "Chrissy" Snow, a
    secretary   Suzanne Somers
Jack Tripper (a chef in
    later episodes)   John Ritter
Stanley Roper, their landlord   Norman Fell
Helen Roper, Stanley's wife   Audra Lindley
Ralph Furley, the landlord in
    later episodes   Don Knotts
Larry, Jack's friend, a used
    car salesman   Richard Kline
Lana Shields, the woman with
    eyes for Jack   Ann Wedgeworth
Jim, the bartender at the Regal Beagle,
    the local hangout   Paul Ainsley
Rev. Luther Snow, Chrissy's
    father   Peter Mark Richman
Dean Travers, the head of Jack's
    cooking school   William Pierson
J. C. Braddock, Chrissy's
    employer   Emmaline Henry
Waitress at the Regal Beagle   Isabel Wolfe
Cindy Snow, Chrissy's
    cousin   Jenilee Harrison
Music: Joe Raposo.
Theme Vocal: Ray Charles, Julia Rinker.
Executive Producer: Don Nicholl, Michael Ross, Bernie West, Budd Grossman.
Producer: Bill Richmond, Gene Perrett, George Burditt, George Sunga.
Associate Producer: Wendy Blair.

Director: Bill Hobin, Dave Powers (most of the series), Sam Gray.

Art Director: Don Roberts.

THREE'S COMPANY — 30 minutes — ABC — March 15, 1977 – April 21, 1977. Returned: Premiered: August 11, 1977.

1224   THUNDARR THE BARBARIAN

Animated Cartoon. In the year 1994, a runaway planet crosses between the Earth and the moon and unleashes a cosmic chain reaction that destroys both worlds. Two thousand years later, the planet Earth is reborn, but a strange new world emerges from the old: a world of savagery, super science, sorcery and evil beings bent on ruling the universe. The series depicts the exploits of Thundarr, a slave who broke his bonds and now battles the evils that exist on Earth. His assistants: Princess Ariel and Oukla.

Voices: Michael Bell, Rachel Baker, Marilyn Schreffler, Julie McWhirter, Stacy Keach, Sr., Henry Corden, Alan Dinehart, Shep Menkin, Joan Van Ark, Alan Oppenheimer.

Music: Dean Elliott.

Executive Producer: Joe Ruby, Ken Spears.

Producer: Jerry Eisenberg.

Director: Rudy Larriva, Charles A. Nichols, John Kimball.

THUNDARR THE BARBARIAN — 25 minutes — ABC — Premiered: October 4, 1980.

1225   THUNDER

Adventure. The story of a semi-wild black stallion named Thunder and the adventures of the young girl, Cindy Prescott, who befriends him.

CAST
Cindy Prescott	Melora Hardin
Bill Prescott, her father	Clint Ritchie
Ann Prescott, her mother	Melissa Converse
Willie Williams, Cindy's friend	Justin Randi
Sam Williams, Willie's father	Ray Girardin

Also: Cupcake the mule.

Music: Ray Ellis.

Producer: Irving Cummings, Charles Marion.

Director: Sigmund Neufeld, Jr., William Beaudine, Jr.

Creator: Irving Cummings, Charles Marion.

THUNDER — 30 minutes — NBC — September 10, 1977 – September 2, 1978.

1226   TIC TAC DOUGH

Game. The basic format calls for two contestants, Player X and Player O, to fill in a tic-tac-toe board by answering questions.

Each correct response awards a player a box and the first contestant to acquire three boxes in a row, up and down or diagonally, is the winner and receives a cash prize.

Version 1:

Host: Jay Jackson, Jack Barry.

Organist: Paul Taubman.

Producer: Stan Greene, Hudson Faussett, Robert Noah, Howard Flesher.

TIC TAC DOUGH — 30 minutes — NBC — July 30, 1956 – October 30, 1959.

Version 2:

Host: Wink Martindale.

Announcer: Jay Stewart.

Music: Hal Hidey, Bob Cobert.

Executive Producer: Ron Greenberg, Jack Barry, Dan Enright.

Producer: Allan Koss.

Director: Richard S. Kline.

TIC TAC DOUGH — 30 minutes — CBS — July 3, 1978 – September 1, 1978. 45 programs. Syndicated first run.

1227   TILL DEATH US DO PART

Comedy. The British series on which America's *All in the Family* is based. The program, which has not been broadcast in the United States, follows the life of Alf Garnett, a super bigot who lives in the heart of London's cockney East End docks area.

CAST
Alf Garnett	Warren Mitchell
Elsie Garnett, his wife	Dandy Nichols
Rita, their daughter	Una Stubbs
Mike, Rita's husband	Anthony Booth
Minnie, Alf's neighbor	Patricia Hayes
Bert, Minnie's husband	Alfie Bass

TILL DEATH US DO PART — 30 minutes — Produced by the BBC from 1964 through 1974.

1228   THE TIM CONWAY COMEDY HOUR

Variety. Music, songs and comedy sketches.

Host: Tim Conway.

Regulars: Sally Struthers, McLean Stevenson, Art Metrano, Bonnie Boland, Belland and Somerville, The Tom Hanson Dancers.

Orchestra: Nelson Riddle.

Producer: Bill Hobin, Ron Clark, Sam Bobrick.

Writer: Ron Clark, Sam Bobrick, William Raynor, Myles Wilder, Fred S. Fox, Seaman Jacobs, Douglas Arango, Barry Levinson, Craig Nelson, Rudy DeLuca, Tim Conway.

Director: Bill Hobin.

THE TIM CONWAY COMEDY HOUR — 60 minutes — CBS — September 20, 1970 – December 28, 1970.

1229   THE TIM CONWAY SHOW

Comedy. The series, set at Crawford Airport in Los Angeles, follows the misadventures of Timothy "Spud" Barrett, pilot, and Herbert Kenworth, executive officer, who own the *Lucky Linda*, a decrepit plane that comprises Triple A Airlines. Unable to pay creditors and threatened by eviction, they struggle to acquire passengers, relieve monetary burdens and maintain an airline.

CAST
Timothy "Spud" Barrett	Tim Conway
Herbert Kenworth	Joe Flynn
Mrs. Crawford, the owner of the airport	Anne Seymour
Ronnie Crawford, her son	Johnnie Collins III
Becky, the airlines reservations clerk	Emily Banks
Sherman, the control tower operator	Dennis Robertson
Harry, the owner of the coffee shop	Fabian Dean

Music: Harry Geller.

Producer: Burt Nodella.

Director: Alan Rafkin, Harry Falk.

THE TIM CONWAY SHOW — 30 minutes — CBS — January 30, 1970 – June 19, 1970.

1230   THE TIM CONWAY SHOW

Variety. Music, songs and comedy sketches.

Host: Tim Conway.

Regulars: Maggie Roswell, Kelly Garrett, Jack Riley, Dick Orkin, Harvey Korman, Miriam Flynn, Bert Berdis, Eric Boardman, The Don Crichton Dancers.

Orchestra: Peter Matz.

Executive Producer: Joe Hamilton.

Producer: Bill Richmond, Gene Perrett.

Associate Producer: Robert Wright.

Writer: Bill Richmond, Gene Perrett, Tim Conway, Maggie Roswell, Kelly Garrett, Jack Riley, Dick Orkin, Miriam Flynn, Bert Berdis, Eric Boardman.

Director: Roger Beatty.

Choreographer: Don Crichton.

Art Director: Bob Sanson.

THE TIM CONWAY SHOW — 60 minutes — CBS — March 22, 1980 – May 17, 1980. 9 programs. 30 minutes: Premiered: August 30, 1980.

1231   TIME EXPRESS

Anthology. Adventure stories about people who board the *Time Express*, a special train that takes them back in time to alter important moments in their pasts. People selected to ride the *Time Express* are chosen by an unknown and unseen person (the head of the train line). He bases his selection on one factor: the need for an individual to return to and change his past. Selected people anonymously receive a time ticket stating the date at which he is to return. Each departs at Gate Y, Track 13, at Union Station.

CAST
Jason Winters, the Time Express host	Vincent Price
Margaret Winters, his wife	Coral Browne
Richard Jefferson Walker (R. J.), the porter on the train	James Reynolds
E. Patrick Callahan, the engineer	William Edward Phipps
The Ticket Agent at Union Station (shows Time Express travelers the way)	Woodrow Parfrey

Music: Richard Hazard.

Executive Producer: Ivan Goff, Ben Roberts.

Producer: Leonard Kaufman.

Director: Arnold Laven, Cliff Bole, Michael Caffey, Alan J. Levi.

Creator: Ivan Goff, Ben Roberts.

TIME EXPRESS — 60 minutes — CBS — April 26, 1979 – May 17, 1979. 4 episodes.

1232 THE TODAY SHOW

Information. News, interviews, fashion, sports, politics, weather and entertainment.

Hosts: Dave Garroway (1952 – 61), John Chancellor (1961 – 62), Hugh Downs (1962 – 71), Frank McGee (1971 – 74), Jim Hartz (1974 – 76), Lloyd Dobbins (1976), Tom Brokaw (1976 –).

Hostesses: Barbara Walters, Jane Pauley.

Substitute Host: Jim Backus.

Substitute Hostess for Barbara Walters: Betty Furness.

Substitute Hostess for Jane Pauley: Mariette Hartley.

Regulars: Estelle Parsons, Lee Meriwether, Helen O'Connell, Betsy Palmer, Florence Henderson, Beryl Pfizer, Anita Colby, Robbin Bain, Louise King, Pat Fontaine, Maureen O'Sullivan, Gene Shalit, Betty Furness, Dr. Art Ulene, Floyd Kalber, Lew Wood, Katie Kelly, Candice Bergen, Ron Hendren, Phil Donahue, Bob Ryan, Willard Scott, Spencer Christian, Candace Hasey, Charles Van Doren, Paul Cunningham, Edwin Newman, Robin Chandler, Judith Crist, Frank Blair, Louise O'Brien, Bob Elliott, Ray Goulding, Martin Agronsky, Joe Garagiola, James Fleming, Jack Lescoulie, Roberta MacDonald, J. Fred Muggs.

Music Theme: "This Is Today" by Ray Ellis.

Producer: Mort Werner, Robert Bendick, Gerald Green, Jack Hein, Robert Northshield, Fred Freed, Al Morgan, Stuart

Schulberg, Dick Pinkham, Paul Friedman.

THE TODAY SHOW—2 hours—NBC—Premiered: January 14, 1952.

1233   TOMA

Crime Drama. The exploits of Dave Toma, an undercover agent with the Newark, New Jersey, Police Department. A master of disguise, he attempts to infiltrate and expose the "Organization" which is responsible for numerous illegal rackets. Based on the real-life exploits of David Toma, a Newark detective.

CAST

Det. Dave Toma (Badge No. 150)	Tony Musante
Patty Toma, his wife	Susan Strasberg
Donna Toma, their daughter	Michele Livingston
Jimmy Toma, their son	Sean Mannering
Inspector Spooner, Dave's superior	Simon Oakland
Various roles	David Toma

Music: Mike Post and Pete Carpenter.
Executive Producer: Roy Huggins.
Producer: Stephen J. Cannell.
Director: Michael Schultz, Joseph Hardy, Charles S. Dubin, Jeannot Szwarc, Gary Nelson, Alex Grasshoff.

TOMA—60 minutes—ABC—October 4, 1973–September 6, 1974. The 90-minute pilot film aired on ABC on March 21, 1973.

1234   TOM AND JERRY

Animated Cartoon. The misadventures of two nontalking animals: Tom the cat and Jerry the mouse.

Version One:

Vocal Effects: Paul Frees, Mel Blanc, June Foray, Allen Swift.
Music: Scott Bradley, Eugene Poddany, Carl Brandt.
Producer: Fred Quimby, Chuck Jones, William Hanna, Joseph Barbera.
Director: Chuck Jones, William Hanna, Joseph Barbera, Tom Washman, George Deitch.

THE TOM AND JERRY SHOW—30 minutes—CBS—September 10, 1966–September 17, 1972. Syndicated.

Version Two:

Voice Characterizations: Frank Welker.
Producer: Norm Prescott, Lou Scheimer.
Director: Don Christensen.
Art Director: Robert Kline.

THE TOM AND JERRY COMEDY SHOW—25 minutes—CBS—Premiered: September 6, 1980.

1235   THE TOM AND JERRY/GRAPE APE/MUMBLY SHOW

Animated Cartoon.

Segments:

Tom and Jerry. The misadventures of Tom the cat and Jerry the mouse, two nonspeaking animals who delight in annoying each other.

The Grape Ape. The misadventures of a 40-foot purple ape, the Grape Ape, and his fast-talking friend, Beagle the dog.

Mumbly. The fumbling investigations of Lieutenant Mumbly, a snickering canine detective.

Voices: Daws Butler, Henry Corden, Joan Gerber, Bob Hastings, Bob Holt, Marty Ingels, Cathy Gori, Virginia Gregg, Don Messick, Alan Oppenheimer, Allan Melvin, Hal Smith, Joe E. Ross, John Stephenson, Lurene Tuttle, Jean VanderPyl, Janet Waldo, Lennie Weinrib, Paul Winchell, Frank Welker.
Music: Hoyt Curtin, Paul DeKorte.
Executive Producer: William Hanna, Joseph Barbera.
Producer: Iwao Takamoto.
Director: Charles A. Nichols.

THE TOM AND JERRY/GRAPE APE/MUMBLY SHOW—55 minutes—ABC—September 6, 1975–September 4, 1976.

1236   THE TOMORROW SHOW

Discussion. Interviews with people rarely seen on television and for the most part non-show business who have a story to tell.

Host: Tom Snyder.
Co-Host: Rona Barrett.
Announcer: Frank Barton, Bill Wendell.
Producer: Pamela Burke, Bruce McKay.
Director: George Paul.

THE TOMORROW SHOW—60 minutes—NBC—October 15, 1973–September 15, 1980. 90 minutes; premiered: September 16, 1980.

1237   THE TONIGHT SHOW

Talk-Variety. Television's first late-night entertainment series.

Version 1:

Host: Steve Allen.
Regulars: Steve Lawrence, Helen Dixon, Pat Kirby.
Announcer: Gene Rayburn.
Orchestra: Bobby Byrne.

THE TONIGHT SHOW—40 minutes—Local New York (WNBT-TV)—July 27, 1953–September 24, 1954.

Version 2:

Host: Steve Allen.
Regulars: Steve Lawrence, Eydie Gormé, Pat Marshall, Helen Dixon, Andy Williams.
Announcer: Gene Rayburn.
Orchestra: Skitch Henderson.

THE TONIGHT SHOW—105 minutes—NBC—September 27, 1954–January 25, 1957.

Version 3:

Host: Ernie Kovacs.
Vocalists: Maureen Arthur, Pete Hanley.
Announcer: Bill Wendell.
Orchestra: Leroy Holmes.

THE TONIGHT SHOW—105 minutes—NBC—October 1, 1956–January 22, 1957. Broadcast twice a week for a period of four months, preempting version two (above) on Monday and Tuesday evenings.

Version 4:

Host: Jack Lescoulie, Al "Jazzbo" Collins.
Vocalist: Judy Johnson.
Newscasters: Hy Gardner, Bob Considine, Earl Wilson, Irv Kupcinet, Vernon Scott, Paul Coates, Lee Giroux.
Music: The Lou Stein Trio, The Mort Lindsey Quartet, The Johnny Guarnieri Quartet.

TONIGHT! AMERICA AFTER DARK—105 minutes—NBC—January 28, 1957–July 26, 1957.

Version 5:

Host: Jack Paar.
Regulars: Cliff Arquette (as Charlie Weaver), Pat Harrington, Jr. (as Guido Panzini), Peggy Cass, Alexander King, Mary Margaret McBride, Dody Goodman, Betty Johnson, Elsa Maxwell, Tedi Thurman (the weather girl), The Bil and Cora Baird Puppets.
Announcer: Hugh Downs, Art James.
Orchestra: Jose Melis.

THE TONIGHT SHOW—105 minutes—NBC—July 29, 1957–March 30, 1962.

Version 6: (Interim series with guests hosting)

Announcer: Hugh Downs, Ed Herlihy.
Orchestra: Skitch Henderson.

THE TONIGHT SHOW—105 minutes—NBC—April 2, 1962–September 28, 1962.

Version 7:

Host: Johnny Carson.
Regular: Carol Wayne.
Announcer: Jack Haskell, Durward Kirby, Ed McMahon.
Orchestra: Skitch Henderson, Milton DeLugg, Doc Severinsen.

Substitute Orchestra Leader: Tommy Newson.
Producer: Fred DeCordova.

THE TONIGHT SHOW—105, then 90 minutes—NBC—October 1, 1962–September 15, 1980. 60 minutes—Premiered: September 16, 1980.

1238   THE TONI TENNILLE SHOW

Variety. Music, songs and celebrity interviews.

Hostess: Toni Tennille.
Regulars: Daryl Dragon (Toni's husband), Melissa Tennille (Toni's sister).
Orchestra: Ira Newborn.
Supervising Producer: Walt Case.
Executive Producer: Bob Eubanks, Michael Hill.
Producer: Earl Durham.
Writer: Earl Durham, Michael Hill.
Director: Bruce Gowers.
Art Director: Ed Flesh.

THE TONI TENNILLE SHOW—60 minutes—Syndicated 1980.

1239   TONY ORLANDO AND DAWN

Variety. Various comedy sketches and musical numbers.

Host: Tony Orlando.
Co-Host: Dawn, his backup vocal duo (Joyce Vincent Wilson, Telma Hopkins).
Regulars: Steve Franken, Susan Tolsky, George Carlin, Bob Holt, Susan Lancer, Jimmy Martinez, Edie McClurg, Adam Wade.
Announcer: Roger Carroll, Dick Tufeld.
Orchestra: Bob Rozario.
Producer: Saul Ilson, Ernest Chambers.
Director: Peter Calabrese, Bill Foster, Jeff Margolis.
Choreographer: Walter Painter, Jerry Jackson.

TONY ORLANDO AND DAWN—60 minutes—CBS—July 3, 1974–July 24, 1974; December 4, 1974–December 28, 1976. Also titled *The Tony Orlando and Dawn Rainbow Hour.*

1240   THE TONY RANDALL SHOW

Comedy. The home and working life of Walter O. Franklin, a less-than-magisterial judge of the Court of Common Pleas in Philadelphia.

CAST

Walter Franklin, a widower	Tony Randall
Roberta "Bobby" Franklin, his daughter	Devon Scott Penny Peyser
Oliver Franklin, Jr., his son	Brad Savage
Janet Reubner, his secretary	Allyn Ann McLerie

Bonnie McClellan, his
housekeeper — Rachel Roberts
Jack Terwilliger, the court
stenographer — Barney Martin
Judy Trowbridge, Walter's law
clerk — Brooke Adams
Mario Lanza, Walter's law
associate — Zane Lasky
Wyatt Franklin, Walter's
father — Hans Conried

Music: Patrick Williams.
Producer: Tom Patchett, Jay
Tarses, Gary David Goldberg,
Hugh Wilson.
Director: Jay Sandrich, James
Burrows, Hugh Wilson, Tony
Mordente.
Creator: Tom Patchett, Jay Tarses.

THE TONY RANDALL SHOW — 30
minutes — ABC — September 23,
1976 – March 10, 1977. CBS — 30
minutes — September 24, 1977 –
March 25, 1978.

1241 TONY THE PONY

Children. The story of Tony, a
magic pony who can grant children any wish. The book of magic
decreed that a colt named Tony
be endowed with magic powers
and be given to Jonathan, a lonely
boy. The series depicts their adventures as they help children in
need and shows that having the
impossible is not always the best.

CAST
Jonathan, Tony's master — Poindexter
G. G., the wizard who gave Tony
his power — Sterling Holloway
Agnes, the witch — Barbara Cason

Music: Horace Taylor, Sy Miller,
Win Opie.
Theme Vocal: "Tony the Pony" by
Jill Jackson.
Producer: James Lowe.
Associate Producer: Jackie
Beavers.
Director: James Lowe.

TONY THE PONY — 30 min-
utes — Syndicated 1979.

1242 TOP OF THE MONTH

Variety. Highlights of the months
of the year are saluted through
songs, sketches and dances.

Host: Tony Randall.
Co-Host: E. J. (Edra Jeanne)
Peaker.
Regulars: Anson Williams, Tina
Andrews, The Anita Mann
Dancers, The Alan Copeland
Singers.
Orchestra: Alan Copeland.

TOP OF THE MONTH — 30 minutes — Syndicated 1972.

1243 THE TOP OF THE HILL

Drama. The story of Michael
Stone, a successful businessman
who escapes from the tedium of
his business by recklessly pursu-

ing danger. Based on an original
story by Irwin Shaw.

CAST
Michael Stone — Wayne Rogers
Elizabeth Stone, his wife — Adrienne Barbeau
Eva Heggener, the wife of the
owner of Lake Placid Mirror
Mountain Lodge — Elke Sommer
Andreas Heggener, Eva's
husband — Mel Ferrer
Bobby Antoine, Mike's friend — Sonny Bono
Dave Cully, the ski
instructor — Gary Lockwood
Norma Cully, Dave's wife — Paula Prentiss
Maria Vontan, a skier
competing in the 1980
Winter Olympics — Denise DuBarry
Frank Langrock, Mike's
employer — J. D. Cannon
"Mitch" Mitchell, works for the
Langrock Corp. — Macdonald Carey
Herb Ellsworth, Mike's
friend — Richard O'Brien
Minna Ellsworth, Herb's
wife — Carmen Mathews
McCain, the sky diving
instructor — Peter Brown
Josie, the bar pickup — Janice Lynde
Allison, Elizabeth's friend — Allison Carroll
Police Sergeant — Barry Snyder

Music: George Duning.
Executive Producer: Arthur Fel-
lows, Terry Keegan.
Producer: John Cutts.
Writer: Eric Bercovici.
Director: Walter Grauman.

THE TOP OF THE HILL — 2 hours
— Operation Prime Time — February 1980. 2 episodes.

1244 TO ROME WITH LOVE

Comedy. The series, set in Rome,
follows the trials and tribulations
of Michael Endicott, an Iowa
school professor hired to teach at
the American School, as he and
his family struggle to adjust to a
new homeland.

CAST
Michael Endicott, a
widower — John Forsythe
Alison Endicott, his
daughter — Joyce Menges
Penny Endicott, his
daughter — Susan Neher
Jane "Pokey" Endicott,
his daughter — Melanie Fullerton
Andy Pruitt, the girls'
grandfather — Walter Brennan
Harriet Endicott, Mike's
sister — Kay Medford
Gino Mancini, their friend, the
cab driver — Vito Scotti
Mama Vitale, Mike's
landlady — Peggy Mondo
Nico, a friend of
Penny's — Gerald Michenaud
Margot, a friend — Brioni Farrell
Tina, Alison's friend — Brenda Benet

Music: Frank DeVol.
Theme: Jay Livingston, Ray Evans.
Executive Producer: Don Fed-
derson.
Producer: Edmund Hartman.

Director: Fred DeCordova, Earl
Bellamy, James Sheldon.
Creator: Joan O'Brien.

TO ROME WITH LOVE — 30
minutes — CBS — September 28,
1969 – September 1 1971. 48
episodes.

1245 TO SAY THE LEAST

Game. Two teams, each composed of three players — two
celebrities and one noncelebrity
contestant — compete. Two players from each team are isolated
backstage. A phrase is shown to
the on-stage players (e.g. "Dutch
girls clop around in them"), and
on an alternating basis, the players eliminate words from it. At
any time, the contestant at play
can challenge or take out a word.
When a challenge is made, the
opposing team must attempt to
identify the meaning of the
phrase. The backstage players are
brought out and the challenged
player's teammates are shown the
remaining words to the phrase. If
they can identify it ("Wooden
shoes" in the example), they
score one point; if not, the opposing team scores the point. The
first team to score two points
is the winner and the noncelebrity player receives merchandise
prizes.

Host: Tom Kennedy.
Announcer: Kenny Williams.
Music: Stan Worth.
Executive Producer: Merrill Heat-
ter, Bob Quigley.
Producer: Robert Noah.
Director: Jerome Shaw.

TO SAY THE LEAST — 30 minutes — NBC — October 3, 1977 –
April 21, 1978. 135 programs.

1246 TO TELL THE TRUTH

Game. Through a series of
question-and-answer probe
rounds, a celebrity panel of four
must determine which of three
guests, each of whom claims to
be the same person, is telling the
truth. Cash prizes are awarded to
players based on the number of
incorrect guesses on the part of
the panel.

Version 1:

Host: Clayton "Bud" Collyer.
Regular Panelists: Phyllis New-
man, Peggy Cass, Sally Ann
Howes, Tom Poston, Orson
Bean, Kitty Carlisle, Milt Ka-
men, Bess Myerson, Joan Fon-
taine, Sam Levenson, Barry
Nelson, Dr. Joyce Brothers,
Polly Bergen, Dick Van Dyke,
John Cameron Swayze, Hildy
Parks.
Announcer: Johnny Olsen.

TO TELL THE TRUTH — 30 min-

utes — CBS. Evening run: January
1, 1957 – May 22, 1967. Daytime
run: June 18, 1962 – September
6, 1968.

Version 2:

Host: Garry Moore, Joe Garagiola.
Regular Panelists: Orson Bean,
Bill Cullen, Kitty Carlisle,
Peggy Cass.
Announcer: Johnny Olsen, Bill
Wendell, Alan Calter.
Music: Score Productions.
Producer: Bruno Zirato.
Director: Lloyd Gross.

TO TELL THE TRUTH — 30 minutes — Syndicated 1969 – 1978.

Version 3:

Host: Robin Ward.
Regular Panelists: Soupy Sales,
Peggy Cass.
Announcer: Alan Calter.
Music: Score Productions.
Executive Producer: Gil Fates.
Producer: Mimi O'Brien.
Director: Lloyd Gross.
Art Director: Ronald Baldwin.

TO TELL THE TRUTH — 30 minutes — Syndicated 1980.

1247 A TOUCH OF GRACE

Comedy. The series, set in Oakland, California, follows the life of
Grace Sherwood, a 65-year-old
widow, as she struggles to make a
life for herself at the home of her
married daughter, Myra Bradley,
a beautician, and her husband,
Walter Bradley, the manager of
the Penny Mart Supermarket.

One day, while tending her
husband's grave, Grace meets
and falls in love with Herbert
Morrison, a widowed grave
digger.

Believing Herbert is not a gentleman, Myra disapproves of him.
A family crisis ensues when
Grace, feeling her life is unful-
filled because Myra and Walter
are childless, states her intent to
continue seeing him.

Serial-type episodes relate
Grace and Herbert's courtship,
Myra's final acceptance of Herbert when she realizes her mother's feelings, and Herbert's proposal to Grace. Based on the
British series, *For the Love of Ada.*

CAST
Grace Sherwood (a.k.a. Grace
Simpson) — Shirley Booth
Herbert Morrison — J. Pat O'Malley
Myra Bradley, Grace's
daughter — Marian Mercer
Walter Bradley, Myra's
husband — Warren Berlinger

Music: Pete Rugolo.
Producer: Saul Turteltaub, Bernie
Orenstein.
Director: Carl Reiner.

A TOUCH OF GRACE — 30 minutes — ABC — January 20, 1973 –
June 16, 1973.

TOURIST

See *Operation Prime Time: Tourist*.

1248 TOWARDS THE YEAR 2000

Documentary. Films exploring the technological advances that will mark the twenty-first century.

Narrator: Henry Ramcer.
Music: George Greeley.
Executive Producer: Philip S. Habel, Douglas Leiterman.
Producer: John R. Smith, Beryl L. Fox.
Director: Timothy Howard.

TOWARDS THE YEAR 2000 — 30 minutes — Syndicated 1977.

1249 TRAPPER JOHN, M.D.

Drama. The experiences of Dr. "Trapper" John McIntyre, a Korean War M*A*S*H* veteran who is now chief surgeon of San Francisco Memorial Hospital. A spin-off from *M*A*S*H* that is set 28 years later (1979).

CAST
Dr. "Trapper" John McIntyre	Pernell Roberts
Dr. G. Alonzo "Gonzo" Gates	Gregory Harrison
Nurse "Starch" Willoughby	Mary McCarty
Dr. Stanley Riverside II	Charles Siebert
Dr. "Jackpot" Jackson	Brian Mitchell
Nurse Gloria "Ripples" Brancusi	Christopher Norris
Melanie McIntyre, John's ex-wife	Jessica Walter
Dr. Gallant	Marvin Sternhauser
Hospital Receptionist	Karen Glow Carr
Emergency Room Nurse	Blake Harris
Nurse	Jennifer Davis
Nurse	Brenda Elder
Anesthesiologist	Ned Wilson
	Frank Coppola
	Laurence Haddon
	Maurice Hill
	Mel Carter
Scrub Nurse Ernestine Shoop	Madge Sinclair
Dr. Slocum	Simon Scott
Dr. Clark	Norman Gibbs

Gonzo's mobile home: *Titanic*.

Music: John Parker.
Music Supervision: Lionel Newman.
Executive Producer: Frank Glicksman.
Producer: Don Brinkley.
Director: Jackie Cooper, Murray Golden, Joseph Pevney, Corey Allen, Ralph Senensky, Barry Crane, Bernard McEveety, Alex March, Robert Douglas, Ralph Levy, Alf Kjellin.
Art Director: David M. Huber.
Director of Photography: William Jurgensen, Marvin Summerfield.
Medical Adviser: Walter D. Dishell, Chris Hutson.

TRAPPER JOHN, M.D. — 60 minutes — CBS — Premiered: September 23, 1979.

TREASURE HUNT

See *The New Treasure Hunt*.

1250 THE TROUBLE WITH TRACY

Comedy. The series, set in Toronto, Canada, follows the misadventures of the Youngs: Douglas, an executive with the advertising firm of Hutton, Dutton, Sutton and Norris; and his well-meaning, but scatterbrained wife, Tracy. Produced in Canada.

CAST
Tracy Young	Diane Nyland
Douglas Young	Steve Weston
Sally Anderson, Doug's secretary	Bonnie Brooks
Paul Sherwood, Tracy's unemployed brother	Franz Russell
Jonathan Norris, Doug's employer	Ben Lennick
Margaret Norris, Jonathan's wife	Sandra Scott

Producer: Seymour Berns.
Writer: Goodman Ace.
Director: Seymour Berns.

THE TROUBLE WITH TRACY — 30 minutes — Syndicated 1971.

1251 TRUTH OR CONSEQUENCES

Game. Selected contestants (numbers vary) are first interviewed, then asked to answer a nonsense riddle. If they are unable to answer it before Beulah the Buzzer sounds, they have to pay the consequences and perform stunts. Prizes are awarded in accord with the success of their performances.

Version 1:

Host: Ralph Edwards, Jack Bailey, Bob Barker.
Announcer: Ken Carpenter.
Music: Buddy Cole, Jack Fascinato.
Producer: Ralph Edwards, Ed Bailey.

TRUTH OR CONSEQUENCES — 30 minutes — NBC — July 5, 1950 — September 25, 1965.

Version 2:

Host: Bob Barker.
Announcer: Charles Lyon.
Music: Dave Bacoll, Hal Hidy.
Producer: Ralph Edwards, Ed Bailey.
Director: Bill Chestnut.

TRUTH OR CONSEQUENCES — 30 minutes — Syndicated 1967.

Version 3:

Host: Bob Hilton.
Announcer: John Harlan.

Music: Bruce Belland, Gary Edwards.
Executive Producer: Jon Ross.
Producer: Ralph Edwards, Bruce Belland.
Director: Richard Gottlieb, Arthur Forrest.

THE NEW TRUTH OR CONSEQUENCES — 30 minutes — Syndicated 1977.

1252 TURNABOUT

Comedy. The series, set in Los Angeles, follows the lives of Penny Alston, an Aura Cosmetics Company vice president, and Sam Alston, her husband, a writer for *Sports Life* magazine. Problems befall them when each believes the other's life is better and Penny idly wishes they could trade places — in front of an impish statue purchased from a Gypsy that grants her wish. Now, with his personality in her body, and her's in his, and unable to reverse the wish, each struggles to adjust — and live as the other.

CAST
Penny Alston (Sam Alston)	Sharon Gless
Sam Alston (Penny Alston)	John Schuck
Judy Overmeyer, their neighbor	Bobbi Jordan
Jack Overmeyer, Judy's husband	Richard Stahl
Al Brennan, Sam's publisher	Bruce Kirby
Geoffrey St. James, Penny's employer	James Sikking

Opening Theme Narration: Sterling Holloway.
Music: Jack Elliott, Allyn Ferguson.
Supervising Producer: Michael Rhodes.
Executive Producer: Sam Denoff.
Producer: Arnold Kayne.
Director: Richard Crenna, Arnold Laven, Alex March, William P. D'Angelo.

TURNABOUT — 30 minutes — NBC — January 26, 1979 – March 30, 1979. 7 episodes.

1253 THE $20,000 PYRAMID

Game. Two teams compete, each composed of one celebrity and one noncelebrity contestant. One team chooses a subject from six categories that appear on a board (e.g., "Sleepy Head"). A question is read that relates its purpose ("Describe things that are associated with sleep") and one player has to relate clues to the identity of seven objects (that appear on a monitor) within 30 seconds. Each correct identification scores one point and each team competes in three rounds (alternating turns at guessing and giving clues) with the highest scoring team being declared the winners.

The Championship Round:

One member of the winning team sits facing a pyramid of six categories; his partner sits with his back to the board. Within 60 seconds, the player seated with his back to the board must identify all six categories from clues given to him by his partner. Success earns him $10,000. (In *The $20,000 Pyramid*, the player has to win three games and faces the pyramid at least three times to win $20,000; in *The $25,000 Pyramid*, the player has to win two games and face and successfully guess the pyramid twice to win $25,000. If a player fails to guess a pyramid, he wins what money is represented by the individual categories.)

Host: Dick Clark.
Announcer: Bob Clayton, Steve O'Brien.
Executive Producer: Bob Stewart.
Producer: Anne Marie Schmitt, Jane Rothchild.
Director: Mike Gargiulo.

THE $20,000 PYRAMID — 30 minutes — ABC — January 19, 1976 – June 27, 1980. As *The $10,000 Pyramid* — 30 minutes — CBS — March 26, 1973 – March 29, 1974; ABC — May 6, 1974 – January 16, 1976. 1,808 programs.

1254 THE $25,000 PYRAMID

Game. A syndicated version of the previous title.

Host: Bill Cullen.
Announcer: Bob Clayton.
Executive Producer: Bob Stewart.
Producer: Anne Marie Schmitt.
Director: Mike Gargiulo.

THE $25,000 PYRAMID — 30 minutes — Syndicated 1974 – 1977.

1255 TWIGGY'S JUKE BOX

Music. Performances by Rock musicians.

Hostess: Twiggy (Leslie Hornby).
Music: Recorded and/or provided by guests.
Theme Music: Kenny Lynch.
Executive Producer: Malcolm Gold.
Producer-Director: Mike Mansfield.

TWIGGY'S JUKE BOX — 30 minutes — Syndicated 1978 – 1979. See also *Britt Ekland's Juke Box*, the revised version of the series.

1256 240-ROBERT

Adventure. The series follows the search and rescue operations of Dwayne Thibideaux, T. R. "Trap" Applegate and Morgan Wainwright, Los Angeles County Sheriff's Emergency Service Detail Deputies who operate under the code name 240-Robert.

That's Incredible! John Davidson, at right, with insets of Fran Tarkenton and Cathy Lee Crosby.

Three's Company. At left, Norman Fell. Center, from bottom, Suzanne Somers, John Ritter and Joyce DeWitt. Right, Audra Lindley.

To Rome with Love. Joyce Menges and John Forsythe.

Turnabout. Sharon Gless and John Schuck. Courtesy of the *Call-Chronicle Newspapers,* Allentown, Pa.

CAST

Deputy Dwayne "Thib" Thibideaux	Mark Harmon
Deputy Morgan Wainwright	Joanna Cassidy
Deputy T. R. "Trap" Applegate	John Bennett Perry
Deputy C. B. Harris	Lew Saunders
Deputy Roverino	JoeAl Nicassio
Deputy Terry Caster	Thomas Babson
Deputy Kestenbaum	Steve Tanner
Sheriff	Peter J. Pitchess

Music: Mike Post, Pete Carpenter, Murray MacLeod.
Executive Producer: Rick Rosner.
Producer: Richard M. Rosenbloom.
Writer: James Schmerer, Glen Olson, Rod Baker, Lew Hunter, Simon Muntner, L. Ford Neale, John Huff, Rudy Dochtermann, Patrick Mathews, Anthony Yerkovich, Charlene Bralver, Robert Specht.
Director: Phil Bondelli, Ric Rondell, Sigmund Neufeld, Jr., Christian I. Nyby II, Sutton Roley, John Florea, Bruce Kessler.
Creator: Rick Rosner.

240-ROBERT — 60 minutes — ABC — September 3, 1979 – December 10, 1979. 13 episodes. Rebroadcasts: May 31, 1980 – August 23, 1980.

1257 THE TWO RONNIES

Satire. The series, which stars two men named Ronnie (hence the title), features offbeat satirizations of whatever is considered funny to the show's writers — from real life to story-telling. Produced in England.

Hosts: Ronnie Barker, Ronnie Corbett.
Regulars: Julia McKenzie, Janet Webb, Joyce Windsor, Chaz Chase, Sue Lloyd, The Fred Tomalson Singers.
Music: Ronnie Hazelhurst.
Producer-Director: Terry Hughes.

THE TWO RONNIES — 30 minutes — Syndicated to PBS in 1978.

U

1258 U.F.O.

Science Fiction. As Unidentified Flying Objects (U.F.O.'s) become established and are believed to be a threat to the safety of Earth, world governments unite and sponsor the construction of S.H.A.D.O. (Supreme Headquarters, Alien Defense Organization). Closely guarded under a veil of deep secrecy, it is housed beneath the Harlington-Straker film studios in London.

Establishing bases on both the Earth and the Moon, and incorporating highly complex defense equipment, S.H.A.D.O.'s battle of secrecy* against alien invaders is dramatized as it attempts to discover who they are, where they come from, and what they want.

CAST

Edward Straker, the commander of S.H.A.D.O.	Ed Bishop
Col. Alec Freeman, his assistant	George Sewell
Lt. Gay Ellis, the commander of Moon Base	Gabrielle Drake
Col. Paul Foster, Straker's assistant	Michael Billington
Lt. Nina Barry, a space tracker	Dolores Mantez
Lt. Joan Harrington, a space tracker	Antoni Ellis
Col. Virginia Lake	Wanda Ventham
Capt. Peter Karlin	Peter Gordeno
Miss Eland, Straker's secretary	Norma Roland
Douglas Jackson, the psychiatrist	Valdek Sheybol
Lt. Keith Ford	Keith Alexander
Gen. James Henderson, Straker's superior	Grant Taylor
Miss Holland, Straker's secretary (later episodes)	Lois Maxwell
Miss Scott, Henderson's secretary	Louise Pajd
Pilot Lew Waterman	Garry Myers
Pilot Mark Bradley	Harry Baird
Radio Operator Tunner	Patrick Allen
Skydiver operator	Georganna Moon
Skydiver navigator	Jeremy Wilkin
Skydiver captain	David Warbeck
Skydiver engineer	Jon Kelly
Moon Base operator	Andrea Allan
Mobile Officer	Hugh Armstrong
S.H.A.D.O. operative	Penny Spencer
S.H.A.D.O. operative	Ayshea
Radar Technician	Michael Ferrand

Music: Barry Gray.
Producer: Reg Hill, Gerry Anderson.
Director: Ken Turner, David Bell, Alan Perry, David Lane, Jeremy Summers, Gerry Anderson, David Tomblin, Cyril Frankel.

U.F.O. — 60 minutes — Syndicated 1972. 26 episodes.

*It is feared that public awareness of U.F.O.'s would cause a worldwide panic.

1259 UNCLE CROC'S BLOCK

Children. A spoof of children's television programs. Set in a television studio, the series focuses on the antics of Uncle Croc, the costumed (as a crocodile) host of *Croc's Block,* a kids' show he detests doing. Live-action segments are coupled with short cartoons.

CAST

Uncle Croc	Charles Nelson Reilly
Basil Bitterbottom, the director	Jonathan Harris
Rabbit Ears, Croc's assistant	Johnny Silver
	Alfie Wise
The $6.95 Man	Robert Ridgely

Voices (for the cartoon segments): Allan Melvin, Kenneth Mars, Alan Oppenheimer, Robert Ridgely, Lennie Weinrib.
Music: Yvette Blais, Jeff Michael.
Producer: Mack Bing, Don Christensen.
Director: Mack Bing.

Cartoon Segments:
Fraidy Cat. The misadventures of a cat who, having lost eight of his nine lives, struggles to protect his last remaining life.

The Mush Puppies. The hectic exploits of MUSH (Mangy Unwanted Shabby Heroes), Northwest Mounted Canadian Police dogs.

Wacky and Packy. The story concerns the misadventures of a caveman named Packy and his pet elephant, Wacky, who were caught in an earthquake and transported to modern times.

UNCLE CROC'S BLOCK — 55 minutes — ABC — September 6, 1975 – October 18, 1975. 30 minutes — October 25, 1975 – February 14, 1976.

1260 UNICORN TALES

Children. Modern adaptations of classic fairy tales.

Music: Jack Feldman.
Executive Producer: Nick DeNoia.
Producer: William P. Milling.

UNICORN TALES — 30 minutes — Syndicated 1977.

1261 UNITED STATES

Comedy-Drama. A very talkative, no-action series about the daily events that affect the lives of Richard and Libby Chapin, a well-to-do married couple, and their sons, Dylan and Nicky.

CAST

Richard Chapin, the father	Beau Bridges
Libby Chapin, his wife	Helen Shaver
Dylan Chapin, their son	Rossie Harris
Nicky Chapin, their son	Justin Dana

Music (Closing Theme Only): Jack Elliott.
Supervising Producer: Chuck Kalish.
Executive Producer: Larry Gelbart.
Producer: Gary Markowitz.
Writer: Larry Gelbart, Cathy Gilbert, Everett Greenbaum.
Director: Will MacKenzie, Nick Havinga.
Creator: Larry Gelbart.

UNITED STATES — 30 minutes — NBC — March 11, 1980 – April 29, 1980. 8 episodes (includes one unscheduled episode broadcast on April 2, 1980 that aired in place of *Hello, Larry*).

1262 UNIVERSAL STAR TIME

Anthology. Retitled episodes of *The Bob Hope Chrysler Theatre.* See any of the following titles for examples of the type of programs that comprise the series: *The NBC Action Playhouse, The NBC Adventure Theatre,* or *The NBC Comedy Theatre.*

UNIVERSAL STAR TIME — 60 minutes — Syndicated 1971.

1263 UPSTAIRS, DOWNSTAIRS

Drama. A depiction of life in a fashionable London townhouse as seen through the interactions of two classes: the Bellamys, who live upstairs, and their servants, who form a family of their own downstairs.

CAST

Richard Bellamy	David Langton
James Bellamy	Simon Williams
Hazel Bellamy	Meg-Wynn Owen
Virginia Bellamy	Hannah Gordon
Rose, the maid	Jean Marsh
Hudson, the butler	Gordon Jackson
Mrs. Bridges, the head servant	Angela Baddeley
Alfred, the footman	George Innes
Edward, the footman	Christopher Beeny
Daisy, the maid	Jacqueline Tong
Lady Georgina Worsley	Lesley-Anne Down
Sarah	Pauline Collins
Watkins	John Alderton
Emily	Evin Crowley
Lady Marjorie	Rachel Gurney
Lil	Angela Brown
Dolly	Madeline Cannon
Frederick	Gareth Hunt
Alice	Anne Yarker
Lily	Karen Dotrice

The Bellamys' address: 165 Eaton Place.

Music: Alexander Faris.
Producer: John Hawkesworth, Rex Firkin.
Director: Derek Bennett.
Creator: Jean Marsh, Eileen Atkens.

UPSTAIRS, DOWNSTAIRS — 60 minutes — PBS — 1974 – 1977. 57 episodes.

1264 THE U.S. OF ARCHIE

Animated Cartoon. The series features the Archie Gang (Archie Andrews, Betty Cooper, Veronica Lodge, Reggie Mantle and Jughead Jones) as great American heroes in stories that detail their achievements throughout history.

VOICES

Archie Andrews	Dallas McKennon
Betty Cooper	Jane Webb
Veronica Lodge	Jane Webb
Jughead Jones	Howard Morris
Reggie Mantle	Dallas McKennon

Music: George Blais, Jeff Michael.

Music Supervision: Don Kirshner.
Producer: Norm Prescott, Lou Scheimer.
Director: Don Towsley, Lou Zukor, Rudy Larriva, Bill Reed.

THE U.S. OF ARCHIE — 30 minutes — CBS — September 7, 1974 – September 5, 1976.

1265 THE VAL DOONICAN SHOW

Variety. Music, songs and comedy sketches.

Host: Val Doonican.
Regulars: Bob Todd, Bernard Cribbins, The Norman Maen Dancers, The Mike Sammes Singers.
Announcer: Paul Griffith.
Orchestra: Jack Parnell, Kenny Woods.
Producer: Bernie Kukoff, Jeff Harris.
Writer: Tom Waldman, Frank Waldman, Bryan Blackburn, Derek Collyer, Bernie Kukoff, Jeff Harris.
Director: Bill Hitchcock.
Choreographer: Norman Maen.

THE VAL DOONICAN SHOW — 60 minutes — ABC — June 5, 1971 – August 14, 1971.

1266 VALLEY OF THE DINOSAURS

Animated Cartoon. While exploring an uncharted river canyon in the Amazon, a twentieth-century family, the Butlers, are engulfed by a whirlpool, propelled through an underground cavern and transported to the prehistoric era, where they befriend a cave family parallel to them. Stories depict their struggles for survival. Scientific principles are illustrated as both families assist and learn from one another.

VOICES

John Butler, the modern
 family father   Mike Road
Kim Butler, his wife   Shannon Farnon
Katie Butler, their
 daughter   Margene Fudenna
Greg Butler, their son   Jackie Haley
Gorak, the prehistoric family
 father   Alan Oppenheimer
Gera, his wife   Joan Gardner
Tana, their daughter   Melanie Baker
Lock, their son   Steacy Bertheau

Music: Hoyt Curtin.
Executive Producer: William Hanna, Joseph Barbera.
Producer: Iwao Takamoto.
Director: Charles A. Nichols.

VALLEY OF THE DINOSAURS — 25 minutes — CBS — September 7, 1974 – September 4, 1976. 16 episodes. Syndicated.

1267 VAN DYKE AND COMPANY

Variety. Music, songs and comedy sketches.

Host: Dick Van Dyke.
Regulars: Lois January, Marilyn Soko, Mickey Rose, Pat Proft, Andy Kaufman, Al Bloomfield, Bob Einstein, Chuck McCann, Tom Kelly, Barry Van Dyke, Bill Engeser, Michael Wheeler, The Los Angeles Mime Company.
Orchestra: Lex De Avezedo.
Musical Coordinator: D'Vaughn Pershing.
Executive Producer: Byron Paul.
Producer: Allan Blye, Bob Einstein.
Director: John Moffitt.
Choreographer: Lester Wilson.

VAN DYKE AND COMPANY — 60 minutes — NBC — September 20, 1976 – December 30, 1976.

1268 VAUDEVILLE

Variety. Performances by Vaudeville comedians and re-creations of its associated comedy by new talent discoveries.

Guest Hosts: Milton Berle, Steve Allen and Jayne Meadows, Edgar Bergen and Charlie McCarthy, Eddie Foy, Jr., Rudy Vallee, Jack Carter, Red Buttons, Gordon MacRae.
The Card Girl: Donna Jean Young.
Orchestra: George Wyle.
Executive Producer: Burt Rosen.
Producer: Mort Green.
Director: Jack Scott.

VAUDEVILLE — 60 minutes — Syndicated 1975.

1269 VEGA$

Crime Drama. The series, set in Las Vegas, details the exploits of Dan Tanna, a macho private investigator with an eye for finding — and helping — beautiful women in trouble.

CAST

Dan Tanna   Robert Urich
Bea Travis, a showgirl/Dan's
 secretary   Phyllis Elizabeth Davis
Angie Turner, a showgirl
 /Dan's secretary, early
 episodes   Judy Landers
Binzer, Dan's legman   Bart Braverman
Lt. David Nelson, Las Vegas Metropolitan
 Police Dept.   Greg Morris
Sgt. Bella Archer, supplies Dan
 with information   Naomi Stevens
Philip "Slick" Roth, the
 casino owner   Tony Curtis
Harlan Two Leaf, Dan's
 legman (originally
 Eli Two Leaf)   Will Sampson
Julie Travis, Bea's daughter   Heather Hobbs
Burt M. Cohen, the owner of the
 Desert Inn Casino (where the
 series is filmed)   Himself
Various roles   Heather Menzies
Diamond Jim, Dan's information
 man   Victor Buono

Music: Dominic Frontiere, Shorty Rogers, Artie Kane, John Beal.
Supervising Producer: E. Duke Vincent.
Executive Producer: Aaron Spelling, Douglas S. Cramer.
Producer: Alan Godfrey, Phil Fherle, Larry Forrester, Herman Groves, Jeffrey Hayes.
Director: Harry Falk, Sutton Roley, Bernard McEveety, Don Chaffey, Marc Daniels, Lawrence Doheny, Lawrence Dobkin, Paul Stanley, Bob Kelljan, Curtis Harrington, George McCowan, Cliff Bole, Phil Bondelli, Alf Kjellin, Lewis Teague, Michael S. McLean.
Creator: Michael Mann.

VEGA$ — 60 minutes — ABC — Premiered: September 20, 1978. The 90-minute pilot film aired on ABC on April 25, 1978.

1270 THE VEIL

Anthology. Dramatizations based on incredible but true phenomena.

Host-Performer: Boris Karloff.
Music: Edwin Astley.
Producer: Hal Roach, Jr.
Director: David MacDonald, Herbert L. Strock.
Program Open:
Announcer: Presenting *The Veil* and Boris Karloff.
Boris Karloff: How do you do? The story you are about to see actually happened and is completely documented. It's one of those strange events that seems to defy all explanations; they lie beyond the veil of human knowledge and yet they happen. Science has many terms for these strange occurrences, but no explanations, as yet. But then, not too long ago, they had no explanation for a bolt of lightning or a falling star. They too seemed to come from beyond the Veil.

THE VEIL — 30 minutes — Syndicated 1958. Resyndicated in 1978 as *Mystery Adventure: The Veil.*

1271 THE VIC DAMONE SHOW

Musical Variety.

Host: Vic Damone.
Regulars: Carol Lawrence, Gail Martin.
Orchestra: Les Brown.
Producer-Director: Greg Garrison.

THE VIC DAMONE SHOW — 60 minutes — NBC — July 8, 1971 – August 19, 1971.

1272 VIENNA 1900

Anthology. A series of dramas of love set in Vienna in 1900. Adapted from the stories by Arthur Schnitzler.

Mother and Son. The story of a widow who attempts to end her son's affair with an older woman.

Cast: Widow: Dorothy Tutin.

The Man of Honour. The story of Alfred Beratoner as he attempts to free himself of his present girlfriend to marry the daughter of a wealthy factory owner.

Cast: Alfred: Norman Eshley; Elsie: Cheryl Murray; Adele: Vanessa Miles.

The Confirmed Bachelor. A two-part story about a middle-aged confirmed bachelor who finds solace in the companionship of a younger woman after the death of his sister.

Cast: Dr. Graesler: Robert Stephens; Sabine: Fiona Walker; Karl: Christopher Gable; Dr. Bohlinger: John Bennett; Katharina: Susan Littler.

The Gift of Life. The story of two lovers who promise to live and die together, but then find their vow difficult to keep when one is stricken with a terminal illness.

Cast: Karl: Christopher Gable; Marie: Maureen O'Brien; Dr. Graesler: Robert Stephens.

The Spring Sonata. The story of a young widow whose dream of romance is fulfilled when she hears from a former lover.

Cast: Berta: Lynn Redgrave; Emil: Sandor Eles; Dr. Graesler: Robert Stephens; Anna: Jacqueline Pearce.

VIENNA 1900 — 60 minutes — PBS — March 2, 1975 – April 6, 1975. 6 episodes. Produced in England.

1273 THE VIN SCULLY SHOW

Variety. Music, guests and celebrity interviews.

Host: Vin Scully.
Announcer: Harry Blackstone, Jr.
Orchestra: H. B. Barnum.
Producer: Paul W. Keyes, Armand Grant.
Writer: Bob Howard, Sidney Reznick, Bruce Taylor, Brad Lachman.
Director: Bill Foster.
Art Director: Don Roberts.

THE VIN SCULLY SHOW — 30 minutes — CBS — January 15, 1973 – March 23, 1973.

1274 THE VIRGINIA GRAHAM SHOW

Talk-Variety.

Hostess: Virginia Graham.
Music: The Ellie Frankel Quintet, The Jimmy Rowles Quartet.
Producer: Forrest Fraser.

THE VIRGINIA GRAHAM SHOW—
60- and 30-minute versions—
Syndicated 1970.

1275   THE VIRGINIAN

Western. Events in the shaping of
Wyoming during the 1880s as
seen through the eyes of The Virginian, the foreman of the Shiloh
Ranch in Medicine Bow.

CAST

The Virginian	James Drury
Judge Henry Garth, the first owner of the ranch	Lee J. Cobb
Morgan Starr, the temporary owner of the ranch	John Dehner
John Grainger, the second owner of the ranch	Charles Bickford
Clay Grainger, the third owner of the ranch	John McIntire
Trampas, the assistant foreman	Doug McClure
Molly Wood, the newspaper publisher	Pippa Scott
Betsy Garth, Henry's daughter	Roberta Shore
Steve Hill, a ranch hand	Gary Clarke
Emmett Ryker, the deputy sheriff	Clu Gulager
Randy Garth, Henry's son	Randy Boone
Belden, a ranch hand	L. Q. Jones
Jennifer Garth, Henry's niece	Diane Roter
Sheriff Mark Abbott	Ross Elliott
Elizabeth Grainger, John's niece	Sara Lane
Stacy Grainger, John's grandson	Don Quine
Holly Grainger, Clay's wife	Jeanette Nolan
David Sutton, a ranch hand	David Hartman
Jim Horn, a ranch hand	Tim Matheson
Sheriff Brannon	Harlan Warde
Gene, a ranch hand	Jean Peloquin
The bartenders	The Irish Rovers

Music: Leonard Rosenman, Percy
Faith, Hans Salter, Leo Shuken.
The Virginian Theme: Percy Faith.
Executive Producer: Norman
MacDowell, Leslie Stevens,
Herbert Hirschman.
Producer: James McAdams, James
Duff, Howard Christie, Roy
Huggins, Jules Schermer, Rich-
ard Irving, Winston Miller,
Frank Price.
Director: Robert Gist, Charles S.
Dubin, Leo Penn, Don Weis,
Roy Huggins, David Friedkin,
Jeannot Szwarc, Andrew V.
McLaglen, Thomas Carr, John
Brahm, Stuart Heisler, William
Witney, Joseph Pevney, Earl
Bellamy, Abner Biberman,
Richard Benedict, Alan Cros-
land, Jr., John Florea, Samuel
Fuller, Ida Lupino, Paul Hen-
ried, Robert Totten, Paul Stan-
ley, Seymour Robbie, James
Sheldon, John Peyser, Don
Richardson, Anton Leader,
Bernard McEveety, Russ May-
berry, Gerald Mayer, James
Neilson, Gene L. Coon, Jack
Arnold, Philip Leacock, Marc
Daniels, Harry Harris, Hollings-
worth Morse, Don McDougall.

THE VIRGINIAN—90 minutes—

NBC—September 19, 1962–Sep-
tember 9, 1970. 225 episodes.
Syndicated. Spin-off series: *The
Men from Shiloh.*

1276   VISIONS

Anthology. Dramatizations of
American plays written especially
for television.

Music: Mark Snow.
Music Theme: Joe Raposo.
Producer: Barbara Schultz.
Director: Paul Bogart.

Included:

Prison Game. An unusual story
that takes place on a TV game
show where panelists must determine which of three contestants is truthfully confessing to
the murder of her husband.

Cast: Anna I: Edith Diaz; Anna II:
Jessica Walter; Anna III: Cara
Williams; Henry Stokes: Peter
Bonerz; Marion Kostine: Neva
Patterson; Marvin Stirling; Se-
veren Darden; Moderator: Bo
Kaprall.

The War Widow. The story centers on the love between two
young women: Amy, a lonely girl
living with her mother while her
husband is serving overseas during World War I; and Jenny, an
independent woman struggling
to succeed as a photographer.

Cast: Amy: Pamela Bellwood;
Jenny: Frances Lee McCain;
Sarah: Katherine Bard; Emily:
Maxine Stuart; Kate: Barbara
Cason; Annie: Nan Martin;
Voice of Leonard (Amy's hus-
band): Tim Matheson.

Lisa's Pioneer Diary. A drama that
chronicles the journey of a young
pioneer woman through Oregon
in 1848.

Cast: Liza Stedman: Ayn Ruymen;
Eben Stedman: Dennis Red-
field; Aunt Sara: Katherine
Helmond; Martha Stedman:
Fran Ryan; Hiram Stedman:
Patrick Burke; Kate Scofield:
Andra Akers.

Two Brothers. The story focuses
on the relationship between two
brothers: David Morris, a young,
withdrawn doctor, and his older,
understanding brother, Joe.

Cast: David Morris, David Spiel-
berg; Joe Morris: Judd Hirsch;
Dr. Markle: Stephen Elliott;
Agnes: Diane Shalet; Mrs. Mor-
ris: Sarah Cunningham; Sylvia:
Zina Jasper.

VISIONS—60 minutes—PBS—
October 21, 1976–February 10,
1977.

1277   VIVA VALDEZ

Comedy. The trials and tribulations of the Valdezes, a Mexican-
American family living in East Los

Angeles, as they strive to maintain
their traditional values in a
rapidly changing world.

CAST

Sophie Valdez, the mother	Carmen Zapata
Luis Valdez, the father, a plumber	Rodolfo Hoyos
Victor Valdez, their son	James Victor
Connie Valdez, their daughter	Lisa Mordente
Ernesto Valdez, their son	Nelson D. Cuevas
Pepe Valdez, their son	Claudio Martinez
Jerry Ramerez, their cousin	Jorge Cervera, Jr.

The Valdezes' address: 363-1/2 La
Hamber Street.

Music: Shorty Rogers.
Executive Producer: Stan Jacob-
son, Bernard Rothman, Jack
Wohl.
Director; Alan Rafkin.

VIVA VALDEZ—30 minutes—
ABC—May 31, 1976–September
6, 1976.

1278   WACKO

Variety. A series of unrelated, outlandish comedy and musical skits
geared to children.

Starring: Julie McWhirter, Bo
Kaprall, Charles Fleischer.
Regulars: Millicent Crisp, Doug
Cox, Bob Comfort, Rick Kel-
lard.
Music: Stu Gardner.
Executive Producer: Chris
Bearde, Bob Wood.
Producer: Coslough Johnson,
Richard Adamson.
Director: Stanley Dorfman.
Animation: John Wilson.

WACKO—25 minutes—CBS—
September 17, 1977–November
12, 1977. 9 episodes.

1279   THE WACKY RACES

Animated Cartoon. The saga of a
cross-country automobile race.
Episodes depict the endless and
devious efforts of the evil Dick
Dastardly to secure the prize and
title as "The World's Wackiest
Racer."

Competitors: Pat Pending, who
drives the *Convert-A-Car;*
Rufus Ruftut and Sawtooth,
drivers of the *Buzz Wagon;*
Penelope Pitstop, who drives
the *Compact Pussycat;* The
Slag Brothers, Rock and Gravel,
drivers of the *Boulder Mobile;*
The Ant Hill Mob, drivers of
the *Bulletproof Bomb;* The Red
Max, pilot of the *Crimson
Haybailer;* The Gruesome
Twosome, drivers of the
Creepy Coupe; Luke and Blub-
ber Bear, drivers of the *Arkan-*

sas Chugabug; and Dick Das-
tardly and his aide Muttley (a
snickering dog), who com-
mand the *Mean Machine.*
Voices: Mel Blanc, Don Messick,
Janet Waldo, Paul Winchell,
John Stephenson.
Music: Hoyt Curtin.
Narrator: Dave Willcock.
Producer-Director: William Han-
na, Joseph Barbera.

THE WACKY RACES—30 minutes
—CBS—September 14, 1968–
September 5, 1970. Syndicated.

1280   THE WACKY WORLD OF JONATHAN WINTERS

Comedy. Unrehearsed comedy
skits that utilize Jonathan Winter's
greatest gift: his ability to im-
provise.

Host: Jonathan Winters.
Regulars: Marian Mercer, Mary
Gregory, Ronnie Graham, The
Soul Sisters.
Orchestra: Van Alexander.
Producer: Hal Parets.
Director: Buddy Bergman.

THE WACKY WORLD OF JONA-
THAN WINTERS—30 minutes—
Syndicated 1972.

1281   WAIT TIL YOUR FATHER GETS HOME

Animated Cartoon. The trials and
tribulations of Harry Boyle, president of the Boyle Restaurant Supply Company in Los Angeles, as
he, an old-fashioned father, struggles to bridge his generation gap with his progressive
children.

VOICES

Harry Boyle, the father	Tom Bosley
Irma Boyle, his wife	Joan Gerber
Alice Boyle, their daughter	Kristina Holland
Chet Boyle, their son	David Hayward
Jaimie Boyle, their son	Jackie Haley
Ralph, their neighbor	Jack Burns

Boyle family dog: Julius.

Additional Voices: Pat Harrington,
Jr., Gil Herman.
Music: Richard Bowden.
Producer-Director: William Han-
na, Joseph Barbera.

WAIT TIL YOUR FATHER GETS
HOME—30 minutes—Syndi-
cated 1972.

1282   WALLY'S WORKSHOP

Advice. Home repair instructions,
tips and advice.

Host: Wally Bruner.
Assistant: Natalie Bruner.
Announcer: Johnny Olsen.
Music: A recorded opening and
closing theme.

WALLY'S WORKSHOP—30 min-
utes—Syndicated 1972.

240-Robert. From left, Mark Harmon, Joanna Cassidy and John Bennett Perry.

United States. Front, from left, Justin Dana and Rossie Harris. Top, Beau Bridges and Helen Shaver.

Vega$. From left, Tony Curtis (bottom), Judy Landers, Phyllis Elizabeth Davis and Robert Urich.

W.E.B. Pamela Bellwood. Courtesy of the *Call-Chronicle Newspapers,* Allentown, Pa.

1283 WALT DISNEY'S WONDERFUL WORLD

Anthology. Excursions into the realm of reality and fantasy. Various types of presentations, including: cartoon, drama, mystery, adventure, educational, comedy and nature and science studies.

Host: Walt Disney.
Announcer: Gary Owens.

Included:

My Dog, the Thief. The misadventures that befall Jack Crandall, the owner of a kleptomaniac St. Bernard, when the dog steals a million-dollar necklace from jewel thieves.

Cast: Jack Crandall: Dwayne Hickman; Kim Lawrence: Mary Ann Mobley; Mrs. Formby: Elsa Lanchester; P. J. Applegate: Joe Flynn; Travell: John van Dreelen; McClure: Roger C. Carmel.

The Mystery of Dracula's Castle. The story of two boys whose attempts to make a film involve them with jewel thieves.

Cast: Alfie Booth: Johnny Whitaker; Leonard Booth: Scott Kolden; Marsha Booth: Mariette Hartley; Keith Raynor: Clu Gulager; Noah Baxter: Mills Watson; Jean Wyndham: Maggie Wellman.

Summer Magic. The heartwarming story of a penniless Boston family and their struggles to survive during the pre-World War I era.

Cast: Nancy Corey: Hayley Mills; Osh Popham: Burl Ives; Mrs. Corey: Dorothy McGuire; Gilly Corey: Eddie Hodges; Peter Corey: Jimmy Mathers; Maria Popham: Una Merkel; Julia Corey: Deborah Walley.

Babes in Toyland. A musical fantasy based on the operetta by Victor Herbert.

Cast: Mary Contrary: Annette Funicello; Mr. Barnaby: Ray Bolger; Tom: Tommy Sands; Gonzorgo: Henry Calvin; Rodrigo: Gene Sheldon.

The Young Runaways. The story of a 12-year-old girl and her 5-year-old brother, and their efforts to remain a family by kidnapping their brother and sister from a foster home.

Cast: Rosebud Doyle: Alicia Fleer; Eric Doyle: Chip Courtland; Lt. Ray Phillips: Gary Collins; Marian Lockhart: Anne Francis; Fred Lockhart: Robert Webber; Joseph T.: Tommy Crebbs.

WALT DISNEY'S WONDERFUL WORLD — 60 minutes — NBC — Premiered: September 9, 1979. Also titled *Disney's Wonderful World*.

Prior Broadcasts:

DISNEYLAND — 60 minutes — ABC — October 27, 1954 — September 3, 1958.

WALT DISNEY (*TV Guide* title) — 60 minutes — ABC — September 12, 1958 — September 10, 1961.

WALT DISNEY'S WONDERFUL WORLD OF COLOR — 60 minutes — NBC — September 17, 1961 — September 2, 1979.

1284 THE WALTONS

Drama. The series, set in Jefferson County, Virginia, during the 1930s, depicts events in the lives of the Waltons, a poor, rural family and operators of a sawmill. Focus is as seen through the sentimental eyes of John Boy, the eldest son, a high school (later college) student who hopes to become a writer. John Boy's fond recollections of his youth and his family's struggles to survive during the Depression extol the simple virtues of chastity, honesty, thrift, family unity and love.

CAST

John Walton, the father (series)	Ralph Waite
John Walton (pilot film)	Andrew Duggan
Olivia Walton, the mother (series)	Michael Learned
Olivia Walton (pilot film)	Patricia Neal
Zeb (Grandpa) Walton, John's father (series)	Will Geer
Zeb Walton (pilot film)	Edgar Bergen
Esther (Grandma) Walton, John's mother	Ellen Corby

The Walton Children:

John Boy Walton	Richard Thomas
	Robert Wightman
Mary Ellen Walton	Judy Norton-Taylor
Jason Walton	Jon Walmsley
Erin Walton	Mary Elizabeth McDonough
Ben Walton	Eric Scott
Jim-Bob Walton	David S. Harper
Elizabeth Walton	Kami Cotler

Also:

Ike Godsey, the general store owner	Joe Conley
Corabeth Godsey, Ike's wife	Ronnie Claire Edwards
Aimee Godsey, their daughter	Rachel Longaker
Dr. Curtis Willard, married Mary Ellen Walton on Nov. 14, 1976	Tom Bower
John Curtis Walton-Willard, Mary Ellen's son	Marshall & Michael Reed
Mamie Baldwin, a friend of the Waltons (series)	Helen Kleeb
Mamie Baldwin (pilot film)	Josephine Hutchinson
Emily Baldwin, Mamie's sister (series)	Mary Jackson
Emily Baldwin (pilot film)	Dorothy Stickorey
Reverend Matthew Fordwick	John Ritter
Rosemary Fordwick, Matthew's wife	Mariclare Costello
Sheriff Ep Bridges	John Crawford
Yancy Tucker, a friend of the Waltons	Robert Donner
Sissy Tucker, Yancy's wife, married on Nov. 11, 1977	Cissy Williams
Flossie Brimmer, the owner of the rooming house	Norma Marlowe
Maude Gromley, a friend of Esther's	Merie Earle
Rose Burton, Olivia's aunt	Peggy Rea
Serena, Rose's granddaughter	Martha Nix
Jeffrey, Rose's grandson	Keith Mitchell
Cindy, married Ben Walton on March 1, 1979	Leslie Winston
Patsy Brimmer, Flossie's niece	Eileen McDonough
Professor Parks, John Boy's English instructor at Boatwright University	Paul Jenkins
Nora, the county nurse	Kaiulani Lee
Clarence Johnson, publisher of the *Jefferson County Times*	Walter Brooke
Fannie Tatum, Erin's employer at the phone company	Sheila Allen
Thelma, the owner of the Dew Drop Inn, where Jason works	Dorothy Shay
J. D. Pickett, Erin's employer at Pickett Metal Products (W.W. II episodes)	Lewis Arquette
George "G. W." Haines, Erin's friend	David Doremus
Verdie Foster, the Walton's friend	Lynn Hamilton
Harley Foster, Verdie's husband	Hal Williams
Reverend Andrew March	Sean Roche
Daisy Garner, John Boy's friend in New York City	Deirdre Lenihan
Reverend Hank Buchanan	Peter Fox

Prototypes for the Walton Children (the series is based on the childhood memories of Earl Hamner, Jr.):

Earl Hamner, Jr., the model for John Boy.
Nancy Hamner Jamerson, the model for Elizabeth.
James Hamner, the model for Jim-Bob.
Marion Hamner Hoggs, the model for Mary Ellen.
Audrey Hamner Hankins, the model for Erin.
Bill and Paul Hamner, the models for Ben.
Cliff Hamner, the model for Jason.

Walton family dog: Reckless.

Narrator: Earl Hamner, Jr.
Music: Jerry Goldsmith, Arthur Morton, Alexander Courage.
Executive Producer: Lee Rich, Earl Hamner, Jr.
Producer: Robert Jacks, Andy White, Rod Peterson.
Director: Harry Harris, Ralph Senensky, Harvey Laidman, Ralph Waite, Lawrence Dobkin, Richard Bennett, Ivan Dixon, Philip Leacock, Lee Philips, Vincent Sherman, Robert Butler, Walter Alzmann, Fiedler Cooke, Jack Shea, Herbert Hirschmann, Gwen Arner, Stan Lathan.

THE WALTONS — 60 minutes — CBS — Premiered: September 14, 1972. The two-hour pilot film, "The Homecoming," aired on CBS on December 19, 1971.

1285 WAR AND PEACE

Drama. A tableau of Russian society during the turbulent era of the Napoleonic Wars (1805 – 1820). Based on the novel by Leo Tolstoy and produced in England.

CAST

Natasha	Morag Hood
Prince Andre Balonsky	Alan Dobie
Nikolai Bolonsky	Anthony Jacobs
Maria Bolonsky	Angela Down
Anatole Kuragin	Colin Baker
Napoleon Bonaparte	David Swift
Prince Vasili Kuragin	Basil Henson
Helene Kuragin	Fiona Gaunt
Pierre Bezuhov	Anthony Hopkins
Dolohov	Donald Burton
Count Ilya Rostov	Rupert Davies
Natalia Rostov	Faith Brook
Sonya	Joanna David
Nicolai Rostov	Sylvester Morand
Denisov	Gary Watson
Boris Drubetskoy	Neil Stacy
Tzar Alexander I	Donald Douglas
Kutuzov	Frank Middleman

Producer: David Conroy.
Writer: Jack Pulman.
Director: John Davies.

WAR AND PEACE — PBS — November 20, 1973 – January 15, 1974. Broadcast in seven 90-minute and two 2-hour installments.

1286 WASHINGTON: BEHIND CLOSED DOORS

Drama. A six-part miniseries loosely based on John Ehrlichman's political novel, *The Company*. The complex story, which centers on the life and rise to power of Richard Monckton from senator to the President of the United States, exposes the public and intimate lives of the people who control our nation — lives filled with greed, lust and corruption.

CAST

Richard Monckton	Jason Robards
William Martin, the C.I.A. director	Cliff Robertson
Linda Martin, William's wife	Lois Nettleton
Sally Whalen, the spy	Stefanie Powers
Frank Flaherty, the Chief of Staff	Robert Vaughn
Esker Anderson, the retiring President	Andy Griffith
Bob Bailey, the Press Secretary	Barry Nelson
Carl Tessler, the Foreign Affairs Advisor	Harold Gould
Adam Gardiner, the idealist	Tony Bill

Also:

Myron Dunn	John Houseman
Roger Castle	David Selby
Jennie Jameson	Meg Foster
Eli McGinn	Peter Coffield
Paula Gardiner	Frances Lee McCain
Joe Wisnovsky	Barry Primus
Kathy Ferris	Diana Ewing
Wanda Elliott	Lara Parker

Tucker Tallford	John Lehne
Simon Cappell	Alan Oppenheimer
Hank Ferris	Nicholas Pryor
Peter Ozymandias	Joseph Sirola
Jack Atherton	Linden Chiles
Lawrence Allison	Frank Marth
Elmer Morse	Thayer David
Bennett Lowman	John Randolph
Mrs. Monckton	June Dayton
Marta Anderson	Danna Hansen
Dorothy Kemp	Jean Cameron Howell
Walter Tullock	Phillip Allen
Lars Haglund	Skip Homeier
Jimmy Bird	Joseph Hacker
Brewster Perry	George Gaynes
Anne Marie Lowman	Mary LaRoche
Ashton	John Kerr

Music: Dominic Frontiere.
Executive Producer: Stanley Kallis.
Supervising Producer: Eric Bercovici, David Rintels.
Producer: Norman S. Powell.
Writer: Eric Bercovici, David Rintels.
Director: Gary Nelson.

WASHINGTON: BEHIND CLOSED DOORS—12 hours (total)—ABC—September 6, 1977–September 11, 1977.

1287   WATCH ME

Human Interest. The program focuses on ordinary people as they appear on camera for the first time and display some hidden talent.

Host: Robert King.
Music: Stan Tarner.
Theme: Stan Tarner and Jess Korman.
Executive Producer: Bob Schwartz.
Producer: John Horvath.
Director: John Horvath.

WATCH ME—30 minutes—Syndicated 1980.

1288   THE WAVERLY WONDERS

Comedy. The series concerns itself with the misadventures of Joe Casey, a washed-up professional basketball player who now coaches basketball and teaches history at Waverly High School.

CAST

Joe Casey (originally Harry Casey)	Joe Namath
Linda Harris, the principal	Gwynne Gilford
George Benton, a teacher	Ben Piazza
Students Comprising The Waverly Wonders Team:	
Connie Rafkin	Kim Lankford
Tony Faguzzi	Joshua Grentock
Hasty	Tierre Turner
John Pate	Charles Bloom

Music: Fred Karlin.
Executive Producer: Lee Rich, Marc Merson.
Producer: Bruce Kane, Steve Zacharias.
Director: Bill Persky, Dick Martin.

THE WAVERLY WONDERS—30

minutes—NBC—September 22, 1978–October 6, 1978. 4 episodes. The series was "sneak previewed" on September 7, 1978.

1289   WAY OUT GAMES

Game. Two three-member teams of junior high school students compete in various contests of skill to complete stunts in the quickest time. Points are awarded after each of the three rounds and the team that scores the highest receives the opportunity to compete in the quarter finals—a tournament for prizes.

Host: Sonny Fox.
Assistant: Mark Smith.
Music: Mort Lindsey.
Producer: Jack Barry, Dan Enright.
Director: Richard S. Kline.

WAY OUT GAMES—25 minutes—CBS—September 11, 1976–September 3, 1977.

1290   W.E.B.

Drama. A behind-the-scenes look at the world of television as seen through the experiences of Ellen Cunningham, an up-and-coming programming executive with the Trans-Atlantic Broadcasting Company (TAB) in New York City.

CAST

Ellen Cunningham	Pamela Bellwood
Jack Kiley, the programming chief	Alex Cord
Dan Costello, the sales executive	Andrew Prine
Gus Dunlap, the news director	Richard Basehart
Walter Matthews, the director of operations	Howard Witt
Harvey Pearlstein, the head of research	Lee Wilkof
Harry Brooks, the board chairman	Stephen McNally
Christine Nichols, Ellen's secretary	Tish Raye
Kevin, Ellen's assistant	Peter Coffield

Music: Jerry Fielding, David Rose, Morton Stevens.
Music Supervision: Lionel Newman.
Executive Producer: Lin Bolen.
Producer: Christopher Morgan.
Director: Harvey Hart, Ray Austin, Alex March.
Creator: David Karp.

W.E.B.—60 minutes—NBC—September 13, 1978–October 5, 1978. 5 episodes.

1291   WELCOME BACK, KOTTER

Comedy. The trials and tribulations of Gabe Kotter, a graduate of the James Buchanan High School in Bensonhurst, Brooklyn, New York, who returns to the school ten years later. His assignment is to teach Special Guidance Remedial Academics to

a class of incorrigible students known as "Sweat Hogs," teenagers who resemble the way he was when he was attending the same school.

CAST

Gabe Kotter	Gabriel Kaplan
Julie Kotter, his wife	Marcia Strassman
Michael Woodman, the vice principal	John Sylvester White
Voice of the Principal, John Lazarus	James Komack
Judy Borden, a student	Helaine Lembeck
Todd Ludlow, a student	Dennis Bowen
Jenny Henson, Julie's sister	Susan Pratt
Jean Tremaine, English teacher	Della Reese
The Sweat Hogs:	
Vinnie Barbarino	John Travolta
Juan Epstein	Robert Hegyes
Frederick "Boom Boom" Washington	Lawrence-Hilton Jacobs
Arnold Horshack	Ron Palillo
Rosalie "Hotsie" Totzi	Debralee Scott
Vernajean Williams	Vernee Watson
Angie Graboski	Melonie Haller
Carvelli	Charles Fleischer
Beau DeLabarre	Stephen Shortridge
Wilbur Murray	Bob Harchum
Bambi Foster	Susan Lanier
Maria	Caterina Cellino
Wendy	Wendy Rastatter
Laura	Sally Hightower
Doris	Judy Young
Also:	
Mary Johnson, Arnold's girlfriend	Irene Arranga
Carmine Epstein, Juan's sister	Lisa Mordente
Kelly, the Kotters' babysitter	Georganne LaPiere
Mo Epstein, Juan's uncle and Gabe's landlord	Herb Edelman
Robin and Rachel Kotter, Gabe and Julie's twins (grown; flash forwards)*	Beth and Kay Kearney
Sally, Vinnie's girlfriend	Linda McCullough

Gabe's address: 711 East Ocean Parkway (later, after the birth of the twins, 1962 Linden Blvd., Apt. 409).

Announcer: Gabriel Kaplan.
Music: John B. Sebastian.
Theme Vocal: "Welcome Back" by John B. Sebastian.
Supervising Producer: Ed Simmons, Peter Meyerson.
Executive Producer: James Komack.
Producer: Bill Richmond, Gene Perrett, Nick Arnold, Alan Sacks, Eric Cohen, George Yanok, George Bloom.
Writer: Peter Meyerson, Beverly Bloomberg, Jerry Ross, Jerry Rannow, Jewel Jaffe Rannow, George Yanok, Myles Wilder, Michael Weinberger, Eric Cohen, Pat Proft, Bo Kaprall, Neil Rosen, George Tricker, Ira Miller, Gabriel Kaplan.
Director: Norman Abbott, Bob Claver, James Komack, Bob LaHendro, Gary Shimokawa, Bill Persky, Al Schwartz, Robert Hegyes.

Creator: Gabriel Kaplan, Alan Sacks; developed by Peter Meyerson.

WELCOME BACK, KOTTER—30 minutes—ABC—September 9, 1975–March 17, 1979; May 25, 1979–August 3, 1979. Syndicated.

*The infants who play the part are not credited.

1292   WE'LL GET BY

Comedy. The series, set in suburban New Jersey, depicts events in the lives of the Platt family: George, a lawyer; his wife, Liz; and their three bright children, Muff, Andrea and Kenny.

CAST

George Platt, the father	Paul Sorvino
Liz Platt, his wife	Mitzi Hoag
Michael "Muff" Platt, their son	Jerry Houser
Andrea Platt, their daughter	Devon Scott
Kenny Platt, their son	Willie Aames

Music: Joe Raposo, Sheldon Harnick.
Executive Producer: Marc Merson, Alan Alda.
Producer: Alan Alda, Allan Katz, Don Reo.
Director: Jack Shea, Jay Sandrich.
Creator-Writer: Alan Alda.

WE'LL GET BY—30 minutes—CBS—March 6, 1975–May 30, 1975.

1293   WESTSIDE MEDICAL

Drama. The personal and professional lives of Doctors Sam Lanagan, Janet Cottrell and Phil Parker, staff physicians at Westside Memorial Hospital in California.

CAST

Dr. Sam Lanagan	James Sloyan
Dr. Janet Cottrell	Linda Carlson
Dr. Phil Parker	Ernest Thompson
Carrie, the woman who assists them in the clinic	Alice Nunn

Music: Billy Goldenberg.
Executive Producer: Martin Starger.
Producer: Alan A. Armer.
Director: Leo Penn, Gerald Mayer, Ralph Senensky, Larry Elikann, Vincent Sherman, Paul Stanley.
Creator: Barry Oringer.

WESTSIDE MEDICAL—60 minutes—ABC—March 15, 1977–April 14, 1977; July 20, 1977–August 24, 1977.

1294   THE WESTWIND

Adventure. The series, set in Hawaii, follows the adventures of Steve Andrews, an underwater photographer, and his wife, Kate, a marine biologist, as they travel through the various islands seeking to further man's knowledge of the sea.

CAST

Steve Andrews	Van Williams
Kate Andrews, his wife	Niki Dantine
Robin Andrews, their daughter	Kimberly Beck
Tom Andrews, their son	Steve Burns

Their yacht: The *Westwind*.

Music: Richard La Salle.
Executive Producer: William P. D'Angelo.
Producer: Norm Prescott, Lou Scheimer, Dick Rosenbloom, Richard Bluel.
Director: Christian I. Nyby II, Richard L. Bare.

THE WESTWIND—30 minutes—NBC—September 6, 1975–September 4, 1976.

1295   WE'VE GOT EACH OTHER

Comedy. The series, set in California, focuses on the chaotic misadventures of the Hibbards: Judy, a not-so-attractive, lanky photographer's assistant, and her husband, Stuart, who works at home as a copywriter for bizarre devices advertised in the Herman Gutman Mail Order Catalogue.

CAST

Judy Hibbard	Beverly Archer
Stuart Hibbard	Oliver Clark
Damon Jerome, Judy's employer	Tom Poston
Dee Dee, Damon's top model	Joan Van Ark
Donna, Damon's secretary	Ren Woods
Ken Redford, the Hibbard's neighbor	Martin Kove
Damon's Model	Reba Waters
Damon's Model	Anitra Ford

Music and Theme Vocal: Nino Candido.
Executive Producer: Tom Patchett, Jay Tarses.
Producer: Jack Burns.
Director: James Burrows, Will MacKenzie.
Creator: Tom Patchett and Jay Tarses.
Art Director; Sydney Z. Litwack.

WE'VE GOT EACH OTHER—30 minutes—CBS—October 1, 1977–January 7, 1978. 12 episodes.

1296   WHAT REALLY HAPPENED TO THE CLASS OF '65?

Anthology. Dramatizations that update the lives of the 1965 graduating class of the fictitious Bret Harte High School in Los Angeles. Stories open with the commentary by Sam Ashley, a '65 grad and now a teacher at Bret Harte High, as he recalls his fellow classmates. The program then chronicles the life of a particular grad from 1965 to 1977. Based on the book by Michael Medved and David Wallechinsky.

Starring: Tony Bill as Sam Ashley.
Music: Don Costa, Jimmie Has-

kell, Stu Phillips, James Di Pasquale.
Executive Producer: Richard Irving.
Producer: Richard Irving, James M. Miller, Rick Husky, Jack Laird, Ron Satlof, Jules Irving, Jon Epstein, Robert L. Crawford.
Director: Harry Falk, Richard Irving, James M. Miller, Edward Parone, Lawrence Dobkin, Seymour Robbie, Ron Satlof, Leo Penn, Jack Starrett, James Sheldon, Alan J. Levi, Jules Irving.

Included:

Everybody's Girl. The story of Kathy Adams, the girl with the worst reputation in class. Now wed, she finds her happy marriage threatened by a renewed inclination to promiscuity—a condition that brings on serious anxiety attacks. The episode focuses on her attempts to resolve the situation.

Cast: Kathy Adams Miller: Annette O'Toole; Jay Miller: Tim Matheson; Samantha: Valorie Armstrong; Dane: Charles Frank.

Class Dreamers. The story focuses on graduates Soldado and Sook—the class dreamers—and their desperate attempts to begin a roadside restaurant.

Cast: Soldado: Gilbert Garcia; Sook: Richard Stanley; Wanda: Judy Landers; Lloyd Casty: Eugene Roche; Hornblower: Alex Rocco; Sunshine: Jewel Blanche.

The Girl Nobody Knew. The story of Cynthia Keller, the shy, sensitive, nondistinctive girl in high school, and the changes that affect her when, after graduating, she meets a songwriter who sets her poems to music—and her on the road to musical stardom.

Cast: Cynthia Keller: Kim Cattrall; Fran: Jessica Walter; Jack Miller: John Rubinstein; Gene: Larry Hagman.

Mr. Potential. The story of Robert Spencer, the class underachiever, now a park athletic director being pressured by his father and girlfriend to improve his situation in life.

Cast: Robert Spencer: Richard Hatch; Nancy: Rosanna Arquette; G. A. Malone: Maggie Wellman; Frank Spencer: John Marley; Elgin: Erin Blunt; Gary Lowen: Jack Ging; Cheryl Lynn: Pat Anderson.

WHAT REALLY HAPPENED TO THE CLASS OF '65?—60 minutes—NBC—December 8, 1977–March 9, 1978; June 6, 1978–July 27, 1978. 14 episodes.

1297   WHAT'S HAPPENING!!

Comedy. The series, set in Southern California, follows the antics of three black teenagers: Roger Thomas, Dwayne Clemens and Freddie Stubbs, nicknamed "Rerun" for his constant habit of repeating in summer school what he should have learned during the school year.

CAST

Roger Thomas	Ernest Thomas
Dwayne Clemens	Haywood Nelson
Freddie "Rerun" Stubbs	Fred Berry
Mabel Thomas, Roger's mother	Mabel King
Dee Thomas, Roger's sister	Danielle Spencer
Shirley Wilson, the waitress at Robert's Place, the soda shop hangout	Shirley Hemphill
Bill Thomas, Roger's father	Thalmus Rasulala
Rob, the owner of Robert's Place	Earl Billings

Music: Henry Mancini.
Executive Producer: Saul Turteltaub, Bernie Orenstein, Bud Yorkin.
Producer: Dee Caruso, Gerald Bardner, Sidney Miller.
Director: Dennis Steinmetz, Bud Yorkin, Jack Shea, Mark Warren, Dick Harwood, Alan Rafkin, Hal Alexander, Mark Warren.

WHAT'S HAPPENING!!—30 minutes—ABC—August 5, 1976–August 26, 1976; November 13, 1976–April 28, 1979.

1298   WHAT'S NEW MR. MAGOO?

Animated Cartoon. The misadventures of the nearsighted Quincy Magoo and his equally nearsighted dog, McBarker.

VOICES

Quincy Magoo	Jim Backus
McBarker	Frank Welker

Additional Voices: Hal Smith.
Music: Doug Goodwin, Eric Rogers, Dean Elliott.
Producer: David DePatie, Friz Freleng.
Director: Sid Marcus, Bob McKimson, Spencer Peel.

WHAT'S NEW MR. MAGOO?—30 minutes—CBS—September 10, 1977–September 2, 1978.

1299   WHEELIE AND THE CHOPPER BUNCH

Animated Cartoon. The adventures of Wheelie, an almost human Volkswagen and the world's greatest stunt-racing car. He and his girlfriend, Rota Ree, a convertible, struggle to overcome the evils of the Chopper Bunch, daredevil motorcycles led by Chopper, who plots to acquire Rota's affections.

VOICES

Wheelie	Frank Welker
Rota Ree	Judy Strangis
Chopper	Frank Welker
Revs, Chopper's cohort	Paul Winchell
Hi Riser, Chopper's cohort	Lennie Weinrib

Music: Hoyt Curtin.
Executive Producer: William Hanna, Joseph Barbera.
Producer: Iwao Takamoto.
Director: Charles A. Nichols.

WHEELIE AND THE CHOPPER BUNCH—30 minutes—NBC—September 7, 1974–August 30, 1975.

1300   WHEEL OF FORTUNE

Game. A line of blank spaces, which represents the letters in a famous name, place or event, is displayed. One of the three players who compete spins a large wheel that pinpoints a money amount, and suggests a letter of the alphabet that might be contained in the mystery phrase. If the letter is contained in the phrase, it is revealed in its appropriate position and the player receives a chance to identify the phrase. If he is stumped, he spins again and suggests another letter (each correct letter awards the player the money the wheel pinpoints). When an incorrect letter is suggested, the next player receives a turn, and the game continues in this manner until the phrase is identified. The player who makes the identification is the winner and receives what money he has accumulated, which he uses to purchase merchandise gifts from a series of showcases that are displayed on stage.

Host: Chuck Woolery.
Hostess: Susan Stafford.
Substitute Hostess: Summer Bartholomew.
Announcer: Charlie O'Donnell.
Substitute Announcer: John Harlan.
Producer: Nancy Jones.
Associate Producer: David Williger.
Director: Dick Carson.

WHEEL OF FORTUNE—30 minutes—NBC—Premiered: January 6, 1975.

1301   WHEELS

Drama. A five-part miniseries, set against the background of Detroit, Michigan, in the late 1960s, that focuses on the personal and public lives of the members of National Motors, a large auto corporation. Based on the novel by Arthur Hailey.

CAST

Adam Trenton	Rock Hudson
Erica Trenton	Lee Remick
Barbara Lipton	Blair Brown

Greg Trenton	Howard McGillin
Peter Flodenhale	Johh Beck
Lowell Baxter	Ralph Bellamy
Matt Zaleski	Scott Brady
Merv Rucks	John Durren
Caroline Horton	Marj Dusay
Jody Horton	Lisa Eilbacher
Smokey Stevenson	Tony Franciosa
Kirk Trenton	James Carroll Jordan
Teresa Chapman	Adele Mara
Hub Hewitson	Tim O'Connor
Rusty Horton	Gerald S. O'Loughlin
Waggoner	Allan Rich
Dr. Patterson	David Spielberg
Rollie Knight	Harold Sylvester
Ursula	Jessica Walter
Leonard Wingate	Fred Williamson
Emerson Vale	Anthony Costello
Val	Debbie Ritcher
Bob Nessell	Bob Hastings
Arnold Beecham	James Ray
Sir Philip Sturdevant	James Booth
Newkirk	Al C. White

Music: Morton Stevens.
Executive Producer: Roy Huggins.
Producer: Robert F. O'Neill.
Writer: Millard Lampell, Hank Searls, Robert Hamilton, Nancy Lynn Schwartz.
Director: Jerry London.
Director of Photography: Jacques Marquette.

WHEELS — 2 hours — NBC — May 7, 1978 — May 15, 1978. 5 episodes.

1302 WHEN HAVOC STRUCK

Documentary. The series examines twentieth-century disasters through old newsreel film footage and interviews with eyewitnesses.

Host-Narrator: Glenn Ford.
Music: Harry Robinson.
Executive Producer: Martin McKeand.
Producer: David C. Rae.
Director: David C. Rae.

WHEN HAVOC STRUCK — 30 minutes — Syndicated 1978. 12 episodes.

1303 WHEN THE WHISTLE BLOWS

Comedy. The on-and-off the job antics of a group of hard-living construction workers for the Tri-State Construction Company in Los Angeles.

CAST

Darlene, the owner of Darlene's Place, the bar hangout	Sue Ane Langdon
"Big" Buzz Dillard, a construction worker	Doug Barr
Lucy, a construction worker	Susan Buckner
Norm Jenkins, a construction worker	Dolph Sweet
Randy Harford, a construction worker	Philip Brown
Martin "Hunk" Kincaid, a construction worker	Tim Rossovich

Bulldog, the assistant foreman	Noble Willingham
Ted Hanrahan, the foreman	Gary Allen
Dottie Jenkins, Norm's wife	Alice Hirson
Sharon Jenkins, Norm's daughter	Talia Balsam
Jill Macklin, Randy's girlfriend	Stacey Kuhne
Tuey Wy, the Korean girl adopted by Buzz, Norm, Randy and Hunk	Sally Imamura

Music: Mark Snow.
Theme: "When the Whistle Blows" sung by Jerry Whitman and the Sweet Inspirations.
Supervising Producer: Rick Husky.
Executive Producer; Leonard Goldberg, Jerry Weintraub.
Producer: Gerald Sanford, Carroll Newman.
Director: Michael Preece, Allen Baron, Christian I. Nyby II, Edward Parone.
Art Director: Richard B. Lewis.

WHEN THE WHISTLE BLOWS — 60 minutes — ABC — March 14, 1980 — April 25, 1980; June 7, 1980 — June 14, 1980; July 6, 1980 — July 27, 1980. 12 episodes.

1304 WHEN TELEVISION WAS LIVE

Nostalgia. Through the use of kinescopes, the television careers of Peter Lind Hayes and Mary Healy are recalled.

Hosts: Peter Lind Hayes, Mary Healy.
Producer: Peter Lind Hayes.
Director: Debra Gangnebin.

WHEN TELEVISION WAS LIVE — 30 minutes — PBS — August 6, 1975 — September 17, 1975. 7 episodes.

1305 WHEN THINGS WERE ROTTEN

Comedy. A satire based on the legend of Robin Hood. The series, set in twelfth-century England, depicts Robin Hood, the man who stole from the rich to give to the poor, as a birdbrain. His Merry Men, free-born Englishmen loyal to the king, are shown as bumbling klutzes; and Maid Marian, Robin's romantic interest, as a sexy dumb blonde. When Prince John usurps the throne of his brother, Richard the Lionhearted, he provokes hatred between Normans and Saxons by imposing a tax on the Saxons. When Sir Robin of Locksley, a Saxon, opposes this, he is declared a criminal. Retreating to Sherwood Forest, Robin Hood establishes a base near the Gallows Oak with his Merry Men (Alan-A-Dale, Friar Tuck, Renaldo and Little John). Episodes depict Robin's efforts to return the throne to its rightful king, protect the weak, avenge the oppressed,

and foil the evils of the Sheriff of Nottingham, who acts on behalf of Prince John.

CAST

Robin Hood	Dick Gautier
Maid Marian, his girlfriend	Misty Rowe
Alan-A-Dale, one of his Merry Men	Bernie Kopell
Friar Tuck, one of his Merry Men	Dick Van Patten
Renaldo, one of his Merry Men	Richard Dimitri
Little John, one of his Merry Men	David Sabin
Lord Hubert, the Sheriff of Nottingham	Henry Polic II
Betram, the Sheriff's aide	Richard Dimitri
Prince John	Ron Rifkin
Princess Isabelle	Jane Johnston
Sylvester, a peasant	Jimmy Martinez

Music: Artie Butler.
Executive Producer: Mel Brooks.
Producer: Norman Steinberg.
Writer: Mel Brooks, John Boni, Norman Steinberg.
Director: Jerry Paris, Joshua Shelley, Marty Feldman, Peter H. Hunt, Bruce Bilson.
Creator: Mel Brooks, John Boni.

WHEN THINGS WERE ROTTEN — 30 minutes — ABC — September 10, 1975 — December 24, 1975.

1306 WHERE'S HUDDLES

Animated Cartoon. The misadventures of Ed Huddles and Bubba McCoy, quarterback and team center for the Rhinos, a disorganized professional football team.

VOICES

Ed Huddles	Cliff Norton
Bubba McCoy	Mel Blanc
Marge Huddles, Ed's wife	Jean VanderPyl
Penny McCoy, Bubba's wife	Marie Wilson
Claude Pertwee, their neighbor	Paul Lynde
The Coach	Alan Reed
Freight Train, a team member	Herb Jeffries

Additional Characters: Fumbles, the Huddles dog; and Beverly, Claude's cat.
Announcer: Dick Enberg.
Music: Hoyt Curtin.
Executive Producer: William Hanna, Joseph Barbera.
Producer: Alex Lovy.
Director: William Hanna, Joseph Barbera.

WHERE'S HUDDLES — 30 minutes — CBS — July 1, 1970 — September 10, 1971; July 11, 1971 — September 5, 1971. 17 episodes.

1307 WHERE THE HEART IS

Serial. The conflicts, tensions and drives of the close-knit Hathaway family, residents of Northcross, Connecticut.

CAST

Julian Hathaway	James Mitchell
Mary Hathaway	Diana Walker
Michael Hathaway	Greg Abels
Vicky Hathaway	Lisa Richards
Kate Prescott	Diana van der Vlis
Alison Jessup	Louise Shaffer
Dr. Hugh Jessup	David Cryer
Dr. Joe Prescott	Bill Post, Jr.
Nancy Prescott	Katherine Meshill
Ed Lucas	Joe Mascolo
Stella O'Brien	Bibi Osterwald
Christine Cameron	Delphi Harrington
Loretta Jorden	Alice Drummond
Peter Jorden	Mike Bersell
Carol Gault	Janet League
Elizabeth Rainey	Tracy Brooks Swope
John Rainey	Peter MacLean
Dr. Adrienne Harris	Priscilla Pointer
Lt. Hayward	Philip Sterling
Amy Snowden	Clarice Blackburn
Dr. Jim Hudson	Ruben Greene
Terry Stevens	Ted LaPlatt
Will Watts	Robert Symonds
Detective Munford	Gil Rogers
Lt. Fenelli	Ted Beniodes
Dr. Homes Rayburn	Alan Manson
Margaret Jordas	Rue McClanahan
	Barbara Baxley
Daniel Hathaway	Joseph Dolen
Ellie Jordas	Zohra Lampert
Mrs. Harrison	Caroline Coates
Lois Snowden	Jeanne Ruskin
Judge	William Prince
Ben Jessup	Daniel Keyes
Steve Prescott	Laurence Luckinbill
	Ron Harper
Baby Katina	Kara Fleming
Judge Halstad	Mason Adams
Dave	Charles Dobson
Bill Conway	Barton Hayman
Mrs. Pangborn	Paula Truman

Music: Eddie Layton.

WHERE THE HEART IS — 30 minutes — CBS — September 8, 1969 — March 23, 1973.

1308 WHEW!

Game. Two players compete. One player, the winner of a toss of the coin, chooses one of two positions: the Blocker or the Charger. The Charger is taken offstage to a soundproof room. A large board, which contains six lines (five lines of five boxes each and one line of three boxes) is displayed. Each of the boxes in the first five lines is valued at $10, $20, $30, $40 and $50; the sixth line of three boxes is valued at $200, $350 and $500. The Blocker selects any six boxes, which become five-second penalty blocks. The Charger is brought on stage and begins the game by calling a line (beginning with line one) and a money amount. A blooper is read, which the Charger must correct before he can proceed to the next line. Each correct response wins him a line and the associated money amount. The object is for the Charger to correct six bloopers, one for each line, within a 60-second time limit (if a block is called, it deducts five seconds from the Charger's time). The round is won by either the Charger if he successfully answers six bloopers, or by the Blocker, if the Charger fails. In round two, the players change position and the game is played in the same manner. The first player to win two games is the champion.

Host: Tom Kennedy.
Announcer: Rod Roddy.
Music: Alan Thicke, Michael Malone.
Executive Producer: Bud Austin, Burt Sugarman.
Producer: Jay Wolpert.
Director: Bill Carruthers, Dick Darley.
Art Director: James Agazzi.
First Champion: Annie Brown.

WHEW!—25 minutes—CBS—April 23, 1979–May 30, 1980. 280 programs. Also titled *Celebrity Whew!*

1309   THE WHITE SHADOW

Drama. The story of Ken Reeves, a former pro basketball player (washed up when he injured his knee) who acquires a job as athletic coach for Carver High School in Los Angeles. His attempts to manage the losing and unruly team are the focal point of the series. (The title is derived from a remark made by Reeves, saying after his team's first win, "I'll be behind you like a White Shadow.")

CAST

Ken Reeves	Ken Howard
Jim Willis, the principal	Jason Bernard
	Ed Bernard
Sybil Buchanan, the vice principal	Joan Pringle
Katie Donohue, Ken's sister	Robin Rose
Bill Donohue, Katie's husband	Jerry Fogel

The High School Team:

Morris Thorpe	Kevin Hooks
Warren Coolidge	Byron Stewart
Curtis Jackson	Eric Kilpatrick
Mario "Salami" Petrino	Timothy Van Patten
Milton Reese	Nathan Cook
James Hayward	Thomas Carter
Ricardo Gomez	Ira Augustain
Abner Goldstein	Ken Michelman
Nick Vitaglia	John Mengatti
Jessie B. Mitchell	Stoney Jackson
Wardell Stone	Larry Flash Jenkins
Patrick Falahey	John Laughlin
Eddie Franklin	Art Holliday
Teddy Rutherford	Wolfe Perry

Also:

Harold Witherspoon, the school reporter	David Hubbard
Phil Jeffers, the team manager	Russell Phillip Robinson
The Referee	Dick Baker
The P.A. Announcer	Billy Crawford
Edward Thorpe, Morris' father	Herbert Jefferson, Jr.
Pamela Thorpe, Morris' mother	Hazel Medina
Gwen Thorpe, Morris' sister	Crystal Makes

Music: Mike Post and Pete Carpenter.

Executive Producer: Bruce Paltrow.
Producer: Mark Tinker.
Director: Jackie Cooper, Bruce Paltrow, Victor Lobl, Michael Zinberg, Ernest Pintoff, Mark Tinker, Betty Goldberg, Thomas Carter, Marc Norman, LeRoy McDonald.
Creator: Bruce Paltrow.

THE WHITE SHADOW—60 minutes—CBS—Premiered: November 27, 1978.

1310   WHITNEY AND THE ROBOT

Children. An unusual series in which aspects of the adult world are explained to children through the adventures of Whitney, a cab driver, and 4-U-2. A robot, 4-U-2 is from the planet Zeda and was sent to Earth to study our ways.

CAST

Whitney	Whitney Rydbeck
4-U-2	Buddy Douglas
Corky, Whitney's friend	Corky Greene

Music Director: Corky Greene.
Musical Arrangements: Erich Bulling.
Executive Producer: Stephanie B. Gray.
Producer: Dave Bell, Dan Gomez.
Director: John W. Mitchell.
Art Director: Carlos Berben.

WHITNEY AND THE ROBOT—30 minutes—Syndicated 1979.

1311   WHODUNIT?

Mystery-Game. A staged crime, in which a murder is committed, is enacted. Based on the clues and suspects presented in the dramatization, three celebrity guests and three studio audience contestants have to figure out Whodunit. Before the second commercial break (midway in the police investigation of the crime), the dramatization is stopped and the studio audience panelists receive the opportunity to win $10,000 by identifying the killer at this point. If a player decides to do so, he secretly writes his answer on a card and cannot change his answer later on. Following the dramatization, the suspects are brought on stage and, for the benefit of the panelists, the three celebrity guests cross-examine them in an attempt to uncover the culprit. Each of the celebrity experts chooses the subject he believes is the killer; the panelists lock in their choices. Excluding the $10,000 situation (which is awarded if the player's early prediction is correct), money is scored as follows: $2,500 if a player agrees with the panel (and the panel is correct), or $5,000 if a player's choice is different than

the majority of the panel—and correct.

Host: Ed McMahon.
Regular Celebrity Expert: F. Lee Bailey.
Music: Fred Werner.
Supervising Producer: Bill Carruthers.
Executive Producer: Martin Starger.
Producer: Doris Quinlan, Joel Stein.
Director: Bill Carruthers, Don Wallace.
Creator: Jeremy Lloyd, Lance Percival.

WHODUNIT?—30 minutes—NBC—April 12, 1979–May 17, 1979. 6 episodes. Based on the British series of the same title.

1312   WHODUNIT?

Mystery-Game. The British series on which the American series of the same title is based. The format has a panel of celebrity sleuths attempt to solve a re-enacted crime.

Host: Jon Pertwee.
Producer-Director: Anthony Parker.
Designer: Frank Gillman.
Creator: Jeremy Lloyd, Lance Percival.

WHODUNIT?—30 minutes—Produced and aired by Thames TV in 1978.

1313   WHO'S WATCHING THE KIDS?

Comedy. The series, set in Las Vegas, focuses on the misadventures of Stacy Turner and Angie Vitola, two luscious showgirls at the seedy Club Sand Pile. The girls share an apartment with Frankie, Angie's mischievous 16-year-old brother, and Melissa, Stacy's know-it-all 9-year-old sister. The series title is derived from the problem the girls have: who can watch their kids when they are working? Their solution: Larry Parnell, a KVGS-TV newscaster, and Burt Gunkel, his cameraman, neighbors who, to impress Angie and Stacy, babysit when they are able.

CAST

Stacy Turner, a showgirl	Caren Kaye
Angie Vitola, a showgirl	Lynda Goodfriend
Frankie Vitola, Angie's brother	Scott Baio
Melissa Turner, Stacy's sister	Tammy Lauren
Larry Parnell, their neighbor	Larry Breeding
Burt Gunkel, Larry's roommate	James Belushi
Mitzi Logan, the landlady	Marcia Lewis
Memphis, a showgirl	Lorrie Mahaffey
Cochise, a showgirl	Shirley Kirkes
Bridget, a showgirl	Elaine Bolton

Music: Charles Bernstein.
Executive Producer: Garry Mar-

shall, Tony Marshall, Don Silverman.
Producer: Martin Nadler, Gary Menteer.
Director: John Thomas Lenox, Ray DeVally, Jr., David Ketchum.

WHO'S WATCHING THE KIDS?—30 minutes—NBC—September 22, 1978–December 15, 1978. 9 episodes.

1314   THE WHO, WHAT, OR WHERE GAME

Game. A category topic is revealed, followed by three questions: the Who (even money), the What (2 to 1) and the Where (3 to 1). Each player, of the three who compete, secretly lock in a "W" of their choice and a cash wager ($50 minimum of the $125 each receives at the beginning of the game). Players' choices are revealed and the highest wagerer receives the "W" of his choice and its cash value, added to his score, if he correctly answers it (a wrong answer deducts the bet amount from his score). If two players choose the same "W" a verbal auction is held and the highest bidder receives it; if all three select the same "W" it is an automatic cancellation and a new category is introduced. The winner, the highest cash scorer, receives what money he has accumulated.

Host: Art James.
Announcer: Mike Darrow.
Music: George David Weiss.

THE WHO, WHAT, OR WHERE GAME—25 minutes—NBC—December 29, 1969–January 4, 1974.

1315   WILD KINGDOM

Documentary. Films depicting animals' struggle for survival.

Hosts: Marlin Perkins, Jim Fowler, Stan Brock, Tom Allen.
Narrator: Joe Slattery.
Music: James Bourgeois.
Producer-Director: Don Meier.

WILD KINGDOM—30 minutes—NBC—January 6, 1963–September 5, 1973. Syndicated first run.

1316   WILD TIMES

Western. A two-part miniseries, based on the novel by Brian Garfield, that details the exploits of Hugh Cardiff, a sharpshooter who became a frontier legend during the 1860s.

CAST

Hugh Cardiff	Sam Elliott
John Tyree	Leif Erickson
Vern Tyree	Bruce Boxleitner
Libby Tyree	Penny Peyser
Caleb Rice	Timothy Scott
Doc Bogardus	Ben Johnson
Bob Halburton	Pat Hingle

Harry Dreier	Cameron Mitchell
Jeannette Fowler	Trish Stewart
Fitz Bragg	Harry Carey, Jr.
Wild Bill Hickok	L. Q. Jones
Celetus Hatch	Gene Evans
Joe McBride	Buck Taylor
Doc Holliday	Dennis Hopper
Dolly	Chris Noel
Ibran	Geno Silva
Drifter	Arthur Wagner

Music: Jerrold Immel.
Executive Producer: Douglas Netter.
Supervising Producer: Jim Byrnes.
Producer: Les Sheldon.
Writer: Don Balluck.
Director: Richard Compton.

WILD TIMES — 2 hours — Golden Circle — January 1980. 2 episodes.

1317   THE WILD WILD WEST

Western. The series, set during the 1870s, follows the investigations of James T. West and Artemus Gordon, United States government Secret Service agents, as they use ingenious scientific weapons to battle diabolical villains.

CAST

Agent James T. West	Robert Conrad
Agent Artemus Gordon	Ross Martin
Jeremy Pike, West's assistant for a short period	Charles Aidman
President Ulysses S. Grant, their superior	James Gregory
	Roy Engle
Dr. Miguelito Loveless, an enemy agent	Michael Dunn
Count Manzeppi, the evil magician	Victor Buono
Colonel Richmond, head of the Secret Service	Douglas Henderson
Colonel Armstrong, head of the California Secret Service	Harry Ellerbe
President Juarez, head of the Mexican Secret Service	Frank Sorello
Colonel Crockett, head of the Denver Secret Service	Walter Sande
Tennison, West and Gordon's manservant	Charles Davis
Voltaire, Dr. Loveless' assistant	Richard Kiel
Antoinette, one of Dr. Loveless' ladies	Phoebe Dorin
Dr. Loveless' attendant	Leonard Falk
Professor Montague, a Secret Service school instructor	Arthur Malet
Frank Harper, an agent, Jim's partner	William Schallert
Bosley Cranston, an agent, Jim's partner	Pat Paulsen

Artemus' pigeons: Annabella, Arabella, Henry and Henrietta. West and Gordon's Service car: The *Nimrod*.

Music: Richard Shores, Richard Markowitz, Morton Stevens.
Executive Producer: Philip Leacock, Michael Garrison.
Producer: Richard Landau, Leonard Katzman, Fred Freiberger, Collier Young, John Mantley, Gene L. Coon, Bruce Lansbury.
Writer: George Schenik, Bill Marks, Gilbert Ralston, John Kneubuhl, Oliver Crawford, Bob Barbash, Preston Wood, Henry Sharp, Edmund Morris, Fred Freiberger, Bill Tunberg, Stephen Kandel, Richard Landau, Stanford Whitmore, Norman Katkov, Philip Saltzman, Jason Wingreen, Bob Barron, Jack Marlowe, Calvin Clements, Steve Fisher, Kevin DeCourcey, Bob Hamner, Don Mullally, Jackson Gillis, Leigh Chapman, Bob Wright, Gene L. Coon, Ken Kolb, Edward D. Lorenzo, Don Ullman, Michael Edwards, Robert C. Dennis, Earl Barrett, Simon Wincelberg, Elon Packard, Norman Hudis, Daniel Mainwaring, Digby Wolfe, David Moessinger, Denne Bart Petticlerc, Peter Robinson, Ron Silverman, Max Ehrlich, Arthur Weingarten, Robert E. Kent, Edward J. Lakso, Ken Pettus, Max Hodge, Samuel Newman, Paul Playdon, Joel Kane, Jerry Thomas, Shirl Hendryx, Leonard Katzman, Alf Harris, Louis Vitters, Barney Slater, Frank Moss, Ed Adamson.
Director: Bill Witney, Richard Sarafian, Bernard L. Kowalski, Don Taylor, Irving J. Moore, Harvey Hart, Alvin Ganzer, Justis Addiss, Alan Copeland, Jr., Paul Wendkos, Richard Whorf, Lee H. Katzin, Mark Rydell, Ed Dein, Ralph Senensky, Richard Donner, Robert Sparr, Sherman Marks, Jesse Hibbs, Charles R. Rondeau, Leon Benson, Gunnar Hellstrom, James B. Clark, Marvin Chomsky, Alex Nicol, Mike Moder, Lawrence Dobkin, Michael Caffey, Vincent McEveety, Paul Stanley, Bernard McEveety, Herb Wallerstein.
Creator: Michael Garrison.

THE WILD WILD WEST — 60 minutes — CBS — September 17, 1965 – September 19, 1969; July 6, 1970 – September 7, 1970. 104 episodes. Syndicated.

1318   THE WILD WILD WEST: EXTENSION EPISODES

Western. The casts, story lines and credits to the two extension episodes, based on *The Wild Wild West* series, that were broadcast in 1979 and 1980.

The Wild Wild West Revisited. The first extension episode, set in 1885, reunites former Secret Service agents James West, who had retired to Mexico, and Artemus Gordon, who had become an actor with the Deadwood Shakespearian Strolling Players traveling tent show. Their assignment: stop Michelito Loveless, Jr., the son of their old adversary, from controlling the world with perfect clones of heads of state — "people" who will be responsible only to him.

CAST

Agent James T. West	Robert Conrad
Agent Artemus Gordon	Ross Martin
Robert T. Malone, the head of the Secret Service	Harry Morgan
Michelito Loveless, Jr., their adversary	Paul Williams
Carmelita Loveless, Michelito's sister	Jo Ann Harris
Hugo Kaufman, Malone's assistant	Jeff McKay
Sir David Edney, the British Intelligence agent	Rene Auberjonois
Penelope, Edney's assistant	Trisha Noble
Gabrielle Jackson, the dance hall girl	Susan Blu
Alan, Michelito's $600 bionic man	Robert Shields
Sonia, Michelito's $600 bionic woman	Lorene Yarnell
Showgirl	Joyce Jameson
The kid gunning for West	Jeff Redford

Music: Jeff Alexander.
The Wild Wild West Theme: Richard Markowitz.
Executive Producer: Jay Bernstein.
Producer: Robert L. Jacks.
Writer: William Bowers.
Director: Burt Kennedy.
Director of Photography: Robert Houser.

More Wild Wild West. The second extension episode, set circa 1890, once again reunites former Secret Service agents James West and Artemus Gordon to combat Professor Albert Paradine II, a daft megalomaniac who seeks to rule the world through his ingenious and diabolical weapons of doom.

CAST

James T. West	Robert Conrad
Artemus Gordon	Ross Martin
Robert T. Malone, the head of the Secret Service	Harry Morgan
Capt. Sir David Edney, the head of British Intelligence	Rene Auberjonois
Prof. Albert Paradine II	Jonathan Winters
Dr. Messenger, the Secretary of State	Victor Buono
Juanita, the woman gunning for Jim	Liz Torres
Yvonne, Albert's assistant	Randi Brough
Daphne, Albert's assistant	Candi Brough
Mirabelle	Emma Samms
Bystander	Joyce Brothers
Jack LaStrange	Jack LaLanne
Russian Ambassador	Avery Schreiber
French Ambassador	Gino Conforti
German Ambassador	Dave Madden
Italian Ambassador	Joe Alfasa
Spanish Ambassador	Hector Elias

Music: Jeff Alexander.
The Wild Wild West Theme: Richard Markowitz.
Executive Producer: Jay Bernstein.
Producer: Robert L. Jacks.
Writer: William Bowers, Tony Kayden.
Director: Burt Kennedy.
Director of Photography: Charles G. Arnold.

THE WILD WILD WEST REVISITED — 2 hours — CBS — May 9, 1979 (repeated on May 17, 1980).

MORE WILD WILD WEST — 2 hours (total) — CBS — October 7 and October 8, 1980. 2 one-hour episodes.

1319   WILD WILD WORLD OF ANIMALS

Documentary. Films depicting the animals' struggle for survival.

Narrator: William Conrad.
Additional Narration: Hugh Faulk, Mary Batten.
Music: Gerherd Trede, Beatrice Witkin.
Executive Producer: Jonathan Donald.
Producer: Wolfgang Bayer, Dieter Franck, Jurgen Birth, Jurgen Voight.
Director: Peter Fera.

WILD WILD WORLD OF ANIMALS — 30 minutes — Syndicated 1973.

1320 WINNING STREAK

Game. Sixteen letters of the alphabet, each representing a different point value, are displayed on a large board. One player, of two who compete, chooses one letter and its point value is revealed. A player wins the point by correctly answering a question that corresponds to that letter (e.g., if the letter S is chosen, the answer will begin with the letter S). Turns alternate and the first contestant to reach the goal (varies from 250 to 350 points) is the winner.

The champion and the previous winner now compete. A board that contains eighteen numbers is displayed. One player chooses one number, from one to six. A cash amount is revealed, which becomes the value of each number from seven through eighteen. One player selects a number, which reveals a letter of the alphabet, and has to give a word using that letter. If an acceptable word is given, the money is placed in a jackpot. The opponent selects a number and has to give a word using the two letters that are now exposed. The game continues in this manner; for each additional number that is selected, the player has to give a word using all the exposed letters. When a player is stumped or gives an unacceptable word, he is defeated. The opponent becomes the champion and receives whatever money has been accumulated in the jackpot.

Host: Bill Cullen.
Announcer: Don Pardo.

Music: Score Productions.
Executive Producer: Bob Stewart.
Producer: Bruce Burmester.
Director: Mike Gargiulo.

WINNING STREAK — 30 minutes — NBC — July 1, 1974 — January 3, 1975.

1321   THE WIZARD OF ODDS

Game. Selected studio audience members compete in greatly varying contests designed to test their knowledge of national odds and averages and bring forth a "Wizard's Champion."

Regular Segments:

The Elimination Round. Three contestants compete. Clues to the identity of a mystery celebrity appear on a board, one at a time, to a maximum of five clues. The first player to correctly identify the personality is the winner and receives a merchandise prize. Three such rounds are played and the two highest scoring players remain.

The Odds and Averages Board. Two players compete. Three items are displayed on a board, one of which is the odd item. The first player to identify the odd item receives one point. The first player to score three points is the winner and receives a merchandise prize.

Before the final round is played the names of all the players who have competed are placed on a large spinning wheel. The player whose name is selected by the wheel when it stops receives the opportunity to play "Wizard's Wheel of Fortune."

One figure is displayed on the top of a large board. Below it are seven questions, each of which are answerable by a number, but only four of which will total just less than the established figure. If the player can select the correct four items, he wins a new car. If he fails, he receives merchandise prizes according to his correct number selections.

Host: Alex Trebek.
Assistant: Mary Pom.
Announcer: Owen Spam, Charlie O'Donnell.
Music: Stan Worth.
Executive Producer: Burt Sugarman.
Producer: Perry Cross, Neal Marshall, Alan Thicke.
Director: Terry Kyne.

THE WIZARD OF ODDS — 30 minutes — NBC — June 17, 1973 — June 28, 1974.

1322   WKRP IN CINCINNATI

Comedy. The series focuses on the antics of the management and

staff of WKRP, a five-thousand watt, Rock format radio station in Cincinnati, Ohio.

CAST
Andy Travis, the program director	Gary Sandy
Jennifer Marlowe, the receptionist	Loni Anderson
Arthur Carlson, the station manager	Gordon Jump
Bailey Quarters, the continuity writer	Jan Smithers
Johnny Caravella, the D.J. who works as Dr. Johnny Fever	Howard Hesseman
Les Nessman, the news director	Richard Sanders
Herb Tarlek, the sales manager	Frank Bonner
Gordon Sims, the night D.J. who works as Venus Flytrap	Tim Reid
Mrs. Carlson, Arthur's mother	Sylvia Sidney Carol Bruce
Carmen Carlson, Arthur's wife	Allyn Ann McLerie

WKRP Studios: The 9th floor of the Flimm Building.

Music: Tom Wells.
Supervising Producer: Rod Daniel.
Executive Producer: Hugh Wilson.
Producer: Rod Daniel, Hugh Wilson, Bill Dial, Blake Hunter, Steven Kampmann, Peter Torokvei.
Writer: Hugh Wilson, Dan Guntzelman, Steve Marshall, Blake Hunter, Peter Torokvei, Steven Kampmann, Tim Reid.
Director: Jay Sandrich, Michael Zinberg, Asaad Kelada, Hugh Wilson, Will MacKenzie, Rod Daniel, Linda Day.
Creator: Hugh Wilson.
Art Director: Jacqueline Webber.

WKRP IN CINCINNATI — 30 minutes — CBS — September 17, 1978 — November 6, 1978. 13 episodes produced; 8 aired. Returned: CBS — 30 minutes — Premiered: January 15, 1979.

1323   WODEHOUSE PLAYHOUSE

Comedy. A series of humorous stories based on the prolific pen of P. G. Wodehouse.

Introduced By: P. G. Wodehouse.
Regular Performers: Pauline Collins, John Alderton.
Music: Raymond Jones.
Producer: Michael Mills.

WODEHOUSE PLAYHOUSE — 30 minutes — Syndicated 1977. Produced in England.

1324   THE WOLFMAN JACK SHOW

Variety. A mixture of music, songs and comedy sketches.

Host: Wolfman Jack.

Regulars: Peter Cullen, Murray Langston, John Harris, The Incredible Puppets, and Vivian, the talking mule.
Orchestra: Jimmy Dale.
Executive Producer: Don Kelley.
Producer: Rif Markowitz.
Director: Mark Warren.

THE WOLFMAN JACK SHOW — 30 minutes — Syndicated 1977.

1325   WOMEN IN WHITE

Drama. The series, set in Florida, follows the personal and professional lives of the doctors and nurses attached to Biscayne General Hospital.

CAST
Dr. Jill Bates	Kathryn Harrold
Dr. Rebecca Dalton	Susan Flannery
Nurse Cathy Payson	Patty Duke Astin
Dr. Mike Rayburn	David Ackroyd
Dr. Karen Fletcher	Laraine Stephens
Anthony Broadhurst	Robert Culp
Nurse Lisa Gordon	Sheree North
Kevin Haggerty	Scott Brady
Deena Tyndall	Dena Crowder
Dr. Ken Dalton	Stuart Whitman
Virginia Tyndall	Tracy Reed
Ellen Rayburn	Caroline Smith
Frederick Thaler	Aldo Ray
Priscilla Harper	Maggie Cooper
Richard Payson	Gerald S. O'Loughlin
Dr. Frank Evanhauer	Howard McGillin
Mary Haskell	Carol Baxter
Nurse	Gloria Delaney
Nurse Jean Robinson	June Witney Taylor
Admitting Nurse	Janet Winter
Helen Thaler	Linda Ryan
Valerie	Harriet Karr

Music: Morton Stevens.
Executive Producer: David Victor.
Producer: Robert F. O'Neill.
Writer: Robert Malcolm Yates.
Director: Jerry London.

WOMEN IN WHITE — 4 hours total (2 one-hour episodes; 1 two-hour episode) — NBC — February 8, 1979 — February 22, 1979. The series was repeated as 2 two-hour segments on NBC on June 9 and June 10, 1980.

1326   WONDERBUG

Comedy. Seeking a used car, three teenagers, Susan, Barry and C. C. find, in a junkyard, Schlep Car, a conglomeration of several wrecked cars. However, when pretty Susan places what turns out to be a magic horn on the car, it becomes Wonderbug, an automobile that is capable of fantastic feats. Stories depict the group's battle against evil.

CAST
Susan	Carol Anne Seflinger
Barry Buntrock	David Levy
C. C.	John Anthony Bailey
Voice of Wonderbug	Frank Welker

Music: Jimmie Haskell.
Executive Producer: Sid and Marty Krofft.

Producer: Al Schwartz.
Director: Art Fisher, Bob La-Hendro.

WONDERBUG — 15 minutes — ABC — September 11, 1976 — September 2, 1978 (as part of *The Krofft Supershow*).

1327   WONDER WOMAN

Adventure. Around 200 B.C., when the rival gods Mars and Aphrodite ruled the Earth, Aphrodite, who was unable to defeat Mars, organized a group of superwomen called Amazons and retreated to Paradise Island, an uncharted land mass within what is now called the Bermuda Triangle. There, she selected Hippolyte as her queen and presented her with the magic girdle, a gold belt that produces superhuman strength. However, still determined to defeat his adversary, Mars retreated to skullduggery and used love, Hippolyte's own weapon, against her to snatch the magic girdle. Though displeased, Hippolyte received forgiveness from Aphrodite but had to, as all Amazons, wear special wrist bracelets made of feminum to remind them always of the dangers of submitting to men's domination. To further show her sorrow, Hippolyte fashioned a small statue that, when offered to Aphrodite, was brought to life as the baby Diana.

The time: World War II. Crashlanding on Paradise Island when his plane is hit by enemy gunfire, U.S. Fighter Pilot Steve Trevor is found by Diana, now grown, and nursed back to health. An olympic games competition is held and Diana, who proves herself superior, is chosen to escort Steve back to civilization and to assist America in the war effort.

From the Queen Mother, Diana receives the gold belt (to maintain her cunning and strength away from Paradise Island) and the magic lariat, which compels people to tell the truth. Diana then chooses a revealing red, white and blue costume to signify her allegiance to freedom and democracy. With the final words of her mother, "In the words of ordinary mortals you are a Wonder Woman," Diana leaves Paradise Island, and flies Steve back to Washington, D.C., in her invisible plane. (Prior to their departure, Steve had been given a special drug from the Hybernia tree to erase all memory of Paradise Island.)

In order to be with Steve, Diana adopts the guise of Diana Prince and, after achieving remarkably high scores on Army aptitude tests, she is made Yeoman First Class and assigned to the U.S. War Department as

The Wild Wild West. Ross Martin, at left, with Robert Conrad.

WKRP in Cincinnati. Bottom, from left, Jan Smithers, Loni Anderson and Howard Hesseman. Middle, from left, Frank Bonner and Gary Sandy. Back, from left, Richard Sanders, Gordon Jump and Tim Reid.

Wonder Woman. Lynda Carter.

A Year at the Top. The original cast. Front, from left, Phil Leeds, Mickey Rooney, Vivian Blaine and Robert Alda. Back, from left, Paul Shaffer, Kelly Bishop, Judith Cohen and Greg Evigan.

Major Trevor's secretary. Stories depict Diana's crusade, as Wonder Woman, against Nazi activities in America. (By doing a twirling striptease, the plain-looking Diana emerges into the beautiful Wonder Woman.)

CAST

Diana Prince/Wonder Woman	Lynda Carter
Major Steve Trevor	Lyle Waggoner
Gen. Phillip Blankenship, Steve's superior	Richard Eastham
Yeoman Etta Candy, Phillip's secretary	Beatrice Colen
Drusilla/Wonder Girl, Diana's sister	Debra Winger
The Queen Mother	Cloris Leachman Carolyn Jones
Magda, an Amazon	Pamela Shoop
Dalma, an Amazon	Erica Hagen
Lynda Carter's stand-in	Adina Ross

Music: Artie Kane, Charles Fox.
Wonder Woman Theme: Norman Gimbel (lyrics), Charles Fox (music).
Executive Producer: Douglas S. Cramer.
Producer: Wilfred Baumes.
Director: Stuart Margolin, Bruce Bilson, Herb Wallerstein, Charles R. Rondeau, Richard Kinon, Leonard Horn, Alan Crosland, Jr., Barry Crane.
Creator: Charles Moulton.

WONDER WOMAN — 60 minutes — ABC. Broadcast dates as a series of specials: November 7, 1975, March 31, 1976, April 21, 1976, April 28, 1976, August 21, 1976, September 11, 1976, September 18, 1976, October 31, 1976, November 6, 1976, November 8, 1976, December 18, 1976, December 25, 1976, January 1, 1977, January 8, 1977, January 15, 1977, January 17, 1977, January 22, 1977, January 29, 1977, February 16, 1977. *As a weekly series:* May 14, 1977 – July 30, 1977. Spin-off series: *The New Adventures of Wonder Woman.* Original title, *The New, Original Wonder Woman.* See also, *Wonder Woman* in the pilot film section.

1328   WOOBINDA — ANIMAL DOCTOR

Adventure. The series, set in Gottens Creek, Australia, follows the life and work of Dr. John Stevens, a veterinary surgeon.

CAST

Dr. John Stevens	Don Pascoe
Tiggie Stevens, his daughter	Sonia Hofmann
Kevin Stevens, his adopted son	Bindi Williams
Jack Johnson, his retainer	Slim Degrey
Peter Fischer, his assistant	Lutz Hochstraate

Producer: Roger Mirams (for Ajax Films, Ltd., NLT Productions, Ltd., and Fremantle International Productions, Ltd.).

WOOBINDA — ANIMAL DOCTOR — 30 minutes — Syndicated 1978. 39 episodes.

1329   THE WORD

Drama. A four-part miniseries, based on the novel by Irving Wallace, that follows the exploits of Steve Randall, a public relations executive and representative of a religious publisher. He seeks to discover if Resurrection Two, a top-secret project involving a new Bible based on the discovery of an ancient manuscript (said to be a lost gospel written by Jesus' brother and liable to change the course of Christianity) is authentic or a hoax.

CAST

Steve Randall	David Janssen
George Wheeler	James Whitmore
Angela Monti	Florinda Bolkan
Ogden Towery	Eddie Albert
Naomi Dunn	Geraldine Chaplin
Cedric Plummer	Hurd Hatfield
Nathan Randall	John Huston
Florian Knight	John McEnery
Claire Randall	Diana Muldaur
Tony Nicholson	Kate Mulgrew
LeBrun	Ron Moody
Barbara Randall	Janice Rule
Sarah Randall	Martha Scott
Maertin de Vroome	Nicol Williamson
Tom Carey	David Ackroyd
Maria	Laura Betti
Heldering	Bo Brundin
Hennig	Walter Gottell
Judy Randall	Alexa Kenin
Thad Crawford	John Korkes
Abbot Petropolous	Nehemiah Persoff
Henri Aubert	Donald Moffat
Dr. Oppenheim	Alan Miller
Lori Cook	Catherine Burns
Peter Ajemian	Nicholas Coster
Valerie Hughs	Lynn Farleigh
Tessie O'Shea	Herself
Dr. Fass	John Van Dreeland

Music: Alex North.
Executive Producer: Dick Berg, Charles Fries.
Producer: David Manson.
Writer: Dick Berg, Robert L. Joseph, S. S. Schweitzer, Richard Fielder.
Director: Richard Lang.
Art Director: Herman Zimmerman.

THE WORD — 2 hours — CBS — November 12, 1978 – November 14, 1978. 4 episodes.

1330   WORDS AND MUSIC

Game. A large board that contains 16 squares is displayed on stage. Each square contains a clue that is associated with a particular word in a particular song. One player, of the three who compete, chooses one square. A clue is read (e.g., "The very yeast"), and a song is sung ("The Sound of Music"). The player who is first to associate the clue with the word

in the song presses a button to identify himself. If he gives a correct response ("Rise" — "Of the wings of the birds that rise"; rise being the key word to the clue word yeast), he receives a cash award. The person with the last correct response selects the next clue. The player with the highest cash score is the winner and vies to win three straight games and a new car.

Host: Wink Martindale.
Announcer: Johnny Gilbert.
Vocalists: Peggy Connelly, Bob Marlo, Katie Grant, Don Minter, Pat Henderson.
Orchestra: Bob Alberti.
Producer: Armand Grant.

WORDS AND MUSIC — 30 minutes — NBC — September 28, 1970 – February 12, 1971.

1331   WORKING STIFFS

Comedy. The story of Ernie and Mike O'Rourke, two incompetent brothers, and their misadventures working as janitors in the O'Rourke Building, a Chicago establishment owned by the only man who would hire them — their uncle Harry.

CAST

Ernie O'Rourke	Jim Belushi
Mike O'Rourke	Michael Keaton
Harry O'Rourke, their uncle	Michael Conrad
Charles Pressman, the building manager (first episode)	Neil Thompson
Al Steckler, the building manager (several episodes)	Val Bisoglio
Frank Falzone, the building manager (remainder of series)	Phil Rubenstein
Mitch Hannigan, the owner of the Playland Café, over which Ernie and Mike live	Allan Arbus
Nikki Evashevsky, Mitch's waitress	Lorna Patterson
Ralph Evashevsky, Nikki's husband	Thomas Calloway

Music: John Cacavas.
Working Stiffs Theme: Jack Carone.
Supervising Producer: Marc Sotkin, David W. Duclon.
Executive Producer: Arthur Silver, Bob Brunner.
Producer: Harry Colomby, Nick Abdo.
Writer: Marc Sotkin, E. Jack Kaplan, Alan Adekman, Gail Hoingberg, David W. Duclon.
Director: Penny Marshall, Norman Abbott, Arthur Silver, Greg Antonacci.
Art Director: James F. Claytor, Monty Elliott.
Director of Photography: William Mendenhall.

WORKING STIFFS — 30 minutes — CBS — September 15, 1979 – October 6, 1979. 4 episodes aired (of 5 that were scheduled).

1332   A WORLD APART

Serial. The dramatic story of Betty Kahlam, a serial writer and the unwed mother of two children, Patrice and Chris. Against a plaguing generation gap, she struggles to achieve their love and foster a sense of family unity and togetherness.

CAST

Betty Kahlam	Augusta Dabney
Patrice Kahlam	Susan Sarandon
Chris Kahlam	Matthew Cowles
Dr. John Karr	Robert Gentry
T. D. Drinkard	Tom Logan
Matilda	Rosetta LaNoire
Nancy Condon	Susan Sullivan Judith Barcroft
Linda Peters	Heather MacRae
Russell Barry	William Prince
Sara Sims	Kathy Parker
Dr. Edward Sims	James Noble
Thomas Walsh	Roy Shuman

Also: M'el Dowd, Elizabeth Lawrence.

A WORLD APART — 30 minutes — ABC — March 30, 1970 – June 25, 1971.

1333   THE WORLD AT WAR

Documentary. The history of World War II is traced through newsreel film — from the rise of Hitler to Allied victory.

Narrator (1973): Sir Laurence Olivier.
Narrator (1978): Burt Lancaster.
Music: Carl Davis.
Producer: Jeremy Isaacs.

THE WORLD AT WAR — 60 minutes — Syndicated 1973 (resyndicated in 1978).

1334   WORLD WAR II: G.I. DIARY

Documentary. Former servicemen recount their experiences during World War II — the highlights of which are seen through newsreel film footage.

Narrator: Lloyd Bridges.
Music: Score Productions.
G.I. Voices: Bob McFadden, Peter Edens, Steve Rolland.
Producer: Arthur Holch, Anne Chambers.
Production Executive: Peter Hansen.

WORLD WAR II: G.I. DIARY — 30 minutes — Syndicated 1978. 25 episodes.

Y

1335   THE YEAGERS

Drama. The series, set in MacKenzie County, Washington, follows the life of Carroll Yeager, the owner of the Yeager Logging and Mining Company, and his family, as they struggle to operate and maintain the family-owned business.

CAST

Carroll Yeager (series)	Andy Griffith
Carroll Yeager (pilot film)	Eddie Albert
Willie Yeager, Carroll's son (series)	James Whitmore, Jr.
Willie Yeager (pilot film)	Martin Kove
John David Yeager, Carroll's son (series)	David Ackroyd
John David Yeager (pilot film)	James Sloyan
Joanna Yeager, Carroll's daughter (series)	Deborah Shelton
Joanna Yeager (pilot film)	Robin Dearden
Carrie Yeager, John's wife (series)	Molly Cheek
Carrie Yeager (pilot film)	Belinda J. Montgomery
Tony Yeager, Carroll's nephew	Kevin Brophy
Kyle Yeager, Carroll's son (series)	Gregg Henry
Kyle Yeager, (pilot film)	Steve Doubet
Scotty Yeager, Carrie's son	Jimmy Mair
Timmy Yeager, Carrie's son	Bob Olidi
Roy, works for Carroll	John Quade
Sheriff (series)	William Stratton
Sheriff (pilot film)	John Lupton

Music: George Tipton.
Executive Producer: Paul Junger Witt, Tony Thomas.
Producer: Robert Papazian.
Writer: Joel Steiger, Jeb Rosebrook.
Director: Winrich Kolbe, Arnold Laven.
Creator: Paul Junger Witt, Jeb Rosebrook.

THE YEAGERS — 60 minutes — ABC — June 1, 1980 – June 8, 1980. 2 episodes. The two-hour pilot film, "Trouble in High Timber Country," aired on ABC on June 27, 1980.

1336   A YEAR AT THE TOP

Comedy. The story of Greg and Paul, two unknown songwriters, who sell their souls to Paragon Records president Frederick J. Hanover — the devil's son — in return for a year at the top in the music world.

CAST

Greg	Greg Evigan
Paul	Paul Shaffer
Mickey Durbin, their uncle	Mickey Rooney
Frederick J. Hanover, the devil's son	Gabriel Dell
Linda, Greg's girlfriend	Priscilla Lopez
Miss Worley, Hanover's secretary	Priscilla Morrill
Grandma Bell Durbin, Mickey's mother	Nedra Volz
Trish, Greg and Paul's friend	Julie Cobb

Music Supervision: Don Kirshner.
Executive Producer: Norman Lear.
Producer: Darryl Hickman, Patricia Fass Palmer.

Director: Alan Rafkin, Marlena Laird.
Creator: Woody Kling.

A YEAR AT THE TOP — 30 minutes — CBS — August 5, 1977 – September 4, 1977. 5 episodes.

Original Format:
Originally, the series was scheduled to air beginning January 19, 1977, but was canceled at the last moment, then revised, supposedly to improve it. Following are the cast and credits to the original version which never aired. An aging musical trio (elderly Lillian, Cliff and Studly) sell their souls to the devil for a year at the top in the music business as the Rock group Top (young Lillian, Cliff and Studly).

CAST

Mickey	Mickey Rooney
Elder Lillian	Vivian Blaine
Elder Cliff	Robert Alda
Elder Studly	Phil Leeds
Young Lillian	Judith Cohen
Young Cliff	Greg Evigan
Young Studly	Paul Shaffer
Dee Dee	Kelly Bishop
Stage Manager	Kay Dingle

Music Supervision: Don Kirshner.
Musical Coordinator: Jay Siegel.
Special Musical Material: Earl Brown.
Musical Staging: Kevin Carlisle.
Executive Producer: Norman Lear.
Producer: Darryl Hickman.
Director: Jim Drake, Alan Myerson.
Creator: Woody Kling, Don Kirshner.
Art Director: Don Roberts.

A YEAR AT THE TOP — Scheduled, but never aired on CBS.

1337   YOGI'S GANG

Animated Cartoon. As living conditions become intolerable, Yogi (the ingenious Jellystone Park bear) and his friends decide to do something about it and commission inventor Noah Smith to construct a flying ark. Beginning a crusade to protect the environment, they travel throughout the country and attempt to battle the enemies of man and nature — polluters.

VOICES

Yogi Bear	Daws Butler
Boo Boo Bear	Don Messick
Doggie Daddy	John Stephenson
Augie Doggie	Daws Butler
Paw Ruggs	Henry Corden
Huckleberry Hound	Daws Butler
Snagglepuss	Daws Butler
Quick Draw McGraw	Daws Butler
Peter Potamus	Daws Butler
Wally Gator	Daws Butler
Touche Turtle	Don Messick
Squiddly Diddly	Don Messick
Ranger Smith	Don Messick

Magilla Gorilla	Allan Melvin
Atom Ant	Don Messick

Music: Hoyt Curtin.
Executive Producer: William Hanna, Joseph Barbera.
Producer: Iwao Takamoto.
Director: Charles A. Nichols.

YOGI'S GANG — 30 minutes — ABC — September 8, 1973 – August 30, 1975.

1338   YOGI'S SPACE RACE

Animated Cartoon. The format finds Yogi Bear and his friend, Scarebear, as astronauts who compete in various space races for prizes.

Other Competitors: The Jabberjaws and Buford; Wendy, Rita and Nugget Nose; Huckleberry Hound and Quackup; Captain Good and Kleen Cat; and the evil Phantom Fink and Sludge.
Voices: Daws Butler, Don Messick, Gary Owens, Pat Parris, Hal Peary, Tommy Cook, Barry Gordon, Gay Hartwig, Casey Kasem, Julie McWhirter, Vic Perrin, Barney Phillips, Janet Waldo, Hattie Lynn Hunt, Hal Smith, John Stephenson, Virginia Gregg.
Narrator: Gary Owens.
Music: Hoyt Curtin.
Executive Producer: William Hanna, Joseph Barbera.
Creative Producer: Iwao Takamoto.
Producer: Art Scott.
Director: Ray Patterson.

YOGI'S SPACE RACE — 90 minutes — NBC — September 9, 1978 – October 28, 1978; 60 minutes — November 4, 1978 – January 27, 1979.

1339   YOU ARE THERE

Historical Dramatizations. Through reenactments and present-day interviews, America's past is brought to life. The people and events that contributed to its founding and growth are seen through eyewitness accounts.

Host-Narrator: Walter Cronkite.
Reproters-Interviewers: CBS News correspondents.
Music: Glenn Paxton.
Executive Producer: Burton Benjamin.
Producer: Vern Diamond.
Director: Burt Brinkerhoff.

Program Open:
Announcer: The time ... ; the place .... All things are as they were then, except, YOU ARE THERE.

Program Close:
Host: What kind of day was it? A day like all days, filled with those unexpected events which alter our lives — and you were there.

YOU ARE THERE — 30 minutes — CBS — September 11, 1971 – September 2, 1972. An earlier version, with Walter Cronkite as host, appeared on CBS from November 4, 1953 through October 13, 1957.

1340   YOU BET YOUR LIFE

Game. Three players compete, one at a time. Each contestant is asked five questions based on a category he selects and receives money as follows: $25 for the first two correct answers; $100 for three correct replies; and $400 for four correct responses. If the player answers the fifth segment of his questions correctly, he triples his winnings up to that point (an incorrect response at any stage cuts a player's earnings in half). The winner is the highest cash scorer.

Host: Buddy Hackett.
Announcer-Assistant: Ron Hussmann.
Music: The Robert Ivie Organization.
Music Coordinator: Lee Ringuette.
Supervising Producer: Walt Case.
Executive Producer: Bob Eubanks, Michael Hill.
Producer: Earl Durham.
Director: Chris Darley.

YOU BET YOUR LIFE — 30 minutes — Syndicated 1980.

1341   YOU DON'T SAY

Game. Two teams compete, each composed of one celebrity captain and one noncelebrity contestant. One member on each team receives the name of a famous person or place. The player makes up and relates a sentence to his partner wherein he leaves the last word, which sounds like part of the name, unsaid. If his partner is able to identify the name, the team scores one point; if not, the opponent receives a turn. A two-out-of-three match competition is played and the winning contestant receives $100.

Host: Tom Kennedy.
Announcer: John Harlan.
Music: Recorded.
Producer: Bill Yagemann, Ralph Andrews.

YOU DON'T SAY — 30 minutes — NBC — April 1, 1963 – September 26, 1969.

1342   YOU DON'T SAY

Game. A revised version of the previous title. Four guest celebrities and two contestants are involved. The celebrities are each given the name of a famous person or place. One contestant chooses a celebrity who must then give him a clue to its identity by making up a sentence and leaving the last word, which sounds like a part of the name, unsaid. If the contestant identifies the name within five seconds he scores $200; if not, his opponent chooses a celebrity and receives a chance at play. The clue is worth $150 and decreases to $100 and finally $50 if the remaining two clues are needed for one player to identify the name. The first player to score $600 is the winner.

Host: Tom Kennedy.
Announcer: John Harlan.
Music: Stan Worth.
Executive Producer: Bill Carruthers.
Producer: John Harlan, Mike Henry.
Director: Tom Cole.

YOU DON'T SAY — 30 minutes — ABC — July 7, 1975 – November 26, 1975. 90 programs.

1343 YOU DON'T SAY

Game. A syndicated version of the ABC version of the game. See prior title for format.

Host: Jim Peck.
Announcer: John Harlan.
Executive Producer: Ralph Edwards.
Producer: Bill Yagemann.
Director: Tom Cole.

YOU DON'T SAY — 30 minutes — Syndicated 1978.

1344 THE YOUNG AND THE RESTLESS

Serial. The story of the new morality as seen through the lives of several young people, upper-middle-class adults in Genoa City.

CAST

Brad Eliot	Tom Hallick
Stuart Brooks	Robert Colbert
Jennifer Brooks	Dorothy Green
Peggy Brooks	Pamela Peters
	Pamela Solow
Liz Foster	Julianna McCarthy
Victor Neuman	Eric Braeden
Pierre Rolland	Robert Clary
Sally McGuire	Lee Crawford
Jill Foster	Brenda Dickson
	Bond Gideon
Leslie Brooks	Janice Lynde
	Victoria Mallory
Chris Brooks Foster	Trish Stewart
	Lynne Topping
April Stevens	Cynthia Eilbacher
	Janet Wood
Greg "Snapper" Foster	James Houghton
	Brian Kerwin
	Wings Hauser
Larry Larkin	Gary Giem
Nikki Reed	Erica Hope
	Melody Thomas
Laurie Brooks Prentiss	Jaime Lyn Bauer
	Victoria Thompson*
	Lezlie Dalton*
Nancy Becker	Cathy Carricaburu
Ron Becker	Dick DeCoit
Marion Reeves	Carolyn Conwell

Scott Adams	Jack Stauffer
Barbara Anderson	Deidre Hall
Marianne	Lilyan Chauvan
Gwen Sherman	Jennifer Leak
Philip Chancelor	Donnelly Rhodes
Kay Chancelor	Jeanne Cooper
Jed Andrews	Tom Selleck
Brock Reynolds	Beau Kayzer
Sam Powers	Barry Cahill
Bruce Henderson	Paul Stevens
Mark Henderson	Steve Carlson
Lance Prentiss	John McCook
Vanessa Prentiss	K. T. Stevens
Cynthia Harris	Lori Saunders
Michael Scott	Nick Benedict
Julia Newman	Meg Bennett
Rose DeVille	Darlene Conley
Carl Williams	Brett Hadley
Jake	Paul Jenkins
Jonas	Jerry Lacy
Derek Thurston	Joe LaDue
Casey Reed	Roberta Leighton
Lucas Prentiss	Tom Ligon
Vince Holliday	Alex Rebar
Suzanne Lynch	Ellen Weston
Jim Davis	Michael Forest
Maestro Fausch	Karl Bruck

Music: David McGinnis, J. Wood, B. Todd.
Music Coordinator: Jez Davidson, Mary Stewart.
Theme: "Theme from The Young and the Restless" by Barry DeVorzon and Perry Botkin.
Executive Producer: John Conboy.
Producer: Patricia Wenig, Edward Scott, Cathy Abbi.
Writer: William J. Bell, Kay Alden, Elizabeth Harrower, John F. Smith, Jim Inman, Mark Waxman.
Director: Richard Dunlap, Bill Glenn.
Creator: William J. Bell, Lee Philip Bell.

THE YOUNG AND THE RESTLESS — 30 minutes — CBS — March 26, 1973 – February 1, 1980; 60 minutes — Premiered: February 4, 1980.

*Temporarily replaced Jaime Lyn Bauer.

1345 YOUNG DAN'L BOONE

Adventure. The series, set in Kentucky during the nineteenth century, details the exploits of Daniel Boone, the frontiersman-pioneer, as a young man (age 25), before he became a legend.

CAST

Dan'l Boone	Rick Moses
Rebecca Bryan, his girlfriend	Devon Ericson
Peter Dawes, the young boy who tags along with Dan'l	John Joseph Thomas
Hawk, the ex-slave	Ji-Tu Cumbuka

Music: Earle Hagen.
Music Supervision: Lionel Newman.
Theme Vocal: The Mike Curb Congregation.

Executive Producer: Ernie Frankel.
Producer: Jimmy Sangster.
Director: Earl Bellamy, Ernest Pintoff, Don McDougall, Arthur Marks.
Creator: Ernie Frankel.

YOUNG DAN'L BOONE — 60 minutes — CBS — September 12, 1977 – October 4, 1977. 4 episodes.

1346 YOUNG DOCTOR KILDARE

Drama. An updated version of *Doctor Kildare*. The experiences, defeats and victories of James Kildare, a young resident intern at Blair General Hospital.

CAST

Dr. James Kildare	Mark Jenkins
Dr. Leonard Gillespie, his mentor	Gary Merrill
Nurse Marsha Lord	Marsha Mason
Nurse Ferris	Dixie Marquis
Nurse Newell	Olga James
Orderly	Dennis Robinson

Music: Harry Lojewski.
Producer: Joseph Gantman.
Director: Glenn Jordan.

YOUNG DOCTOR KILDARE — 30 minutes — Syndicated 1972.

1347 THE YOUNG LAWYERS

Drama. The cases and courtroom defenses of David Barrett, the senior lawyer of the Neighborhood Law Office (N.L.O.), a legal-aid service in Boston, Massachusettes, and his two protégés, Aaron Silverman and Pat Walters, Bercol University law students.

CAST

David Barrett	Lee J. Cobb
Aaron Silverman	Zalman King
Pat Walters	Judy Pace

Music: Lalo Schifrin, Leith Stevens.
Producer: Matthew Rapf.
Associate Producer: Jerry Briskin.
Director: Jud Taylor, John Newland, Harvey Hart, Gene Levitt.

THE YOUNG LAWYERS — 60 minutes — ABC — September 21, 1970 – May 5, 1971.

1348 YOUNG MAVERICK

Western. A continuation of the *Maverick* series, which ran on ABC from 1957 to 1962 and dealt with the exploits of three slick gamblers, brothers Bret and Bart Maverick (James Garner and Jack Kelly) and their suave British cousin, Beau (Roger Moore). Although there is a 17-year gap between series, the new version continues the same story line and again details the exploits of a Maverick — Beau's son Ben, a

suave, fast-talking gambler who roams throughout the West seeking rich prey.

CAST

Ben Maverick	Charles Frank
Nell McGarrahan, Ben's lady friend	Susan Blanchard
Edge Troy, the U.S. Marshal	John Dehner

Music: Lee Holdridge, Lex DeAvezedo.
Theme: "Maverick" by Jay Livingston and Ray Evans.
Supervising Producer: Andy White.
Executive Producer: Robert Van Scoyk.
Producer: Chuck Bowan.
Writer: David Peckinpah, Norman Leibmann, Robert Van Scoyk, Jerry Ross.
Director: Bernard McEveety, Don McDougall, Leslie H. Martinson, Hy Averback, Ralph Senensky, Bob Claver.

YOUNG MAVERICK — 60 minutes — CBS — November 28, 1979 – January 16, 1980. 8 episodes. The two-hour pilot film, "The New Maverick," aired on ABC on September 3, 1978.

1349 THE YOUNG PIONEERS

Drama. The series, set in Dakota during the 1870s, follows the enduring hardships of Molly and David Beaton, young newlyweds who are struggling to make a new life for themselves on the hostile frontier.

CAST

Molly Beaton	Linda Purl
David Beaton	Roger Kern
Dan Grey, their neighbor	Robert Hays
Mr. Peters, their neighbor	Robert Donner
Nettie Peters, his daughter	Shelly Juttner
	Kay Kimler
	Mare Winningham
Flora Peters, his daughter	Sherri Wagner
	Michelle Stacy
Charlie Peters, his son	Brian Melrose
	Jeff Cotler

Narrator: Linda Purl.
Music: Dominic Frontiere, Laurence Rosenthal.
Executive Producer: Earl Hamner, Lee Rich, Ed Friendly.
Producer: Robert L. Jacks.
Director: Harry Harris, Alf Kjellin, Irving J. Moore.

THE YOUNG PIONEERS — 60 minutes — ABC — April 2, 1978 – April 16, 1978. 3 episodes. The first pilot, "The Young Pioneers," aired on ABC on March 1, 1976. The second pilot film, "The Young Pioneers Christmas," aired on ABC on December 17, 1976.

1350 THE YOUNG REBELS

Adventure. The series, set in Chester, Pennsylvania, in 1777, follows the exploits of the Yankee

Doodle Society, a secret organization comprised of four people: Jeremy Larken, a man who is regarded as the town fool; Henry Abington, a chemist and explosives expert; Isak Poole, a blacksmith; and Elizabeth Coates, their one-woman auxiliary. Pretending to be indifferent to the American cause and considered worthless, they struggle to foil British advances on the Colonies.

CAST

Jeremy Larken	Rick Ely
Isak Poole	Lou Gossett
Henry Abington	Alex Henteloff
Elizabeth Coates	Hilarie Thompson
General Lafayette, their ally	Philippe Forquet

Music: Dominic Frontiere.
Music Supervision: Lionel Newman.
Executive Producer: Aaron Spelling.
Producer: Jon Epstein.
Program Open:
Announcer (over "Yankee Doodle" theme music):
This is the Yankee Doodle Society, a secret organization like those that operated during the American Revolution, young patriots determined to help mold their own future by fighting for freedom behind British lines.

THE YOUNG REBELS — 60 minutes — ABC — September 20, 1970 – January 15, 1971. 13 episodes.

1351   THE YOUNG SENTINELS

Animated Cartoon. At a time when the Earth was young, Sentinel One, an intelligent life force from another galaxy, carefully selected three young people for training on his planet. Granting them astounding powers and eternal youth, the three earthlings (Hercules, with the strength of a hundred men; Astria, a beautiful woman capable of assuming any life form; and Mercury, able to move with the speed of light) were returned to their native planet to watch over the human race and help the good survive and flourish. Now, with the guiding influence of Sentinel One and his maintenance robot, Mo, the series details the exploits of the Young Sentinels as they battle evil on Earth.

VOICES

Hercules	George DiCenzo
Astria	Dee Timberlake
Mercury	Evan Kim
Sentinel One	George DiCenzo
Mo	Evan Kim

Music: Yvette Blais, Jeff Michael.
Executive Producer: Norm Prescott, Lou Scheimer.
Producer: Don Christensen.
Director: Hal Sutherland.

THE YOUNG SENTINELS — 30 minutes — NBC — September 10, 1977 – November 12, 1977. As *The Space Sentinels* — November 19, 1977 – September 2, 1978.

1352   YOUR HIT PARADE

Variety. America's taste in popular music is dramatized. The top songs of the day, which are played from No. 12 to "the song that's No. 1 all over America," are determined by surveys of the best sellers, sheet music and phonograph record sales, juke box selections and songs played over the radio.

Program Open:
Announcer: Ladies and gentlemen, presenting America's award winning musical show, *Your Hit Parade.* Tonight, *Your Hit Parade* presents the pop tunes of yesterday and today. America's most popular music as determined by *Your Hit Parade* survey, featuring the best sellers in phonograph records, sheet music, songs most played on automatic coin machines, and the songs most played on the air all over America.

Version 1:
Starring: Eileen Wilson, June Valli, Dorothy Collins, Snooky Lanson, Russell Arms, Gisele MacKenzie, Tommy Leonetti, Jill Corey, Alan Copeland, Virginia Gibson.
Regulars: Niles and Fosse (dancers), The Hit Parade Singers, The Hit Parade Dancers.
Announcer: Andre Baruch, John Laing.
Orchestra: Raymond Scott, Peter Van Steeden, Dick Jacobs, Harry Sosnik.
Choreographer: Tony Charmoli. Ernest Flatt, Peter Gennaro.
Producer: Dan Lounsbury, Ted Fetter.
Director: Clark Jones.

YOUR HIT PARADE — 60- and 30-minute versions — NBC — July 10, 1950 – June 17, 1958.

Version 2:
Starring: Dorothy Collins, Johnny Desmond, Virginia Gibson, Jill Corey.
Regulars: The Hit Parade Singers and Dancers.
Announcer: Art Gilmore.

Orchestra: Harry Sosnik.
Producer: Dan Lounsburg, Perry Lafferty.

YOUR HIT PARADE — 30 minutes — CBS — October 10, 1958 – April 14, 1959.

Version 3:
Starring: Kelly Garrett, Sheralee, Chuck Woolery.
Regulars: The Tom Hanson Dancers (who are referred to as The Hit Parade Dancers).
Announcer: Art Gilmore.
Orchestra: Milton DeLugg.
Executive Producer: Chuck Barris.
Producer: Bill Hobin.

YOUR HIT PARADE — 30 minutes — CBS — August 2, 1974 – August 30, 1974. 5 programs.

1353   YOUR NEW DAY

Variety. A daily series of consumer tips, beauty advice, exercise, and related information geared to women.

Host: Vidal Sassoon.
Regulars: Suzy Prudden, Nina Blanchard.
Announcer: John Harlan.
Executive Producer: John E. Ringel, Stanley H. Moger.
Producer: Beth Forcelledo.
Director: Jim Crum.
Art Director: Brian Bartholomew.

YOUR NEW DAY — 30 minutes — Syndicated 1980.

1354   YOUR SHOW OF SHOWS

Comedy. A syndicated version of the 1950s program of the same title that consists of new opening and closing themes and introductions by Sid Caesar and Imogene Coca. Kinescope clips (of outrageous comedy spoofs) from the original series are shown.

Host: Sid Caesar.
Regulars: Imogene Coca, Carl Reiner, Howard Morris, Judy Johnson, Cliff Norton, Robert Merrill, Marguerite Piazza, Bill Hayes, Nellie Fisher, Bambi Linn, Rod Alexander, The Chandra Kaly Dancers, The Bob Hamilton Trio, The Billy Williams Quartet.
Announcer: Vaughn Monroe.
Orchestra: Charles Sanford, Tony Romano, Irwin Kostal.
Producer: Max Liebman.
Director: Hal Keith, Bill Hobin.
Choral Director: Clay Warnick.
Narrator: Ed Herlihy.
Creator: Pat Weaver.

YOUR SHOW OF SHOWS — 60 minutes — Syndicated 1976. Original broadcast: 90 minutes — NBC — February 25, 1950 – June 5, 1954.

Z

1355   THE ZOO GANG

Crime Drama. The story of four World War II resistance fighters known as the Zoo Gang, who reunite 28 years later to battle crime in Europe.

CAST

Steven Halliday, an antique dealer, code name: The Fox	Brian Keith
Manouche Roget, the owner of the Les Pêcheurs Bar in France, code name: The Leopard	Lilli Palmer
Tom Devon, a jeweler, code name: The Elephant	John Mills
Alec Marlowe, a mechanic, code name: The Tiger	Barry Morse
Police Lt. Georges Roget, Manouche's son	Michael Petrovitch
Jill Barton, Tom's niece	Seretta Wilson

Music: Ken Thorne.
The Zoo Gang Theme: Paul and Linda McCartney.
Producer: Herbert Hirschman.
Director: Sidney Hayers, John Hough.

THE ZOO GANG — 60 minutes — NBC — July 16, 1975 – August 6, 1975. 6 episodes.

1356   ZOOM

Children. Nonprofessional preteen children relate stories, songs, dances, games and jokes either written by themselves or submitted by home viewers. The program represents a television framework for the creative efforts of children.

Hosts: Seven children at a time host, but are identified and credited by a first name only: Nancy, Maura, David, Ann, Kenny, Tracy, Jay, Bernadette, Luiz, Edith, Tommy, Jon, Lori, Danny, Neil, Nina, Donna, Mike, Leon, Timmy, Jennifer, Chris, Karen, Ron, Shawn, Arcadio, Carmen, Red, Harvey, Nell, Levell.
Orchestra: Newton Wayland.
Producer: Cheryl Bibbs, Sushiel Bibbs, Payne Francis.

ZOOM — 30 minutes — PBS — January 9, 1972 – June 23, 1975. Syndicated to PBS stations.

CBS

Circus of the Stars. Actress and model Brooke Shields, the youngest performer to risk her life in the potentially hazardous series.

ABC

Here We Go Again. Nita Talbot.

NBC

Shirley. From left, Shirley Jones, Rosanna Arquette and guest star Edward Winter.

CBS

The Sonny and Cher Show. Cher and Sonny Bono.

Section 2
Pilot Films
January 1, 1970– October 31, 1980

Each year more than one thousand ideas are proposed to both network officials and independent producers for development into potential series. From this number, about five hundred scripts will be commissioned, but only between 90 and one hundred will actually be made into pilot films (at a cost of $500,000 for a half hour of comedy and more than one million dollars per hour of dramatic film). From these filmed or taped pilots the network officials select the programs they feel are worthy of becoming full-fledged weekly series.

While most of the pilot films that sell a series are broadcast as part of that series, unsold pilot films are not always televised and the few that are—those that are considered worthwhile—are aired on a sporadic basis, usually during the summer months when TV viewing is down and ratings are not critical.

As production costs continue to rise, fewer pilot films of the thirty- and sixty-minute variety will be produced each year. With television's growing dependence on feature films, many pilot ideas will be made into a ninety-minute or two-hour TV movie (as has already been done a number of times). The pilot can now serve as both a pilot and a feature film—and the film can earn back production costs through syndication—something that cannot be done, for example, with a thirty-minute comedy pilot because there would be no market for it.

The pilot films listed here are those televised from January 1, 1970 through October 31, 1980 and consist of both the standard thirty- and sixty-minute variety and those produced as TV movies/pilot films. Where possible, cast listings have been divided into two categories: Regular Cast, which indicates the proposed regulars had the series sold, and the Guest Cast, which indicates the guests for that particular episode. In cases where a pilot film has been broadcast apart from a series (e.g., *Charlie's Angels*) and contains almost identical information (to the series it became) the information has been listed with the series and cross-referenced where appropriate. In situations where a pilot film's information differs considerably from the series it became (e.g., *The Love Boat*), the information has been included in both the series and pilot film sections and cross-referenced. All other entries, unless otherwise noted, are unsold pilot films.

The Daughters of Joshua Cabe. From left, Lesley Ann
Warren, Karen Valentine, Buddy Ebsen and Sandra Dee.

America 2100. Karen Valentine (foreground), Mark King
(at left) and Jon Cutler. The guard, who has a nonspeaking part, is not identified.

The Four of Us. From bottom left, Kathy Jo Kelly, Will
McMillan, Barbara Feldon and Vicky Dawson.

A

1357   ABC'S MATINEE TODAY

Pilot (Anthology). A proposed series of daily 90-minute dramas.

The Series:

I Never Said Goodbye (Dec. 3, 1973). The story of a doctor who is accused of hastening the death of a woman afflicted with a terminal disease.

CAST

Katherine Telford	June Lockhart
David Laughton	Jack Staufford
Alice Laughton	Renne Jarrett
Dr. Morton	John Lupton
Mike Rodman	Philip Clark
John Rodman	John Howard
Dr. Goldstone	DeForest Kelley
Judge Micklin	Anne Seymour

The Other Woman (Dec. 4, 1973). The story of a pregnant, unwed librarian who wants to keep her child despite the embarrassment the action will bring to her and the child's married father.

CAST

Liz Cunningham	Katherine Helmond
Dr. Miller	Pat O'Brien
Davie Collins	Joel Fabiani
Lorraine Collins	Beverlee McKensey

Alone With Terror (Dec. 5, 1973). The story of a police lieutenant's widow who risks her own life to prove that her husband was not on the take at the time of his apparent suicide.

CAST

Susan Maroni	Juliet Mills
Marian Webb	Virginia Vincent
Leonard Walters	Colby Chester
Sam Vickers	Joseph Bernard
Capt. John Ryan	Charles Schull
Lt. Joe Maroni	Paul Shenar

My Secret Mother (Dec. 6, 1973). The story of Nora Sells, 18, adopted, unwed and pregnant, and her search to find her real mother—who gave her up for adoption and disappeared.

CAST

Nora Sells	Sondra Locke
Mary Fiske	Lola Albright
Carol Babcock	Rue McClanahan
Mrs. Sells	Marge Redmond

A Mask of Love (Dec. 7, 1973). The story of John Connors, a biographer, and his hunt for a deceased novelist's personal papers—now jealously guarded by his last mistress.

CAST

John Connors	Harris Yulin
Tina Bordeaux	Barbara Barrie
Juliana Bordeaux	Cathleen Nesbitt
Mary Prest	Geraldine Brooks
Maria	Naomi Stevens

ABC'S MATINEE TODAY—90 minutes (each episode)—ABC—December 3, 1973–December 7, 1973. 5 programs.

1358   ACE

Pilot (Comedy). The misadventures of Edward R. Ace, an eccentric private detective facing bankruptcy. In the pilot, Ace seeks to relieve some of his monetary burdens by attempting to find the source of a security leak in a large corporation.

REGULAR CAST

Edward R. Ace	Bob Dishy
Gloria Ross, his secretary	Rae Allen

GUEST CAST

Janet Slade	Barbara Brownell
Alice Slade	Ruth Manning
Mr. Mason	Dick Van Patten
Mr. Strutt	Liam Dunn

Music: Pat Williams.
Producer: Larry White.
Writer: Jerry Davis.
Director: Gary Nelson.

ACE—30 minutes—NBC—July 26, 1976.

1359   ACES UP

Pilot (Comedy). The misadventures of Jose and Raul, two spirited Puerto Ricans, and their struggles to run the Ace Moving and Hauling Service, a trucking outfit.

REGULAR CAST

Jose	Jose Perez
Raul	Raul Julia

GUEST CAST

Father	Ron Steinberg
Daughter	Carol Bagdasarian
Son	Paul Michael Glaser

Music: Earle Hagen.
Producer: Sheldon Leonard, Danny Arnold.

Writer: Bob Klane.
Director: Sheldon Leonard.
Director of Photography: Brick Marquand.

ACES UP—30 minutes—CBS—March 29, 1974.

1360   ADDIE AND THE KING OF HEARTS

Pilot (Drama). The fourth of four pilot films about the Mills family, who live in a small town in Nebraska during the 1940s (see also "The Easter Promise," "The House Without a Christmas Tree," and "The Thanksgiving Treasure" in the pilot film section). The story details a young girl's handling of the emotion of love when she (Addie Mills, age 13) discovers that her father (James, a widower) is dating Irene Davis, the local beautician. Her adolescent shock, jealously and shattered security later teach her that love has many faces and that telling them apart is a function of growing up.

REGULAR CAST

James Mills, the father	Jason Robards
Addie Mills, his daughter	Lisa Lucas
Grandma Mills	Mildred Natwick

GUEST CAST

Irene Davis	Diane Ladd
Mr. Davenport	Richard Hatch
Miss Collins	Hope Alexander Willis
Kathleen Tate	Christina Hart
Danny	Michael Morgan
Terry	Vicki Schreck

Music: Arthur Rubinstein.
Producer: Alan Shayne.
Writer: Gail Rock.
Director: Joseph Hardy.
Associate Producer: Annabelle Davis-Goff.
Art Director: Ben Edwards, Jack Stewart.
Costumes: Jane Greenwood, Orpha Barry.

ADDIE AND THE KING OF HEARTS—60 minutes—CBS—January 25, 1976.

1361   ADVENTURING WITH THE CHOPPER

Pilot (Comedy). The misadventures of Arnold "The Chopper" Jackson and Leonard Jones, two dimwitted private detectives who,

in the pilot episode, become the dupes for a racketeer's protection racket.

CAST

Arnold "The Chopper" Jackson	Harrison Page
Leonard Jones	Antonio Fargas
Cousin Bea	Ketty Lester
Lieutenant Hoover	Lawrence Cook

Producer: Norman Steinberg.
Director: Hy Averback.

ADVENTURING WITH THE CHOPPER—30 minutes—NBC—August 7, 1976.

1362   THE ADVENTURES OF NICK CARTER

Pilot (Crime Drama). The story, set in the 1900s, follows the exploits of Nick Carter, a private detective working out of New York City. In the pilot, Carter attempts to discover the whereabouts of a playboy's missing wife.

REGULAR CAST

Nick Carter	Robert Conrad
Captain Dan Keller	Neville Brand

GUEST CAST

Bess Tucker	Shelley Winters
Otis Duncan	Broderick Crawford
Freddie Duncan	Dean Stockwell
Hallelujah Harry	Pat O'Brien
Neal Duncan	Pernell Roberts
Lloyd Deems	Sean Garrison
Joyce Jordan	Laraine Stephens
Roxy O'Rourke	Brooke Bundy
Singer	Jaye P. Morgan

Music: John Andrew Tartaglia.
Producer: Stanley Kallis.
Writer: Ken Pettus.
Director: Paul Krasny.
Director of Photography: Alric Edens.

THE ADVENTURES OF NICK CARTER—90 minutes—ABC—February 20, 1972.

A.E.S. HUDSON STREET

The pilot episode broadcast on ABC on July 21, 1977, for the series of the same title (see regular program section).

1363   ALEX AND THE DOBERMAN GANG

Pilot (Crime Drama). The exploits of Alexander Parker, a private detective who uses five smart Doberman pinschers he inherited from a carnival performer to help him solve crimes. In the pilot, Alex attempts to prove that his client, Susan Hamilton, is innocent of the murder of an art dealer.

CAST

Alexander Parker	Jack Stauffer
The diner owner, his friend	Taurean Blaque
The diner waitress	Lane Binkley
Susan Hamilton (guest role)	Martha Smith

Guests: Bill Lucking, Jerry Orbach, Burt Edwards, Alan Gibbs, Harriet Gibson, James Jeter, Jerry Maren, Sari Price, Don Starr, Sandy Acker, Cindy Acker, Doug Bank, James Espinoza, David Griffith, Tim Rossovich.

The dogs (Trained by Cindy James-Cullen): Duke, Rocky, Harlow, Little Bogie and Gabel. Alex's license plate number: 352 4ZS.

Music: Earle Hagen.
Supervising Producer: James D. Parriott, Richard Chapman.
Executive Producer: Harve Bennett, Harris Katleman.
Producer: Ralph Sariego.
Writer: James D. Parriott, Richard Chapman.
Director: Byron Chudnow.
Art Director: Ross Bellah, Russell Menzer.
Director of Photography: Travers Hill.

ALEX AND THE DOBERMAN GANG — 60 minutes — NBC — April 11, 1980. See also "Nick and the Doberman Gang" in the pilot film section.

ALIAS SMITH AND JONES

The pilot film broadcast on ABC on January 5, 1971, for the series of the same title (see regular program section).

ALICE

The pilot episode, broadcast on CBS on August 31, 1976, for the series of the same title (see regular program section).

1364 THE ALIENS ARE COMING

Pilot (Science Fiction). The story of disembodied extraterrestrials who land in southern Nevada to begin their colonization of Earth. The would-be series was to depict the exploits of Dr. Scott Dryden, an astrophysicist, as he battles the aliens who, to survive on Earth, inhabit the bodies of people most able to fulfill their needs. In the pilot, Dryden attempts to foil an alien plot to take over Hoover Dam. The aliens require the dam's hydroelectric power to sustain themselves.

REGULAR CAST

Dr. Scott Dryden	Tom Mason
Gwendelyn O'Brien, his assistant	Melinda Fee
Leonard Nero, the head of Nero International, for which Scott works	Eric Braeden

GUEST CAST

Russ Garner	Max Gail
Sue Garner	Caroline McWilliams
Timmy Garner	Matthew Laborteaux
Joyce Cummings	Fawne Harriman
Harve Nelson	Ron Masak
Eldon Gates	John Milford
Bert Fowler	Laurence Haddon
Colonel John Sebastian	Hank Brandt
Patrolman Strong	Richard Lockmiller
Dr. Conley	Sean Griffin

Music: William Goldstein.
Producer: Philip Saltzman.
Writer: Robert Lenski.
Director: Harvey Hart.
Art Director: George B. Cahn, Norman Newburg.
Director of Photography: Jacques R. Marquette.

THE ALIENS ARE COMING — 2 hours — NBC — March 2, 1980.

1365 THE ALL-AMERICAN COLLEGE COMEDY SHOW

Pilot (Variety-Comedy). The program features college students performing their own original material.

Hostess: Jaye P. Morgan.
Executive Producer: Mike Gargiulo.
Producer: Chuck Horner, Bob Lane.
Director: Mike Gargiulo.
Art Director: Jim Ryan.
Performers:
Princeton University's Triangle Club: Creigh Duncan, Jane Abernathy, Gallia Kuharsky, Hilary Meserole, Molly Groton, Cinny Strickland, Alyson Wood, Anne Goodale, Kathy Hov, Larry Robinson, Joe Quinn, Len Galla, Bob Brisk.
Northwestern University's Waamu Show: Winifred Freedman, Eric Kincaid, Mark D. Kaufmann, Richard Kind, Dana Olsen, Tom Virtue, Michael Spound.
Indiana University's Laugh Tracks: Kelli Bixler, Kathy Hutsen, Elizabeth Kay, John Garvey, Michael Weisman, Paul W. Shapiro.
University of Pennsylvania's Mask and Wig Club: Paul Provenza, Rich Werblin, Ron Alper, Joe Fillip, Jeff Younger, Mark Kuhn, Ken Olshansky, Mich Canelos, Steve Schwartzberg, Murray Indick, Perry Perretz, Dan Helming, Ira Bleiweiss, Bill Shore, Brett Hellerman.

THE ALL-AMERICAN COLLEGE COMEDY SHOW — 60 minutes — CBS — December 14, 1979.

1366 ALL-AMERICAN PIE

Pilot (Human Interest). The program spotlights the activities of ordinary people at work and play.

Host: Joe Namath.
Music: Billy Goldenberg.
Supervising Producer: Caryn Sneider.
Executive Producer: Bernie Kukoff, Jeff Harris.
Writer-Director: Bernie Kukoff, Jeff Harris.

ALL-AMERICAN PIE — 60 minutes — ABC — August 17, 1980.

1367 ALLAN

Pilot (Comedy). The story of the relationship between Harold Fisher, a hard-working father, and his son, Allan, a hippie. In the pilot, Harold, who wants his son to join him in the hardware business, seeks a way to discourage Allan from leaving home to join a hippie commune.

REGULAR CAST

Harold Fisher, the father	Lou Jacobi
Allan Fisher, his son	Mark Jennings
Blanche Fisher, Harold's wife	Florence Halop

GUEST CAST

Doris	Barbara Press
Ted	Victor Brandt
Alice	Brioni Farrell
Franny	Connie Sawyer

ALLAN — 30 minutes — NBC — August 23, 1971.

1368 ALMOST HEAVEN

Pilot (Comedy). The misadventures of a group of deceased souls who are relegated to Almost Heaven, a place where they have to remain until they can earn their way through the Pearly Gates by encouraging good deeds among the living.

CAST

Lydia	Eva Gabor
Dave	Robert Hays
Annie	Laurie Heinemann
George	Larry Gelman
Randall	Richard Roat

Also: Jay Leno, Anne Schedeen, Ellen Regan.
Music: Paul Chihara.
Executive Producer: Dale McRaven.
Producer: David Pollack, Elias Davis.
Writer: Dale McRaven.
Director: Bill Persky.
Director of Photography: Lester Shorr.

ALMOST HEAVEN — 30 minutes — ABC — December 28, 1978.

1369 ALONE AT LAST

Pilot (Comedy). The story lines, casts and credits for two unsold pilot films about the lives of the Elliotts, a family of four living in California.

First Pilot:
As Greg Elliott and his wife Laurie prepare for a trip to Europe, Greg attempts to solve his latest problem: his son Michael's announcement that he is marrying a woman twice his age.

CAST

Greg Elliott, the father	Bill Daily
Laurie Elliott, his wife	Virginia Vestoff
Nancy Elliott, their daughter	Kerry Sherman
Michael Elliott, their son	Michael Horton
Agnes Bernoski, Greg's mother	Francine Beers
Jack Bernoski, Agnes' husband	Martin Garner
Sherry, the woman Michael loves	Elaine Joyce
Lisa, Sherry's daughter	Melissa Sherman
Harry Elliott, Greg's brother	Howard Platt

Music: Joe Harnell.
Executive Producer: Bob Sweeney, Edward H. Feldman.
Producer: Larry Rosen.
Writer: Larry Tucker.
Director: Hy Averback.
Art Director: Ross Bellah.

ALONE AT LAST — 30 minutes — NBC — June 24, 1980.

Second Pilot:
Larry Elliott, the chief of radiology at Memorial General Hospital, struggles to cope with his son Michael's uncaring attitude and teach him the meaning of the word responsibility.

CAST

Larry Elliott, the father	Eugene Roche
Maureen Elliott, his wife	Susan Bay
Nancy Elliott, their daughter	Lilibet Stern
Michael Elliott, their son	Dana Carvey
Agnes Bernoski, Larry's mother	Florence Halop
Jack Bernoski, Agnes' husband	Martin Garner

Music: Joe Harnell.
Producer: Larry Tucker, Larry Rosen.
Writer: Larry Tucker, Larry Rosen.
Director: Peter Baldwin.
Art Director: Ross Bellah, Zoltan Muller.
Director of Photography: Jack Engel.

ALONE AT LAST — 30 minutes — NBC — November 3, 1980 (an unscheduled air date).

1370 AN AMATEUR'S GUIDE TO LOVE

Pilot (Comedy). Glimpses of unsuspecting individuals caught in prearranged romantic situations by hidden cameras.

Host: Joe Flynn.
Guests: Dick Martin, Rose Marie, Michael Landon, Peter Marshall.

AN AMATEUR'S GUIDE TO LOVE — 30 minutes — CBS — August 8, 1971.

1371 AMANDA FALLON

Pilot (Drama). The story, set in Los Angeles, follows the work of Amanda Fallon, a female pediatrician. In the pilot film she seeks to comfort and help a 14-year-old boy who is suffering from bleeding ulcers.

REGULAR CAST

Dr. Amanda Fallon	Jane Wyman
Dr. Vic Wheelwright	Mike Farrell
Nurse Crawford	Lillian Lehman

GUEST CAST

Dee Merlino	Lynnette Mettey
Peter Merlino	Jim Davis
Cory Merlino (the boy)	Ronny Howard
Jack Merlino	Robert Hogan
Girl	Jill Banner
Jonathan	Michael Laird

Music: Richard Clements.
Producer: Jack Laird.
Writer: Robert Malcolm Young.
Director: Don Taylor.

AMANDA FALLON — 60 minutes — NBC — March 5, 1972.

1372 AMERICA 2100

Pilot (Comedy). The story follows the misadventures of Chester Barnes and Phil Keese, two unsuccessful comics who, through a freak accident,* were in suspended animation for 120 years and awoke in the year 2100 (in America's capital — Newark, New Jersey).

CAST

Dr. Karen Harland, the girl who wakes them	Karen Valentine
Chester Barnes	Jon Cutler
Phil Keese	Mark King
Max, the computer (voiced by)	Sid Caesar

Music: Jonathan Tunick.
Executive Producer: Austin and Irma Kalish.
Producer: Gary Menteer.
Director: Joel Zwick.

AMERICA 2100 — 30 minutes — ABC — July 24, 1979.

*In a freezing hotel room, Chester and Phil each took a sleeping pill, but neglected to turn off the oven, on which warm milk had begun to boil. The fumes from the oven eventually killed them, but a split second before they died, the cold air froze and suspended them; it took scientists 120 years to master the process of cell rejuvenation, at which time they could be thawed out.

1373 THE AMERICAN BAG

Pilot (Comedy). The pilot, set in mythical small town locales, presents a satirical look at life in the United States.

Host: Dennis Weaver.
Guest: McLean Stevenson.
Producer: Chris Bearde, Allan Blye.

THE AMERICAN BAG — 60 minutes — NBC — February 26, 1974.

1374 ANN IN BLUE

Pilot (Comedy). The story of Ann Neal, the head of a four-woman police unit in New York City.

CAST

Sgt. Ann Neal	Penny Fuller
Officer Bea Russo	Mary Elaine Monte
Officer Elizabeth Jensen	Maybeth Hart
Officer Jessie Waters	Hattie Winston

Music: Jack Elliott, Allyn Ferguson.
Producer: Danny Arnold.
Director: Theodore J. Flicker.

ANN IN BLUE — 30 minutes — ABC — August 8, 1974.

1375 ANNIE FLYNN

Pilot (Comedy). The story of Annie Flynn, a former nurse trying to succeed in medical school. In the pilot episode, Annie attends a faculty-student reception and meets Paul Lucas, whom she believes is a fellow student and starts a promising romance with him. When she discovers that he is to be her anatomy professor, she seeks a subtle way to break off their relationship, fearing her grade in class may depend on how well she performs in bed.

REGULAR CAST

Annie Flynn	Barrie Youngfellow
C. C., her neighbor	Carol Potter
Elliott Hoag, a medical student	Harvey Lewis
Hoyt Kosloff, Annie's landlord	Louis Guss

GUEST CAST

Paul Lucas	Charles Frank
Mr. Braden	Jack Fletcher
Sherry	Lisa Loring
Marty Trellis	Josh Grenrock
Stephanie Pilzcyk	Renee Lippin

Producer: Coleman Mitchell, Geoffrey Neigher.
Writer: Coleman Mitchell, Geoffrey Neigher.
Director: Robert Moore.
Art Director: Ross Bellah, John Beckman.
Director of Photography: Meredith Nicholson.
Music: Gene Page.

ANNIE FLYNN — 30 minutes — CBS — January 21, 1978.

ANOTHER APRIL

See "Marriage Times Four" in the pilot film section.

1376 ARCHIE

Pilot (Comedy). The series, set in the mythical town of Riverdale, follows the misadventures of the Archie Gang: Archie Andrews, Betty Cooper, Veronica Lodge, Jughead Jones and Reggie Mantle. Based on the comic strip by Bob Montana.

CAST

Archie Andrews	Dennis Brown
Betty Cooper	Audrey Landers
Veronica Lodge	Hilary Thompson
Reggie Mantle	Mark Winkworth
Jughead Jones	Derrel Maury
Mr. Andrews, Archie's father	Gordon Jump
Mr. Weatherbee, the school principal	Byron Webster
Miss Grundy, a teacher at Riverdale High	Jane Lambert
Big Ethel, a friend of the Archies	Tifni Twitchell
Midge, a friend	Susan Blu
Moose, a friend	Jim Boelsen
Mr. Lodge, Veronica's father	Whit Bissell
Mrs. Lodge, Veronica's mother	Amzie Strickland
Little Jinx	Michelle Stacy
Larry, a friend	Billy Mumy
Phil	Paul Gordon
Aunt Helen	Mae Marmy

Music: Stu Gardner, Larry Farrow.
Executive Producer: James Komack.
Producer: Perry Cross.
Co-Producer: George Yanok.
Writer: Eric Cohen, George Yanok, Beverly Bloomberg, Peter Galley, Mickey Rose, Neil Rosen, George Tricker.
Director: Robert Scheerer.

ARCHIE — 60 minutes — ABC — December 19, 1976.

1377 ARNOLD'S CLOSET REVIEW

Pilot (Comedy). A series of blackouts and sketches that satirize various aspects of everyday life.

Host: Arte Johnson.
Regulars: Bonnie Boland, Joyce Bulifant, Jim Connell, Joan Gerber, Harvey Jason, Chuck McCann, Carol Robinson, Fred Smott, Frank Welker.
Music: Ian Bernard.
Executive Producer: George Schlatter.
Producer: Carolyn Raskin.
Writer: Chris Bearde, Coslough Johnson.
Director: Alan J. Levi.

ARNOLD'S CLOSET REVIEW — 30 minutes — NBC — August 30, 1971.

1378 THE ART OF CRIME

Pilot (Crime Drama). The story, set in New York City, follows the exploits of Roman Grey, a Gypsy antique dealer and amateur sleuth. The pilot, based on the novel, *Gypsy in Amber* by Martin Smith, depicts Grey's efforts to solve the murder of a friend.

REGULAR CAST

Roman Grey	Ron Leibman
Dany, his girlfriend	Jill Clayburgh
Sgt. Harry Isadore	Eugene Roche
Gypsy Queen	Tally Brown

GUEST CAST

Beckwith Sloan	Jose Ferrer
Parker Sharon	David Hedison
Hilary	Diane Kagan
Madame Vera	Dimitra Arliss
Kore	Mike Kellin

Music: Gil Mellé.
Executive Producer: Richard Irving.
Producer: Jules Irving.
Writer: Martin Smith, Bill Davidson.
Director: Richard Irving.
Art Director: William Campbell, May Callas.

THE ART OF CRIME — 90 minutes — NBC — December 3, 1975.

1379 ASSIGNMENT: MUNICH

Pilot (Adventure). The story of Jake Webster, a U.S. government undercover agent for the Internal Central Bureau, who operates in Munich, Germany, under the guise of a bar and grill owner. In the pilot, Webster seeks to help Cathy Lange, a beautiful girl who is being pursued by three men seeking $500,000 — money stolen by her father who was killed before he could reveal its location to his three accomplices. The men think Cathy knows its whereabouts.

REGULAR CAST

Jake Webster	Roy Scheider
Major Bernard Caldwell, his superior	Richard Basehart

GUEST CAST

Cathy Lange	Lesley Ann Warren
Inspector Hoffman	Werner Klemperer
Mitch	Robert Reed
C. C. Bryan	Pernell Roberts
George	Keenan Wynn
Gus	Mike Kellin

Music: George Romanis.
Executive Producer: Robert H. Justman.
Producer: Jerry Ludwig, Eric Berovichi.
Writer: Jerry Ludwig, Eric Berovichi.
Director: David Lowell Rich.
Director of Photography: Mike Marszalek.

ASSIGNMENT: MUNICH — 2 hours — ABC — April 30, 1972. Became the basis for the series *Assignment: Vienna.*

1380 AT EASE

Pilot (Comedy). The story, set at an Army post on Staten Island, New York, follows the misadventures of Sgt. Henry Rumsey, a 27-year Army veteran, as he struggles to bridge his generation gap with young recruits of today's Army. The pilot episode revolves around Henry's immediate problem: whether or not to re-enlist for his last three-year hitch — a problem that is complicated by his assistants: Cpl. Green, a pizza freak who hates the Army; Lt. Block, a newly minted ROTC officer still wet behind the ears; and Pvt. Franklin, a chronic insubordinate.

REGULAR CAST

Sgt. Henry Rumsey	Richard O'Neill
Agnes Rumsey, his wife	Peg Shirley
Stacy Rumsey, their daughter	Kathleen Beller
Cpl. Harvey Green	Danny Goldman
Lt. Block	Ken Gilman
Pvt. Albert Franklin	Roy Applegate

GUEST CAST

M.P.	Rod McCary
WAC Carol	Amanda Jones
Soldier	Kenneth Martinez
Soldier's mother	Rita Conde
Soldier's bride	Roxanna Bonilla-Giannini

Executive Producer: Jay Benson.
Producer: Bob Shayne, Eric Cohen.
Associate Producer: Norm Gray.
Writer: Eric Cohen, Bob Shayne.
Director: Bob Claver.
Art Director: Steven Moore.

AT EASE—30 minutes—CBS—September 7, 1976.

B

1381 BACHELOR AT LAW

Pilot (Comedy). The misadventures of Ben Sikes, a recent law school graduate, as he begins his career as an attorney.

REGULAR CAST

Ben Sikes	John Ritter
Ellen Brandon, his girlfriend	Sarah Kennedy
Matthew Brandon, Ellen's father	Harold Gould

GUEST CAST

Gloria Farrell	Betsy von Furstenburg
Mr. Woodward	Bill Zuckert
Mrs. Woodward	Kathleen O'Malley
Mr. Pierce	Craig Nelson
Prison Guard	David Frank
Phil	Richard Schaal
Judge	Curt Conway
Bailiff	Richard Gittings
Convict	Wayne Heffley
Assistant D.A.	Ron Rifkin

Producer: Ed Weinberger.
Writer: Ed Weinberger.
Director: Jay Sandrich.

BACHELOR AT LAW—30 minutes—CBS—June 5, 1973.

1382 BACHELORS 4

Pilot (Comedy). The overall title for four pilot films about single men.

Friends and Lovers. The story of Robert Dreyfuss (Paul Sand), a bass violinist, as he struggles to prepare for an audition with the Boston Symphony Orchestra and contend with his girlfriend Maggie (Lynn Lipton), who hates classical music. Produced by Robert H. Precht, written by Allan Burns and James L. Brooks, and directed by Jay Sandrich. Became the basis for the *Paul Sand in Friends and Lovers* series.

The Boys. See title "The Boys" in the pilot film section.

Jerry. The story of Jerry Edwards (Robert Walden), a 30-year-old bachelor who yearns for an exciting romance. Also cast: Linda Lavin (as a not-so-gay divorcée), Beatrice Colen and Bob Hastings (as Jerry's married neighbors), Norman Alden (as Jerry's employer at the bank), and Keone Young (as Jerry's lady-killer friend). Produced by Edward H. Feldman, written by Hal Dresner, and directed by Hal Cooper.

Sonny Boy. The story of Sonny Waller (Allen Garfield), a 35-year-old, frustrated mama's boy. Also cast: Florence Stanley as Marjorie Waller, Sonny's mother. Produced and written by Rob Reiner and Phil Mishkin, and directed by Rob Reiner and Bob LaHendro.

BACHELORS 4—2 hours (30 minutes each pilot)—CBS—May 16, 1974.

1383 BAFFLED

Pilot (Mystery). The story of Tom Kovack, a race car driver who acquires mysterious occult powers as the result of the impact of a crash—powers that enable him to envision and help people in trouble.

REGULAR CAST

Tom Kovack	Leonard Nimoy
Michele Brent, an expert on the occult; his assistant	Susan Hampshire
Hopkins, Tom's chauffeur	Ewan Roberts

GUEST CAST

Andrea Glenn	Vera Miles
Jennifer Glenn	Jewel Blanch
Mrs. Farraday	Rachel Roberts
Louise Sanford	Valerie Taylor
Parrish/Sanford	Mike Murray
Mr. Verelli	Christopher Benjamin
Peggy Tracewell	Angharad Rees

Music: Richard Hill.
Executive Producer: Norman Felton.
Producer: Philip Leacock.
Writer: Theodore Apstein.
Director: Michael Dryhurst.

BAFFLED—2 hours—NBC—January 30, 1973.

1384 THE BAIT

Pilot (Crime Drama). The exploits of Tracy Fleming, an undercover policewoman. The pilot depicts her attempts to apprehend a rapist-murderer.

REGULAR CAST

Tracy Fleming	Donna Mills
Captain Maryk	Michael Constantine

GUEST CAST

Earl Stokey	William Devane
Nora	June Lockhart
Solomon	Noam Pitlik
Nugent	Thalmus Rasulala
Liz Fowler	Arlene Golonka

Music: Jack Elliott, Allyn Ferguson.
Executive Producer: Aaron Spelling, Leonard Goldberg.
Producer: Peter Nelson
Writer: Don Mankiewicz.
Director: Leonard J. Horn.
Director of Photography: Gert Andersen.

THE BAIT—90 minutes—ABC—March 13, 1973.

BANACEK

The pilot film broadcast on NBC on March 20, 1972, for the series of the same title (see regular program section).

1385 THE BANANA COMPANY

Pilot (Comedy). The story, set in the South Pacific during World War II, follows the misadventures of the Banana Company, a group of combat correspondents who go to outrageous lengths to acquire stories for their press service.

CAST

Major Platt	Ted Gehring
Capt. Harry Gill	John Reilly
Peebles	Gailard Sartain
Segal	Sam Chew, Jr.
Muldoon	Ron Masak
Seebring	Eddie Quillan
"Front Line" Turner (guest role)	Bob Brown

Executive Producer: Carroll O'Connor.
Producer: Ron Rubin.
Writer: Bob Klane, Ron Rubin, Bernard Kahn.
Director: Bruce Bilson.
Art Director: Perry Ferguson.
Director of Photography: Dennis Dalzell.

THE BANANA COMPANY—30 minutes—CBS—August 25, 1977.

1386 BANJO HACKETT

Pilot (Western). The story, set in the Old West of the 1880s, follows the exploits of Banjo Hackett, an easygoing horse trader, and his nephew, Jubal Winter, an orphan who is now his ward and traveling companion. The pilot depicts their attempts to find Jubal's valuable Arabian mare, which was stolen from him when his widowed mother died.

REGULAR CAST

Banjo Hackett	Don Meredith
Jubal Winter	Ike Eisenmann

GUEST CAST

Flora	Anne Francis
Sam Ivory	Chuck Connors
Mollie Brannan	Jennifer Warren
Tip Conacher	Dan O'Herlihy
Lijah Tuttle	Slim Pickens
Judge Janeway	Jeff Corey
Sheriff Tadlock	J. D. Cannon
Lady Jane Grey	Gloria De Haven

Music: Morton Stevens.
Producer: Bruce Landsbury.

Writer: Ken Trevey.
Director: Andrew V. McLaglen.
Art Director: Ross Bellah, Carl Braunger.

BANJO HACKETT—2 hours—NBC—May 3, 1976.

BARNEY AND ME

See "Triple Play '73" in the pilot film section for information.

1387 BATTLES: THE MURDER THAT WOULDN'T DIE

Pilot (Crime Drama). The story of William F. Battles, a former Los Angeles policeman turned football coach and security chief for Hawaii State University in Aloha, Hawaii. In the pilot, Battles attempts to resolve a 38-year-old mystery, Hawaii's famous but unsolved "Chambers Murder Case" (in which an American woman named Pamela Chambers was supposedly raped by four young Hawaiians, one of whom was killed; the other three were rapidly acquitted).

REGULAR CAST

William Battles	William Conrad
Shelby Battles, his niece	Robin Matson
Joe "Deacon" Johnson, Shelby's boyfriend	Lane Caudell
Nancy Phillips, the college dean	Marj Dusay
Tuliosis (Tuli), a member of the college football team	Tommy Aguilar
Jack Spaulding, the head coach	Roger Bowen
Lt. Frank Fowler, H.P.D.	Jimmy Bowles

GUEST CAST

Alan Battles (William's brother)	Edward Binns
Jeff Briggs	Jose Ferrer
Gen. Rocky Jensen	Don Porter
Paul Harrison	John Hillerman
Chuck Parks	Kenneth Tobey
Dr. John Spencer	Ben Piazza
Jill Spencer	Sharon Acker

Narrator: William Conrad.
Music: Joe Harnell, Glen A. Larson, Stu Phillips.
Music Conductor-Arranger: John Andrew Tartaglia.
Executive Producer: Glen A. Larson.
Producer: Ben Kadish.
Writer: Glen A. Larson, Michael Sloan.
Director: Ron Satlof.
Art Director: Loyd S. Papez.
Director of Photorpahy: Harry Wolf.

BATTLES: THE MURDER THAT WOULDN'T DIE—2 hours—NBC—March 9, 1980.

BATTLESTAR GALACTICA

The pilot film broadcast on ABC on September 17, 1978, for the series of the same title (see regular program section).

1388 THE BAY CITY AMUSEMENT COMPANY

Pilot (Comedy). A behind-the-scenes look at life in a television station as seen through the antics of the creative staff of *The Bay City Amusement Company*, a local series in San Francisco.

CAST

Bradshaw	Ted Gehring
Alan	Dennis Howard
Ann	Barrie Youngfellow
Clifford	Terry Kiser
Howie	Pat McCormick
Gail	June Gable
Warren	Jim Scott

Executive Producer: Norman Steinberg.
Producer: Bo Kaprall.
Writer: Ken Levine, David Isaacs.
Director: Norman Steinberg, Gary Shimokawa.

THE BAY CITY AMUSEMENT COMPANY—30 minutes—NBC—July 28, 1977.

1389 THE B.B. BEEGLE SHOW

Pilot (Variety). A proposed series, similar to *The Muppet Show*, wherein 51 puppets join guests in comedy sketches.

Host: B.B. Beegle (a puppet dog voiced by Michael Bell).
Voices: Michael Bell, Marilyn Schreffler, Norman Grohmann.
Puppeteers: Pat Bryne, Jeanne Engelbright, Fran Dowie, Judy Anderson, Terry Hardin, Nina Koegh, Greg Deadler, David Janzow.
Music: Bob Buckley.
Executive Producer: Joseph Barbera, Arthur Weinthel, W. C. Elliott.
Producer: Stan Jacobson, John Joachims.
Writer: Dick Robbins, Duane Poole.
Director: Stan Jacobson.
Art Director: Graeme Murray.
Guests: Joyce DeWitt, Arte Johnson.

THE B.B. BEEGLE SHOW—30 minutes—Syndicated January 1980.

1390 THE BEACH GIRLS

Pilot (Comedy). The story, set in Los Angeles, follows the struggles of Ginny, Sue and Abby, three aspiring singers who comprise the group, "The Beach Girls," as they seek stardom.

CAST

Ginny	Rita Wilson
Sue	Kim O'Brien
Abby	Ava Lazar
Sonny Pink, their agent	Don Calfa

Music: Dick Smedley.
Executive Producer: Joseph Barbera.
Producer: Walter deFaria.
Writer: Marion C. Freeman.
Director: Stanley Z. Cherry.
Choreographer: Larry Merritt.

THE BEACH GIRLS—30 minutes—Syndicated December 1977.

1391 BEACH PATROL

Pilot (Crime Drama). The exploits of Jan Plumer, Marty Green, Earl Hackman and Russ Patrick, members of the San Gabriel Police Department, as they patrol the beaches of Southern California.

REGULAR CAST

Officer Jan Plumer	Christine DeLisle
Officer Marty Green	Jonathan Frakes
Officer Earl Hackman	Richard J. Hill
Officer Russ Patrick	Robin Strand
Sgt. Lou Markowski, their superior	Michael Gregory

GUEST CAST

Wes Dobbs	Paul Burke
Wanda	Mimi Maynard
Tall Girl	Princess Mahoney

Also: Lillian Adams, Bella Brick, X Brands, Michael V. Gazzo.
Music: Barry DeVorzon.
Executive Producer: Aaron Spelling, Leonard Goldberg.
Supervising Producer: Ronald Austin, James David Buchanan.
Writer: Ronald Austin, James David Buchanan.
Director: Bob Kelljan.

BEACH PATROL—90 minutes—ABC—April 30, 1979.

1392 BEANE'S OF BOSTON

Pilot (Comedy). The antics of the staff and management of Beane's of Boston, an old-line department store.

REGULAR CAST

Frank Beane, the owner	Tom Poston
Mr. Peacock, the floorwalker	John Hillerman
Mrs. Slocombe, in charge of women's wear	Charlotte Rae
Franklyn Beane, Frank's nephew, the manager	George O'Hanlon, Jr.
Shirley Brahms, Mrs. Slocombe's assistant	Lorna Patterson
Mr. Humphries, the men's wear dept. salesman	Alan Sues

GUEST CAST

Mr. Granger	Morgan Farley
Mr. Lucas	Larry Bishop
Mr. Johnson	Don Bexley
Ingrid	Dana House

Music: Don Peake.
Supervising Producer: Bill Idelson, Sheldon Bull.
Executive Producer: Garry K. Marshall, Tony Marshall.
Producer: Jeremy Lloyd.
Writer: Jeremy Lloyd, David Croft, Bill Idelson, Sheldon Bull.
Director: Jerry Paris.
Art Director: Jim Claytor.
Director of Photography: Robert Hager.
Set Decorator: Andy Nealis.

BEANE'S OF BOSTON—30 minutes—CBS—May 5, 1979.

1393 BELL, BOOK, AND CANDLE

Pilot (Comedy). The story, adapted from the 1958 feature film of the same title, follows the life of Alex Brandt, a publisher who moves into a flat above a curio shop that is run by Gillian Holroyd, a beautiful young witch, and her aunt, Enid, also a sorceress. In the pilot, Brandt first meets—and falls in love with—Gillian.

REGULAR CAST

Gillian Holroyd	Yvette Mimieux
Alex Brandt	Michael Murphy
Aunt Enid	Doris Roberts
Nicky Holroyd, Gillian's brother	John Pleshette

GUEST CAST

Lois	Bridget Hanley
Rosemary	Susan Sullivan
Bishop Fairbarn	Edward Andrews
Melissa	Dori Whitaker

Producer: Bruce Lansbury.
Writer: Richard DeRoy.
Director: Hy Averback.

BELL, BOOK, AND CANDLE—30 minutes—NBC—September 8, 1976.

1394 BENDER

Pilot (Crime Drama). The exploits of Bender, a tough, ex-New York police executive who becomes the chief of police in Tamarisk Wells, a rich California desert resort community targeted by clever criminals as "easy pickings."

REGULAR CAST

Chief of Police Bender	Harry Guardino
Bert Arkins, the city manager	Nicholas Coster
Wade Rawlings, the deputy police chief	Joe Burke
Joanne Clark, Bender's secretary	Susan Damante Shaw
R. J. Phillips, the mayor	Stephen Elliott

GUEST CAST

Vincent Farragut	Ben Piazza
Zachary Wilson	Will Hare
Raker	Robert Phalen
Bill Wilson	Sean Thomas Roche
Jim Wilson	Chad Roche
Pat Farragut	Nancy Bleier
Desk Sgt. Johnson	James Jeter
H. H. Dodd	Art Kassul
Doyle	Joe Bratcher
Maid	Margarita Cordova

Music: Ralph Ferraro.
Executive Producer: Carroll O'Connor, Terry Becker.
Producer: Cy Gomberg.
Writer: Cy Gomberg.
Director: Ray Danton.
Art Director: Fred Price.
Director of Photography: Leonard J. South.

BENDER—60 minutes—CBS—September 12, 1979.

1395 BENNY AND BARNEY, LAS VEGAS UNDERCOVER

Pilot (Crime Drama). The exploits of Benny Kowalski and Barney Tuscom, two Las Vegas Police Department officers who moonlight as nightclub singer-musicians. In the pilot, they attempt to solve the mysterious kidnapping of a big-name entertainer.

REGULAR CAST

Benny Kowalski	Terry Kiser
Barney Tuscom	Timothy Thomerson
Lieutenant Callan	Jack Colvin

GUEST CAST

Davis	Hugh O'Brian
Margie	Jane Seymour
Rosent	Jack Cassidy
Jake	Ted Cassidy

Music: Stu Phillips.
Executive Producer: Glen A. Larson.
Producer: Ron Satlof.
Writer: Glen A. Larson.
Director: Ron Satlof.

BENNY AND BARNEY, LAS VEGAS UNDERCOVER—90 minutes—NBC—January 19, 1977.

1396 BEST FRIENDS

Pilot (Comedy). The misadventures of a group of teenagers from varying backgrounds who scheme, dream and plan their futures while hanging around together in the basement of an apartment building on Chicago's northwest side.

CAST

Nick, the group leader	James Canning
Kathy, his cousin	Sherry Hursey
Arthur, a member of the gang	Bill Henry Douglas
Mountain Man, a member of the gang	Gary Epp
Gypsy, a member of the gang	Barry Pearl
Maggie, Kathy's aunt	Gloria LeRoy
Ouspensky, the building superintendent	Cliff Osmond
Lionel "Big O" Lapidus, a tough character with a reputation for revenge at pool	Ray Sharkey

Producer: Alan Sacks.
Writer: Stanely Ralph Ross, Peter Meyerson.
Director: Jerry Paris.

BEST FRIENDS—30 minutes—CBS—July 19, 1977.

1397 BETWEEN THE LINES

Pilot (Comedy). The antics of the staff of the *Back Bay Mainline*, an underground newspaper in Boston.

REGULAR CAST

Harry, a reporter	Kristoffer Tabori
Abbie, a reporter	Susan Krebs
Stanley, the advertising head	Sandy Helberg
Lynn, the secretary	Nancy Lane

Frank, the editor	Squire Fridel
David, a reporter	Charley Lang
Max, a reporter	Adam Arkin

GUEST CAST

The Perfect Teacher	Gino Conforti
Mrs. Boudry	Peggy Pope
Mr. Boudry	Henry Hoing

Music: Kenny Loggins, Richard Stekol.
Music Arranger: Billy Byers.
Executive Producer: Philip Mandelker.
Producer: Patricia Mardo.
Co-Producer: Russ Petranto.
Writer: Fred Barron.
Director: Charlotte Brown.
Art Director: René Lagler.

BETWEEN THE LINES — 30 minutes — ABC — July 7, 1980.

1398 BIG BOB JOHNSON AND HIS FANTASTIC SPEED CIRCUS

Pilot (Adventure). The exploits of Big Bob Johnson, Vikki Lee Sanchez and Julie Hunsacker, three daredevil race car drivers. The pilot depicts Johnson's efforts to win the title to an eccentric's estate by defeating two competitors in a cross-country auto race.

REGULAR CAST

Big Bob Johnson	Charles Napier
Vikki Lee Sanchez, his assistant	Maud Adams
Julie Hunsacker, his assistant	Constance Forslund

GUEST CAST

Timothy Stepwell	Rick Hurst
Lawrence Stepwell	William Daniels
W. G. Blazer	Robert Stoneman
Jesse	James Bond III
Half Moon Muldoon	Burton Gilliam

Music: Mark Snow.
Executive Producer: Bob Goodwin, Edward L. Rissien.
Producer: Joseph Gantman.
Writer: Bob Comfort, Rick Kellard.
Director: Jack Starrett.

BIG BOB JOHNSON AND HIS FANTASTIC SPEED CIRCUS — 2 hours — NBC — June 27, 1978.

1399 BIG CITY BOYS

Pilot (Comedy). The story of Harry Buckman, a public relations man and a disorganized free spirit who shuns responsibility. He suddenly finds his life changed when his sister and brother-in-law are sentenced to one-to-three years for tax evasion, and their son, Peter, is sent to live with him. The episode depicts Harry's attempts to change his life-style to accommodate his nephew.

CAST

Harry Buckman	Austin Pendleton
Peter, his nephew	Chris Barnes
Emily, Harry's girlfriend	Laurie Heineman
Susan, Peter's girlfriend	Francesca Bill
Pancho, Peter's friend	David Yanez

Executive Producer: Franklin Konigsberg.
Producer: Bruce Paltrow, Stephanie Sills.
Writer: Bob De Laurentis.
Director: Bill Persky.
Associate Producer: Harry Waterson.
Associate Director: Bob Lally.
Art Director: Don Roberts, Hub Braden.
Creator: Bruce Paltrow.

BIG CITY BOYS — 30 minutes — CBS — April 11, 1978.

BIG DADDY

See title "Triple Treat" in the pilot film section.

BIG EDDIE

The pilot episode broadcast on CBS on May 2, 1975, for the series of the same title (see regular program section).

1400 BIG ROSE

Pilot (Crime Drama). The cases of Rose Winters, a female private detective working out of Los Angeles. In the pilot, she and her colleague, Ed Mills, attempt to expose a team of con artists who are blackmailing a wealthy contractor.

REGULAR CAST

Rose Winters	Shelley Winters
Ed Mills	Barry Primus
Lieutenant Moore	Lonny Chapman

GUEST CAST

Gunther	Michael Constantine
Nina	Joan Van Ark
Troy	Paul Mantee
Blass	Paul Picerni
Marian	Peggy Walton
Mayhew	Yale Summers
Waitress	Lenore Kasdorf

Music: Robert Prince.
Producer: Joel Rogosin.
Writer: Andy Lewis.
Director: Paul Krasny.

BIG ROSE — 90 minutes — CBS — March 26, 1974.

1401 THE BILLION DOLLAR THREAT

Pilot (Adventure). The exploits of Robert Sands, a U.S. government super-spy. In the pilot, Sands seeks to stop Horatio Black, a mad scientist, from carrying out his threat: unless he is paid one billion dollars, he will blow a hole in the ozone layer which protects the Earth from the sun's rays, and expose millions of people to radioactive poisoning.

REGULAR CAST

Robert Sands	Dale Robinette
Miles Larson, his superior	Ralph Bellamy
Harry Darling, Larson's assistant	Stephen Keep
Marcia Buttercup, a government scientist	Ronnie Carol

GUEST CAST

Horatio Black	Patrick Macnee
Ely	Keenan Wynn
Holly	Beth Specht
Ivy	Karen Specht

Music: Morton Stevens.
Executive Producer: David Gerber.
Producer: Jay Daniel.
Writer: Jimmy Sangster.
Director: Barry Shear.
Director of Photography: Jack Woolf.

THE BILLION DOLLAR THREAT — 2 hours — ABC — April 15, 1979.

1402 BIZARRE

Pilot (Satire). A series of unusual comedy sketches. For example, a father, played by Richard Dawson, and his 10-year-old son, played by Eric Taslitz, ponder the question as to why the boy was expelled from school while both smoke and sip cocktails. Or, Nancy Steen as a concert pianist who appears to explain her recent surgery: her hand was enlarged to improve her keyboard reach.

Host: Richard Dawson.
Regulars: Tanya Boyd, Melissa Steinberg, Eric Taslitz, Nancy Steen, George Allen, Bill Decker.
Music: D'Vaughn Pershing.
Producer: Bob Einstein, Allan Blye.
Director: Bill Carruthers.

BIZARRE — 30 minutes — ABC — March 20, 1979.

B.J. AND THE BEAR

The pilot film broadcast on NBC on October 4, 1978, for the series of the same title (see regular program section).

1403 BLACK BART

Pilot (Comedy). The story, set in the Old West, follows the misadventures of Black Bart, the black sheriff in the bigoted town of Paris, Arizona. In the pilot, Bart arrests the mayor's nephew for "toe shooting," then tries to find a judge who will deliver a fair trial in a town completely owned and dominated by the mayor.

REGULAR CAST

Sheriff Black Bart	Lou Gossett
Reb Jordan, his deputy	Steve Landesberg
Belle Buzzer, the owner of the saloon	Millie Slavin
Fern B. Malaga, the mayor	Noble Willingham

GUEST CAST

Moonwolf	Ruben Moreno
Mr. Swenson	Ted Lehmann
Curley (the mayor's nephew)	Gerrit Graham
Jennifer	Brooke Adams

Porter	Rand Bridges
Mrs. Swenson	Tamar Cooper
Hughie	Poindexter

Executive Producer: Mark Tuttle.
Producer: Michael Elias, Frank Shaw, Robert Butler.
Writer: Michael Elias, Frank Shaw.
Director: Robert Butler.
Art Director: Arch Bacon.
Director of Photography: Michael Margulies.

BLACK BART — 30 minutes — CBS — April 4, 1975.

1404 BLUE JEANS

Pilot (Comedy). The story, set in Boston, follows the misadventures of Jimmy Scanlon, Vickie Gardner, Miles Savatini and Beethoven Zwirko, four young adults who comprise the struggling Rock group Blue Jeans.

CAST

Jimmy Scanlon	Paul Provenza
Vickie Gardner	Elissa Leeds
Miles Savatini	Charles Fleischer
Beethoven Zwirko	Jay Fenichel
Mr. Zwirko, Beethoven's father	George S. Irving
Molly Zwirko, Beethoven's mother	Ruth Manning
Club owner	Michael Aliamo

Music: Don Foliart, Howard Pearl.
Theme: "Blue Jeans Song" arranged by Bob Esty.
Executive Producer: Jerry Weintraub, Leonard Goldberg.
Producer: Alan Eisenstock, Larry Mintz, Gene Marcione.
Associate Producer: Denny King.
Writer: Alan Eisenstock, Larry Mintz.
Director: J. D. Lobu.
Art Director: Charles Koon.

BLUE JEANS — 30 minutes — ABC — July 26, 1980.

THE BLUE KNIGHT

The pilot film broadcast on CBS on May 9, 1975, for the series of the same title (see regular program section).

1405 BOBBY JO AND THE BIG APPLE GOODTIME BAND

Pilot (Comedy). The misadventures of a Country and Western Rock group called Bobby Jo and the Big Apple Goodtime Band. In the pilot, Bobby Jo, the band's pretty, but naive singer, writes a hit song that embroils the group in an unexpected legal hassle.

CAST

Bobby Jo, the singer	Season Hubley
Cousin Jack, the manager	Forrest Tucker

The Band:

Augie	Robert Walden
Jeff	John Bennett Perry
Virgil	Ed Begley, Jr.
Brian	Michael Gray

Also (guests): Tom Bosley (the mayor) and Pat Harrington, Jr.
Music: Jerry Fuller, Michael Murphy.
Producer: Paul Junger Witt.
Writer: Bernard Slade.
Director: Hal Cooper.

BOBBY JO AND THE BIG APPLE GOODTIME BAND—30 minutes—CBS—March 31, 1972.

BOBBY PARKER AND COMPANY

See title "Three-In-One" in the pilot film section.

1406   BOSTON AND KILBRIDE

Pilot (Crime Drama). The story of Tom Boston and Jim Kilbride, a pair of freewheeling private detectives. In the pilot, Boston and Kilbride team with Jill Miller, a pilot, in a mission that takes them to Central America where they seek to snatch a stolen jet and return it to its rightful owner in the States.

REGULAR CAST

Tom Boston	Tom Selleck
Jim Kilbride	James Whitmore, Jr.

GUEST CAST

Jill Miller	Jaime Lyn Bauer
Armand Beller	Don Ameche
Maria Sangria	Marlena Amey
C. Donald Devlin	William Daniels
Louise	Lane Bradbury
Toby Nash	Kathryn Leigh Scott
Turgeyev	David Palmer
Markov	George Fisher
Manolito	Walt Davis
Dianne	Elizabeth Halliday
Vince	Michael Brick
Mrs. Beller	June Whitley Taylor

Executive Producer: Stephen J. Cannell.
Supervising Producer: Alex Beaton.
Writer: Stephen J. Cannell.
Director: Lou Antonio.
Art Director: David Marshall.
Director of Photography: Dennis Dalzell.
Set Decorator: Steve Palmer.

BOSTON AND KILBRIDE—60 minutes—CBS—March 3, 1979.

1407   THE BOYS

Pilot (Comedy). The misadventures of comedy writers Eddie Ryan and Harry Rufkin. The pilot episode finds Eddie contemplating remarriage—but still finding his life being run by his ex-wife, Cassie.

CAST

Eddie Ryan	Tim Conway
Harry Rufkin	Herb Edelman
Cassie, Eddie's ex-wife	Esther Sutherland
Alice, Eddie's fiancée	Gwynne Gilford
Vicki (guest role)	Phyllis Elizabeth Davis
Dr. Ferguson (guest role)	Richard Stahl

Producer: Bill Persky, Sam Denoff.

Writer: Bill Persky, Sam Denoff.
Director: Bill Persky.

THE BOYS—30 minutes—CBS—May 23, 1975. Originally presented on May 16, 1974, as part of "Bachelors 4."

1408   BRAVO TWO

Pilot (Adventure). The exploits of Wiley Starrett and Bud Wizzer, the crew of the *Bravo Two* patrol boat, a unit of the Los Angeles Harbor Patrol. In the pilot, the Harbor Patrol attempts to locate an amphibious plane that has been forced down at sea in a dense fog.

REGULAR CAST

Wiley Starrett	Bruce Fairbairn
Bud Wizzer	David Gilliam
Lt. O'Brien, the commander of the *Bravo One* patrol boat	James Hampton
T. J. Phillips, O'Brien's aide	Cooper Huckabee

GUEST CAST

Mr. Morgan	Don Matheson
Mrs. Morgan	Lynn Carlin
Eddie Morgan	Matthew Laborteaux
Lucy	Lucy Saroyan

Executive Producer: Lee Rich, Philip Capice.
Producer: Robert Stambler, Guerdon Trueblood.
Writer: Leo Gordon, Guerdon Trueblood.
Director: Ernest Pintoff.
Creator: Guerdon Trueblood.

BRAVO TWO—30 minutes—CBS—March 25, 1977.

1409   BRENDA STARR

Pilot (Drama). The exploits of Brenda Starr, a crusading journalist. In the first pilot film (see following title) Brenda attempts to prove that the murder of her close friend is linked to the mysterious death of an eccentric billionaire, a man who was involved in foreign intrigue, blackmail and voodoo.

REGULAR CAST

Brenda Starr	Jill St. John
A. J. Livwright, her publisher	Sorrell Booke

GUEST CAST

Roger Randall	Jed Allan
Lance O'Toole	Victor Buono
Kentucky	Marcia Strassman
Luisa Santamaria	Barbara Luna
Carlos Varga	Joel Fabiani
Hank O'Hare	Tabi Cooper

Music: Lalo Schifrin.
Executive Producer: Paul Mason.
Producer: Bob Larson.
Writer: George Kirgo.
Director: Mel Stuart.

BRENDA STARR—90 minutes—ABC—May 8, 1976.

1410   BRENDA STARR, REPORTER

Pilot (Drama). The exploits of Brenda Starr, a beautiful newspaper reporter for the *Daily Flash*. In the pilot, Brenda seeks to help free a hostage who is being held for ransom by a madman.

CAST

Brenda Starr	Sherry Jackson
A. J. Livwright, the managing editor of the *Flash*	Shelly Berman

Music: Richard La Salle.
Producer: Jerry Harrison.
Director: Lawrence Dobkin.

BRENDA STARR, REPORTER—30 minutes—Syndicated January 1979.

1411   BRIDGER

Pilot (Adventure). The exploits of Jim Bridger, the legendary pioneer mountain man who opened the West for settlement in the 1830s. In the pilot, Bridger seeks to blaze a trail from Wyoming to the California coast to prove President Andrew Jackson's theory that the territory is accessible, and thwart the plan by Senator Daniel Webster to give the Pacific Northwest to England in exchange for fishing rights for New Englanders in Newfoundland coastal waters.

REGULAR CAST

Jim Bridger	James Wainwright
Joe Meek, his sidekick	Dirk Blocker

GUEST CAST

Kit Carson	Ben Murphy
Jennifer Medford	Sally Field
Daniel Webster	William Windom
Andrew Jackson	John Anderson
David Bridger	Claudio Martinez
Shoshone Woman	Margarita Cordova
Crow Chief	X Brands
Paiute Chief	Skeeter Vaughn

Music: Elliot Kaplan.
Producer: David Lowell Rich.
Writer: Merwin Gerard.
Director; David Lowell Rich.

BRIDGER—2 hours—ABC—September 10, 1976.

1412   BROCK'S LAST CASE

Pilot (Crime Drama). The story of Max Brock, a retired New York police detective, as he attempts to begin a new life in California as a rancher. The pilot, which depicts Brock's move from New York to California, focuses on his attempts to clear his ranch foreman, Arthur Goldencorn, an Indian, who has been charged with a series of bow and arrow murders.

REGULAR CAST

Max Brock	Richard Widmark
Arthur Goldencorn, his foreman	Henry Darrow
Ellen Ashley, his neighbor	Beth Brickell

GUEST CAST

Dawson	David Huddleston
Jake	Henry Beckman
Smiley	Will Geer
Cuspis	John Anderson
Stretch	Michael Burns
Sam Wong	Pat Morita

Music: Charles Gross.
Executive Producer: Leonard B. Stern.
Producer: Roland Kibbee.
Writer: Martin Donaldson.
Director: David Lowell Rich.

BROCK'S LAST CASE—2 hours—NBC—March 5, 1973.

BRONK

The pilot film broadcast on CBS on April 17, 1975, for the series of the same title (see regular program section).

1413   BROTHERS

Pilot (Comedy). The story of Michael and Allan Radford, two adopted and unlikely brothers—one of Jewish and the other of Irish ancestry—who pick up their lives together in San Francisco after many years of separation. In the pilot, Michael moves his family from the Bronx to San Francisco, where he sets up housekeeping in Allan's spacious bachelor apartment. The episode depicts the efforts of the two brothers to blend their clashing life-styles.

REGULAR CAST

Michael Radford	Charles Levin
Allan Radford	James O'Sullivan
Sheri Radford, Michael's wife	Dori Brenner
Horatio Beckett, the owner of the law office employing Allan	Bobby Ramsen
Lee On Wong, the owner of the Chinese Grocery employing Michael	James Hong
Rhonda, the law office receptionist	Jeanetta Arnette
Ellen, Beckett's legal secretary	Chip Fields

GUEST CAST

Mr. Hu	Keye Luke
Mother	Frances Fong
Daughter	Christiana Wu
Delivery Man	Alvin Ing
Arguing Lady	Lang Yun

Music: Hod-David Schudson.
Executive Producer: Ric Podell, Michael Preminger.
Producer: Norman Stiles, Charles Raymond.
Writer: Rick Podell, Michael Preminger.
Director: Will MacKenzie.
Art Director: Ken Reid.
Director of Photography: George LaFountaine.
Set Decorator: Katherine Arnold.

BROTHERS—30 minutes—CBS—July 30, 1980.

BUCK ROGERS IN THE 25th CENTURY

The pilot film broadcast on NBC on September 20, 1979, for the series of the same title (see regular program section).

1414   BUCKSHOT

Pilot (Comedy). The program explores comedy via film clips of comedians at work.

Hosts: Karen Breen, Ned Townsend.
Regulars: Deborah Harmon, David Rupprecht, Paul Reubens, Susan Elliot, William Schallert, Nancy Steen, Muffy Durham.
Executive Producer: Bernie Billerstein, Mitzi Shor, Howard West, George Shapiro.
Producer: John Aylesworth, Bernard Rothman, Jack Wohl, Pat Croft.
Director: Paul Miller, Dick Carson, Dan Smith, Bill Foster, Barry Glazer.

BUCKSHOT — 60 minutes — ABC — July 18, 1980.

1415   THE BUFFALO SOLDIERS

Pilot (Western). The story, set in the year 1867, follows the exploits of the U.S. Army's 10th Cavalry ("The Buffalo Soldiers"), a mostly black unit patrolling the West.

CAST

Col. Frank "Buckshot" O'Connor	John Beck
Sgt. Joshua Haywood	Stan Shaw
Caleb Holiday, the scout	Richard Lawson
Willie, a private	Hilly Hicks
Oakley, a private	Ralph Wilcox
Private Wright	Charles Robinson

Also: Ernest Harden, Jr., Carl Lumbly, Philip Michael Thomas, Angel Tompkins, L. Q. Jones, Don Knight, Ivan Naranjo, Don Collier, Marla Pennington, Rockne Tarkington.
Music: Jerrold Immel.
Executive Producer: Douglas Netter, Jim Byrnes.
Producer: Les Sheldon.
Writer: Jim Byrnes.
Director: Vincent McEveety.
Art Director: Joseph M. Altadonna.
Director of Photography: Robert L. Morrison.

THE BUFFALO SOLDIERS — 60 minutes — NBC — May 26, 1979.

1416   BUMPERS

Pilot (Comedy). The story, set in Detroit, Michigan, follows the misadventures of Joey Webber, a car assemblyline worker. In the pilot, Joey tries to raise $600 to help put his wife through dental school.

CAST

Joey Webber	Richard Masur
Rozzie Webber, his wife	Stephanie Faracy
Murphy, their friend	Jack Riley
Andy, Joey's friend	Michael L. McManus
Jay, Joey's friend	Tim Reid
Jennifer, Rozzie's friend	Zane Buzby

Music: The Brecker Brothers.
Producer: David Davis, Charlotte Brown.
Director: James Burrows.

BUMPERS — 30 minutes — NBC — May 16, 1977.

1417   BUNCO

Pilot (Crime Drama). The exploits of Ben Gordean and Ed Walker, plainclothes police officers attached to the Los Angeles Police Department's Bunco Squad. In the pilot, Gordean and Walker team with Frankie Dawson, an undercover policewoman, to expose a ruthless swindler's "college for con artists."

REGULAR CAST

Officer Ben Gordean	Tom Selleck
Officer Ed Walker	Robert Urich
Officer Frankie Dawson	Donna Mills
Lieutenant Hyatt, their superior	Milt Kogan

GUEST CAST

Dixon, the con artist	Michael Sacks
Winky	Will Geer
Yousha	Arte Johnson

Executive Producer: Lee Rich, Philip Capice.
Producer: Jerry Ludwig.
Director: Alexander Singer.

BUNCO — 60 minutes — NBC — January 13, 1977.

1418   THE BUREAU

Pilot (Comedy). The exploits of Peter Davlin, a bungling federal investigator. In the pilot, Davlin attempts to crack an interstate hijacking operation.

CAST

Sub Chief Peter Davlin	Henry Gibson
Agent Katie Peterson	Barbara Rhoades
Agent Paul Browning	Richard Gilliland
Charlie Sunglasses	Arnold Stang
"Combat" Cummings	Beeson Carroll
Agent Butterfield	John Lawlor

Music: Peter Matz.
Executive Producer: Gerald I. Isenberg.
Producer: Gerald W. Abrams.
Writer: Charles Sailor, Eric Kalder.
Director: Hy Averback.

THE BUREAU — 30 minutes — NBC — July 26, 1976.

1419   THE BUSTERS

Pilot (Adventure). The story of two cowboys, Chad Kimbrough, a seasoned veteran, and Albie McRae, an ambitious tenderfoot, as they team up to tackle the rough but remunerative professional rodeo circuit.

REGULAR CAST

Chad Kimbrough	Bo Hopkins
Albie McRae	Brian Kerwin

GUEST CAST

Wister Kane	Slim Pickens
Marti Hamilton	Devon Ericson
Billy Burnet	Buck Taylor
Joanna Bailey	Susan Howard
Nick Carroll	Chris Robinson
Mel Drew	Lance Le Gault

Music: Jerrold Immel.
Executive Producer: Stu Erwin.
Producer: Jim Byrnes.
Writer: Jim Byrnes.
Director: Vincent McEveety.

THE BUSTERS — 60 minutes — CBS — May 28, 1978.

1420   BUT MOTHER!

Pilot (Comedy). The story of the relationship between a former madam and her daughter. In the pilot, Billie Barkley, the mother, begins her new life — and seeks to re-establish a relationship with her daughter Sharon, a writer.

CAST

Billie Barkley	Dena Dietrich
Sharon Barkley	Amy Johnston
Trixie, Billie's friend	Gloria LeRoy
Harold, Trixie's husband	Phil Bruns
Carl Henry Dockstedder, Sharon's agent	Allan Rich
The Psychiatrist (guest role)	Harry Gold

Music: Jeff Alexander, Larry Orenstein.
Theme Vocal: Amy Johnston.
Producer: Bob Weiskopf, Bob Schiller.
Director: Jack Shea.

BUT MOTHER! — 30 minutes — NBC — June 27, 1979.

1421   BUTTERFLIES

Pilot (Comedy). Incidents in the lives of marrieds Rea and Ben Parkinson. The pilot episode focuses on the changes that occur in Rea, a bored housewife, when she meets a handsome stranger who sparks new life in her. (The title is derived from the saying, "We are like kids chasing butterflies — we see it, we want it.")

CAST

Rea Parkinson	Jennifer Warren
Ben Parkinson, her husband	John McMartin
Russell Parkinson, their son	Craig Wasson
Adam Parkinson, their son	Robert Doran
Leonard Dean, the stranger (guest)	Jim Hutton

Supervising Producer: Conrad Holzgang.
Executive Producer: Roger Gilbel, Tony Converse.
Producer: Milt Josefsberg, Carla Lane.
Writer: Carla Lane.
Director: James Burrows.

BUTTERFLIES — 30 minutes — NBC — August 1, 1979.

C

1422   THE CABOT CONNECTION

Pilot (Adventure). The story of Marcus Cabot, a jet-set socialite whose avariciousness forces him into a reluctant partnership, as a U.S. government agent, when he is caught red-handed in an illicit business deal and agrees to work for Uncle Sam rather than face imprisonment.

REGULAR CAST

Marcus Cabot	Craig Stevens
Olivia Cabot, his daughter and assistant	Cathee Shirriff
Muffin Cabot, his daughter and assistant	Jane Actman
Stephen Kordiak, the government agent who poses as Cabot's chauffeur	Chris Robinson
Harold O'Hara, Cabot's superior	Warren Kemmerling
Essie, Cabot's maid	Matilda Calnan

GUEST CAST

Dolly Foxworth	Gloria De Haven
Heinz Vogel	Alf Kjellin
Victor Kreindler	Curt Lowens
Brom Loomis	Dirk Benedict
Bozuffi	James Luisi
Rosenfeld	Frank Downing
Wendell	Ivor Barry
Clerk	Lynn Storer
Wharfman	Glen R. Wilder

Music: George Romanis.
Executive Producer: Barry Weitz.
Producer: Robert Mintz.
Writer: George Kirgo.
Director: E. W. Swackhamer.
Art Director: John Beckman.
Director of Photography: Jules Brenner.
Set Decorator: Fred Goetz.

THE CABOT CONNECTION — 60 minutes — CBS — May 10, 1977.

1423   CALL HER MOM

Pilot (Comedy). The story, set at Beardsley College, a small university in Chattanooga, Tennessee, follows the experiences of Angela Bianco, a beautiful ex-waitress who acquires a job as housemother at A.P.E. (Alpha Rho Epsilon), an unruly fraternity house.

REGULAR CAST

Angela Bianco	Connie Stevens
Chester Hardgrove, the college president	Van Johnson
Helen Hardgrove, Chester's wife	Gloria De Haven
College Dean Calder	Charles Nelson Reilly
Prof. Jonathan Calder, the faculty advisor	Jim Hutton
Ida, the frat house cook	Thelma Carpenter
Randall Feigelbaum, a student	Steve Vinovich
Woody Guinness III, a student	John David Carson
Wilson, a student	Mike Evans
Roscoe, a student	William Tepper
Jeremy, a student	Alfie Wise

GUEST CAST

Mr. Feigelbaum	William Benedict
Mrs. Feigelbaum	Thelma Pelish
Jeremy's father	Alfie Wise
Woman in restaurant	Kathleen Freeman
Woody's father	Herbert Rudley
Bruno	Corbett Monica

Music: Theme only ("Come on a My House"); vocal by Connie Stevens.

Executive Producer: Douglas S. Cramer.
Producer: Herb Wallerstein.
Writer: Gail Parent, Kenny Solms.
Director: Jerry Paris.
Art Director: Ross Bellah, John Beckman.
Director of Photography: Emil Oster.

CALL HER MOM—90 minutes—ABC—February 15, 1972.

CALL HOLME

See title "Triple Play '72" in the pilot film section.

1424   CALLING DR. STORM, M.D.

Pilot (Comedy). The story of Jim Storm, a physician who is dedicated to work, seldom at home, and uncaring as to whether patients pay their hospital bills or not.

CAST

Dr. Jim Storm	Larry Linville
Patti Storm, his wife	Sharon Spelman
Paul Storm, their son	Stephen Parr
Dr. Stendak, the hospital administrator	Bruce Gordon
Dr. Nate Nateman	Richard Libertini

Executive Producer: Stirling Silliphant.
Producer: Frank Konigsberg.
Director: James Burrows.

CALLING DR. STORM, M.D.—30 minutes—NBC—August 25, 1977.

1425   CALL TO DANGER

Pilot (Crime Drama). The exploits of Douglas Warfield, an inspector for the Department of Justice. In the pilot, Warfield engineers a bold attempt to rescue a kidnapped underworld informer.

CAST

Douglas Warfield	Peter Graves
Carrie Donovan	Diana Muldaur
Emmett Jergens	Clu Gulager
April Tierney	Tina Louise
Joe Barker	Stephen McNally
Marla Hays	Ina Balin
Tony Boyd	William Jordan
Frank Mulvey	Michael Ansara
Dave Falk	Roy Jenson
Edward McClure	John Anderson

Music: Laurence Rosenthal.
Producer: Lawrence Heath.
Writer: Lawrence Heath.
Director: Tom Gries.
Director of Photography: Ronald W. Browne.

CALL TO DANGER—90 minutes—CBS—February 28, 1973.

1426   CAMP GRIZZLY

Pilot (Comedy). Life at "Uncle Bernie's Camp Grizzly," a rundown summer camp with decrepit facilities and incompetent counselors. In the pilot, Nick, a counselor, wants his group of kids to win a swimming contest so he can spend time with Missy, the beautiful (and only) female counselor, and her girls on a camping trip.

CAST

Uncle Bernie, the camp owner	Carl Ballantine
Missy, a counselor	Hilary Thompson
Nick Nickerson, a counselor	Richard Cox
Furman, a counselor	Demetre Phillips
Garafala, a counselor	Jay Fenichel

The Kids: Joey Coleman, Charles Wilhite, Brian Scott, Timothy Roesch, Steve Pollick, Reed Diamond, Jeannette Arnette, Donna Mason, Christine Richards, John Robert Yates, Dennis Dooder.
Music: Ken Lauber.
Executive Producer: Nick Vanoff.
Producer: Nick Vanoff, Robert Klane.
Writer: Robert Klane.
Director: Steve Stern.
Art Director: David Hamber.
Director of Photography: John Jones.

CAMP GRIZZLY—30 minutes—ABC—June 30, 1980.

1427   CAPTAIN AMERICA

Pilot (Adventure). During World War II, Steve Rogers, a scientist, developed FLAG (Full Latent Ability Gain), a special serum that, taken from his cells, produced super-human strength and transformed him into Captain America, a daring and courageous war hero. More than 25 years later, when his son, Steve Rogers, Jr., is injured in an accident, he is given the special serum in an attempt to save his life when all other methods fail. Not only does FLAG save his life, but Steve Rogers, like his father, becomes Captain America, now a daring crime fighter. In the first pilot (see following title), Steve attempts to thwart a madman who is threatening to destroy mankind with a neutron bomb.

REGULAR CAST

Steve Rogers/ Captain America	Reb Brown
Dr. Simon Mills, the scientist in charge of FLAG research	Len Birman
Dr. Wendy Day, Simon's assistant	Heather Menzies

GUEST CAST

Brackett	Steve Forrest
Harley	Lance Le Gault
Charles Barber	Frank Marth
Tina Hayden	Robin Mattson
Sandrini	Joseph Ruskin
Jeff Hayden	Dan Barton
Lester Wayne	James Ingersol
Barber's assistant	Jim B. Smith
Sergeant	Jason Wingreen
Secretary	June Dayton

Music: Mike Post, Pete Carpenter.
Executive Producer: Allan Balter.
Producer: Martin Goldstein.
Writer: Don Ingalls (story by Don Ingalls and Chester Krumholz).
Director: Rod Holcomb.

CAPTAIN AMERICA—2 hours—CBS—January 19, 1979.

1428   CAPTAIN AMERICA

Pilot (Adventure). See previous title for background information. In the second pilot film, Captain America searches for a kidnapped scientist who has the ability to accelerate the aging process.

REGULAR CAST

Steve Rogers/ Captain America	Reb Brown
Dr. Simon Mills, the scientist in charge of FLAG research	Len Birman
Dr. Wendy Day, Simon's assistant	Connie Sellecca

GUEST CAST

Miguel	Christopher Lee
Yolanda	Lana Wood
Heflin	Katherine Justice
Professor Ilson	Christopher Cary
Peter Moore	John Waldron
Jane Cullen	June Dayton
Dr. J. Brenner	Bill Mims

Music: Mike Post, Pete Carpenter.
Executive Producer: Allan Balter.
Writer: Wilton Schiller, Patricia Payne.
Director: Ivan Nagy.

CAPTAIN AMERICA—60 minutes—CBS—November 23, 1979 (part one), November 24, 1979 (part two).

THE CAPTAIN AND TENNILLE

The pilot (videotape) broadcast on ABC on August 17, 1976, for the series of the same title (see regular program section).

1429   CAR WASH

Pilot (Comedy). The antics of the crew of the Great American Car Wash, a gas station-garage car wash in Los Angeles.

CAST

The Car Wash Crew:

Frank Ravelli	Danny Aiello
Last Chance	Stuart Pankin
Rocky	Matt Landers
Viva	Pepe Serna
Floyd	T. K. Carter
Lloyd	John Anthony Bailey
Fingers	Lefty Pedroski
Charlie	Hilary Beanne

Music: Dave Fisher.
Executive Producer: Leonard B. Stern.
Producer: Bill Dana.
Director: Alan Myerson.

CAR WASH—30 minutes—NBC—May 24, 1979.

1430   CARLTON YOUR DOORMAN

Pilot (Animated Comedy). The story of Carlton, a New York City apartment house doorman, a misfit who seeks to better himself and his position in society. In the pilot, which presents viewers with a first look at Carlton, who was only heard on the *Rhoda* series, Carlton looks for a replacement for his boss's wife's dog, Punkin, who died while in his care.

REGULAR CAST (VOICES)

Carlton	Lorenzo Music
Charles Shaftman, Carlton's boss	Jack Somack
Mrs. Shaftman, Charles's wife	Lucille Meredith
Carlton's Mother	Lurene Tuttle
Darlene, Carlton's girlfriend	Kay Cole

GUEST CAST (VOICES)

Mr. Gleason	Paul Lichtman
Fat Man	Paul Lichtman
Dog Catcher	Alan Barzman
Parrot	Bob Arbogast
Pop	Charles Woolf
D. J.'s voice	Roy West

Music: Stephen Cohn.
Producer: Lorenzo Music, Barton Dean.
Writer: Lorenzo Music, Barton Dean.
Director: Charles Swenson, Fred Wolf.
Animation By: Murakami Wolf Swenson.
Animators: Bob Bachman, Joan Case, Barrie Nelson, Mike Sanger, Bob Zamboni, Bill Wolf, John Kafka, Hank Tucker, Mike Kaweski, Nelson Rhodes, Pat Shinagawa, Nancy Avery.
Based on the Character Created By: James L. Brooks, Alan Burns, David Davis, Lorenzo Music.

CARLTON YOUR DOORMAN—30 minutes—CBS—May 21, 1980.

1431   CASINO

Pilot (Drama). The story of Nick (no last name), the owner of the S.S. *Mardi Gras,* a fourteen million dollar seagoing gambling casino. The pilot, which is an update of the *Mr. Lucky* series (1959), depicts Nick's attempts to solve a series of baffling and violent acts of sabotage that are aimed at destroying his ship on her maiden voyage. Based on characters created by Blake Edwards.

REGULAR CAST

Nick	Mike Connors
Edge, his assistant	Barry Van Dyke
K. L. "Fitz" Fitzgerald, the captain	Gene Evans
Foxworth, the bartender	Hedley Mattingly
Sam, the piano player	Don Pedro Colley
Harry, works for Nick	Harry Townes
Andre, the maitre d'	Neil Flanagan
Andrews, works for Nick	James Murtaugh

GUEST CAST

Jennifer	Sherry Jackson
Sam Fletcher	Barry Sullivan
Ed Booker	Joseph Cotten
Carol	Lynda Day George
John Stonewall Jackson	Bo Hopkins
Bill Taylor	Gary Burghoff
Darius	Robert Reed
Faber	Conrad Roberts
Packard	Austin Willis
Tour Officer	Thomas W. Bobsin

Music: Mark Snow.
Music Supervision: Rocky Moriana.
Executive Producer: Aaron Spelling, Douglas S. Cramer.
Producer: E. Duke Vincent.
Associate Producer: Elaine Rich, Shelley Hull.
Writer: Richard Carr.
Director: Don Chaffey.
Art Director: James Agazzi, Paul Sylos.
Director of Photography: Arch Dalzell.

CASINO — 2 hours — ABC — August 1, 1980.

1432   CAT BALLOU

Pilot (Comedy). The first pilot (see following title also), adapted from the movie of the same title, depicts the adventures of Cat Ballou, a rather outrageous Old West heroine, as she attempts to start a school against the wishes of a boneheaded sheriff and a foppish land developer.

CAST

Cat Ballou	Lesley Ann Warren
Kid Sheleen, the boozing ex-gunman	Jack Elam
Jackson Two Bears, Cat's aide	Tom Nardini
The Sheriff	Joel Higgins
The Land Developer	Laurie Main
Clay, Cat's friend	Bo Hopkins

Director: Jerry Paris.

CAT BALLOU — 30 minutes — NBC — September 5, 1971.

1433   CAT BALLOU

Pilot (Comedy). In this second pilot based on the film of the same title, Cat Ballou hires Kid Sheleen, the frequently soused ex-gunfighter, to protect her from a land-hungry rancher trying to gain control of the land she recently inherited — and which brought her West to take ownership.

CAST

Cat Ballou	Jo Ann Harris
Kid Sheleen	Forrest Tucker
Jackson Two Bears, Kid's aide	Lee J. Casey
The Rancher	Harry Morgan
Clay, Cat's friend	Bryan Montgomery
Spider Levinsky	Jim Luisi
Loopy	Bill Calloway
Indian Chief	Jay Silverheels

Director: Bob Claver.

CAT BALLOU — 30 minutes — NBC — September 6, 1971.

1434   THE CATCHER

Pilot (Crime Drama). The story of Noah Hendrix, a former cop turned Catcher (a missing persons investigator) for the *New Journal,* a newspaper run by his friend. In the pilot, Hendrix searches for a missing coed and becomes involved in murder.

REGULAR CAST

Noah Hendrix	Michael Witney

GUEST CAST

Sam	Jan-Michael Vincent
Joe Cade	Tony Franciosa
Sara	Catherine Burns
Armand Faber	David Wayne
Captain Mike Keller	Mike Kellin
Kate	Anne Baxter
Wes Watkins	Kiel Martin
Amy Lee	Jackie DeShannon
Andy	Andy Robinson

Music: Bill Walker.
Theme Vocal: Jackie DeShannon.
Executive Producer: Stanley Neufeld.
Producer: Herbert B. Leonard.
Writer: David Freeman.
Director: Allen H. Miner.

THE CATCHER — 2 hours — CBS — June 2, 1972.

1435   CBS COMEDY TRIO

Pilot (Comedy). The overall title for three comedy pilot films.

The Living End. The misadventures of Doug Newman, an aging football player.

CAST

Doug Newman	Lou Gossett
Nancy Newman, his wife	Diana Sands
Bullets	Dick O'Neill
Mickey	Paul Cavonis
Stan	Don Sherman
Henry	Roger Mosley
Richie	John Calvin

Credits: Producer-Writer: Saul Ilsen, Ernest Chambers; Director: Peter Baldwin.

Oh, Nurse! The story depicts the comic frustrations of live-in student nurses.

CAST

Kathi	Susan Foster
LuAnn	Heather Young
Maria	Lori Saunders
Gail	Judy Pace
Jimmy	Stephen Young
Miss Conklin	Pat Carroll
Steve	Norman Grabowski

Credits: Executive Producer: David Gerber; Producer: Charles Fitzsimons; Writer: Stan Hart, Larry Siegel, Treva Silverman; Director: Bob Sweeney.

Singles. The misadventures of two working girls (Michele and Ruth).

CAST

Michele	Michele Lee
Ruth	Ruth Buzzi

Freddy	John Byner
Sidney	Henry Jones
Officer Foley	Jerry Fogel

Also: David Doyle, William Elliott.

Credits: Producer-Director: Sheldon Leonard.

CBS COMEDY TRIO — 90 minutes (30 minutes each segment) — CBS — March 17, 1972.

1436   CBS DAYTIME 90

Pilot (Anthology). A proposed daily series of original dramas.

The Series:

Legacy of Fear (Feb. 11, 1974). The story of an innocent girl who becomes the target of revenge against her underworld family.

Starring: Katherine Houghton (as Gabby); Peter Coffield (Peter); Scott McKay (Frank); and Rae Allen (Dommy).

Trio for Lovers (Feb. 12, 1974). The story of a retired concert artist who is jolted out of his loneliness by a beautiful woman seeking to escape her loveless marriage.

Starring: Herbert Berghof.

The Guest Room (Feb. 13, 1974). An unusual story about a young woman who makes a pact with a ghost to help save her rocky marriage.

Starring: Gilmer McCormick (as Susan Banks); and Frank Converse (as John Banks).

Once in Her Life. (Feb. 14, 1974). The story focuses on Joan Baldwin, an estranged wife who finds herself being blackmailed by the young beachcomber with whom she had an affair.

Starring: Constance Towers (as Joan Baldwin); Brett Halsey (as Martin Baldwin).

My Little Love (Feb. 15, 1974). The story of a happily remarried widow who suspects that her emotionally disturbed daughter is guilty of murder.

Starring: Julia Meade and Dick Shawn.

CBS DAYTIME 90 — 90 minutes — February 11, 1974 – February 15, 1974. 5 programs.

1437   CBS TRIPLE PLAY

Pilot (Comedy). The overall title for three comedy pilots.

The Nancy Dussault Show. The story of Nancy Clancy, a Broadway understudy who becomes an instant star when her leading lady becomes ill. Written by Carl Reiner and directed by Dick Van Dyke.

CAST

Nancy Clancy	Nancy Dussault
Charlie	Karen Morrow
Bill	Lawrence Pressman

The Ted Bessell Show. The story of Ted Harper, a married magazine editor who is sorely tempted by all the girls in his office.

CAST

Ted Harper	Ted Bessell
Dianne Harper, his wife	Barra Grant
Barney Raider	Robert Walden
Margaret	Beth Howland
Amy	Karen Jensen
Mario	Mark Gordon

Two's Company. The misadventures of a pro football player with numerous female fans.

Starring: John Amos as the football star; Diana Sands as his wife; and Vic Tayback as Bullets.

CBS TRIPLE PLAY — 90 minutes (30 minutes each segment) — CBS — May 8, 1973.

1438   THE CHADWICK FAMILY

Pilot (Comedy-Drama). Events in the hectic lives of the Chadwicks, a family of six living in San Diego, California.

REGULAR CAST

Ned Chadwick, the father	Fred MacMurray
Valerie Chadwick, his wife	Kathleen Maguire
Joan Chadwick, their daughter	Darleen Carr
Lisa Chadwick, their daughter	Jane Actman
Tim Chadwick, their son	Stephen Nathan
Duffy Chadwick, their son	Barry Bostwick

GUEST CAST

Alex	Alan Fudge
Eileen	Lara Parker
Lee	Frank Michael Liu
Cindy	Carlena Gower
Sari	Kim Durso
Jimmy	Eben George

Music: Hal Mooney.
Executive Producer: David Victor.
Producer: David J. O'Connell.
Writer: David Victor.
Director: David Lowell Rich.

THE CHADWICK FAMILY — 90 minutes — ABC — April 17, 1974.

CHANGE AT 125th STREET

See title "4 Funny Families" in the pilot film section.

1439   CHARACTERS

Pilot (Comedy). The misadventures of Carol Goodman and Jack Elmendorf, students at the Work Shop, a theatrical acting school in Chicago.

CAST

Carol Goodman	Maggie Roswell
Jack Elmendorf	Philip Charles MacKenzie

Leila Flynn, the director of the
    Work Shop   Marcia Wallace
Steve Tucker, Carol's friend   Terry Lester

NBC Announcer: Peggy Taylor.
Music: Hod David Schudson.
Music Supervision: Lionel Newman.
Executive Producer: Ken Levine, David Isaacs.
Producer: Gene Marcione.
Writer: Ken Levine, David Isaacs.
Director: Will MacKenzie.
Art Director: David Haber.
Director of Photography: Keith Smith.

CHARACTERS — 30 minutes — NBC — October 26, 1980.

1440 CHARLIE COBB: NICE NIGHT FOR A HANGING

Pilot (Western). The story, set in the West of the 1870s, follows the exploits of Charles A. "Charlie" Cobb, a private investigator for the Chicago-based Hodgeside Security Agency. In the pilot, Cobb seeks to clear himself of a murder charge when, after he finds the long-lost daughter of his client (rancher Noah McVea), the rancher is killed and he is blamed for the crime.

REGULAR CAST

Charlie Cobb   Clu Gulager
Angelica Adams, a Pinkerton Detective,
   his assistant   Tricia O'Neil

GUEST CAST

Charity McVea/Loretta Lee Blair Brown
Martha McVea   Stella Stevens
Noah McVea   Ralph Bellamy
Wakeo Burns   Christopher Connelly
Sheriff Josh Yates   Pernell Roberts
Tobias Conroy   George Furth
Hotel Clerk   Olan Soule
Mrs. Cumberland Carmen Mathews

Music: Mike Post and Pete Carpenter.
Executive Producer: Richard Levinson, William Link.
Producer: Peter S. Fischer.
Writer: Peter S. Fischer.
Director: Richard Michaels.
Art Director: Arch Bacon.
Director of Photography: Andrew Jackson.

CHARLIE COBB: NICE NIGHT FOR A HANGING — 2 hours — NBC — June 9, 1977.

CHARLIE'S ANGELS

The pilot film broadcast on ABC on March 2, 1976, for the series of the same title (see regular program section).

1441 CHARO AND THE SERGEANT

Pilot (Comedy). The story of Charo, a beautiful Spanish entertainer who marries Hank Palmer, a U.S. Marine sergeant. Charo's attempt to adjust to the American way of life is the focal point of the pilot episode.

CAST

Charo Palmer   Charo
Sgt. Hank Palmer   Tom Lester
Sergeant Turkel,
   Hank's friend   Noam Pitlik
Chaplain (guest role) Dick Van Patten

Producer: Aaron Ruben, John Rich.
Writer: Aaron Ruben.
Director: John Rich.

CHARO AND THE SERGEANT — 30 minutes — ABC — August 24, 1976.

CHASE

The pilot film broadcast on NBC on March 24, 1973, for the series of the same title (see regular program section).

1442 THE CHEAP DETECTIVE

Pilot (Comedy). The story of Eddie Krowder, a private detective who works out of Los Angeles and charges $19.95 a day, plus expenses (hence the title). In the pilot, Eddie tries to recover more than $300,000 stolen from a friend.

REGULAR CAST

Eddie Krowder   Flip Wilson
Inez Krowder, his ex-wife Paula Kelly
Ricky, Eddie's
   assistant Richard Beauchamp

GUEST CAST

Ralph Garvey   Murray Hamilton
Arloe Fairweather Michael Keenan
Big Sam   John Quade
Elvis   Franklin Ajae
Fogerty   David Morick
Carlton Fairweather Daniel Thorpe

Inez' dog: Tommy.

Music: Don Costa.
Executive Producer: Restar Television.
Producer: Stanley, Rosen and Feldman Productions.
Writer: Richard M. Powell.
Director: Edward H. Feldman.
Art Director: Ross Bellah, Carl Anderson.
Director of Photography: Robert Hoffman.

THE CHEAP DETECTIVE — 30 minutes — NBC — June 3, 1980.

1443 THE CHEERLEADERS

Pilot (Comedy). The misadventures of Snowy, B. J. and Beverly, three fun-loving high school girls. The pilot episode focuses on the girls, members of the cheerleading team, as they perform embarrassing pledge week antics for a sorority house they hope to join.

CAST

Snowy   Kathleen Cody
B. J.   Debbie Zipp
Beverly   Teresa Medaris
Margie, a cheerleader Mary Kay Place
Howard, a student   Darel Glaser

Dorothy Snow, Snowy's
   mother   Susan Quick
Snowy's father   George Wallace
Snowy's grandmother Ruth McDevitt
Terry Sears, the sorority house
   president   Robin Mattson
Joe King, a student   Ronald Roy
Cheerleader   Janis Lynn
Cheerleader   Rita Wilson

Music: Earle Hagen.
Producer: Jerome Zeitman.
Writer: Monica McGowan Johnson.
Director: Richard Crenna.

THE CHEERLEADERS — 30 minutes — NBC — August 2, 1976.

1444 THE CHOPPED LIVER BROTHERS

Pilot (Comedy). The misadventures of Tom Van Broklin and Jay Luckman, two stand-up comics struggling to become headliners.

REGULAR CAST

Tom Van Broklin Tom Patchett
Jay Luckman   Jay Tarses
Sally Van Broklin, Tom's
   wife   Gwynne Gilford

GUEST CAST

Ruth   Phil Bruns
Duffy   Robert Emhardt
Kelso   Michael Pataki
Nathan Brailoff   Philip Roth

Executive Producer: Tom Patchett, Jay Tarses.
Producer: Michael Zinberg.
Director: Hugh Wilson.

THE CHOPPED LIVER BROTHERS — 30 minutes — ABC — June 20, 1977.

1445 A CHRISTMAS FOR BOOMER

Pilot (Drama). The pilot film for the series *Here's Boomer*. The story of a shaggy, adorable and abandoned stray dog named Boomer. The pilot episode retitled "Boomer in Love" for a repeat showing on the series (March 18, 1980) details Boomer's misadventures as he tries to win the affection of a French poodle named Celeste; and his adventures with the Sinclairs, the first family to temporarily adopt him. (Boomer received his name from the Sinclair children — "he looks like a Boomer.")

CAST

Dan Sinclair, the father Lawrie Driscoll
Marsha Sinclair, his wife Margie Impert
Jaime Sinclair, their
   daughter   Gillian Grant
Their son   Jonathan Ward
Lila Manchester, Celeste's
   owner   Joyce Van Patten
Dorothy, Lila's maid Sheree North
Jack, Lila's butler   Larry Linville
Casey, the delivery man Al Molinaro
Helen Sinclair, Dan's
   mother   Harriet Nelson

Music: David Frank.
Producer: A. C. Lyles.
Writer: Bethel Leslie, Gerry Day.
Director: William Asher.

A CHRISTMAS FOR BOOMER — 60 minutes — NBC — December 6, 1979.

THE CITY

The pilot film, broadcast on ABC on May 17, 1971, for *The Man and the City* (see regular program section).

1446 THE CITY

Pilot (Crime Drama). The exploits of Lieutenant Matt Lewis and Sergeant Brian Scott, Los Angeles police detectives. The pilot episode depicts their efforts to apprehend a crazed man bent on murdering a famous Country and Western entertainer.

REGULAR CAST

Lt. Matt Lewis   Robert Forster
Sgt. Brian Scott   Don Johnson
Capt. Lloyd Decker Ward Costello
Sgt. Burt Frescara Paul Cavonis

GUEST CAST

Eugene Banks   Mark Hamill
Wes Collins   Jimmy Dean
Carol Carter   Susan Sullivan
Mel Greenwall   Joby Baker

Music: John Elizalde.
Executive Producer: Quinn Martin.
Producer: John Wilder.
Writer: John Wilder.
Director: Harvey Hart.

THE CITY — 90 minutes — NBC — January 12, 1977.

1447 CLINIC ON 18th STREET

Pilot (Crime Drama). The exploits of Abe Strayhorn, Lynn Carmichael and Gino Bardi, agents for M.F.C.P. (Major Frauds and Consumer Protection), a new legal department of the Los Angeles District Attorney's office that investigates frauds.

REGULAR CAST

Abe Strayhorn, the D.A. Ed Nelson
Lynn Carmichael, his
   assistant   Sharon Gless
Gino Bardi, his assistant Frank Sinatra, Jr.

GUEST CAST

Dr. Elroy Guntham Dick Haymes
Don Bates   Kenneth Tobey
Marian Fenton Virginia Vincent

Music: Frank Comstock.
Executive Producer: Jack Webb.
Producer: Robert H. Forward.
Writer: Joseph Calvelli.
Director: Paul Krasny.
Director of Photography: Enzo A. Martinelli.

CLINIC ON 18th STREET — 30 minutes — NBC — March 13, 1974 (as a segment of *Adam-12*).

1448 CODE NAME: DIAMOND HEAD

Pilot (Adventure). The exploits of Johnny Paul, a U.S. Intelligence agent working out of Hawaii (based at Diamond Head). In the pilot, Paul attempts to prevent

Sean Donovan, a ruthless spy, from stealing the formula for a deadly gas.

REGULAR CAST

Johnny Paul	Roy Thinnes
Tso-Tsing, the owner of the Dragon Lady Saloon	France Nuyen
Zulu, Paul's assistant	Himself

GUEST CAST

Sean Donovan	Ian McShane
Captain MacIntosh	Ward Costello
H.K. Muldoon	Don Knight
Ernest Graeber	Eric Braeden
Cmdr. Yarnell	Dennis Patrick

Music: Morton Stevens.
Executive Producer: Quinn Martin.
Producer: Paul King.
Writer: Paul King.
Director: Jeannot Szwarc.
Art Director: George B. Chan.

CODE NAME: DIAMOND HEAD — 90 minutes — NBC — May 3, 1977.

1449   COLORADO C.I.

Pilot (Crime Drama). The exploits of brothers Mark and Pete Gunnison, members of the Criminal Investigation Unit of the Colorado Police Department, an elite, statewide force of plainclothes detectives who specialize in criminal cases that cross city and county lines. In the pilot, the Gunnisons seek to crack a multimillion dollar real estate swindle.

REGULAR CAST

Mark Gunnison	John Elerick
Pete Gunnison	Marshall Colt
Hoyt Gunnison, their father	L. Q. Jones
Chris Morrison, the police lab technician	Laurette Spang

GUEST CAST

Carla Winters	Christine Belford
David Royce	David Hedison
Niles	Bill Lucking
Piper Collins	Chris De Lisle
Capt. Cochran	Van Williams
Stan Cusek	Randy Powell
Frank Bannock	Lou Frizzell
Kessler	John Karlen
George Hopkins	George Wallace
Phone Operator	Joan Roberts
Hazel Bicker	Anne H. Bradley

Music: Dave Grusin.
Executive Producer: Philip Saltzman.
Producer: Christopher Morgan.
Writer: Robert W. Lenski.
Director: Virgil W. Vogel.
Art Director: George B. Chan.
Director of Photography: Jacques R. Marquette.

COLORADO C.I. — 60 minutes — CBS — May 26, 1978.

1450   COMEDY NEWS

Pilot (Comedy). A satirization of TV news shows and newscasts.

Comedy News Staff: Stan Freberg, Bob and Ray (Bob Elliott and Ray Goulding), Richard Pryor, Kenneth Mars, Fannie Flagg, Marian Mercer, Anthony Holland, Carmen Zapata, R.G. Brown, Richard Dawson, Andrew Duncan, Melodie Johnson, Lawrence Pressman.
Guests: Mort Sahl, Robert Klein, Dick Gregory.
Executive Producer: Sylvester (Pat) Weaver.
Producer: Bernie Kukoff, Jeff Harris.
Writer: Mort Green.

COMEDY NEWS — 90 minutes — ABC — November 28, 1972.

1451   COMPLETELY OFF THE WALL

Pilot (Comedy). The program spotlights the comedy troupe, Completely Off the Wall, as members perform unrehearsed skits based on audience suggestions.

Host: John Ritter.
Completely Off the Wall: Wendy Cutler, Tony Delia, Rod Gist, Andy Goldberg, Nancy Steen, Paul Wilson, Susan Elliot, Dee Marcus.
Music: Carol Weiss and the Weiss Man.
Executive Producer: Devere Marcus.
Producer: George Van Noye.
Director: Jim Drake.

COMPLETELY OFF THE WALL — 30 minutes — ABC — September 7, 1979.

1452   CONSPIRACY OF TERROR

Pilot (Crime Drama). The cases of Jacob and Helen Horowitz, husband and wife police detectives. In the pilot, Jacob and Helen try to break up a deadly satanist cult.

REGULAR CAST

Jacob Horowitz	Michael Constantine
Helen Horowitz, his wife	Barbara Rhoades
Arthur Horowitz, Jacob's father	David Opatoshu
David Horowitz, Jacob's brother	Jed Allan
Leslie Horowitz, David's wife	Arlene Martell

GUEST CAST

Mrs. Warnall	Mariclare Costello
Mr. Warnall	Roger Perry
Dale	Logan Ramsey
Slate	John Lormer

Music: Neil Hefti.
Executive Producer: Lee Rich.
Producer: Charles B. Fitzsimons.
Writer: Howard Rodman.
Director: John Llewellyn Moxey.

CONSPIRACY OF TERROR — 90 minutes — NBC — April 10, 1975.

1453 CONSTANTINOPLE

Pilot (Variety). Performances by guest personalities from the music world.

Pilot Guests: Lance LeGault, John Valenti, The Manhattan Transfer, Doug Kershaw, Ian Whitcomb, Tina Turner.
Music: Ray Pohlman.
Music Conductor: H. B. Barnum.
Executive Producer: Grant Tinker.
Producer: Jack Good.
Writer: Jack Good.
Director: Rita Gillespie.
Choreographer: Andre Tayir.

CONSTANTINOPLE — 30 minutes — ABC — July 25, 1977.

COOL MILLION

The pilot film broadcast on NBC on October 16, 1972, for the series of the same title (see regular program section).

1454   COPS

Pilot (Comedy). The story of Sonny Miglio, a hardboiled city police captain, as he struggles to adjust to his new position in a quiet suburban precinct.

REGULAR CAST

Capt. Sonny Miglio	Vincent Gardenia
Det. Dennis Till	Bruce Davison
Sgt. Monroe Dupree	Scoey Mitchlll
Det. Ed Carter	Britt Leach
Capt. Irving Ho	Pat Morita

GUEST CAST

Wanda Burke	Ruth Roman
Benny the Squealer	Stuart Margolin
Coach	Vic Tayback
Winston	Little Dion
Donna Jo	Betty Aidman
Mrs. Wilcox	Royce Wallace

Executive Producer: Meta Rosenberg.
Producer: Charles Shyer, Alan Mandel.
Writer-Director-Creator: Jerry Belson.

COPS — 30 minutes — CBS — June 5, 1973.

THE COPS AND ROBIN

See title *Future Cop* in the regular program section for information.

1455   COREY: FOR THE PEOPLE

Pilot (Crime Drama). The cases of Dan Corey, a Los Angeles County assistant district attorney. In the pilot, Corey investigates the case of a renowned doctor's battered wife who claims she killed her husband in self-defense.

REGULAR CAST

Dan Corey	John Rubinstein
Judy Corey, his wife	Deborah Ryan
District Attorney Shannon	Eugene Roche

GUEST CAST

Harriet Morgan	Carol Rossen
Gilman	Wynn Irwin
Dr. Hanley	Ronny Cox
Laurie Casey	Ann Sweeny
Nick Wolf	Steve Pearlman
Judge Taylor	Frank Campanella
Janet Hanley	Lana Wood
Katie Ryan	Joan Pringle

Music: Ed Kalehoff.
Executive Producer: Buzz Kulick.
Producer: Tay Daniel.
Writer: Alvin Boretz.
Director: Buzz Kulick.

COREY: FOR THE PEOPLE — 90 minutes — NBC — June 12, 1977.

1456   COUSINS

Pilot (Comedy). The misadventures of Gail Raymond and Barbara Donohue, secretaries in a large New York advertising agency.

CAST

Gail Raymond	Lisa Mordente
Barbara Donohue	Deedee Rescher
Leonard Mandroff, their employer	David Ogden Stiers
Alan Peters, works in the agency	Ray Buktenica

Executive Producer: Bob Ellison.
Producer: Pat Nardo, Gloria Banta.
Writer: Pat Nardo, Gloria Banta.
Director: Tony Mordente.

COUSINS — 30 minutes — ABC — August 10, 1976.

1457   COVER GIRLS

Pilot (Crime Drama). The exploits of Linda Allen and Monique Lawrence, two beautiful fashion models who double as undercover agents for the C.I.U. (Criminal Intelligence Unit) of the U.S. government. In the pilot, Linda and Monique attempt to break up a kidnapping ring.

REGULAR CAST

Linda Allen	Cornelia Sharpe
Monique Lawrence	Jayne Kennedy
James Andrews, their superior	Don Galloway

GUEST CAST

Bradner	Vince Edwards
Michael	George Lazenby
Paul Reynolds	Michael Baseleon
Fritz Porter	Jerry Douglas
Johnny Wilson	Don Johnson
Ziggy	Ellen Travolta

Music: Richard Shores.
Executive Producer: David Gerber.
Producer: Charles B. Fitzsimons.
Writer: Mark Rodgers.
Director: Jerry London.
Art Director: Ross Bellah, Robert Peterson.

COVER GIRLS — 90 minutes — NBC — May 18, 1977.

1458   THE CRIME CLUB

Pilot (Crime Drama). The exploits of Paul Cord, a Los Angeles-based private detective who works for Roger Knight, a retired judge and founder of the Crime Club. The organization unites various law-enforcement officials to solve crimes. In the pilot, Cord investigates the mysterious death of an old friend.

ABC

Go West Young Girl. Karen Valentine.

ABC

Having Babies III. From left, Beverly Todd, Susan Sullivan and Mitchell Ryan.

ABC

The Hustler of Muscle Beach. Kay Lenz.

REGULAR CAST
Paul Cord	Lloyd Bridges
Judge Roger Knight	Victor Buono

GUEST CAST
Denise London	Barbara Rush
Robert London	Paul Burke
Hilary Kelton	Cloris Leachman
Nick Kelton	David Hedison
Anne Dryden	Belinda J. Montgomery
Deputy Wilson	Martin Sheen
Sheriff Baird	Frank Marth
Parrish	Mills Watson
Kilburn	William Devane

Music: George Romanis.
Executive Producer: Frank Glicksman.
Producer: Charles Larson.
Writer: Charles Larson.
Director: David Lowell Rich.

THE CRIME CLUB — 90 minutes — CBS — March 6, 1973.

1459   THE CRIME CLUB

Pilot (Crime Drama). The exploits of a group of detectives, lawyers and writers who have formed a society (the Crime Club) to prevent and solve crimes. In the pilot, they seek to solve a series of ice-pick murders.

CAST
Alex Norton	Robert Lansing
Daniel Lawrence	Eugene Roche
John Keesey	Scott Thomas
Byron Caine	Biff McGuire
Angela Swoboda	Barbara Rhoades
Frank Swoboda	Michael Cristofer
Peter Karpf	David Clennon
Pam Agostino	Kathleen Beller
Mary Jo	Jennifer Shaw
Lt. Doyle	M. Emmet Walsh
Dr. Schroeder	Martine Beswick

Music: Gil Mellé.
Executive Producer: Matthew Rapf.
Producer: James McAdams.
Writer: Gene Kearney.
Director: Jeannot Szwarc.

THE CRIME CLUB — 90 minutes — CBS — March 3, 1975.

1460   CRISIS IN SUN VALLEY

Pilot (Crime Drama). The story of Bill Stedman, sheriff of Sun Valley, a small, sleepy ski town in Idaho. In "Outward Bound," the first of two one-hour episodes aired back-to-back, Stedman struggles to safeguard a group of New York students who are planning a dangerous mountain climb; and in "The Vanishing Kind," the second story, Stedman investigates reports of sabotage in a newly developed condominium.

REGULAR CAST
Sheriff Bill Stedman	Dale Robinette
Deputy Archie Sykes	Taylor Lacher

GUEST CAST
Buchanan	Bo Hopkins
Sheila	Tracy Brooks Swope
Thorndike	Ken Swofford
Poole	Paul Brinegar
Derry	Jason Johnson
Hubbard	John McIntire
Eva	Susan Adams
Jenny	Julie Parsons

Music: Dick De Benedictis.
Producer: Barry Weitz.
Writer: Carl Gottlieb, Alvin Buretz.
Director: Paul Stanley.

CRISIS IN SUN VALLEY — 2 hours — NBC — March 29, 1978.

1461   CROSSFIRE

Pilot (Crime Drama). The exploits of Vince Rossi, an undercover police detective. The pilot depicts Rossi's attempts to apprehend a syndicate chieftain.

REGULAR CAST
Vince Rossi	James Farentino
Captain McCardle	Ramon Bieri
Dave Ambrose, Rossi's partner	John Saxon

GUEST CAST
Lane Fielding	Patrick O'Neal
Sheila Fielding	Pamela Franklin
Bert Ganz	Herb Edelman
Albert Ambrose	Frank de Kova
Arthur Peabody	Lou Frizzell
Bartender	Ned Glass

Music: Pat Williams.
Executive Producer: Quinn Martin.
Producer: Philip Saltzman.
Writer: Philip Saltzman.
Director: William Hale.

CROSSFIRE — 90 minutes — NBC — March 24, 1975.

1462   CUTTER

Pilot (Crime Drama). The exploits of Frank Cutter, a Chicago-based private detective, who, in the pilot episode, searches for a missing pro quarterback.

REGULAR CAST
Frank Cutter	Peter DeAnda

GUEST CAST
Riggs	Cameron Mitchell
Linda	Barbara Rush
Leone	Gabriel Dell
Meredith	Robert Webber
Susan Macklin	Marlene Warfield
Ray Brown	Archie Moore
Macklin	Herbert Jefferson, Jr.
Miss Aguilera	Anna Navarro
Shineman	Stephin Fetchit

Executive Producer: Richard Irving.
Producer: Dean Hargrove.
Writer: Dean Hargrove.
Director: Richard Irving.
Director of Photography: Jack Priestly.

CUTTER — 90 minutes — NBC — January 26, 1972.

D

DADDY'S GIRL

See title "Triple Treat" in the pilot film section.

1463   THE DALLAS COWBOYS CHEERLEADERS

Pilot (Drama). The first of two unsold pilot films that were to star the Dallas Cowboys Cheerleaders (see also "The Dallas Cowboys Cheerleaders II"). The first pilot tells how the cheerleaders are chosen (through open auditions each season) and follows the experiences of Laura Coleman, an investigative reporter, who auditions for the cheerleaders in an attempt to get a behind-the-scenes story on what it is like to be a cheerleader for the Dallas Cowboys football team.

REGULAR CAST
Suzanne Mitchell, the cheerleaders' coordinator	Laraine Stephens
Texie Waterman, the cheerleaders' choreographer	Herself
Jessie Mathews, a featured cheerleader	Lauren Tewes
Betty Denton, same as Jessie	Pamela Susan Shoop
Kim Everly, same as Jessie	Jennifer Shaw
Joanne Vail, same as Jessie	Ellen Bry

The Dallas Cowboys Cheerleaders: Laurie Murdock, Debbie Brooks, Robin Sindor, Angel Bland, Debbie White, Suzette Russell, Vanessa Baker, Susan Jones, Lauren Moss, Pam Davis, Denise Doran, Tammy Roberts, Debbie Wagner, Connie Dolan, Jeannie McKelvey, Terry Richardson, Cindy Sykes, Christine Mathews, Jill Wagner, Vanetta Briggs, Kim McKinney, Suzette Schultz.

GUEST CAST
Laura Coleman	Jane Seymour
Lyman Spencer	Bert Convy
Kyle Jessup	Bucky Dent
J. R. Denton	Terry Cook

Music: Jimmie Haskell.
Executive Producer: James T. Aubrey, Robert Hamner.
Producer: Bruce Bilson.
Writer: Rober Hamner.
Director: Bruce Bilson.
Art Director: Ray Beal.

THE DALLAS COWBOYS CHEERLEADERS — 2 hours — ABC — January 14, 1979.

1464   THE DALLAS COWBOYS CHEERLEADERS II

Pilot (Drama). In the second pilot film (see previous title) that was to star the Dallas Cowboys football team cheerleaders, the girls prepare for a Far East U.S.O. tour.

REGULAR CAST
Texie Waterman, the cheerleaders' choreographer	Herself
Suzanne Mitchell, the cheerleaders' coordinator	Laraine Stephens
Diane Tyler, a cheerleader	Roxanne Gregory
Patti Ames, a cheerleader	Julie Hill
Candy Beaumont, a cheerleader	Candy Ann Brown

The Dallas Cowboys Cheerleaders: Terry Richardson, Karen Baker, Cindy Garger, Jane Porter, Angela Parnell, Lucille Baker, Debbie White, Tammy Barnes, Pinelle Waggoner, Kim Trueway, Pam Richards, Stephanie Schultz, Suzette Schultz, Jeannie Montford, Kim Kilway.

GUEST CAST
Terry Killain, the TV producer	John Davidson
Capt. James Webner, the man who organizes the U.S.O. tour	Ray Wise
Tim, Candy's romantic interest	Duane Thomas

Music: Jimmie Haskell.
Executive Producer: James T. Aubrey, Robert Hamner, Joey Tata.
Producer: Alan Godfrey.
Writer: Stephen Kandel.
Director: Michael O'Herlihy.
Director of Photography: Robert Jessup.

THE DALLAS COWBOYS CHEERLEADERS II — 2 hours — ABC — January 13, 1980.

DANGER IN PARADISE

The pilot film for *Big Hawaii,* see regular program section.

1465   DANNY AND THE MERMAID

Pilot (Comedy). The story of Danny Stevens, a budding oceanographer who is working his way through school as an underwater observer. In the pilot, Danny first sees Aqua, a beautiful mermaid (blond hair, blue eyes, lithe legs and iridescent scales), swim by the portholes of his underwater habitat and later meets and befriends her. She is the daughter of a human man and a mermaid — hence the legs and scales — who speaks English and Dolphinese. The basis of the would-be-series, as depicted in the first episode, would have focused on Danny's misadventures as he, a bumbling klutz, struggles to conceal Aqua's presence and successfully complete experiments, with the help of Aqua, for his mentor, Professor Stoneham.

CAST
Danny Stevens	Patrick Collins
Aqua	Harlee McBride
Professor Stoneham	Ray Walston
Turtle, Danny's aide	Rick Fazel

Psychiatrist (guest role)　　Conrad Janis
Pilot (guest role)　　Ancel Cook

Producer: Ivan Tors.
Writer: Budd Grossman.
Director: Norman Abbott.

DANNY AND THE MERMAID—30 minutes—CBS—May 17, 1978.

1466　DAUGHTERS

Comedy. The story of a widowed policeman and his attempts to raise his three mischievous daughters.

CAST

Dominick, the father　Michael Constantine
Cookie, his daughter　Judy Landers
Diane, his daughter　Olivia Barash
Terry, his daughter　Robin Groves
Rosa, his aunt　Julie Bovasso

Executive Producer: Paul Junger Witt, Tony Thomas.
Producer: Susan Harris.
Writer: Susan Harris.
Director: Bob Claver.

DAUGHTERS — 30 minutes — NBC—July 20, 1977.

1467　THE DAUGHTERS OF JOSHUA CABE

Pilot (Western). The first of three unsold pilot films about a fur trapper and his daughters (see also "The Daughters of Joshua Cabe Return" and "The New Daughters of Joshua Cabe").

When Congress passes the homesteading law (1870s) which requires Wyoming squatters to file a claim, Joshua Cabe, a widower, travels east to St. Louis to find his three long-lost daughters, whom he hopes to take back west so each can file a claim and help him gain control of the valley he loves. Amos Wetherall, a land baron, is also seeking the land. Meeting with his youngest daughter, Katie, now a nun (Sister Mary Robert), he learns that his other daughters are married and living in New York. Unable to bring his own daughters back with him, he decides to "adopt" three girls — Charity, a con artist; Ada, a pickpocket; and Mae, a lady of the evening — and pass them off as his daughters. The story depicts their efforts to win the homesteading claim — and keep it once they acquire it.

REGULAR CAST

Joshua Cabe　Buddy Ebsen
Charity, his daughter　Karen Valentine
Mae, his daughter　Lesley Ann Warren
Ada, his daughter　Sandra Dee
Bitterroot, Joshua's friend　Jack Elam

GUEST CAST

Amos Wetherall　Leif Erickson
Blue Wetherall　Don Stroud
Codge Collie　Henry Jones
Cole Wetherall　Michael Anderson, Jr.
Deke Wetherall　Paul Koslo
Sister Mary Robert　Julie Mannix
Arnie　Ron Soble

Billy Jack Wetherall　Bill Katt
Warden Tippet　Claude Bryar
Telegrapher　Doodles Weaver

Music: Jeff Alexander.
Music Supervision: Rocky Moriana.
Executive Producer: Aaron Spelling, Leonard Goldberg.
Producer: Richard E. Lyons.
Associate Producer: Robert Monroe.
Writer: Philip Savage.
Director: Philip Leacock.
Art Director: Bud Brooks.
Director of Photography: Arch Dalzell.

THE DAUGHTERS OF JOSHUA CABE — 90 minutes — ABC — September 13, 1972.

1468　THE DAUGHTERS OF JOSHUA CABE RETURN

Pilot (Western). The second of three unsold pilot films about a fur trapper and his daughters (see also "The Daughters of Joshua Cabe" and "The New Daughters of Joshua Cabe"). The revised story line has three shady ladies — Charity (a con artist), Ada (a pickpocket) and Mae (a prostitute) — agreeing to pose for one year as the respectful daughters of homesteader Joshua Cabe, a widower, so he can win the title to his farm.

REGULAR CAST

Joshua Cabe　Dan Dailey
Ada, his daughter　Ronne Troup
Charity, his daughter　Christina Hart
Mae, his daughter　Brooke Adams
Bitterroot, Joshua's friend　Dub Taylor

GUEST CAST

Essie　Kathleen Freeman
Will　Carl Betz
Miner　Arthur Hunicutt
Jim Finch　Randall Carver
Sgt. Maxwell　Terry Wilson
Jenny Finch　Jane Alice Brandon
Claver　Robert Burton
Vickers　Greg Leydig

Music: Jeff Alexander.
Executive Producer: Aaron Spelling, Leonard Goldberg.
Producer: Richard E. Lyons.
Writer: Kathleen Hite.
Director; David Lowell Rich.

THE DAUGHTERS OF JOSHUA CABE RETURN — 90 minutes — ABC—January 28, 1975.

THE DEADLY GAME

The pilot film broadcast on NBC on April 24, 1976, for the series *Serpico* (see regular program section).

1469　THE DEADLY TRIANGLE

Pilot (Crime Drama). The exploits of Bill Stedman, the newly elected sheriff of Sun Valley, a ski resort town in Idaho. The pilot depicts Stedman's attempts to

solve the murder of an aspiring skier who was shot while practicing the biathlon.

REGULAR CAST

Sheriff Bill Stedman　Dale Robinette
Deputy Archie Sykes　Taylor Lacher

GUEST CAST

Joanne Price　Linda Scruggs Bogart
Charles Cole　Robert Lansing
Edith Cole　Diana Muldaur
Red Bayliss　Geoffrey Lewis
Merrie Leonard　Maggie Wellman

Music: Dick De Benedictis.
Producer: Robert Stambler.
Writer: Carl Gottlieb.
Director: Charles S. Dubin.

THE DEADLY TRIANGLE — 90 minutes—NBC—May 19, 1977.

1470　DEAD MAN ON THE RUN

Pilot (Crime Drama). The exploits of Jim Gideon, the head of an elite team of U.S. Justice Department investigators. In the pilot, Gideon, just appointed to his new position, seeks to discover if his predecessor's murder is somehow linked to the assassination of a presidential aspirant.

REGULAR CAST

Jim Gideon　Peter Graves
Meg, his assistant　Diana Douglas

GUEST CAST

Brock Dillon　Pernell Roberts
Libby Stockton　Katherine Justice
Fletcher　Tom Rosqui
Flanagan　Jack Knight
DiMosco　Joe E. Tata
Jason Monroe　John Anderson
Father Sebastian　Mills Watson

Music: Harry Geller.
Executive Producer: Bob Sweeney.
Producer: William Finnegan.
Writer: Ken Pettus.
Director: Bruce Bilson.

DEAD MAN ON THE RUN — 90 minutes—ABC—April 2, 1975.

1471　DEATH AMONG FRIENDS

Pilot (Crime Drama). The exploits of Lt. Shirley Ridgeway, called Mrs. R., an L.A.P.D. homicide detective. The pilot depicts Mrs. R.'s attempts to solve the murder of a financier.

REGULAR CAST

Lt. Shirley Ridgeway　Kate Reid
Officer Manny Reyes　A Martinez
Captain Lewis　John Anderson

GUEST CAST

Buckner　Martin Balsam
Chico Donovan　Jack Cassidy
Otto Schiller　Paul Henreid
Lisa Manning　Lynda Day George
Sheldon Casey　William Smith
Connie　Pamela Hensley
Carol　Katherine Baumann
Nancy　Robyn Hilton

Music: Jim Helms.

Executive Producer: Douglas S. Cramer.
Producer: Alex Beaton.
Writer: Stanley Ralph Ross.
Director: Paul Wendkos.

DEATH AMONG FRIENDS—90 minutes—NBC—May 20, 1975. Also titled: *Mrs. R.: Death Among Friends.*

1472　DEAN'S PLACE

Pilot (Variety). The program, set in a nightclub called Dean's Place, spotlights new talent discoveries. Videotaped at the Cave de Roys, a private club in Beverly Hills.

CAST

Dean, the owner　Dean Martin
Club Maitre d'　Jack Cassidy
Italian Chef　Vincent Gardenia
Bartender　Guy Marks
Intoxicated Customer　Foster Brooks

Club Entertainers: Jessi Colter, The Golddiggers, Kelly Monteith.
Hotel Guests (first pilot): Angie Dickinson, Robert Mitchum, Ronald Reagan, Nancy Reagan, Georgia Engel, Sherman Hemsley, Isabel Sanford.
Hotel Guests (second pilot): Peter Graves, Freddy Fender.
Music Conductor: Les Brown.
Music Director: Lee Hale.
Producer: Greg Garrison.
Director: Greg Garrison.
Choreographer: Ed Kerrigan.

DEAN'S PLACE — 60 minutes — NBC—September 6, 1975 (first pilot); January 13, 1976 (second pilot).

1473　DELANCEY STREET: THE CRISIS WITHIN

Pilot (Drama). The story of Robert Holtzman, John McCann and Otis James, the operators of Delancey Street, a halfway house in San Francisco that is devoted to rehabilitating junkies, ex-cons and other noncopers. Based on the work of John Maher, the founder of Delancey Street (an actual halfway house in California).

REGULAR CAST

John McCann　Walter McGinn
Robert Holtzman　Michael Conrad
Otis James　Lou Gossett, Jr.

GUEST CAST

Philip Donaldson　Mark Hamill
Copell　John Karlen
Joe　Carmine Caridi
Rudolfo　Hector Elias
Suzie Franklin　Jeri Woods
Mary　Leigh French
Mrs. Donaldson　Barbara Babcock
Ms. Somerville　Barbara Cason
Ruby James　Sylvia Soames

Music: Lalo Schifrin.
Executive Producer: Emmet G. Larvey, Jr.
Producer: Anthony Wilson.

Writer: Robert Foster.
Director: James Frawley.

DELANCEY STREET: THE CRISIS WITHIN — 90 minutes — NBC — April 19, 1975.

THE DELPHI BUREAU

The pilot film broadcast on ABC on March 6, 1972, for the series of the same title (see regular program section).

1474 DELTA COUNTY, U.S.A.

Pilot (Drama). A depiction of small-town life as seen through the experiences of the people of Delta County, a rural Southern community.

CAST

John McCain, Jr.	Peter Donat
Jack the Bear	Jim Antonio
Terry Nicholas	Jeff Conaway
Joe Ed	Joe Penney
Robbie Jean	Tisch Raye
Billy Wangate	Peter Masterson
Kate McCain Nicholas	Joanna Miles
Dossie Wilson	Lola Albright
Val Nicholas	Ed Power
Josie Wilson	Michele Carey
Vonda	Leigh Christian
Captain McCain	John McLiam
Doris Ann	Morgan Brittany
Biggie	Dennis Burkley
McCain	Doney Oatman

Music: Jack Elliott and Allyn Ferguson.
Executive Producer: Leonard Goldberg.
Producer: Robert Greenwald, Frank Von Zerneck.
Writer: Thomas Rickman.
Director: Glenn Jordan.
Art Director: Jack Collins.

DELTA COUNTY, U.S.A. — 2 hours — ABC — May 20, 1977.

1475 THE DETECTIVE

Pilot (Comedy). The exploits of Dennis O'Finn, a not-too-bright private detective who, in the pilot film, seeks to solve the mysterious murders of four elderly women.

REGULAR CAST

Det. Dennis O'Finn	Larry Hagman

GUEST CAST

Miss Hiddy-Lou	Helen Kleeb
Miss Bessie	Hope Summers
Miss Amantha	Helen Craig
Miss Birdie	Shirley O'Hara

Producer: Jules Irving.
Writer: Sarett Rudley.
Director: Jules Irving.

THE DETECTIVE — 30 minutes — NBC — October 12, 1975.

1476 D.H.O.

Pilot (Drama). The story of Sam Delaney, the head of a District Health Office (D.H.O.), a doctor who is responsible twenty-four hours a day, seven days a week, for the health of the people of his community. In the pilot, Delaney investigates the tragic death of a diabetic girl, a death he believes was related to an outbreak of drinking among neighborhood teenagers.

REGULAR CAST

Dr. Sam Delaney	Frank Converse
Dr. Levine, the medical examiner	Luther Adler
Dr. Bianca Pearson, a staff member	Ruby Dee
Axel Thorson, the community worker	Ed Grover

GUEST CAST

Mr. Randall	Jack Weston
Milo	Richard Gere

Executive Producer: Herman Rush, Ted Bergmann.
Producer: William Finnegan.
Writer: Alvin Boretz.
Director: John Trent.

D.H.O. — 60 minutes — ABC — June 17, 1973.

DIAL HOT LINE

The pilot film broadcast on ABC on March 8, 1970, for *Matt Lincoln* (see regular program section).

1477 DID YOU HEAR ABOUT JOSH AND KELLY?!

Pilot (Comedy). The misadventures of Josh Fowler and Kelly Porter, a newly divorced couple who discover they still love each other and decide to live together so each can pursue a career without the hassles of a marriage.

REGULAR CAST

Josh Fowler, a writer for *Modern Female* magazine	Dennis Dugan
Kelly Porter, a department store purchaser	Jane Daly
Rick Mannings, their friend, an insurance salesman	Jimmie Samuels
Jennifer Mannings, Rick's wife	Denise Galik

GUEST CAST

Deke Bradshaw	Dawson Mays
Mr. Clay	Cliff Norton

Music: Rod Parker, Hal Cooper.
Producer: Rod Parker, Hal Cooper.
Writer: Rod Parker.
Director: Hal Cooper.
Art Director: Chuck Murawski.

DID YOU HEAR ABOUT JOSH AND KELLY?! — 30 minutes — CBS — October 13, 1980.

DOCTOR DAN

See title "Three-In-One" in the pilot film section.

1478 DOCTOR MAX

Pilot (Drama). The story of Dr. Max Gordon, a Baltimore-based physician fraught with professional crises and family problems.

REGULAR CAST

Dr. Max Gordon	Lee J. Cobb
Alex Gordon, his son	Robert Lipton
Gloria Gordon, his wife	Janet Ward

GUEST CAST

Lester Oppel	David Sheiner
Libby Oppel	Katherine Helmond
Dr. Scott Herndon	Sorrell Booke
Mrs. Camacho	Miriam Colon
Rafel Camacho	Panchito Gomez
Dr. Poole	Granville van Dusen
Dr. Grogin	John Lehne

Music: Billy Goldenberg.
Producer: James Goldstone.
Writer: Robert L. Joseph.
Director: James Goldstone.

DOCTOR MAX — 90 minutes — NBC — April 4, 1974.

1479 DOCTOR SCORPION

Pilot (Adventure). The story of Jonathan Shackelford, a former secret agent turned marine biologist who occasionally undertakes assignments for his former organization, "The Company." In the pilot, Shackelford seeks to end the reign of Dr. Cresus, a power broker who is selling death-dealing devices to nations. (The title is derived from Dr. Cresus' hobby: scorpions.) Originally titled "Shack."

REGULAR CAST

Jonathan Shackelford	Nick Mancuso
Sharon Shackelford, his wife	Sandra Kerns
Tania, his assistant	Christine Lahti

GUEST CAST

Dr. Cresus	Roscoe Lee Browne
Worthington	Richard Herd
The Dane	Denny Miller
Whitey	Michael Cavanaugh

Music: Mike Post and Pete Carpenter.
Executive Producer: Stephen J. Cannell.
Producer: Alex Beaton.
Writer: Stephen J. Cannell.
Director: Richard Lang.
Art Director: John Lloyd.
Director of Photography: Charles Correll.

DOCTOR SCORPION — 90 minutes — ABC — February 24, 1978.

1480 DOCTOR STRANGE

Pilot (Fantasy). The story of Dr. Stephen Strange, a psychiatrist who is in reality a sorcerer, a magical champion of good over evil. The pilot episode depicts how Strange is endowed with the Hermedic Arts, the ability to control the elements of the universe, from Thomas Lindmer, an aging sorcerer who is no longer able to continue his battle against evil; and how Morgan Le Fay, the beautiful Dark Queen of Evil, seeks to destroy Lindmer before he can transfer his powers to Strange. Based on the *Marvel* comic book stories.

REGULAR CAST

Dr. Stephen Strange	Peter Hooten
Wong, his aide	Clyde Kusatsu
Morgan Le Fay, the evil sorceress	Jessica Walter
Dr. Frank Taylor, the head of the psychiatric ward at Eastside Hospital in New York	Philip Sterling
The Nameless One, Morgan's evil master	David Hooks
Voice of the Ancient One, the ruler of the Hermedic Arts	Michael Ansara

GUEST CAST

Thomas Lindmer	John Mills
Clea Lake	Eddie Benton
Sarah	June Barnett
Head Nurse	Diane Webster
Nurse	Sarah Rush
Magician (at end of program)	Larry Anderson
Taxi Driver	Michael Clark

Stephen's address: 22 Bleecker Street in Greenwich Village.

Music: Paul Chichara.
Executive Producer: Philip DeGuere.
Producer: Alex Beaton.
Writer: Philip DeGuere.
Director: Philip DeGuere.
Art Director: William Tunkle.
Director of Photography: Enzo A. Martinelli.

DOCTOR STRANGE — 90 minutes — CBS — September 6, 1978.

DOCTORS' PRIVATE LIVES

The pilot film broadcast on ABC on March 20, 1978, for the series of the same title (see regular program section).

1481 A DOG'S LIFE

Pilot (Comedy). The program features actors dressed as dogs and presents man as seen through the eyes of his best friend. Originally titled "McGurk."

CAST

McGurk, the dog whose life we see	Barney Martin
Iris, his lady friend	Beej Johnson
Camille, Iris' daughter	Sherry Lynn
Tucker, the other dog owned by McGurk's masters	Charlie Martin Smith
Spike, McGurk's friend	Hamilton Camp
Turk, McGurk's friend	Michael Huddleston

Producer: Charlie Hauck.
Associate Producer: Ken Stump.
Director: Peter Bonerz.

A DOG'S LIFE — 30 minutes — NBC — June 15, 1979.

DOMINICK'S DREAM

See title "4 Funny Families" in pilot film section.

1482   DON'T CALL US

Pilot (Comedy). The misadventures of brothers Marty and Larry King, the owners of Talent Unlimited, a small theatrical agency in Philadelphia. The focal point of the program is the relationship between the two brothers: Larry, who is inefficient and hopelessly intrigued by odd-ball acts and out-of-work actors; and Marty, who is all business and efficient to a fault.

REGULAR CAST

Larry King	Jack Gilford
Marty King	Allan Miller
Rene Patterson, their receptionist	Leland Palmer
Jackie Nakamura, a client	Richard Narita
Sylvia, a client	Patty Maloney
Lloyd, a client	Billy Barty

GUEST CAST

Tolanda Gelman	Tina Louise
Gus DeMarco	James Luisi
One Man Band	Don Davis

Music: Pat Williams.
Producer: Ed Weinberger, Stan Daniels.
Writer: David Lloyd.
Director: Robert Moore.
Creator: Ed Weinberger, Stan Daniels, David Lloyd.
Art Director: Ken Reid.
Set Director: Earl Carlson.

DON'T CALL US—30 minutes—CBS—August 13, 1976.

1483   THE DOOLEY BROTHERS

Pilot (Comedy). A satirization of the Old West as seen through the antics of George and Billy Dooley, bumbling brothers who, though unable to ride, shoot or rope, seek to dispense justice to all deserving inhabitants. In the pilot, they try to help Cool Sam Bennett, an aging sheriff who is the target of revenge of the notorious Simond Gang.

REGULAR CAST

George Dooley	Garrett Brown
Bill Dooley	Robert Peirce
Jack Black, the journalist who invented the legend of the Dooleys	John Myhers

GUEST CAST

Cool Sam Bennett	Dub Taylor
Lucy Bennett	Shelly Long
Bear Breath	Pete Schrum
Zeke	Rusty Lee
Zack	Grizzly Green
Gilbert	Charles Julian
Doctor	Allen Wood

Music: Murry McCloud, Jac Redford, Herb Martin.
Producer: Arnold Margolin.
Writer: Arnold Margolin.
Director: Don Weis.
Art Director: Frank Smith.
Director of Photography: Michael Joyce.
Associate Producer: William Green.
Set Director: Robert Gullickson.

THE DOOLEY BROTHERS—30 minutes—CBS—July 31, 1979.

1484   DOWN HOME

Pilot (Drama). The story of Priscilla and Nate Simmons, a couple who move from Detroit to a small town in the South to find a more peaceful and meaningful life.

REGULAR CAST

Priscilla Simmons, the mother	Madge Sinclair
Nate Simmons, her husband	Robert Hooks
Darlene Simmons, their daughter	Tia Rance
Junior Simmons, their son	Kevin Hooks
"Highpockets" Simmons, their son	Eric Hooks
Aunt Velvet, the woman who helps the Simmons	Beah Richards

GUEST CAST

Joe Mayfield	Lincoln Kilpatrick
Helen Mayfield	Beverly Hope Atkinson
Trunk	Sonny Jim Gaines
Sarah Claypool	Anne Seymour
Mrs. Winston	Norma Connolly
Julie Mayfield	Dena Crowder
Abner Claypool	Edward Binns
Burt Pritchard	William Watson
Benjamin Pritchard	Paul Koslo
Bobby Pritchard	Timothy Scott
Mr. Winston	Woodrow Parfrey
Frank Simmons	Boyd Bodwell
Billy Joe Pritchard	Mickey Jones
Jeeter Simmons	John Gilgreen
Dr. Johnson	George McDaniel
Sheriff	Andrew Duggan

Producer: Philip Barry.
Writer: Melvin Van Peebles.
Director: Fielder Cook.
Art Director: Dick Haman.
Director of Photography: Michael Hugo.

DOWN HOME—60 minutes—CBS—August 16, 1978.

1485   A DREAM FOR CHRISTMAS

Pilot (Drama). The story, set in Los Angeles in 1950, follows the struggles of the Douglases, a poor black family. The pilot depicts the efforts of Will Douglas, the father, a minister, as he attempts to rebuild his congregation, having just moved from Arkansas to California. Based on characters created by Earl Hamner, Jr.

REGULAR CAST

The Rev. Will Douglas	Hari Rhodes
Sarah Douglas, his wife	Lynn Hamilton
Grandma Douglas	Beah Richards
Joey Douglas, his son	George Spell
Bradley Douglas, his son	Marlin Adams
Emmarine Douglas, his daughter	Ta Ronace Allen
Becky Douglas, his daughter	Bebe Redcross

GUEST CAST

George Briggs	Robert Do Qui
Arthur Rogers	Joel Fluellen
Fannie	Juanita Moore

Music: David Rose.
Executive Producer: Lee Rich.
Producer: Walter Coblenz.

Writer: John McGreevey.
Director: Ralph Senensky.

A DREAM FOR CHRISTMAS—2 hours—ABC—December 24, 1973.

1486   DRIBBLE

Pilot (Comedy). The story, set in New York City, presents a behind-the-scenes look at the antics of a professional basketball team (unnamed). The pilot depicts the team's efforts to adjust to Pete Terry, a new member whose professional status causes undue unrest with the team.

REGULAR CAST

Anne Harrelson, the sportswriter	Dee Wallace
Red Arnold, the coach	Dan Frazier
John Raider, a team member	Joseph Hacker
Lou Jamison, a team member	Julius J. Carry III
Pete Terry, a team member	Larry Anderson
Will Herb, a team member	Edward Edwards
Ginny Jamison, Lou's wife	Vernee Watson
Sarabeth Herb, Will's wife	Amy Stryker
Sal, a team member	Lewis Arquette

GUEST CAST

Countess	Yula Gavala
Fred	Basil Hoffman
Bert	Danny Goldman

Music: Joey Levine.
Executive Producer: Jim Green, Allen Epstein.
Producer: Linda Bloodworth.
Writer: Linda Bloodworth.
Director: Charles S. Dubin.
Art Director: Ross Bellah.

DRIBBLE—30 minutes—NBC—August 21, 1980.

1487   DUFFY

Pilot (Comedy). The misadventures of Duffy, a nondescript dog with almost human qualities, who is the adopted mascot of a junior high school.

REGULAR CAST

Cliff Sellers, Duffy's master	Fred Grandy
Thomas N. Tibbles, the principal	Roger Bowen
Marty Carter, Tibbles' secretary	Lane Binkley
Happy Jack, the owner of the local hamburger stand	George Wyner
Nick, a student	John Sheldon
Craig, a student	John Herbsleb
Josh, a student	Stephen Manley
Danny, a student	Jarrod Johnson

GUEST CAST

Friendly Bum	Robert E. Ball
Neighbor	Jane Dulo
Mrs. Dreifuss	Jane Lambert
Postman	Dick Yarmy

Producer: George Eckstein.
Writer: Richard DeRoy.
Director: Bruce Bilson.
Art Director: Dave Marshall.
Director of Photography: John Nickolaus.

DUFFY—30 minutes—CBS—May 6, 1977.

1488   DYNASTY

Pilot (Drama). The story, set in Westmore, Ohio, follows the experiences of the Blackwoods, pioneering scrub farmers, from 1820 to their emergence as a ruthless family dynasty in the early 1860s. Based on the story by James Michener and also titled *James Michener's Dynasty*. Originally titled (and the potential series title) *James Michener's The Americans.*

REGULAR CAST

Jennifer Blackwood, the power behind the dynasty	Sarah Miles
John Blackwood, her husband	Harris Yulin
Matt Blackwood, John's brother	Stacy Keach
Amanda Blackwood, Jennifer's daughter	Amy Irving
Mark Blackwood, Jennifer's son	Harrison Ford
Harry Blackwood, Jennifer's son	Tony Swartz
Carter Blackwood, Jennifer's son	Garret Graham
Creed Vauclose, the plantation owner	Granville Van Dusen
Sam Adams, the ex-slave who works for Jennifer	Charles Weldon
Lucinda Adams, Sam's wife	Stephanie Faulkner
Young Sam Adams, Sam's son	Stanley Clay
Pelly, Creed's servant	J. Jay Saunders

GUEST CAST

Margaret McCullum	Sari Price
Benjamin McCullum	John Carter
Amanda Blackwood, as a young girl	Michelle Stacy
Amanda Blackwood, older	Debbie Fresh
Albert Brinkerhoff	James Houghton
Rev. Wheatley	Francis DeSales
Daughter Slate	Brent Jones
McHenry	Guy Raymond
Majors	Rayford Barnes

Music: Gil Mellé.
Executive Producer: David Frost.
Producer: Buck Houghton.
Writer: Sidney Carroll.
Director: Lee Philips.
Art Director: Perry Ferguson.

DYNASTY—2 hours—NBC—March 13, 1976.

E

1489   THE EASTER PROMISE

Pilot (Drama). The third of four pilot films about the Mills family and life in Nebraska during the 1940s (see also: "Addie and the King of Hearts," "The House Without a Christmas Tree," and "The Thanksgiving Treasure"). The story focuses on Addie, the 12-year-old daughter of widower James Mills, and her experiences with Constance Payne, a visiting actress who overcomes great difficulties due to Addie's caring and understanding. The title is derived from a promise Constance made to Addie, but was unsure of keeping: to spend Easter with her family.

REGULAR CAST

James Mills, the father	Jason Robards
Addie Mills, his daughter	Lisa Lucas
Grandmother Mills	Mildred Natwick

GUEST CAST

Constance Payne	Jean Simmons
Mrs. Coyne	Elizabeth Wilson
Cora Sue	Franny Michael
Terry	Vicki Schreck
Linda	Lori Ann Rutherford

Music: Arthur Rubinstein.
Producer: Alan Shayne.
Writer: Gail Rock.
Director: Paul Bogart.
Art Director: Ben Edwards.
Costumes: Jane Greenwood.
Set Decorator: Robert Checchi.

THE EASTER PROMISE—90 minutes—CBS—March 26, 1975.

1490 EBONY, IVORY, AND JADE

Pilot (Crime Drama). The story of a trio of private detectives who pose as a nightclub act to cover for their assignments for the Central Service Agency, a unit of the U.S. government. (The nightclub act: Ebony and Ivory, two beautiful singers, and Jade, who acts as their manager.)

REGULAR CAST

Nick Jade	Bert Convy
Claire (Ebony)	Debbie Allen
Maggie (Ivory)	Martha Smith

GUEST CAST

Blair	Claude Akins
Cabot	Donald Moffat
Adele Teba	Nina Foch
David Brenner	Himself
Franki Valli	Himself

Music: Earle Hagen.
Executive Producer: Ernie Frankel.
Producer: Jimmy Sangster.
Writer: Jimmy Sangster (from a story by Anne Beckett and Mike Farrell).
Director: John Llewellyn Moxey.
Choreographer: Lester Wilson.

EBONY, IVORY, AND JADE—90 minutes—CBS—August 3, 1979.

1491 EDDIE

Pilot (Comedy). The dealings of Eddie Skinner, a private patrolman in a posh residential area who manipulates both men and machines for his own profit.

CAST

Eddie Skinner	Phil Silvers
Chief Pike, his superior	Fred Clark
Sylvia, the society woman	Joanna Barnes
Patrolman Callahan	Frank Faylen
Milburn	Edward Andrews

EDDIE—30 minutes—CBS—September 5, 1971.

1492 EDDIE AND HERBERT

Pilot (Comedy). The story of the friendship between two blue collar workers: Eddie Scanlon, who is pompous and opinionated; and his co-worker Herbert Draper, who is naive and worships Eddie. The episode focuses on Eddie's attempts to grab the brass ring of life, and the turmoil he causes for all concerned because of his philosophies.

CAST

Eddie Scanlon	Jeffrey Tambor
Herbert Draper	James Cromwell
Madge Scanlon, Eddie's wife	Marilyn Meyer
Dorine Draper, James's wife	Candice Azzara

Music: Ray Charles.
Supervising Producer: E. Duke Vincent.
Executive Producer: Perry Lafferty.
Producer: Richard Rosenbloom.
Writer: Sam Bobrick.
Director: Robert Scheerer.
Art Director: Ray Klausen.

EDDIE AND HERBERT—30 minutes—CBS—May 30, 1977.

1493 EGAN

Pilot (Crime Drama). The exploits of Eddie Egan, a former New York City detective turned private investigator. The pilot, based on Egan's real life experiences, follows Eddie's attempts to solve the syndicate murder of his ex-partner.

REGULAR CAST

Eddie Egan	Eugene Roche
Captain Jones	Dabney Coleman
Detective Burke	Glenn Corbett

GUEST CAST

J. R. King	John Anderson
Deveaux	John Carlin
Woman in shower	Marian Collier
Bobby	Michael Bell
Desk Clerk	Fred Holliday
Cab Driver	Ian Sander

Producer: Thomas L. Miller.
Writer: Abram S. Ginnes.
Director: Jud Taylor.

EGAN—30 minutes—ABC—September 18, 1973.

1494 ELKE

Comedy. The story of Elke, a beautiful German girl who marries a homely American—and the ensuing complications, especially in her new husband's family.

CAST

Elke Stefan	Elke Sommer
Peter Stefan, her husband	Peter Bonerz
Mrs. Stefan, Peter's mother	Kay Medford
Dodie Stefan, Peter's sister	Debi Storm
Charlie Stefan, Peter's brother	Paul Petersen

ELKE—30 minutes—CBS—August 22, 1971.

ELLERY QUEEN

The pilot film for the series of the same title aired on NBC on March 23, 1975. See *Ellery Queen* in the regular program section. The pilot, which is syndicated as a movie, has been retitled "Too Many Suspects."

1495 ELLERY QUEEN: DON'T LOOK BEHIND YOU

Pilot (Crime Drama). The exploits of Ellery Queen, a gentleman detective and writer working out of New York City. In the pilot film, he attempts to catch an elusive strangler. Based on the 1949 novel *Cat of Many Tails* by Frederick Danny and Manfred B. Lee.

REGULAR CAST

Ellery Queen	Peter Lawford
Inspector Richard Queen, his father	Harry Morgan

GUEST CAST

Dr. Cazalis	E. G. Marshall
Celeste	Stefanie Powers
Christy	Skye Aubrey
Mrs. Cazalis	Coleen Gray
Commissioner	Morgan Stere

Music: Jerry Fielding.
Executive Producer: Edward J. Montagne.
Producer: Leonard J. Ackerman.
Writer: Ted Leighton.
Director: Barry Shear.

ELLERY QUEEN: DON'T LOOK BEHIND YOU—2 hours—NBC—November 14, 1971.

EMERGENCY!

The pilot film broadcast on NBC on January 15, 1972, for the series of the same title (see regular program section).

1496 ENIGMA

Pilot (Adventure). The exploits of Andrew Icarus, a daring agent for Triangle, a sophisticated crime-fighting organization based in the Caribbean. In the pilot, Icarus seeks to end the reign of a dangerous band of fanatics who are building a secret army financed by stolen diamonds.

REGULAR CAST

Agent Andrew Icarus	Scott Hylands
Baron Maurice Mockcastle, Icarus' superior	Guy Doleman
Princess Miranda Larawa, Maurice's assistant	Barbara O. Jones
Mei San Gow, Icarus' partner	Soon-Teck Oh

GUEST CAST

Dora Herren	Melinda Dillon
Peter McCauley	Peter Coffield
Idi Ben Youref	Percy Rodrigues

Kate Valentine	Sherry Jackson
Col. Valentine	Jim Davis
Wolf	Bill Fletcher
Benjamin Herren	Morgan Farley
Dr. Beverly Golden	Melodie Johnson
Marsha	Judith Brown

Producer: Sam H. Rolfe.
Writer: Sam H. Rolfe.
Director: Michael O'Herlihy.
Creator: Sam H. Rolfe.

ENIGMA—60 minutes—CBS—May 27, 1977.

1497 ERNIE, MADGE, AND ARTIE

Pilot (Comedy). The story of Madge and Artie, a middle-aged newlywed couple who are plagued by Ernie, the ghost of Madge's first husband, who has come back to haunt her.

CAST

Madge	Cloris Leachman
Artie	Dick Van Patten
Ernie	Frank Sutton
Blanche	Susan Sennett
Charlie	William Molloy

ERNIE, MADGE, AND ARTIE—30 minutes—ABC—August 15, 1974.

1498 ESCAPADE

Pilot (Adventure). The exploits of Joshua Rand, a U.S. government secret agent, who takes his orders from an ingenious computer named Oz. In the pilot, Rand and his beautiful assistant, Suzy, attempt to stop a foreign invasion by putting an end to the operations of Arnold Tulliver, a freelance agent who steals top government secrets from countries and sells them to the highest bidder.

REGULAR CAST

Joshua Rand	Granville Van Dusen
Suzy, his assistant	Morgan Fairchild

GUEST CAST

Arnold Tulliver	Len Birman
Paula	Janice Lynde
Wences	Alex Henteloff
Seaman	Gregory Walcott
Charlie Webster	Dennis Rucker

Music: Pat Williams.
Executive Producer: Philip Saltzman.
Producer: Brian Clemens.
Writer: Brian Clemens.
Director: Jerry London.

ESCAPADE—60 minutes—CBS—May 19, 1978.

1499 ESCAPE

Pilot (Adventure). The exploits of Cameron Steele, an escape artist who specializes in helping people in trouble. The pilot depicts Steele's efforts to rescue Dr. Henry Walding, a kidnapped scientist who holds the key to synthesized life.

REGULAR CAST

Cameron Steele	Christopher George
Nicholas Slye, his assistant, the owner of the Crystal Ball Bar	Avery Schreiber

GUEST CAST

Susan Walding	Marlyn Mason
Dr. Henry Walding	William Windom
Rodger Clifton	George Clifton
Evelyn Harrison	Gloria Grahame
Lewis Harrison	William Schallert
Gilbert	Huntz Hall

Music: Lalo Schifrin.
Producer: Bruce Landsbury.
Writer: Paul Playdon.
Director: John Llewellyn Moxey.
Art Director: Walter M. Jeffries.
Director of Photography: Al Francis.

ESCAPE — 90 minutes — ABC — April 6, 1971.

1500   ETHEL IS AN ELEPHANT

Pilot (Comedy). While walking home on a New York Street, photographer Eugene Henderson removes a painful nail from the foot of an abandoned baby elephant (from a bankrupt carnival). The grateful elephant, named Ethel, follows him home and creates a problem when Eugene takes her in and tries to conceal her from his landlord. The story depicts the courtroom battle that ensues when Harold Brainer, the landlord, tries (but fails) to evict Eugene and Ethel from the apartment house. The would-be series was to depict Eugene's misadventures — as the owner of a half-ton baby elephant in Manhattan.

REGULAR CAST

Eugene Henderson	Todd Susman
Howard Dimitri, his friend	Steven Peterman
Dr. Diane Taylor, the vet	Liberty Godshall
Harold Brainer, the landlord	Eddie Barth
Ethel	Ethel

GUEST CAST

Prosecutor	Stephen Pearlman
Judge	John C. Becher
Keeper	Ed Call
Woman in court	Nora Denney
Police Officer	Bernie McInerney
Cab driver	Ralph Monaco
Man in court	Guy Remsen

Music: Ken Harrison.
Theme: "Ethel's Song" by Marilyn Messina Tucker and Larry Tucker.
Executive Producer: Bob Sweeney, Edward H. Feldman.
Producer: Larry Rosen.
Writer: Larry Tucker.
Director: John Astin.
Art Director: Ross Bellah, Robert Purcell.
Director of Photography: Al Francis.

ETHEL IS AN ELEPHANT — 30 minutes — CBS — June 18, 1980.

1501   EVEL KNIEVEL

Pilot (Adventure). The exploits of thrill-seeker Evel Knievel. In the pilot, the motorcycle daredevil pits his skills against a female cyclist.

REGULAR CAST

Evel Knievel	Sam Elliott
Gene Ray Stone, Evel's manager	Gary Barton

GUEST CAST

Female cyclist	Karen Philipp
Decataur	Noble Willingham
Pettet	Michael Anderson, Jr.
Newsman	Edward Ansara
Hymie	Herbie Faye

Music: Gil Mellé.
Executive Producer: Robert E. Relyea.
Producer: John Strong.
Writer: Richard Adams.
Director: Michael O'Herlihy.

EVEL KNIEVEL — 30 minutes — CBS — March 29, 1974.

1502   EVIL ROY SLADE

Pilot (Comedy). A wagon train, traveling to California, is attacked and burned to the ground by Apache Indians. The lone survivor, an infant boy, somehow manages to survive and grows up as one mean man, loving no one and expecting neither love nor respect. Adopting the name Evil Roy Slade (Slade for Sneaking, Lying, Arrogance, Dirtiness and Evil) he becomes the leader of an outlaw gang and one of the most wanted men in the Old West — with lawmen from every state seeking to end his life of evil doing.

The pilot episode, which is actually two story lines in one, is set in the town of Willow Bend and opens with Nelson L. Stool, the owner of the Western Express and Stage Lines, hiring ex-San Francisco Marshal Bing Bell, "The Singing Lawman," to stop Slade from robbing his stages and trains ("Why he's so mean he even steals the locomotive whistles because he likes the toot toot sound"). The second story line, which is interwoven into the first, depicts Slade's first taste of decency when he meets Betsy Potter, a school teacher who becomes attracted to him and sets out to reform him so they can marry and settle down in peace.

REGULAR CAST

Evil Roy Slade	John Astin
Nelson L. Stool, the train and stage line owner	Mickey Rooney
Betsy Potter, the school teacher	Pamela Austin
Marshal Bing Bell	Dick Shawn
Aggie Potter, Betsy's mother	Connie Sawyer
Clifford Stool, Nelson's nephew	Henry Gibson
Flossie, a member of Slade's gang	Edie Adams
Preacher, same as Flossie	Robert Liberman
Smith, same as Flossie	Larry Hankin
Snake, same as Flossie	Edmund Cambridge
Turhan, Bing's servant	Pat Morita
Nelson's telegrapher	Milton Frome

GUEST CAST

Harry Fern	Milton Berle
Alice Fern	Luana Anders
Logan Delp	Dom DeLuise
Bank teller	Penny Marshall
Minister	John Ritter
Souvenir salesman	Jerry Paris

Nelson's dog: Custer.

Narrator: Pat Buttram.
Music: Stuart Margolin, Murray McLeod, Jerry Riopelle.
Producer: Jerry Belson, Garry Marshall.
Writer: Jerry Belson, Garry Marshall.
Director: Jerry Paris.
Art Director: Alexander A. Mayer.
Director of Photography: Sam Leavitt.

EVIL ROY SLADE — 2 hours — NBC — February 18, 1972.

1503   THE EYES OF CHARLES SAND

Pilot (Drama). The story of Charles Sand, a man who possesses a special power called "The Sight," which enables him to see what others cannot. In the pilot, Sand investigates a girl's story about her brother's alleged murder.

REGULAR CAST

Charles Sand	Peter Haskell

GUEST CAST

Katherine	Barbara Rush
Emily Parkhurst	Sharon Farrell
Jeffrey Winslow	Bradford Dillman
Aunt Alexandria	Joan Bennett
Dr. Paul Scott	Adam West
Raymond	Gary Clarke

Music: None credited due to a musician's strike; Henry Mancini's score to the feature film "Wait Until Dark" was apparently used.
Producer: Hugh Benson.
Writer: Henry Farrell, Stamford Whitmore.
Director: Reza S. Badiyi.

THE EYES OF CHARLES SAND — 90 minutes — ABC — February 29, 1972.

1504   THE EYES OF TEXAS

Pilot (Crime Drama). The misadventures of Heather Fern and Caroline Capoty, two beautiful rookie private detectives who work for Mort Jarvis, the head of Texas International, a two-bit investigative organization. In the pilot, which aired as a segment of the *B.J. and the Bear* series, the girls travel to New Orleans to apprehend a con man who preys on elderly, wealthy women.

REGULAR CAST

Heather Fern	Rebecca Reynolds
Caroline Capoty	Lorrie Mahaffey
Mort Jarvis, their employer	Roger C. Carmel

GUEST CAST

B. J. McKay	Greg Evigan
Jay Michael Lawrence (the con man)	Peter Haskell
Laura Forrester	Anna Lee
Bradley	Raymond St. Jacques
Frieda	Mitzi Hoag
Benji	Marcia Morgan
Miss	Beth Grant

Music: Stu Phillips.
Theme Vocal: "The Eyes of Texas" by Greg Evigan.
Executive Producer: Glen A. Larson, Michael Sloan.
Producer: John Peyser.
Writer: Glen A. Larson.
Director: Bruce Bilson.

THE EYES OF TEXAS — 60 minutes — NBC — May 24, 1980.

1505   EXO-MAN

Pilot (Adventure). The exploits of Nick Conrad, a crippled physics professor who develops an exo suit, a device that revitalizes his limbs, making him mobile again, and endows him with superhuman abilities, which he uses to battle crime.

REGULAR CAST

Nick Conrad	David Ackroyd

GUEST CAST

Emily Frost	Anne Schedeen
Raphael	A Martinez
Kermet Haas	Jose Ferrer
D. A. Kaminski	Kevin McCarthy

Music: Dana Kaproff.
Executive Producer: Richard Irving.
Producer: Lionel E. Segal.
Writer: Martin Caidin, Howard Rodman.
Director: Richard Irving.

EXO-MAN — 2 hours — NBC — June 8, 1977.

F

1506   THE FABULOUS DR. FABLE

Pilot (Crime Drama). The story of Dr. Justin Darius Fable, a brilliant, but eccentric diagnostician and teacher with an uncanny knack for perceiving ailments that are the results of criminal actions. In the pilot, Fable attempts to uncover the reason and culprit responsible for the poisonings of several people at the university where he teaches.

REGULAR CAST

Dr. Justin Fable	W. B. Brydon
June Fable, his wife	Jane Elliot
Police Lt. DeLusso	Jack Ging

GUEST CAST

Elliot Borden — William Daniels
Marilla — Cynthia Hall

Producer: Robert Christiansen, Rick Rosenberg.
Writer: George Wells.
Director: Bernard Girard.

THE FABULOUS DR. FABLE — 60 minutes — ABC — June 17, 1973.

1507 FAMILY FUNTIME, U.S.A.

Pilot (Variety). Tours of various U.S. locales. In the pilot, a visit to the Marine World/Africa U.S.A. Park in Redwood City, California.

Hosts: Joey Heatherton, Harvey Korman.
Music: Ed Bogas, Judy Munson.
Producer: Lee Mendleson, Karen Crommie.
Director: Lee Mendleson.

FAMILY FUNTIME, U.S.A. — 30 minutes — Syndicated July 1979.

1508 THE FAMILY KOVACK

Pilot (Drama). Events in the lives of the Kovacks, a close-knit family of five.

REGULAR CAST

Vinnie Kovack, the father — James Sloyan
Ma Kovack, his wife — Sarah Cunningham
Lennie Kovack, their son — Richard Gilliland
Karen Kovack, their daughter — Tammi Bula
Butch Kovack, their son — Andy Robinson

GUEST CAST

Jill Linsen — Renne Jarrett
Mrs. Linsen — Mary La Roche
Jo Jo Linsen — Phil Bruns

Music: Harry Sukman.
Producer: Ron Roth.
Writer: Adrian Spies.
Director: Ralph Senensky.

THE FAMILY KOVACK — 90 minutes — NBC — April 5, 1974.

FANTASY ISLAND

The first pilot film (the second, "Return to Fantasy Island") broadcast on ABC on January 14, 1977, for the series *Fantasy Island* (see regular program section).

1509 FATHER O FATHER

Pilot (Comedy). The misadventures of Father Flicker, a conservative Boston Pastor, and his liberal assistant, Father Morgan.

CAST

Father Flicker — Iggie Wolfington
Father Morgan — Dennis Dugan
Parishioner — Richard Stahl

Executive Producer: Jerry Weintraub.
Producer: Rich Eustis, Al Rogers, Ron Clark.
Director: Peter Bonerz, Lee H. Bernhardi.

FATHER O FATHER — 60 minutes — ABC — June 26, 1976.

1510 FATHER ON TRIAL

Pilot (Comedy). The romantic misadventures of Mike Bryan, a widowed judge, and his girlfriend, Billie Roman.

CAST

Judge Mike Bryan — Darren McGavin
Billie Roman, his girlfriend — Barbara Feldon
Stevie Bryan, Mike's son — Moosie Drier
Mike Bryan, Jr., Mike's son — Kieran Mullaney
Maggie, Mike's secretary — Joan Tompkins

Music: Walter Marks.
Producer: Mel Shavelson.
Writer: Mel Shavelson.
Director: Mel Shavelson.

FATHER ON TRIAL — 30 minutes — NBC — September 3, 1972.

THE FEATHER AND FATHER GANG: NEVER CON A KILLER

The pilot film aired on ABC on May 13, 1977, for the series *The Feather and Father Gang* (see regular program section).

1511 FEATHERSTONE'S NEST

Pilot (Comedy). The story of Charlie Featherstone, a pediatrician, as he struggles to run a house and cope with two lively daughters, Kelly and Courtney, while his wife is away studying at law school. In the pilot, Charlie struggles to cope with a nasty new housekeeper and Kelly's, his 13-year-old daughter, decision to sleep with a boy — her initiation to join a high school sorority.

REGULAR CAST

Dr. Charlie Featherstone — Ken Berry
Kelly Featherstone, his daughter — Susan Swift
Courtney Featherstone, his daughter — Dana Hill
Bella Beacham, his housekeeper — Virginia Capers
Everett Buhl, Charlie's friend — Phil Leeds
Dr. John Q. A. DeMott, Charlie's assistant — Fred Morsell

GUEST CAST

Hedwig — Kate Zentall
Thurgood Ludlow — Shane Sinutko
Mrs. Ludlow — Jessica Rains
Dee Dee — Anita Jodelsohn
Sue Sue — Rhonda Foxx

Music: Earle Hagen.
Executive Producer: Danny Thomas, Ronald Jacobs.
Producer: Michael Norell.
Writer: Michael Norell.
Director: James Drake.
Co-Producer: Jack Thompson.
Art Director: Bob Keene.

FEATHERSTONE'S NEST — 30 minutes — CBS — August 1, 1979.

THE FESS PARKER SHOW

See title "4 Funny Families" in the pilot film section.

1512 THE FIGHTING NIGHTINGALES

Pilot (Comedy-Drama). The story, set in Korea during the war, depicts the lives and experiences of combat-weary army nurses.

REGULAR CAST

Major Kate Steele — Adrienne Barbeau
Col. H. Jonas Boyette — Kenneth Mars
Lt. Angie Finelli — Livia Genise
Capt. Margaret "Irish" McCall — Erica Yohn
Lt. Hope Phillips — Stephanie Faracy
Pvt. Tyrone Vallone — Randy Stumpf
Sgt. Baker — George Whiteman

GUEST CAST

Capt. Jules Meyer — Jerry Houser
Chaplain Billy Joe Lee — Rod McCary
Patient — Jonathan Banks
Driver — Frank Whiteman
North Korean soldier — Kim Kahana
Patient — Lawrence Rosenberg

Music: Steven Kagen.
Music Supervision: Lionel Newman.
Writer: Alan Uger, Barry Sand.
Director: George Tyne.
Art Director: Dave Haber.
Director of Photography: Joseph M. Wilcots.
Associate Producer: Tom Lisi.

THE FIGHTING NIGHTINGALES — 30 minutes — CBS — January 16, 1978.

1513 FIREHOUSE

Pilot (Drama). The pilot film for the series of the same title. While both the series and pilot film depict the work of fire fighters in Los Angeles, the pilot presents the original story line, which was later dropped: the experiences of Shelly Forsythe, a rookie fireman, as he struggles to cross the color line in an all-white fire company.

CAST

Capt. Spike Ryerson — Vince Edwards
Fireman Shelly Forsythe — Richard Roundtree
Michelle Forsythe, Shelly's wife — Sheila Frazier
Captain Parr — Andrew Duggan
Fireman Hank Myers — Richard Jaeckel
Fireman Sonny Caputo — Val Avery
Fireman Billy Dalzell — Paul Le Mat
Fireman Ernie Bush — Michael Lerner

Music: Tom Scott.
Executive Producer: Dick Berg.
Producer: Joe Manduke.
Writer: Frank Lucci.
Director: Alex March.

FIREHOUSE — 90 minutes — ABC — January 2, 1973.

1514 FIRST TIME, SECOND TIME

Pilot (Comedy). The misadventures of Doug Fitzpatrick, a think-tank management executive whose personal and professional worlds merge to cause unusual and insoluble problems. In the pilot, he seeks a way to cope with his son David's inability to accept Karen (Doug's new wife) as his mother.

REGULAR CAST

Doug Fitzpatrick — Ronny Cox
Karen Fitzpatrick, his wife — Julie Cobb
David Fitzpatrick, his son — David Hollander
Jhampur Nehrudi, the deposed minister from Central Asia who resides with the Fitzpatricks — Sumant
Joan Armstrong, Doug's associate — Mary Frann

GUEST CAST

Lester Brotman — David Clennon
Pretty girl — Robyn Blythe
Brian — Todd Starks
Mrs. Redack — Joan Crosby
Young man — Richard Marcus

The Fitzpatricks' dog: Edison.

Music: Cort Casady, Michael Cannon.
Executive Producer: Bob Comfort, Rick Kellard.
Producer: Ron Bloomberg, Charles Raymond, Karyl Geld Miller.
Writer: Bob Comfort, Rick Kellard.
Director: Asaad Kelada.
Art Director: Ken Reid.
Director of Photography: George La Fountaine.

FIRST TIME, SECOND TIME — 30 minutes — CBS — October 25, 1980.

1515 THE FIRST 36 HOURS OF DR. DURANT

Pilot (Drama). The challenges, struggles, defeats and victories of Dr. Chris Durant, a surgical resident in a teaching hospital. The pilot depicts his hectic initiation into the hospital (hence the title).

REGULAR CAST

Dr. Chris Durant — Scott Hylands
Dr. Konrad Zane — Lawrence Pressman
Nurse Katherine Gunther — Katherine Helmond
Nurse Olive Olin — Karen Carlson
Dr. Baxter — James Naughton
Dr. Atkinson — David Doyle
Dr. Bryce — Peter Donat
Dr. Lynn Peterson — Renne Jarrett
Surgical secretary — Janet Brandt

GUEST CAST

Alex Keefer — Alex Henteloff
Dr. Hutchins — Dana Andrews
Graham — Michael Conrad
Mrs. Graham — Joyce Jameson

Music: Leonard Rosenman.
Executive Producer: Stirling Silliphant.
Producer: James H. Brown.
Writer: Stirling Silliphant.
Director: Alexander Singer.

THE FIRST 36 HOURS OF DR. DURANT — 90 minutes — ABC — May 13, 1975.

1516   FLAMINGO ROAD

Pilot (Drama). The story, set in Truro County, a small Southern community, depicts events in the lives of the Weldons, a wealthy family whose lives are corrupted by power and passion. The pilot episode for a proposed 1980 NBC series.

CAST

Titus Semple, the sheriff	Howard Duff
Claude Weldon, the mill owner	Kevin McCarthy
Eudora Weldon, Claude's wife	Barbara Rush
Constance Weldon, Claude's daughter	Morgan Fairchild
Lane Ballou, the ex-carnival dancer who rises to prominence	Cristina Raines
Lute Mae Saunders, the owner of the brothel	Stella Stevens
Fielding Carlyle, the deputy sheriff	Mark Harmon
Sam Curtis, the land developer	John Beck
Skip Semple, Titus' son	Woody Brown
Elmo Tyson, the newspaper editor	Mason Adams
Jasper, the Weldon's butler	Glen Richards
Pete, the owner of the Eagle Cafe	Norman Alden
Tom Coin, the carnival barker	Michael Delano
Annabelle Troy, the waitress	Dianne Kay
Elma, Lane's friend	Melba Moore

Also: Daniel Torppe, Paul Sorenson, Ted Lehmann, Tom Regan, John Furlong, Ben Young, Ed Kenney, Bill McLaughlin, Karen Rushmore.

Music: Gerald Fried.
Executive Producer: Michael Filerman, Lee Rich.
Producer: Edward H. Feldman.
Writer: Rita Lakin (based on the novel by Robert Wilder).
Director: Gus Trikonis.
Art Director: Charles M. Zacha, Jr.

FLAMINGO ROAD — 2 hours — NBC — May 12, 1980.

1517   FLANNERY AND QUILT

Pilot (Comedy). The story of Luke Flannery and Samuel Quilt, two argumentative senior citizens who share an apartment (at 365 West 73rd Street) and struggle to live with each other.

CAST

Luke Flannery	Red Buttons
Samuel Quilt	Harold Gould
Rose Caselli, Samuel's married daughter	Pat Finley
Kevin Caselli, Rose's husband	Howard Storm

Music: Jack Elliott, Allyn Ferguson.

Producer: Carl Reiner.
Writer: Carl Reiner, Marty Feldman.
Director: Carl Reiner.

FLANNERY AND QUILT — 30 minutes — NBC — February 1, 1976.

1518   FLATBED ANNIE AND SWEETIEPIE: LADY TRUCKERS

Pilot (Adventure). The lighthearted misadventures of Flatbed Annie, a feisty, rough-and-tumble lady trucker who can "push any rig" on the road, and her partner, Ginny "Sweetiepie" La Rosa, a naive, "wet behind the ears" beginner. The pilot episode, which teams the two lady truckers for the first time, depicts their efforts to save Jack La Rosa's (Ginny's husband) near-bankrupt trucking firm from C. W. Douglas, a persistent creditor who, because of unpaid bills, seeks to repossess Jack's rig.

REGULAR CAST

Flatbed Annie	Annie Potts
Ginny "Sweetiepie" La Rosa	Kim Darby
C. W. Douglas, the creditor	Harry Dean Stanton
Ginny's Uncle Wally	Arthur Godfrey
Jack La Rosa, Ginny's husband	Fred Willard

GUEST CAST

Mr. Munroe	Avery Schreiber
Deputy Miller	Billy Carter
Farmer	Rory Calhoun
Mr. Murray	Rance Howard
Georgina	Julie Mannix
Al	Don Pike

Annie and Ginny's truck: A 1978 blue and white Sturdy Built Superliner, license plate number 2T1 395.

Music: Don Peake.
Flatbed Annie & Sweetiepie Vocal: Marshall Chapman.
Producer: Frank von Zerneck.
Writer: Robie Robinson.
Director: Robert Greenwald.
Art Director: Jack Bissell.
Director of Photography: William K. Jurgensen.

FLATBED ANNIE AND SWEETIE-PIE: LADY TRUCKERS — 2 hours — CBS — February 10, 1979.

1519   FLATBUSH/ AVENUE J

Pilot (Comedy). The misadventures of newlyweds Stanley and Frannie Rosello, who live on Avenue J in Flatbush, Brooklyn, New York.

CAST

Stanley Rosello	Paul Sylvan
Frannie Rosello	Brooke Adams
Annie Yukaminelli, their friend	Jamie Donnelly
Wimpy Morzallo, their friend	Paul Jabara

Music: Paul Jabara.

Executive Producer: Martin Davidson, Stephen Verona.
Producer: Lee Miller.
Writer: Martin Davidson.
Director: Martin Davidson.

FLATBUSH/AVENUE J — 30 minutes — ABC — August 24, 1976.

1520   FLO'S PLACE

Pilot (Comedy). The story, set in Flo's Place, a small dockside hotel and restaurant, follows the misadventures of the staff and customers who inhabit the establishment.

CAST

Flo, the owner	Della Reese
Louie	Eric Laneuville
Beito	Art Metrano
Eddie	Johnny Silver
Abner	Danny Wells
Al Held	Michael Bell
Hoffman	Bernie Kopell

Producer: Stanley Ralph Ross.
Writer: Stanley Ralph Ross.
Director: Don Weis.

FLO'S PLACE — 30 minutes — NBC — August 9, 1976.

FLYING HIGH

The pilot film broadcast on CBS on August 28, 1978, for the series of the same title (see regular program section).

1521   FORCE FIVE

Pilot (Crime Drama). The story of a group of five ex-cons who become special police officers and use their unique skills to solve baffling crimes.

REGULAR CAST

Lt. Roy Kessler, the group leader	Gerald Gordon
James T. O'Neil, a con	Nicholas Pryor
Vic Bauer, a con	William Lucking
Lester White, a con	James Hampton
Arnie Kogan, a con	Roy Jenson
Norman Ellsworth, a con	David Spielberg

GUEST CAST

Cal Newkirk	Leif Erickson
Arthur Haberman	Normann Burton
Michael Dominick	Bradford Dillman
Frankie Hatcher	Victor Argo
Ginger	Belinda Balaski
Patty	Nancy Fuller

Music: James DiPasquale
Producer: Michael Gleason, David Levinson.
Writer: Michael Gleason, David Levinson.
Director: Walter Grauman.

FORCE FIVE — 90 minutes — CBS — March 28, 1975.

1522   4 FUNNY FAMILIES

Pilot (Comedy). The overall title for four unsold comedy pilots.

The Fess Parker Show. The story of Fess Hamilton, a widowed fa-

ther and his attempts to raise his three mischievous daughters.

CAST

Fess Hamilton	Fess Parker
Susie Hamilton, his daughter	Cynthia Eilbacher
Beth Hamilton, his daughter	Dawn Lyn
Holly Hamilton, his daughter	Michelle Stacy
Their housekeeper	Florence Lake
Fess's girlfriend	Linda Dano

Credits: Music: Frank DeVol; Executive Producer: Don Fedderson; Producer: George Tibbles; Writer: John McGreevey; Director: Bruce Bilson.

Dominick's Dream. The story revolves around Dominick and Anita Benete, a Manhattan couple who move from the city to suburban Los Angeles and their struggles to adjust to a new lifestyle.

CAST

Dominick Benete	Joseph Mascolo
Anita Benete	Rita Moreno
Marie Benete, their daughter	Toni Kalem
Mrs. Hendrickson, their neighbor	Marjorie Battles
Mr. Hendrickson, her husband	Burt Heyman
Their son	Dennis Kort

Credits: Music: Buzz Cohen; Executive Producer: William P. D'Angelo, Garry Marshall; Producer: Tony Marshall; Writer-Creator: Garry Marshall; Director: Garry Marshall.

Pete 'N' Tillie. The misadventures of a welfare worker (Tillie) who plagues her husband (Pete) by bringing her work home from the office.

CAST

Pete	Carmine Caridi
Tillie	Cloris Leachman
Their housekeeper	Mabel Albertson

Credits: Music: Michael Melvoin; Producer: Carl Kleinschmitt; Writer: Carl Kleinschmitt; Director: Jerry Belson.

Change At 125th Street. The story of a Harlem family's misadventures when their son John, a Harvard graduate, is hired by an all-white Wall Street bank.

CAST

John	Ron Glass
John's mother	Roxie Roker
John's sister	Chip Fields
John's uncle	Vernon Washington

Also: Terry Kiser, Frank Cover, Garrett Morris.

Credits: Producer: Ernest Kinoy; Writer: Ernest Kinoy; Director: Michael Schultz, Bob LaHendro.

4 FUNNY FAMILIES — 2 hours (30 minutes each segment) — CBS — March 28, 1974.

1523   THE FOUR OF US

Pilot (Comedy). The story of Julie Matthews, a widow, and her struggles to raise her three mischievous children.

CAST

Julie Matthews	Barbara Feldon
Chrissie Matthews, her daughter	Vicky Dawson
Caroline Matthews, her daughter	Kathy Jo Kelly
Andy Matthews, her son	Will McMillan
Annie Ray, Julie's friend	Heather MacRae
Mrs. Reilly, Julie's housekeeper	Sudie Bond
Marie, Julie's friend	K Callan
Walter, Julie's romantic interest	Laurence Keith
Estelle, Julie's friend	Marcia Jean Kurtz

Music: Morton Gould.
Executive Producer: Herbert Brodkin.
Producer: Robert Berger.
Writer: Reginald Rose.
Director: James Cellan Jones.

THE FOUR OF US — 30 minutes — ABC — July 18, 1977.

1524   THE 416th

Pilot (Comedy). The story, set in 1968 (during the height of the Vietnam War), follows the misadventures of Rick Michaels, a talent agent, Myron Kowalski, an accountant, Carmine Pompinece, a mechanic, and Billy Henderson, a college dropout. The four are Army reservists who are called up and assigned to combat training as part of the 416th Medical Detachment-Supply Distribution Team — the U.S. Army's smallest and most confused unit (composed of only six members with no knowledge of what the unit is supposed to do or how it is supposed to do it).

REGULAR CAST

Colonel Davis, the base commander	Raymond St. Jacques
Lt. Jackson MacCalvey, his assistant	John Larroquette
Rick Michaels	Richard Lewis
Carmine Pompinece	Richard Dimitri
Billy Henderson	Donald Petrie
Myron Kowalski	Bo Kaprall
Iris Michaels, Rick's mother	Joan Hotchkis

GUEST CAST

Phyllis Shankman	Louise Hoven
Heather Hanley	Susan Lanier

Music: Mike Post, Pete Carpenter.
Executive Producer: Rick Bernstein.
Producer: Peter H. Engel, Eric Cohen.
Writer: Eric Cohen.
Director: Buddy Tyne.
Art Director: Seymour Klate.
Director of Photography: Irving Lippman.
Set Decorator: Ernie Bishop.
Costumes: Bill Jobe.

THE 416th — 30 minutes — CBS — August 25, 1979.

1525   FRANKIE AND ANNETTE: THE SECOND TIME AROUND

Pilot (Comedy). The story reunites Annette Funicello and Frankie Avalon, the stars of a number of "Beach Party" feature films throughout the 1960s. The would-be series focuses on the experiences of Dolores (Dee Dee), now a sorority housemother at a campus near Malibu — where she and Frankie used to frolic some dozen years ago. Dee Dee and Frankie, now a singer, meet by accident — and Frankie wants to pick up where he left off with his teenage sweetheart.

REGULAR CAST

Dolores (Dee Dee)	Annette Funicello
Frankie	Frankie Avalon
Dean Burroughs, the head of the school	Don Porter
Tiki, one of Dee Dee's students	Helaine Lembeck

GUEST CAST

Sharkey	Herb Edelman
Nick	Taurean Blacque
Bradley	Doug Rowe

Executive Producer: Dick Clark.
Producer: Arthur Alsberg, Don Nelson.
Writer: Arthur Alsberg, Don Nelson.
Director: Bob LaHendro.

FRANKIE AND ANNETTE: THE SECOND TIME AROUND — 60 minutes — NBC — November 18, 1978.

1526   FREEMAN

Pilot (Comedy). The story, set in Connecticut, is about a ghost named Freeman who haunts the new occupants of the Colonial house he cherished when alive — and now refuses to vacate. The focal point of the program is the attempts of both the ghost and the family to adjust to each other.

CAST

Freeman, the ghost	Stu Gilliam
Dwight Wainwright, the father	Linden Chiles
Helen Wainwright, his wife	Beverly Sanders
Timmy Wainwright, their son	Jimmy Baio

Producer-Writer: Bernie Kukoff, Jeff Harris.
Director: Hal Cooper.

FREEMAN — 30 minutes — ABC — June 19, 1976.

1527   FRIENDS

Pilot (Comedy). The story of Teddy Serrano and Scott Rollins, a once-popular team of Rock singers who forsake the "road" and become staff songwriters for a Hollywood record company. The episode depicts the misadventures that occur as a result of their differing points of view (Teddy, a bachelor, longs for the glamour of performing and looks for ways to get himself and Scott back on stage; and Scott, who likes songwriting because it gives him more time to spend with his family).

REGULAR CAST

Teddy Serrano	Michael Tucci
Scott Rollins	Darrell Fetty
Susan Rollins, Scott's wife	Susan Buckner
Kevin Rollins, Scott's son	Stephen Mond
J. B. Henderson, the president of the record company	Brian Cutler
Leslie Frankel, the company secretary	Dori Brenner

GUEST CAST

Mike	George Wyner
Diane Miller	Rae Dawn Chong
Gordon Bass	Larry Cedar

Music Director: Gene Page.
Producer: Lorenzo Music, Steve Pritzker.
Writer: Lorenzo Music, Steve Pritzker.
Director: Hy Averback.
Art Director: Tho. E. Azzari.
Director of Photography: F. Budd Mautino.
Set Decorator: Robert G. Freer.

FRIENDS — 30 minutes — CBS — August 19, 1978.

FRIENDS AND LOVERS

See title "Bachelors 4" in the pilot film section.

1528   FROM CLEVELAND

Pilot (Comedy). The program, videotaped in Cleveland, Ohio, presents a satirical look at modern life through sketches and blackouts.

Starring: Bob Elliott, Ray Goulding.
Regulars: Catherine O'Hara, Andrea Martin, Joe Flaherty, Dave Thomas, Eugene Levy.
Producer: Rocco Urbisci.
Associate Producer: Ellen Rucker.
Writer: Rod Warren, Bob Elliott, Ray Goulding, Andrea Martin, Dave Thomas, Catherine O'Hara, Eugene Levy, Rocco Urbisci.
Director: Bob Bowker.
Art Director: Eldon Murray.

FROM CLEVELAND — 60 minutes — CBS — October 24, 1980.

1529   FROM SEA TO SHINING SEA

Pilot (Drama). One man's odyssey through Colonial America as seen through the experiences of John Freeborn, "an American Everyman," who is presented in various periods in our nation's history. In the pilot, Freeborn, a peddler in 1775, becomes involved in the fight for independence from British rule.

REGULAR CAST

John Freeborn	Robert Culp

GUEST CAST

George Washington	Fritz Weaver
Robertson	Richard Kiley
Sara	Sheila Sullivan
John Adams	Richard Venture
John Hancock	Phil Pleasants
Gannett	Will Hare
Krantz	Kenneth Tigar

FROM SEA TO SHINING SEA — 90 minutes — Syndicated 1974.

1530   FULL HOUSE

Pilot (Comedy). The misadventures that befall the three generations of one family living in the same house in Iowa. In the pilot, Frank attempts to cope with the announcement that his parents are divorcing.

CAST

Frank Campbell, the husband	Kenneth Mars
Pauline Campbell, his wife	Aneta Corsaut
Eloise Campbell, Frank's mother	Nora Marlowe
Henry Campbell, Frank's father	Liam Dunn
Willard Campbell, Frank's son	Basil Hoffman

Music: Harper McKay.
Executive Producer: Charles Fries.
Producer: Bill Foster.
Writer: Budd Grossman.
Director: Bill Foster.

FULL HOUSE — 30 minutes — NBC — August 2, 1976.

THE FUNNY SIDE

The pilot episode broadcast on NBC on October 29, 1971, for the series of the same title (see regular program section).

1531   THE FUNNY WORLD OF FRED AND BUNNI

Pilot (Variety). Animation coupled with live action comedy skits and musical numbers.

Host: Fred Travalena and the animated Bunni.
Regulars: Sandy Duncan, Vicki Lawrence, Pat Harrington, Jr.
Music: Jack Elliott, Allyn Ferguson.
Producer: Joseph Barbera.
Writer: John Aylesworth, Frank Peppiatt, Barry Adelman, Barry Silver, Pat Harrington, James Burr Johnson.
Director: Bill Davis.

THE FUNNY WORLD OF FRED AND BUNNI — 60 minutes — CBS — August 30, 1978.

1532   THE FURST FAMILY OF WASHINGTON

Pilot (Comedy). The story, set in Washington, D.C., follows the experiences of Oscar Furst, the owner of a barber shop that doubles as the local men's community center. Served as the basis for the *That's My Mama* series.

CAST

Oscar Furst	Godfrey Cambridge
Eloise "Mama" Furst, his mother	Thelma Merritt
Earl Jefferson, a friend	Theodore Wilson
King Osborne, a friend	Eddy C. Dyer
Low Lead, a friend	Dewayne Jessie
Junior, a friend	Eric Laneuville

Producer: Norman Campbell.
Writer: Stanley Ralph Ross.
Director: Norman Campbell.

THE FURST FAMILY OF WASH-INGTON — 30 minutes — ABC — September 11, 1973.

1533   THE FURTHER ADVENTURES OF WALLY BROWN

Pilot (Comedy). The misadventures of Wally Brown, a sensational track star for Stephen Foster High School whose mouth is as fast as his feet.

REGULAR CAST

Wally Brown	Clinton Derricks-Carroll
Douglas Burdett, his friend	Peter Scolari
Warren Burdett, Douglas' father	Ron Masak
May Burdett, Douglas' mother	Arlene Golonka
Arlene Burdett, Douglas' sister	Sally Hightower
Coach Fleischman	Marvin Braverman
Bernstein, Douglas' friend	Gilbert Gotfried

GUEST CAST

Automat chef (Bruno)	Richard Karron
Kline	Bobby Ellerbee
Also	Robert Wise

Music: Don Peake.
Executive Producer: Mark Rothman, Lowell Ganz.
Producer: John C. Chauly.
Associate Producer: Linda Solomon.
Writer: Barbara Mandell.
Director: Lowell Ganz.
Art Director: Sidney Litwick.

THE FURTHER ADVENTURES OF WALLY BROWN — 30 minutes — NBC — August 21, 1980.

FUTURE COP

The pilot film broadcast on ABC on May 1, 1976, for the series of the same title (see regular program section).

1534   THE FUZZ BROTHERS

Pilot (Comedy). The misadventures of brothers Francis and Luther Fuzz, two black detectives working out of Los Angeles. In the pilot, they seek to apprehend a master jewel thief.

REGULAR CAST

Francis Fuzz	Lou Gossett
Luther Fuzz	Felton Perry
Police Captain Lean	Jeff Corey

GUEST CAST

Flowers	Don Porter
Sonny	William Smith
Trina	Nira Barab
Andy	Mario Riccuzzo
Ben	Mitchell Ryan

Music: J. J. Johnson.
Producer: Joel D. Freeman, John D. F. Black.
Writer: John D. F. Black.
Director: Don Medford.

THE FUZZ BROTHERS — 60 minutes — ABC — March 5, 1973.

G

THE GEMINI MAN

The pilot film broadcast on NBC on May 10, 1976, for the series of the same title (see regular program section).

1535   GENESIS II

Pilot (Science Fiction). On February 14, 1979, in a secret underground N.A.S.A. lab in the Carlsbad Caverns in New Mexico, an experiment to discover a form of suspended animation to allow astronauts to travel further into space is conducted on Dylan Hunt, a scientist. Shortly after he is placed in the Zeon Pressure Chamber, an earthquake triggers an avalanche of rock, caused by a flaw in the rock strata, and buries the experimental chamber under tons of stone. One hundred and fifty years later, Dylan is found alive, perfectly suspended, by a group of explorers and learns from Lyra-a that it is the year A.D. 2133 and that the world, which was destroyed by a nuclear war, is just not revitalizing itself. In his first adventure in his new world, Dylan becomes involved in a power struggle between the Pax, a people of peace, and the Terrania, a ruthless race of human beings.

REGULAR CAST

Dylan Hunt	Alex Cord
Harper-Smythe, a Pax	Lynne Marta
Isiah, a Pax	Ted Cassidy
Astrid, a Pax	Linda Grant
Primus Isaac Kimbridge, a Pax leader	Percy Rodrigues

GUEST CAST

Lyra-a	Mariette Hartley
Primus Dominic	Majel Barrett
Brian	Tom Pace
Slan-U	Harry Raybould
Overseer	Leon Askin
Princess Lu Chun	Beulah Quo
Janos	Liam Dunn
Weh-r	Ed Ashley
Yuloff	Tito Vandis
Singh	Harvey Jason
General	Dennis Young

Music: Harry Sukman.

Producer: Gene Roddenberry.
Writer: Gene Roddenberry.
Director: John Llewellyn Moxey.
Art Director: Hilyard Brown.
Director of Photography: Gerald Finnerman.

GENESIS II — 90 minutes — ABC — March 23, 1973. See also "Planet Earth" in the pilot film section for the sequel episode.

GET CHRISTIE LOVE!

The pilot film broadcast on ABC on January 22, 1974, for the series of the same title (see regular program section).

1536   GETTING THERE

Pilot (Comedy). The story of Harry and Rose Miller, husband and wife partners in Harry and Rose's West-East Auto Delivery Firm who seldom agree on how to run their business. Episodes were to depict incidents in the lives of the people who agree to transport cars from California to the East Coast.

REGULAR CAST

Harry Miller	George S. Irving
Rose Miller	Brett Somers

GUEST CAST

Agatha*	Hermione Baddeley
Emily*	Imogene Coca
Grandma	Jane Connell
Mary	Cathryn Damon
Jim	Norman Fell
Jerome	Todd Susman
Ben	Dub Taylor
Lester	Tim Thomerson
Melanie	Diane Venora
Tricia	Kelly Mohre
Joey	Steven Mond
Julie	Kristi Jill Wood

Music: Jeff Barry.
Executive Producer: Lila Garrett.
Producer: John Whittle.
Writer: Lila Garrett, Sandy Krinski.
Director: John Astin.
Art Director: Stephen Berger.
Set Decorator: John Franco, Jr.
Creator: Lila Garrett, Sandy Krinski.

GETTING THERE — 30 minutes — CBS — February 12, 1980 (originally scheduled as an hour pilot that was to air on February 27, 1980, but was pushed forward to make room for an hour pilot called "Pottsville").

*Sequences were cut in the half-hour version — of the hour pilot — that was finally shown on television.

1537   GHOST OF A CHANCE

Pilot (Comedy). The program, set in New York City, follows the marital misadventures of Jenny and Wayne Clifford, a couple whose life is plagued by the ghost of Jenny's first husband, Tom Chance, who returns to haunt her and voice his objections to her remarriage.

CAST

Jenny Clifford	Shelley Long
Wayne Clifford, Jenny's husband	Barry Van Dyke
Tom Chance, the ghost	Steven Keats
Frances, Jenny's mother	Gretchen Wyler
Michael, Wayne's friend	Archie Hahn
Leslie, Jenny's friend	Rosalyn Kind
Minister (guest role)	John O'Leary

Music: Earle Hagen.
Executive Producer: Austin and Irma Kalish.
Producer: Gene Marcione.
Writer: Austin and Irma Kalish.
Director: Nick Havigna.
Art Director: Charles Hughes.

GHOST OF A CHANCE — 30 minutes — ABC — July 7, 1980.

GHOST STORY

The pilot film broadcast on NBC on March 17, 1972, for the series of the same title (see regular program section).

1538   G.I.'S

Pilot (Comedy). The program, set during World War II, follows the misadventures of a squad of American servicemen who serve as a "mop-up" troup during the Italian Campaign.

REGULAR CAST

Cpl. Peter Buchanan	Kenneth Gilman
Sgt. John Vitella	Jonathan Banks
Pvt. T. J. Witherspoon	Gregg Berger
Pvt. Leroy Lumpkin	Michael Binder
Pvt. Harry Freedman	Lorry Goldman
Pvt. Joseph Battaglia	Chick Vennera

GUEST CAST

Peasant Lady	Lillian Garrett-Bonner
British Soldier	Lew Horn
British Officer	Patrick Gorman

Music: Jack Elliott.
Producer: Bernard Rothman, Jack Wohl.
Writer: Jack Wohl, Bernard Rothman, Phil Hahn.
Director: Peter Bonerz.
Art Director: Frank T. Smith.
Director of Photography: Robert E. Collins.
Creator: Bernard Rothman, Jack Wohl, Phil Hahn.

G.I.'S — 30 minutes — CBS — July 29, 1980.

1539   GO WEST YOUNG GIRL

Pilot (Western Comedy). The story, set in the Old West, follows the misadventures of Netty Booth, a beautiful female newspaper reporter who turns things topsy-turvey to get her stories. In the pilot, the inexperienced Netty tries to get an interview with Billy the Kid.

REGULAR CAST

Netty Booth	Karen Valentine
Gilda Corin, her assistant	Sandra Will
Deputy Sheriff Shreeve	Stuart Whitman

GUEST CAST

Billy the Kid	Richard Jaeckel
Chato	Michael Bell
Reverend Crane	David Dukes
Captain Anson	Charles Frank
Griff	Richard Kelton
Payne	Griff Palmer

Music: Jerrold Immel.
Executive Producer: Harve Bennett, Harris Katleman.
Producer: George Yanok.
Writer: George Yanok.
Director: Alan J. Levi.

GO WEST YOUNG GIRL — 90 minutes — ABC — April 27, 1978.

GOING PLACES

See title "Triple Play '73" in the pilot film section.

1540   THE GOLDEN AGE OF TELEVISION

Pilot (Anthology). A projected series of kinescopes recalling the medium's golden age of live television programs (1950s). The pilot program features the first repeat telecast of "Requiem for a Heavyweight," first broadcast on CBS on *Playhouse 90* on October 11, 1956, and which tells the story of four people: Harlan "Mountain" McClintock, a proud, but punch-drunk fighter; Maish, his ruthless manager; Army, his trainer; and Grace Carney, the sympathetic woman who gives Harlan a job.

Requiem Credits:
Cast: Harlan McClintock: Jack Palance; Maish: Keenan Wynn; Army: Ed Wynn; Grace: Kim Hunter; Also: Maxie Rosenbloom, Max Baer, Sr., Stanley Adams.
Producer: Martin Manulis; *Associate Producer:* Julian Claman; *Writer:* Rod Serling; *Director:* Ralph Nelson.

Golden Age Credits:
Host: Jack Klugman.
Guests (Interview Segments): Jack Palance, Martin Manulis, Keenan Wynn.
Executive Producer: Sonny Fox.
Producer: David Eagle.

THE GOLDEN AGE OF TELEVISION — 90 minutes — PBS — August 22, 1980.

1541   GOOBER AND THE TRUCKERS' PARADISE

Pilot (Comedy). A spin-off from *The Andy Griffith Show,* in which the character of Goober Pyle, a garage mechanic, was first introduced. In the pilot, Goober moves to a small town outside of Atlanta where he and his sister Pearl open a truck-stop café. Their misadventures as they attempt to remain solvent are the basis of the story.

REGULAR CAST

Goober Pyle	George Lindsey
Pearl Pyle, his sister	Leigh French
Charlene, the waitress	Sandie Newton
Becky Pyle, Goober's niece	Audrey Landers
Toni Pyle, Goober's sister	Lindsay Bloom

GUEST CAST

Deputy Eagle Keyes	John Chappell
Bible Bill	Bill Medley
T-Bone	Brion James
Catfish	Bruce Fisher
Elwood Gunnite	Robert Towers
Troll	Mickey Jones
Bud	Ken Johnson

Theme: Ray Stevens.
Executive Producer: Rich Eustis.
Writer: Rich Eustis, George Lindsey, April Kelly.
Director: Rich Eustis, Bill Wyse.

GOOBER AND THE TRUCKERS' PARADISE — 30 minutes — CBS — May 17, 1978.

1542   GOOD AGAINST EVIL

Pilot (Thriller). The story of Father Kemschler, a Catholic priest who battles the powers of darkness. The pilot depicts his attempts to exorcise the evil from Jessica Gordon, a woman who has been chosen by a satanic cult to bear the Devil's child.

REGULAR CAST

Father Kemschler	Dan O'Herlihy
Father Weathley	John Harkins

GUEST CAST

Jessica Gordon	Elyssa Davalos
Andy Stuart	Dack Rambo
Mr. Rimmin	Richard Lynch
The Woman	Jenny O'Hara
Lt. Taggart	Sandy Ward
Sister Monica	Leila Goldoni
Irene	Peggy McCay
Linda Isley	Kim Cattrall

Music: Lalo Schifrin.
Producer: Lin Bolen, Ernest Frankel.
Writer: Jimmy Sangster.
Director: Paul Wendkos.
Art Director: Richard Haman.

GOOD AGAINST EVIL — 90 minutes — ABC — May 22, 1977.

THE GOOD LIFE

The pilot film broadcast on NBC on March 22, 1971, for the series of the same title (see regular program section).

1543   GOOD OL' BOYS

Pilot (Comedy). The story of Traveler and Cooter, two would-be Country music stars marking time as vending machine company maintenance men.

CAST

Traveler	Jerry Reed
Cooter	Lance Caudell
Isaac, their employer	Mel Stewart
Mary, Traveler's girlfriend	Linda Thompson
Forklift, a co-worker	Dennis Harrison

Music: Jack Elliott, Allyn Ferguson.
Theme Vocal: Jerry Reed.
Executive Producer: Perry Lefferty.
Producer: William Ferguson, Ted Bergman.
Director: Harry Falk.

GOOD OL' BOYS — 30 minutes — NBC — June 7, 1979.

1544   GOOD PENNY

Pilot (Comedy). The misadventures of Penny, an emotionally disturbed woman who joins an outlandish therapy group.

CAST

Penny	Renee Taylor
Al	Scott Brady
Pauline	Gloria LeRoy
Jerry	Carmine Caridi
Dr. Frostman	Roger Bowen

Producer: Joseph Bologna, Richard Harwood.
Writer: Renee Taylor, Joseph Bologna.

GOOD PENNY — 30 minutes — NBC — September 1, 1977.

1545   GOSSIP

Pilot (Comedy). The misadventures of the editorial staff of the *National Gossip,* a Hollywood-based scandal sheet.

CAST

Office Secretary Goldie	Judy Landers
Milton, a reporter	Jeff Altman
April James, a reporter	Sarah Daly
Mac, a reporter	Charles Levin
Leech, the bookkeeper	Raymond Singer
Ed Stone, the editor	Thomas Hill
Luanda Neester, the society reporter	Fern Fitzgerald

Music: Art Twain.
Executive Producer: Roger Gimbel.
Producer: Mort Lachman.
Co-Producer: Michael Shamberg.
Writer: Bernie Kukoff, Jeff Harris.
Director: Bernie Kukoff, Jeff Harris.

GOSSIP — 30 minutes — NBC — June 10, 1979.

1546   GOSSIP

Pilot (Comedy). The less than believable antics of the staff of the *National Gossip,* a national scandal sheet.

CAST

Mr. Dempster, the editor	John Hillerman
Mrs. Gallup, the secretary	Dena Dietrich
Jeb, a reporter	Charles Levin
Mittie, a reporter	Mary Catherine Wright
Flash, the photographer	Jeff Altman
Tip, the psychic predictor	Robbie Rist

Music: Art Twain.
Executive Producer: Roger Gimbel, Tony Comberse.
Producer: Michael Shamberg, Jerry McPhie.
Director: Peter Baldwin.

GOSSIP — 30 minutes — NBC — July 10, 1979.

1547   GRANDPA MAX

Pilot (Comedy). A story of the generation gap between middle age and old age as seen through the bickering relationship of "Grandpa" Max Sherman, a crusty, caustic Jewish widower, and Paul Sherman, his overly protective son, who treats his father, who considers himself young at heart, like an old man.

CAST

Grandpa Max Sherman	Larry Best
Paul Sherman, his son	Michael Lerner
Liz Sherman, Paul's wife	Suzanne Astor
Michael Sherman, Paul's son	Brad Savage
Louis Yates, Max's friend	Shimen Ruskin
Mr. Unger (guest role)	Dick Van Patten
Betty (guest role)	Susan Alpern

Producer: Aaron Ruben, John Rich.
Writer: Aaron Ruben.
Director: John Rich.
Art Director: Ed Stephenson.

GRANDPA MAX — 30 minutes — CBS — March 28, 1975.

1548   GREAT DAY

Pilot (Comedy). The misadventures of a group of skid-row derelicts living at an inner-city mission in Los Angeles.

CAST

Peavey	Al Molinaro
Boomer	Guy Marks
Doc	Dub Taylor
Billy	Billy Barty
Moose	Josip Elic
Jabbo	Spo-Dee-Odee

Producer: Aaron Ruben.
Director: Peter Baldwin.

GREAT DAY — 30 minutes — ABC — May 23, 1977.

THE GREATEST GIFT

The pilot film broadcast on NBC on November 4, 1974, for the series *The Family Holvak* (see regular program section).

1549   GUESS WHO'S COMING TO DINNER?

Pilot (Comedy). A story of an interracial marriage. In the pilot, the newlyweds, Joanna Prentiss (white) and her husband John (black), face the prospect of having their respective families meet for the first time.

REGULAR CAST

Joanna Prentiss	Leslie Charleson
John Prentiss	Bill Overton
Christine Drayton, Joanna's mother	Eleanor Parker
Matt Drayton, Christine's father	Richard Dysart
Ralph Prentiss, John's father	Lee Weaver
Sarah Prentiss, John's mother	Madge Sinclair

GUEST CAST

Tillie	Rosetta Le Noir
Joe Delaney	William Calloway
Orville Peacock	Joseph R. Sicari

Producer: Stanley Cramer.
Writer: Bill Idelson.
Director: Stanley Cramer.

GUESS WHO'S COMING TO DINNER? — 30 minutes — ABC — May 28, 1975.

1550 THE GUN AND THE PULPIT

Pilot (Western). The story, set in the Old West, depicts the exploits of Ernie Parsons, a gunfighter who masquerades as a preacher and fights for right in both guises.

REGULAR CAST

Ernie Parsons	Marjoe Gortner

GUEST CAST

Ross	David Huddleston
Billy One-eye	Slim Pickens
Sally	Pamela Sue Martin
Sadie	Estelle Parsons
Adam	Karl Swenson
Tom	Robert Phillips

Music: George Tipton.
Executive Producer: Paul Junger Witt.
Producer: Paul Maslansky.
Writer: William Bowers.
Director: Daniel Petrie.

THE GUN AND THE PULPIT — 90 minutes — ABC — April 3, 1974.

1551 THE GYPSY WARRIORS

Pilot (Adventure). The story, set during World War II, follows the exploits of Shelly Alhern and Ted Brinkerhoff, U.S. Army captains who undertake dangerous assignments behind enemy lines. Their cover: posing as Gypsies with a man named Ganault, his daughter Lela, and his son Androck. In the pilot, Alhern and Brinkerhoff seek to retrieve a deadly toxin, which is capable of killing millions of people, from French scientists.

REGULAR CAST

Capt. Shelly Alhern	James Whitmore, Jr.
Capt. Ted Brinkerhoff	Tom Selleck
Ganault, the Gypsy father	Joseph Ruskin
Lela, Ganault's daughter	Lina Raymond
Androck, Ganault's son	Michael Lane

GUEST CAST

Bruno Schlagel	Albert Paulsen
Schulman	Kenneth Tiger
Ramon Pierre Cammus	William Wheatley
Henry Deseau	Hubert Noel
Lady Britt Austin-Forbes	Kathryn Leigh Scott

Executive Producer: Stephen J. Cannell.
Producer: Alex Beaton.
Writer: Stephen J. Cannell, Philip DeGuere.
Director: Lou Antonio.
Art Director: John D. Jeffries.
Director of Photography: Enzo A. Martinelli.
Set Decorator: Robert Freer.

THE GYPSY WARRIORS — 60 minutes — CBS — May 12, 1978.

1552 HANDLE WITH CARE

Pilot (Comedy). The story, set during the Korean War, follows the experiences of Liz Baker and Jackie Morse, two beautiful Army nurses, part of an all-female M*A*S*H unit assigned to the war front.

CAST

Liz Baker, a nurse	Marlyn Mason
Jackie Morse, a nurse	Didi Conn
Major Hinkley, a nurse	Mary Jo Catlett
Shirley "Scoop" Nichols, a nurse	Betsy Slade
Turk, a nurse	Jeannie Wilson
Col. Marvin Richardson	Brian Dennehy
Corporal Carp	Bob Lussier

Producer: Lew Gallo.
Writer: Woody Kling, Dawn Aldredge, Marion Freeman, Jim Parker.
Director: Alan Rafkin.

HANDLE WITH CARE — 30 minutes — CBS — May 9, 1977. Originally titled "Nurses."

HAPPY DAYS

The pilot film broadcast on ABC on February 25, 1972 (as a segment of *Love, American Style*) for the series of the same title (see regular program section).

1553 HARRY AND MAGGIE

Pilot (Comedy). A story of clashing life-styles as seen through the bickering relationship between Harry Kellogg, a grumpy Iowa widower, and Maggie Sturdivant, his aggressive, flamboyant and sophisticated sister-in-law, who lives with him and takes charge of his life. The episode follows Harry's attempts to arrange a romance for Maggie and marry her out of his life.

CAST

Harry Kellogg	Don Knotts
Maggie Sturdivant	Eve Arden
Clovis Kellogg, Harry's daughter	Kathy Davis
Arlo Wilson, Harry's friend	Tom Poston
Thelma	Lucille Benson
Max Lovechild	Eddie Quillan

Producer: James Parker, Arnold Margolin.
Writer: James Parker, Arnold Margolin.
Director: Jay Sandrich.
Art Director: Perry Ferguson.

HARRY AND MAGGIE — 30 minutes — CBS — April 25, 1975.

HARRY O

The first pilot film broadcast on ABC on March 11, 1973, for the series of the same title (see regular program section).

HART TO HART

The pilot film aired on ABC on August 25, 1979, for the series of the same title (see regular program section).

THE HARVEY KORMAN SHOW

The pilot episode (videotape) aired on ABC on May 19, 1977, for the series of the same title (see regular program section).

1554 HAVING BABIES I

Pilot (Drama). The story interweaves the personal dramas of three couples and an expectant mother who are preparing for childbirth through the Lamaze method, a technique for natural delivery. The first of three pilot films that eventually led to the *Julie Farr, M.D.* series. See also "Having Babies II" and "Having Babies III" in the pilot film section.

CAST

Allie Duggan	Adrienne Barbeau
Sally McNamara	Jessica Walter
George McNamara	Ronny Cox
Laura Gorman	Linda Purl
Frank Gorman	Desi Arnaz, Jr.
Grace Fontrelli	Vicki Lawrence
Beth Pertano	Karen Valentine
Mickey Pertano	Greg Mullavey
Max Duggan	Richard Masur
Ralph Bancini	Harry Guardino
Al Schneider	Abe Vigoda

Music: Earle Hagen.
Theme: "Paper Bridges" by Al Fasha and Joel Hirschhorn.
Theme Vocal: Maureen McGovern.
Executive Producer: Gerald I. Isenberg, Gerald Abrams.
Producer: Lew Gallo.
Writer: Peggy Elliott.
Director: Robert Day.

HAVING BABIES I — 2 hours — ABC — October 17, 1976. Original title: "Giving Birth."

1555 HAVING BABIES II

Pilot (Drama). A sequel to "Having Babies I" and the second pilot film that led to the *Julie Farr, M.D.* series. The story interweaves the personal dramas of three expectant couples, a teenager in love, and a doctor (Julie Farr) torn between her career and a romantic involvement. See also "Having Babies I" and "Having Babies III" in the pilot film section.

CAST

Dr. Julie Farr	Susan Sullivan
Aaron Canfield	Tony Bill
Trish Canfield	Paula Prentiss
Arthur McGee	Cliff Gorman
Sally McGee	Carol Lynley
Martha Cooper	Lee Meriwether
Jenny Cooper	Tracy Marshak
Jeff Kramer	Nicholas Pryor
Lou Plotkin	Wayne Rogers
Paula Plotkin	Cassie Yates
Danny McGee	Robbie Rist
Chris	Michael LeClair

Music: Fred Karlin.
Executive Producer: Gerald W. Abrams.
Producer: Richard Briggs.
Writer: Elizabeth Clark.
Director: Richard Michaels.
Art Director: William M. Hiney.
Director of Photography: Michael Joyce.

HAVING BABIES II — 2 hours — ABC — October 28, 1977.

1556 HAVING BABIES III

Pilot (Drama). The third of three pilot films that fostered the *Julie Farr, M.D.* series (see also "Having Babies I" and "Having Babies II" in the pilot film section). The story chronicles a work day in the life of Julie Farr, a dedicated obstetrician who is often embroiled in the personal lives of her patients.

REGULAR CAST

Dr. Julie Farr	Susan Sullivan
Dr. Blake Simmons	Mitchell Ryan
Dr. Ron Daniels	Dennis Howard
Kelly Williams, Julie's receptionist	Beverly Todd

GUEST CAST

Leslie Wexler	Patty Duke Astin
Dawn Roberts	Kathleen Beller
Gloria Miles	Rue McClanahan
Jim Wexler	Richard Michaels
Marnie Bridges	Jamie Smith Jackson
Russ Bridges	Michael Lembeck
Chuck	Phil Foster

Music: Lee Holdridge.
Theme: "There Will Be Love" by Alan and Marilyn Bergman.
Executive Producer: Gerald W. Abrams.
Producer: B. W. Sandefur, James Heinz.
Writer: Pamela Chais.
Director: Jackie Cooper.

HAVING BABIES III — 2 hours — ABC — March 3, 1978.

HAWKINS
ON MURDER

The pilot film broadcast on CBS on March 13, 1973, for the series *Hawkins* (see regular program section).

1557   HAZARD'S
PEOPLE

Pilot (Crime Drama). The story of John Hazard, a renowned criminal attorney whose style and flair, as well as his inherent sense of larceny in the pursuit of justice, sets him apart from his peers in the legal profession. In the pilot, Hazard and his three associates seek to help Dr. Carl DeLacy, a noted surgeon who is accused of murdering his mistress.

REGULAR CAST

John Hazard	John Houseman
Michael Crowder, his associate	John Elerick
Trish Corelli, his associate	Jesse Welles
Ernest Clay, his associate	Roger Hill
Sylvia Freed, the office secretary	Doreen Lang
Robert F. Powell, the D.A.	Stefan Gierasch

GUEST CAST

Dr. Carl DeLacy	Michael Tolan
Mrs. DeLacy	Hope Lange
Sam Colby	Cliff Emmich
Howard Frederickson	Richard Herd
Court Clerk	R. A. Sirianni
Deputy D.A.	Eric Server
David Stock	James Whitmore, Jr.

Music: John Cacavas.
Executive Producer: Jo Swerling, Jr.
Producer: Roy Huggins.
Writer: Heywood Gould, Roy Huggins, Jo Swerling, Jr.
Director: Jeannot Szwarc.
Art Director: Jack Chilberg.
Director of Photography: Charles Correll.
Set Decorator: Rick Goddard.

HAZARD'S PEOPLE — 60 minutes — CBS — April 9, 1976.

1558   THE HEALERS

Pilot (Drama). The story of Dr. Robert Kier, the director of the Institute for Medical Research in California. The pilot episode depicts several problems that are facing the institute: a lack of funds, a threat of rebellion by members of the research staff, and a doctor who is using an untested drug without permission. Proposed series title: *Crisis!*

REGULAR CAST

Dr. Robert Kier	John Forsythe
Joe Tate, the hospital's financial director	Pat Harrington
Claire, a research doctor	Kate Woodville
Laura Kier, Robert's ex-wife	Beverly Garland
Nikki Kier, Robert's daughter	Shelly Juttner
Vince Kier, Robert's son	Christian Jettner
Barbara, Robert's secretary	Ellen Weston

GUEST CAST

Ann Kilmer	Season Hubley
Dr. Ernest Wilson	John McIntire
Al Scanlon	Anthony Zerbe
Dr. Anton Balinowski	Michael C. Gwynne
Kennedy Brown	Lance Kerwin
Mr. Brown	Bill McKinney
Mrs. Brown	Jay W. McIntosh
Mr. Addison	Liam Dunn

Music: David Shire.
Executive Producer: Jerry Thorpe.
Producer: John Furia, Jr.
Writer: John Furia, Jr., Howard Dimsdale.
Director: Tom Gries.
Art Director: Walter Scott Herndon.
Director of Photography: Jack Woolf.

THE HEALERS — 90 minutes — NBC — May 22, 1974.

1559   HEAT
OF ANGER

Pilot (Crime Drama). The story of Jessica Fitzgerald, a prominent Los Angeles attorney. In the pilot, Jessica defends Frank Galvin, a building contractor who is accused of pushing an iron worker off a girder 21 stories up. Potential series title: *Fitzgerald and Pride*.

REGULAR CAST

Jessica Fitzgerald	Susan Hayward
Gus Pride, her associate	James Stacy

GUEST CAST

Frank Galvin	Lee J. Cobb
Stella Galvin	Bettye Ackerman
Chris Galvin	Jennifer Penny
Vincent Kagel	Fritz Weaver
Jean Carson	Tyne Daly
Obie	Mills Watson
Fran	Lynnette Mettey
Ray Carson	Ray Sims
Police Sergeant	Ron Masak

Music: None credited due to a musician's strike.
Executive Producer: Dick Berg.
Producer: Ron Roth.
Writer: Fay Kanin.
Director: Don Taylor.
Art Director: Lawrence Paull.
Director of Photography: Robert Moreno.

HEAT OF ANGER — 90 minutes — CBS — March 3, 1972.

1560   HEAVEN
ON EARTH

Pilot (Comedy). The story of Roxy and Karen, two beautiful girls who are allowed to return to their earthly status when bungling celestial powers caused a fatal car accident that claimed their lives. The episode focuses on their efforts to repay the kindness by performing good deeds.

CAST

Roxy	Carol Wayne
Karen	Donna Ponterotto
Sebastian Parnell, the celestial messenger	William Daniels

Music: Stephen Cohn.
Executive Producer: Peter Meyerson.
Producer: Richard Caffey.
Director: Lou Antonio.

HEAVEN ON EARTH — 30 minutes — NBC — June 28, 1979.

1561   HECK'S ANGELS

Pilot (Comedy). The story, set in France in 1917, follows the misadventures of Colonel Gregory Heck and his Aero Squadron 35, a group of inferior aviators who battle the Huns during World War I.

CAST

Col. Gregory Heck	William Windom
Lt. David Webb	Joe Barrett
Lt. Billy Bowling	Christopher Allport
Lt. George MacIntosh, a woman who is masquerading as a male pilot to avenge her brother's death	Jillian Kesner
Odette, the German spy	Susan Silo
Pierre Ritz, the flying officer/cook	Henry Polic II
Lt. Eddy Almont	Chip Zien
Ludwig von Stratter, the squadron's prisoner of war	Arnold Soboloff

Music: Jack Elliott, Allyn Ferguson.
Theme: "Heck's Angels March" by Frank Peppiatt and John Aylesworth.
Executive Producer: Frank Peppiatt, John Aylesworth.
Producer: Lew Gallo.
Writer: Frank Peppiatt, John Aylesworth, Jay Burton.
Director: Richard Kinon.
Art Director: Jack Stewart.

HECK'S ANGELS — 30 minutes — CBS — August 31, 1976.

1562   THE HEE HAW
HONEYS

Pilot (Comedy). The misadventures of Chrissy, Lee Anne and Toby, three former bit regulars from the *Hee Haw* television series, who are struggling to achieve success as a singing trio. "The Hee Haw Honeys" travel about the country in a motor home and hope to one day become important regulars on *Hee Haw*.

CAST

Chrissy	Kathie Lee Johnson
Toby	Catherine Hickland
Lee Anne	Muffy Durham
Kenny, their motor home driver	Kenny Price

Music: Charlie McCoy.
Executive Producer: Sam Louvello.
Producer: Barry Adelman.
Director: Ron Kantor.

THE HEE HAW HONEYS — 30 minutes — Syndicated 1978. Served as the basis for the series, *The Hee Haw Honeys*.

1563   HELLZAPOPPIN

Pilot (Variety). An unsold variety revue based on Olsen and Johnson's 1938 Broadway hit *Hellzapoppin* (also a 1941 movie). The program blends vaudeville and burlesque: zany one-liners, sight gags, walk-ons and variety acts.

Starring: Jack Cassidy, Ronnie Schell.
Guests: Lynn Redgrave, The Jackson Five, Rex Reed, Bob Williams and his dog Louie, The Volantes (unicyclists).
Cameos: Ruth Buzzi, Peter Lupus, Lyle Waggoner.
Orchestra: Nick Perito.
Executive Producer: Alexander H. Cohen.
Producer: Carolyn Raskin.
Writer: Sheldon Keller, Kenny Solms, Gail Parent, Howard Albrecht, Sol Weinstein, Gene Perrett, John Rappaport, Dan Shapiro, Mark Richards.
Director: Clark Jones.

HELLZAPOPPIN — 60 minutes — ABC — March 1, 1972.

1564   HERNANDEZ:
HOUSTON P.D.

Pilot (Crime Drama). The exploits of a Chicago police detective with the Houston Police Department.

REGULAR CAST

Detective Hernandez	Henry Darrow
Sergeant Lukas	Desmond Dhooge

GUEST CAST

Jackman	Dana Elcar
Roper	Ronny Cox
Penner	G. D. Spradlin
Mamacita	Amapola del Vando

HERNANDEZ: HOUSTON P.D. — 60 minutes — NBC — January 16, 1973.

1565   HIGH RISK

Pilot (Adventure). The exploits of a group of six ex-circus performers who become expert thieves, but use their unique skills to aid the U.S. government. The pilot depicts their attempts to steal a national treasure, the Mask of the Sun, to win the freedom of four American medical missionaries sentenced to death in a Latin American country.

REGULAR CAST

Sebastian	Victor Buono
Sandra	JoAnna Cameron
Guthrie	Joseph Sirola
Daisy	Ronne Troup
Walker-T	Don Stroud
Erik	Wolf Roth

GUEST CAST

Ambassador Henriques	Rene Enriquez
Quincey	John Fink
Aide	George Skaff
Butler	William Beckley

Music: Billy Goldenberg.

Executive Producer: Paul Junger Witt.
Producer: Robert E. Relyea.
Writer: Robert Carrington.
Director: Sam O'Steen.

HIGH RISK — 90 minutes — ABC — May 15, 1976.

1566 HITCHED

Pilot (Western Comedy-Drama). The story of Jenny and Clare Bridgeman, newlyweds struggling to begin a new life in the Old West. A sequel to the pilot film "Lock, Stock, and Barrel."

REGULAR CAST

Jenny Bridgeman	Sally Field
Clare Bridgeman	Tim Matheson

GUEST CAST

Barnstable	Henry Jones
Banjo Riley	Neville Brand
Cruett	John Anderson
Dawson Brothers	Slim Pickens
Henry	John Fielder
Hunter	John McLiam

Music: Pat Williams.
Producer: Richard Alan Simmons.
Writer: Richard Alan Simmons.
Director: Boris Sagal.
Director of Photography: Gerald Perry Finnerman.

HITCHED — 90 minutes — NBC — March 31, 1973.

1567 HOLLYWOOD HIGH

Pilot (Comedy). The misadventures of Phoebe and Dawn, two Hollywood High School students. The pilot episode depicts the problems that befall Phoebe and Dawn when they reluctantly accept a dance invitation from the class undesirables, then scheme to get out of the dates.

CAST

Phoebe	Annie Potts
Dawn	Kim Lankford
Wheeler, a student	Chris Pina
Bill, a student	Rory Stevens
Icky, the undesirable	John Megna
Dr. Bad, the other undesirable	Sam Kwasman

Executive Producer: Gerald I. Isenberg.
Producer: Gerald W. Abrams.
Director: Peter Baldwin.

HOLLYWOOD HIGH — 30 minutes — NBC — July 21, 1977.

1568 HOLLYWOOD HIGH

Pilot (Comedy). The misadventures of Paula Lindell, a Hollywood High School student studying to become a journalist. The pilot episode depicts the problems that arise when Paula and Eugene, a male student, assigned to cover an out-of-town story, are forced to spend one night together in a motel room.

CAST

Paula Lindell	Annie Potts
Eugene Langley	Darren O'Connor
Allison, a student	Roberta Wallach
Judith, a student	Beverly Saunders
Janet, a student	Janet Wood
Stu, a student	John Guerrasio
Blaine, a student	Dick O'Neill

Executive Producer: Gerald I. Isenberg, Gerald W. Abrams.
Producer: Elias Davis, David Pollock.
Director: Burt Brinkerhoff.

HOLLYWOOD HIGH — 30 minutes — NBC — July 21, 1977 (aired back-to-back with the previous title).

1569 HOME COOKIN'

Pilot (Comedy). The misadventures of Adelle and Ernie, a married couple who run a truck stop diner. The pilot episode centers on the problems that occur when Ernie hires Dinette, a pretty waitress who sparks Adelle's jealous streak.

CAST

Adelle	Fannie Flagg
Ernie	Wynn Irwin
Dinette, the waitress	Nancy Fox
Jammer, a trucker	Burton Gilliam
Bevo, a diner customer	Frank McRay
Trooper, a diner customer	Walker Edmiston
Shorty, a diner customer	Bill McLean

Executive Producer: Lawrence Gordon.
Producer: Don Van Atta.
Writer: Tom Rickman.
Director: Herb Kenwith.

HOME COOKIN' — 30 minutes — ABC — July 11, 1975.

1570 THE HOME FRONT

Pilot (Drama). The story, set in Shelter Cove, Massachusetts, during World War II, follows the lives of John Travis, a shipyard owner, and his wife, Enid, and the problems they and their friends and family face during wartime.

REGULAR CAST

Enid Travis	Jean Simmons
John Travis	Craig Stevens
Kate Travis, their daughter	Martina Deignan
Christopher Travis, their son	Dane Witherspoon
Cynthia Travis, their daughter	Maylo McCaslin
Jack Travis, their son	Nicholas Hammond
Leona Spinelli, their neighbor	Eunice Christopher
Angela Spinelli, her daughter	Delta Burke
Rocco Spinelli, her son	Joe Penny
The Travis housekeeper	Janice Carroll
Helen Maddox, John's secretary	Christine DeLisle

GUEST CAST

Birch	Ivor Francis
Bradley Parker	John Furey
Stebbins	Steve Marlo
Johnson	Mike Stroka

Music: Pete Rugolo.
Executive Producer: Charles Fries, Malcolm Stuart.
Supervising Producer: Rita Lakin.
Producer: Buck Houghton.
Writer: Rita Lakin.
Director: Harry Harris.
Art Director: Philip Barber.
Director of Photography: Richard L. Rawlins.

THE HOME FRONT — 60 minutes — CBS — October 9, 1980.

THE HOMECOMING: A CHRISTMAS STORY

The pilot film broadcast on CBS on December 19, 1971, for the series *The Waltons* (see regular program section).

1571 HONEST AL'S A-OK USED CAR AND TRAILER RENTAL TIGERS

Pilot (Comedy). The misadventures of "Honest" Al, a used car salesman who undertakes sponsorship of the Tigers, a youth league football team.

CAST

"Honest" Al	Herb Edelman
Franklin ("Hot Wheels"), his mechanic	Danny Bonaduce
Ethel, Franklin's aunt	Zoey Wilson
Moody, a Tiger	Kyra Stempel
Doc, a Tiger	Marc Jason
Chicago, a Tiger	J. R. Miller

Al's dog: Ugly.

Music: Solen/Weber.
Executive Producer: Daniel Wilson.
Producer: Frank Sears.
Director: Jeff Bleckner.

HONEST AL'S A-OK USED CAR AND TRAILER RENTAL TIGERS — 30 minutes — Syndicated January 1978.

1572 HONEYMOON SUITE

Pilot (Anthology). Comedy vignettes that depict brief incidents in the lives of couples who check into Room 300 of the plush Honeymoon Suite of the Beverly Hills Hotel.

REGULAR CAST

Maggie, the maid	Rose Marie
Charlie, the bellboy (first pilot)	Morey Amsterdam
Charlie (second pilot)	Henry Gibson
Duncan, the hotel manager	Richard Deacon

GUEST CAST (FIRST PILOT)

Kim	Dianne Hill
Jeff	Brad David
Marge	Gloria De Haven
Weaver	Alan Oppenheimer
Harry	Arthur O'Connell
Eleanor	Martha Scott
Jean	June Lockhart
Cathy	Anne Lockhart

GUEST CAST (SECOND PILOT)

Brenda	Elaine Giftos
Phyllis	Tami Shaw
Bob	Ronnie Schell
Darren	Bruce Kimmel

Also: Gavin MacLeod, Mitzi McCall, Roger Perry, Jo Anne Worley.
Music: Jack Elliott, Allyn Ferguson.
Producer: Aaron Spelling.
Director: Jack Regas.

HONEYMOON SUITE — 90 minutes — ABC. First pilot: July 26, 1972; second pilot: January 30, 1973.

1573 HONKY TONK

Pilot (Western). The lighthearted misadventures of Candy Johnson, a sweet-talking con man, and Lucy Cotton, a beautiful con gal, as they travel throughout the boom towns of the Old West seeking rich prey.

REGULAR CAST

Candy Johnson	Richard Crenna
Lucy Cotton	Margot Kidder

GUEST CAST

Gold Dust	Stella Stevens
Roper	Geoffrey Lewis
Judge Cotton	Will Geer
Slade	Gregory Sierra
Brazos	John Dehner

Music: Jerry Fielding.
Executive Producer: Douglas Heyes.
Producer: Hugh Benson.
Writer: Douglas Heyes.
Director: Don Taylor.
Director of Photography: Joseph Biroc.

HONKY TONK — 90 minutes — NBC — April 1, 1974.

1574 THE HOUSE WITHOUT A CHRISTMAS TREE

Pilot (Drama). The first of four pilot films about the Mills, a family living in Nebraska during the 1940s (see also "Addie and the King of Hearts," "The Easter Promise," and "The Thanksgiving Treasure" in the pilot film section). The story of Addie Mills, a precocious tomboy; her stern, widowed father, James; and her compassionate grandmother. The episode depicts Addie's attempts to convince her unsentimental father that, with Christmas Day approaching, their house needs a Christmas tree.

REGULAR CAST

James Mills	Jason Robards
Addie Mills	Lisa Lucas
Grandmother	Mildred Natwick

GUEST CAST

Carla Mae	Alexia Kenin
Miss Thompson	Kathryn Walker
Billy Wild	Brady MacNamara
Mrs. Cott	Baya Kenin Ryan
Gloria Cott	Gail Dusome

Producer: Alan Shayne.

Writer: Eleanor Perry.
Director: Paul Bogart.

THE HOUSE WITHOUT A CHRISTMAS TREE—90 minutes —CBS—December 3, 1972.

1575   HOW TO SUCCEED IN BUSINESS WITHOUT REALLY TRYING

Pilot (Comedy). The story of J. Pierpont Finch, an ambitious window washer who is determined to make it in the business world—even if it means starting at the bottom.

CAST

J. Pierpont Finch	Alan Bursky
Rosemary	Susan Blanchard
Smitty	Marcella Lowery
Bratt	Larry Haines
J. B. Biggley	Max Showalter
Frump	Jim Jansen
Miss Jones	Polly Rowles
Twimble	Sam Smith
Peterson	Alan Resin

Producer: Abe Burrows.
Writer: Abe Burrows.
Director: Burt Brinkerhoff.

HOW TO SUCCEED IN BUSINESS WITHOUT REALLY TRYING —30 minutes—ABC—June 27, 1975.

1576   HOWDY

Pilot (Variety). Music and comedy acts set against the background of fictional Mildew, Arkansas.

Host: Ferlin Husky.
Regulars: Chanin Hale, Sidney Blackmer, Bob Hastings, Lyle Talbot, Gene Sheldon, William Sylvester.
Guests: Barbara Eden, Glenn Ford, Nanette Fabray, Terry Thomas, Eddie Albert, Eva Gabor, Jimmy Durante, Henry Fonda, Pat Buttram, Jack Jones.
Orchestra: Alan Copeland.
Producer: Jay Sommers.
Writer: Jay Sommers, Dick Chevillat.
Director: Seymour Berns.

HOWDY—60 minutes—ABC— September 26, 1970.

1577 HUMAN FEELINGS

Pilot (Comedy). Angry at the crime, divorce rate and general disgustingness of Las Vegas, God decides to give the city one chance to redeem itself before She destroys it. Myles Gordon, an angel, is dispatched to find six righteous people within one week. The story depicts Myles's efforts to find the six people to appease God and save the city.

REGULAR CAST

God	Nancy Walker
Angel Myles Gordon	Billy Crystal
Verna Gold, the human who befriends Myles	Pamela Sue Martin
Lester, God's secretary	John Fiedler
Angel Garcia	Richard Dimitri

GUEST CAST

Gloria	Donna Pescow
Robin Dennis	Jack Carter
Phil	Squire Fridell
Johnny Turner	Armand Assante
Sinbad Hotel Waiter	Pat Morita
Cab Driver	Art Metrano
Detective	James Whitmore, Jr.

Music: John Cacavas.
Executive Producer: Charles Fries, Malcolm Stuart.
Producer: Herbert Hirschmann.
Writer: Henry Bloomstein.
Director: Ernest Pintoff.
Art Director: Bill Ross.

HUMAN FEELINGS—90 minutes—NBC—October 16, 1978. Repeated as a two-hour pilot (30 minutes of new material were added) on NBC on April 18, 1980 (an unscheduled airing).

1578   HUNTER

Pilot (Adventure). The exploits of Hunter, a chameleonic agent for a U.S. government security agency. In the pilot, Hunter seeks to obtain a deadly germ virus that is capable of destroying half of America, from a criminal.

CAST

Hunter	John Vernon
Alain Pratorius	Steve Ihnat
Cirrak	Fritz Weaver
Larkdale	Edward Binns
Anne Novak	Sabrina Scharf
Mishani	Ramon Bieri
McDaniel	John Schuck
Girl	Barbara Rhoades

Music: Lalo Schifrin.
Producer: Bruce Geller.
Writer: Cliff Gould.
Director: Leonard J. Horn.
Creator: Bruce Geller.
Art Director: Allen Smith.

HUNTER—90 minutes—CBS— January 9, 1973.

HUNTER

The pilot film, with James Franciscus and Linda Evans, aired on CBS on September 14, 1976, for the series of the same title (see regular program section).

1579 HUNTER'S MOON

Pilot (Adventure). The story, set in Wyoming during the range wars between cattlemen and sheepherders at the turn of the century, follows the exploits of Fayette Randall, a mysterious figure for justice. In the pilot, Randall begins a vendetta against a man called the Captain, who murdered his family.

REGULAR CAST

Fayette Randall	Cliff De Young
Isham Hart, his friend	Robert DoQui

GUEST CAST

The Captain	Alex Cord
George Randall	Leif Erickson
Hobble	Dan O'Herlihy
Kels Johansen	John Ericson

Marshal	Ty Hardin
Ora Bowen	John Quade
Senator Terry	Morgan Ramsey
Peter Randall	Morgan Stevens

Music: Harry Sukman.
Music Supervision: Lionel Newman.
Executive Producer: David Dortort.
Producer: Ken Annakin.
Writer: David Dortort.
Director: Ken Annakin.

HUNTER'S MOON—60 minutes—CBS—December 1, 1979.

HUSBANDS AND WIVES

The pilot eipsode (videotape) broadcast on CBS on July 18, 1977, for the series *Husbands, Wives, and Lovers* (see regular program section).

1580   THE HUSTLER OF MUSCLE BEACH

Pilot (Comedy). The story of Nick Dominick, a con artist who devises elaborate schemes to make money. In the pilot, set in California, Nick stages a body building contest with an unlikely entrant at incredible odds.

REGULAR CAST

Nick Dominick	Richard Hatch
Jenny O'Rourke, his partner	Kay Lenz

GUEST CAST

Rose McIntosh	Jeanette Nolan
Mancusco	Jack Carter
Todd Nash	Tim Kimber
Mr. Davidson	Patty Jerome
Uncle Sam	Paul Bryar

Also (portraying themselves): Franco Columbia, Bobby Van, Frank Zane, Stacy Bently, Claudia Stern, Larry Jacobs, Ken Rockland, Lisa Lyons.
Music: Earle Hagen.
Executive Producer: John Furia, Jr., Barry Oringer.
Producer: Neil Maffeo.
Writer: David Smilow.
Director: Jonathan Kaplan.
Art Director: Arch Bacon.
Director of Photography: Chuck Arnold.

THE HUSTLER OF MUSCLE BEACH—2 hours—ABC—May 16, 1980.

I

1581   IF I LOVE YOU, AM I TRAPPED FOREVER?

Pilot (Comedy). The misadventures of Alan Bennett, a nonconformist high school student touting the joys of unrequited love.

REGULAR CAST

Alan Bennett	Ted Eccles
Leah Pennington, his girlfriend	Tannis G. Montgomery

Alice Bennett, Alan's mother	Elinor Donahue
Sophie Pennington, Leah's mother	Denise Nickerson
Grandfather Bennett	Liam Dunn
Doomed, Alan's friend	Rob Berger
Murray, Alan's friend	Mike Robelo
Lucius Luther, the coach	Joe Di Reda

GUEST CAST

Gwendolyn Graney	Vicky Huxtable
Carleton Penner	Paul Clemens
Dave McKee	Michael Talbott
Simon	Kevin McCarley
Mrs. Tompkins	Rachel Bard

Music: Benny Golson.
Producer: Gene Reynolds, Larry Gelbart.
Writer: Larry Gelbart.
Director: Gene Reynolds.
Director of Photography: William Jurgensen.

IF I LOVE YOU, AM I TRAPPED FOREVER?—30 minutes—CBS —March 22, 1974.

1582   I LOVE A MYSTERY

Pilot (Mystery). The exploits of Jack Packard, Doc Long and Reggie York, private detectives who roam the world solving crimes. The pilot depicts their efforts to escape from Randy Cheyene, an eccentric who, having lured them to her mysterious castle, plans to kill them.

REGULAR CAST

Doc Long	David Hartman
Jack Packard	Les Crane
Reggie York	Hogan Beggs

GUEST CAST

Randy Cheyene	Ida Lupino
Job Cheyene	Jack Weston
Gordon Elliott	Terry Thomas
Archer	Don Knotts
Faith	Karen Jensen
Hope	Deanna Lund
Charity	Melodie Johnson

Also: Francine York, Joseph Perry, Val Avery.
Music: Oliver Nelson.
Producer: Frank Price.
Writer: Leslie Stevens.
Director: Leslie Stevens.
Art Director: John J. Lloyd.

I LOVE A MYSTERY—2 hours— NBC—February 27, 1973. Filmed in 1966 and based on the radio series of the same title.

1583   THE IMPOSTER

Pilot (Crime Drama). The exploits of Joe Tyler, a former army intelligence officer who possesses a unique talent for impersonation. The pilot depicts Tyler's attempts to safeguard an intended murder victim, a wealthy businessman, by standing in for him.

REGULAR CAST

Joe Tyler	Paul Hecht

GUEST CAST

Julie	Meredith Baxter
Barney West	Edward Asner
Sheriff Turner	John Vernon
Rennick	Jack Ging
Margaret Elliott	Barbara Baxley
Victoria Kent	Nancy Kelly

Music: Gil Mellé.
Executive Producer: Richard Bluel.
Producer: Robert Stambler.
Writer: Ken August, Jon Sevorg
Director: Edward Abroms.

THE IMPOSTER — 90 minutes — NBC — March 18, 1975.

THE INCREDIBLE HULK

The pilot film broadcast on CBS on November 4, 1977, for the series of the same title (see regular program section). A second pilot film, titled "The Incredible Hulk, Part 2," aired on CBS on November 28, 1977.

1584   INSIDE O.U.T.

Pilot (Comedy). The exploits of Pat Bouillon and Ron Hart, the chief operatives of O.U.T. (the Office of Unusual Tactics), a semi-official agency devoted to helping people cope with our complex society. In the pilot, O.U.T. seeks to recover $2 million in counterfeit bills for the U.S. government.

CAST

Pat Bouillon	Farrah Fawcett
Ron Hart	Bill Daily
Agent Winston	Alan Oppenheimer
Agent Dandy	Mike Henry
Finance Director (guest)	Edward Andrews

Executive Producer: Harry Ackerman.
Producer: Lawrence J. Cohen, Fred Freeman.
Writer: Lawrence J. Cohen, Fred Freeman.
Director: Reza S. Badiyi.

INSIDE O.U.T. — 30 minutes — NBC — March 22, 1971; repeated May 9, 1977.

1585   INSTANT FAMILY

Pilot (Comedy). The story of Clifford Beane and Frank Boyle, two single fathers who pool their resources to share an apartment and save on rent. The episode depicts the efforts of the two families to adjust to living together.

CAST

Clifford Beane	William Daniels
Frank Boyle	Lou Criscuolo
Lisa Boyle, Frank's daughter	Wendy Fredericks
Robbie Boyle, Frank's son	Brad Wilkin
Kevin Beane, Clifford's son	Jeff Harlan
Ernie Beane, Clifford's son	Robbie Rist

Producer: Lila Garrett.
Director: Russ Petranto.

INSTANT FAMILY — 30 minutes — NBC — July 28, 1977.

1586   INSTITUTE FOR REVENGE

Pilot (Adventure). The exploits of John Schroeder, an agent for the Wyatt Foundation for Human Rights. The Palm Springs-based organization, run by the IFR 7000 Computer, is nicknamed the Institute for Revenge and is dedicated to righting nonviolent wrongs. In the pilot, Schroeder seeks to apprehend Alan Roberto, a swindler who has fleeced both the rich and poor out of $20 million.

REGULAR CAST

Agent John Schroeder	Sam Groom
Lilah Simms, his assistant	Lauren Hutton
Mr. Wellington, the head of the foundation	Robert Coote
JoAnn Newcombe, an agent	Lane Binkley
T. J. (Terence James) Bradley, an agent	T. J. McCavitt
Voice of the IFR 7000	John Hillerman
IFR Operative	Harlee McBride
IFR Operative	Dawn Hutchinson

GUEST CAST

Alan Roberto	George Hamilton
Frank Anders	Ray Walston
Hollis Barnes	Leslie Nielsen
Senator	Robert Emhardt
Powerbroker	James Karen

Music: Lalo Schifrin.
Executive Producer: Bill Driskill, Otto Salomon.
Producer: Bert Gold.
Writer: Bill Driskill, Otto Salamon.
Director: Ken Annakin.
Art Director: Ross Bellah, Richard Lawrence.
Director of Photography: Roland Smith.

INSTITUTE FOR REVENGE — 90 minutes — NBC — January 22, 1979.

IN TANDEM

The pilot film broadcast on NBC on May 8, 1974, for the series *Movin' On* (see regular program section).

1587   INTERTECT

Pilot (Crime Drama). The exploits of Intertect, an international investigative agency founded and directed by John McKennon, a former F.B.I. agent. The pilot episode depicts McKennon's efforts to free the wife and son of a wealthy industrialist from a kidnapper who is holding them for $1 million ransom.

REGULAR CAST

John McKennon	Stuart Whitman

GUEST CAST

Amanda Hollister	Pamela Franklin
Curt Lowens	David Soul
Barrett	Bernard Fox
Emhardt	Eric Braeden

Blake Hollister	Robert Reed
Sylvia Doyle	Sherry Alberoni

Executive Producer: Quinn Martin.
Producer: Philip Saltzman.
Writer: Philip Saltzman.
Director: Lawrence Dobkin.
Creator: Philip Saltzman.

INTERTECT — 60 minutes — ABC — March 11, 1973.

THE INVISIBLE MAN

The pilot film broadcast on May 6, 1975, for the series of the same title (see regular program section).

1588   IS THERE A DOCTOR IN THE HOUSE

Pilot (Comedy). The story, set in Wendell Falls, a small New England town, follows the experiences of Dr. Tim Newly, a G.P., and his female assistant, Dr. Michael Griffin. The pilot episode depicts Michael's attempts to prove her abilities to Newly — who is opposed to having a female assistant — when he sprains his wrist and she fills in for him.

CAST

Dr. Tim Newly	William Windom
Dr. Michael Griffin	Rosemary Forsyth
Emma Procter, Tim's housekeeper	Margaret Hamilton

Producer: Lawrence J. Cohen.
Writer: Bernard Slade.

IS THERE A DOCTOR IN THE HOUSE — 30 minutes — NBC — March 22, 1971.

1589   THE ISLANDER

Pilot (Drama). The story of Gabe McQueen, a Los Angeles lawyer who retires to Hawaii where, in Honolulu, he purchases the Queen Kulani, a hotel fraught with problems. The would-be series was to depict Gabe's attempts to run the hotel and his involvement with and attempts to help people in trouble. In the pilot, Gabe's life of serenity is disrupted when he becomes involved with three people: Senator Jerry Stratton, a friend who is seeking his help to clear him of a set up attempted murder; Trudy Engels, a beautiful runaway grand jury witness; and Paul Lazarro, an underworld figure who seeks Gabe's help in acquiring an extension on an upcoming trial.

REGULAR CAST

Gabe McQueen	Dennis Weaver
Shauna Cooke, the hotel manager	Sharon Gless
Lieutenant Larkin	Peter Mark Richman
Kimo, works in the hotel	Ed Kaahea
Al Kahala, Larkin's assistant	Dick Jenson

GUEST CAST

Trudy Engels	Bernadette Peters
Jerry Stratton	Robert Vaughn

Paul Lazarro	Sheldon Leonard
Noel Hatch	John S. Ragin
Arnie Simms	George Wyner
Henchman	Moe Keale
Sgt. Chow	Jimmy Rogers
Wallace	Glenn Cannon

Music: John Andrew Tartiglia.
Theme Vocal: "My Islander" by Shelby Flint.
Producer: Glen A. Larson.
Writer: Glen A. Larson.
Director: Paul Krasny.
Art Director: Ira Diamond.

THE ISLANDER — 2 hours — CBS — September 16, 1978.

J

1590   JACKIE AND DARLENE

Pilot (Comedy). The chaotic misadventures of policewomen Jackie Clifton and Darlene Shilton.

CAST

Officer Jackie Clifton	Sarina Grant
Officer Darlene Shilton	Anna L. Pagan
Sergeant Guthrie, their superior	Lou Frizzell

Executive Producer: Aaron Ruben.
Producer: Gene Marcione.
Director: Russ Petranto.

JACKIE AND DARLENE — 30 minutes — ABC — July 8, 1978.

1591   JAKE'S WAY

Pilot (Crime Drama). The exploits of Jake Rudd, sheriff of Fox County, a rural town near San Antonio, Texas. In the pilot, Jake investigates the slaying of his friend Tom Ross, an attorney who was about to divulge some important information to him.

REGULAR CAST

Sheriff Jake Rudd	Robert Fuller
Sam Hargis, his assistant	Slim Pickens
Deputy Daniel "Dogg" Doggett	Steve McNaughton
Deputy Steve "Dude" Cantwell	Ben Lemon
Christina O'Toole, the dispatcher	Lisa LeMole

GUEST CAST

Mace Kaylor	Andrew Duggan
Luana Kaylor	Kristin Griffith
Tom Ross	Michael Jaynes
Corrine Burke	Suzie Humphreys
Billy Jean	Chris Godfredson
Judge Pettibone	Merill Connally
Maybelle	Donna Marie Awtrey

Music: Frank Lewin.
Music Supervision: Lionel Newman.
Executive Producer: Richard Lewis.
Producer: S. Bryan Hickox.
Writer: Richard Fielder.
Director: Richard Colla.
Art Director: Peter Wooley.
Director of Photography: Robert Jessup.

JAKE'S WAY — 60 minutes — CBS — June 28, 1980.

JAMES AT 15

The pilot film broadcast on NBC on September 5, 1977, for the series of the same title (see regular program section).

1592 JARRETT

Pilot (Crime Drama). The exploits of Sam Jarrett, a private detective who specializes in cases involving fine arts thefts. In the pilot, Jarrett is hired to recover a collector's stolen rare scrolls.

REGULAR CAST

Sam Jarrett .... Glenn Ford

GUEST CAST

Cosmo .... Anthony Quayle
Simpson .... Forrest Tucker
Sigrid .... Laraine Stephens
Luluwa .... Yvonne Craig
Loomis .... Richard Anderson
Dr. Carey .... Elliott Montgomery

Music: Jeff McDuff.
Executive Producer: David Gerber.
Producer: Richard Maibaum.
Writer: Richard Maibaum.
Director: Barry Shear.

JARRETT — 90 minutes — NBC — August 11, 1973.

1593 JEREMIAH OF JACOB'S NECK

Pilot (Comedy). The story, set in the town of Jacob's Neck, New England, follows the misadventures of Tom Rankin, the police chief, and his family, when they move into a decrepit beach house. The residence is haunted by the spirit of Jeremiah Starbuck, an eighteenth-century ghost who refuses to depart from his once earthly dwelling.

REGULAR CAST

Jeremiah Starbuck .... Keenan Wynn
Tom Rankin .... Ron Masak
Anne Rankin, Tom's wife .... Arlene Golonka
Clay Rankin, Tom's son .... Brandon Cruz
Tracy Rankin, Tom's daughter .... Quinn Cummings
Wilbur Swift, Tom's deputy chief .... Elliott Street

GUEST CAST

Mayor Dick Barker .... Pitt Herbert
Abby Penrose .... Amzie Strickland
Leonard .... Alex Henteloff
Max .... Les Lannom
Crabtree .... Tom Palmer
Bob Peabody .... Don Burleson

Music: Harry Sukman.
Producer: Edgar J. Scherick, Art Stolnitz.
Writer: Peter Benchley.
Director: Ralph Senensky.
Art Director: Dick Haman.
Director of Photography: Jack Woolf.
Creator: Peter Benchley.
Set Decorator: Rich Gentz.

JEREMIAH OF JACOB'S NECK — 30 minutes — CBS — August 13, 1976.

JERRY

See title "Bachelors 4" in the pilot film section.

JIGSAW

The pilot film broadcast on ABC on March 26, 1972, for the series of the same title (see regular program section). For syndication purposes, the pilot film has been retitled "Man On the Move."

JOE AND SONS

The pilot episode (videotape) broadcast on CBS on April 18, 1975, for the series of the same title (see regular program section).

JOHN O'HARA'S GIBBSVILLE

The pilot film broadcast on NBC on April 12, 1975, for the series *Gibbsville* (see regular program section).

1594 THE JORDAN CHANCE

Pilot (Crime Drama). The story of Frank Jordan, an attorney who was once wrongly imprisoned for murder and who now helps others who are falsely convicted. In the pilot, Jordan tries to help a young woman who was set up for the murder of her lover.

REGULAR CAST

Frank Jordan .... Raymond Burr
Brian Klosky, his assistant .... Ted Shackelford
Karen Wagner, his assistant .... Jeannie Fitzsimmons
Jimmy Foster, his assistant .... James Canning

GUEST CAST

Elena Delgado .... Maria-Elena Cordero
Virna Stewart .... Stella Stevens
Sheriff DeVega .... George DiCenzo
Joseph Colton .... John McIntire
Lee Southland .... Peter Haskell
Lew Mayfield .... John Dennis Johnson

Music: Pete Rugolo.
Executive Producer: Roy Huggins.
Producer: Jo Swerling, Jr.
Writer: Stephen J. Cannell.
Director: Jules Irving.

THE JORDAN CHANCE — 2 hours — CBS — December 12, 1978.

1595 JOSHUA'S WORLD

Pilot (Drama). The story, set in the small town of Strawee, Arkansas, during the 1930s, follows the experiences of Joshua Torrance, a doctor whose practice is jeopardized by his opposition to racism as he attempts to treat blacks as equals.

REGULAR CAST

Dr. Joshua Torrance (a widower) .... Richard Crenna
Thorpe Torrance, his daughter .... Tonya Crowe
James Torrance, his son .... Randy Gray
Donie, his housekeeper .... Mary Alice
Caroline Morgan, the school teacher .... Carol Vogel
Dawn Starr, a friend of Thorpe and James .... Alexandra Pauley
Josie, same as Dawn .... LaShana Dendy

GUEST CAST

Nathaniel .... Carl Franklin
Thee .... Chez Lister
Billy Bob .... Hunter Von Leer
Shug .... Brion James
Tiny .... Ray Girardin
Viola .... Roberta Jean Williams
Waitress .... Sharon Madden

Music: Leonard Rosenman.
Executive Producer: Lee Rich, Earl Hamner, Michael Filerman.
Producer: Claylene Jones.
Writer: Earl Hamner (based on *Thorpe* by Mary Dutton).
Director: Peter Levin.
Art Director: Ed Graves.
Director of Photography: Serge Haignere.

JOSHUA'S WORLD — 60 minutes — CBS — August 21, 1980.

1596 THE JUDGE AND JAKE WYLER

Pilot (Crime Drama). The story of a retired judge who operates a private detective agency.

REGULAR CAST

Judge Meredith .... Bette Davis
Jake Wyler, her legman .... Doug McClure

GUEST CAST

Anton Granicek .... Eric Braeden
Alicia Dodd .... Joan Van Ark
Frank Morrison .... Gary Conway
James Rockmore .... John Randolph
Lt. Wolfson .... Lou Jacobi
Chloe Jones .... Barbara Rhoades
Caroline Dodd .... Lisabeth Rush
Robert Dodd .... Kent Smith

Music: Gil Mellé.
Producer: Richard Levinson, William Link.
Writer: Richard Levinson, William Link, David Shaw.
Director: David Lowell Rich.
Director of Photography: William Margulies.

THE JUDGE AND JAKE WYLER — 2 hours — NBC — December 2, 1972.

1597 JUDGE DEE IN THE MONASTERY MURDERS

Pilot (Mystery). The exploits of Judge Dee, a seventh-century Chinese magistrate turned detective. In the pilot, Judge Dee attempts to solve the mysterious deaths of three young women. Based on the stories by Robert Van Gulick.

REGULAR CAST

Judge Dee .... Khigh Dhigh

GUEST CAST

Pure Faith .... Yuki Shimoda
Lord Sun Ming .... Keye Luke
Jade Mirror .... Miiko Taka
Kang I-Te .... Soon-Tech Oh
Tao Gan .... Mako
Miss Ting .... Susie Elene
Prior .... James Hong
Celestial Image .... Irene Tsu

Music: Leonard Rosenman.
Producer: Gerald I. Isenberg.
Writer: Nicholas Meyer.
Director: Jeremy Kagan.

JUDGE DEE IN THE MONASTERY MURDERS — 2 hours — ABC — December 29, 1974.

K

1598 KATE BLISS AND THE TICKER TAPE KID

Pilot (Comedy-Western). The lighthearted misadventures of Kate Bliss, a beautiful turn-of-the-century private detective. The pilot depicts Kate's attempts to solve the problems of Lord Devery, a land baron who is being terrorized by a gang of outlaws led by Clint Allison, an ex-Wall Street businessman turned Robin Hood whom Kate calls "The Ticker Tape Kid."

REGULAR CAST

Kate Bliss .... Suzanne Pleshette

GUEST CAST

Lord Devery .... Tony Randall
Clint Allison .... Don Meredith
William Blackstone .... Burgess Meredith
Hugo Peavy .... Harry Morgan
Sheriff .... David Huddleston

Music: Jeff Alexander.
Executive Producer: Aaron Spelling, Douglas S. Cramer.
Producer: Richard E. Lyons.
Writer: William Bowers, John Zodoron.
Director: Burt Kennedy.

KATE BLISS AND THE TICKER TAPE KID — 2 hours — ABC — May 26, 1978.

KATE McSHANE

The pilot film broadcast on CBS on April 11, 1975, for the series of the same title (see regular program section).

1599 THE KEEGANS

Pilot (Crime Drama). Events in the lives of the Keegan family. In the pilot, Larry Keegan, an investigative reporter, sets out to prove that his brother Pat, a professional football player, is innocent of a charge that he murdered his sister's brutal attacker.

REGULAR CAST

Larry Keegan	Adam Roarke
Pat Keegan, his brother	Spencer Milligan
Brandy Keegan, his sister	Heather Menzies
Tim Keegan, their father	Tom Clancy
Mary Keegan, their mother	Joan Leslie
Penny Voorhees Keegan,	
Pat's wife	Penelope Windust

GUEST CAST

Rudi Portinari	Paul Shenar
Helen Hunter McVey	Priscilla Pointer
Lt. Mario Giardi	Judd Hirsch
Tracy McVey	Janet Baldwin
Vince Cavell	Robert Yurin
Martha Carechal	Anna Navarro
Don Carechal	George Skaff

Music: Paul Chihara.
Producer: George Eckstein.
Writer: Dean Riesner.
Director: John Badham.

THE KEEGANS — 90 minutes — CBS — May 3, 1976.

KEEP AN
EYE ON DENISE

See title "Triple Treat" in the pilot film section.

1600   KEEP
THE FAITH

Pilot (Comedy). The story of two rabbis, Miller and Mossman, and their various misadventures. In the pilot, the rabbis attempt to discharge the temple's long established, but ill-tempered caretaker.

CAST

Rabbi Miller	Bert Convy
Rabbi Mossman	Howard Di Silva
Hosenthal, the caretaker	Henry Corden
Pink	Milton Selzer
Sophie	Nancy Walker
Judy	Linda March

Writer: Ed Simmons.
Director: Jackie Cooper.

KEEP THE FAITH — 30 minutes — CBS — April 14, 1972.

1601   KEEPER
OF THE WILD

Pilot (Drama). The story, set in Africa, depicts the experiences of Jim Donaldson, Holly James and Paul Limkula, the owner-operators of an animal preserve.

CAST

Jim Donaldson	Denny Miller
Holly James	Pamela Shoop
Paul Limkula	James Reynolds

Music: Bill Marx.
Producer: Leonard B. Kaufman.
Director: Dick Moder.

KEEPER OF THE WILD — 30 minutes — Syndicated January 1977.

KEEPING UP
WITH THE JONESES

See title "Triple Play '72" in the pilot film section.

1602   KEY WEST

Pilot (Adventure). The exploits of Steve Cutler, a retired C.I.A. agent, living in Key West, Florida, who aids people in distress. The pilot episode depicts Steve's attempts to stop Prescott Webb, an eccentric tycoon he once sent to prison, from carrying out his deadly plan of revenge.

REGULAR CAST

Steve Cutler	Stephen Boyd
Candy, his sidekick	Woody Strode
Brandi, Steve's girlfriend, a	
bar owner	Sheree North
Sam, Steve's friend	George Fisher
Police Chief Jim Miller	Don Collier

GUEST CAST

Ruth Frazier	Tiffany Bolling
Prescott Webb	Ford Rainey
General Luker	Simon Oakland
Senator	William Prince
Rick	Earl Hindman
George	Stephen Mendillo
Carol Luker	Virginia Kiser

Music: Frank DeVol.
Producer: Anthony S. Martin.
Writer: Anthony S. Martin.
Director: Philip Leacock.
Director of Photography: Ted Voigtlander.
Creator: Anthony S. Martin.

KEY WEST — 2 hours — NBC — December 10, 1973.

1603 KILLER BY NIGHT

Pilot (Crime Drama). The story, set in Los Angeles, depicts the exploits of two harried police servants: Dr. Larry Ross, a health officer, and George Benson, a police captain — men who work together to insure the public's safety. In the pilot, Ross and his assistant, Tracey Morrow, join with police to apprehend two killers: an armed robber infected with diphtheria.

REGULAR CAST

Dr. Larry Ross	Robert Wagner
Capt. George Benson	Greg Morris
Dr. Tracey Morrow	Diane Baker
Sgt. Phil Gold	Theodore Bikel

GUEST CAST

Warren Claman	Robert Lansing
Sister Sarah	Mercedes McCambridge
Dr. Madera	Pedro Armendariz, Jr.

Music: Quincy Jones.
Producer: Fred Engel.
Writer: David P. Harmon.
Director: Bernard McEveety.
Director of Photography: Robert B. Hauser.

KILLER BY NIGHT — 2 hours — CBS — January 7, 1972.

1604   THE KILLER
WHO WOULDN'T DIE

Pilot (Crime Drama). The story of Kirk Ohanian, a former homicide detective, now the operator of the *Quest*, a charter boat service in Hawaii. The pilot, which begins with Ohanian resigning from the force after the unsolved bombing murder of his wife, depicts his efforts to solve the murder of a close friend, an undercover agent who was killed by an assassin. Potential series title: *Ohanian*.

REGULAR CAST

Kirk Ohanian	Mike Connors
Uncle Ara, Kirk's mate on the	
Quest	Gregoire Aslan

GUEST CAST

Anne Roland	Samantha Eggar
Heller	Clu Gulager
Commissioner Moore	Patrick O'Neal
Commissioner Wharton	Robert Hooks
Heather	Mariette Hartley
David Lao	James Shigeta
Soong	Philip Ahn
Flo	Lucille Benson

Music: Georges Garvarentz.
Producer: Ivan Goff, Ben Roberts.
Writer: Cliff Gould.
Director: William Hale.
Art Director: Joseph R. Jennings.
Director of Photography: Gert Andersen.

THE KILLER WHO WOULDN'T DIE — 2 hours — ABC — April 4, 1976.

1605   KING OF
THE ROAD

Pilot (Comedy). The story of Cotton Grimes, a semi-retired Country and Western singer who runs a motel in Muscle Shoales, Alabama. The program, which depicts Cotton's misadventures as he operates the motel, also spotlights the performances of guest entertainers.

CAST

Cotton Grimes	Roger Miller
Maureen Kenney, his	
girlfriend	Lee Crawford
Sam Braffman, Cotton's	
partner	Larry Haines
Mildred Braffman, Sam's	
wife	Marian Mercer
Billy Dee Huff, works in	
the motel	R. G. Brown
Rick, works in the motel	Ric Carrott
Mrs. Hickey (guest)	Nedra Volz
Eddie, the drunk (guest)	Eddie Foy, Jr.

Also: John Davidson (as himself), and Karen Specht, Beth Specht and Jenny Neumann as the Kleegle Sisters.
Music: Larry Cansler, Don Piestrup.
Executive Producer: Norman Lear, Jerry Weintraub.
Producer: Rod Parker, Hal Cooper.
Writer: Rod Parker.
Director: Hal Cooper.
Art Director: Chuck Murawski.
Creator: Rod Parker.

KING OF THE ROAD — 60 minutes — CBS — May 10, 1978.

KINGSTON:
THE POWER PLAY

The pilot film broadcast on NBC on September 15, 1976, for the series *Kingston: Confidential* (see regular program section).

1606   KISS ME,
KILL ME

Pilot (Crime Drama). The cases of Stella Stafford, a beautiful investigator for the Los Angeles County District Attorney's Office. In the pilot, Stella seeks to prove that an ex-con is not responsible for the murder of a young schoolteacher.

REGULAR CAST

Stella Stafford	Stella Stevens
Edward Fuller, the D.A.	Robert Vaughn
Captain Logan, L.A.P.D.	Dabney Coleman

GUEST CAST

Dan Hodges	Michael Anderson, Jr.
Harry Grant	Claude Akins
Maureen	Tisha Sterling
Jimmy	Pat O'Brien
Douglas	Bruce Boxleitner
Murry	Steve Franken

Music: Richard Markowitz.
Producer: Stanley Kallis.
Writer: Robert Thompson.
Director: Michael O'Herlihy.

KISS ME, KILL ME — 90 minutes — ABC — May 8, 1976.

1607 KOMEDY TONITE

Pilot (Variety). Music, songs and comedy sketches enacted mostly by black performers.

Starring: Cleavon Little, Paula Kelly, Marion Ramsey, Shon Vaughn, Charles Valentino.
Orchestra: H. B. Barnum.
Executive Producer: Raymond Katz.
Producer: Lawrence Kasha.
Director: Mark Warren.
Choreographer: Donald McKayle.

KOMEDY TONITE — 60 minutes — NBC — May 9, 1978.

1608   KOSTA AND
HIS FAMILY

Pilot (Comedy Drama). The misadventures of Herb Kosta, an unemployed aerospace technician too qualified for the jobs he might find, and his slightly wacky family.

CAST

Herb Kosta, the father	Herb Edelman
Isabel Kosta, his wife	Barbara Barrie
Gina Kosta, their daughter	Ellen Sherman
Jimmy Kosta, their son	Jack David Walker
Al Kosta, their son	Albert Henderson

Executive Producer: Leonard B. Stern.
Producer: Ted Rich.
Writer: Roger Price.
Director: Dan Dailey.

KOSTA AND HIS FAMILY — 60 minutes — NBC — December 31, 1973.

1609   THE KOWBOYS

Pilot (Musical Comedy). The story, set in the Old West, follows the exploits of the Kowboys, four children (Matthew, Zak, Sweetwater and Smitty), a Rock group that dispenses justice where needed. In the pilot, the Kowboys, composed of three boys and one girl, seek to rescue the town of Civilization from a power-hungry boss.

CAST

Matthew	Boomer Castleman
Zak	Michael Martin Murphey
Sweetwater	Jamie Carr
Smitty	Joy Bang
Captain Walker, the power boss	Edward Andrews
Clem, his assistant	Frank Welker

Music: Don Kirshner, Jeff Barry.
Director: Ernest Pintoff.

THE KOWBOYS — 30 minutes — NBC — July 13, 1970.

1610   THE KROFFT COMEDY HOUR

Pilot (Variety). Various comedy sketches.

Host: Patty Harrison, Robin Tyler.
Regulars: Bart Braverman, Sheryl Lee Ralph, Deborah Malone, Kaptain Kool and the Kongs.
Guests: Redd Foxx, Sha Na Na.
Supervising Producer: Bonny Dore.
Executive Producer: Sid and Marty Krofft.
Writer: Michael Kagan, Dick Robins, Duane Poole, William Bickley, Michael Warren.
Director: Jack Regas, Howard Storm, Alan Myerson.

THE KROFFT COMEDY HOUR — 60 minutes — ABC — July 29, 1978.

KUNG FU

The pilot film broadcast on ABC on February 22, 1972, for the series of the same title (see regular program section).

L

1611   LACY AND THE MISSISSIPPI QUEEN

Pilot (Comedy-Western). The story, set in the Old West, follows the lighthearted misadventures of Kate Lacy, a level-headed cowgirl, and Queenie Lacy, her free-living sister. The pilot episode depicts their attempts to apprehend their father's murderer.

REGULAR CAST

Kate Lacy	Kathleen Lloyd
Queenie Lacy	Debra Feuer

GUEST CAST

Willie	Jack Elam
Isaac Harrison	Edward Andrews
Parker	James Keach
Jennings	Christopher Lloyd
Webber	Les Lannom
Sam Lacy	Anthony Palmer

Music: Barry De Vorzon.
Executive Producer: Lawrence Gordon.
Producer: Lew Gallo.
Writer: Kathy Donnell, Madeline DiMaggio Wagner.
Director: Robert Butler.

LACY AND THE MISSISSIPPI QUEEN — 90 minutes — NBC — May 17, 1978.

1612   LADIES IN BLUE

Pilot (Crime Drama). The exploits of Casey Hunt and Britt Blackwell, two beautiful policewomen with the San Francisco Police Department. In the pilot episode, broadcast as a segment of Vega$, the girls seek to apprehend a psychotic police killer.

REGULAR CAST

Officer Casey Hunt	Michelle Phillips
Officer Britt Blackwell	Tanya Roberts
Captain Turner	Peter Haskell
Sergeant Culley	Bruce Kirby
Mrs. Hunt, Casey's mother	Natalie Schafer

GUEST CAST

Derek	Andrew Robinson
Dottie	Peggy Cass
Sam	Peter Mark Richman
Dan Tanna	Robert Urich
Binzer	Bart Braverman
Bea Travis	Phyllis Elizabeth Davis
Lt. Dave Nelson	Greg Morris

Music: John Beal.
Supervising Producer: E. Duke Vincent.
Executive Producer: Aaron Spelling, Douglas S. Cramer.
Producer: Phil Fherle, Larry Forrester.
Director: Lewis Teague.

LADIES IN BLUE — 60 minutes — ABC — March 19, 1980.

1613   LADY LUCK

Pilot (Comedy). The story of a beautiful, but mysterious woman who magically appears to assist people who are in need of a little Lady Luck. The pilot depicts Lady Luck's efforts to help a hotel employee who is about to miss out on a promotion.

REGULAR CAST

Lady Luck (Laura)	Valerie Perrine

GUEST CAST

Roger	Paul Sand
Clay	Bert Convy
Penny	Sallie Shockley
Walter	J. D. Cannon
Fran	Carole Cook

Music: Hal Mooney.
Producer: James Komack.
Writer: Dean Hargrove, Charles Shyer, Alex Mandel.
Director: James Komack.

Director of Photography: Emil Oster.

LADY LUCK — 30 minutes — NBC — February 12, 1973.

1614   LAND OF HOPE

Pilot (Drama). The story of the Barskys, an immigrant family living on New York's Lower East Side. In the pilot, the Barskys face their first crisis as they battle a disreputable uncle to keep the foundling they've cared for.

REGULAR CAST

The Barsky Family:

Reva Barsky	Marian Winters
Isaac Barsky	Phil Fisher
Devvie Barsky	Roberta Wallach
Herschel Barsky	Richard Liberman
Benji Barsky	Joseph Miller

The Gottschalk Family (their neighbors):

Gerda Gottschalk	Ariane Munker
Gustav Gottschalk	Roy Poole
Kathi Gottschalk	Carol Williard
Ernst Gottschalk	Donald Warfield

GUEST CAST

Rafe Pavlin	Anthony Cannon
Kevin Dwyer	Colin Duffy
Lea Gianni	Maria Tucci
Labe Ravitz	Michael Lombard

Music: Morton Gould.
Executive Producer: Herbert Brodkin.
Producer: Robert Berger.
Writer: Rose Leiman Goldberg.
Director: George Schaefer.

LAND OF HOPE — 60 minutes — CBS — May 13, 1976.

1615   LANDON, LANDON, AND LANDON

Pilot (Comedy-Mystery). The story of Ben Landon, a former private detective, murdered while investigating a case, who returns as a ghost* to assist his children, Holly and Nick, now the operators of their father's Hollywood investigative agency. In the pilot, Holly and Nick, assisted by their father's ghost, investigate Ben's murder.

REGULAR CAST

Ben Landon	William Windom
Holly Landon	Nancy Dolman
Nick Landon	Daren Kelly
Judith Saperstein, Ben's secretary; now assistant to Holly and Nick	Millie Slavin
Police Inspector Ulysses Barnes	Richard O'Brien

GUEST CAST

George Rumford	Norman Bartold
Billie	Sudie Bond
Darryl P. Goren	Jason Wingreen
Coroner	Arthur Adams
Reggie Ozer	Wil Albert
Captain Nestor	Pat Studstill
White Suit	Paul Tuerpe
Cy Vorpal	Maurice Hill

Music: Perry Botkin, Jr.
Executive Producer: Don Reo.

Producer: Bruce Kalish, Philip John Taylor.
Writer: Bruce Kalish, Philip John Taylor.
Director: Don Reo.
Art Director: George B. Chan.
Director of Photography: Robert Caramico.

LANDON, LANDON, AND LANDON — 60 minutes — CBS — June 14, 1980.

*Ben, who appears only to Holly and Nick, returns to Earth to be the father he never was to his children, and to help operate the newly formed Landon, Landon, and Landon Private Detective Agency.

LANIGAN'S RABBI

The pilot film broadcast on NBC on June 17, 1976, for the series of the same title (see regular program section).

1616   LASSIE: THE NEW BEGINNING

Pilot (Drama). The story follows the new adventures of Lassie, the beautiful collie, and her new masters, Samantha and Chip Stratton, two orphans who live with their uncle, Stuart Stratton, the editor of the *Lake Pines Journal* in Lake Pines, California. The pilot follows the journey of Samantha and Chip after their grandmother's death from Arizona to California to find their only living relative.

CAST

Stuart Stratton, the uncle	John Reilly
Samantha Stratton, his niece	Sally Boyden
Chip Stratton, his nephew	Shane Sinutko
Kathy McKendrick, Stuart's friend	Lee Bryant
Dr. Amos Rheams	David Wayne
Sheriff J. D. Marsh	Gene Evans
Buzz McKendrick, Kathy's son	Jeff Harlan
The Grandmother (guest)	Jeanette Nolan

Music: Jerrold Immel.
Music Supervision: Alfred Perry.
Executive Producer: Tom McDermott.
Producer: Jack Miller, William Beaudine, Jr.
Director: Don Chaffey

LASSIE: THE NEW BEGINNING — 60 minutes — ABC. Part one aired on September 17, 1978; part two on September 24, 1978; repeated as a two-hour movie on June 3, 1979.

1617   THE LAST ANGRY MAN

Pilot (Drama). The story, set in Brooklyn, New York, in 1936, follows the life of Sam Abelman, a doctor who involves himself in his patients' private lives.

REGULAR CAST

Dr. Sam Abelman	Pat Hingle
Sarah Abelman, his wife	Lynn Carlin

Eunice Abelman, his
daughter   Tracy Bogart
Nurse   Ann Doran

GUEST CAST

Myron	Paul Jabara
Frankie Parelli	Michael Margotta
Max Vogel	Sorrell Booke
Petey Parelli	David Roy
Paul Parelli	Paul Henry Itkin

Music: Gil Mellé.
Executive Producer: Gerald Isenberg.
Producer: Jerrold Freedman, Ernest Losso.
Writer: Gerald Green.
Director: Jerrold Freedman.

THE LAST ANGRY MAN — 90 minutes — ABC — April 16, 1974.

1618   LAST CHANCE

Pilot (Comedy). The antics of five mischievous juveniles who are serving time at a county probation camp.

CAST

Pat Gilhooley, the supervisor	Sorrell Booke
Counselor Crosby	Will MacKenzie
Meredith Gilhooley, Pat's daughter	Debi Richter
Counselor Feinberg	Lauren Frost
The Juveniles:	
Ludlam	Steve Guttenberg
Angie	Albert Insinnia
Tim Honeywood	J. Andrew Kenny
Farkas	Alvin Kupperman
Cromwell	Jaison Walker

Executive Producer: Lee Rich, Philip Capice.
Producer: Lew Gallo.
Writer: Hal Dresner.
Director: Robert Moore.

LAST CHANCE — 30 minutes — NBC — April 21, 1978.

1619   LAST HOURS BEFORE MORNING

Pilot (Crime Drama). The story, set in Los Angeles in the 1940s, follows the exploits of Bud Delaney, a house detective in a residential hotel. The pilot depicts Delaney's efforts to solve the theft of jewels from a penthouse and the murder of a gangster — both of which occurred on the same night.

REGULAR CAST

Bud Delaney	Ed Lauter

GUEST CAST

Yolanda Marquez	Victoria Principal
Mrs. Pace	Rhonda Fleming
Shirley	Sheila Sullivan
Bruno	Michael Baseleon
Max	Philip Bruns
Lucky English	Robert Alda
Justice	Thalmus Rasulala
Ty Randolph	Kaz Garas
Peter Helms	Peter Donat

Music: Pete Rugolo.
Executive Producer: Charles Fries.
Producer: Malcolm Stuart.

Writer: Robert Garland, George Yanok.
Director: Joseph Hardy.

LAST HOURS BEFORE MORNING — 90 minutes — NBC — April 19, 1975.

1620   LAW OF THE LAND

Pilot (Western). The story, set in the Old West of the 1870s, follows the exploits of Sheriff Pat Lambrose, a Denver lawman. The pilot depicts Lambrose's attempt to track down a crazed killer of prostitutes.

REGULAR CAST

Sheriff Pat Lambrose	Jim Davis

GUEST CAST

Jane Adams	Barbara Parkins
Tim Condor	Cal Bellini
Quirt	Don Johnson
Jacob	Moses Gunn
Travis Carrington	Andrew Prine
Selena Jensen	Darleen Carr
Andy Hill	Glenn Corbett
Brad Jensen	Nicholas Hammond

Music: John Parker.
Executive Producer: Quinn Martin.
Producer: John Wilder.
Writer: John Wilder, Sam Rolfe.
Director: Virgil W. Vogel.
Art Director: Al Heschong.

LAW OF THE LAND — 2 hours — NBC — April 29, 1976.

1621   LEGEND OF THE GOLDEN GUN

Pilot (Western). The story, set in the Old West, depicts the exploits of John Colton, a gunfighter for hire. The pilot episode follows Colton's efforts to end the reign of William Quantrill, a Confederate guerilla leader.

REGULAR CAST

John Colton	Jeffrey Osterhage
J. R. Swackhamer, the gunfighter who trains Colton	Hal Holbrook

GUEST CAST

William Quantrill	Robert Davi
General Custer	Keir Dullea
Maggie	Michele Carey
Jake Powell	John McLiam
Sara	Elissa Leeds
Judge Harding	R. G. Armstrong

Music: Jerrold Immel.
Executive Producer: Harve Bennett, Harris Katleman.
Producer: B.W. Sandefur.
Writer: James D. Parriott.
Director: Alan J. Levi.

LEGEND OF THE GOLDEN GUN — 2 hours — NBC — April 10, 1979.

1622   LEGS

Pilot (Comedy). The misadventures of a company of entertainers who are struggling to make ends meet by working in a not-so-posh Las Vegas Hotel. With

some revisions, it became the pilot for the series *Who's Watching the Kids?*

CAST

Stacy Turner, a showgirl	Caren Kaye
Angie Bates, a showgirl	Lynda Goodfriend
Melissa Turner, Stacy's sister	Tammy Lauren
Frankie Bates, Angie's brother	Scott Baio
Cochise, a showgirl	Shirley Kirkes
Bridget, a showgirl	Elaine Bolton
Memphis Blake, a showgirl	Lorrie Mahaffey
Dixie, a showgirl	Sayra Hammel
Major Putnam, the hotel owner	David Ketchum
Norma Kay	Marcia Lewis
Rimshot	Dawson Mays
Billy Joe	Marv Daniels

Executive Producer: Garry K. Marshall, Tony Mordente.
Writer: Walter Kempley, Marty Nadler.
Director: Alan Rafkin.

LEGS — 60 minutes — NBC — May 19, 1978.

1623   THE LETTERS

Pilot (Anthology). The first of two pilot films (see following title) about the effects letters, delayed one year in transit due to a plane crash, have on the people to whom they were addressed once they are delivered.

REGULAR CAST

The Postman	Henry Jones

GUEST CAST

Paul Anderson	John Forsythe
Elaine Anderson	Jane Powell
Laura Reynolds	Lesley Ann Warren
Geraldine Parkington	Barbara Stanwyck
Penelope Parkington	Dina Merrill
Derek Childs	Leslie Nielsen
Karen Forrester	Pamela Franklin
Mrs. Forrester	Ida Lupino
Joe Randolph	Ben Murphy
Paul Anderson, Jr.	Gary Dubin
Stewardess	Trish Mahoney

Music Supervision: Rocky Moriana.
Executive Producer: Aaron Spelling, Leonard Goldberg.
Producer: Paul Junger Witt.
Writer: James Hirsch, Ellis Marcus, Hal Sitowitz.
Director: Gene Nelson, Paul Krasny.

THE LETTERS — 90 minutes — ABC — March 6, 1973.

1624   LETTERS FROM THREE LOVERS

Pilot (Anthology). The second of two pilot films (see previous title) about the effects letters (in this instance, written from one lover to another), delayed one year in transit, have on the recipients when they are delivered.

REGULAR CAST

The Postman	Henry Jones

GUEST CAST

Monica	June Allyson
Maggie	Juliet Mills
Angie	Belinda J. Montgomery
Jack	Ken Berry
Bob	Robert Sterling
Joshua	Barry Sullivan
Vincent	Martin Sheen
Sam	Lyle Waggoner
Wilson	Logan Ramsey
Eddie	Lou Frizzell
Donna	Ellen Weston

Music: Pete Rugolo.
Producer: Aaron Spelling, Leonard Goldberg.
Writer: Ann Marcus, Jerome Kass.
Director: John Erman.

LETTERS FROM THREE LOVERS — 90 minutes — ABC — October 3, 1973.

THE LIFE AND TIMES OF CAPTAIN BARNEY MILLER

The pilot episode (videotape) broadcast on ABC on August 22, 1974, for the series *Barney Miller* (see regular program section).

1625   LIGHTS' OUT

Pilot (Anthology). A would-be series of mystery-suspense presentations based on the old radio and television series of the same title.

The Pilot Episode:
When Widows Weep. An occult drama about a doll maker whose creations trigger a series of bizarre deaths.

Cast: Sabina: Joan Hackett; Howard: Laurence Luckinbill; Karen: Louisa Horton; State Trooper: Michael McGuire; Helen: Kathryn Walker.
Producer: Herbert Brodkin.
Writer: Alvin Boretz.

LIGHTS' OUT — 60 minutes — NBC — January 15, 1972.

1626   LI'L ABNER

Pilot (Musical Comedy). The misadventures of the hillbilly residents of Dogpatch, U.S.A. In the pilot, the citizens battle pollution in the form of deadly glops.

CAST

Li'l Abner	Ray Young
Daisy Mae	Nancee Parkinson
Mammy Yokum	Billie Hayes
Pappy Yokum	Billy Bletcher
Nightmare Alice	Bobo Lewis

Music: Earl Brown, Jimmy Dale.
Producer: Allan Blye, Chris Bearde.
Writer: Coslough Johnson, Ted Zeigler, Allan Blye, Chris Bearde.
Director: Gordon Wiles.

LI'L ABNER — 60 minutes — ABC — April 26, 1971.

1627   THE LISA HARTMAN SHOW: HOT STUFF

Pilot (Variety). A look at various aspects of American culture. The pilot, subtitled "Hot Stuff," spotlights the activities in which people engage for fun.

Hostess: Lisa Hartman.
Guests: Andy Kaufman, Ruci Martin, Karen Turner, Bill Kirkenbauer.
Orchestra: Johnny Harris.
Theme Vocal: "Hot Stuff" by Lisa Hartman.
Executive Producer: George Schlatter.
Producer: Rod Warren, David Winters.
Director: Tim Kiley.
Choreographer: David Winters.

THE LISA HARTMAN SHOW: HOT STUFF — 60 minutes — ABC — June 30, 1979 (an unscheduled airing).

LITTLE HOUSE ON THE PRAIRIE

The pilot film broadcast on March 30 1974, for the series of the same title (see regular program section).

LITTLE WOMEN

The pilot film aired on NBC on October 2, 1978 (part 1) and October 3, 1978 (part 2), for the series of the same title (see regular program section).

1628   THE LIVES OF JENNY DOLAN

Pilot (Crime Drama). The exploits of Jenny Dolan, a beautiful investigative reporter for the *News World Journal.* In the pilot, Jenny seeks to solve the murder of her husband, Wes, a murder she believes is connected with her investigation of a conspiracy involving a political assassination.

REGULAR CAST

Jenny Dolan	Shirley Jones
Joe Rossiter, her editor	Stephen Boyd

GUEST CAST

Wes Dolan	David Hedison
Andrea Hardesty	Dana Wynter
Nancy Royce	Lynn Carlin
Orlando	James Darren
Dave Ames	Farley Granger
Lt. Nesbitt	Stephen McNally
Store owner	Pernell Roberts
Mr. Springfield	Alan Oppenheimer
Dr. Lawrence Mallen	Percy Rodrigues
E. Norris Wilde	Hayden Rorke

Music: Pat Williams.
Executive Producer: Ross Hunter.
Producer: Jacques Mapes.
Writer: Richard Alan Simmons, James Lee.
Director: Jerry Jameson.
Art Director: Preston Ames.
Director of Photography: Matthew Leonetti.

THE LIVES OF JENNY DOLAN — 2 hours — NBC — October 27, 1975.

THE LIVING END

See title "CBS Comedy Trio" in the pilot film section.

1629   LOCAL 306

Pilot (Comedy). The misadventures of Harvey Gordon, the newly appointed chief steward of Plumber's Local 306. In the pilot, Harvey seeks a way to overcome his fear of flying to attend a distant union meeting.

CAST

Harvey Gordon	Eugene Roche
Rose Gordon, his wife	Miriam-Byrd Nethery
Helene Gordon, their daughter	Susan Sennett
Hutchings, a union member	Milton Parsons
Rocco, a union member	Roy Stewart

Executive Producer: Mark Carliner.
Producer: Stanley Ralph Ross.
Writer: Stanley Ralph Ross.
Director: Alan Rafkin.

LOCAL 306 — 30 minutes — NBC — August 23, 1976.

1630   LOCK, STOCK, AND BARREL

Pilot (Western Comedy-Drama). The misadventures of newlyweds Roselle and Clare Bridgeman as they seek to begin a new life in Colorado during the nineteenth century. See also "Hitched," the sequel pilot film.

REGULAR CAST

Rosella Bridgeman	Belinda J. Montgomery
Clare Bridgeman	Tim Matheson

GUEST CAST

Punch Logan	Claude Akins
Brucker	Jack Albertson
Sergeant Markey	Neville Brand
Pursle	Burgess Meredith
Micah	John Beck
Corporal Fowler	Charles Dierkop

Music: Pat Williams.
Producer: Richard Alan Simmons.
Writer: Richard Alan Simmons.
Director: Jerry Thorpe.
Director of Photography: Russell Metty, Harry May.

LOCK, STOCK, AND BARREL — 2 hours — NBC — September 24, 1971.

1631   THE LONG DAYS OF SUMMER

Pilot (Drama). An unsold pilot based on the successful made-for-television movie, *When Everyday Was the Fourth of July.* The story recreates the mood of America during the turbulent years just prior to World War II as seen through the eyes of Daniel Cooper, a 13-year-old Jewish boy growing up in Bridgeport, Connecticut.

REGULAR CAST

Ed Cooper, the father, a lawyer	Dean Jones
Millie Cooper, the mother	Joan Hackett
Daniel Cooper, their son	Ronnie Scribner
Sarah Cooper, their daughter	Louanne
Frances Haley, their married daughter	Leigh French
Duane Haley, Frances' husband	John Karlen
Freddy Landauer, Jr., Daniel's friend	David Baron
Fred Landauer, Sr., Freddy's father	Lee deBroux

GUEST CAST

Joseph Kaplan	Donald Moffat
Sam Wiggins	Andrew Duggan
Charlie Wilson	Tiger Williams
Coach Dowd	Joe Medals
Lt. O'Hare	Michael McGuire

Narrator: Charles Aidman.
Executive Producer: Dan Curtis.
Producer: Joseph Stern, Lee Hutson.
Writer: Lee Hutson.
Director: Dan Curtis.
Art Director: Trevor Williams.
Director of Photography: Charles Correll.

THE LONG DAYS OF SUMMER — 90 minutes — ABC — May 23, 1980.

LONGSTREET

The pilot film broadcast on ABC on September 9, 1971, for the series of the same title (see regular program section).

1632   LOOK WHAT THEY'VE DONE TO MY SONG

Pilot (Musical Comedy). Spoofs of popular melodies via sketches based on the song (includes impersonations of the actual recording artists).

Guest Host: Norman Fell.
Repertory Company: Dimitra Jo Freeman, Gale Garnet, Howard Iskowitz, Marsha Myers, Joe Ristivo, Karen Rushmore, Sherry Worth, Ty Witney.
Cameo Guests: Hal Linden, The Captain and Tennille.
Orchestra: Bob Rosario.
Executive Producer: Ernest Chambers.
Producer: Jack Watson, James Ritz.
Writer: James Ritz, Ian Bernard, Dick Rosen, Bob Silberg.
Director: Joshua White.
Choreographer: Scott Salmon.
Art Director: Kerry Joyce.
Costumes: Ret Turner.
Creator: Ernest Chambers.

LOOK WHAT THEY'VE DONE TO MY SONG — 30 minutes — Syndicated July 1980.

1633   LOVE AND LEARN

Pilot (Comedy). The misadventures of Jason Brewster, a college English professor, and his wife, Holly, a beautiful showgirl, as they seek to live a normal life despite the problems the differences in their occupations cause.

CAST

Professor Jason Brewster	Lawrence Pressman
Holly Brewster, his wife	Candy Clark
Mark Brewster, Jason's brother	Jimmy Van Patten
Harvey, Jason's friend	Eric Boen
Jason's landlady	Natalie Core
Denise Pfeiffer, a student of Jason's	Kelly Bishop

Music: Dick De Benedictis, Paul Wayne.
Producer: Paul Wayne, George Burditt.
Writer: Paul Wayne, George Burditt.
Director: Jack Shea.

LOVE AND LEARN — 30 minutes — NBC — August 1, 1979.

1634   LOVE AT FIRST SIGHT

Pilot (Comedy). The problems of a not-so-typical marriage as seen through the experiences of Karen Alexander and her husband, Jonathan, a blind jingles writer for the Fame Advertising Agency. The pilot depicts Jonathan's fears as he and Karen's parents prepare to meet for the first time.

CAST

Karen Alexander	Susan Bigelow
Jonathan Alexander	Philip Levien
Francis Fame, the agency owner	Pat Cooper
Genevieve Lamont, the stylish jingle writer	Deborah Baltzell
Denise, the agency's buxom receptionist	Angela Aames
Mr. Bellamy, Karen's father	Robert Rockwell
Mrs. Bellamy, Karen's mother	Peggy McCay

Music Performed, Composed, and Arranged By: Jose Feliciano.
Music Producer: Rick Jarrard.
Executive Producer: Nick Arnold.
Producer: Peter Locke.
Writer: Nick Arnold.
Director: Bill Persky.
Art Director: Ken Johnson.

LOVE AT FIRST SIGHT — 30 minutes — CBS — October 13, 1980.

1635   THE LOVEBIRDS

Pilot (Comedy). The story, set in Baltimore, follows the misadventures of marrieds Janine and Al Burley. The pilot episode depicts Janine's attempts to fulfill herself by finding a job — and Al's attempts, believing her place is at home, to discourage her.

CAST

Janine Burley	Lorna Patterson
Al Burley	Louis Welch
Patricia Wexelblatt, their neighbor	Ellen Regan
Fred Wexelblatt, Patricia's husband	Eugene Levy

Music: Peter Matz.
Theme Vocal: "The Lovebirds" by Bobby Van; written by Mark Rothman.
Executive Producer: Mark Rothman, Lowell Ganz.
Associate Producer: Leslie Fritz.
Writer-Creator: Mark Rothman, Lowell Ganz.
Director: Peter Baldwin.
Art Director: John Vallone.
Director of Photography: Robert G. Hager.
Set Decorator: Rich Reams.

THE LOVEBIRDS — 30 minutes — CBS — July 18, 1979.

1636   THE LOVE BOAT I

Pilot (Comedy-Drama). The first of three pilot films that eventually launched *The Love Boat* series (see also "The Love Boat II" and "The Love Boat III"). The anthology-type program interweaves four romantic stories that take place aboard the *Sun Princess,* a luxury cruise ship bound for Acapulco.

REGULAR CAST

Captain Thomas Allenford III	Ted Hamilton
Dr. Adam O'Neal	Dick Van Patten
Jeri Landers, the cruise director	Teri O'Mara
"Gopher," the yeoman purser	Sandy Helberg
Isaac, the bartender	Theodore Wilson
Nino, the steward	Joseph Sicari
Dena DeMarco, the lounge entertainer	Kathryn Ish
Danny DeMarco, Dena's husband and partner	Richard Stahl

GUEST CAST

George Havlicek	Tom Bosley
Iris Havlicek	Cloris Leachman
Juanita Havlicek	Laurette Spang
Donald Richardson	Don Adams
Monica Richardson	Florence Henderson
Ellen Carmichael	Karen Valentine
Andrew Kannan	Hal Linden
Stan Nichols	Gabe Kaplan
Richard Garnett III	Ric Carrott
Willard	Harvey Korman
Louella	Joyce Jameson
Bianca	Jette Seear
Arnold	Jimmy Baio

Stories:

Mona Lisa Speaks. The story of an awkward salesman (Gabe Kaplan) who falls for a sexy model (Jette Seear).

'Til Death Us Do Part. A philandering husband (Don Adams) plans the untimely demise of his wife (Florence Henderson) to save money on an expensive divorce.

Mr. and Mrs. Havlicek Aboard. The story of rich, obnoxious parents (Tom Bosley, Cloris Leachman) who object to their daughter's (Laurette Spang) heartthrob (Ric Carrott).

Are There Any Real Love Stories? The story of a smooth-talking business executive (Hal Linden) who is attracted to a pretty, but shy woman (Karen Valentine).

Music: Charles Fox.
Producer: Douglas S. Cramer.
Writer: Carl Kleinschmitt, Robert Ilkes, James R. Stein, Dawn Aldredge, Marion Freeman.
Director: Richard Kinon, Alan Myerson.

THE LOVE BOAT I — 2 hours — ABC — September 17, 1976.

1637   THE LOVE BOAT II

Pilot (Comedy-Drama). The second of three pilot films about the romantic misadventures that occur aboard a ship bound for Acapulco that led to *The Love Boat* series. See also "The Love Boat I" and "The Love Boat III."

REGULAR CAST

Captain Tom Madison	Quinn Redeker
Sandy Summers, the cruise director	Diane Stilwell
Amy Mitchell, the lounge entertainer	Candice Azzara
Burl Smith, the yeoman purser	Fred Grandy
Dr. Adam Bricker, the physician	Bernie Kopell
Isaac Washington, the bartender	Ted Lange

GUEST CAST

Elaine Palmer	Hope Lange
Steve Palmer	Robert Reed
Donna Marley	Diana Canova
Dr. Jim Berkley	Ken Berry
Roger	Lyle Waggoner
Ralph Manning	Bert Convy
Pat McFarland	Marcia Strassman
Robert Grant	Craig Stevens
Linda Marley	Kristy McNichol
Eva McFarland	Celeste Holm
Angela	Tracy Brooks Swope

Stories:

Unfaithfully Yours. The story of a dissatisfied housewife (Hope Lange) who runs away with her tennis pro (Lyle Waggoner) to spite her philandering husband (Robert Reed).

For the Love of Sandy. The story of a playboy CPA who sets his sights on the pretty cruise director (Diane Stilwell).

The Heckler. The story of a shy psychiatrist (Ken Berry) who falls for the ship's wise-cracking entertainer (Candice Azzara).

Here's Looking at You. A gentle tale of how romantic feelings are rekindled between a divorced matron (Celeste Holm) and her old flame (Craig Stevens).

Music: Charles Fox.
Executive Producer: Aaron Spelling, Douglas S. Cramer.
Producer: Henry Colman.
Writer: Carl Kleinschmitt, Steve Pritzker, Dawn Aldridge.
Director: Hy Averback.
Art Director: Roger Maus.
Director of Photography: Arch Dalzell.

THE LOVE BOAT II — 2 hours — ABC — January 21, 1977.

1638   THE LOVE BOAT III

Pilot (Comedy-Drama). The actual pilot film for *The Love Boat* series, about the romantic misadventures that occur aboard the *Pacific Princess,* a luxury cruise ship. See also "The Love Boat I" and "The Love Boat II."

REGULAR CAST

Captain Merrill Stubing	Gavin MacLeod
Julie McCoy, the cruise director	Lauren Tewes
Dr. Adam Bricker, the physician	Bernie Kopell
Burl Smith, the yeoman purser	Fred Grandy
Isaac Washington, the bartender	Ted Lange

GUEST CAST

Cleo	Georgia Engel
Leonora Klopman	Stella Stevens
Ernie Klopman	Pat Harrington
Morris Beckman	Phil Silvers
Mae Allen	Audra Lindley
Stanley Adams	Gary Frank
Joyce Adams	Melanie Mayron

Stories:

The story of a stowaway (Georgia Engel) who complicates the life of the crew.

A story of a nervous bride whose sudden rashes wreak havoc on her honeymoon cruise (starring Melanie Mayron and Gary Frank).

The story of a couple (Stella Stevens and Pat Harrington) who seek to patch up their marital difficulties.

A tender story of the chance meeting between a brassy older woman (Audra Lindley) and a morose widower (Phil Silvers).

Music: Charles Fox.
Executive Producer: Aaron Spelling, Douglas S. Cramer.
Producer: Henry Colman.
Director: Richard Kinon.

THE LOVE BOAT III — 60 minutes — ABC — May 5, 1977.

1639   LOVE, NATALIE

Pilot (Comedy). The story, set in California, satirizes family life as seen through the eyes of Natalie Miller, wife, mother and overall problem solver. The title is derived from Natalie's closing in her letter, which she reads during the opening theme. The program is also unique inasmuch as Natalie speaks directly to the audience and relates her feelings regarding the situations that develop.

REGULAR CAST

Natalie Miller	Judy Kahan
Peter Miller, her husband	Christopher Allport
Nora Miller, their daughter	Kimberly Woodward
Franklin Miller, their son	Corey Feldman
Ruth Newman, Natalie's friend	Jean DeBaer
Mel Orlorfsky, Peter's live-in friend; Natalie's live-in headache	Kenneth Tigar

GUEST CAST

Pretty High School Girl	Darian Mathias
Brownie Scout	Becky Michelle
Moving Man	Terry Wells

The Miller's address: 16 Valley Hart Drive.

Music: John Foster.
Conductor: Billy Byers.
Executive Producer: Judy Kahan.
Producer: Patricia Rickey.
Writer: Judy Kahan, Merrill Maroke.
Director: Peter Bonerz.
Director of Photography: Larry Boelens.

LOVE, NATALIE — 30 minutes — NBC — July 11, 1980.

1640   LOVE NEST

Pilot (Comedy). The misadventures of Ned Cooper and Jenny Ludlow, widowed senior citizens who live together in a Florida trailer court.

CAST

Ned Cooper	Charles Lane
Jenny Ludlow	Florida Friebus
Mort Cooper, Ned's son	Dana Elcar
Dorothy Ludlow, Jenny's daughter	Dee Carroll
Dickie Ewing, Ned's friend	Burt Mustin
Mary Francis, Jenny's friend	Alice Nunn

Producer: Saul Ilson, Ernest Chambers.
Writer: Austin and Irma Kalish.
Director: Mel Ferber.

LOVE NEST — 30 minutes — CBS — March 14, 1975.

1641   THE LOW MOAN SPECTACULAR

Pilot (Comedy). A satirization of life as seen through the eyes of the comedy group, Low Moan.

Starring: Low Moan (Brandis Kemp, Diz White, Alan Sherman, Mitch Kreindel, Ron House, Mark Blankfield).
Featured: The Bob Talmage Dancers.
Music Director: Alan Sherman.
Executive Producer: Diz White, Ron House, Alan Sherman.
Producer: Bill Lee, John Moffitt.
Associate Producer: Vic Kaplan.
Director: John Moffitt.

Choreographer: Bob Talmage.
Art Director: Bob Rang.

THE LOW MOAN SPECTACULAR
— 70 minutes — ABC — August 21, 1979.

LUCAN

The pilot film broadcast on May 22, 1977, for the series of the same title (see regular program section).

LUCAS TANNER

The pilot film broadcast on NBC on May 8, 1974, for the series of the same title (see regular program section).

1642   LUCY MOVES TO NBC

Combination Comedy Special and Pilot Film. An unusual story line in which Fred Silverman, the president of NBC, talks Lucille Ball out of retirement and back into television (and away from CBS) to develop a comedy series for the network. Now, as executive producer, she and her production assistant, Gale Gordon, devise "The Music Mart," a would-be series about Wally and Carol Coogan, a retired song and dance team who run a music store called "Coogan's Music Mart." (The pilot is presented as the last 30 minutes of the 90-minute program.)

COMEDY SPECIAL CAST

Lucille Ball	Herself
Gale Gordon	Himself
Wanda Clark, Lucy's secretary	Doris Singleton
Ruta Lee, Lucy's friend	Herself
Choo Choo, Lucy's maid	Takayo Doran
Fred Silverman	Gary Imhoff
Mr. Luder, the lawyer	Robert Alda

Guests: Jack Klugman, Johnny Carson, Bob Hope, Gene Kelly, Gary Coleman.

MUSIC MART CAST

Wally Coogan	Donald O'Connor
Carol Coogan	Gloria De Haven
Scotty Coogan, their son	Scotty Plummer
Lola, the Coogan's bookkeeper	Micki McKenzie
Al Coody, Wally's friend	Sidney Miller
Sister Hitchcock (guest)	Lucille Ball

Music: Morton Stevens.
Executive Producer: Lucille Ball.
Producer: Hal Kanter.
Director: Jack Donohue.
Choreographer: Louis DaPron.

LUCY MOVES TO NBC — 90 minutes — NBC — February 8, 1980.

1643   LYNDA CARTER'S SPECIAL

Combination Variety Special and Pilot. The program, a variety outing that spotlights Lynda Carter's talents as a singer and dancer, is also a proposed series idea that did not materialize.

Hostess: Lynda Carter.
Guests: Kenny Rogers, Leo Sayer.
Also: Richard Rizzo.
Announcer: Dick Tufeld.
Orchestra: John Harris.
Executive Producer: Ron Samuels.
Producer: Saul Ilson.
Associate Producer: Patti Person.
Director: Stan Harris.
Choreographer: Lester Wilson.
Art Director: Ray Klausen.

LYNDA CARTER'S SPECIAL — 60 minutes — CBS — January 12, 1980.

M

THE MACAHANS

The pilot film broadcast on ABC on January 19, 1976, for the series *How the West Was Won* (see regular program section).

McCLOUD: WHO KILLED MISS U.S.A.?

The pilot film broadcast on NBC on February 17, 1970, for the series *McCloud* (see regular program section).

1644   McLAREN'S RIDERS

Pilot (Adventure). The story of Sam Downing and T. Wood, two highly trained policemen, members of the McLaren Project, a federally sponsored loan-out law-enforcement program that assists understaffed small-town police departments around the country. The pilot episode depicts their efforts to assist Sheriff Bill Willett in his investigation of a cattle rustling operation in Arizona.

REGULAR CAST

Sam Downing	George DiCenzo
T. Wood	Ted Neeley

GUEST CAST

Sheriff Bill Willett	Harry Morgan
Bobby John Britain	Brad Davis
Lamarr Skinner	James Best
Kate Britain	Hilary Thompson
Wanda	Joan Goodfellow
Pete Sunfighter	Geno Silva

Music: Fred Karlin.
Producer: Herbert F. Solow.
Writer: Cliff Gould.
Director: Lee H. Katzin.
Art Director: Joseph Altadonna.
Director of Photography: Hector Figueroa.
Stunt Coordinator: Bill Catching.

McLAREN'S RIDERS — 60 minutes — CBS — May 17, 1977.

1645   McNAMARA'S BAND

Pilot (Comedy). The misadventures of a bumbling group of undercover agents who are sent to occupied Norway during World War II. In the first of two pilot films, Johnny McNamara and his band attempt to silence a disc jockey broadcasting secret messages to German U-boats; the second pilot depicts the band's efforts to rescue a scientist kidnapped by the Nazis.

REGULAR CAST

The Band:

Johnny McNamara	John Byner
Gaffney	Bruce Kirby, Sr.
Zoltan	Sid Haig
Aggie	Lefty Pedroski
Milgrim	Joseph R. Sicari

GUEST CAST

Hedy	Denise Galick
Schnell	Henry Polic II
Jovan	Albert Salmi
Olga	Janice Heiden
Dr. Beshnokov	Peter Elbing

Executive Producer: Jeff Harris, Bernie Kukoff.
Producer: Darrell Hollenbeck.
Writer: Jeff Harris, Bernie Kukoff.
Director: Hal Cooper.

McNAMARA'S BAND — 30 minutes — ABC — first pilot: May 14, 1977; second pilot: December 5, 1977.

McNAUGHTON'S DAUGHTER

The pilot film broadcast on NBC on March 4, 1976, for the series of the same title (see regular program section).

MA AND PA

See title "Marriage Times Four" in the pilot film section.

1646   MADAME SIN

Pilot (Adventure). The exploits of Madame Sin, a female Fu Manchu type of character, as she sets out to rule the world. The pilot depicts her efforts to steal a polaris submarine and ransom it for one billion dollars.

REGULAR CAST

Madame Sin	Bette Davis
DeVere, her aide	Denholm Elliott

GUEST CAST

Anthony Lawrence	Robert Wagner
Cavendish	Gordon Jackson
Monk	Dudley Sutton
Barbara	Catherine Schell
Connors	Paul Maxwell

Music: Michael Gibbs.
Executive Producer: Robert Wagner.
Producer: Lou Morheim, Julian Wintle.
Writer: Barry Oringer.
Director: David Greene.

MADAME SIN — 90 minutes — ABC — January 15, 1972.

THE MAGICIAN

The pilot film broadcast on NBC on March 17, 1973, for the series of the same title (see regular program section).

1647   MAKING IT

Pilot (Comedy). The struggles and misadventures of four law students.

CAST

Steve	Ed Begley, Jr.
Pete	Benjamin Masters
Jay	Alvin Kupperman
Greg	Evan Kim
Cloris	Jeanne Arnold
Janice	Sandy Faison

Executive Producer: Lee Rich, Lawrence Marks.
Producer: Gene Marcione, Burt Metcalfe.
Writer: John Regier.
Director: Peter Baldwin.

MAKING IT — 30 minutes — NBC — August 30, 1976.

1648   MALLORY: CIRCUMSTANTIAL EVIDENCE

Pilot (Crime Drama). The exploits of Daniel Mallory, a once celebrated attorney whose reputation and practice have been tarnished by unfounded perjury charges. The pilot depicts his attempts to defend a young man who is jailed for a car theft — but charged with murder.

REGULAR CAST

Daniel Mallory	Raymond Burr
Joe Celli, his assistant	Mark Hamill

GUEST CAST

Angelo Rondello	Robert Loggia
Roberto Ruiz	A Martinez
Tony Garcia	Victor Mohica

Music: James Di Pasquale.
Producer: William Sackheim.
Writer: Joel Oliansky.
Director: Boris Sagal.

MALLORY: CIRCUMSTANTIAL EVIDENCE — 2 hours — NBC — February 8, 1976.

1649   MANDRAKE

Pilot (Crime Drama). The exploits of Mandrake, a magician knowledgeable in the lore and magic of the ancient (twelfth century) Egyptians and Chinese — secrets he learned in the College of Magic, in an unknown Tibetan valley — secrets he now uses to battle crime. The pilot depicts Mandrake's attempts to apprehend a madman who is trying to blackmail a businessman for $10 million.

REGULAR CAST

Mandrake	Anthony Herrera
Lothar, his servant/ assistant	Ji-Tu Cumbuka

GUEST CAST

Stacy	Simone Griffeth
Jennifer Lindsay	Gretchen Corbett
William Romero	Peter Haskell
Dr. Malcolm Lindsay	David Hooks
Dr. Nolan	Harry Blackstone, Jr.

NBC

Inside O.U.T. Farrah Fawcett.

ABC

The Lisa Hartman Show. Lisa Hartman.

NBC

Frankie and Annette: The Second Time Around. Annette Funicello.

NBC

The Many Loves of Arthur. Caroline McWilliams.

Music: Morton Stevens.
Producer: Rick Husky.
Writer: Rick Husky.
Director: Harry Falk.

MANDRAKE — 2 hours — NBC — January 24, 1979.

THE MAN FROM ATLANTIS

The pilot film broadcast on NBC on March 4, 1977, for the series of the same title (see regular program section).

1650   MAN IN THE MIDDLE

Pilot (Comedy). The misadventures of a conservative family man who is caught between a left-wing daughter, a right-wing mother and a middle-aged business partner on a youth trip.

CAST

Norman, the father	Van Johnson
Harriet, his wife	Nancy Malone
Debbie, his daughter	Heather Menzies
Belle, his mother	Ruth McDevitt
Kirk, his son	Michael Brandon
Harvey, his business partner	Allan Melvin

Music: Jerry Fielding.
Producer: Harvey Bullock, Ray Allen.
Writer: Harvey Bullock, Ray Allen.
Director: Herb Kenwith.

MAN IN THE MIDDLE — 30 minutes — CBS — April 14, 1972.

1651   MAN ON A STRING

Pilot (Crime Drama). The exploits of Pete King, an undercover police lieutenant who undertakes hazardous assignments for the U.S. government. The pilot depicts King's efforts to infiltrate and break up a crime ring.

REGULAR CAST

Lt. Pete King	Christopher George
William Connaught, his superior	William Schallert

GUEST CAST

Mickey Brown	Michael Baseleon
Jake Moniker	Jack Warden
Danny Brown	Keith Carradine
Joe Brown	Joel Grey
Angela Canyon	Kitty Winn
Cowboy	Paul Hampton
Carlo Buglione	J. Duke Russo
Billy Prescott	Lincoln Demyan

Producer: Douglas S. Cramer.
Writer: Peter Madden.
Director: Joseph Sargent.
Director of Photography: Ed Rosson.

MAN ON A STRING — 90 minutes — CBS — February 18, 1972.

MAN ON THE OUTSIDE

The pilot film broadcast on ABC on June 29, 1975, for the series *Griff* (see regular program section).

1652   THE MAN WITH THE POWER

Pilot (Adventure). The exploits of Eric Smith, a Milwaukee high school teacher and the scion of an alien father and Earth mother, who uses his psychokinetic abilities to aid the U.S. government. In the pilot, Smith attempts to protect an oil-rich visiting princess from kidnappers.

REGULAR CAST

Eric Smith	Bob Neill

GUEST CAST

Princess Siri	Persis Khambatta
Paul	Vic Morrow
Shanda	Noel de Souza
Sajid	Rene Assa
Agent Bloom	Tim O'Connor
Farnsworth	Roger Perry

Music: Pat Williams.
Producer: Allan Balter.
Writer: Allan Balter.
Director: Nicholas Sgarro.

THE MAN WITH THE POWER — 2 hours — NBC — May 24, 1977.

MANHUNTER

The pilot film broadcast on CBS on February 26, 1974, for the series of the same title (see regular program section).

1653   THE MANY LOVES OF ARTHUR

Pilot (Comedy). The misadventures of Arthur Murdock, a veterinarian who relates better to animals than people.

CAST

Dr. Arthur Murdock	Richard Masur
Gail	Caroline McWilliams
Karen	Constance McCashin
Mendoza	Silvana Gallardo
Dr. Chase	David Dukes
Michelle	Linda Lukens
Peg	Paddy Edwards

Music: Pat Williams.
Producer: Philip Barry.
Writer: Gerald Di Pego.
Director: Bill Bixby.
Director of Photography: Chuck Arnold.

THE MANY LOVES OF ARTHUR — 60 minutes — NBC — May 23, 1978.

THE MARCUS-NELSON MURDERS

The pilot film broadcast on CBS on March 8, 1973, for the series *Kojak* (see regular program section).

1654   MARIE

Pilot (Comedy). The story of Marie Owens, a beautiful 20-year-old Nebraskan girl who comes to New York to break into show business, and her misadventures as she encounters setback after setback.

CAST

Marie Owens	Marie Osmond
Carla Coburn, Marie's dancing instructor	Ellen Travolta
K. C. Jones, Marie's roommate	Telma Hopkins
Sandra, Marie's other roommate	Zan Charisse
Pancho, Marie's neighbor	Tony Ramierz
Edgar Merton, Marie's landlord	Bruce Kirby, Sr.
Detective Driscoll (guest)	Stephen Shortridge
Sergeant Dryer (guest)	Cliff Pellow

Music: Denny Crockett.
Theme Vocal: Marie Osmond.
Executive Producer: Norman Paul, Joseph Bonaduce.
Producer: Dennis Johnson.
Director: Richard Crenna.

MARIE — 30 minutes — ABC — December 1, 1979.

1655   MARRIAGE IS ALIVE AND WELL

Pilot (Anthology). Incidents in the lives of married couples as seen through the eyes of Bryan Fish, a wedding photographer.

REGULAR CAST

Bryan Fish	Joe Namath
Sarah Fish, his wife	Susan Sullivan

GUEST CAST

Herb Rose	Judd Hirsch
Rachel Satowitz	Gee Gee Vorgan
Jeannie	Melinda Dillon
Corky Dennis	Deborah Baltzell
Chris Dennis	Fred McCarren
Manny Wax	Jack Albertson
LuAnn Brightly	Jeannie Wilson
Judge Elton Sheffield	Mel Stewart
Sunny Delmar	John Harkins
Larry Wax	Nicholas Pryor
Jane Tremont	Swoosie Kurtz
Hop Joe	Erica Yohn
Owen	Jack Riley
Fritz	Jordan Charney

Music: Fred Karlin.
Executive Producer: Marc Merson, Lee Rich.
Producer: Paul Waigner.
Writer: Lee Kalcheim.
Director: Russ Mayberry.
Art Director: John Kuri.
Director of Photography: Hector Figueroa.

MARRIAGE IS ALIVE AND WELL — 2 hours — NBC — January 25, 1980.

1656   MARRIAGE TIMES FOUR

Pilot (Comedy). The overall title for four comedy pilot films.

We'll Get By. The pilot for the series of the same title (see regular program section).

Mo and Jo. Louise Lasser and Michael Tolan as a middle-aged couple caught in the generation gap.

Ma and Pa. The misadventures of a young-at-heart elderly couple,

played by Mary Wickes and Arthur Space.

Another April. The misadventures of April (Leslie Charleson), a young divorcée trying to find peace in the home of her parents (Barnard Hughes and Elizabeth Wilson).

MARRIAGE TIMES FOUR — 2 hours (30 minutes each segment) — CBS — March 7, 1974.

1657   MASON

Pilot (Comedy). The misadventures of a precocious boy named Mason Bennett. In the pilot, Mason's parents attempt to discover why he lacks friends.

CAST

Mason Bennett	Mason Reese
Howard Bennett, his father	Barry Nelson
Peggy Bennett, his mother	Barbara Stuart
Joyce Bennett, his sister	Lee Lawson

Producer: Ira Barmak.
Director: Jack Shea.

MASON — 30 minutes — ABC — July 4, 1977.

THE MASK OF MARCELLA

The syndicated title for the pilot film to the *Cool Million* series (which aired, as "Cool Million," on NBC on October 16, 1972).

MATT HELM

The pilot film broadcast on ABC on May 7, 1975, for the series of the same title (see regular program section).

1658   A MATTER OF WIFE AND DEATH

Pilot (Crime Drama). The story of a rugged police detective named Shamus and his attempts, in the pilot film, to find those responsible for the bombing murder of an old friend, a small-time investigator seemingly not worth the cost of the explosives that killed him. Based on the motion picture *Shamus*.

REGULAR CAST

Detective Shamus	Rod Taylor
Lt. Vince Promuto	Joe Santos

GUEST CAST

Blinky	Eddie Firestone
Snell	Luke Askew
Joe Ruby	John Colicos
Helen Baker	Anita Gillette
Paulie Baker	Tom Drake
Carol	Anne Archer
Springy	Larry Block
Zelda	Lynda Carter
Heavy	Dick Butkus

Music: Richard Shores.
Producer: Robert M. Weitman.
Writer: Don Ingalls.
Director: Marvin Chomsky.

A MATTER OF WIFE AND DEATH — 90 minutes — NBC — April 10, 1975.

1659 MAUREEN

Pilot (Comedy). The misadventures of Maureen Langaree, a middle-aged department store lingerie saleswoman. In the pilot, Maureen, who has always lived her life to help others, seeks to change her boring, monotonous routine by taking a trip to the Virgin Islands—despite the objections of her boss, her mother and her son.

CAST

Maureen Langaree	Joyce Van Patten
Ruth, her mother	Sylvia Sidney
Mr. Frederick, her employer	Alan Oppenheimer
Alice, her friend	Karen Morrow
Damon	Jack Bannon
Trudy	Leigh French
Harvey	Ron Roy

Music: Arthur Rubinstein.
Executive Producer: Mark Carliner.
Producer: Marty Cohan.
Writer: Marty Cohan.
Director: Jay Sandrich.
Art Director: Bill Bonhert.
Associate Producer: Hal Schaffel.

MAUREEN—30 minutes—CBS—August 24, 1976.

1660 ME AND DUCKY

Pilot (Comedy). The misadventures of Carol Munday and her friend Ducky, two glamorous teenagers attending San Francisco High School.

CAST

Carol Munday	Linda Cook
Cidra Hopnagel (Ducky)	Jayne Modean
Dawn Duvall, their friend	Dawn Dunlap
Babs Hulet, their friend	Valerie Landsburg
Toby Wells, a friend	Susan Duvall
Rims, a student	Gary Imhoff
Carol's mother	Kathleen Doyle
Carol's father	James Karen

Music: Larry Weiss.
Executive Producer: Lee Rich, Marc Merson.
Producer: Steve Zacharias.
Director: Bill Persky.

ME AND DUCKY—30 minutes—NBC—June 21, 1979.

1661 MELVIN PURVIS—G-MAN

Pilot (Crime Drama). The story, set in the 1930s, follows the exploits of Melvin Purvis, a ruthless F.B.I. agent (then called G-Men) with an appetite for publicity. The pilot depicts Purvis' relentless pursuit of the notorious mobster, Machine Gun Kelly.

REGULAR CAST

Melvin Purvis	Dale Robertson
Sam Cowley, his assistant	Steve Kanaly
	John Karlen*

GUEST CAST

George "Machine Gun" Kelly	Harris Yulin
Katherine Ryan	Margaret Blye
Thatcher Covington	Dick Sargent
Charles Parlmetter	Matt Clark
Anthony Redecci	John Karlen
Thomas Longaker	Elliott Street
Eugene Farber	David Canary
Nash Covington	Woodrow Parfrey

Narrator: Dale Robertson.
Music: Robert Cobert.
Executive Producer: Paul R. Picard.
Producer: Dan Curtis.
Writer: John Milius.
Director: Dan Curtis.
Director of Photography: Jacques Marquette.

MELVIN PURVIS—G-MAN—90 minutes—ABC—April 9, 1974.

*Replaced Kanaly in a sequel television movie, but not a pilot titled *The Kansas City Massacre* (ABC, September 19, 1975) in which Dale Robertson again portrayed Melvin Purvis, this time in pursuit of mobsters Charles "Pretty Boy" Floyd (Bo Hopkins), Frank "Jelly" Nash (Mills Watson) and Adam Richetti (Robert Walden).

1662 MEN OF THE DRAGON

Pilot (Adventure). The exploits of Jan, Lisa and Li-Teh, three karate experts who use their unique skills to battle crime. In the pilot, they seek to stop a ring of modern slave marketeers operating in Hong Kong.

REGULAR CAST

Jan	Jared Martin
Lisa	Kati Saylor
Li-Teh	Robert Ito

GUEST CAST

Balashev	Joseph Wiseman
Sato	Lee Tit War
Madame Wu	Hsai Ho Lan
O-Lan	Nang Sheen Chiou
Endacott	Bill Jervis

Music: Elmer Bernstein.
Executive Producer: Stan Margulies.
Producer: Barney Rosenzweig.
Writer: Denne Bart Petitclere.
Director: Harry Falk.

MEN OF THE DRAGON—90 minutes—ABC—March 20, 1974.

1663 THE MICHELE LEE SHOW

Pilot (Comedy). The story of Michele Burton, a pretty newsstand clerk at the Beverly Wilshire Hotel in Beverly Hills, California. The pilot episode depicts her misadventures as she attempts to impress a young intern by preparing him a home cooked dinner—despite the fact that she can't cook.

REGULAR CAST

Michele Burton	Michele Lee
Mr. Zelensky, her neighbor	Herbie Faye
Gladys Gooch, her friend	Joyce Bulifant

GUEST CAST

Dr. Steven Mayhill	Stephen Collins
Customer	Sidney Clute

Music: Stephen Lawrence.
Theme Vocal: Michele Lee.
Producer: Fred Coe.
Writer: Robert Klane.
Director: Peter Baldwin.
Director of Photography: Paul Uhl.

THE MICHELE LEE SHOW—30 minutes—CBS—April 5, 1974.

1664 THE MILLIONAIRE

Pilot (Drama). An update of the 1950s television series about people who are surprised with a gift of one million dollars from an anonymous benefactor.* In the pilot episode, Kate Mathews, Arthur Haines and the Reardon brothers each receive a million-dollar, tax-free check. The story details how the money helps or hinders the recipients (for Kate, it brings a new life for a group of children whose lives have been a nightmare; for Arthur, the money brings a new lease on life; and for Eddie, Mike and Harold Reardon, the money brings a high-rolling fling in Las Vegas).

REGULAR CAST

Michael Anthony, the man who, on behalf of the estate of John Beresford Tipton, distributes the checks .... Robert Quarry

GUEST CAST

Kate Mathews	Pamela Toll
Arthur Haines	Martin Balsam
Eddie Reardon	Bill Hudson
Mike Reardon	Mark Hudson
Harold Reardon	Brett Hudson
Maggie Haines	Patricia Crowley
Paul Mathews	Edward Albert, Jr.
Wayburn	John Ireland

Music: Frank DeVol.
Producer: Don Fedderson.
Director: Don Weis.
Art Director: David Scott.
Creator: Don Fedderson.

THE MILLIONAIRE—2 hours—CBS—December 19, 1978.

*In the original series, a man named John Beresford Tipton, a multimillionaire, made it a hobby to give to people selected by a means known only to him, a cashier's check for $1 million. Marvin Miller portrayed Michael Anthony in the original series.

1665 MISS STEWART, SIR

Pilot (Comedy). The story of Kate Stewart, a boys' school housemother. In the pilot, Kate meets her first challenge: to teach her charges the art of playing football.

CAST

Kate Stewart	Joanna Pettet
Buzz	Gary Vinson
Joe	Michael Witney
Principal Prentiss	Murray Matheson
Hannah	Nora Marlowe
George	Don Clarke
Mike	Lee Hollingshead

Producer: Peter Tewksbury.
Writer: A. J. Carothers.
Director: Peter Tewksbury.

MISS STEWART, SIR—30 minutes—CBS—March 31, 1972.

1666 MIXED NUTS

Pilot (Comedy). The comic conflicts between patients and staff at a mental institution.

CAST

Dr. Sara Allgood	Zohra Lampert
Dr. Folder	Emory Bass
Nurse Cassidy	Conchata Ferrell
Moe	Morey Amsterdam
Bugs	Dan Barrows
Jamie	Ed Begley, Jr.
Logan	Richard Karron

Executive Producer: Jerry Belson, Mark Carliner.
Producer: Michael Leeson.
Writer: Jerry Belson, Mark Carliner.
Director: Peter H. Hunt.

MIXED NUTS—30 minutes—ABC—May 12, 1977.

MO AND JO

See title "Marriage Times Four" in the pilot film section.

1667 MOBILE MEDICS

Pilot (Drama). The exploits of Liz, Robb, Bryant and Paco, four doctors who operate a sophisticated mobile medical unit, a mini-lab and operating room that they use to assist people who don't have the time to make it to a hospital.

CAST

Liz	Ellen Weston
Robb	Jack Stauffer
Bryant	Ben Masters
Paco	Jaime Tirelli

Executive Producer: Bruce Lansbury.
Producer: Bob Hamilton.
Writer: Bob Hamilton.
Director: Paul Krasny.

MOBILE MEDICS—30 minutes—CBS—May 10, 1977.

MOBILE 2

The pilot film broadcast on ABC on September 2, 1975, for the series *Mobile 1* (see regular program section).

MOST WANTED

The pilot film broadcast on ABC on March 21, 1976, for the series of the same title (see regular program section).

1668 MOTHER AND ME, M.D.

Pilot (Comedy). The story follows the life of Barrie Tucker, a young female doctor, as she begins her internship in a New York hospital where her mother, Lil Brenner, works as the head nurse.

CAST

Lil Brenner	Rue McClanahan
Barrie Tucker	Leah Ayres
Evan Murray, Lil's neighbor	Jack Riley
Dr. Mace Oatfield	Ken Gilman
Dr. Sam Kanin	Howard Witt

Music: Patrick Williams.
Executive Producer: Michael Zinberg.
Producer: Jennie Blacton, Charles Raymond.
Director: Michael Zinberg.

MOTHER AND ME, M.D.—30 minutes—NBC—June 14, 1979.

1669 MOTHER, JUGGS, AND SPEED

Pilot (Comedy). The story of a near-bankrupt ambulance service whose proprietor, Harry Fishbine, seeks to beat the competition and still make a buck off muggings, malnutrition and disease. His angels of mercy are: Mother, a hard-drinking driver; Juggs, the well-endowed switchboard girl who longs to be a paramedic; and Speed, an embittered, suspended police officer.

CAST

Mother	Ray Vitte
Juggs	Joanne Nail
Speed	Joe Penny
Harry Fishbine	Harvey Lembeck
Mrs. Fishbine	Barbara Minkus
Murdock	Rod McCary

Producer: John Rich.
Writer: Tom Mankiewicz.
Director: John Rich.

MOTHER, JUGGS, AND SPEED—30 minutes—ABC—August 17, 1978. Based on the 1976 feature film of the same title.

1670 MOVIN' ON

Pilot (Adventure). The story of Clint Daniels, a stock car racer, and Johnny Lake, a cycle racer, two clean-cut young men who decide to pool their resources and travel around the country to see America. The would-be series, which was to depict their adventures with the people they encounter, involves Clint and Johnny with Cory, a beautiful Mormon, and a death-defying race for the girl's affections.

REGULAR CAST

Clint Daniels	Patrick Wayne
Johnny Lake	Geoffrey Deuel

GUEST CAST

Cory	Kate Jackson
Jeff	David Soul
Mrs. Lake (Johnny's mother)	Meg Wyllie
Clint's father	Walter Barnes

Music: Dominic Frontiere.
Theme: "Movin' On" by Dominic Frontiere (music) and Sally Stevens (lyrics).
Executive Producer: Douglas S. Cramer.
Producer: Jerome Courtland.

Writer: Stirling Silliphant.
Director: E. W. Swackhamer.
Creator: Stirling Silliphant.

MOVIN' ON—65 minutes—NBC—July 24, 1972.

1671 MR. & MRS. & MR.

Pilot (Comedy). A year after her husband, Jimmy York, an ex-quarterback for the New York Jets, is reported killed in a plane crash in the Caribbean, widow Jenny Collins (who retained her maiden name) marries Jeff Zelinka, a sportswriter. Shortly after, her life is complicated when Jimmy shows up alive, having been nursed back to health by an Indian fisherman. The would-be series focuses on the problems series focuses on the problems that exist as Jenny, now with two husbands who each dispute the other's claim on his wife, desperately seeks a way to resolve the situation and live a normal, happy married life—with one husband.

CAST

Jenny Collins	Rebecca Balding
Jimmy York	Kale Browne
Jeff Zelinka	Patrick Collins
Susan Waters, Jenny's friend	Eda Zahl

Music: Bill Byers.
Theme: "Mr. & Mrs. & Mr." by Rod Parker and Hal Cooper.
Theme Vocal: Joannie Sommers.
Executive Producer: Rod Parker, Hal Cooper.
Producer: Rob Dames, Bob Fraser, Rita Dillon.
Writer: Rod Parker.
Director: Hal Cooper.
Art Director: Chuck Murawski.

MR. & MRS. & MR.—30 minutes—CBS—September 1, 1980.

1672 MR. AND MRS. COP

Pilot (Crime Drama). The story chronicles a newlywed couple's adjustment to marriage, made more difficult by their demanding jobs as police officers.

REGULAR CAST

Officer Paul Roscommon	Anthony Costello
Officer Nancy Roscommon, his wife	Marianne McAndrew
Lieutenant Ocala	Richard Angarola
Sergeant Baum	William Campbell

GUEST CAST

Al Johnson	Tom Falk
Chester	Howard Platt
Albanel	Max Gail
Mrs. Salmon	Holly Near
Irv Pyle	Redmond Gleeson
Minister	Alan Dexter

Producer: Leonard B. Kaufman.
Writer: Howard Rodman.
Director: Harvey Hart.

MR. AND MRS. COP—30 minutes—CBS—April 1, 1975.

1673 MR. AND MRS. DRACULA

Pilot (Comedy). After 618 years of marriage, Vladimir Dracula, a vampire, and his wife Sonia, relocate from their castle in Transylvania to the Bronx, New York, when angry villagers force them to leave their homeland. The pilot episode depicts their struggles to adjust to life in America and Vladimir's efforts to provide a happy anniversary celebration for Sonia.

CAST

Vladimir Dracula, the father	Dick Shawn
Sonia Dracula, his wife	Carol Lawrence
Minna Dracula, their daughter	Gail Mayron
Sonny Dracula, their son	Anthony Battaglia
Voice of Gregor, the bat who forgot how to turn back into a vampire	Johnny Haymer
Vladimir's Cousin Anton	Barry Gordon
Mario, the building janitor	Rick Aviles

Music: Ken Lauber.
Executive Producer: Robert Klane.
Producer: Stanley Korey.
Writer-Creator: Robert Klane.
Director: Doug Rogers.

MR. AND MRS. DRACULA—30 minutes—ABC—September 5, 1980.

MRS. COLUMBO

The pilot film broadcast on NBC on February 26, 1979, for the series of the same title (see regular program section).

1674 M STATION: HAWAII

Pilot (Adventure). The exploits of a five-person oceanographic team attached to M (Makai) Station: Hawaii, a privately funded research development company working off the Hawaiian coast. In the pilot, the team, hired by the U.S. government, attempts to retrieve secret information contained in a sunken Soviet submarine. (Makai is Hawaiian for "Towards the Sea.")

REGULAR CAST

The M Station Team:

Dana Ryan	Jared Martin
Andrew McClelland	Andrew Duggan
Karen Holt	Jo Ann Harris
Luana Sorel	Elissa Dulce
Truck Kealoha	Moe Keale

GUEST CAST

Margaret Michaels	Dana Wynter
Billy Jim Whitney	Tom McFadden
Vasily Litvak	Ted Hamilton
Admiral Henderson	Jack Lord
Capt. Ben Galloway	Andrew Prine
Admiral Lincoln	Lyle Bettger

Music: Morton Stevens.
Executive Producer: Jack Lord.
Producer: Frank Baum.

Writer: Robert Janes.
Director: Jack Lord.

M STATION: HAWAII—2 hours—CBS—June 10, 1980.

MULLIGAN'S STEW

The pilot film broadcast on NBC on June 20, 1977, for the series of the same title (see regular program section).

1675 MURDER CAN HURT YOU!

Pilot (Comedy). A would-be series in which television's famous detectives ban together to solve crimes. In the pilot presentation, the clones of TV detectives, members of "The Best Cops in the World Club," join forces to apprehend "The Man in White," an archvillain who is planning to kill each one of them.

CAST

Lt. Nojack (clone of Lt. Kojak)	Gavin MacLeod
Sgt. Salty Sanderson (clone of Sgt. Pepper Anderson)	Connie Stevens
Chief Ironbottom (clone of Chief Ironside)	Victor Buono
Detective Studsky (clone of Det. Starsky)	Jamie Farr
Detective Hatch (clone of Det. Hutch)	John Byner
Pony Lambretta (clone of Tony Baretta)	Tony Danza
Sheriff Tim MacSkye (clone of Sam McCloud)	Buck Owens
Inspector Palumbo (clone of Lt. Columbo)	Burt Young
Sarafina Palumbo (clone of Kate Columbo)	Liz Torres
Parks, Ironbottom's aide (clone of Mark on *Ironside*)	Jimmie Walker
Det. Starkos (clone of Stavros on *Kojak*)	Marty Allen
Chickie Baby (clone of Baretta's cockatoo Fred); voiced by	Mel Blanc
The Man in White, the villain	Mitch Kreindel
Raquel Sophia, Pony's informant, a hooker	Gunilla Hutton
Virginia Trickwood, the madam	Roz Kelly
Willie the wino	Mason Adams
Hooker (Pony's informant)	Muffy Durham
Woman whose purse is snatched	Iris Adrian

Narrator: Don Adams.
Music: Artie Kane.
Supervising Producer: E. Duke Vincent.
Executive Producer: Aaron Spelling, Douglas S. Cramer.
Writer: Ron Friedman.
Director: Roger Ducovny.

MURDER CAN HURT YOU!—2 hours—ABC—May 21, 1980.

1676 MURDER IN MUSIC CITY

Pilot (Crime Drama). The story of Sonny Hunt, a songwriter, and his wife, Samantha, newlyweds who become private detectives. The head of the investigative agency in which Sonny has a vested interest has been murdered and the Hunts assume ownership. The pilot episode depicts their efforts to find the agency owner's killer. Potential series title: *Sonny and Sam*.

REGULAR CAST

Sonny Hunt	Sonny Bono
Samantha Hunt	Lee Purcell
Mrs. Bloom, the agency secretary	Lucille Benson

GUEST CAST

Billy West	Claude Akins
Peggy Ann	Belinda J. Montgomery
Dana	Morgan Fairchild
Lt. Culver	Tommy Cutrer
Barbara Mandrell	Herself
Charlie Daniels	Himself
Mel Tillis	Himself
Ray Stevens	Himself

Music: Earle Hagen.
Producer: Jimmy Sangster.
Writer: Jimmy Sangster, Ernie Frankel.
Director: Leo Penn.
Director of Photography: Alan Stensvold.

MURDER IN MUSIC CITY — 2 hours — NBC — January 16, 1979.

1677 THE MURDOCKS AND THE McCLAYS

Pilot (Comedy). A hillbilly-accented comedy about a feud that exists between two rival families, the Murdocks and the McClays. In the pilot, Calvin Murdock and Angus McClay, the family leaders, seek a way to discourage a romance between their children, Junior Murdock and Julianna McClay — a romance that could lead to marriage and an unwanted peace between the two families (and "hate ain't no good 'less it's likewise").

CAST

Angus McClay	Dub Taylor
Julianna McClay	Kathy Davis
Calvin Murdock	Noah Beery
Calvin Murdock, Jr.	John Carson
Ira Murdock	Judy Canova
Grandpa Murdock	William Fawcett
Grandma Murdock	Nydia Westman
Sheriff Bates	James Westerfield
Turkey	George C. Fisher

Producer: Jerry Belson, Garry Marshall.
Writer: Jerry Belson, Garry Marshall.
Director: Charles R. Rondeau.

THE MURDOCKS AND THE McCLAYS — 30 minutes — ABC — September 2, 1970.

1678 MURDOCK'S GANG

Pilot (Crime Drama). The story, set in California, follows the exploits of Bartley James "B.J." Murdock, a disbarred criminal attorney (falsely accused of allowing a witness to purjure himself).

After serving a two-year prison term, he begins a private investigative service by hiring a staff of ex-cons. In the pilot, Murdock attempts to track the missing accountant of a millionaire — a case that leads to murder (the accountant), an uncovered love affair (the millionaire's wife and friend), and a murder attempt on the millionaire, Harold Talbot, by two of his staff.

REGULAR CAST

Bradley James Murdock	Alex Drier
Bat Collins, one of Murdock's Gang	Walter Burke
Terry, Murdock's secretary	Donna Benz
Lawrence Devans, Murdock's lawyer	Colby Chester
Denver Briggs, same as Bat	Charles Dierkop
Ed Lyman, same as Bat	Ed Bernard
Mickey Carr, same as Bat	Dave Morrick
Red Harris, same as Bat	Norman Alden

GUEST CAST

Harold Talbot (the millionaire)	Murray Hamilton
Laura Talbot (his wife)	Janet Leigh
Frank Winston (the accountant)	Milton Selzer
Roger Bates	William Daniels
Dave Ryker	Harold Gould
Barney Parelli	Frank Campanella
Glenn Dickson	Don Knight
Ryker's secretary	Karen Arthur
Deputy	Larry McCormick
Dr. Barkis	Fred Sadoff

Music: Frank DeVol.
Executive Producer: Don Fedderson.
Producer: Edward H. Feldman.
Writer: Edmund North.
Director: Charles S. Dubin.
Art Director: Perry Ferguson.
Director of Photography: Michael Joyce.

MURDOCK'S GANG — 90 minutes — CBS — March 20, 1973.

THE MUSIC MART

See title "Lucy Moves to NBC" in the pilot film section.

1679 MUSICAL COMEDY TONIGHT

Combination Variety Special and Pilot. The program highlights memorable moments from the American music theatre. In the pilot, a recreation of twelve songs and dances from four Broadway hits.

Hostess: Sylvia Fine Kaye.
Guests: Ethel Merman, Rock Hudson, Bernadette Peters, Sandy Duncan, John Davidson, Bobby Van, Richard Chamberlain, Agnes de Mille, Carol Burnett.
Orchestra: Peter Matz.
Music Coordinator: David Baker.
Executive Producer: Sylvia Fine Kaye.
Producer: Eric Lieber.
Writer: Sylvia Fine Kaye.
Director: Stan Harris.

Choreographer: Walter Painter.
Art Director: Romain Johnston.
Creator: Sylvia Fine Kaye.

The Broadway Plays and Songs/Dances:

Good News (1927): "The Best Things in Life Are Free" (Bernadette Peters, Bobby Van); "The Varsity Drag" (Sandy Duncan).

Anything Goes (1934): "I Get a Kick Out of You" (Ethel Merman); "You're the Top" (Ethel, Rock Hudson); "Anything Goes" (Ethel).

Oklahoma (1943): "Oh What a Beautiful Mornin'" (John Davidson); "I Can't Say No" (Carol Burnett); "Oklahoma" (John).

Company (1970): "Another Hundred People" (Sandy); "Barcelona" (Richard Chamberlain, Bernadette); "The Ladies Who Lunch" (Carol); "Side by Side" (Richard).

MUSICAL COMEDY TONIGHT — 90 minutes — PBS — October 1, 1979.

1680 MY BUDDY

Pilot (Comedy). The story of Woodrow "Buddy" Johnson, an average guy and owner of Buddy's Bar in San Francisco, and his misadventures when he inherits, from a late friend, the multimillion dollar Worth Enterprises and enters high society.

CAST

Woodrow "Buddy" Johnson	Redd Foxx
Catherine Worth, the sister of the late owner of Worth Enterprises	Pamela Mason
Slappy, Buddy's bartender	Slappy White

Also: Basil Hoffman, Irwin C. Watson.
Music: Gerald Wilson.
Executive Producer: Redd Foxx.
Producer: Norman Hopps.
Director: Gerren Keith.

MY BUDDY — 30 minutes — NBC — July 3, 1979 (an unscheduled air date).

1681 MY SISTER HANK

Pilot (Comedy). The misadventures of Hank Bennett, a pretty teenage tomboy. In the pilot, Hank faces and attempts to overcome discrimination when, because of her sex, she is kept from joining the Little League team.

CAST

Henrietta "Hank" Bennett	Jodie Foster
Eunice Bennett, her mother	Pippa Scott
Willis Bennett, her father	Jack Ging
Grandpa Bennett	Edgar Bergen
Dianne Bennett, her sister	Suzanne Hillard
Arthur, Hank's friend	Todd Bass

Producer: Norman Tokar.
Writer: Ben Starr.
Director: Norman Tokar.

MY SISTER HANK — 30 minutes — CBS — March 31, 1972.

1682 MY WIFE NEXT DOOR

Pilot (Comedy). The story of Suzy and George Bassett, a newly separated young couple, awaiting a divorce settlement, who become sparring partners again when they accidentally rent neighboring apartments.

CAST

Suzy Bassett	Julie Sommars
George Bassett	James Farentino
Suzy's mother	Martha Scott
Ronnie	Jordan Crittenden

Producer: Bill Persky, Sam Denoff.
Writer: Bill Persky, Sam Denoff.
Director: Bill Persky.

MY WIFE NEXT DOOR — 30 minutes — NBC — December 31, 1975.

1683 MY WIFE NEXT DOOR

Pilot (Comedy). The story of Paul Gilmore, a big league ball player, and Lisa Pallick, his ex-wife, a producer of television commercials, and their misadventures when, after accidentally renting adjoining apartments in San Francisco, they again become sparring partners.

CAST

Paul Gilmore	Granville Van Dusen
Lisa Pallick	Lee Purcell
Jan Pallick, Lisa's sister	Desiree Boschetti
Vinnie Messina, Paul's friend	Michael DeLano
Lionel, Lisa's co-worker	Frank Dent
Artie, the apartment building super	Phil Rubinstein

Theme Music: Rich Fatah, Ian LeFrenais.
Executive Producer: Martin Starger.
Producer: Allan McKeown, Ian LeFrenais.
Writer: Dick Clement, Ian LeFrenais.
Director: Bill Persky.
Art Director: Chuck Murawski.

MY WIFE NEXT DOOR — 30 minutes — CBS — September 11, 1980.

1684 MY WIVES JANE

Pilot (Comedy). The misadventures of Jane Franklin, an actress, married to a doctor, who also portrays a doctor's wife on a television serial. In the pilot, Jane seeks to ease the tension her dual roles cause by convincing her husband that she can handle both careers — actress and housewife — efficiently.

CAST

Jane Franklin	Janet Leigh
Dr. Nat Franklin, her	
husband	Barry Nelson
Vic Semple, the serial star	John Dehner
Dirk Bennett	McLean Stevenson
Molly	Mia Bendixsen
Magda	Nora Marlowe

Producer: Edward H. Feldman.
Writer: Larry Gelbart.
Director: Edward H. Feldman.

MY WIVES JANE — 30 minutes — CBS — August 1, 1971.

N

NAKIA

The pilot film broadcast on April 17, 1974, for the series of the same title (see regular program section).

THE NANCY DUSSAULT SHOW

See title "CBS Triple Play" in the pilot film section.

1685   THE NATURAL LOOK

Pilot (Comedy). The misadventures that befall the newlywed Harrisons: Bud, a doctor, and Edie, a cosmetics executive. The pilot depicts Edie's feelings as she prepares to meet Bud's ex-flame, a glamorous girl who exhibits a domestic flair she feels she can't match.

CAST

Bud Harrison	Bill Bixby
Edie Harrison	Barbara Feldon
Jane	Caren Kaye
Countess	Brenda Forbes

Music: Charles Fox.
Producer: Leonora Thuna.
Director: Robert Moore.

THE NATURAL LOOK — 30 minutes — NBC — July 6, 1977.

1686   NERO WOLFE

Pilot (Crime Drama). The exploits of Nero Wolfe, gourmet, connoisseur, and a sometimes detective who tangles with — and helps — the police and F.B.I. Based on the character created by Rex Stout.

REGULAR CAST

Nero Wolfe	Thayer David
Archie Goodwin, his assistant	Tom Mason

GUEST CAST

Rachel Bruner	Anne Baxter
Sarah Dacos	Brooke Adams
Inspector Cramer	Biff McGuire
Mr. Althaus	Sarah Cunningham
Lon Cohen	John Randolph

Executive Producer: Emmett Larvey, Jr.
Producer: Everett Chambers.
Writer: Frank Gilroy.

Director: Frank Gilroy.
Director of Photography: Ric Waite.

NERO WOLFE — 2 hours — ABC — December 18, 1979 (originally filmed in 1977).

1687   NEVADA SMITH

Pilot (Western). The story, set in the Old West, follows the adventures of Nevada Smith, a half-breed gunslinger, and Jonas Cord, his mentor, men who join forces to enforce law and order on the ruthless frontier. The pilot depicts their efforts to escort a shipment of explosives across the Utah territory. Based on the 1966 feature film of the same title.

REGULAR CAST

Nevada Smith	Cliff Potts
Jonas Cord	Lorne Greene

GUEST CAST

Frank Hartlee	Adam West
Red Fickett	Warren Vanders
Two Moon	Jorge Luke
Brill	Jerry Gatlin
Davey	Eric Cord

Music: Lamont Dozier.
Producer: Martin Rackin, John Michael Hayes.
Writer: Martin Rackin, John Michael Hayes.
Director: Gordon Douglas.

NEVADA SMITH — 90 minutes — NBC — May 3, 1975.

1688   NEVER SAY NEVER

Pilot (Comedy). The story of Harry Walter, a widowed, middle-aged (54) plumbing supply company businessman, who falls in love with Dr. Sarah Keaton, a poised, young (32), and beautiful pediatrician. The pilot depicts Sarah's efforts to convince Harry that, before they marry, they should first live together.

REGULAR CAST

Harry Walter	George Kennedy
Dr. Sarah Keaton	Anne Schedeen
Florence, Harry's	
mother-in-law	Irene Tedrow
Paul Walter, Harry's son	Bruce Kimmel
Ronnie, Sarah's friend	Rick Podell
Sarah's nurse	Maidie Norman

GUEST CAST

DeMarco	Ric Mancini
Mother	Jan Jorden
Little boy	Danny Gellis
Jimmy	Jayson Naylor

Music: Danny Wells.
Executive Producer: Leonard A. Rosenberg.
Producer: Elliot Shoenman.
Co-Producer: Lee Miller.
Writer: Elliot Shoenman.
Director: Charles S. Dubin.
Art Director: Frank Swig.
Director of Photography: Bob Caramico.
Set Decorator: Solomon Brewer.
Creator: Leonard A. Rosenberg.

NEVER SAY NEVER — 30 minutes — CBS — July 11, 1979.

1689   THE NEW DAUGHTERS OF JOSHUA CABE

Pilot (Western Comedy-Drama). The third of three unsold pilot films about Joshua Cabe, a fur trapper who passes off three shady ladies as his daughters (see also "The Daughters of Joshua Cabe" and "The Daughters of Joshua Cabe Return"). The story focuses on an elaborate plan by Bitterroot, Cabe's friend, and Charity, Ada and Mae, Cabe's three daughters, to clear Joshua of a murder charge for which he was unjustly accused — and save him from the hangman's noose.

REGULAR CAST

Joshua Cabe	John MacIntire
Bitterroot, his friend	Jack Elam
Charity, his daughter	Liberty Williams
Ada, his daughter	Renne Jarrett
Mae, his daughter	Lezlie Dalton

GUEST CAST

Essie Cargo	Jeanette Nolan
Warden Mannering	John Dehner
Dutton	Geoffrey Lewis
Codge Collier	Sean McClory
Matt Cobley	Joel Fabiani
Judge	Ford Rainey
Billy Linaker	Randall Carver

Music: Jeff Alexander.
Executive Producer: Aaron Spelling, Leonard Goldberg.
Producer: Paul Savage.
Writer: Paul Savage.
Director: Bruce Bilson.

THE NEW DAUGHTERS OF JOSHUA CABE — 90 minutes — ABC — May 29, 1976.

1690   THE NEW HEALERS

Pilot (Drama). The story of three people, Calvin Briggs and Jimmy Martin, ex-Vietnam medics, and Michelle Johnson, an ex-nurse, who join forces to help Dr. Simmons, an aging physician, care for the people of Hope, a rural community in California. The pilot depicts their efforts to gain the confidence of the people who are distrustful of the young medics.

REGULAR CAST

Dr. Calvin Briggs	Robert Foxworth
Nurse Michelle Johnson	Kate Jackson
Dr. Jimmy Martin	Jonathan Lippe
Dr. Simmons	Burgess Meredith
Dr. Victor Briggs,	
Calvin's father	Leif Erickson

GUEST CAST

Mr. Farrigan	William Windom
Mr. Fisherman	Karl Swenson
Terri	Susan Moffatt
Mrs. Spencer	Barbara Baldavin
Mr. McDermott	William Bryant

Music: Kenyon Hopkins.
Producer: Stirling Silliphant.

Writer: Stirling Silliphant.
Director: Bernard L. Kowalski.
Art Director: John M. Elliott.
Director of Photography: Howard Schwartz.
Set Decorator: Dorcy Howard.

THE NEW HEALERS — 60 minutes — ABC — March 27, 1972.

1691   THE NEW LORENZO MUSIC SHOW

Pilot (Comedy). The misadventures of Lorenzo Music, a nervous, anxiety-ridden writer who hosts a talk-variety series on television.

Starring: Lorenzo and Henrietta Music (Mr. and Mrs.).
Guests: David Ogden Stiers, Jack Eagle, Steve Anderson, Roz Kelly, Lewis Arquette.
Executive Producer: Lorenzo Music.
Producer: Carl Gottlieb.
Writer: Lorenzo Music, Carl Gottlieb, James L. Brooks, Jerry Davis, Allan Burns.
Director: Tony Mordente.

THE NEW LORENZO MUSIC SHOW — 30 minutes — ABC — August 10, 1976.

THE NEW MAVERICK

The pilot film broadcast on ABC on September 3, 1978, for the series *Young Maverick* (see regular program section).

THE NEW, ORIGINAL WONDER WOMAN

The pilot film broadcast on ABC on November 7, 1975, for the series *Wonder Woman* (see regular program section).

1692   NEWMAN'S DRUGSTORE

Pilot (Comedy). The story, set in Brooklyn, New York, during the Depression, follows the life of Charles Newman, a druggist who, despite hard times, is overly generous with his hard-luck customers — a generosity that threatens to sink his business.

CAST

Charles Newman	Herschel Bernardi
Woody Newman	Michael LeClair
Leon Rossoff	Allan Rich
Shirley Tinker	June Gable
Murray Tinker	Robert Lussier
Dora Goldman	Fritzi Burr
Marcy Goldman	Dominique Pinassi

Music: Charles Fox.
Executive Producer: Bob Lovenheim, Mitchell Brower.
Producer: Hy Averback.
Director: Hy Averback.

NEWMAN'S DRUGSTORE — 30 minutes — NBC — August 30, 1976.

1693   NICK AND THE DOBERMANS

Pilot (Crime Drama). The story of Nick Macazie, a private detective who is assisted by three Doberman pinschers. The pilot episode depicts Nick's attempts to safeguard an accountant who witnessed a murder and now fears for her life.

REGULAR CAST

| Nick Macazie | Michael Nouri |
| Lieutenant Elbone | Robert Davi |

GUEST CAST

Barbara Gateon (the accountant)	Judith Chapman
Roger Vincent	John Cunningham
Speed Queen	Vivian Bonnell
Speedy Man	Chris Hayward

The Dobermans: Duke, Pee Wee and Erskine.

Music: Jerrold Immel.
Executive Producer: Harve Bennett, Harris Katleman.
Producer: James D. Parriott, Richard Chapman.
Writer: James D. Parriott, Richard Chapman.
Director: Bernard L. Kowalski.
Art Director: Ross Bellah.

NICK AND THE DOBERMANS — 60 minutes — NBC — April 25, 1980. See also "Alex and the Doberman Gang" in the pilot film section.

1694   THE NIGHTENGALES

Pilot (Crime Drama). The exploits of Jenny Palermo and Cotton Gardner, two beautiful Los Angeles undercover policewomen who work the Hollywood beat at night (they ride in a patrol car and are called the Nightengales, an experimental two-girl team). The pilot depicts their efforts to nab a criminal posing as Humphrey Bogart; apprehend thieves who make their getaways in a souped-up van; and reform Fingernail Dolly, a famous thief.

REGULAR CAST

Officer Jenny Palermo	Marcia Strassman
Officer Cotton Gardner	Colette Blonigan
Big Duane, their contact, a D.J. at radio station KIRA	James Spinks
Sergeant Donovan, their superior	Richard Hatch

GUEST CAST

Fingernail Dolly	Sheree North
Ice	Dennis Redfield
James	Ji-Tu Cumbuka
Jumbo	Eugene Butler
Ray Sikora	Mark Schneider
Humphrey Bogart criminal	Jerry Lacy

Music: Barry De Vorzon.
Executive Producer: Lawrence Gordon.
Producer: Jay Benson.
Writer: Christian Danus.
Director: Charles S. Dubin.
Director of Photography: Dennis Dalzell.

THE NIGHTENGALES — 60 minutes — NBC — May 19, 1979.

NIGHT GAMES

The pilot film broadcast on NBC on March 16, 1974, for the series *Petrocelli* (see regular program section).

1695   THE NIGHT RIDER

Pilot (Adventure). The story, set in New Orleans in the 1870s, follows the exploits of Sir Thomas Earl, a dandy by day, a daring and powerful figure for justice by night. (Shortly after the murder of his parents, a wealthy British woman adopts the surviving son, Charles Hollister. Raised and educated in the finest schools, hence his British title, Hollister, now Sir Thomas Earl, returns to New Orleans to become the mysterious Night Rider to avenge the death of his parents by avenging the wrongs done to innocent people.)

REGULAR CAST

| Sir Thomas Earl | David Selby |
| Robert, Earl's companion | Percy Rodrigues |

GUEST CAST

Alex Sheridan	Pernell Roberts
Dan Keaton	George Grizzard
Regina	Kim Cattrall
Hollister	Van Williams

Music: Mike Post and Pete Carpenter.
Supervising Producer: William Phillips.
Executive Producer: Stephen J. Cannell.
Producer: J. Rickley Dunn.
Director: Hy Averback.

THE NIGHT RIDER — 90 minutes — ABC — May 11, 1979.

1696   NIGHTSIDE

Pilot (Drama). The story of Carmine Kelly, a press agent who covers the midnight action in New York City. In the pilot, Kelly attempts to help protect his friend Smitty from the impending destruction of her restaurant — a hangout for actors, writers, businessmen, "and other folk who brighten up when the sun goes down" — by a ruthless realtor. He also tries to help Vantura Davis, a faded movie star who has come to New York to appear on *The Dick Cavett Show* to promote an awful movie, which, unfortunately, is her attempt at a comeback.

REGULAR CAST

Carmine Kelly	John Cassavetes
Smitty, the owner of the restaurant hangout	Alexis Smith
Aram Bessoyggian, the private detective	Mike Kellin

GUEST CAST

Vantura Davis	June Havoc
Grudin	Joseph Wiseman
Gable	Richard Jordan
Ralph	Seymour Cassell
Jabbo	Joe Santos
Shane	Seth Allen
Acky	F. Murray Abraham
Dick Cavett	Himself

Producer: Herbert B. Leonard.
Writer: Pete Hamill.
Director: Richard Donner.
Creator: Pete Hamill.

NIGHTSIDE — 60 minutes — ABC — April 15, 1973.

1697   NIGHTSIDE

Pilot (Crime Drama). The story of Danny Dandoy and Ed Macey, two less-than-perfect Los Angeles police officers who patrol the city at night.

REGULAR CAST

Officer Danny Dandoy	Doug McClure
Sgt. Ed Macey	Michael Cornelison
Sgt. Duckman, the watch commander	Roy Jenson
Janie Moody, the night D.J. at radio station KDEV	Melinda Naud
Lily, the police radio dispatcher	Janice Lynde
Eddie Kopeck, the free-lance reporter	Danny Wells
Greenlight, the ambulance driver	Michael D. Roberts
Redlight, Greenlight's partner	Michael Winslow
Dr. Willy Pitts	John de Lancie
Dr. Samuel Hicks	Jason Kincaid

GUEST CAST

Redhead	Patch MacKenzie
Smitty	Doug Hume
Bones	Doug Cox
Slow Boy, the pimp	Timothy Carey
Sharon, the hooker	Susan Plumb
Rusty, the hooker	Karen Newell
Vanilla, the hooker	Louie Ellis
Michael Vincent	Joe Spinell
President	Sid Conrad
Maggie	Sondra Blake
Sgt. Treetorn	Wayne Hefly

Music: John Andrew Tartaglia.
Executive Producer: Glen A. Larson, Stephen J. Cannell.
Producer: Alex Beaton.
Writer: Stephen J. Cannell, Glen A. Larson.
Director: Bernard L. Kowalski.
Art Director: John Leimanis.
Director of Photography: Arthur Botham.

NIGHTSIDE — 90 minutes — ABC — June 8, 1980.

1698   THE NIGHT STALKER

Pilot (Thriller). The first of two pilot films that eventually led to *The Night Stalker* series (see also "The Night Strangler"). The story, set in Las Vegas, follows the experiences of Carl Kolchak, a reporter for the *Daily News*, as he seeks to prove that the murders of several young women were the act of a vampire.

REGULAR CAST

| Carl Kolchak | Darren McGavin |
| Anthony Vincenzo, the managing editor | Simon Oakland |

GUEST CAST

Gail Foster	Carol Lynley
Sheriff Warren Butcher	Claude Akins
Captain Ed Masterson	Charles McGraw
D. A. Thomas Paine	Kent Smith
Bernie Jenks	Ralph Meeker
Dr. Robert McKenzie	Larry Linville
Janos Skorzeny, the vampire	Barry Atwater
Fred Herlihy	Stanley Adams

Narrator: Darren McGavin.
Music: Robert Cobert.
Producer: Dan Curtis.
Writer: Richard Matheson.
Director: John Llewellyn Moxey.
Art Director: Trevor Williams.
Director of Photography: Michel Hugo.

THE NIGHT STALKER — 90 minutes — ABC — January 11, 1972.

1699   THE NIGHT STRANGLER

Pilot (Thriller). The second pilot film for the series *The Night Stalker* (see previous title). The story, set in Seattle, Washington, follows Carl Kolchak, a reporter for the *Daily Chronicle*, as he seeks to solve a bizarre series of murders of young women: since 1889 and every 21 years thereafter, and during an 18-day period (March 29 through April 16), six women have been murdered — found with crushed necks and partially drained of blood. He discovers the crimes were committed by Richard Malcolm, a doctor who perfected a means for immortality that requires human blood.

REGULAR CAST

Carl Kolchak	Darren McGavin
Anthony Vincenzo, the managing editor	Simon Oakland
Louise Harper, Carl's girlfriend	Jo Ann Pflug

GUEST CAST

Llwellyn Crossbinder	John Carradine
Titus Berry	Wally Cox
Richard Malcolm	Richard Anderson
Charisma Beauty (a.k.a. Gladys Weems)	Nina Wayne
Capt. Roscoe Schubert	Scott Brady
Dr. Christopher Webb	Ivor Francis
Hester Crabwell	Margaret Hamilton

Narrator: Darren McGavin.
Music: Robert Cobert.
Producer: Dan Curtis.
Associate Producer: Robert Singer.
Writer: Richard Matheson.
Director: Dan Curtis.

THE NIGHT STRANGLER — 90 minutes — ABC — January 6, 1973.

1700   NO PLACE LIKE HOME

Pilot (Comedy). The overall title for three unsold comedies focusing on family life.

Hello Mother, Goodbye. The story of an indomitable matriarch (Bette Davis) who plagues the life of her grown son (Kenneth Mars). Also starring Ellen Weston and Dran Hamilton.

Where's Momma? The story of a young father (Richard Mulligan) whose life is changed when the spirit of his dead wife Lina (Michele Carey) returns and appears and speaks only to him. Also starring Richard Stahl and Peggy Rea.

Grandpa, Mom, Dad and Richie. The misadventures of a sprightly grandfather (John Marley). Also starring Scott Jacoby as Richie, his grandson.

NO PLACE LIKE HOME—2 hours —NBC—May 15, 1974.

1701 THE NORLISS TAPES

Pilot (Thriller). The story of David Norliss, a San Francisco-based writer who investigates supernatural occurrences. In the pilot, Norliss attempts to solve a series of murders that were seemingly committed by a zombie-like reincarnation of a deceased sculptor. (The title is derived from the fact that David records his notes on audio tape, then transcribes them for a book.)

REGULAR CAST

David Norliss	Roy Thinnes
Sanford Evans, his publisher	Don Porter

GUEST CAST

Ellen Cort	Angie Dickinson
Marsha Sterns	Michele Carey
Sheriff Tom Hartley	Claude Akins
James Cort (the sculptor)	Nick Dimitri
Madame Jechiel	Vonetta McGee
Charles Langdon	Hurt Hatfield
David's attorney	Robert Mandan
Sid Phelps	Edmond Gilbert
Sara Dobkins	Jane Dulo
Truck Driver	Stanley Adams

Music: John Mick.
Executive Producer: Charles Fries.
Producer: Dan Curtis.
Writer: William Nolan.
Director: Dan Curtis.
Director of Photography: Ben Colman.

THE NORLISS TAPES—90 minutes—NBC—February 21, 1973.

1702 NOT UNTIL TODAY

Pilot (Comedy). The story depicts events in the life of Jason Swan, a police chief. The pilot focuses on the complications that ensue when a young man named Jake Warren shows up claiming to be Jason's illegitimate son.

CAST

Jason Swan	Darren McGavin
Jake Warren	Michael Horton
Father Francis Dacey, Jason's friend	Dick Sargent
Sally, the waitress	Alexandra Stoddard
Mae, Jason's sister	Lynn Carlin

Music: Johnny Mandel.
Executive Producer: Michael Zinberg, David Lloyd.
Producer: Charles Raymond.
Director: Michael Zinberg.

NOT UNTIL TODAY—30 minutes—NBC—June 27, 1979. Originally titled "Home Again."

1703 NO WHERE TO HIDE

Pilot (Crime Drama). The exploits of Joey Faber, an agent for the U.S. Marshals Service. The pilot episode depicts his efforts to protect a government witness, a hit man, from a racketeer seeking to kill him.

REGULAR CAST

Joey Faber	Tony Musante
Linda Faber, his wife	Lelia Goldoni
Frankie Faber, their son	Noel Fournier

GUEST CAST

Ike Scanlon	Lee Van Cleef
Deputy Ted Willoughby	Charlie Robinson
Alberto Amarici	Edward Anhalt
Vittorio	John Aderman

Music: Ray Ellis.
Executive Producer: Mark Carliner.
Producer: Rift Fournier, Edward Anhalt.
Writer: Edward Anhalt.
Director: Jack Starrett.

NO WHERE TO HIDE—90 minutes—NBC—June 5, 1977.

1704 THE OATH

Pilot (Anthology). A would-be series of medical dramas.

First Pilot:
33 Hours in the Life of God. The story of Dr. Simon Abbott, a cold, impersonal cardiologist whose total dedication to work begins to affect his health and marriage.

CAST

Dr. Simon Abbott	Hal Holbrook
Alison Abbott	Carol Rossen
Dr. Jaffe	Hume Cronyn
Nurse Levitt	Louise Latham
Dr. Watt	John Devlin
Freddie	Michael O'Keefe
Paula Handy	Doris Roberts

Producer: Aaron Spelling, Leonard Goldberg.
Writer: Hal Sitowitz.
Director: Glenn Hordan.

Second Pilot:
The Sad and Lonely Sundays. The story of George Sorenson, an aging doctor who decides to re-enter medical school and catch up on 40 years of medical progress.

CAST

Dr. George Sorenson	Jack Albertson
Lucas Wembly	Will Geer
Dr. Frankman	Ed Flanders
Bainbridge	Eddie Firestone
Dr. Sweeny	Sam Jaffe
Hester	Doreen Lang
Gloria Evans	Dorothy Tristan
Dean Miller	Jeff Corey
Sandy	Dori Brenner
Mort Cooper	Bert Remsen

Producer: Aaron Spelling, Leonard Goldberg.
Writer: Rod Serling.
Director: James Goldstone.

THE OATH—60 minutes—ABC. First pilot: August 24, 1976; second pilot: August 26, 1976.

1705 OFF CAMPUS

Pilot (Comedy). A comic look at life in a coed rooming house as seen through the eyes of a group of college students as they prepare for adulthood and graduation.

CAST

Janet	Marilu Henner
Steve	Josh Mostel
Bonnie	Ann Risley
Stanley	Peter Reigert
Josh	Chip Zien

Also: Joe Bova, Alexia Kenin, Rober Hitt, James Gallery.
Producer: Gil Cates.
Writer: Marshall Brickman.
Director: Burt Brinkerhoff.

OFF CAMPUS—30 minutes—CBS—June 8, 1977.

1706 OFF THE WALL

Pilot (Comedy). The program, set against the background of Ohio Western College, presents a comic look at life in Hokins Hall, a coed dormitory.

CAST

Matt Bozeman	Todd Susman
Jeannie	Dana House
Flash	Harry Gold
Mother, the cook	Hal Williams
Lennie	Cindy Helberg
Gordon	Sean Roche
Melvin	Sandy Helberg
Arthur	Frank Helberg

Also: Sally Hightower, Frank O'Brien.
Music: Mike Post and Pete Carpenter.
Theme Vocal: Harry Gold.
Executive Producer: Franklin Barton.
Producer: George Tricker, Neil Rosen.
Director: Bob LaHendro.

OFF THE WALL—30 minutes—NBC—May 7, 1977.

OH, NURSE!

See title "CBS Comedy Trio" in the pilot film section.

1707 OMNIBUS

Pilot (Variety). An updated version of the 1950s series of the same title: a TV forum for the fine arts.

Host: Hal Holbrook.
Orchestra: Peter Matz.
Omnibus Theme: Marvin Hamlisch.
Executive Producer: Martin Starger.
Producer: Bob Shanks.
Writer: Leonard Harris, Frank Rich.
Director: Don Mischer.
Art Director: Ray Klausen.

Included Segments/Guests: Sandy Duncan in a scene from her Broadway play, *Peter Pan*; movie and TV fashion with designers Edith Head and Bob Mackie, and models Ann-Margret, Carol Burnett, Cher, Lola Falana, Linda Gray, Cheryl Ladd, Carol Lynley, Yvette Mimieux, Valerie Perrine, Victoria Principal, Jill St. John, Toni Tennille, Cindy Williams; and Luciano Pavarotti and Loretta Lynn in a discussion on grand opera and the Grand Ole Opry.

OMNIBUS—60 minutes—ABC—June 15, 1980.

1708 ON TRIAL

Pilot (Anthology). Re-enactments of actual courtroom cases.

Music: John Parker.
Executive Producer: Alan P. Sloan.
Producer: Robert H. Justman.
Director: Joseph Scanlan.

ON TRIAL—30 minutes—Syndicated January 1978.

ONCE UPON A DEAD MAN

The pilot film broadcast on NBC on September 17, 1971, for the series *McMillan and Wife* (see regular program section).

1709 ONCE UPON A SPY

Pilot (Adventure). The exploits of Jack Chenault, a computer genius, and Paige Tannehill, a K-12 Agent, both of whom are operators for The Operation, a secret investigative agency of the U.S. government. The pilot depicts their efforts to stop Marcus Valorium, a scientific genius, from controlling the world through his molecular condenser beam, which rearranges molecules and reduces matter.

REGULAR CAST

The Lady, the head of	
The Operation	Eleanor Parker
Jack Chenault, an agent	Ted Danson
Paige Tannehill, an	
agent	Mary Louise Weller
Berkle, The Lady's aide	Burke Byrnes

GUEST CAST

Marcus Valorium	Christopher Lee
Dr. Charlie Webster	Leonard Stone
Susan Webster	Jo McDonnell
Rudy	Terry Lester
Chief	John Hostetter
Greta	Irene Serris

Music: John Cacavas.
Executive Producer: David Gerber.
Producer: Jay Daniel.
Writer: Jimmy Sangster.
Director: Ivan Nagy.
Art Director: Ross Bellah.
Director of Photography: Dennis Dalzell.

ONCE UPON A SPY — 2 hours — ABC — September 19, 1980.

1710   ONE OF MY WIVES IS MISSING

Pilot (Crime Drama). The exploits of Murray Levine, a small-town police inspector. In the pilot, Levine investigates a strange missing persons case: that of a vacationer who reports his wife missing, then claims she's an imposter when she suddenly turns up.

REGULAR CAST

Inspector Murray Levine	Jack Klugman

GUEST CAST

Elizabeth Corban	Elizabeth Ashley
Daniel Corban	James Franciscus
Father Kelleher	Joel Fabiani
Mrs. Foster	Ruth McDevitt
Sidney	Milton Seltzer

Music: Billy Goldenberg.
Executive Producer: Aaron Spelling, Leonard Goldberg.
Producer: Barney Rosenzweig.
Writer: Pierre Marton.
Director: Glenn Jordan.
Art Director: Paul Sylos.

ONE OF MY WIVES IS MISSING — 90 minutes — ABC — March 5, 1976.

ONE OF OUR OWN

The pilot film broadcast on NBC on May 5, 1975, for the series *Doctor's Hospital* (see regular program section).

1711   OPERATING ROOM

Pilot (Comedy). The antics of three doctors attached to Los Angeles Memorial Hospital.

CAST

Dr. Jim Lawrence	David Spielberg
Dr. Charles Webner	Oliver Clark
Dr. Robert Robinson	James Sutorius
Jean Lawrence, Jim's wife	Barbara Babcock

Also: Trish and Cyb Barnstable.
Music: Mike Post and Pete Carpenter.
Producer: Mark Tinker.
Writer: Bruce Paltrow.
Director: Bruce Paltrow.

OPERATING ROOM — 60 minutes — NBC — October 4, 1979.

THE OREGON TRAIL

The pilot film broadcast on NBC on January 10, 1976, for the series of the same title (see regular program section).

1712   THE ORPHAN AND THE DUDE

Pilot (Comedy). The misadventures of Oliver Smith, a mild-mannered garage mechanic; Curtis Brown, his feisty roommate; and Leonard Brown, Curtis' adopted son.

CAST

Oliver Smith	Oliver Clark
Curtis Brown	Art Evans
Leonard Brown	Todd Bridges
Sam Brodsky	Ed Barth
Amber	Lynne Holmes
Fast Freddie	Frank McRae
Dan	David Moody

Producer: Jim Parker, Arnold Margolin.
Director: James Frawley.

THE ORPHAN AND THE DUDE — 30 minutes — ABC — July 18, 1975.

1713   THE OUTSIDE MAN

Pilot (Crime Drama). The exploits of Richie Martinelli, a street-wise federal agent who goes undercover to apprehend criminals (thus making him the "outside man" in dangerous situations). The pilot depicts Martinelli's attempts to apprehend the bank robbers responsible for the deaths of two police officers.

REGULAR CAST

Richie Martinelli	Ron Leibman
Shaker Thompson, his	
assistant	Woody Strode

GUEST CAST

Rosalie	Janet Margolin
Stalio	Nicholas Colasanto
Sal	Al Ruscio
Leo	Pepper Martin
Armand	Robert Donner
Sally	Pat Corley
Bank manager	Fred Stuthman
Ellsworth	Nicholas Pryor
Morgan	William Wintersole
Roger Elks	Michael Frost

Music: Tom Scott.
Executive Producer: Paul Magistretti.
Producer: William F. Phillips.
Writer: Paul Magistretti.
Director: Russ Mayberry.
Director of Photography: Jacques Marquette.

THE OUTSIDE MAN — 60 minutes — CBS — April 8, 1977.

1714   OVER AND OUT

Pilot (Comedy). The story, set during World War II, follows the antics of five female communications officers stranded on an all-male Army base in the South Pacific.

CAST

Capt. Betty Jack Daniels	Michele Lee
Sgt. Cookie Dobson	Susan Lanier
Lt. Paula Rabinowitz	Pat Finley
T/Sgt. "Lizard" Gossamer	Alice Playten
Sgt. Alice Pierson	Mary Jo Catlett
Capt. Paddy Patterson	Ken Berry
Sgt. Travis	Stewart Moss

Music: Peter Matz.
Executive Producer: Bob Claver.
Producer: Mark Carliner.
Writer: Linda Bloodworth.
Director: Bob Claver.

OVER AND OUT — 30 minutes — NBC — August 11, 1976.

1715   THE OVER-THE-HILL GANG RIDES AGAIN

Pilot (Western). An unsold pilot based on the successful made-for-television movie *The Over-the-Hill Gang*. The story, set in the Old West, follows the exploits of Nash Crawford, "Gentleman" George Agnew, Jason Fitch, and The Baltimore Kid, four former and aging Texas Rangers who ban together to help each other in times of need. The pilot depicts their efforts to clean up Waco, a ruthless, lawless town in Texas.

REGULAR CAST

Nash Crawford	Walter Brennan
George Agnew	Chill Wills
Jason Fitch	Edgar Buchanan
The Baltimore Kid	Fred Astaire

GUEST CAST

Amos Polk	Andy Devine
Mayor	Parley Baer
Sam Braham	Paul Richards
Kate Whelan	Lana Wood
Tom	Walter Burke
Mrs. Murphy	Lillian Bronson
Jason's friend	Burt Mustin

Music: David Raksin.
Executive Producer: Danny Thomas.
Producer: Aaron Spelling, Shelly Hull.
Associate Producer: Andrew Brennan.
Writer: Richard Carr.
Director: George McCowan.

THE OVER-THE-HILL GANG RIDES AGAIN — 90 minutes — ABC — November 17, 1970.

OWEN MARSHALL: COUNSELOR AT LAW

The pilot film broadcast on ABC on September 12, 1971, for the series of the same title (see regular program section).

OZZIE'S GIRLS

The pilot episode (videotape) broadcast on NBC on September 10, 1972, for the syndicated series of the same title (see regular program section).

1716   PANACHE

Pilot (Adventure). The exploits of Panache, a poet, lover and dashing swordsman involved in the intrigue and romance of seventeenth-century France.

CAST

Panache	Rene Auberjonois
Donat	David Healy
Alain	Charles Frank
King Louis XIII	Harvey Solin
Treville	John Doucette
Anne	Amy Irving
Cardinal Richelieu	Joseph Ruskin
M. Durant/Pere Joseph	Liam Dunn
Laval	Peggy Wilton
Chevreuse	Marjorie Battles
Lisa	Lisa Eilbacher
Dutchess	Judith Brown

Music: Frank De Vol.
Executive Producer: E. Duke Vincent.
Producer: Robert E. Rlyea.
Writer: E. Duke Vincent.
Director: Gary Nelson.

PANACHE — 90 minutes — ABC — May 15, 1976.

1717   PARTNERS IN CRIME

Pilot (Crime Drama). The exploits of Meredith Leland, a judge turned private detective. The pilot depicts her efforts to recover $750,000 in stolen bank money.

REGULAR CAST

Meredith Leland	Lee Grant
Charles Leland, her father	John Randolph

GUEST CAST

Sam	Lou Antonio
Connors	Harry Guardino
Jordan	Richard Jaeckel
Elsworth	Bob Cummings
Mrs. Jordan	Lorraine Gray

Music: Gil Mellé.
Executive Producer: Richard Levinson, William Link.
Producer: Jon Epstein.
Writer: David Shaw.
Director: Jack Smight.

PARTNERS IN CRIME — 90 minutes — NBC — March 24, 1973.

1718   THE PAUL WILLIAMS SHOW

Pilot (Comedy). The misadventures of Paul Hamilton, an aspiring TV personality who portrays Marvin the Martian, the host of a kid show on station KFAP in Denver, Colorado.

CAST

Paul Hamilton	Paul Williams
Denny Morton, Paul's agent	Rick Poddell
Deborah, Paul's neighbor	Dana Hill
Victoria Woodbridge, the program director	
at KFAP	Amanda McBroom
Barbara, Paul's girlfriend	Sandra Kearns

Music: Paul Williams.
Executive Producer: Peter H. Engel.
Producer: Dennis M. Bond.
Director: Dennis Steinmetz.

THE PAUL WILLIAMS SHOW—30 minutes—NBC—June 27, 1979.

1719   PEOPLE LIKE US

Pilot (Drama). The story of the Allmans, a contemporary American family, and their struggles to retain their close ties amid economic instability and a changing moral climate.

REGULAR CAST

Davy Allman, the father	Eugene Roche
Irene Allman, his wife	Katherine Helmond
Sharon Allman, their	
daughter	Eileen McDonough
Lennie Allman, their son	Grant Goodeve
Anna Allman, Davy's mother	Irene Tedrow

GUEST CAST

Elgin	Stock Pierce
Ray	Richard Foronjy
Sesser	William Flately

Executive Producer: Lee Rich.
Producer: Gene Reynolds.
Writer: Howard Storm.
Director: Gene Reynolds.

PEOPLE LIKE US—60 minutes—NBC—April 19, 1976.

PETE 'N' TILLIE

See title "4 Funny Families" in the pilot film section.

1720   PETER LUNDY AND THE MEDICINE HAT STALLION

Pilot (Drama). The story, set in the Nebraska Territory just prior to the Civil War (1861), follows the exploits of Peter Lundy, a teenager (15) and rider for the Pony Express. Based on the novel, *San Domingo—The Medicine Hat Stallion*.

REGULAR CAST

Peter Lundy	Leif Garrett
Jethro Lundy, his father	Mitchell Ryan
Emily Lundy, his mother	Bibi Besch
Mr. Majors, the head of	
the Pony Express	John Anderson
Peter's Grandmother	Ann Doran
Adam, the town blacksmith	John Quade

GUEST CAST

Brisly	Milo O'Shea
Slade	Charles Tyner
Jim Baxter	Brad Rearden
Muggerdige	James Lydon

Music: Morton Stevens.
Producer: Ed Friendly
Writer: Jack Turley
Director: Michael O'Herlihy.

PETER LUNDY AND THE MEDICINE HAT STALLION—2 hours—NBC—November 6, 1977.

1721   PHILLIP AND BARBARA

Pilot (Comedy). The misadventures of Phillip and Barbara Logan, a married couple who are employed as TV comedy script writers.

CAST

Barbara Logan	Patty Duke Astin
Phillip Logan	John Astin
Edna	Rosemary DeCamp
George	Leonard Frey
Shirley	Ann Prentiss
Secretary	Patti Jerome

Producer: Leonard B. Stern.
Writer: Jerry Mayer.
Director: Leonard B. Stern.

PHILLIP AND BARBARA—30 minutes—NBC—August 13, 1976.

1722   PINE CANYON IS BURNING

Pilot (Drama). The story of William Stone, a widowed Los Angeles fire captain who takes to the wilds of Pine Canyon, California, to become the operator of a one-man fire rescue station.

REGULAR CAST

Capt. William Stone	Kent McCord
Margaret Stone, his	
daughter	Megan McCord
Michael Stone, his son	Shane Sinutko
Capt. Ed Wilson, a	
fireman	Andrew Duggan
Anne Walker, the schoolteacher	Brit Lind

GUEST CAST

Edna Wilson	Doreen Long
Sandra	Diana Muldaur
Charlie Edison	Dick Bakalyan

Music: Lee Holdridge.
Executive Producer: Robert A. Cinader.
Producer: Gino Grimaldi, Hannah Shearer.
Writer: Robert A. Cinader.
Director: Christian I. Nyby II.

PINE CANYON IS BURNING—90 minutes—NBC—May 18, 1977.

1723   PIPER'S PETS

Pilot (Comedy). The misadventures of Dr. Piper, a veterinarian, and his not-too-bright assistant, Lester.

CAST

Dr. Piper	Don Knotts
Lester	Peter Isacksen
Maggie, Lester's wife	Maggie Roswell
Thelma, Piper's	
receptionist	Jacque Lynn Colton

Music: Jack Elliott, Allyn Ferguson.
Executive Producer: Aaron Ruben.
Producer: Gene Marcione.
Director: Russ Petranto.

PIPER'S PETS—30 minutes—NBC—May 31, 1979 (an unscheduled air date. "Piper's Pets" replaced a scheduled pilot called "Faculty Lounge," which never aired).

1724   THE PLANT FAMILY

Pilot (Comedy). Events in the lives of the Plant family, residents of a run-down house in a borderline neighborhood in Southern California.

REGULAR CAST

Lyla Plant, the mother	Joyce Van Patten
Augie Plant, the father	Norman Alden
Geneva, Lyla's friend, who lives in	
the same house	Jo Marie Payton
Leo Harrell, Geneva's brother	Jesse White
Ava, Lyla's married daughter	Kay Heberle
Art, Ava's husband	Larry Hankin
Homer Jay, Geneva's son	DeWayne Hessie

GUEST CAST

Aerilio	Peter Elbling
Patty	Willie Tjan
Eddie	Anthony Sirico

Executive Producer: Bud Austin, Robert D. Wood.
Producer: Monica Johnson.
Writer: Monica Johnson, Jordan Tabat.
Director: James Burrows.
Art Director: Jim Claytor.
Director of Photography: Meredith Nicholson.

THE PLANT FAMILY—30 minutes—CBS—September 2, 1978.

1725   PLANET EARTH

Pilot (Science Fiction). A sequel to "Genesis II" (see pilot film section). The story of Dylan Hunt, a scientist who, lost in 1979 during a suspended animation accident, was found 154 years later (A.D. 2133) by the people of a civilization called Pax (peace), the one area on Earth that escaped a nuclear war in the twentieth century. The would-be series was to depict Dylan's exploits, as the leader of a Pax science team, as he seeks to help rebuild the Earth into a newer and wiser civilization. In the pilot, Dylan and Harper-Smithe, his assistant, travel to Ruth, a female-run empire, to find a kidnapped member of their group—the only person who can save the life of Patar Kimbridge, a Pax leader.

REGULAR CAST

Dylan Hunt	John Saxon
Harper-Smithe	Janet Margolin
Isiah, a Pax	Ted Cassidy
Patra Kimbridge, a Pax leader	Rai Tasco

GUEST CAST

Jonathan Connor	Jim Antonio
Marg	Diana Muldaur
Villar	Johana DeWinter
Baylok	Christopher Carey
Yuloff	Majel Barrett
Treece	Sally Kemp
Delba	Claire Brennan
Sklar	Patricia Smith
Gorda	Aaron Kincaide
Kyla	John Crosby
Thetis	Sara Chattin
Bronta	Corrine Camacho

Music: Harry Sukman.
Executive Producer: Gene Roddenberry.
Producer: Robert H. Justman.
Writer: Gene Roddenberry, Juanita Bartlett.
Director: Marc Daniels.
Creator: Gene Roddenberry.

PLANET EARTH—90 minutes—ABC—April 23, 1974.

1726   PLEASURE COVE

Pilot (Comedy-Drama). A series of interwoven vignettes that depict brief incidents in the lives of the guests at the Pleasure Cove, a posh resort that is operated as part of the Xavier Hotel Chain.

REGULAR CAST

Henry Sinclair, the	
manager	James Murtaugh
Julie, the reservations	
clerk	Melody Anderson
Kim Parker, the assistant	
manager	Constance Forslund
Osaki, the desk clerk	Ernest Harada
Chip Garvey, the gambler	Jerry Lacy

GUEST CAST

Raymond Gordon	Tom Jones
Bert Harrison	Harry Guardino
Martha Harrison	Joan Hackett
Joe	Ron Masak
Helen	Shelley Fabares
Sally	Tanya Roberts
Scott	David Hasselhoff

Music: Perry Botkin, Jr.
Executive Producer: Lou Shaw.
Producer: Mel Swope.
Writer: Lou Shaw.
Director: Bruce Bilson.
Director of Photography: Jack A. Whitman, Jr.

PLEASURE COVE—2 hours—NBC—January 3, 1979.

THE POLICE STORY

The pilot film broadcast on NBC on March 20, 1973, for the series *Police Story* (see regular program section).

1727   POOR DEVIL

Pilot (Comedy). The story of Sammy, a bumbling, soft touch disciple from hell. The pilot depicts Sammy's attempts, after 1,400 years of failure, to redeem himself by securing a soul for Satan, that of Burnett Emerson, a mortal fumbler.

REGULAR CAST

Disciple Sammy	Sammy Davis, Jr.
Lucifer, the Devil	Christopher Lee
Mr. Bligh, Lucifer's aide	Gino Conforti

GUEST CAST

Burnett Emerson	Jack Klugman
Crawford	Adam West

Frances   Madelyn Rhue
Chelsey   Emily Yancy

Music: Morton Stevens.
Executive Producer: Arne Sultan, Earl Barrett.
Producer: Robert Stambler.
Writer: Arne Sultan, Richard Bare, Earl Barrett.
Director: Robert Scheerer.

POOL DEVIL—90 minutes—NBC—February 14, 1973.

1728 THE POSSESSED

Pilot (Drama). The story of Kevin Leahy, an ex-minister fallen from the grace of God and expelled from the church. After a fatal automobile accident, Leahy is brought back to life. To gain salvation, he is ordered to seek out and destroy evil. In the pilot, set at the Helen Page School for Girls in Salem, Massachussetts, Leahy battles demonic forces that are threatening the lives of the students.

REGULAR CAST
Kevin Leahy   James Farentino

GUEST CAST
Ellen Summer   Claudette Nevins
Police Sgt. Taplinger   Eugene Roche
Louise Gelson   Joan Hackett
Weezie Summer   Ann Dusenberry
Paul Winjam   Harrison Ford
Lane   Diana Scarwid
Celia   Dinah Manoff
Alex   Carol Jones
Marty   P. J. Soles

Music: Leonard Rosenman.
Executive Producer: Jerry Thorpe.
Producer: Philip Mandelker.
Writer: John Sacret Young.
Director: Jerry Thorpe.
Director of Photography: Charles Arnold.

THE POSSESSED—90 minutes—NBC—May 1, 1977.

1729 POTTSVILLE

Pilot (Comedy). The story of Bulldog O'Halloran, a harassed labor leader and the president of Local 605 of the National Factory Workers Union in Pottsville, a small manufacturing town. The pilot depicts Bulldog's efforts to contend with a feminist rebellion within his own ranks and avert a strike against his company, the Farraday Sandpaper Corporation.

REGULAR CAST
Bulldog O'Halloran   Forrest Tucker
Grace O'Halloran, his wife   Jan Miner
Tinker O'Halloran, their
     son   George O'Hanlon Jr.
Bill Gentry, Bulldog's union
     assistant   Richard Brestoff
Holden Farraday, the owner of the
     sandpaper company   John Lawlor
Gardy Farraday, Holden's wife   Nina Foch
Ted Farraday, Holden's
     son   Jimmie Samuels

Randy, one of the office girls   Jane Daly
Snell, Holden's aide   Hamilton Camp
Pippa, same as Randy   Heidi Gold
Helen, same as Randy   Edie McClurg
Sue, same as Randy   Lynne Thigpen

GUEST CAST
Sundance Ewbanks   Rory Calhoun
Benny Haucke   Christopher Murney
Frank   James Cromwell
Guido   Luke Andreas

Music: Larry Camsler.
Theme: "Pottsville" by Rod Parker and Hal Cooper.
Executive Producer: Rod Parker, Hal Cooper,
Producer: Gene Marcione.
Writer: Rod Parker.
Director: Hal Cooper.
Art Director: Chuck Murawski.

POTTSVILLE—60 minutes—CBS—February 27, 1980 (an unscheduled airing; repeated August 6, 1980).

POWDERKEG

The pilot film broadcast on CBS on April 16, 1971, for the series *The Bearcats* (see regular program section).

1730 POWDER ROOM

Pilot (Comedy). A series of vignettes that explore the feminine point of view.

Included:

The Militant. Joey Heatherton as a coed determined to seduce her professor (Jack Cassidy).

The Affair. The story of an over-30 housewife (Jeanine Burnier) as she attempts to revive her husband's (Jack Cassidy) romantic appetite.

The Mourner. Elaine Stritch as an over-40 widow seeking a new mate (Jack Cassidy).

Host: Dean Martin.
Producer: Rod Parker.
Writer: Robert Hilliard, George Bloom, Rod Parker.
Director: Jonathan Lucas.

POWDER ROOM—30 minutes—NBC—August 26, 1971.

1731 THE POWER WITHIN

Pilot (Adventure). The story of Chris Darrow, a young daredevil pilot who acquires incredible powers after a freak accident: during an electrical storm, Darrow is struck by lightning and transformed into a virtual human dynamo, energy he uses to battle evil. (It is explained that before Darrow's birth, his mother had been exposed to an accidental overdose of radiation, which had been absorbed by Chris, and years later saved his life when struck by the lightning.)

REGULAR CAST
Chris Darrow   Art Hindle
Bill Carmalie, his mechanic   Joe Rossulo
General Darrow, U.S.A.F., Chris's
     father   Edward Binns

GUEST CAST
Capt. Ed Holman   Dick Sargent
Dr. Joanne Miller   Susan Howard
Danton   David Hedison

Music: John Addison.
Supervising Producer: E. Duke Vincent.
Producer: Alan S. Godfrey.
Writer: William Clark.
Director: John Llewellyn Moxey.

THE POWER WITHIN—90 minutes—ABC—May 11, 1979. Originally titled "Power Man."

1732 THE PRIMARY ENGLISH CLASS

Pilot (Comedy). The story of Sandy Lambert, an English teacher in a night school for foreign students.

CAST
Sandy Lambert   Valerie Curtin
Chuma, a student   Freeman King
Hal, a student   Murphy Dunne
Yosef Ari, a student   Harvey Jason
Rosa, a student   Lupe Ontiveros
Sergio, a student   Joe Bennett
Ritteman, a student   Robert Holt

Music: Joe Hamilton, Peter Matz.
Producer: Joe Hamilton.
Director: Tom Conway.

THE PRIMARY ENGLISH CLASS—30 minutes—ABC—August 15, 1977.

PROBE

The pilot film broadcast on NBC on February 21, 1972, for the series *Search* (see regular program section).

1733 PRUDENCE AND THE CHIEF

Pilot (Comedy). The story, set in the Old West, follows the adventures of Prudence MacKenzie, widow, teacher and missionary, who, on behalf of the United Council of Churches, establishes a school on a Cheyenne Indian reservation. The would-be series was to depict her experiences teaching the Indian children. The pilot depicts Prudence's efforts to convince Snow Eagle, chief of the Cheyenne, that a school is necessary for his people.

CAST
Prudence MacKenzie   Sally Ann Howes
Chief Snow Eagle   Rick Jason
Letitia MacKenzie, Prudence's
     mother   Kathryn Givney
Gavin MacKenzie, Prudence's
     son   Teddy Quinn
Fergus MacKenzie, Prudence's
     son   Johnny Lee
Major O'Toole   Rhoades Reason

Lieutenant Burns   Mac Krell
Sergeant   Troy Melton

Creator: Jean Holloway.
Director: Marc Daniels.

PRUDENCE AND THE CHIEF—30 minutes—ABC—August 26, 1970.

THE PSYCHIATRIST: GOD BLESS THE CHILDREN

The pilot film broadcast on NBC on May 24, 1971, for the series *The Psychiatrist* (see regular program section).

Q

QUARK

The pilot film broadcast on NBC on May 7, 1977, for the series of the same title (see regular program section).

THE QUEST

The pilot film broadcast on NBC on May 13, 1976, for the series of the same title (see regular program section).

1734 THE QUESTOR TAPES

Pilot (Adventure). The unsold pilot film for a proposed series about the exploits of Questor, a robot whose mental processes are programmed by tape with human emotional factors. The pilot depicts Questor's awakening to the world and his first assignment: to locate his missing creator.

REGULAR CAST
Questor   Robert Foxworth
Jerry Robinson, Questor's
     programmer   Mike Farrell
Dr. Vaslovik, Questor's creator   Lew Ayres

GUEST CAST
Lady Trimbal   Dana Wynter
Darrow   John Vernon
Allison Sample   Ellen Weston
Dr. Chen   James Shigeta
Dr. Bradley   Majel Barrett
Dr. Michaels   Robert Douglas

Music: Gil Mellé.
Executive Producer: Gene Roddenberry.
Producer: Howie Horwitz.
Writer: Gene Roddenberry, Gene L. Coon.
Director: Richard A. Colla.

THE QUESTOR TAPES—2 hours—NBC—January 23, 1974.

1735 THE QUINNS

Pilot (Drama). The story, set in New York City, follows the lives of the Quinns, a close-knit Irish-American family.

CAST

Sean Quinn, Sr.	Liam Dunn
Peggy Quinn	Geraldine Fitzgerald
Elizabeth Quinn	Susan Browning
Laurie Quinn	Penny Peyser
Bill Quinn	Barry Bostwick
Rita Quinn	Pat Elliott
Michael Quinn	Peter Masterson
Tom Quinn	William Sweetland
Renee Carmody	Virginia Vestoff
Eugene Carmody	Pat Corley
Millicent Priestly	Blair Brown

Music: John Scott.
Producer: Daniel Wilson.
Writer: Sidney Carroll.
Director: Daniel Petrie.

THE QUINNS — 90 minutes — ABC — July 1, 1977.

R

1736   THE RAG BUSINESS

Pilot (Comedy). The story, set against the background of the Los Angeles garment industry, follows the antics of a group of dressmakers.

CAST

Fisher	Dick O'Neill
Connie	Conchetta Ferrell
Jackie	Sarina Grant
Dennis	Fred McCarren
Alma	Sudie Bond
Coco	Jeannine Linero
Rita	Peggy Pope

Executive Producer: Aaron Ruben.
Producer: Gene Marcione.
Director: Russ Petranto.

THE RAG BUSINESS — 30 minutes — ABC — July 8, 1978.

THE RANGERS

The pilot film broadcast on NBC on December 24, 1974, for the series *Sierra* (see regular program section).

1737   RANSOM FOR ALICE

Pilot (Crime Drama). The exploits of Jenny Cullen and Clint Kirby, law enforcement officers in the Old West of the 1890s. The pilot depicts their efforts to end a white slavery ring that is operating out of Seattle.

REGULAR CAST

Jenny Cullen	Yvette Mimieux
Clint Kirby	Gil Gerard
Pete Phalan, their superior	Charles Napier

GUEST CAST

Alice Halliday	Laurie Prange
Jess Halliday	Barnard Hughes
Yankee Sullivan	Gavin MacLeod
Harry Darew	Gene Barry
Whitaker Halliday	Robert Hogan
Isaac Pratt	Harris Yulin
Toby	Mills Watson

Music: David Rose.
Producer: Franklin Barton.
Writer: Jim Byrnes.
Director: David Lowell Rich.
Art Director: David Marshall.

RANSOM FOR ALICE — 90 minutes — NBC — June 2, 1977.

READY AND WILLING

See title "Three-in-One" in the pilot film section.

1738   REAR GUARD

Pilot (Comedy). The antics of an American Civil Defense volunteer group during World War II. Based on the British series *Dad's Army* (see regular program section).

CAST

Raskin	Lou Jacobi
Rosatti	Cliff Norton
Wayne	Eddie Foy, Jr.
Crawford	John McCook
Muldoon	Arthur Peterson
Colonel Walsh	James McCallion
Henderson	Dennis Kort
German captain (guest)	Conrad Janis

Executive Producer: Herman Rush.
Producer: Arthur Julian.
Writer: Arthur Julian.
Director: Hal Cooper.

REAR GUARD — 30 minutes — ABC — August 10, 1976.

1739   RELENTLESS

Pilot (Crime Drama). The exploits of Sam Watchman, a Navaho Indian who is also an Arizona State Trooper. The pilot depicts Sam's efforts to track down Major Leo Hargit, the military-minded leader of a group of bank robbers.

REGULAR CAST

Sam Watchman	Will Sampson
Buck, his deputy	Larry Wilcox

GUEST CAST

Major Leo Hargit	John Hillerman
Paul Vickers	Monte Markham
Annie Lansford	Marianne Hill
Jack Hanratty	Anthony Ponzini
Dan Barraclough	Ted Markland
Dwayne Terry	David Pendleton
Ed Kleber	Ron Foster

Music: John Cacavas.
Producer: Fred Baum.
Associate Producer: Sy Kasoff.
Writer: Sam H. Rolfe.
Director: Lee H. Katzin.
Art Director: Albert Heschong.
Director of Photography: Jack Whitman.

RELENTLESS — 100 minutes — CBS — September 14, 1977.

1740   RENDEZVOUS HOTEL

Pilot (Comedy). The misadventures of Walter Grainger, the owner and manager of the Rendezvous, a resort hotel in California.

REGULAR CAST

Walter Grainger	Bill Daily
Barbara Clairborne, the social director	Bobbie Mitchell
Jerry Greenwood, the desk clerk	Jeff Redford
Cleveland Jennings, the cook	Theodore Wilson
Conchetta Jennings, the housekeeper	Talya Ferro
Lucille Greenwood, Jerry's mother	Carole Cook

GUEST CAST

Anne Jones	Kathryn Witt
Mr. Church	Severn Darden
Sherry Leonard	Nellie Bellflower
Daley	Emory Bass
Harvey	Dolph Sweet
Jim Becker	Edward Winter
Mrs. Williams	Jeff Donnell
Frank	Bruce French
Guy	Sean Garrison
Texas waitress	Jane Abbott
Dr. Coleman	Diane Lander
Kiki	Brooke Kaplan

Music: Jonathan Tunick.
Executive Producer: Austin and Irma Kalish.
Producer: Mark Carliner.
Writer: Austin Kalish, Irma Kalish, Clayton Baxter.
Director: Peter H. Hunt.
Art Director: Ray Storey.
Director of Photography: William K. Jurgensen.

RENDEZVOUS HOTEL — 2 hours — CBS — July 11, 1979.

1741   THE RETURN OF CHARLIE CHAN

Pilot (Crime Drama). The exploits of Charlie Chan, a Chinese private detective. The pilot, which brings Chan, past 60 and the owner of a pineapple plantation in Hawaii, out of retirement after ten years, depicts his efforts to solve a series of mysterious attacks on Alexander Hadrachi, an aging Greek tycoon with a heart condition.

REGULAR CAST

Charlie Chan	Ross Martin
Peter Chan, his number 8 son	Rocky Gunn
Doreen Chan, his daughter	Virginia Lee

GUEST CAST

Alexander Hadrachi	Leslie Nielsen
Ariane Hadrachi	Louise Sorel
Irene Hadrachi	Kathleen Widdoes
Andrew Kidder	Richard Hydn
Paul Hadrachi	Joseph Hindy
Lambert	Don Gordon
Richard Lovell	Neil Oaniard
Noel Adamson	Peter Donat
Anton Grombach	Otto Lowy
Sylvia Grombach	Patricia Gage
Dr. Howard Jamison	Ted Greenhalgh
Fielding	William Nunn
Stephen Chan	Soon-Tech Oh
Jan Chan	Pearl Hong
Oliver Chan	Ernest Harada
Mai-Ling Chan	Adele Yoshioka
Inspector McKenzie	Graeme Campbell

Music: Robert Prince.
Executive Producer: John J. Cole.
Producer: Jack Laird.
Writer: Gene Kearney.
Story By: Simon Last, Gene Kearney.
Director: Daryl Duke.
Art Director: Frank Arrigo.
Director of Photography: Richard C. Glouner.

THE RETURN OF CHARLIE CHAN — 90 minutes (actual running time less commercials) — ABC — July 17, 1979. Filmed in 1971 and originally titled "Happiness Is a Warm Clue."

RETURN TO FANTASY ISLAND

The second pilot film (the first, "Fantasy Island") broadcast on ABC on November 20, 1977, for the series *Fantasy Island* (see regular program section).

1742   REWARD

Pilot (Crime Drama). The story of Michael Dolan, a former San Francisco police officer turned relentless bounty hunter. The pilot depicts his efforts to find his former partner's murderer.

REGULAR CAST

Michael Dolan	Michael Parks
Captain Randolph	Richard Jaeckel
Christine, Dolan's girlfriend	Annie McEncroe
Dutch, Dolan's friend	Louis Giambalvo

GUEST CAST

Marie Morrella	Bridget Hanley
Jimmy Moran	Malachy McCourt
Steven Rawlin	David Clennon
Frank Morrella	Andrew Robinson

Music: Barry De Vorzon.
Executive Producer: Lee Rich.
Producer: Jerry Adler.
Writer: Jason Miller.
Director: E. W. Swackhamer.
Art Director: Lee Fischer.
Director of Photography: Fred Jackman.

REWARD — 90 minutes — ABC — May 23, 1980.

RICHIE BROCKELMAN, PRIVATE EYE

The pilot film broadcast on NBC on October 27, 1976, for the series of the same title (see regular program section).

1743   RIDDLE AT 24,000

Pilot (Crime Drama). The story of Dr. Domingo, a small-town physician with a knack for finding trouble. In the pilot, broadcast as a segment of *Ironside*, Domingo joins forces with his friend, chief of detectives Robert Ironside, to solve a baffling, carefully designed murder.

REGULAR CAST

Dr. Domingo   Desi Arnaz

GUEST CAST

Robert Ironside   Raymond Burr
Big Sue   Linda Foster
Laura   Patricia Smith
Westcott   Ralph Meeker
Cardiff   L. Q. Jones
Mrs. Wescott   Dolores Dorn

Music: Quincy Jones.
Producer: Cy Chermak.
Writer: Larry Slate.
Director: Don Weis.

RIDDLE AT 24,000 — 60 minutes — NBC — March 14, 1974.

1744   RIDING FOR THE PONY EXPRESS

Pilot (Western). The story, set in the Old West, follows the adventures of Jed Beechum and Albie Foreman, riders for the Pony Express. In the pilot, Jed and Albie become involved in a venture to find water for the drought-stricken town of Layover.

REGULAR CAST

Jed Beechum   John Hammond
Albie Foreman   Harry Crosby
I. G. Peacock, the express
    agent   Victor French
Billy Bloss, an
    express rider   Glenn Withrow
Willy Gomes, an express
    rider   Richard Lineback

GUEST CAST

Nancy Durfee   Susan Myers
Rev. Slaughter   Byron Morrow
Mr. Durfee   Philip Baker Hall
Blue Hawk   Alex Kubik
Seth Coleman   Del Hinkley

Music: Ralph Ferraro.
Producer: Terry Becker.
Writer: James Menzies.
Director: Don Chaffey.
Art Director: Seymour Klate.
Director of Photography: Vincent Martinelli.

RIDING FOR THE PONY EXPRESS — 60 minutes — CBS — September 3, 1980.

1745   RIDING HIGH

Pilot (Comedy). The story, set in Hollywood in the early 1930s, follows the misadventures of Lewis Tater, a fledgling screenwriter, who takes a job as a stuntman with Tumbleweed Productions to make ends meet.

CAST

Lewis Tater   Charles Frank
Wendy Trout, his girlfriend Wendy Phillips
Howard Pike, the studio
    head   Lonny Chapman
Bert Kessler, Pike's assistant Allan Miller
Sid, a stuntman   Don Calfa
Wally, a stuntman   Bill Hart

Producer: Marc Merson.
Writer: Larry Gelbart.
Director: Lee Philips.

RIDING HIGH — 30 minutes — NBC — August 25, 1977.

1746   RISKO

Pilot (Crime Drama). The story of Joe Risko, a street-wise ex-convict, working as the leg man for a lawyer. He holds a correspondence school law degree and hopes to get a waiver of his criminal record and be permitted to take the bar exam. The pilot depicts Risko's attempts to create a courtroom defense for Tom Grainger, a young racing driver charged with the murder of a girl he allegedly picked up in a singles bar.

REGULAR CAST

Joe Risko   Gabriel Dell
Allen Burnett, his employer Joel Fabiani

GUEST CAST

Pollack   Peter Haskell
Max   Norman Fell
Sharon   Joyce DeWitt
Marie   Karen Machon
Maggie   Hilary Thompson
Jenny   Barbara Sharma
Bartender   Jack Knight
Tom Grainger   Paul Hampton
Susan Grainger   Laraine Stephens
Harkavy   John Durren

Executive Producer: Larry White.
Producer: Robert Stambler.
Writer: Adrian Spies; revised story and screenplay: Bill Driskill.
Director: Bernard L. Kowalski.
Art Director: Leroy Dean.
Director of Photography: Howard Schwartz.
Set Decorator: Ted Lake.

RISKO — 60 minutes — CBS — May 9, 1976.

1747   THE RITA MORENO SHOW

Pilot (Comedy). The story of Marie Constanzo, the owner of a hotel fraught with problems. In the pilot, Marie attempts to adjust to her new responsibilities, having just inherited the hotel from its late owner and her former employer.

REGULAR CAST

Marie Constanza   Rita Moreno
Leo, the chef   Victor Buono
Mr. Gladstone, the owner of the
    adjoining hotel   Louis Nye
Carol Constanza, Marie's
    sister   Kathy Bendett

GUEST CAST

Esteban   Bert Rosario
Miss Forbush   Kit McDonough
Mr. Leopold   Ron Vernan
Doris   Shirley Mitchell
Mrs. Kleppner   Lee Bryant

Music: Peter Matz.
Executive Producer: Mark Rothman, Lowell Ganz.
Writer: Mark Rothman, Lowell Ganz.
Director: Tony Mordente.

THE RITA MORENO SHOW — 30 minutes — CBS — May 2, 1978.

THE ROCKFORD FILES

The pilot film broadcast on NBC on March 27, 1974, for the series of the same title (see regular program section). The 90-minute episode, with guest star Lindsay Wagner, has been re-edited to 60 minutes and is syndicated as part of *The Rockford Files* series.

1748   ROGER AND HARRY

Pilot (Crime Drama). The exploits of Roger Quentin and Harry Jaworsky, two flamboyant operators who specialize in recovering stolen valuables. In the pilot, the duo attempt to recover a tycoon's daughter who was kidnapped along with the priceless necklace she wore.

REGULAR CAST

Roger Quentin   John Davidson
Harry Jaworsky   Barry Primus

GUEST CAST

Sylvester March   Biff McGuire
Arthur Pennington   Harris Yulin
Joanna March   Ann Randall Stewart
Blair   Richard Lynch

Music: Jack Elliott, Allyn Ferguson.
Executive Producer: Bruce Landsbury.
Producer: Anthony Spinner.
Writer: Alvin Sapinsley.
Director: Jack Starrett.

ROGER AND HARRY — 90 minutes — ABC — May 2, 1977.

THE ROOKIES

The pilot film broadcast on ABC on March 7, 1972, for the series of the same title (see regular program section).

1749   ROOSEVELT AND TRUMAN

Pilot (Comedy). The misadventures of Roosevelt and Truman, the owner-operators of the Roosevelt and Truman Bail Bond and Security Guard Agency — "We Nail 'em, We Bail 'em." In the pilot, Roosevelt and Truman, whose agency has a perfect record, seek to re-establish that record when a client flies the coop and leaves them facing bankruptcy.

REGULAR CAST

Roosevelt   Art Evans
Truman   Philip Michael Thomas
Juanita, their secretary   Ilka Payan
Richie, the doughnut
    shop owner   Richard Karron

GUEST CAST

Reverend Davis   Hank Rolike
Mrs. Tilson   Minnie S. Lindsey
Rodriguez   Danny Mora
Garcia   Bert Rosario
Quinn   Michael Keaton
Crawford   Tim Pelt

Executive Producer: Norman Steinberg.
Producer: Richard Dimitri.
Writer: Norman Steinberg, Richard Dimitri.
Director: James Burrows.
Art Director: Serge Krizman.

ROOSEVELT AND TRUMAN — 30 minutes — CBS — April 29, 1977.

1750   ROSENTHAL AND JONES

Pilot (Comedy). The misadventures of Nate Rosenthal and Henry Jones, two retired widowers who share a low-rent apartment as the only alternative to living a miserable existence with their grown children.

CAST

Nate Rosenthal   Ned Glass
Henry Jones   George Kirby
David Rosenthal, Nate's son Jerry Fogel
Marge Rosenthal, David's wife Nedra Deen
Lucille Jones, Henry's
    daughter   Dee Timberlake

Music: Al Kasha, Joel Hirschhorn.
Theme Vocal: "All Kinds of People" by Phyllis McGuire.
Executive Producer: Ira Barmak.
Producer: Lawrence Kasha.
Associate Producer: Robert Williams.
Writer: Robert Klane.
Director: H. Wesley Kenney.
Art Director: Charles Lisanby.

ROSENTHAL AND JONES — 30 minutes — CBS — April 11, 1975.

ROSETTI AND RYAN: MEN WHO LOVE WOMEN

The pilot film broadcast on NBC on May 23, 1977, for the series *Rosetti and Ryan* (see regular program section).

1751   THE ROWAN AND MARTIN REPORT

Pilot (Comedy). A satirization of TV news shows and news reporters.

Anchormen: Dan Rowan and Dick Martin.
Reporters: Cindi Haynie, Judy Pace, Carolyn Calcote, Jim Connell, Dick Stewart, Robbie Rist, Marcia Lewis.
Producer: Paul W. Keyes.
Writer: Marc London, Bill Larkin, Terry Hart, Ed Hider, Bob Keane, Bruce Taylor, Dawn Aldredge, Marion Freeman, Ed Monaghan.
Director: Martin Morris.
Art Director: E. Jay Krause.

THE ROWAN AND MARTIN REPORT — 30 minutes — ABC — November 5, 1975.

1752 ROXY PAGE

Pilot (Comedy). The misadventures of Roxy Hagopian, an ambitious young singer who, while working as a page at the Roxy Theater, is determined to make it to the Broadway stage.

CAST

Roxy Hagopian	Janice Lynde
Sylvia Hagopian, her sister	Leslie Ackerman
Anna Hagopian, her mother	Rhoda Gimignani
Alex Hagopian, her brother	Jeff Corey
Charlie Martin, her friend	Jim Catusi
Broadway director	Ken Olfson

Executive Producer: Don Kirshner, Allan Manings.
Producer: Jack Shea.
Director: Jack Shea.

ROXY PAGE — 30 minutes — NBC — September 6, 1976.

1753 ROYCE

Pilot (Western). The exploits of Royce, a strong, silent man who lived with the Comanche Indians and learned well how to deal with the harsh realities of 1870 frontier life. In the pilot, Royce guides a young woman and her two children, abandoned in the Kansas wasteland by the woman's husband, on a dangerous journey to California.

REGULAR CAST

Royce	Robert Forster

GUEST CAST

Susan Mabry (the woman)	Marybeth Hurt
Stephen Mabry (her son)	Moosie Drier
Heather Mabry (her daughter)	Terri Lynn Wood
Blair Mabry (her husband)	Michael Parks
White Bull	Eddie Little Sky
Dent	Dave Cass

Music: Jerrold Immel.
Executive Producer: Jim Byrnes.
Producer: William F. Phillips.
Writer: Jim Byrnes.
Director: Andrew V. McLaglen.
Art Director: Al Heschong.
Director of Photography: Ed Plante.
Set Director: Robert Bradfield.

ROYCE — 60 minutes — CBS — May 21, 1976.

1754 THE RUBBER GUN SQUAD

Pilot (Comedy). The misadventures of Chopper and Eddie, two misfit policemen working out of New York's Central Park Precinct.

CAST

Chopper	Andy Romano
Eddie	Lenny Baker
Sergeant O'Leary	Tom Signorelli
Rosie	Betty Buckley
Jerome	Alan Weeks
Austin	Paul Jabara

Executive Producer: Philip D'Antoni.

Producer: Sonny Grosso.
Director: Hy Averback.

THE RUBBER GUN SQUAD — 30 minutes — NBC — September 1, 1977.

1755 RUN JACK RUN

Pilot (Comedy). During a retirement party for underworld figure Smiley John Grazioni, a girl approaches hotel waiters Chester Blinsol and Jack Perry and, posing as a newspaper photographer, pays them $50 to take a picture of the gangster. Using her camera, Chester presses the shutter button and a bullet fires and wounds the guest of honor. The story depicts Jack and Chester's efforts to escape from Grazioni and his hit men.

CAST

Jack Perry	Dave Astor
Chester Blinsol	Adam Keefe
Smiley John Grazioni	Robert Middleton
Lefty, his aide	Anthony Caruso
The Girl	Marilyn Hanold

RUN JACK RUN — 30 minutes — NBC — July 20, 1970.

1756 RX FOR THE DEFENSE

Pilot (Crime Drama). The story of Zach Clinton, a former doctor turned attorney who works for a law firm that specializes in cases involving the medical world. In the pilot, Clinton attempts to help free Daniel Kemper, a famous professor from a psychiatric hospital after his wife has him committed following an alleged suicide attempt.

REGULAR CAST

Zach Clinton	Tim O'Connor

GUEST CAST

Laura Masters	Nancy Malone
Al Moore	Ronny Cox
Daniel Kemper	Fritz Weaver
Hilda Kemper	Kathryn Walker
Dr. Schwartz	Milton Selzer
Dr. Packer	Kevin Conway
D. A. Horn	Charles Durning
Marge	Marge Eliot

Executive Producer: Herbert Brodkin.
Producer: Robert Buzz Berger.
Writer: Ernest Kinoy.
Director: Ted Kotcheff.

RX FOR THE DEFENSE — 60 minutes — ABC — April 15, 1973.

S

1757 SALT AND PEPE

Pilot (Comedy). The misadventures of Jeremiah Salt, a prejudiced black businessman (the owner of a window washing firm) and his son-in-law and employee, Pepe, a Puerto Rican.

CAST

Jeremiah Salt	Mel Stewart
Pepe	Frank La Loggia
Abigail Salt, Jeremiah's wife	Dorothy Meyer
Yolanda Salt, Jeremiah's daughter	Diane Sommerfield
Millie, Jeremiah's secretary	Clarice Taylor
Nadine Salt	Sharon Brown

Executive Producer: E. Duke Vincent.
Producer: Frank Gertz.
Writer: E. Duke Vincent, Bob Arnott.
Director: Jack Shea.
Creator: E. Duke Vincent, Bob Arnott.

SALT AND PEPE — 30 minutes — CBS — April 18, 1975.

SLAVAGE

The pilot film broadcast on ABC on January 20, 1979, for the series *Salvage 1* (see regular program section).

1758 SAM HILL: WHO KILLED THE MYSTERIOUS MR. FOSTER?

Pilot (Western). The story, set in the Old West, follows the exploits of Sam Hill, an alcoholic drifter who runs for and is elected the sheriff of King City. In the pilot, Sam seeks to solve the mysterious poisoning death of the Reverend Mr. Foster, who was collecting $10,000 for a new church just before he was killed.

REGULAR CAST

Sheriff Sam Hill	Ernest Borgnine
Jethro, the boy who tags along with Sam	Stephen Hudis

GUEST CAST

Simon Anderson	Will Geer
Jody Kenyon	Judy Geeson
Doyle Pickett	Bruce Dern
Mal Yeager	J. D. Cannon
Doc Waters	Woodrow Parfrey
Reverend Mr. Foster	C. D. Spardlin
Abigail Booth	Carmen Mathews
Toby	Sam Jaffe
Judge	John McGiver
Mr. Kilpatrick	Slim Pickens
Mr. Fletcher	George Furth
Banker	Milton Selzer
Reed	Dub Taylor
Lucas	Ted Gehring
Hotel Clerk	Dennis Fimple
Telegraph Operator	Robert Gooden

Music: Pete Rugolo.
Producer: Jo Swerling, Jr.
Writer: Richard Levinson, William Link.
Director: Fielder Cook.
Art Director: Robert E. Smith.
Director of Photography: Gene Polito.

SAM HILL: WHO KILLED THE MYSTERIOUS MR. FOSTER? — 2 hours — NBC — February 1, 1971.

1759 SAMURAI

Pilot (Adventure). The story of Lee Cantrell,* a lawyer with the San Francisco County Prosecutor's Office, who lives by the code of the Samurai — a code by which he has sworn to defend those who are unable to defend themselves.

REGULAR CAST

Lee Cantrell	Joe Penny
Takeo Chisato, his martial arts instructor	James Shigeta
Hannah Cantrell, his mother	Beulah Quo
Frank Boyd, Lee's employer	Dana Elcar
Lt. Al DeNisco, S.F.P.D.	Norman Alden

GUEST CAST

Amory Bryson	Charles Cioffi
Harold Tigner	Geoffrey Lewis

Music: Fred Karlin.
Executive Producer: Danny Thomas, Ronald Jacobs, Fernando Lamas.
Producer: Allan Balter.
Writer: Jerry Ludwig.
Director: Lee H. Katzin.

SAMURAI — 90 minutes — ABC — April 30, 1979.

*Cantrell, born in Japan, was taught the martial arts and at the age of 10 had earned the red belt. Shortly thereafter, his parents moved to San Francisco where he later became a lawyer — his cover by day for his true purpose at night: to use his Oriental martial arts to battle injustice.

1760 SANCTUARY OF FEAR

Pilot (Mystery). The pilot film for the proposed but unsold *Father Brown, Detective* series. The story of Father Brown, an eccentric Manhattan priest and amateur detective. In the pilot, based on the stories by G.K. Chesterton, Father Brown, pastor of St. Eustacious Parish, attempts to help Carol Bain, a pretty young actress who is the subject of a mysterious campaign of terror after she witnesses a shooting — but can't convince anyone it happened.

REGULAR CAST

Father Brown	Barnard Hughes
Father William Wembley, his assistant	Robert Schenkkan
Mrs. Glidden, the church fund raiser	Elizabeth Wilson
Police Lt. Bellamy	Michael McGuire

GUEST CAST

Carol Bain	Kay Lenz
Jack Collins	David Rascher
Russell Heyman	Donald Symington
Whitney Fowler	Jeffrey DeMann
Beth Landau	Mareen Silliman
Eli Clay	Peter Maloney
Judge Potter	Fred Gwynne
Grace	Alice Drummond
Annie	Sudie Bond

Father Brown's dog: Rebley.

Music: Jack Elliott, Allyn Ferguson.

Supervising Producer: Gordon Cotler.
Executive Producer: Martin Starger.
Producer: Philip Barry.
Writer: Don Mankiewicz, Gordon Cotler.
Director: John Llewellyn Moxey.
Art Director: Robert Gundlash.

SANCTUARY OF FEAR — 2 hours — NBC — April 23, 1979. Repeated on June 12, 1980, as "Girl in the Park." Originally titled "Sanctuary of Death," then "Father Brown, Detective," "Sanctuary of Fear," and finally "Girl in the Park."

SAN FRANCISCO INTERNATIONAL AIRPORT

The pilot film broadcast on NBC on September 29, 1970, for the series of the same title (see regular program section).

THE SAN PEDRO BUMS

The pilot film broadcast on ABC on April 1, 1977, for the series *The San Pedro Beach Bums* (see regular program section).

SARGE

The pilot film broadcast on NBC on February 22, 1971, for the series of the same title (see regular program section).

1761   SAVAGE

Pilot (Crime Drama). The exploits of Paul Savage, a TV journalist and investigative reporter. The pilot episode depicts Savage's investigation of a scandal involving a Supreme Court nominee.

CAST

Paul Savage	Martin Landau
Gail Abbott	Barbara Bain
Joel Ryker	Will Greer
Brooks	Paul Richards
Allison	Michele Carey
Judge Stern	Barry Sullivan
Marion Stern	Louise Latham
Russell	Pat Harrington, Jr.
Lee Reynolds	Susan Howard

Music: Gil Mellé.
Executive Producer: William Link, Richard Levinson.
Producer: Paul Mason.
Writer: Mark Rodgers, William Link, Richard Levinson.
Director: Steven Spielberg.

SAVAGE — 90 minutes — NBC — March 31, 1973.

1762   SCALPELS

Pilot (Comedy). The story, set in San Francisco, comically depicts the public and private lives of a group of less-than-believable doctors.

CAST

Dr. Carl Jerrett, a psychiatrist	Rene Auberjonois
Dr. Betty Hacker, a neurologist	Marilyn Sokol
Dr. Nicole Tessier, a surgeon	Livia Genise
Dr. Bob Hobart, a surgeon	Simon MacCorkindale
Dr. Lawrence "Red" Hacker, Betty's husband, an anesthesiologist	Charles Haid
Connie Primble, a nurse	Kimberly Beck

NBC Announcer: Peggy Taylor.
Music: John LaSandra.
Supervising Producer: Bruce Johnson.
Executive Producer: Steve Zacharias.
Producer: Robert Keats.
Writer: Steve Zacharias, Robert Keats.
Director: John Tracy.
Director of Photography: George Dibie.

SCALPELS — 30 minutes — NBC — October 26, 1980.

1763   SCOTT FREE

Pilot (Crime Drama). The exploits of Tony Scott, a professional hustler who uses his unique skills to combat crime. The pilot depicts his attempts to expose a syndicate front for the U.S. government in exchange for a break on his IRS hassles.

REGULAR CAST

Tony Scott	Michael Brandon

GUEST CAST

Holly Morrison	Susan Saint James
Ed McGraw	Ken Swofford
Tom Little Lion	Cal Bellini
Joseph Donaldson	Robert Loggia
George Running Bear	Dehl Berti

Music: Mike Post and Pete Carpenter.
Executive Producer: Meta Rosenberg, Stephen J. Cannell.
Producer: Alex Beaton.
Writer: Stephen J. Cannell.
Director: William Wiard.

SCOTT FREE — 90 minutes — NBC — October 13, 1976.

1764   THE SECOND TIME AROUND

Pilot (Comedy). The misadventures of Joanne and David Norman, a husband and wife team of marriage counselors who, after two years of separation, decide to live together again.

CAST

Dr. Joanne Norman	Mariette Hartley
Dr. David Norman	Edward Winter
Mark Norman, their son	Brad Savage
Robin, their secretary	Simone Griffith
Bert, their friend	Jim Staahl

Music: Don Costa.
Theme Vocal: "The Second Time Around" by Steve Lawrence.
Producer: Jerry Tokofsky.
Director: Robert Drivas.

THE SECOND TIME AROUND — 30 minutes — ABC — July 24, 1979.

SEMI TOUGH

The pilot (videotape) broadcast on ABC on January 6, 1980, for the series of the same title (see regular program section).

SENIOR YEAR

The pilot film broadcast on CBS on March 22, 1974, for the series *Sons and Daughters* (see regular program section).

1765   SGT. T. K. YU

Pilot (Crime Drama). The exploits of Sgt. T. K. Yu, a Korean detective, working out of the Los Angeles Police Department, who moonlights as a nightclub comic. The pilot depicts Yu's efforts to adjust to his new surroundings, just having been transferred from Korea as part of an exchange program.

CAST

Sgt. T. K. Yu	Johnny Yune
Lt. Robert Ridge, his superior	John Lehne
Sam Palfy, Yu's friend, the owner of the Horn Night Club	Martin Brill

Music: Al Kasha.
Executive Producer: Joseph Barbera.
Producer: Terry Morse, Jr.
Writer: Gordon Dawson.
Director: Paul Stanley.

SGT. T. K. YU — 60 minutes — NBC — April 19, 1979.

1766   A SHADOW IN THE STREETS

Pilot (Drama). The story of Pete Mackey, an ex-con who serves as a paraprofessional deputy parole agent while on parole himself. The pilot depicts Mackey's attempts to adjust to his new position, which is an experimental state program, and contend with the pressures from his fellow parolees, as he uses his experience as an ex-con to make the program work.

REGULAR CAST

Pete Mackey	Tony LoBianco
Gina Polaski, his parole officer	Sheree North
Len Raeburn, the deputy director of state parole services	Dana Andrews

GUEST CAST

Debby	Jesse Welles
Siggie	Ed Lauter
Leroy Benson	Bill Henderson
Bense	Dick Balduzzi
Mr. Cavelli	John Sylvester White

Music: Charles Bernstein.
Executive Producer: Hugh Hefner.
Producer: John D. F. Black.
Writer: John D. F. Black, Edward L. Rissien.

Director: Richard Donner.

A SHADOW IN THE STREETS — 90 minutes — NBC — January 28, 1975. Also titled "Shadow in the Street."

1767   THE SHAMEFUL SECRETS OF HASTINGS CORNERS

Pilot (Comedy). A spoof of television serials as seen through the activities of the Honker and Fandango families, residents of Hastings Corners, and their continual feud.

CAST

Dr. Byron Dorman, the psychiatrist	Alan Oppenheimer
Ta Ta Honker, head of the Honkers	Woodrow Parfrey
Corey Honker, his son, the D.A.	Hal Linden
Morey Honker, Corey's twin brother	Hal Linden
Jenny Honker, Corey's wife	Karen Black
Charlotte Honker, Ta Ta's daughter	Ann Willis
Pa Fandango, head of the Fandangos	Hoke Howell
Brett Fandango, Pa's son	Peter Brocco
Tina Fandango, Pa's daughter	Stefani Warren
Junior Fandango, Pa's son	Barry Williams
Frieda Bindel, the woman who holds various shameful secrets in her memory	Madge Blake
Stacy Bindel, Frieda's niece	Robyn Millan

Music: George Duning.
Executive Producer: Harry Ackerman.
Producer: Lawrence J. Cohen, Fred Freeman.
Writer: Lawrence J. Cohen, Fred Freeman.
Director: Bob Claver.

THE SHAMEFUL SECRETS OF HASTINGS CORNERS — 30 minutes — NBC — January 14, 1970.

1768   SHAUGHNESSEY

Pilot (Comedy). The misadventures of the drivers and garage crew of the Morgan Cab Company in Chicago.

CAST

Eddie Shaughnessey, the dispatcher	Pat McCormick
Doris Shaughnessey, his wife	Nita Talbot
Mona Phillips, a driver	Sally Kirkland
Banners, the mechanic	Warren Berlinger
Steve Williams, a driver	Jack Mullaney
Phil Jenkins, a driver	Ralph Wilcox
Mr. Morgan, the auditor (guest)	David Doyle

Producer: Elliott Kozan.
Director: Hy Averback.

SHAUGHNESSEY — 30 minutes — NBC — September 6, 1976.

1769   S*H*E

Pilot (Adventure). The exploits of Lavinia Kean, an American secret agent and a member of S*H*E (Securities Hazards Expert), a

U.S. intelligence agency. The pilot episode depicts Lavinia's attempts to stop Cesare Magnasco, an international criminal who has schemed to contaminate the world's oil supply.

REGULAR CAST

Lavinia Kean	Cornelia Sharpe
Lacey, her assistant	William Traylor

GUEST CAST

Cesare Magnasco	Omar Sharif
Hunt	Robert Lansing
Fanya	Isabella Rye
Elsa	Anita Ekberg
Bronzi	Tom Christopher
Caserta	Fabio Testi
Alfredo Mucci	Mario Colli
Larue	Claudio Ruffini
Paesano	Fortunato Arena

Music: Michael Kamen.
Theme Vocal: Linda Gaines.
Producer: Martin Bergman.
Writer: Richard Maibaum.
Director: Robert Lewis.
Associate Producer: Michael Economou.
Director of Photography: Jules Brenner.
Costumes: Nadia Vitali.

S*H*E — 2 hours — CBS — February 23, 1980.

1770   SHEEHY AND THE SUPREME MACHINE

Pilot (Comedy). The misadventures of Jack Sheehy, an ex-Marine turned apartment building manager. In the pilot, Sheehy attempts to cope with a mischievous group of teenagers who are disrupting the tranquility of the apartment building.

CAST

Jack Sheehy	John Byner
Mr. Cagle, the building owner	Tige Andrews
Bogen, one of the teenagers	Jimmy Baio
Loretta Bogen, Bogen's mother	Gwynne Gilford
Ted, Bogen's friend	Pierre Daniel

Executive Producer: Harry Colomby.
Producer: Bernie Kukoff, Jeff Harris.
Director: Howard Storm.

SHEEHY AND THE SUPREME MACHINE — 30 minutes — ABC — August 22, 1977.

1771   SHEILA

Pilot (Comedy). The story of Sheila Levine, a young, somewhat bewildered, marriage-minded city girl of the 1970s, and her misadventures. She is employed by Marty Rose, a Broadway composer-producer who has an eye for the ladies and a never-failing lust for life.

CAST

Sheila Levine	Dori Brenner
Marty Rose	Milton Berle
Kate, Sheila's roommate	Barbara Trentham
Stewart Rose, Marty's son	George Wyner
Joshua	Larry Breeding
Brad Wooly	Philip R. Allen

Executive Producer: Gail Parent.
Producer: Martin Cohan.
Writer-Creator: Gail Parent, Kenny Solms.
Director: Peter Bonerz.
Art Director: Joe Jennings.
Director of Photography: Edward Nugent.
Set Decorator: Ira Bates.

SHEILA — 30 minutes — CBS — August 29, 1977.

1772   SHEPHERD'S FLOCK

Pilot (Comedy). The story of Jack Shepherd, an ex-football player turned minister, and his misadventures as he attempts to control his quick temper and adjust to a new life and responsibilities.

CAST

Jack Shepherd	Kenneth Mars
Abby Scoffield, his assistant	Jill Jaress
Dr. Hewitt, the head of the church	Don Ameche

SHEPHERD'S FLOCK — 30 minutes — CBS — August 29, 1971 (repeated August 11, 1972).

1773   SHERLOCK HOLMES: THE HOUNDS OF THE BASKERVILLES

Pilot (Mystery). The exploits of Sherlock Holmes, a consulting detective (a man who intervenes in baffling police matters) and his roommate and biographer, Dr. John H. Watson. The pilot episode, based on the story by Sir Arthur Conan Doyle, depicts Holmes's attempts to uncover the source of a supposed family curse that is killing members of the Baskerville family; and a vicious dog that prowls the moors near Baskerville Hall.

REGULAR CAST

Sherlock Holmes	Stewart Granger
Dr. John H. Watson	Bernard Fox
Police Inspector Lestrade	Alan Caillou

GUEST CAST

Dr. Mortimer	Anthony Zerbe
Sir Henry Baskerville	Ian Ireland
Stapleton	William Shatner
Laura Baskerville	Sally Ann Howes
Beryl Stapleton	June Merrow
Frankland	John Williams

Producer: Stanley Kallis.
Writer: Robert E. Thompson.
Director: Barry Crane.
Director of Photography: Harry Wolf.

SHERLOCK HOLMES: THE HOUND OF THE BASKERVILLES — 90 minutes — ABC — February 12, 1972.

1774   SHIPSHAPE

Pilot (Comedy). The story of Leslie O'Hara, an ambitious young Navy ensign, assigned to train a group of misfit sailors.

REGULAR CAST

Ensign Leslie O'Hara	Deborah Ryan
Captain Latch	Earl Boen
Yeoman Rita Sweetzer	Shell Kepler
Seaman Howard Beltzman	Andrew Bloch
Seaman House	Lorenzo Lamas
Seaman Harold Kozak	Demetre Phillips
Seaman Watkins	Gary Veney

GUEST CAST

Congressman Nelson	Ted Hartley
Mrs. Nelson	Kristin Larkin

Music: Michael Lloyd.
Executive Producer: James Komack.
Producer: Al Gordon, Jack Mendelsohn.
Supervising Producer: Stan Cutler, George Tricker, Neil Rosen.
Associate Producer: Claire Barrett Young.
Writer: George Tricker, Neil Rosen, Gary Belkin, Stan Cutler.
Director: James Komack, Gary Shimokawa.
Art Director: Roy Christopher, Jim Shanahan.

SHIPSHAPE — 30 minutes — CBS — August 1, 1978.

1775   SIDE BY SIDE

Pilot (Comedy). The misadventures of four couples, boxed together in a housing development: Charlie and Connie Ryan, a conservative couple who are enjoying their retirement; Carmine and Luis Rivera, a Latin duo; Sally and Dick Stern, young liberals with unconventional lives; and Billy Joe and Hadley Pearson, a transplanted couple from the South.

CAST

Charlie Ryan	Stubby Kaye
Connie Ryan	Peggy Pope
Carmine Rivera	Barbara Luna
Luis Rivera	Luis Avalos
Sally Stern	Janie Sell
Dick Stern	Keith Charles
Hadley Pearson	Diane Stilwell
Billy Joe Pearson	Don Scardino

Title Song: Stephen Schwartz.
Producer: Darryl Hickman.
Creator-Writer: Robert Kimmel Smith.
Director: H. Wesley Kenney.
Associate Producer: George Choderker.
Art Director: Jim Ryan.

SIDE BY SIDE — 30 minutes — CBS — July 27, 1976.

1776   SIDEKICKS

Pilot (Comedy-Western). The misadventures of Quince Drew and Jason O'Rourke, two inept con men who roam throughout the post-Civil War West seeking rich prey. The pilot depicts their misadventures when they become involved with an inept outlaw gang (and their disastrous attempts to rob a bank) and a pretty sheriff's daughter (Prudy) who knows they are con artists but can't prove it.

REGULAR CAST

Quince Drew	Larry Hagman
Jason O'Rourke	Lou Gossett

GUEST CAST

Boss	Jack Elam
Prudy	Blythe Danner
Sheriff Jenkins	Harry Morgan
Sam	Gene Evans
Drunk	Denver Pyle
Tom	Noah Beery

Music: David Shire.
Producer: Burt Kennedy.
Writer: William Bowers.
Director: Burt Kennedy.
Director of Photography: Robert Hauser.

SIDEKICKS — 90 minutes — CBS — March 21, 1974.

1777   THE SINGLE LIFE

Pilot (Comedy). The story, set in New York City, follows the misadventures of Barrie Shepherd, a beautiful writer for "The Single Life," a lonely-hearts column for *Manhattanite* magazine.

CAST

Barrie Shepherd	Barrie Youngfellow
Stephanie, Barrie's friend	Ceila Weston
Rocky, Barrie's friend	Paul Regina
Doris, Barrie's friend	Joyce Reehling
John Muller (guest role)	Fred McCarren
Waiter (guest role)	John Wyler

Music: David Frank.
Theme Vocal: Phyllis Brown.
Executive Producer: Bob Ellison.
Producer: Steve Pritzker.
Writer: Saura Sevine.
Director: Bill Persky.
Art Director: Frank Smith.

THE SINGLE LIFE — 30 minutes — NBC — August 21, 1980.

SINGLES

See title "CBS Comedy Trio" in the pilot film section.

1778   SISTER TERRI

Pilot (Comedy). The story of Sister Terri, a street-wise nun who works with inner-city children.

CAST

Sister Terri	Pam Dawber
Samantha, her sister	Robbie Lee
Mother Helen	Allyn Ann McLerie
Sister Agatha	Amy Johnston
Angel, one of the children	Scott Colomby
Boots, same as Angel	Kimberly LaPage
Franco, same as Angel	Derrel Maury

Music: Donald Peake.
Theme: "Sister Terri" by Stephanie E. Bernstein, Donald Peake.
Theme Vocal: Shelby Flint.

Executive Producer: Bob Brunner, Arthur Silver.
Producer: Jeffrey Ganz.
Writer: Bob Brunner, Arthur Silver.
Art Director: Jim Clayton.
Director of Photography: Meredith Nicholson.
Director: Jerry Paris.

SISTER TERRI—30 minutes—ABC—May 27, 1978.

THE SIX MILLION DOLLAR MAN

The pilot film broadcast on ABC on March 7, 1973, for the series of the same title (see regular program section).

1779 SLITHER

Pilot (Comedy). The hectic misadventures of Dick Kanipsia, a likeable young man who gets involved in unusual situations. In the pilot, Dick tries to profit from a plan to sell produce salvage from a train wreck. Based on the feature film of the same title.

REGULAR CAST

Dick Kanipsia	Barry Bostwick
Ruthie, his girlfriend	Patti Deutsch

GUEST CAST

Fat stranger	Cliff Emmich
Skinny stranger	Michael C. Gwynne
Farmer	Seaman Glass
First seller	Louis Quinn
Second seller	Robert Stiles
Driver	Johhn Delgado

Producer: Jack Shea.
Writer: W. D. Richter.
Director: Daryl Duke.

SLITHER—30 minutes—CBS—March 21, 1974.

SMILE JENNY, YOU'RE DEAD

The second pilot film (the first, "Harry O") broadcast on ABC on February 3, 1974, for the series *Harry O* (see regular program section).

1780 SNAFU

Pilot (Comedy). A humorous look at the insanity of combat as seen through the eyes of battleweary G.I.'s spending World War II in the muddy trenches of Italy.

CAST

Sgt. Mike Conroy	Tony Roberts
Capt. Billy Kaminski	James Cromwell
Lt. Hemsley Hauser	Kip Niven

Executive Producer: Leonard B. Stern.
Producer: Arnie Rosen.
Director: Jackie Cooper.

SNAFU—30 minutes—NBC—August 23, 1976.

THE SNOOP SISTERS

The pilot film broadcast on NBC on December 18, 1972, for the series of the same title (see regular program section).

1781 THE SON-IN-LAW

Pilot (Comedy). The story of Cindy Sugarman, an American girl who marries Johnny Quan, an unemployed Korean comedian. The pilot depicts their misadventures when they move in with and encounter the objections of Cindy's father, who is unable to fully accept their marriage.

CAST

Cindy Sugarman Quan	Judith-Marie Bergman
Johnny Quan	Johnny Yune
Charlotte Sugarman, Cindy's mother	Rue McClanahan
Manny Sugarman, Cindy's father	Pat Cooper
Mr. Muirfield, their landlord	Bernard Fox

NBC Announcer: Peggy Taylor.
Music: Pete Rugolo.
Executive Producer: Martin Starger.
Producer: Arthur Julian.
Writer: Arthur Julian, William Davenport.
Director: Gary Shimokawa.
Art Director: Chuck Murawski.

THE SON-IN-LAW—30 minutes—NBC—October 26, 1980.

SONNY BOY

See title "Bachelors 4" in the pilot film section.

1782 SORORITY '62

Pilot (Comedy). The story, set in Stafford College in northern Indiana in 1962, focuses on the experiences of Vickie, Cindy, Sheila and Gloria, Gamma Gamma Fi sorority sisters.

CAST

Vickie	Marcie Hanson
Cindy	Karen Bercovici
Sheila	Marya Small
Gloria	Suzanne Wishner
Miss Fletcher, the den mother	Marj Dusay
The Coach	Joey Bishop
Roger, Cindy's boyfriend	John Torp

Producer: Dick Clark, Jerry Frank.
Director: Tony Csiki.

SORORITY '62—30 minutes—Syndicated January 1978.

1783 SPACE FORCE

Pilot (Comedy). The misadventures that befall a crew of astronauts assigned to man a remote military space station.

CAST

Cmdr. Irving Hinkley	William Phipps
Capt. Thomas Woods	Fred Willard
Pvt. Arnold Fleck	Larry Block
Capt. Leon Stoner	Jimmy Boyd
Capt. Robert Milford	Hilly Hicks
Sgt. Eve Bailey	Maureen Mooney
Lt. Kabar	Joe Medalis

Producer: John Boni, Norman Stiles.
Writer: John Boni, Norman Stiles.
Director: Peter Baldwin.

SPACE FORCE—30 minutes—NBC—April 28, 1978.

1784 SPARROW

Pilot (Crime Drama). The exploits of Jerry Sparrow, a mailroom clerk in a detective agency. In the first of two unsold pilots (see following title), Sparrow attempts to solve a series of seemingly senseless and unrelated murders.

REGULAR CAST

Jerry Sparrow	Randy Herman
Mr. Medwick, his employer	Don Gordon
Tammy, Medwick's secretary	Beverly Sanders
Harriet, Sparrow's girlfriend	Karen Sedgley

GUEST CAST

Karen	Dori Brenner
Bruce	Jeff Holland
Bennett	Jack Wallace
Marty	Lenny Baker

Executive Producer: Herbert B. Leonard.
Producer: Sam Manners, Charles Russell.
Writer-Creator: Larry Cohen, Paul Bauman; revised story and screenplay: Walter Bernstein.

SPARROW—60 minutes—CBS—January 12, 1978.

1785 SPARROW

Pilot (Crime Drama). The exploits of Jerry Sparrow, a private investigator with a large detective agency in New Orleans. In the second pilot (see previous title also), Sparrow attempts to recover the missing bird of a wealthy woman.

REGULAR CAST

Jerry Sparrow	Randy Herman
Mr. Medwick, his employer	Gerald S. O'Loughlin
Valerie, Jerry's neighbor	Catherine Hicks

GUEST CAST

Mrs. Benet	Lillian Gish
Dory	Jonelle Allen
Rhino	Kurt Knudsen
Landon	Dolph Sweet

Theme Music: Paul Williams.
Executive Producer: Herbert B. Leonard.
Producer: Walter Bernstein.
Writer: Walter Bernstein.
Director: Jack Sold.
Art Director: Trevor Williams.
Director of Photography: Irving Lippman.

SPARROW—60 minutes—CBS—August 11, 1978.

SPENCER'S PILOTS

The pilot film broadcast on CBS on April 9, 1976, for the series of the same title (see regular program section).

1786 THE SPECIALISTS

Pilot (Drama). The exploits of the doctors attached to the Public Health Epidemic Intelligence Service Division as they seek to locate carriers of highly communicable diseases.

REGULAR CAST

Dr. William Nugent	Robert Urich
Dr. Christine Scholfield	Maureen Reagan
Dr. Edward Grey	Jack Hogan
Dr. Al Marsdan	Alfred Ryder
Dr. Burkhart	Harry Townes

GUEST CAST

Dick Rowdon	Jed Allan
Eileen	Anne Whitefield
Ruth Conoyer	Corinne Camacho
Resident doctor	Lillian Lehman

Music: Billy May.
Producer: Robert A. Cinader.
Writer: Preston Wood, Robert A. Cinader.
Director: Richard Quine.

THE SPECIALISTS—90 minutes—NBC—January 6, 1975.

1787 SPECTRE

Pilot (Thriller). The exploits of Dr. William Sebastian, a criminologist, and Dr. Hamilton, a physician, who team to battle supernatural forces. The pilot depicts their attempts to uncover the source of a powerful financier whose home in England is fraught with strange occurrences.

REGULAR CAST

Dr. William Sebastian	Robert Culp
Dr. Hamilton	Gig Young

GUEST CAST

Inspector Cabell	Gordon Jackson
Cyon	James Villiers
Anita	Ann Bell
Lilith	Majel Barrett
Mitri	John Hunt
Maid	Linda Benson

Music: John Cameron.
Producer: Gordon Scott.
Writer: Gene Roddenberry, Sam Peeples.
Director: Clive Donner.

SPECTRE—2 hours—NBC—May 21, 1977.

SPIDER-MAN

The pilot film broadcast on CBS on September 14, 1977, for the series *The Amazing Spider-Man* (see regular program section).

1788 STARSTRUCK

Pilot (Comedy). The story, set in the twenty-second century, follows the misadventures of the McCallister family, the owner-operators of McCallister's Midway Inn, a hotel-restaurant-saloon on an orbiting way station somewhere between Earth and Pluto.

REGULAR CAST

Ben McCallister, the father	Beeson Carroll
Kate McCallister, his daughter	Tania Myren
Mark McCallister, his son	Meegan King
Rupert McCallister, his son	Kevin Brando
Ezra McCallister, Ben's father	Guy Raymond
Abigail McCallister, Ben's mother	Elvia Allman
Amber LaRue, the lounge singer	Lynne Lipton
Delight, the waitress	Sarah Kennedy

GUEST CAST

Chance	Robin Strand
Max	Joe Silver
Orthwaite Frodo	Roy Brocksmith
Dart	Herb Kaplowitz
Hudson	Robert Short
Mrs. Bridges	Buddy Douglas
Tashko	J. C. Wells
Mary-John	Chris Walas
Madame Dumont	Cynthia Latham

Music: Alan Alper.
Executive Producer: Herbert B. Leonard.
Producer: Bob Kiger.
Associate Producer: Ed Forsyth.
Writer-Creator: Arthur Kopit.
Director: Al Viola.
Art Director: Kirk Axtell.
Director of Photography: Craig Greene.

STARSTRUCK — 30 minutes — CBS — June 9, 1979.

STARSKY AND HUTCH

The pilot film broadcast on ABC on April 30, 1975, for the series of the same title (see regular program section).

1789   STARTING FRESH

Pilot (Comedy). The story of Maggie Harris, a 36-year-old divorcée who enrolls at the same college as her 17-year-old daughter, Stephanie, and the mild misadventures that occur when they both share the same classes.

CAST

Maggie Harris	Lynnette Mettey
Stephanie Harris	Kimberly Beck
Phoebe Johnson, the dean of admissions	Janie Sell
Judy, Stephanie's friend	Susan Duvall
Cliffie, the son of Maggie's landlord	Ike Eisenman

Music: Norman Sacs.
Producer: Danny Thomas, Ronald Jacobs.
Director: Bob Claver.

STARTING FRESH — 30 minutes — NBC — June 27, 1979.

1790   STAT!

Pilot (Drama). The story of a harried medical staff forced to cope with a physically and emotionally exhausting daily routine.

REGULAR CAST

Dr. Ben Voorhees	Frank Converse
Dr. Nick Candros	Michael Delano
Nurse Ellen Quayle	Marian Collier
Dr. Jan Cavanaugh	Casey MacDonald

GUEST CAST

Dr. Neil Patricks	Henry Brown
Mary Ann Murphy	Monika Henreid
Doris Runyon	Peggy Rea
Dolores Payne	Marcy Lafferty

Producer: E. Jack Neuman.
Writer: E. Jack Neuman.
Director: Richard Donner.

STAT! — 30 minutes — CBS — July 31, 1973.

1791   STATE FAIR

Pilot (Drama). The story, set against the background of a state fair, follows the life of Wayne Bryant, a talented farm boy who dreams of becoming a Country music star.

CAST

Melissa Bryant	Vera Miles
Jim Bryant	Tim O'Connor
Wayne Bryant	Mitch Vogel
Karen Bryant Miller	Julie Cobb
Chuck Bryant	Dennis Redfield
Bobbie Jean Shaw	Linda Purl
Tommy Miller	Jeff Cotler
Catfish McKay	W. T. Zacha
Mr. Grant	Jack Garner
Miss Detweiler	Virginia Gregg
Ben Roper	Harry Moses
David Clemmans	Joel Stedman
Marnie	Dina K. Ousley
Deputy	Rance Howard
Judge	Ivor Francis

Music: Laurence Rosenthal.
Songs: "Carousel Love" and "Wind in the Trees" by Harriet Schock; "Everything Reminds Me of You" by Mitch Vogel.
Executive Producer: M. J. Frankovich, William Self.
Producer: Robert L. Jacks.
Associate Producer: Peter Frankovich.
Writer: Richard Fielder.
Director: David Lowell Rich.
Based On: The novel *State Fair* by Philip Stong.
Art Director: Archie Bacon.
Set Decorator: Cheryl Kearney.

STATE FAIR — 60 minutes — CBS — May 14, 1976.

1792   STEELTOWN

Pilot (Drama). The story of Modge Modgelewsky, a steelworker with the Riverbend Steel Company in Riverbend, Pennsylvania. The pilot focuses on Modge's clash with Bill Anderson, the company president, as he seeks to negotiate for higher wages, new safety conditions, and a postponement of the plant's automation plans.

REGULAR CAST

Modge Modgelewsky, a widower	Frank Converse
Aggie Modgelewsky, his daughter	Mare Winningham
Stevie Modgelewsky, his son	Justin Randi
Chris Modgelewsky, his son	Kraig Cassity
Bill Anderson, the company president	James Carroll Jordan
Janet Anderson, Bill's mother	Bibi Besch
Gibby Anderson, Bill's brother	Michael Biehn

GUEST CAST

Terri	Wendy Rastatter
Alma	Anna Garduno
Ed Lemke	Trevor Henley
Charley Lemke	Charles Cooper
Joe Falcone	Kevin Geer

Executive Producer: Gerald W. Abrams, Bruce J. Sallan.
Producer: Erv Zavada.
Writer: Laurence Heath.
Director: Robert Collins.
Art Director: Charles Hughes.
Director of Photography: Ric Waite, Gil Hubbs.

STEELTOWN — 60 minutes — CBS — May 19, 1979.

1793   STICK AROUND

Pilot (Comedy). The story, set in the year A.D. 2055, follows the misadventures of Elaine and Vance Keefer, a space-age family.

CAST

Elaine Keefer	Nancy New
Vance Keefer	Fred McCarren
Andy, their robot helper	Andy Kaufman
Burkus, their landlord	Cliff Norton
Earl	Craig Richard Nelson
Ed	Jeffrey Kramer

Producer: Fred Freeman, Lawrence J. Cohen.
Director: Bill Hobin.

STICK AROUND — 30 minutes — ABC — May 30, 1977.

STICKIN' TOGETHER

The pilot film broadcast on ABC on May 30, 1977, for the series *The MacKenzies of Paradise Cove* (see regular program section).

1794   STONESTREET: WHO KILLED THE CENTERFOLD MODEL?

Pilot (Crime Drama). The exploits of Liz Stonestreet, a beautiful private detective. The pilot depicts Liz's probe of a missing person's case which involves her with blackmail and murder.

REGULAR CAST

Liz Stonestreet	Barbara Eden

GUEST CAST

Max Pierce	Joseph Mascolo
Elliott Osborn	Richard Basehart
Jessica Hilliard	Joan Hackett
Arlene	Elaine Giftos
Mrs. Shroeder	Louise Latham
Chuck Voit	Val Avery
Amory Osborn	Ann Dusenberry
Della	Sally Kirkland
Dale Anderson	Robert Burton

Music: Pat Williams.
Producer: Leslie Stevens.
Writer: Leslie Stevens.
Director: Russ Mayberry.

STONESTREET: WHO KILLED THE CENTERFOLD MODEL? — 90 minutes — NBC — January 16, 1977.

1795   STRANDED

Pilot (Drama). The story, set on an isolated island in the South Pacific, depicts the hardships faced by a group of air-crash survivors from an Australia-bound airplane.

CAST

Sgt. Rafe Harder	Kevin Dobson
Crystal Norton	Lara Parker
Rose Orselli	Marie Windsor
Julie Blake	Devon Ericson
Tim Blake	Jimmy McNichol
John Rados	Rex Everhart
Ali Baba	Erin Blunt
Burt Hansen	Lal Baum
Jerry Holmes	James Cromwell
Charley Lee	John Fujioka

Music: Gordon Jenkins.
Executive Producer: David Victor.
Producer: Howie Horowitz.
Writer: Anthony Lawrence.
Director: Earl Bellamy.
Art Director: David Marshall.
Director of Photography: Alan Davey.

STRANDED — 60 minutes — CBS — May 26, 1976.

1796   THE STRANGER

Pilot (Science Fiction). The story of Neil Stryker, a U.S. astronaut, stranded on Terra, the twin planet of Earth, when his spacecraft passes through a vortex and later crash-lands. The would-be series, which was to focus on Stryker's adventures as he seeks a way to return to Earth, depicts, in the pilot, his efforts to escape from a mysterious dictatorship that has ordered his extermination.

REGULAR CAST

Neil Stryker	Glenn Corbett

GUEST CAST

Dr. Bettina Cooke	Sharon Acker
Benedict	Cameron Mitchell
Professor MacAuley	Lew Ayres
Max Greene	George Coulouris
Henry Maitland	Steve Franken
Steve Perry	Jerry Douglas
Mike Frome	Arch Whiting
Carl Webster	Dean Jagger
Dr. Revere	Tim O'Connor
Tom Nelson	Buck Young

Music: Richard Markowitz.
Executive Producer: Andrew J. Fenady.
Producer: Alan A. Armer.
Writer: Gerald Sanford.
Director: Lee H. Katzin.
Art Director: Stan Jolley.
Director of Photography: Keith C. Smith.

THE STRANGER — 2 hours — NBC — February 26, 1973.

1797   STREET KILLING

Pilot (Crime Drama). The exploits of Gus Brenner, a hard-driving, high-principled New York City prosecutor. In the pilot, Brenner seeks to prove that an underworld big shot is responsible for the death of a jewel importer.

REGULAR CAST

Gus Brenner	Andy Griffith
Susan Brenner, his wife	Sandy Faison
Kitty Brenner, their daughter	Gigi Semone

GUEST CAST

Howard Bronstein	Bradford Dillman
Al Lanier	Harry Guardino
Joe Spillane	Robert Loggia
Darlene Lawrence	Debbie White
Bud Schiffman	Don Gordon
Dr. Najukian	Raymond Singer
Ace Hendricks	Randy Martin
J. D. Johnson	Adam Wade

Music: J. J. Johnson.
Producer: Richard Rosenbloom.
Writer: William Driskell.
Director: Harvey Hart.

STREET KILLING—90 minutes—ABC—September 12, 1976.

1798   STRIKE FORCE

Pilot (Crime Drama). The exploits of Joey Gentry, a New York City detective; Jerome Ripley, a federal agent; and Walter Spenser, a state trooper, three men who are teamed to battle highly dangerous crimes. The pilot depicts their efforts to crack a narcotics case.

CAST

Joey Gentry	Cliff Gorman
Jerome Ripley	Donald Blakely
Walter Spenser	Richard Gere
Captain Peterson, their superior	Edward Grover
Sol Terranova (guest)	Joe Spinell

Producer: Philip D'Antoni, Barry Weitz.
Writer: Roger Hirson.
Director: Barry Shear.
Creator: Sonny Grosso.

STRIKE FORCE—90 minutes—NBC—April 12, 1975.

1799   STUNT SEVEN

Pilot (Adventure). The exploits of seven stunt people who team to solve complex, high-risk crimes. The pilot depicts their efforts to rescue Rebecca Wayne, a beautiful actress from Maximillian Bourdeaux, a ruthless kidnapper.

REGULAR CAST

The Stunt 7:

Hill Singleton	Christopher Connelly
Skip Hartman	Christopher Lloyd
Eleana Sweet	Morgan Brittany
Dinah Lattimore	Juanin Clay
Wally Ditweller	Bob Seagren
Ken Uto	Soon-Tech Oh
Horatio Jennings	Brian Brodsky

GUEST CAST

Rebecca Wayne	Elke Sommer
Maximillian Bourdeaux	Patrick Macnee

Music: Jack Eskew.
Theme Music: Bill Conti.

Producer: Martin Poll.
Co-Producer: William Carver.
Associate Producer: Ralph Singleton.
Director: John Peyser.

STUNT SEVEN—2 hours—CBS—May 30, 1979.

1800   STUNTS UNLIMITED

Pilot (Adventure). The exploits of Matt, C.C. and Bo (no last names), three Hollywood stunt performers who are united by the C.I.A. to perform top-secret missions. In the pilot, they use their incredible skill to penetrate a madman's fortress and recover a deadly laser weapon from a gun runner.

REGULAR CAST

Matt	Chip Mayer
Cecilia "C.C."	Susanna Dalton
Bo	Sam J. Jones
"Mac" Macauley, the head of Stunts Unlimited	Glenn Corbett
Jody, Mac's assistant	Linda Grovernor

GUEST CAST

Fernando Castilla	Alejandro Rey
Tallia	Victor Mohica
Hal Needham	Himself
Stuntman	Charles Picerni
Horse Gilbert	Mickey Gilbert

Music: Barry De Vorzon.
Executive Producer: Lawrence Gordon.
Producer: Lionel E. Siegel.
Writer: Laurence Heath.
Director: Hal Needham.
Art Director: Hilyard Brown.
Director of Photography: Mike Shea.

STUNTS UNLIMITED—90 minutes—ABC—January 4, 1980.

1801   THE SUNDAY GAMES

Pilot (Game). Ordinary people compete in various games for the sheer enjoyment the sport offers.

Host: Bruce Jenner.
Announcer: Gary Owens.
Music: Don Great.
Supervising Producer: Don Azaros.
Executive Producer: Don Ohlmeyer.
Producer: Howard Katz.
Writer: Norman Bleichman.
Director: Jim Cross.
Art Director: Bob Keene.
Field Producer: Kim Dawson, Chris Pyne.

THE SUNDAY GAMES—2 hours—NBC—April 27, 1980. Originally titled "The Friday Games" and scheduled for April 18, 1980. The pilot for *The Games People Play*.

SUNSHINE

The pilot film broadcast on NBC on November 9, 1973, for the series of the same title (see regular program section).

1802   THE SUNSHINE BOYS

Pilot (Comedy). The story of Willie Clark and Al Lewis, two retired vaudevillians who share an apartment—and struggle to get along with each other.

CAST

Willie Clark	Red Buttons
Al Lewis	Lionel Stander
Ben Clark	Michael Durrell
Myrna Navazio	Bobbi Mitchell
Muriel Green	Sarina Grant

Executive Producer: Michael Levee.
Producer: Sam Denoff.
Director: Robert Moore.

THE SUNSHINE BOYS—60 minutes—NBC—June 9, 1977.

1803   SUPERCOPS

Pilot (Crime Drama). The exploits of Dave Greenberg and Bobby Hantz, two New York City police officers, known as "Batman and Robin" for their daring tactics and record number of arrests and convictions. The pilot depicts their efforts to apprehend a thief who sadistically victimizes only big-time gambling winners.

REGULAR CAST

Dave Greenberg	Steven Keats
Bobby Hantz	Alan Feinstein
Captain McLain, their superior	Dick O'Neill

GUEST CAST

Bessie	Peggy Rea
Lt. Gorney	Bryon Morrow
Lt. Vanesian	Tony Brande
Sgt. Falcone	Lou Tiano
Delgado	George Loros

Music: Jack Urbont.
Executive Producer: Bruce Geller.
Producer: James David Buchanan, Ronald Austin.
Writer: Austin and Irma Kalish.
Director: Bernard L. Kowalski.
Art Director: Robert E. Smith.
Director of Photography: Howard Schwartz.

SUPERCOPS—30 minutes—CBS—March 21, 1975.

1804   SUSAN AND SAM

Pilot (Comedy). The romantic misadventures of Susan Foster and Sam Denton, magazine writers who find their romance is floundering on the rocks of professional competition and vastly different tastes.

REGULAR CAST

Susan Foster	Christine Belford
Sam Denton	Robert Foxworth
Doug Braden, the editor	Lee Bergere

GUEST CAST

Percy	Jack Bannon
Lionel	Rod McCary
Hilly	Alan Oppenheimer

Producer: Alan Alda, Marc Merson.
Writer: Alan Alda.
Director: Jay Sandrich.

SUSAN AND SAM—30 minutes—NBC—July 13, 1977.

1805   SWEET, SWEET RACHEL

Pilot (Mystery). The pilot film for *The Sixth Sense* with Gary Collins in the title role. The story of Dr. Lucas Darrow, a professor of parapsychology who aids people threatened by ghosts and attempts to solve crimes that are associated with the supernatural. In the pilot, Darrow seeks to find a psychic who uses his telepathic power to commit murder.

REGULAR CAST

Dr. Lucas Darrow	Alex Dreier

GUEST CAST

Rachel Stanton	Stefanie Powers
Arthur Piper	Pat Hingle
Lillian Piper	Louise Latham
Nora Piper	Brenda Scott
Carey	Chris Robinson
Dr. Tyler	Steve Ihnat
Houseman	Mark Tapscott

Music: Lawrence Rosenthal.
Producer: Stan Shpetner.
Writer: Anthony Lawrence.
Director: Sutton Roley.

SWEET, SWEET RACHEL—90 minutes—ABC—October 2, 1971.

SWISS FAMILY ROBINSON

The pilot film broadcast on ABC on April 15, 1975, for the series of the same title (see regular program section).

SWITCH

The pilot film broadcast on CBS on March 21, 1975, for the series of the same title (see regular program section).

T

TABITHA

The pilot film broadcast on ABC on April 24, 1976, for the series of the same title (see regular program section).

1806   TARGET RISK

Pilot (Crime Drama). The exploits of Lee Driscoll, a bonded courier. The pilot depicts Driscoll's attempts to save the life of his girlfriend by unwittingly participating in a jewel robbery to raise the two million dollars in ransom for her.

REGULAR CAST

Lee Driscoll	Bo Svenson
Linda Frayly, his girlfriend	Meredith Baxter Birney

Marie. Marie Osmond.

Stonestreet: Who Killed the Centerfold Model?
Barbara Eden.

The Three Wives of David Wheeler. Cathy Lee Crosby.

Wonder Woman. Cathy Lee Crosby. Costume differences
can be compared with photos for *The New Adventures of
Wonder Woman* and *Wonder Woman.*

GUEST CAST

Ralph Sloan	John P. Ryan
Julian Ulrich	Robert Coote
Simon Cusack	Keenan Wynn
Marty	Philip Bruns
Harry	Lee Paul
Bill Terek	Charles Shull

Music: Emvir Deodato.
Executive Producer: Jo Swerling, Jr.
Producer: Robert F. O'Neil.
Writer: Don Carlos Dunaway.
Director: Robert Scheerer.

TARGET RISK — 90 minutes — NBC — January 6, 1975.

THE TED BESSELL SHOW

See title "CBS Triple Play" in the pilot film section.

1807 TERRACES

Pilot (Drama). The story, set in a luxury high-rise apartment, depicts the social and sexual entanglements of the people who share adjoining terraces.

CAST

Chalan Turner	Julie Newmar
Julie Borden	Kit McDonough
Gregg Loomis	Bill Gerber
Beth Loomis	Eliza Garrett
Roberta Robbins	Jane Dulo
Martin Robbins	Arny Freeman
Dr. Roger Cabe	Lloyd Bochner
Dorothea Cabe	Lola Albright
Steve	Timothy Thomerson
Vogel	Allan Rich
Alex	James Phipps

Music: Peter Matz.
Producer: Charles Fries.
Writer: Lila Garrett, George Kirgo.
Director: Lila Garrett.

TERRACES — 90 minutes — NBC — June 27, 1977.

1808 THE THANKSGIVING TREASURE

Pilot (Drama). The second of four pilot films about life in Nebraska during the 1940s as seen through the experiences of the Mills family (see also "Addie and the King of Hearts," "The Easter Promise" and "The House Without a Christmas Tree"). The story follows Addie Mills, the 11-year-old daughter of widower James Mills, as she attempts to befriend Mr. Rhenquist, a bitter old man who is an enemy of her gruff father. (The title is derived from Addie's experiences, winning Rhenquist's friendship just before Thanksgiving, as she cares for his horse, Treasure.)

REGULAR CAST

James Mills, the father	Jason Robards
Addie MIlls, his daughter	Lisa Lucas
Grandmother Mills	Mildred Natwick

GUEST CAST

Mr. Rhenquist	Barnard Hughes
Miss Thompson	Kathryn Walker
Uncle Will	Larry Reynolds
Aunt Nora	Kay Hawtry
Aaron Burkhart	Cec Linder

Producer: Alan Shayne.
Writer: Eleanor Perry.
Director: Paul Bogart.

THE THANKSGIVING TREASURE — 90 minutes — CBS — November 18, 1973.

1809 THERE'S ALWAYS ROOM

Pilot (Comedy). The misadventures of Madelyn Fairchild, a middle-aged free spirit, and the owner of a once-fashionable Los Angeles home that has become a haven for a variety of eccentric guests.

REGULAR CAST

Madelyn Fairchild	Maureen Stapleton
Stewart Dennis, the greeting card businessman	Conrad Janis
Annette Ederby, the girl who resides with Madelyn while attending school	Debbie Zipp

GUEST CAST

Bob Ederby (Annette's father)	Barry Nelson
Valerie	Leland Palmer
Buck Burke	Royce Applegate
Mr. McRaven	Woody Chambliss

Music: Bill Conti.
Executive Producer: Robert W. Christiansen, Rick Rosenberg.
Producer: Michael Leeson.
Writer: Michael Leeson.
Director: Robert Moore.
Art Director: Ken Johnson.
Director of Photography: Ken Peach.
Set Decorator: Bob Checchi.

THERE'S ALWAYS ROOM — 30 minutes — CBS — April 24, 1977.

1810 THEY CALL IT MURDER

Pilot (Mystery). The exploits of Doug Selby, a small-town district attorney. Based on the character created by Erle Stanley Gardner.

CAST

Doug Selby	Jim Hutton
A. B. Carr	Lloyd Bochner
Jane Antrim	Jessica Walter
Rona Corbin	Nita Talbot
Sylvia Martin	Jo Ann Pflug
Chief Larkin	Edward Asner
Doris Kane	Carmen Mathews
Frank Antrim	Leslie Nielsen
Sheriff Brandon	Robert J. Wilke

Music: Robert Drasnin.
Producer: Walter Grauman.
Writer: Sam Rolfe.
Director: Walter Grauman.

THEY CALL IT MURDER — 2 hours — NBC — December 17, 1971.

THEY ONLY COME OUT AT NIGHT

The pilot film broadcast on April 29, 1975, for the series *Jigsaw John* (see regular program section).

1811 THE 13th DAY: THE STORY OF ESTHER

Pilot (Anthology). The Old Testament story of Esther, the beautiful Jewish girl who is wrested from her fiancé by the King of Persia to become his reluctant queen. A potential series of Biblical stories.

CAST

Esther	Olivia Hussey
King	Tony Musante
Haman	Harris Yulin
Mordecai	Nehemiah Persoff
Simon	Ted Wass
Sura	Erica Yohn
Dalphon	Kurio Salem

Narrator: Raymond Burr.
Music: Morton Stevens.
Executive Producer: David Victor.
Writer: Norman Hurdis.
Director: Leo Penn.

THE 13th DAY: THE STORY OF ESTHER — 60 minutes — ABC — November 18, 1979.

1812 THIS BETTER BE IT

Pilot (Comedy). The story of Annie and Harry Bell, newlyweds who each have a grown child from a previous marriage that ended in a divorce.

CAST

Annie Bell	Anne Meara
Harry Bell	Alex Rocco
Diana Bell, Harry's daughter	Baillie Gersten
Flower, Annie's daughter	Linda Conrad
Paul, Diana's fiancé	David Pollack

Music: David Shire.
Executive Producer: Charles Fries.
Producer: Lila Garrett.
Creator-Writer: Lila Garrett, Lynn Roth.
Director: Richard Kinon.
Art Director: Jack Stewart.

THIS BETTER BE IT — 30 minutes — CBS — August 10, 1976.

1813 THIS WEEK IN NEMTIN

Pilot (Comedy). A satirical survey of events that occur in the fictional country of Nemtin.

CAST

Newscaster	Alex Dreier
Wiseman	Carl Reiner

Producer-Writer: Saul Turteltaub, Bernie Orenstein, Ron Clark, Sam Bobrick.
Director: Bill Foster.

THIS WEEK IN NEMTIN — 30 minutes — CBS — April 14, 1972.

1814 THREE COINS IN THE FOUNTAIN

Pilot (Comedy). The romantic misadventures of Maggie Wilson, an American girl living in Rome and working as a secretary.

CAST

Maggie Wilson	Cynthia Pepper
Dorothy, her roommate	Yvonne Craig
Ruth, her roommate	Joanna Moore
Gino, the waif taken in by the girls	Antony Alda
Count Giorgio (guest)	Nino Castelnuovo

Maggie's address: 27 Verda La-Cruca.

Music: Jeff Alexander.
Theme Vocal: "Three Coins In The Fountain" by Trini Lopez.
Executive Producer: Hal Kanter.
Producer: Robert L. Jacks.
Writer: Melville Shavelson.
Director: Hal Kanter.

THREE COINS IN THE FOUNTAIN — 30 minutes — NBC — August 10, 1970. Based on the 1954 movie of the same title.

THREE FOR THE ROAD

The pilot film broadcast on CBS on September 4, 1975, for the series of the same title (see regular program section).

1815 THREE FOR TAHITI

Pilot (Comedy). The story of three men, Kelly, Muk and Jay, plagued by life's endless problems, who decide to get away from it all and purchase, sight unseen, a hotel in Tahiti. The episode focuses on their misadventures as they attempt to operate what turns out to be a hotel fraught with problems.

CAST

Kelly	Robert Hogan
Muk	Bob Einstein
Jay	Steve Franken
Cecil Barrett, their friend	Alan Oppenheimer
Longet, the local police chief	Marcel Hillaire

Music: Jack Elliott, Allyn Ferguson.
Producer: Bill Persky, Ken Kragen, E. W. Swackhamer.
Director: E. W. Swackhamer.

THREE FOR TAHITI — 30 minutes — ABC — August 19, 1970.

1816 THREE-IN-ONE

Pilot (Comedy). The overall title for three comedies.

Doctor Dan (1970). The misadventures of a child psychologist (Jackie Cooper) with distrustful patients.

Bobby Parker and Company (1970). The story of Bobby Parker (Ted Bessell), a man whose hangups follow him around in imaginary forms.

Ready and Willing (1966). The misadventures of a mismatched team of crime fighters: Pamela (Melodie Johnson), a rich girl with a degree in criminology, and her partners, misfits Ready (Joe Flynn) and Willing (Jack Weston).

THREE-IN-ONE — 90 minutes (30 minutes each segment) — CBS — April 22, 1974.

1817   THREE TIMES DALEY

Pilot (Comedy). The misadventures of Bob Daley, a divorced newspaper columnist; his father, Alex; and his son, Wes — three generations of a family trying to live together under one roof.

CAST

Bob Daley	Don Adams
Alex Daley	Liam Dunn
Wes Daley	Jerry Houser
Stacy	Bibi Besch
Jenny	Ayn Ruyman

Music: Don Costa.
Executive Producer: Leonard B. Stern.
Producer: John Rappaport.
Writer: John Rappaport.
Director: Jay Sandrich.
Art Director: Ray Beal.

THREE TIMES DALEY — 30 minutes — CBS — August 3, 1976.

1818   THE THREE WIVES OF DAVID WHEELER

Pilot (Comedy). The misadventures of David Wheeler, owner of Wheeler Graphic Arts, and a man with three wives: Ginger, his first ex-wife and still his business partner; Bibi, his second ex-wife, a model he still employs; and Julia, his current wife, a girl who understands — usually.

CAST

David Wheeler	Art Hindle
Ginger Wheeler	Cathy Lee Crosby
Bibi Wheeler	Sherril Lynn Katzman
Julia Wheeler	Nancy Grigor
Vinnie, the photographer	Archie Hahn
Debbie, David's secretary	Susan Tolsky

Music: Jack Elliott, Allyn Ferguson.
Supervising Producer: Norman S. Powell.
Producer: Jay Folb.
Director: Burt Brinkerhoff.

THE THREE WIVES OF DAVID WHEELER — 30 minutes — NBC — August 1, 1979.

1819   A TIME FOR LOVE

Pilot (Anthology). A would-be series about people of opposite interests meeting on love's common ground. In the first pilot (of two that were aired back-to-back), John Davidson stars as a straight-laced junior executive who falls for a free-spirited convention hostess (Lauren Hutton). In the second, Bonnie Bedelia stars as a shy teacher whose life is disrupted when a Rock singer, seeking to escape from his hectic world, enters her life.

CAST (Story 1)

Larry	John Davidson
Darleen	Lauren Hutton
Tom Pierson	Jack Cassidy

CAST (Story 2)

Kitty	Bonnie Bedelia
Mark	Christopher Mitchum
Patricia	Jennifer Leak
Jamison May	Malachi Throne
Mini	JoAnna Cameron
Seabrook	Joseph Hindy

Music: Pat Williams.
Producer: Stirling Silliphant.
Writer: Stirling Silliphant.

A TIME FOR LOVE — 2 hours (one hour each story) — NBC — March 3, 1973.

1820   TIME TRAVELERS

Pilot (Science Fiction). The exploits of Clinton Earnshaw and Jeff Adams, a doctor and a scientist, who travel through time for purposes of helping mankind. In the pilot, Earnshaw and Adams return, via a time machine, to Chicago in 1871 to find a doctor who can help cure a disease that has broken out in the New Orleans of their own era.

REGULAR CAST

Dr. Clinton Earnshaw	Sam Groom
Jeff Adams	Tom Hallick

GUEST CAST

Dr. Henderson	Richard Basehart
Jane Henderson	Trish Stewart
Dr. Cummings	Booth Colman
Dr. Helen Sanders	Francine York
Dr. Stafford	Walter Burke
Chief Williams	Baynes Barron
Sharkey	Dort Clark

Music: Morton Stevens.
Producer: Irwin Allen.
Writer: Jackson Gillis.
Director: Alex Singer.

TIME TRAVELERS — 90 minutes — ABC — March 19, 1976.

TO KILL A COP

The pilot film broadcast in two parts on NBC on April 10, 1978, and April 11, 1978, for the series *Eischied* (see regular program section).

1821   TOM AND JOANN

Pilot (Drama). The story of Tom and Joann, a divorced couple who explore new relationships while maintaining their mutual affection a year after their 16-year marriage has ended.

REGULAR CAST

Joann	Elizabeth Ashley
Tom	Joel Fabiani
Amy, their daughter	Jennifer Cook
T. C., their son	Colin McKenna

GUEST CAST

Lou	Bibi Besch
Gabe	David Ackroyd
Beth	Marie McCann
Kenny	Tim Okon
Helene	Brenda Donohue
Norman	Louis Del Grande

Music: Hagood Hardy.
Executive Producer: David Susskind.
Producer: Frederick Brogger, Diana Kerew.
Writer: Loring Mandel.
Director: Delbert Mann.
Director of Photography: Ronald M. Latoure.

TOM AND JOANN — 60 minutes — CBS — July 5, 1978.

TOMA

The pilot film broadcast on ABC on March 21, 1973, for the series of the same title (see regular program section).

1822   TONI'S BOYS

Pilot (Crime Drama). The story of Antonia "Toni" Blake, the owner of a private detective agency, who solves crimes with the help of three handsome operatives and a butler. The pilot, which was broadcast as a segment of *Charlie's Angels*, teams Toni's Boys (Bob Sorensen, Cotton Harper and Matt Parrish) with Charlie's Angels (Kris Munroe, Kelly Garrett and Tiffany Welles) to find Michael Durano, an assassin who is plotting to kill the Angels and get even for putting him behind bars.

REGULAR CAST

Antonia Blake	Barbara Stanwyck
Bob Sorensen, an Olympic champion	Bob Seagren
Cotton Harper, a rodeo champion	Stephen Shortridge
Matt Parrish, a master of disguise	Bruce Bauer
Rolph, Toni's butler	James E. Broadhead

GUEST CAST

Kris Munroe	Cheryl Ladd
Kelly Garrett	Jaclyn Smith
Tiffany Welles	Shelley Hack
John Bosley	David Doyle
Voice of Charlie Townsend	John Forsythe
Michael Durano	Robert Loggia

Toni's address: 612 Essex Road, Los Angeles, California.

Music: Jack Elliott, Allyn Ferguson.
Executive Producer: Aaron Spelling, Leonard Goldberg.
Producer: Robert Janes.
Writer: Kathryn Powers.
Director: Ron Satlof.

TONI'S BOYS — 60 minutes — ABC — April 2, 1980.

TOO MANY SUSPECTS

The syndicated title for the "Ellery Queen" pilot episode (which was broadcast on NBC on March 23, 1975).

1823   TOPPER

Pilot (Comedy). The story of two ghosts, the spirits of George and Marian Kerby, a wealthy, irresponsible young couple who were killed in an automobile accident and now haunt Cosmo Topper, their lawyer, in an attempt to bring some fun into his dreary life. Based on characters created by Thorne Smith.

REGULAR CAST

Marian Kerby	Kate Jackson
George Kerby	Andrew Stevens
Cosmo Topper	Jack Warden
Clara Topper, Cosmo's wife	Rue McClanahan
Wilkins, Cosmo's butler	Macon McCalman
Fred Korbell, Cosmo's business partner	James Karen

GUEST CAST

Stan Ogilvy	Charles Siebert
Lingerie saleswoman	Gloria LeRoy
Auto mechanic	Larry Gelman
Charlene	Lois Areno
Nurse	Jane Wood
Man in disco	Marshall Teague

The Kerby's dog: Sam.

Music: Fred Karlin.
Executive Producer: Kate Jackson, Andrew Stevens.
Producer: Robert Papazin.
Director: Charles S. Dubin.
Art Director: Allen Smith.
Director of Photography: Robert Caramico.

TOPPER — 2 hours — ABC — November 9, 1979.

1824   TOPPER RETURNS

Pilot (Comedy). An update of the Topper story in which Cosmo Topper, Jr., the nephew of the late Cosmo Topper, finds his life plagued when he inherits his uncle's possessions, including the spirits of George and Marian Kerby. The ghosts who appeared and spoke only to his uncle now appear and speak only to him in an attempt to bring some excitement into his dull life.

CAST

Cosmo Topper, Jr.	Roddy McDowall
Marian Kerby	Stefanie Powers
George Kerby	John Fink
Jones, Cosmo's butler	Reginald Owen

Also: John Randolph, Jeanne Bates, Ed Peck, Amzie Strickland, Arthur Lewis, Ralph Manza.
Music: Pat Williams.
Executive Producer: Arthur P. Jacobs.
Producer: Walter Bien.
Writer: A. J. Carothers.
Director: Hy Averback.

TOPPER RETURNS — 30 minutes — NBC — March 19, 1973.

1825   TOP SECRET

Pilot (Adventure). The exploits of Aaron Strickland, a U.S. government secret agent. In the pilot, Strickland seeks to trace the whereabouts of one hundred pounds of plutonium stolen from a U.S. army depot in Italy.

REGULAR CAST

Aaron Strickland	Bill Cosby
McGee, his assistant	Tracy Reed

GUEST CAST

Carl Vitale	Sheldon Leonard
Judith	Gloria Foster
Murphy	George Brenlin
Sgt. Kwitney	Nat Bush
Brigitte	Francesca DeSaplo

Music: Teo Macero, Stu Gardner.
Producer: Sheldon Leonard.
Writer: David Levinson.
Director: Paul Leaf.

TOP SECRET — 2 hours — NBC — June 4, 1978.

1826   TRAVIS LOGAN, D.A.

Pilot (Crime Drama). The exploits of Travis Logan, a district attorney. In the pilot, Logan's prosecution of a case involving a routine homicide and a plea of temporary insanity, reveals an almost perfect crime and a premeditated murder when he discovers an odd-sized shotgun pellet.

REGULAR CAST

Travis Logan	Vic Morrow

GUEST CAST

Mark	Chris Robinson
Sand	Hal Holbrook
Jerry	James Callahan
Eve	Brooke Bundy
Lucille Sand	Brenda Vaccaro
Bender	George Grizzard
George Carnera	Scott Marlowe
Judge Rose	Edward Andrews
Dr. Reichert	Michael Strong
Mrs. Tice	Josephine Hutchinson
Tony Carnera	Richard Angarola

Music: Pat Williams.
Executive Producer: Quinn Martin.
Producer: Adrian Samish, Arthur Fellows.
Writer: Adrian Samish, Arthur Fellows.
Director: Paul Wendkos.

TRAVIS LOGAN, D.A. — 2 hours — CBS — March 11, 1971.

1827   A TREE GROWS IN BROOKLYN

Pilot (Drama). The story, set in Brooklyn, New York, in 1912, follows the lives of the Nolans, a poor family living in a tenement: Johnny, the charming but alcoholic father; Katie, his strong-willed wife who supports the family; and their resourceful children, Francie and Neely. Based on the book by Betty Smith.

CAST

Johnny Nolan, the father	Cliff Robertson
Katie Nolan, the mother	Diane Baker
Francie Nolan, their daughter	Pamelyn Ferdin
Neely Nolan, their son	Michael-James Wixted
Sissy, Katie's sister	Nancy Malone
Officer McShane	James Olson
Mr. Barker, the rent collector	Liam Dunn
Miss Tillford	Anne Seymour
Miss Martin	Allyn Ann McLerie

Music: Jerry Goldsmith.
Producer: Norman Rosemont.
Writer: Blanche Hanalis, Tess Slesinger, Frank Davis.
Director: Joseph Hardy.

A TREE GROWS IN BROOKLYN — 90 minutes — NBC — March 27, 1974.

1828   TRIPLE PLAY '72

Pilot (Comedy). The overall title for three unsold comedies.

Host: Arte Johnson.

Call Holme. The story of a private detective who uses his mastery of disguises to apprehend criminals.

CAST

Detective Holme	Arte Johnson
Miss Musky, his secretary	Arlene Golonka
Lieutenant	Jim Hutton
Phadera	Linda Cristal
Von Klug	Helmut Dantine
Miss Paperman	Rosemary De Camp
Lester	Noel Harrison

Music: Johnny Mandel.
Executive Producer: Douglas S. Cramer.
Producer: W. L. Baumes.
Writer: Gerald Gardner.
Director: Gary Nelson.

Keeping Up with the Joneses. The story of a white couple who share a New York brownstone with a black couple—both of whom have the surname Jones.

Cast: White couple: Warren Berlinger (a construction supervisor) and Pat Finley (his wife); black couple: John Amos (a cop) and Teresa Graves (his wife).

Executive Producer: Douglas S. Cramer.
Producer-Writer: Gordon Farr, Arnold Kane.
Director: Jerry Paris.

Wednesday Night Out. The story focuses on three suburban couples and a divorcée who take turns inviting one another to theme parties on Wednesday evenings.

CAST

Jim	Jim Hutton
Tess	Kathleen Nolan
Paula	Gloria De Haven
Tom	Robert Sampson
Anna Marie	Brenda Benet
Frank	Pat Harrington, Jr.
David	Greg Mullavey
Sandy	Marcia Strassman
Dr. Rogers	Cicely Tyson

Music: Jerry Fielding.
Executive Producer: Douglas S. Cramer.
Producer: Larry Rosen.
Writer: Garry Marshall.
Director: Jerry Paris.

TRIPLE PLAY '72 — 90 minutes (30 minutes each segment) — NBC — April 24, 1972.

1829   TRIPLE PLAY '73

Pilot (Comedy). The overall title for three unsold comedies.

Hostess: Ruth Buzzi.

Barney and Me. The misadventures of Pete Richards, a kiddie show host who uses a talking bear to zap up his faltering ratings.

CAST

Pete Richards	Soupy Sales
Barney, the bear	Janos Prohaska
Barney's voice	Shepherd Menkin
Pete's girlfriend	Udana Power
Jungle Johnny, a regular on Pete's show	Joey Forman

Also: Bonnie Boland, Dave Morrick, Leonard Ross, Dick Wilson, Trent Lehman, Ceil Cabot, Cherie Foster, Bobbie Hall.
Music: Jeff Alexander.
Executive Producer: Arthur P. Jacobs.
Producer: Walter Bien.
Writer: Allan Blye, Chris Bearde, A. J. Carothers.
Director: Bruce Bilson.

Topper Returns. See title in the pilot film section.

Going Places. The misadventures of West Tucker, a small-town novelist struggling to make a living in New York City.

CAST

West Tucker	Todd Susman
Gloria	Jill Clayburgh
Mr. Shaw	Norman Fell
Steve	Jed Allan
Ellen	Judith DeHart

Music: Charles Fox.
Executive Producer: Grant Tinker.
Producer: Arnold Margolin, Jim Parker.
Writer: James L. Brooks, Michael Zagor.
Director: Lee Philips.

TRIPLE PLAY '73 — 90 minutes (30 minutes each segment) — NBC — March 19, 1973.

1830   TRIPLE TREAT

Pilot (Comedy). The overall title for three unsold comedies.

Keeping an Eye on Denise. Jackie Cooper is a happy single who is suddenly saddled with the care of an uninhibited teenage daughter he never knew he had (from a Korean War romance).

Also: Lynne Frederick (his daughter), Richard Dawson (his

friend), Rae Allen, Ernie Anderson, Carmen Zapata, Sheila Wells, Barney Phillips, Joshua Shelley, Elaine Church, Diana Chesney, Shirley Mitchell, Gloria Manners.
Executive Producer: Harry Ackerman.
Writer: Stanley Roberts.
Director: Hy Averback.

Big Daddy. The misadventures of a one-time football hero (Rosey Grier) turned cook show chef.

Also: Helen Martin (his mother), Shari Frees (his daughter), Deirdre Smith (his daughter), Nick Stewart (his uncle), Patti Deutsch, Edward Winter, Lennie Weinrib.
Music: H. B. Barnum.
Theme Vocal: O. C. Smith.
Producer: Norman Tokar.
Writer: Perry Grant, Dick Bensfield.
Director: Norman Tokar.

Daddy's Girl. The story of Bob Randall, the widowed father of a junior miss fascinated by nudism.

CAST

Bob Randall	Eddie Albert
Flossie Randall, his daughter	Dawn Lyn
Diane, his neighbor	Della Reese
Aunt Mary, his housekeeper	Helen Page Camp
Bennett, his friend	Alan Oppenheimer

Music: Vic Mizzy.
Producer: Jay Sommers.
Writer: Jay Sommers.
Director: Alan Rafkin.

TRIPLE TREAT — 90 minutes (30 minutes each segment) — CBS — June 19, 1973.

TROUBLE IN HIGH TIMBER COUNTRY

The pilot film broadcast on ABC on June 27, 1980, for the series *The Yeagers* (see regular program section).

1831   TRUE GRIT (A FURTHER ADVENTURE)

Pilot (Western). The story, set in the Old West, follows the exploits of Rooster Cogburn, a crusty, one-eyed lawman, and Mattie Ross, his pretty teenage charge, "the strangest team ever to fight for justice on the untamed frontier." The pilot depicts Cogburn's attempts to escort Mattie to her grandparents' home in California—despite a run of bad luck at cards that separates him from the train fare. Based on the feature film of the same title.

REGULAR CAST

Rooster Cogburn	Warren Oates
Mattie Ross	Lisa Pelikan

GUEST CAST

Annie	Lee Meriwether
Christopher	Jeff Osterhage
Joshua	James Stephens
Daniel	Lee H. Montgomery

| Rollins | Parley Baer |
| Sheriff | Ramon Bieri |

Music: Earle Hagen.
Producer: Sandor Stern.
Writer: Sandor Stern.
Director: Richard Heffron.
Art Director: Arch Bacon.

TRUE GRIT (A FURTHER ADVENTURE) — 2 hours — ABC — May 19, 1978.

1832 TURNOVER SMITH

Pilot (Crime Drama). The story of Professor Thaddeus "Tee" Smith, a criminologist instructor at Wellington University in San Francisco, who uses advanced scientific methods and computer technology to help police solve baffling crimes. The pilot depicts Smith's desperate efforts to find a psycho who is murdering women — and not leaving any clues behind. (The title refers to Smith's nickname: "Turnover" — for his ability to take evidence others have overlooked or not seen and turn it into a conviction.)

REGULAR CAST

Professor Thaddeus Smith	William Conrad
Kelly Kellogg, his	
assistant	Belinda J. Montgomery
Eddy, his assistant	Hilly Hicks
Lieutenant Brophy	Michael Parks
Sergeant McCallister	Nita Talbot
Smith's lab assistant	Brianne Leary
Rita Downey, the coroner	Gail Landry

GUEST CAST

George Green (the killer)	James Darren
Colonel Simmons	Cameron Mitchell
Ashmid Hamid	Nehemiah Persoff
Bob Faud	Adam Ageli
Franz Gerhard	Ben Wright
Anini	Tracy Reed
Shariff	Richard Dimitri
Victoria Simmons	Sondra Blake

Smith's French poodle: Tiger.

Music: Bernard Segall.
Executive Producer: William Conrad.
Producer: Everett Chambers.
Writer: Richard Jessup.
Director: Bernard L. Kowalski.
Art Director: William Hanney.
Director of Photography: Matthew Leonetti.

TURNOVER SMITH — 90 minutes — ABC — June 8, 1980.

1833 THE TV SHOW

Pilot (Comedy). A satirization of television and its programs via comedy sketches.

Cast: Rob Reiner, Billy Crystal, Martin Mull, Christopher Guest, Tom Leopold, Johnny Brown, Kres Mersky, Deborah Harmon, Harry J. Shearer, Michael McKean.

Music: Steve Cagan.
Executive Producer: Rob Reiner, Phil Mishkin.
Producer: Harry Shearer.
Director: Tom Trbovichi.

THE TV SHOW — 70 minutes — ABC — July 24, 1979.

1834 THE TV TV SHOW

Pilot (Comedy). A satirization of local TV newscasters and newscasts via comedy sketches.

CAST

Ralph Buckler, the	
anchorman	Howard Hesseman
Mary Kay, the co-anchorman	Mary Frann
News editor	Rene Auberjonois
George	Carl Gotlieb
Father	Garry Goodrow
Billy Bud	Gerrit Graham
Mother	Mina Kolb
Nancy	Annie Roth
Tommy	Mike Darnell

Producer: Michael Shamberg.
Director: Alan Myerson.

THE TV TV SHOW — 90 minutes — NBC — April 30, 1977.

1835 TWICE IN A LIFETIME

Pilot (Comedy-Drama). The story of Vince Boselli, an ex-Navy cook who buys a tugboat and begins a salvage business.

CAST

Vince Boselli	Ernest Borgnine
Flo	Della Reese
Lewis	Eric Laneuville
Pete Lazich	Slim Pickens
Ron Talley	Arte Johnson
Carlos	Vito Scotti

Music: Al Capps.
Producer: Martin Rackin.
Writer: Martin Rackin, Robert Pirosh.
Director: Herschel Daugherty.

TWICE IN A LIFETIME — 90 minutes — NBC — March 16, 1974.

1836 TWIN DETECTIVES

Pilot (Crime Drama). The exploits of Tony and Shep Thomas, twins who are also police detectives. The pilot depicts their efforts to expose a ring of phony psychics.

REGULAR CAST

Tony Thomas	Jim Hager
Shep Thomas	Jon Hager
Lieutenant Martinez	James Victor

GUEST CAST

Billy Jo Haskins	Lillian Gish
Rainer	Patrick O'Neal
Sheila Rainer	Barbara Rhoades
Nancy	Lynda Day George
Sampson	Michael Constantine
Jennie	Randi Oakes
Telford	David White

Music: Tom Scott.
Vocals: The Hudson Brothers.

Executive Producer: Charles Fries.
Producer: Everett Chambers.
Writer: Robert Specht.
Director: Robert Day.

TWIN DETECTIVES — 90 minutes — ABC — May 1, 1976.

1837 TWO BOYS

Pilot (Comedy). The story, set in a small town in Wisconsin, follows the misadventures of Jud Thomas and Billy Beckett, two enterprising 15-year-old boys.

CAST

Jud Thomas	Mitch Vogel
Billy Beckett	Mark Kearney
William Beckett, Billy's	
father	William Schallert
Mr. Landers (guest role)	Dabbs Greer

TWO BOYS — 30 minutes — NBC — July 6, 1970.

1838 THE TWO-FIVE

Pilot (Crime Drama). The story, spiced with light humor, follows the less than perfect exploits of Charlie Morgan and Frank Sarno, two police officers with a knack for being in the wrong place at the wrong time.

REGULAR CAST

Charlie Morgan	Don Johnson
Frank Sarno	Joe Bennett
Chief Johnson	Richard O'Brien
Captain Carter	John Crawford
Detective Lombardo	Michael Durrell

GUEST CAST

Iron Mike Malloy	George Murdock
Dale Von Krieg	Charlene Watkins
Pierre Menoir	Jacques Aubuchon
Waldo	Marty Zagon
Cliff Roberts	Curtis Credel

Music: Peter Matz.
Executive Producer: Robert A. Cinader.
Producer: Gian Grimaldi, Hannah Shearer.
Writer: Robert A. Cinader, Joseph Polizzi.
Director: Bruce Kessler.

THE TWO-FIVE — 90 minutes — ABC — April 14, 1978.

1839 TWO FOR THE MONEY

Pilot (Crime Drama). The exploits of Larry Dean and Chip Bronx, two police officers who resign from the force to become private detectives. The pilot depicts their efforts to apprehend a mass murderer who has evaded police capture for years.

REGULAR CAST

| Larry Dean | Robert Hooks |
| Chip Bronx | Stephen Brooks |

GUEST CAST

Cody Guilford	Walter Brennan
Judith Gap	Catherine Burns
Harley	Neville Brand
Bethany Hagen	Shelley Fabares

Mrs. Castle	Mercedes McCambridge
Mrs. Gap	Anne Revere
Morris Gap	Richard Dreyfuss

Producer: Aaron Spelling.
Writer: Howard Rodman.
Director: Bernard L. Kowalski.
Director of Photography: Arch Dalzell.

TWO FOR THE MONEY — 90 minutes — ABC — February 26, 1972.

U

1840 THE UGILY FAMILY

Pilot (Comedy). The story of Sal Ugily (pronounced U-giel-ie), a Global Can Company employee who receives a promotion and moves from New Jersey to Southern California where he and his family struggle to adjust to new surroundings. In the pilot, the Ugilys, who are not overly attractive, struggle to cope with their first exposure to the "beautiful people" of Southern California and the inferiority complexes the situation causes.

CAST

Sal Ugily, the father	Al Molinaro
Verna Ugily, his wife	Mimi Hines
Susan Ugily, their daughter	Susan Elliot
Bradley Ugily, their son	Stephen Myers
Tillie Brock, Verna's mother	Bella Bruck
Kenny Bing, their neighbor, a	
yacht broker	Lyle Waggoner
Babs Bing, Kenny's wife	Elaine Joyce
Bambi Bing, Kenny's daughter	Lory Walsh
Jeffrey, Bradley's	
friend	Bumper (as credited)
Photographer (guest)	Patti Gilbert

Music: Michael Leonard.
Theme Vocal: Al Molinaro, Mimi Hines.
Executive Producer: Walter Kempley.
Producer: Don Silverman.
Writer: Walter Kempley, Gregory Pistole.
Director: Robert Drivas.
Art Director: Bobby Bacon.

THE UGILY FAMILY — 30 minutes — ABC — July 26, 1980.

1841 THE ULTIMATE IMPOSTER

Pilot (Adventure). The exploits of Frank Monihan, an American secret agent with a specially implanted brain that can be programmed like a computer. (Monihan, captured by the enemy during an assignment, is treated with a chemical that erases 90 percent of his memory. When he is returned to the U.S., Dr. Jake McKeever implants an experimental Alpha Computer in Frank's brain to re-create his mind and memory.)

REGULAR CAST

Frank Monihan	Joseph Hacker
Eugene Danzinger, his superior	Keith Andes
Beatrice "Bucky" Tate, an agent, Frank's girlfriend	Erin Gray
Dr. Jake McKeever, Eugene's assistant	Macon McCalman

GUEST CAST

Danielle Parets	Tracy Brooks Swope
Rubin Papich	Normann Burton
Cottle	Robert Phillips
Bobby Riggs	Himself
Chinese girl	Rosalind Chao
Weeks	W. T. Zacha
Joe Mason	Thomas Berlin
Eddie	Joseph Hardin

Music: Dana Kaproff.
Producer: Lionel E. Siegel.
Writer: Lionel E. Siegel.
Director: Paul Stanley.
Art Director: Lou Montejo.
Director of Photography: Vincent A. Martinelli.

THE ULTIMATE IMPOSTER — 2 hours — CBS — May 12, 1980.

1842   THE UNDERGROUND MAN

Pilot (Crime Drama). The pilot film for the *Archer* series. The exploits of Lew Archer, a private detective who, in the pilot, seeks to find the kidnapped son of an old girlfriend.

REGULAR CAST

Lew Archer	Peter Graves

GUEST CAST

Sheriff Tremaine	Jack Klugman
Sue Crandall	Kay Lenz
Beatrice Broadhurst	Celeste Holm
Jean Broadhurst	Jo Ann Pflug
Marty Nickerson	Sharon Farrell
Stanley Broadhurst	Jim Hutton

Music: Marvin Hamlisch.
Executive Producer: Howard W. Koch.
Producer: Philip Parslow.
Writer: Douglas Heyes.
Director: Paul Wendkos.

THE UNDERGROUND MAN — 2 hours — NBC — May 6, 1974.

1843   UPTOWN SATURDAY NIGHT

Pilot (Comedy). The misadventures of two Harlem go-getters: Wardell Washington and Monroe Hoover.

CAST

Wardell Washington	Cleavon Little
Monroe Hoover	Adam Wade
Sarah Washington, Wardell's wife	Starletta DuPois
Geechy Dan, the hoodlum	Julius Harris
Janitor	Don Bexley

Music: Gary Lemel.
Producer: Eric Cohen.
Director: Bill Davis.

UPTOWN SATURDAY NIGHT — 30 minutes — NBC — June 28, 1979.

1844   VALENTINE MAGIC ON LOVE ISLAND

Pilot (Anthology). A proposed but unsold series in which romance-seeking singles find not only romance but misadventure at a tropical resort called Love Island.

REGULAR CAST

Madge, the mysterious owner of Love Island	Janis Paige
Cheryl, her niece/assistant	Dominique Dunne
Jimmy, Cheryl's brother	Christopher Knight

GUEST CAST

Beverly McGraw	Adrienne Barbeau
Charles	Bill Daily
Denise	Mary Louise Weller
Alfred Jerome	Howard Duff
Billy Colorado	Bob Seagren
Crystal Kramer	Lisa Hartman
Ida Kramer	Dody Goodman
Robert Murphy	Rick Hurst
Harvey	Stuart Pankin
Bellboy	Ivan Philpot
Nurse	Rosalyn Royce
Bishop	Norm Montgomery

Music: Peter Matz.
Theme Vocal: Bernard Ighner.
Executive Producer: Dick Clark, Paul Klein.
Producer: Pat and Bill Finnegan.
Writer: Madelyn David, Bob Hillyard.
Director: Earl Bellamy.
Director of Photography: Ken Lemkin.

VALENTINE MAGIC ON LOVE ISLAND — 2 hours — NBC — February 15, 1980.

1845   VARIETY

Pilot (Variety). Performances by top-name entertainment acts; an attempt to re-create the feeling of the golden age of television's variety series.

Host: Hugh Downs.
Guests: David Merrick, Roberta Peters, Evel Knievel, Jim Stafford, Gabe Kaplan, Rodney Allen Rippy.
Producer: Norman Rosemont.
Writer: Ron Clark, Jack Burns.
Director: Bill Davis.

VARIETY — 60 minutes — ABC — March 31, 1974.

VEGA$

The pilot film broadcast on ABC on April 25, 1978, for the series of the same name (see regular program section).

1846   A VERY MISSING PERSON

Pilot (Mystery). The exploits of Hildegarde Withers, a retired schoolteacher and amateur sleuth. The pilot depicts Hildegarde's efforts to help the New York City Police Department solve a missing person's case. Based on the novels by Stuart Palmer.

REGULAR CAST

Hildegarde Withers	Eve Arden
Oscar Piper, her assistant	James Gregory

GUEST CAST

Aletha	Julie Newmar
Isobel	Skye Aubrey
Captain Westering	Ray Danton
Onofre	Robert Easton
Al Fisher	Dennis Rucker
Eberhardt	Woodrow Parfrey
Malloy	Bob Hastings

Music: Vic Mizzy.
Producer: Edward J. Montagne.
Writer: Philip H. Reisman.
Director: Russ Mayberry.
Director of Photography: William Margulies.

A VERY MISSING PERSON — 90 minutes — ABC — March 4, 1972.

1847   WAIKIKI

Pilot (Crime Drama). The exploits of Ronnie Browning and David King, two reckless private detectives based in Waikiki, Hawaii. In the pilot, Ronnie and Dave team with Cassie Howard, a beautiful policewoman, in an attempt to find "The Cane Field Killer," a murderer-rapist.

REGULAR CAST

Ronnie Browning	Dack Rambo
David King	Steve Marachuk
Cassie Howard	Donna Mills
Rex, their friend, the owner of Rex's Bar	Cal Bellini
Kahona, the bartender	Jack Hisatake
Police Captain McGuire (Oahu, P.D.)	Darren McGavin

GUEST CAST

Mark Barrington	Robert F. Lyons
Lloyd Barrington	Mark Slade
Walter Kahmonhu	Branscombe Richmond
Anne Kahmonhu	Betty Carvalho
Carol	Tanya Roberts
Joe Farnsworth	Angus Duncan

Music: Stu Phillips.
Executive Producer: Aaron Spelling, Douglas S. Cramer.
Supervising Producer: E. Duke Vincent
Producer: Robert Janes.
Writer: Robert Janes, Curtis Kenyon.
Director: Ron Satlof.
Art Director: Paul Sylos, Arch Bacon.
Director of Photography: Robert L. Morrison.

WAIKIKI — 2 hours — ABC — April 21, 1980.

1848   WALKIN' WALTER

Pilot (Comedy). The story of Walkin' Walter, a free-spirited ex-vaudevillian songwriter who moves in with and freeloads off his long-lost brother's wife and her two foster children.

CAST

Walkin' Walter	Spo-De-Odee
Rosabell "Mama" Hoxie	Madge Sinclair
Booker Brown	Christoff St. John
Jackie Onassis Orlando	Denise Marcia
Loud Leon	David Yanez
Wendell Henderson	Jack Dodson
Rev. Tucker Tooley	Theodore Wilson

Executive Producer: Garry Marshall, Edward Milkis, Thomas L. Miller.
Producer: Arnold Margolin.
Writer: Lowell Ganz, Mark Rothman.
Director: Arnold Margolin.

WALKIN' WALTER — 30 minutes — ABC — June 13, 1977.

WEDNESDAY NIGHT OUT

See title "Triple Play '72" in the pilot film section.

WE'LL GET BY

The pilot (videotape) broadcast on CBS, for the series of the same title (see regular program section).

1849   WHATEVER HAPPENED TO DOBIE GILLIS?

Pilot (Comedy). The story, an update of the 1959 – 1963 series *Dobie Gillis*, reunites the original cast in an unsold pilot that continues to depict events in the life of Dobie Gillis, a once indecisive teenager who is now married, the father of a teenage son, and partners with his father in an expanded Gillis Grocery Store. In the pilot, which is basically a reintroduction of the cast, Dobie's friend Maynard G. Krebs, the former beatnik, is now an entrepreneur and returns to help celebrate Dobie's 40th birthday.

CAST

Dobie Gillis	Dwayne Hickman
Maynard G. Krebs	Bob Denver
Zelda Gilroy Gillis, Dobie's wife	Sheila James
Herbert T. Gillis, Dobie's father	Frank Faylen
Georgie Gillis, Dobie's son	Steven Paul
Lucky, Georgie's friend	Lorenzo Lamas

Music: Randy Newman
Executive Producer: James Komack, Paul Mason.
Writer: Peter Meyerson, Nick Arnold.
Director: James Komack.

WHATEVER HAPPENED TO DOBIE GILLIS? — 30 minutes — CBS — May 10, 1977.

1850 WHAT'S UP?

Pilot (Comedy). A satirization of the contemporary scene through sketches, blackouts, interviews and newsreel footage.

Host: Jackie Cooper.
Guests: Tom Bosely, Marian Mercer, Bill Zuckert, Phil Leeds, John Ritter, Lee Montgomery.
Producer: Ed Weinberger.
Writer: Rod Parker, Robert Hilliard, George Bloom.
Director: Jonathan Lucas.

WHAT'S UP?—30 minutes—NBC—August 26, 1971.

1851 WHAT'S UP DOC?

Pilot (Comedy). The story, based on 1972 feature film of the same title, follows the further misadventures of brash Judy Maxwell and timid Howard Bannister.

CAST

Judy Maxwell	Harriet Hall
Howard Bannister	Barry Van Dyke
Claudia	Caroline McWilliams
Urban Wyatt	Don Porter
Amanda Wyatt	Neva Patterson
Fabian Leek	Jeffrey Kramer

Music: Ian Freebairn-Smith.
Executive Producer: Hal Kanter.
Producer: Charles B. Fitzsimmons, Mike Norell.
Writer: Mike Norell.
Director: E. W. Swackhamer.

WHAT'S UP DOC?—30 minutes—ABC—May 27, 1978.

1852 WHEELER AND MURDOCH

Pilot (Crime Drama). The exploits of Sam Wheeler and Terry Murdoch, Seattle-based private detectives. The pilot episode depicts their efforts to solve a syndicate murder-robbery.

REGULAR CAST

Sam Wheeler	Jack Warden
Terry Murdoch	Christopher Stone

GUEST CAST

Buddy Shore	Van Johnson
Karen	Diane Baker
DeNisco	Charles Cioffi
Dorcie	Jane Powell
Travanty	Dewey Martin
Galvin	Robert Ellenstein
Weston	Woodrow Parfrey
Turk	Michael Conrad

Narrator: Jack Warden.
Music: Robert Drasnin.
Executive Producer: Eric Bercovici, Jerry Ludwig.
Producer: Joseph Sargent.
Writer: Eric Bercovici, Jerry Ludwig.
Director: Joseph Sargent.
Director of Photography: Howard Schwartz.

WHEELER AND MURDOCH—60 minutes—ABC—May 9, 1973.

1853 WHERE'S POPPA?

Pilot (Comedy). The story, based on the 1970 feature film of the same title, about a somewhat senile widow whose demands on her son are wrecking his social life and his law practice.

CAST

Momma Hockheiser	Elsa Lanchester
Gordon Hockheiser, her son	Steven Keats
Louise Hamelin, Momma's nurse	Judith-Marie Bergen
Sid Hockheiser, Gordon's brother	Allan Miller

Music: Alan Douglas, Ken Lauber.
Executive Producer: Robert Klane, Marvin Worth.
Producer: Patricia Rickey.
Director: Richard Benjamin.

WHERE'S POPPA?—30 minutes—ABC—July 17, 1979.

1854 WHERE'S THE FIRE?

Pilot (Comedy). The antics of a group of firefighters. In the pilot, the firemen's efforts to hold a beauty contest—to lure women into the station—involves them with a local gangster who demands that his plain-looking daughter win the contest.

REGULAR CAST

Captain O'Hara	Dave Ketchum
Fire Chief	Roger Bowen
Renaldo	Gregory Sierra
Stanley	Danny Fortus
Skipper	J. Pat O'Malley
Roscoe	Johnny Brown
Buck	John Fink

GUEST CAST

Acropolis, the gangster	Carl Ballantine
Angelina, his daughter	Leigh French

Producer: Douglas S. Cramer.
Director: Jerry Paris.

WHERE'S THE FIRE?—30 minutes—ABC—May 17, 1975.

1855 WHO'S ON CALL?

Pilot (Comedy). The story focuses on the shenanigans of medical students at Manhattan General Hospital in New York City.

CAST

Dr. Liz Spencer	Forbesy Russell
Dr. Leland Forsythe	Jim McKrell
Nurse Bremmer	Fran Ryan
Marsha Stone	Melissa Steinberg
Eddie Grado	Matt Landers
Neil Goggini	Frank Covsentino

Music: Glen Page.
Producer: Coleman Mitchell, Geoffrey Neigher.
Writer: Laura Levine.
Director: Tony Mordente.
Art Director: Ross Bellah.

WHO'S ON CALL?—30 minutes—ABC—December 16, 1979.

1856 WILD ABOUT HARRY

Pilot (Comedy). The story of Harry Baxter, a 45-year-old architect who falls in love with a girl (Vickie) who is 20.

CAST

Harry Baxter	Efrem Zimbalist, Jr.
Vickie Knowles	Andrea Howard
Don	Bernie Kopell
Maggie	Elaine Giftos
Jennie	Stephanie Zimbalist
Delia	Reva Rose
Sophie	Ruth Manning
Sheila Marshall	Gloria Stroock
Larry Marshall	George Sperdakos
Frank Knowles	Dick Yarmy
Molly Knowles	Emmaline Henry

Producer: George Eckstein, Leonard B. Stern.
Writer: Richard Waring.
Director: Robert Moore.

WILD ABOUT HARRY—30 minutes—NBC—May 26, 1978.

1857 WILD AND WOOLY

Pilot (Western). The story, set in the West in 1903, follows the exploits of Liz, Lacey, Shiloh and Megan, four beautiful undercover law-women. The pilot depicts their efforts to expose a plot to kill the President of the United States.

REGULAR CAST

Liz Hannah	Susan Bigelow
Shiloh	Elyssa Davalos
Lacey Somers	Chris De Lisle
Megan	Jessica Walter

GUEST CAST

Tobias Singleton	Paul Burke
Otis Bergen	Ross Martin
Delaney Burke	Doug McClure
Warden Wills	Vic Morrow
Sean	Charles Siebert
Teddy Roosevelt	David Doyle

Music: Charles Bernstein.
Executive Producer: Aaron Spelling, Douglas S. Cramer.
Producer: Earl W. Wallace.
Writer: Earl W. Wallace.
Director: Philip Leacock.

WILD AND WOOLY—2 hours—ABC—February 20, 1978.

1858 WILDER AND WILDER

Pilot (Comedy). The misadventures of marrieds Steffi and Sam Wilder, a television writing team often plagued by a clash of identical careers.

REGULAR CAST

Steffi Wilder	Meredith MacRae
Sam Wilder	Greg Mullavey
Tina Chambers, Steffi's sister	Susan Lanier

GUEST CAST

Al Meredith	Lou Criscoulo
Jason	T. K. Carter
Roger Bacon	Lonnie Shorr
Phil Crawford	Warren Burton
Joel	Vaughn Armstrong

Executive Producer: Mark P. Carliner.
Producer: Austin and Irma Kalish.
Writer: Austin and Irma Kalish.
Director: Peter Hunt.
Art Director: Don Roberts.

WILDER AND WILDER—30 minutes—CBS—August 26, 1978.

1859 THE WILDS OF TEN THOUSAND ISLANDS

Pilot (Drama). The story of the Wilds, a contemporary family of animal behaviorists living and working in the wilderness wetlands (the Ten Thousand Islands) of western Florida along the Gulf of Mexico.

REGULAR CAST

Dr. Jeff Wild, the father	Chris Robinson
Dr. Barbara Wild, his wife	Julie Gregg
Sara Wild, their daughter	Mary Ellen McKeon
Jeff Wild, their son	Charles Aiken

GUEST CAST

Clara Mooney	Rachel Roberts
Fred Osceola	John Kauffman
Miss Kathy	Monica Gayle
Orville	John Ashton

Music: Dominic Frontiere.
Executive Producer: Lee Rich, Philip Capice.
Producer-Creator: Andy White.
Writer: Andy White, Paul West.
Director: Charles S. Dubin.
Art Director: James H. Spencer.
Director of Photography: Jim Pergola.
Associate Producer: Ricou Browning, Ted Swanson.

THE WILDS OF TEN THOUSAND ISLANDS—60 minutes—CBS—February 24, 1978.

1860 WILLOW B: WOMEN IN PRISON

Pilot (Drama). Life in the El Camino Institution for women as seen through the eyes of Kim Kavanaugh, a socialite who finds herself behind bars (in section Willow B) when she is convicted of felony manslaughter (driving while intoxicated and killing a pedestrian).

CAST

Prisoners:

Kim Kavanaugh (No. 28912)	Debra Clinger
Chris Bricker (No. 25428)	Trisha Noble
Kate Stewart (No. 26458)	Sally Kirkland
Sabrina (No. 26128)	Sarah Kennedy
Claire Hastings (No. 26812)	Carol Lynley
Helen (No. 28456)	Elizabeth Hartman
Trini Santos (No. 26421)	Liz Torres
T.J. (No. 22168)	Susan Tyrell
Prisoner (No. 26054)	Lynne Moody
Francine (No. 26509)	Saundra Sharpe
Eloise Baker	Virginia Capers

Other Prisoners: Edith Diaz, Sarina Grant, Isobel Wolfe.

Prison Staff:

Sgt. Pritchett, the sadistic guard in
    charge of Willow B   Ruth Roman
Mrs. McAllister, the
    governor   Norma Donaldson
Guard Dave Tyree   Jared Martin
Guard Mr. Canady   John P. Ryan

Music: James Di Pasquale.
Executive Producer: Lee Rich,
Michael Filerman.
Producer: Lawrence Kasha.
Writer: Gerry Day.
Director: Jeff Bleckner.

WILLOW B: WOMEN IN PRISON
— 60 minutes — ABC — June 29,
1980. An American version of the
syndicated Australian series *Prisoner: Cell Block H.*

1861   WINNER TAKE ALL

Pilot (Crime Drama). The exploits of Allison Nash, a stunning,
free-lance insurance investigator,
and Charlie Quigley, a cracker-
jack police lieutenant, agents who
are often pitted against each
other, but who work in tandem,
to solve crimes—Allison for her
company, Charlie for the L.A.P.D.
The pilot depicts their efforts to
recover five perfectly matched
emeralds they believe were stolen by a notorious cat burglar.

REGULAR CAST

Allison Nash   Joanna Pettet
Lt. Charlie Quigley   Michael Murphy
E. P. Woodhouse, Allison's
    collaborator   Clive Revill
Mo Rellis, Charlie's
    assistant   Mark Gordon

GUEST CAST

Hiram Yerby   David Huddleston
Swenson   Loni Anderson
Maria von Alsburg   Signe Hasso
Solange Dupree   Martine Beswick
Room clerk   John Fiedler
Clarence Woo   James Hong
Hank   James McCallion
Mae Burt   Dorothy Meyer

Music: John Elizalde.
Executive Producer: Quinn
Martin.
Producer: John Wilder.
Writer: Cliff Gould.
Director: Robert Day.
Art Director: Herman Zim-
merman.
Director of Photography: Jacques
Marquette.
Set Decorator: Ruby Levitt.

WINNER TAKE ALL — 60 min-
utes — CBS — April 1, 1977.

1862   WINTER KILL

Pilot (Crime Drama). The pilot
film for *Adams of Eagle Lake.* The
story of Sam McNeill, a sheriff in
the resort town of Eagle Lake,
California. The pilot episode depicts Sam's efforts to unravel a
sudden series of murders that are
plaguing the ski resort town.

REGULAR CAST

Sheriff Sam McNeill   Andy Griffith
Deputy Jerry Troy   John Calvin
Betty, Sam's girlfriend   Sheree North
Doris, the police radio
    dispatcher   Louise Latham

GUEST CAST

Cynthia Howe   Elayne Heilveil
Dave Michaels   Nick Nolte
Dr. Hammond   John Larch
Bill Carter   Tim O'Connor
Grace Lockwood   Joyce Van Patten
Peter Lockwood   Lawrence Pressman
Elaine Carter   Devra Korwin
Mayor Clint Bickford   Eugene Roche
Charley Eastman   Charles Tyner
Mildred Young   Ruth McDevitt

Music: Jerry Goldsmith.
Executive Producer: Richard O.
Linke.
Producer: Burt Nodella.
Associate Producer: Alan Godfrey.
Writer: John Michael Hayes.
Director: Jud Taylor.
Art Director: Albert Brenner.
Director of Photography: Frank
Stanley.
Set Decorator: Harry Reif.

WINTER KILL — 2 hours — ABC —
April 15, 1974.

1863   WIVES

Pilot (Comedy). The story revolves around the daily routines
and misadventures of five married women.

REGULAR CAST

Connie   Penny Marshall
Doris   Phyllis Elizabeth Davis
Frannie   Janie sell
Mary Margaret   Candice Azzara
Lillian   Jacque Lynn Colton

GUEST CAST

Miss Chin   Barbara Luna
Waiter   Pat Morita
Man   Billy Sands

Music: Buzz Kohen.
Executive Producer: Garry
Marshall.
Producer; Tony Marshall.
Writer-Creator: Garry Marshall.
Director: Jay Sandrich.
Art Director: Monte Elliot.
Set Decorator: Andy Neelis.

WIVES — 30 minutes — CBS —
March 21, 1975.

1864   THE WOLFMAN JACK RADIO SHOW

Pilot (Music). Performances by
recording artists.

Host: Wolfman Jack.
Guests: The Captain and Tennille,
The Village People, Leif Gar-
rett, Peaches and Herb,
Michael Jackson, Chuck Berry,
Nick Gilder.
Music Coordinator: Walter
Stewart.
Supervising Producer: Lou Smith.
Executive Producer: Jerry Harri-
son, Joel Siegman.
Producer: Scott Steinberg.

Writer: Phil Kellard, Scott Stein-
berg.
Director: Paul Miller.
Art Director: Bill Bohnert.

THE WOLFMAN JACK RADIO
SHOW — 60 minutes — Syndicated 1980.

1865   WONDER WOMAN

Pilot (Adventure). On Paradise Island, which is inhabited by a race
of superhuman women, the
beautiful Diana stands before her
Queen Mother, who speaks: "The
world would one day require a
unique woman, a Wonder Woman. You are that unique woman,
Diana. You are endowed with
extraordinary wisdom, love, and
strength ... and now you are
charged with a mission. To accomplish that mission you must
leave this island. You must adopt
other ways [and take] our pure
and true love of justice and right
to that world beyond ours here.
There's deep sadness in having
you leave us, but there's also joy;
the hope that your presence in
the world of man will open
closed eyes to the genuine value
of women; that you'll never lose
the sensitivity that is our real
strength. You carry with you our
love." Shortly after leaving Paradise Island, Diana adopts the alias
of Diana Prince and acquires a
job as secretary to Steve Trevor,
an agent of the U.S. government,
in Washington, D.C.

In the pilot, Diana, as Wonder
Woman, attempts to recover ten
top-secret books that contain
the names of America's top
agents from Abner Smith, a diabolical criminal who seeks $5
million ransom for them.

REGULAR CAST

Diana Prince/
    Wonder Woman   Cathy Lee Crosby
Steve Trevor   Kaz Garas
Ahnjayla, Diana's nemesis, a
    woman of Paradise Island who
    turned renegade   Anitra Ford
Hippolyte, the Queen
    Mother   Charlene Holt

GUEST CAST

Abner Smith   Ricardo Montalban
George Calvin   Andrew Prine
Cass   Donna Garrett
Joey   Robert Porter
Colonel   Richard X. Slattery
Big Spender   Ronald Long
Thug   Steve Mitchell
Ting   Sandy Gabiola
Captain   George Diaga
Waiter   Mario Roccuszo
Bob   Jordan Rhodes
Dia   Beverly Gill

Music: Artie Butler.
Executive Producer: John D.F.
Black.
Producer: John G. Stevens.
Writer: John D.F. Black.
Director: Vincent McEveety.

Art Director: Phillip Bennett.
Costumes: Bill Thomas.

WONDER WOMAN — 90 min-
utes — ABC — March 12, 1974. See
also *The New Adventures of
Wonder Woman* and *Wonder
Woman* in the regular program
section for information (and photographs depicting the costume
styles) for the version of the series starring Lynda Carter.

1866   THE WORLD BEYOND

Pilot (Thriller). The second of
two pilots (see following title,
"The World of Darkness") about
Paul Taylor, a sportswriter who,
after a motorcycle accident, dies
on the operating table. After two
and one half minutes of clinical
death, he is revived by doctors.
Taylor, however, retains a thread
tying him to the world of beyond — a connection through
which the dead can compel him
to seek out people he has never
seen and protect them from the
deadly forces of the occult. In the
second suspenseful story, a
supernatural inner voice brings
Taylor to a remote island in
Maine to seek out Marian Faber
and protect her and her brother
Frank from a "golem," an eerie
spirit Frank created from mud
and now seeks only to kill.

REGULAR CAST

Paul Taylor   Granville Van Dusen

GUEST CAST

Marian Faber   Jo-Beth Williams
Frank Faber   Richard Fitzpatrick
Andy Borchard   Barnard Hughes
Sam Barker   Jan Van Evera

Music: Fred Karlin.
Executive Producer: David
Susskind.
Producer: Fred Brogger.
Writer: Art Wallace.
Director: Noel Black.
Creator: Art Wallace.

THE WORLD BEYOND — 60 minutes — CBS — January 27, 1978.

1867   THE WORLD OF DARKNESS

Pilot (Thriller). The first of two
pilot films (see previous title)
about Paul Taylor, a sportswriter
who dies on the operating table
and is then brought back from
the brink of death. Though in a
world of the living, Taylor still
holds a connection to the world
beyond, one that commands him
to help people who are threatened by the occult. In the first
story, a supernatural inner voice
brings Taylor to Woodvale, a
small New England town, to seek
out Clara Sanford and solve the
mystery of an eerie presence that
has her and her Aunt Joanna in a
grip of fear.

REGULAR CAST

Paul Taylor   Granville Van Dusen

GUEST CAST

Clara Sanford   Tovah Feldshuh
Joanna Sanford   Beatrice Straight
Dr. Thomas Madsen   Gary Merrill
John Sanford   James Austin
Matty Barker   Shawn Mcann
Helen   Jane Eastwood
Max   Al Bernardo

Music: Fred Karlin.
Executive Producer: David Susskind.
Producer: Diana Kerew.
Writer-Creator: Art Wallace.
Director: Jerry London.
Art Director: Karen Bromley.
Director of Photography: Zale Magder.

THE WORLD OF DARKNESS — 60 minutes — CBS — April 17, 1977.

Y

1868   YOUNG GUY CHRISTIAN

Pilot (Comedy). A spoof of superspy dramas as seen through the exploits of Guy Christian, a playboy who combats international evil in his spare time.

CAST

Guy Christian   Barry Bostwick
Professor Mishugi, his superior   Pat Morita
Mia Mishugi, the professor's
daughter   Shelley Long
Junkman, the professor's
assistant   Richard Karron

Music: Murray MacLeod
Producer: Jerry Belson, Michael Lesson.
Director: Stuart Margolin.

YOUNG GUY CHRISTIAN — 30 minutes — ABC — May 24, 1979.

THE YOUNG PIONEERS

The pilot film broadcast on ABC on March 1, 1976, for the series of the same title (see regular program section).

1869   YOU'RE GONNA LOVE IT HERE

Pilot (Comedy). The misadventures of Lolly Rogers, a Broadway star who is suddenly saddled with the temporary care of her 11-year-old grandson, Peter, when the boy's parents are jailed for tax evasion.

CAST

Lolly Rogers   Ethel Merman
Peter Rogers   Chris Barnes
Harry Rogers, Lolly's son   Austin Pendleton

Also: Mathew Anton, Jerome Dempsey, Tony Holmes, Joanne Jonas, Glenn Scarpelli.
Music: Peter Matz.
Theme Vocal: "You're Gonna Love It Here" by Ethel Merman.
Executive Producer: Franklin Konigsberg.
Producer: Mel Farber.
Director: Bud Paltron.

YOU'RE GONNA LOVE IT HERE — 30 minutes — CBS — June 1, 1977.

1870   YOU'RE JUST LIKE YOUR FATHER

Pilot (Comedy). The misadventures of Harry Toffler, Sr., a businessman who believes in the great American dream that success is just around the corner; and his son, Harry, Jr., his partner in the near-bankrupt Toffler Enterprises, who is following in his misguided footsteps.

CAST

Harry Toffler, Sr.   Dick Shawn
Harry Toffler, Jr.   Barry Gordon
Cheryl Toffler, Harry,
Jr.'s wife   Nellie Bellflower
Claudine, Harry, Sr.'s
girlfriend   Maureen Arthur

Music: Harry Geller.

Executive Producer: Lee Rich, Laurence Marks.
Producer: Alan J. Levitt, Gene Marcione.
Writer: Alan J. Levitt.
Director: Noam Pitlik.
Art Director: Ed Graves.
Creator: Alan J. Levitt.

YOU'RE JUST LIKE YOUR FATHER — 30 minutes — CBS — August 13, 1976.

1871   YOUR PLACE OR MINE

Pilot (Comedy). The story of Kelly Barnes, an attractive editorial assistant on a magazine, who works in Manhattan but lives in Queens. Jeff Burrell is a young free-lance writer who lives in Manhattan but longs for the tranquility of the country for his writing. Their misadventures begin when they meet, fall in love and decide to swap residences to be closer to what they each require.

CAST

Kelly Barnes   Jane Actman
Jeff Burrell   Stuart Gillard
Frances Barnes, Kelly's mother   Alice Hirson
Ernie Barnes, Kelly's father   Peter Hobbs
Linda Hiller, Kelly's
neighbor   Judy Graubart
Mrs. Hicks, Kelly's employer   Elizabeth Kerr

Also: George Pentecost, Elizabeth Halliday.
Producer: Bob Ellison, David Lloyd.
Writer: Bob Ellison, David Lloyd.
Director: James Burrows.

YOUR PLACE OR MINE — 30 minutes — CBS — May 27, 1978.

1872   YUMA

Pilot (Western). The story, set in the Old West, follows the exploits of Dave Harmon, a U.S. marshal. In the pilot, Harmon attempts to clean up a frontier town filled with bitter cattlemen and crooked businessmen.

REGULAR CAST

Marshal Dave Harmon   Clint Walker

GUEST CAST

Nels Decker   Barry Sullivan
Julie Williams   Kathryn Hays
Mules McNeil   Edgar Buchanan
Arch King   Morgan Woodward
Major Lucas   Peter Mark Richman
Captain White   John Kerr
Sanders   Robert Phillips
Anders   Miguel Aleiandro
Rolking   Neil Russell
Sam King   Bruce Glover

Music: George Duning.
Producer: Aaron Spelling.
Writer: Charles Wallace.
Director: Ted Post.

YUMA — 90 minutes — ABC — March 2, 1971.

Z

1873   ZERO INTELLIGENCE

Pilot (Comedy). A lighter side of the Cold War as seen through the comic adventures of a group of servicemen stationed at a top-secret radar station in Alaska in 1959.

CAST

Higgins   Don Galloway
Deerfield   Sorrell Booke
Fred   Tom Rosqui
Arnold   Michael Huddleston
Ruben   Chu Chu Malave
Mo   Clyde Kusatsu

Producer: Saul Ilson, Ernest Chambers.
Writer: Lee Kalcheim.
Director: Jack Shea.
Creator: Saul Ilson, Ernest Chambers.

ZERO INTELLIGENCE — 30 minutes — ABC — August 10, 1976.

CBS

ABC

Hot l Baltimore. Front row, from left, Robin Wilson and Conchata Ferrell. Middle row, from left, Stan Gottlieb, Gloria LeRoy, Richard Masur, Al Freeman, Jr., and Jeannie Linero. Back row, from left, James Cromwell, Lee Bergere and Henry Calvert.

Dallas. Seated, from left, Charlene Tilton, Barbara Bel Geddes, Linda Gray, Patrick Duffy and Victoria Principal. Standing, Larry Hagman and Jim Davis.

NBC

ABC

Dinah in Search of the Ideal Man. Dinah Shore.

Julie! Julie Andrews.

CBS

Lynda Carter's Special. Lynda Carter.

Section 3
Variety Specials

An alphabetical listing of 425 variety specials broadcast from
January 1, 1970 through January 1, 1981.

ABC Presents Tomorrow's Stars (John Ritter, host), ABC, June 17, 1978.

Acts of Love—and Other Comedies (Marlo Thomas, star), ABC, March 16, 1973.

Alan King Goes Nashville, ABC, Oct. 17–20, 1977.

Alan King Inside Las Vegas, ABC, Jan. 29, 1973.

Alan King Looks Back in Anger, ABC, Jan. 3, 1973.

Alan King Salutes the Turkeys of the Year, NBC, Nov. 25, 1980.

Alan King's Energy Crisis, Rising Prices, and Assorted Vices Comedy Hour, ABC, April 5, 1974.

Alan King's Final Warning, ABC, April 12, 1977.

Alan King Special, ABC, May 13, 1978.

Alan King's Third Annual Final Warning!!, ABC, May 24, 1979.

All Commercials—A Steve Martin Special, NBC, Sept. 30, 1980.

All Kindsa Stuff (Dick Clark, Steve Jamison, Fran Druscher, Lencola Sullivan, Kevin Breslin, hosts), NBC, Dec. 27, 1980.

And Now . . . The Bay City Rollers, Syndicated November 1975.

Andy Griffith's Uptown/Downtown Show, CBS, Feb. 21, 1970.

Andy's Fun House (Andy Kaufman), ABC, Aug. 28, 1979.

Andy Williams Christmas Show, NBC, Dec. 14, 1971; Dec. 11, 1974.

Andy Williams Presents, NBC, Sept. 7, 1974.

Andy Williams Special, NBC, Jan. 2, 1971.

An Evening with Diana Ross, NBC, March 6, 1977.

An Evening with John Denver, ABC, March 10, 1975.

An Evening with Julie Andrews and Harry Belafonte, NBC, Sept. 9, 1971.

Anita Bryant Spectacular, Syndicated March 1980.

Anne Bancroft Show, CBS, Feb. 18, 1970.

Annie and the Hoods (Anne Bancroft), ABC, Nov. 2, 1974.

Annie, the Woman in the Life of a Man (Anne Bancroft), CBS, May 8, 1972.

Ann-Margret Olsson, NBC, Jan. 23, 1975.

Ann-Margret . . . Rhinestone Cowgirl, NBC, April 26, 1977.

Ann-Margret's Hollywood Movie Girls, ABC, May 3, 1980.

Ann-Margret Smith Show, NBC, Nov. 20, 1975.

Ann-Margret—When You're Smiling, NBC, April 16, 1973.

Anne Murray's Ladies' Night, Syndicated May 1979.

Anthony Newley Show, Syndicated February 1972.

Arthur Godfrey Special, NBC, March 28, 1972.

Barbi Doll for Christmas (Barbi Benton), Syndicated December 1977.

Barbra Streisand and Other Musical Instruments, CBS, Nov. 2, 1973.

Barry Manilow . . . One Voice, ABC, May 19, 1980.

Barry Manilow Special, ABC, March 2, 1977; ABC, May 23, 1979.

Baryshnikov on Broadway (Mikhail Baryshnikov), ABC, April 24, 1980.

Beach Party with the Doodletown Pipers, Syndicated July 1971.

The Beatles Forever (Bernadette Peters, Tony Randall, hosts), NBC, Nov. 24, 1977.

Beatrice Arthur Special, CBS, Jan. 19, 1980.

The Bee Gees (Barry, Robin, and Maurice Gibb), NBC, Nov. 21, 1979.

Ben Vereen . . . His Roots, ABC, March 2, 1978.

Bette Midler in Concert, Syndicated July 1980.

Bette Midler Special, NBC, Dec. 7, 1977.

Bing! A 50th Anniversary Gala (Bing Crosby), CBS, March 20, 1977.

Bing Crosby and His Friends, NBC, Feb. 27, 1972; CBS, Oct. 9, 1974; CBS, Dec. 1, 1976.

Bing Crosby and the Sounds of Christmas, NBC, Dec. 14, 1971.

A Bing Crosby Christmas . . . Like the Ones We Used to Know (Kathryn Crosby, host), NBC, Dec. 6, 1979.

Bing Crosby Christmas Show, CBS, Dec. 3, 1975.

Bing Crosby—The Christmas Years (Kathryn Crosby, host), CBS, Dec. 6, 1978.

Bing Crosby—Cooling It, Syndicated Oct. 1971.

Bing Crosby's Merrie Olde Christmas, CBS, Nov. 30, 1977.

Bing Crosby's Sun Valley Christmas Show, NBC, Dec. 9, 1973.

Bob and Ray and Jane, Laraine, and Gilda (Bob Elliott, Ray Goulding, Jane Curtin, Laraine Newman, Gilda Radner, hosts), NBC, March 31, 1979.

Bob Dylan Special, NBC, Sept. 14, 1976.

Bob Hope Special, NBC. Dates: *1970:* Feb. 7; *1971:* Sept. 13, Nov. 7, Dec. 9; *1972:* Jan. 17, March 13, April 10, Oct. 5; *1973:* Jan. 17, Feb. 8, March 7, April 19, Sept. 26, Nov. 13, Dec. 9; *1974:* Jan. 24, March 1, April 19, Sept. 25, Dec. 15; *1975:* March 5, April 17, Oct. 24, Dec. 14; *1976:* Feb. 13, March 5, April 7, April 21, July 4, Oct. 29, Dec. 13; *1977:* Jan. 21, March 25, Oct. 28, Dec. 19; *1978:* Jan. 8, Feb. 13, May 29, Oct. 18, Dec. 22; *1979:* Jan. 28, March 2, May 14, May 30, Sept. 16, Nov. 19, Dec. 13; *1980:* Jan. 21, Feb. 3, March 17, May 28, Sept. 6, Nov. 1, Dec. 16.

Bobbie Gentry Show, Syndicated May 1971.

Bobbie Gentry Special, Syndicated February 1970.

Bobby Sherman Show, ABC, June 4, 1971.

Bobby Van and Elaine Joyce Show, CBS, Dec. 17, 1973.

Bobby Vinton's Rock 'N Rollers, CBS, Nov. 20, 1978.

A Boy from New Orleans—Louis Armstrong, Syndicated August 1972.

The Brass Are Coming (Herb Alpert), NBC, March 31, 1970.

Bravo Julie (Julie Andrews), Syndicated October 1975.

Broadway! My Street (Florence Henderson), Syndicated April 1974.

Buddy Greco Show, Syndicated June 1972.

Burt and the Girls (Burt Reynolds), NBC, Dec. 8, 1973.

Burt Bacharach: Close to You, ABC, April 23, 1972.

Burt Bacharach—Opus No. 3, ABC, Feb. 28, 1973.

Burt Bacharach Special, NBC, Jan. 10, 1974.

Burt Reynolds' Late Show, NBC, March 9, 1974.

The Captain and Tennille (Toni Tennille, Daryl Dragon), ABC, April 3, 1978; May 5, 1978.

The Captain and Tennille Songbook (Toni Tennille, Daryl Dragon), ABC, March 26, 1979.

Carol Channing Show, NBC, Sept. 9, 1970.

The Carpenters (Karen and Richard Carpenter), ABC, Dec. 8, 1976; May 16, 1980.

The Carpenters: A Christmas Portrait (Karen and Richard Carpenter), ABC, Dec. 19, 1978.

The Carpenters at Christmas (Karen and Richard Carpenter), ABC, Dec. 9, 1977.

The Carpenters—Space Encounters (Karen and Richard Carpenter), ABC, May 17, 1978.

Cass Elliot Special, CBS, Sept. 28, 1973.

Caterina Valente Special, Syndicated June 1971.

Charo, ABC, May 24, 1976.

Cher!, CBS, Feb. 12, 1975; March 7, 1979.

Cheryl Ladd . . . Looking Back: Souvenirs, ABC, May 19, 1980.

Cheryl Ladd Special, ABC, April 9, 1979.

Chevrolet Presents Burt Bacharach, ABC, Nov. 15, 1972.

Chevrolet Presents the Very First Glen Campbell Special, NBC, Sept. 16, 1973.

Chevy Chase's National Humor Test, NBC, May 10, 1979.

Chevy Chase Special, NBC, May 5, 1977.

Christmas at the Grand Ole Opry (John Ritter, host), ABC, Dec. 14, 1978.

A Christmas Special . . . With Love, Mac Davis, NBC, Dec. 24, 1979.

Christmas with the Bing Crosbys, NBC, Dec. 10 1972; Dec. 15, 1974.

Chuck Barris Special, NBC, Dec. 20, 1977.

Cliff Robertson at Squaw Valley, Syndicated November 1973.

Clown Around (Ed Sullivan, host), CBS, March 26, 1972.

Cole Porter in Paris, NBC, Jan. 17, 1973.

The Comedians: Love and Marriage (Carl Reiner, host), ABC, April 23, 1972.

Como Country—Perry and His Nashville Friends (Perry Como), CBS, Feb. 17, 1975.

The Confessions of Dick Van Dyke, ABC, April 10, 1975.

A Country Christmas (Barbi Benton, Loretta Lynn, hosts), CBS, Dec. 12, 1979.

A Country Christmas (Minnie Pearl, host), CBS, Dec. 1, 1980.
Country Comes Home (Johnny Cash, host), NBC, April 26, 1974.
Country Music Hit Parade (Eddy Arnold, host), CBS, Feb. 4, 1974.
Country Night of Stars (Charley Pride, host), NBC, May 23, 1978.
Country Night of Stars (Crystal Gayle, host), NBC, May 30, 1978.
Country Super Stars of the '70s (Dolly Parton, host), NBC, Oct. 16, 1979.
A Couple of Dons (Don Adams, Don Rickles), NBC, Sept. 8, 1973.
Crystal (Crystal Gayle), CBS, Dec. 4, 1980.
Crystal Gayle Special, CBS, Dec. 12, 1970.

Danny Kaye's Look-in at the Opera, CBS, April 27, 1975.
Darin Invasion (Bobby Darin), Syndicated August 1972.
David Soul and Friends, ABC, Aug. 18, 1977.
Dean Martin Celebrity Roast. See program No. 283.
Dean Martin's Christmas in California, NBC, Dec. 18, 1977; Dec. 9, 1978; Dec. 13, 1979.
Dean Martin Christmas Show, NBC, Dec. 14, 1975; Dec. 16, 1980.
Dean Martin Comedy Special, NBC, Nov. 8, 1976; April 4, 1977.
Dean Martin's Red Hot Scandals of 1926, NBC, Nov. 8, 1976.
Dean Martin's Red Hot Scandals, Part 2, NBC, April 4, 1977.
Debby Boone ... The Same Old Brand New Me, NBC, June 23, 1980.
Dinah in Search of the Ideal Man (Dinah Shore), NBC, Nov. 18, 1973.
Dinah Won't You Please Come Home! (Dinah Shore), NBC, April 7, 1974.
Dolly and Carol in Nashville (Dolly Parton, Carol Burnett), CBS, Feb. 14, 1979.
Don Knotts' Nice Clean, Decent, Wholesome Hour, CBS, April 3, 1970.
Don Rickles—Alive and Kicking, CBS, Dec. 12, 1972.
Don Rickles Special, CBS, Nov. 19, 1975.
Donald's Dublin (Donald O'Connor), Syndicated March 1972.
Donna Summer Special, ABC, Jan. 27, 1980.
Donny and Marie Christmas Show (Marie and Donny Osmond), ABC, Dec. 4, 1979.
Donny and Marie Osmond Special, ABC, Nov. 16, 1975.
Dora's World (Dora Hall), Syndicated August 1974.
Doris Day Special, CBS, March 14, 1971.

Doris Day Today, CBS, Feb. 19, 1975.
Dorothy Hamill's Corner of the Sky, ABC, April 23, 1979.
Dorothy Hamill Special, ABC, Nov. 17, 1976; April 28, 1978.
Dorothy Hamill Winter Carnival Special, NBC, March 2, 1977.
Doug Henning's World of Magic, NBC, Dec. 23, 1976; Dec. 15, 1977; Feb. 15, 1980.
Duke Ellington ... We Love You Madly, CBS, Feb. 11, 1973.

Eddy Arnold Show, Syndicated October 1971.
Eddie Rabbitt Special, NBC, July 10, 1980.
Ed McMahon and His Friends, NBC, March 12, 1972.
Elvis: Aloha from Hawaii (Elvis Presley), NBC, April 4, 1973.
Elvis in Concert (Elvis Presley), CBS, Oct. 3, 1977.
Engelbert Humperdinck in Bermuda, Syndicated August 1974.
Ernie Ford's White Christmas, NBC, Dec. 23, 1972.

Family Night with Horace Heidt, Syndicated August 1971.
5th Dimension Travelling Sunshine Show, ABC, Aug. 18, 1971.
50 Years of Country Music (Dolly Parton, host), NBC, Jan. 22, 1978.
Flip Wilson .. Of Course, NBC, Oct. 18, 1974.
Flip Wilson Special, NBC, Dec. 11, 1974; Feb. 27, 1975; May 7, 1975; CBS, Nov. 11, 1975.
Frank Sinatra Special, NBC, Nov. 18, 1973.
From Raquel with Love (Raquel Welch), ABC, Nov. 23, 1980.
From This Moment On ... Cole Porter (Steve Lawrence, host), Syndicated May 1979.
Funny Girl to Funny Lady (Barbra Streisand), ABC, March 9, 1975.

Gabriel Kaplan Presents the Future Stars, ABC, April 14, 1977.
Gabriel Kaplan Presents the Small Event, ABC, Oct. 23, 1977.
Gene Kelly: An American in Pasadena, CBS, March 13, 1978.
Gene Kelly's Wonderful World of Girls, NBC, Jan. 14, 1970.
George Burns Comedy Special, CBS, Dec. 1, 1976.
George Burns in Nashville, NBC, Nov. 13, 1980.
George Burns' 100th Birthday, CBS, Jan. 22, 1979.
George Burns' One Man Show, CBS, Nov. 23, 1977.
George Carlin Special, ABC, Jan. 2, 1973.
George Kirby Special, NBC, Oct. 2, 1973.
George Segal Special, NBC, Oct. 26, 1974.
Gladys Knight and the Pips, NBC, June 21, 1974.
Glen Campbell: Back to Basics, NBC, May 20, 1979.

Glen Campbell—Down Home and Down Under, CBS, May 20, 1976.
Glen Campbell Special: The Musical West, NBC, March 8, 1974.
Goldie and Liza Together (Goldie Hawn, Liza Minnelli), CBS, Feb. 19, 1980.
Goldie: The Goldie Hawn Special, CBS, March 1, 1978.
Gypsy in My Soul (Shirley MacLaine), CBS, Jan. 20, 1976.

Hal Linden's Big Apple, ABC, June 1, 1980.
Hal Linden Special, ABC, April 11, 1979.
Happy Days Are Here Again (Fred and Mickie Finn), Syndicated October 1971.
Helen Reddy Special, ABC, May 22, 1979.
Henry Fonda Special, Syndicated April 1973.
Henry Mancini Special, ABC, Dec. 3, 1971.
Herb Alpert and the Tijuana Brass, ABC, Oct. 13, 1974.
Hi-Ho Steverino (Steve Allen), ABC, Jan. 16, 1974.
Hi, I'm Glen Campbell, ABC, July 7, 1976.
Hollywood Palladium (John Davidson, host), NBC, Sept. 6, 1974.
Hooray for Hollywood (Don Adams, Don Rickles, Edie Adams, hosts), CBS, Feb. 26, 1970.
How to Handle a Woman (Dinah Shore), NBC, Oct. 20, 1972.

I Believe in Music (Mac Davis), NBC, Nov. 24, 1973.
I Love You (Edgar Bergen, host), NBC, Feb. 14, 1978.
I'm a Fan (Carol Channing, Dick Van Dyke), CBS, Jan. 25, 1972.

Jack Benny's First Farewell Show, NBC, Jan. 18, 1973.
Jack Benny's Second Farewell Show, NBC, Jan. 24, 1974.
Jack Benny's 20th TV Anniversary, NBC, Nov. 16, 1970.
Jackie Gleason Special, CBS, Oct. 11, 1973.
Jack Jones Show, CBS, May 30, 1971.
Jack Lemmon—Get Happy: A Tribute to Composer Harold Arlen, NBC, Feb. 25, 1973.
Jimmy McNichol Special, CBS, April 30, 1980.
John Davidson Christmas Show, ABC, Dec. 9, 1977; Dec. 22, 1978.
John Denver and Friend: Frank Sinatra, ABC, March 29, 1976.
John Denver and the Ladies, ABC, March 8, 1979.
John Denver and the Muppets: A Christmas Together, ABC, Dec. 5, 1979.
John Denver—Rocky Mountain High Down Under, ABC, Feb. 16, 1978.
John Denver Show, ABC, March 11, 1974; Nov. 17, 1976.

John Denver Show: A Family Event, ABC, Dec. 1, 1974.
John Denver Special, ABC, March 10, 1975.
John Denver's Rocky Mountain Christmas, ABC, Dec. 14, 1976.
John Denver—Thank God I'm a Country Boy, ABC, March 2, 1977.
John Lennon and Yoko Ono, ABC, Dec. 15, 1972.
Johnny Carson Presents the Sun City Scandals '72, NBC, March 13, 1972.
Johnny Cash Christmas Show, CBS, Nov. 30, 1977; Dec. 6, 1978; Dec. 6, 1979; Dec. 3, 1980.
Johnny Cash's Country Music, NBC, Feb. 23, 1974.
Johnny Cash Spring Special, CBS, May 9, 1979.
Johnny Cash: The First 25 Years, CBS, May 8, 1980.
Johnny Mathis in the Canadian Rockies, Syndicated December 1975.
Johnny Mathis Session, Syndicated March 1975.
John Ritter, Being of Sound Mind and Body, ABC, May 4, 1980.
John Schneider—Back Home, CBS, Sept. 24, 1980.
John Wayne's First TV Special: Swing Out, Sweet Land, NBC, Nov. 29, 1970.
Jonathan Winters Presents 200 Years of American Humor, NBC, Jan. 21, 1976.
Jubilee (Bing Crosby, Liza Minnelli), NBC, March 26, 1976.
Jud Strunk Show, ABC, Aug. 17, 1972.
Julie! (Julie Andrews), ABC, Aug. 24, 1972.
Julie and Carol at Lincoln Center (Julie Andrews, Carol Burnett), CBS, Dec. 7, 1971.
Julie and Dick in Covent Garden (Julie Andrews, Dick Van Dyke), ABC, April 21, 1974.
Julie and Jackie ... How Sweet it Is (Julie Andrews, Jackie Gleason), ABC, May 22, 1974.
Julie Andrews: One Step into Spring, CBS, March 9, 1978.
Julie London Show, Syndicated May 1971.
Julie, My Favorite Things (Julie Andrews), ABC, April 18, 1975.
Julie on Sesame Street (Julie Andrews), ABC, Nov. 23, 1973.
Just Friends (John Hartford), ABC, Sept. 13, 1970.

Kate Smith Show, Syndicated July 1973.
Kaye Stevens Show, Syndicated August 1971.
Kenny Rogers' America, CBS, Nov. 20, 1980.
Kenny Rogers and the American Cowboy, CBS, Nov. 28, 1979.
Kenny Rogers Special, CBS, April 12, 1979.

Ladies and Gentlemen ... Bob Newhart, CBS, Feb. 19, 1980.

Las Vegas Palace of Stars (Gene Kelly, host), CBS, Aug. 16, 1979.

Leif Garrett Special, CBS, May 18, 1979.

Leslie Gore Show, Syndicated March 1970.

Liberace: A Valentine Special, CBS, Feb. 3, 1979.

Lights, Camera, Monty! (Monty Hall), ABC, April 24, 1975.

Like Magic (Chris Kirby, host), CBS, Feb. 12, 1980.

Lily (Lily Tomlin), CBS, Nov. 2, 1973; ABC, Feb. 21, 1975; ABC, July 25, 1975.

Linda in Wonderland (Linda Lavin), CBS, Nov. 27, 1980.

Lindsay Wagner—Another Side of Me, ABC, Nov. 7, 1977.

Listen ... That's Love (Helen Reddy, Olivia Newton-John, Paul Williams), ABC, Nov. 30, 1974.

Liza (Liza Minnelli), NBC, June 29, 1970.

Liza With a Z (Liza Minnelli), NBC, Sept. 10, 1972.

Lola (Lola Falana), ABC, Dec. 18, 1975; Jan. 29, 1976; March 9, 1976; March 23, 1976.

Love from A to Z (Liza Minnelli), NBC, April 30, 1974.

Love Is ... Barbara Eden, ABC, Dec. 15, 1972.

A Lucille Ball Special Starring Lucille Ball and Dean Martin, CBS, March 1, 1975.

Lucy Goes to Nashville (Lucille Ball), CBS, Nov. 19, 1978.

Lynda Carter: Encore, CBS, Sept. 16, 1980.

Lynda Carter's Special, CBS, Jan. 12, 1980.

Lynn Anderson, Country Welcome, NBC, Sept. 20, 21, 1977.

Mac (Mac Davis), ABC, May 28, 1975.

Mac Davis Christmas Show, NBC, Dec. 14, 1975.

Mac Davis—I'll Be Home for Christmas, NBC, Dec. 23, 1980.

Mac Davis: I Still Believe in Music, NBC, May 20, 1980.

Mac Davis's Christmas Odyssey, ABC, Dec. 19, 1978.

Mac Davis ... Sounds Like Home, NBC, April 26, 1977.

Mac Davis Special, NBC, Nov. 13, 1975; Dec. 7, 1977; May 11, 1978.

McLean Stevenson Show, NBC, Nov. 2, 1975.

Magic of David Copperfield, CBS, Oct. 27, 1978; Oct. 24, 1979; Sept. 25, 1980.

Magic of Sammy Davis, Jr., Syndicated July 1973.

Make Mine Red, White and Blue (Fred Astaire), NBC, Sept. 9, 1972.

Many Faces of Comedy (Alan King), ABC, Dec. 4, 1973.

Many Sides of Don Rickles, ABC, Sept. 17, 1970.

Marlo Thomas and Friends: Free to Be You and Me, ABC, March 11, 1974.

Mary's Incredible Dream (Mary Tyler Moore), CBS, Jan. 22, 1976.

Mary Tyler Moore's How to Survive the '70s, CBS, Feb. 22, 1978.

Memories of Elvis (Ann-Margret, host), NBC, Nov. 20, 1977.

Men Who Rate a "10" (Brooke Shields, Barbara Eden, Gloria Swanson, hosts), NBC, Oct. 7, 1980.

Merry Christmas from the Grand Ole Opry (Loni Anderson, Robert Urich, hosts), ABC, Dec. 14, 1979.

Merry Christmas ... With Love, Julie (Julie Andrews), Syndicated December 1979.

Mitzi and a Hundred Guys (Mitzi Gaynor), CBS, March 24, 1975.

Mitzi Gaynor—A Tribute to the American Housewife, CBS, Feb. 4, 1974.

Mitzi Gaynor—Swinging into Spring, CBS, March 29, 1977.

Mitzi ... The First Time (Mitzi Gaynor), CBS, March 28, 1973.

Mitzi ... Roarin' in the '20s (Mitzi Gaynor), CBS, March 14, 1976.

Mitzi ... What's Hot? What's Not? (Mitzi Gaynor), CBS, April 6, 1978.

Mitzi Zings into Spring (Mitzi Gaynor), CBS, March 29, 1977.

Monsanto Night Presents Benny Goodman, NBC, March 31, 1974.

Monsanto Night Presents Burl Ives, Syndicated June 1972.

Monsanto Night Presents Dionne Warwick, Syndicated March 1975.

Monsanto Night Presents Henry Mancini, Syndicated December 1971.

Monsanto Night Presents Jack Jones, Syndicated December 1974.

Monsanto Night Presents Jose Feliciano, Syndicated December 1972.

Monsanto Night Presents Nancy Wilson, Syndicated March 1972.

Monty Hall at Sea World, ABC, May 31, 1974.

Monty Hall's Smokin'-Stokin'-Fire Brigade, ABC, June 5, 1972.

Monty Hall Special, ABC, Aug. 7, 1976.

Muhammad Ali Special, ABC, Sept. 13, 1975.

The Music of Paul McCartney, ABC, April 16, 1973.

Nancy Sinatra Show, CBS, April 4, 1971.

Nashville Palace (Roy Clark, host), ABC, Oct. 27, 1980.

Nashville Remembers Elvis on His Birthday (Jimmy Dean, host), NBC, Jan. 8, 1978.

Natalie Cole Special, CBS, April 27, 1978.

Neil Diamond Special, NBC, Feb. 21, 1977; Nov. 17, 1977.

Neil Sedaka, Steppin' Out, NBC, Sept. 17, 1976.

Olivia (Olivia Newton-John), ABC, May 17, 1978.

Olivia Newton-John's Hollywood Nights, ABC, Arpil 14, 1980.

One More Time (Carol Channing, Pearl Bailey), CBS, Jan. 10, 1974.

Opryland, U.S.A. (Ernie Ford, Petula Clark), NBC, Oct. 22, 1973.

Opryland, U.S.A. (Sandy Duncan, Dennis Weaver), ABC, May 14, 1975.

The Osmonds, CBS, Nov. 20, 1974.

Osmond Brothers Special, ABC, May 26, 1978; Oct. 14, 1978.

Osmond Family Christmas Show, NBC, Dec. 15, 1980.

Out to Lunch (Barbara Eden, Rita Moreno, Elliot Gould), ABC, Dec. 10, 1974.

Pat Boone and Family, ABC, April 8, 1978; Nov. 12, 1978.

Pat Boone and Family Christmas Show, ABC, Dec. 8, 1979.

Pat Boone and Family Easter Special, ABC, April 15, 1979.

Paul Anka in Monte Carlo, CBS, Aug. 27, 1978.

Paul Anka, Music My Way, NBC, April 25, 1977.

Paul Lynde at the Movies, ABC, March 24, 1979.

Paul Lynde Comedy Hour, ABC, Nov. 6, 1975; Oct. 29, 1976; April 23, 1977; May 20, 1978.

Paul Lynde Goes Ma-a-a-ad, ABC, May 12, 1979.

Paul Lynde: 'Twas the Night Before Christmas, ABC, Dec. 7, 1977.

Paul Simon Special, NBC, Dec. 8, 1977.

Peggy Fleming Visits the Soviet Union, NBC, Oct. 28, 1973.

Peggy Fleming with Holiday on Ice at Madison Square Garden, NBC, Oct. 26, 1976.

Perry Como: An Olde English Christmas, ABC, Dec. 14, 1977.

Perry Como ... Bahama Holiday, ABC, May 21, 1980.

Perry Como—Las Vegas Style, NBC, Sept. 11, 1976.

Perry Como Special, NBC, Feb. 22, 1970; CBS, April 10, 1974; CBS, Dec. 17, 1974; ABC, May 21, 1980.

Perry Como's Christmas in Austria, NBC, Dec. 13, 1976.

Perry Como's Christmas in Mexico, NBC, Dec. 15, 1975.

Perry Como's Christmas in New Mexico, ABC, Dec. 14, 1979.

Perry Como's Christmas in the Holy Land, ABC, Dec. 13, 1980.

Perry Como's Early American Christmas, ABC, Dec. 13, 1978.

Perry Como's Easter by the Sea, ABC, March 22, 1978.

Perry Como's Hawaiian Holiday, NBC, Feb. 22, 1976.

Perry Como's Lake Tahoe Holiday, NBC, Oct. 28, 1975.

Perry Como's Music from Hollywood, ABC, March 28, 1977.

Perry Como's Spring in New Or-

leans, NBC, April 7, 1976.

Perry Como's Spring Time Special, CBS, March 27, 1975; ABC, April 9, 1979.

Perry Como's Summer of '74, CBS, Sept. 12, 1974.

Perry Como's Winter Show, NBC, Dec. 9, 1971; CBS, Dec. 4, 1972; CBS, Dec. 10, 1973.

Petula Clark in Concert, Syndicated March 1977.

Petula Clark Show, ABC, Dec. 9, 1970.

Polly Bergen Show, Syndicated June 1971.

Pop! (Davey Jones, host), ABC, July 15, 1972.

Pure Goldie (Goldie Hawn), NBC, Feb. 15, 1971.

Raquel Welch Show, CBS, April 26, 1970.

Raquel Welch Special, Syndicated August 1974.

Ray Conniff Christmas Show, Syndicated December 1971.

Real George Carlin, Syndicated August 1973.

Really Raquel (Raquel Welch), CBS, March 8, 1974.

Red Skelton Special, CBS, Feb. 24, 1970.

Rich Little Special, NBC, Sept. 3, 1975; May 13, 1978.

Richard Pryor Special, NBC, May 5, 1977.

Roberta Flack ... The First Time Ever, ABC, June 19, 1973.

Robert Goulet and Carol Lawrence Show, Syndicated November 1973.

Robert Young with the Young, ABC, May 6, 1973.

The Rock and Roll Years (Dick Clark), ABC, Sept. 27, 1973.

Rockette: A Holiday Tribute to the Radio City Music Hall (Gregory Peck, host; Ann-Margret, star), NBC, Dec. 14, 1978.

Rod McKuen's Christmas in New England, Syndicated December 1978.

Roger Miller Special, ABC, Jan. 1, 1973.

Rowan and Martin Bite the Hand That Feeds Them (Dan Rowan, Dick Martin), NBC, Jan. 14, 1970.

Rowan and Martin Report (Dan Rowan, Dick Martin), NBC, Nov. 5, 1975.

Rowan and Martin Special (Dan Rowan, Dick Martin), NBC, Sept. 13, 1973.

Roy Clark Special, ABC, May 5, 1979.

Roy Clark's Ranch Party, Syndicated January 1978.

Sandy (Sandy Duncan), CBS, Nov. 13, 1974.

Sandy Duncan at the American Ice Spectacular, CBS, Jan. 16, 1976.

Sandy in Disneyland (Sandy Duncan), CBS, April 10, 1974.

Scoey Mitchlll Show, Syndicated April 1972.

Seasons Greetings from Mike Douglas, CBS, Dec. 18, 1972.

Sea World – Country Style (Charley Pride, host), Syndicated July 1979.

Second Barry Manilow Special, ABC, Feb. 24, 1978.

Sensational, Shocking, Wonderful, Wacky '70s (Dick Clark, host), NBC, Jan. 4, 1980.

Shani Wallis Show, Syndicated September 1970.

Shelley Berman Show, Syndicated May 1970.

Shirley Bassey Special, Syndicated January 1980.

Shirley MacLaine at the Lido, CBS, May 20, 1979.

Shirley MacLaine ... Every Little Movement, CBS, May 22, 1980.

Shirley MacLaine: If They Could See Me Now, CBS, Nov. 28, 1974.

Shirley MacLaine – Where Do We Go from Here?, CBS, March 12, 1977.

Siegfried and Roy – Superstars of Magic (Lorne Greene, host), NBC, Nov. 14, 1980.

Siegfried and Roy – Thrills and Illusions (Eddie Albert, host), NBC, Feb. 1, 1980.

Sills and Burnett at the Met (Beverly Sills, Carol Burnett), CBS, Nov. 25, 1976.

Sinatra and Friends (Frank Sinatra), ABC, April 21, 1977.

Sinatra – The Main Event (Frank Sinatra), ABC, Oct. 13, 1974.

Smokey Robinson Show, Syndicated August 1972.

Sonny and Cher Nitty Gritty Hour, Syndicated September 1974.

Sonny and Cher's Rock 'N' Roll Years, Syndicated August 1980.

A Special Kenny Rogers, CBS, April 12, 1979.

A Special Olivia Newton-John, ABC, Nov. 17, 1976.

Steve Lawrence and Eydie Gormé: From This Moment on, NBC, Aug, 22, 1978.

Steve Lawrence and Eydie Gormé on Stage, NBC, Sept. 16, 1973.

Steve Lawrence and Eydie Gormé: Our Love Is Here to Stay, CBS, Nov. 27, 1975.

Steve Martin: A Wild and Crazy Guy, NBC, Nov. 22, 1978.

Strolling with Al Hirt, Syndicated November 1972.

The Sullivan Years (Dick Cavett, host), CBS, Feb. 2, 1975.

Sun City Scandals (Johnny Carson, host), NBC, Dec. 7, 1970.

Ted Knight Musical Comedy Variety Special, CBS, Nov. 30, 1976.

Tell Me on a Sunday (Marti Webb), Syndicated April 1980.

Telly Savalas – Who Loves Ya Baby?, CBS, Feb. 18, 1976.

Tennessee Ernie Ford's Nashville – Moscow Express, NBC, Jan. 8, 1975.

Tennessee Ernie Ford Special, NBC, May 19, 1971.

The 36 Most Beautiful Girls in Texas (Hal Linden, host), ABC, Sept. 4, 1978.

Three Dog Night, ABC, Aug. 24, 1972.

Tim Conway Special, CBS, Jan. 15, 1979.

To Europe with Love (Peggy Fleming), NBC, Jan. 23, 1972.

Tom and Dick Smothers Special, NBC, Nov. 1, 1980.

Tom and Dick Smothers Special II, NBC, Nov. 11, 1980.

Tom Jones Special, ABC, May 15, 1971; June 17, 1971.

Tony Bennett Special, Syndicated November 1974.

Tony Bennett Super Special, Syndicated December 1971; May 1973.

Tony Bennett: This Is Music, Syndicated August 1974.

Tony Martin Show, Syndicated December 1972.

Tony Orlando Special, NBC, Jan. 3, 1979.

Top Ten (Bill Saluga, host), NBC, July 10, 1980.

Touch of Gold (Mac Davis, host), NBC, Oct. 13, 1974.

Trini Lopez Show, Syndicated Febuary 1970.

Unbroken Circle (Kris Kristofferson, host), CBS, Nov. 28, 1979.

Uncle Tim Wants You (Tim Conway), CBS, Sept. 17, 1977.

Waylon! (Waylon Jennings), ABC, Oct. 23, 1980.

Wayne Newton: A Christmas Carol, Syndicated December 1976.

Wayne Newton Special, Syndicated September 1974.

Wayne Newton Special, NBC, Sept. 26, 1977.

When the West Was Fun (Glenn Ford, host), ABC, June 5, 1979.

Willie Nelson Singing to the Country, Syndicated July 1980.

Wonderful World of Aggravation (Alan King), ABC, Nov. 15, 1972.

Words and Music (Danny Thomas), Syndicated November 1974.

World of Magic (Bill Cosby, host), NBC, Dec. 26, 1975.

World's Largest Indoor Country Music Show (Dottie West, Kenny Rogers, hosts), NBC, April 5, 1978.

Yesterday, Today and Tomorrow (Danny Thomas, Carol Channing, Juliet Prowse, Marjorie Lord), CBS, Jan. 28, 1970.

Section 4
Program Addendum

Series and pilot films broadcast from October 27, 1980 through March 1, 1981.

1874 THE ASPHALT COWBOY

Pilot (Crime Drama). The exploits of Max Caulpepper, the owner-operator of the Los Angeles-based Caulpepper Security Service. In the pilot, Max attempts to solve the murder of a friend. He believes it is linked to the theft of $20,000 from the Van Heuran Aircraft Company. Originally titled *Caulpepper*.

REGULAR CAST

Max Caulpepper (a widower)	Max Baer
Molly Caulpepper, his daughter	Lory Walsh
Meg Caulpepper, his daughter	Lori Lowe
Rosie Caulpepper, his daughter	Robin Dearden
Sergeant Brown, Max's housekeeper	Noah Beery
Lieutenant Lassiter, L.A.P.D.	James Luisi

GUEST CAST

Charles Van Heuran	Richard Denning
Candy Man	James Sloyan
Vincent "Buster" Bustermonte	Cal Bellini
Annie Van Heuran	Jennifer Holmes
Richie Bancroft	Michael Mullins
Rita	Kathy Shea

Meg's horses: Toby and Last Chance.

Max's license plate number: 38983Q

Music: Ken Harrison.
Executive Producer: Michael Fisher.
Producer: Mike Vejar.
Writer: Michael Fisher.
Director: Cliff Bole.
Art Director: Robert Crawley.

THE ASPHALT COWBOY — 60 minutes — NBC — December 7, 1980.

1875 BARBARA MANDRELL AND THE MANDRELL SISTERS

Variety. An entertaining, well-coordinated series that spotlights the musical talents of singer Barbara Mandrell and her sisters, Irlene and Louise.

Hostess: Barbara Mandrell.
Co-Hostesses: Irlene and Louise Mandrell.
Regulars: Georgi Irene (as Barbara as a girl), Melanie Griffin, Bobby Salter, Ray Stewart, The Krofft Puppets (as Truck Shackley and the Critters, a hillbilly Rock group).

Orchestra: Dennis McCarthy.
Barbara's Band: The Do-Rights.
Executive Producer: Sid and Marty Krofft.
Producer: Ernest Chambers.
Writer: Al Gordon, Peter Galley, Phil Hahn, Ernest Chambers, Jeremy Stevens, Lisa Medway, Cord Casady, Sam Greenbaum.
Director: Bob Henry.
Art Director: Romain Johnston.
Puppets Design/Director: Tony Urbano.

BARBARA MANDRELL AND THE MANDRELL SISTERS — 60 minutes — NBC — Premiered: November 18, 1980.

1876 B.J. AND THE BEAR

Adventure. A revised version of Program No. 137. When Trans-Cal, a powerful California trucking syndicate, threatens to ruin his independent transport company, Dave Chaffey seeks the help of his friend, trucker B.J. McKay. In Hollywood, B.J. becomes involved in the dangerous conflict between the syndicate and independents when Trans-Cal arranges an accident that puts Chaffey in the hospital. Bitter, B.J. decides to take matters in his own hands and make Chaffey Enterprises solvent again. Despite constant harassment, B.J. hires seven beautiful lady truckers and reestablishes operations. The series depicts B.J.'s efforts to run the transport company against the wishes of Rutherford T. Grant, a corrupt S.C.A.T.* police captain who wants to stop B.J. before he unites the independent truck drivers and cuts off Grant's lucrative illegal dealings with the syndicate. (After completing their first successful operation, Chaffey renames the company Bear Enterprises — after B.J.'s simian companion.)

CAST

B.J. McKay	Greg Evigan
Stacy, his Girl Friday	Susan Woollen
Capt. Rutherford T. Grant	Murray Hamilton
Bear	Sam

The Lady Killers (B.J.'s truckers):

Stacks	Judy Landers
Teri	Candi Brough
Geri	Randi Brough
Samantha	Barbra Horan
Callie	Linda McCullough
Angie	Sheila DeWindt
Cindy	Sherilyn Wolter

Also:

Jason T. Willard, the head of Trans-Cal	Jock Mahoney
Dave Chaffey, B.J.'s partner	Neil Zevnik
Lt. Jim Steiger, Grant's aide	Eric Server
Nick, the bartender at Phil's Disco	John Dullagan

B.J. and the Bear Theme Vocal: Greg Evigan.
Executive Producer: Glen A. Larson, Michael Sloan.
Producer: Richard Lindheim, Robert F. O'Neill.

B.J. AND THE BEAR — 60 minutes — NBC — Premiered: January 13, 1981.

*The Special Crime Action Team of the L.A.P.D.

1877 BLOCKBUSTERS

Game. One solo player competes against a family pair. A board with twenty letters, each contained in a hexagon, is displayed on stage. One player selects a letter and a question, whose answer will begin with that letter, is read. The first player to answer correctly wins that space and the opportunity to select another letter. The object is for the solo player to acquire four red hexagons (from top to bottom) and for the family pair to acquire five white hexagons (from side to side). The first player or players to do so wins the game and cash prizes.

Host: Bill Cullen.
Announcer: Bob Hilton.
Music: Bob Cobert.
Executive Producer: Mark Goodson, Bill Todman.
Producer: Robert Sherman.
Director: Ira Skutch.
Art Director: Dennis Roof.

BLOCKBUSTERS — 30 minutes — NBC — Premiered: October 27, 1980.

1878 BOSOM BUDDIES

Comedy. When Henry Desmond and Kip Wilson are evicted and find they have no place to live, they accept the hospitality of a female friend and move into the Susan B. Anthony, a hotel for women only. Episodes depict their misadventures as they struggle to stay in their low-rent New York bachelor's paradise by parading as women. (Henry, an ad agency copywriter, poses as his sister, Hildegarde; and Kip, also a copywriter, poses as his sister, Buffy.)

CAST

Henry Desmond/Hildegarde Desmond	Peter Scolari
Kip Wilson/Buffy Wilson	Tom Hanks
Ruth Dunbar, their employer at the Livingston, Gentry and Mishkin Ad Agency	Holland Taylor
Amy Cassidy, their coworker	Wendie Jo Sperber
Sonny, a dancer, Amy's roommate	Donna Dixon
Isabelle, a model, a hotel resident	Telma Hopkins
Lilli Sinclair, the hotel manager	Edie Adams Lucille Benson
Dawn Steekovitch, works in the agency	Linda Lawrence
Lee Anne, a hotel resident	Samantha Fox
Marty Bursky, an agency executive	Patrick Quinn

Music: Dan Foliart, Howard Pearl.
Exeuctive Producer: Edward K. Milkis, Thomas L. Miller, William Boyett, Chris Thompson.
Producer: Chris Thompson, Don Van Atta.
Director: Joel Zwick, Chris Thompson, Don Van Atta, Herbbert Kenwith, John Bowab.

BOSOM BUDDIES — 30 minutes — ABC — Premiered: November 27, 1980.

1879 BOWZER

Pilot (Comedy-Variety). A proposed extension series based on *Sha Na Na*. The story, set at the shabby night club Chez Bowzer, follows the misadventures of Bowzer J. Bowzer, the owner, as he struggles to keep his establishment operating — despite rotten food, awful entertainment, and long overdue bills. In the pilot, Bowzer seeks to raise the rent money by conning Barbi Benton into performing at the club.

CAST

Bowzer J. Bowzer	Jon Bauman
Victoria, his girlfriend	Susan Lawrence
Barney Sheldon, his landlord	Bruce Kirby

Jason, Bowzer's piano teaching
student   Tony Christopher
Barbi Benton (guest role)   Barbi Benton

Bowzer Theme: Scott Simon, Jon Bauman.
Music: Lenny Stack.
Executive Producer: Pierre Cosette.
Producer: Walter C. Miller.
Writer: Gary Jacobs, Gary Burns, P.G. Burnstein, Walter C. Miller.
Director: Walter C. Miller.
Choreographer: Walter Painter.
Art Director: John McAdam.

BOWZER — 30 minutes — Syndicated January 1981.

1880   BREAKING AWAY

Comedy-Drama. The series, set in Bloomington, Indiana, follows the experiences of Dave, Mike, Cyril and Moocher, four new high school graduates, as they attempt to "break away" from their childhood and find a place for themselves in the adult world. Based on the feature film of the same title.

CAST

Dave Stohler   Shaun Cassidy
Mike Carnahan   Tom Wiggins
Cyril (no last name)   Thom Bray
Moocher (George; no last
name)   Jackie Earle Haley
Evelyn Stohler, Dave's
mother   Barbara Barrie
Ray Stohler,
Dave's father   Vincent Gardenia
Nancy, Moocher's
girlfriend   Shelly Brammer
Paulina, Dave's friend   Dominique Dunne

Music: Lance Rubin.
Music Supervision: Lionel Newman.
Executive Producer: Frank Konigsberg, Peter Yates, Herbert B. Leonard.
Supervising Producer: Jerry McNeely, Glen Gordon Caron, Frank Konigsberg.
Producer: Sam Manners, Herbert B. Leonard.
Writer: Steve Tesich, Charles Rosin, Caroline Elias.
Director: Joseph Ruben, Stan Lathan, Jack Bender.

BREAKING AWAY — 60 minutes — ABC — November 29, 1980 – January 10, 1981. 7 of 8 filmed episodes aired.

1881   BUCK ROGERS

Science Fiction. A revised version of *Buck Rogers in the 25th Century.* The further adventures of William "Buck" Rogers, the twentieth century astronaut suspended in time to awaken five hundred years later, as he explores the universe aboard the space ship *Searcher,* seeking the lost tribes of Earth.

CAST

Capt. William "Buck" Rogers   Gil Gerard
Col. Wilma Deering, his aide   Erin Gray

Dr. Goodfellow, the
scientist   Wilfrid Hyde-White
Admiral Asimov, commander of
Searcher   Jay Garner
Twiki, Buck's droid (robot)   Felix Silla
Voice of Twiki   Mel Blanc
Lt. Devlin   Paul Carr
Lt. Moore   Alex Hyde-White

Also: Crichton, the robot who refuses to believe it is manmade.
Music: Bruce Broughton, John Cacavas.
Executive Producer: John Mantley.
Supervising Producer: Calvin Clements.
Producer: John G. Stephens, David J. O'Connell.

BUCK ROGERS — 60 minutes — NBC — Premiered: January 15, 1981.

1882   CAMP WILDERNESS

Adventure. The exploits of a group of teenage campers as they explore the natural wonders of the United States.

CAST

Franci, a counselor at
Camp Wilderness   Franci Hogle
Stefan, a counselor   Stefan Hayes
Ruth, a camper   Ruth Ingersoll
Matt, a camper   Matt Boston
Lisa, a camper   Lisa Catalli
Nora, a camper   Nora Lester
Phil, a camper   Phil Catalli
Jeff, a camper   Jeff Kurtz
Scott, a camper   Scott Monti
Korry, a camper   Korry Blakemor
Dan, a camper   Dan Smith
Steve, a camper   Steve Abbott
Will, a camper   Raymond Roy
Swift Eagle, the guide   Wallace Eddy

Music: William Loose, Michael Tschedin, Don Peake.
Producer: David E. Jackson.
Writer: James T. Flocker, Rex Wilder, Augie Kribach.
Director: James T. Flocker.

CAMP WILDERNESS — 30 minutes — Syndicated December 1980.

1883   CONDOMINIUM

Drama. A two-part miniseries based on the novel by John D. MacDonald. The story, set at the Silver Sands Condominium in Fiddler Key, Florida, depicts events in the lives of its residents — retired people who are being fleeced by corrupt city officials and builders who cut corners when constructing the complex. The program's main action centers on the problems that occur when Hurricane Ella strikes Fiddler Key and threatens to destroy Silver Sands.

CAST

Barbara Messenger   Barbara Eden
Sam Harrison   Dan Haggerty
Gus Garver   Steve Forrest
Thelma Messenkott   Ana Alicia
Henry Churchbridge   Richard Anderson

Lee Messenger   Ralph Bellamy
Julian Higbee   Larry Bishop
Dr. Arthur Castor   Macdonald Carey
Pete McGinnity   Dane Clark
Carlotta Churchbridge   Linda Cristal
Audrey Ames   Elinor Donahue
Jack Messenkott   Don Galloway
Drusilla Byrne   Pamela Hensley
Brooke Ames   Arte Johnson
Cole Kimber   Jack Jones
Molly Denniver   Dorothy Malone
Lorrie Higbee   Mimi Maynard
Vic York   Lee Paul
Conlaw   Nehemiah Persoff
Mrs. Conlaw   Nedra Volz
Roberta Fish   Carlene Watkins
Marty Liss   Stuart Whitman
Tom Forrester   Richard Eastham
Martha Cook   Danna Hansen
David Dow   Harry Townes
Frank Branhammer   Bill Zuckert
Carolyn Garver   Virginia Leith
Doris Branhammer   Lyndel Stuart

Music: Gerald Fried.
Executive Producer: R. A. Cinader.
Producer: Gian Grimaldi, Hannah L. Shearer.
Writer: Steve Hayes.
Director: Sidney Hayers.
Art Director: William Campbell.

CONDOMINIUM — 2 hours — Operation Prime Time — November 1980. 2 episodes. Originally presented on Home Box Office, a cable system, during April 1980.

1884   THE DAY THE WOMEN GOT EVEN

Pilot (Comedy). The story of Dee Dee Fields, Martha Jo Alfieri, Evelyn Michaels and Kathy Scott, four dauntless Westchester (New York) housewives who ban together to help victims of crime. In the pilot, they attempt to help Lisa Harris, an innocent victim of three ruthless blackmailers.

REGULAR CAST

Dee Dee Fields   Barbara Rhoades
Martha Jo Alfieri   Tina Louise
Evelyn Michaels   Jo Ann Pflug
Kathy Scott   Georgia Engel
Pancho Diaz, the cab driver
who assists them   Rick Aviles
Mark Fields, Dee Dee's
husband   Vincent Cobb
Dr. Bill Scott, Kathy's
husband   Andrew Duncan
Steve Michaels, Evelyn's
husband   Rex Robbins
Tony Alfieri, Martha Jo's
husband   Tom Keena
Dee Dee's daughter   Sue Kennedy
Kathy's daughter   Elizabeth Ward
Dee Dee's son   Lawrence Holcomb
Evelyn's son   Justin Frieman

GUEST CAST

Lisa Harris   Julie Hagerty
Marden (the blackmailer)   Gerald Gordon
Marden's receptionist   Harriet Hall
Marden's associate (Ed)   Ed O'Neill
Marden's associate (Joey)   Henry Madsen
Father O'Shea   Charles White
Jill Larson   Rolla Robertson

Narrator: Rick Aviles.
Music: Brad Fiedel.
Executive Producer: Paul Klein, Deann Burkley.
Producer: Otto Salamon.
Writer: Judy Scott, Gloria Gonzalez.
Director: Burt Brinkerhoff.
Art Director: Edward Burbridge.
Director of Photography: Brian West.

THE DAY THE WOMEN GOT EVEN — 2 hours — NBC — December 4, 1980.

1885   DYNASTY

Drama. Serial-type episodes that explore the conflicts, drives, and tensions of two strong-willed Denver oil families: the rich, powerful and greedy Carringtons; and the struggling, middle-class Blaisdels. The series, a take-off on *Dallas,* was originally titled *Oil.*

CAST

Blake Carrington, the
oil baron   John Forsythe
Krystle Jennings Carrington,
Blake's wife   Linda Evans
Fallon Carrington, Blake's
daughter   Pamela Sue Martin
Steven Carrington, Blake's son   Al Corley
Matthew Blaisdel, a geologist   Bo Hopkins
Claudia Blaisdel, Matthew's
wife   Pamela Bellwood
Lindsay Blaisdel, Matthew's
daughter   Katy Kurtzman
Cecil Colby, Blake's friend   Lloyd Bochner
Jeff Coly, Cecil's nephew   John James
Walter Lankershim, an
oil wildcatter   Dale Robertson
Andrew Laird, Blake's
associate   Peter Mark Richman
Michael, Blake's
chauffeur   Wayne Northrop
Joseph, Blake's butler   Lee Bergere

Music: Bill Conti.
Executive Producer: Richard and Esther Shapiro.
Supervising Producer: E. Duke Vincent.
Producer: Philip Parslow.

DYNASTY — 60 minutes — ABC — Premiered: January 12, 1981.

1886   ENOS

Crime Drama. A spin-off from *The Dukes of Hazzard.* The somewhat comical exploits of police officers Enos Strate, a naive deputy,* and Turk Adams, a tough, ghetto-bred black. They work for the Los Angeles Police Department's Metro Squad.

CAST

Officer Enos Strate   Sonny Shroyer
Officer Turk Adams   Samuel E. Wright
Lt. T. J. Broggi   John Dehner
Captain Dempsey   John Milford
Sgt. T. Kick   Leo V. Gordon

Announcer: William Schallert.
Music: Dennis McCarthy.
Executive Producer: Gy Waldron.

Supervising Producer: Rod Amateau.
Producer: Jim Heinz, B. W. Sandefur, George Lehr.
Director: Rod Amateau, Michael Caffey, Hollingsworth Morse, Bruce Kessler, Bernard McEveety, Robert Totten.

ENOS—60 minutes—CBS—Premiered: November 12, 1980.

*When Strate, a deputy sheriff in Hazzard County, Georgia, single-handedly captures two of America's most wanted felons, he is recruited by the L.A.P.D.

1887 THE FACTS OF LIFE

Comedy. A revised version of Program No. 374. Continued events in the lives of Edna Garrett, now the dietitian at the Eastland School for Girls in Peekskill, New York, and four teenage students who are struggling to cope with the facts of life.

CAST

Edna Garrett	Charlotte Rae
Blair Warner, a student	Lisa Whelchel
JoAnn "Jo" Polniachek, a student	Nancy McKeon
Tootie Ramsey, a student	Kim Fields
Natalie Green, a student	Mindy Cohn
Howard, the school chef	Hugh Gillin
Mr. Harris, the headmaster	Kenneth Mars

Semiregular Students:

Sue Anne Weaver	Julie Piekarski
Cindy Webster	Julie Anne Haddock
Nancy Moore	Felice Schacter

Music: Alan Thicke, Gloria Loring, Al Burton.
Executive Producer: Jack Elinson.
Producer: Jerry Mayer.
Director: Bob Claver, Asaad Kelada, John Bowab.

THE FACTS OF LIFE—30 minutes—NBC—Premiered: November 19, 1980.

1888 FLAMINGO ROAD

Drama. The series, set in Truro County, a small Southern community, depicts events in the lives of the Weldons, a wealthy family whose lives are corrupted by power and passion.

CAST

Titus Semple, the corrupt sheriff	Howard Duff
Claude Weldon, the papermill owner	Kevin McCarthy
Eudora Weldon, Claude's wife	Barbara Rush
Constance Weldon Carlyle, Claude's married daughter	Morgan Fairchild
Lute Mae Saunders, the owner of the brothel	Stella Stevens
Lane Ballou, a singer at Lute Mae's	Cristina Raines
Fielding Carlyle, Constance's husband, the deputy sheriff	Mark Harmon
Sam Curtis, the land developer	John Beck
Skipper Semple, Titus' son	Woody Brown

Jasper, the Weldon's butler	Glen Richards
Elmo Tyson, publisher of *The Clarion*	Peter Donat

Music: Gerald Fried.
Flamingo Road Theme: Gerald Fried.
Executive Producer: Michael Filerman, Lee Rich.
Supervising Producer: Rita Lakin.
Producer: Edward H. Feldman.

FLAMINGO ROAD—60 minutes—NBC—Premiered: January 6, 1981. The pilot film, based on the movie of the same name, aired on May 12, 1980.

1889 FONZ AND THE HAPPY DAYS GANG

Animated Cartoon. An extension series based on *Happy Days*. When Cup Cake, a girl from the twenty-fifth century lands in Milwaukee in 1957, she befriends the main characters from *Happy Days* (Fonzie, Richie and Ralph) and takes them aboard her slightly defective time machine. During a demonstration, they become lost in time. The series depicts their adventures as they struggle to find a way back to 1957 Milwaukee.

VOICES

Fonzie (Arthur Fonzerelli)	Henry Winkler
Richie Cunningham	Ron Howard
Ralph Malph	Donny Most
Cup Cake	Didi Conn
Announcer	Wolfman Jack
Mr. Cool, Fonzie's dog	Frank Welker

Music: Hoyt Curtin.
Executive Producer: William Hanna, Joseph Barbera.
Producer: Art Scott, Don Jurwich.
Director: Ray Patterson, George Gordon, Rudy Zamora.

FONZ AND THE HAPPY DAYS GANG—30 minutes—ABC—Premiered: November 8, 1980.

1890 FREEBIE AND THE BEAN

Crime Drama. The lighthearted exploits of Tim "Freebie" Walker and Dan "The Bean" Delgado, plainclothes police sergeants who work as a team to gather evidence against underworld figures scheduled for prosecution by the San Francisco District Attorney's office. Based on the movie of the same name.

CAST

Sgt. Tim "Freebie" Walker	Tom Mason
Sgt. Dan "The Bean" Delgado	Hector Elizondo
Walter A. Cruikshank, the D.A.	William Daniels
Rodney Axel, the police garage mechanic	Mel Stewart
Walter's secretary	Rosanna Huffman
Wally the wino, Tim and Dan's friend	Carmen Filpi

Music: Dominic Frontiere.

Theme: "You and Me Babe" sung by Bobby Hart.
Executive Producer: Philip Saltzman.
Producer: Robert Sherman, Norman Jolley, Robert Singer, Jay Folb, Hy Averback.
Writer: Dick Nelson, Jay Folb, Robert Lenski, Rick Mittleman.
Director: Lawrence Dobkin, Bruce Kessler, Jay Folb, Hy Averback, Arnold Laven, Michael Preece.

FREEBIE AND THE BEAN—60 minutes—CBS—December 6, 1980–January 24, 1981. 8 episodes.

1891 THE GEORGIA PEACHES

Pilot (Adventure). The exploits of Lorette Peach, her sister Sue Lynn Peach, and Dusty Tyree, three friends who are recruited as undercover agents by the U.S. Treasury Department. In the pilot, they attempt to break up a ring of cigarette bootleggers operating out of their home state of Georgia.

REGULAR CAST

Lorette Peach, a country singer	Tanya Tucker
Sue Lynn Peach, the owner of the Georgia Peaches Garage	Terri Nunn
Dusty Tyree, a stock car racer	Dirk Benedict
Randolph Dukane, their Treasury Dept. contact	Lane Smith

GUEST CAST

Vivian Stark	Sally Kirkland
Wade Holt	Dennis Patrick
Jarvis Wheeler	Noble Willingham
Delbart Huggins	Burton Gilliam

Music: R. Donovan Fox.
Vocals: Tanya Tucker.
Executive Producer: Roger Corman.
Producer: James Sbardellati, Thomas Hammel.
Writer: Michael Benderoth, Monte Stettin, Lois Luger.
Director: Daniel Haller.
Art Director: Michael Erler.
Director of Photography: David Sanderson.

THE GEORGIA PEACHES—2 hours—CBS—November 8, 1980.

1892 HARPER VALLEY P.T.A.

Comedy. Following the death of her husband, Stella Johnson, a beautiful and outspoken mother, moves to Harper Valley, Ohio, a hotbed of hypocrisy. Because of her flamboyant style and independent attitude, she encounters the objections of the P.T.A., a group of stuffed shirts who believe she is a bad influence and seek ways to discredit her in hopes she'll leave town. Episodes relate Stella's efforts to remain in

Harper Valley by "teaching her neighbors some lessons" and showing them off as the hypocrites they are. Based on the motion picture of the same title.

CAST

Stella Johnson, a saleswoman for Angel Glow Cosmetics	Barbara Eden
Dee Johnson, her daughter	Jenn Thompson
Cassie Bowman, Stella's friend, a beautician	Fannie Flagg
Otis Harper, the mayor	George Gobel
Flora Simpson Reilly, the P.T.A. president	Anne Francine
Wanda Reilly Taylor, Flora's daughter	Bridget Hanley
Scarlett Reilly, Wanda's daughter	Suzi Dean
Bobby Taylor, Wanda's husband	Rod McCary
Vivian Washburn, a P.T.A. board member	Mari Gorman
Willa Mae Jones, the recording secretary of the P.T.A.	Edie McClurg
Cliff Willoughby, a P.T.A. member	Robert Gray
George Kelly, the owner of Kelly's Bar	Vic Dunlop
Norman Clayton, school board member	Gary Allen
Eunice Clayton, Norman's wife	Joan Kjan

Stella's address: 769 Oakwood Street

Harper Valley P.T.A. Theme Vocal: Jeannie C. Riley.
Music: Nelson Riddle.
Executive Producer: Sherwood Schwartz.
Producer: Gordon Mitchell, Jerry Ross.

HARPER VALLEY P.T.A.—30 minutes—NBC—Premiered: January 16, 1981.

1893 HILL STREET BLUES

Crime Drama. The series is set at the Hill Street police station, located in the worst neighborhood of a large, unidentified urban community. It depicts the experiences of the men and women who place their lives on the line each day to protect the innocent.

CAST

Capt. Frank Furillo	Daniel Travanti
Joyce Davenport, the attorney	Veronica Hamel
Sgt. Phillip Esterhaus	Michael Conrad
Detective Mike Belker	Bruce Weitz
Officer Andy Renko	Charles Haid
Officer Bobby Hill	Michael Warren
Detective Ray Calletano	Rene Enriquez
Detective John LaRue	Kiel Martin
Officer Lucy Bates	Betty Thomas
Fay Furillo, Frank's ex-wife	Barbara Bosson
Sgt. Howard Hunter	James Sikking
Detective Henry Goldblume	Joe Spano
Officer Washington	Taurean Blacque

Hill Street Blues Theme: Mike Post.
Music: Mike Post.

Executive Producer: Steven Bochco, Michael Kozoll.
Producer: Gregory Hoblit.
Writer: Steven Bochco, Michael Kozoll.
Director: Robert Butler.
Art Director: Jeff Goldstein.

HILL STREET BLUES—60 minutes—NBC—January 15, 1981– January 31, 1981. 5 episodes.

1894   I'M A BIG GIRL NOW

Comedy. The story of Diana Cassidy, a divorcée, and Benjamin Douglas, her father, just divorced after thirty-four years of marriage, as they attempt to share an apartment and help each other through the difficult times. Episodes depict Diana's efforts to prove to her intrusive and acerbic father, who still treats her like a child, that she's a big girl now.

CAST

Diana Cassidy, works for the Kramer Research and Testing Co. in Washington, D.C.	Diana Canova
Benjamin Douglas, a dentist	Danny Thomas
Rebecca Cassidy, Diana's daughter	Rori King
Edie, Diana's employer	Sheree North
Walter Douglas, Diana's brother	Michael Durrell
Karen Hawks, Diana's coworker	Deborah Baltzell
Neal Stryker, Diana's coworker	Martin Short
Polly Douglas, Walter's wife	Joan Welles
Preston Kramer, the owner of the company	Richard McKenzie

Music: George Tipton.
Theme Vocal: "I'm a Big Girl Now" by Diana Canova; written by Leslie Bricusse.
Executive Producer: Paul Junger Witt, Tony Thomas.
Producer: Don Richetta, Marc Sotkin, Judi Pioli.
Writer: Susan Seeger, Judy Pioli, Paula Roth, Barbara Benedek, Marc Sotkin, Deborah Leschin.
Director: John Bowab, Doug Rogers.

I'M A BIG GIRL NOW—30 minutes—ABC—Premiered: October 31, 1980.

1895   IT'S A LIVING

Comedy. The experiences of Lois Adams, Jan Hoffmeyer, Dot Higgins, Cassie Cranston and Vickie Allen, five waitresses in the posh Los Angeles Above the Top Restaurant, as they tackle customers and life head on.

CAST

Lois Adams, the level-headed waitress	Susan Sullivan
Jan Hoffmeyer, the student and mother	Barrie Youngfellow
Cassie Cranston, the brassy, sexy waitress	Ann Jillian
Vickie Allen, the virtuous waitress	Wendy Schaal
Dot Higgins, the hopeful actress	Gail Edwards
Nancy Beebee, the maitre d'	Marian Mercer
Sonny Mann, the piano player	Paul Kreppel
Mario, the chef	Bert Remsen
Ellen Hoffmeyer, Jan's daughter	Lili Haydn

Vickie's parakeet: Squeaky.

Music: George Tipton.
Theme Vocal: "It's a Living" by Leslie Bricusse.
Executive Producer: Paul Junger Witt, Tony Thomas.
Supervising Producer: Joel Zwick.
Producer: Gloria Banta, Greg Antonacci.
Writer: Stu Silver, Wally Dalton, Shelley Zellman, Sheldon Bull, Mark Rothman, Greg Antonacci.
Director: John Tracy, Joel Zwick, Jay Sandrich.

IT'S A LIVING—30 minutes—ABC—Premiered: October 30, 1980.

1896   KEEP IT IN THE FAMILY

Comedy. The British series on which America's *Too Close for Comfort* is based (see Program No. 1911). The series, which has not been broadcast in the United States, follows the misadventures of Dudley Rush, a strip cartoonist, as he struggles to keep tabs on his daughters when they move out on their own and into the basement apartment of the Rush home. (Dudley draws *Barney*, the adventures of a bionic bulldog.)

CAST

Dudley Rush	Robert Gillespie
Muriel Rush, his wife	Pauline Yates
Jacqui Rush, their daughter	Jenny Quayle
Susan Rush, thir daughter	Stacy Dorning

Producer: Mark Stuart.
Writer: Brian Cooke.
Director: Mark Stuart.

KEEP IT IN THE FAMILY—30 minutes. Produced in England by Thames Television Ltd. in 1980.

1897   LADIES' MAN

Comedy. The misadventures of Alan Thackeray, a bachelor father and the token male writer on *Woman's Life*, a New York-based magazine whose staff is totally female.

CAST

Alan Thackeray	Lawrence Pressman
Amy Thackeray, his daughter	Natasha Ryan
Elaine Holstein, the managing editor	Louise Sorel
Andrea Gibbons, a staff writer	Betty Kennedy
Gretchen, a researcher	Simone Griffeth
Susan, a staff writer	Allison Argo
Betty Brill, Alan's neighbor	Karen Morrow
Reggie, the magazine's accountant	Herbert Edelman
Various nonspeaking roles	Mitzi McCall

Music: Jack Elliott.
Executive Producer: Herbert B. Leonard.
Supervising Producer: Michael Loman.
Producer: Lee Miller.
Writer: David Wiltse, Michael Loman, John Owen, Beverly Bloomberg, Chip and Doug Keyes, Anne Convy, Mitzi McCall, Michael Weinberger.
Director: H. Wesley Kenney, John Tracy.

LADIES' MAN—30 minutes—CBS—Premiered: October 27, 1980.

1898   LASSITER

Pilot (Crime Drama). The exploits of Pete Lassiter, a tough investigative reporter for *Contrast* magazine. In the pilot, Lassiter travels to Grand Lake, a Midwestern city, to investigate reports of corruption within the police department.

REGULAR CAST

Pete Lassiter	Burt Reynolds

GUEST CAST

D.A. Stan Marchek	Cameron Mitchell
Joanie Mears	Sharon Farrell
Lt. Dave Brandon	Gerald S. O'Loughlin
Officer Russ Faine	James MacArthur
Kramer	Lloyd Haynes
Jerry Burns	Lawrence Haddon

Producer: Richard Alan Simmons.
Writer: Richard Alan Simmons.
Director: Sam Wanamaker.
Art Director: Bill Ross.
Director of Photography: Kenneth Peach.

LASSITER—60 minutes—NBC—November 6, 1980. Originally broadcast by CBS in 1968.

1899   THE LIVES WE LIVE

Serial. An unusual "soap opera" that features true stories, loves, concerns and triumphs of three real-life women: Nancy Tigue, a divorced mother of four who lives in Westchester; Joyce Spector, a Manhattan businesswoman; and Linda Tarry, a social worker. The program, which is unscripted, is set in a living room and features the women discussing various matters with their actual friends and family, who appear as guests.

Starring: Nancy Tigue, Joyce Spector, Linda Tarry.
Executive Producer: Hilary Schacter.
Producer: Joanne Roberts.
Director: Michael Albanse.

THE LIVES WE LIVE—30 minutes—CBS Owned and Operated Stations—Premiered: October 27, 1980.

1900   LOBO

Crime Drama. A spin-off from *The Misadventures of Sheriff Lobo*. When the governor of Georgia discovers that Orly County, Georgia, is virtually crime free due to what he believes is the honest work of the larcenous Sheriff Elroy P. Lobo, he hires Lobo and his deputies to help curb the rising crime rate. The series follows the adventures of Sheriff Lobo as he and his deputies, Perkins and Hawkins, attempt to do for Atlanta what they did in Orly.

CAST

Sheriff Elroy P. Lobo	Claude Akins
Deputy Perkins	Mills Watson
Deputy Birdwell "Birdie" Hawkins	Brian Kerwin
John Carson, Chief of Detectives, Metro Atlanta Police	Nicholas Coster
Officer Brandy Kravits	Tara Buckman
Officer Peaches Douglas	Amy Botwinick
Sgt. Hildy Jones	Nell Carter
Voice of the Governor of Atlanta	William Schallert

Music: John Tartiglia.
Executive Producer: Glen A. Larson.
Supervising Producer: Jo Swerling, Jr.
Producer: Frank Lupo, Bill Dial.

LOBO—60 minutes—NBC—Premiered: December 30, 1980.

1901   MAGNUM, P.I.

Crime Drama. The exploits of Thomas Magnum, a former Naval Intelligence officer turned private investigator. (Magnum, whose reasons for leaving the Navy are not explained, lives on the fabulous Hawaiian estate of Robin Masters, a never-seen, successful pulp writer, in return for providing its security.)

CAST

Thomas Magnum	Tom Selleck
Higgins, the retired British Army officer and major-dommo of the estate	John Hillerman
T. C., Magnum's aide	Roger E. Mosley
Rick, Magnum's aide, the owner of the Rick's Place Disco	Larry Manetti
Sam, the D.J. at Rick's Place	Mel Carter

Higgins' Doberman pinschers: Apollo and Zeus.

Narrator: Tom Selleck.
Music: Ian Freebairn-Smith.
Executive Producer: Donald Bellisario, Glen A. Larson.
Producer: J. Rickley Dumm.
Director: Roger Young, Donald

Happy Days are Here Again. Fred and Mickie Finn.

It's a Living. From left: Gail Edwards, Marian Mercer, and
Barrie Youngfellow.

Bellisario, Bruce Green, Lawrence Doheny.

MAGNUM, P.I.—60 minutes—CBS—Premiered: December 11, 1980.

1902 MARIE

Variety. A comedy-accented series that spotlights the many talents of actress-singer Marie Osmond.

Hostess: Marie Osmond.
Regulars: Shirley Mitchell, Melissa Multray, Greg Norberg, Scott Mullaney, Howard It-kowitz, Steve Stucker, Jim Hudson, Charles Graves, Doris Hess, Kathy Primby, The Carl Jablonski Dancers.
Orchestra: Bob Rozario.
Special Musical Material: Earl Brown.
Executive Producer: Alan Os-mond, Jay Osmond, Jerry McPhie.
Producer: Neal Isreal, Pat Proft.
Writer: Bob Arnott, Nancy Steen, Gina Goldman, Jeff Richman, Jim Staahl, Earl Brown, Joyce Gitlan, Mike McManus.
Director: Jeff Margolis.
Choreographer: Lester Wilson, Carl Jablonski.
Art Director: Rene Lagler.

MARIE—60 minutes—NBC—December 12, 1980–January 2, 1981. 4 programs.

1903 MOMMA THE DETECTIVE

Pilot (Crime Drama). The story of Momma Sykes, a housekeeper with an uncanny knack for solving crimes. In the pilot, Momma attempts to solve the mysterious murder of a man in a hotel room—despite the objections of her son, a New York police sergeant who balks at her intervention.

REGULAR CAST
Momma Sykes	Esther Rolle
Sgt. Alvin Sykes, her son	Kene Holliday

GUEST CAST
Mrs. Hackman	Jean Marsh
Tom Hackman	Frank Converse
Edward Forbes	Andrew Duggan
Dr. Glickman	Lawrence Luckinbill
Mr. Foster	Fritz Weaver

Music: Joey Levine, Chris Palermo.
Executive Producer: Hal Schaffel.
Producer-Writer-Director: Larry Cohan.
Art Director: Ed Burbridge.
Director of Photography: Paul Glickman.

MOMMA THE DETECTIVE—60 minutes—NBC—January 9, 1981. An unscheduled air date.

1904 NERO WOLFE

Crime Drama. The story of Nero Wolfe, a reclusive, master criminologist who solves baffling crimes from his home. He works through the eyes and ears of others—namely Archie Goodwin, his trusted associate, and Saul Panzer, his field operative. Based on the character created by Rex Stout. See also Program No. 1686 for the unsold pilot version of the series.

CAST
Nero Wolfe	William Conrad
Archie Goodwin, his assistant	Lee Horsley
Fritz Brenner, his gourmet chef	George Voskovec
Saul Panzer, his associate	George Wyner
Inspector Cramer, N.Y.P.D. 8th Precinct	Allan Miller
Theodore Hortsmann, Nero's horticulturist	Robert Coote

Nero's address: 918 West 35th Street in New York City.

Music: John Addison.
Executive Producer: Ivan Goff, Ben Roberts.
Associate Producer: John Fegan.

NERO WOLFE—60 minutes—NBC—Premiered: January 16, 1981.

1905 NUMBER 96

Comedy-Drama. The outrageous sexual activities of a group of people who reside at Number 96 Pacific Way, a Los Angeles apartment building. Based on the Australian series of the same title (see following title for information).

CAST
Lou Sugarman, the bar owner	Eddie Barth
Rita Sugarman, Lou's sister and partner	Ellen Travolta
Max Quintzel, an architect	Greg Mullavey
Marion Quintzel, Max's wife	Randee Heller
Mark Keaton, a baseball player with the Bullets	Howard McGillin
Jill Keaton, Mark's wife	Sherry Hussey
Sharon St. Clair, an aspiring actress	Hilary Thompson
Ginny Ramirez, Sharon's roommate	Maria O'Brien
Anthea Bryan, a boutique shop owner	Rosine Widdowson-Reynolds
Horace Batterson, a retired army officer	Barney Martin
Sandy Galloway, a nurse	Jill Choder
Maureen Galloway, Sandy's mother	Betsy Palmer
Nathan Sugarman, Lou's brother, a cop	Todd Susman
Chick Walden, a movie director	John Reilly
Lisa Brendon, a resident	Christine Jones
Roger Busky, a resident	James Murtaugh
Robert Leon, a doctor	Brian Curran
Dorothy, Roger's ex-wife	Sharon Spelman
Lyle Bixler, the janitor	Charles Bloom
Hildy, Roger's girlfriend	Elaine Giftos
Mel, Dorothy's new husband	Graham Jarvis
Donald, Dorothy's son	Christian Zika
Lt. Tim McGavin, Nathan's superior	Andrew Block

Music: Gerald Fried.
Executive Producer: Bob Ellison.
Supervising Producer: Allan Manings.
Producer: Mitchell Gamson.
Writer: David Lloyd, Lloyd Garver, Richard Baer, Howard Ostroff.
Director: Robert Scheerer.
Art Director: Brian Bartholomew.

NUMBER 96—60 minutes—NBC—December 10, 1980–January 2, 1981. 6 episodes.

1906 NUMBER 96

Serial. The Australian series on which America's *Number 96* is based. The series, which is not likely to be broadcast in the United States, explores the human foibles and sexual hang-ups of the people who reside in a block of flats in Sydney, Australia. The 0-10 network series brought nudity to Australian TV "and viewers were treated to dozens of bare breasts and naked bottoms." When *Number 96*, called "a salacious Peyton Place" by *Time* magazine, made its debut in 1972, it was trumpeted as "the night television lost its virginity."* The following cast is a listing of the original regulars—only a handful of the 1,350 actors who have appeared on the series.

CAST
Aldo Godolfus	Johnny Lockwood
Roma Lubinski	Philippa Baker
Dorrie Evans	Pat McDonald
Herb Evans	Ron Shand
Les Whittaker	Gordon McDougall
Norma Whittaker	Sheila Kennelly
Bev Houghton	Abigail
Jack Sellers	Tom Oliver
Vera Collins	Elaine Lee
Don Finlayson	Joe Hasham
Arnold Feather	Jeff Kevin
Maggie Cameron	Bettina Welch
Janie	Robyn Gurney
Georgina Carter	Susannah Piggott
Chad	Ronnie Arnold
Sonia	Lynn Rainbow
Bruce Taylor	Paul Weingott
Mark Eastwood	Martin Harris
Helen Eastwood	Briony Behets
Rose Godolfus	Vivienne Garrett

NUMBER 96—30 minutes. Produced and broadcast in Australia from March 13, 1972–August 11, 1977. 1,218 episodes.

*For example: "A startled Australia watched a sex-starved Mark Eastwood groping vainly at the underclothes of his eight-month pregnant wife Helen and in frustration, bedding neighbor Rose.... The busty Abigail ... was lighting up the screen in various stages of undress. Sometimes it was in a see-through blouse, sometimes no blouse at all.... The pack rape of Rose by Cliff and his hippie friends ... was one of the program's more seamy segments—and drew few protests for its starkness. But possibly no segment was more 'way out' than the black mass in which both Vera and Abigail—the latter destined to be a sacrificial virgin—appeared nude."

1907 SATURDAY NIGHT LIVE—THE NEXT GENERATION

Comedy-Variety. A revised version of *Saturday Night Live* that features a new group of regulars in various and sometimes tasteless comedy sketches.

Included Guest Hosts: Jamie Lee Curtis, David Carradine, Elliott Gould, Karen Black.
Regulars: Denny Dillon, Gilbert Gottfried, Gail Matthius, Joe Piscopo, Ann Risley, Charles Rocket, Yvonne Hudson, Eddie Murphy.
Announcer: Don Pardo.
Music: Kenny Vance.
Producer: Jean Doumanian.
Director: Dave Wilson.

SATURDAY NIGHT LIVE—THE NEXT GENERATION—90 minutes—NBC—Premiered: November 15, 1980. Also titled *Saturday Night Live '80*.

1908 SECRETS OF MIDLAND HEIGHTS

Drama. A prime-time serial that explores the dreams, frustrations, hidden secrets, and shames of the people who live and work in Midland Heights, a small Midwestern college town.

CAST
Margaret Millington, a descendant of the town's founders	Martha Scott
Dorothy Wheeler, Margaret's friend	Bibi Besch
Guy Millington, Margaret's son	Jordan Christopher
Holly Wheeler, Dorothy's daughter	Linda Grovenor
	Marilyn Jones
Ann Dulles, Margaret's niece	Doran Clark
Prof. Nathan Welsh, Dorothy's romantic interest	Robert Hogan
Teddy Welsh, Nathan's son	Daniel Zippi
Danny Welsh, Nathan's son	Stephen Manley
Burt Carroll, the town's football star	Lorenzo Lamas
Lisa Rogers, Burt's girlfriend	Linda Hamilton
Micki Carroll, Burt's sister	Melora Hardin
John Grey, Burt's friend	Jim Youngs
Lucy Dexter, the diner owner	Jenny O'Hara
Calvin Richardson, a teacher at Midland Heights College	Mark Pinter
Sue, a friend of Ann's	Irene Arranga
Mrs. Grey, John's mother	Arlene Golonka

Music: Jerrold Immel.
Secrets of Midland Heights Theme: Jerrold Immel.
Executive Producer: Lee Rich, Michael Filerman, David Jacobs.
Producer: Joseph Wallerstein, Paul Waigner, Sally Robinson.
Writer: David Jacobs, Caroline Ellis, Elizabeth Quicksilver.

Director: Robert Lewis, Fernando Lamas, Alexander Singer, Gabriel Beaumont, Rick Rosenthal.

SECRETS OF MIDLAND HEIGHTS — 60 minutes — CBS — December 6, 1980 – January 24, 1981. 8 episodes.

1909 THE SECRET WAR OF JACKIE'S GIRLS

Pilot (Adventure). When England enters the Second World War in 1939, Jackie Scott, an American, forms a squadron of five female helicopter pilots to aid the British in the war effort. The pilot episode depicts their exploits as they perform several hazardous missions. (The title is derived from the fact that "Jackie's Girls" officially do not exist. The girls, who pose as American nurses, are stationed near Darwell in the South of England.)

REGULAR CAST

Jackie Scott, the leader*	Mariette Hartley
Russ Hamilton, the RAF Squadron leader	John Reilly
Cpl. Mabel Wheeton, the girls' den mother	Marilyn Chris
Phillis, the bartender at The Pub	Sheila MacRae
Jackie's Girls:	
Casey McCann	Lee Purcell
Donna	Ann Dusenberry
Zimmy	Tracy Brooks Swope
Patti	Caroline Smith
Maxine	Dee Wallace

GUEST CAST

Buck	Ben Murphy
Sgt. McPherson	Don Knight
Dr. Kruger	Curt Lowens

Dieter	Henry Olek
Brewer	Edward Bell

Narrator: Lee Purcell.
Music: Fred Karlin.
Executive Producer: Florence Small, John Surgall.
Producer: Dorothy J. Bailey.
Writer: Theodore Jonas, D. Guthrie.
Director: Gordon Hessler.
Art Director: Sherman Loudermilk.
Director of Photography: William Cornjager.

THE SECRET WAR OF JACKIE'S GIRLS — 2 hours — NBC — November 29, 1980.

*In the pilot, Jackie's helicopter is shot down and she is reported killed in action. Though her fate is not shown, it is questionable as to whether or not Mariette would have been a regular had the pilot sold.

1910 THE STEVE ALLEN COMEDY HOUR

Comedy. Various comedy sketches.

Host: Steve Allen.
Regulars: Catherine O'Hara, Bill Saluga, Joe Baker, Tom Leopold, Bob Shaw, Joey Forman, Fred Smoot, Nancy Steen, Dorothy Hess.
Orchestra: Terry Gibbs.
Executive Producer: Frank Peppiatt, William O. Harbacht.
Producer: Carl Gibson.
Writer: Steve Allen, Tom Moore, Tom Leopold, Jay Burton, Jeremy Stevens, Bob Shorr.

Director: Bob Bowker, Russ Petranto
Art Director: Bill Bonhert.

THE STEVE ALLEN COMEDY HOUR — 60 minutes — NBC — October 18, 1980 – January 10, 1981. 5 programs.

1911   TOO CLOSE FOR COMFORT

Comedy. The misadventures of Henry Rush, an overprotective father, as he struggles to keep tabs on his two beautiful daughters who have moved out on their own — and into the funky downstairs apartment of the Rushes' San Francisco duplex. (Henry illustrates the children's comic strip, *Cosmic Cow*, which is published by Random Comics, a division of Wainwright Publishing.) Based on the British series *Keep It in the Family* (see program No. 1896).

CAST

Henry Rush	Ted Knight
Muriel Rush, his wife, a photographer	Nancy Dussault
Jackie Rush, their daughter, a bank teller	Deborah Van Valkenburgh
Sarah Rush, their daughter, a college student	Lydia Cornell
Monroe Ficus, Sarah's friend	Jim B. Bullock
Arthur Wainwright, Henry's employer	Hamilton Camp

Music: Johnny Mandel.
Executive Producer: Arne Sultan, Earl Barret.
Supervising Producer: Austin and Irma Kalish.

Producer: Jerry McPhie.
Writer: Arne Sultan, Earl Barret, Mitch Markowitz, Richard Reinhart.
Director: Will MacKenzie, Howard Storm.
Art Director: Ken Reid.

TOO CLOSE FOR COMFORT — 30 minutes — ABC — Premiered: November 11, 1980.

1912   WALKING TALL

Crime Drama. The exploits of Buford Pusser, the heroic sheriff of McNeal County, Tennessee, as he battles lawlessness. Based on the real-life exploits of Buford Pusser, a fearless Southern lawman. Based also on three feature films (*Walking Tall, Walking Tall, Part 2,* and *Walking Tall, the Final Chapter*) and one TV movie (*The Great American Hero*).

CAST

Sheriff Buford Pusser (a widower)	Bo Svenson
Carl Pusser, Buford's father	Walter Barnes
Dwana Pusser, Buford's daughter	Heather McAdam
Michael Pusser, Buford's son	Rad Daly
Deputy Joan Litton, the dispatcher	Courtney Pledger
Deputy Aaron Fairfax	Harold Sylvester
Deputy Grady Spooner	Jeff Lester

Music: Ed Kalehoff.
Executive Producer: David Gerber.
Producer: Mel Swope.

WALKING TALL — 60 minutes — NBC — Premiered: January 17, 1981.

Index of Performers

Program numbers, not *page numbers, are listed in this index.*

See also Section 3: Variety Specials on pages 291 – 294

Index of Directors

Program numbers, not *page numbers, are listed in this index.*